What they're saying about

The Complete Guide to Bed & Breakfasts, Inns & Guesthouses . . .

. . . all necessary information about facilities, prices, pets, children, amenities, credit cards and the like. Like France's Michelin . . .

—New York Times

Definitive and worth the room in your reference library.

—Los Angeles Times

. . . innovative and useful . . .

—Washington Post

A must for the adventurous . . . who still like the Hobbity creature comforts.

—St. Louis Post-Dispatch

What has long been overdue: a list of the basic information of where, how much and what facilities are offered at the inns and guesthouses.

—San Francisco Examiner

Standing out from the crowd for its thoroughness and helpful cross-indexing . . .

—Chicago Sun Times

A quaint, charming and economical way to travel—all in one book.
—Waldenbooks (as seen in USA Today)

Little descriptions provide all the essentials: romance, historical landmarks, golf/fishing, gourmet food, or, just as important, low prices. Take your pick!

—National Motorist

For those travelling by car, lodging is always a main concern . . . The Complete Guide to Bed & Breakfasts, Inns & Guesthouses provides listings and descriptions of more than 1,200 inns.

—Minneapolis Star & Tribune

. . . the most complete compilation of bed and breakfast data ever published.

—Denver Post

Unique and delightful inns . . .

—Detroit Free Press

. . . lists more than 260 places in California alone . . .

—Oakland Tribune

. . . I've got just the book for you . . . settle back and picture yourself lapping discount luxury.

—Washington Times

The book may give . . . readers everything they ever wanted to know . . .

—Dallas Morning News

A state-by-state and city-by-city guide . . . researched listings . . . an impressive number.

—San Francisco Chronicle

. . . comprehensive . . .

—Atlanta Journal

It is a good basic resource for inn fanciers.

—Indianapolis Star

. . . a worthwhile addition to libraries.

—Library Journal

. . . a concise guide. .thousands of hotels, inns & guesthouses . . .

—Los Angeles Herald-Examiner

. . . access to more than 10,000 private guesthouses . . .

—Chicago Tribune

. . . the best so far.

—Whole Earth Review

The joy of the Complete Guide to BBIG is that it compromises neither description nor practical info . . . an essential reference.

—Midwest Book Review

. . . excellent guide book.

—Focus, Philadelphia, PA

. . . well coded and full of practical information.

—Diversion

THE COMPLETE GUIDE TO

BED &
BREAKFASTS,
INNS & GUESTHOUSES
IN THE UNITED STATES AND CANADA

PAMELA LANIER

Other Books By Pamela Lanier

All-Suite Hotel Guide	(Lanier Publishing Int., Ltd.)
Elegant Small Hotels	(Lanier Publishing Int., Ltd.)
Elegant Hotels—Pacific Rim	(Lanier Publishing Int., Ltd.)
Condo Vacations: The Complete Guide	(Lanier Publishing Int., Ltd.)
Golf Resorts: The Complete Guide	(Lanier Publishing Int., Ltd.)
Golf Resorts International	(Lanier Publishing Int., Ltd.)
22 Days in Alaska	(John Muir Press)
Bed & Breakfast Cookbook	(Running Press)
Cinnamon Mornings	(Running Press)

For further information, please contact:
  The Complete Guide to Bed & Breakfasts,
    Inns and Guesthouses
  P.O. Box 20467
  Oakland, CA 94620-0467

© 1994 by Lanier Publishing Int., Ltd.
All rights reserved. Published 1994

1994 edition. First printing

ISBN 0-89815-582-7

Distributed to the book trade by:
  Ten Speed Press
  P.O. Box 7123
  Berkeley, CA 94707

Cover by Jim Wood

Design & Production by J.C. Wright

Typeset by Futura Graphics

Printed in the United States of America on recycled paper

Rated #1 GUIDEBOOK *by Innkeepers nationwide*

In a nationwide survey of innkeepers conducted by *Innsider Magazine*

For J.C. Dolphin Valdés

Acknowledgements

Corrine Rednour and George Lanier for your help, love, and support—thank you.

For Eleanor Rush and Mariposa Valdés, Project Coordinators, who gave their all to this update, many many thanks.

To my friends who were so generous with their time and skills:

Venetia Young, Carol McBride, Marianne Barth, Vincent Yu, Madelyn Furze, Rus Quon, Terry Lacey, John Garrett, Chris Manley, Mary Kreuger, Mr. Wiley, Adele Novelli, Ruth Young, Mrs. Gieselman (the best English teacher ever), Mary Institute, Ingrid Head, Sumi Timberlake, Marvin Downey, Marguerite Tafoya, Peggy Dennis, Judy Jacobs, Derek Ng, Katherine Bertolucci, Margaret Callahan, Mary Ellen Callahan, Glenna Goulet, Lisa Ruffin, Hal Hershey, Leslie Chan and Jane Foster.

Special thanks to Richard Paoli

To the great folks in the Chambers of Commerce, State and Regional Departments of Tourism, I am most grateful.

To the innkeepers themselves who are so busy, yet found the time to fill out our forms and provide us with all sorts of information, I wish you all great success.

Contents

VOTE

FOR YOUR CHOICE OF
INN OF THE YEAR

Did you find your stay at a Bed & Breakfast, Inn or Guesthouse listed in this Guide particularly enjoyable? Use the form in the back of this page or just drop us a note and we'll add your vote for the "Inn of the Year."

The winning entry will be featured in the next edition of **The Complete Guide to Bed & Breakfasts, Inns and Guesthouses in the U.S. and Canada.**

Please base your decision on:

- Helpfulness of Innkeeper   • Quality of Service
- Cleanliness   • Amenities   • Decor   • Food

Look for the winning Inn in the next Updated & Revised edition of **The Complete Guide to Bed & Breakfasts, Inns and Guesthouses in the U.S. and Canada.**

VOTE

FOR YOUR CHOICE OF
INN OF THE YEAR

To the editors of **The Complete Guide to Bed & Breakfasts, Inns and Guesthouses in the U.S. and Canada:**

I cast my vote for "Inn of the Year" for:

Name of Inn _____

Address _____

_____

Phone _____

Reasons _____

_____

_____

I would also like to (please check one):

___ Recommend a new Inn   ___ Comment
___ Critique   ___ Suggest

Name of Inn _____

Address _____

_____

Phone _____

Comment _____

_____

Please send your entries to:
**The Complete Guide to Bed & Breakfast Inns
P.O. Box 20467
Oakland, CA 94620-0467**

1994 INN OF THE YEAR

THE CAPTAIN FREEMAN INN
BREWSTER, CAPE COD, MASSACHUSETTS

The Inn, a charming old sea captain's mansion, was built in 1860 on the original town square for Captain William Freeman, an aristocratic shipmaster. After an extensive renovation, the innkeepers, Carol Covitz and Tom Edmondson, brought back to life the beautiful Victorian that once was.

Before becoming innkeepers, Carol and Tom worked in high-tech marketing for more than 20 years. Their gregarious personalities and many interests helped them to decide that running a B&B would be perfect for them. For Carol, who is a professionally trained chef, it is an opportunity to combine two of her favorite things—cooking and meeting people. The B&B gave Tom a chance to create a magnificent garden and raise orchids. Elegant architectural details abound throughout the house. Each guest room is beautifully decorated with antiques and canopy beds and a 140 ft. wraparound porch has its original mahogany.

Most of all, guests appreciate the little things—the beach only minutes away, the cool pitcher of lemonade by the entrance, the basket of menus from nearby restaurants, the marble fireplace, romantic guestrooms, and, of course, the excellent gourmet food (especially those elaborate breakfasts!).

INNS OF THE YEAR
HONOR ROLL

1985 Joshua Grindle Inn,
Mendocino CA

1986 Carter House, Eureka, CA

1987 Governor's Inn, Ludlow, VT

1988 Seacrest Manor, Rockport, MA

1989 Wedgewood Inn,
New Hope, PA

1990 The Veranda,
Senoia, GA

1991 Kedron Valley Inn,
South Woodstock, VT

1992 The Lamplight Inn
Lake Luzerne, NY

1993 The Whalewalk Inn
Eastham, Cape Cod, MA

Introduction

There was a time, and it wasn't so long ago, when bed and breakfast inns were a rarity in the United States. Travelers made do at a hotel or motel; there was no alternative. The few bed and breakfast inns were scattered across the rural areas of New England and California. They were little known to most travelers; often their only advertisement was by word of mouth.

But in a few short years that has changed, and changed in a way that could only be called dramatic. There has been an explosion in the number of bed and breakfast inns. Today, inns can be found in every state, and often in cities; they have become true alternatives to a chain motel room or the city hotel with its hundreds of cubicles.

This sudden increase in bed and breakfast inns started less than two decades ago when Americans, faced with higher costs for foreign travel, began to explore the backroads and hidden communities of their own country.

Other factors have influenced the growth and popularity of bed and breakfast inns. Among them, the desire to get away from the daily routine and sameness of city life; the desire to be pampered for a few days; and also the desire to stay in a place with time to make new friends among the other guests.

The restored older homes that have become bed and breakfast inns answer those desires. The setting most often is rural; the innkeepers provide the service—not a staff with name tags—and the parlor is a gathering place for the handful of guests. They are a home away from home.

The proliferation of these inns as an alternative lodging has created some confusion. It's been difficult to find—in one place—up-to-date and thorough information about the great variety of inns.

Some books published in the past five or six years have tried to provide this information. But those books focused on one region of the country or named too few inns. While some earlier books gave detailed descriptions of the inns, few bothered to provide information about the type of breakfast served, whether there are rooms for non-smokers, and such things as whether the inn offered free use of bicycles or whether it had a hot tub.

An effort to collect as much information about as many inns as possible in one book has been overdue. Now that has been remedied. You hold a copy of the result in your hands.

Richard Paoli,
Travel Editor
San Francisco Examiner

How to Use this Guide

Organization

This book is organized alphabetically by state and, within a state, alphabetically by city or town. The inns appear first. More inns are listed after the featured inns. At the back of the guide are listings of the reservation service organizations serving each state and inns with special characteristics.

Three Types of Accommodations

Inn: Webster's defines an inn as a "house built for the lodging and entertainment of travelers." All the inns in this book fulfill this description. Many also provide meals, at least breakfast, although a few do not. Most of these inns have under 30 guest rooms.

Bed and Breakfast: Can be anything from a home with three or more rooms to, more typically, a large house or mansion with eight or nine guest accommodations where breakfast is served in the morning.

Guest House: Private homes welcoming travelers, some of which may be contacted directly but most of which are reserved through a reservation service organization. A comprehensive list of RSOs appears toward the back of this guide.

Breakfasts

We define a **full breakfast** as one being along English lines, including eggs and/or meat as well as the usual breads, toast, juice and coffee.

Continental plus is a breakfast of coffee, juice, and choice of several breads and pastry and possibly more.

Continental means coffee, juice, bread or pastry

Meals

Bear in mind that inns that do not serve meals are usually located near a variety of restaurants.

Can We Get a Drink?

Those inns without a license will generally chill your bottles and provide you with set-ups upon request.

Prices

We include a price code to give you an idea of each inn's rates. Generally, the coded prices indicate a given lodging's lowest priced double room, double occupancy rate as follows:

$—under $50 $$—$50-$75 $$$—$75 plus

Appearing to the right of the price code is a code indicating the type of food services available:

B&B: Breakfast included in quoted rate

EP (European Plan): No meals

MAP (Modified American Plan): Includes breakfast and dinner

AP (American Plan): Includes all three meals

All prices are subject to change. Please be sure to confirm rates and services when you make your reservations.

Credit Cards and Checks

If an establishment accepts credit cards, it will be listed as VISA, MC or AmEx, etc. Most inns will accept your personal check with proper identification, but be sure to confirm when you book.

Ratings

One of the beauties of bed & breakfast travel is the individual nature of each inn. And innkeepers thrive on their independence! Some inns are members of their local, state or national inn association (most of which have membership requirements), and/or are members of or are rated by AAA, Mobil and others. Each of these rating systems relies upon different inspection protocol, membership and evaluative criteria. We use * Rated * in the listings to designate inns which have informed us that they have been rated by or are affiliated with any of these groups. If ratings are important to you, we suggest that you call and inquire of the specific inn for details. We continue to find, however, that some very good inns remain unrated, simply because of their size or idiosyncratic nature.

Reservations

Reservations are essential at most inns, particularly during busy seasons, and are appreciated at other times. Be sure to reserve, even if only a few hours in advance, to avoid disappointment. When you book, feel free to discuss your requirements and confirm prices, services and other details. We have found innkeepers to be delightfully helpful.

Most inns will hold your reservation until 6 p.m. If you plan to arrive later, please phone ahead to let them know.

A deposit or advance payment is required at some inns.

Children, Pets and Smoking

Children, pets, smoking and physical handicaps present special considerations for many inns. Whether or not they can be accommodated is generally noted as follows:

	Yes	Limited	No
Children	C-yes	C-ltd	
Pets	P-yes	P-ltd	P-no
Smoking	S-yes	S-ltd	S-no
Handicapped	H-yes	H-ltd	H-no

However, many inns with limited facilities for children will often have one or two rooms set aside for families. Be sure to inquire when you book your room.

Accessibility for the Handicapped

Because many inns are housed in old buildings, access for handicapped persons in many cases is limited. Where this information is available, we have noted it as above. Be sure to confirm your exact requirements when you book.

Big Cities

In many big cities there are very few small, intimate accommodations. We have searched out as many as possible. We strongly advise you to investigate the guest house alternative, which can provide you with anything from a penthouse in New York to your own quiet quarters with a private entrance in the suburbs. See our RSO listings at the back of the book.

Farms

Many B&Bs are located in a rural environment, some on working farms. We have provided a partial list of farm vacation experiences. What a restorative for the city-weary. They can make a great family vacation—just be sure to keep a close eye on the kids around farm equipment.

Bathrooms

Though shared baths are the norm in Europe, this is sometimes a touchy subject in the U.S.A. We list the number of private baths available directly next to the number of rooms. Bear in mind that those inns with shared baths generally have more than one.

Manners

Please keep in mind when you go to an inn that innkeeping is a very hard job. It is amazing that innkeepers manage to maintain such a thoroughly cheerful and delightful presence despite long hours. Do feel free to ask your innkeepers for help or suggestions, but please don't expect them to be your personal servant. You may have to carry your own bags.

When in accommodations with shared baths, be sure to straighten the bathroom as a courtesy to your fellow guests. If you come in late, please do so on tiptoe, mindful of the other patrons visiting the inn for a little R&R.

Special Offers

Many of our featured inns wish to make our readers special offers—discounts, bonuses, etc., which appear at the end of the inns' listing. To redeem the special offer be sure to confirm its availability—some are limited ("ltd.")—when you reserve your room and then you must present the Guide when you check in. And enjoy! with our compliments.

Sample Bed & Breakfast Listing

Price and included meals
Numbers of rooms and private baths
Credit cards accepted
Name of inn — Travel agent commission •
Street address and zip code — Limitations:
Phone number — Children (C), Pets (P)
Name of innkeeper — Smoking (S), Handicapped Access (H)
Dates of operation — Foreign languages spoken

Name of city or town — Extra charge for breakfast

ANYPLACE ——————————————————————————

Any Bed & Breakfast	$$ B&B	Full breakfast ($)
Any Street, ZIP code	8 rooms, 6 pb	Lunch, dinner
555-555-5555	Visa, MC •	sitting room
Tom & Jane Innkeeper	C-12+ /S-ltd/P-no/H-ltd	library, bicycles
All year	French, Spanish	antiques

*Large Victorian country house in historic village. Hiking, swimming and golf nearby. Old-fashioned comfort with modern conveniences. **Third night 50% off.***

Description given by the innkeeper about the original characteristics of his establishment

Meals and drinks — Special offer
Amenities

6 How to Use this Guide

Ejemplo de una entrada para las posadas con cama & desayuno

Ciudad ó pueblo nombre

Nombre de la posada
Dirección
Teléfono
Fechas de temporada

Precio del alojamiento
Qué comidas van incluídas
Número de cuartos y número de cuartos
  con baño privado
Tarjetas de crédito aceptables
Agente de viaje comisión •
Limitaciones:
  niños (C); animales domésticos (P);
  prohibido fumar (S); entradas para
  minusválidos (H)
Se habla idiomas extranjeros

Comidas y bebidas

Entretenimientos

ANYPLACE ——————————————————————————

Any Bed & Breakfast $$ B&B Full breakfast ($)
Any Street, ZIP code 8 rooms, 6 pb Lunch, dinner
555-555-5555 Visa, MC • sitting room
Tom & Jane Innkeeper C-12+ /S-ltd/P-no/H-ltd library, bicycles
All year French, Spanish antiques

Large Victorian country house in historic village. Hiking, swimming and golf nearby. Old-fashioned comfort with modern conveniences. ***Third night 50% off.***

Descripción proporcionada por el dueño de
la posada sobre las características
especiales y originales de establecimiento

Oferta especial

Mode d'emploi

Nom de ville

Prix des chambres Repas
  inclus ou non
Nombre de chambres et
  chambres avec salle de bain
  privées
Cartes de crédit acceptées

Repas, boissons possibles

Commodités

ANYPLACE ——————————————————————————

Any Bed & Breakfast $$ B&B Full breakfast ($)
Any Street, ZIP code 8 rooms, 6 pb Lunch, dinner
555-555-5555 Visa, MC • sitting room
Tom & Jane Innkeeper C-12+ /S-ltd/P-no/H-ltd library, bicycles
All year French, Spanish antiques

Large Victorian country house in historic village. Hiking, swimming and golf nearby. Old-fashioned comfort with modern conveniences.

Nom de l'auberge
Addresse
Téléphone
Dates d'ouverture s'il n'y
  a pas de dates ouvert
  toute l'année

Restrictions—
  Enfants (C); Animaux (P);
  Fumeurs (S); Handicappés (H)
On parle les langues étrangères

L'aubergiste décrit ce qui rend
son auberge unique

Erläuterung der Eintragungen der Unterkunfsstätte

Preis für die Unterkunft, und
welche Mahlzeiten im Preis
Name der Stadt oder　　einbegriffen sind
　Ortschaft　　　　Reisebüro-Kommission ●
　　　　　　　Anzahl der Zimmer, und wieviel mit
　Name der Unterkunft　eigenem
　Adresse　　　　Badezimmer (=pb)
　Telefon-Nummer　Beschränkungen in Bezug auf
　Zu welcher　　　Kinder, Haustiere, Rauchen,　Was für ein Frühstück?
　　Jahreszeit offen?　oder für Behinderte geeignet　Andere Mahlzeiten und Bars
　　　　　　　(yes=ja; ltd=beschränkt;
　　　　　　　no=nicht zugelassen)　　　Was gibt's sonst noch?
　　　　　　　Man spricht Fremdsprachen

ANYPLACE

Any Bed & Breakfast　　$$ B&B　　　　Full breakfast ($)
Any Street, ZIP code　　8 rooms, 6 pb　　Lunch, dinner
555-555-5555　　　　Visa, MC ●　　　sitting room
Tom & Jane Innkeeper　C-12+ /S-ltd/P-no/H-ltd　library, bicycles
All year　　　　　French, Spanish　antiques

Large Victorian country house in historic village. Hiking, swimming and golf nearby.
Old-fashioned comfort with modern conveniences.

Beschreibung des Gastwirts, was an
diesem Gästehaus einmalig oder
besonders bemerkenswert ist

旅館名
住所
電話番号
利用期間。　　　　　朝食のタイプ
　　　　　　　　　その他の設備
都市又は町の名　　　　昼食、夕食、アルコールのサービス

ANYPLACE

Any Bed & Breakfast　　$$ B&B　　　　Full breakfast ($)
Any Street, ZIP code　　8 rooms, 6 pb　　Lunch, dinner
555-555-5555　　　　Visa, MC ●　　　sitting room
Tom & Jane Innkeeper　C-12+ /S-ltd/P-no/H-ltd　library, bicycles
All year　　　　　French, Spanish　antiques

Large Victorian country house in historic village. Hiking, swimming and golf nearby.
Old-fashioned comfort with modern conveniences.

Alabama

FLORENCE

River Park B&B
Route 7, Box 123G, 35630
205-757-8667
Edith & Buddy Meeks
All year

1 room, 1 pb
Rated, •
C-ltd/S-ltd/P-no/H-no

Continental plus
Snacks
Comp. wine
sitting room
decks overlooking river

New contemporary home, professionally designed & decorated, on Tennessee River. Enjoy decks, porches, swing hammocks. Watch pleasure barge cruisers. Near Natchez Trace.

MENTONE

Mentone Inn B&B
P.O. Box 284, 35984
Hwy 117
205-634-4836
Amelia Kirk
End April–end October

$$ B&B
15 rooms, 15 pb
Rated, •
C-ltd/S-no/P-no/H-no

Full breakfast
Afternoon tea
Catering, sitting room
golf, hike, trail rides
video, spa, sun deck

*Country mountain hideaway, antiques. Relax. Near shops, restaurants. Fly into Ft. Payne airport. On Alabama Historical Register. **3rd night 50% off***

MONTGOMERY

Red Bluff Cottage
P.O. Box 1026, 36101
551 Clay St., 36104
205-264-0056 FAX:262-1872
Mark & Anne Waldo
All year

$$ B&B
4 rooms, 4 pb
Visa, MC, *Rated*, •
C-yes/S-no/P-no/H-no

Full breakfast
Deep porches
gazebo, gardens

Two-story raised cottage in historic district. Panoramic view of river plain and state capitol. Family antiques, gazebo and gardens. Within blocks of I65 & I85

ORANGE BEACH

Original Romar House B&B
23500 Perdido Beach Blv, 36561
205-981-6156 800-487-6627
Burke & Roxanne Chance
All year

$$$ B&B
6 rooms, 6 pb
Visa, MC, •
C-yes/S-no/P-no/H-no

Full breakfast
Comp. wine and cheese
Bar service, library
sitting room, hot tubs
two-seater bicycles

Quiet ambiance, comfort, quaint surrounding, friendly service and white sandy beaches for romantic weekends. Restaurants, golf, sailing, fishing discounts.

TALLADEGA

Historic Oakwood B&B
715 E. North St., 35160
205-362-0662
Al & Naomi Kline
All year

$$ B&B
4 rooms, 2 pb
Rated
C-ltd/S-no/P-no/H-no

Full breakfast
TV room
badminton, horseshoes
sitting room

Oakwood, commissioned in 1847, is on the National Historic Register and furnished with many heirloom antiques. A heart southern breakfast is served.

More Inns . . .

Noble-McCaa-Butler House, 1025 Fairmont, Anniston, 36201, 205-236-1791
Victoria, 1604 Quintard Ave., Anniston, 36201, 205-236-0503
Stamps Inn, 100 First Ave. N.E., Arab, 35016, 205-586-7038
Citronella B&B Inn, 19055 S. Main St., Citronelle, 36522, 205-866-2849

Dancy-Polk House, 901 Railroad St., Decatur, 35601, 205-353-3579
Hearts and Treasures, 911 Seventh Ave.,S.E., Decatur, 35601, 205-353-9562
St. Mary's B&B, 206 Rivers Ave., Eufaula, 36027, 205-687-7195
Kirkwood, 111 Kirkwood Dr., Eutaw, 35462, 205-372-9009
Away At The Bay, 557 North Mobile St., Fairhope, 36532, 000-928-9725
Barons on the Bay Inn, 701 S. Mobile Ave., Fairhope, 36532, 205-928-8000
Doc & Dawn's Garden B&B, 314 De La Mare Ave., Fairhope, 36532, 000-928-0253
Marcella's Tea Room & Inn, 114 Fairhope Ave., Fairhope, 36532, 000-928-9212
Mershon Court B&B Inn, 203 Fairhope Ave., Fairhope, 36532, 205-928-7398
Rutherford Johnson House, P.O. Box 202, Main St., Franklin, 36444, 205-282-4423
Blue Shadows B&B, Box 432, RR2, Greensboro, 36744, 205-624-3637
Wandlers Inn B&B, 101 Shawnee Dr. N.W., Huntsville, 35806, 205-895-0847
Hill-Ware Dowdell Mansion, Lafayette, 205-864-7861
B&B Birmingham, RR 2, Box 275, Leeds, 35094, 205-699-9841
Country Sunshine, Rte 2, Box 275, Leeds, 35094,
Madaperca Inn, HC 68, Box 20, Mentone, 35984, 205-634-4792
Malaga Inn, 359 Church St., Mobile, 36602, 205-438-4701
Colonel's Rest-East Fork, 11091 Atlanta Hwy., Montgomery, 36117, 000-279-0380
Plantation House, The, 752 Loder St., Prattville, 36067, 000-316-0442
Brunton House, 112 College Ave., Scottsboro, 35768, 205-259-1298
Grace Hall, 506 Lauderdale St., Selma, 36701, 205-875-5744
Veranda, 416 Cherry St., Talladega, 35160, 000-362-0548

Alaska

ANCHORAGE

Glacier Bear B&B	$$ B&B	Continental plus
4814 Malibu Rd., 99517	5 rooms, 2 pb	Snacks
907-243-8818 FAX:248-4532	Visa, MC, •	Hiking & biking trails
Linda & Daniel Truesdell	C-ltd/S-ltd/P-no/H-no	restaurants nearby
All year		sitting room

First class accommodations at reasonable rates. Our location; 1.2 mi. from airport, 3 miles to downtown. Public transportation. **3rd night 50% off.**

Green Bough Inn, The	$ B&B	Continental plus
3832 Young St., 99508	3 rooms	Sitting room
907-562-4636	•	TV, radio, piano
Phyllis & Jerry Jost	C-yes/S-no/P-ltd/H-no	outdoor deck
All year		

Anchorage's oldest independent B&B, located midtown—close to everything. Comfortable, relaxed living. Mountain view. Your hosts are 20-year Alaskans. **2nd. night free, ltd.**

Lynn's Pine Point B&B	$$$ B&B	Full breakfast
3333 Creekside Dr., 99504	2 rooms, 2 pb	Comp. wine, snacks
907-333-2244	Visa, MC, *Rated*, •	Sitting room
Lynnette Stouff	C-yes/S-no/P-no/H-yes	VCR with 500 movies
All year		gazebo, laundry

Lovely cedar retreat with all the comforts of home. Queen beds, private baths, VCRs. Complimentary cocktails and hors d'oeuvres. Views of mountain. Tour planning.

Walkabout Town B&B	$$ B&B	Full breakfast
1610 "E" St., 99501	3 rooms	Deck, cable TV
907-279-2918	•	freezer, free laundry
Sandra & Terry Stimson	C-yes/S-no/P-no/H-no	parking
April—October		

Downtown convenience with beautiful park and coastal trail. Hearty Alaskan breakfast of sourdough waffles, reindeer sausage. **Reduced rate after 3 days.**

10 Alaska

FAIRBANKS

Alaska's 7 Gables B&B
P.O. Box 80488, 99708
4312 Birch Ln.
907-479-0751 FAX:479-2229
Paul & Leicha Welton
All year

$$ B&B
11 rooms, 6 pb
Visa, MC, *Rated*, •
C-yes/S-ltd/P-ask/H-yes
Spanish, German

Full gourmet breakfast
Comp. refreshments
Sitting room, library
Cable TV, phone in room
bikes, jacuzzis, canoes

Spacious Tudor estate with floral solarium entrance and waterfall. Each room follows a stained glass icon theme. 4 apartments, conference/reception room. Excellent location.

GUSTAVUS

Glacier Bay Country Inn
P.O. Box 5, 99826
Mile 1 Tong Rd.
907-697-2288 FAX:697-2289
Al & Annie Unrein
All year

$$$ AP
8 rooms, 7 pb
Rated, •
C-yes/S-no/P-no/H-no

Full breakfast
All meals included
Library, sitting room
bicycles, hiking
Glacier Bay yacht tours

Idyllic homestead blends country living w/Alaskan wilderness. Yacht tours of Glacier Bay. A fisherman's dream, traveler's paradise, professional's retreat. **$5 off cookbook**

Gustavus Inn
P.O. Box 60, 99826
1 mi. Gustavus Rd.
907-697-2254 FAX:697-2291
JoAnn & David Lesh
May 1-September 15

$$$ AP
13 rooms
Rated, •
C-yes/S-ltd/P-ltd/H-yes
French, Spanish

Full breakfast
Lunch & dinner included
Bar, tea, bicycles
fishing poles
courtesy van

Original homestead, completely updated 1993. Garden & ocean harvest family-style dining. Glacier Bay boat tours, bicycling, charter & stream fishing, kayaking, whalewatching.

A Puffin's B&B
P.O. Box 3, 99826
907-697-2260 FAX:697-2258
Sandy & Chuck Schroth
Mid-April—September

$$ B&B
3 rooms, 3 pb
Visa, MC, AmEx, *Rated*,
•
C-yes/S-yes/P-yes/H-yes

Full breakfast
Dinner, coffee, tea
Separate lodge, bicycles
antiques, picnic area
travel service

Modern cabins with Alaskan art, quiet country atmosphere, hearty homestead breakfast; fishing, wildlife; photography-charters, Glacier Bay tours. **Free dessert at the cafe**

HOMER

Home B&B/Seekins
P.O. Box 1264, 99603
2 mi. E. Hilli Roca Rd.
907-235-8996 FAX:235-2625
Floyd & Gert Seekins
All year

$$ B&B
9 rooms, 7 pb
Visa, MC, •
C-yes/S-ltd/P-no/H-ltd

Continental plus
Kitchen facilities
Snacks, sitting room
outdoor sauna, BBQ grill
tours arranged, TV

Fantastic view of bay, mountains & glaciers. Clean, quiet Alaskan hospitality. Cabin & guest houses. Moose wander into the yard. Referrals for B&B. Salmon & halibut fishing.

Magic Canyon Ranch
40015 Waterman Rd., 99603
907-235-6077
Davis & Betsy Webb
All year

$$ B&B
4 rooms, 1 pb
Rated, •
C-yes/S-ltd/P-no/H-no

Full breakfast
Sundeck, telescope
stereo, llamas, Model T
nature trails, hot tub

Superb views of Kachemak Bay & glaciers in country seclusion, only 5 miles from Homer. Elegant rooms with Alaskan antiques & quilts. Farm-fresh breakfasts. Naturalist owner.

JUNEAU

Pearson's Pond Luxury Inn
4541 Sawa Circle, 99801
907-789-3772
Steve & Diane Pearson
All year

$$ B&B
3 rooms, 1 pb
Most CC, *Rated*, •
C-ltd/S-no/P-no/H-ltd

Full breakfast
Afternoon tea, snacks
Comp. wine for occasions
sitting room, library
bicycles, hot tubs

Alaska charm at its best. Capture majestic glaciers as background to hot tub on pond. Suite retreat for privacy & quality. Ski packages. **Free travel/booking service.**

SKAGWAY

Skagway Inn B&B
P.O. Box 500, 99840
Broadway and 7th.
907-983-2289
Suzanne Mullen
All year

$ B&B
14 rooms
Visa, MC
C-yes/S-ltd/P-no/H-yes

Continental plus
Piano
sitting room

Operated as an inn since the 1920s—all rooms are decorated in period style. Right in historic district.

WASILLA

Yukon Don's B&B Inn
HC 31 5086, 2221 Macabon
Circle, 99654
907-376-7472
Art/Diane Mongeau & Children
All year

$$ B&B
6 rooms
Rated, •
C-yes/S-no/P-yes/H-no

Continental plus
Restaurant nearby
Sitting room
library
exercise room

Extraordinary view; 30-year Alaskan resident; great collection of Alaskana; each room has unique Alaskan decor. "One of the Top 50 Inns in America"—Inn Times, July 1991

More Inns . . .

42nd Avenue Annex, 410 W. 42nd Ave., Anchorage, 99503, 907-561-8895
A Log Home B&B, 2440 Sprucewood St., Anchorage, 99508, 907-276-8527
Adams House B&B, 700 W. 21st, #A, Anchorage, 99508, 907-274-1944
Alaskan Comfort, 2182 Stanford Dr., Anchorage, 99508, 907-258-7500
Alaskan Frontier Gardens, 1011 E. Tudor Rd. #160, Anchorage, 99503, 907-345-6556
All The Comforts of Home, 12531 Turk's Turn St., Anchorage, 99516, 907-345-4279
Anchorage Eagle Nest Hotel, 4110 Spenard Rd. (BB), Anchorage, 99503, 907-243-3433
Chugach View B&B, 1639 Sunrise Dr., Anchorage, 99508, 907-279-8824
Country Garden, 8210 Frank St., Anchorage, 99518, 907-344-0636
Country Style B&B, P.O. Box 220986, Anchorage, 99522, 907-243-6746
Darbyshire House B&B, 528 "N" St., Anchorage, 99501, 907-279-0703
Denali Cabins Inc., 200 W. 34th. Ave. #362, Anchorage, 99503, 907-683-2643
Fay's B&B, P.O. Box 2378, Anchorage, 99510, 907-243-0139
Grandview Gardens B&B, 1579 Sunrise Dr., Anchorage, 99508, 907-277-7378
Hillcrest Haven, 1455 Hillcrest Dr., Anchorage, 99503, 907-274-3086
Pilot's Row B&B, 217 East 11th Ave., Anchorage, 99501, 907-274-3305
Wright's Bed & Breakfast, 1411 Oxford, Anchorage, 99503, 907-561-1990
Favorite Bay Inn, P.O. Box 101, Angoon, 99820, 907-788-3123
Whaler's Cove Lodge, Box 101-VP, Angoon, 99820, 907-788-3123
Bentley's Porterhouse B&B, 62 First Ave. Box 529, Bethel, 99559,
Wilson's Hotel, P.O. Box 969, Bethel, 99559, 907-543-3841
Jeanie's on Big Lake, Box 520598, Big Lake, 99652,
Adventures Unlimited Lodge, Box 89-RD, Cantwell, 99729,
Arctic Circle Hot Springs, P.O. Box 69, Central, 99730, 907-520-5113
Reed's End Lounge, Box 5629, Mile 42, Chiniak, 99615,
Peters Creek Inn, P.O. Box 671487, Chugiak, 99576, 907-688-2776
Reluctant Fisherman Inn, Box 150, Cordova, 99574, 907-424-3272
North Face Lodge, Denali National Park, Denali, 99755,
Camp Denali, Box 67 - RD, Denali National Park, 99755, 907-683-2290
Carlo Creek Lodge, Box 890, Denali National Park, 99755, 907-683-2512
Denali Crow's Nest, P.O. Box 700, Denali National Park, 99756, 907-683-2321
Kantishna Roadhouse, Box 397-TD, Denali National Park, 99755, 907-345-1160
Fairbanks B&B, Box 74573, Fairbank, 99707,
AAA Care B&B, 557 Fairbanks St., Fairbanks, 99709, 907-479-2447
B&B at Bev & John's, Box 75269, Fairbanks, 99707, 907-456-7351
Beaver Bend B&B, 231 Iditarod, Fairbanks, 99701, 907-452-3240
Blue Goose B&B, The, 4466 Dartmouth, Fairbanks, 99709, 907-479-6973

Borealis Hotel, 700 Fairbanks St., Fairbanks, 99709,
Goldstream B&B, P.O. Box 80090, Fairbanks, 99708, 907-455-6550
Iniakeek Lake Lodge, Box 80424, Fairbanks, 99701, 907-479-6354
Sophie Station Hotel, 1717 University Ave., Fairbanks, 99701, 907-479-3650
Summit Lake Lodge, P.O. Box 1955, Fairbanks, 99707, 907-822-3969
Tolovan B&B, 4538 Tolovan, Fairbanks, 99701, 907-479-6004
Wild Iris Inn, P.O. Box 73246, Fairbanks, 99707, 907-479-4062
Chistochina Trading Post, Mile 32, Tok/Slann Hwy, Gakona, 99586, 907-822-3366
Bear Creek Camp/Youth Hstl, Box 1158, Haines, 99827, 907-766-2259
Cache Inn Lodge, Box 441-VP, Haines, 99827, 907-766-2910
Fort Seward B&B, House #1, Box 5, Haines, 99827, 907-766-2856
Jotel Halsingland, P.O. Box 1589, Haines, 99827, 907-766-2000
Summer Inn B&B, P.O. Box 1198, Haines, 99827, 907-766-2970
Quiet Place Lodge, Box 6474, Halibut Cove, 99603, 907-296-2212
Brass Ring B&B, 987 Hillfair Court, Homer, 99603,
Driftwood Inn, 135 W. Bunnell Ave., Homer, 99603, 907-235-8019
Halibut Cove Cabins, P.O. Box 1990, Homer, 99603, 907-296-2214
JP B&B, Box 2256, Homer, 99603,
Kachemak Bay Wilderness, Box 956-VP, Homer, 99603, 907-235-8910
Lakewood Inn, 984 Ocean Dr., #1, Homer, 99608, 907-235-6144
Sadie Cove Wilderness Ldge, Box 2265-VP, Homer, 99603, 907-235-7766
Seaside Farm, HCR 58335 East End Rd., Homer, 99603,
Tutka Bay Lodge, Box 960 F, Homer, 99603, 907-235-3905
Wild Rose B&B, Box 665, Homer, 99603, 907-235-8780
Willard's Moose Lodge, SRA Box 28, Homer, 99603, 907-235-8830
Admiralty Inn, 9040 Glacier Hwy., Juneau, 99801, 907-789-3263
Alaskan Hotel, 167 S. Franklin, Juneau, 99801, 800-327-9347
B&B Inn - Juneau, 1802 Old Glacier Hwy, Juneau, 99801, 907-463-5855
Dawson's B&B, 1941 Glacier Hwy, Juneau, 99801, 907-586-9708
Juneau Hostel, 614 Harris St., Juneau, 99801, 907-586-9559
Lost Chord, The, 2200 Fritz Cove Rd., Juneau, 99801,
Louie's Place-Elfin Cove, P.O. Box 020704, Juneau, 99802, 907-586-2032
Mullins House, 526 Seward St., Juneau, 99801, 907-586-2959
Pearson's Pond, 4541 Sawa Circle, Juneau, 99801, 907-789-3772
Silver Bow Inn, 120 Second St., Juneau, 99801, 907-586-4146
Tenakee Inn, 167 S. Franklin, Juneau, 99801, 907-586-1000
Daniels Lake Lodge B&B, Box 2939 - BW, Kenali, 99611, 907-776-5578
Hidden Inlet Lodge, Box 3047-VP, Ketchikan, 99901, 907-225-4656
North Tongas, Box 684, Ketchikan, 99828,
Tongass View B&B, 415 Front St., Ketchikan, 99901,
Waterfall Resort, P.O. Box 6440, Ketchikan, 99901, 800-544-5125
Fireweed Lodge, Box 116-VP, Klawock, 99925, 907-755-2930
Kalsin Inn Ranch, Box 1696 VP, Kodiak, 99615,
Evergreen Lodge, HC 1 Box 1709 GennAllen, Lake Louise, 99588, 907-822-3250
Manley Lodge, 100 Landing Rd.-VP, Manley Hot Springs, 99756, 907-672-3161
Aurora House B&B, 562 E. 3rd., Nome, 99762, 907-443-2100
Oceanview Manor B&B, Box 65, 490 Front St., Nome, 99762, 907-443-2133
Hatcher Pass Lodge, Box 2655-BB, Palmer, 99645, 907-745-5897
Pollens B&B, HC01, Box 60052, Palmer, 99645,
Sheep Mountain Lodge, Star Route C, Box 4890, Palmer, 99645, 907-745-5121
Weathervane House, SRD 9589x, Palmer, 99645, 907-745-5168
Paxson Lodge, 1185 TD Richardson Hwy, Paxson, 99737, 907-822-3330
Beachcomber Inn, Box 1027, Petersburg, 99833, 907-772-3888
Heger Haus B&B, P.O. Box 485, Petersburg, 99833, 907-772-4877
Little Norway Inn B&B, Box 192-BW, Petersburg, 99833,
Scandia House, P.O. Box 689, Petersburg, 99833, 907-772-4281
Afognak Wilderness Lodge, Seal Bay, 99697, 907-486-6442
High Tide Originals, Main St., Seldonia, 99663, 907-234-7850
Annie McKenzie's Boardwalk, P.O. Box 72, Seldovia, 99663, 907-234-7816
Seldovia Rowing Club Inn, P.O. Box 41, Bay St., Seldovia, 99663, 907-234-7614
Swiss Chalet B&B, P.O. Box 1734, Seward, 99664, 907-224-3939
Helga's B&B, Box 1885, Sitka, 99835,
Karras B&B, 230 Kogwanton St., Sitka, 99835, 907-747-3978
Sitka Youth Hostel, P.O. Box 2645, Sitka, 99835, 907-747-6332
Golden North Hotel, P.O. Box 431, Skagway, 99840, 907-983-2294
Irene's Inn, Box 538-VP, Skagway, 99840, 907-983-2520
Mary's Bed & Breakfast, Box 72, Skagway, 99840, 907-983-2875
Sgt. Preston's Lodge, P.O. Box 538, Skagway, 99840,
Wind Valley Lodge, Box 354-VP, Skagway, 99840, 907-983-2236
Skwentna Roadhouse, 100 Happiness Ln., Skwentna, 99667,
Internat'l Riverside Inn, Box 910-VP, Soldotna, 99669, 907-262-4451
Soldotna B&B Inn, 399 Lover's Ln., Soldotna, 99669, 907-262-4779
Fairview Inn, P.O. Box 379-VP, Talkeetna, 99676, 907-733-2423
River Beauty B&B, P.O. Box 525, Talkeetna, 99676, 907-733-2741
Twister Creek Union, Talkeetan Span, Talkeetna, 99676, 907-258-1717
Stage Stop B&B, The, P.O. Box 69, Tok, 99780, 907-883-5338
Reflection Pond B&B, Mile 11 Petersville Rd., Trapper Creek, 99683, 907-733-2457
Trapper Creek B&B, P.O. Box 13068, Trapper Creek, 99683, 907-733-2220
B&B—Valdez, Box 442, Valdez, 99686, 907-835-4211
Garden House, The, Box 2017, Valdez, 99686,
Johnson House, Box 364, Valdez, 99686,
Lake House, P.O. Box 1499, Valdez, 99686, 907-835-4752

Rainbow Lodge, Mile 4, Richardson Hwy., Valdez, 99686,
Totem Inn, P.O. Box 648 BB, Valdez, 99686, 907-835-4443
1260 Inn, Mile 1260 AK Hwy, Via Tok, 99780, 907-778-2205
Mat-Su Resort, Bogard Rd. - Mile 1.3, Wasilla, 99687, 907-376-3228
Sportman's Inn, Box 698-VP, Whittier, 99693,
Willow Trading Post, Willow Station Rd., Willow, 99688,
Clarke B&B, Box 1020, Wrangell, 99686, 907-874-2125 0
Yes Bay Lodge, Yes Bay, 99950, 907-247-1575

Arizona

AJO

Guest House Inn	$$ B&B	Full breakfast
3 Guest House Rd., 85321	4 rooms, 4 pb	Sitting room, library
602-387-6133	Most CC, *Rated*, •	hiking trails
Norma & Mike Walker	C-yes/S-no/P-no/H-no	bird-watching
All year	Spanish, French	

Sonoran Desert retreat with excellent hiking, bird-watching, relaxation and spectacular desert vistas. Near Organ Pipe Cactus National Monument. Sumptuous breakfasts.

Mine Managers House B&B	$$ B&B	Full breakfast
One Greenway Rd., 85321	5 rooms, 5 pb	Snacks, tea, ice cream
602-387-6505 FAX:387-6508	Visa, MC, *Rated*, •	Sitting room, library
Jean & Micheline Fournier	C-ltd/S-ltd/P-no/H-yes	tennis courts, hot tubs
All year		coin laundry, gift shop

Copper Mine Manager's Hilltop Mansion, circa 1919, overlooks town and Open Pit Mine. Near Organ Pipe National Monument. Generous Southwestern hospitality.

BISBEE

Bisbee Grand Hotel B&B Inn	$ B&B	Full breakfast
P.O. Box 825, 85603	11 rooms, 7 pb	Bar service
61 Main St	Most CC, *Rated*, •	Sitting room, library
602-432-5900 800-421-1909	C-ltd/S-ltd/P-no/H-no	
Bill Thomas & Gail Waid		
All year		

Romantic Victorian decor, family heirlooms, turn-of-the-century rooming house. Old Western saloon, downtown historic Bisbee. Escape the modern world, relax.

Greenway House, The	$$$ B&B	Continental plus
401 Cole Ave., 85603	8 rooms, 8 pb	Comp. wine, snacks
602-432-7170 800-253-3325	Visa, MC, *Rated*	Sitting room, library
Joy O'Clock, Dr. George Knox	C-ltd/S-ltd/P-no/H-yes	billiard room, A/C
All year		game room, barbecues

Picturesque copper mining town in mile-high setting. Luxury accommodations in 1906 mansion. Craftsman architecture, furnished with antiques.

FLAGSTAFF

Birch Tree Inn
824 W. Birch Ave., 86001
602-774-1042
The Pettingers, The Znetkos
All year

$$ B&B
5 rooms, 3 pb
Visa, MC, *Rated*, •
C-ltd/S-no/P-no/H-no

Full breakfast
Afternoon tea, snacks
Sitting room, piano
pool table, bicycles
tennis court nearby

Comfortable, country charm; savory, down-home, hearty breakfasts. A four season retreat in the magnificent beauty of Northern Arizona.

GOLD CANYON

Sinelli's B&B
5605 South Sage Way, 85219
602-983-3650
Carl & Patricia Sinelli
All year

$ B&B
3 rooms, 1 pb
•
C-yes/S-yes/P-no/H-no

Continental plus wkdays
Full breakfast wkends
Lunch & dinner by req.
snacks, comp. wine
sitting room

Two bedrm. apt., completely furnished, short or long stays. Casual southwest living in foot-hills of the Superstition Mtns. Outdoor recreation abundant. **Free bottle of wine**

ORACLE

Villa Cardinale
P.O. Box 649, 85623
1315 W. Oracle Ranch Rd.
602-896-2516
Judy & Ron Schritt
All year

$$ B&B
4 rooms, 4 pb
Rated, •
C-ltd/S-ltd/P-ltd/H-no
German

Full breakfast
Snacks
Courtyard w/fountain
360 degree views
high desert, hiking

High country hacienda under clear, starry skies. Cozy fireplaces in every room. Near Tucson: Biosphere II, Aravaipa Canyon. Birdwatching, hiking. **10% off on 2+ nights**

PHOENIX

Maricopa Manor
P.O. Box 7186, 85011
15 W. Pasadena Ave.
602-274-6302
Mary Ellen, Paul Kelley
All year

$$ B&B
5 rooms, 5 pb
Rated, •
C-yes/S-yes/H-yes

Continental plus
Comp. wine
Sitting room
library
hot tubs

Old World charm, elegant urban setting. Central and Camelback, close to everything. Luxury suites, secluded, gardens, patios, and palm trees.

Westways "Private" Resort
P.O. Box 41624, 85080
602-582-3868
Darrell Trapp
All year

$$ B&B
6 rooms, 6 pb
Visa, MC, Disc, *Rated*, •
C-ltd/S-yes/P-no/H-ltd
French, Spanish

Full breakfast-Limited
Welcome refreshment
Library, sitting room
hot tub, tennis courts
swimming pool, bicycles

Deluxe small oasis resort w/Southwest contemporary decor. Golf, tennis, swimming, biking & exercise equipment available. Beautiful desert landscape. **Extended stays discount. Ask**.

PRESCOTT

Lynx Creek Farm B&B
P.O. Box 4301, 86302
602-778-9573
Greg & Wendy Temple
All year

$$$ B&B
6 rooms, 6 pb
Visa, MC, •
C-yes/S-ltd/P-yes/H-no
Spanish

Full breakfast
Comp. wine, appetizers
Bicycles, pool, croquet
hot tubs, volleyball
wood stoves, romance

Charming retreat on 25-acre apple farm. Log cabin avail. Spacious antique-filled suites. Beautiful views & climate. Gourmet breakfasts include our own fruits and vegetables.

PRESCOTT

Prescott Pines Inn B&B
901 White Spar Rd., Hwy 89
South, 86303
602-445-7270 800-541-5374
Jean & Mike
All year. FAX:778-3665

$$ EP
13 rooms, 13 pb
Visa, MC, *Rated*
C-ltd/P-no/H-ltd
some French & German

Full breakfast $4
Kitchenettes, gardens
Sitting room, library
porches, ceiling fans
games, patio with BBQ

Country-Victorian rooms in 4 guesthouses, including one chalet for up to 8 people, all under Ponderosa pines near National Forest. Gourmet breakfasts. Ideal 4-season climate.

SEDONA

"A Touch of Sedona" B&B
595 Jordan Rd., 86339
602-282-6462
Dick & Doris Stevenson
All year

$$$ B&B
4 rooms, 4 pb
Visa, MC, *Rated*
C-yes/S-ltd/P-no/H-no

Full breakfast
Afternoon tea
Snacks

Eclectic elegance...furnished with stained-glass lamps, antiques, but with a mix of contemporary. Just walking distance to uptown. Homemade breads.

B&B at Saddle Rock Ranch
P.O. Box 10095, 86339
255 Rock Ridge Dr.
602-282-7640
Fran & Dan Bruno
All year

$$$ B&B
3 rooms, 3 pb
Rated
C-ltd/S-no/P-no/H-no
Spanish, French, Italian

Full Breakfast
Comp. wine, snacks
Sitting room, library
jacuzzi, pool, gardens
decks, hiking, wildlife

History. Romance. Elegance. Old West movie ranch. Antique-filled rooms feature native rock, adobe, timber beams, fireplaces. **Comp. jeep tour for two after a five night stay**

Briar Patch Inn
Star Route 3, Box 1002, Hwy
89A N., Oak Creek Cyn, 86336
602-282-2342
Jo Ann & Ike Olson
All year

$$$ B&B
15 rooms, 15 pb
Visa, MC, *Rated*, •
C-yes/S-ltd/P-no/H-ltd
German, French, Spanish

Full breakfast
Fireplaces, hiking
bird-watching, fishing
Classical music by creek

One of the most beautiful spots in Arizona! Cottages nestled on 8½ acres along lush banks of sparkling Oak Creek. Warm, generous hospitality. Masseuse on staff!

CasaLea Country Inn, A
P.O. Box 552, 86336
95 Portal Lane
602-282-2833
Lea Pace, Vincent Mollan
All year

$$ B&B
10 rooms, 10 pb
Rated, •
C-ltd/S-ltd/P-no/H-yes

Full breakfast
Dinner Fri. & Sat.
Aft. tea, snacks
sitting room, library
hot tubs, sauna

We feature Arizona's past: Sunken Kiva, Old West dining area, A CasaLea creek. Each guest room touches a moment of history. Massage fac. **Special discounts w/extended stay**

Cozy Cactus B&B
80 Canyon Circle Dr., 86336
602-284-0082 800-788-2082
Lynne & Bob Gillman
All year

$$$ B&B
5 rooms, 5 pb
Visa, MC, *Rated*, •
C-yes/S-ltd/P-no/H-yes
Some Italian, Sign

Full breakfast
Snacks
Library, bicycles
tennis, golf nearby
hiking nearby, sitt. rm.

Cozy home furnished with heirlooms, theatrical memorabilia, fireplaces. Patios border national forest and spectacular Red Rock views. Old-fashioned hospitality.

SEDONA ———

Garland's Oak Creek Lodge | $$$ MAP | Full breakfast
P.O. Box 152, 86339 | 16 rooms, 16 pb | Dinner included, bar
8067 N. Hwy 89A | Visa, MC, *Rated* | Comp. tea daily
602-282-3343 | C-yes/S-ltd/P-no/H-ltd | Sitting room, piano
Mary & Gary Garland | German | clay tennis court (fee)
End March–mid-November

Lovely historic lodge nestled in gorgeous red rock setting of Oak Creek Canyon. Rustic log cabins, excellent gourmet meals, friendly staff.

Graham B&B Inn | $$$ B&B | Full breakfast
P.O. Box 912, 86336 | 6 rooms, 6 pb | Afternoon refreshments
150 Canyon Circle Dr. | Visa, MC, *Rated* | Sitting room, games
602-284-1425 FAX:284-1627 | C-yes/S-no/P-no/H-no | Golf nearby
Roger & Carol Redenbaugh | | Hot tub & swimming pool
All year

Comfortable elegance; unmatched red rock views; fireplaces; jacuzzis. Choose Southwest, antique, art deco, contemporary or American heritage room decor. Mobil Four-Star.

Rose Tree Inn | $$$ EP | Kitchenettes
376 Cedar St., 86336 | 4 rooms, 4 pb | In-room coffee & tea
602-282-2065 | Visa, MC, *Rated*, • | Patios, library
Rachel M. Gillespie | C-yes/S-yes/P-no/H-no | courtyard, jacuzzi
All year | | bicycles

Sedona's "best-kept secret"! Quaint, quiet accommodations nestled in a gorgeous English garden environment within walking distance of "Old Town."

Slide Rock Cabins | $$$ B&B | Continental breakfast
Star Route 3, Box 1140, Hwy | 4 rooms, 4 pb | Easy access to the creek
89A/6 mi. N of Sedona, 86336 | Visa, MC | hosts pleased to advise
602-282-6900 | C-ltd/S-ask/P-no/H-ltd | you on local activities
Milena Pfeifer & Mike Smith | Slovenian

In spectacular Oak Creek Canyon. Cabins have full kitchen, firepl., jacuzzi, decks. Most have open lofts. Romantic getaways are Slide Rock Cabins' specialty! **7th night free.**

Slide Rock Lodge | $$ B&B | Continental breakfast
Star Route 3, Box 1141, 86336 | 24 rooms, 24 pb | Comp. coffee & pastry
Hwy 89A/6 mi N. of Sedona, | Visa, MC | Picnic area, BBQ grills
602-282-3531 | C-yes/S-ltd/P-no/H-no | fireplaces
Bogomir & Milena Pfeifer | Slovenian (Yugoslavia) | no TV or phones
All year

20 comfortable, clean, knotty pine paneled rooms, some with fireplaces. Advance reservations recommended. **Seventh night free.**

TOMBSTONE —————————————————————————————————————

Buford House B&B | $$ B&B | Full breakfast
P.O. Box 38, 85638 | 4 rooms, 1 pb | Afternoon tea, snacks
113 E. Safford St. | C-ltd/S-no/P-ltd/H-ltd | Sitting room, bicycles
602-457-3168 | | hot tub, piano
Jeanne & Chuck Hagel | | mystery wkends, ask
All year

An 1880 adobe in National Register of Historic Homes. Territorial style, porch & herb gardens. Antique furnishings & country hospitality. **3rd Night 40% Off**

TUCSON ———

Arizona Inn
2200 E. Elm St., 85719
602-325-1541 800-933-1093
Patty Doar
All year, FAX: 881-5830

$$ EP
83 rooms, 83 pb
Visa, MC, AmEx, *Rated*,
•
C-yes/S-yes/P-no/H-yes
Spanish, French, German

Full breakfast $, snacks
Restaurant, bar, lunch
Dinner, lounge
sitting room,library
tennis courts, htd pool

National Register of Historic Places, family owned & operated since 1930. Spanish Colonial Casitas w/individually decorated guest rooms. 1991 "Ten Best Country Inns."

———

Casa Alegre
316 E. Speedway, 85705
602-628-1800 FAX:792-1880
Phyllis Florek
All year

$$ B&B
4 rooms, 4 pb
Visa, MC, *Rated*, •
C-ltd/S-no/P-no/H-no

Full breakfast
Afternoon tea, snacks
Sitting room, library
swimming pool
public tennis courts

Beautiful 1915 Craftsman bungalow near University of AZ, metropolitan Tucson, golf & mountain & desert attractions. Scrumptious breakfast, poolside refreshments.

———

Lodge on the Desert, The
306 North Alvernon, 85711
602-325-3366 800-456-5634
Schuyler W. Lininger
All year

$ EP/B&B/MAP/AP
40 rooms, 40 pb
Visa, MC, AmEx, DC, CB, •
C-yes/S-yes/P-ask/H-yes
French

Continental
Restaurant, bar
All meals available
sitting room, library
swimming pool, games

A garden resort hotel established over fifty years ago, with the atmosphere of a Mexican ranch house. Relax! Lots of indoor & outdoor games. **2 for 1 dining rm, ltd**

———

Mariposa
940 N. Olsen Ave., 85719
602-322-9157
Maria Morgan
July/August closed

$$$ B&B
3 rooms, 3 pb
•
C-ltd/S-ltd/P-no/H-ltd

Full breakfast
Tennis court nearby
swimming pool
sitting room

After a busy day, relax by the pool of this classic Southwestern adobe. Complete privacy w/unpretentious elegance and serenity.

———

Peppertrees B&B Inn
724 E. University Blvd., 85719
602-622-7167 800-348-5763
Marjorie G. Martin
All year

$$$ B&B
9 rooms, 3 pb
Rated, •
C-ltd/S-no/P-no/H-no

Full gourmet breakfast
Picnic lunch to go
Afternoon tea
library, TV, VCR
walk to restaurants

Warm, friendly territorial home. Antiques; memorable gourmet breakfasts. Walk to U. of Arizona, downtown, shopping. 2-two bdrm guesthouses. **Homemade shortbread 3rd night**

———

La Posada del Valle Inn
1640 N. Campbell Ave., 85719
602-795-3840
Charles & Debbi Bryant
All year

$$$ B&B
5 rooms, 5 pb
Visa, MC, *Rated*, •
C-ltd/S-no/P-no/H-no
Spanish

Continental plus (wkdys)
Full breakfast (wkends)
Afternoon tea
library, sitting room
courtyard, patios

Elegant 1920s inn nestled in the heart of the city, offering gourmet breakfast, afternoon tea; catering available for special functions. Privileges at raquet & swim club.

TUCSON

El Presidio B&B Inn	$$$ B&B	Full elaborate breakfast
297 N. Main Ave., 85701	4 rooms, 4 pb	Afternoon tea, snacks
602-623-6151	*Rated*, •	Comp. wine, juice, soda
Patti & Jerry Toci	C-ltd/S-no/P-no/H-no	kitchenettes, phones, TV
All year except July		nearby health club

Historic Victorian adobe with Old-Mexico ambiance. Spacious suites open to large court-yards, gardens, fountains. Antique decor. Walk to sights. **7th night free weekdays**

Tucson Mountain Hideaway	$ B&B	Continental plus
3212 W. Holladay St., June's	3 rooms	Sitting room, piano
B&B, 85746	C-ltd/S-no/P-no/H-no	heated swimming pool
602-578-0857		art studio, exercise rm.
June Henderson		
All year		

Mountainside home with pool. Majestic towering mountains. Hiking in the desert. Sparkling city lights. Beautiful backyard & patio. Owner's artwork for sale. **7th night free**

More Inns . . .

Manager's House Inn, #1 Greenway Dr., Ajo, 85321, 602-387-6505
Bisbee Inn, The, Box 1855, Bisbee, 85603, 602-432-5131
Inn at Castle Rock, P.O. Box 161, Bisbee, 85603, 602-432-7195
Judge Ross Home, 605 Shattuck St., Bisbee, 85605,
Park Place B&B, 200 East Vista, Bisbee, 85603, 800-388-4388
Cone's Tourist Home, 2804 W. Warner Rd., Chandler, 85224, 602-839-0369
Cochise Hotel, Box 27, Cochise, 85606, 602-384-3156
Pumpkinshell Ranch, HC 66, Box 2100, Cornville, 86325, 602-634-4797
Arizona Mountain Inn, 685 Lake Mary Rd., Flagstaff, 86001, 602-774-8959
Cedar B&B, 425 W. Cedar, Flagstaff, 86001, 602-774-1636
Dierker House B&B, 423 W. Cherry, Flagstaff, 86001, 602-774-3249
Walking L Ranch, RR 4, Box 721B, Flagstaff, 86001, 602-779-2219
Villa Galleria B&B, 16650 E. Hawk Dr., Fountain Hills, 85268, 602-837-1400
Ramsey Canyon Inn, 85 Ramsey Canyon Rd., Hereford, 85615, 602-378-3010
Sun Catcher, The, 105 N. Avenida Ave., Javalina, 85748,
Bartram's Bed & Breakfast, Route 1, Box 1014, Lakeside, 85929,
Triangle L Ranch B&B, P.O. Box 900, Oracle, 85623, 602-896-2804
Villa Cardinale, P.O. Box 649, Oracle, 85603,
Grapevine Canyon Ranch, P.O. Box 302, Pearce, 85625, 602-826-3185
B&B in Arizona, 5995 E. Orange Blossom, Phoenix, 85018, 602-994-3759
Charlotte White & Assoc.s, P.O. Box 15828, Phoenix, 85060, 602-230-8668
Gerry's B&B, 5150 37th Ave, Phoenix, 85019, 602-973-2542
Benson's B&B, 4016 N. LaJolla Dr., Prescott, 86314, 602-772-8358
Hotel Vendome, 230 Cortez St., Prescott, 86301, 602-776-0900
Juniper Well Ranch, P.O. Box 10623, Prescott, 86304, 602-442-3451
Marks House Inn, The, 203 E. Union, Prescott, 86303, 602-778-4632
Victorian Inn of Prescott, 246 South Cortez St., Prescott, 86303, 602-778-2642
Azura East, 3703 N. 69th St., Scottsdale, 85251,
Casa de Mariposa, 6916 E. Mariposa, Scottsdale, 85251, 602-947-9704
Valley 'O the Sun B&B, P.O. Box 2214, Scottsdale, 85252, 602-941-1281
Cathedral Rock Lodge, SR 2, Box 836, Red Rock, Sedona, 86336, 602-282-7608
L'Auberge de Sedona Resort, P.O. Box B, Sedona, 86336, 602-282-7131
Lantern Light Inn B&B, 3085 W. Hwy 89A, Sedona, 86336, 602-282-3419
Leduc's B&B, 41 Arrow Dr., Sedona, 86336,
Bird In Hand B&B, 529 S. Meyer, Tucson, 85701,
Casa Suecia B&B, P.O. Box 36883, Ste 181, Tucson, 86704,
Casa Tierra, 11155 West Calle Pima, Tucson, 85743, 602-578-3058
Copper Bell B&B, 25 N. Westmoreland Ave., Tucson, 85745,
Florence A. Ejrup, 941 W. Calle Dadivosa, Tucson, 85704,
Hacienda del Sol Ranch, 5601 N Hacienda del Sol, Tucson, 85718, 602-299-1501
La Madera Ranch & Resort, 9061 E. Woodland Rd., Tucson, 85749, 602-749-2773
Myer's Blue Corn House, 4215 E. Kilmer, Tucson, 85711, 602-327-4663
Paz Entera B&B & Beyond, 7501 No. Wade Rd., Tucson, 85743, 800-356-9104
SunCatcher, 105 N. Avenida Javalina, Tucson, 85748, 800-835-8012
Tanque Verde Ranch, 14301 E. Speedway, Tucson, 85748, 602-296-6275
Tucson Old Pueblo, 4201 N. Saranac Dr., Tucson, 85718,
Kay El Bar Ranch, Box 2480, Wickenburg, 85358, 602-684-7593
Rancho De Los Caballeros, Box 1148, Wickenburg, 85358, 602-684-5484
Canyon Country Inn, 442 W. B. Williams Ave., Williams, 86046,

Arkansas

EUREKA SPRINGS

5 Ojo Inn B&B	$$ B&B	Full breakfast
5 Ojo St., 72632	10 rooms, 10 pb	Snacks
501-253-6734	Visa, MC, Disc., •	Library, hot tub, gazebo
Paula Kirby Adkins	C-ltd/S-ltd/P-no/H-ltd	jacuzzis, fireplaces
All year		fresh flowers, deck

Award winning restoration of Victorian home says "stay here and revive." Historic District. 8 min. walk to shops and galleries. **3rd night 50% off Dec-April**

Bonnybrooke Farm	$$$ EP	Muffins/fruit upon arriv
Rt 2, Box 335A, 72632	5 rooms, 5 pb	Books & games, fireplace
501-253-6903	C-ltd/S-ltd/P-no/H-no	jacuzzi, glass showers
Bonny & Josh		basketball court
All year		

Sweet quiet & serenity atop Misty Mountain. Fireplace, jacuzzi (for 2), shower under the stars in your glass shower. You're gonna love it! Mountain views. 5 cottages

Bridgeford House	$$$ B&B	Full breakfast
263 Spring St., 72632	4 rooms, 4 pb	Coffee in rooms
501-253-7853	Visa, MC, *Rated*, •	Sitting room
Denise & Michael McDonald	C-yes/S-no/P-no/H-no	garden, flowers in rooms
All year		3 private porches

An 1884 antique-filled Victorian cottage located on a quiet tree-lined street in the historic district. Close to shops. **$10.00 off Sun.-Thur., Ltd.**

Crescent Cottage Inn	$$$ B&B	Full breakfast
211 Spring St., 72632	4 rooms, 4 pb	Coffee on verandas
501-253-6022	Visa, MC, Disc, *Rated*	Sitting room, verandas
Dr. Ralph and Phyllis Becker	C-ltd/S-no/P-no/H-no	2 rooms w/dbl jacuzzis
All year		all queen-sized beds

Premier class oldest (1881) historic Victorian house w/superb views. Walk to town. Newly redecorated, antiques. Featured in magazines & books.

Dairy Hollow House	$$$ B&B	Full breakfast to room
515 Spring St., 72632	6 rooms, 6 pb	Restaurant, dinner
501-253-7444 800-562-8650	Most CC, *Rated*, •	Beverage upon check-in
N. Shank, C. Dragonwagon	C-ltd/S-no/P-no/H-no	sitting room, hot tub
All year	some French	fireplaces in rooms

Restored Ozark farmhouse. Great breakfast-in-a-basket, fireplaces, hot tub. Six course "Nouveau Zarks" dinners. Murder mystery weekends. Best Inn Awards, 1989 & 1990.

Heart of the Hills Inn	$$ B&B	Full gourmet breakfast
5 Summit, 62 Business, 72632	4 rooms, 4 pb	Comp. beverage, dessert
501-253-7468 800-253-7468	Visa, MC, *Rated*, •	Sitting room, jacuzzi
Jan Jacobs Weber	C-ltd/S-no/P-no/H-no	suite w/dbl jacuzzi
All year		cottage, crib, porches

Historic home furnished in genuine antiques; gourmet breakfast served on deck and porches. Gorgeous Victorian in a unique town. Trolly stops in front. **3rd night 20% off**

EUREKA SPRINGS

Heartstone Inn & Cottages

35 Kingshighway, 72632	$$ B&B	Full gourmet breakfast
501-253-8916	9 rooms, 9 pb	Comp. beverages
Iris & Bill Simantel	Visa, MC, *Rated*, •	Sitting room, cable TVs
February–mid December	C-ltd/S-yes/P-no/H-no	wedding gazebo, decks
		massage/reflexology

Award-winning. Antique furniture, prvt baths & entrances, some queen beds. Historic district by attractions. "Best breakfast in the Ozarks"-NY Times 1989. **10% off 4+ nights**

Ridgeway House

28 Ridgeway St., 72632	$$ B&B	Full breakfast
501-253-6618	5 rooms, 2 pb	Guest kitchens
Linda Kerkera	Visa, MC, AmEx, *Rated*,	Comp. wine, snacks
All year	•	sitting room, porches
	C-yes/S-no/P-no/H-no	jacuzzi in garden suite

"Fun, Fancy & Formal" sumptuous breakfasts, homemade desserts, luxurious rooms, wide porches & decks. Be pampered–my guests are V.I.P.'s!! **10% discount Sun.-Thur., ask**

Scandia B&B Inn

P.O. Box 166, 72632	$$$ B&B	Full breakfast
33 Avo, Hwy 62 West	7 rooms, 7 pb	Tea & homemade treats
501-253-8922 800-523-8922	Visa, MC, *Rated*	Sitting room w/fountain
Cynthia L. Barnes	C-yes/S-yes/P-no/H-yes	woodland patio, hot tub
All year		wedding services avail.

Delightful cottages feature private baths, TV, designer bed & bath linens, woodland views, private jaccuzi. Honeymoon suite. Gourmet breakfast served with crystal and china.

Singleton House B&B

11 Singleton, 72632	$$ B&B	Full breakfast
501-253-9111 800-833-3394	5 rooms, 5 pb	Dinner on train (RSVP)
Barbara Gavron	Visa, MC, AmEx, •	Passion play (RSVP)
All year	C-yes/S-ltd/P-no/H-no	honeymoon cottage
		Sunday hiking club

C.1894 antiques, folk art; breakfast balcony overlooks magical garden & pond; in historic district. Walk to shops & cafes. Passion play–RSVP, dinner on train. **5+ days disc't**

Tweedy House B&B

16 Washington St., Historic	$$ B&B	Full breakfast
Loop, 72632	Visa, MC, Disc, *Rated*, •	Continental upon request
501-253-5435 800-346-1735	C-ltd/S-ltd	Off-street parking
Lillian L. Freeman		semi-private bath
All year		sunroom w/microwave, TV

Old fashioned charm w/ modern convenience. Beautiful antique furnishings, fine stained glass, honeymoon suite w/jacuzzi, private decks & porches. **Comp. wine. 3rd nite 25% off**

HARDY

Olde Stonehouse B&B Inn

511 Main St., 72542	$$ B&B	Full breakfast
501-856-2983	5 rooms, 5 pb	Evening snack
Peggy & David Johnson	Visa, MC, *Rated*, •	Sitting room, library
All year	C-ltd/S-ltd/P-no/H-no	A/C, ceiling fans
		Breakfast in bed

Two-story native rock home with large porches, antiques. Near quaint shops, sparkling Spring River, golf, water sports, antique auctions. **3rd night 50% off.**

HARRISON

Mountain Pines Cabin
P.O. Box 1355, 72602
501-420-3575
Karin & Mike Nabors
All year

$$$ B&B
1 rooms, 1 pb
Rated
C-yes/S-no/P-no/H-no

Continental plus
Snacks
Bicycles

Romantic mountain-top hideaway. Restored 1850s handhewn cabin. Antiques and primitives throughout. Full kitchen, fireplace. Trails, waterfalls, views. **7th night free**

HEBER SPRINGS

Anderson House Inn, The
P.O. Box 630, 72543
201 E. Main
501-362-5266 800-264-5279
Peggy L. Ward
February—November

$$ B&B
16 rooms, 16 pb
Visa, MC, *Rated*
C-ltd/S-ltd/P-no/H-no

Full breakfast
Afternoon tea
Sitting room, iron beds
quilts, city park
with tennis courts

Country inn furnished in American antiques available for purchase. Porch and upstairs balcony overlooks park. Summer paradise for water sports and fishing. **3rd. night 50% off**

HELENA

Edwardian Inn
317 S. Biscoe, 72342
501-338-9155
Jerri Steed
All year

$$ B&B
18 rooms, 18 pb
Most CC, *Rated*
C-yes/S-yes/P-yes/H-yes

Continental plus
Wine & cheese sometimes
Sitting room
cable, phones
conference room

The Edwardian Inn offers twelve antique guest rooms, private bath and continental breakfast. Elegance and romance from the turn of the century.

HOT SPRINGS

Vintage Comfort B&B Inn
303 Quapaw Ave., 71901
501-623-3258
Helen R. Bartlett
All year

$$ B&B
4 rooms, 4 pb
Visa, MC, *Rated*, •
C-ltd/S-no/P-no/H-no

Full breakfast
Comp. wine & beverages
Sitting room
antique reed organ

1903 Queen Anne home decorated with antiques, soft, light colors; featuring Southern hospitality. Romantic atmosphere ideal for weddings and honeymoons.

HOT SPRINGS NAT'L PARK

Dogwood Manor
906 Malvern Ave., 71901
501-624-0896 405-321-0099
Lady Janie Wilson
All year

$$ B&B/EP
5 rooms, 5 pb
Visa, MC, •
C-yes/S-ltd/P-yes/H-no

Continental plus
Bar service, comp. wine
Sitting room, fireplace
transportation provided
to spa & racetrack

Lovely 3-story Victoriani National Registry. Architects dream, 5 gables, lead glass, gingerbread, custom draped, wonderful wall covering from China. **3rd night 50% off**

Williams House B&B Inn
420 Quapaw St., 71901
501-624-4275
Gary & Mary Riley
All year

$$ B&B
6 rooms, 4 pb
Visa, MC, AmEx, Optima,
•
C-ltd/S-ltd/P-ask/H-no

Continental plus
Spring water, iced tea
Sitting rooms, fireplace
piano, picnic tables
BBQ, hiking trail maps

Williams House shows Victorian flair for convenience and elegance. Your home away from home, nestled in Oachita Mountains. Romantic atmosphere. Mystery weekends.

MOUNTAIN VIEW

Wildflower B&B	$ B&B	Continental plus
P.O. Box 72, 72560	8 rooms, 6 pb	Bakery on premises
100 Washington St.	AmEx, *Rated*	Sitting room
501-269-4383 800-362-2632	C-yes/S-no/P-no/H-no	Suite w/ kitchenette
Todd & Andrea Budy		entertainment, porch
All year, Nov-Mar res.		

Restored country inn on historic Courthouse Square; close to Ozark Folk Center and Blanchard Springs Caverns. Old-time music on our porch. Breakfast served daily.

Inn at Mountain View, The	$$ B&B	Full breakfast
P.O. Box 812, 72560	10 rooms, 10 pb	Sitting room, sun room
307 Washington St.	Most CC, *Rated*, •	music room, antiques
800-535-1301	C-ltd/S-no/P-no/H-no	evening live folk music
All year	Spanish	

Luxuriously refurbished Victorian home; antiques, fireplace, music and sun rooms. Large front porch overlooks historic courthouse square; famous country breakfast.

WOOSTER

Patton House B&B Inn	$ B&B	Full buffet breakfast
P.O. Box 61, 72181	3 rooms, 1 pb	Wraparound front porch
Highway 25, 14 Reed Rd.	Visa, MC, •	upstairs balcony
501-679-2975	C-yes/S-yes/P-ltd/H-no	library porch, TV, VCR
Mary Lee Patton Shirley		
All year		

Rural Victorian hideaway furnished antiques. Sausage souffle inn specialty. Nearby restaurants, parks, antique stores, other shopping. **10% disc't for res. 3 wks ahead**

More Inns . . .

Iron Mountain Lodge, 1 Marina Dr., Arkadelphia, 71923, 501-246-4310
Great Southern Hotel, 127 W. Cedar, Brinkley, 72021, 501-734-4955
May House, 101 Railroad Ave., Clarksville, 72830, 501-754-6851
5-B's, The, P.O. Box 364, Des Arc, 72040, 501-256-4789
Bass Haven Resort, HCR 1, Box 4480E, Eureka Springs, 72632, 417-858-6401
Bell Spring Cottage, Roiute 1, Box 981, Eureka Springs, 72632, 501-253-8581
Blue John's Log Cabin, 303 P. Square, B'ville, Eureka Springs, 72632, 501-423-3478
Bodie House, 247 Spring St., Eureka Springs, 72632,
Brackenridge Lodge & Gifts, Rt. 4 Box 60, Eureka Springs, 72632,
Brownstone Inn, 75 Hillside, Eureka Springs, 72632, 501-253-7505
Candlestick Cottage, 6 Douglas, Eureka Springs, 72632, 501-253-6813
Carriage House, 75 Lookout Ln., Eureka Springs, 72632, 501-253-8310
Cedarberry Cottage, 3 Kings Highway, Eureka Springs, 72632,
Cliff Cottage B&B Inn, 42 Armstrong St., Eureka Springs, 72632, 501-253-7409
Coach House Inn, 140 S. Main, Eureka Springs, 72632,
    501-253-8099
Cobblestone Guest Cottage, 29 Ridgeway, Eureka Springs,
    72632, 501-253-8105
Cottage Inn, Route 2, Box 429, Eureka Springs, 72632,
    501-253-5282
Crescent Moon, P.O. Box 429, Eureka Springs, 72632,
    501-253-9463
Elmwood House, 110 Spring, Eureka Springs, 72632,
    501-253-7227
Enchanted Cottages, 18 Nut St., Eureka Springs, 72632,
    501-253-6790
Eureka Springs & Arkansas, P.O. Box 310, Eureka Springs,
    72632, 501-253-9623
Fairwinds Mountain Cottges, RR 2 Box 425, Eureka
    Springs, 72632,
Flatiron Flats, 25 Spring St., Eureka Springs, 72632,
    501-253-9434
Fletcher's Devil's Dive, HCR 01, Box 8/23N, Eureka Springs,
    72632, 417-271-3396
Four Winds B&B, 3 Echols St., Eureka Springs, 72632,
    501-253-9169
Greenwood Hollow Ridge, 23 S. Greenwood Hollow,
    Eureka Springs, 72632, 501-253-5283

Dogwood Manor, Hot Springs, AR

Harvest House B&B, 104 Wall St., Eureka Springs, 72632, 501-253-9363
Hidden Valley Guest Ranch, Rural Rt. 2, Box 45, Eureka Springs, 72632, 501-253-9777
Hillside Cottager, 23 Hillside, Eureka Springs, 72632, 501-253-8688
Johnson's Hilltop Cabin, Route 1, Box 503, Eureka Springs, 72632, 501-253-9537
Lake Chalet, Inn, Eureka Springs, 72632, 501-253-9210
Lake Lucerne Resort, P.O. Box 441, Eureka Springs, 72632, 501-253-8085
Lazee Daze, Route 1, Box 196, Eureka Springs, 72632, 501-253-7026
Lookout Cottage, 12 Lookout Circle, Eureka Springs, 72632, 501-253-9545
Magnolia Guest Cottage, 180 Spring St., Eureka Springs, 72632, 501-253-9463
Maple Ridge, 2 First St., Eureka Springs, 72632, 501-253-5220
Maplewood B&B, 4 Armstrong St., Eureka Springs, 72632, 501-253-8053
Miss Annie's Garden Cttges, c/o 24 Armstrong, Eureka Springs, 72632, 501-253-8356
New Orleans Hotel, 63 Spring St., Eureka Springs, 72632, 501-253-8630
Oak Crest Cottages, Route 2, Box 26, Eureka Springs, 72632, 501-253-9493
Old Homestead, The, 82 Armstrong, Eureka Springs, 72632, 501-253-7501
Palace Hotel & Bathhouse, 135 Spring St., Eureka Springs, 72632, 501-253-7474
Piedmont House, 165 Spring St., Eureka Springs, 72632, 501-253-9258
Primrose Place, 39 Steele St., Eureka Springs, 72632, 501-253-9818
Queen Anne Mansion, 207 Kings Highway, Eureka Springs, 72632,
Red Bud Manor, 7 Kingshighway, Eureka Springs, 72632, 501-253-9649
Red Bud Valley Resort, RR 1, Box 500, Eureka Springs, 72632, 501-253-9028
Riverview Resort, RR 2 Box 475, Eureka Springs, 72632, 501-253-8367
Roadrunner Inn, Route 2, Box 158, Eureka Springs, 72632, 601-253-8166
Rock Cabins, 10 Eugenia, Eureka Springs, 72632, 501-253-8659
Rosewood Guest Cottage, One Kings Highway, Eureka Springs, 72632, 501-253-7674
Rustic Manor, Route 4, Box 66, Eureka Springs, 72632, 501-253-8128
School House Inn, 15 Kansas St., Eureka Springs, 72632, 501-253-7854
Shady Rest Cottages, One Magnetic, Eureka Springs, 72632, 501-253-8793
Sleepy Hollow Inn, 92 S. Main, Eureka Springs, 72632, 501-253-7448
Spider Creek Resort, Route 2, Box 418, Eureka Springs, 72632, 501-253-9241
Sunnyside B&B Inn, 5 Ridgeway, Eureka Springs, 72632, 501-253-6638
Sweet Seasons Cottages, P.O. Box 642, Eureka Springs, 72632, 501-253-7603
Tatman-Garret House, P.O. Box 171, Eureka Springs, 72632, 501-253-7617
Valais-Hi, 33 Van Buren, Eureka Springs, 72632, 501-253-5140
White Flower Cottage, 62 Kings Hwy, Eureka Springs, 72632, 501-253-9636
White River Oaks B&B, Rt. 2, Box 449, Eureka Springs, 72632, 501-253-9033
Corn Cob Inn, Route 1, Box 183, Everton, 72633, 501-429-6545
Eton House, 1485 Eton, Fayetteville, 72703, 501-521-6344
Mount Kessler Inn, P.O. Box 3033, Fayetteville, 72701,
McCartney House, 500 S. 19th St., Fort Smith, 72901, 501-782-9057
Merry Go Round Cottage, 412 N. 8th, Fort Smith, 72901, 501-783-3472
Thomas Quinn Guest House, 815 N. "B" St., Fort Smith, 72901, 501-782-0499
Dogwood Inn B&B, U.S. 62, Garfield, 72732, 604-287-4213
Anna's House, P.O. Box 58, Gilbert, 72636, 501-439-2888
Oak Tree Inn, Vinegar Hill, 110 W., Heber Springs, 72543, 501-362-6111
Betty Robertson's B&B, P.O. Box 933, Hot Spring Nat'l Park, 71902, 501-624-6622
Stillmeadow Farm, Route 1, Box 434-D, Hot Springs, 71913, 501-525-9994
Woodbine Place B&B, 213 Woodbine, Hot Springs, 71901, 501-624-3646
Snowden House B&B, Hwy. 147, P.O. Box 486, Hughes, 72348, 501-339-3414
Carol's Place, HCR 31, Box 78, Jasper, 72641, 501-446-5144
Cliff House Inn, Scenic Ark., Highway 7, Jasper, 72641, 501-446-2292
Johnson House 1882, P.O. Box 431, Johnson, 72741, 501-756-1095
Dr. Witt's Quapaw Inn, 1868 S. Gaines, Little Rock, 72206, 501-376-6873
Tanyard Springs, Route 3, Box 335, Morrilton, 72110, 501-727-5200
Margland B&B, P.O. Box 8594, Pine Bluff, 71601, 501-536-6000
Coppermine Lodge, Rt. 6 Box 575, Rogers, 72756,
Hammons Chapel Farm, 1 mile of Ark. 5, Romance, 72136, 501-849-2819
Washington Street B&B, 1001 South Washington, Siloam Springs, 72761, 501-524-5669
Old Washington Jail, P.O. Box 157, Washington, 71862, 501-983-2790
Red Raven Inn, P.O. Box 1217, Yellville, 72687, 501-449-5168

California

ALAMEDA

Garratt Mansion
900 Union St., 94501
510-521-4779 FAX:521-6796
Royce & Betty Gladden
All year

$$ B&B
6 rooms, 3 pb
Rated, •
C-ltd/S-no/P-no/H-no

Full breakfast
Cookies, hot/cold drinks
Sitting room
phones in 4 rooms

An elegant Victorian in a quiet island community just 20 min. from downtown San Francisco, offering personalized attention.

ALAMEDA

Webster House B&B Inn
1238 Versailles Ave., 94501
510-523-9697
Andrew & Susan McCormack
All year

$$$ B&B
5 rooms, 3 pb
Rated, •
C-yes/S-ltd

Full breakfast
Comp. afternoon tea
Snacks, Teahouse-public
deck, sun porch, library
waterfall, garden, games

22nd City Historical Monument. Quaint, enchanting Gothic Revival Cottage is oldest house in Alameda. Walk to beach, shops, golf. San Francisco 20 min. away. 3rd night 50% off

ALBION

Fensalden Inn
P.O. Box 99, 95410
33810 Navarro Ridge Rd.
707-937-4042 800-959-3850
Scott & Frances Brazil
All year

$$$ B&B
7 rooms, 7 pb
Visa, MC, •
C-ltd/S-ltd/P-ltd/H-ltd

Full breakfast
Wine & hors d'oeuvres
Sitting room
parlor, library
library

On 20 acres of Mendocino Coast. Historic country inn with spectacular ocean views—and only ten minutes from the village of Mendocino. One bungalow sleeps 4. 7th night free.

AMADOR CITY

Mine House Inn
P.O. Box 245, 95601
14125 Hwy 49
209-267-5900 800-646-3673
Peter Daubenspeck
All year

$$ B&B
7 rooms, 7 pb
•
C-yes/S-yes/P-no/H-no
Portuguese

Continental breakfast
Art gallery
swimming pool, Air Cond.
gift shop, sitting room

Former Keystone Gold Mining Company office building, all rooms furnished in Victorian antiques. Relive a night from the gold rush days. 3rd. night 50% off Sun.-Thur.

ANAHEIM

Anaheim Country Inn
856 S. Walnut St., 92802
714-778-0150 800-755-7801
Lois Ramont, Marilyn Watson
All year

$$ B&B
8 rooms, 4 pb
Visa, MC, Disc., •
C-ltd/S-ltd/P-no/H-no

Full breakfast
Comp. beverages & snacks
Sitting room
organ, hot tub

Large historic house near Disneyland. Garden & trees, off-street parking, antiques, warm homey atmosphere. Complimentary appetizers before dinner. 3rd night 50% off

ANGWIN—NAPA VALLEY

Forest Manor
415 Cold Springs Rd., 94508
707-965-3538 800-788-0364
Harold & Corlene Lambeth
All year

$$$ B&B
3 rooms, 3 pb
Visa, MC, •
C-ltd/S-ltd/P-no/H-no
Thai, French

Full breakfast
Comp. beverages & snacks
Jacuzzi, refrig., limo
sitting room, piano
organ, 53' pool & spa

Beautiful secluded 20-acre English Tudor forested estate in Napa Wine Country. Massive carved beams, fireplaces, decks, air-conditioning, game rooms. Off-season rates, ask

APTOS

Apple Lane Inn
6265 Soquel Dr., 95003
408-475-6868
Doug & Diana Groom
All year

$$ B&B
5 rooms, 3 pb
Visa, MC, *Rated*, •
C-ltd/S-ltd/P-no/H-no

Full breakfast
Comp. cookies & milk
Sitting room, library
player piano
Weddings to 175 people

Victorian farmhouse furnished w/beautiful antiques offers country charm. Quiet, yet close to everything, incl. fine restaurants. Romantic Victorian gazebo. Midweek disc't $15

Forest Manor, Angwin–Napa Valley, CA

APTOS

Mangels House
P.O. Box 302, 95001
570 Aptos Creek Rd.
408-688-7982
Jacqueline Fisher
All year exc. Christmas

$$$ B&B
5 rooms, 5 pb
Visa, MC, *Rated*, •
C-ltd/S-ltd/P-no/H-no
French, Spanish

Full breakfast
Comp. wine, piano
Sitting room, fireplace
table tennis and darts
english garden, nursery

Casual elegance in country setting, 5 minute drive to Hwy 1. 4 acres of lawn and woodland on edge of Redwood State Park. 1 mi. from beach, golf, Monterey Bay. **3rd night 50%**

AVALON

Gull House
P.O. Box 1381, 90704
344 Whittley Ave.
310-510-2547
Bob & Hattie Michalis
April–October

$$$ B&B
5 rooms, 4 pb
Rated, •
C-yes/S-no/P-no/H-no

Continental plus
Comp. fruit basket
Refrigerator, whirlpool
pool, BBQ, all king beds
taxi to boat terminal

Deluxe suites in quiet residential area. Breakfast on patio. Beach, sights & activities on this beautiful island. Perfect for couples. RSVP well in advance. **Taxi service**

BAYWOOD PARK

Baywood B&B Inn
1370 Second St., 93402
805-528-8888
Ms. Barbie Porter
All year

$$$ B&B
15 rooms, 15 pb
Visa, MC, *Rated*, •
C-yes/S-no/P-no/H-yes
British

Continental plus
Restaurant, lunch
Comp. wine
sitting room, fireplaces
bay views, 11 suites

Bayfront Inn on South Morro Bay. 15 unique rooms…each with its own personality. Suites have many amenities. Near Hearst Castle, San Luis Obispo, Montano De Oro State Park.

BEN LOMOND ───────────────────────────

Fairview Manor	$$$ B&B	Full breakfast
P.O. Box 74, 95005	5 rooms, 5 pb	Comp. wine
245 Fairview Ave.	Visa, MC, *Rated*, •	Sitting room
408-336-3355	C-ltd/S-yes/P-no/H-yes	
Nancy Glasson		

Romantic country-styled redwood home, majestic stone fireplace, 2.5 wooded acres of Santa Cruz Mountains. Total privacy. Walk to town. Champagne. **3rd night 50% off.**

BERKELEY ───────────────────────────

Gramma's Rose Garden Inn	$$$ B&B	Full breakfast
2740 Telegraph Ave., 94705	40 rooms, 38 pb	Evening wine & cheese
510-549-2145 FAX:549-1085	Visa, MC, *Rated*, •	Sunday brunch $
Barry Cleveland/Kathy Kuhner	C-yes/S-ltd/P-no/H-yes	Full in-house catering
All year		sitting room, piano

Two beautiful turn-of-the-century mansions with lovely gardens. Individual guest rooms with antique furnishings, color TV. Close to UC Berkeley; 20 min. to San Francisco.

BIG BEAR LAKE ───────────────────────────

Gold Mountain Manor B&B	$$$ B&B	Full breakfast
P.O. Box 2027, 92314	7 rooms, 3 pb	Comp. beverages, snacks
1117 Anita	*Rated*, •	Poor table, fireplaces
909-585-6997	C-ltd/S-ltd/P-ltd/H-no	veranda, hot tub
Conny Ridgway	French	parlor w/large fireplace
All year		

Magnificent, historic and very romantic 1920s log mansion featured in Ralph Lauren ads. Gourmet country breakfast. Near National Forest. **Midwk specials up to 30% off**

───────────────────────────

Knickerbocker Mansion	$$$ B&B	Full breakfast
Box 3661, 869 S. Knickerbocker,	10 rooms, 5 pb	"Grandma's kitchen"
92315	*Rated*, •	Sitting room
714-866-8221	C-yes/H-no	library
Phyllis Knight		hot tubs
All year		

Peaceful retreat at a historic inn; pampering & spoiling. Hiking, water sports, skiing or reading & quiet meditation in a forest setting.

BIG BEND ───────────────────────────

Royal Gorges Rainbow	$ B&B	Full breakfast
Lodge	32 rooms, 12 pb	Restaurant, lunch/dinner
Hampshire Rocks Rd., M.A.:	Visa, MC, •	Sitting room, library
P.O. Box 1100, 95728	C-yes/S-yes/P-no/I I-no	river, fishing
916-426-3661 916-426-3871		cross-country skiing
Jacqui James		
All year		

Beautiful old mountain hotel, guests' lounge with fireplace. Nestled in a bend of the Yuba river with mountains around. Ride to Summit Station on the shuttle bus and ski back!

BISHOP ───────────────────────────

Matlick House, The	$$$ B&B	Full breakfast
1313 Rowan Ln., 93514	4 rooms, 4 pb	Picnic lunches
619-873-3133	*Rated*, •	Wine, bedside cookies
Nanette Robidart	C-ltd/S-ltd/P-no	hors d'oeuvres, antiques
All year		sitting room, bicycles

1906 ranch house; picturesque views of the eastern Sierra Nevadas. Minutes from skiing, fishing, hiking & other outdoor sports. **Special occasion wine.**

BLUE JAY ───────────────────────

Eagles Landing B&B	$$$ B&B	Full breakfast on Sunday
P.O. Box 1510, 92317	4 rooms, 4 pb	Continental Mon. - Sat.
27406 Cedarwood	Most CC, *Rated*, •	Picnic area, boat rides
714-336-2642	C-ltd/S-no/P-no/H-no	Catered dinner in suite
Dorothy & Jack Stone		sitting room, fireplace
All year		

Enjoy home-style hospitality in atmosphere reminiscent of cozy European mountain inns. Decks view beautiful Lake Arrowhead. Yr-round fun. Prvt beach club. **2 day pkg. avail.**

BRIDGEPORT ───────────────────────

Cain House, The	$$$ B&B	Full breakfast
P.O. Box 454, 93517	7 rooms, 6 pb	Comp. wine, cheese
11 Main St.	Most CC, Rated-, •	Sitting room
619-932-7040 800-433-CAIN	C-yes/S-no/P-no/H-no	tennis courts
Chris & Marachal Gohlich		1 rm. w/private entrance
All year		

The grandeur of the eastern Sierras is the perfect setting for evening wine and cheese. Quiet, romantic, peaceful getaway. **Mon-Thurs, 2nd night free**

CALISTOGA ───────────────────────

Calistoga Country Lodge	$$$ B&B	Continental plus
2883 Foothill Blvd., 94515	6 rooms, 4 pb	Snacks, Comp. wine
707-942-5555	Most CC, *Rated*,	Sitting room
February - December	C-ltd/S-no/P-no/H-no	swimming pool

1917 ranchouse restored in Southwest style offering country solitude, spacious common area, views of valley & open land. 1 mile from Calistoga spas. **Comp. bottle of wine**

Calistoga Wayside Inn	$$$ B&B	Full breakfast
1523 Foothill Blvd., 94515	3 rooms, 3 pb	Afternoon tea
707-942-0645 800-845-3632	Visa, MC, AmEx, •	Comp. wine & cheese
Jan & Tom Balcer	C-ltd/S-no/P-no	parlor, library
All year		fireplace, sherry

1920s Spanish-style home in park-like setting w/fountains and fish pond. Gourmet breakfast served on lower patio in the summer. **In-week specials**

Calistoga Wishing Well Inn	$$$ B&B	Full country breakfast
2653 Foothill Blvd., Hwy 128,	3 rooms, 3 pb	Complimentary wine
94515	Visa, MC, •	Hors d'oeuvres
707-942-5534	C-ltd/S-no/P-no/H-yes	fireplace, hot tubs
Marina & Keith Dinsmoor	Russian	swimming pool, bikes, TV
All year		

Elegant country farmhouse on four historical areas. Full breakfast served on deck overlooking orchard or poolside with view of Mount Saint Helena. Fireplace in cottage.

Christopher's Inn	$$$ B&B	Continental plus
1010 Foothill Blvd., 94515	10 rooms, 10 pb	Fireplaces, TV, croquet
707-942-5755	Most CC, *Rated*, •	small conference space
Christopher Layton	C-ltd/S-no/P-no/H-no	concierge service
All year		

Elegant new country inn. Walk to Calistoga, Laura Ashley interiors. Fireplaces, garden patios, breakfast brought to your room.

CALISTOGA ————————————————————————————————

Culver's, A Country Inn
1805 Foothill Blvd, 94515
707-942-4535
Meg & Tony Wheatley
All year

$$$ B&B
7 rooms
Visa, MC, *Rated*, •
C-ltd/S-ltd/P-no/H-yes

Full breakfast
Comp. sherry, beverages
Fresh fruit, piano
living room w/fireplace
pool, hot tub, sauna

Comfortable, elegant Victorian home circa 1875, restored historical landmark in Napa. Easy access to wineries, spas, gliding, ballooning, restaurants. $20.00 cancellation fee.

Elms B&B, The
1300 Cedar St., 94515
800-235-4316
Elaine Bryant
All year

$$$ B&B
7 rooms, 7 pb
Most CC, *Rated*, •
C-ltd/S-no/P-no/H-yes

Full breakfast-3 courses
Snacks, comp. wine
Sitting room, bicycles
Wine & cheese in p.m.
choclates at bedtime

Step into the past where life was quieter and the pace relaxed. Enjoy the romance and intimacy of this 1871 French Victorian.

Foothill House B&B Inn
3037 Foothill Blvd, 94515
707-942-6933 800-942-6933
Doris & Gus Beckert
All year

$$$ B&B
3 rooms, 3 pb
Visa, MC, *Rated*, •
C-ltd/S-no/P-no/H-no

Continental plus
Comp. wine & cheese
Turndown service: sherry
Whirlpool bath in suite
sitting room, A/C

In a country setting, Foothill House offers 3 spacious rooms individually decorated with antiques, each with private bath, entrance & fireplace. **Free bottle wine each night.**

Pink Mansion, The
1415 Foothill Blvd., 94515
707-942-0558 800-942-PINK
Jeff Seyfried, Mr. Toppa Epps
All year

$$$ B&B
5 rooms, 5 pb
Visa, MC, AmEx, *Rated*,
•
C-ltd/S-no/P-no/H-yes
Spanish

Full breakfast
Lunch, dinner
Comp. wine with cheese
library, parlor
A/C, bicycles

Restored 1875 home combines turn-of-the-century elegance with modern amenities to provide our wine country travelers with old-fashioned comfort.

Quail Mountain B&B Inn
4455 N. St. Helena Hwy, 94515
707-942-0316
Don & Alma Swiers
All year

$$$ B&B
3 rooms, 3 pb
Visa, MC, *Rated*, •
C-ltd/S-no/P-no/H-no

Full breakfast-champagne
Private decks, hot tub
swimming pool, gardens
comp. wine in afternoon

26 acre secluded luxury, heavily wooded country estate with vineyard on property. Comtemporary architecture with rooms individually decorated with artworks and antiques.

Scarlett's Country Inn
3918 Silverado Tr., 94515
707-942-6669
Scarlett Dwyer
All year

$$$ B&B
3 rooms, 3 pb
•
C-yes/S-yes/P-no/H-no
Spanish

Continental plus
Comp. wine & cheese
Sitting room, A/C
microwaves & frigdes
coffee makers, pool

Secluded French country farmhouse overlooking vineyards in famed Napa Valley. Breakfast served by woodland swimming pool. Close to spas and wineries. **3rd night 50% off**

CALISTOGA ————————————————————————————

Silver Rose Inn $$$ B&B   Continental plus
351 Rosedale Rd., 94515   9 rooms, 9 pb   Comp. wine, snacks
707-942-9581 800-995-9381   Visa, MC, AmEx, *Rated*,   Fireplace, jacuzzi
Sally Dumont   •   swimming pool, library
All year   C-ltd/S-no/P-no/H-no   sitting room
                             French

*Quiet elegance in a country setting. Walk or jog through adjacent vineyards & enjoy
Calistoga's famous mud & mineral baths. Guests are welcomed with a bottle of wine.*

Zinfandel House $$ B&B   Full breakfast
1253 Summit Dr., 94515   3 rooms, 2 pb   Comp. wine
707-942-0733   C-ltd/S-no/P-no/H-no   Library
Bette & George Starke   sitting room
All year   hot tub

*Beautiful home situated on wooded hillside overlooking vineyards and mountains. Lovely
breakfast served on outside deck or in dining room.*

CAMBRIA ————————————————————————————

Beach House, The $$$ B&B   Continental plus
6360 Moonstone Beach Dr,   7 rooms, 7 pb   Aftn. tea, comp. wine
93428   Visa, MC, •   Sitting room, fireplace
805-927-3136 800-549-6789   C-ltd/S-no/P-no/H-no   patios, 3 outside decks
Penny Hitch & Kernn   mountain bikes
MacKinnon
All year

*Oceanfront home with antique oak furniture, queen and king-size beds, ocean views. Visit
Hearst Castle, beach, wineries, shops. Rural atmosphere, gorgeous sunsets.*

Cambria Landing Inn $$$ B&B   Continental plus
6530 Moonstone Beach Dr,   20 rooms, 20 pb   Comp. wine/champagne
93428   Visa, MC, Disc. *Rated*, • Hot tubs, jacuzzi room
805-927-1619 800-549-6789   C-yes/S-yes/P-no/H-yes   oceanfront rooms, bikes
Kernn MacKinnon, Joni Apathy   common living room
All year

*Romantic country inn set on ocean bluff near rocky beaches. Oceanfront rms with TV, refers.,
VCR, private decks/patios, fireplaces & "breakfast in bed"!* **Free wine/champagne**

Pickford House B&B $$$ B&B   Full breakfast
2555 MacLeod Way, 93428   8 rooms, 8 pb   Afternoon wine
805-927-8619   Visa, MC, *Rated*,   Hors d'oeuvres, cookies
Anna Larsen   C-yes/S-ltd/P-no/H-yes   sitting room
All year   piano, hot tub

*All rooms named after silent film-era stars and furnished with genuine antiques. Full breakfast
included. All rooms have showers, TV and tubs. Homemade fruit breads and cakes.*

CAPITOLA-BY-THE-SEA ————————————————————————

Inn at Depot Hill, The $$$ B&B   Full breakfast
P.O. Box 1934, 95010   8 rooms, 8 pb   Aftn. tea/hors d'oeuvres
250 Monterey Ave.   Most CC, *Rated*, •   Evening dessert & wine
408-462-3376   C-ltd/S-no/P-no/H-yes   sitting room, library
Suzie Lankes   Croatian   private garden patios
All year

*Near sandy beach, stately 1901 railway station lavishly offers Orient-Express-style sophisti-
cated charm, timeless beauty, and upscale classical European elegance. AAA 3 stars.*

CARLSBAD ───────────────────────────────

Pelican Cove B&B Inn
320 Walnut Ave., 92008
619-434-5995
Scott & Betsy Buckwald
All year

$$$ B&B
8 rooms, 8 pb
Visa, MC, *Rated*, •
C-ltd/S-no/H-yes

Continental plus
Comp. sherry
Beach nearby
beach chairs, towels
picnic baskets

Feather beds/fireplaces in every room. Jacuzzis in 2 rooms. Private tiled baths, private entries, fruit, flowers, candy in every room. Comp. Amtrak pickup. **3rd night 50% off**

CARMEL ───────────────────────────────

Carriage House Inn
P.O. Box 1900, 93921
Junipero btwn 7th & 8th
408-625-2585 800-433-4732
Raul Lopez
All year

$$$ B&B
13 rooms, 13 pb
Most CCs, *Rated*, •
C-ltd/S-yes/P-no/H-no

Continental plus
Wine, hors d'oeuvres
Sitting room, library
some rooms w/jacuzzi tub

Intimate, romantic. King-size beds, down comforters, fireplaces, some sunken tubs. Within walking distance of shops, galleries, restaurants, and white beaches.

Cobblestone Inn
P.O. Box 3185, 93921
Junipero btwn 7th & 8th
408-625-5222
Ray Farnsworth
All year

$$$ B&B
24 rooms, 24 pb
AmEx, Visa, MC, *Rated*,
•
C-yes/S-ltd/P-no/H-no

Full breakfast
Wine & hors d'oeuvres
Sitting room
terrace, bicycles
picnics avail.

Charming country inn nestled in English garden. Each room has a fireplace and country decor, turndown service, beverages and morning paper. **Breakfast in bed**

Happy Landing Inn
P.O. Box 2619, 93921
Monte Verde at 5th & 6th
408-624-7917
Robert Ballard & Dick Stewart
All year

$$$ B&B
7 rooms, 7 pb
Visa, MC, *Rated*,
C-ltd/S-no/P-no/H-yes

Continental plus
Comp. sherry
Sitting room
Gazebo, gardens, pond
Honeymoon cottage avail.

Hansel & Gretel cottages in the heart of Carmel, like something from a Beatrix Potter book. Surrounds a central flowering garden; breakfast is served in your room.

Holiday House
P.O. Box 782, 93921
Camino Real at 7th Ave.
408-624-6267
Dieter & Ruth Back
All year

$$$ B&B
6 rooms, 4 pb
•
C-ltd/S-ltd/P-no/H-no
German

Full breakfast
Afternoon sherry
Colorful garden
sitting room, library

Lovely inn personifying Carmel charm, in quiet residential area. A short walk to beautiful Carmel beaches, quaint shops, restaurants. Ocean views, beautiful garden.

Homestead, The
P.O. Box 1285, 93921
8th & Lincoln Sts.
408-624-4119
Kim & Gina Weston
All year

$$ EP
12 rooms, 12 pb
Rated
C-yes/S-yes

Comp. coffee in rooms
4 cottages w/kitchens
2 cottages w/fireplaces

A unique inn nestled in the heart of Carmel. Rooms and cottages with private baths, some kitchens & fireplaces. Reasonably priced and close to town.

CARMEL

Lincoln Green Inn
P.O. Box 2747, 93921
Carmelo btwn 15th & 16th
408-624-1880 800-262-1262
Hollace Thompson
All year

$$$ B&B
4 rooms, 4 pb
Visa, MC, AmEx, •
C-yes/S-yes/P-yes/H-yes

Continental breakfast
Comp. tea
English garden

Four charming English country-style cottages set in a formal English garden behind a white picket fence; nestled in a quaint residential area near ocean.

San Antonio House
P.O. Box 3683, 93921
San Antonio
@ Ocean & 7th
408-624-4334
Sarah & Rick Lee
All year

$$$ B&B
4 rooms, 4 pb
Visa, MC, AmEx, •
C-ltd/S-no/P-no/H-no

Continental plus
Comp. tea
Sitting room, fireplaces
flower gardens, patios
private entrances

Private 2- and 3-room suites decorated with antiques and art. One block from famous Carmel Beach. Sounds of surf and sense of yesteryear melt tensions away.

Sea View Inn
P.O. Box 4138, 93921
Camino Real @ 11th & 12th
408-624-8778
Marshall & Diane Hydorn
All year

$$$ B&B
8 rooms, 6 pb
Visa, MC
C-ltd/S-no/P-no/H-no

Continental plus
Afternoon tea & coffee
Comp. evening wine
sitting room
library, garden

Small, intimate, cozy Victorian, near village and beach. Enjoy breakfast and evening wine served by the fireside, or relax in secluded garden. **20% off Nov-March, ltd.**

Tally Ho Inn
P.O. Box 3726, 93921
Monte Verde at 6th St.
408-624-2232
Barbara & Erven Torell
All year

$$$ B&B
14 rooms, 14 pb
Most CC, *Rated*, •
C-yes/S-yes/P-no/H-no
some French

Continental plus
Aft. tea, brandy
Floral garden, sun deck
fireplaces, ocean views
close to beach

This English country inn has bountiful gardens with sweeping ocean views from individually appointed rooms and sun decks. Former home of cartoonist Jimmy Hatlo.

Vagabond's House
P.O. Box 2747, 93921
4th & Dolores
408-624-7738 800-262-1262
Honey Spence
All year

$$$ B&B
11 rooms, 11 pb
Visa, MC, •
C-ltd/S-yes/P-yes/H-no
French

Continental plus
Sitting room w/fireplace
library, courtyard
2 blocks to downtown

Antique clocks and pictures, quilted bedspreads, fresh flowers, plants, shelves filled with old books. Sherry by the fireplace; breakfast served in your room.

CARMEL BY-THE-SEA

Sandpiper Inn at-the-Beach
2408 Bay View Ave., 93923
408-624-6433 FAX:624-5964
G. & I. MacKenzie, K. Roberts
All year

$$$ B&B
16 rooms, 16 pb
Most CC, *Rated*, •
C-ltd/S-ltd/P-no/H-no
French, German

Continental plus
Coffee, tea, sherry
Library, flowers
fireplace lounge
tennis, golf, bicycles

Fifty yards from Carmel Beach. European-style country inn, filled with antiques and fresh flowers. Ocean views, fireplaces, garden. Mobil 2 star rating.

CARMEL VALLEY

Valley Lodge
P.O. Box 93, 93924
8 Ford Rd.
408-659-2261 800-641-4646
Peter & Sherry Coakley
All year

$$$ B&B
35 rooms, 35 pb
Most CC, *Rated*, •
C-yes/S-yes/P-yes/H-yes
French, Spanish

Continental plus
Library, hot tub, sauna
pool, fitness center, TV
conf. fac., comp. paper

Quiet, lovely spot. Romantic setting for lovers of privacy, nature, hiking, golf, tennis, swimming, riding & just plain lovers. Cozy fireplace cottages. **20% off Sun.—Th.**

CAZADERO

Cazanoma Lodge
P.O. Box 37, 95421
1000 Kidd Creek Rd.
707-632-5255
Randy & Gretchen Neuman
March—November

$$$ B&B
5 rooms, 5 pb
Visa, MC, AmEx, •
C-yes/S-yes/P-ltd/H-yes

Continental plus
Comp. wine, bar
Comp. cheese, crackers
entertainment, swimming
hiking trails

Secluded lodge on 147 acres of Redwood Forest. Two creeks, trout pond and waterfall. Near the ocean and beautiful Russian River. **Bottle wine/champagne on check-in**

Timberhill Ranch Resort
35755 Hauser Bridge Rd., 95421
707-847-3258
Barbara Farrell, Frank Watson
All year

$$$ MAP
15 rooms, 15 pb
Visa, MC, *Rated*, •
C-ltd/S-ltd/P-no/H-yes

Continental plus
Lunch, 6-course dinner
Bar, sitting rm, hot tub
heated swimming pool
tennis courts, jacuzzi

Romantic 80-acre resort featuring gourmet dining, 15 secluded cottages, fireplaces, private baths and decks. World-class tennis courts. Conference facility.

CLOVERDALE

Abrams House Inn
314 N. Main St., 95425
707-894-2412 800-764-4466
Betsy Fitz-Gerald
All year

4 rooms, 2 pb
Visa, MC, AmEx, *Rated*,
•
C-ltd/S-no/P-no/H-no

Full breakfast
Snacks, comp. wine
Sitting room, library
hot tub, eve. sweets
aft. appetizers

1870's Victorian home. Antiques, garden, gazebo, hot tub, near wineries, lake and river. Small weddings and seminars. **3rd night 20% off**

Vintage Towers B&B Inn
302 N. Main St., 95425
707-894-4535
Jane Patton
All year exc. December

$$$ B&B
7 rooms, 5 pb
Visa, MC, AmEx, •
C-ltd/S-ltd/P-ask/H-yes

Full breakfast
Afternoon snacks
3 sitting rms., piano
bicycles, gazebo, TV
veranda & gardens

A towered mansion on the national register, on a quiet tree-lined street in a wine country town. Walk to river, wineries and fine dining.

Ye Olde Shelford House
29955 River Rd., 95425
707-894-5956 800-833-6479
Ina & Al Sauder
All year

$$$ B&B
6 rooms, 6 pb
Visa, MC, Disc., •
C-ltd/S-ltd/P-no/H-no

Full breakfast
Comp. beverages, snacks
Sitting rm, rec. room
hot tub, pool, bicycles
antique car wine tour

Stately 1880s Victorian, genuine antiques, wraparound porch overlooking vineyards. Delicious brkfst in formal dining rm, porch. "Surry & Sip" winery ride. **10% disc't, ltd**

COLOMA ——————————————————

Coloma Country Inn, The	$$$ B&B	Full breakfast
P.O. Box 502, 95613	5 rooms, 3 pb	Comp. wine, beverages
345 High St.	•	Sitting room, bicycles
916-621-6919	C-ltd/S-no/P-no/H-no	Victorian tea, rafting
Alan & Cindi Ehrgott	Spanish, French	2 new suites
All year		

Country Victorian built in 1856, set among rose and flower gardens and pond on 5 acres. Half a block to Sutter's Mill and American River. **10% off on balloon flight**

COLUMBIA ——————————————————

Columbia City Hotel	$$ B&B	Continental plus
P.O. Box 1870, 95310	10 rooms, 10 pb	French restaurant
Columbia State Park	Visa, MC, AmEx, *Rated*,	Sitting room, piano
209-532-1479	•	Anchor Steam beer on
Tom Bender	C-yes/S-ltd/P-no/H-no	draft in saloon
All year		

Historical location in a state-preserved Gold Rush town; 9 antique-appointed rooms; small elegant dining room and authentic saloon.

Fallon Hotel	$$ B&B	Continental plus
P.O. Box 1870, 95310	14 rooms, 14 pb	Sitting room
Washington St.	Visa, MC, *Rated*, •	rose garden
209-532-1470	C-ltd/S-ltd/P-no/H-yes	avail. for receptions
Tom Bender		
All year		

Restored Victorian hotel, full of antiques in state-preserved Gold Rush town. Elegant and intimate. Near Yosemite. Many historic family fun events throughout the year.

CROWLEY LAKE ——————————————————

Rainbow Tarns	$$$ B&B	Full breakfast
Rt 1, P.O. Box 1097,	3 rooms, 3 pb	Aft. tea, snacks
Rainbow Tarns Rd., 93546	*Rated*, •	Comp. wine
619-935-4556	C-ltd/S-no/P-no	sitting rm. w/library
Lois Miles		whirlpool & jacuzzi
All year		

Indulge yourself in a unique experience at 7000 ft. in the glorious High Sierras. Native trees & flowers, 3 ponds, your own horses welcome. **7th night free w/wk stay**

DANA POINT ——————————————————

Blue Lantern Inn	$$$ B&B	Full breakfast
34343 Blue Lantern St., 92629	29 rooms	Comp. wine, tea, fruit
714-661-1304	Visa, MC, AmEx, *Rated*,	Sitting room, library
Tom Taylor	•	bicycles, exercise room
All year	C-yes/S-no/P-no/H-yes	hot tub in rooms

Cape Cod inn with a dramatic location overlooking the Pacific Ocean. Rooms have fireplaces, jacuzzi, decks and are individually decorated. Breakfast in bed.

DAVENPORT ——————————————————

New Davenport B&B Inn	$$ B&B	Continental plus
P.O. Box J,	12 rooms, 12 pb	Full breakfast $ midwk
31 Davenport Ave., 95017	Visa, MC, AmEx, *Rated*,	Restaurant, gift shop
408-425-1818 408-426-4122	C-ltd/S-no/P-no/H-yes	champagne on arrival
Bruce & Marcia McDougal		sitting room, gallery
All year		

Charming ocean-view rooms decorated w/antiques, handcrafts & ethnic treasures. Comp. champagne. Artist/owners. Beach access. **3rd night 50%**

DAVIS

University Inn B&B
340 "A" St., 95616
916-756-8648
Lynda & Ross Yancher
All year

$$ B&B
4 rooms, 4 pb
Most CC, •
C-yes/S-no/P-no/H-yes

Continental plus
Comp. beverages
Microwave
bicycles
airport shuttle

A great taste of Davis, ten steps from the University. Quiet location. Rooms with private bath, private phone, Cable TV, refrigerator, micro wave use. **Free Cookies, Ltd.**

DEL MAR

Rock Haus Inn
410 - 15th St., 92014
619-481-3764
Doris Holmes
All year

$$$ B&B
10 rooms, 4 pb
Visa, MC, •
C-ltd/S-no/P-no/H-no

Continental plus
Tea time
Sitting room, piano
player piano, veranda

Romantic getaway to quaint seaside village. Most rooms have ocean views in this historic landmark. Goosedown comforters, Amtrak 2 blocks. **$10 off weekdays off-season**

DULZURA

Brookside Farm B&B Inn
1373 Marron Valley Rd., 91917
619-468-3043
Edd & Sally Guishard
All year

$$ B&B
11 rooms, 8 pb
MC, Visa, *Rated*, •
C-ltd/S-ltd/P-no/H-ltd

Full breakfast
4-course dinner by RSVP
Hot tub, piano
terraces, gardens
new rm. w/2-sided frplc.

Quaint farmhouse nestled in mountain setting w/ stream. Handmande quilts and rugs, fireplace and farm animals. Gourmet dinners on weekends. **$15.00 off 2 night stay (weekends)**

ELK

Elk Cove Inn
P.O. Box 367, 95432
6300 S. Hwy. 1
707-877-3321
Hildrun-Uta Triebess
All year

$$$ B&B
16 rooms, 10 pb
Rated
C-ltd/S-no/P-no/H-ltd
Ger., Span., Fr., Ital.

Full breakfast
Dinner included Saturday
Comp. sherry or port
Bar, sitting room, deck
piano, library, stereo

1883 Victorian—original old-fashioned country inn, outstanding dramatic ocean views; specializing in German and French cuisine and personal service. **Disc't Mon. to Th.**

Harbor House
P.O. Box 369, 95432
5600 S. Hwy 1
707-877-3203
Helen & Dean Turner
All year

$$$ MAP
10 rooms, 10 pb
Rated
C-ltd/S-ltd/P-no/H-no
French, Spanish

Full breakfast
Full dinner, wine list
Sitting room, piano
fireplaces, parlor stove
gardens, private beach

Spectacular north coast vistas of the sea. Renowned country gourmet cuisine. Wine lover's paradise. Rooms include original artwork, fireplaces or parlor stoves, and decks.

Sandpiper House Inn
P.O. Box 49, 95432
5520 S. Hwy 1
707-877-3587
Richard & Claire Melrose
All year

$$$ B&B
4 rooms, 4 pb
Visa, MC, *Rated*,
C-ltd/S-no/P-no/H-no

Full breakfast
Aft. tea, snacks
Comp. sherry
breakfast in dining rm.
living room for guests

Seaside country inn built in 1916. Rich redwood panelling, European charm, lush perrenial gardens, stunning ocean views, private beach access.

ELKCREEK ─────────────────────────────────

Stony Creek Retreat B&B	$$ B&B	Full breakfast
P.O. Box 205, 95939	4 rooms, 1 pb	Lunch, dinner
3145 Glenn Cty. Rd. 306	Visa, MC, *Rated*,	Afternoon tea, snacks
916-968-5178 800-643-7183	C-ltd/S-ltd/P-ltd/H-no	sitting room, bicycles
Ted & Norma Arnold		near lakes, bass pond
All year		

Country hideaway on 67 acres. Quiet room with view balcony, beautiful lakes, wildlife, near national forest. Romantic, secluded getaway place to rest. **3rd night 50%**

EUREKA ─────────────────────────────────

Carter House	$$$ B&B	Full breakfast
1033 3rd St., 301 L St., 95501	5 rooms, 5 pb	Dinner (by reservation)
707-445-1390 707-444-8062	Most CC, *Rated*, •	Wine, hors d'oeuvres
Mark & Christi Carter	C-ltd/S-no/P-no/H-no	sitting rooms, gardens
All year		corporate rates

New Victorian. Enjoy wines & appetizers before dinner, cordials or teas & cookies at bedtime. Warm hospitality; award-winning breakfasts. OUR 1986 INN OF THE YEAR.

Daly Inn, The	$$ B&B	Full breakfast
1125 H St., 95501	5 rooms, 3 pb	Afternoon tea, snacks
707-445-3638 800-321-9656	Visa, MC, AmEx, •	Comp. wine
Sue & Gene Clinesmith	C-ltd/S-ltd/P-no/H-no	sitting room, library
All year		Victorian gardens, pond

A beautifully restored turn of the century mansion. One of Eureka's finest examples of Victorian elegance. Should not be missed. 1 room w/twin beds, 4 rooms w/queen.

Elegant Victorian Mansion	$$$ B&B	Full breakfast
1406 "C" St., at 14th. St., 95501	3 rooms, 2 pb	Comp. ice cream sodas
707-444-3144 707-442-5594	Visa, MC, *Rated*, •	Sauna, massage, croquet
Doug & Lily Vieyra	C-ltd/S-no/P-no/H-no	parlors, cable TV, bikes
All year	French, Dutch, German	antique autos, bay views

"Victorian opulence, grace, grandeur-a most elegant home in Eureka. Spirited, eclectic innkeepers share regal splendor of a NAT'L HISTORIC LANDMARK." **3rd nite carriage ride.**

Hotel Carter, The	$$$ B&B	Continental plus/full
301 L St., 95501	23 rooms, 23 pb	Dinner (by reservation)
707-444-8062 707-445-1390	Most CC, *Rated*, •	Wine & hors d'oeuvres
Mark & Christi Carter	C-yes/S-no/P-no/H-yes	sitting room, jacuzzi
All year		luxury suites w/frplcs.

Luxury full-service small hotel; attentive staff. Sophisticated blend of Old World elegance and modern amenities; antiques and art, in-room phones. Intimate hotel of quality.

Old Town B&B Inn	$$$ B&B	Full country breakfast
1521 Third St., 95501	7 rooms, 5 pb	Afternoon refreshments
707-445-3951 800-331-5098	Most CC, *Rated*, •	Comp. wine, some phones
Leigh & Diane Benson	C-ltd/S-no/P-no/H-no	sitting room w/fireplace
All year		feather beds, cable TV

Historic 1871 home, graciously decorated w/ antiques. Historical landmark. Original home of the Williams Carson family. Close to Old Town. Teak hot tub. **Discounts, ask**

EUREKA

A Weaver's Inn	$$ B&B	Full breakfast
1440 "B" St., 95501	4 rooms, 2 pb	Afternoon tea or coffee
707-443-8119	Visa, MC, •	Sitting room
Bob & Dorothy Swendeman	C-yes/S-no/P-ask/H-no	hot tub in one room
All year		Japanese garden

Stately 1883 home of weaver; quiet, spacious flower/herb garden; full breakfast; afternoon tea; historic town in heart of Redwoods.

FERNDALE

Gingerbread Mansion, The	$$$ B&B	Continental plus
P.O. Box 40, 95536	9 rooms, 9 pb	Afternoon tea & cake
400 Berding St.	Visa, MC, *Rated*, •	4 guest parlors
707-786-4000 800-952-4136	C-ltd/S-no/P-no/H-no	library w/fireplace
Kenneth W. Torbert	Port., Span., Fr., Jap.	English gardens, bikes
All year		

Northern California's most photographed inn! Large, elegant rooms. Victorian splendor, twin clawfoot tubs ("his & her bubble baths"). Turndown w/chocolate. **3rd night 50%**

Shaw House B&B	$$$ B&B	Continental plus
P.O. Box 1125, 95536	9 rooms, 9 pb	Aft. tea, cookies
703 Main St.	Visa, MC, *Rated*, •	Sittng room, library
707-786-9958	C-ltd/S-no/P-no/H-no	gazebo, yard, organ
Norma & Ken Bessingpas		robes, umbrellas
All year		

Ferndale's elegant inn—first house built in Ferndale (1854). Antiques, fresh flowers. Join other guests in library or parlor. **Discounts to all returning guests**

Shaw House B&B	$$$ B&B	Continental plus
P.O. Box 1125, 95536	6 rooms, 6 pb	Comp. beverages/cookies
703 Main St.	*Rated*, •	Sitting room, library
707-786-9958	C-ltd/S-ltd/P-no/H-no	gazebo, yard
Norma & Ken Bessingpas		
All year		

Ferndale's elegant inn—first house built in Ferndale (1854). Antiques, fresh flowers; join other guests in library, parlor. **Discounts to returning guests**

FISH CAMP

Karen's B&B Yosemite Inn	$$$ B&B	Full breakfast
P.O. Box 8, 93623	3 rooms, 3 pb	Afternoon tea, snacks
1144 Railroad Ave.	•	Sitting room, library
209-683-4550 800-346-1443	C-yes/S-ltd/P-no/H-no	private baths
Karen Bergh & Lee Morse		individual heating
All year		

Enjoy cozy country comfort, nestled in the pines. 2 mi. from Yosemite National Park. Skiing, golfing, horseback riding, fine dining. **Free night for 2 with 5 room referrals.**

FORT BRAGG

Avalon House	$$ B&B	Full breakfast
561 Stewart St., 95437	6 rooms, 6 pb	Comp. sherry/port
707-964-5555	Visa, MC, AmEx, Disc., •	Fireplaces in rooms
Anne Sorrells	C-yes/S-no/P-no/H-no	whirlpool tubs in rooms
All year		

1905 Craftsman house in a quiet neighborhood close to ocean and Skunk Train Depot. Fireplaces. Romantic Mendocino Coast retreat.

FORT BRAGG

Glass Beach B&B Inn
726 N. Main St., 95437
707-964-6774
Nancy Cardenas/Rich Fowler
All year

$$ B&B
9 rooms, 9 pb
Visa, MC, •
C-yes/S-yes/P-no/H-yes

Full breakfast
Snacks
Sitting room
hot tubs

Glass Beach is a small, gracious guest house where we offer you elegance, relaxation, and the comforts of home.

Grey Whale Inn, The
615 N. Main St., 95437
707-964-0640 800-382-7244
John & Colette Bailey
All year

$$$ B&B
14 rooms, 14 pb
Most CC, *Rated*, •
C-ltd/S-no/P-no/H-yes

Full buffet breakfast
Aft. tea, fresh fruit
Parlor, TV-VCR, fireplc.
game rm., mini conf. rm.
gift shop, art gallery

Mendocino coast landmark since 1915. Spacious rooms; ocean, town or garden views. Honeymoon suite w/jacuzzi & pvt. sundeck. Stroll to beach, shopping & dining.

Noyo River Lodge
500 Casa del Noyo Dr., 95437
707-964-8045 800-628-1126
Ellie Sinsel
All year

$$$ B&B
16 rooms, 16 pb
Rated, •
C-ltd/S-no/P-no/H-yes

Continental plus
Comp. wine
Sitting room
charter fishing
charter whale watch

Secluded country inn overlooks river and harbor. Fireplaces, decks. "Mendocino coast's best kept secret." **3rd Night 50% Off, Ltd; 10% off to readers—any time**

Pudding Creek Inn
700 N. Main St., 95437
707-964-9529
G. & C. Anloff & J. Woltman
All year

$$ B&B
10 rooms, 10 pb
Visa, MC, AmEx, *Rated*, •
C-ltd/S-no/P-no/H-no

Full buffet breakfast
Afternoon refreshments
Victorian parlor
lush garden
TV/game room

1884 Victorian built by Russian count. Enclosed garden court fuchsias, begonias, ferns. Restaurants, beaches, tennis courts nearby. **Free bottle wine & 50% off 3rd night**

FREESTONE

Green Apple Inn
520 Bohemian Hwy., 95472
707-874-2526
Rogers & Rosemary Hoffman
All year

$$$ B&B
4 rooms, 4 pb
Visa, MC, •
C-ltd/H-yes
Spanish

Full breakfast
Complimentary wine
Sitting room w/fireplace
bicycles

1860 farmhouse in a sunny meadow backed by redwoods. Located in a designated historic village near coast and wine country. **3rd night 50% off.**

FREMONT

Lord Bradley's Inn
43344 Mission Blvd., Mission
San Jose, 94539
415-490-0520
Keith & Anne Medeiros
All year

$$ B&B
8 rooms, 8 pb
Visa, MC, *Rated*, •
C-yes/S-ltd/P-ltd/H-yes
Spanish

Continental plus
Comp. tea
Sitting room

Adjacent to historic Mission San Jose de Guadalupe; nestled below Mission Peak. Kite fliers' paradise; Victorian antiques and decorations; gourmet breakfasts.

GEORGETOWN

American River Hotel	$$$ B&B	Full breakfast
P.O. Box 43, 95634	18 rooms, 12 pb	Evening refreshments
Main at Orleans St.	Visa, MC, AmEx, *Rated*,	Barbecue, games, aviary
916-333-4499 800-245-6566	•	player piano, bicycles
Will & Maria Collin, Helene	C-ltd/P-no/H-yes	hot tubs, swimming pool
All year		

An enchanting setting for weddings, honeymoons, anniversaries, corporate getaways or just a weekend away from the world. Putting green, mini-driving range. **3rd night 50%, ltd**

GEYSERVILLE

Campbell Ranch Inn	$$$ B&B	Full breakfast from menu
1475 Canyon Rd., 95441	5 rooms, 5 pb	Evening dessert
707-857-3476 800-959-3878	Visa, MC, Dis, *Rated*, •	Living room, A/C
Mary Jane & Jerry Campbell	C-ltd/S-no/P-no/H-no	family rm w/TV, VCR
All year		hilltop views, gardens

35-acre rural setting in heart of Sonoma County's wine country with tennis court, swimming pool & spa. Private cottage unit. Fresh flowers, evening dessert, and homemade pie.

Hope-Merrill/Hope-Bosworth	$$$ B&B	Full country breakfast
P.O. Box 42, 95441	12 rooms, 7 pb	Picnic lunches, pool
21253/38 Geyserville Ave.	Visa, MC, AmEx, *Rated*,	Beer & wine license
707-857-3356 800-825-4BED	•	sitting room, library
Bob & Rosalie Hope/Kim Taylor	C-yes/H-ltd	large Sterling Suite
All year		

Victorians in Sonoma County's wine country. Old-fashioned hospitality; delicious food. Stage-A-Picnic in the vineyards. Award-winning restoration. **Free bottle wine**

GILROY

Country Rose Inn B&B	$$$ B&B	Full breakfast
P.O. Box 1804, 95021	5 rooms, 5 pb	Library
455 Fitzgerald Ave. #E	Visa, MC, *Rated*, •	suite w/jet tub
408-842-0441	C-ltd/S-no/P-no/H-no	sitting room
Rose Hernandez	Spanish	
All year		

A surprise at the end of the private lane. An Oasis between San Jose and Monterey. Restful, gracious, centrally located. **3rd night 50% off**

GROVELAND

Groveland Hotel, The	$$$ B&B	Continental plus
P.O. Box 289, 95321	17 rooms, 17 pb	Restaurant-lunch/dinner
18767 Main St.	Visa, MC, AmEx, *Rated*,	Conf. fac., comp. wine
209-962-4000 800-273-3314	•	bar service, sitting rm.
Peggy A. Mosley	C-yes/S-ltd/P-ltd/H-yes	library, hot tubs
All year, Fax: 962-6674	AT&T interpreter service	

Beautifully restored Gold Rush hotel, w/incomparable hospitality. Restaurant & outdoor dining in Victorian garden. Near Yosemite National Park. **Off-season, midwk specials**

GUALALA

Gualala Hotel	$ EP	Dinner
P.O. Box 675, 95445	19 rooms, 5 pb	Sitting room
39301 S. Hwy. 1	Most CC, *Rated*,	piano
707-884-3441	C-yes/S-yes/P-no/H-no	
Howard Curtis		
All year		

Historic 1903 hotel, overlooking the ocean, furnished with original antiques. Extensive wine shop, family-style meals.

North Coast Country Inn, Gualala, CA

GUALALA

North Coast Country Inn
34591 S. Highway 1, 95445
707-884-4537 800-959-4537
Loren & Nancy Flanagan
All year

$$$ B&B
4 rooms, 4 pb
Visa, MC, AmEx, *Rated*,
•
C-ltd/S-no/P-no/H-no

Full breakfast to room
Wet bar in all rooms
Hot tub, library, gazebo
antique shop, fireplaces
beach access

A cluster of weathered redwood buildings on a forested hillside overlooking the Pacific Ocean. Close to golf, tennis and riding facilities. **Mid-week "Pamela Lanier special"**

GUERNEVILLE

Ridenhour Ranch House Inn
12850 River Rd., 95446
707-887-1033
Diane & Fritz Rechberger
Exc. January & February

$$$ B&B
8 rooms, 8 pb
Visa, MC, *Rated*, •
C-ltd/S-ltd/P-no/H-yes

Full gourmet breakfast
Dinner $ weekends
Comp. port or sherry
picnic lunches, hot tub
sitting room, fireplace

Country inn on the Russian River in the heart of the lush and lovely Sonoma wine country. Adjacent to historic Korbel Champagne Cellars. Fresh flowers.

HALF MOON BAY

Old Thyme Inn, The
779 Main St., 94019
415-726-1616
George & Marcia Dempsey
All year

$$$ B&B
7 rooms, 7 pb
Most CC, *Rated*, •
C-ltd/S-ltd/P-yes/H-no
French

Full breakfast
Comp. wine
Library
sitting room
herb garden

1890 Victorian with herb garden on historic Main Street. Some private baths with large whirlpool tubs, fireplaces. Great breakfasts.

Zaballa House
324 Main St., 94019
415-726-9123 800-77-BNB4U
Kerry Pendercast
All year

$$ B&B
9 rooms, 9 pb
Most CC, *Rated*, •
C-ltd/S-no/P-yes/H-no

"All-you-can-eat"
Full breakfast
Comp. wine and beverages
sitting room, gardens
near fine restaurants

First house built in town (1859). Garden setting by creek. Fireplaces, double whirlpool baths. Friendly and knowledgeable innkeeper. **Reduced rates midweek**

HANFORD

Irwin Street Inn, The
522 N. Irwin St., 93230
209-583-8000
Bruce Evans-Luci Burnworth
All year

$$ B&B
31 rooms, 31 pb
Visa, MC, •
C-yes/S-yes/P-no/H-yes

Continental breakfast
On site restaurant
Lunch, dinner available
afternoon tea
sitting room, hot tub

Four Victorian houses fully restored. 32 rooms, 4 meeting rooms. Run as an inn with breakfast & lunch served daily. Room service available.

HEALDSBURG

Calderwood Inn
P.O. Box 967, 95448
25 W. Grant St.
707-431-1110
Chris & Bob Maxwell
All year

$$$ B&B
6 rooms, 6 pb
Rated, •
C-ltd/S-no/P-no/H-no

Full breakfast
Comp. wine
Afternoon tea, dessert
sitting room
spa tub room

Restored Victorian, furnished with antiques. Serving a gourmet breakfast. Close to many wineries, restaurants, shopping and the Russian River. **Off-season discounts**

Camellia Inn
211 North St., 95448
707-433-8182 800-727-8182
Ray, Del & Lucy Lewand
All year

$$ B&B
9 rooms, 9 pb
Visa, MC, *Rated*, •
C-ltd/S-yes/P-no/H-ltd

Full breakfast
Comp. beverage & snacks
Sitting room
swimming pool
4 rms. w/whirlpool tub

Elegant Italianate Victorian built in 1869, near Sonoma's finest wineries—beautifully restored and furnished with antiques, oriental rugs.

Frampton House B&B
489 Powell Ave., 95448
707-433-5084
Paula D. Bogle
All year

$$ B&B
3 rooms, 3 pb
Visa, MC
C-ltd/S-no/P-no/H-no
Spanish

Full breakfast
Snacks, comp. wine
Library, sitting room
hot tub, sauna, pool
bicycles, entertainment

An escape from the ordinary. Emphasis on privacy and service. Centrally located for wine country and Sonoma coast. Lavish breakfast. **3rd night 50%, Sun.-Thur., Nov.-Apr.**

Calderwood Inn, Healdsburg, CA

HEALDSBURG

George Alexander House
423 Matheson St., 95448
707-433-1358
C. & P. Baldenhofer
All year

$$$ B&B
4 rooms, 4 pb
Visa, MC, *Rated*, •
C-yes/S-no/P-no/H-no

Full breakfast
Snacks
Sitting rooms
jacuzzi in 1 rm.
fireplaces 2 rms.

Charming 1905 Victorian. Interesting art, Oriental rugs. 4 rooms, private baths (one Jacuzzi), fireplaces, parlors. Walk to town, Russian River. Air conditioning.

Grape Leaf Inn
539 Johnson St., 95448
707-433-8140
Karen & Terry Sweet
All year

$$$ B&B
7 rooms, 7 pb
Visa, MC, *Rated*, •
C-ltd/S-no/P-no/H-no

Full country breakfast
Comp. wine & cheese
Jacuzzi tub/showers for
two in five guest rooms

Victorian elegance amidst Sonoma County's finest wineries. Generous full breakfast, complimentary premium wines, all private baths, and more!

Healdsburg Inn @ the Plaza
P.O. Box 1196, 95448
110 Matheson St.
707-433-6991
Genny Jenkins
All year

$$$ B&B
9 rooms, 9 pb
Visa, MC, *Rated*,
C-ltd/S-no/P-no/H-no

Full breakfast
Comp. wine, eve. dessert
Champagne brunch
(wkend)
rooftop garden, gallery
2 gift shops, fireplaces

Individually appointed Victorian rooms decorated with antiques and sunrise/sunset colors. Centrally located overlooking old town plaza. Breakfast served on airy roof garden.

Madrona Manor,
Country Inn
P.O. Box 818, 95448
1001 Westside Rd.
707-433-4231 800-258-4003
John & Carol Muir
All year, FAX:433-0703

$$$ B&B
21 rooms, 21 pb
Most CC, *Rated*, •
C-ltd/S-yes/P-ltd/H-yes
Spanish

Full breakfast
Gourmet restaurant
Music room, robes
antique rosewood piano
swimming pool, billiards

Circa 1881, furnished with antiques. All rooms with private baths. Carriage house. Wine country, canoeing, bicycling, historical points of interest. February "daffodil" month.

Raford House, The
10630 Wohler Rd., 95448
707-887-9573
Gina & Vince Velleneuve
All year

$$$ B&B
7 rooms, 5 pb
Visa, MC, *Rated*, •
C-ltd/S-ltd/P-no/H-ltd

Full breakfast
Comp. wine
Porch, vineyards, patio
some fireplaces, roses

Victorian farmhouse overlooks the vineyards of Sonoma County. Country setting just a half hour away from San Francisco. County historical landmark. **3rd night 50%**

HOMEWOOD

Rockwood Lodge
P.O. Box 226, 96141
5295 W. Lake Blvd.
916-525-5273 800-538-2463
Louis Reinkens
All year

$$$ B&B
4 rooms, 2 pb
Visa, MC, •
C-ltd/S-no/P-no/H-no

Continental
Comp. cordials & sweets
  wine
Sitting room, game room

"Old Tahoe" estate nestled in pine forest; Lake Tahoe within 100 feet. Breakfast served in guest rooms. Many fine appointments. 800 LE TAHOE.

Wilkum Inn, Idyllwild, CA

IDYLLWILD ────────────────

Wilkum Inn	$$ B&B	Continental plus
P.O. Box 1115, 92549	5 rooms, 3 pb	Aft./evening snacks
26770 Hwy. 243	*Rated*, •	Guest frig/microwave
909-659-4087	C-ltd/S-no/P-no/H-yes	common room, fireplace
A. Chambers & B. Jones	Basic Sign Language	Max. 2 persons per room
All year		

Warm hospitality enhanced by handmade quilts, antiques and collectibles. Shop, hike and relax in a pine-forested mountain village. **3rd night 50% off Mon.-Thrus.**

INVERNESS ────────────────

Blackthorne Inn	$$$ B&B	Full breakfast
P.O. Box 712, 94937	5 rooms, 2 pb	Comp. tea, dessert
266 Vallejo Ave.	Visa, MC, *Rated*, •	Wet bar sink area
415-663-8621	C-ltd/S-ltd/P-no/H-no	sitting room w/fireplace
Susan Wigert		hot tub
All year		

Sunset Magazine (April 1983) describes the Blackthorne Inn as "a carpenter's fantasy, with decks, hot tub, fireman's pole, and spiral staircase." **3rd. night free, Ltd. ask**

Dancing Coyote Beach	$$$ B&B	Continental plus
P.O. Box 98, 94937	3 rooms, 3 pb	Coffee & tea
12794 Sir Francis Drake	Visa, MC	Popcorn poppers
415-669-7200	C-yes/P-no/H-no	fireplace, kitchen, deck
Sherry King & Bobbi Stumpf		living room, library
All year		

The best of both worlds...Privacy while being catered to. 3 lovely, fully equipped cottages nestled among pines on secluded beach. **Jan-March whale-watching special, ask**

INVERNESS ————————————————————————————————

Fairwinds Farm B&B Cottage
P.O. Box 581, 94937
82 Drake's Summit
415-663-9454
Joyce H. Goldfield
All year

$$$ B&B
1 rooms, 1 pb
Rated
C-yes/S-no/P-no/H-no
Sign language

Continental plus
Desserts, snacks
Full kitchen, library
TV, VCR and movies
hot tubs, garden w/pond

Lg. cottages sleep 6. Ridge-top cottage adjoins 68,000-acre Nat'l Seashore. Ocean view from hot tub. Firepl., garden w/ponds & swing. Barnyard animals. **8th night free**

Hotel Inverness
P.O. Box 780, 94937
25 Park Aven.
415-669-7393
Susan & Thomas Simms
All year

$$$ B&B
5 rooms, 5 pb
Visa, MC, *Rated*, •
C-yes/S-no/P-no/H-no

Continental plus
Picnics
croquet
lawn for lounging

1906 shingle-style hotel in village's historical section. Upstairs rooms, queen beds, some private decks. Walk to shops, restaurants and bay.

Manka's Inverness Lodge
P.O. Box 126, 94937
Argyle & Calender Way
415-669-1034
Judy & Rob Prokupek
All year

$$$ EP
9 rooms, 9 pb
Major Cre.Cards,*Rated*,
C-ltd/S-no/P-no/H-no
Czech

Full breakfast ($)
Dinner

Secluded family-operated country hideaway in old world atmosphere; gourmet Czech cuisine, extensive wine list, Czech & Viennese background music; romantic.

Moorings B&B
P.O. Box 35, 94937
8 Pine Hill Dr.
415-669-1464
Lee & John Boyce-Smith
All year

$$ B&B
1 rooms, 1 pb
•
C-ltd/S-no/P-no/H-no
German

Full breakfast
Outdoor deck off suite
restaurants nearby, TV
Pt. Reyes Park nearby

A guest said, "The serene beauty of your home and surroundings was matched only by your warm spirits." **7th night free in week's stay.**

Rosemary Cottage
Box 619, 75 Balboa Ave., 94937
415-663-9338
Suzanne Storch
All year

$$$ B&B
1 rooms, 1 pb
•
C-yes/S-yes/P-no/H-no

Full breakfast
Comp. tea, coffee
Kitchen
fireplace
decks, garden

Charming, romantic French country cottage nestled in secluded garden with dramatic forest views. Close to beaches; families welcome.

Ten Inverness Way B&B
P.O. Box 63, 94937
10 Inverness Way
415-669-1648
Mary E. Davies
All year

$$$ B&B
4 rooms, 4 pb
Rated, •
C-ltd/S-ltd/P-no/H-no
French, Spanish

Full breakfast
Comp. sherry
Sitting room
library, piano
hot tub (by appointment)

A classic bed and breakfast inn for lovers of handmade quilts, hearty breakfasts, great hikes and good books.

INVERNESS-PT. REYES STA.

Marsh Cottage B&B
P.O. Box 1121, 94956
12642 Sir Francis Drake
415-669-7168
Wendy Schwartz
All year

$$$ B&B
1 rooms, 1 pb
C-yes/S-no/P-no/H-no

Full breakfast
Comp. coffee/tea/wine
Kitchen, library
sitting room, fireplace
porch, sun deck

Cheerful, carefully appointed private cottage along bay. Kitchen, fireplace, queen bed, desk; extraordinary setting for romantics and naturalists. **3rd night 50%, Ltd.**

IONE

Heirloom B&B Inn, The
P.O. Box 322, 95640
214 Shakeley Ln.
209-274-4468
Pat Cross, Melisande Hubbs
All year

$$ B&B
6 rooms, 4 pb
Rated, •
C-ltd/S-no/P-no/H-yes

Full gourmet breakfast
Comp. Wine/Beverages
Dinner, sitting room
piano, bicycles, croquet
fireplaces, balconies

Petite 1863 colonial mansion—private garden setting, verandas, fireplaces, heirloom antiques, French country breakfast, comfort, gracious hospitality. Private dinners.

JACKSON

Wedgewood Inn, The
11941 Narcissus Rd., 95642
209-296-4300 800-WEDGEWD
Vic & Jeannine Beltz
All year

$$$ B&B
6 rooms, 6 pb
Visa, MC, *Rated*, •
C-ltd/S-no/P-no/H-no

Full gourmet breakfast
Snacks, cheese, beverage
Sitting room, porch
terraced garden park w/
gazebo & fountains

Charming replica Victorian on wooded acreage. Antique decor, queen-size beds, porch swing, gardens, wood burning stoves. InnTimes readers' Top 50 Inns 1991, Mobil: 3 stars.

The Wedgewood Inn, Jackson, CA

JAMESTOWN

Historic National Hotel
P.O. Box 502, 95327
77 Main St.
209-984-3446
Stephen & Pamela Willey
All year

$$$ B&B
11 rooms, 5 pb
Visa, MC, Disc.,*Rated*, •
C-ltd/S-ltd/P-yes/H-no
Spanish, French

Continental plus
Full restaurant, bar
Champagne brunch
Sundays
library, antiques
courtyard dining

Restored 1859 hotel in center of Gold Rush town. Original saloon. Many outdoor activities. Outstanding restaurant—recognized in Bon Appetit. Near Yosemite. **Midwk discounts.**

Royal Hotel
P.O. Box 219, 95327
18239 Main St.
209-984-5271
Don & Joyce Chitty
All year

$ B&B
19 rooms, 12 pb
Visa, MC, AmEx, •
C-yes/S-yes/P-no/H-yes

Continental plus
Sitting room
library

Historic Victorian gold country hotel in second oldest gold town in U.S. Steam powered train rides, antiquing and great restaurants. **Mid-week specials**

JENNER

Murphy's Jenner Inn
P.O. Box 69, 95450
10400 Coast Hwy 1
707-865-2377 800-732-2377
Jenny Carroll
All year

$$ B&B
11 rooms, 11 pb
Visa, MC, AmEx, •
C-yes/S-no/P-no/H-yes

Continental plus
Comp. teas & aperitifs
Port & sherry available
sitting room
pvt. separate cottages

Coastal retreat inn—antiques, lots of character, peaceful, romantic, river and ocean views. Sunset weddings by the sea, wineries, redwoods nearby, 8 beautiful sandy beaches.

JULIAN

Julian Gold Rush Hotel
P.O. Box 1856, 92036
2032 Main St.
619-765-0201 800-734-5854
Steve & Gig Ballinger
All year

$$ B&B
18 rooms, 5 pb
Visa, MC, AmEx, *Rated*,
•
C-yes/S-yes/P-no/H-no

Full breakfast
Afternoon tea
Sitting room, library
piano, cottage

Surviving 1897 hotel in southern Mother Lode of CA, restored to full glory w/American antiques. Nat'l Register. "CA Point of Historical Interest" **3rd night 25% off, ltd**

Julian Lodge
P.O. Box 1930, 92036
2720 C. St.
619-765-1420 800-542-1420
Jim & Linda Huie
All year

$$ B&B
23 rooms, 23 pb
Visa, MC, AmEx, •
C-yes/S-ltd/P-no/H-ltd

Continental plus

A mountain inn 60 miles north of San Diego. Antique furnishings, Victorian charm in the gold mining town of Julian. AAA rated 2 diamonds.

KELSEY

Mountainside B&B
P.O. Box 165, 95643
5821 Spanish Flat Rd.
916-626-1119 800-237-0832
Paul & Mary Mello
All year

$$ B&B
4 rooms, 3 pb
•
C-ltd/S-ltd/P-no/H-no

Full breakfast
Comp. beverage
Sitting room
library
hot tubs

1929 country home, 80-acre wooded retreat. 180-degree view of Sacramento Valley. Dorm for groups available. River rafting, ballooning, gold country. **3rd. night 50% off**

KERNVILLE ──────────────────────────────

Kern River Inn B&B	$$$ B&B	Full breakfast
P.O. Box 1725, 93238	6 rooms, 6 pb	Afternoon tea
119 Kern River Dr.	Visa, MC, *Rated*,	Comp. wine, champagne
619-376-6750	C-ltd/S-no/P-no/H-yes	riverviews, fireplaces
Mike Meehan & Marti Andrews		whirlpool tubs, TV
All year		

New country inn on the Kern River. Mountain setting. Fishing, golf, antique shops, giant redwoods. Whitewater rafting/skiing pkgs. Year-round getaway. **Many disc'ts, ask**

Whispering Pines	$$$ B&B	Full breakfast
Lodge B&B	11 rooms, 11 pb	Lunch, dinner
Rt. 1, Box 41, 13745 Sierra Way,	Most CC, *Rated*,	Aft. tea
93238	C-yes/S-no/P-no/H-no	swimming pool
619-376-3733		jacuzzi
All year		

Romantic country getaway featuring Roman jacuzzis, fireplaces, gourmet breakfast on patio w/view of Sequoia Forest & the wild and scenic Kern River. AAA 3 diamonds.

KLAMATH ──────────────────────────────

Requa Inn	$$ B&B	Full breakfast
451 Requa Rd., 95548	15 rooms, 15 pb	Restaurant, dinner
707-482-8205	Visa, MC, AmEx,	Afternoon tea
Paul & Donna Hamby	C-ltd/S-no/P-no/H-no	sitting room
March–October		

Located on majestic Klamath River in Redwood National Park. A relaxing, romantic retreat. Stroll through woods, swim, boat, or fish. Wonderful dining.

LAGUNA BEACH ──────────────────────────────

Carriage House, The	$$$ B&B	Continental plus
1322 Catalina St., 92651	10 rooms, 10 pb	Comp. wine, cheese
714-494-8945	*Rated*, •	fruit in room
Dee Taylor-Vernon/Thom Taylor	C-yes/S-yes/P-ltd/H-no	courtyard
All year		ocean swimming

Colonial New Orleans-style carriage house with central brick courtyard, tropical landscaping. Six suites each with sitting room, bedroom, bath.

Casa Laguna Inn	$$ B&B	Continental plus
2510 Coast Hwy, 92651	21 rooms, 21 pb	Aft. tea, snacks
714-494-2996 800-233-0449	Most CC, -CLIA, •	Comp. wine, galleries
Louise Gould	C-yes/S-yes/P-no/H-no	library, boutiques
All year	Spanish	heated swimming pool

Romantic country inn on terraced hillside overlooking ocean. 21 rms. individually decorated w/antiques, collectables. Kitchen suites & cottages for families. Near beach.

LAKE ARROWHEAD ──────────────────────────────

Bluebelle House B&B	$$$ B&B	Full breakfast
P.O. Box 2177, 92352	5 rooms, 3 pb	Evening hors d'oeuvres
263 S. State Hwy 173	Visa, MC, *Rated*, •	Comp. wine, sitting room
909-336-3292	C-ltd/S-no/P-no/H-no	library, darts on deck
Rick & Lila Peiffer		private beach club
All year exc. Dec 24-27		

Elegant, cozy European decor in Alpine setting. Exquisite brkfsts, warm hospitality. Near lake, village, shops, restraunts. **10% midwk Sr disc't free lunch at local restaurant**

LAKE ARROWHEAD

Carriage House B&B, The	$$$ B&B	Full gourmet breakfast
P.O. Box 982, 92352	3 rooms, 3 pb	Comp. wine, snacks
472 Emerald Dr.	Visa, MC, Disc.,*Rated*, •	Sitting rm, deck w/swing
909-336-1400	C-ltd/S-no/P-no/H-no	all rooms have lake view
Lee & Johan Karstens	Dutch	room w/private balcony
All year		

Our home is furnished in French country style, very warm & cozy. 5 min. walk to lake. Featherbeds w/down comforters. We pamper our guests. **10% discount 2+ nights, midweek**

Chateau Du Lac	$$$ B&B	Full breakfast
P.O. Box 1098, 92352	6 rooms, 4 pb	Comp. wine, tea, snacks
911 Hospital Rd.	Visa, MC, AmEx, •	Dinner by appointment
909-337-6488 Fax:337-6746	C-ltd/S-no/P-no/H-no	sitting room, library
Jody & Oscar Wilson		hot tubs in room
All year		

The Chateau du Lac overlooks a beautiful view of Lake Arrowhead. It's a warm and friendly place to stay. We do weddings, showers, and birthday parties, too. **3rd. night 50%**

Prophet's Paradise B&B Inn	$$$ B&B	Full breakfast
P.O. Box 2116, 92352	3 rooms, 3 pb	Snacks, Comp. wine
26845 Modoc Lane	Visa, MC, •	Bicycles, 1 hot tub
909-336-1969	C-yes/S-no/P-yes/H-no	gym/billiard rm.
Tom & LaVerne Prophet		2 rms. TV/VCR
All year		

Multi-level home exudes country charm w/stained glass, antiques, film memorabilia, warm colors. 2 suites. Shopping, dining, restaurants nearby.

LAKEPORT

Forbestown Inn	$$$ B&B	Pool, spa, veranda
825 Forbes St., 95453	4 rooms, 1 pb	free ride to airport
707-263-7858	Visa, MC, AmEx, *Rated*,	corporate rates
Nancy & Jack Dunne	•	
All year	C-ltd/S-no/P-no/H-no	

1869 quaint victorian inn. Country breakfast, refreshments, gardens, pool, spa, robes, bicycles, walking distance to the lake, water sports, restaurants, wineries.

LEGGETT

Sky Canyon Ranch	$$$ EP	4 cottages w/kitchens
P.O. Box 160, 95585	4 rooms, 4 pb	Comp. sparkling cider
66000 Dr. Thru Tree Rd.	*Rated*, •	Horseback riding
707-925-6415	C-yes/S-no/P-no/H-yes	swimming, hiking
Barbara Burke		rafting on river
All year		

Idyllic 250 acres on 1.5 miles of pristine river. Contemporary cottages w/all amenities. Includes therapeutic massage. Fine horseback riding. **Free bottle of wine**

LITTLE RIVER

Victorian Farmhouse	$$$ B&B	Full breakfast
P.O. Box 357, 95456	10 rooms, 7 pb	Comp. wine & sherry
7001 N. Hwy 1	Visa, MC, AmEx, *Rated*,	Sitting room
707-937-0697	•	7 rooms w/fireplace
George & Carol Molnar	C-yes/S-no/P-no/H-no	
All year	Hungarian	

Built in 1877; short walk to the ocean. Enjoy deer, flower gardens, creek, or sitting in our small orchard. Quiet atmosphere.

LODI

Wine & Roses Country Inn
2505 W. Turner Rd., 95242
209-334-6988
K. Cromwell, D. & S. Smith
All year

$$$ B&B	Full breakfast
10 rooms, 10 pb	Restaurant, lunch
Visa, MC, AmEx, *Rated*,	Dinner, snacks
•	comp. wine, bar service
C-ltd/S-ltd/P-no/H-yes	sitting room, lake

Charming historical manor sequestered on 5 acres of towering trees & gardens. "Casually elegant" restaurant. Enjoyed by leisure & business travelers. **Surprise gift basket**

LONG BEACH

Lord Mayor's B&B Inn
435 Cedar Ave., 90802
310-436-0324
All year

$$$ B&B	Full breakfast
5 rooms, 5 pb	Snacks, tea, sherry
Visa/MC/AmEx,	Library, sitting room
Rated, •	porches, sundecks
C-yes/S-no/P-no/H-no	IBM PC on request
Dutch, Danish	

Award-winning restored 1904 Edwardian home of Long Beach's first mayor. Spacious rooms with antiques, library, gardens, porches, parking.

LOS ANGELES

Channel Road Inn
219 Channel Rd., Santa Monica, 90402
310-459-1920 FAX:454-9920
Kathy Jensen
All year

$$$ B&B	Continental plus (wkdys)
14 rooms, 14 pb	Full breakfast (Sunday)
Visa, MC, *Rated*, •	Aftn. tea, comp. wine
C-yes/S-yes/P-no/H-yes	sitting room, library
Spanish, French, German	bicycles, hot tubs

Elegant historic home converted to luxury inn. Located one block from the sea and furnished in period antiques. Historic and intimate...so romantic. Outstanding location.

Salisbury House B&B
2273 W. 20th St., 90018
213-737-7817 800-373-1778
Sue & Jay German
All year

$$$ B&B	Full gourmet breakfast
5 rooms, 3 pb	Comp. tea, shortbread
Most CC, *Rated*, •	Sitting room
C-yes/S-ltd/P-no/H-no	

Experience the ultimate in bed and breakfast luxury and turn-of-the-century charm. Has been used as location for movies and commercials.

LUCERNE

Kristalberg B&B
P.O. Box 1629, 95458
715 Pearl Ct.
707-274-8009
Merv Myers
All year

$$ B&B	Continental plus
3 rooms, 2 pb	Afternoon tea
AmEx, •	Complimentary wine
C-ltd/S-no/P-no/H-no	sitting room, library
German, Spanish, French	bicycles, 1 rm w/whirlpl

Awe-inspiring view of Clear Lake. Euorpean/Victorian ambience, country tranquility, gourmet breakfast, canoe, hike. Congenial, multi-lingual host. **3rd night 50% off**

MALIBU

Malibu Beach Inn
22878 Pacific Coast Hwy, 90265
213-456-6444
Dan Ferrante
All year

$$$ B&B	Continental plus
47 rooms, 47 pb	Snacks
Visa, MC, AmEx, *Rated*,	Some rooms w/jacuzzis
•	horse & jet ski rentals
C-yes/S-yes/P-no/H-yes	fishing, water sports
Spanish	

On the beach. Rooms beautifully decorated in mission style: Mexican tile, textured stucco, fireplaces, private balconies with ocean view, honor bar, remote TV, VCR.

MAMMOTH LAKES ───────────────────────────────

Snow Goose Inn	$$ B&B	Full breakfast
P.O. Box 946, 93546	20 rooms, 20 pb	Comp. wine, appetizers
57 Forest Trail	Visa, MC, AmEx, *Rated*,	Sitting room
619-934-2660 800-874-7368	•	bicycles
Bob & Carol Roster	C-yes/S-yes/P-no/H-no	hot tubs
All year		

Winter ski resort/Sierra's summer getaway. European-style deluxe mountain bed and break-fast. Offering special ski packages midweek. **10% off w/mention of ad**

───────────────────────────────

Tamarack Lodge Resort	$$ EP	Full breakfast $
P.O. Box 69, 93546	37 rooms, 31 pb	Restaurant, lunch/dinner
Twin Lakes Rd.	Visa, MC, *Rated*, •	Afternoon tea, snacks
619-934-2442	C-yes/S-ltd/P-no/H-ltd	sitting room
Carol & David Watson		boats (summ), ski (wint)
All year		

Historic High Sierra lakeside lodge; regionally acclaimed Lakefront Restaurant. Major cross-country ski resort; four-season fishing, hiking, biking. **Free house wine w/dinner**

MARINA DEL RAY ───────────────────────────────

Mansion Inn	$$ B&B	Continental plus
327 Washington Blvd., 90291	43 rooms, 43 pb	Bicycle rentals nearby
310-821-2557 800-828-0688	Most CC, *Rated*, •	tennis court nearby
Richard Hunnicutt	C-yes/S-yes/P-no/H-yes	walk to shops, cafes
All year	Spanish	

Comfortable French-style rooms, p/baths. Walk to Venice Beach. Continental breakfast served daily in cobblestone courtyard. Venice beach one block.

MARIPOSA ───────────────────────────────

Dubord's Restful Nest	$$$ B&B	Full breakfast
4274 Buckeye Creek Rd., 95338	3 rooms, 3 pb	Dinner by request
209-742-7127 FAX:742-6888	C-yes/S-ltd/P-no/H-no	Comp. wine, snacks
Huguette Dubord	French	sitting room, library
All year		swimming pool, pond

Cozy accomodations on 11 wooded acres near Yosemite National Park. French Canadian breakfast served buffet style. 2 day min. Relax and be pampered. **3rd night 10% discount**

───────────────────────────────

Oak Meadows, too B&B	$$ B&B	Continental plus
P.O. Box 619, 95338	6 rooms, 6 pb	Sitting room
5263 Hwy 140 N.	Visa, MC, *Rated*, •	
209-742-6161 FAX:966-2320	C-ltd/S-no/P-no/H-no	
Frank Ross and Kaaren Black	French, German	
All year		

Relax in luxury. Located in town. Near Yosemite. Rooms decorated with brass beds and hand-made quilts. All private baths. **3rd Night 50% Off, Ltd**

───────────────────────────────

Pelennor B&B, The	$ B&B	Full breakfast
3871 Hwy 49 South, 95338	4 rooms,	Kitchen
209-966-2832	•	Sitting room, sauna
Dick & Gwen Foster	C-yes/S-ltd/P-ltd/H-ltd	spa & lap pool
All year		Sauna

Quiet country accommodations at economical rates. Enjoy the stars while listening to a tune on the bagpipes.

McCLOUD ─────────────────────────────────

McCloud Guest House
P.O. Box 1510, 96057
606 W. Colombero Dr.
916-964-3160
The Leighs & The Abreus
All year

$$$ B&B
5 rooms, 5 pb
Visa, MC
C-ltd/S-ltd/P-no/H-no

Continental plus
Restaurant, dinner
Evening sherry
antique pool table
library, bicycles

Completely restored 1907 country inn & restaurant near Mt. Shasta. Warm, country inn charm. Former guests include: President Hoover, Jean Harlow and the Hearst Family.

MENDOCINO ───────────────────────────────

Agate Cove Inn B&B
P.O. Box 1171, 95460
11201 Lansing St.
707-937-0551 800-527-3111
Sallie & Jake McConnell-Zahvi
All year

$$$ B&B
10 rooms, 10 pb
Visa, MC, AmEx, *Rated*,
C-ltd/S-ltd/P-no/H-no

Full country breakfast
Comp. sherry in room
Common room w/antiques
spectacular ocean views
whale watching Dec-Mar

*Romantic cottages w/fireplaces, spectacular ocean views. Full country breakfast served in 1860s farmhouse viewing ocean. Beautifully landscaped garden. **Winter rates avail.***

──

Brewery Gulch Inn
9350 Coast Highway 1, 95460
707-937-4752
Linda & Bill Howarth
All year

$$$ B&B
5 rooms, 4 pb
Visa, MC
C-ltd/S-no/P-no/H-ltd

Full country breakfast
Fireplaces, sitting room
down pillows
gardens

*Brewery Gulch is an unhurried authentic pre-Victorian farm surrounded by two acres of flowers & tree gardens. Full country brkfast. **2nd night 50%, Ltd***

──

Glendeven Inn & Gallery
8221 N. Hwy 1, 95456
707-937-0083 800-822-4536
Jan & Janet deVries
All year, FAX:707-6108

$$$ B&B
10 rooms, 10 pb
Rated
C-ltd/S-ltd/P-no/H-no

Continental plus
Comp. wine
Sitting room
baby grand piano
Comp. tennis

*A special country inn with lovely gardens and bayviews near Mendocino village and adjacent to state park trails and beach. **3rd night 50% off***

──

Headlands Inn, The
P.O. Box 132, 95460
Howard St. at Albion St.
707-937-4431
David & Sharon Hyman
All year

$$$ B&B
5 rooms, 5 pb
Rated
C-ltd/S-no/P-no/H-ltd

Gourmet breakfast to rm.
Aftn. tea, mineral water
Comp. paper, 2 parlors
antiques, flowers in rm.
English-style garden

Restored 1868 Victorian w/antiques in picturesque Mendocino Village. All rooms have private baths, fireplaces, Q/K beds many have ocean views. Fruit & candy in parlor.

──

John Dougherty House
P.O. Box 817, 95460
571 Ukiah St.
707-937-5266
David & Marion Wells
All year

$$$ B&B
6 rooms, 6 pb
●

C-ltd/S-no/P-no/H-no

Full breakfast
Comp. wine
Sitting room, verandas
ocean views, near tennis
antiques, English garden

Historic 1867 house in Village center. All private baths. Large verandas with ocean views; quiet peaceful nights; walk to shops and dining. Woodburning stoves in 5 rooms.

MENDOCINO ─────────────────────────

Joshua Grindle Inn
P.O. Box 647, 95460
44800 Little Lake Rd.
707-937-4143
Jim & Arlene Moorehead
All year

$$$ B&B
10 rooms, 10 pb
Rated
C-ltd/S-no/P-no/H-yes

Full breakfast
Comp. sherry, min. water
Sitting room
piano
Near shops, restaurants

*Historic country charm in coastal village of Mendocino. Antiques, fireplaces, private baths.
OUR 1985 INN OF THE YEAR!* **Comp. bottle of wine with mention of Guide**

MacCallum House Inn
P.O. Box 206, 95460
45020 Albion St.
707-937-0289
Nick Reding
All year

$$ B&B
20 rooms, 8 pb
Visa, MC, •
C-yes/S-yes/P-no/H-no

Continental breakfast
Restaurant, bar
Sitting room

The MacCallum House provides friendly, personal attention to guests in a handsome, authentically restored Victorian home in the village of Mendocino.

Mendocino Farmhouse
P.O. Box 247, 95460
43410 Comptche-Ukiah Rd.
707-937-0241 FAX:937-1086
Margie & Bud Kamb
All year

$$$ B&B
5 rooms, 5 pb
Visa, MC, *Rated*,
C-yes/S-no/P-no/H-no

Full breakfast
Sitting room, library
fireplaces
deep tubs in bathrooms

*Secluded in a redwood forest close to Mendocino Village. Comfortable rooms with fireplaces,
antique furnishings. Quiet and away from the real world.*

Stanford Inn by the Sea
P.O. Box 487, 95460
Hwy 1, Comptche-Ukiah Rd.
707-937-5026 800-331-8884
Joan & Jeff Stanford
All year

$$$ B&B
25 rooms, 25 pb
Most CC, *Rated*,
C-yes/S-yes/P-yes/H-yes
French, Spanish

Full breakfast
Wine, organic vegetables
Indoor pool, hot tub
decks, nurseries, llamas
bicycles, canoe rentals

*A truly elegant country inn in a pastoral setting. All accommodations with ocean views,
fireplaces, decks, antiques, four-posters and TVs.*

Stevenswood Lodge
P.O. Box 170, 95460
8211 N. Hwy 1
707-937-2810 800-421-2810
Robert & Vera Zimmer
All year

$$$ B&B
10 rooms, 10 pb
Visa, MC, *Rated*, •
C-yes/S-no/P-no/H-yes

Full gourmet breakfast
Bar service, comp. wine
Coffee, snacks
sitting room, library
lounge, conference room

*Distinctive ocean view suites in "old growth" forest. Beach access, fireplaces, fine art decor,
gallery. Mendocino's only AAA four diamond rating.*

Whitegate Inn B&B
P.O. Box 150, 95460
499 Howard St.
707-937-4892
Carol and George Bechtloff
All year

$$$ B&B
5 rooms, 5 pb
Rated
C-ltd/S-no/P-no/H-no

Full breakfast
Complimentary wine
Sitting room
organ
deck with gazebo

*Located in historic Mendocino. All rooms furnished with French or Victorian antiques. Sit
down breakfast in dining room.* **Winter disc'ts.; box of chocolates**

MILL VALLEY

Mountain Home Inn
810 Panoramic Hwy, 94941
415-381-9000
Lynn M. Saggese
All year

$$$ B&B
10 rooms, 10 pb
Visa, MC, *Rated*, •
C-ltd/S-yes/P-no/H-yes

Full breakfast
Lunch, dinner
Jacuzzis
hiking trails
telephones in rooms

Two-and-a-half-million-dollar restored classic California luxury inn. Adjacent to parklands, Muir Woods. Panoramic S.F. Bay views; jacuzzis, fireplaces, terraces.

MONTARA

Goose & Turrets B&B
P.O. Box 370937, 94037
835 George St.
415-728-5451
Raymond & Emily Hoche-Mong
All year

$$$ B&B
5 rooms, 5 pb
Most CC, *Rated*, •
C-yes/S-no/P-no, French
spoken

Full 4-course breakfast
Afternoon tea, snacks
Sitting room w/woodstove
gardens, fireplaces
local airport pickup

*Solitude. Bonhomie. Cozy down comforters, towel warmers, and fantastic breakfasts. 30 minutes from San Francisco; 0.5 mile from Pacific Ocean. **5 nights, 10% off***

MONTEREY

Jabberwock, The
598 Laine St., 93940
408-372-4777
Jim & Barbara Allen
All year

$$$ B&B
7 rooms, 3 pb
Rated
C-ltd/S-ltd/P-no/H-no
Spanish, French, Danish

Full breakfast
Sherry & hors d'ouevres
Sitting room
sun porch

Once a convent, this Victorian home is above Cannery Row. Sherry on the sun porch overlooking Monterey Bay, gardens & waterfalls. Near Monterey Bay Aquarium.

MOSS BEACH

Seal Cove Inn
221 Cypress Ave., 94038
415-728-7325 FAX:728-4116
Karen & Rick Herbert

$$$ B&B
10 rooms, 10 pb
Visa, MC, AmEx, *Rated*,
•
C-ltd/S-no/P-no/H-yes

Full breakfast
Comp. wine, snacks
Afternoon tea
2 rooms have jacuzzis
private terraces

A romantic European-style country inn on the coast south of San Francisco. Ten charming guest rooms, all with fireplaces, overlook wildflowers, cypress trees and ocean.

MOUNT SHASTA

Mount Shasta Ranch B&B
1008 W.A. Barr Rd., 96067
916-926-3870
Mary & Bill Larsen
All year

$$ B&B
10 rooms, 4 pb
Visa, MC, AmEx, *Rated*,
•
C-ltd/S-no/P-no/H-no

Full breakfast
Afternoon tea
Comp. wine, snacks
sitting room, hot tub
library

Affordable elegance in historical setting. Enjoy the country charm of the Main Lodge, Cottage and Carriage House. Nearby lake fishing, year-round golf and winter skiing.

MUIR BEACH

Pelican Inn
10 Pacific Way, 94965
415-383-6000
Barry Stock
X-mas day closed

$$$ B&B
7 rooms, 7 pb
Visa, MC
C-yes/S-yes/P-no/H-ltd

Full English breakfast
Comp. sherry
Sitting room
restaurant
British pub/bar, darts

Romantic English inn capturing the spirit of the 16th century. Between ocean & redwoods, surrounded by countryside. Hiking, cycling trails. 20 min. from Golden Gate Bridge.

MURPHYS

Dunbar House, 1880
P.O. Box 1375, 95247
271 Jones St.
209-728-2897 800-225-3764
Barbara & Bob Costa
All year

$$$ B&B
4 rooms, 4 pb
Visa, MC, *Rated*, •
C-ltd/S-no/P-no/H-no

Full country breakfast
Comp. bottle of wine
Sitting room, library
wood-burning stoves
clawfoot tubs, TVs, VCRs

Restored 1880 home w/historical designation located in Murphys, Queen of the Sierra. 2 person luxury spa bath. Walking distance to Main Street. A place to be pampered.

NAPA

Beazley House
1910 First St., 94559
707-257-1649 800-559-1649
Jim & Carol Beazley
All year

$$$ B&B
9 rooms, 9 pb
MC, Visa, *Rated*, •
C-ltd/S-ltd/P-no/H-yes

Full gourmet breakfast
Comp. wine, wine list
Private spas/fireplaces
entertainment, sunroom
sitting room, library

The Beazley House is a Napa landmark. Relax in old-fashioned comfort. Breakfast, complimentary sherry. Personal wine tour orientation. **3rd night 50% off, Ltd**

La Belle Epoque
1386 Calistoga Ave., 94559
707-257-2161
Claudia & Merlin Wedepohl
All year

$$$ B&B
6 rooms, 6 pb
Most CC, *Rated*, •
C-yes/S-no/P-no/H-no

Full breakfast
Comp. wine, snacks
Sitting room, wine
tasting room and cellar
fully air-conditioned

Historic Victorian bejeweled in stained glass, antique furnishings, gourmet breakfasts by the fireside. Walk to wine train depot, restaurant and shops. **3rd night 50% off, ltd**

Blue Violet Mansion
443 Brown St., 94559
707-253-2583
Bob & Kathy Morris
All year

$$$ B&B
6 rooms, 6 pb
Visa, MC, AmEx, •
C-yes/S-no/P-no/H-no

Full breakfast
Aft. tea, snacks, dinner
Comp. wine, sitting room
bicycles, gazebo w/swing
grape-arbored deck

Historic 1886 Queen Anne Victorian in "American Painted Ladies." Antiques, romantic getaway, wine and evening desserts served. Near wine train. In National Register.

Churchill Manor
485 Brown St., 94559
707-253-7733
Joanna Guidotti, Brian Jensen
All year exc. Christmas

$$$ B&B
8 rooms, 8 pb
Visa, MC, AmEx, •
C-ltd/S-ltd/P-no/H-ltd

Full breakfast
Comp. wine, tea, snacks
Sitting room, pianos
sauna, side garden
croquet, bicycles

Grand beyond compare, this 1889 mansion, filled w/antiques & surprises, is listed in Nat'l Historic Register. Offseason pkgs. **10% off 2nd night, ltd.**

Country Garden Inn
1815 Silverado Trail, 94558
707-255-1197 FAX:255-3112
Lisa & George Smith
All year

$$$ B&B
13 rooms, 9 pb
Visa, MC, AmEx, *Rated*,
•
C-ltd/S-no/P-no/H-yes

Full breakfast
Comp. wine, tea, dessert
Sitting room
private jacuzzis & decks
rose garden, terrace

1.5 acres of woodland riverside property. Decorated in English style with antiques and heirlooms, and of course, true English hospitality. **3rd night 50% off, Nov-June, ltd**

NAPA ———————————————————————————————————

Hennessey House
1727 Main St., 94559
707-226-3774
A. Weinstein, L. Delay
All year

$$$ B&B
10 rooms, 10 pb
Most CC, *Rated*, •
C-ltd/S-no/P-no/H-no

Full breakfast
Comp. wine
Sitting room w/TV, bikes
sauna
near the Wine Train

1889 Queen Anne Victorian boasts original architectural details and a spectacular, hand-painted, tin ceiling in the dining room.

Napa Inn, The
1137 Warren St., 94559
707-257-1444
Doug & Carol Morales
All year

$$$ B&B
6 rooms, 6 pb
C-ltd/S-no/P-no/H-no

Full breakfast
Afternoon refreshments
Homebaked breads & cakes
sitting room w/fireplace
antiques, gardens

Beautiful, old Queen Anne Victorian home built in 1899. Quiet location in historic section of the town of Napa. Appropiately furnished with turn-of the century antiques.

Oak Knoll Inn
2200 E. Oak Knoll Ave., 94558
707-255-2200
Barbara Passino, John Kuhlman
All year

$$$ B&B
3 rooms, 3 pb
Visa, MC, *Rated*, •
C-ltd/S-no/P-no/H-no

Full breakfast
Afternoon tea, snacks
Complimentary wine
spa, swimming pool
fireplaces in all rooms

Romantic, elegant stone country inn surrounded by vineyards. Spacious rooms with fire-places. Sip wine watching the sunset over the mountains. **3rd night 50%, Ltd.**

Old World Inn
1301 Jefferson St., 94559
707-257-0112 800-966-6624
Daine M. Dumaine
All year

$$$ B&B
8 rooms, 8 pb
Visa, MC, AmEx, *Rated*,
•
C-ltd/S-no/P-no/H-no

Continental plus
Comp. wine & cheese
Afternoon tea
evening dessert buffet
sitting room, jacuzzi

Run with Old World hospitality by its English innkeepers, this Victorian inn is uniquely deco-rated throughout in bright Scandinavian colors.

Oak Knoll Inn, Napa, CA

NAPA

La Residence Country Inn
4066 St. Helena Hwy., 94558
707-253-0337
David Jackson, Craig Claussen
All year

$$$ B&B
20 rooms, 18 pb
Visa, MC, *Rated*, •
C-ltd/S-no/P-no

Full breakfast
Complimentary wine
Sitting room
swimming pool, hot tub
two acres of grounds

For the sophisticated traveler who enjoys an elegant yet intimate style, La Residence is the only choice in Napa Valley. Mobil rated 3 stars.

Stahlecker House B&B Inn
1042 Easum Dr., 94558
707-257-1588
Ron & Ethel Stahlecker
All year

$$$ B&B
4 rooms, 4 pb
Visa, MC, AmEx, •
C-ltd/S-ltd/P-no/H-no

Full candlelight bkfast
Beverages & cookies
Sitting room, fireplaces
piano, antiques, sundeck
ping-pong, croquet, AirC

A secluded, romantic, quiet, country inn located just minutes from wineries, the Wine Train & fine restaurants. The entire inn & beautiful gardens open to guests. **50% off ask**

Trubody Ranch B&B
5444 St. Helena Hwy, 94558
707-255-5907 Fax-255-7254
Jeff & Mary Page
Exc. Christmas & January

$$$ B&B
2 rooms, 2 pb
Visa, MC
C-yes/S-no/P-no/H-no

Continental plus
Sitting room
air conditioned rooms

1872 Victorian home & water tower nestled in 120 acres of family-owned vineyard. Stunning views from the water tower rooms.

NAPA VALLEY

Crossroads Inn
6380 Silverado Trail, 94558
707-944-0646
Nancy & Sam Scott
All year

$$$ B&B
3 rooms, 3 pb
Visa, MC, •
C-ltd/S-no/P-no/H-no

Full breakfast
Comp. wine, host bar
Aftn. tea, eve. brandies
library, game room, deck
hot tubs, bikes, gardens

Sweeping Napa Valley views; custom 2-person spas; complete privacy; king-sized beds, wine bars and full baths complement each suite.

NEVADA CITY

Downey House B&B
517 W. Broad St., 95959
916-265-2815 800-258-2815
Miriam Wright
All year

$$$ B&B
6 rooms, 6 pb
Visa, MC, •
C-ltd

Full breakfast
Comp. wine, soft drinks
Coffee, cookies, fruit
common area, veranda
library, garden, arbor

Light, comfortable view rooms. Lovely garden and terrace. Near restaurants, shops, theaters, galleries, museums & outdoor recreational facilities. **10% off midwk**

Flume's End B&B Inn
317 S. Pine St., 95959
916-265-9665
Terrianne Straw, Steve Wilson
All year

$$$ B&B
6 rooms, 6 pb
Visa, MC, *Rated*, •
C-ltd/S-no/P-no/H-no

Full breakfast
Snacks
Sitting room, library
two jacuzzis

Charming Victorian on Gold Run Creek. Easy walk to shopping and restaurants in historical town. Gourmet breakfast in serene natural setting.

NEVADA CITY

Grandmere's Inn
449 Broad St., 95959
916-265-4660
Doug & Geri Boka
All year

$$$ B&B
7 rooms, 7 pb
Visa, MC, *Rated*, •
C-ltd/S-no/P-no/H-ltd

Full breakfast
Dinner by arrangement
soft drinks, cookies
sitting room

Historic landmark with country French decor in the heart of Nevada City. Lovely grounds suitable for weddings and private parties.

Red Castle Inn, The
109 Prospect St., 95959
916-265-5135
Conley and Mary Louise Weaver
All year

$$ B&B
7 rooms, 7 pb
Visa, MC, *Rated*, •
C-ltd/S-ltd/P-no/H-no

Full candlelight bkfst.
Comp. beverages/desserts
Afternoon tea & sweets
parlor, antique organ
flowers in every room

State Historic Landmark 4-story brick mansion. Elegant, homey, lush grounds, a nature lover's dream. Vegetarian breakfasts and horse & buggy rides available. Dinner by res.

NEWPORT BEACH

Portofino Beach Hotel
2306 W. Oceanfront, 92663
714-673-7030
Christine Luetto
All year

$$$ B&B
12 rooms, 12 pb
Most CC, *Rated*, •
C-ltd/S-ltd/P-no/H-no
Italian, French, Spanish

Continental plus
Comp. wine & cheese
Antique beer & wine bar
Catalina Isl. day trips
sightseeing, boating

Nestled in the sand in beautiful Newport Beach. Enjoy our European hideaway, furnished in antiques. Complimentary wine and cheese included. AAA—3 star rating, ABBA—excellent

NIPTON

Hotel Nipton
HCI, Box 357, 72 Nipton Rd.,
92364
619-856-2335
Gerald & Roxanne Freeman
All year

$ B&B
5 rooms
Visa, MC, *Rated*, •
C-ltd/S-yes/P-no/H-no
Spanish

Continental breakfast
Lunch, dinner, snacks
Comp. brandy, BBQ
sitting room, hot tub
horse trails, picnic tbl

19th-century desert hideaway w/antiques; home cooked breakfast from our cafe next door; in east Mojave Desert nat'l scenic area; horses stay free. **3rd night 50% off**

OAKHURST

Chateau du Sureau
P.O. Box 577, 93644
48688 Victoria Ln.
209-683-6860
Kathryn Kincannon
All year

$$$ B&B
9 rooms, 9 pb
Most CC, Rated-,
C-ltd/S-no/P-no/H-yes
German, French, Italian

Full breakfast
Lunch, dinner, aft. tea
Snacks, comp. wine, bar
sitting room, library
pool, outdoor chess

At our "Estate by the Elderberries"—Ernas Elderberry House Restaurant & Chateau du Sureau—you will take a step back in time—into a world of gracious service & romance.

OCCIDENTAL

Heart's Desire Inn
P.O. Box 857, 95465
3657 Church St.
707-874-1047 FAX:874-1078
R. Jewell, H. & J. Selinger
All year

$$$ B&B
8 rooms, 8 pb
Visa, MC, AmEx, *Rated*,
•
C-ltd/S-no/P-no/H-yes
German

Full breakfast
Comp. evening sherry
Sitting room, library
courtyard garden, aviary
bicycles, tennis nearby

Renovated 1867 Victorian with European ambience. Antique furnishings, goose down comforters, elegant appointments, sumptuous breakfasts. **20% off restaurant**

OJAI ──

Ojai Manor Hotel
P.O. Box 608, 93023
210 E. Matilija
805-646-0961
Mary Nelson
All year

$$$ B&B
6 rooms
Visa, MC, *Rated*,
C-ltd/S-ltd/P-no/H-no
Spanish

Continental plus
Comp. wine, biscotti
Sitting room
bicycles
health club nearby

1874 schoolhouse, now a B&B in the heart of town. Walk to shops, restaurants, golf and tennis. Minutes drive to Los Padres National Forest and hot springs.

OLEMA ──

Pt. Reyes Seashore Lodge
P.O. Box 39, 94950
10021 Highway 1
415-663-9000
Judi Burkes
All year

$$$ B&B
21 rooms, 21 pb
Most CC, *Rated*, •
C-yes/S-ltd/P-no/H-yes

Continental plus
Antique pool table
game & sitting room
Meeting facility

A unique re-creation of a turn-of-the-century lodge. Many rooms with whirlpool tubs and fireplaces. Next to the Point Reyes National Seashore Park. **Free wine**

OROVILLE ──

Jean's Riverside B&B
P.O. Box 2334, 95965
45 Cabana Dr.
916-533-1413
Jean Pratt
All year

$$ B&B
11 rooms, 11 pb
Visa, MC, *Rated*, •
C-ltd/S-ltd/P-ltd/H-yes

Full breakfast
Comp. wine
River waterfront
deck overlooking river
lawn games, golfing

Romantic waterfront hideaway w/private jacuzzis, fishing, goldpanning, birdwatching, historical sites. Near hiking, Feather River Cyn, Oroville Dam, Sac. **3+ nites 10% disc't**

PACIFIC GROVE ──

Centrella Hotel
612 Central Ave., 93950
408-372-3372 800-233-3372
Canan Bariman
All year

$$$ B&B
26 rooms, 25 pb
Visa, MC, AmEx, *Rated*,
•
C-ltd/S-ltd/P-no/H-yes
Italian

Continental plus
Tea/wine/hors d'oeuvres
Parlor, dining room
beveled glass, gardens
weekly specials

Restored Victorian—award winner for interior design. Ocean, lovers' point and many attractions of the Monterey Peninsula. Fireplaces in suites. Take a trip back in time.

──

Gosby House Inn
643 Lighthouse Ave., 93950
408-375-1287
Jillian Brewer
All year

$$$ B&B
22 rooms, 20 pb
AmEx, Visa, MC, *Rated*,
•
C-yes/S-ltd/P-no/H-no

Full gourmet breakfast
Wine and hors d'oeuvres
Sitting room
bicycles
turndown service

Romantic Victorian mansion. Antique furniture, cheerful pastel fabrics & fireplaces abound. Turndown service, morning paper. Part of Four Sisters' Inns. **Breakfast in bed**

──

Green Gables Inn
104 Fifth St., 93950
408-375-2095
Shirley Botts
All year

$$$ B&B
11 rooms, 7 pb
AmEx, Visa, MC, •
C-yes/S-ltd/P-no/H-no

Full breakfast
Wine and hors d'oeuvres
Sitting room, bathrobes
bicycles, newspapers
coffee/breakfast in bed

Spectacular Victorian mansion with views of Monterey Bay. Individually decorated rooms with antiques and beautiful fabrics. The most romantic inn around. Mobil 3-Stars.

PACIFIC GROVE

Maison Bleue French B&B
P.O. Box 51371, 93950
157 - 15th St.
408-373-2993
Jeanne E. Coles
All year

$$$ B&B
5 rooms, 1 pb
Visa, MC, AmEx, DC, •
C-ltd/S-ltd

Full breakfast
Afternoon tea
Sitting room
hot outside showers for
divers

For the truly romantic—canopy queen and king beds. French antiques. Breakfast in the privacy of your room or charming parlor. **Discounts for special events, Ask**

Martine Inn, The
255 Ocean View Blvd., 93950
408-373-3388
Marion & Don Martine
All year

$$$ B&B
19 rooms, 19 pb
Visa, MC, AmEx, *Rated*,
•
C-yes/S-yes/P-no/H-yes
Italian, Russian, Span.

Full breakfast
Picnic basket lunches
Comp.wine/hors d'oeuvres
sitting room, game room
bicycles, conf. room

12,000-square-foot mansion on Monterey Bay. Elegant museum quality American antiques. Breakfast served on old Sheffield silver, crystal, Victorian china, and lace.

Roserox Country Inn
557 Ocean View Blvd., 93950
408-373-7673
Dawn Vyette Browncroft
All year

$$$ B&B
8 rooms, 4 pb
Rated, •
C-yes/S-ltd/P-no/H-no

Full breakfast
Comp wine/hors d'oeuvres
Bar, library, horseshoes
croquet, bicycles
sitting room w/fireplace

Intimate historic Victorian on shores of Pacific. Honeymoon Suite, antique brass beds, feather quilts, clawfoot tubs, breakfast in bed, spectacular views. **Comp. slipper socks**

Ross Cottage
122 18th St., 93950
800-729-7677
Paula DiCarlo & Brian M. Ross
All year

$ EP
1 rooms, 1 pb
•
C-yes/S-no/P-no/H-no
Italian

Snacks
Comp. sherry
Sitting room
hot tubs
fireplace, deck w/view

Charming 109-year-old Victorian, furnished period & contemporary w/all amenities. Steps from Monterey Bay and town. Minutes to all major attractions. **10% off when 6+ nights**

Seven Gables Inn
555 Ocean View Blvd., 93950
408-372-4341
The Flatley Family
All year

$$$ B&B
14 rooms, 14 pb
Rated, •
C-ltd/S-no/P-no/H-no
French, Spanish

Full breakfast
High tea
Grand Victorian parlor
aquarium tickets
ocean views in rooms

Elegant Victorian mansion at the very edge of Monterey Bay. Fine antique furnishings throughout. Incomparable ocean views from all rooms.

PALM SPRINGS

Casa Cody B&B Country Inn
175 S. Cahuilla Rd., 92262
619-320-9346
Frank Tysen, Therese Hayes
All year

$ B&B
17 rooms, 17 pb
Most CC, *Rated*, •
C-ltd/S-ask/P-ask/H-yes
French, Dutch, German

Continental breakfast
Library, bicycles
hot tubs, swimming pools
hiking, horseback riding

Romantic hideaway in the heart of Palm Springs Village. One or two bedrooms w/kitchens & wood-burning fireplace. Beautifully restored in Santa Fe style. **3rd night 50% off**

PALM SPRINGS

Orchid Tree Inn
261 S. Belardo Rd., 92262
619-325-2791 800-733-3435
Karen Prince, Bob Weithorn
All year

$$ B&B
40 rooms, 40 pb
Visa, MC, AmEx, *Rated*,
•
C-ltd/S-ltd/P-no/H-no
Some Spanish

Continental plus
Tennis court, not tubs
2 pools, sitting room
golf packages, tours

Beautifully restored historic desert garden retreat. Rooms, suites, villas. Rediscover Old Palm Springs through this picturesque & convenient inn-site. **3rd night 50% off, ltd**

PALO ALTO

Victorian on Lytton, The
555 Lytton Ave., 94301
415-322-8555
Susan Maxwell Hall
All year

$$$ B&B
10 rooms, 10 pb
Visa, MC, *Rated*, •
C-ltd/S-no/P-no/H-yes

Continental
Comp. appetizers
port & sherry
occasional entertainment

A lovely Victorian built in 1895 offering a combination of forgotten elegance with a touch of European grace. Near Stanford University, charming shops, cafes.

PLACERVILLE

Chichester-McKee House
800 Spring St., 95667
916-626-1882 800-831-4008
Doreen & Bill Thornhill
All year

$$$ B&B
3 rooms, 3 pb
Most CC, *Rated*, •
C-ltd/S-no/P-no/H-no

Special full breakfast
Comp. soft drinks, mixes
Parlor, large library
queen-size beds
gardens & porches

Feel pampered in our elegant 1892 Victorian home filled with antique family treasures. Gourmet breakfasts served above our gold mine. Music & doll collection. **Business rate**

Combellack-Blair House
3059 Cedar Ravine, 95667
916-622-3764
Al & Rosalie McConnell
All year

$$$ B&B
2 rooms,
•
C-ltd/S-no/P-no/H-no

Continental plus
Comp. tea, coffee
Baked goods
sitting room

Elaborate 1895 Queen Anne Victorian furnished in genuine antiques. Original stained glass windows and free-standing spiral staircase.

River Rock Inn
1756 Georgetown Dr., 95667
916-622-7640
Dorothy Irvin
All year

$$$ B&B
4 rooms, 2 pb
Rated, •
C-yes/S-ltd/P-no/H-ltd

Full breakfast
Comp. sherry
Sitting room
hot tub, TV lounge
antiques

Relax on the 110' deck overlooking the American River, fish and pan for gold in the front yard. Quiet and beautiful.

POINT ARENA

Coast Guard House
695 Arena Cove, 95468
707-882-2442 800-524-9320
M. Whatley, R. Wasserman
All year

$$ B&B
6 rooms, 4 pb
Visa, MC, Pers. checks,
C-ltd/S-yes/P-ltd

Full breakfast
Comp. beverages
Hot tub, beaches
whale watching, theater
fishing pier, tide pools

Historic Coast Guard House, built by the Life-Saving Service in 1901, was eventually taken over by the U.S. Coast Guard and became officially known as the Life-Saving Station.

60 California

POINT REYES STATION ————————————————————————

Cricket Cottage	$$$ B&B	Full breakfast
P.O. Box 627, 94956	1 rooms, 1 pb	Comp. sparkling juice
18 Cypress Rd.	C-yes/P-ltd/H-yes	Library, private hot tub
415-663-9139		private garden
Penelope Livingston		Franklin fireplace
All year		

A garden cottage with private hot tub. Cozy, romantic furnishings; original art. Located near Point Reyes National Seashore and Tomales Bay Headlands. **6th night free**

Ferrando's Hideaway	$$$ B&B	Full breakfast
P.O. Box 688, 94956	3 rooms, 3 pb	Aft. tea, comp. wine
12010 Hwy. 1	*Rated*	Sitting room, library
415-663-1966 FAX:663-1825	C-yes/S-no/P-no/H-no	hot tubs
Greg & Doris Ferrando	German	
All year		

One cozy, private cottage with full kitchen sleeps 3. 2 rooms in main house, hot tub, vegetable garden, view. **3rd night 50% off, midweek, Jan-March**

Holly Tree Inn	$$$ B&B	Hearty country breakfast
P.O. Box 642, 94956	5 rooms, 5 pb	Comp. refreshments
3 Silverhills Rd.	Visa, MC, •	Sitting room
415-663-1554	C-ltd/S-ltd/P-no/H-no	fireplaces
Diane & Tom Balogh		garden hot tub
All year		

Romantic country inn on 19 acres in a coastal valley near San Francisco. Breakfast by the curved hearth. Herb gardens. Also a cottage in the woods near the waterfront.

Jasmine Cottage	$$$ B&B	Full breakfast
P.O. Box 56, 94956	1 rooms, 1 pb	Comp. teas & coffee
11561 Coast Route 1	*Rated*, •	Large naturalist library
415-663-1166	C-yes/S-no/P-yes/H-no	picnic area, patio
Karen Gray		garden hot tub, Cable TV
All year		

Secluded country cottage sleeps 4. Fully equipped kitchen, writing desk, library, woodburning stove, queen-sized bed, sun room, patio, garden, laundry. **3rd night 50% off**

Thirty-Nine Cypress	$$$ B&B	Full breakfast
P.O. Box 176, 94956	3 rooms, 1 pb	Hot tub w/great view
39 Cypress Way	C-ltd/S-no/P-no/H-yes	140 mi. of hiking trails
415-663-1709	French	bicycles, sitting room
Kate Howan & Julia Bartlett		
All year		

Antiques, original art, oriental rugs, spectacular view! Close to beaches. Horseback riding arrangements available. **3rd night off except at holiday times**

POINT RICHMOND ————————————————————————

East Brother Light Station	$$$ MAP	Continental plus
117 Park Place, 94801	4 rooms, 2 pb	Dinner, lunch, aft. tea
510-233-2385	*Rated*	Snacks, sitting room
Cliff & Ruth Benton	C-yes/S-no/P-no/H-no	library, horseshoes
All year		fishing, bird watching

Experience the panorama of San Francisco–Marin skylines from East Brother island & lighthouse. Multi-course dinner w/wine. **Free book on lighthouses.**

QUINCY ——————————

Feather Bed, The	$$ B&B	Full breakfast
P.O. Box 3200, 95971	6 rooms, 6 pb	Sitting room, gazebo
542 Jackson St.	Visa, MC, AmEx, *Rated*,	Victorian garden
916-283-0102	•	fountain, bicycles
Bob & Jan Janowski	C-ltd/S-no/P-no/H-yes	
All year		

Country Victorian in forested surroundings, relaxing our specialty, antiques in individually decorated rooms, located on Heritage Walk. Recreation area. Four rooms with A/C.

RED BLUFF ——————————

Faulkner House, The	$$ B&B	Full breakfast
1029 Jefferson St., 96080	4 rooms, 4 pb	Complimentary beverage
916-529-0520	MC, Visa, AmEx, *Rated*,	Sitting room
Harvey & Mary Klingler	•	bicycles
All year	C-ltd/S-no/P-no/H-no	

1890s Queen Anne Victorian furnished in antiques. Screened porch on quiet street, hiking and skiing nearby. Visit Ide Adobe or Victorian Museum, Sacramento River.

REDDING ——————————

Cabral House on Chestnut	$$ B&B	Full breakfast
1752 Chestnut St., 96001	3 rooms, 3 pb	Hors d'oeuvres, wine
916-244-3766	MC, Visa, *Rated*, •	Patio gazebo, porch
Ann & Louie Cabral, Jr.	C-ltd/S-no/P-no/H-no	flowering garden
All year		household cat & dog

The nostalgic era of the "golden years," 1920's–1940's. Residential setting, vintage furnishings, Big Band music, memories of a vanished time, and warm hospitality await you.

Palisades Paradise B&B	$$ B&B	Full breakfast (wkends)
1200 Palisades Ave., 96003	2 rooms	Continental plus (wkdys)
916-223-5305 800-382-4649	Visa, MC, *Rated*, •	Comp. wine, snacks, TV
Gail Goetz	C-ltd/S-ltd/P-no/H-ltd	fireplace, porch swing
All year		hot tubs, garden spa

Breathtaking view of Sacramento River, mountains, and city from a secluded contemporary home in Redding. Gateway to the Shasta-Cascade Wonderland.

Tiffany House B&B Inn	$$ B&B	Full breakfast
1510 Barbara Rd., 96003	4 rooms, 4 pb	Comp. refreshments
916-244-3225	Visa, MC, AmEx, *Rated*,	Sitting room, library
Susan & Brady Stewart	•	1 rm w/spa, gazebo
All year	C-yes/S-ltd/P-no/H-ltd	swimming pool, parlor

Romantic Victorian w/in minutes of beautiful lakes, championship golf and Sacto River. Elegant view of Lassen mountain range. Music in parlor & drawing room.

REDLANDS ——————————

Morey Mansion B&B Inn	$$$ B&B	Continental
190 Terracina Blvd., 92373	7 rooms, 3 pb	Comp. tea, wine
909-793-7970	Visa, MC, AmEx, *Rated*,	Sitting room, library
Dolly Travares Wimer	•	2 pianos, 2 organs
All year	C-yes/S-ltd/P-no/H-no	bicycles, phone in rm.

*Historic landmark Victorian home. Onion dome, beveled and leaded windows, interior abounds with antiques. Near mountain, lake and ski resorts. **3rd night 25% off***

RUTHERFORD

Rancho Caymus Inn
P.O. Box 78, 94573
1140 Rutherford Rd.
707-963-1777
Tony Prince
All year

$$$ B&B
26 rooms, 26 pb
Visa, MC, *Rated*, •
C-ltd/S-yes/P-no/H-yes

Continental breakfast
Comp. wine
Sitting room, piano
Jacuzzi

Located in the "Heart of the Napa Valley," this Spanish-style inn, with 26 suites encircling private gardens, captures the rustic spirit of early California.

SACRAMENTO

Abigail's B&B Inn
2120 "G" St., 95816
916-441-5007 800-858-1568
Susanne & Ken Ventura
All year FAX:441-0621

$$$ B&B
5 rooms, 5 pb
Most CC, *Rated*, •
C-ltd/S-no/P-no/H-no

Full breakfast
Comp. beverages
Secluded garden, piano
sitting rooms, fireplace
hot tub, games

Grand old mansion in the heart of the State Capitol. Large & comfortable, delicious breakfasts, A/C. Ideal for business travelers & romantic escapes. **Comp. wine w/dinner-Ltd**

Amber House B&B Inn
1315 - 22nd St., 95816
916-444-8085 800-755-6526
Michael & Jane Richardson
All year

$$$ B&B
8 rooms, 8 pb
Visa, MC, AmEx, *Rated*, •
C-ltd/S-ltd/P-no/H-no

Full gourmet breakfast
Comp. wine, tea, coffee
4 suites with jacuzzi
tandem bicycle, phones
new "Monet Room"

Luxury guest rooms offer ultimate comfort for the business traveler and the perfect setting for a romantic escape. Phones, cable TV, in-room jacuzzis, breakfasts in room.

Power's Mansion Inn
1910 Rockwood Dr., 164
Cleveland Ave, Auburn, 95864
916-885-1166
Tony & Tina Verhaart
All year

$$$ B&B
13 rooms, 13 pb
Rated, •
C-yes/S-no/P-no/H-yes
French, Spanish

Full breakfast
Comp. wine, snacks
Deluxe amenities
fireplaces, patios/decks
terry robes

1885 mansion, 10,000 sq. ft. built from gold-mining fortune. Has elegance of detailed restoration & antique furnishings w/queen beds & central air & heat. **3rd night 50% off.**

Savoyard
3322 H St., 95816
916-442-6709
Bruce & Pat Ansell
All year

$$$ B&B
2 rooms, 2 pb
Visa, MC, DC, •
C-ltd/S-no/P-no/H-no

Full breakfast
Aft. tea
Sitting room
library, hot tubs
bicycles, tennis nearby

Across the street from Sacramento's most romantic park. Exceptional breakfast to please your taste. Call or write for brochure. **Reduced rate for long stays**

SAINT HELENA

Bartels Ranch/Country Inn
1200 Conn Valley Rd., 94574
707-963-4001 800-932-4002
Jami E. Bartels
All year, FAX:963-5100

$$$ B&B
3 rooms, 3 pb
Most CC, *Rated*, •
C-ltd/S-yes/P-no/H-yes
Spanish, German

Hearty continental plus
Catered lunch & dinner
Comp. wine/fruit/cheese
library, sauna, jacuzzi
darts, horseshoes, golf

Elegant, secluded romantic wine country estate. Award-winning. Ideal honeymoon: 10,000-acre view, firepl., billiards, bicycles. Champagne under stars. **3rd night free, Ltd**

SAINT HELENA

Bylund House B&B Inn
2000 Howell Mtn. Rd., 94574
707-963-9073
Bill & Diane Bylund
All year

$$$ B&B
2 rooms, 2 pb
•
C-ltd/S-ltd/P-no/H-no

Continental plus
Wine & hors d'oeuvres
Sitting room w/fireplace
swimming pool, bicycles
spa w/deck

Wine country villa designed by owner-architect in secluded valley with sweeping views. 2 private rooms with views, balconies and European feather beds! **3rd night 50% off**

Cinnamon Bear B&B
P.O. Box 1196, 95448
1407 Kearney St.
707-963-4653
Genny Jenkins
All year

$$$ B&B
3 rooms, 3 pb
Visa, MC, *Rated*,
C-ltd/S-no/P-no/H-no

Full breakfast
Comp. snacks
Sitting room, games
fireplace, piano
classical music or swing

Homesick for a visit to your favorite aunt's house? Bring your teddy and come to the Napa Valley wine country. **Midweek rates discounted**

Creekside Inn
945 Main St., 94574
707-963-7244
J. Nicholson, V. Toogood
All year

$$$ B&B
3 rooms
Rated
C-ltd/S-no/P-no/H-no

Full breakfast
Sitting room

Country French atmosphere in the very heart of St. Helena, yet peacefully sheltered. White Sulphur Creek ripples past secluded rear patio garden. **3rd night 50% off**

Deer Run Inn
3995 Spring Mountain Rd, 94574
707-963-3794
Tom & Carol Wilson
All year

$$$ B&B
3 rooms, 3 pb
AmEx, •
C-ltd/S-no/P-no/H-no

Full breakfast
Comp. wine
Library
swimming pool
horseshoes, Ping Pong

Romantic, cozy country hideaway, furnished in antiques, wrapped in treed deckings on four acres of forest. Situated in the heart of the Napa Valley wine country.

Elsie's Conn Valley Inn
726 Rossi Rd., 94574
707-963-4614
Elsie Asplund Hudak
All year

$$$ B&B
3 rooms, 1 pb
AmEx, Visa, MC, •
C-yes/S-ltd/P-no/H-no
Finnish

Full breakfast
Comp. wine, fruit basket
  with cheese, library
sitting room, fireplace
extensive gardens & yard

Peaceful country hideaway, vineyards, lake trails. Genuine antiques. Continental plus breakfast served indoors or in the garden. **3rd night 50% off**

Erika's—Hillside
285 Fawn Park, 94574
707-963-2887
Erika Cunningham
All year

$$ B&B
3 rooms, 2 pb
Rated, •
C-yes/S-ltd/P-no/H-no
German

Continental breakfast
Comp. sparkling water
Sitting room

Enjoy a peaceful and romantic retreat nestled on a hillside overlooking the Silverado Trail with inspiring views of the Napa Valley and its vineyards. **3rd Night 50% Off**

SAINT HELENA ───

Harvest Inn
One Main St., 94574
707-963-9463 800-950-8466
Steacy Drew
All year

$$$ B&B
54 rooms
Most CC, *Rated*, •
C-yes/S-yes/P-yes/H-yes
Spanish

Continental breakfast
Bar service, snacks
Hot tubs
swimming pool
VCR & movie rentals

Cozy English Tudor cottages are set amidst 7 acres of lovely gardens; an anniversary or honeymoon paradise. AAA—Four diamond rating.

Hilltop House B&B
P.O. Box 726, 94574
9550 St. Helena Rd.
707-944-0880
Annette Gevarter
All year

$$$ B&B
3 rooms, 3 pb
Visa, MC, *Rated*, •
C-yes/S-no/P-no/H-yes

Full breakfast
Comp sherry after dinner
Guest refrigerator
sitting room, hot tub
hiking trails

Secluded mountain hideaway in romantic setting on 135 acres of unspoiled wilderness, offers a hang glider's view of Mayacamas Mountains. **3rd night 50% off**

Oliver House Country Inn
2970 Silverado Tr., 94574
707-963-4089
Richard & Clara Oliver
All year

$$$ B&B
4 rooms, 4 pb
Visa, *Rated*, •
C-ltd/S-ltd/P-no/H-no
German

Continental plus
Sitting room
walk to wineries
balconies w/view

Warm intimate country atmosphere. Picturesque Swiss chalet overlooking acres of vineyard. Fireplaces, private baths, queen-sized beds. **3rd night 50% off ltd.**

Shady Oaks Country Inn
399 Zinfandel Ln., 94574
707-963-1190
John & Lisa Wild-Runnells
All year

$$$ B&B
4 rooms, 4 pb
Rated, •
C-ltd/S-no/P-no/H-yes

Full gourmet breakfast
Picnic basket, garden
Wine & hors d'oeuvres
horseshoes, croquet
sightseeing tips

Romantic, secluded on 2 acres among finest wineries in Napa Valley. Elegant ambience; country comfort; antiques; warm hospitality. **Offseason midweek rates available.**

Villa St. Helena
2727 Sulphur Springs Av, 94574
707-963-2514
Ralph Cotton
All year

$$$ B&B
3 rooms, 3 pb
Visa, MC, AmEx, *Rated*,
•
C-ltd/S-ltd/P-no/H-no

Continental breakfast
Comp. wine
Swimming pool
library, hiking
walking trails

Secluded hilltop Mediterranean villa overlooking Napa Valley. Romantic antique-filled rooms, fireplaces, private entrances; elaborate breakfast. Country elegance.

Wine Country Inn, The
1152 Lodi Ln., 94574
707-963-7077 800-473-3463
Jim Smith
Exc. December 12-26

$$$ B&B
25 rooms, 25 pb
Visa, MC. *Rated*, •
C-ltd/S-yes/P-no/H-yes

Continental plus buffet
Patios, balconies
swimming pool
whirlpool

Beautiful country inn furnished with antiques and nestled in the heart of the wine country.

SAINT HELENA

Wine Country Victorian
P.O. Box 295, 94574
709-963-0852
Jan Strong
All year

$$$ B&B
3 rooms, 3 pb
C-ltd/S-yes/P-no/H-no

Continental plus
Wine tasting seminar

Relax in this cozy cottage secluded in a private woodland setting of several acres. Victorian charm and beauty surround you.

SAN DIEGO

Blom House B&B
1372 Minden Dr., 92111
619-467-0890
Bette Blom
All year

$ B&B
2 rooms, 2 pb
Rated, •
C-yes/S-ltd/P-no/H-no
Dutch, Spanish

Full breakfast-4 courses
Comp. cheese & soda
Sitting room, video lib.
bathrobes, hot tubs
after dinner drinks

Elegant cottage on bluffs overlooking lights of Hotel Circle. 65' deck w/spa. Antique furnishings, refrigerators, phones, color TV, all attractions nearby. **3rd night 50% off**

Carole's B&B Inn
3227 Grim Ave., 92104
619-280-5258 619-280-7162
C. Dugdale, M. O'Brien
All year

$$ B&B
8 rooms, 3 pb
Rated, •
C-yes/S-yes/P-no/H-no

Continental plus
Comp. wine & cheese
Sitting room
swimming pool, spa
player piano, cable TV

Historical site, antiques, lrg pool. Close to zoo, Balboa Park. Centrally located. Friendly, congenial atmosphere. House built in 1904 & tastefully redecorated. **3rd nite 50%**

Cottage, The
3829 Albatross St., 92103
619-299-1564
Carol & Robert Emerick
All year

$ B&B
2 rooms, 2 pb
Visa, MC, *Rated*, •
C-yes/S-no/P-no/H-no

Continental breakfast

Relaxation in a garden setting with turn-of-the-century ambiance is offered in a residential downtown San Diego neighborhood.

Harbor Hill Guest House
2330 Albatross St., 92101
619-233-0638
Dorothy A. Milbourn
All year

$$ B&B
5 rooms, 5 pb
Rated, •
C-yes/S-yes/P-no/H-no

Continental breakfast
Kitchens on each level
Large sun deck & garden
barbecue, TV, phones
rooms with harbor views

Private entrances & kitchens on each level. Near Balboa Park, zoo, museums, Sea World, Old Town, harbor, shopping, theater. Families welcome. **4+ night stay special rates.**

La Jolla Oasis B&B
P.O. Box 99666, 92169
619-456-1776
Winifred Krause
All year

$$$ B&B
2 rooms, 2 pb
•
C-ltd/S-no/P-no/H-no

Full breakfast
Snacks
Library, bicycles
hot tubs, swimming pool
indoor jacuzzi, sitt. rm

Private residence in the hills above La Jolla Village. Near all. Very quiet. Luxurious accommodations, gourmet breakfast. Let us spoil you.

SAN DIEGO ───────────────────────────────────────

Keating House Inn
2331 Second Ave., 92101
619-239-8585
Ruth Babb
All year

$$ B&B
6 rooms, 2 pb
Visa, MC, AmEx, •
C-ltd/S-ltd/P-no/H-no

Full breakfast
Comp. wine
Fireplaces
sitting room
Gardens

Historically designated Queen Anne Victorian home. Walk to Balboa Park, zoo, museums, Gaslamp Quarter; near restaurants, beaches, shopping, Sea World. **$20. for 3rd. person**

Sea Breeze B&B Inn
121 N. Vulcan Ave., Encinitas, 92024
619-944-0318
Kristen Richter
All year

$$$ B&B
5 rooms, 5 pb
Rated, •
C-yes/S-yes/P-no/H-no

Continental plus
Comp. wine & cheese
Wet bar, kitchenette
sitting room
near beach and tennis

N. San Diego quiet beach town. Contemporary B&B w/ocean view. Penthouse Boudoir w/private 8' hot tub. Intimate oceanview wedding grotto. Squeaky clean. **3rd night 50% off**

SAN FRANCISCO ───────────────────────────────────

Alamo Square Inn
719 Scott St., 94114
415-922-2055 800-345-9888
Klaus E. May, Wayne M. Corn
All year

$$$ B&B
5 rooms
Visa, MC, AmEx, *Rated*, •
C-yes/S-ltd/P-no/H-no
German, French

Full breakfast
Comp. tea, wine
Sitting room
bicycles
entertainment (harpist)

Fine restoration of a magnificent mansion. Graced by European furnishings and Oriental rugs, flowers from the garden and host committed to excellence.

Albion House Inn, The
135 Gough St., 94102
415-621-0896 FAX:621-0154
Aziz & Regina Bouagou
All year

$$$ B&B
8 rooms, 8 pb
Visa, MC, AmEx, *Rated*, •
C-ltd/S-yes/P-no/H-no
Spanish

Full breakfast
Comp. wine
Sitting room

An elegant city hideaway conveniently located near the Opera House, just moments away from Union Square & other tourist attractions. **Free bottle wine or champagne**

Amsterdam Hotel, The
749 Taylor St., Fax: 415-673-3277, 94108
415-673-3277 800-637-3444
Harry
All year

$$ B&B
30 rooms, 22 pb
Visa, MC, AmEx, *Rated*, •
C-yes/S-yes/P-no/H-no

Continental breakfast
Sitting room, library
sunny patio
color TV & phones in rms

Located on Nob Hill. Quality accommodations and friendly service provided at modest rates. A little bit of Europe in America. Near Union Square, Financial District, Cable Car.

Andrews Hotel, The
624 Post St., Between Jones & Taylor, 94109
415-563-6877 800-926-3739
Paula Forselles
All year

$$$ B&B
48 rooms, 48 pb
Visa, MC, AmEx, *Rated*, •
S-ltd/P-no/H-no
some Ital, Fr, Jap, Span

Continental plus
Restaurant, bar
Comp. wine, coffee, tea

European-style charm in the heart of Union Square shopping and theater district. Just two blocks from cable cars.

SAN FRANCISCO ───

Anna's Three Bears
114 Divisadero St., 94117
415-255-3167 800-428-8559
Anna & Frank Pope
All year

$$$ B&B
3 rooms, 3 pb
Visa, MC, AmEx, •
C-ltd/S-no/P-no/H-no

Continental plus
3 fully equipped flats
kitchen, living room
bedroom, dining room

Edwardian splendor. Your own flat. Gorgeous views, antique furnishings, fireplaces. 2-bdrm. apts. w/living room, dining room & kitchen. **frequent guest specials, ask**

Ansonia-Cambridge Hotel
711 Post St., 94109
415-673-2670
All year

$ MAP
150 rooms, 90 pb
Visa, MC, AmEx, •
C-yes/S-yes/P-no/H-no
Fr., Ital., Sp., Ger.

Full breakfast
Dinner included

Neat, clean, budget hotel, 5 min. walk to Union Square & Powell St. cable cars. Family owned & operated. Complimentary full breakfast and dinner.

Archbishop's Mansion Inn
1000 Fulton St., 94117
415-563-7872 800-543-5820
Kathleen Austin
All year

$$$ B&B
15 rooms, 15 pb
Visa, MC, AmEx, *Rated*,
•
C-yes/S-no/P-no/H-no

Continental breakfast
Comp. wine, tea, coffee
Sitting room, piano
reception & conference
facilities

Historic French chateau. Luxurious lodging in the "Belle Epoque" style. "Arguably the most elegant, in-city small hotel on the West Coast if not the USA," USA TODAY.

Art Center B&B
1902 Filbert at Laguna, 94123
415-567-1526 800-821-3877
George, Helvi & Brian
All year

$$$ B&B
5 rooms, 5 pb
Visa, MC, *Rated*, •
C-yes/S-no/P-no/H-no
Finnish

Stocked kitchen, picnics
Pastry & fruit on deck
Studio room, art gallery
art classes, city tours
enclosed patio, gardens

Art shows, classes, garden art, workroom & art materials. We offer an Art Package—Includes 3 days lodging, museum tour, buffet. Suites w/ whirlpool & easels. **Discounts**

Casa Arguello
225 Arguello Blvd., 94118
415-752-9482
Emma Baires, Marina McKenzie
All year

$ B&B
5 rooms, 5 pb
Rated
C-ltd/S-no/P-no/H-no
Spanish

Continental plus
Sitting room, TV

An elegant townhouse near Golden Gate Park, the Presidio, Golden Gate Bridge, 10 min. to Union Square.

Casita Blanca
330 Edgehill Way, 94127
415-564-9339
Joan Bard
All year

$$$ B&B
2 rooms, 1 pb
•
C-ltd/S-yes/P-no/H-no
Spanish

Continental breakfast
Homes avail. in Tahoe
Maui, Palm Desert, and
Carmel. Request brochure

Casita Blanca is a detached cottage in a secluded forest area. View of Golden Gate. Fireplace, patio, completely furnished. Other homes in California & Hawaii available.

SAN FRANCISCO ——

Chateau Tivoli B&B, The $$$ B&B   Continental plus (wkday)
1057 Steiner St., 94115   7 rooms, 5 pb   Full breakfast (wkend)
415-776-5462 800-228-1647   Visa, MC, AmEx, *Rated*, Comp. wine, aftn. tea
Rodney Karr, Willard Gersbach •   double parlors, library
All year   C-yes/S-ltd/P-no/H-no   new suite

A stay at the Victorian townhouse, Chateau Tivoli, provides guests a time travel experience back to San Francisco's Golden Age of Opulence, the 1890s. **3rd night free**

Edward II B&B Inn & Suites $$$ B&B   Continental plus
3155 Scott St., at Lombard St., 31 rooms, 20 pb   Italian dinner, pub
94123   Visa, MC, •   Parlour, conference room
415-922-3000   C-yes/S-ltd/P-no/H-no luxury suites available
Bob & Denise Holland   Spanish, Italian   phones & cable TV in rms
All year

Perched atop a delightful Italian restaurant and an old English- style pub. Full refurbished 1914 European-style hotel in San Francisco's Marina district. Suites w/whirlpool.

Garden Studio, The $$ EP   Coffee
1387 Sixth Ave., 94122   1 rooms, 1 pb   Garden, private entrance
415-753-3574   C-yes/S-no/P-no/H-no   full kitchen
Alice & John Micklewright   French   TV, radio
All year

On lower level of charming Edwardian home; 2 blocks from Golden Gate Park. Studio opens to garden, has private entrance, private bath, fully equipped kitchen, queen-sized bed.

Golden Gate Hotel, The $$ B&B   Continental breakfast
775 Bush St., 94108   23 rooms, 14 pb   Afternoon tea
415-392-3702 800-835-1118   Most CC, *Rated*, •   Sitting room
John & Renate Kenaston   C-yes/S-yes/P-ltd/H-no sightseeing tours
All year   German, French

Charming turn-of-the-century hotel. Friendly atmosphere. Antique furnishings, fresh flowers. Ideal Nob Hill location. Corner cable car stop. Guest rooms newly restored.

Grove Inn, The $ B&B   Continental breakfast
890 Grove St., 94117   16 rooms, 9 pb   Sitting room
415-929-0780 800-829-0780   Visa, MC, AmEx, •   bicycles
Klaus & Rosetta Zimmermann   C-yes/S-ltd/P-no/H-no laundry
All year   Italian, German

Turn-of-the-century Victorian, fully restored, simply furnished. Community kitchen, refrigerator. Part of Alamo Square Historic district.

Inn at Union Square, The $$$ B&B   Continental plus
440 Post St., 94102   30 rooms, 30 pb   Comp. wine, aftn. tea
415-397-3510 800-288-4346   Visa, MC, AmEx, *Rated*, Hors d'oeuvres
Brooks Bayly-General Manager •   comp. shoe shine & paper
All year   C-yes/S-no/P-no/H-yes turn-down, meeting room
                             French, Spanish

Rooms are individually decorated with Georgian furniture and warm colorful fabrics by noted San Francisco interior designer Nan Rosenblatt.

SAN FRANCISCO ————————————————————————

Inn San Francisco, The	$$$ B&B	Full breakfast buffet
943 S. Van Ness Ave., 94110	22 rooms, 17 pb	Sun deck, gazebo, garden
415-641-0188 800-359-0913	Visa, MC, AmEx, •	hot tub, phones, TV's
Marty Neely, Jane Bertorelli	C-yes/S-yes/P-no/H-no	off-street parking
All year		

A grand 27-room 1872 Victorian mansion furnished in 19th-century antiques. Garden room, hot tub, fresh flowers in rooms. Jacuzzi, fireplace available. **10% discount, ltd**

Jackson Court	$$$ B&B	Continental breakfast
2198 Jackson St., at Buchanan	10 rooms, 10 pb	Comp. sherry
St., 94115	Visa, MC, AmEx, *Rated*,	Sitting room
415-929-7670	C-ltd/S-yes/P-no/H-no	
Pat Cremer	Spanish	
All year		

An elegant brick mansion built in 1901 in the heart of San Francisco, distinguished by its luxurious amenities and attention to comfort and hospitality.

Mansions Hotel, The	$$$ B&B	Full breakfast
2220 Sacramento St., 94115	29 rooms, 29 pb	Dinner, tea, wine
415-929-9444 800-826-9398	Visa, MC, AmEx, DC, •	Sitting room, pianos
Robert C. Pritikin	C-yes/S-yes/P-yes/H-no	park next door
All year		Mansion Magic Concerts

Breakfast in bed, fresh flowers in your room, nightly concerts, billiard room, Bufano Gardens, superb dining. San Francisco landmark. Close to all S.F. main attractions.

Moffatt House	$ B&B	Continental plus
431 Hugo St., Near 5th Ave.,	4 rooms	Hot beverages, kitchen
94122	*Rated*, •	Tennis, bicycles nearby
415-661-6210 FAX:564-2480	C-yes/S-yes/P-yes/H-no	Japanese Tea Garden
Ruth Moffatt	Spanish, French, Italian	runner's discount
All year		

Walk to Golden Gate Park's major attractions from our Edwardian home. Safe location for active, independent guests. Excellent public transportation.

Monte Cristo, The	$$ B&B	Continental plus buffet
600 Presidio Ave., 94115	14 rooms, 12 pb	Comp. tea, wine
415-931-1875	Visa, MC, AmEx, •	Parlor w/fireplace
George	C-yes/S-yes/P-no/H-yes	phones, TV
All year	French, Spanish	

1875 hotel-saloon-bordello, furnished with antiques. Each room uniquely decorated—Georgian four-poster, Chinese wedding bed, spindle bed, etc. **10% off 5 nights or more.**

No Name Victorian B&B	$$$ B&B	Full breakfast
P.O. Box 420009, 94142	5 rooms, 3 pb	Afternoon tea, snacks
847 Fillmore St., 94117	Visa, MC, AmEx, •	Comp. wine, sitting room
415-479-1913	C-yes/S-no/P-no/H-no	tennis courts
Susan or Richard Kreibich	German	hot tubs
All year		

Victorian in the heart of San Francisco. Enjoy the great hospitality of the innkeepers and the city. **3rd night free.**

SAN FRANCISCO —————————————————————————————————————

Obrero Hotel & Restaurant $ B&B Full European breakfast
1208 Stockton St., 94133 12 rooms Basque dinners
415-989-3960 C-ltd/S-no/P-no/H-no
Bambi McDonald Fr., Ger., It., Canton.
All year

Friendly slice of life in bustling Chinatown adjacent to North Beach, within walking distance of Union Square and Fisherman's Wharf. **3rd night 50% off Sept.-March**

Petite Auberge $$$ B&B Full breakfast
863 Bush St., 94108 26 rooms, 26 pb Wine and hors d'oeuvres
415-928-6000 AmEx, Visa, MC, *Rated*, Sitting room
Rich Revaz • near Cable Car line
All year C-yes/S-ltd/P-no/H-no

Romantic French country inn near Union Square in San Francisco. Turndown service, robes, afternoon wine. Honeymoon packages. One of the Four Sisters' Inns. Breakfast in bed.

Sherman House, The $$$ EP Continental plus $
2160 Green St., 94123 15 rooms, 15 pb Lunch, dinner, beer/wine
415-563-3600 Major credit cards, Sitting room, piano
Gerard Lespinette C-ltd/S-yes/P-no/H-yes
All year Fr, Sp, It, Ger, Portug.

Luxury, full-service hotel. Superb appointments, formal gardens, garage, full concierge and valet services, 24-hour room service, view of bay.

Spencer House $$$ B&B Full elegant breakfast
1080 Haight St., 94117 6 rooms, 6 pb Comp. wine
415-626-9205 • Sitting rooms
Jack & Barbara Chambers C-ltd/S-no/P-no/H-no All rooms have phones
All year

Elegant Queen Anne mansion near Golden Gate Park. Antique furnishings, feather mattresses, crystal and silver breakfast service. All private baths. Parking

---

Victorian Inn on the Park $$$ B&B Continental plus
301 Lyon St., 94117 12 rooms, 12 pb Comp. wine
415-931-1830 800-435-1967 Most CC, *Rated*, • Homemade breads, cheeses
Lisa and William Benau C-yes/S-yes/P-no/H-no library, phones in rooms
All year TV on request, parlor

1897 Queen Anne Victorian near Golden Gate Park, downtown. Each room has antiques, flowers, beautiful comforters, down pillows, phones. Historic landmark. **3rd night 50%, Ltd**

Washington Square Inn, The $$$ B&B Continental plus
1660 Stockton St., 94133 15 rooms, 11 pb Comp. wine & beer
415-981-4220 800-388-0220 Visa, MC, AmEx, *Rated*, Sitting room
Brooks Bayly • furnished with English
All year C-yes/S-no/P-no/H-no and French antiques

In San Francisco's North Beach—the essence of San Francisco. Near all attractions and many fine restaurants.

SAN FRANCISCO

White Swan Inn	$$$ B&B	Full breakfast
845 Bush St., 94108	26 rooms, 26 pb	Hors d'oeuvres, wine
415-775-1755	Visa, MC, AmEx, *Rated*,	Library, sitting room
Rich Revaz	•	English garden
All year	C-yes/S-ltd/P-no/H-no	near Cable Car line
	Fr., Cantonese, Tagalog	

English garden, in cosmopolitan San Francisco; built in 1908. Business conference facilities; country breakfast; afternoon appetizers. 2 honeymoon suites. Breakfast in bed.

SAN GREGORIO

Rancho San Gregorio	$$ B&B	Full country breakfast
Route 1, Box 54, 5086 La Honda	5 rooms, 4 pb	Comp. beverages, snacks
Rd.(Hwy 84), 94074	Most CC, *Rated*, •	Sitting room, library
415-747-0810 FAX:747-0184	C-yes/S-ltd	antiques, gazebo
Bud & Lee Raynor		gardens, orchards
All year		

California Mission-style coastal retreat; serene; spectacular views of wooded hills; friendly hospitality; hearty breakfast; Near Año Nuevo. **10% discount midwk**

SAN JOSE

Briar Rose B&B Inn, The	$$ B&B	Full breakfast
897 E. Jackson St., 95112	5 rooms, 3 pb	Afternoon tea, gardens
408-279-5999	Visa, MC, AmEx, •	Comp. wine/snacks, porch
James & Cheryl Fuhring	C-ltd/S-ltd/P-no/H-no	sitting room, library
All year		Period furnishings rms.

An 1875 Victorian once a flourishing walnut orchard restored to its former grandeur. Rooms fabulously wallpapered with Bradbury & Bradbury papers. **3rd. night 50% off.**

Hensley House, The	$$$ B&B	Full gourmet breakfast
456 N. 3rd St., 95112	5 rooms, 5 pb	Lunch/dinner by reserv.
408-298-3537 800-498-3537	Visa, MC, AmEx, *Rated*,	Comp. wine, tea, snacks
Sharon Layne, Bill Priest	•	sitting room, library
All year, FAX: 298-4676	C-ltd/S-no/P-no/H-no	2 rms w/whirlpool, patio

Elegant city Queen Anne Victorian, near everything. TV/VCR each room. Business services, FAX, phone, PC, conference, meetings, airport service. Historic Register. **High tea.**

SAN LUIS OBISPO

Adobe Inn	$ B&B	Full homemade breakfast
1473 Monterey St., 93401	15 rooms, 15 pb	Picnic baskets
805-549-0321	Visa, MC, AmEx, *Rated*,	Afternoon tea (Thur-Sat)
Michael & Ann Dinshaw	•	travel arrangements
All year	C-yes/S-ltd/P-no/H-yes	wine tours

Cozy, comfortable, congenial southwestern-style inn, in the heart of this charming town. Near Hearst Castle, beaches, restaurants. **Hearst Castle Pkg; 2 nts. fr. $69 pp.**

Apple Farm Inn	$$$ EP	Restaurant
2015 Monterey St., 93401	67 rooms, 67 pb	All meals served
805-544-2040 800-374-3705	Most CC, *Rated*, •	Swimming pool, hot tubs
Bob & Kathleen Davis	C-yes/S-ltd/P-no/H-yes	gift shop, mill house
All year		working water wheel

Memorable lodging experience; uniquely appointed rooms—canopy beds, fireplaces, turrets, cozy window seats. Working water wheel. Mill house. Rated Four Diamond.

SAN LUIS OBISPO

Garden Street Inn
1212 Garden St., 93401
805-545-9802
Dan & Kathy Smith & Mozart

$$$ B&B
13 rooms, 13 pb
Visa, MC, AmEx, *Rated*,
•
C-ltd/S-ltd/P-no/H-yes

Full breakfast
Comp. wine, snacks
Sitting room, library
fireplaces, board games
hot tubs, decks

1887 Victorian lovingly restored. Romantic get-away in the heart of an old-fashioned downtown. Antiques, expansive decks, jacuzzis, homemade breakfast, genuine hospitality.

SAN RAFAEL

Casa Soldavini
531 "C" St., 94901
415-454-3140
Linda Soldavini-Cassidy
All year

$$ B&B
3 rooms, 2 pb
•
C-ltd/S-no/P-yes/H-no

Continental
Afternoon tea, snacks
Sitting room, piano
TV, VCR, patio w/swing
lush gardens, bicycles

1932 winemaker's home, in a quaint Italian neighborhood near Mission San Rafael. Close to everything. Enjoy 1930s movies & melodies or just relax. **2 for 1 rest. disc'ts**

SANTA BARBARA

B&B at Valli's View
340 N. Sierra Vista Rd., 93108
805-969-1272
Valli & Larry Stevens
All year

$$$ B&B
2 rooms, 2 pb
•
C-yes/P-ltd/H-yes

Full breakfast
Comp. wine
Train/airport pickup
garden swing, patios
deck, mountain views

A secluded home nestled in Montecito foothills provides peace and tranquillity, yet near city. Gourmet breakfast on patio or by fireplace. **7th night free.**

Bath Street Inn
1720 Bath St., 93101
805-682-9680 800-788-BATH
Susan Brown
All year

$$ B&B
10 rooms, 10 pb
Visa, MC, AmEx, *Rated*,
•
C-yes/S-no/P-no/H-no

Full breakfast
Evening refreshments
Sitting & dining rooms
TV room, library
bicycles

Luxurious 3-story Victorian, panoramic views, balconies, brick courtyards. Lovely gardens create country inn environment; blocks from downtown.

Blue Quail Inn & Cottages
1908 Bath St., 93101
800-549-1622 800-676-1622
Jeanise Suding Eaton
All year exc. Dec 24-25

$$ B&B
9 rooms, 9 pb·
Visa, MC, AmEx, *Rated*,
•
C-yes/S-ltd/P-no/H-no

Full breakfast
Picnic lunches, cider
Comp. wine, eve. sweets
sitting room, garden
brick patio, bicycles

Guest rooms, suites and private cottages filled with country charm in a delightfully quiet and relaxing country setting. Close to town and beaches. Scrumptious full breakfast.

Casa Del Mar
18 Bath St., 93101
805-963-4418 800-433-3097
Mike & Becky Montgomery
All year

$$ B&B
20 rooms, 22 pb
Most CC, *Rated*, •
C-yes/S-yes/P-ask/H-yes
Spanish & German

Continental breakfast
Afternoon tea
Sitting room, hot tub
beach towels, umbrellas
Comp. wine & cheese

Spanish-style villa, quiet, charming. One block from beach. Courtyard jacuzzi. Several units with fireplaces and kitchens. **3rd night free, November-March**

SANTA BARBARA ———————————————————————

Cheshire Cat Inn, The
36 W. Valerio St., 93101
805-569-1610 FAX:682-1876
C. Dunstan, M. Goeden
All year

$$$ B&B
14 rooms, 14 pb
Visa, MC, *Rated*, •
C-ltd/S-no/P-no/H-no

Full breakfast
Comp. wine (Sat. eve)
Library, sitting room
bicycles, hot tub
cooking school

Victorian elegance, uniquely decorated in Laura Ashley & English antiques; kitchenettes, private baths, jacuzzis, balconies, fireplaces, gardens. **3rd night 50% off**

Glenborough Inn B&B
1327 Bath St., 93101
805-966-0589 800-962-0589
Michael Diaz
All year

$$ B&B
11 rooms, 5 pb
Most CC, *Rated*, •
C-ltd/S-ltd/P-no/H-no

Full gourmet breakfast
Wine & hors d'oeuvres
Bedtime snacks, jacuzzi
parlor with fireplace
refrigerator available

Lovely grounds, elegant antique-filled rooms and suites, breakfast in bed, enclosed jacuzzi create a relaxing romantic holiday or business trip. **Comp. desserts, ltd.**

Long's Seaview B&B
317 Piedmont Rd., 93105
805-687-2947
LaVerne M. Long
All year

$$ B&B
1 rooms, 1 pb
C-ltd/S-no/P-no/H-no

Full breakfast
King size bed
Gardens, patio

Home with a lovely view, furnished with antiques. Quiet neighborhood. Full breakfast served on the patio. Homemade jams and fresh fruits.

Ocean View House
P.O. Box 3373, 93105
Shoreline & Cliff
805-966-6659
Carolyn & Bill Canfield
All year

$$ B&B
2 rooms, 1 pb
Rated
C-yes/S-ltd/P-ltd/H-no

Continental plus
Stocked refrigerator
Beach towels & chairs
2 room suite available
w/den, private entry

Breakfast on the patio while viewing sailboats and the Channel Islands. Private home in a quiet neighborhood. $10 extra for single night stay. Fruit trees in yard.

Old Yacht Club Inn, The
431 Corona Del Mar Dr., 93103
805-962-1277 800-676-1676
N.Donaldson, S.Hunt, L.Caruso
All year, 800-549-1676

$$$ B&B
9 rooms, 9 pb
Most CC, *Rated*, •
C-yes/S-ltd/P-no/H-no
Spanish

Full breakfast
Dinner (weekends)
Comp. evening beverage
beach chairs & towels
bicycles

A 1912 California classic. Beautifully decorated antique-filled rooms. Gourmet breakfast. Dinner on weekends. Half block to beautiful beach. **10% disc't. on direct res.**

Olive House, The
1604 Olive St., 93101
805-962-4902 800-786-6422
Lois Gregg
All year

$$$ B&B
6 rooms, 6 pb
Visa, MC, *Rated*, •
C-ltd

Continental plus
Afternoon refreshments
Sitting room, library
bicycles, fireplace
studio grand piano

Quiet comfort in lovingly restored CA Craftsman pattern home. Bay windows, ocean views. Large sunny dining room setting for lively brkfast conversation. **3rd night 50%, Ltd**

SANTA BARBARA ───────────────────────────────

Parsonage B&B	$$$ B&B	Full breakfast
1600 Olive St., 93101	6 rooms, 6 pb	Comp. wine
805-962-9336	*Rated*, •	Sitting room
Holli Harmon	C-ltd/S-ltd/P-no/H-no	
All year	German	

A beautifully restored Queen Anne Victorian. An atmosphere of comfort, grace and elegance; with ocean and mountain views. Close to shops, dining, sightseeing.

Simpson House Inn	$$$ B&B	Full breakfast
121 E. Arrellaga, 93101	13 rooms, 13 pb	Comp. wine, beverages
805-963-7067 800-676-1280	Visa, MC, *Rated*, •	Sitt. rm, library, patio
G. Wilson, G. & L. Davies	C-yes/S-ltd/P-no/H-yes	veranda, garden, jacuzzi
All year	Spanish, French, Danish	bicycles, fireplaces

1874 Victorian estate secluded on an acre of English garden. Cottages & barn suites. Elegant antiques, art. Delicious leisurely brkfast on verandas. Walk to historic downtown.

Upham Hotel & Cottages	$$$ B&B	Continental plus
1404 De La Vina St., 93101	39 rooms, 39 pb	Comp. wine, coffee, tea
805-962-0058	Most CC, *Rated*, •	Newspaper, lobby
Jan Martin Winn	C-yes/S-yes/P-no/H-no	garden veranda, gardens
All year	Spanish	valet laundry, phones

California's oldest Victorian hotel. Cottage rooms with patios and fireplaces, lawn, flowers. Complimentary wine and cheese by the lobby fireplace. Corporate rates available.

SANTA CLARA ───────────────────────────────

Madison Street Inn	$$ B&B	Full breakfast
1390 Madison St., 95050	5 rooms, 3 pb	Lunch, dinner w/notice
408-249-5541 FAX:249-6676	Visa, MC, AmEx, *Rated*,	Comp. wine & beverages
Ralph & Theresa Wigginton	•	library, sitting room
All year	C-yes/S-ltd/P-no/H-no	hot tub, bicycles, pool
	French	

*Santa Clara's only inn! A beautiful Victorian; landscaped gardens. Eggs Benedict is a brkfast favorite. Near Winchester Mystery House. Weekend dinner pkg. **2nd night 50% off***

SANTA CRUZ ───────────────────────────────

Babbling Brook Inn	$$$ B&B	Full buffet breakfast
1025 Laurel St., 95060	12 rooms, 12 pb	Comp. wine, refreshments
408-427-2437 800-866-1131	Most CC, *Rated*, •	Picnic baskets
Helen King	C-ltd/S-ltd/P-no/H-ltd	phone & TV in rooms
All year		romantic garden gazebo

*Secluded inn among waterfalls, gardens, gazebo, Laurel Creek, pines and redwoods. Complimentary wine, fireplaces. 12 rooms in country French decor. **Comp. Champagne***

Chateau Victorian, B&B Inn	$$$ B&B	Continental plus
118 First St., 95060	7 rooms, 7 pb	Comp. wine & cheese
408-458-9458	Visa, MC, AmEx	Sitting room
Franz & Alice-June Benjamin	C-ltd/S-no/P-no/H-no	2 decks, patio
All year	German	fireplaces in rooms

*One block from the beach and the boardwalk, in the heart of the Santa Cruz fun area. All rooms have queen-size beds with private bathrooms. **7th Night Free (Mult. stays O.K.)***

SANTA CRUZ

Cliff Crest B&B Inn
407 Cliff St., 95060
408-427-2609
Bruce & Sharon Taylor
All year

$$$ B&B
5 rooms, 5 pb
Visa, MC, AmEx, *Rated*,
•
C-ltd/S-no/P-no/H-yes

Full gourmet breakfast
Evening wine & tidbits
Sitting room, library

Romantic Victorian mansion. Five unique rooms w/private baths, fireplaces, solarium, belvedere, breakfast in bed. One block to beach, boardwalk.

Darling House, The
314 W. Cliff Dr., 95060
408-458-1958
Darrell & Karen Darling
All year

$$$ B&B/MAP
8 rooms, 2 pb
Visa, MC, AmEx, *Rated*,
•
C-ltd/S-ltd/P-no/H-ltd

Continental plus
Comp. dinner-wknite pkg.
Beverage, orchids in rm.
library, hot tub spa
double size bathtubs

*1910 ocean side mansion with beveled glass, Tiffany lamps, Chippendale antiques, open hearths and hardwood interiors. Walk to beach. **Dinner for 2—limitations.***

Pleasure Point Inn
2-3665 East Cliff Dr., 95062
408-475-4657
Margaret & Sal Margo
All year

$$$ B&B
3 rooms, 3 pb
Visa, MC, *Rated*, •
C-ltd

Continental plus
Comp. wine & cheese
Fireplace in suite
fishing charters
day cruises on yacht

On beach, overlooking beautiful Monterey Bay. Walk to beach & shopping village. Rooms include private bath, sitting room & deck. Motor yacht available for fishing or cruises.

SANTA CRUZ—BEN LOMOND

Chateau des Fleurs
7995 Hwy 9, 95005
408-336-8943
Lee & Laura Jonas
All year

$$$ B&B
3 rooms, 3 pb
Visa, MC, AmEx, Disc.,
C-yes/S-no/P-no/H-no
German

Full breakfast
Comp. wine
Sitting room, organ
antique piano, hiking
swimming, tennis nearby

A Victorian mansion once owned by the Bartlett (pear) family, this inn is spacious, special, sensational, historic, quiet, unforgettable, surrounded by evergreens & wineries.

SANTA CRUZ—FELTON

Hanna's Guest House
780 El Solyo Heights Dr, 95018
408-335-4011 408-336-8943
Hannelore Peters
All year

$$$ B&B
2 rooms, 2 pb
C-yes/S-yes/P-yes/H-no
German

Full breakfast
Afternoon tea
Hot tubs

Overlooking the San Lorenzo Mountains. Close to Beach Boardwalk, Big Basin, Roaring Camp, Henry Cowell State Park. Fireplace, large deck, jacuzzi, big screen TV, VCR.

SANTA CRUZ-SOQUEL

Blue Spruce B&B Inn
2815 Main St., 95073
408-464-1137
Pat & Tom O'Brien
All year

$$$ B&B
6 rooms, 6 pb
Visa, MC, AmEx, *Rated*,
•
C-ltd/S-ltd/P-no/H-no
Spanish

Full breakfast
Snacks
Sitting room
library, hot tubs
gas fireplaces

*Award-winning inn that's fresh and unpretentious as a sea breeze. Explore Monterey Bay! Enjoy jacuzzis, fireplaces, original local art. **3rd night 25% off***

SANTA ROSA

Gables B&B Inn, The
4257 Petaluma Hill Rd., 95404	$$$ B&B	Full breakfast
707-585-7777	7 rooms, 7 pb	Lunch, dinner, snacks
Michael & Judith Ogne	Visa, MC, AmEx, *Rated*,	Sitting room, piano
All year	•	parking, fireplaces
	C-ltd/S-yes/P-ltd/H-yes	conferences, weddings

Built in 1877, National Register of Historic Places; museum-quality restoration; European-Victorian decor. Gateway to wine country; elegant, rural location. Cottage w/jacuzzi.

Melitta Station Inn
5850 Melita Rd., 95409	$$ B&B	Full breakfast
707-538-7712	6 rooms, 4 pb	Comp. wine
Diane Crandon & Vic Amstadter	Visa, MC, *Rated*, •	Sitting room
All year	C-ltd/S-ltd/P-no/H-no	

Restored railroad station in a beautiful country setting across the road from parks. Wineries nearby. Elegant country breakfast. **Discounts during the week, ask**

Pygmalion House B&B
331 Orange St., 95407	$$ B&B	Full breakfast
707-526-3407	5 rooms, 5 pb	Sparkling cider & snacks
Lola L. Wright	*Rated*, •	Sitting room, fireplace
All year	C-ltd/S-ltd/P-no/H-no	television
		central A/C & heat

Delightfully restored Queen Anne cottage central to Northern California wine country, San Francisco Bay area and North Coast resort areas.

Vintner's Inn
4350 Barnes Rd., 95403	$$$ B&B	Continental plus
707-575-7350 800-421-2584	44 rooms, 44 pb	Restaurant, bar
Cindy Young	Most CC, *Rated*, •	Sitting room
All year	C-yes/S-yes/P-no/H-yes	hot tubs, wine touring
	Spanish	nearby tennis, pool

European-styled country inn surrounded by a 50-acre vineyard. Antique furniture, conference facilities. Home of John Ash & Co. Restaurant. AAA Four Diamond rating.

SAUSALITO

Casa Madrona Hotel
801 Bridgeway, 94965	$$$ B&B	Continental breakfast
415-332-0502 800-288-0502	34 rooms, 34 pb	Restaurant
John Mays	Visa, MC, AmEx, •	Wine & cheese hour
All year	C-ltd/S-yes/P-no/H-ltd	outdoor dining
	German, French, Spanish	spa

Casa Madrona offers the privacy and coziness of a European country inn with individually decorated rooms, spectacular views of S.F. Bay & yacht harbor.

Sausalito Hotel
16 El Portal, 94965	$$$ B&B	Continental plus
415-332-4155 FAX:332-3542	15 rooms, 9 pb	Adjacent to ferry
Liz MacDonald, Gene Hiller	Visa, MC, AmEx, *Rated*,	walk to shops, harbors
All year	•	restaurants
	C-ltd/S-yes/P-ltd/H-no	

Intimate European-style hotel furnished in Victorian antiques. Rooms have color TVs and phones. Located in heart of Sausalito and adjacent to San Francisco ferry.

SEAL BEACH

Seal Beach Inn & Gardens
212 - 5th St., 90740
310-493-2416
Marjorie Bettenhausen
All year

$$$ B&B
23 rooms, 23 pb
Visa, MC, AmEx, *Rated*,
•
C-ltd/S-ltd/P-no/H-no

Lavish full breakfast
Comp. wine and cheese
Fruit, tea, coffee
sitting rooms, library
swimming pool

Charming French Mediterranean inn, antique lights, ornate fences, brick courtyard, private pool, exquisite gardens, near Disneyland & Long Beach. **Free gift with 3 nite stay.**

SKYFOREST

Storybook Inn
P.O. Box 362, 92385
28717 Highway 18
909-336-1483
Kathleen & John Wooley
All year

$$$ B&B
9 rooms, 9 pb
Most CC, *Rated*, •
C-yes/S-no/P-no/H-yes
French, Italian, German

Full breakfast
Aft. tea, snacks
Comp. wine, sitting room
library, hot tubs
gazebo for weddings, etc

Mountain inn designed w/theme of storybook. Rustic cabin w/fireplc. Spectacular views, gourmet breakfasts, comp. hors d'oeurves, wine, hot choc. cookies. **Getaway packages**

SODA SPRINGS

Rainbow Lodge
P.O. Box 1100, 95728
916-426-3661
All year

$
33 rooms, 10 pb
Visa, MC, •
C-yes/S-yes/P-no/H-yes

Full breakfast
Restaurant, lunch
Dinner, snacks
bar service, library
sitting room

A year-round Sierra hideaway. Cozy & romantic with Swiss-Italian cuisine. Enjoy a winter skiers paradise or summer serenity by the Yuba River. Hiking, biking, fishing areas.

SOLVANG

Danish Country Inn
1455 Mission Dr., 93463
805-688-2018
Mr. Darcy Rust
All year

$$$ B&B
82 rooms, 82 pb
Most CC, *Rated*, •
C-yes/S-yes/P-no/H-yes

Full breakfast
Aft. tea, snacks
Comp. wine, sitting room
hot tubs
swimming pool

Nestled in the Santa Ynez Valley wine country. See Solvang w/unique shops and delicious pastry, all in country comfort.

SONOMA

Sonoma Chalet B&B
18935 Fifth St. W., 95476
707-938-3129
Joe Leese
All year exc. Christmas

$$$ B&B
7 rooms, 4 pb
Visa, MC, AmEx, *Rated*,
•
C-ltd/S-ltd/P-ltd/H-no

Continental plus
Comp. sherry, tea/coffee
Sitting room, fireplaces
wood burning stoves
garden, spa, bicycles

Swiss-style chalet & country cottages located in the beautiful Sonoma Valley. Romantic, antique filled rooms. Wonderful country farm setting near historic plaza and wineries.

Sonoma Hotel
110 W. Spain St., 95476
707-996-2996 800-468-6016
Dorene & John Musilli
All year

$$$ B&B
17 rooms, 5 pb
Visa, MC, AmEx, *Rated*,
•
C-yes/S-yes

Continental breakfast
Comp. wine, snacks
Restaurant, bar
lunch, dinner
garden patio

Vintage hotel nationally acclaimed; bed & breakfast ambiance, exceptional dining amidst antiques or on the garden patio. Sunday brunch. **Winter packages available**

SONOMA

Thistle Dew Inn
171 W. Spain St., 95476
707-938-2909
Larry & Norma Barnett
All year

$$$ B&B
6 rooms, 4 pb
Visa, MC, AmEx, •
C-ltd/S-ltd/P-no/H-ltd

Full breakfast
Comp. wine & appetizers
Sitting room, spa
picnic baskets, bicycles
rare plant/cactus coll.

Two Victorian homes near Sonoma's historic plaza. Collector pieces of Stickley furniture; fresh-cut flowers; extensive collection of rare plants and cactus.

Victorian Garden Inn
316 E. Napa St., 95476
707-996-5339 800-543-5339
Donna Lewis
All year

$$$ B&B
4 rooms, 3 pb
Visa, MC, AmEx, *Rated*,
•
C-ltd/S-ltd/P-no/H-no
Spanish

Continental plus
Sitting room
piano
swimming pool

Secluded, large 1870 Greek revival farmhouse. Antiques, private entrances, fireplaces, Victorian rose gardens, winding paths, near plaza. Gracious hospitality.

SONORA

Lavender Hill B&B
683 S. Barretta St., 95370
209-532-9024
Alice J. Byrnes
All year

$$ B&B
4 rooms, 2 pb
C-ltd/S-ltd/P-no/H-no

Full breakfast
Comp. coffee or tea
Sitting room
porch swing

Restored Victorian in historic Gold Country. Antique furnishings, lovely grounds, porch swing and unmatched hospitality. Walk to town. Near Yosemite.

Lulu Belle's B&B
85 Gold St., 95370
209-533-3455 800-538-3455
Janet & Chris Miller
All year

$$$ B&B
5 rooms, 5 pb
Most CCs, *Rated*, •
C-yes/S-ltd/P-no/H-ltd
German, Spanish

Full breakfast
Comp. tea, coffee
Porch, gardens, A/C
sitting room w/fireplace
Dinner/theatre packages

*Historic 107-year-old Victorian with beautiful gardens and Lulu Belle's famous hospitality. Enjoy nearby theater, antiquing, boating, horseback riding. **3rd night 30% off***

Ryan House, The
153 S. Shepherd St., 95370
209-533-3445
Nancy & Guy Hoffman
All year

$$$ B&B
3 rooms, 3 pb
Visa, MC, *Rated*, •
C-yes/S-no/P-no/H-no

Full breakfast
Aftn. tea, comp. wine
Sitting room
queen-sized beds
2 parlors, new suite

*Gold Rush romance in historic Mother Lode, nearby fine dining & antique shops. Suite available w/parlor, 2 person bathtub. We make you kindly welcome!!! **3rd night 50%, Ltd***

Serenity-A B&B Inn
15305 Bear Club Dr., 95370
209-533-1441 800-426-1441
Fred & Charlotte Hoover
All year

$$$ B&B
4 rooms, 4 pb
Most CC, *Rated*, •
C-ltd/S-ltd/P-no/H-no

Full breakfast
Comp. tea/wine/lemonade
Sitting room, library
queen/twin beds, veranda
beautiful grounds

Enjoy relaxed elegance in 19th-century-styled home. Large rooms, library, veranda, and 6 acres of wooded grounds with pines, wildflowers and wildlife add to the ambiance.

SONORA—TUOLUMNE

Oak Hill Ranch B&B
P.O. Box 307, 95379
18550 Connally Ln.
209-928-4717
Sanford & Jane Grover
All year

$$ B&B
5 rooms, 3 pb
Rated
C-ltd/S-no/P-no/H-yes

Full gourmet breakfast
Comp. tea, coffee
Gazebo
player piano, organ
sitting room, fireplaces

"For a perfect sojourn into the past," spacious rural Victorian on 56 acres, near three state parks and Yosemite. 3000 ft. elevation in California Gold Country. 10th year!

SPRINGVILLE

Annie's B&B
33024 Globe Dr., 93265
209-539-3827
Annie & John Bozanich
All year

$$$ B&B
3 rooms, 3 pb
Most CC, *Rated*, •
C-ltd/S-no/P-no/H-no

Full breakfast
Dinner, afternoon tea
Snacks, comp. wine, pool
sitting room, hot tubs
Cancellation policy

Quiet, beautifully furnished w/ antiques, on 5 acres in the Sierra foothills. Full breakfast cooked on a wood stove. Relax on deck overlooking pool/spa. **3rd nite 50% off**

STINSON BEACH

Casa Del Mar
P.O. Box 238, 94970
37 Belvedere Ave.
415-868-2124
Rick Klein
All year

$$$ B&B
5 rooms, 5 pb
Visa, MC, AmEx, *Rated*,
•
C-yes/S-no/P-no/H-no

Full breakfast
Comp. wine, juice
Hors d'oeuvres
sitting room, library
garden, near ocean

Romantic ocean views; historic garden; delicious breakfasts; colorful artwork; and you can hear the waves break all day long.

SUMMERLAND

Inn on Summer Hill
2520 Lillie Ave., 93067
805-969-9998 800-845-5566
Verlinda Richardson
All year

$$$ B&B
16 rooms, 16 pb
Visa, MC, AmEx, *Rated*,
•
C-ltd/S-no/P-no/H-yes
Spanish

Full breakfast
Afternoon tea & wine
Sitting room, library
room service, jacuzzi
fireplaces, canopy beds

Elegant, romantic European inn. VCR, stereo, antiques, decks & balconie overlooking Pacific. Outdoor spa, gourmet breakfast. ABBA top rated inn. **3rd night 50% off, Ltd**

SUTTER CREEK

Gold Quartz Inn
15 Bryson Dr., 95685
209-267-9155 800-752-8738
Wendy Woolrich
All year

$$$ B&B
24 rooms, 24 pb
Visa, MC, •
S-no/P-no/H-yes

Full breakfast
Afternoon tea, beverages
Food catered for groups
porch, picnics, A/C
TV in rm, conference rm.

Tucked away in charming Gold Country town. Step back 100 years. Rooms are decorated with antique furniture, prints and charming small touches, and have private porches.

TAHOE CITY

Chaney House
P.O. Box 7852, 96145
4725 W. Lake Blvd.
916-525-7333
Gary & Lori Chaney
All year

$$$ B&B
4 rooms, 2 pb
Rated
C-ltd/S-no/P-no/H-no

Full breakfast
Sitting room, bicycles
private beach and pier

Unique stone lakefront home. Gourmet breakfast on patios overlooking the lake in season. Private beach and pier. Close to ski areas.

TAHOE CITY ─────────────────────

Mayfield House B&B	$$$ B&B	Full breakfast
P.O. Box 5999, 96145	6 rooms	Comp. wine, brandy
236 Grove St.	Visa, MC, *Rated*, ●	cheese & crackers
916-583-1001	C-ltd/S-ltd/P-no/H-yes	
Bruce & Cynthia Knauss		
All year		

Within walking distance to shops and restaurants—each room individually decorated—"spit-spat" clean—convenient shuttle to skiing. **10% discount for five or more nights**

TEMPLETON ─────────────────────

Country House Inn	$$ B&B	Full breakfast
91 Main St., 93465	6 rooms, 4 pb	Comp. refreshments
805-434-1598 800-362-6032	*Rated*, ●	Picnic lunches w/notice
Dianne Garth	C-yes/S-no/P-no/H-no	dining & sitting room
All year		player piano

Home built in 1886 by founder of Templeton. 6 spacious bedrooms with antiques, fresh flowers, beautiful gardens. Near 30 wineries, Hearst Castle. **2nd night 50% Off**

TOMALES ─────────────────────

Tomales Country Inn	$$ B&B	Continental plus
P.O. Box 376, 94971	5 rooms, 2 pb	Kitchen use
25 Valley St.	*Rated*	Sitting room, piano
707-878-2041 800-547-1463	C-ltd	
JoAnne Wallace/J. McChesney		
All year		

Quiet, privacy on dead-end street; large garden, patios, etc. Newly refurbished and decorated.

TRINIDAD ─────────────────────

Trinidad B&B	$$$ B&B	Continental plus
P.O. Box 849, 95570	4 rooms, 4 pb	Comp. beverages & snacks
560 Edwards St.	Visa, MC, Disc.,	Sitting rooms
707-677-0840	C-ltd/S-no/P-no	walk to beaches and
Paul & Carol Kirk		redwoods
All year		

Sitting high above the rugged North Coast, this Cape Cod house provides the most picturesque view of the Pacific to be seen anywhere! Minutes to Redwook National Park.

UKIAH ─────────────────────

Vichy Hot Springs Resort	$$$ B&B	Continental plus
2605 Vichy Springs Rd., 95482	14 rooms, 14 pb	Restaurant, lunch/dinner
707-462-9515 FAX:462-9516	Most CC, *Rated*, ●	Sitting room, library
Gilbert & Marjorie Ashoff	C-yes/S-no/P-no/H-yes	mineral baths, pool
All year	Spanish	sauna, 700-acre ranch

Vichy Springs is a true historic country inn—quiet, elegant, and charming. The baths are incomparable memories for a lifetime. Swedish massage. **3rd night 50%(no holidays)**

VALLEY FORD ─────────────────────

Inn at Valley Ford	$$ B&B	Continental plus
P.O. Box 439, 94972	4 rooms	Comp. tea
14395 Hwy 1	Visa, MC, *Rated*, ●	Hot tub
707-876-3182	C-ltd/S-ltd/P-no/H-ltd	bicycles
N. Balashov, S. Nicholls	French	sitting room
All year		

Comfortable Victorian farmhouse furnished w/antiques, books & flowers. Located in rolling, pastoral hills, minutes from the Pacific & Sonoma Wine Country. **3rd night 50% off.**

VENICE

Venice Beach House, The
15 30th Ave., 90291
310-823-1966
Betty Lou Weiner
All year

$$$ B&B
9 rooms, 4 pb
Visa, MC, AmEx, •
C-yes/S-no/P-no/H-no

Continental plus
Sitting room, piano

A world of warmth and hospitality offered at this elegant 1911 historic landmark; secluded, but close to beach, galleries and restaurants.

VENTURA

"La Mer"
411 Poli St., 93001
805-643-3600
Gisela Flender Baida
All year

$$$ B&B
5 rooms, 5 pb
Visa, MC, *Rated*, •
C-ltd/S-no/P-no/H-no
German, Spanish

Bavarian full breakfast
Comp. wine or champagne
Picnic baskets, library
therapeutic massages
antique carriage rides

Authentic European style in old Victorian. Ocean view. Three blocks to beach. Private entrances and private baths. **Free bottle wine/ 3rd night 50% off midweek**

Bella Maggiore Inn
67 S. California St., 93001
805-652-0277 800-523-8479
Thomas Wood
All year

$$$ B&B
32 rooms, 32 pb
AmEx, Visa, MC, *Rated*,
•
C-ltd/S-yes/P-no/H-no

Full breakfast
Comp. wine, snacks
Sitting room, piano
spas in some rooms
sundeck, conference room

Enjoy European elegance—garden courtyard, chandeliers, antiques, original artwork, grand piano in lobby and downstairs shops. **Midweek discounts & free wine/special occasions**

VOLCANO

St. George Hotel
P.O. Box 9, 95689
#2 Main St.
209-296-4458
Marlene & Charles Inman
Wed-Sun, mid-Feb–Dec

$$$ EP/$$$ MAP
20 rooms, 6 pb
C-ltd/S-no/P-ltd/H-ltd

Full breakfast
Dinner included, bar
Sitting room
pianos, new porches
meeting facilities

Elegant Mother Lode hotel built in 1862. Maintains a timeless quality. Quiet, uncommercialized town. Brand new back-to-1862 porches and balausters. **3rd night 50% off**

WESTPORT

Howard Creek Ranch
P.O. Box 121, 95488
40501 N. Hwy 1
707-964-6725
Charles & Sally Grigg
All year

$$ B&B
10 rooms, 8 pb
Rated
C-ltd/S-ltd/P-ltd/H-ltd
German, Italian, Dutch

Full ranch breakfast
Comp. tea
Piano, hot tub, cabins
sauna, massage by resv.
horses, a working ranch

Historic farmhouse filled with collectibles, antiques & memorabilia, unique health spa with privacy and dramatic views adjoining a wide beach. Award-winning flower garden.

WHITTIER

Coleen's California Casa
P.O. Box 9302, 90608
310-699-8427
Coleen Davis
All year

$$ B&B
3 rooms, 3 pb
Rated, •
C-ltd/S-ltd/P-no/H-yes
some Spanish

Full gourmet breakfast
Lunch & dinner on requ.
Comp. wine, tea, snacks
sitting room, patio
jacuzzi in suite

Beautifully decorated hillside home with sweeping view; lush landscaping. Wine & cheese on your return from sightseeing. Minutes from the 605 freeway. **7th night free**

WINDSOR

Country Meadow Inn
11360 Old Redwood Hwy, 95492
707-431-1276
Susan Hardesty
All year

$$$ B&B
5 rooms, 5 pb
Visa, MC, *Rated*, •
C-ltd/S-ltd/P-no/H-yes

Full breakfast
Refreshments, wet bar
Sitting room, library
games, hot tubs in room
pool, Victorian garden

Romantic and comfortable. Fireplaces, whirlpool tubs, decks, flower gardens, swimming and a freshness that extends to the abundant gourmet breakfast. **20% Off 3rd night**

YOSEMITE NAT'L PARK

Waldschloss B&B
7486 Henness Circle, Yosemite
West, 95389
209-372-4958
John & Betty Clark
Dec. - Feb., closed

$$$ B&B
2 rooms, 2 pb
Rated, •
C-ltd/S-no/P-no/H-no
German, ltd

Full breakfast
Afternoon tea, snacks
Sitting room

Minutes to wonders of Yosemite National Park. Starry nights, old toys, home cooked breakfasts and hospitality await guests. 2 night min, wkends & holidays. **3rd night 50% Off**

YOUNTVILLE

Burgundy House
P.O. Box 3156, 94599
6711 Washington St.
707-944-0889
Deanna Roque
All year

$$$ B&B
5 rooms, 5 pb
Rated, •
C-ltd/S-no/P-no/H-no
French, German

Full breakfast
Comp. wine
Air conditioned
Mobil 4-star rated

1870 rustic country French stone house with Old World appeal. Furnished with country antiques. Perfect location in beautiful Napa Valley.

Oleander House
P.O. Box 2937, 94599
7433 St. Helena Hwy
707-944-8315
John & Louise Packard
All year

$$$ B&B
4 rooms, 4 pb
Visa, MC, *Rated*, •
C-ltd/S-no/P-no/H-no
Spanish

Full breakfast
Comp. soft drinks
Sitting room, spa, patio
near ballooning, tennis
golf, dining, shops

Country French charm. Antiques. Spacious rooms with brass beds, private decks, fireplaces, central A/C, and Laura Ashley fabrics and wallpapers. Beautiful rose garden.

Sybron House
7400 St. Helena Hwy., Napa,
94558
707-944-2785
Cheryl Maddox
All year

$$$ B&B
4 rooms, 4 pb
Rated, •
C-ltd/S-no/P-no/H-no

Continental plus
Comp. wine
Hot tub
tennis courts
sitting room, piano

New Victorian on hill commanding best view of Napa Valley. First-class tennis court and spa.

More Inns . . .

Ol-Nip Gold Town B&B Inn, 49013 Highway 49, Ahwahnee, 93601, 209-683-2155
Albion River Inn, P.O. Box 100, Albion, 95410,
Wool Loft, 32751 Navarro Ridge Rd., Albion, 95410, 707-937-0377
Kenton Mine Lodge, P.O. Box 942, Alleghany, 95910, 916-287-3212
Cedar Creek Inn, P.O. Box 1466, Alpine, 92001, 619-445-9605
Dorris House B&B, P.O. Box 1655, Alturas, 96101, 916-233-3786
Anaheim B&B, 1327 S. Hickory, Anaheim, 92805, 714-533-1884
Plantation House, The, 1690 Ferry St., Anderson, 96007, 916-365-2827
Cooper House B&B Inn, P.O. Box 1388, Angels Camp, 95222, 209-736-2145
Bayview Hotel B&B Inn, 8048 Soquel Dr., Aptos, 95003, 408-688-8654

Chihuahua Valley Inn, 30247 Chihuahua Valley,
Aquanga, 92302, 714-766-9779
Lady Anne Victorian Inn, 902 - 14th St., Arcata,
95521, 707-822-2797
Lodge at Manuel Mill, P.O. Box 998, Arnold, 95223,
209-795-2622
Guest House, 120 Hart Ln., Arroyo Grande, 93420,
805-481-9304
Rose Victorian Inn, 789 Valley Rd., Arroyo Grande,
93420, 805-481-5566
Dry Creek Inn, 13740 Dry Creek Rd., Auburn,
95603, 916-878-0885
Lincoln House B&B Inn, The, 191 Lincoln Way,
Auburn, 95603, 916-885-8880
Old Auburn Inn, 149 Pleasant, Auburn, 95603,
916-885-6407
Powers Mansion Inn, 164 Cleveland Ave., Auburn,
95603, 916-885-1166
Victoria Inn, P.O. Box 9097, Auburn, 95603,
Hotel Monterey, 108 Summer Ave., Avalon, 90704,
Hotel Villa Portofino, P.O. Box 127, Avalon, 90704,
213-510-0555

Mangels House, Aptos, CA

Inn at Mt. Ada, P.O. Box 2560, Avalon, 90704, 213-510-2030
Mavilla Inn, P.O. Box 2607, Avalon, 90704, 213-510-1651
Seacrest Inn, P.O. Box 128, Avalon, 90704, 213-510-0196
Zane Grey Pueblo Hotel, P.O. Box 216, Avalon, 213-510-0966
Garden House Inn, P.O. Box 1881, Avalon, Catalina Island, 90704, 310-510-0356
San Luis Bay Inn, Box 188, Avila Beach, 93424, 805-595-2333
Helen K Inn, 2105 - 19th St., Bakersfield, 93301, 805-325-5451
Ballard Inn, 2436 Baseline, Ballard, 93463, 805-688-7770
Altamira Ranch, Box 875, 6878 Hwy 82, Basalt, 81621, 303-927-3309
Bayview House, 1070 Santa Lucia Ave., Baywood Park, 93402, 805-528-3098
Chateau des fleurs, 7995 Hwy. 9, Ben Lomond, 95005, 408-336-8943
Capt. Walsh House B&B, 235 E. "L" St., Benicia, 94510, 707-747-5653
Captain Dillingham's Inn, 145 East "D" St., Benicia, 94510, 707-746-7164
Painted Lady, The, 141 E. F St., Benicia, 94510, 707-746-1646
Union Hotel, 401 First St., Benicia, 94510, 707-746-0100
B&B Accomm. in Berkeley, 2235 Carleton St., Berkeley, 94704, 510-548-7556
Delphinus B&B, Berkeley Marina, Berkeley, 94530, 510-527-9622
Elmwood House, 2609 College Ave., Berkeley, 94704, 510-540-5123
Flower Garden B&B, 2341 5th. St., Berkeley, 94710, 510-644-9530
French Hotel, 1538 Shattuck Ave., Berkeley, 94709, 510-548-9930
Hillegass House, 2834 Hillegass Ave., Berkeley, 94705,
Ray Abrams c/o Heitman Prp, 9601 Wilshire Blvd. 200, Beverly Hills, 90210,
Eagle's Nest B&B, 41675 Big Bear Blvd., Big Bear Lake, 92315, 714-866-6465
Janet Kay's, P.O. Box 3874, Big Bear Lake, 92315, 800-243-7031
Moonridge Manor, P.O. Box 6599, Big Bear Lake, 92315,
Wainwright Inn B&B, 43113 Moonridge Rd., Big Bear Lake, 92315, 714-585-6914
Deetjen's Big Sur Inn, Hwy 1, Big Sur, 93920, 408-667-2377
Lucia Lodge, Big Sur, 93920, 408-667-2391
River Inn, Pheneger Creek, Big Sur, 93920,
Chalfant House, 213 Academy St., Bishop, 93514, 619-872-1790
Graeagle Lodge, P.O. Box 38, Blairsden, 96103, 916-836-2511
Bodega Vista Inn, P.O. Box 362, Bodega, 94922, 707-876-3300
School House Inn, 17699 Hwy.1, Box 255, Bodega, 94922,
Taylor's Estero Vista Inn, P.O. Box 255, Bodega, 94922, 707-876-3300
Bodega Harbor Inn, P.O. Box 161, Bodega Bay, 94923, 707-875-3594
Holiday Inn - Bodega Bay, P.O. Box 55, Bodega Bay, 94923, 707-875-2217
Bolinas Villa, 23 Brighton Ave., Bolinas, 94924, 415-868-1650
Star Route Inn, 825 Olema-Bolinas Rd., Bolinas, 94924, 415-868-2502
Thomas' White House Inn, 118 Kale Rd., Bolinas, 94924, 415-868-0279
Wharf Road B&B, 11 Wharf Rd., Bolinas, 94924, 415-868-1430
Anderson Creek Inn, P.O. Box 217, Boonville, 95415, 707-895-3091
Bear Wallow Resort, P.O. Box 533, Boonville, 95415, 707-895-3335
Boonville Hotel, P.O. Box 326, Boonville, 95415, 707-895-2210
Colfax's Guest House, Redwood Ridge Rd., Boonville, 95415, 707-895-3241
Furtado's Hideaway, P.O. Box 650, Boonville, 94515, 707-895-3898
Toll House Restaurant/Inn, P.O. Box 268, Boonville, 95415, 707-895-3630
Diablo Vista B&B, 2191 Empire Ave., Brentwood, 94513, 510-634-2396
Bridgeport Hotel, Main St., Bridgeport, 93517, 619-932-7380
Burbank/Belair, 941 N. Frederic, Burbank, 91505, 818-848-9227
Burlingame B&B, 1021 Balboa Ave., Burlingame, 94010, 415-344-5815
Cora Harschel, 8 Mariposa Ct., Burlingame, 94010, 415-697-5560
Madrone Lane B&B, HCR #34, Burnt Ranch, 95527, 916-629-3642
Brandy Wine Inn, 1623 Lincoln Ave., Calistoga, 94515, 707-942-0202
Brannan Cottage Inn, 109 Wapoo Ave., Calistoga, 94515, 707-942-4200
Brannan's Loft, P.O. Box 561, Calistoga, 94515, 707-963-2181
Calistoga Inn, 1250 Lincoln Av., Calistoga, 94515, 707-942-4101
Golden Haven Hot Springs, 1713 Lake St., Calistoga, 94515, 707-942-6793
Hideaway Cottages, 1412 Fairway, Calistoga, 94515, 707-942-4108
Hillcrest B&B, 3225 Lake Co. Hwy., Calistoga, 94515, 707-942-6334
Larkmead Country Inn, 1103 Larkmead Ln., Calistoga, 94515, 707-942-5360

Le Spa Francais, 1880 Lincoln Ave., Calistoga, 94515, 707-942-4636
Meadowlark Country House, 601-605 Petr. Forest Rd, Calistoga, 94515, 707-942-5651
Mount View Hotel, 1457 Lincoln Ave., Calistoga, 94515, 707-942-6877
Mountain Home Ranch, 3400 Mountain Home, Calistoga, 94515, 707-942-6616
Old Toll Road Inn, 3875 Old Toll Rd., Calistoga, 94515,
Pine Street Inn, 1202 Pine St., Calistoga, 94515, 707-942-6829
Trailside Inn, 4201 Silverado Trail, Calistoga, 94515, 707-942-4106
Village Inn & Spa, 1880 Lincoln Ave., Calistoga, 94515, 707-942-0991
Washington Street Lodging, 1605 Washington St., Calistoga, 94515, 707-942-6968
Wine Way Inn, 1019 Foothill Blvd., Calistoga, 94515, 707-942-0680
Blue Whale Inn, The, 6736 Moonstone Beach Dr, Cambria, 93428, 805-927-4647
Olallieberry Inn, The, 2476 Main St., Cambria, 93428, 805-927-3222
Sylvia's Rigdon Hall Inn, 4036 Burton Dr., Cambria, 93428, 805-927-5125
Camino Hotel, P.O. Box 1197, Camino, 95709, 916-644-7740
Country Bay Inn, 34862 S. Coast Hwy, Capistrano Beach, 92624, 714-496-6656
Summer House B&B, 216 Monterey Way, Capitola Valley, 95010, 408-475-8474
Cardiff by the Sea B&B, 1487 San Elijo, Cardiff by the Sea, 92007,
Candle Light Inn, Box 101, Carmel, 93921,
Colonial Terrace Inn, P.O. Box 1375, Carmel, 93921, 408-624-2741
Cypress Inn, P.O. Box Y, Carmel, 93921, 408-624-3871
Dolphin Inn, Box 101, Carmel, 93921,
Green Lantern Inn, P.O. Box 2619, Carmel, 93921, 408-624-4392
Mission Ranch, 26270 Dolores, Carmel, 93923, 408-624-6436
Monte Verde Inn, P.O. Box 3373, Carmel, 93921, 408-624-6046
Pine Inn, Ocean and Monte Verde, Carmel, 93921,
Stonehouse Inn, P.O. Box 2517, Carmel, 93921, 408-624-4569
Sundial Lodge, P.O. Box J, Carmel, 93921, 408-624-8578
Sunset House, P.O. Box 1925, Carmel, 93921, 408-624-4884
Svensgaards Inn, Box 101, Carmel, 93921,
Wayside Inn, Box 101, Carmel, 93921,
Los Laureles Lodge, 300 Carmel Valley Rd., Carmel Valley, 93924, 408-659-2233
Robles del Rio Lodge, 200 Punta Del Monte, Carmel Valley, 93924, 408-659-3705
Stonepine, 150 East Carmel Valley , Carmel Valley, 93924,
Forest Lodge, Ocean Ave. and Torres, Carmel-By-The-Sea, 95903, 408-624-7023
Pines Inn, P.O. Box 250, Carmel-By-The-Sea, 93921, 408-624-3851
Hofsas House, 3rd & San Carlos,Box 11, Carmel-by-the-Sea, 93921,
Chibchas Inn, P.O. Box 127, Cathey's Valley, 95306,
Ten Aker Wood, P.O. Box 208, Cazadero, 95421, 707-632-5328
Oakridge Manor B&B, 9525 Oakridge Pl., Chatsworth, 91311, 818-998-7547
Bidwell House, 1 Main St., Chester, 96020, 916-258-3338
Drakesbad Guest Ranch, Warner Valley Rd.,
    Chester, 96020, 916 Drakes
Bullard House B&B Inn, 256 E. 1st Ave., Chico,
    95926, 916-342-5912
Esplenade B&B, The, 620 The Esplenade, Chico,
    95926, 916-345-8084
Johnson's Country Inn, 3935 Morehead Ave.,
    Chico, 95928, 916-345-STAY
Music Express Inn, 1091 El Monte Ave., Chico,
    95928, 916-345-8376
O'Flaherty House, 1462 Arcadian, Chico, 95926,
Palms of Chico, 1525 Dayton Rd., Chico, 95726,
    916-343-6868
Kim DuBois, 15 Malibu Court, Clayton, 94517,
    415-672-4400
White Sulphur Springs B&B, P.O. Box 136, Clio,
    96106, 916-836-2387
Crocker Country Inn, 26532 River Rd.,
    Cloverdale, 95425, 707-894-3911
Brookhill, Box 1019, 17655 Hwy 17S, Cobb, 95426,
    707-928-5029
Bear River Mt. Farm, 21725 Placer Hills Rd.,
    Colfax, 95713, 916-878-8314
Sierra Nevada House, P.O. Box 268, Coloma,
    95613, 916-622-5856
Vineyard House, P.O. Box 176, Coloma, 95613,
    916-622-2217
O'Rourke Mansion, 1765 Lurline Rd., Colusa,
    95932, 916-458-5625

The Healdsburg Inn, Mendocino, CA

Carolyn's B&B Homes, P.O. Box 943, Coronado,
    92118, 207-548-2289
Coronado Victorian House, 1000 Eighth St.,
    Coronado, 92118, 619-435-2200
Coronado Village Inn, 1017 Park Pl., Coronado, 92118, 619-435-9318
Jeffrey Hotel, P.O. Box 4, Coulterville, 95311, 209-878-3400
Davis Bed 'N Breakfast Inn, 422 A St., Davis, 95616,
Partridge Inn, 521 First St., Davis, 95616, 916-753-1211
Travelers Repose, P.O. Box 655, Desert Hot Springs, 92240,
Country Living B&B, 40068 Rd. 88, Dinuba, 93618, 209-591-6617
Dorrington Hotel, P.O. Box 4307, Dorrington, 95223, 209-795-5800
Hospitality Inn, 200 S. California St., Dorris, 96023,
Lamplighters, 7724 E. Cecilia St., Downey, 90241, 213-928-8229

Sierra Shangri-La, P.O. 285, Route 49, Downieville, 95936, 916-289-3455
Dunsmuir Inn, 5423 Dunsmuir Ave., Dunsmuir, 96025,
Lion's Head Guest House, Box 21203, El Cajon, 92021, 619-463-4271
Green Dolphin Inn, P.O. Box 132, Elk, 95432, 707-877-3342
Greenwood Pier Inn, P.O. Box 36, Elk, 95432, 707-877-9997
Griffin House at Greenwood, P.O. Box 172, Elk, 95432, 707-877-3422
Castle Creek Inn, 29850 Circle R Way, Escondido, 92026, 619-751-8800
Halbig's Hacienda, 432 S. Citrus Ave., Escondido, 92927, 619-745-1296
Scott Valley Inn, P.O. Box 261, Etna, 96027, 916-467-3229
Chalet de France, SR Box 20A, Kneeland PO, Eureka, 95549, 707-443-6512
Eagle House Victorian Inn, 139 2nd St., Eureka, 95501, 707-442-2334
Heuer's Victorian Inn, 1302 "E" St., Eureka, 95501, 707-445-7334
Hollander House, 2436 E. St., Eureka, 95501, 707-443-2419
Iris Inn, 1134 "H" St., Eureka, 95501, 707-445-0307
Freitas House Inn, 744 Jackson St., Fairfield, 94533, 707-425-1366
Inn at Fawnskin, P.O. Box 378, Fawnskin, 92333,
Felton Crest Hanna's B&B, 780 El Solyo Hts. Dr., Felton, 95018, 408-335-4011
Ferndale Inn, P.O. Box 887, Ferndale, 95536, 707-786-4307
Apple Tree Inn, P.O. Box 41, Fish Camp, 93623, 209-683-5111
Narrow Gauge Inn, 48571 Hwy. 41, Fish Camp, 93623, 209-683-7720
Folsom Hotel, 703 Sutter St., Folsom, 95630,
Plum Tree Inn, 307 Leidesdorff St., Folsom, 95630, 916-351-1541
Farmhouse Inn, 7871 River Rd., Forest Ville, 95436, 707-887-3300
Fort Bidwell Hotel, Main & Garrison, Fort Bidwell, 96112,
Blue Rose Inn, 520 N. Main St., Fort Bragg, 95437, 707-961-3477
Cleone Lodge, 24600 N Hwy. #1, Fort Bragg, 95437, 707-964-2788
Colonial Inn, P.O. Box 565, Fort Bragg, 95437, 707-964-9979
Country Inn, 632 N. Main St., Fort Bragg, 95437, 707-964-3737
Jughandle Beach Country I, 32980 Gibney Ln., Fort Bragg, 95437, 707-964-1415
Oceanview Lodge, 1141 N. Main St., Fort Bragg, 95437, 707-964-1951
Old Stewart House Inn, 511 Stewart St., Fort Bragg, 95437, 707-961-0775
Orca Inn, 31502 N. Hwy 1, Fort Bragg, 95437, 707-964-5585
Pine Beach Inn, P.O. Box 1173, Fort Bragg, 95437, 707-964-5603
Roundhedge Inn, 159 N. Whipple St., Fort Bragg, 95437, 707-964-9605
Marlahan House, 9539 North Hwy 3, Fort Jones, 96032, 916-468-5527
Circle Bar B Guest Ranch, 1800 Refugio Rd., Galeta, 93117, 805-968-1113
Benbow Inn, 445 Lake Benbow Dr., Garberville, 95542, 707-923-2124
Hidden Valley B&B, 9582 Halekulani Dr., Garden Grove, 92641, 714-636-8312
Patrick Creek Lodge, Gasquet, 95543, Dial 0 Idlew
Isis Oasis Lodge, 20889 Geyserville Ave., Geyserville, 95441, 707-857-3524
Beltane Ranch, P.O. Box 395, Glen Ellen, 95442,
Gaige House, 13540 Arnold Dr., Glen Ellen, 95442, 707-935-0237
Glenelly Inn, 5131 Warm Springs Rd., Glen Ellen, 95442, 707-996-6720
Jack London Lodge, P.O. Box 300, Glen Ellen, 95442, 707-938-8510
Stonetree Ranch, 7910 Sonoma Mt. Rd., Glen Ellen, 95442, 707-996-8173
Tanglewood House, 250 Bonnie Way, Glen Ellen, 95442, 707-996-5021
Top O'The World Lodge, 4614 Cavedale Rd., Glen Ellen, 95442, 707-938-4671
Annie Horan's B&B, 415 W. Main St., Grass Valley, 95945, 916-272-2418
Domike's Inn, 220 Colfax Ave., Grass Valley, 95945, 916-273-9010
Golden Ore House B&B, 448 S. Auburn St., Grass Valley, 95945, 916-272-6872
Holbrooke Hotl/Purcell Hse, 212 W. Main St., Grass Valley, 95945, 916-273-1353
Murphy's Inn, 318 Neal St., Grass Valley, 95945, 916-273-6873
Swan-Levine House, 328 S. Church St., Grass Valley, 95945, 916-272-1873
Lodge, The, 33655 Green Valley Lake, Green Valley, 92341, 909-867-5410
McCracken's B&B Inn, 1835 Sycamore Ln., Gridley, 95948, 916-846-2108
Berkshire Inn, P.O. Box 207, Groveland, 95321, 209-962-6744
Hotel Charlotte, Route 120, Groveland, 95321, 209-962-6455
Lee's Middle Fork Resort, 11399 Cherry Oil Rd., Groveland, 95321,
Old Milano Hotel, The, 38300 Hwy 1, Gualala, 95445, 707-884-3256
Saint Orres, P.O. Box 523, Gualala, 95445, 707-884-3303
Whale Watch Inn by the Sea, 35100 Hwy 1, Gualala, 95445, 707-884-3667
Applewood Inn, 13555 Hwy 116, Guerneville, 95446, 707-869-9093
Camelot Resort, P.O. Box 467 4th & Mill, Guerneville, 95446, 707-869-2538
Creekside Inn & Resort, P.O. Box 2185, Guerneville, 95446, 707-869-3623
Fern Grove Inn, 16650 River Rd., Guerneville, 95446, 707-869-9083
River Lane Resort, 16320 First St., Guerneville, 95446, 707-869-2323
Santa Nella House, 12130 Hwy. 116, Guerneville, 95446, 707-869-9488
Willows, The, 15905 River Rd, Box 465, Guerneville, 95446, 707-869-3279
Cypress Inn—Miramar Beach, 407 Mirada Rd., Half Moon Bay, 94019, 415-726-6002
Mill Rose Inn, 615 Mill St., Half Moon Bay, 94019, 415-726-9794
San Benito House, 356 Main St., Half Moon Bay, 94019, 415-726-3425
Belle de Jour Inn, 16276 Healdsburg Ave., Healdsburg, 95448, 707-433-7892
Calistoga Silver Rose Inn, P.O. Box 1376, Healdsburg, 95448, 707-942-9581
Haydon House, The, 321 Haydon St., Healdsburg, 95448, 707-433-5228
L'Auberge du Sans-Souci, 25 W. Grant St., Healdsburg, 95448, 707-431-1110
Hudson, 1740 N. Hudson Ave., Hollywood, 90028, 213-469-5320
Sorensen's Resort, 14255 Hwy 88, Hope Valley, 96120, 916-694-2203
Hopland House, P.O. Box 310, Hopland, 95449, 707-744-1404
Thatcher Inn, 13401 Hwy. 101, Hopland, 95449, 707-744-1890
Strawberry Creek Inn, P.O. Box 1818, Idyllwild, 92349, 714-659-3202
Winnedumah Hotel, P.O. Box 147, Independence, 93526, 619-878-2040
Alder House, 105 Vision Rd., Box 6, Inverness, 94937, 415-669-7218

Ark, The, P.O. Box 273, Inverness, 94937, 415-663-9338
Gray Whale Upstairs, 12781 Sir Francis Drake, Inverness, 94937, 415-669-1330
Inverness Valley Inn, 13275 Sir Francis Drake, Inverness, 94937, 415-669-7250
Laurels, The, P.O. Box 394, Inverness, 94937,
MacLean House, P.O. Box 651, Inverness, 94937, 415-669-7392
Delta Daze Inn, P.O. Box 607, Isleton, 95641, 916-777-7777
Ann Marie's Lodging, 410 Stasel St., Jackson, 95642, 209-223-1452
Court Street Inn, 215 Court St., Jackson, 95642, 209-223-0416
Gate House Inn, 1330 Jackson Gate Rd., Jackson, 95642, 209-223-3500
Windrose Inn, 1407 Jackson Gate Rd., Jackson, 95642, 209-223-3650
Jamestown Hotel, P.O. Box 539, Jamestown, 95327, 209-984-3902
Palm B&B, 10382 Willow St., Jamestown, 95327, 209-984-3429
Sheets N' Eggs B&B, P.O. Box 675, Jamestown, 95327, 209-984-0915
River's End, No. Coast Hwy 1, Jenner, 95450,
Salt Point Lodge, 23255 Coast Hwy 1, Jenner, 95450, 707-847-3234
Sea Coast Hideaways, 21350 N. Coast Hwy 1, Jenner, 95450, 707-847-3278
Stillwater Cove Ranch, 22555 Coast Hwy. 1, Jenner, 95450, 707-847-3227
Timber Cove Inn, 21780 North Coast Hwy, Jenner, 95450,
Butterfield B&B, P.O. Box 1115, Julian, 92036, 619-765-2179
Julian White House, The, 3014 Blue Jay Dr., Julian, 92036, 619-765-1764
Mountainside, 3955 Deer Lake Park Rd., Julian, 92036, 619-765-1295
Pine Hills Lodge, P.O. Box 701, Julian, 92036, 619-765-1100
Pinecroft Manor, P.O. Box 665, Julian, 92036, 619-765-1611
Shadow Mountain Ranch, 2771 Frisius Rd., Julian, 92036, 619-765-0323
Villa Idalene, P.O. Box 90, Julian, 92036, 619-765-1252
Kenwood Inn, 10400 Sonoma Hwy., Kenwood, 95452, 707-833-1293
Kenwood Inn, The, 10400 Sonoma Hwy, Kenwood, 95452, 707-833-7293
Neill House, The, P.O. Box 377, Kernville, 93238,
Montecito-Sequoia Lodge, Box 858, Grant Grove, Kings Canyon Nat'l Park, 93633, 209-565-3388
Kingsburg's Swedish Inn, 401 Conejo St., Kingsburg, 93631, 209-897-1022
B&B Inn at La Jolla, The, 7753 Draper Ave., La Jolla, 92037, 619-456-2066
Irish Cottage, 5623 Taft Ave., La Jolla, 92037, 619-454-6075
Prospect Park Inn, 1110 Prospect St., La Jolla, 92037, 619-454-0133
Scripps Inn, 555 Coast Blvd. S., La Jolla, 92037, 619-454-3391
Sea Lodge, 8110 Camino Del Oro, La Jolla, 92037,
Lost Sierra Country Inn, P.O. Box 57, La Porte, 95981,
Eiler's Inn, 2891 Chateau Way, Laguna Beach, 92651, 714-494-3004
Hotel California, 1316 S. Coast Hwy, Laguna Beach, 92651, 714-497-1457
Hotel San Maarten, 696 S. Coast Hwy, Laguna Beach, 92651, 714-494-9436
Spray Cliff, P.O. Box 403, Laguna Beach, 92677, 714-499-4022
Lakeview Lodge, P.O. Box 189, Lake Arrowhead, 92352, 714-337-6633
Romantique Lakeview Lodge, P.O. Box 128, Lake Arrowhead, 92352, 714-337-6633
Saddleback Inn, 300 S. State Hwy 173, Lake Arrowhead, 92352, 714-336-3571
Storybrook Inn, P.O. Box 362, Lake Arrowhead-Skyforest, 92385, 714-336-1483
Wooden Bridge B&B, 1441 Oakwood Ct., Lakeport, 95453, 707-263-9125
Bell Glen Eel River Inn, 70400 Highway 101, Leggett, 95455, 707-925-6425
Lewiston B&B, P.O. Box 688, Lewiston, 96052, 916-778-3385
Fools Rush Inn, 7533 N. Highway 1, Little River, 95456, 707-937-5339
Heritage House, Little River, 95456, 707-937-5885
Appleton Place B&B Inn, 935 Cedar Ave., Long Beach, 90813, 310-432-2312
Crane's Nest, 319 W. 12th St., Long Beach, 90813, 310-435-4084
Union Hotel, P.O. Box 616, Los Alamos, 93440, 805-344-2744
Eastlake Victorian Inn, 1442 Kellam Ave., Los Angeles, 90026, 213-250-1620
Secret Garden B&B, The, 8039 Selma Ave., Los Angeles, 90046,
Suzanne Multout, 449 N. Detroit St., Los Angeles, 90036, 213-938-4794
Terrace Manor, 1353 Alvarado Terrace, Los Angeles, 90006, 213-381-1478
West Adams B&B Inn, 1650 Westmoreland Blvd., Los Angeles, 90006, 213-737-5041
Mercy Hot Springs, P.O. Box 1363, Los Banos, 93635,
Courtside, 14675 Winchester Blvd., Los Gatos, 95030, 408-395-7111
La Hacienda Inn, 18840 Los Gatos Rd., Los Gatos, 95030, 408-354-9230
Los Gatos Hotel, 31 E. Main St., Los Gatos, 95030, 408-354-4440
Country Cottage, 2920 Grand Ave., Box 26, Los Olivos, 93441, 805-688-1395
Los Olivos Grand Hotel, P.O. Box 526, Los Olivos, 93441, 800-446-2455
Red Rooster Ranch, P.O. Box 554, Los Olivos, 93441, 805-688-8050
Zaca Lake, P.O. Box 187, Los Olivos, 93441, 805-688-4891
Geralda's B&B, 1056 Bay Oaks Dr., Los Osos, 93402, 805-528-3973
Big Canyon Inn, P.O. Box 1311, Lower Lake, 95457, 707-928-5631
J & J's B&B, P.O. Box 1059, Magalia, 95954, 916-873-4782
Boulder Creek B&B, 4572 Ben Hur Rd., Maiposa, 95338, 209-742-7729
White Horse Inn, P.O. Box 2326, Mammoth Lakes, 93546, 619-924-3656
Wildasinn House, The, 26 Lupin St., Box 8026, Mammoth Lakes, 93546, 619-934-3851
Blueroses, P.O. Box 338, Manchester, 95459, 707-882-2240
Chalet on the Mount, 4960 Usona Rd., Mariposa, 95338, 209-966-5115
Dick & Shirl's B&B, 4870 Triangle Rd., Mariposa, 95338, 209-966-2514
Granny's Garden B&B, 7333 Hwy. 49 N., Mariposa, 95338, 209-377-8342
Meadow Creek Ranch B&B Inn, 2669 Triangle & Hwy 49S, Mariposa, 95338, 800-955-3843
Poppy Hill B&B, 5218 Crystal Aire Dr., Mariposa, 95338, 209-742-6273
Schlageter House, P.O. Box 1202, Mariposa, 95338, 209-966-2471
Vista Grande B&B, 4160 Vista Grande Way, Mariposa, 95338, 209-742-6206
Joanie's B&B, P.O. Box 924, McCloud, 96057, 916-964-3106
Stoney Brook Inn, P.O. Box 1860, McCloud, 96057, 916-964-2300
1021 Main St. Guest House, P.O. Box 803, Mendocino, 95460,

B.G. Ranch & Inn, 9601 N. Hwy 1, Mendocino,
  95460, 707-937-5322
Blackberry Inn, 44951 Larkin Rd., Mendocino,
  95460, 707-937-5281
Blue Heron Inn B&B, 390 Kasten St, Box 1142,
  Mendocino, 95460, 707-937-4323
Cypress House, P.O. Box 303, Mendocino, 95460,
  707-937-1456
Hill House Inn, P.O. Box 625, Mendocino, 95410,
  707-937-0554
Mama Moon Gardens, P.O. Box 994, Mendocino,
  95460, 707-937-4234
Mendocino Hotel, P.O. Box 587, Mendocino, 95460,
  707-937-0511
Mendocino Tennis Club/Ldge, 43250 Little Lake
  Rd., Mendocino, 95460, 707-937-0007
Mendocino Village Inn, P.O. Box 626, Mendocino,
  95460, 707-937-0246
Osprey Hill, Box 1307, Mendocino, 95460,
  707-937-4493
Rachel's Inn, Box 134, Mendocino, 95460,
  707-937-0088
S.S. Seafoam Lodge, P.O. Box 68, Mendocino,
  95460,
Sea Gull Inn, P.O. Box 317, Mendocino, 95460,
  707-937-5204
Sears House Inn, Main St., P.O. Box 844,
  Mendocino, 95460, 707-937-4076
Big Canyon Inn, P.O. Box 1311, Middletown, 95461,
  707-928-5631

Ross Cottage, Pacific Grove, CA

Harbin Hot Springs, P.O. Box 782, Middletown, 95461, 707-987-2477
Nethercott Inn, P.O. Box 671, Middletown, 95461, 707-987-3362
Happy Medium, P.O. Box 10, Midpine, Midpine, 95345, 209-742-6366
Aviary, The, 4954 Pondersoa Way, Midpines, 95345,
Homestead Guest Ranch B&B, P.O. Box 13, Midpines, 95345, 209-966-2820
Sierra B&B, Box 221, Midpines, 95345, 209-966-5478
St. Bernard Lodge, Rt. 5, Box 550, Mill Creek, 96061,
Sycamore House, 99 Sycamore Ave., Mill Valley, 94941, 415-383-0612
Malaga House B&B, 2828 Maloga Way, Modesto, 95355,
Hotel Leger, P.O. Box 50, Mokelumne Hill, 95245, 209-286-1401
Farallone Hotel, 1410 Main, Montara, 94037, 415-728-7817
Highland Dell Inn, P.O. Box 370, Monte Rio, 95462, 800-767-1759
House of a 1000 Flowers, P.O. Box 369, Monte Rio, 95421, 707-632-5571
Huckleberry Springs Inn, P.O. Box 400, Monte Rio, 95462, 707-865-2683
Rio Villa Beach Resort, 20292 Hwy 116, Monte Rio, 95462, 707-865-1143
Village Inn, P.O. Box 850, Monte Rio, 95462, 707-865-2304
Carter Art Galleries B&B, 44 Sierra Vista Dr., Monterey, 93940,
Charlaine's Bay View B&B, 44 Sierra Vista Dr., Monterey, 93940, 408-655-0177
Del Monte Beach Inn, 780 Munras, Monterey, 93940, 408-649-4410
Merritt House, 386 Pacific St., Monterey, 93940, 408-646-9686
Monterey, The, 406 Alvarado St., Monterey, 93940, 408-375-3184
Old Monterey Inn, 500 Martin St., Monterey, 93940, 408-375-8284
Ward's Bigfoot Ranch B&B, 1530 Hill Rd., Mount Shasta, 96064,
Murphys Hotel, P.O. Box 329, 457 Main, Murphys, 95247, 209-728-3444
Arbor Guest House, 1436 G St., Napa, 94559, 707-252-8144
Black Surrey Inn, 1815 Silverado Tr., Napa, 94558, 707-255-1197
Brookside Vineyard B&B, 3194 Redwood Rd., Napa, 94558, 707-944-1661
Candlelight Inn, 1045 Easum Dr., Napa, 94558, 707-257-3717
Chateau, The, 4195 Solano Ave., Napa, 94558, 707-253-9300
Coombs Residence Inn, 720 Seminary St., Napa, 94559, 707-257-0789
Crystal Rose Victorian Inn, 7564 St. Helena Hwy, Napa, 94558, 707-944-8185
Elm House, 800 California, Napa, 94559, 707-255-1831
Goodman House, 1225 Division St., Napa, 94559, 707-257-1166
John Muir Inn, The, 1998 Trower Ave, Napa, 94558, 707-257-7220
Magnolia Hotel, 6529 Yount St., Napa, 94599, 707-944-2056
Rockhaven, 7774 Silverado Trail, Napa, 94558, 707-944-2041
Tall Timber Chalets, 1012 Darms Ln., Napa, 94558, 707-252-7810
Yesterhouse Inn, 643 Third St., Napa, 94559, 707-257-0550
Dickinson/Boal Mansion, 1433 E. 24th St., National City, 92050,
Deer Creek Inn, The, 116 Nevada St., Nevada City, 95959, 916-265-0363
Kendall House, The, 534 Spring St., Nevada City, 95959, 916-265-0405
National Hotel, 211 Broad St., Nevada City, 95959, 916-265-4551
Piety Hill Inn, 523 Sacramento St., Nevada City, 95959, 916-265-2245
US Hotel, 233 B Broad St., Nevada City, 95959, 916-265-7999
Victorian Manor, 482 Main St., Newcastle, 95658,
Doryman's Inn, 2102 W. Oceanfront, Newport Beach, 92663, 714-675-7300
LITTLE INN on the Bay, The, 617 Lido Park Dr., Newport Beach, 92663, 714-673-8800
Feather Bed Railroad Co., 2870 Lakeshore Blvd., Nice, 95864,
Norden Inn, Box 94, Norden, 95724, 916-426-3326
Ye Olde South Fork Inn, P.O. Box 731, North Fork, 93643, 209-877-7025
La Maida House, 11154 La Maida St., North Hollywood, 91601, 818-769-3857
Bayside Boat & Breakfast, 49 Jack London Square, Oakland, 94607, 510-444-5858

Bedside Manor, P.O. Box 93, Oakland, 94604, 510-452-4550
Rockridge B&B, 5428 Thomas Ave., Oakland, 94618, 510-655-1223
Washington Inn, 495 - 10th St., Oakland, 94607, 510-452-1776
Ojai B&B, 921 Patricia Ct., Ojai, 93023, 805-646-8337
Theodore Woolsey House, 1484 E. Ojai Ave., Ojai, 93023, 805-646-9779
Bear Valley Inn, P.O. Box 33, Olema, 94950, 415-663-1777
Olema Inn, P.O. Box 37, Olema, 94950, 415-663-9559
Roundstone Farm, P.O. Box 217, Olema, 94950, 415-663-1020
Christy Hill Inn, Box 2449, Olympic Valley, 95730, 916-583-8551
Dolphin's Home, P.O. Box 3724, Olympic Valley, 95730, 916-581-0501
Palm Shadow Inn, 80-761 Hwy. 111, Ondio, 92201, 619-347-3476
Red Lion Inn, 222 N. Vineyard Rd., Ontario, 91764, 714-983-0909
Inn at Shallow Creek Farm, Route 3, Box 3176, Orland, 95963, 916-865-4093
Valley View Citrus Ranch, 14801 Ave. 428, Orosi, 93647, 209-528-2275
Andril Fireplace Cottages, 569 Asilomar Blvd., Pacific Grove, 93950, 408-375-0994
Down Under Inn, 157 15th St., Pacific Grove, 93950, 408-373-2993
Old St. Angela Inn, 321 Central Ave., Pacific Grove, 93950, 408-372-3246
Ross Cottage, 121 18th St., Pacific Grove, 93950, 800-729-7677
Ingleside Inn, 200 W. Ramon Rd., Palm Springs, 92262, 619-325-0046
Le Petit Chateau, 1491 Via Soledad, Palm Springs, 92262, 619-325-2686
Raffles Palm Springs Hotel, 280 Mel Ave., Palm Springs, 92262, 619-320-3949
Villa Royale Inn, 1620 Indian Trail, Palm Springs, 92264, 619-327-2314
Adella Villa, P.O. Box 4528, Palo Alto, 94027, 415-321-5195
Cowper Inn, 705 Cowper St., Palo Alto, 94301, 415-327-4475
Patricia Mendenhall B&B, P.O. Box 236, Palomar Mountain, 92060,
Crown B&B Inn, 530 S. Marengo, Pasadena, 91101, 818-792-4031
Roseleith Bed & Breakfast, 1415 Vine St., Paso Robles, 93446,
Cavanagh Inn, 10 Keller St., Petaluma, 94952, 707-765-4657
Seventh St. Inn, The, 525 Seventh St., Petaluma, 94952, 707-769-0480
Philo Pottery Inn, P.O. Box 166, Philo, 95466, 707-895-3069
Pismo Landmark B&B, 701 Price St., Pismo Beach, 93449, 805-773-5566
Fleming Jones Homestead, 3170 Newtown Rd., Placerville, 95667, 916-626-5840
James Blair House, 2985 Clay St., Placerville, 95667, 916-626-6136
Rupley House Inn, P.O. Box 1709, Placerville, 95667, 916-626-0630
Amador Harvest Inn, 12455 Steiner Rd., Plymouth, 95664, 209-245-5512
Shenandoah Inn, 17674 Village Dr., Plymouth, 95669, 209-245-4491
Estate, The, 13555 Hwy 116, Pocket Canyon, 95446, 707-869-9093
Point Arena Lighthouse, Box 11, Point Arena, 95468, 707-882-2777
Carriage House B&B, 325 Mesa Rd., Point Reyes Station, 94956, 415-663-8627
Country House, The, P.O. Box 98, Point Reyes Station, 94956, 415-663-1627
Eureka House, P.O. Box 660, Point Reyes Station, 94956,
Gallery Cottage, P.O. Box 118, Point Reyes Station, 94956,
Horseshoe Farm Cottage, P.O. Box 332, Point Reyes Station, 94956, 415-663-9401
Knob Hill, P.O. Box 1108, Point Reyes Station, 94956, 415-663-1784
Neon Rose, P.O. Box 632, Point Reyes Station, 94956,
Terris Homestay, P.O. Box 113, Point Reyes Station, 94956,
Tree House Bed & Breakfast, P.O. Box 1075, Point Reyes Station, 94956, 415-663-8720
Quinta Quetzalcoati, P.O. Box 27, Point Richmond, 94807, 415-235-2050
James Creek Ranch B&B, 2249 James Crk., Pope Valley, 94567,
Burlington Hotel, 2 Canyon Lake Dr., Port Costa, 94569,
Upper Feather B&B, 256 Commercial St., Portola, 96122,
Road's End at Paso Creek, RR #1, Box 450, Posey, 93260, 805-536-8668
Pillar Point Inn, 380 Capristrano Rd., Princeton By-The-Sea, 94018, 415-728-7377
Windsong Cottage, P.O. Box 84, Pt. Reyes Station, 94956, 415-663-9695
Christmas House B&B Inn, 9240 Archibald Ave., Rancho Cucamonga, 91730, 714-980-6450
Buttons and Bows B&B, 427 Washington St., Red Bluff, 96080, 916-527-6405
Jeter Victorian, The, 1107 Jefferson, Red Bluff, 96080, 916-527-7574
Claassen B&B, P.O. Box 1625, Red Way, 95560,
Redding's Bed & Breakfast, 1094 Palisades Ave., Redding, 96003,
Magnolia House, 222 S. Buena Vista St, Redlands, 92373, 414-798-6631
Ocean Breeze Inn, 122 S. Juanita Ave., Redondo Beach, 90277, 310-316-5123
Olson Farmhouse B&B, 3620 Road B, Redwood Valley, 95470, 707-485-7523
Hotel Burgess, 1726 11th St., Reedley,
Reedley Country Inn B&B, 43137 Rd 52, Reedley, 93654, 209-638-2585
Spring Oaks B&B, P.O. Box 2918, Running Springs, 92382, 714-867-9636
Auberge du Soleil, 180 Rutherford Hill Rd., Rutherford, 94573, 707-963-1211
Rosi's of Rutherford B&B, P.O. Box 243, Rutherford, 94573, 707-963-3135
Hartley House Inn, 700 - 22nd St., Sacramento, 95816, 916-447-7829
River Rose, 8201 Freeport Blvd., Sacramento, 95832,
Riverboat Delta King, 1000 Front St., Sacramento, 95814,
Sterling Hotel, 1300 "H" St., Sacramento, 95814,

Orchid Tree Inn, Palm Springs, CA

Vizcaya B&B, 2019 21st St., Sacramento, 95818,
916-455-5243
Ambrose Bierce House, 1515 Main St., Saint Helena,
94574, 707-963-3003
Chalet Bernensis, 225 St. Helena Hwy, Saint Helena,
94574, 707-963-4423
Creekwood, 850 Conn Valley Rd., Saint Helena,
94574, 707-963-3590
Hotel St. Helena, 1309 Main St., Saint Helena, 94574,
707-963-4388
Ink House B&B, The, 1575 St. Helena Hwy., Saint
Helena, 94574, 707-963-3890
Courtyard B&B, 334 W. St. Charles, San Andreas,
95249, 209-754-1518
Robin's Nest, The, P.O. Box 1408, San Andreas,
95249, 209-754-1076
Thorn Mansion, P.O. Box 1437, San Andreas, 95249,
209-754-1027
Casa Tropicana, 610 Avenida Victoria, San
Clemente, 92672, 714-492-1234
Casa de Flores B&B, 184 Ave. La Cuesta, San
Clemente, 92672,
San Clemente Hideaway, 323 Cazador Ln., San
Clemente, 92672, 714-498-2219
Britt House 1887, The, 406 Maple St., San Diego,
92103, 619-234-2926
Burley B&B, 6500 San Miguel Rd., San Diego, 92002,
619-479-9839
Castaway Inn, The, 1220 Rosecrans St., San Diego,
92106, 619-298-5432

The Chichester House, Placerville, CA

Heritage Park B&B Inn, 2470 Heritage Park Row, San
Diego, 92110, 619-299-6832
Hill House B&B Inn, 2504 "A" St., San Diego, 92102, 619-239-4738
Hotel Churchill, 827 C St., San Diego, 92101,
Monets Garden, 7039 Casa Ln., San Diego, 91945, 619-464-8296
Quince St. Trolley B&B, P.O. Box 7654, San Diego, 92167, 619-226-8454
Skyview II, 2156 Becky Place, San Diego, 92104, 619-584-1548
Surf Manor & Cottages, P.O. Box 7695, San Diego, 92167, 619-225-9765
1818 California, 1818 California St., San Francisco, 94109,
Adelaide Inn, 5 Adelaide Place, San Francisco, 94102, 415-441-2261
Alexander Inn, 415 O'Farrell St., San Francisco, 94102,
American Family Inn, P.O. Box 349, San Francisco, 94101, 415-931-3083
Aurora Manor, 1328 16th Ave., San Francisco, 94122, 415-564-2480
Bed & Breakfast Inn, 4 Charlton Court, San Francisco, 94123, 415-921-9784
Bock's B&B, 1448 Willard St., San Francisco, 94117, 415-664-6842
Clementina's Bay Brick, 1190 Folsom St., San Francisco, 94103, 415-431-8334
Comfort B&B, 1265 Guerrero St., San Francisco, 94110, 415-641-8803
Commodore International, 825 Sutter St. at Jones, San Francisco, 94109, 415-885-2464
Dolores Park Inn, 3641 - 17th St., San Francisco, 94114, 415-621-0482
Emperor Norton Inn, 615 Post St., San Francisco, 94109, 415-775-2567
Fay Mansion Inn, 834 Grove St., San Francisco, 94117, 415-921-1816
Hotel Louise, 845 Bush St., San Francisco, 94108, 415-775-1755
Hyde Park Suites, 2655 Hyde St., San Francisco, 94123,
Inn at the Opera, 333 Fulton St., San Francisco, 94102, 415-836-8400
Inn on Castro, 321 Castro St., San Francisco, 94114, 415-861-0321
Le Petit Manoir, 468 Noe St., San Francisco, 94114, 415-864-7232
Lyon Street B&B, 120 Lyon St., San Francisco, 94117, 415-552-4773
Majestic, The, 1500 Sutter St., San Francisco, 94109, 415-441-1100
Marina Inn, 3110 Octavia St., San Francisco, 94123, 415-928-1000
Masonic Manor, 1468 Masonic Ave., San Francisco, 94117, 415-621-3365
Millefiori Inn, 444 Columbus, San Francisco, 94133, 415-433-9111
Nolan House, 1071 Page St., San Francisco, 94117, 415-863-0384
Pacific Bay Inn, 520 Jones St., San Francisco, 94102, 800-445-2631
Pacific Heights Inn, 1555 Union St., San Francisco, 94123, 415-776-3310
Pension San Francisco, 1668 Market St., San Francisco, 94102, 415-864-1271
Queen Anne Hotel, The, 1590 Sutter St., San Francisco, 94109, 415-441-2828
Red Victorian Inn B&B, 1665 Haight St., San Francisco, 94117, 415-864-1978
Riley's B&B, 1322-24 6th Ave., San Francisco, 94122, 415-731-0788
Sarah T. Crome, 789 Wisconsin St., San Francisco, 94107,
St. Francis Yacht Club, P.O. Box 349, San Francisco, 94101, 415-931-3083
Stanyan Park Hotel, 750 Stanyan St., San Francisco, 94117, 415-751-1000
Stewart-Grinsell House, 2963 Laguna St., San Francisco, 94123, 415-346-0424
Union Street Inn, 2229 Union St., San Francisco, 94123, 415-346-0424
Willows B&B Inn, 710 - 14th St., San Francisco, 94114, 415-431-4770
La Chaumiére, 1336 Cerro Verde, San Jose, 94515, 707-942-5139
O'Neill's Private Accom., 11801 Sharon Dr., San Jose, 95129, 408-996-1231
B&B San Juan, P.O. Box 613, San Juan Bautista, 95045, 408-623-4101
Forster Mansion Inn, 27182 Ortega Hwy., San Juan Capistrano, 92675, 714-240-7414
Best House B&B, 1315 Clarke St., San Leandro, 94577, 415-351-0911
Arroyo Village Inn, 407 El Camino Real, San Luis Obispo, 93420, 805-489-5926
Heritage Inn, 978 Olive St., San Luis Obispo, 93401, 805-544-2878
Darken Downs Equestre-Inn, Star Route Box 4562, San Miguel, 93451, 805-467-3589

Ranch B&B, R.R. Box 3653, San Miguel, 93451,
Grand Cottages, 809 S. Grand Ave., San Pedro, 90731, 213-548-1240
Ole Rafael B&B, 528 C St., San Rafael, 94901, 415-453-0414
Panama Hotel & Restaurant, 4 Bayview St., San Rafael, 94901, 415-457-3993
Old Oak Table, 809 Clemensen Ave., Santa Ana, 92701, 714-639-7798
Arlington Inn, The, 1136 De La Vina St., Santa Barbara, 93101, 805-428-3912
Bayberry Inn B&B, The, 111 W. Valerio St., Santa Barbara, 93101, 805-682-3199
Brinkerhoff B&B Inn, 523 Brinkerhoff Ave., Santa Barbara, 93101, 805-963-7844
Eagle Inn, 232 Natoma Ave., Santa Barbara, 93101, 800-767-0030
Harbour Carriage House, 420 W. Montecito St., Santa Barbara, 93101, 805-962-8447
Inn at Two Twenty Two, 222 W. Valerio, Santa Barbara, 93101, 805-687-7216
Tiffany Inn, 1323 De La Vina, Santa Barbara, 93101, 805-963-2283
Villa Rosa, 15 Chapala St., Santa Barbara, 93101, 805-966-0851
Villa d'Italia, 780 Mission Canyon Rd., Santa Barbara, 93105, 805-687-6933
Inn Laguna Creek, 2727 Smith Grade, Santa Cruz, 95060, 408-425-0692
Queen Anne, 407 Cliff St., Santa Cruz, 95060,
Sea and Sand Inn, 201 W. Cliff Dr., Santa Cruz, 95060, 408-427-3400
Santa Maria Inn, 801 S. Broadway, Santa Maria, 93454, 805-928-7777
Shutters On The Beach, 1 Pico Blvd., Santa Monica, 90405, 800-334-9000
Sovereign at Santa Monica, 205 Washington Ave., Santa Monica, 90403, 800-331-0163
Fern Oaks Inn, 1025 Ojai Rd., Santa Paula, 93060, 805-525-7747
Lemon Tree Inn, 299 W. Santa Paula St., Santa Paula, 93060, 805-525-7747
Belvedere Inn, 727 Mendocino Ave., Santa Rosa, 95401, 707-575-1857
Cooper's Grove Ranch, 5763 Sonoma Mountain Rd, Santa Rosa, 95404, 707-571-1928
Eden Valley Place, 22490 Mt. Eden Rd., Saratoga, 95070, 408-867-1785
Inn at Saratoga, 20645 Fourth St., Saratoga, 95070, 617-232-8144
Alta Mira Continental Htl, P.O. Box 706, Sausalito, 94966, 415-332-1350
Butterfly Tree, P.O. Box 790, Sausalito, 94966, 415-383-8447
Scotia Inn, P.O. Box 248, Scotia, 95565, 707-764-5683
Sea Ranch Lodge, P.O. Box 44, Sea Ranch, 95497, 707-785-2371
O'Hagin's Guest House, P.O. Box 126, Sebastopol, 95472, 707-823-4771
Strout House, 253 Florence Ave., Sebastopol, 95472, 707-823-5188
Lemon Cove B&B Inn, 33038 Sierra Dr., Sequoia Nat'l Park, 93244, 209-597-2555
Spring Creek Inn, 15201 Hwy 299 W., Box 1, Shasta, 96087, 916-243-0914
Shelter Cove B&B, 148 Dolphin, Shelter Cove, 95589, 707-986-7161
Busch & Heringlake Inn, P.O. Box 68, Sierra City, 96125,
High Country Inn, HCR 2, Box 7, Sierra City, 96125,
Consciousness Village, Box 234, Sierraville, 96126,
    916-994-8984
Serene Lakes Lodge, P.O. Box 164, Soda Springs, 95728,
    916-426-9001
Sunflower House, 243 Third St., Solvang, 93463,
    805-688-4492
Fitzpatrick Winery Lodge, 7740 Fairplay Rd., Somerset,
    95684, 209-245-3248
Ranch at Somis, 6441 La Cumbre Rd., Somis, 93066,
    805-987-8455
Au Relais Inn, 681 Broadway, Sonoma, 95476,
    707-996-1031
Austin Street Cottage, 739 Austin St., Sonoma, 95476,
    707-938-8434
Country Cottage, 291 1st St. East, Sonoma, 95476,
    707-938-2479
El Dorado Inn, 405 First St. W., Sonoma, 95476,
    707-996-3030
Hidden Oak, 214 E. Napa St., Sonoma, 95476,
    707-996-9863
Kate Murphy's Cottage, 43 France St., Sonoma, 95476,
    707-996-4359
Magliulo's Pensione, 691 Broadway, Sonoma, 95476,
Trojan Horse Inn, 19455 Sonoma Hwy, Sonoma, 95476,
    707-996-2430
Vineyard Inn, P.O. Box 368, Sonoma, 95476,
    707-938-2350
JVB Vineyards B&B, P.O. Box 997, Sonoma—Glen Ellen,
    95442, 707-996-4533
Barretta Gardens Inn, 700 S. Barretta St., Sonora,
    95370, 209-532-6039
Gunn House, 286 S. Washington, Sonora, 95370,
    209-532-3421
La Casa Inglesa B&B, 18047 Lime Kiln Rd., Sonora,
    95370, 209-532-5822
Sonora Inn, 160 S. Washington, Sonora, 95370,
    209-532-7468
Via Serena Ranch, 18007 Via Serena Dr., Sonora, 95370,
    209-532-5307
Willow Spgs. Country Inn, 20599 Kings Ct.,
    Soulsbyville, 95372, 209-533-2030
Christiana Inn, Box 18298, South Lake Tahoe, 95706,
    916-544-7337
Richardson's Resort, P.O. Box 9028, South Lake Tahoe,
    96158, 800-544-1801

Rancho Caymus Inn, Rutherford, CA

Strawberry Lodge, Hwy 50, South Lake Tahoe, 95720, 916-659-7200
Bale Mill Inn, 3431 N St. Helena Hwy., St. Helena, 94574, 707-963-4545
Bell Creek B&B, 3220 Silverado Tr., St. Helena, 94574, 707-963-2383
Chestelson House, 1417 Kearney St., St. Helena, 94574, 707-963-2238
Farmhouse, 300 Turpin Rd., St. Helena, 94574, 707-944-8430
Judy's Ranch House, 701 Rossi Rd., St. Helena, 94574, 707-963-3081
Meadowood Resort, 900 Meadowood Ln., St. Helena, 94574, 707-963-3646
Prager Winery B&B, 1281 Lewelling Ln., St. Helena, 94574, 707-963-3713
Spanish Villa Inn, 474 Glass Mtn. Rd., St. Helena, 94574, 707-963-7483
Toller's Guest Cottage, 917 Charter Oak, St. Helena, 94574,
Valley Knoll Vineyard, Highway 29, St. Helena, 94574, 707-963-7770
White Ranch, 707 White Ln., St. Helena, 94574, 707-963-4635
Old Victorian Inn, 207 W. Acacia St., Stockton, 95203, 209-462-1613
Figs Cottage, 3935 Rhodes Ave., Studio City, 91604, 818-769-2662
Summerland Inn, 2161 Ortega Hill Rd,B12, Summerland, 93067, 805-969-5225
Sunnyside Inn, 435 E. McKinley, Sunnyvale, 94086, 408-736-3794
Harbour Inn, 16912 Pacific Coast Hwy, Sunset Beach, 90742, 310-592-3547
Sunset B&B Inn, P.O. Box 1202, Sunset Beach, 90742, 213-592-1666
Roseberry House, 609 North St., Susanville, 96130,
Hanford House, P.O. Box 1450, Sutter Creek, 95685, 209-267-0747
Nancy & Bob's Inn, P.O. Box 386, Sutter Creek, 95685, 209-267-0342
Sutter Creek Inn, P.O. Box 385, Sutter Creek, 95685, 209-267-5606
Chateau Place, P.O. Box 5254, Tahoe City, 96145, 800-773-0313
Cottage Inn at Lake Tahoe, P.O. Box 66, Tahoe City, 95730, 916-581-4073
Lakeside House, P.O. Box 7108, Tahoe City, 95730, 916-683-8796
River Ranch, P.O. Box 197, Tahoe City, 95730, 916-583-4264
Captain's Alpenhaus, The, P.O. Box 262, Tahoma, 96142, 916-525-5000
Loma Vista Bed & Breakfast, 33350 La Serena Way, Temecula, 92390
Sandra Spence, 2410 Markham Ave., Thousand Oaks, 91360
Cort Cottage, P.O. Box 245, Three Rivers, 93271, 209-561-4671
Lost Whale Inn, The, 3452 Patrick's Pt. Dr., Trinidad, 95570, 707-677-3425
Carrville Inn, Star Rt. 2, Box 3536, Trinity Center, 96091
Donner Country Inn, 10070 Gregory Ln., Truckee, 95734
Hilltop at Truckee, Box 8579, Hwy. 267, Truckee, 95737, 916-587-2545
Mountain View Inn, P.O. Box 2011, Truckee, 95734, 916-587-5388
Twain Harte's B&B, P.O. Box 1718, Twain Harte, 95383, 209-586-3311
Sanford House, 306 S. Pine, Ukiah, 95482, 707-462-1653
E. Daday, P.O. Box 8774, Universal City, 91608
Narrows Lodge, 5670 Blue Lake Rd., Upper Lake, 95485, 707-275-2718
Rose Inn, The, 2435 Lincoln Blvd, Venice, 90291
Baker Inn, 1093 Poli St., Ventura, 93001, 805-652-0143
Clocktower Inn, The, 181 E. Santa Clara St., Ventura, 93001, 805-652-0141
Roseholm, 51 Sulphur Mt. Rd., Ventura, 93001, 805-649-4014
Spalding House, 631 E. Encine, Visalia, 93291
Volcano Inn, P.O. Box 4, Volcano, 95689, 209-296-4959
Gasthaus zum Baren, 2113 Blackstone Dr., Walnut Creek, 94598, 510-934-8119
Mansion at Lakewood, The, 1056 Hacienda Dr., Walnut Creek, 94598, 510-945-3600
Chihuahua Valley Inn, P.O. 99, Warner Springs, 92086, 714-766-9779
Warner Springs Ranch, Box 10, Warner Springs, 92086, 619-782-4219
Granny's House, P.O. Box 31, Weaverville, 96093, 916-623-2756
Hendrick Inn, 2124 E. Merced Ave., West Covina, 91791, 818-919-2125
Bowen's Pelican Lodge, P.O. Box 35, Westport, 95488, 707-964-5588
DeHaven Valley Farm, 39247 N. Hwy 1, Westport, 95488, 707-961-1660
Westport Inn B&B, Box 145, Westport, 95488, 707-964-5135
Wilbur Hot Springs, Star Route, Williams, 95987, 916-473-2306
Doll House B&B, 118 School St., Willits, 95490, 707-459-4055
Napa Valley Railway Inn, 6503 Washington St., Yountville, 94559, 707-944-2000
Webber Place, 6610 Webber St., Yountville, 94599, 707-944-8384
Harkey House B&B, 212 C St., Yuba City, 95991, 916-674-1942
Moore Mansion Inn, 560 Cooper Ave., Yuba City, 95991, 916-674-8559
Wick's, 560 Cooper Ave., Yuba City, 95991, 916-674-7951

Colorado

ALAMOSA

Cottonwood Inn B&B
123 San Juan Ave., 81101
719-589-3882 800-955-2623
Julie Ann Mordecai-Sellman
All year

$$ B&B
7 rooms, 7 pb
Visa, MC, *Rated*, •
C-yes/S-ltd/Spanish

Full gourmet breakfast
Library
Neutrogena soaps/creams
turn-down service

Charming inn. Artwork & antiques adorn cozy guest rooms. Biking, hiking, dune walking, fishing, bird-watching, skiing. Historically furnished dining room. **3rd night 30% off.**

ASPEN

Crestahaus Lodge
1301 E. Cooper Ave., 81611
303-925-7081 800-344-3853
Melinda Goldrich
All year

$$$ B&B
31 rooms, 31 pb
Visa, MC, *Rated*, •
C-yes/S-yes/P-yes/H-yes

Continental plus
Afternoon tea, snacks
Comp. wine (winter)
Sitting room, library
bicycles, hot tubs

European charm and comfort ¼ mi. from downtown Aspen; decorated rooms, perfect for singles, couples or families. Fireplace lounges & spectacular views. **Discounts, ask.**

Hearthstone House
134 E. Hyman St., 81611
303-925-7632
Irma Prodinger
Summer & winter

$$$ B&B
17 rooms, 17 pb
Visa, MC, AmEx, •
C-ltd/S-ltd/P-no/H-no
French, German

Full breakfast
Afternoon tea, cookies
Hot tub, bed turndown
service, sitting room
fireplace, herbal bath

The preferred place to stay! Distinctive lodge with the hospitality and services in the finest tradition of European luxury inns.

Innsbruck Inn
233 W. Main St., 81611
303-925-2980
Karen & Heinz Coordes
6/1–10/15, 11/23–4/15

$$ B&B
30 rooms, 30 pb
Most CC, *Rated*, •
C-yes/S-yes/P-no/H-no
German

Continental plus
Comp. wine (winter)
Afternoon tea (winter)
sitt. rm, hot tub, sauna
heated outdoor pool

Tyrolean charm and decor; located at ski shuttle stop, 4 blocks from malls. Sunny breakfast room, generous breakfast buffet, après-ski refreshments, fireside lobby.

Little Red Ski Haus
118 E. Cooper, 81611
303-925-3333 303-925-9000
Marjorie Bobcock
Summer, Thkgvng–Easter

$ B&B
21 rooms, 5 pb
•
C-yes/S-yes/P-no/H-yes
Spanish, German

Full breakfast (winter)
Continental (summer)
Sitting room
piano

Historic 1888 Victorian house. Full breakfast (winter) or continental (summer), complimentary wine. In town, 2 blocks from chair lift. Recent renovations.

Snow Queen Victorian B&B
124 E. Cooper St., 81611
303-925-8455 303-925-6971
Norma Dolle
FAX:925-8455 All year

$ B&B
7 rooms, 5 pb
AmEx, Visa, MC, •
C-yes/S-yes/P-no/H-no
Spanish

Continental plus
Weekly party
Parlor w/fireplace
TV, outdoor hot tub
walk to ski lifts

Quaint, family-oriented Victorian lodge built in 1880s. Parlor w/fireplace & color TV. 2 rms. w/kitchens. Walk to restaurants, shops & ski area. **Free bottle wine**

BASALT

Shenandoah Inn
P.O. Box 578, 81621
0600 Frying Pan Rd.
303-927-4991
Bob & Terri Ziets
All year

$$ B&B
4 rooms
Rated, •
C-ltd/S-ltd/P-no/H-no
French, Spanish

Full breakfast
Dinner, snacks, wine
Sitting room, library
bicycles, skiing, rafts
golf, tennis closeby

Contemporary Colorado B&B, situated on 2 riverfront acres on premier gold-medal trout stream. 20 min. to Aspen. Warm, friendly atmosphere, exceptional cuisine. **Midwk specials**

BOULDER

Briar Rose B&B Inn
2151 Arapahoe Ave., 80302
303-442-3007
Margaret & Bob Weisenbach
All year

$$$ B&B
9 rooms, 9 pb
Most CC, *Rated*, •
C-yes/S-ltd/P-yes/H-no
Polish, Tibetan

Continental plus
Comp. sherry, port
High tea - chamber music
poetry, drama readings
bicycles

Entering the Briar Rose is like entering another time when hospitality was an art and the place for dreams was a feather bed. Three rooms with fireplaces. AAA rated 3 diamond

---

Pearl Street Inn
1820 Pearl St., 80302
303-444-5584 800-232-5949
Theresa Schuller
All year

$$$ B&B
7 rooms, 7 pb
Visa, MC, AmEx, *Rated*,
•
C-yes/S-yes/P-yes/H-no
French

Full breakfast
Comp. wine/cheese/tea
Sitting room, bar
entertainment, TV/room
Dinner served $ Wed.-Sat

A rare combination of a European inn and luxury hotel. Near Boulder's pedestrian mall. Refreshing breakfast and evening bar in garden courtyard.

BRECKENRIDGE

Allaire Timbers Inn
P.O. Box 4653, 80424
9511 Hwy #9/So. Main St.
303-453-7530 800-624-4904
Jack & Kathy Gumph
All year

$$$ B&B
10 rooms, 10 pb
Visa, MC, AmEx, *Rated*,
•
C-ltd/S-no/P-no/H-yes

Continental breakfast
Winter full breakfast
Snacks, comp. wine
Sitting room, fireplaces
hot tubs

Newly constructed log and stone Inn; suites with private hot tub and fireplace; spectacular mountain views; quiet luxury; personalized hospitality.

Cotten House B&B
P.O. Box 387, 80424
102 S. French St.
303-453-5509
Peter & Georgette Contos
All year

$$ B&B
3 rooms, 1 pb
Rated
C-ltd/S-no/P-no/H-no
Greek, French

Full breakfast
Afternoon tea
Sitting room, library
cable TV, VCR
local recreation center

Genuine Breckenridge in a restored 1886 Victorian home. Central to Historic District and winter and summer activities. "Home away from home."

Ridge Street Inn
P.O. Box 2854, 80424
212 N. Ridge St.
303-453-4680
Carol Brownson
All year

$$ B&B
6 rooms, 4 pb
Visa, MC, •
C-ltd/S-no/P-no/H-no

Full breakfast
Aft. tea, snacks
Sitting room
fireplace, guest phone
kitchen facilities

*1890 Victorian B&B in heart of Historic District. Spacious, comfortable rooms. Antiques, home-cooked breakfast. **Innkeeper hosted biking/hiking/ski tours.***

Williams House B&B, c.1885
P.O. Box 2454, 80424
303 N. Main St.
303-453-2975 800-795-2975
Diane Jaynes, Fred Kinat
All year exc. May & Oct

$$ B&B
4 rooms, 4 pb
AmEx, *Rated*, •
C-ltd/S-no/P-no/H-no

Full breakfast
Apres-ski treat
Afternoon tea, deck
sitting room, sun room
TV, VCR, mountain views

Step back in time to gold fever Breckenridge. Restored historic mining home furnished w/antiques. 2 romantic fireplaced parlours. Homemade baked goods. Large outdoor hot tub.

Holden House—1902 B&B Inn, Colorado Springs, CO

BUENA VISTA

Adobe Inn, The
P.O. Box 1560, 81211
303 N. Hwy 24
719-395-6340
Paul, Marjorie & Mike Knox
All year

$$ B&B
5 rooms, 5 pb
Visa, MC, *Rated*,
C-yes/S-no/P-no/H-no
some Spanish

Full gourmet breakfast
Comp. beverages
Restaurant, sitting room
library, piano, solarium
2 suites, jacuzzi

Santa Fe-style adobe hacienda. Indian, Mexican, antique, wicker & Mediterranean rooms. Indian fireplaces. Gourmet breakfast. Jacuzzi. Majestic mountain & river scenery.

CLARK

Home Ranch
Box 822, 80428
303-879-1780
Ken & Cile Jones
All year

$$$ EP/AP
14 rooms, 14 pb
●
C-yes/S-yes/P-no/H-no

Full breakfast
Lunch, dinner
Sitting room, piano
Herds of Llamas
sleigh rides

What's special? The food, the horses, the fishing, and the company. Mobile 4 star rating. Relais & Chateux, Colo. Dune Ranch. Yes!

COLORADO SPRINGS

Holden House—1902 B&B Inn
1102 W. Pikes Peak Ave., 80904
719-471-3980
Sallie & Welling Clark
All year

$$ B&B
5 rooms, 5 pb
Most CC, *Rated*, ●
C-ltd/S-no/P-no/H-no

Full gourmet breakfast
Comp. coffee, tea, snack
Parlor w/TV, fireplaces
living room w/ fireplace
"Tubs for Two", veranda

Charming 1902 Victorian home filled with antiques and family heirlooms located in Historic District. Suites w/fireplaces. Conveniently located. Friendly resident cats.

COLORADO SPRINGS

Painted Lady B&B Inn	$$ B&B	Full breakfast
1318 W. Colorado Ave., 80904	4 rooms, 2 pb	Afternoon tea
719-473-3165	Visa, MC, Disc.,*Rated*, •	Bicycles
Kenneth & Stacey Kale	C-yes/S-no/P-no/H-no	sitting room
All year		

1894 Victorian home nestled in historic Old Colorado City. Guest rooms feature Victorian furnishings. Hearty, healthy breakfasts begin your day.

CRESTED BUTTE

Alpine Lace B&B	$$$ B&B	Full gourmet breakfast
P.O. Box 2183, 81224	4 rooms, 2 pb	Afternoon tea, snacks
726 Maroon	Visa, MC, *Rated*,	Sitting room, ski room
303-349-9857	C-ltd/S-no/P-no/H-no	hot tub, bikes, library
Ward Weisman & Loree Mulay		Balconies off all rooms
Nov.–April, May–Oct.		

Mountain paradise located in historic district. Wildflower capital, skier haven. Gourmet breakfasts, informal elegance, great views! Come visit.

Purple Mountain Lodge	$$ B&B	Full breakfast (winter)
P.O. Box 897, 81224	5 rooms, 3 pb	Cont. breakfast (summer)
714 Gothic Ave.	Visa, MC, SkiAm, DC, •	Sitting room
303-349-5888	C-yes/S-yes/P-no/H-no	
Walter & Sherron Green	Swiss	
Summer & winter		

Victorian home in historic town. Relax by the massive stone fireplace in the living room; breakfast with view of Mt. Crested Butte.

DENVER

Castle Marne—Urban Inn	$$$ B&B	Full gourmet breakfast
1572 Race St., 80206	9 rooms, 9 pb	Aftn. tea
303-331-0621 800-92-MARNE	Visa, MC, AmEx, *Rated*,	Library, gift shop
The Peiker Family	•	game room w/pool table
All year	C-ltd/S-no/P-no/H-no	computer, fax, copier
	Spanish, Hungarian	

Luxury urban inn. Minutes from airport, convention center, business district, shopping, fine dining. Local & National Historic Structure. Guest office. Candlelight dinners.

Haus Berlin B&B	$$$ B&B	Continental plus
1651 Emerson St., 80218	4 rooms, 4 pb	Comp. wine
303-837-9527	Visa, MC, AmEx, *Rated*,	Sitting room
Christiana Brown	C-ltd/S-no/P-no/H-no	library
All year	German	

Beds are dressed in luxurious European linens. Urban, conveniently located uptown for tourists and business travelers. **3+ nights 10% discount**

Queen Anne B&B Inn	$$ B&B	Full breakfast
2147 Tremont Pl., Clements	14 rooms, 14 pb	Afternoon beverages
Historic Dist., 80205	Most CC, *Rated*, •	Fresh flowers
303-296-6666 800-432-INNS	C-ltd/S-no/P-no/H-no	4 suites w/sitting rm.
Tom King		flower garden, patio
All year, FAX:296-2151		

Colorado's most (16) award winning inn. Located in beautiful, residential 1870s district facing park, heart of downtown. **Ask about special packages, Nov.-May**

DURANGO

Blue Lake Ranch
16919 State Hwy 140, Hesperus, 81326
303-385-4537
Shirley & David Alford
All year

$$$ B&B
8 rooms, 8 pb
Rated, •
C-yes/S-no/P-no/H-no

Full European breakfast
Afternoon tea
Sitting room, sauna
bicycles, lake, gardens
Cabin is available

Victorian farmhouse surrounded by gardens of flowers, vegetables herbs. Spectacular lake & mountain views, trout-stocked lake, meals of homegrown ingredients. **10% off 7+ nights**

Country Sunshine B&B
35130 Hwy. 550 N., 81301
303-247-2853 800-383-2853
Jill & Jim Anderson
All year

$$ B&B
5 rooms, 3 pb
Most CC, *Rated*, •
C-yes/S-no/P-yes/H-ask

Full breakfast
Afternoon tea
Comp. wine, snacks
sitting room
library

Spacious ranch-style house on 3 acres of Pine Oak forest. Abundant wildlife, skiing, fishing, golf, mountain biking, hot springs outdoor spa.

Logwood B&B
35060 Hwy. 550N, 81301
303-259-4396
Greg & Debby Verheyden
All year

$$ B&B
6 rooms, 6 pb
Visa, MC, *Rated*, •
C-ltd/S-no/P-no/H-no

Full country breakfast
Aft. tea, snacks
Lunch box by request
sitting room, library
swimming pool nearby

Large, 3-story red cedar log home w/wrap-around porch on 15 acres viewing animals, river valley and San Juan Mtns. Award-winning desserts. **Free beverages & flowers**

Riverhouse B&B
495 Animas View Dr., 81301
303-247-4775 800-544-0009
C. Carroll, K. & L. Enggren
Exc. Oct 15–Nov 15, Apr

$$ B&B
6 rooms, 6 pb
Visa, MC, Disc.,*Rated*, •
C-yes/S-no/P-no/H-no

Full gourmet breakfast
Comp. wine, juice/snacks
Massage & hypnosis sess.
exercise rm, hot springs
fish pond, hot tub

Dine in a spacious skylighted atrium. View the Animas River Valley. Hear the haunting whistle of historic narrow-gauge train. Vegetarian meals avail. **Massage discounts**

Queen Anne B&B, Denver, CO

DURANGO

Vagabond Inn B&B
P.O. Box 2141, 81301
2180 Main Ave.
303-259-5901 ext. 23
Ace & Mary Lou Hall
All year

$$$ B&B/EP
28 rooms, 24 pb
Most CC, *Rated*, •
C-yes/S-yes/P-no/H-yes

Continental breakfast
Comp. wine
Sitting room, hot tubs
BBQ grill, deck, patio
fireplaces, bridal suite

Attractions include the historic train, Purgatory Ski Area, Mesh Verde National Park, a national scenic highway, many other activities, fine dining, and entertainment.

EATON

Victorian Veranda B&B Inn
P.O. Box 361, 80615
515 Cheyenne Ave.
303-454-3890
Dick & Nadine White
All year

$ B&B
3 rooms, 1 pb
•
C-yes/S-no/P-no/H-no

Continental breakfast
Cookout on grill
Afternoon tea, fruit
baby grand player piano
whirlpool, near tennis

The beautifully restored 1894 Queen Anne 12-room home is furnished with antiques in each large bedroom, with fireplace and balcony in one room. **3rd night 50% off**

ESTES PARK

Anniversary Inn B&B, The
1060 Mary's Lake Rd., Moraine
Route, 80517
303-586-6200
Don & Susan Landwer
All year

$$ B&B
4 rooms, 4 pb
Visa, MC, *Rated*, •
C-ltd/S-no/P-no/H-ltd

Full gourmet breakfast
Snacks, dinner by req.
Sitting room, library
"Sweetheart" cottage
2 rms w/jacuzzi tubs

Cozy, turn-of-the-century log home one mile from Rocky Mountain National Park. Come and be pampered. Member of BBCI and PAII. **Special chocolate basket**

Black Dog Inn B&B
P.O. Box 4659, 80517
650 S. St. Vrain Ave.
303-586-0374
Pete & Jane Princehorn
All year

$$ B&B
4 rooms, 2 pb
Visa, MC, *Rated*, •
C-ltd/S-no/P-no/H-no

Full breakfast
Afternoon tea, snacks
Special occasion wine
sitting room,library
bicycles, piano, games

1910 Rambling mountain home snuggled among towering aspen and pine. View, antiques, cozy fireplace. Western hospitality makes your stay memorable. **2nd night 50% off Nov-Ap**

FRISCO

Galena St. Mountain Inn
P.O. Box 417, 80443
106 Galena St.
303-668-3224 800-248-9138
Brenda McDonnell
All year

$$ B&B
14 rooms, 14 pb
Most CC, *Rated*, •
C-yes/S-no/P-no/H-yes

Full breakfast (winter)
Con. Plus bkfst (summer)
Aft. tea, sitting room
library, hot tubs
sauna, meeting rooms

Striking Neo-mission-style furnishing, down comforters, windowseats, mountain views. Located minutes from Breckenridge, Keystone, Copper Mt. Catered meals for groups.

Mar Dei's Mountain Retreat
P.O. Box 1767, 80443
221 S. 4th Ave.
303-668-5337
All year

$ B&B
5 rooms, 2 pb
C-yes/S-no/P-no

Continental plus
Aft. tea, snacks
Comp. wine
library, hot tubs
sitting room

Mar Dei's is a cozy European-style B&B, surrounded by 80 pines. Enjoy outside hot tub, bike path. 2 blocks to boat dock.

FRISCO

Twilight Inn
P.O. Box 397, 80443
308 Main St.
303-668-5009 800-262-1002
J. Harrington & R. Ahlquist
All year

$$ B&B
12 rooms, 8 pb
Visa, MC, AmEx, Disc., •
C-yes/S-ltd/P-ltd/H-ltd

Continental plus
Aft. tea, use of kitchen
Sitting room, library
hot tubs, steam room
laundry, guest storage

Country antiques and modern conveniences are combined for your comfort and relaxation. Make yourself at home in the Colorado Rockies.

GREEN MOUNTAIN FALLS

Outlook Lodge B&B
P.O. Box 5, 80819
6975 Howard St.
719-684-2303
Hayley & Patrick Moran
All year

$ B&B
8 rooms, 2 pb
Visa, MC, *Rated*, •
C-yes/S-no/H-yes
German

Full gourmet breakfast
BBQ
Piano, organ, sitt. rm.
fishing, tennis, hiking
horseback ride, library

Historic Victorian inn located in secluded mountain village at foot of Pikes Peak. Reminiscences of the past rekindled to the present. German atmosphere in decor & breakfast.

GUNNISON

Mary Lawrence Inn, The
601 N. Taylor, 81230
303-641-3343
Jan Goin
All year

$$ B&B
5 rooms, 5 pb
Visa, MC, •
C-yes/S-no/P-no/H-no

Full breakfast
Sack lunch ($)
Two suites
sitting room, many books
tandem bicycles

Our renovated home is inviting and comfortable; delectable breakfasts. Gunnison country offers marvelous outdoor adventures; super Crested Butte ski package.

LAKE CITY

Old Carson Inn
P.O. Box 144, 81235
8401 HC 30
303-944-2511
Don & Judy Berry
May–March

$$ B&B
6 rooms
Visa, MC, •
C-yes/S-no/P-no/H-ltd

Full breakfast
Snacks
Sitting room
hot tubs

A warm and cozy inn, nestled among aspen and spruce below the "divide." A wilderness experience with the comforts of home.

LEADVILLE

Wood Haven Manor
P.O. Box 1291, 80461
809 Spruce
719-486-0109 800-748-2570
Bobby & Jolene Wood
All year

$ B&B
8 rooms, 7 pb
Most CC, *Rated*, •
C-ltd/S-no/P-no/H-no

Full breakfast
Afternoon tea, snacks
Sitting room, library
hot tubs, 1 whirlpool
sleighrides

1890s Victorian home, spacious and comfortable living room with massive wood carved fireplace, cable TV & VCR. Each room furnished with antiques. **3rd night 50% off**

LIMON

Midwest Country Inn
P.O. Box 550, 80828
795 Main St.
719-775-2373
Harold & Vivian Lowe
All year

$ EP
32 rooms, 32 pb
Most CC, *Rated*, •
C-yes/S-yes/P-no/H-no

Coffee & tea available
Restaurant - 1 block
Sitting room, gift shop
"listening" waterfall
and "watching" fountain

Beautiful rooms, oak antiques, stained glass, elegant wallpapered bathrooms, near I-70, 1.5 hours from Denver and Colorado Springs. Train rides available Saturday evenings.

LOVELAND

Lovelander B&B Inn, The	$$$ B&B	Full gourmet breakfast
217 W. 4th St., 80537	9 rooms, 9 pb	Comp. beverages
303-669-0798	Most CC, *Rated*, •	Meeting & reception ctr.
Marilyn & Bob Wiltgen	C-ltd/S-no/P-no/H-ltd	sitting room, library
All year		1 whirlpool/deluxe room

Victorian grace and old-fashioned hospitality from the heart of the Sweetheart City: a community of the arts. Gateway to the Rockies.

LYONS

Inn at Rock 'n River	$$$ B&B	Full breakfast
P.O. Box 829, 80540	9 rooms, 9 pb	Restaurant, lunch/dinner
16858 N. St. Vrain Dr.	Visa, MC, *Rated*, •	Snacks, hot tubs
303-443-4611	C-yes/S-yes/P-no/H-yes	ponds, trout farm
Marshall & Barbara		trout fishing
McCrummen		
All year		

*Country inn & trout farm, 18 acres on river. Covered bridges, waterfalls. Fish private ponds, license & tackle provided. Restaurant—"we'll cook your catch!" **Fishing discount.***

MANITOU SPRINGS

Two Sisters Inn-a B&B	$$ B&B	Full gourmet breakfast
Ten Otoe Place, 80829	5 rooms, 3 pb	Comp. wine, snacks
719-685-9684	Visa, MC, *Rated*, •	Picnic lunches
Sharon Smith, Wendy Goldstein	C-ltd/S-no/P-no/H-no	Sitting room
All year		library

Gracious Victorian nestled at base of Pikes Peak in historic district. Garden honeymoon cottage. Mineral springs, art galleries, shops, restaurants.

MINTURN

Eagle River Inn	$$$ B&B	Full breakfast
P.O. Box 100, 81645	12 rooms, 12 pb	Comp. wine & cheese
145 N. Main St.	Visa, MC, AmEx, *Rated*,	Sitting room, patio
303-827-5761 800-344-1750	•	hot tub, backyard
Jane Leavitt	C-ltd/S-no/P-no/H-no	conference/banquet room
Exc. May & mid-October		

Quiet mountain inn nestled alongside the Eagle River minutes from Vail Ski Resort. Furnished in southwest decor. Romantic riverside setting catering especially to couples.

OURAY

St. Elmo Hotel	$$ B&B	Full breakfast
P.O. Box 667, 81427	9 rooms, 9 pb	Restaurant
426 Main St.	Visa, MC, *Rated*, •	Comp. wine, coffee, tea
303-325-4951	C-yes/S-ltd/P-no/H-no	piano, outdoor hot tub
Sandy & Dan Lingenfelter		sauna, meeting room
All year		

Hotel & Bon Ton Restaurant surrounded by beautiful, rugged 14,000-ft. peaks. Furnished with antiques, stained glass & brass; honeymoon suite. Hot springs, jeeping, cross-country skiing.

PUEBLO

Abriendo Inn	$$ B&B	Full gourmet breakfast
300 W. Abriendo Ave., 81004	7 rooms, 7 pb	Comp. wine, snacks
719-544-2703	Most CC, *Rated*, •	Cater groups for lunch
Kerrelyn Trent	C-ltd/S-no/P-no/H-no	and dinner, sitting room
All year		non-smoking inn

A classic B&B on the National Register of Historic Places. The comfortable elegance and luxury of the past. Taste-tempting breakfasts. Nearby attractions & recreational areas.

SALIDA

Poor Farm Country Inn
8495 C.R. 160, 81201
719-539-3818
Herb & Dottie Hostetler
All year

$ B&B
5 rooms, 2 pb
Visa, MC, *Rated*,
C-yes/S-ltd/P-no/H-no

Full country breakfast
Comp. tea
Library
piano, bicycles

Secluded area on the Arkansas River. Furnished in antiques and 100-year-old library. Country breakfast, close to everything to enjoy the four seasons. R&R time.

SILVERTON

Alma House Hotel
P.O. Box 359, 81433
220 East 10th St.
303-387-5336 303-249-4646
Christine & Terry Payne
Mem. Day—Labor Day

$ B&B
10 rooms, 1 pb
Most CC, *Rated*, •
C-yes/S-no/P-no/H-no

Continental breakfast
Comp. coffee, tea
Sitting room
in-house movies
honeymoon suite

Beautifully restored 1898 mountain town hotel features in each room soft water, huge towels, clock-radio, color cable TV, queenbed. Beautiful views. **3rd night 50% Nov.—Mar.**

SNOWMASS

Starry Pines B&B
2262 Snowmass Creek Rd.,
81654
303-927-4202
Shelley Burke. All year

$$$ B&B
2 rooms, 2 pb
•
C-ltd/S-no/P-no/H-no

Continental plus
Aft. tea, snacks
Sitting room
hot tubs

Enjoy contemporary comfort on 70 acres w/trout stream and panoramic views. 25 minutes to Aspen's year-round activities. **5th night 50% off, 7th night free**

STEAMBOAT SPRINGS

Sky Valley Lodge
P.O. Box 3132, 80477
31490 E. U.S. Hwy 40
303-879-7749
Steve Myler
All year

$$ B&B
24 rooms, 24 pb
Visa, MC, AmEx, *Rated*,
•
C-yes/S-yes/P-yes/H-no

Continental, summer
Continental plus, winter
Restaurant, bar, library
sitting room, hot tub
sauna, shuttle in winter

Nestled in the side of the mountains, this English country manor-style lodge affords a sweeping view of the valley below. Nearby skiing, dining, shopping, hiking.

Steamboat Springs B&B
P.O. Box 773815, 80477
1245 Crawford Ave.
303-870-9017 800-530-3866
George & Alice Lund
All year

$$ B&B
4 rooms, 4 pb
Visa, MC, *Rated*, •
C-ltd/S-no/P-no/H-no

Full breakfast
Aft. tea
Library, Hot air ballons
swim, bike nearby, golf
public hot springs, ski

Hilltop log house. Scandinavian decor, charming wallpapers & antiques, spectacular views, fireplace, TV, piano. Homemade breakfasts. **Seniors (over 62) 10% off**

TELLURIDE

Johnstone Inn
P.O. Box 546, 81435
403 W. Colorado Ave.
303-728-3316 800-752-1901
Bill Schiffbauer
Ski season & summer

$$$ B&B
8 rooms, 8 pb
Visa, MC, AmEx, •
C-ltd/S-no/P-no/H-no

Full breakfast
Comp. refreshments
  in ski season
sitting room w/fireplace
games, outdoor hot tub

A true, 100 year old, restored Victorian boarding house, located in the center of Telluride & the spectacular San Juan mountains. Rooms are warm, romantic w/Victorian marble.

WINTER PARK

Beau West B&B	$$$ B&B	Continental plus
P.O. Box 587, 80482	3 rooms, 3 pb	Sitting room
148 Fir Dr.	Visa, MC, *Rated*, •	library
303-726-5145 800-473-5145	C-ltd/S-no/P-no/H-no	hot tubs
Bobby Goins		
Nov 20-Apr 20, June-Sept		

Your bed and breakfast stay includes a dreamy bedroom, gourmet continental breakfast, fireplace and jacuzzi—all at our slopeside location! **3rd night 50% off, ltd**

Engelmann Pines	$$ B&B	Full breakfast
P.O. Box 1305, 80482	6 rooms, 2 pb	Comp. wine
1035 Cranmer	Visa, MC, AmEx, *Rated*,	Snacks, sitting room
303-726-4632	•	library, bicycles
Margaret & Heinz Engel	C-yes/S-no/P-no/H-no	jacuzzi, kitchen, TV
All year	German	

Spectacular mountain getaway furnished with antiques, down comforters & handmade quilts. Near Winter Park Ski Resort, Rocky Mountain National Park, Pole Creek Golf Course.

More Inns . . .

Allenspark Lodge, Colorado Hwy. 7 - Bus. , Allenspark, 80510, 303-747-2552
Lazy H Ranch, Box 248, Allenspark, 80510, 303-747-2532
Tarado Mansion, Route 1, Box 53, Arriba, 80804, 719-768-3468
On Golden Pond B&B, 7831 Eldridge, Arvada, 80005, 303-424-2296
Treehouse, The, 6650 Simms, Arvada, 80004, 303-431-6352
Alpina Haus, 935 E. Durant, Aspen, 81611, 800 24A-SPEN
Aspen Ski Lodge, 101 W. Main St., Aspen, 81611, 303-925-3434
Brass Bed Inn, 926 E. Durant, Aspen, 81611, 303-925-3622
Copper Horse Guest House, 328 W. Main, Aspen, 81611, 303-925-7525
Hotel Lenado, 200 S. Aspen St., Aspen, 81611, 303-925-6246
Inn at Aspen, The, 38750 Highway 82, Aspen, 81611
Molly Gibson Lodge, 120 W. Hopkins, Aspen, 81611, 303-925-2580
Mountain House B&B, 905 East Hopkins, Aspen, 81611, 303-920-2550
Pomegranate Inn, Box 1368, Aspen, 81612, 800-525-4012
Sardy House, 128 E. Main St., Aspen, 81611, 303-920-2525
Tipple Inn, 747 S. Galena St., Aspen, 81611, 800-321-7025
Ullr Lodge, 520 W. Main St., Aspen, 81611, 303-925-7696
Eastridge Farms, 38634B Weld Cty. Rd# 39, Ault, 80610, 303-834-2617
Altamira Ranch, Box 875, 23484 Hwy. 82, Basalt, 81621, 303-927-3309
Deer Valley Resorts, P.O. Box 796, Bayfield, 81122, 303-884-2600
Parrish's Country Squire, 2515 Parrish Rd., Berthoud, 80513, 303-772-7678
Boulder Victorian Historic, 1305 Pine St., Boulder, 80302, 303-938-1300
Gunbarrel Inn, 6901 Lookout Rd., Boulder, 80301
Magpie Inn, The, 1001 Spruce St., Boulder, 80302, 303-449-6528
Salina House, 365 Gold Run, Boulder, 80302, 303-442-1494
Lark, The, P.O., Box 1646, 80443, 303-668-5237
Fireside Inn, P.O. Box 2252, Breckenridge, 80424, 303-453-6456
Swiss Inn B&B, P.O. Box 556, Breckenridge, 80424, 303-453-6489
Blue Sky Inn, 719 Arizona St., Buena Vista, 81211, 303-395-8865
Trout City Inn, Box 431, Buena Vista, 81211, 719-495-0348
Ambiance Inn, 66 N. 2nd. St., Carbondale, 81623, 303-963-3579
Ambiance Inn B&B, 66 N. 2nd Street, Carbondale, 81623, 303-963-3597
Biggerstaff House B&B, The, 0318 Lions Ridge Rd., Carbondale, 81623, 303-963-3605
Eastholme, Box 98, 4445 Haggerman , Cascade, 80809, 719-684-9901
Sue's Guest House, P.O. Box 483, Cascade, 80809, 303-684-2111

Haus Berlin, Denver, CO

Cedar' Edge Llamas B&B, 2169 Hwy. 65, Cedaredge, 81413, 303-856-6836
Golden Rose Hotel, P.O. Box 127, 102 Main, Central City, 80427, 303-825-1413
Winfield Scott Guest Qtrs., P.O. Box 369, Central City, 80427, 303-582-3433
Inn at Hahn's Peak, Box 867, Clark, 80486
1894 Victorian, P.O. Box 9322, Colorado Springs, 80932, 719-630-3322
Black Forest B&B, 11170 Black Forest Rd., Colorado Springs, 80908, 719-495-4208
Griffin's Hospitality Hse, 4222 N Chestnut, Colorado Springs, 80907, 303-599-3035
Hearthstone Inn, 506 North Cascade, Colorado Springs, 80903, 719-473-4413
Pikes Peak Paradise, Box 5760, Woodland Park, Colorado Springs, 80866, 719-687-6656
Wedgewood Cottage B&B, 1111 W. Pikes Peak Ave., Colorado Springs, 80904, 719-636-1829
Brumder Hearth, P.O. Box 1152, Crested Butte, 81224, 303-349-6253
Claim Jumper, 704 Whiterock, Box 1181, Crested Butte, 81224, 303-349-6471
Cristiana Guesthaus, P.O. Box 427, Crested Butte, 81224, 303-349-5326
Forest Queen Hotel, Box 127, 2nd & Elk Ave., Crested Butte, 81224, 303-349-5336
Nordic Inn, P.O. Box 939, Crested Butte, 81224, 303-349-5542
Tudor Rose B&B, Box 1995, 429 Whiterock,
     Crested Butte, 81224, 303-349-6253
Imperial Hotel, 123 N. Third St., Cripple Creek,
     80813, 303-689-2713
Greg Rhodes / Hostmark, 1125 - 17th St, Ste 820,
     Deaver, 80202
Balloon Ranch, Box 41, Del Norte, 81132,
     303-754-2533
Windsor Hotel B&B Inn, P.O. Box 762, Del Norte,
     81132, 719-657-2668
Delta-Escalante Ranch, 701-650 Rd., Delta, 81416,
     303-874-4121
Escalante Ranch, 701-650 Rd., Delta, 81416,
     303-874-4121
Cambridge Club Hotel, 1560 Sherman, Denver,
     80203, 303-831-1252
Merritt House B&B, 941 E. 17th Ave., Denver,
     80218, 303-861-5230
Victoria Oaks Inn, 1575 Race St., Denver, 80206,
     303-355-1818
Annabelle's B&B, 382 Vail Circle, Dillon, 80435,
     303-468-8667
Silverheels, Box 367, 81 Buffalo Dr., Dillon, 80435,
     303-468-2926
Swan Mountain Inn, P.O. Box 2900, Dillon, 80424,
     303-453-7903

Logwood B&B, Durango, CO

Blue Valley Guest House, Blue River Rt. 26R, Dillon (Silverthorne), 80435, 303-468-5731
Little Southfork B&B, 15247 County Rd. 22, Dolores, 81323, 303-882-4259
Lost Canyon Lake Lodge, P.O. Box 1289, Dolores, 81323, 303-882-4913
Edgemont Ranch, 281 Silver Queen, Durango, 81301, 303-247-2713
Pennys Place, 1041 County Rd. 307, Durango, 81301, 303-247-8928
Scrubby Oaks B&B Inn, P.O. Box 1047, Durango, 81302, 303-247-2176
Tall Timber, Box 90G, Durango, 81301, 303-259-4813
Victorian Inn, 2117 W. 2nd Ave., Durango, 81301, 303-247-2223
Historic Western B&B, P.O. Box 726, Duray, 81427, 303-325-4645
Lodge at Cordillera, P.O. Box 1110, Edwards, 81632, 303-926-2200
Mad Creek B&B, P.O. Box 404, Empire, 80438, 303-569-2003
Aspen Lodge & Guest Ranch, Longs Peak Route 7, Estes Park, 80517, 303-586-8133
Baldpate Inn, P.O. Box 4445, Estes Park, 80517, 303-586-6151
Big Horn Guest House, P.O. Box 4486, Estes Park, 80517, 303-586-4175
Cottenwood House, P.O. Box 1208, Estes Park, 80517, 303-586-5104
Eagle Cliff House, P.O. Box 4312, Estes Park, 80517, 303-586-5425
Emerald Manor, P.O. Box 3592, Estes Park, 80517, 303-586-8050
Inn at Rock 'n River, P.O. Box 4644, Estes Park, 80517, 303-443-4611
Riversong, P.O. Box 1910, Estes Park, 80517, 303-586-4666
Wanek's Lodge at Estes, P.O. Box 898, Estes Park, 80517, 303-586-5851
Wind River Ranch, P.O. Box 3410, Estes Park, 80517, 303-586-4212
Elizabeth St. Guest House, 202 E. Elizabeth St., Fort Collins, 80524, 303-493-2337
Helmshire Inn, 1204 S. College, Fort Collins, 80524, 303-493-4683
West Mulberry Street B&B, 616 W. Mulberry St., Fort Collins, 80521, 303-221-1917
Lark B&B, P.O. Box 1646, Frisco, 80443, 303-668-5237
MarDel's Mountain Retreat, P.O. Box 1767, Frisco, 80443, 303-668-5337
Hardy House B&B Inn, P.O. Box 0156, Georgetown, 80444, 303-569-3388
Hideout, 1293 - 117 Rd., Glenwood Springs, 81601, 303-945-5621
Kaiser House, The, 932 Cooper Ave., Glenwood Springs, 81602, 303-945-8827
Talbott House, 928 Colorado Ave., Glenwood Springs, 81601, 303-945-1039
Dove Inn, 711 - 14th St., Golden, 80401, 303-278-2209
Drowsy Water Ranch, Box 147A, Granby, 80446, 303-725-3456
Gatehouse B&B, The, 2502 N. First St., Grand Junction, 81501, 303-242-6105
Junction Country Inn B&B, 861 Grand Ave., Grand Junction, 81501, 303-241-2817
Terrace Inn, The, P.O. Box 647, Grand Lake, 80447, 303-627-3079
Winding River Resort, P.O. Box 629, Grand Lake, 80447, 303-627-3215
Tumbling River Ranch, Grant, 80448, 303-838-5981
Columbine Lodge, P.O. Box 267, Green Mountain Falls, 80819, 719-684-9062
Lakeview Terrace Hotel, Box 115, Green Mountain Falls, 80819, 719-684-9119
Waunita Hot Springs Ranch, 8007 Country Rd. 877, Gunnison, 81230, 303-641-1266
7-W Guest Ranch, 3412 County Rd. 151, Gypsum, 81637, 303-524-9328

Sweetwater Creek Ranch, 2650 Sweetwater Rd., Gypsum, 81637, 303-524-7949
Blue Lake Ranch, 16919 Hwy. 140, Hesperus, 81326, 303-385-4537
Midway Inn, 1340 Hwy 133, Hotchkiss, 81419, 303-527-3422
Ye Ole Oasis, 3142 "J" Rd., Box 609, Hotchkiss, 81419, 303-872-3794
Kelsall's Ute Creek Ranch, 2192 County Rd. 334, Ignacio, 81137, 303-563-4464
Ski Tip Lodge, Box 38, Keystone, 80435, 303-468-4202
1899 Inn, 314 S. Main, La Veta, 81055, 303-742-3576
Cinnamon Inn B&B, The, 426 Gunnison Ave., Lake City, 81235, 303-944-2641
Crystal Lodge, Lake City, 81235, 303-944-2201
Moncrief Mountain Ranch, Slumgullion Pass, Lake City, 81235, 303-944-2796
Moss Rose B&B, P.O. Box 910, Lake City, 81235, 303-366-4069
Ryan's Roost, P.O. Box 218, Lake City, 81235, 303-944-2339
Trailshead Lodge, P.O. Box 873, Lead, 80754, 605-584-3464
Apple Blossom Inn, The, 120 W. 4th St., Leadville, 80461, 719-486-2141
Delaware Hotel, 700 Harrison Ave., Leadville, 80461, 800-748-2004
Leadville Country Inn, 127 E. 8th St, Box 1989, Leadville, 80461, 719-486-2354
Mountain Mansion Inn B&B, P.O. Box 1229, Leadville, 80461, 719-486-0655
Gray's Avenue Hotel, 711 Manitou Ave., Manitou Springs, 80829, 719-685-1277
On a Ledge, 336 El Paso Blvd., Manitou Springs, 80829
Peaceful Place B&B, 1129 Manitou Ave., Manitou Springs, 80829, 719-685-1248
Red Crags B&B, 302 El Paso Blvd, Manitou Springs, 80829, 719-685-1920
Red Eagle Mountain B&B, 616 Ruxton Ave., Manitou Springs, 80829, 719-685-4541
Sunnymede B&B, 106 Spencer Ave., Manitou Springs, 80829, 719-685-4619
Inn At Raspberry Ridge, 5580 Country Rd. 3, Marble, 81623, 303-963-3025
Diamond J Guest Ranch, 26604 Frying Pan Rd., Meredith, 81642, 303 927 3222
Fryingpan River Ranch, 32042 Fryingpan Rd., Meredith, 81642, 303-927-3570
Cliff House Lodge B&B, 121 Stone St., Morrison, 80465, 303-697-9732
Great Sand Dunes Inn, 5303 Hwy 150, Mosca, 81146, 719-378-2356
Deer Valley Ranch, Box Y, Nathrop, 81236, 303-395-2353
Baker's Manor, 317 Second St., Ouray, 81427, 303-325-4574
Damn Yankee B&B Inn, The, 100 6th Ave., Ouray, 81427, 800-842-7512
Kunz House, The, Box 235, 723-4th St., Ouray, 81427, 303-325-4220
Manor B&B, The, 317 2nd St., Ouray, 81427, 303-325-4574
Weisbaden Spa & Lodge, Box 349, Ouray, 81427, 303-325-4347
Davidson's Country Inn B&B, Box 87, Pagosa Springs, 81147, 303-264-5863
Echo Manor Inn, 3366 Hwy 84, Pagosa Springs, 81147, 303-264-5646
Royal Pine Inn B&B, P.O. Box 4506, Pagosa Springs, 81157, 800-955-0274
Orchard House, The, 3573 E-1/2 Rd., Palisade, 81526, 303-464-0529
E.T.'s B&B, 1608 Sage Ln., Paonia, 81428, 303-527-3300
Aspen Canyon Ranch, 13206 Country Rd. #3, Parshall, 80468, 303-725-3518
Bar Lazy J Guest Ranch, Box N, Parshall, 80468, 303-725-3437
Meadow Creek B&B Inn, 13438 US Hwy 285, Pine, 80470, 303-838-4167
Jackson Hotel, 220 S. Main St., Poncha Springs, 81242, 303-539-3122
Pilgrim's Inn, The, P.O. Box 151, Red Cliff, 81649, 303-827-5333
Avalanche Ranch, 12863 Hwy 133, Redstone, 81623, 303-963-2846
Cleveholm Manor, 0058 Redstone Blvd., Redstone, 81623, 303-963-3463
Historic Redstone Inn, 82 Redstone Blvd., Redstone, 81623, 303-963-2526
MacTiernan's San Juan, 2882 Highway 23, Ridgway, 81432, 303-626-5360
Pueblo Hostel & Cantina, P.O. Box 346, Ridgway, 81432, 303-626-5939
Coulter Lake Guest Ranch, P.O. Box 906, Rifle, 81650, 303-625-1473
Gazebo Country Inn, The, 507 E. Third, Salida, 81201, 719-539-7806
North Fork Ranch, Box B, Shawnee, 80475, 303-838-9873
Brewery Inn B&B, P.O. Box 473, Silver Plume, 80476, 303-674-5565
Alpen Hutte, 471 Rainbow Dr., Box 91, Silverthorne, 80498, 303-468-6336
Christopher House B&B, 821 Empire St., Box 241, Silverton, 81433, 303-387-5857
Fool's Gold B&B, P.O. Box 603, Silverton, 81433, 303-387-5879
Teller House Hotel, P.O. Box 2, Silverton, 81433, 303-387-5423
Wingate House, PO Box 2, Silverton, 81433
Wyman Hotel, 1371 Greene St., Silverton, 81433, 303-387-5372
Bear Pole Ranch, Star Rt. 1, Box BB, Steamboat Springs, 80487, 303-879-0576
Country Inn at Stmbt Ranch, 46915 County Rd. 129, Steamboat Springs, 80487, 303-879-5767
Crawford House, Box 775062, Steamboat Springs, 80477, 303-879-1859
Harbor Hotel, P.O. Box 4109, Steamboat Springs, 80477, 800-543-8888
House on the Hill, P.O. Box 770598, Steamboat Springs, 80477, 303-879-1650
Inn at Steamboat, The, 3070 Columbine Dr., Steamboat Springs, 80477, 303-879-2600
Steamboat B&B, Box 772058, Steamboat Springs, 80477, 303-879-5724
Vista Verde Guest Ranch, Box 465, Steamboat Springs, 80477, 303-879-3858
Scandinavian Lodge, Box 5040, Steamboat Village, 80449, 303-879-0517
Crest House, 516 S. Division St., Sterling, 80751, 303-522-3753
Alpine Inn, The, P.O. Box 546, Telluride, 81435, 303-728-6282

Steamboat Valley Guest House,
Steamboat Springs, CO

Bear Creek Inn, P.O. Box 1797, Telluride, 81423, 303-728-6681
Cimarron Lodge, 568 W. Pacific Ave., Telluride, 81435, 303-728-3803
Dahl Haus B&B, 122 S. Oak St., Box 695, Telluride, 81435, 303-728-4158
Manitou Hotel, 627 W.Pacific Ave,Box 7, Telluride, 81435, 800-237-0753
New Sheridan Hotel, The, P.O. Box 980, Telluride, 81435, 303-728-4351
Oak Street Inn, 134 N. Oak St., Telluride, 81435
San Sophia, 330 W. Pacific Ave., Telluride, 81435, 303-728-3001
Skyline Guest Ranch, 7214 Highway 145, Telluride, 81435, 303-728-3757
Black Bear Inn of Vail, 2405 Elliot Rd., Vail, 81657, 303-476-1304
Mountain Weavery, 1119 E. Ptarmigan Rd., Vail, 81657, 303-476-5539
Portland Inn, 412 W. Portland, Box 32, Victor, 80860, 719-689-2102
Rainbow Inn, 104 Main, Box 578, Westcliffe, 81252, 719-783-2313
Angelmark B&B, 50 Little Pierre Ave., Winter Park, 80482, 303-726-5354
Outpost Inn, P.O. Box 41, Winter Park, 80482, 303-726-5346
Something Special, P.O. Box 800, Winter Park, 80482, 303-726-5346
Hackman House B&B, Box 6902, Woodland Park, 80866, 719-687-9851
Woodland Hills Lodge, P.O. Box 276, Woodland Park, 80863, 800-621-8386
Wilson's Pinto Bean Farm, House No. 21434 Rd. 16, Yellowjacket, 81335

Connecticut

BRISTOL

Chimney Crest Manor B&B
5 Founders Dr., 06010
203-582-4219
Dante & Cynthia Cimadamore
All year

$$$ B&B
4 rooms, 4 pb
Visa, MC, *Rated*, •
C-ltd/S-ltd/P-no/H-no

Full breakfast
Sitting room, piano
wading pool, 3 mi. to
Hershey, Lake Compounce

32-rm Tudor mansion w/National Historic listing. 6 fireplaces. 20 min. from Hartford, Litchfield & Waterburg. Unique architecture. Balloon packages. **10% off 2+ nights, ltd.**

CHESTER

Inn at Chester, The
318 W. Main St., 06412
203-526-9541 800-949-7829
Deborah L. Smith
All year

$$$ B&B
48 rooms, 48 pb
Visa, MC, AmEx, *Rated*,
•
C-yes/S-yes/P-ltd/H-yes

Continental breakfast
Lunch, dinner, tavern
Bicycles, tennis, sauna
sitting room, library
piano, entertainment

The inn, on 15 acres centered around a 1776 farmhouse, abounds with fireplaces, antiques, and public areas for resting, reading, refreshment. **3rd. night free, Ltd.**

CLINTON

Captain Dibbell House
21 Commerce St., 06413
203-669-1646
Helen & Ellis Adams
All year exc. January

$$$ B&B
4 rooms, 4 pb
Visa, MC, *Rated*, •
C-ltd/S-ltd/P-no/H-no

Full breakfast
Comp. refreshments
Sitting room, gazebo
bicycles, horseshoes
beach chairs & towels

Our 1866 sea captain's Victorian offers comfortable lodging and home-baked savories to guests while they discover the charms of our coastal towns.

CORNWALL BRIDGE

Cornwall Inn, The
Route 7, 06754
203-672-6884 800-786-6884
Lois, Emily, Robyn & Ron
All year

$ B&B/MAP
13 rooms, 12 pb
Visa, MC, AmEx, Disc., •
C-yes/S-yes/P-yes/H-yes

Full breakfast
Lunch, dinner, snacks
Restaurant, bar service
sitting room, library
swimming pool

An inn dating back to 1810. Nestled in the Hitchfield Hills. Open year-round for weekend getaways or retreats. **3rd night 50% off. 10% off lunch or dinner**

COVENTRY

Maple Hill Farm B&B
365 Goose Ln., 06238
203-742-0635 800-742-0635
Tony & MaryBeth Gorke-Felice
All year

$$ B&B
4 rooms
Visa, MC, *Rated*
C-ltd/S-no/P-no/H-no
Spanish

Full breakfast
Hot tubs, herb garden
pool, picnic areas
hammocks, horses

A warm friendly home circa 1731 filled with antiques. Unique mixture of old and new. Room for relaxation or recreation. Amish wedding buggy. **Discount after 4 nights**

DEEP RIVER

Riverwind Inn
209 Main St., 06417
203-526-2014
Barbara Barlow, Bob Bucknall
All year

$$$ B&B
8 rooms, 8 pb
Visa, MC, *Rated*,
C-ltd/S-yes/P-no/H-no

Full breakfast
Comp. sherry
8 common rooms
piano, classic British
limousine service

Furnished in country antiques. Smithfield ham with breakfast, fireplace in dining room. New England charm and southern hospitality.

EAST HADDAM

Bishopsgate Inn
P.O. Box 290, 06423
7 Norwich Rd.
203-873-1677
Dan & Molly Swartz
All year

$$$ B&B
6 rooms, 6 pb
•
C-ltd/S-yes/P-no/H-ltd

Full breakfast
Comp. wine
Dinner
piano, sauna
sitting room

1818 colonial home with 6 charming guest rooms, open fireplaces, period pieces and fine antiques, near famous Goodspeed Opera House.

EAST WINDSOR

Stephen Potwine House, The
84 Scantic Rd., 06088
203-623-8722
Bob & Vangi Cathcart
All year

$$ B&B
3 rooms, 1 pb
C-ltd/S-no/P-no/H-no

Full breakfast
Afternoon tea
Sitting room
library
jacuzzi

Rural country setting surrounded by farmland, only 15 minutes from Hartford and Springfield. Picturesque, peaceful and charming. Overlooking pond, flowers, and willow trees.

ESSEX

Griswold Inn, The
36 Main St., 06426
203-767-1776
William Winterer
All year

$$$ B&B
25 rooms, 25 pb
Visa, MC, AmEx, *Rated*,
C-yes/S-yes/P-ask/H-yes

Continental breakfast
Restaurant, bar service
Lunch & dinner available
sitting room, library

Located in center of historic Essex; renowned marine art collection; entertainment nightly from Griswold Inn Banjo Band to Cliff Haslem's Sea Chantys.

GLASTONBURY

Butternut Farm
1654 Main St., 06033
203-633-7197 FAX:633-7197
Don Reid
All year

$$ B&B
4 rooms, 2 pb
Visa, MC, AmEx, *Rated*,
C-yes/S-ltd/P-no/H-no

Full breakfast
Comp. wine, chocolates
Piano, 8 fireplaces
sitting rooms, library
bicycle

An 18th-century jewel furnished with period antiques. Attractive grounds with herb gardens and ancient trees, dairy goats and prize chickens. 10 minutes from Hartford.

The Copper Beech Inn, Ivoryton, CT

GREENWICH

Homestead Inn
420 Field Point Rd., 06830
203-869-7500
Lessie Davison, Nancy Smith
All year

$$$ B&B
23 rooms, 23 pb
Major credit cards, •
C-ltd/S-yes/P-no/H-ltd
Sp., Fr., It., Ger., Ch.

Continental plus
Lunch, dinner, bar
Sitting room
turn-down service
meeting rms. up to 20

Sophisticated country inn; 45 min. from NYC; built 1799, completely restored 1979; superb French cuisine for lunch and dinner; full breakfast available. Many antiques.

IVORYTON

Copper Beech Inn, The
46 Main St., 06442
203-767-0330
Eldon & Sally Senner
All year exc. Mondays

$$$ B&B
13 rooms, 13 pb
Most CC, *Rated*,
C-ltd/S-ltd/P-no/H-ltd

Continental plus
Dinner, bar
TV, Jacuzzi
gardens
porcelain gallery

A hostelry where even a short visit is a celebration of good living. One of few 4-star restaurants in Connecticut. The feel of country elegance. **Room upgrade weekdays.**

MADISON

Madison Beach Hotel
94 West Wharf Rd., 06443
203-245-1404
The Cooneys, The Bagdasarians
April–December

$$ B&B
32 rooms, 32 pb
Visa, MC, AmEx, DC, •
C-yes/S-ask/P-no/H-ask

Continental breakfast
Lunch, dinner, bar
Sitting room
entertainment
right on beach

Victorian beach hotel furnished with oak and wicker antiques. Seafood tops the menu at the attached restaurant. Weekend entertainment.

MIDDLEBURY

Tucker Hill Inn	$$ B&B	Full breakfast
96 Tucker Hill Rd., 06762	4 rooms, 2 pb	Hot & cold drinks
203-758-8334 FAX:598-0652	Visa, MC, *Rated*, •	Sitting room
Susan & Richard Cebelenski	C-yes/S-ltd/P-no/H-no	library
All year		TV room

Large colonial-style inn near Village Green. Large, spacious period rooms. Hearty brkfast. Near sights & sports. **Discount tickets for Quassy Amusememt Park.**

MYSTIC

Comolli's Guest House	$$$ B&B	Continental breakfast
36 Bruggeman Place, 06355	2 rooms, 1 pb	Kitchen privileges
203-536-8723	C-ltd/S-no/P-no/H-no	TV in rooms
Dorothy M. Comolli		
All year		

Country setting on top of dead-end street overlooking Mystic seaport; immaculate and quiet. Within walking distance of everything.

Harbor Inne & Cottage	$ EP	Kitchen privileges
RFD #1, Box 398, Edgemont St.,	5 rooms, 5 pb	Sitting room, A/C
06355	*Rated*, •	canoe & boats, cable TV
203-572-9253	C-yes/S-yes/P-yes/H-no	Fireplaces, hot tub
C. Lecouras, R. Morehouse	Greek	
All year		

Small inn plus 3-room cottage on Mystic River. Walk to seaport & all attractions. Waterfront tables, cable TV, kitchen privileges, canoeing and boating. Cottage w/fireplace.

Inn at Mystic	$$$ EP	Restaurant, bar
Junction Rts. 1 & 27, 06355	68 rooms, 68 pb	Tennis, hot tubs
203-536-9604	Most CC, Rated-, •	swimming pool, sitt. rm.
All year	C-yes/S-yes/P-no/H-yes	boating available
	French, Spanish	

Overlooking Mystic Harbor and Sound. Varied accommodations with antiques, reproductions, canopied beds, balconies, fireplaces, jacuzzis, gourmet restaurant, tennis, boating.

Red Brook Inn	$$$ B&B	Full country breakfast
P.O. Box 237, 06372	9 rooms, 9 pb	Comp. wine, tea, cider
2750 Gold Star Hwy	Visa, MC, *Rated*,	Sitting room, library
203-572-0349	C-yes/S-no/P-no/H-no	bicycles, patio
Ruth Keyes		whirlpool
All year		

The inn strikes a nice balance between authentic handsome furnishings & comfort. Surrounded by wooded acres, convenient to old New England sights. **Midweek 3rd night 50% off**

MYSTIC—NOANK

Palmer Inn, The	$$$ B&B	Continental plus
25 Church St., 06340	6 rooms, 6 pb	Comp. sherry, tea
203-572-9000	Visa, MC, *Rated*,	Sitting room, fireplaces
Patricia Ann White	C-ltd/S-ltd/P-no/H-no	bicycles, games, flowers
All year		Antique & gift shop

Elegant 1907 mansion w/antique furnishings. Quiet charm of New England fishing village, 2 mi. to historic Mystic. Holiday wkends. **20% off 3 nights, weekdays, ltd**

NEW LONDON

Queen Anne Inn
265 Williams St., 06320
203-447-2600 800-347-8818
Ray & Julie Rutledge
All year

$$$ B&B
9 rooms, 9 pb
Most CC, *Rated*, •
C-ltd/S-ltd/P-no/H-no

Full breakfast
Comp. tea, refreshments
Sitting room, hot tub
sauna, nearby tennis
massage, health club

Elegant lodging near the historically rich Mystic-Groton-New London waterfront resort area. Tennis, massage, health & racquet club are available. **Progressive midwk disc't.**

NEW MILFORD

Homestead Inn, The
5 Elm St., 06776
203-354-4080
Rolf & Peggy Hammer
All year

$$ B&B
14 rooms, 14 pb
Visa, MC, AmEx, *Rated*,
•
C-yes/S-ltd/P-no/H-no

Continental plus
Sitting room, piano
front porch, gardens
near trout fishing

Small country inn in picturesque New England town next to village green, near shops, churches, restaurants, antiques, galleries, hiking, crafts.

NEW PRESTON

Boulders Inn, The
P.O. Box 2575, 06777
Route 45, E. Shore Rd.
203-868-0541
Kees & Ulla Adema
All year

$$$ B&B/MAP
17 rooms, 17 pb
Visa, MC, AmEx, •
C-ltd/S-yes/P-no/H-yes
German, Dutch, French

Full breakfast
Restaurant, bar, dinner
Sitting room, bicycles
tennis, private beach
boats, hiking trail

Exquisitely furnished country inn in spectacular location, viewing Lake Waramaug. Lakeview dining inside or on terrace. **4th. night 50% off, 7th. night free**

Inn on Lake Waramaug, The
107 North Shore Rd., 06777
203-868-0563 800-LAKE-INN
Chip & Meg Chapell
All year

$$$ MAP
23 rooms, 23 pb
Most CC, *Rated*, •
C-yes/S-yes/P-no/H-yes

Full breakfast
Dinner, bar
Pool, sauna, tennis
sitting room, piano
entertainment

Authentic colonial (1790) restored & furnished w/pine & cherry antiques. Complete resort, private beach, indoor pool, Showboat Cruises, sleigh rides. **3rd night 50% off, ltd.**

NORFOLK

Manor House
P.O. Box 447, 06058
69 Maple Ave.
203-542-5690
Hank & Diane Tremblay
All year

$$$ B&B
9 rooms, 9 pb
Visa, MC, *Rated*, •
C-ltd/S-ltd/P-no/H-ltd
French

Full breakfast (to room)
Comp. tea, coffee, cocoa
Sitting room, library
piano, sun porch, gazebo
bicycles, gardens, lake

Historic Victorian mansion furnished w/genuine antiques, on 5 acres. Romantic, elegant bdrms some w/fireplaces. Sleigh/carriage rides. Concert series. Suites w/2 person tub.

Mountain View Inn
P.O. Box 467, 06058
Route 272
203-542-6991
Michele Sloane
All year

$$ B&B
10 rooms, 7 pb
Visa, MC, AmEx, *Rated*,
•
C-yes/S-yes/P-ltd/H-yes

Full breakfast (ex. Sun)
Gourmet restaurant
Lunch, tea, dinner, bar
sitting room, piano
outdoor dining deck

Romantic 1875 Victorian country inn located in picture perfect village. Central to musical concerts, antiquing, skiing and hiking. Guest room fireplaces. **3rd night 50% off**

NORWALK

Silvermine Tavern
194 Perry Ave., 06850
203-847-4558
Frank Whitman, Jr.
All year

$$$ B&B
12 rooms, 12 pb
Most CC, *Rated*, •
C-yes/S-yes/P-no/H-no

Continental breakfast
Restaurant, bar
Lunch, dinner
sitting room

Charming 225-year-old country inn only an hour from New York City. Decorated with hundreds of antiques. Overlooking the Tranquil Millpond. AAA 3-Diamond. Mobil 3-Star.

OLD LYME

Bee and Thistle Inn
100 Lyme St., 06371
203-434-1667 800-622-4946
Penny & Bob Nelson
All year

$$$ EP
11 rooms, 9 pb
Most CC, *Rated*, •
C-ltd/S-yes/P-no/H-no

Lunch, dinner, bar
Bicycles, phone in room
2 parlors, piano
harpist Saturdays

An inn on 5.5 acres in historic district. On the Lieutenant River set back amidst majestic trees. Sophisticated country cuisine. **3rd night 20% off (not incl. Sat.)**

Old Lyme Inn
P.O. Box 787, 06371
85 Lyme St.
203-434-2600
Diana Field Atwood
All year

$$$ B&B
13 rooms, 13 pb
Most CC, •
C-yes/S-yes/P-ltd/H-yes

Continental plus
Lunch, dinner
Sitting room
telephones/clock radios
bannister porch

An 1850 Victorian inn in Old Lyme's historic district. Restaurant was given three stars by the New York Times on three separate visits. Empire and Victorian furnishings.

OLD MYSTIC

Old Mystic Inn, The
P.O. Box 634, 06372
52 Main St
203-572-9422
Mary & Peter Knight
All year

$$$ B&B
8 rooms, 8 pb
Visa, MC, AmEx, *Rated*,
•
C-ltd/S-no/P-no/H-no

Full country breakfast
Afternoon tea
Sat. eve. wine & cheese
sitting room
bicycles

Located minutes from Mystic Seaport and Aquarium, this charming inn offers a complete country breakfast to guests. **Free bottle of wine**

PLAINFIELD

French Renaissance House
550 Norwich Rd., Route 12,
06374
203-564-3277
Lucile Melber
All year

$ B&B
4 rooms, 1 pb
Visa, MC, DC
C-yes/S-no

Full breakfast
Comp. wine & beverages
Sitting room, library
near antique shops and
restaurants, large rooms

1871 Victorian French Renaissance Second Empire architecture; Historic Register listed. Round arched windows; high ceilings; charming atmosphere. **10% disc't for 3+ nights**

POMFRET

Clark Cottage, Wintergreen
Box 94, Rt. 44 & 169, 06258
203-928-5741
Doris & Stanton Geary
All year

$$ B&B
5 rooms, 3 pb
Visa, MC, •
C-yes/S-no/P-no/H-no

Full breakfast
Restaurant nearby
Aftn. tea, comp. wine
sitting room, library
screened porch, bicycles

1890 cottage on 4 acres of lawn, extensive flower and rose gardens, and vegetable gardens overlooking an undeveloped valley which is magnificent when the leaves turn.

PUTNAM

Felshaw Tavern, The
Five Mile River Rd., 06260
203-928-3467
Herb & Terry Kinsman
All year

$$$ B&B
2 rooms, 2 pb
•
C-ltd/P-no/H-no

Full breakfast
Comp. wine & drinks
Sitting room, library
5 miles to golf, tennis
and swimming

Noble center-chimney Colonial, built as tavern in 1742, lovingly restored, antiques, rich in history. In rural setting, accessible to Boston, Providence, Hartford, Worcester.

RIDGEFIELD

Elms Inn, The
500 Main St., 06877
203-438-2541
Violet & Robert Scala
All year

$$$ EP
20 rooms, 20 pb
Most CC, *Rated*,
C-yes/S-yes/P-no/H-no
Spanish

Continental breakfast
Restaurant, bar
Lunch, dinner
sitting room

Park your car and stroll along our tree-lined main street.

West Lane Inn
22 West Ln., Route 35, 06877
203-438-7323
M. M. Mayer
All year

$$$ B&B
20 rooms, 20 pb
Most CC, *Rated*, •
C-yes/S-yes/P-no, Spanish

Continental plus
Full breakfast $
Comp. whiskey or julep
bicycles, tennis nearby

Colonial elegance framed by majestic old maples and flowering shrubs. Breakfast served on the veranda. Always a relaxing atmosphere. Newly decorated lobbies & rooms.

RIVERTON

Old Riverton Inn
P.O. Box 6, 06065
Rt. 20
203-379-8678
All year

$$ B&B
12 rooms, 12 pb
Most CC, *Rated*,
C-yes/S-yes/P-no/H-yes

Full breakfast
Lunch, dinner, bar
Sitting room

Hospitality for the hungry, thirsty and sleepy since 1796. Originally a stagecoach stop. Overlooks West Branch of Farmington River. Listed on Nat'l Register Historic Places.

SALISBURY

White Hart, The
P.O. Box 385, 06068
The Village Green
203-435-0030
Juliet & Terry Moore
All year

EP
26 rooms, 26 pb
Most CC, *Rated*, •
C-yes/S-yes/P-yes/H-ltd
Span, Swedish, Fr, Germ

Breakfast/lunch/dinner
Sunday brunch
Sea Grill restaurant
Historic Tavern
garden court, weddings

19th century gracious inn and restaurants. "chinz covered dream of an inn"—Berkshire Magazine, rated "excellent" by NY Times. Weddings/corp. meetings.

SIMSBURY

Simsbury 1820 House
731 Hopmeadow St., Rte. 10 &
202, 06070
203-658-7658 800-TRY-1820
Kelly Hohengarten
All year

$$$ B&B
34 rooms, 34 pb
Visa, MC, AmEx, *Rated*,
•
C-yes/S-yes/P-no/H-yes

Continental plus
Lunch, dinner
Restaurant, bar
sitting room
picnic hampers

*A graciously restored 34 room 19th-century mansion in period decor with 20th-century amenities. Noted dining room serves daily. Brochure available. **Seasonal discounts***

The Tolland Inn, Tolland, CT

THOMPSON

A Taste of Ireland B&B
47 Quaddick Rd., 06277
203-923-2883
Jean & Elaine Murphy-Chicoine
All year

$$ B&B
2 rooms, 2 pb
Rated, •
C-yes/S-no/P-no/H-no

Full Irish breakfast
Afternoon tea, snacks
Sitting room, porch
library, gift shop
whirlpool bath

Circa 1780 cottage serving imported breakfast food from Ireland, Barry's Teas. Irish hospitality; Celtic music. Near Quaddick State Park, golfing, hiking. **3rd night 50% off**

TOLLAND

Tolland Inn, The
P.O. Box 717, 06084
63 Tolland Green
203-872-0800
Susan & Steve Beeching
All year

$$ B&B
8 rooms, 6 pb
Visa, MC, AmEx, *Rated*,
•
C-ltd/S-no/P-no/H-no

Full breakfast
Comp. wine, aftern. tea
Winter/summer sunporch
sitting rm., bridal room
guest room w/fireplace

Historic inn on New England village green. Short drive from I-84; convenient to Hartford, Sturbridge, Brimfield & U. of Connecticut. Sunken tub in bridal. **3rd night 50%, Ltd**

TORRINGTON

Yankee Pedlar Inn Hotel
93 Main St., 06790
203-489-9226
Christopher J. Bolan
All year

$$ EP
60 rooms, 60 pb
Most CC, *Rated*, •
C-yes/S-yes/P-no/H-ltd

Full breakfast $
Restaurant, bar
Comp. drink/chocolates
bicycles, pool
comp. passes to YMCA

100-year-old hotel in the heart of Litchfield and Berkshire Foothills. Old fashioned country charm surrounded by skiing, golf, antiques and breathtaking scenery.

Yankee Pedlar Inn, Torrington, CT

WESTPORT

Cotswold Inn
76 Mrytle Ave., 06880
203-226-3766
Lorna & Richard Montanaro
All year

$$$ B&B
4 rooms, 4 pb
Visa, MC, AmEx, •
C-ltd/S-ltd/P-no/H-no

Continental plus
Snacks, comp. wine
Comp. brandy, sitting rm
bicycles, land
some canopy beds

Authentic, private country charm in cheerful, pleasant new inn. Walking distance to Westport's fine restaurants, shops, theatres, recreational facilities.

WOODBURY

Curtis House, Inc.
506 Main St. South, 06798
203-263-2101
The Hardisty Family
All year exc. Christmas

$ EP
18 rooms, 12 pb
Most Cred/Card, *Rated*,
•
C-yes/S-yes/P-no/H-yes

Continental breakfast $
Luncheon, dinner, bar

Connecticut's oldest Inn, most rooms with canopied beds, in heart of antique country.

More Inns . . .

Henrietta House, 125 Ashford Center Rd., Ashford, 06278
Buck Homestead, 630 Westford Rd., Rt.89, Ashford Stafford Springs, 06076
Jared Cone House, 25 Hebron Rd., Bolton, 06043, 203-643-8538
Sandford/Pond House, P.O. Box 306, Bridgewater, 06752, 203-355-4677
Barrett Hill Farm, 210 Barrett Hill Rd., Brooklyn, 06234
Friendship Valley, Route 169, Brooklyn, 06234
Golden Lamb Buttery, Bush Hill Rd., Brooklyn
Tannerbrook, 329 Pomfret Rd., Brooklyn, 06234
Fine Bouche Inn, 23 Main St., Box 121, Centerbrook, 06409
Issac Shepard House, 165 Shepard Hill, Bx503, Central Village, 06322
Moorings, The, Blaisdell Point, Box 45, Clinton, 06413
Hayward House Inn, 35 Hayward Ave., Colchester, 06415, 203-537-5772
Cornwall Inn, The, Cornwall Bridge, 06754, 203-672-6884
Mill Brook Farm, 110 Wall St., Coventry, 06238
Special Joys B&B, 41 N. River Rd., Coventry, 06238
Quiet Waters, 465 Cook Hill Rd., Danielson, 06239
Selden House, 20 Read St., Deep River, 06417
Austin's Stonecroft Inn, 17 Main St., East Haddam, 06423, 203-873-1754
Gelston House, Goodspeed Landing, East Haddam, 06423, 203-873-1411
Mount Parnassus View, 122 Shanaghan Rd., East Haddam, 06423
Stonecroft Inn, 17 Main St., East Haddam, 06423, 203-873-1754
Whispering Winds Inn, 93 River Rd., East Haddam, 06423, 203-526-3055
Island, The, 20 Island Dr., Box 2, East Lyme, 06333
Red House, 365 Boston Post Rd., East Lyme, 06333
Barney House, 11 Mountain Spring Rd., Farmington, 06032, 203-677-9735

Shore Inne, 54 E. Shore Rd., Groton Long Point, 06340, 203-536-1180
Ivoryton Inn, 115 Main St., Ivoryton, 06442
1741 Saltbox Inn, P.O. Box 677, Kent, 06757, 203-927-4376
Country Goose B&B, 211 Kent-Cornwall Rd., Kent, 06757
Flanders Arms, Box 393, Kent-Cornwall, Kent, 06757
Fife'n Drum Inn, Main St., Route 7, Kent (Litchfield Hills), 06757, 203-927-3509
B&B at Laharan Farm, 350 Route 81, Killingworth, 06417, 203-663-1706
Killingworth Inn, 249 Rt. 81, Killingworth, 06417, 203-663-1103
Wake Robin Inn, Route 41, Lakeville, 06039, 203-435-2515
Applewood Farms Inn, 528 Col. Ledyard Hwy., Ledyard, 06355, 203-536-2022
Tollgate Hill Inn, P.O. Box 1339, Litchfield, 06759, 203-567-4545
Dolly Madison Inn, 73 W. Wharf Rd., Madison, 06443, 203-245-7377
Fowler House, P.O. Box 340, Plains Rd, Moodus, 06469, 203-873-8906
Adams House, The, 382 Cow Hill Rd., Mystic, 06355, 203-572-9551
Whaler's Inn, P.O. Box 488, Mystic, 06355, 800-243-2588
Corttis Inn, 235 Corttis Rd., N. Grosvenordale, 06255
Maples Inn, 179 Oenoke Rd., New Canaan, 06840, 203-966-2927
Roger Sherman Inn, 195 Oenoke Ridge Rt. 12, New Canaan, 06840
Cobbie Hill Farm, Steele Rd (off Rte. 44), New Hartford, 06057, 203-379-0057
Highland Farm B&B, Highland Ave., New Hartford, 06057, 203-379-6029
Inn at Chapel West, 1201 Chapel St., New Haven, 06511, 203-777-1201
Heritage Inn, 34 Bridge St., New Milford, 06776, 203-354-8883
Birches Inn, West Shore Rd., New Preston, 06777, 203-868-0229
Hopkins Inn, Hopkins Rd., New Preston, 06777, 203-868-7295
Hawley Manor Inn, 19 Main St., Newtown, 06470, 203-426-4456
Blackberry River Inn, Route 44, Norfolk, 06058, 203-542-5100
Greenwoods Gate B&B Inn, P.O. Box 662, Norfolk, 06058, 203-542-5439
Weaver's House, P.O. Box 336, Route 44, Norfolk, 06058, 203-542-5108
Randall's Ordinary, P.O. Box 243, North Stonington, 06359, 203-599-4540
Harbor House Inn, 165 Shore Rd., Old Greenwich, 06870, 203-637-0145
Old Mystic Inn, The, 58 Main St., Box 634, Old Mystic, 06372, 203-572-9422
Castle Inn, 50 Hartlands Dr., Old Saybrook, 06475
Saybrook Point Inn, 2 Bridge St., Old Saybrook, 06475, 800-243-0212
Cobbscroft, Rts. 169 & 44, Pomfret, 06258
Inn at Gwyn Careg, Route 44, Box 96, Pomfret, 06230
Croft B&B, The, 7 Penny Corner Rd, Portland, 06480, 203-342-1856
Thurker House, 78 Liberty Way, Putman, 06260, 203-928-6776
Thurber House, 78 Liberty Hwy., Rt. 21, Putnam Heights, 06260
Epenetus Horne House, 91 N. Salem Rd., Ridgefield, 06877
Stonehenge Inn, P.O. Box 667, Ridgefield, 06877, 203-438-6511
Ragamont Inn, Main St., Salisbury, 06068
Under Mountain Inn, 482 Under Mountain Rd., Salisbury, 06068, 203-435-0242
Yesterday's Yankee, Route 44 East, Box 442, Salisbury, 06068, 203-435-9539
Nathan Fuller House, 147 Plains Rd., Box 257, Scotland, 06264
Inn at Villa Bianca, Rt. 34, 312 Roosevelt, Seymour, 06483
Alexander's B&B, 17 Rhynus Rd., Sharon, 06069, 800-727-7592
Barnes Hill Farm B&B, Route 37, Sherman, 06784, 203-354-4404
Old Mill Inn, 63 Maple St., Somersville, 06072
Cumon Inn, 130 Buckland Rd., South Windsor, 06074, 203-644-8486
Inn at Woodstock Hill, P.O. Box 98, South Woodstock, 06267, 203-928-0528
Chaffee's, 28 Reussner Rd., Southington, 06489
Winterbrook Farm, Beffa Rd., Staffordville, 06076, 203-684-2124
Farnan House, 10 McGrath Court, Stonington, 06378
Lasbury's B&B, 24 Orchard St., Stonington Village, 06378, 203-535-2681
Altnaveigh Inn, 957 Storrs Rd., Storrs, 06268
Diesel Home, 92 East Rd., Storrs, 06268
Farmhouse on the Hill, 418 Gurleyville Rd., Storrs, 06268, 203-429-1400
Spring Gardens, 359 Spring Hill Rd., Storrs, 06268
Hedgerow House, Box 265, Thompson, 06227, 203-923-9073
Hickory Ridge, 1084 Quaddick Tn.Fm.Rd., Thompson, 06277, 203-928-9530
Lord Thompson Manor, Rt. 200, Box 428, Thompson, 06277
Samuel Watson House, P.O. Box 86, Thompson, 06277, 203-923-2491
Old Babcock Tavern, 484 Mile Hill Rd.,Rt.31, Tolland, 06084, 203-875-1239
1851 House, 1851 Route 32, Uncasville, 06382
Evie's Turning Point Farm, Rte 45, Cornwall Bridge, Warren, 06754, 203-868-7775
Mayflower Inn, Route 47, Washington, 06793, 213-868-0515
Boulevard B&B, 15 Columbia Blvd., Waterbury, 06710
House on the Hill, 92 Woodlawn Terrace, Waterbury, 06710
Hilltop Haven, Rte 7 Dibble Hill Rd, West Cornwall, 06796
Mohawk Mtn Country Lodge, Rte 4, West Goshen, 06756
Ebenezer Stoddard House, Rt. 171, Perrin Rd., West Woodstock, 06281
Captain Stannard House, 138 S. Main St., Westbrook, 06498, 203-399-4634
Talcott House B&B, 161 Seaside Ave., Westbrook, 06498
Chester Bulkley House B&B, 184 Main St., Wethersfield, 06109, 203-563-4236
Provincial House, 151 Main St., Winsted, 06098, 203-379-1631
Beaver Pond, 68 Cutler Hill Rd., Woodstock, 06281

Delaware

LAUREL ————————————————————————————————————

Spring Garden $$ B&B   Full breakfast
RD 1, Box 283A, Delaware Ave. 6 rooms, 2 pb   Comp. wine, snacks
Extended, 19956   •   Bar service set-ups
302-875-7015   C-ltd/S-ltd/H-yes   sitting room, library
Gwen North   Spanish   bicycles, historic tours
All year

Get away to a Colonial National Registry country plantation home near Atlantic beaches & Chesapeake Bay. State Tourism Award for Excellence in Hospitality. Antique shop.

NEW CASTLE ————————————————————————————————

Jefferson House B&B $$ B&B   Continental
5 The Strand, 19720   3 rooms, 3 pb   Restaurant, lunch/dinner
302-325-1025 302-322-8944 *Rated*, •   Afternoon tea, jacuzzi
Debbie   C-yes/S-yes   room w/porch river view
All year   room w/kitchen available

Charming 200-yr-old riverfront hotel, historic district center. Furnished w/antiques, country motif. Orig. wood floors/millwork. William Penn landed here. **10% off 3+ nights.**

——

Terry House B&B $$ B&B   Continental plus
130 Delaware St., 19720   5 rooms, 5 pb   Near tennis, park
302-322-2505   Visa, MC, AmEx, Disc., •   bike path, library
Brenda Rogers   C-ltd/S-no/P-no/H-no   sitting room
All year   German

A pleasant place to relax and enjoy historic New Castle. 1869 Federal townhouse with 12-foot ceilings, period antiques & reproductions. Step back into the past.

——

William Penn Guest House $ B&B   Continental breakfast
206 Delaware St., 19720   4 rooms   Living room
302-328-7736   C-ltd/S-no/P-no/H-no
Mr. and Mrs. Richard Burwell Italian
All year

This house was built about 1682, and William Penn stayed overnight! Restored and located in the center of the Square.

REHOBOTH BEACH ——————————————————————————————

Corner Cupboard Inn, The $$$ MAP/B&B   Full breakfast
50 Park Ave., 19971   18 rooms, 18 pb   Dinner included
302-227-8553   Visa, MC, AmEx, *Rated*,   Restaurant
Elizabeth G. Hooper   C-yes/S-yes/P-yes/H-no   sitting room, piano
All year   beach

The inn that was in before inns were in! Fifty years at 50 Park Ave. as a summer retreat for Baltimore and Washington. B&B mid-Sept. to Mem. Day, MAP otherwise.

REHOBOTH BEACH ——————————————

Tembo B&B	$$ B&B	Continental
100 Laurel St., 19971	6 rooms, 1 pb	Use of kitchen
302-227-3360	*Rated*	Sitting room w/fireplace
Don & Gerry Cooper	C-ltd/S-no/P-ask/H-no	A/C, enclosed porch
All year		refrigerator in rooms

Warm hospitality in cozy beach cottage furnished with antiques, fine art, braided rugs. Short walk to beach, quality shops, restaurants. Nonsmoking.

More Inns ...

Addy Sea, P.O. Box 275, Bethany Beach, 19930, 302-539-3707
Homestead Guests, 721 Garfield Pkwy, Bethany Beach, 19930, 302-539-7244
Journey's End Guest House, 101 Parkwood St., Bethany Beach, 19930
Sea-Vista Villas, Box 62, Bethany Beach, 19930, 302-539-3354
Buckley's Tavern, 5812 Kennett Pike, Centreville, 19807, 302-656-9776
Biddles B&B, 101 Wyoming Ave., Dover, 19901, 302-736-1570
Inn @ Meeting House Square, 305 S. Governors Ave., Dover, 19901, 302-678-1242
Noble Guest House B&B, 33 S. Bradford St., Dover, 19901, 302-674-4084
Savannah Inn B&B, 330 Savannah Rd., Lewes, 19958, 302-645-5592
Towers B&B, The, 101 N.W. Front St., Milford, 19963, 302-422-3814
Drawing Room, The, 6 Main Sail Dr., Milton, 19968, 302-684-0339
Janvier-Black House, 17 The Strand, New Castle, 19720
Ross House B&B, 129 E. 2nd St., New Castle, 19720, 302-322-7787
Terry House, The, 130 Delaware St., New Castle, 19720, 302-322-2505
Cantwell House, 107 High St., Odessa, 19730
Cantwell House B&B, 107 High st., Odessa, 19730, 302-378-4179
Beach House, The, 15 Hickman St., Rehoboth Beach, 19971, 302-227-7074
Drift Inn, 16 Brooklyn Ave., Rehoboth Beach, 19971
Gladstone Inn, 3 Olive Ave., Rehoboth Beach, 19971, 302-227-2641
Lord & Hamilton Seaside In, 20 Brooklyn Ave., Rehoboth Beach, 19971, 302-227-6960
Lord Baltimore Lodge, 16 Baltimore Ave., Rehoboth Beach, 19971, 302-227-2855
O'Connor's Guest House B &, 20 Delaware Ave., Rehoboth Beach, 19971, 302-227-2419
Pleasant Inn Lodge, 31 Olive Ave. @ 1st St., Rehoboth Beach, 19971, 302-227-7311
Victorian Rose B&B, 22 Church St, Selbyville, 19975, 302-436-2558
A Small Wonder B&B, 213 W. Crest Rd., Wilmington, 19803, 302-764-0789
Boulevard B&B, The, 1909 Baynard Blvd., Wilmington, 19802, 302-656-9700
Creek View B&B, 2901 Faulkland Rd., Wilmington, 19808, 302-994-5924
Pink Door, The, 8 Francis Ln., Wilmington, 19803

District of Columbia

WASHINGTON ——————————————

Adams Inn	$$ B&B	Continental plus
1744 Lanier Pl. NW, 20009	11 rooms, 6 pb	Coffee, tea, donuts
202-745-3600 800-578-6807	Visa, MC, AmEx, •	Sitting room
Gene & Nancy Thompson	C-yes/S-no/P-no/H-no	library, TV lounge
All year		gardens, deck

Restored Edwardian townhouse; enjoy charm and quiet of residential street in the heart of the famous Adams-Morgan neighborhood. Shops and restaurants nearby. Walk to zoo.

Capitol Hill Guest House	$$ B&B	Continental breakfast
101 Fifth St. NE, 1801 Lamont St.,	10 rooms	Comp. sherry
NW, 20002	Visa, MC, AmEx, •	Sitting room
202-547-1050	C-ltd/S-no/P-no/H-no	maid service daily
Mark Babich		
All year		

Formerly home to US Congressional pages. Turn-of-the-century Victorian rowhouse with original woodwork and appointments. Ten moderately priced rooms in historic district.

WASHINGTON ———————————————————————————

Connecticut-Woodley House
2647 Woodley Rd. NW, 20008
202-667-0218
Ray Knickel
All year

$ EP
15 rooms, 7 pb
C-yes/S-yes/P-no/H-no

Restaurants nearby
TV lounge, family rates
laundry facilities, A/C
convention ctr. nearby

Comfortable, convenient, and inexpensive accommodations. Walk to restaurants, shops, Metro, bus transportation, Smithsonian museums, and other points of interest.

Embassy Inn, The
1627 16th St. NW, 20009
202-234-7800 800-423-9111
Jennifer Schroeder
All year

$$ B&B
38 rooms, 38 pb
Most CC, *Rated*, •
C-yes/S-yes/P-no/H-no
Spanish

Continental breakfast
Comp. wine
Afternoon tea, snacks
sitting room
walk to Metro

Near Metro, White House, restaurants and shops with knowledgeable and helpful staff. Colonial style, in renovated 1920's boarding house. **Bottle of Windsor wine**

Kalorama Guest House
1854 Mintwood Place, NW,
20009
202-667-6369
Tami & John
All year

$ B&B
19 rooms, 12 pb
Most CC, *Rated*, •
C-yes/S-yes/P-no/H-no

Continental plus
Comp. wine, lemonade
Parlor, sun room
24-hour message service
free local phone calls

Victorian townhouse decorated in period furnishings. Antique-filled, spacious rooms. Beautiful sun room for your morning breakfast. Charming, unique & inexpensive.

*The Reeds,
Washington, D.C.*

WASHINGTON ─────────────────────────────

Kalorama Guest House, The $$ B&B
2700 Cathedral Ave., NW, 20008   50 rooms, 50 pb
202-328-0860 FAX:319-1262   Visa, MC, AmEx, DC, •
Michael & Maryanne   C-ltd/S-yes/P-no/H-no
All year

Continental plus
Comp. wine, lemonade
Sitting room
conference room avail.

Charming European-style bed & breakfast in six turn-of-the-century townhouses. Period art, furnishings, brass beds, plants, outdoor landscaped garden, and hospitality.

Reeds, The $$ B&B
P.O. Box 12011, 20005   6 rooms, 1 pb
c/o Bed & Breakfast, Ltd.   *Rated*, •
202-328-3510 FAX:332-3885   C-yes/S-yes/P-no/H-no
Jackie Reed   French, Spanish
All year

Continental breakfast
Sitting room, gardens
library, Victorian porch
piano, antiques

Spacious rooms with wood-burning fireplaces and crystal chandeliers bring a bit of the Nineteenth Century to historic downtown Washington.

Windsor Inn, The $$ B&B
1842 16th St., NW, 20009   46 rooms, 46 pb
202-667-0300 800-423-9111   Most CC, *Rated*, •
Jennifer Schroeder   C-yes/S-yes/P-no/H-no
All year   French, Spanish

Continental breakfast
Comp. sherry, snacks
5-10 p.m. in lobby
TV, radio alarm clock in
rooms

Relaxing and charming haven in heart of nation's capitol. Art deco flair. Close to Metro and many restaurants. 11 blocks north of White House. **Free bottle of Windsor wine**

More Inns . . .

B&B Accom. of Washington, 3222 Davenport St. NW, Washington, 20008, 202-363-8909
Castlestone Inn, 1918 17th St. NW, Washington, 20009, 202-483-4706
Clifton Inn, 1507 - 28th St. N.W., Washington, 20007
Meg's International House, 1315 Euclid St., NW, Washington, 20009, 202-232-5837
Morrison-Clark Inn, 1015 "L" St. N.W., Washington, 20001, 202-898-1200
Swiss Inn, 1204 Massachusetts NW, Washington, 20005, 202-371-1816
Victorian Accommodations, 1304 Rhode Island Av NW, Washington, 20005, 202-234-6292

Florida

AMELIA ISLAND ─────────────────────────

1735 House, The $$$ B&B
584 S. Fletcher Ave., 32034   5 rooms, 5 pb
904-261-5878 800-872-8531   Visa, MC, AmEx, *Rated*,
Gary & Emily Grable   •
All year   C-ltd/S-yes/P-no/H-no

Continental plus
In-room coffee service
beach towel, comp. paper
Units have mini-kitchen

White frame house overlooking Atlantic Ocean. Breakfast served with morning paper. Stay in suites (up to 4) or lighthouse (up to 6). Golf, tennis, fishing, riding, sailing.

AMELIA ISLAND ──────────────────────────────

Elizabeth Pointe Lodge $$$ B&B Full breakfast
98 S. Fletcher Ave., 32034 20 rooms, 20 pb Comp. wine, snacks
904-277-4851 Visa, MC, AmEx, *Rated*, Sitting room, library
David & Susan Caples • bicycles, oceanfront
All year C-yes/S-yes/P-no/H-yes

Reminiscent of a turn-of-the-century lodge; oceanfront on a small Florida barrier island; bike to historic seaport village nearby. Hearty breakfast, newspaper, fresh flowers.

Florida House Inn $$ B&B Full breakfast
P.O. Box 688, 32034 12 rooms, 12 pb Restaurant, bar
22 S. Third St. Visa, MC, AmEx, *Rated*, Sitting room, library
904-261-3300 800-258-3301 • bicycles, near beaches
Bob & Karen Warner C-yes/S-no/P-no/H-yes golf, tennis, fishing
All year, FAX:277-3831 some Spanish

Florida's oldest continually operating tourist hotel, circa 1857, in 50-block historic district. Country antiques, quilts, wide shady porches, courtyard with fountain.

APALACHICOLA ──────────────────────────────

Gibson Inn, The $$ EP All meals available
P.O. Box 221, 32320 30 rooms, 30 pb Bar service
51 Ave C Visa, MC, AmEx, *Rated*, Special weekend packages
904-653-2191 904-653-8282 • lounge, entertainment
J.A. Dearing, M. Koon C-yes/S-ask/P-ask/H-no bicycles, tennis courts
All year

30-room historic inn where true southern hospitality can be found. Enjoy the Victorian dining room and the spacious verandas. Downtown Apalachicola.

APOLLO BEACH ──────────────────────────────

B & B of Apollo Beach $ B&B Continental plus
6350 Color Lane, 33572 3 rooms, 1 pb Comp. wine
813-645-2471 • Sitting room
Joseph R. Molnar C-yes/S-ltd/P-no/H-yes laundry available
All year German, Hungarian tennis nearby

*Waterfront, Spanish-style residence. Near Busch Gardens, Dali Museum, Disney World, Adventure Island. Dockside fishing, pelicans, dolphins, sunsets. **Catamaran available, ltd.***

BAY HARBOR ISLAND ──────────────────────────────

Bay Harbor Inn $$ B&B Continental plus
9660 E. Bay Harbor Dr., 33154 38 rooms, 38 pb Lunch, dinner
305-868-4141 Visa, MC, AmEx, *Rated*, Snacks, comp. wine
Sandy & Celeste Lankler • restaurant, bar service
All year C-yes/S-yes/P-yes/H-ltd sitting room, pool
  Spanish

*Award-winning water-front inn, adjacent to Bal Harbour shops. Beautiful tropical setting w/world famous Palm Restaurant & B.C. Chong's Seafood. **Frequent guests 10% off***

BIG PINE KEY ──────────────────────────────

Barnacle B&B, The $$$ B&B Full breakfast
Route 1 Box 780A, Long Beach 4 rooms, 4 pb Comp. wine
Rd., 33043 • Hot tub, bicycles
305-872-3298 C-ltd/S-yes/P-no/H-no fishing poles
Wood & Joan Cornell French refrigerators
All year

Barefoot living with panache. Secluded area on ocean in fabulous Florida Keys. Private cottage and efficiency unit.

BIG PINE KEY ———————————————————————————

Deer Run B&B	$$ B&B	Full breakfast
P.O. Box 431, 33043	3 rooms, 3 pb	Bicycles, beach
Long Beach Drive	•	hot tubs, library
305-872-2015	C-ltd/S-no/P-no/H-yes	
Sue Abbott		
All year		

Ocean front hideaway—quiet, serene. Breakfast is served on the veranda overlooking the ocean. 33 miles to Key West

BRADENTON BEACH ———————————————————————

Duncan House B&B	$$ B&B	Full breakfast
1703 Gulf Dr., 34217	4 rooms, 4 pb	Comp. wine
813-778-6858	Visa, MC, AmEx, •	Sitting room
Becky Kern & Joseph Garbus	C-ltd/S-no/P-no/H-no	sun deck
All year		hot tub

Turn-of-the-century Victorian. Located on beautiful Anna Maria Island. Steps away from white sandy beaches. **10% off week stay**

CEDAR KEY ———————————————————————————

Historic Island Hotel	$$$ B&B	Full breakfast
P.O. Box 460, 32625	10 rooms, 6 pb	Full menu, cafe
2nd. and B St.	Visa, MC, *Rated*, •	Natural foods restaurant
904-543-5111	C-ltd/S-no/P-no/H-ltd	comp. wine, draft beer
Tom & Alison Sanders	Spanish	sitting & dining room
All year		

1850 Jamaican architecture in historic district. Antiques. Gourmet natural foods specializing in original recipes, seafood and vegetarian, poppy-seed bread. **25% off wkdays.**

DAYTONA BEACH ———————————————————————

Captain's Quarters Inn	$$ B&B	Full breakfast
3711 S. Atlantic Ave., 32127	25 rooms, 25 pb	Lunch, comp. wine
904-767-3119	Visa, MC, AmEx, *Rated*,	Cheese, crackers
Becky Sue Morgan & Family	•	All suites
All year	C-yes/S-yes/P-ask/H-yes	heated pool, bicycles

Daytona's first new B&B inn, directly on the world's most famous beach. Old-fashioned coffee shop. Unique antique shoppe, all-suite inn, private balconies. AAA "excellent."

EDGEWATER ——————————————————————————

Colonial House, The	$ B&B	Full breakfast
110 E. Yelkca Terr., 32132	5 rooms, 4 pb	Comp. snacks on arrival
904-427-4570	•	Guest refrigerator, A/C
Eva Brandner	C-ltd/S-yes/German,	washing machine, TV
All year	French, Italian	pool, hot tub

Colonial-style home with year-round heated pool and hot tub close to one of Florida's finest beaches and attractions. **3rd night 30% off**

FERNANDINA BEACH ———————————————————————

Greyfield Inn	$$$ AP	Full breakfast
P.O. Box 900, 32034	11 rooms, 3 pb	Lunch & dinner included
Cumberland Island, GA	Visa, MC, *Rated*,	Comp. boat to island
904-261-6408	C-ltd/S-ltd/P-no/H-no	sitting room, Bar
Mary Jo & Mitty Ferguson		hot tub, bicycles
All year		

House built 1904 for Margaret Carnegie. Original furnishings and unspoiled island—no telephone, TV, etc. Beach. Seafood; everything homemade. Naturalist outing.

FORT MYERS

Drum House Inn B&B
2135 McGregor Blvd., 33901
813-332-5668
James W. & Shirley Drum
All year

$$$ B&B
6 rooms, 6 pb
•
C-ltd/S-no/P-no/H-yes

Continental plus
Comp. wine, snacks
Sitting room
library
bicycles

Romantic Florida style. Uniquely decorated with antiques and period furniture. Walk to Ford & Edison homes. Shopping and restaurants nearby. Comp. champagne & hors d'oeuvres.

GAINESVILLE

Magnolia Plantation B&B
309 SE 7th St., 32601
904-375-6653
Joe & Cindy Montalto
All year

$$ B&B
6 rooms, 4 pb
Visa, MC, *Rated*, •
C-ltd/S-no/P-ltd/H-no

Full breakfast
Lunch by res., snacks
Comp. beverages, library
sitting room, bicycles
60-feet pond, gazebo

Restored 1885 Victorian in downtown. Two miles from Univ. of Florida. Beautifully land-scaped gardens, pond, waterfalls & gazebo. **Special rates after 3 nights.**

Sweetwater Branch Inn B&B
625 E. University Ave., 32601
904-373-6760 800-451-7111
Cornelia Holbrook
All year

$$ B&B
7 rooms, 7 pb
Visa, MC, AmEx, •
C-yes/S-no/P-no/H-yes
Spanish, Itaian, French

Full breakfast
Dinner avlb., comp. wine
Afternoon tea, snacks
sitting room, bicycles
airport/univ. transport

Enjoy a piece of the past; restored 1880 Victorian with antiques, English garden/patio. Walk to historic district's fine dining, Hippodrome Theatre; 1.5 mi. to Univ. of Fla.

HOLMES BEACH

Harrington House B&B
5626 Gulf Dr., 34217
813-778-5444
Jo & Frank Davis
All year

$$ B&B
8 rooms
Visa, MC *Rated*, •
C-ltd/S-no/P-no

Full gourmet breakfast
Comp. iced tea, popcorn
Sitting room
bicycles
swimming pool

Charming restored 1920s home directly on Gulf of Mexico reflects "casual elegance." Antiques, balconies, great rooms, swimming pool, peace and quiet. Near major attractions.

HOMESTEAD

Room at the Inn
15830 SW 240 St., 33031
305-246-0492 FAX:246-0492
Sally Robinson
All year

$ B&B
4 rooms, 3 pb
C-yes/S-no/P-ltd/H-no

Continental plus
Great room w/fireplace
heated pool with spa
sitting room, hot tub

Relax, refresh, meditate, grow. A country retreat on a country estate furnished in period antiques. Convenient to South Florida and the Florida Keys. **3rd night 20% off**

INDIAN SHORES

Meeks B&B on the Gulf
19418 Gulf Blvd. #407, 34635
813-596-5424
Greta & Bob Meeks
All year

$ B&B
3 rooms, 2 pb
•
C-yes/S-no/P-no/H-no

Full breakfast
Swimming pool
Tennis court
beach
outdoor grill

Beach! Pool! Sunsets! Enjoy our beach condo or cottage overlooking The Gulf of Mexico. Close to Florida attractions. Located between Clearwater & St. Petersburg Beach.

JACKSONVILLE

House on Cherry Street
1844 Cherry St., 32205
904-384-1999
Carol Anderson
All year

$$ B&B
4 rooms, 4 pb
Visa, MC, *Rated*, •
C-ltd/S-yes/P-no/H-no

Full breakfast
Comp. wine, snacks
Sitting room, color TV
air conditioned
porch, bicycles, fax

In historic Riverside, a restored colonial house filled with period antiques, decoys, four poster beds and country collectibles. On beautiful St. John's River. **3rd night 50%**

Plantation Manor Inn
1630 Copeland St., 32204
904-384-4630
Jerry & Kathy Ray
All year

$$$ B&B
8 rooms, 8 pb
Visa, MC, AmEx, *Rated*,
•
C-ltd/S-yes/P-no/H-no

Continental plus
Comp. refreshments
sitting room, spa
swimming pool

Restored 1905 Southern Mansion with antique furnishings and oriental carpets. 2 blocks from river, restaurants, antique shops. Convenient to Cummer Art Museum, downtown.

KEY WEST

Blue Parrot Inn
916 Elizabeth St., 33040
305-296-0033 800-231-2473
Rick Scrabis, Ed Lowery
All year

$$$ B&B
9 rooms, 9 pb
Visa, MC, AmEx, Disc., •
C-ltd/S-yes/P-no/H-no

Continental plus
Library
swimming pool
A/C, private bath

Classic Bahamian Conch house built in 1884 with major renovations in 1989. In the heart of Old Town Key West. Walk to beaches, shopping, restaurants, clubs.

Duval House
815 Duval St., 33040
305-294-1666 800-22D-UVAL
James Brown Jr.
All year

$$$ B&B
27 rooms, 25 pb
Most CC, *Rated*, •
C-ltd/S-yes

Continental plus
2 apts. with kitchenette
Sitting room
TV lounge, sun decks
swimming pool, gardens

A restored guest house (circa 1885). Ideally located in historic Old Key West. Tropical gardens and a laid-back atmosphere. Walk to beaches, restaurants. New Victorian gazebo.

Eden House, The
1015 Fleming St., 33040
305-296-6868 800-533-KEYS
Stephan Clement
All year

$ EP
41 rooms, 41 pb
Visa, MC, •
C-yes/S-yes/P-no/H-no
Spanish, French, German

Restaurant, cafe
Free happy hour
Swimming pool, jacuzzi
snorkeling, scuba diving
sailing & jet ski nearby

In old Key West. Ceiling fans, white wicker. Sip a cool drink under a poolside gazebo, lounge on veranda, dine in garden cafe, join us on a sunset sail. **Packages, wkly rates**

Heron House
512 Simonton St., 33040
305-294-9227 800-937-5656
Fred Geibelt
All year

$$$ B&B
23 rooms, 21 pb
Visa, MC, AmEx, *Rated*,
•
C-ltd/S-yes/P-no/H-yes

Continental breakfast
Full breakfast
Gardens, sun deck
gym, swimming pool

Old island charm situated in location central to all the main tourist attractions. Pool, sun deck, gardens and gym. Continual renovation.

Key West B&B, Key West, FL

KEY WEST

Incentra Carriage House
729 Whitehead St., 33040
305-296-5565
Maryanna Mike & John Sumner
All year

$$$ B&B
7 rooms, 3 pb
Visa, MC, AmEx, •
C-yes/S-yes/P-yes/H-yes

Continental plus
Private decks w/hammock
tropical garden
sitting room

*Charming, personalized cottages in tropical garden setting in heart of "Old Town." Extremely private property that takes you back in time. **Wine for special occasions***

Island City House Hotel
411 William St., 33040
305-294-5702 800-634-8230
All year

$$$ B&B
24 rooms, 24 pb
Visa, MC, *Rated*, •
C-yes/S-yes/Spanish

Continental breakfast
Rooftop sun deck w/view
bicycles, hot tub
swimming pool, garden

A Victorian mansion, a historic Carriage house and a Cypress Cigar house accommodate guests with parlor suites and share exotic tropical gardens.

KEY WEST ───────────────────────────────

Key West B&B/Popular House
415 William St., 33040
305-296-7274 800-438-6155
Jody Carlson
All year

$$ B&B
8 rooms, 4 pb
Visa, MC, AmEx, •
C-ltd/S-ltd

Continental plus
1 room w/private deck
hot tubs, sauna
sun deck, sitting room

In heart of Historic District, restored 100-yr-old Victorian. Breakfast at your leisure. Caribbean casual. Sun deck, sauna, jacuzzi for your relaxation. **10% off 3+ nights**

Marquesa Hotel & Cafe
600 Fleming St., 33040
305-292-1919 800-869-4631
Carol Wightman
All year

$$$ EP
15 rooms, 15 pb
Visa, MC, AmEx, *Rated*,
•
C-yes/S-yes/H-ltd

Continental plus $6
Comp. wine at check-in
Restaurant, sitting room
swimming pool
parking lot

Impeccably restored Victorian hotel with 15 rooms & suites, pool and exceptional restaurant, "Mira," in the heart of Old Key West.

Merlinn Guesthouse
811 Simonton St., 33040
305-296-3336
Pat Hoffman
All year

$$ B&B
18 rooms, 18 pb
Visa, MC, AmEx, *Rated*,
•
C-ltd/S-yes/P-ltd/H-yes

Full breakfast
Comp. rum punch, snacks
Sitting room, library
garden, swimming pool
Wheelch. to prvt. patio

Magical, secluded retreat in the heart of Old Town. Homemade quiche & muffins. You'll love the leisurely breakfast in the lush, tropical oriental garden. **7th night free, Ltd**

Papa's Hideaway Guesthouse
309 Louisa St., 33040
305-294-7709
S. McBratnie & Sandy Islands
All year

$$$ B&B
5 rooms, 5 pb
Visa, MC, •
C-yes/S-yes/P-no/H-yes

Continental breakfast
Comp.
champagne/newlywed
Hot tubs, pool, bicycles
one cottage

Secluded private getaway. Lush tropical gardens. Breezy spacious studios. Quaint cottage house. Walking distance from historic Old Town and beaches. **Attraction discounts**

Pilot House Guest House
414 Simonton St., 33040
305-294-8719 800-648-3780
Ed
All year

$$$ EP
8 rooms, 8 pb
Visa, MC, AmEx, •
C-ltd/S-ltd/P-no/H-no

Fully equipped kitchens
Hot tubs, marble baths
verandas, private garden
courtyard with gas grill

The 19th-century Victorian Guest House is conveniently located in the heart of Historic Old Town Key West. Suites have A/C, TV and phones. Jacuzzi pool and grill in garden.

Seascape
420 Olivia St., 33040
305-296-7776
Alan D. Melnick
All year

$$ B&B
5 rooms, 5 pb
Visa, MC, AmEx
C-ltd/S-yes/P-no/H-no

Continental breakfast
Sunset wine hr-seasonal
Heated pool-spa
sun decks, wicker
A/C, TVs, Bahama fans

C.1889, listed on National Historic Register. Intimate pool in tropical garden setting. Royal blue & white wicker motif. Center of Old Town Key West. **10% off 7+ nights, Ltd**

KEY WEST ─────────────────────────────────────

Watson House, The | $$$ B&B | Continental breakfast
525 Simonton St., 33040 | 3 rooms, 3 pb | Heated pool & spa, A/C
305-294-6712 800-621-9405 | Visa, MC, AmEx, *Rated*, | cableTV, phones, veranda
Joe Beres & Ed Czaplicki | • | wicker/rattan furniture
All year | C-ltd/S-yes/P-no, Spanish |

Small, quaint award-winning inn with fully furnished guest suites in a lush, tropical garden setting. Located in the Historic Preservation District.

─────────────────────────────────────

Whispers B&B Inn | $$ B&B | Full gourmet breakfast
409 William St., 33040 | 6 rooms | Rooms have A/C and TVs
305-294-5969 | Visa, MC, AmEx | walk to all activities
John Marburg | C-ltd/S-ltd/P-no/H-no | old town, swimming, fans
All year | |

Historic Register. Victorian old town inn. Breakfast in tropical garden. Beer or wine on arrival. Antiques throughout. Quiet and romantic. **Free bottle wine w/2+ night stay**

KISSIMMEE ─────────────────────────────────────

Unicorn Inn | $$ B&B | Continental breakfast
8 S. Orlando Ave., 34741 | 7 rooms, 7 pb | TV in rooms
407-846-1200 | *Rated* | coffee makers
Don & Fran Williamson | C-yes/S-yes/P-no/H-no | in all rooms
All year | |

Located in beautiful downtown Kissimmee, minutes from Disney World, Gatorland Zoo, Wet & Wild Boardwalk & baseball. British innkeepers. Right across from Police Headquarters!

LAKE BUENA VISTA-ORLANDO ─────────────────────────────────────

PerriHouse B&B Inn | $$ B&B | Continental plus
P.O. Box 22005, 32830 | 4 rooms, 4 pb | Private entrance to room
10417 State Rd. 535 | All major CC's, *Rated*, • | swimming pool, jacuzzi
407-876-4830 800-780-4830 | C-yes/S-ltd | bird sanctuary project
Nick & Angi Perretti | |
All year, FAX:876-0241 | |

A private & secluded country estate on 20 acres conveniently nestled right in Disney's "backyard." All Orlando & Disney attractions minutes away. Boutique shopping nearby.

LAKE WALES ─────────────────────────────────────

Chalet Suzanne Country Inn | $$$ B&B | Full breakfast
3800 Chalet Suzanne Dr., 33853 | 30 rooms, 30 pb | Restaurant, lounge
813-676-6011 800-433-6011 | Most CC, *Rated*, • | Comp. sherry in room
Carl & Vita Hinshaw | C-yes/S-yes/P-yes/H-ltd | pool on lake, airstrip
All year | German, French | 3 rooms w/pvt. jacuzzi

Unique country inn centrally located for Florida attractions. Gourmet meals; award-winning restaurant. Ranked one of 10 most romantic spots in Florida. Uncle Ben's Top 10.

MAITLAND ─────────────────────────────────────

Thurston House | $$ B&B | Continental plus
851 Lake Ave., 32751 | 4 rooms, 4 pb | Comp. wine, snacks
407-539-1911 | Visa, MC, *Rated*, • | Sitting room
Carole Ballard | C-ltd/S-no/P-no/H-no | screened porches
All year | | lake front, bicycles

Newly renovated 1885 Queen Anne Victorian home. Hidden away in a country setting but moments from downtown Orlando. Come experience the "old Florida."

MARATHON

Hopp-Inn Guest House	$$ B&B	Full breakfast
500 Sombrero Beach Rd., 33050	5 rooms, 5 pb	No breakfasts in villas
305-743-4118 FAX:743-9220	*Rated*, •	Televisions
Joe & Joan Hopp	C-ltd/S-yes/P-no/H-ltd	Bahama fans
October–August	German	air conditioning

Three rooms w/private entrances & baths. Located on the ocean w/tropical plants & many palm trees. Two ocean view villas sleep 2-6 with kitchens. **Attraction discounts**

MICANOPY

Herlong Mansion	$$ B&B	Full breakfast (wkends)
P.O. Box 667, 32667	10 rooms, 10 pb	Aftn. tea, comp. wine
402 N.E. Cholokka Blvd.	Visa, MC, *Rated*, •	sitting room
904-466-3322	C-yes/S-no/P-no/H-no	library
H.C. (Sonny) Howard, Jr.		
All year		

Twenty antique and craft shops one block away. Historic Greek Revival house, circa 1845. Moss draped oaks, pecans and dogwoods. **3rd night free, Sun.-Th.**

NAPLES

Inn by the Sea	$$ B&B	Continental plus
287 - 11th Ave. S., 33940	5 rooms, 5 pb	Bicycles, sitting room
813-649-4124	Visa, MC, *Rated*, •	beach just 700 feet away
Catlin Maser	C-ltd/S-no/P-no/H-no	2 suites
All year		

Tropical beach house just 700 feet from beach. Walk to fabulous shopping, art galleries, restaurants. Located in Old Naples Historic District. **3rd night 50%, Ltd.**

OCALA

Seven Sisters Inn	$$$ B&B	Full breakfast
820 SE Fort King St., 34471	7 rooms, 7 pb	Dinner sometimes
904-867-1170	Most CC, *Rated*,	Aft. tea, snacks
Bonnie Morehardt & Ken Oden	C-ltd/S-ltd/P-no/H-yes	sitting room
All year		bicycles

Come back in time!- sip rasberry tea on the veranda, enjoy flowering walkways, play croquet on the lawn. Many special package weekends. **3rd night 50% off**

ORANGE PARK

Club Continental Suites	$$ B&B	Continental plus
P.O. Box 7059, 32073	37 rooms, 37 pb	Lunch, dinner, bar serv.
2143 Astor St.	Visa, MC, AmEx, *Rated*,	Restaurant, sitting room
904-264-6070 800-877-6070	•	tennis court, pool
Caleb Massee	C-yes/S-yes/P-ltd/H-yes	entertainment
All year		

Florida riverfront inn with giant live oaks, gardens & fountains. Historical Palmolive Estate, superior suites, jacuzzis, tennis, marina priviledges and fine dinning.

ORLANDO

Courtyard at Lake Lucerne	$$ B&B	Continental plus
211 N. Lucerne Cir. E., 32801	22 rooms, 22 pb	Comp. wine or cocktails
407-648-5188 800-444-5289	Visa, MC, AmEx, *Rated*,	Sitting rooms
Charles Meiner & Paula Bowers	•	Courtyard & Gardens
All year	C-yes/S-yes/P-no/H-no	Meeting room

Three unique and historic buildings surrounding a lush tropical garden in the heart of the City. Walk to shopping and restaurants. **AAA, AARP & Corp. rates available.**

Five Oaks Inn, Palmetto, FL

PALM BEACH

Plaza Inn
215 Brazilian Ave., 33480
407-832-8666
Ajit Asrani
All year

$$$ B&B
50 rooms, 50 pb
Visa, MC, AmEx, *Rated*,
•
C-yes/S-yes/Spanish

Full breakfast
Bar service
Free parking
bicycles, tennis nearby
sitting room, pool

Romantic, intimate hideaway. Uniquely affordable w/European ambience. Heated pool, jacuzzi. Canopy & four-poster beds. One block to ocean.

PALMETTO

Five Oaks Inn
1102 Riverside Dr., 34221
813-723-1236 800-658-4167
Colorito & Kreissler Families
All year

$$ B&B
4 rooms, 4 pb
Visa, MC, *Rated*, •
C-ltd/S-ltd/P-no/H-no

Full breakfast
Aft. tea, snacks
Comp. wine, bar service
sitting room, library
bicycles, tanning beach

*Magnificent Southern estate. River setting, a taste of Florida elegance & grace. Antiques, history & hospitality. Near shops, restaurants, beach. **50% off 3rd night, ltd***

PENSACOLA

Homestead Village
7830 Pine Forest Rd., 32526
904-944-4816
Jeanne Liechty
All year

$$ B&B
6 rooms, 6 pb
AmEx, Visa, MC, *Rated*,
C-ltd/S-no/P-no/H-no

Full 6-course breakfast
Dessert, ice cream, pie
Sitting room
Restaurant
Complimentary desserts

Featuring Lancaster Pennsylvania Amish-Mennonite recipes at our restaurant. Our rooms have wood floors, poster beds, fireplaces and garden tubs.

RUSKIN

Ruskin House B&B | $ B&B | Continental plus
120 Dickman Dr. S.W., 33570 | 4 rooms, 1 pb | Full breakfast (arrange)
813-645-3842 | Visa, MC | Sitting room, library
Dr. Arthur M. Miller | C-ltd/S-ltd/P-ask/H-yes | health club nearby ($)
All year | French, some Spanish |

Gracious 1910 waterfront home with period (1860-1920) antiques, between Tampa & Sarasota on west coast. Three minutes from I-75. Friendly!

SAINT AUGUSTINE

Westcott House | $$$ B&B | Continental plus
146 Avenida Menendez, 32084 | 8 rooms, 8 pb | Comp. wine, brandy
904-824-4301 | Visa, MC, *Rated*, • | Sitting room
David & Sharon Dennison | C-ltd/S-ltd/P-no/H-no | 3 Victorian porches
All year | | courtyard

Built in 1880s, beautifully decorated Victorian home furnished w/European antiques, located in historic district overlooking Matanzas Bay for a breathtaking view.

SANFORD

Higgins Hosue, The | $$ B&B | Continental plus
420 Oak Ave., 32771 | 3 rooms, 1 pb | Snacks, Comp. wine
407-324-9238 | Visa, MC, *Rated*, • | Sitting room, bicycles
Roberta & Walter Padgett | C-ltd/S-no/P-no/H-no | outdoor hot tub, deck
All year | | gardens, tennis nearby

Romantic Victorian inn close to the St. Johns River and Lake Monroe in the Historic District. Quiet, relaxing, very elegant. Cottage w/2 bdrm., 2 bath, living rm., kitchen.

SANIBEL ISLAND

Sanibel's Song of the Sea | $$$ B&B | Continental breakfast
863 East Gulf Dr., 33957 | 30 rooms, 30 pb | Comp. wine
813-472-2220 800-231-1045 | Visa, MC, AmEx, *Rated*, | Bicycles, hot tubs
Mrs. Patricia Slater | • | tennis nearby, library
All year | C-yes/S-yes/P-no/H-no | swimming pool

European-style, seaside inn located on Sanibel Island & the Gulf of Mexico. Complimentary continental breakfast, wine, fresh flowers, bikes & whirlpool. **Ask about packages**

ST. AUGUSTINE

Casa de La Paz | $$ B&B | Full breakfast
22 Avenida Menendez, 32084 | 6 rooms, 6 pb | Comp. sherry, champagne
904-829-2915 | Most CC, *Rated*, • | Sitting room, library
Sandy Upchurch | C-ltd/S-no/P-no/H-no | room service, courtyard
All year | Spanish | veranda, carriage tours

On the Historic District's bayfront, this elegant Mediterranean-style home (1915) offers fine accommodations in a beautiful, central location. **Comp. sherry, 7th night free.**

Castle Garden B&B | $$ B&B | Full breakfast
15 Shenandoah St., 32084 | 6 rooms, 6 pb | Snacks, comp. wine
904-829-3839 | Most CC, *Rated*, • | Sitting room, antiques
Bruce & Joyce Kloeckner | C-ltd/S-ltd/P-no/H-no | bicycles, fresh flowers
All year | | two bridal suites w/spa

St. Augustine's only Moorish Revival dwelling, former Castle Warden Carriage House, built 1800's. Restored, lush landscape, beautiful gardens, hideaway. **3rd nite 50%, ltd.**

ST. AUGUSTINE

Kenwood Inn, The
38 Marine St., 32084
904-824-2116
M. K. & C. Constant
All year

$$ B&B
15 rooms, 15 pb
Visa, MC, Disc, *Rated*,
C-ltd/S-ltd/P-no/H-no

Continental breakfast
Sitting room, piano
swimming pool
walled in courtyard

Lovely old 19th-century Victorian inn located in historic district of our nation's oldest city. Walk to attractions; beautiful beaches 5 minutes away. **Sun-Th 10% disc't., ask**

Old City House Inn & Rest.
115 Cordova St., 32084
904-826-0113
Alice & Bob Compton
All year

$$ B&B
5 rooms, 5 pb
Visa, MC, AmEx, *Rated*,
•
C-yes/S-no/P-no/H-no

Full breakfast
Restaurant, bar
Comp. wine
veranda, bicycles
6 mi. to beach

Newly renovated Colonial Revival house in heart of nation's oldest city. Queen-size beds, private entrances. Award-winning restaurant. Walk to historical attractions, shops.

Secret Garden Inn, The
56½ Charlotte St., 32084
904-829-3678
Nancy Noloboff
All year

$$$ B&B
3 rooms, 3 pb
Visa, MC, *Rated*, •
C-yes/S-no/P-no/H-no

Continental plus
Kitchens
Decks, patio, sitt. room
block from the bay
carriage rides nearby

Three very private suites in a garden setting. Secluded historic district hideaway—great for honeymoons. Walk to restaurants, shops and attractions. **20% off mid-wk**

Southern Wind B&B
18 Cordova St., 32084
904-825-3623
Jeanette & Dennis Dean
All year

$$ B&B
7 rooms, 7 pb
Visa, MC, AmEx, *Rated*,
•
C-ltd/S-no/P-no/H-ltd

Full breakfast
Comp. wine
Sitting room
large verandas
cable TV, bicycles

On the Carriage Trail through historic district, Southern Wind offers an elegant 1916 columned masonry home with exceptional buffet breakfast. Separate guest inn for families.

St. Francis Inn
279 St. George St., 32084
904-824-6068
Stan & Regina Reynolds
All year

$ B&B
11 rooms, 11 pb
Visa, MC, *Rated*, •
C-ltd/S-yes/P-no/H-no

Continental plus
Iced tea & lemonade
Sunday nite music
free passes to Oldest
House, bicycles

Built in 1791, located in Historic District, one block west of the "Oldest House in USA." New owner, many improvements. **Free admission to "Oldest House"**

ST. PETERSBURG

Bayboro House on Tampa Bay
1719 Beach Dr. SE, 33701
813-823-4955
Gordon & Antonia Powers
All year

$$$ B&B
4 rooms, 4 pb
Visa, MC, •
C-ltd/S-ltd/P-no/H-no

Continental plus
Comp. wine/cocktails
Veranda
player piano

Walk out the door to sunning and beachcombing from a turn-of-the-century Queen Anne house. Florida B&B-ing at its best. 1991 St. Petersburg Historical Preservation Award.

ST. PETERSBURG

Mansion House	$$ B&B	Full English breakfast
105 5th Ave., N.E., 33701	6 rooms, 6 pb	English tea, snacks
813-821-9391 FAX:821-9754	Visa, MC, *Rated*, •	Sitting room
Alan & Suzanne Lucas	C-ltd/S-no/P-no/H-no	picnic baskets, patio
All year		

Turn-of-the-century Southern home; renowned Welsh hospitality and hearty breakfast. Beaches, marina, baseball, festivals and many other attractions. **10% off room rate**

VENICE

Banyan House, The	$$ B&B	Continental plus
519 S. Harbor Dr., 34285	9 rooms, 7 pb	Sitting room
813-484-1385	*Rated*	bicycles, hot tubs
Chuck & Susan McCormick	C-ltd/S-ltd/P-no	swimming pool
All year		

Historic Mediterranean-style home. Enormous banyan tree shades courtyard, pool and spa. Centrally located to shopping, restaurants, beaches and golfing.

More Inns ...

Seaside Inn, 1998 South Fletcher, Amelia Island, 32034
Pink Camellia Inn, The, 145 Ave. E, Apalachicola, 32320, 904-653-2107
Gasparilla Inn, Boca Grande, 33921, 813-964-2201
Mary Lee B&B, 717 Sunlit Court, Brandon, 33511, 813-653-3807
Cabbage Key Inn, Cabbage Key, 33924, 813-283-2278
Cedar Key B&B, P.O. Box 700, Cedar Key, 32625, 904-543-9000
Clewiston Inn, The, 108 Royal Palm Ave., Clewiston, 33440, 813-983-8151
Colonial River House, 607 N. Indian River Dr., Cocoa, 32922, 407-632-8780
Hotel Place St. Michel, 162 Alcazar Ave., Coral Gables, 33134, 305-444-1666
Nick and Ann Perretti, 8151 N.W. 12th Ct., Coral Springs, 33071, 305-752-2355
Sprague House Inn, 125 Central Ave., Crescent City, 32112, 904-698-2430
Coquina Inn B&B, 544 S. Palmetto Ave., Daytona Beach, 32114, 904-254-4969
Live Oak Inn, 444-448 South Beach St., Daytona Beach, 32114, 904-252-4667
Mrs. W.L. Bishop, 401 Bay Ave., De Funiak Springs, 32433
Sunbright Manor, 606 Live Oak, De Funiak Springs, 32433, 904-892-0656
DeLand Country Inn, 228 W. Howry Ave., DeLand, 32720, 904-736-4244
Hutch's Haven, 811 N.W. 3rd Ave., Delray Beach, 33444, 407-276-7390
Lemon Bay B&B, 12 Southwind Dr., Englewood, 33533, 813-474-7571
Manasota Beach Club, 7660 Manasota Key Rd., Englewood, 34223, 813-474-2614
Ivey House, The, P.O. Box 5038, Everglades City, 33929, 813-695-3299
Rod & Gun Club, P.O. Box G, Everglades City, 33929, 813-695-2101
Bailey House, P.O. Box 805, Fernandina Beach, 32034, 904-261-5390
Grandma Newton's B&B, 40 N.W. 5th Ave., Florida City, 33034, 305-247-4413
Casa Alhambra B&B Inn, 3029 Alhambra St., Fort Lauderdale Beach, 33304, 305-467-2262
Embe's Hobby House, 5570-4 Woodrose Ct., Fort Meyers, 33907, 813-936-6378
Drum House Inn, 2135 McGregor Blvd., Fort Myers, 33901, 813-332-5668
Windsong Garden, 5570-4 Woodrose Court, Fort Myers, 33907, 813-936-6378
Dolan House, The, 1401 N.E. 5 Ct., Ft. Lauderdale, 33301, 305-462-8430
Yearling Cabins, Route 3, Box 123, Hawthorne, 32640, 904-466-3033
Bloomsbury, P.O. Box 2567, High Springs, 32643, 904-454-4040
Maison Harrison House, 1504 Harrison St., Hollywood, 33020, 604-922-7319
Seminole Country Inn, 15885 Warfield Blvd., Indiantown, 33456, 305-597-3777
Crown Hotel, 109 N. Seminole Ave., Inverness, 32650, 904-344-5555
B&B of Islamorada, 81175 Old Highway, Islamorada, 33036, 305-664-9321
1217 On the Bouelvard, 1217 Boulevard St., Jacksonville, 32206, 904-354-6959
Judge Gray's House, 2814 St. Johns Ave., Jacksonville, 32205, 904-388-4248
Willows on the St. Johns, 1849 Willow Branch Ter., Jacksonville, 32205, 904-387-9152
Jules' Undersea Lodge, P.O. Box 3330, Key Largo, 33037, 305-451-2353
Alexander's, 1118 Fleming St., Key West, 33040, 305-294-9919
Angelina, 302 Angela St., Key West, 33040, 305-294-4480
Artist House, 534 Easton St., Key West, 33040, 305-296-3977
Authors, 725 White St., Key West, 33040, 305-296-3977
Big Ruby's Guesthouse, 409 Appelrouth Ln., Key West, 33040, 305-296-2323
Borg's, 712 Amelia St., Key West, 33040, 305-296-3671
Brass Key Guesthouse, 412 Frances St., Key West, 33040, 305-296-4719
Chelsea House, 707 Truman Ave., Key West, 33040, 305-296-2211
Coconut Grove Guest House, 817 Fleming St., Key West, 33040, 305-296-5107
Colours The Guest Mansion, P.O. Box 738, Key West, 33119, 305-294-6977
Cottages, 1512 Dennis St., Key West, 33040, 305-294-6003
Curry Mansion Inn, 511 Caroline St., Key West, 33040, 305-294-5349
Curry Mansion Inn, 511 Caroline St., Key West, 33040
Cypress House, 601 Caroline St., Key West, 33040, 305-294-6969
E.H. Gato Jr. Guesthouse, 1327 Duval St., Key West, 33040, 305-294-0715
Early House, 507 Simonton St., Key West, 33040, 305-296-0214

B&B of Apollo Beach, Apollo Beach, FL

Eaton Lodge, 511 Eaton St., Key West, 33040, 305-294-3800
Ellie's Nest, 1414 Newton St.,, Key West, 33040, 305-296-5757
Fogarty House, 227 Duval St., Key West, 33040, 305-296-9592
Garden House, 329 Elizabeth St., Key West, 33040, 305-296-5368
Hollinsed House, 611 Southard St., Key West, 33040, 305-296-8031
La Te Da, 1125 Duval St., Key West, 33040
Lamp Post House, 309 Louisea St., Key West, 33040, 305-294-7709
Lighthouse Court, 902 Whitehead St., Key West, 33040, 305-294-9588
Mermaid & The Alligator, 729 Truman Ave., Key West, 33040, 305-294-1894
Nassau House, 1016 Fleming St., Key West, 33040, 305-296-8513
Oasis Guest House, 823 Fleming St., Key West, 33040, 305-296-2131
Old Town Garden Villas, 921 Center St., Key West, 33040, 305-294-4427
Orchid House, 1025 Whitehead St., Key West, 33040, 305-294-0102
Palm's Guesthouse, The, 820 White St., Key West, 33040, 305-294-3146
Papa's Hideaway Guesthouse, 309 Louisa St., Key West, 33040, 305-294-7709
Pilot House Guest House, 414 Simonton St., Key West, 33040, 305-294-8719
Pines of Key West, 521 United St., Key West, 33040, 305-296-7467
Rainbow House, 525 United St., Key West, 33040, 305-292-1450
Sea Isle Resort, 915 Windsor Ln., Key West, 33040, 305-294-5188
Simonton Court, 320 Simonton St., Key West, 33040, 305-294-6386
Sunrise Sea House B&B, 39 Bay Dr., Bay Point, Key West, 33040, 305-745-3525
Sweet Caroline, 529 Caroline St., Key West, 33040, 305-296-5173
Tilton Hilton, 511 Angela St., Key West, 33040, 305-294-8697
Tropical Inn, 812 Duval St., Key West, 33040, 305-294-9977
Walden House, 717 Caroline St., Key West, 33040, 305-296-7161
Westwinds, 914 Eaton St., Key West, 33040, 305-296-4440
Wicker Guesthouse, 913 Duval St., Key West, 33040, 305-296-4275
Clauser's Bed & Breakfast, 201 E. Kicklighter Rd., Lake Helen, 32744, 904-228-0310
Breakaway Guest House, 4457 Poinciana, Lauderdale By The Sea, 33308, 305-771-6600
Jim Hollis River Rendevous, Route 2, Box 60, Mayo, 32066, 904-294-2510
Miami River Inn, 118 SW S. River Dr., Miami, 33130, 305-325-0045
Roberts Ranch, 6400 SW 120 Ave., Miami, 33183, 305-598-3257
Cavalier Hotel/Cabana Club, P.O. Box 1157, Miami Beach, 33139, 305-534-2135
Essex House, 1001 Collins Ave., Miami Beach, 33139, 305-534-2700
Penguin Hotel, 1418 Ocean Dr., Miami Beach, 33139, 305-534-9334
Peppermill B&B, 625 East Washington St., Monticello, 32344, 904-997-4600
Lakeside Inn, Box 1390, Mount Dora, 32757, 800-556-5016
Feller House, 2473 Longboat Dr., Naples, 33942, 813-774-0182
Doll House B&B, 719 S.E. 4th St., Ocala, 32671, 904-351-1167
Lake Weir Inn, Rt. 2, 12660 SE Hwy 25, Ocklawaha, 32179, 904-288-3723
Orange Springs, One Main St., Box 550, Orange Springs, 32682, 904-546-2052
Alpen Gast Haus, 8328 Curry Ford Rd., Orlando, 32822, 305-277-1811
Avonelle's, 4755 Anderson Rd., Orlando, 32806, 305-275-8733
Briercliff, 1523 Briercliff Dr., Orlando, 32806, 407-894-0504
Esther's B&B, 2411 Virginia Dr., Orlando, 32803, 407-896-9916
Meadow Marsh, 940 Tildenville School , Orlando, 32787, 305-656-2064
Rinaldi House, 502 Lake Ave., Orlando, 32801, 407-425-6549
Rio Pinar House, The, 532 Pinar Dr., Orlando, 32825
Robin Dodson, 11754 Ruby Lake Rd., Orlando, 32819, 305-239-0109
Spencer Home B&B, 313 Spencer St., Orlando, 32809, 407-855-5603
Florida Suncoast B&B, 119 Rosewood Dr., Palm Harbor, 34685, 813-787-3500
Homestead Inn, The, 7830 Pine Forest Rd., Pensacola, 32506
New World Inn, 6000 South Palafox St., Pensacola, 32501, 904-432-4111
North Hill Inn, 422 N. Baylen St., Pensacola, 32501, 904-432-9804
Sunshine, 508 Decatur Ave., Pensacola, 32507, 904-455-6781
Knightswood, Box 151 Summerland Key, Ramrod Key, 33042
La Belle Francaise, 101 Oriole Ct, Royal Palm Beach, 33411, 407-793-3550
Bay View House, Rt 1, Box 2120, Santa Rosa Beach, 904-267-1202
Gary Cooper, 6863 Old Ranch Rd., Sarasota, 34241
Josephine's B&B, 101 Seaside Ave., Seaside, 32459, 800-848-1840
Crescent House, 459 Beach Rd., Siesta Key, 33578
Tara Oaks, P.O. Box 836, Sparr, 32192, 904-622-8990
Carriage Way B&B, 70 Cuna St., St. Augustine, 32084, 904-829-2467
Casa de Solana, B&B Inn, 21 Aviles St., St. Augustine, 32084, 904-824-3555
Victorian House B&B, 11 Cadiz St., St. Augustine, 32084, 904-824-5214
Homeplace, The, 501 Akron, Stuart, 34994, 407-220-9148
Mrs. Joyce Jenks, 9131 Otter Pass Rd., Tampa, 33626
East Lake B&B, 421 Old East Lake Rd., Tarpon Springs, 34689, 813-937-5487
Kathy Carbaugh Inn, 928 Bayshore Dr, Tarpon Springs, 34689
Spring Bayou Inn, 32 W. Tarpon Ave., Tarpon Springs, 34689, 813-938-9333
"Key West Style", P.O. Box 078581, W. Palm Beach, 407-848-4064
Wakulla Springs Lodge, #1 Springs Dr., Wakulla Springs, 32305, 904-224-5950
Hibiscus House B&B, 501 30th St., West Palm Beach, 33407, 407-863-5633
West Palm Beach B&B, PO Box 8581, West Palm Beach, 33407, 407-848-4064
Casa Adobe, P.O. Box 770707, Winter Garden, 34777, 407-876-5432
Fortnightly Inn, 377 E. Fairbanks Ave., Winter Park, 32789, 407-645-4440
Double M Ranch B&B, Route 1, Box 292, Zolfo Springs, 33890, 813-735-0266

Georgia

ATLANTA

Beverly Hills Inn
65 Sheridan Dr. N.E., 30305
404-233-8520 800-331-8520
Mit Amin
All year

$$$ B&B
18 rooms, 18 pb
Most CC, *Rated*, •
C-yes/S-yes/P-no/H-no

Continental plus
Comp. wine, courtyard
Sitting room, library
piano, health club priv.
London taxi shuttle

Charming city retreat, fine residential neighborhood. Close to Lenox Square, Historical Society and many art galleries. 15 min. to downtown. **4th night free**

Oakwood House B&B
951 Edgewood Ave., N.E., 30307
404-521-9320
Judy & Robert Hotchkiss
All year

$$ B&B
4 rooms, 4 pb
Visa, MC, *Rated*, •
C-yes/S-no/P-no/H-no

Continental plus
Exercise bike, library
front porch, back deck
garden, one child free

Comfortable Craftsman home in Atlanta's first suburb. Interesting art; substantial library. Privacy (owners next door) & close to city. **Discounts for 3+ nights**

Shellmont B&B Lodge
821 Piedmont Ave. NE, 30308
404-872-9290
Ed & Debbie McCord
All year

$$$ B&B
4 rooms, 4 pb
Visa, MC, AmEx, *Rated*,
•
C-ltd/S-ltd/P-no/H-yes

Continental plus
Beverages, chocolates
Sitting room, bicycles
ice, coffee/tea area
near restaurants

Classic Victorian home; guest suites; private baths; authentic furnishings; magnificent woodwork. Located near historic district. National Register; City Of Atlanta Landmark.

Woodruff B&B Inn, The
223 Ponce de Leon Ave., 30308
404-875-9449 800-473-9449
Joan & Douglas Jones
All year

$$$ B&B
11 rooms, 6 pb
Rated, •
C-yes/S-yes/P-no/H-no

Full Southern breakfast
Comp. soda
Sitting room
hot tubs, porches
movies/TV in parlor

Southern hospitality in the heart of Atlanta! Old Victorian, former bordello. Antiques, hot tubs, hot-air ballooning available. **Free bottle wine 2nd night stay**

Woodruff Cottage
100 Waverly Way, NE, 30307
404-688-9498
Eleanor Matthews
All year

$$ B&B
3 rooms
Visa, MC, •
S-no/P-no/H-no

Continental plus
Private garden
Screened porch
fireplaces

Totally restored Victorian located in historic Inman Park. 1 block to subway, close to restaurants. 12-ft ceilings, heart-pine woodwork, antiques.

AUGUSTA

Oglethorpe Inn
836 Greene St., 30901
706-724-9774 FAX:724-4200
D. Lee Edwards
All year

$$$ B&B
20 rooms
AmEx, Visa, MC, DC, •
C-yes/S-yes/P-sml/H-yes

Full breakfast
Restaurant, bar
Cocktails, concierge
conference ctr, hot tub
tennis courts, pool

Historic District; near downtown and airports; restored houses; full complimentary breakfast, whirlpool baths, canopied beds. Special packages.

BRUNSWICK ─────────────────────────────

Brunswick Manor | $$ B&B | Full gourmet breakfast
825 Egmont St., 31520 | 9 rooms, 8 pb | Comp. wine, high tea
912-265-6889 | Visa, MC, *Rated*, ● | Sitting room, library
Harry and Claudia Tzucanow | C-ltd/S-ltd/P-ltd/H-ltd | bicycles, tennis courts
All year | some Spanish | airport pick-up

Elegant Olde Towne historic 1886 inn near Golden Isles. Gourmet breakfast; afternoon high tea. Boat chartering avail. Gracious hospitality. **Honeymoon pkg w/champaign**

CLARKESVILLE ─────────────────────────────

Burns-Sutton House | $$ B&B | Full breakfast
P.O. Box 992, 30523 | 7 rooms, 4 pb | Snacks
124 S. Washington St. | Visa, MC, AmEx, *Rated*, | Restaurant on premises
706-754-5565 | C-yes/S-no/P-no/H-no | sitting room
John & JoAnn Smith | | cable TV
All year

Historic Victorian home elegantly restored. Furnished in antiques. At the foothills of the mountains, close to nature activities and antiquing. AAA 4 stars. **3rd night 50% off**

Glen-Ella Springs | $$$ B&B | Continental plus
Route 3, Box 3304, Bear Gap | 16 rooms, 16 pb | Lunch, dinner, beverages
Rd., Turnerville, 30523 | Visa, MC, AmEx, *Rated*, | Restaurant, conf. room
706-754-7295 800-552-3479 | ● | sitting room, library
Barrie & Bobby Aycock | C-ltd/S-yes/P-no/H-yes | pool, hiking, gardens
All year

100-year-old inn in NE Georgia. Award-winning 1987 restoration. Gourmet dining room features fresh seafood, prime rib & many specialties. Cottage garden shop newly opened.

CLAYTON ─────────────────────────────

English Manor Inns | $$ B&B/$$$ AP | Full breakfast
P.O. Box 1605, 30525 | 60 rooms, 60 pb | Sunday brunch, high tea
US Hwy. 76 East | Visa, MC, *Rated*, ● | Dinner, comp. wine
800-782-5780 706-782-5789 | C-ltd/S-yes/P-yes, French, | setups, pool, hot tubs
Susan & English Thornwell | Spanish, German | tennis courts, croquet
All year, FAX:782-4810

Seven inns furnished in exquisite antiques, reflecting the charm of an earlier era w/ all of today's amenities. Jacuzzis available. Mystery weekends. **10% discount**

CLEVELAND ─────────────────────────────

RuSharon B&B | $$ B&B | Full breakfast
Rt. 7, Box 7202, Old Clarksville | 2 rooms, 2 pb | Snacks
Rd., 30528 | Visa, MC, *Rated*, | Sitting room
706-865-5738 | C-yes/S-no/P-no/H-no
Rush & Sharon Mauney
All year

1890s home in north Georgia mountains. Rooms furnished in antiques with fireplaces, TV & A/C. Quiet, casual elegance in a garden setting.

COMMERCE ─────────────────────────────

Pittman House, The | $$ B&B | Full breakfast
81 Homer Rd., 30529 | 4 rooms, 2 pb | Snacks
706-335-3823 | Visa, MC, Disc.,*Rated*, ● | Sitting room
Tom & Dot Tomberlin | C-yes/S-no/P-no/H-no | library
All year | | tennis court nearby

The Pittman House is a restored 1890 Colonial with wrap-around rocking porch. Completely furnished with antiques. Great sports & shopping nearby. **10% off 3+ nights**

DAHLONEGA

Royal Guard Inn	$$ B&B	Full breakfast
203 South Park St., 30533	5 rooms, 5 pb	Afternoon tea & wine
706-864-1713	Visa, MC, *Rated*, •	Sitting room
The Vanderhoff's	C-ltd/S-no/P-no/H-no	reading material
All year		large wrap-around porch

Historic home in N.E. Georgia mountains. Site of the first gold rush! Gourmet breakfast & wine & cheese on great wrap-around porch. Close to town.

Smith House, The	$$ B&B	Continental breakfast
202 S. Chestatee St., 30533	18 rooms, 18 pb	Restaurant
706-864-3566 800-852-9577	Most CC, *Rated*, •	Country store
Resv's made by Hotel Clerk	C-yes/S-yes/P-no/H-ltd	sitting room
All year		

All-you-can-eat family-style dining for over 50 years. A stay at Smith House Inn is one of old-fashioned nostalgic character.

DARIEN

Open Gates B&B	$ B&B	Full breakfast
Box 1526, Vernon Sq., Exit 10,	5 rooms, 3 pb	Boxed lunch, comp. wine
I-95, 31305	•	Library, Steinway piano
912-437-6985	C-ltd/S-no/P-no/H-no	bicycles, pool, antiques
Carolyn Hodges		sailing, boat tours
All year		

Timber baron's gracious home on oak-shaded historic square. Access to untrammeled barrier islands, including Sapelo and the Altamaha Delta rice culture. **10% off 4+ nights.**

FORT OGLETHORPE

Captain's Quarters B&B	$$ B&B	Full breakfast
13 Barnhardt Circle, 30742	7 rooms, 4 pb	1 suite w/full kitchen
706-858-0624	Visa, MC, AmEx, *Rated*,	Sitting room
Pam Humphrey & Ann Gilbert	•	
All year	C-ltd/S-no/P-no/H-no	

Fully restored 1902 home, carefully appointed for your comfort and convenience. Adjacent to Chickamauga-Chattanooga National Military Park and close to all attractions.

GAINESVILLE

Dunlap House, The	$$$ B&B	Continental plus
635 Green St., 30501	9 rooms, 9 pb	Comp. tea/refreshments
706-536-0200	Most CC, *Rated*, •	Sitting room
Ann & Ben Ventress	C-ltd/S-yes/P-no/H-yes	wedding facilities
All year		

Luxurious historic accommodations. Breakfast in bed or on the veranda. Restaurant and lounge across the street. Lodging and dining excellence. AAA rating 3 diamonds.

HAWKINSVILLE

Black Swan Inn	$$ B&B	Continental breakfast
411 Progress Ave., 31036	6 rooms, 6 pb	Restaurant, lunch
912-783-4466	Visa, MC, AmEx, DC, •	Dinner, bar service
Bill & Mary Jean Pace	C-yes/S-yes/P-no/H-no	sitting room
All year		

Southern Colonial-style mansion. Verandas encourage guests to relax in a rocking chair and listen to a southern cricket serenade.

HELEN

Dutch Cottage B&B	$$ B&B	Full breakfast
P.O. Box 757, 30545	4 rooms, 3 pb	Afternoon tea
Ridge Rd.	C-yes/S-ltd/P-no/H-no	Sitting room
706-878-3135	Dutch - a little	hammock
Bill & Jane VanderWerf		bird watching
May - October		

Tranquil waterfall. Ivy covered hillside. Idyllic wooded setting. Large rooms furnished with Dutch antiques. Also charming hillside chalet. Spring water.

Hilltop Haus B&B	$ B&B	Full country breakfast
P.O. Box 154, 30545	2 rooms, 2 pb	Afternoon coffee
Chattahoochee St.	C-ltd/S-ltd/P-no/H-yes	Bicycles
706-878-2388		sitting rooms
Frankie Allen		with fireplaces
All year		

Located within walking distance of alpine village, Helen. Country-style breakfast with buttermilk biscuits, Appalachian Trail nearby. **10% off 4+ days off-season.**

MACON

1842 Inn	$$$ B&B	Continental plus
353 College St., 31201	22 rooms, 22 pb	Tea, coffee, bar service
912-741-1842 800-336-1842	Visa, MC, AmEx, *Rated*,	Morning paper, whirlpool
Phillip Jenkins	•	turn-down/bedtime sweets
All year	C-yes/S-yes/H-yes	overnight shoeshines

Antebellum mansion and Victorian cottage furnished with fine antiques. All rooms have private baths, air conditioning and color televisions. 4 diamond rating w/AAA.

PERRY

Swift Street Inn B&B	$$ B&B	Full breakfast
1204 Swift St., 31069	4 rooms, 4 pb	Afternoon tea, snacks
912-987-3428	Most CC, *Rated*, •	Sitting room, library
Wayne & Jane Coward	C-ltd/S-no/P-ltd/H-no	bicycles
All year		golf at local club

Step back to a time of Southern charm, romance & luxury 135 years ago. Our gourmet breakfast is a special treat! **Nabisco coupons accepted**

SAUTEE

Stovall House, The	$$ B&B	Continental breakfast
Route 1, Box 1476, Hwy 225	6 rooms, 6 pb	Restaurant
North, 30571	*Rated*	Lunch, dinner
706-878-3355	C-yes/S-yes/P-no/H-ltd	sitting room
Ham Schwartz	Spanish	Historic Register
All year		

Award-winning restoration of 1837 farmhouse on 28 serene acres; mountain views; a country experience. One of top 50 restaurants in Georgia. **Restaurant discounts**

SAVANNAH

Ballastone Inn & Townhouse	$$$ B&B	Continental plus
14 E. Oglethorpe Ave., 31401	20 rooms, 20 pb	Comp. sherry, cognac
912-236-1484 800-822-4553	Visa, MC, AmEx, •	Full service bar, parlor
Richard Carlson, Tim Hargus	C-ltd/S-yes/P-no/H-yes	elevator, VCRs, florist
All year		courtyard, gift shop

Closest B&B inn to the Savannah Riverfront. 1835 mansion with beautiful antiques and courtyard. Fireplaces, jacuzzis. Recommended by the New York Times, Gourmet, and Brides.

SAVANNAH ———————————————————————————

Bed & Breakfast Inn, The
117 W. Gordon St., at Chatham Sq., 31401
912-238-0518 FAX:233-2537
Robert McAlister, Pamela Gray
All year

$ B&B
7 rooms, 4 pb
Visa, MC, *Rated*, •
C-yes/S-yes/P-ltd/H-no
German, French, Spanish

Full homestyle breakfast
Library, garden
sitting room

Restored 1853 Federal-style townhouse in heart of historic Savannah; amidst museums, restaurants & antique shops; walk to major attractions. **Special gift, ask**

East Bay Inn
225 East Bay St., 31401
912-238-1225 800-500-1225
Jean Ryerson
All year

$$$ B&B
28 rooms, 28 pb
Most CC, *Rated*, •
C-yes/S-yes/P-no/H-yes

Continental plus
Lunch, dinner
Eve. wine & sherry
turn-down service

Steps away from the bustling riverfront, shops and museums. Original flooring, brick walls, and cast iron columns add true charm to this restored 1853 warehouse.

Eliza Thompson House, The
5 W. Jones St., 31401
912-236-3620 800-348-9378
Lee Smith
All year

$$ B&B
25 rooms, 25 pb
Visa, MC, AmEx, *Rated*,
•
C-yes/S-yes/P-no/H-yes

Continental plus
Sherry on arrival
Evening cordials/sweets
small conference room
imported wine, concierge

Regally restored home in the heart of the Historic District. Elegant parlor, updated furnishings, beautifully landscaped courtyard with splashing fountains. **Comp. beverages**

Foley House Inn
14 W. Hull St., 31401
912-232-6622 800-647-3708
Susan Steinhauser
All year

$$$ B&B
20 rooms, 20 pb
Visa, MC, AmEx, *Rated*,
•
C-yes/S-yes/P-no/H-no

Continental plus
Comp. port, sherry, tea
Hot tub, newspaper
shoes shined on request
VCR & film lib. in rooms

A restored antebellum mansion, furnished with antiques, 5 jacuzzi rooms. Turndown service, fireplace rooms. Truly the best of two worlds. **3rd night free, ltd.**

Forsyth Park Inn, The
102 W. Hall St., 31401
912-233-6800
Virginia & Hal (son) Sullivan
All year

$$$ B&B
10 rooms, 10 pb
Visa, MC, AmEx, *Rated*,
•
C-yes/S-yes/some French

Continental plus
Comp. wine
Sitting room
tennis courts, hot tubs
piano music nightly

An elegantly restored Victorian mansion in the historic district. Rooms feature fireplaces, whirlpool tubs, antiques and 16-foot ceilings. **3rd night free, ltd.**

Gastonian, The
220 E. Gaston St., 31401
912-232-2869 800-322-6603
Hugh & Roberta Lineberger
All year, FAX: 232-0710

$$$ B&B
13 rooms, 13 pb
Visa, MC, AmEx, *Rated*,
•
C-ltd/S-no/P-no/H-yes

Full Southern breakfast
Comp. wine & fruit
Twin parlors, elevator
fireplace in each room
hot tub, private parking

1868 southern elegance! Completely furnished with antiques, Persian rugs, whirlpool baths. Hot tubs on the sun deck. Luxurious. Mobil 4-Star; AAA 4-Diamond.

The Forsyth Park Inn, Savannah, GA

SAVANNAH

Jesse Mount House
209 W. Jones St., 31401
912-236-1774 800-347-1774
Howard Crawford
All year

$$$ B&B
2 rooms, 2 pb
Private garage parking, •
C-yes/S-yes/P-ltd/H-yes

Continental plus
Comp. sherry and candies
Garden with fountains
full kitchen, bicycles
room phones, cable TV

Circa 1854 elegant Greek Revival house. Two luxurious 3-bedroom suites for one to six persons. Cable TV. Rare antiques, gilded harps. 4 person spa, robes. **4 nights disc't**

Joan's on Jones
17 West Jones St., 31401
912-234-3863 FAX:234-1455
Joan & Gary Levy
All year

$$$ B&B
2 rooms, 2 pb
Rated, •
C-yes/S-no/P-ltd/H-yes

Continental
Comp. wine
Sitting room
tennis nearby
golf, fishing by nearby

Victorian townhouse with private entrance to each suite, secluded garden. Here are location, comfort and southern hospitality...amid period antiques. **Free bottle wine**

Lion's Head Inn
120 E. Gaston St., 31401
912-232-4580
Christy Dell'Orco
All year

$$ B&B
6 rooms, 6 pb
Visa, MC, AmEx, *Rated*,
•
C-yes/S-no/P-no/H-yes

Continental plus
Aft. tea, comp. wine
Sitting room, library
bicycles, massage
babysitting services

19th century mansion, proximity to Savannah's amenities, tastefully decorated w/Federal furnishings, unique 19th century lighting, romantic ambiance. **3rd night 50% off**

SAVANNAH

Presidents' Quarters	$$$ B&B	Continental plus
225 E. President St., 31401	16 rooms, 16 pb	Comp. wine, aftn. tea
912-233-1600 800-233-1776	Most CC, *Rated*, •	Ltd. bar, sandwiches
Muril L. Broy	C-ltd/S-ltd/P-no/H-yes	sitting room, courtyard
All year, FAX: 238-0849		jacuzzi, swimming pool

Newly restored 1885 home in heart of Historic District: jacuzzi bathtubs, gas log fireplaces, period reproductions. Deluxe yet affordable. **Wine and fruit in-suite.**

Remshart-Brooks House	$$ B&B	Continental plus
106 W. Jones St., 31401	1 rooms, 1 pb	Sherry in room
912-234-6928 912-234-8165	•	Sitting room
Ewing & Anne Barnett	C-ltd/S-yes/P-no/H-ltd	terrace garden
All year		

Experience the charm and hospitality of historic Savannah while being "at home" in the garden suite of Remshart-Brooks House—built in 1854.

SENOIA

Veranda, The	$$$ B&B	Full breakfast
252 Seavy St., Box 177, 30276	9 rooms, 9 pb	Lunch, dinner by res.
404-599-3905 FAX:599-0806	Visa, MC, AmEx, *Rated*,	Library, conference fac.
Jan & Bobby Boal	•	sitting rm, organ, Fax
All year	C-ltd/S-ltd/P-no/H-yes	tennis, fishing nearby
	German	

Historic inn furnished w/ antiques & fascinating Victorian memorabilia. Delicious meals served in beautiful Old South setting. 1990 INN OF THE YEAR. **$10 certif for gift shop**

ST. SIMONS ISLAND

Little St. Simons Island	$$$ AP	Full breakfast
P.O. Box 1078, 31522	12 rooms, 12 pb	Meals & activities incl.
912-638-7472	Visa, MC, •	Swimming pool
Debbie McIntyre	C-ltd/S-yes/P-no/H-ltd	sitting room
Ind. guests Spring/Fall		bicycles, horses

A 10,000-acre undeveloped barrier island with early 1900s lodge and guest cottages. Southern cuisine. Professional naturalists and activities included. Groups only June-Sept.

THOMASVILLE

Evans House B&B	$$ B&B	Full breakfast
725 S. Hansell St., 31792	4 rooms, 4 pb	Comp. wine, snacks
912-226-1343 800-344-4717	*Rated*, •	Bicycles
Lee & John Puskar	C-yes/S-no/P-ask/H-no	
All year		

Restored Victorian home located in Parkfront historical district across from Paradise Park. Walking distance of historic downtown, tours, antique shops and restaurants.

Susina Plantation Inn	$$$ MAP	Full breakfast
Route 3 Box 1010, 31792	8 rooms, 8 pb	5 course comp. dinner
912-377-9644	*Rated*	Swimming pool, croquet
Anne-Marie Walker	C-yes/S-yes/P-yes/H-no	tennis, bicycles, trails
All year		sitting room

Greek Revival mansion built 1840 and furnished in antiques; a real southern "Tara." AAA & Mobil rate 3 stars. 5 course complimentary dinner with wine included.

THOMSON

1810 West Inn	$ B&B	Continental breakfast
254 No. Seymour Dr. NW, 30824	10 rooms, 10 pb	Afternoon tea
404-595-3156	Visa, MC, AmEx, *Rated*,	Sitting room, library
Virginia White	•	jogging trail, pond
All year	C-ltd/S-no/P-no/H-no	peacocks, 11 acres

Country charm, city amenities in restored antique farm house and renovated folk houses on eleven landscaped acres. Secluded, safe, convenient to I20 and Augusta, Ga.

WARM SPRINGS

Hotel Warm Springs B&B	$$ B&B	Full breakfast
P.O. Box 351, 31830	18 rooms, 18 pb	Restaurant
17 Broad St.	Most CC, •	Comp. wine
706-655-2114	C-yes/S-ltd/P-no/H-no	sitting room, library
Lee & Geraldine Thompson		
All year		

Perfect get-away in 1907 historic hotel, authentically restored, decorated w/Roosevelt furniture & family antiques. Southern breakfast on silver service. **3rd night 50% off**

More Inns . . .

Jesse Lemon B&B, 4965 N. Main St., Acworth, 30101, 404-974-8005
Old Home Place, 764 Union Grove Church, Adairsville, 30103, 404-625-3649
Beggar's Bush-Cane Miller, 615 Mud Creek Rd., Albany, 31707, 912-432-9241
Cottage Inn,The, Box 488, Hwy. 49N, Americus, 31709, 912-924-9316
Hideout B&B, Rt. 2, Americus, 31709, 912-924-9800
Lee Street 1884, 622 S. Lee St., Americus, 31709, 912-924-1290
Merriwood Country Inn, Rt. 6, Box 50, Americus, 31709, 912-924-4992
Morris Manor, The, 425 Timberlane Dr., Americus, 31709, 912-924-4884
Place Away B&B, A, 110 Oglethorpe St., Andersonville, 31711, 912-924-2558
Bramlette B&B, 255 Clarkewoods Rd., Athens, 30607, 404-546-9740
Ansley Inn, 253 Fifteenth St. NE, Atlanta, 30309, 404-872-9000
Halcyon B&B, 872 Euclid Ave., Atlanta, 30307, 404-688-4458
Augusta House, P.O. Box 40069, Augusta, 30904, 404-738-5122
1880 Victorian Inn, Rt. 7, Box 77886, Blairsville, 30512
Maple Bend Inn, Rt. 7, Box 7332A, Blairsville, 30512
Souther Country Inn, P.O. Box 2865, Blairsville, 30512, 706-379-1603
Stonehenge B&B, Rt. 6, Box 6314, Blairsville, 30512
Layside B&B, 611 River St., Blakely, 31723, 912-723-8932
Harry & June's B&B, Box 1247, Blue Ridge, 30513, 404-632-8846
Rose Manor Guest House, 1108 Richmond St., Brunswick, 31520, 912-267-6369
Jenny May & Sapp's B&B, 229 Broad St., Buena Vista, 31803, 912-649-7307
Stoneleigh B&B, 316 Fain St., Calhoun, 30701, 706-629-2093
Adair Inn, The, 602 W. Ave., Cartersville, 30120, 404-382-3662
Hearn Academy Inn, Box 639, Cave Spring, 30124, 404-777-8865
Standifer Inn, Rt. 4, Cherokee Point, 30114, 404-345-5805
Gordon-Lee Mansion, 217 Cove Rd., Chickamauga, 30707, 404-375-4728
LaPrade's, Route 1, Hwy 197N, Clarkesville, 30523, 404-947-3312
Charm House, The, P.O. Box 392, Clarksville, 30523, 706-754-9347
Spring Hill B&B, R. 5, Box 5450, Clarksville, 30523
Kellum Valley Inn, Rt. 3, Box 3610, Cleveland, 30528
Lodge at Windy Acres, The, Rt. 5, Hwy. 75, Cleveland, 30528
Schlemmer's Lodging, The, Rt. 4 Box 4655, Cleveland, 30528
Towering Oaks B&B Lodge, #5 Box 5172, Cleveland, 30528, 404-865-6760
Tyson Homestead, Rt. 5, Box 5130, Cleveland, 30528
Forest Hills Mt. Resort, Route 3, Dahlonega, 30533, 404-864-6456
Laurel Ridge, P.O. Box 338, Dahlonega, 30533, 404-864-7817
Mountain Top Lodge, Route 7, Box 150, Dahlonega, 30533, 404-864-5257
Worley Homestead Inn, 410 W. Main St., Dahlonega, 30533, 404-864-7002
Amy's Place, 217 W. Cuyler St., Dalton, 30720, 404-226-2481
Magnolia Plantation, U.S. 80, Danville, 31017, 912-962-3988
Blackburn Park, Route 3, Box 160, Dawsonville, 30534
Herb Patch Inn, 115 Hwy. 441 Business N, Demorest
Dillard House Inn, P.O. Box 10, Dillard, 30537, 404-746-5349
VIP B&B, 501 N. Dr., Dublin, 31021, 912-275-3739
Dodge Hill Inn, 105 9th Ave. NE, Eastman, 31023, 800-628-3778
Grenoke B&B, 914 Lower Heard St., Elberton, 30635
Elderberry Inn B&B Home, 75 Dalton St., Ellijay, 30540, 404-635-2218
Whitworth Inn, 6593 McEver Rd., Flowery Branch, 30542, 404-967-2386
Country Place, Route 3, Box 290, Forsyth, 31029
Evans House, The, 206 Miller St., Fort Valley, 31030, 912-922-6691
Early Hill, 1580 Lick Skillet Rd., Greensboro, 30648, 404-453-7876

Wedgwood B&B, P.O. Box 115, Hamilton, 31811, 706-628-5659

Hartwell Inn, 504 W. Howell St., Hartwell, 30643

Habersham Hollow Inn, Route 6, Box 6208, Helen, 30523, 706-754-5147

Helendorf Inn, P.O. Box 305, Helen, 30545, 404-878-2271

Blueberry Hill, Rt. 1, Box 253, Hoboken, 31542, 912-458-2605

Helmstead, The, P.O. Box 61, Homerville, 31634, 912-487-2222

Trowell House B&B, 256 E. Cherry St., Jesup, 31545, 912-530-6611

Anapauo Farm, Star Route, Box 13C, Lakemont, 30522, 404-782-6442

Barn Inn, Rt. 1, Lakemont, 30552

Lake Rabun Inn, The, P.O. Box 10, Lakemont, 30552, 706-782-4946

Southern Trace, The, 14 Baker St., Lakemont, 30553

Robert Toombs Inn, 101 South State St., Lyons, 30436, 912-526-4489

Carriage Stop Inn/Antiques, 1129 Georgia Ave., Macon, 31201, 912-743-9740

Stone-Conner House, 575 College St., Macon, 31302, 912-745-0258

Burns-Sutton House, Clarksville, GA

Victorian Village, 1841 Hardeman Ave., Macon, 31302, 912-743-3333

Boat House, 383 Porter St., Madison, 30650, 404-342-3061

Brady Inn, The, 250 N. Second St., Madison, 30650, 706-342-4400

Arden Hall, 1052 Arden Dr. SW, Marietta, 30060, 404-422-0780

Carrie L. Corrion, 1675 Roswell, ND, #1027, Marietta, 30062, 404-565-9425

Marlow House/Stanley House, 192 Church St., Marietta, 30060, 404-426-1887

Suite Revenge, 400 W. Main St., Marshallville, 31057, 912-967-2252

Revel Wylly Hoga, 167 Kenan Dr., Millegeville, 31061

Olena's Guest House, Route 26, Montezuma, 31063, 912-472-7620

Pinefields Plantation, Rt. 2, Box 215, Moultrie, 31768, 912-985-2086

York House, P.O. Box 126, Mountain City, 30068, 404-746-2068

Parrott-Camp-Soucy Home, 155 Greenville St., Newman, 30263, 404-253-4846

Quailridge B&B, Box 155, Norman Park, 31771, 912-985-7262

217 Huckaby, Box 115, Parrott, 31777, 912-623-5545

Mountain Top Inn, Box 147, Pine Mountain, 31822, 800-533-6376

Plains B&B Inn, The, 100 W. Church St., Plains, 31780, 912-824-7252

Moon River B&B, 715 Mt. Zion Rd., Resaca, 30735, 404-629-4305

Buckley's Cedar House, Route 10, Box 161, Ringgold, 30736, 404-935-2619

Karen R. Herman, 1185 Grimes Bridge Rd., Roswell, 30075, 800-533-4332

Beachview Bed & Breakfast, 537 Beachview Dr., Saint Simons Island, 31522, 912-638-9424

Gaubert Bed & Breakfast, 521 Oglethorpe, Saint Simons Island, 31522, 912-638-9424

King's on the March, 1776 Demere Rd., Saint Simons Island, 31522, 912-638-1426

Glen-Kenimer-Tucker House, Hwy. 17, Sautee, 30571

Lumsden Homeplace, The, Guy Palmer Rd., Sautee, 30571, 404-878-2813

Nacoochee Valley House, Box 249, Hwy. 17, Sautee, 30571, 404-878-3830

Woodhaven Chalet, Route 1, Box 39, Sautee, 30571, 404-878-2580

118 West, 118 W. Gaston St., Savannah, 31401, 912-234-8557

17 Hundred 90 Inn, 307 E. President St., Savannah, 31401, 912-236-7122

Barrister House, 25 W. Perry St., Savannah, 31499, 912-234-0621

Charlton Court, 403 Charlton St. E., Savannah, 31401, 912-236-2895

Comer House, 2 East Taylor St., Savannah, 31401, 912-234-2923

Greystone Inn, 214 E. Jones St., Savannah, 31401, 912-236-2442

Guerard-McClellan House, 221 East Gordon St., Savannah, 31401, 912-236-1863

Haslam-Fort House, 417 E. Charlton St., Savannah, 31401, 912-233-6380

Liberty Inn 1834, 128 W. Liberty St., Savannah, 31401, 912-233-1007

Lion's Head Inn, 120 E. Gaston St., Savannah, 31401, 912-232-4580

Magnolia Place Inn, 503 Whitaker St., Savannah, 31401, 912-236-7674

Mulberry, The, 601 E. Bay St., Savannah, 31401, 912-238-1200

Olde Harbour Inn, 508 E. Factors Walk, Savannah, 31401, 912-234-4100

Planters Inn, 29 Abercorn St., Savannah, 31499, 912-232-5678

Pulaski Square Inn, 203 W. Charlton St., Savannah, 31401, 912-232-8055

River Street Inn, 115 E. River St., Savannah, 31499, 912-234-6400

Royal Colony Inn, 29 Abercorn St., Savannah, 31401, 912-232-5678

Timmons House, 407 E. Charlton St., Savannah, 31401, 912-233-4456

Victoria Barie House, 321 E. Liberty St., Savannah, 31499, 912-234-6446

Culpepper House B&B, 35 Broad St., Senoia, 30276, 404-599-8182

Goodbread House, The, 209 Osborne St., St. Marys, 31558, 912-882-7490

Riverview Hotel, 105 Osborne St., St. Marys, 31558, 912-882-3242

Country Hearth Inn, 301 Main St., St. Simons Island, 31522, 800-673-6323

Aldred's Trellis Gardens, 107 S. Main St., Statesboro, 30458

Statesboro Inn, 106 South Main St., Statesboro, 30458, 912-489-8628

Coleman House, 323 N. Main St., Swainsboro, 30401, 912-237-2822

Edenfield House Inn, Box 556, Swainsboro, 30401, 912-237-3007

Tate House, Box 33, Tate, 30177, 404-735-3122

Gordon Street Inn, 403 W. Gordon St., Thomaston, 30286, 404-647-5477

Whitfield Inn, 327 W. Main St., Thomaston, 30286, 404-647-2482

Woodall House, 324 W. Main St., Thomaston, 30286, 404-647-7044

Deer Creek B&B, 1304 S. Broad St., Thomasville, 31792, 913-226-7294
Neel House, 502 S. Broad St., Thomasville, 31792, 912-228-6500
Quail Country B&B, 1104 Old Monticello Rd., Thomasville, 31792, 913-226-7218
Willow Lake, Rt. 4, Box 117, Thomasville, 31792, 913-226-6372
Four Chimneys B&B, 2316 Wire Rd., S.E., Thomson, 30824, 706-597-0220
West Fields B&B, Rt. 3, Box 728, Thomson, 404-595-3156
Myon B&B, 128 1st St., Tifton, 31793, 912-382-0959
Habersham Manor House, 326 W. Doyle St., Toccoa, 30577, 404-886-6496
Simmons-Bond Inn, 130 W. Tugaloo, Toccoa, 30577, 800-533-7693
Robert Toombs Inn, 3401 Lawrenceville Hwy, Tucker, 30084
Hunter House B&B, 1701 Butler Ave., Tybee Island, 31328, 912-786-7515
Magnolia Plantation, 1012 Williamsburg Dr., Valdosta, 31602, 912-247-5318
Twin Oaks, 9565 E. Liberty Rd., Villa Rica, 30180, 404-459-4374
Burress B&B, Box 201, Warm Springs, 31830, 404-655-2168
Little Blue House, Box 566, Warm Springs, 31830, 404-655-3633
Blackmon B&B, 512 N. Alexander Ave., Washington, 30673, 404-678-2278
Colley House B&B, The, 210 S. Alexander Ave., Washington, 30673, 404-678-7752
Holly Ridge Country Inn, Rt. 2, Box 356, Washington, 30673, 404-285-2594
Liberty B&B Inn, 108 W. Liberty St., Washington, 30673, 404-678-3107
Olmstead B&B, Pembroke Dr., Washington, 30673, 404-678-1050
Water Oak Cottage, 211 S. Jefferson St., Washington, 30673, 404-678-3605
Rivendell B&B, 3581 S. Barnett Shoals, Watkinsville, 30677, 706-769-4522
Georgia's Guest B&B, 640 E. 7th St., Waynesboro, 30830, 404-554-4863
Old Winterville Inn, 108 S. Main St., Winterville, 30683, 404-742-7340

Hawaii

AIEA, OAHU

Pear Harbor View B&B | $$ B&B | Continental breakfast
99-442 Kekoa Place, 96701 | • | Suite sleeps 4 or more
808-487-1228 808-486-8838 | C-yes | Large yard
Doris Reichert
All year

Two bedroom suite w/living room, complete kitchen, TV, private bath, private entry, view. Owner downstairs. Residential neighborhood, 3 mi above Pear Harbor. Weekly rate

ANAHOLA, KAUAI

Mahina Kai | $$$ B&B | Continental plus
P.O. Box 699, 96703 | 4 rooms, 2 pb | Kitchenette facilities
4933 Aliomanu | *Rated*, • | Sitting room
808-822-9451 | S-yes/Italian, French | library, bicycles
Mike Williams | | art collection
All year

Asian-Pacific beach villa and tropical gardens overlooking secluded bay. Separate guest wing with ethnic art collected by artist/owner. **8 consecutive nites, 1 nite free**

HANA, MAUI

Hotel Hana-Maui | $$$ | Restaurant - all meals
P.O. Box 8, 96713 | 9 rooms | Coffee grinders
808-248-8211 FAX:808-7264 | Visa, MC, AmEx | Refrigerators
Lisa De Cambra-Shaw | P-no | tennis, croquet, golf
All year | | snorkle, bicycle

Accommodations, including sea ranch cottages are scattered throughout 66 acres of landscaped gardens within a 4,700-acre working ranch. Tropical plants outside and in.

HANALEI, KAUAI

B&B and Beach—Hanalei Bay	$$ B&B	Continental plus
P.O. Box 748, 96714	4 rooms, 4 pb	Restaurant nearby
5095 Opelu Rd.	•	Sitting room, library
808-826-6111	C-yes/S-no/P-no/H-no	television, coolers &
Carolyn Barnes		snorkel equip. available
All year		

Steps to famous Hanalei Bay. Breakfast in view of 1000 foot waterfalls. Antiques and rattan. Hike Na Pali, snorkel, golf, kayak, windsurf, fish and sail.

HILO

Hale Kai B&B	$$$ B&B	Full breakfast
111 Honolii Pali, 96720	5 rooms, 5 pb	Afternoon tea
808-935-6330 FAX:935-8439	*Rated*, •	Hot tubs, pool
Evonne Bjornen	C-ltd/S-no/H-no	faces ocean
All year		Comp. wine & beer

A beautiful and very modern home on the bluff facing the ocean and Hilo Bay. Just 2 miles from downtown Hilo yet quiet & private. Guests are treated as family. Resident cat.

KAILUA

Akamai B&B	$$ B&B	Stocked refrigerator
172 Kuumele Pl., 96734	2 rooms, 2 pb	Restaurant, lunch/dinner
808-261-2227 800-642-5366	*Rated*, •	Aft. tea, snacks
Diane Van Ryzin	C-ltd/S-yes/P-no/H-yes	swimming pool
All year	French	

Hawaiian style B&B. Walking distance to beautiful beach. Private entrance to fully furnished studio. Private poolside garden lanai.

KAILUA-KONA

Hale Maluhia B&B	$$ B&B	Continental plus
76-770 Hualalai Rd., 96740	5 rooms, 4 pb	Snacks, comp. wine
800-559-6627	*Rated*	Sitting room, library
Ken & Ann Smith	C-yes/S-ltd/P-ltd/H-yes	hot tub, pool table
All year	Some German, Japanese	VCR w/movie library

Rambling 5,000 ft. home on 1 acre of coffee land in the beautiful Holualoa fruit belt. In the heart of Kona Hawaii. Use of snorkle/fins/beach equip. **10% off 3+ days**

KANEOHE, OAHU

Emma's Guest Rooms	$ EP	Guest kitchenette
47-600 Hui Ulili St., 96744	3 rooms, 3 pb	Dining room, library
808-239-7248 FAX:239-7224	MC, Visa, AmEx, Disc.,	TV lounge
Emma & Stanley Sargeant	C-ltd/S-no/P-no/H-no	
All year	German	

Cool windward location, private entrance, fully equipped kitchen, tropical garden view dining, convenient shopping, beaches and all Oahu island attractions.

KAPAA, KAUAI

Kay Barker's B&B	$ B&B	Continental plus
P.O. Box 740, 96746	4 rooms, 4 pb	Sitting room, library
5921 Ki'inani Place	*Rated*, •	restaurant, tennis
808-822-3073 800-835-2845	C-yes/S-yes/P-no/H-yes	beaches & river 10 min.
Gordon Barker		
All year		

Lovely home in a garden setting, with mountain and pasture views. Ten minutes from beaches, restaurants, golf, tennis and shopping. **15% off stays over 6 nights.**

KAPAA, KAUAI ———————————————————————————————

Orchid Hut, The	$$$ B&B	Continental plus
6402 Kaahele St., 96746	1 rooms, 1 pb	Kitchenette, sitting rm.
808-822-7201 800-578-2194	•	views, 3-room cottage
Norm & Leonora Ross	C-ltd/S-no/P-no/H-no	beach mats & towels
All year, FAX: 822-7034	French,Danish,Indonesian	

Charming, private, modern cottage. Spectacular view of Wailua River. Beautiful tropical landscaping. Convenient to beaches, restaurants, shopping. 3-day min. **10% off 7+days.**

KILAVEA, KAUAI ———————————————————————————————

Hale Ho'o Maha	$$ B&B	Continental plus
P.O. Box 422, 96754	3 rooms, 1 pb	Comp. wine
4646 Kalihiholo Rd.	Visa, MC, •	Library
808-828-1341 800-851-0291	C-ltd/S-yes/P-no/H-no	boggie/surf boards
Kirby Guyer, Toby Searles	Spanish	beach
All year		

Planation-style home. Fireplace, aquarium, Koa (hardwood) floors, marble baths, 5 acres, gourmet kitchen for guest use. Fun hosts!

KOLOA, KAUAI ———————————————————————————————

Poipu B&B Inn & Rentals	$$ B&B	Tropical breakfast
2720 Hoonani Rd., RR1, Box	7 rooms, 7 pb	Afternoon tea, snacks
308B, 96756	Most CC., *Rated*, •	Sitting room, lanais
808-742-1146 800-227-6478	C-yes/S-no/P-no/H-ltd	tennis & pool free
Dotti Cichon, B. Young	French, German	video library, cable TV
All year, Fax: 742-6843		

Romantic restored 1933 plantation house with the charm of old Hawaii. Also oceanfront condo, cottages, homes. Furnished in white wicker, pine antiques and carousel horses.

KOLOA—POIPU, KAUAI ———————————————————————————

Gloria's Spouting Horn B&B	$$ B&B	Continental plus
4464 Lawai Rd., 96756	4 rooms, 4 pb	Champagne welcome
808-742-6995	*Rated*	beach mats
Gloria & Bob Merkle	C-ltd	& towels provided
All year		

Oceanfront accommodations with surf 40 ft. away; relax in hammocks under coco palms on secluded beach. Charming cottage antiques. Romantic Tea House. Tropical breakfast.

LAHAINA, MAUI ———————————————————————————————

Lahaina Hotel	$$$ B&B	Continental breakfast
127 Lahainaluna Rd., 96761	12 rooms, 12 pb	Restaurant, bar
808-661-0577 800-669-3444	Visa, MC, AmEx, Disc., •	balcony lanais in rooms
Kenneth Eisley	C-ltd/S-ltd/P-no/H-no	ocean & mountain views
All year		

Located in heart of historic Lahaina town. Completely restored & redecorated in 1988-1989. Each guest room is furnished with authentic turn-of-the century antiques.

Plantation Inn, The	$$$ B&B	Continental plus
174 Lahainaluna Rd., 96761	10 rooms, 10 pb	Dinner at (Gerard's)
800-433-6815 808-667-9225	*Rated*, •	Sitting room, TV
Charles Robinson	C-yes/S-no/P-no/H-no	garden, large tiled pool
All year		spa, barbecue area

Spacious, soundproof rooms with oak floors, area carpets, brass beds, 10' ceilings, A/C, lanais (decks), fridges. 1 block from the beach. **Special gourmet package rates**

LAWAI, KAUAI

Victoria Place B&B $$ B&B Continental plus
P.O. Box 930, 96765 4 rooms, 4 pb Lunch & dinner nearby
3459 Lawai Loa Ln. • Large library, pool
808-332-9300 C-ltd/S-no/H-yes lanai overlooking mtns.
Edee Seymour beach mats, snorkel gear
All year

Jungle & ocean views-all rooms open to pool-near beaches, golf course, tennis. We pamper: flowers, homemade muffins, popcorn machine, fridge, microwave at poolside, & aloha.

MAUI, HANA

Kaia Ranch Tropical Garden $$ B&B Continental breakfast
P.O. Box 404, 96713 1 rooms, 1 pb Studios w/bath & kitchen
Ulaino Rd. *Rated*, • Sitting room, library
808-248-7725 C-ltd/S-no/P-no/H-no walk & picnic in flower
JoLoyce & John Kaia & fruit gardens
All year

*Duplex w/2 studios. A country farm. The real Hawaii which few see. Animals, gardens, and friends you'll never forget. Hana is a unique experience. **3rd night 50% off***

PRINCEVILLE, KAUAI

Hale 'Aha $$$ B&B Continental plus
P.O. Box 3370, 96733 4 rooms, 4 pb Many restaurants nearby
3875 Kamehameha *Rated*, • Library, hot tubs
808-826-6733 800-826-6733 C-ltd/S-no/P-no/H-no decks on golf course
Herb & Ruth Bockelman tennis/pool nearby
All year, Fax: 826-9052

*Peaceful resort area w/ocean, mountains, waterfalls, lush hiking trails, hidden beaches, rivers. Plus helicopters, snorkeling, boating & shopping. **Golf, tennis, club disc'ts***

VOLCANO

Kilauea Lodge & Restaurant $$$ B&B Full breakfast
P.O. Box 116, 96785 12 rooms, 12 pb Dinner
Old Volcano Rd Visa, MC, *Rated*, Restaurant, full bar
808-967-7366 FAX:967-7367 C-yes/S-no/P-no, German sitting room
Loma & Albert Jeyte Volcanoes National Park
All year

Mountain lodge with full service restaurant. 6 rooms with fireplace. One mile from spectacular Volcanoes National Park. 28 miles from Hilo. Helicopters and golf nearby.

Lokahi Lodge B&B $$ B&B Continental plus
P.O. Box 7, 96785 4 rooms, 4 pb Afternoon tea
19-450 Kalanikoa Rd. Visa, MC, *Rated*, • Bicycles, sitting room
808-985-8647 800-457-6924 C-yes/S-ltd/P-yes/H-yes wrap-around veranda
P. Dickson, D. deCastro extra long double beds
All year

*Charming, plantation-style home amidst a lush 'ohia forest. Close to Volcanoes National Park and golf course. Truly peaceful, enchanting haven! **10% off for senior citizens***

More Inns ...

Alohaland Guest House, 98-1003 Oliwa St., Aiea, 96701, 808-487-0482
Volcano Heart Chalet, P.O. Box 404, Big Island, 96713, 808-248-7725
Adriennes B&B Paradise, RR 1, Box 8E, Captain Cook, 96704, 808-328-9726
Manago Hotel, Box 145, Captain Cook, 96704, 808-323-2642
Halfway to Hana House, P.O. Box 675, Haiku (Huelo), Maui, 96708, 808-572-1176
Haikuleana B&B Plantation, 555 Haiku Rd., Haiku, Maui, 96708, 808-575-2890
Hamakualoa Tea House, P.O. Box 335, Haiku, Maui, 96708

Heavenly Hana Inn, P.O. Box 146, Hana, Maui, 96713, 808-248-8442
Aha Hui Hawaiian, Box 10, Hawi, 96719, 808-889-5523
Arnott's Lodge, 98 Apapane Rd., Hilo, 96720, 808-969-7097
Holualoa Inn, P.O. Box 222-C, Holualoa, 96725
B&B Waikiki Beach, P.O. Box 89080, Honolulu, 96830, 808-923-5459
John Guild Inn, 2001 Vancouver Dr., Honolulu, 96822, 808-947-6019
Kahala Hibiscus Inn, 1030 Kealaolu Ave., Honolulu, 96816, 808-732-5889
Hale Plumeria B&B, 3044 Hollinger St., Honolulu, Oahu, 96815, 808-732-7719
Manoa Valley Inn, 2001 Vancouver Dr., Honolulu, Oahu, 96822, 808-947-6019
Hale Pau Kala, 33 Kalaka Pl., Kailua, 96734, 808-261-3098
Homer & Mahina Maxey B&B, 1277 Mokulua Dr., Kailua, 96734, 808-261-1059
Sheffield House B&B, 131 Kuulei Rd., Kailua, 96734, 808-262-0721
Pacific-Hawaii B&B, 19 Kai Nani Pl., Kailua, Oahu, 96734, 808-263-4848
Papaya Paradise B&B, 395 Auwinala Rd., Kailua, Oahu, 96734, 808-261-0316
Hale' Maluhia B&B, 76-770 Hualalai Rd., Kailua-Kona, 96740, 808-329-1123
Kailua Plantation House, 75-5948 Alii Dr., Kailua-Kona, 96740, 808-329-3721
Hale Kipa O Kiana, RR 2, Box 4874, Kalapana Shores, 96778, 808-965-8661
Hawaii's Best B&Bs, P.O. Box 563, Kamuela, 96743, 808-885-4550
Paradise Inn B&B, 4540 Fernandes Rd., Kapaa, 96746, 808-822-4104
Lampy's B&B, 6078 Kolopua St., Kapaa Kauai, 96746, 808-822-0478
Keapana B&B, 5620 Keapana Rd., Kapaa, Kauai, 96746, 800-822-7968
Randy Rosario, 6470 Kawaihau Rd., Kapaa, Kauai, 96746, 808-822-1902
Kamalo Plantation, Star Route, Box 128, Kaunakakai, 96748, 808-558-8236
Pau Hana Inn, P.O. Box 546, Kaunakakai, Molokai, 96748, 800-367-8047
Paradise Place, HCR 9558, Keaau, 96749, 808-966-4600
Hale Honua Ranch, P.O. Box 347, Kealakekua, 96750, 808-328-8282
Merryman's, P.O. Box 474, Kealakekua, 96750, 808-323-2276
Whaler's Way B&B, 541 Kupulau Dr, Kihei, Maui, 96753, 808-879-7984
Mahi Ko Inn, General Delivery, Kilauea, 96754, 800-458-3444
Halemanu, P.O. Box 72, Koloa, Kaui, 96756
Hamakua Hideaway, P.O. Box 5104, Kukuihaele, 96727, 808-775-7425
Kula Lodge, RR 1 Box 475, Kula, Maui, 96790, 808-878-2517
Haleakala B&B, 41 Manienie Rd., Makawao, Maui, 96768, 808-572-7988
Nutt House, The, P.O. Box 852, Na'alehu, 96772, 808-929-9940
Coconut Inn, 181 Hui Rd. "F", Napili, Maui, 96761, 808-669-5712
Kalani Honua, Box 4500, Ocean Hwy 137, Pahoa, 96778, 808-965-7828
Oloha B &B, 13-3591 Luana St., Pahoa, 96778, 808-965-9898
Carson's Volcano Cottage, P.O. Box 503, Volcano, 96785, 808-967-7683
Guesthouse at Volcano, P.O. Box 6, Volcano, 96785, 808-967-7775
My Island B&B, P.O. Box 100, Volcano, 96785, 808-967-7110
Fern Grotto Inn, 4561 Kuamoo Rd, Wailua, Kauai, 96746, 808-822-2560

Idaho

COEUR D'ALENE

Greenbriar B&B Inn	$$ B&B	Full 3-course breakfast
315 Wallace, 83814	9 rooms, 7 pb	Gourmet dining by resv.
208-667-9660	Visa, MC, AmEx, *Rated*,	Comp. wine, catering
Kris & Bob McIlvenna	•	library, hot tub
All year	C-ltd/S-no/P-no/H-no	tandem bikes, canoes
	French	

Coeur d'Alene's only historic residence, 4 blocks from lakefront, shopping area. Gourmet cuisine, antiques, down comforters. European-style country inn. **10% off 2 nights**

Warwick Inn B&B	$$$ B&B	Full breakfast
303 Military Dr., 83814	3 rooms, 1 pb	Comp. wine
208-765-6565	Visa, MC, AmEx, •	Sitting room, library
Bonnie Warwick	C-ltd/S-no/P-no/H-no	sports at nearby lake
All year		lake cruising

Nestled among ancient pines in the Old Fort Sherman Grounds—quiet and relaxing. Just steps to Lake Coeur d'Alene—and everything else in town. Small but discriminating.

IRWIN

McBride's B&B Guesthouse $ B&B Full country breakfast
P.O. Box 166, 83428 1 rooms, 1 pb Comp. wine
102 Valley Dr. Visa, MC, • Beautiful yard, grill
208-483-4221 C-yes/S-yes/P-yes maid service daily
Deanna & Craig McBride hiking, fishing, hunting
All year

Private guest house in a high mountain valley. Year-round sportsman's paradise with easy access to Snake River, Tetons, Yellowstone Park. **4th night 50% off.**

KOOSKIA

Three Rivers Resort $ B&B Continental breakfast
HC 75, Box 61, 83539 15 rooms, 15 pb Restaurant - lunch
208-926-4430 Visa, MC, AmEx, Disc., • Dinner, aft. tea
Mike & Marie Smith C-yes/S-yes/P-yes/H-no sitting room, bicycles
All year hot tubs, swimming pool

In the heart of the Idaho wilderness, 70-year old log cabin, fireplace, jacuzzi, private getaway overlooking three wild rivers. Float trips available.

LACLEDE

River Birch Farm B&B $$$ B&B Full breakfast
P.O. Box 0280, 83841 6 rooms, 1 pb Bicycles, hot tubs
208-263-3705 Visa, MC, *Rated*, • lake swimming, sitt. rm.
Charley & Barbro Johnson C-ltd/S-no/P-no/H-no near ski resort, library
All year Swedish

Fish, swim, canoe, hike or ski. Then relax with a refreshing drink and watch the sunset from our spacious hot tub. **Discounts: 5%-3 days, 10%-5 days, 15%-7 days**

LEWISTON

Carriage House B&B $$ B&B Full breakfast
611 - 5th St., 83501 2 rooms, 2 pb Refreshments, seltzers
208-746-4506 Visa, MC Snacks, gift shop
Chuck & Nancy Huff C-ltd/S-no/P-no/H-no indoor spa, bicycles
All year private courtyard

European country guest house; historical neighborhood; tastefully appointed w/antiques; elegant suites; sumptuous breakfasts; near Snake River and Scenic Hells Canyon Tours.

MOSCOW

Beau's Butte B&B $$ B&B Full breakfast
702 Public Ave., 83843 2 rooms, 1 pb Comp. beverage, snacks
208-882-4061 Visa, MC, *Rated*, Sitting room
Joyce & Duane Parr C-ltd/S-no/P-no/H-no fireplace, sun room
All year hot tub, TV, VCR

Tranquil country setting, convenient to university. Locally crafted country decor; fantastic views; scrumptious breakfasts.

SHOUP

Smith House B&B $ B&B Continental plus
49 Salmon River Rd., 83469 5 rooms, 1 pb Comp. wine & snacks
208-394-2121 800-238-5915 Visa, MC, Disc., • Sitting room, library
Aubrey & Marsha Smith C-yes/S-no/P-yes/H-no hot tub, organ
March 15 to November 30 gift shop, float trips

Rustic, country setting with all the comforts of home. Enjoy sightseeing, hunting, hiking or just relaxing. Delicious breakfasts! **3rd nigth 50% off**

Smith House B&B, Shoup, ID

ST. ANTHONY

Riverview B&B
155 South 3rd East, 83445
208-624-4323
Donna Clark
All year

$ B&B
4 rooms, 4 pb
Visa, MC, AmEx, *Rated*,
C-ltd/S-no/P-no/H-yes

Full breakfast
Fishing
National Park
sitting room

Along the Snake River in beautiful St. Anthony. Gorgeous riverview front with fishing available. Close to Yellowstone & Teton Parks. Full breakfast viewing waterfront.

STANLEY

Idaho Rocky Mtn. Ranch
HC 64, Box 9934, Hwy 75, 9
miles-Stanley, 83278
208-774-3544
Bill & Jeana Leavell
June–Sept, Nov–April

$$ B&B
21 rooms, 21 pb
Visa, MC, *Rated*,
C-yes/S-no/P-no/H-no
Spanish

Full breakfast
Picnic lunch, dinner
Restaurant, beer & wine
library, horses
natural hot springs pool

Historic log lodge and cabins; spectacular mountain scenery; gourmet dining in rustic atmosphere; extensive outdoor activities, natural hot springs pool. Weekly rates.

SUN VALLEY–KETCHUM

Idaho Country Inn
P.O. Box 2355, 83353
134 Latigo Lane
208-726-1019
Terry & Julie Heneghan
All year

$$$ B&B
10 rooms, 10 pb
Visa, MC, AmEx, *Rated*,
•
C-ltd/S-no/P-no/H-no

Full breakfast
Comp. wine, snacks
Sitting room, patio
library, sun room, deck
large outdoor hot tub

Rooms reflect the history of Idaho. Wonderful mountain views, log beams, Riverock fireplace, gourmet breakfast in sun room, modern amenities. World-famous Sun Valley.

More Inns ...

Idaho Heritage Inn, 109 W. Idaho, Boise, 83702, 208-342-8066
Littletree Inn, 2717 Vista Ave., Boise, 83703
Sunrise, 2730 Sunrise Rim Rd., Boise, 83705, 208-345-5260
Victoria's White House, 10325 W. Victory Rd., Boise, 83709
Manning House B&B Inn, 1803 S. 10th Ave., Caldwell, 83606
Triple T Ranch, HC 83 & 85, Cascade, 83611

Wapati Meadow Ranch, HC 72, Johnson Creek Rd, Cascade, 83611
Blackwell House, 820 Sherman Ave., Coeur d'Alene, 83814, 208-664-0656
Coeur d'Alene B&B, 906 Foster Ave., Coeur d'Alene, 83814, 208-667-7527
Cricket on the Hearth, 1521 Lakeside Ave., Coeur d'Alene, 83814, 208-664-6926
Gables, The, 916 Foster Ave., Coeur d'Alene, 83814, 208-664-5121
Gregory's McFarland House, 601 Foster Ave., Coeur d'Alene, 83814, 208-667-1232
Inn the First Place, 509 N. 15th St., Coeur d'Alene, 83814, 208-667-3346
Katie's Wild Rose Inn, 1018 Front Ave., Coeur d'Alene, 83814
Sleeping Place of Wheels, P.O. Box 5273, Coeur d'Alene, 83814
Old Heartland Farm, P.O. Box 32, Council, 83612
Tulip House, 403 S. Florence St., Grangeville, 83530, 208-983-1034
Comfort Inn, Box 984, Hailey, 83333, 208-788-2477
Ellsworth Inn, 715 3rd Ave. S., Hailey, 83333, 208-788-2298
MaryAnne's, HCR 1, Box 43E, Harrison, 83833, 208-245-2537
Peg's B&B Place, P.O. Box 144, Harrison, 83833, 208-689-3525
Riverside B&B, Highway 55, Horseshoe Bend, 83629, 208-793-2408
Idaho City Hotel, P.O. Box 70, Idaho City, 83631, 208-392-4290
Indian Valley Inn, P.O. Box 54, Indian Valley, 83632
Montgomery Inn B&B, 305 S. Division, Kellogg, 83837
Busterback Ranch, Star Rt., Ketchum, 83340, 208-774-2217
Lift Haven Inn, Box 21, 100 Lloyd Dr., Ketchum, 83340, 208-726-5601
Powderhorn Lodge, Box 3970, Ketchum, 83340, 208-726-3107
River Street Inn, P.O. Box 182, Sun Vlly, Ketchum, 83353, 208-726-3611
Looking Glass Guest Ranch, HC-75, Box 32, Kooskia, 83539, 208-926-0855
Riverside Inn B&B, 255 Portneuf Ave., Lava Hot Springs, 83246, 208-776-5504
Royal Hotel, 4 E. Main St., Lava Hot Springs, 83246
Harpers Bend River Inn, Rt. 2, Box 7A, Lenore, 83541, 208-486-6666
Bunkhouse, The, 1211 Brideton #481, Lewiston, 83501
Price & Company, 2720 - 6th St., Lewiston, 83501
Sheep Creek Ranch, 717 - 3rd St., Lewiston, 83501, 800-248-1045
Shiloh Rose, 3414 Selway Dr., Lewiston, 83501, 208-743-2482
Hotel McCall, 1101 N. Third St., McCall, 83638, 208-634-8105
Northwest Passage B&B, Box 4208, McCall, 83638, 208-634-5349
Home Place, 415 W Lake Hazel Rd., Meridian, 83642, 208-888-3857
Cottage B&B, The, 318 N. Hayes, Moscow, 83843, 208-882-0778
Peacock Hill, 1245 Joyce Rd., Moscow, 83843, 208-882-1423
Twin Peaks Inn, 2455 W. Twin Rd., Moscow, 83843, 208-882-3898
Van Buren House, The, 220 N. Van Buren, Moscow, 83843, 208-882-8531
Hartland Inn, P.O. Box 215, New Meadows, 83654
Cummings Lake Lodge, Box 810, North Fork, 83466
Indian Creek Guest Ranch, HC 64 Box 105, North Fork, 83466, 208-394-2126
Hillcrest House, 210 Hillcrest Dr., Pinehurst, 83850, 208-682-3911
Bonnie's B&B, Box 258, Plummer, 83851, 208-686-1165
Owl Chalet, Route 1, Box 96A, Plummer, 83851
Rolling Hills B&B, Rt. 1, Box 157, Potlatch, 83855, 208-668-1126
Linger Longer, Route 5, Box 203C, Priest River, 83856
Osprey Nest, The, Rt. 1, Box 105, Priest River, 83856
Lodge B&B, P.O. Box 498, Riggins, 83549
Knoll Hus, P.O. Box 572, Saint Maries, 83861, 208-245-4137
Old McFarland Inn, 227 S. First Ave., Sandpoint, 83864, 208-265-0260
Osprey Cove B&B, 8680 Sunnyside Rd., Sandpoint, 83864, 208-265-4200
Priest Lake B&B, Route 5, Box 150-2A, Sandpoint, 83864
Whitaker House, 410 Railroad Ave, #10, Sandpoint, 83864, 208-263-0816
Loon Cottage Inn, P.O. Box 183, Spirit Lake, 83869
Riverview B&B, 155 E. 3rd So., St. Anthony, 83445
McGowan's Resort, Stanley
Redfish Lake Lodge, P.O. Box 9, Stanley, 83278, 208-774-3536
River Street Inn, P.O. Box 182, Sun Valley, 83353, 208-726-3611
Jameson B&B, 304 Sixth St., Wallace, 83873, 208-556-1554
Pine Tree Inn, 177 King St., Box 1023, Wallace, 83873, 208-752-4391
Bitterroot Mountain Inn, 403 Main St., Wardner, 83837, 208-786-1771
Yellow Pine Lodge, P.O. Box 77, Yellow Pine, 83677

Illinois

CARLYLE

Country Haus B&B	$ B&B	Full breakfast
1191 Franklin, 62231	4 rooms, 4 pb	Evening snacks
618-594-8313 800-279-4486	Visa, MC, AmEx, *Rated*,	Sitting room with TV
Ron & Vickie Cook	C-yes/S-no/P-no/H-no	library, hot tubs
All year		prvt. jacuzzi deck

Informal country hospitality. 1890's Eastlake home. Family-style brkfast. 1 mi. from Carlyle Lake. Chosen for 1994 Olympic Festival sailing. **3rd night 50% off**

CHAMPAIGN ───────────────────────────────────────

Golds B&B, The $ B&B   Continental plus
2065 Cty Rd. 525E, 61821   3 rooms, 1 pb
217-586-4345   *Rated*, •
Rita & Bob Gold   C-yes/S-no/P-no/H-no
All year

Country charm & hospitality in 1874 farmhouse. Handy to interstate & university attractions. Furnished with antiques. Quiet & peaceful.

EVANSTON ───────────────────────────────────────

Homestead, The $$ EP   Comp. coffee
1625 Hinman Ave., 60201   35 rooms, 35 pb   French restaurant
708-475-3300 FAX:570-8100 Visa, MC
David T. Reynolds   C-yes/S-yes/P-no/H-ltd
All year

Historic residential neighborhood; two blocks from Lake Michigan & Northwestern Univ.; 30 minutes from downtown Chicago by car or rail; French restaurant serves dinner.

Margarita European Inn $ B&B   Continental plus
1566 Oak Ave., 60201   32 rooms, 16 pb   Restaurant/lunch, dinner
708-869-2273   Most CC, *Rated*, •   Aft. tea
Barbara & Tim Gorham   C-yes/S-yes/P-no/H-yes sitting room, library
All year   Spanish, some French

Relax to afternoon tea in our Georgian parlor room; snuggle up to a book in our wood-panelled English library.

GALENA ───────────────────────────────────────

Aldrich Guest House $$ B&B   Full breakfast
900 Third St., 61036   5 rooms, 3 pb   Comp. beverages
815-777-3323   Visa, MC, *Rated*,   Sitting room w/fireplace
Sandra & Herb Larson   C-ltd/S-no/P-no/H-no   piano, screened porch
All year   Video/TV in library

Elegant Greek Revival furnished w/fine antiques. Breakfast in dining room or screened porch served formally yet unfussily. Central A/C. **2nd night 25% off midwk**

Country Gardens $$ B&B   Continental plus
Guesthouse   3 rooms, 3 pb   Sitting room w/fireplace
1000 Third St., 61036   Visa, MC   front porch, golf, skii
815-777-3062   C-ltd/S-ltd/P-no/H-no   biking nearby
Sandy & Dave Miller
All year

Riverfront town, home of Ulysses S. Grant. 1856 guest house. Stroll to downtown antique shops. Quilts, country breakfasts. 2 night minimum weekends. **Mdwk & winter discounts**

Goldmoor, The $$$ B&B   Full breakfast
9001 Sand Hill Rd., 61036   6 rooms, 6 pb   Comp. wine
815-777-3925 800-255-3925 Most CC, *Rated*, •   Library, bicycles
James C. Goldthorpe   C-yes/S-ltd/P-ltd/H-yes hot tubs, sauna
All year   TV/VCR, sitting room

Elegant country estate overlooking the Mississippi w/custom decorated suites. Large, 2 person whirlpools & fireplaces. Specialize in Honeymoon, Anniversary packages.

Park Avenue Guest House, Galena, IL

GALENA

Park Avenue Guest House	$$ B&B	Continental plus
208 Park Ave., 61036	4 rooms, 4 pb	Aft. tea, snacks
815-777-1075	Visa, MC, Disc.*Rated*,	Sitting room w/TV
Sharon & John Fallbacher	C-ltd/S-no/P-no/H-no	2 parlours, gazebo, A/C
All year		wrap-around porch

Elegant yet comfortable, located in quiet residential area. Short walk to beautiful Grant Park, Galena River and Main Street shopping and restaurants. **$10 off midwk**

Pine Hollow Inn B&B	$$$ B&B	Continental plus
4700 N. Council Hill Rd, 61036	5 rooms, 5 pb	Comp. wine, snacks
815-777-1071	Visa, MC, *Rated*, •	Afternoon tea
Sally & Larry Priske	C-ltd/S-no/P-no/H-no	cross-country skiing
All year		whirlpool bath

A secluded country inn, surrounded by hundreds of wooded acres. Nestle in front of your own cozy fireplaces. **20% off 2nd night, ltd.**

GENEVA

Oscar Swan Country Inn	$$$ B&B	Full breakfast
1800 W. State St., 60134	7 rooms, 4 pb	Comp. snacks & beverages
708-232-0173	Visa, MC, *Rated*, •	Sitting room, library
Hans & Nina Heymann	C-yes/S-no/P-no/H-no	tennis courts, pool
All year	German	cross-country skiing on 7
		acres

Country hideaway on 7 private acres. Fireplaces, cozy kitchen, hearty breakfast, wonderful River Town, antiques, bike paths. The New England of the Midwest. **3rd night 50% off**

LANARK

Standish House B&B
540 W. Carroll St., 61046
815-493-2307 800-468-2307
Eve Engles
All year

$$ B&B
5 rooms, 1 pb
Visa, MC, *Rated*,
C-ltd/S-no/P-no/H-no

Full breakfast
Restaurants nearby
Sitting room
wildflower gardens
queen-size canopied beds

English antiques, full canopy beds and fine arts. Relaxing country atmosphere within walking distance of business district. Air conditioned.

MAEYSTOWN

Corner George Inn
P.O. Box 103, 62256
1101 Main
800-458-6020
David & Marcia Braswell
All year

$$ B&B
7 rooms, 5 pb
Visa, MC, *Rated*, •
C-ltd/S-no/P-no/H-yes
German

Full breakfast
Aft. tea, restaurant
Sitting room, library
bicycles, bakery, store
horse-drawn carriage

Restored 1880's elegance in historic 19th-century German village, 45 min. south/St. Louis, 45 min. via ferry to Ste. Genevieve.

MORRISON

Hillendale B&B
600 Lincolnway West, 61270
815-772-3454
Barb Winandy
All year

$ B&B
5 rooms, 5 pb
Visa, MC, *Rated*,
C-ltd/S-no/P-no/H-no

Full breakfast
Sitting room

Travel the world in rural America in our international theme rooms. Relax in the Japanese Teahouse while viewing the water gardens with its fish.

ROCK ISLAND

Potter House, The
1906i- 7 Ave., 61201
309-788-1906 800-747-0339
Gary & Nancy Pheiffer
All year

$$ B&B
5 rooms, 5 pb
Most CC, *Rated*, •
C-ltd

Full breakfast
Dinner-theatre nearby
Restaurants nearby
comp. wine, tea, soda
cable TV, phones in room

National Register Colonial Revival c.1907. 7 blocks to Miss. Casino Boats. Stained glass, antiques, player piano. Walking tours of historic Broadway. **Free pass to Casino boat**

Top O' The Morning B&B
1505 - 19th Ave., 61201
309-786-3513
Sam & Peggy Doak
All year

$$ B&B
3 rooms, 3 pb
Rated
C-yes/S-ltd/P-no/H-no

Full breakfast
Piano, tennis nearby
hot tub, sitting room
A/C in all bedrooms

Brick mansion on 3.5 acres in the center of town. Large porch, grand piano, formal dining. Irish hospitality. Champagne, flowers & breakfast in bridal suite for honeymoons.

URBANA

Shurts House B&B
710 W. Oregon St., 61801
217-367-8793 800-339-4156
Bruce & Denni Shurts
All year

$$ B&B
5 rooms, 2 pb
Visa, MC, AmEx, •
C-yes/S-ltd/P-no/H-no
Some Portugese & Span.

Full breakfast
Aft. tea, snacks
Sitting room, library
tandum bikes, pool table
big screen Nintendo

Friendly, fun, comfortable, clean. Each stay with us is special. Rooms are cozy, warm and pretty. Filled w/collections sure to delight. **Special disc'ts., desserts**

WHEATON

Wheaton Inn, The
301 W. Roosevelt Rd., 60187
708-690-2600
Linda Matzen
All year

$$$ B&B
16 rooms, 16 pb
Most CC, *Rated*, •
C-yes/S-yes/P-ask

Full breakfast
Bar Service (some)
Comp. wine, snacks
sitting room, library
near golf, tennis, etc.

Elegant but homey atmosphere in the Williamsburg tradition, 10 rooms with fireplaces, 6 with whirlpools. Weekend getaways or corporate traveler's delight.

WINNETKA

Chateau des Fleurs
552 Ridge Rd., 60093
708-256-7272
Sally H. Ward
All year

$$$ B&B
3 rooms, 3 pb
Rated, •
C-ltd/S-no/P-no/H-no

Full breakfast
Afternoon tea, snacks
Grand piano, 50" TV
VCR with movies, bikes
jacuzzis in 2 rms, pool

Beautiful French country home furnished in rare antiques. Lovely views of magnificent trees, English gardens. Near train & private road for walking/jogging. 2 night minimum.

More Inns . . .

Haagen House B&B, 617 State St., Alton, 62002, 618-462-2419
Goddard Place, The, RR 2, P.O. Box 445G, Anna, 62906, 618-833-6256
Curly's Corner, RR 2, Box 590, Arcola, 61910, 217-268-3352
Flower Patch, The, 225 E. Jefferson, Arcola, 61910, 217-268-4876
Favorite Brother Inn, The, 106 E. Columbia, Arthur, 61911, 217-543-2938
Harshbarger Homestead, RR 1, P.O. Box 110, Atwood, 61913, 217-578-2265
Nostalgia Corner, 115 W. 7th, Beardstown, 62618, 217-323-5382
Enchanted Crest, RR 1, P.O. Box 216, Belle Rive, 62810, 618-736-2647
Holden's Guest House, East Main St., Bishop Hill, 61419, 309-927-3500
Windham, 2606 Washington Ave., Cairo, 62914, 618-734-3247
Wright Farmhouse, RR 3, Carthage, 62321, 217-357-2421
Alice's Place, 1915 Winchester, Champaign, 61821, 217-359-3332
Barb's B&B, 606 S. Russell, Champaign, 61821, 217-356-0376
Davidson Place B&B, 1110 Davidson Dr., Champaign, 61820, 217-356-5915
Glads B&B, The, RR 3, Box 69, Champaign, 61821, 217-586-4345
Grandma Joan's B&B, 2204 Brett Dr., Champaign, 61820, 217-356-5828
Charleston B&B, 814 4th St., Charleston, 61920, 217-345-6463
Betsy's Sugar Wood, 217 E. Buena Vista, Chester, 62233, 618-826-2555
B&B Lincoln Park, 2022 N. Sheffield, Chicago, 60614, 312-327-6546
Hyde Park House, 5210 S. Kenwood, Chicago, 60615, 312-363-4595
Robert Ford, 1860 N. Maud, Chicago, 60614
Maggie's Bed & Breakfast, 2102 North Keebler Rd., Collinsville, 62234, 618-344-8283
1850's Guest House, RR 1, P.O. Box 267, Dallas City, 62330, 217-852-3652
Hamilton House B&B Inn, 500 W. Main St., Decatur, 62522, 217-429-1669
River View Guest House, 507 E. Everett, Dixon, 61021, 815-288-5974
Timbers, The, P.O. Box 339, Dixon Springs, 62330, 618-683-4400
Francie's, 104 S. Line St., Du Quoin, 62832, 618-542-6686
Eagle's Nest, 11125 N. Trigger Rd., Dunlap, 61525, 309-243-7376
La Petite Voyageur B&B, 116 E. South St., Dwight, 60420, 815-584-2239
Hobson's Bluffdale, Eldred-Hillview Rd, Eldred, 62027, 217-983-2854
Locker Knoll Inn, 8833 S. Massbach Rd., Elizabeth, 61028, 815-598-3150
Ridgeview B&B, 8833 S. Massbach Rd., Elizabeth, 61028, 815-598-3150
River Rose Inn, 1 Main St., Elizabeth Town, 62931, 618-287-8811
Corner Nest B&B, P.O. Box 22, Elsah, 62028, 618-374-1892
Green Tree Inn, P.O. Box 96, Elsah, 62028, 618-374-2821
Maple Leaf Cottage B&B, P.O. Box 156, Elsah, 62028
Charles & Barbara Pollard, 2633 Poplar, Evanston, 60201, 312-328-6162
Margarita European Inn, 1566 Oak Ave., Evanstone, 60201, 708-869-2273
Westerfield House, The, RR #2, Box 34, Freeburg, 62243, 618-539-5643
Avery Guest House B&B, 606 S. Prospect St., Galena, 61036, 815-777-3883
Bedford House, Route 20 West, Galena, 61036, 815-777-2043
Belle Aire Mansion, 11410 Route 20 West, Galena, 61036, 815-777-0893
Brierwreath Manor, 216 N. Beach St., Galena, 61036, 815-777-0608
Captain Gear Guest House, 1000 S. Bench St., Galena, 61036, 815-777-0222

The Corner George Inn, Maeystown, IL

Captain Harris Guest Cott., 713 S. Bench St., Galena, 61036
Chestnut Mountain Resort, 8700 W. Chestnut Rd., Galena, 61036, 800-435-2914
De Soto House Hotel, 230 S. Main St., Galena, 61036
DeZoya House, 1203 Third St., Galena, 61036, 815-777-1203
Farmers Home Hotel, 334 Spring St., Galena, 61036
Farster's Executive Inn, 305 N. Main St., Galena, 815-777-9125
Felt Manor Guest House, 125 S. Prospect St., Galena, 61036, 800-383-2830
Gallery Guest Suite, 204-1/2 South Main St, Galena, 61036, 815-777-1222
Grandview Guest Home, 113 S. Prospect St., Galena, 61036, 815-777-1387
Hellman Guest House, 318 Hill St., Galena, 61036, 815-777-3638
Main St. Inn, 404 S. Main St., Galena, 61036, 815-777-3454
Mother's Country Inn, 349 Spring St., Galena, 61036, 815-777-3153
Pat's Country Guest Home, 5148 Hwy. 20 W., Galena, 61036, 815-777-1030
Queen Anne Guest House, 200 Park Ave., Galena, 61036, 815-777-3849
Robert Scribe Harris House, 713 S. Bench St., Galena, 61036, 815-777-1611
Ryan Mansion Inn, Route 20 West, Galena, 61036, 815-777-2043
Stillman's Country Inn, 513 Bouthillier, Galena, 61036, 815-777-0557
Stillwaters Country Inn, 7213 W. Buckhill Rd., Galena, 61036, 312-528-6313
Tripp's Country Home, 1000 Saddleback Rd., Galena, 61036, 312-764-8708
Victorian Mansion, 301 High St., Galena, 61036, 815-777-0675

Shurts House, Urbana, IL

Seacord House, 624 N. Cherry St., Galesburg, 61401, 309-342-4107
Stolz Home, RR 2, Box 27, Gibson City, 60936, 217-784-4502
Mansion of Golconda, P.O. Box 339, Golconda, 62938, 618-683-4400
Brick House B&B, P.O. Box 301, Goodfield, 61742, 309-965-2545
Nancy Kirkpatrick Guest, 210 W. Main, Grafton, 62037, 618-374-2821
Shafer Wharf Inn, 220 W. Main, Grafton, 62037, 618-374-2821
Wildflower Inn B&B, P.O. Box 31, Grafton, 62037, 618-465-3719
Colonial Inn, Rock & Green Sts., Grand Detour, 61021, 815-652-4422
Bennett Curtis House, 302 W. Taylor, Grant Park, 60940, 815-465-6025
Prairie House Country Inn, RR 4, P.O. Box 47AA, Greenville, 62246, 618-664-3003
Sweet Basil Hill Farm, 15937 W. Washington St., Gurnee, 60031, 708-244-3333
McNutt Guest House, 409 W. Main St., Havana, 62644, 309-543-3295
Red Rooster Inn, 123 E. Seward St., Hillsboro, 62049
Croaking Frog, The, 12618 W. Hensel Rd., Huntley, 60142, 708-669-1555
Norma's B&B, 429 So. Fourth Ave., Kankakee, 60901
Bishop's Inn B&B, 223 W. Central Blvd., Kewanee, 61443, 309-852-5201
Woodside B&B, P.O. Box 101, Lawrenceville, 62439, 618-943-2147
Sugar Maple Inn, 607 Maple, Lena, 61048, 815-369-2786
Brockway House, The, 331 E. Carroll, Macomb, 61455, 309-837-2375
Annie Tique's Hotel, 378 Main St., Marseilles, 61341, 815-795-5848
Elizabeth's B&B, 1100 5th St., Mendota, 61342, 815-539-5555
Lord Stocking's, 803 3rd Ave., Mendota, 61342, 815-539-7905
Suprenaut B&B, 304 W. Second St., Momenca, 60954, 815-472-3156
Carr Mansion Guest House, 416 E. Broadway, Monmouth, 61462, 309-734-3654
Linda's Country Loft B&B, R.R.1, Box 198A, Monticello, 61856, 217-762-7316
Old Church House Inn, 1416 E. Mossvill Rd., Mossville/Peoria, 61552, 309-579-2300
Dorsey's B&B, 318 North Belmont, Mount Pulaski, 62548
Living Legacy Homestead, P.O. Box 146A, Mt. Carmel, 62863, 618-298-2476
Farm, The, RR 1, P.O. Box 112, Mt. Carroll, 61053, 815-244-9885
Prairie Path Guest House, RR 3, P.O. Box 223, Mt. Carroll, 61053, 815-244-3462
Kable House, Sunset Hill, Mt. Morris, 61054, 815-734-7297
Round-Robin Guesthouse, 231 East Maple Ave., Mundelein, 60060, 312-566-7664
Die Blaue Gaus, 95265 Route 59, Naperville, 60565, 312-355-0835
Harrison House B&B, 25 W 135 Essex Ave., Naperville, 60540, 708-420-1117
Mill Creek Inn B&B, 504 N. Mill, Nashville, 62263, 618-327-8424
Hotel Nauvoo, Route 96, Town Center, Nauvoo, 62354, 217-453-2211
Mississippi Memories B&B, Box 291, Riverview Hght, Nauvoo, 62354, 217-453-2771
Parley Lane B&B, Route 1, Box 220, Nauvoo, 62354, 217-453-2277
Cheney House, 520 N. E. Ave., Oak Park, 60302, 708-524-2067
Toad Hall, 301 N. Scoville Ave., Oak Park, 60302, 708-386-8623
Under The Ginkgo Tree, 300 N. Kenilworth Ave., Oak Park, 60302, 708-524-2327
Inn-on-the-Square, 3 Montgomery St., Oakland, 61943, 217-346-2289
Johnson's Country Home B&B, 109 E. Main St., Oakland, 61943, 217-346-3274
Welcome Inn, 506 W. Main St., Oblong, 62449, 618-592-3301

Bit of Country B&B, 122 W. Sheridan, Peoria, 61615, 217-632-3771
Ruth's B&B, 1506 W. Alta Rd., Peoria, 61615, 309-243-5971
Carmody's Clare Inn, 207 S. 12th St., Petersburg, 62675, 217-632-2350
Oxbow B&B, Rt. 1, P.O. Box 47, Pinckneyville, 62274, 618-357-9839
Pleasant Haven B&B, 201 E. Quincy, Box 51, Pleasant Hill, 62366, 217-734-9357
Plymouth Rock Resort, 201 W. Summer, Plymouth, 62367, 309-458-6444
Barber House Inn, 410 W. Mason, Polo, 61064, 815-946-2607
Olde Brick House, The, 502 No. High St., Port Byron, 61275, 309-523-3236
La Maison du Rocher Inn, 2 Duclos & Main, Prairie Du Rocher, 62277, 618-284-3463
Yesterday's Memories, 303 East Peru St., Princeton, 61359, 815-872-7753
Kaufmann House, The, 1641 Hampshire, Quincy, 62301, 217-223-5202
Better 'n Grandma's, 102 S. Meyers, Rantoul, 61866, 217-893-0469
Bertram Arms - B&B, RR #3, Box 243, Robinson, 62454, 618-546-1122
Heath Inn, The, P.O. Box 175, Robinson, 62454, 618-544-3410
Victorian Inn B&B, 702 - 20th St., Rock Island, 61201, 309-788-7068
Victoria's B&B, 201 N. Sixth St., Rockford, 61107, 815-963-3232
Stage Coach Inn, 41 W. 278 Whitney Rd., Saint Charles, 60174, 312-584-1263
Hill House, The, 503 S. Locust, Sesser, 62884, 618-625-6064
Corinne's B&B Inn, 1001 S. 6th St., Springfield, 62703, 217-527-1400
Mischler House, 718 South 8th St., Springfield, 62703, 217-523-5616
Maple Lane, 3115 Rush Creek Rd., Stockton, 61085, 815-947-3773
Dicus House B&B, 609 E. Broadway St., Streator, 61364, 815-672-6700
Little House OnThe Prairie, P.O. Box 525, Sullivan, 61951, 217-728-4727
Country Charm Inn, Rt. 2 Box 1, Sycamore, 60178
Stratford Inn, 355 W. State St., Sycamorc, 60178, 815-895-6789
Aunt Zelma's Country Guest, RR 1, Box 129, Tolono, 61880, 217-485-5101
Rockwell Victorian B&B, 404 N. Washington, Toulon, 61483, 309-286-5201
Jefferson House B&B, 305 W. Broadway, Trenton, 62293, 618-224-9733
Nonis Bed & Breakfast, 516 W. Main St., Warren, 61097
Hart of Wenona, 303 North Walnut, Wenona, 61377, 815-853-4778
Ironhedge Inn B&B, 305 Oregon, West Dundee, 60118, 708-426-7777
Thelma's Bed & Breakfast, 201 South Broadway, West Salem, 62476, 618-456-8401
Bundling Board Inn, 222 E. South St., Woodstock, 60098, 815-338-7054

Indiana

BEVERLY SHORES

Dunes Shore Inn
P.O. Box 807, 46301
33 Lakeshore County Rd.
219-879-9029
Rosemary & Fred Braun
All year

$ B&B
12 rooms
Visa, MC, *Rated*,
C-ltd/S-ltd/P-no/H-no
German

Continental plus
Fruit, cider & cookies
Library, sitting room
outdoor grill, tables
bicycles

Located one block from Lake Michigan and surrounded by the National Lakeshore and Dunes State Parks, this inn is an oasis for nature lovers. One hour from Chicago.

BLUFFTON

Wisteria Manor
411 W. Market St., 46714
219-824-4619
Bonnie Harris
All year

$ B&B
5 rooms, 4 pb
Visa, MC, •
C-ltd/S-no/P-no/H-yes

Full breakfast
Lunch, dinner
Aft. tea, snacks
sitting room, pool
meeting facility

*Century old Victorian mansion furnished in period furniture w/private garden & pool. Gracious hospitality and home-cooked meals. **3rd night 50% off***

CHESTERTON

Gray Goose Inn
350 Indian Boundary Rd., 46304
219-926-5781
Timothy Wilk
All year

$$$ B&B
5 rooms, 5 pb
Most CC, *Rated*, •
C-ltd/S-ltd/P-no/H-no

Full gourmet breakfast
Comp. beverages, snacks
Sitting room
telephone in rooms
bicycles, boats

In Dunes Country. English country house on private wooded lake. Charming guest rooms, private baths, fireplaces, gourmet breakfast. Near interstates. **2nd nite $10 off, Ltd**

CORYDON

Kinter House Inn
101 S. Capitol Ave., 47112
812-738-2020
Blaine Waterman
All year

$ B&B
15 rooms, 15 pb
Most CC, *Rated*, •
C-yes

Full breakfast
Comp. coffee, tea, cider
Tennis/swim nearby
golf arrangements
piano organ, 5 fireplcs.

National Historic Registry. 15 guest rms. in Victorian and country decor. In downtown historic Corydon—walk to attractions. 2 miles south of I-64. **Free gift to honeymooners**

CRAWFORDSVILLE

Davis House
1010 W. Wabash Ave., 47933
317-364-0461
Jan & Dave Stearns
All year

$$ B&B
5 rooms, 3 pb
Visa, MC, AmEx, *Rated*,
•
C-yes/S-yes/P-no/H-no

Continental plus
Comp. beverages & snacks
Sitting room
library

Victorian mansion with country atmosphere near canoeing, hiking, and historical sites. Complimentary snacks. Homemade coffee cakes and breads for breakfast.

FORT WAYNE

Candlewyck Inn
331 W. Washington Blvd., 46802
219-424-2643
Jan & Bob Goehringer
All year

$ B&B
5 rooms
Visa, MC, AmEx, *Rated*,
•
C-ltd/S-ltd/P-no/H-no

Continental plus (wkdys)
Full breakfast (wkends)
Cable TV
sun porch
bicycles

Charming, historical inn close to convention center and public library. Five lovely rooms, beautiful decor. Hearty continental breakfast. **10% off to seniors & for 3+ nights.**

GOSHEN

Checkerberry Inn, The
62644 County Rt 37, 46526
219-642-4445
John & Susan Graff
All year exc. January

$$$ B&B
12 rooms, 12 pb
Visa, MC, AmEx, *Rated*,
•
C-ltd/S-ltd/H-yes

Continental plus
Lunch/dinner, restaurant
Sitting room, library
tennis court, pool
croquet court

European-style country inn surrounded by Amish farmland, 100 acres of fields and woods. French country cuisine, luxuriously comfortable decor.

GREENCASTLE

Walden Inn
P.O. Box 490, 46135
2 Seminary Square
317-653-2761
Matthew O'Neill
All year exc. Christmas

$$$ EP
Visa, MC, AmEx, *Rated*,
•
C-yes/S-yes/P-no/H-yes

Breakfast, lunch, dinner
Restaurant, pub
bicycles, pool, sauna
tennis, golf, canoeing
meeting facilities

A warm and unpretentious atmosphere with distinctive cuisine and personalized service. Guest rooms comfortably furnished with Amish furniture. Near quaint shops, restaurants.

HAGERSTOWN ———————————————————————————————————

Teetor House, The $$$ B&B   Full breakfast
300 West Main St., 47346   4 rooms, 4 pb   Lunch & dinner (groups)
317-489-4422 800-824-4319   Visa, MC, *Rated*, •   Comp. soft drinks
Jack & Joanne Warmoth   C-yes/S-ltd   sitting room, library
All year   king size beds

Elegance & charm in a peaceful, rural setting near unique shops & restaurants. A/C. 5 miles from I-70. Golf, tennis, pool nearby. Horse and buggy rides available.

HUNTINGTON ———————————————————————————————————

Purviance House B&B $ B&B   Full breakfast
326 S. Jefferson, 46750   3 rooms, 2 pb   Lunch & dinner by res.
219-356-4218 219-356-9215   C-yes/S-no/P-no/H-no Comp. wine, tea, snacks
Bob & Jean Gernand   sitting room, library
All year   kitchen privileges

Lovingly restored 1859 National Register house furnished w/antiques, offers warm hospitality & homey comforts. Near historic & recreational areas. **3rd. night 50% off**

INDIANAPOLIS ———————————————————————————————————

Hoffman House, The $$ B&B   Continental plus
P.O. Box 906, 46202   2 rooms   Library, sitting room
545 E. 11th St.   Visa, MC, *Rated*, •   fax, copier, modem
317-635-1701   C-ltd/S-no/P-no/H-no laser printer
Laura A. Arnold
May - October

Affordable elegance in 1903 homestay in the heart of downtown. Close to State Capitol, Hoosier Dome and Convention Center. **After 10 nights, 11th night is free**

Nuthatch B&B, The $$ B&B   Full breakfast
7161 Edgewater Place, 46240   2 rooms, 2 pb   Tea, cookies, snacks
317-257-2660   •   Sitting room, deck
Joan H. Morris   C-ltd/S-ltd/P-no/H-no picnic table, swing
All year   canoe rental nearby

1920s country French architecture in resort river setting minutes from downtown Indianapolis. Breakfast is a home-cooked celebration. Herb gardens; herbal classes by request.

KNIGHTSTOWN ———————————————————————————————————

Main Street Victorian B&B $$ B&B   Continental breakfast
130 W. Main St., 46148   3 rooms, 3 pb   Sitting room, library
317-345-2299   Visa, MC, Disc.   bicycles, golf
Don & Ginny Warwick   C-ltd/S-no/P-no/H-no special occ. packages
All year

Antique shops—Coppersmith—Covered Bridges. 1870 restored Victorian. Business traveler friendly. Fax/computer available, resident cat and dog. **3rd. night 50% off**

Old Hoosier House, The $$ B&B   Full breakfast
7601 S. Greensboro Pike, 46148 4 rooms, 3 pb   Cheese, snacks, dessert
317-345-2969 800-775-5315   *Rated*, •   Sitting room
Tom & Jean Lewis   C-yes/S-ltd/P-no/H-no library, bicycles
All year   special golf rates

1840 country home near Indianapolis; popular antique area; comfortable homey atmosphere; delicious brkfasts on patio viewing Royal Hylands Golf Club. **Golfing/antiquing rate**

LA GRANGE

1886 Inn B&B, The
212 W. Factory St., 46761
219-463-4227
D. & G. Billman, K. Shank
All year

$$ B&B
3 rooms, 3 pb
Visa, MC, *Rated*,
C-ltd/S-no/P-no/H-no

Continental plus
Sitting room
bicycles

The 1866 Inn is filled w/historical charm & elegance. Every room aglow w/old fashioned beauty. Finest lodging area, yet affordable. 10 min. from Shipshewana Flea Market.

MICHIGAN CITY

Creekwood Inn
Rt 20-35 at I-94, 46360
219-872-8357
Mary Lou Linnen
All year

$$$ B&B
13 rooms, 13 pb
Most CC, Rated-, •
C-yes/S-yes/P-no/H-yes

Continental plus
Dinner, Fri. & Sat.
Aft. tea, bar service
sitting room, library
bicycles

Deluxe rooms on 33 acres of woods, creeks & gardens. Walking trails, bicycles, paddleboat, fishing. Intimate weekend dining by reservation. Hearty breakfast.

Hutchinson Mansion Inn
220 W. 10th St., 46360
219-879-1700
Ben & Mary DuVal
All year

$$$ B&B
10 rooms, 10 pb
Visa, MC, *Rated*, •
C-ltd/S-ltd/P-no/H-ltd

Full breakfast
Snacks, wineries
Sitting room, piano
whirlpools, Fax
tennis & golf nearby

Elegant Victorian mansion filled with antiques, stained glass, friezes. Near National Lakeshore, dunes, beaches, antique stores, shopping, orchards. **3rd night 50% off**

MIDDLEBURY

Bee Hive B&B
P.O. Box 1191, 46540
51129 CR 35, Bristol
219-825-5023
Herb & Treva Swarm
All year

$$ B&B
3 rooms, 1 pb
Visa, MC, *Rated*,
C-yes/S-no/P-no

Full breakfast
Comp. refreshments
Sitting room
restaurant nearby
guest cottage available

A country home in a relaxing atmosphere. Located in Amish Country with plenty of local attractions. Ski trails nearby. Easy access to Indiana Toll Road.

Patchwork Quilt Inn, The
11748 CR 2, 46540
219-825-2417
Susan Thomas/Maxine Zook
All year

$$ B&B
15 rooms, 15 pb
Rated
C-ltd/S-no/P-no/H-no

Full breakfast
Lunch, dinner available
Sitting room
piano, Amish tours
gift shop

Prepare to be pampered in gracious country home. In Amish country. Near Shipshewana Flea Auction. Closed Sundays.

Varns Guest House
P.O. Box 125, 46540
205 S. Main St.
219-825-9666
Carl & Diane Eash
All year

$$ B&B
5 rooms, 5 pb
Visa, MC, *Rated*, •
C-yes/S-no/P-no/H-no

Continental plus
Whirlpool tub in 1 room
wraparound porch w/swing
TV, golfing, A/C

Beautifully restored turn-of-the-century home in Amish community features modern luxury. Many country shops and fine dining nearby.

Varns Guest House, Middlebury, IN

NASHVILLE

Allison House Inn
P.O. Box 546, 47448
90 S. Jefferson St.
812-988-0814
Tammy Galm
All year

$$$ B&B
5 rooms, 5 pb
Rated
C-ltd/S-no/P-no/H-no

Full breakfast
Library
sitting room

In the heart of Brown County, the center for the arts and craft colony. Coziness, comfort and charm.

PERU

Rosewood Mansion Inn
54 N. Hood, 46970
317-472-5573
Lynn & Dave Hausner
All year

$$ B&B
9 rooms, 9 pb
Most CC, *Rated*, •
C-yes/S-ltd/H-no
Spanish

Full breakfast
Lunch/dinner on request
Comp. beverages & snacks
sitting room, library
bicycles, swimming pool

*Quiet, elegant surroundings. Large, comfortable guest rooms. Gourmet breakfast. Many nearby attractions. Three blocks from downtown. We cater to businessmen. **3rd night 50%***

ROCKVILLE

Suits Us B&B
514 N. College, 47872
317-569-5660
Bob & Ann McCullough
All year

$ B&B
5 rooms, 3 pb
Rated
C-yes/S-no/P-no/H-no

Continental plus
Snacks
Sitting room, library
color TVs, books in rms
bicycles, tennis court

Classic plantation-style home w/beautiful spiral hanging staircase. Large porch w/wicker rockers. Close to Turkey Run State Park, Billie Creek Village & universities.

SOUTH BEND

Book Inn B&B, The
508 West Washington, 46601
219-288-1990
Peggy & John Livingston
All year

$$$ B&B
5 rooms, 5 pb
Visa, MC, AmEx, •
C-ltd/S-no/P-no/H-no

Continental plus
Library, sitting room
quality used bookstore
located downstairs

Designers Showcase Second Empire urban home. Twelve foot ceilings, irreplaceable butternut woodwork, comfortable antiques & fresh flowers welcome you.

Jamison Inn
1404 N. Ivy Rd., 46637
219-277-9682
Janice F. Bella
All year

$$$ B&B
50 rooms, 50 pb
Most CC, *Rated*, •
C-yes/S-yes/P-no/H-yes

Full breakfast
Comp. wine
Sitting room

Full buffet breakfast. Complimentary cocktail party Monday through Thursday. Microwave, refrigerator, coffee maker in each room. At the edge of the Notre Dame campus.

Queen Anne Inn
420 W. Washington, 46601
219-234-5959 800-582-2379
Bob & Pauline Medhurst
All year

$$ B&B
5 rooms, 5 pb
Visa, MC, AmEx, *Rated*,
•
C-yes/S-ltd/P-no/H-no

Full breakfast
Snacks, tea on Thursdays
Sitting room, library
phones, TV in rooms, FAX
conference room (15-25)

Relax in a charming 1893 Victorian home with Frank Lloyd Wright influence—near city center & many restaurants. Victorian getaway package w/carriage ride, dinner, museum.

SYRACUSE

Anchor Inn B&B
11007 N. State Rd. 13, 46567
219-457-4714
Robert & Jean Kennedy
All year

$$ B&B
8 rooms, 5 pb
Visa, MC, *Rated*,
C-ltd/S-no/P-no/H-no

Full breakfast
Comp. coffee and tea
Adjacent to golf course
Across from Lake Wawasee

Turn-of-the-century home filled with period furniture. Close to Amish communities & several antique shops. Many lakes in the area & adjacent to 18-hole public golf course.

TIPPECANOE

Bessinger's Hillfarm B&B
4588 SR 110, 46570
219-223-3288
Wayne & Betty Bessinger
All year

$ B&B
3 rooms, 3 pb
Rated
C-ltd/S-no/P-no/H-no

Full breakfast
Lunch, dinner
Sitting room, ponds
wildlife, birdwatching
cross-country skiing,
canoeing

Bessinger's Hillfarm Wildlife Refuge is a comfortable log home, overlooking water area with many islands. Hiking, canoeing, cross-country skiing, fishing, swimming, or plain relaxing.

WARSAW

White Hill Manor	$$ B&B	Full breakfast
2513 E. Center St., 46580	8 rooms	Suite w/dbl jacuzzi
219-269-6933	Most CC, *Rated*	Conference room
Gladys Deloe	C-yes/S-ltd/P-no/H-yes	sitting room
All year	German	

Restored English Tudor mansion. 8 elegant rooms w/bath, TV, desk, A/C. Adjacent to Wagon Wheel Theater, lake recreation, antique shops. **2 night special, one dinner for 2**

More Inns . . .

Inter Urban Inn, 503 S. Harrison, Alexandria, 46001, 317-724-2001
Sycamore Hill, 1245 S. Golden Lake Rd., Angola, 46703, 219-665-2690
Auburn Inn, 225 Touring Dr., Auburn, 46707
Hill Top Country Inn, 1733 CR 28, Auburn, 46706, 219-281-2529
Hoopis Inn, W. 7th St., Auburn, 46706
Beechwood Inn, County Line Rd., Batesville, 47006
Schug House Inn, 206 West Main St., Berne, 46711
Inn at Bethlehem, 101 Walnut St., Bethlehem, 47104, 812-293-3975
Bauer House, 4595 N. Maple Grove Rd., Bloomington, 47401
Cartwright Home, 2927 N. Bankers Dr., Bloomington, 47401
Quilt Haven B&B, 711 Dittemore Rd., Bloomington, 47404, 812-876-5802
Milburn House, 707 E. Vistula St., Bristol, 46507, 219-848-4026
Open Hearth B&B, 56782 SR 15, Bristol, 46507, 219-825-2417
Overbeck House, 520 E. Church, Cambridge City, 47327
Wingfield's Inn B&B, 526 Indian Oak Mall, Chesterton, 46304, 702-348-0766
Sycamore Spring Farm, Box 224, Churubusco, 46723, 219-693-3603
Columbus Inn, 445 Fifth St., Columbus, 47201, 812-378-4289
Lafayette Street B&B, 723 Lafayette St., Columbus, 47201, 812-372-7245
Maple Leaf Inn B&B, 831 N. Grand Ave., Connersville, 47331, 317-825-7099
Warren Cabin B&B, 1161 Church St., Corydon, 47112, 812-738-2166
Sugar Creek B&B, 901 W. Market St., Crawfordsville, 47933, 317-362-4095
Yount's Mill Inn, 3729 Old State Rd. 32 W, Crawfordsville, 47933, 317-362-5864
Cragwood Inn B&B, 303 N. Second St., Decatur, 46733, 219-728-2000
Eby's B&B, 29168 CR 30, Elkhart, 46517
Brigadoon B&B Inn, 1201 S.E. Second St., Evansville, 47713, 812-422-9635
Roebuck Inn, 2727 St. Joe Rd., Fort Wayne, 46835
Union Chapel B&B, 6336 Union Chapel Rd., Fort Wayne, 46845, 219-627-5663
Pheasant Country B&B, P.O. Box 133, Fowler, 47944, 317-884-0908
Country B&B, 27727 CR 36, Goshen, 46526, 219-862-2748
Flower Patch B&B, 16263 CR 22, Goshen, 46526, 219-534-4207
Lakeside Haven, 63070 Lakeside Dr., Goshen, 46526, 219-642-3678
Timberidge B&B, 16801 SR 4, Goshen, 46526, 219-533-7133
Waterford B&B, 3004 S. Main St., Goshen, 46526, 219-533-6044
Grandview Guest House, Box 311, Grandview, 47615, 812-649-2817
River Belle B&B, The, P.O. Box 669, Grandview, 47615, 800-877-5165
1900 House, The, 50777 Ridgemoor Way, Granger, 46530, 219-277-7783
Brick Inn, 1540 Bloomington St., Greencastle, 46135, 317-653-3267
De'Coy's B&B, 1546 W. 100 N., Hartford City, 47348, 317-348-2164
Applegate Bed & Breakfast, 1817 Applegate St., Indianapolis, 46203
Barn House, 10656 E. 63rd St., Indianapolis, 46236, 317-823-4898
Friendliness With A Flair, 5214 E. 20th Place, Indianapolis, 46218, 317-356-3149
Holland House, 1502 East 10th., Indianapolis, 813-685-9326
Laura Arnold, P.O. Box 906, Indianapolis, 46206
Le Chateau Delaware, 1456 N. Delaware, Indianapolis, 46202
Manor House, 612 E. 13th St., Indianapolis, 46202, 317-634-1711
Pairadux Inn, 6363 N. Guilford Ave., Indianapolis, 46220, 317-259-8005
Artist's Studio B&B, 429 W. Haysville, Jasper, 47546
Hollybeck Inn, 310 N. Riley, Kendallville, 46755
Olde McCray Mansion Inn, 703 E. Mitchell St., Kendallville, 46755, 219-347-3647
Koontz House B&B, 7514 N. Hwy 23, Koontz Lake, 46574, 219-586-7090
Atwater Century Farm B&B, RR 4, Box 307, Lagrange, 46761, 219-463-2743
Weavers Country Oaks, RR 4, Box 193H, Lagrange, 46761, 219-768-7191
Celene Kandis, General Delivery, Lagro, 46941
Thornwood Inn, 211 Rose St., LaPorte, 46350
Folke Family Farm, P.O. Box 66, Lawrenceburg, 47025
Ye Olde Scotts Inn, RR 1, Box 5, Leavenworth, 47137, 812-739-4747
Solomon Mier Manor, 508 S. Cavin St., Ligonier, 46767, 219-894-3668
Snapp Inn, Route 3, Box 102, Limestone, 37681, 615-257-2482
Autumnwood B&B, 165 Autumnwood Ln., Madison, 47250, 812-265-5262
Cliff House B&B, 122 Fairmount Dr., Madison, 47250, 812-265-5272
Clifty Inn, P.O. Box 387, Madison, 47250, 812-265-4135
Elderberry Inn, 411 W. First St., Madison, 47250, 812-265-6856
Heritage House, 705 W. Second St., Madison, 47250, 812-265-2393
Main Street B&B, 739 W. Main St., Madison, 47250
Millwood House, 512 West St., Madison, 47250, 812-265-6780

Publick House, P.O. Box 202, Metamora, 47030, 317-647-6729
Thorpe House, Clayborne St., Metamora, 47030, 317-647-5425
Duneland Beach Inn, 3311 Potawatomi, Michigan City, 46360, 219-874-7729
Plantation Inn, RR2 Box 296-S, Michigan City, 46360, 219-874-2418
Coneygar, 54835 C.R. 33, Middlebury, 46540, 219-825-5707
Essenhaus Country Inn, 240 US 20, Middlebury, 46540, 219-825-9471
Johnson's B&B, 56823 Oak Dale Dr., Middlebury, 46540
Lookout Bed & Breakfast, 14544 CR-12, Middlebury, 46540
Mary's Place, 305 Eugene Dr., PBx 428, Middlebury, 46540, 219-825-2429
Zimmer Haus, 120 Orpha Dr., Middlebury, 46540
Maple Hill, RR 3, Box 76, Middletown, 47356, 317-354-2580
Beiger Mansion Inn, 317 Lincoln Way East, Mishawaka, 46544, 219-256-0365
Zimmer Frei Haus, 409 N. Main St., Monticello, 47960, 219-583-4061
Rock House, The, 380 W. Washington St., Morgantown, 46160, 812-597-5100
Spurgeon Inn, 1101 N. Wheeling Ave., Muncie, 47303
Bob & Arlene Mast, 26206 CR 50, Nappanee, 46550, 219-773-4714
Indiana Amish Country B&B, 1600 W. Market St., Nappanee, 46550, 219-773-4188
Victorian Guest House, 302 E. Market, Nappanee, 46550, 219-773-4383
5th Generation Farm B&B, RR #4, Box 90-A, Nashville, 47448, 812-988-7553
Chestnut Hill Log Home B&B, RR 4, Box 295, Hoover, Nashville, 47448, 812-988-4995
Coffey House B&B, Route 4, Box 179, Nashville, 47448
Fifth Generation Farm, Bear Wallow Hill Rd., Nashville, 800-473-8152
McGinley's Vacation Cabins, Route 3, Box 332, Nashville, 47448, 812-988-7337
Mindheim's Inn, RR 5, Box 592, Nashville, 47448
Plain & Fancy, SR 135 N., RR 3, Box 62, Nashville, 47448, 812-988-4537
Seasons, P.O. Box 187, Nashville, 47448, 812-988-2284
Story Inn, P.O. Box 64, Nashville, 47448, 812-988-6516
Sunset House, Route 3, Box 127, Nashville, 47448, 812-988-6118
Victoria House, Route 4, Box 414, Nashville, 47448, 812-988-6344
Wraylyn Knoll Inn, P.O. Box 481, Nashville, 47448, 812-988-0733
Mrs. Bill Williams, Route 1, Box 167, New Harmony, 47631
Phelps Mansion Inn, 208 State St., Newburgh, 47630, 812-853-7766
Fruitt Basket Inn B&B, 116 W. Main St., North Manchester, 46962, 219-982-2443
Retreat House, 8223 W. 550 North, North Salem, 46165, 317-676-6669
Braxton House Inn, 210 N. Gospel, Paoli, 47454
Driftwood, P.O. Box 16, Plymouth, 46563, 219-546-2274
Sandy Hollow Inn B&B, 935 Sandy Hollow Dr., Portland, 47371, 219-726-9444
Country Homestead Guest Ho, Route 1, Box 353, Richland, 47634, 812-359-4870
Jelley House Country Inn, 222 S. Walnut St., Rising Sun, 47404, 812-438-2319
Victorian House, RR1 Box 27, Roachdale, 46172, 317-522-1225
James and Ann Crawford, 161 W. 4th St., Roanoke, 46783
Minnow Creek Farm, RR 3 Box 381, Rochester, 46975
Rockport Inn, 130 S. Third St., Rockport, 47635
Lanning House, 206 E. Poplar St., Salem, 47167, 812-883-3484
Victorianna Mansion, 1337 Mechanic, Shelbyville, 46176
Country Inn, Route 1, Box 19, Shipshewana, 46565
Green Meadow Ranch, 7905 W. 450 N., Shipshewana, 46565, 219-768-4221
Morton Street B&B, 140 Morton St., Box 3, Shipshewana, 46565
Brenda Rodgers, Route 3, Box 70B, Shoals, 47581
Home B&B, 21166 Clover Hill Ct., South Bend, 46614, 219-291-0535
Lake Breeze, RR 5, Box 169A, Syracuse, 46567, 219-457-5000
Tara B&B, Route 2, Box 276A, Syracuse, 46567
Deere Run B&B, 6218 N. 13th St., Terre Haute, 47805
Embassy B&B, P.O. Box 42, Valparaiso, 46383
Captain's Quarters B&B, 473 Hiway 56, Vevay, 47043, 812-427-2900
Swiss Hills B&B, RR 3, Box 315, Vevay, 47043, 812-427-3882
Mayor Wilhelm's Villa, 428 N. Fifth St., Vincennes, 47591, 812-882-9487
Hilltop House B&B, 88 W. Sinclair St., Wabash, 46992, 219-563-7726
Mrs. Mabel Rumpf, 225 E. Sheridan, Wabash, 46992
Amish Acres, Inc., 160 W. Market, Wappanee, 46550, 219-773-4188
Candlelight Inn, 503 E. Fort Wayne St., Warsaw, 46580, 219-267-2906
Haven B&B, P.O. Box 798, Washington, 46501, 812-254-7770
Julia's Place, P.O. Box 54, Washington, 46501
Mimi's House, 101 W. Maple St., Washington, 47501, 812-254-5562
Camel Lot, 4512 W. 131st St., Westfield, 46074, 317-873-4370
Country Roads Guesthouse, 2731 West 146th St., Westfield, 46074, 317-846-2376
Gunn Guest House, 904 Park Ave., Winona Lake, 46590, 219-267-2023
Four Seasons Farm B&B, RR 1, Box 385, Wolcottville, 46795, 219-854-3993
Brick Street Inn, 175 S. Main St., Zionsville, 46077, 317-873-5895

Iowa

ATLANTIC ────────────────

Chestnut Charm B&B	$$ MAP	Full breakfast
1409 Chestnut St., 50022	5 rooms, 3 pb	Lunch, dinner w/res.
712-243-5652	Visa, MC, *Rated*, •	Sitting room, piano
Barbara Stensvad	C-ltd/S-no/P-no/H-no	A/C, sun rooms, antiques
All year		fountained patio

Enchanting 1898 Victorian mansion on large estate. Be pampered in elegance. Gourmet dining. Experience beauty and fantasy with someone special.

COUNCIL BLUFFS ────────────────

Terra Jane Country Inn	$$ B&B	Full breakfast
Rt 5, Box 69, 51503	5 rooms, 5 pb	Lunch, dinner, snacks
712-322-4200	Visa, MC, •	Restaurant, wine/beer
Jane Connealy	C-yes/S-ltd/H-ltd	sitting/TV room
All year		library/parlor, hot tubs

Lovely Victorian home overlooking lush Iowa farmland. Gourmet cuisine, barn dances, sand volleyball, mile-long exercise trail, hayrides. **2nd night 25% off**

DUBUQUE ────────────────

Mandolin Inn, The	$$ B&B	Full breakfast
199 Loras Blvd., 52001	8 rooms, 4 pb	Aft. tea, comp. wine
319-566-0069	Most CC, *Rated*, •	Sitting room
Jan Oswald	C-yes/S-ltd/P-no/H-no	music room
All year		parlor

1908 Edwardian mansion where pampered service is the norm. Veranda filled w/wicker. Parlors and bedchambers are meticulously decorated w/antiques. **10% off 2 nights stay**

Mandolin Inn, The	$$$ B&B	Full breakfast
199 Loras Blvd., 52001	9 rooms, 7 pb	Comp. wine
319-556-0069	Most CC, *Rated*, •	Sitting room
Jan Oswald	C-yes/S-ltd/P-no/H-no	Comp. sherry at bedtime
All year		

Edwardian elegance, pampered service in antique-filled bed chambers & magnificent dining room. Historic District, downtown shopping & restaurants. **Free champagne, ltd.**

Richards House, The	$ B&B	Full breakfast
1492 Locust St., 52001	5 rooms, 4 pb	Snacks
319-557-1492	Most CC, *Rated*, •	Sitting room, antiques
Michelle Delaney	C-ltd/S-ltd/P-ask/H-no	concealed TV's, phones
All year		fireplaces

1883 Stick-style Victorian mansion with over 80 stained-glass windows. Seven varieties of woodwork and period furnishings. Working fireplaces in guest rooms.

HOMESTEAD ────────────────

Die Heimat Country Inn	$ B&B	Full breakfast
Main St., Amana Colonies,	19 rooms, 19 pb	Occasional beverages
52236	Visa, MC, *Rated*,	Sitting room
319-622-3937	C-yes/S-yes/P-no/H-no	shaded yard
Warren & Jacki Lock		wooden glider
All year		

Stay overnight at our century-old restored inn. All rooms have private baths furnished with Amana furniture and antiques. Colony restaurants and wineries nearby.

The Richards House, Dubuque, IA

MAQUOKETA

Squiers Manor B&B
5547 Caves Rd., 418 West
Pleasant, 52060
319-652-6961
Kathy & Virl Banowetz
All year

$$ B&B
6 rooms, 6 pb
Visa, MC, *Rated*,
C-yes/S-yes/P-no/H-no

Full breakfast
Sitting room, library
bridal suite avail.
fireplaces, whirlpool

Experience Victorian elegance, ambiance & hospitality at its finest. Private whirlpool baths, fireplaces, antique furnishing in this 1882 mansion. Candlelight evening dessert

NEWTON

La Corsette Maison Inn
629 First Ave. E., 50208
515-792-6833
Kay Owen
All year

$$ B&B
5 rooms, 4 pb
Visa, MC, *Rated*, •
C-yes/S-no/P-ask/H-no

Full breakfast
Gourmet dinner
Restaurant
sitting room. Near I-35.
Near Des Moines on I-80.

Turn-of-the-century mission-style mansion. Charming French bedchambers, beckoning hearths. Gourmet Dining 4½ star rating. **2 night stay with wine midweek Nov.15-Mar.15.**

PRINCETON

Woodlands, The $$$ B&B Full breakfast
P.O. Box 127, 52768 2 rooms, 2 pb Lunch, dinner available
319-289-3177 800-257-3177 Visa, MC, • Snacks, sitting room
Wallace/Lindebraekke Family C-yes/S-ltd/P-yes/H-no library, bicycles, pool
All year Span, Norwegian, Port. near Mississippi River

A secluded woodland escape nestled among pines on 26 acres of forest & meadows. Elegant breakfast by pool/cozy fireplace. Skiing, fishing, golf, nature trails. **Free btl. wine**

WATERLOO

Daisy Wilton Inn, The $$ B&B Full breakfast
418 Walnut St., 50703 3 rooms Aft. tea, snacks
319-232-0801 *Rated*, • Sitting room, library
Sue & Al Brase C-ltd/S-no/P-no/H-no guest kitchen & laundry
All year wash basins in rooms

Authentically furnished, turn-of-the-century Victorian. Near downtown antique & specialty shops, will arrange John Deer factory tour. **3rd night 50% off**

More Inns . . .

Walden Acres B&B, RR 1, Box 30, Adel, 50003, 515-987-1567
Addie's Place B&B, 121 Cherokee St., Alta, 51002, 712-284-2509
Inn at Stone City, Anamosa, 52205, 319-462-4733
John James Audubon B&B, P.O. Box 49, Audubon, 50025, 712-563-3674
Inn at Battle Creek, The, 201 Maple St., Battle Creek, 51006, 712-365-4949
Mont Rest, 300 Spring St., Bellevue, 52031, 319-872-4220
Spring Side Inn, P.O. Box 41, RR 2, Bellevue, 52031, 319-872-5452
Abbey Hotel, 1401 Central Ave., Bettendorf, 52722, 319-355-1291
Hallock House B&B, The, P.O. Box 9, Brayton, 50042, 712-549-2449
Hotel Brooklyn, 154 Front St., Brooklyn, 52211, 515-522-9229
Mississippi Manor B&B, The, 809 N. 4th. St., Burlington, 52601, 319-753-2218
Taylor Manor, 919 Washington St., Cedar Falls, 50613, 309-266-0035
Townsend Place B&B, 1017 Washington St., Cedar Falls, 50613, 319-266-9455
Snoozie's B&B, 1570 Hwy. 30 East, Cedar Rapids, 52403, 319-364-2134
Country Gables B&B, P.O. Box 149, Clarinda, 51632, 712-542-5006
Budget Inn, Box 102, Clear Lake, 50428
Larch Pine Inn, 401 N. 3rd St., Clear Lake, 50428, 515-357-7854
Norsk Hus By-The-Shore, 3611 N. Shore Dr., Clear Lake, 50428, 515-357-8368
North Shore House, 1519 N. Shore Dr., Clear Lake, 50428, 515-357-4443
Mill St. B&B, P.O. Box 34, Clermont, 52135, 319-423-5531
Martha's Vineyard, Box 247, Colorado, 50056, 515-377-2586
Robin's Nest Inn B&B, 327 - 9th Ave., Council Bluffs, 51503, 712-323-1649
Bishop's House Inn, 1597 Brady St., Davenport, 52803, 319-324-2454
River Oaks Inn B&B, 1234 E. River Dr., Davenport, 52803, 800-352-6016
Village B&B, The, 2017 E. 13th St., Davenport, 52803, 319-322-4905
Montgomery Mansion, 812 Maple Ave., Decorah, 52101, 319-382-5088
Orval & Diane Bruvold, Route 1, Decorah, 52101, 319-382-4729
Brownswood Country B&B, 5938 S.W. McKinley Ave., Des Moines, 50321, 515-285-4135
Carter House, 640 Twentieth St., Des Moines, 50314, 515-288-7850
Jardin Suite, 6653 NW Timberline Dr., Des Moines, 50313, 515-289-2280
Hancock House, 1105 Grove Terrace, Dubuke, 52001, 319-557-8989
Juniper Hill Farm, 15325 Budd Rd., Dubuque, 52001, 319-582-4405
Kloft House, 459 Lotas Blvd., Dubuque, 52001
L'Auberge Mandolin, 199 Loras, Dubuque, 52001, 319-566-0069
Mississippi Mary's B&B, 175 West 17th St., Dubuque, 52001, 800-723-MARY
Redstone Inn, 504 Bluff St., Dubuque, 52001, 319-582-1894
Stout House B&B, 504 Bluff St. (mail), Dubuque, 52001, 319-582-1890
Get-Away, The, Rt. 2, P.O. Box 109, Dunlap, 51529, 712-643-5584
Another World-Paradise, 16338 Paradise Valley, Durango, 52039, 319-552-1034
Rainbow H. Lodging House, RR 1, Box 89, Elk Horn, 51531, 712-764-8272
Travelling Companion, 4314 Main St., Elk Horn, 51531, 712-764-8932
Little House Vacations, Elkader, 52043, 319-783-7774
Hoffman Guest House, 221 N. 8th Stret, Estherville, 51334, 712-362-5994
Happy Hearth B&B, 400 W. Washington, Fairfield, 52556, 515-472-9386
Cloverleaf Farm, Route 2, Box 140A, Fort Atkinson, 52144, 319-534-7061
LaVerne & Alice Hageman, Route 2, Box 104, Fort Atkinson, 52144, 319-534-7545
Larson House B&B, 300 N. 9th St., Fort Dodge, 50501, 515-573-5733
Pioneer Farm B&B, RR1 Box 96, Galva, 51020
Mrs. B's B&B, 920 Division St., Garner, 50438, 515-923-2390
Wilson Home, The, RR1, Box 132, Greenfield, 50849, 515-743-2031
Spring Valley B&B, RR 4, P.O. Box 47, Hampton, 50441, 515-456-4437
Die Heimat Country Inn, Main St., Homestead, 52236, 319-622-3937

Bella Vista Place B&B, 2 Bella Vista, Iowa City, 52245, 319-338-4129
Golden Haug, The, 517 E. Washington, Iowa City, 52245, 319-338-6452
Haverkamp Linn St Homestay, 619 N. Linn St., Iowa City, 52245, 319-337-4363
Grand Anne B&B, The, 816 Grand Ave., Keokuk, 52632, 319-524-6310
Mason House/Bentonsport, RR 2, Box 237, Keosauqua, 52565, 319-592-3133
Elmhurst, Rt. 1 Box 3, Keota, 52248
FitzGerald's Inn, P.O. Box 157, Lansing, 52151, 319-538-4872
Lansing House, Box 97, 291 N. Front St, Lansing, 52151, 319-538-4263
Brandt's Orchard Inn, RR 1, P.O. Box 224, LaPorte City, 50651, 319-342-2912
The Monarch, 303 Second St., Le Claire, 52753, 319-289-3011
Mississippi Sunrise B&B, 18950 Great River Rd., LeClaire, 52753, 319-332-9203
Heritage House, RR 1, Leighton, 50143, 515-626-3092
Pleasant Country B&B, R.R. #2, Box 23, Malcom, 50157, 515-528-4925
Decker House Inn, 128 N. Main, Maquoketa, 52060, 319-652-6654
Loy's B&B, RR 1, Box 82, Marengo, 52301, 319-642-7787
Evergreen Inn, RR 1, Box 65, Massena, 50853
Boedeker's Bungalow West, 125 7th St. N., Mayward, 50655, 319-637-2711
Little Switzerland Inn, 126 Main St., McGregor, 52157
River's Edge B&B, 112 Main St., McGregor, 52157, 319-873-3501
Rettig House, Middle, 52307, 319-622-3386
Dusk to Dawn B&B, Box 124, Middleamana, 52307
Apple Orchard Inn B&B, RR 3 Box 129, Missouri Valley, 51555, 712-642-2418
Hilltop B&B, RR 3, P.O. Box 126, Missouri Valley, 51555, 712-642-3695
English Valley B&B, RR 2, Montezuma, 50171, 515-623-3663
Varner's Caboose, PO Box 10, 204 E.2nd St, Montpelier, 52759, 319-381-3652
Historic Harlan Hotel, 122 N. Jefferson St., Mount Pleasant, 52641, 319-385-3126
Queen Anne B&B, 1110 9th St., Nevada, 50201, 515-382-6444
Guest House B&B, The, 645 North Court, Ottumwa, 52501, 515-684-8893
Strawtown Inn & Lodge, 1111 Washington St., Pella, 50219, 515-628-2681
Usher's, 711 Corning, Red Oak, 51566, 712-623-3222
Heart & Home B&B, P.O. Box 116, Rutland, 50582, 515-332-3167
Brick Bungalow B&B, 1012 Early St., Sac City, 50583, 800-848-7656
Drewry Homestead, RR2, P.O. Box 98, Sac City, 50583, 712-662-4416
Babi's B&B, Route 1, Box 66, South Amana, 52334, 319-662-4381
Hannah Marie Country Inn, RR 1, Hway. 71 S., Spencer, 51301, 712-262-1286
Old World Inn, The, 331 S. Main St., Spillville, 52168, 319-562-3739
Taylor Made B&B, 330 S. Main, Spillville, 52168, 319-562-3958
Parsonage, The, 227 Lake Ave., Storm Lake, 50588, 712-732-1736
Hook's Point Farmstead B&B, Rt. 1, P.O. Box 222, Stratford, 50249, 515-838-2781
Valkommen House, The, RR 1, P.O. Box 175, Stratford, 50249, 515-838-2440
Summit Grove Inn, 1426 S. Seventh St., Stuart, 50250, 515-523-2147
Terra Verde Farm, Route 1, Box 86, Swisher, 52338, 319-846-2478
Plum Creek Inn, RR 1, P.O. Box 91, Thurman, 51654, 712-628-2191
Victorian House, 508 E. 4th St., Tipton, 52772, 319-886-2633
Antique City Inn B&B, P.O. Box 584, Walnut, 51577, 712-784-3722
Quiet Sleeping Room, 125 Green Meadow Dr., Washington, 52353
Centennial Farm B&B, 1091-220th St., Webster City, 50595, 515-832-3050
Cross Country Traveler, P.O. Box 578, West Branch, 52358, 319-643-2433
Ellendale B&B, 5340 Ashworth Rd., West Des Moines, 50265, 515-225-2219
Lighthouse Marina Inn, RR 1, P.O. Box 72, Whiting, 51063, 712-458-2066
Lucille's B&B, RR 1, Box 55, Williamsburg, 52361, 319-668-1185

Kansas

ABILENE

Balfour's House B&B
Rt 2, Box 143 D, Hwy 15, Mile
Post 168, 67410
913-263-4262
Gil & Marie Balfour
All year

$$ B&B
2 rooms, 2 pb
Visa, MC, *Rated*, •
C-yes/S-ltd/P-ltd/H-no

Continental plus
Hot tubs
indoor pool
sitting room

*Relax in country atmosphere, near town. Suites with private entrances, TV, VCR, stereo.
Indoor pool and spa, fireplace.* **Special Sweetheart Package**

COLUMBUS ————————————————————

Meriwether House B&B
322 W. Pine, 66725
316-429-2812 316-674-3274
M. Meriwether, L. Simpson
All year

$ B&B
7 rooms
Visa, MC, *Rated*
C-yes/S-no/P-no/H-ask

Continental breakfast
Sitting room

Cottage home close to downtown. Furnished with antiques. Decorator shop within. Lace, wallpaper, and many decorating items for sale.

COUNCIL GROVE ————————————————

Cottage House Hotel, The
25 N. Neosho, 66846
316-767-5673 800-727-7903
Connie Essington
All year

$$ B&B
26 rooms
Most Cred.Cds.,*Rated*, •
C-yes/S-yes/P-ltd/H-yes

Continental breakfast
Restaurant nearby
Sitting room, sauna room
6 rooms w/whirlpool tubs
near Hays House Restaur.

*Beautifully renovated Victorian hotel with modern comforts & lovely antique furnishings. Located in historic "Birthplace of the Santa Fe Trail." **3rd. consecutive night 50%***

EUREKA ——————————————————————

123 Mulberry St. B&B
123 S. Mulberry St., 67045
316-583-7515
Jay & Linda Jordan
All year

$ B&B
3 rooms, 1 pb
Visa, MC, *Rated*,
C-ltd/S-no/P-no/H-no

Full breakfast
Hot tub on deck
sitting room

*Nestled in heart of Flint Hills, 1 hr. east of Wichita on State Hwy. 54. Pleasant rooms in fine old 1912 house. Wrap-around porch w/glider. **10% off w/2 nights***

STAFFORD ————————————————————

Henderson House B&B Inn
518 W. Stafford, 551 Woodlawn
Wichita67218, 67578
316-234-6048 800-473-8003
Lee Stalcup, C. & N. Moore
All year

$ B&B
5 rooms, 3 pb
Visa, MC, *Rated*,
C-yes/S-no/P-no/H-no

Continental
Snacks
Bicycles, hot tubs
golf, tennis nearby
limo ride to restaurant

*Grandma's warm hospitality and Victorian elegance exude from this classic 1903 home. Furnished with heirloom antiques and handmade quilts. **3rd night 50% off***

TONGANOXIE ————————————————————

Almeda's B&B Inn
220 S. Main, 66086
913-845-2295
Almeda & Richard Tinberg
All year

$ B&B
7 rooms, 1 pb
Rated
C-ltd/S-ltd/P-no/H-no

Continental plus
Comp. cold drinks
Sitting room
organ, all rooms A/C
suite available

Dedicated as a historical site in 1983; in the '30s was the inspiration for the movie "Bus Stop." Decorated in country style with many antiques. Close to golf courses & pool.

WAKEENEY ————————————————————

Thistle Hill B&B
Rt. 1, Box 93, 67672
913-743-2644
Dave & Mary Hendricks
All year

$$ B&B
4 rooms, 2 pb
Rated, •
C-yes/S-ltd/P-no/H-no

Full breakfast
Aft. tea
Sitting room, library
flower & herb gardens
hiking paths

Nestled halfway between Kansas City & Denver along I-70. A peaceful, modern farm home surrounded by cedars, prairie, wildflowers & herbs.

WAKEFIELD ————————————————————————————

Wakefield Country B&B | $ B&B | Full breakfast
197 Sunflower Rd., RR #1, 67487 | 2 rooms, 2 pb | Waking trail
913-461-5533 | *Rated* | beautiful sunsets
Vernon & Kathy Yenni | C-yes/S-no/P-yes/H-no | sitting room
All year

Country hospitality awaits you at 3rd generation family, working farm. 1930's home lovingly restored and landscaped. Reservations suggested. **Comp. jar of home-raised honey**

WICHITA ————————————————————————————

Inn at the Park | $$$ B&B | Continental plus
3751 E. Douglas, 67218 | 12 rooms, 12 pb | Afternoon tea
316-652-0500 800-258-1951 | Visa, MC, AmEx, *Rated*, | Sitting room
Michelle Hickman | • | library, hot tubs
All year | C-ltd/S-no/P-no/H-yes | tennis and pool nearby
 | Spanish

A 1910 mansion, nestled on the edge of a park. 12 uniquely decorated suites. Close to fine dining, theater, business, shopping. Ideal for vacationers and corporate travelers.

Inn at Willowbend, The | $$$ B&B | Full breakfast
3939 Comotara, 67226 | 22 rooms, 22 pb | Comp. wine
316-636-4032 800-553-5775 | Most Cred. Cds. *Rated*, | Bar service
Gary M. Adamson | • | sitting room, library
All year | C-yes/S-yes/P-no/H-yes | hot tubs in suites

A traditional bed and breakfast with modern conveniences located on a championship golf course.

Max Paul ... An Inn | $$ B&B | Continental plus
3910 E. Kellogg, 67218 | 14 rooms, 14 pb | Group & conf. facilities
316-689-8101 | Most CC, *Rated*, | hot tub, pool, sitt. rm.
Roberta Eaton | C-ltd/S-yes/P-no/H-no | tennis nearby, library
All year

Feather beds and antique furniture; fireplaces, decks, exercise/jacuzzi room opens on gardens and pond; close to park, shops and restaurant.

More Inns ...

Spruce House, 604 N. Spruce, Abilene, 67410, 913-263-3900
Victorian Reflections, 303 N. Cedar, Abilene, 67410, 913-263-7774
Stuewe Place, 617 Nebraska, Alma, 66401, 913-765-3636
Schumann Gast Haus, 615 S. "B" St., Arkansas City, 67005, 316-442-8220
Slaton House, The, 319 W. 7th, Ashland, 67831, 316-635-2290
Wallingford Inn B&B, Box 799, Ashland, 67831, 316-635-2129
Williams House, The, 526 N. 5th, Atchison, 66002, 913-367-1757
Country Corner B&B, South Hiway 25, Box 88, Atwood, 67730, 913-626-9516
Flower Patch, 610 Main, Atwood, 67730, 913-626-3780
Goodnite at Irene's, 703 S. 6th, Atwood, 67730, 913-626-3521
Home on the Range, Atwood, 67730, 913-626-9309
Bedknobs & Biscuits, 15202 Parallel, Basehor, 66007, 913-724-1540
Lois' B&B, Beloit, 67420, 913-738-5869
Lear Acres-B&B on a Farm, Rt. 1 Box 31, Bern, 66408, 913-336-3903
Victorian Memories, 314 N. 4th, Burlington, 66839, 316-364-5752
Caney B&B, Hwy 75, Caney, 67333, 316-879-5478
Sunbarger Guest House, RR 1, Cassoday, 66842, 316-735-4499
Windmill Inn B&B, RR 1, Box 32, Chapman, 67431, 913-263-8755
Cimarron Hotel & Restauran, P.O. Box 633, Cimarron, 67835, 316-855-2244
Clyde Hotel, 420 Washington, Clyde, 66938, 913-446-2231
Crystle's B&B, 508 W. 7th St., Concordia, 66901, 913-243-2192
Flint Hills B&B, 613 W. Main, Council Grove, 66846, 316-767-6655
Country Inn, The, HC 01, Box 59, Dorrance, 67634, 913-666-4468
Dorrance—The Country Inn, HC 01, Box 59, Dorrance, 67634, 913-666-4468
Sage Inn, PO box 24, Dover, 66420
Cimarron, The, P.O. Box 741, Elkhart, 67950, 405-696-4672

Plumb House B&B, The, 628 Exchange, Emporia, 66801, 316-342-6881
123 Mulberry Street B&B, 123 S. Mulberry St., Eureka, 67045, 316-583-7515
Bennington House, 123 Crescent Dr., Fort Scott, 66701, 316-223-1837
Chenault Mansion, The, 820 S. National Ave., Fort Scott, 66701, 316-223-6800
Country Quarters, Route 5, Box 80, Fort Scott, 66701, 316-223-2889
Huntington House, 324 S. Main, Fort Scott, 66701, 316-223-3644
Creek Side Farm B&B, Rt. 1, Box 19, Fowler, 67844, 316-646-5586
Kirk House, 145 W. 4th Ave., Garnett, 66032, 913-448-5813
Heart Haven Inn, 2145 Rd. 64, Goodland, 67735, 913-899-5171
Peaceful Acres B&B, Route 5, Box 153, Great Bend, 67530, 316-793-7527
Walnut Brook B&B, R.R. 3, Box 304, Great Bend, 67530, 316-792-5900
Heritage Inn, 300 Main, Halstead, 67056, 316-835-2118
Nee Murray Way, 220 W. 3rd., Halstead, 67056, 316-835-2027
Dauddy Haus, Route 2, Box 273, Haven, 67543, 316-465-2267
Butterfield B&B, Hays, 67601, 913-628-3908
Pomeroy Inn, Hill City, 67642, 913-674-2098
A Nostalgic B&B Place, 310 South Main, Hillsboro, 67063, 316-947-3519
Dodds House B&B, Hwy 75S, Holton, 66436, 913-364-3172
Hotel Josephine, 5th & Ohio, Holton, 66436, 913-364-3151
Hollyrood House B&B, Route 1, Box 47, Holyrood, 67450, 913-252-3678
Bellmore House B&B, 1500 N. Main St., Hutchinson, 67501, 316-663-5824
Bowman House B&B, 1500 N. Main St., Hutchinson, 67501, 316-663-5824
Auntie Emma's, 318 No. Second, Independence, 67301
Country Pleasures B&B, 1107 S. Bridge St., Lakin, 67860, 316-355-6982
Halcyon House, 1000 Ohio, Lawrence, 66044, 913-841-0314
Kansas City B&B, P.O. Box 14781, Lenexa, 66215, 913-888-3636
Woody House B&B, Route 1, Box 156, Lincoln, 67455, 913-524-4744
Smoky Valley B&B, 2nd & State, Lindsborg, 67456, 913-227-4460
Swedish Country Inn, 112 W. Lincoln, Lindsborg, 67456, 913-227-2985
Holste Homestead, Ludell, 67744, 913-626-3522
Pork Palace, Ludell, 67744, 913-626-9223
Quivira House B&B, 400 E. Commercial St., Lyons, 67554
Kimble Cliff B&B, 6782 Anderson Ave., Manhattan, 66502, 913-539-3816
Country Dreams, Rt. 3, Box 82, Marion, 66861, 316-382-2250
Haven of Rest, Marion, 66861, 316-382-2286
School House Inn, 106 E. Beck, Melvern, 66510, 913-549-3473
Village Inn, RR 2, Box 226D, Meriden, 66512, 913-876-2835
Hawk House B&B Inn, 307 W. Broadway, Newton, 67114, 316-283-2045
Hedrick's B&B Inn, 7910 N. Roy L. Smith Rd, Nickerson, 67561, 316-662-1881
Loft B&B, Osborne, 67473, 913-346-5984
Stone Crest B&B, P.O. Box 394, Oskaloosa, 66066, 913-863-2166
Jones Sheep Farm B&B, Peabody, 66866, 316-983-2815
Cedar Crest, P.O. Box 387, Rt. 1, Pleasanton, 66075, 913-352-6706
Trix's Riley Roomer, 104 N. Hartner, Riley, 66531, 913-485-2654
Queen Anne's Lace B&B, 2617 Queen Anne's Lace, Rose Hill, 67133, 316-733-4075
Country Pleasures B&B, 1107 S. Bridge St., RR1 Box 30 C, 67860, 316-355-6982
Hunters Leigh B&B, 4109 E. North St., Salina, 67401, 913-823-6750
Spillman Creek Lodge, Sylvan Grove, 67481, 913-277-3424
Braddock Ames B&B, P.O. Box 892, Syracuse, 67878, 316-384-5218
Elderberry B&B, The, 1035 S.W. Fillmore St., Topeka, 66604, 913-235-6309
Heritage House, 3535 SW Sixth Ave., Topeka, 66606, 913-233-3800
Sunflower B&B, The, 915 SW Munsion Ave., Topeka, 66604, 913-357-7509
Little Bit Like Home, 323 E. Greeley, Tribune, 67879, 316-376-4776
Fort's Cedar View, RR 3, Box 120B, Ulysses, 67880, 316-356-2570
Barn B&B Inn, RR 2, Box 87, Valley Falls, 66088, 913-945-3303
B&B Still Country, Rt.1 Box 297, Wakefield, 69487
Rest & Relaxation B&B, Rt. 1 Box 297/206 6th, Wakefield, 67487, 913-461-5596
Rock House B&B, 201 Dogwood, Wakefield, 67487, 913-461-5732
Holiday House-Res. B&B, 8406 W. Maple, Wichita, 67209, 316-721-1968
Terradyne, 450 N. 159th East, Wichita, 67230
Iron Gate Inn, The, 1203 E. 9th., Winfield, 67156, 316-221-7202

Kentucky

AUGUSTA

Lamplighter Inn
103 W. 2nd St., 41002
606-756-2603
Kevin & Caroline Froehlich
All year

$$ B&B
9 rooms, 9 pb
Visa, MC, •
C-yes/S-ltd/P-no/H-no

Full breakfast
Restaurant
Bicycles, tennis court
sitting room

Country getaway, antique furnishings, antique shops, quaint town on the Ohio River. All rooms with private baths, cable TV and phone. **Free bottle wine w/dinner for guests**

BARDSTOWN

Jailer's Inn
111 W. Stephen Foster, 40004
502-348-5551
Fran McCoy
March–December

$$ B&B
5 rooms, 5 pb
Visa, MC, *Rated*, •
C-yes/S-ltd/H-yes

Continental breakfast
Comp. wine & cheese
Sitting room
landscaped courtyard
roses, gazebo

*Jailer's Inn was a jail (1819-74), then a jailer's residence (1874-1987), & is now completely remodeled, attractively decorated w/antiques & heirlooms. **Comp. wine/lemonade.***

COVINGTON

Amos Shinkle Townhouse
B&B
215 Garrard St., 41011
606-431-2118
Don Nash & Bernie Moorman
All year

$$ B&B
7 rooms, 7 pb
Most CC, *Rated*, •
C-yes/S-yes/P-no/H-ltd
Some German, French

Full breakfast
Aft. tea
Sitting room, library
whirlpool tub
walk to downtown

Located in Covington's historic district by the Ohio River. Rooms thick w/antiques. Delicious breakfast with "goetta," the area's signature dish. Flower-gardened B&B.

DANVILLE

Twin Hollies Retreat
406 Maple Ave., 40422
606-236-8954
Mary Joe & John Bowling
All year

$$ B&B
3 rooms, 1 pb
Rated, •
C-yes/S-yes/P-yes/H-yes

Continental plus
Afternoon tea
Sitting room, library
bicycles, hot tubs
fireplace, gardens

This fine old antebellum home features spacious rooms, elegant antiques and genuine southern hospitality in the heart of Kentucky's beautiful Bluegrass Region.

GLASGOW

Four Seasons Country Inn
4107 Scottsville Rd., 42141
502-678-1000
Henry Carter
All year

$$ B&B
17 rooms, 17 pb
Most CC, *Rated*, •
C-yes/S-yes/P-no/H-yes

Continental breakfast
Snacks
Sitting room
swimming pool

Charming Victorian-style inn built new in 1989. Modern conveniences and amenities with warm country furnishings and atmosphere. AAA 3 diamond.

LOUISVILLE

Old Louisville Inn
1359 S. Third St., 40208
502-635-1574
Marianne Lesher
All year

$$ B&B
11 rooms, 8 pb
Visa, MC, *Rated*, •
C-yes/S-ltd/P-no/H-no

Continental plus
Afternoon tea
Sitting room, library
bicycles, tennis 1 block
hot tub in one room

"Your home away from home." Wake up to the aroma of freshly baked breads and muffins and Southern hospitality. Children under 12 free.

Victorian Secret B&B, The
1132 South First St., 40203
502-581-1914
Nan-Ellen & Steve Roosa
All year

$$ B&B
6 rooms, 2 pb
Rated, •
C-yes/S-ltd/P-no/H-no

Continental plus
Restaurant
Sitting room
antiques

*Restored to its original elegance, the 110-year-old mansion provides a peaceful setting for enjoying period furnishings. National Register Neighborhood. **7th night free***

The RidgeRunner B&B, Middleborough, KY

MIDDLESBOROUGH

RidgeRunner B&B, The	$ B&B	Full breakfast
208 Arthur Heights, 40965	5 rooms, 2 pb	Comp. tea, refreshments
606-248-4299	Visa, MC, *Rated*,	Sitting room
The RidgeRunner B&B	C-ltd/S-no/P-no/H-no	library
All year		porch

Charming and lovingly restored Victorian mansion. Lovely woodwork, pocket doors, interesting windows, spacious porch. Breathtaking views of mountains. Antique furnishings.

MURRAY

Diuguid House B&B	$ B&B	Full breakfast
603 Main St., 42071	3 rooms	Afternoon tea, snacks
502-753-5470	Visa, MC, *Rated*, •	Sitting room, porch
Karen & George Chapman	C-yes/S-no/P-no/H-no	piano, TV, laundry
All year		

Historic Queen Anne centrally located in beautiful university town; close to Kentucky Lake and many antique shops. Nice retirement area. **7th night free.**

VERSAILLES

B&B at Sills Inn	$$ B&B	Full gourmet breakfast
270 Montgomery Ave., 40383	10 rooms, 10 pb	Snacks
606-873-4478 800-526-9801	Most CC, *Rated*, •	Library
Tony Sills	C-ltd/S-ltd/P-no/H-yes	public tennis courts
All year		5 suites w/jacuzzis

Restored Victorian inn & cottage, jacuzzi suites, full gourmet breakfast, walk to shopping & restaurants.

More Inns ...

Pepper Place, P.O. Box 95, Allensville, 42204, 502-265-9859
Auburn Guest House, 421 W. Main St., Auburn, 40475, 502-542-6019
David Williams Guest House, 421 West Main St., Auburn, 42206, 502-542-6019
1790 House, 110 E. Broadway, Bardstown, 40004, 502-348-7072
Amber LeAnn B&B, 209 E. Stephen Foster, Bardstown, 40004, 800-828-3330
Bruntwood Inn, 714 N. 3rd. St., Bardstown, 40004, 502-348-8218
Coffee Tree Cabin, 980 McCubbin's Lane, Bardstown, 40004, 502-348-1151
Mansion, The, 1003 N. Third, Bardstown, 40004

Talbot Tavern/McLean House, 107 W. Stephen Foster, Bardstown, 40004, 502-348-3494
Weller Haus, 319 Poplar St., Bellevue, 41073, 606-431-6829
Boone Tavern Hotel, CPO 2345, Berea, 40404, 606-986-9358
Vintage Rose, The, 118 Hwy. 62, Bloomfield, 40008, 502-252-5042
Alpine Lodge, 5310 Morgantown Rd., Bowling Green, 42101, 502-843-4846
Bowling Green B&B, 659 E. 14th Ave., Bowling Green, 42101, 502-781-3861
Doe Run Inn, Route 2, Brandenburg, 40108, 502-422-2982
East Hill Inn, 205 LaFayette St., Brandenburg, 40108, 502-422-3047
Annie's of Lake Cumberland, P.O. Box 246, Bronston, 42518, 606-561-9966
Round Oak Inn, P.O. Box 1331, Cadiz, 42211, 502-924-5850
Yellow Cottage, The, 400 N. Central, Campbellsville, 42718, 502-789-2669
P.J. Baker House B&B, The, 406 Highland Ave., Carrolton, 41008, 502-732-4210
Maple Grove Inn, 6100 N. Jackson Hwy., Cave City, 42127, 502-678-7123
Sandford House, 1026 Russell, Covington, 41011, 606-291-9133
Broadwell B&B, Route 6, Box 58, Cynthiana, 41031, 606-234-4255
Seldon Renaker Inn, 24 S. Walnut St., Cynthiana, 41031, 606-234-3752
Heartstone Country Inn, 331 South 4th. St., Danville, 40422
Randolf House, 463 W. Lexington, Danville, 40422, 606-236-9594
Ridley House, 108 W. Walnut St., Dawson Springs, 42408, 502-797-2165
Kenmore Farms, 1050 Bloomfield Rd., E. Bardstown, 40004, 502-348-8023
Cabin Fever, 459 Sportsman Lake Rd., Elizabethtown, 42701, 502-737-8748
Olde Bethlehem Academy, Elizabethtown, 42701, 502-862-9003
Olde Kantucke B&B Inn, 210 E. Fourth St., Frankfort, 40601, 502-227-7389
Taylor-Compton House, 419 Lewis St., Frankfort, 40601, 502-227-4368
College Street Inn, 223 South College, Franklin, 42134, 502-586-9352
Blackridge Hall B&B, 4055 Paris Pike, Georgetown, 40324, 800-768-9308
Breckinridge House B&B, 201 S. Broadway, Georgetown, 40324, 502-863-3163
Log Cabin B&B, 350 N. Broadway, Georgetown, 40324, 502-863-3514
Pineapple Inn, 645 S. Broadway, Rt. 25, Georgetown, 40324, 502-868-5453
Ghent House, P.O. Box 478, Ghent, 41045, 502-347-5807
B&B Country Cottage, 1609 Winn School Rd., Glasgow, 42141, 502-646-2940
Hall Place, 313 S. Green, Glasgow, 42141, 502-651-3176
Petticoat Junction, P.O. Box 36, Glendale, 42740, 502-369-8604
Beaumont Inn, 638 Beaumont Dr., Harrodsburg, 40330, 606-734-3381
Canaan Land Farm B&B, 4355 Lexington Rd., Harrodsburg, 40330, 606-734-3984
Canaan Land Farm B&B, 4355 Lexington Rd., Harrodsburg, 40330, 606-734-3984
Jailhouse B&B, 320 S. Chiles St., Harrodsburg, 40330, 606-743-7012
Shaker Village, 3500 Lexington Rd., Harrodsburg, 40330, 606-734-5411
Outback B&B, Box 4, Hazel, 42049, 502-436-5858
Quilt Maker Inn, P.O. Box 973, Hindman, 41822, 606-785-5622
Oakland Manor, 9210 Newstead Rd., Hopkinsville, 42240, 502-885-6400
Davis House B&B, The, R # 2, Box 21A1, Kuttawa, 42055, 502-388-4468
Perkins Place Farm, P.O. Box 553, Lancaster, 40444, 800-762-4145
Myrtledene, 370 N. Spaulding Ave., Lebanon, 40032, 502-692-2223
547-A B&B, 547 N. Broadway, Lexington, 40508, 606-255-4152
Cherry Knoll Farm B&B, 3975 Lemons Mill Rd., Lexington, 40511, 606-253-9800
Ms. Jesta Belle's, P.O. Box 8225, Lexington, 40533, 606-734-7834
Sycamore Ridge, 6855 Mt. Horeb Rd., Lexington, 40511
Liberty Greystone Manor, P.O. Box 329, Liberty, 42539, 606-787-5444
Angelmelli Inn, 1342 S. 6th St., Louisville, 40208, 800-245-9262
Rose Blossum, 1353 S. 4th St., Louisville, 40203, 502-636-0295
St. James Court, 1436 St. James Court, Louisville, 40208, 502-636-1742
Blair's Country Living, RR #3, Box 865-B, Manchester, 40962, 606-598-2854
LaFayette Club House, 173 LaFayette Hts., Marion, 42064, 502-965-3889
Helm House, 309 S. Tyler, Morgantown, 42261, 800-441-4786
Trimble House, 321 N. Maysville, Mount Sterling, 40353, 606-498-6561
Diuguid House B&B, 603 Main St., Murray, 42071, 502-753-5470
Sherwood Inn, 138 S. Main, New Haven, 40051, 502-549-3386
Getaway B&B, 326 E. 6th St., Newport, 41071, 606-581-6447
Cedar Haven Farm, 2380 Bethel Rd., Nicholasville, 40356, 606-858-3849
Sandusky House, 1626 Delaney Ferry Rd., Nicholasville, 40356, 606-223-4730
Silver Cliff Inn, 1980 Lake Barkley Dr., Old Kuttawa, 42055, 502-388-5858
WeatherBerry B&B, 2731 W. Second St., Owensboro, 42301, 502-684-8760
Ehrhardts B&B, 285 Springwell Dr., Paducah, 42001, 502-554-0644
Paducah Harbor Plaza B&B, 201 Broadway, Paducah, 42001, 502-442-2698
Elmwood Inn, 205 East Fourth, Perryville, 40468, 606-332-2400
Barnes Mill B&B, 1268 Barnes Mill Rd., Richmond, 40475, 606-623-5509
Log House, 2139 Franklin Rd., Russellville, 42276, 502-726-8483
Charlene's Country Inn B&B, HC 75, Box 265, Sandy Hook, 41171, 606-738-5712
Wallace House, 613 Washington St., Shelbyville, 40065, 502-633-4272
Osborne's of Cabin Hollow, 347B Elihu-Cabin Hollow, Somerset, 42501, 606-382-5495
Shadwick House, 411 S Main St., Somerset, 42501, 606-678-4675
Shaker Tavern, P.O. Box 181, Hwy 73, South Union, 42283, 502-542-6801
Shaker Tavern B&B, P.O. Box 181, South Union, 42283, 502-542-6801
Glenmar B&B, Rt. 1, Box 682, Springfield, 40069, 606-284-7791
Maple Hill Manor B&B, 2941 Perryville Rd., Springfield, 40069, 606-366-3075
Marcum-Porter House, P.O. Box 369, Sterns, 42647, 606-376-2242
Bowling's Villa, 1090 Stumps Lane, Taylorsville, 40071, 502-477-2636
B&B at Sills Inn, 270 Montgomery, Versailles, 40383, 800-526-9801
Rosehill Inn, 233 Rose Hill, Versailles, 40383, 606-873-5957
Shepherd Place, 31 Heritage Rd., Versailles, 40383, 606-873-7843
Ditto House Inn, 204 Elm St., West Point, 40177, 502-922-4939
Windswept Farm B&B, 5952 Old Boonesboro Rd., Winchester, 40391, 608-745-1245

Louisiana

CARENCRO

La Maison de Campagne
825 Kidder Rd., 70520
318-896-6529 800-368-3806
Joeann & Fred McLemore
All year

$$$ B&B
3 rooms, 3 pb
Visa, MC, *Rated*, •
C-ltd/S-no/P-no/H-no
Cajun French w/notice

Full breakfast-Cajun
Snacks, lunch w/notice
Sitting room, library
swimming pool
biking, jogging trail

Country setting; 200-year old live oaks & antiques; gourmet "Cajun" breakfast by award winning hostess/chef. 3 minutes from top Cajun restaurants.

MONROE

Boscobel Cottage B&B
185 Cordell Ln., 71202
318-325-1550
Kay & Cliff LaFrance
All year

$$$ B&B
2 rooms, 2 pb
Visa, MC, *Rated*,
C-yes/S-yes/P-yes/H-no

Full plantation brkfast
Comp. wine, snacks
Sitting room, porches
antique comforts
facing Ouachita River

*1820 Cottage listed on National Register. Lovely country hideaway, serene beauty. Stay in historic chapel or garconniere. All creature comforts. **20% off after 1st night.***

NAPOLEONVILLE

Madewood Plantation House
Route 2, Box 478, 4250 Hwy
308, 70390
504-369-7151
David D'Auroy & Janet Ledet
All year

$$$ MAP
8 rooms, 8 pb
•
C-ltd/S-ltd/P-ltd/H-no
some French

Full breakfast
Wine & cheese included
Dinner included
sitting room, piano
canopied beds

Greek Revival mansion. Canopied beds, antiques, fresh flowers, wine and cheese, dinner by candlelight in formal family dining room.

NEW IBERIA

Pourtos House
4018 Old Jeanerette Rd., 70560
318-367-7045 800-336-7317
Emma Fox
All year, FAX:364-8905

$$ B&B
5 rooms, 5 pb
Rated, •
C-ltd/S-ltd/P-no/H-no
Min. French/Spanish

Continental plus
Snacks, comp. wine
Sitting room, tennis
sauna, swimming pool
gym/billiard room, piano

Estate with historic cypress cabin (circa 1850) in Bayou country in the heart of Cajun Culture. Acadian Plantation. Continental plus breakfast. Beautiful!

NEW ORLEANS

623 Ursulines
623 Ursulines St., 70116
504-529-5489
Don Heil
All year

$$ EP
7 rooms, 7 pb
C-ltd/S-yes/P-no/H-no

Owners on premises offer advice on sightseeing, restaurants, tours and public transportation. Easy walking distance to popular attractions. Large, lush courtyard for guests.

Pourtos House, New Iberia, LA

NEW ORLEANS ─────────────────────────

Cornstalk Hotel, The	$$$ B&B	Continental breakfast
915 Royal St., 70116	14 rooms, 14 pb	Comp. tea, wine, paper
504-523-1515	Visa, MC, AmEx, •	Stained-glass windows
Debi & David Spencer	C-yes/S-yes/P-no/H-no	oriental rugs
All year	French, German	fireplaces

Small, elegant hotel in heart of French Quarter. All antique furnishings. Recent renovation.
Complimentary wine/liqueurs upon check in.

Dusty Mansion, The	$ B&B	Continental plus
2231 Gen. Pershing, 70115	4 rooms, 2 pb	Sunday champagne brunch
504-895-4576	•	Comp. wine, beverages
Cynthia Riggs	C-yes/S-yes/P-no/H-no	sitting room, hot tub
All year	Spanish, French	pool table, sun deck

Charming turn-of-the-century home, spacious, comfortable. Near St. Charles Street Car; easy access to French Quarter. Southern hospitality!

A Hotel. . .The Frenchmen	$$$ B&B	Full breakfast
417 Frenchmen St., 70116	25 rooms, 25 pb	Lunch, snacks
504-948-2166 800-831-1781	Visa, MC, AmEx, *Rated*,	Bar, sitting room
John Gipson	•	hot tubs, swimming pool
All year	C-ltd/S-yes/P-no/H-yes	sun deck, books

Each of the rooms is decorated with period furniture, ceiling fan & high ceiling. Classically served Frenchmen breakfast on silver trays in room. **10% disc't off rack rate**

NEW ORLEANS ——————————————————————————————

Lamothe House
621 Esplanade Ave., 70116
504-947-1161 800-367-5858
Carol Chauppette
All year

$$ B&B
20 rooms, 20 pb
Visa, MC, AmEx, •
C-yes/S-yes/P-no/H-no

Continental breakfast
Pralines, comp. beverage
Sitting room, courtyard
newspaper, parking
AAA 4-Diamond rating

An elegantly restored historic old mansion located on the eastern boundary of the French Quarter. This old mansion surrounds a romantic courtyard.

———

La Maison Marigny
B&B/RSO
P.O. Box 52257, 70152
Bourbon at Esplanade
504-488-4640 800-729-4640
Ms Jeremy Bazata
All year

$$$ B&B
2 rooms, 2 pb
Rated, •
C-ltd/S-ltd/P-no/H-no

Continental breakfast
Sitting room

At the edge of the French Quarter. Antique shops, galleries, river boats, music clubs & famous restaurants are a stroll from this historic B&B. **Sightseeing discounts**

———

Marquette House
2253 Carondelet St., 70130
504-523-3014
Steve & Alma Cross
All year

$ EP
12 rooms, 12 pb
Visa, MC, •
C-yes/S-no/P-no/H-no

Kitchenettes
Sitting rooms, veranda
garden-patio, fountain
TV in some rms., laundry

12 guest suites in pre-Civil War brick building. Beautiful garden-patio area with fountain. Kitchenettes in each room. Off-street parking. 12 suites in brick building.

———

Nine-O-Five Royal Hotel
905 Rue Royal St., 70116
504-523-0219
J.M.
All year

$$$ EP
14 rooms, 14 pb
Rated
C-yes/S-yes/P-no/H-no

Kitchens in all rooms
three suite

Quaint guest house built in the 1890s, located in the French Quarter. Nicely furnished, antiques, high ceilings. Kitchenettes and Southern charm.

———

Prytania Inns, The
1415 Prytania St., 2041 Prytania
St., 70130
504-566-1515
Sally & Peter Schreiber
All year

$ EP
17 rooms, 17 pb
Visa, MC, •
C-yes/S-ltd/Arabic, Fr,
Span, Greek

Full gourmet brkfast ($)
Afternoon tea
sitting room, library
parking

Charming Victorian, patio; southern gourmet breakfast, tender care; street car one block. French quarter, Super-Dome 5 minutes. **1 free streetcar pass**

———

Soniat House
1133 Chartres St., 70116
504-522-0570 800-544-8808
Rodney Smith
All year

$$$ EP
24 rooms, 24 pb
Visa, MC, AmEx, *Rated*,
•
C-ltd/S-yes/P-no/H-no
Spanish

Continental breakfast-$
Bar service
Jacuzzis
suites available

A private hotel in the residential area of the French Quarter, furnished in period antiques offering modern amenities. 1991 One of 10 Best Small Hotels in America—Traveler.

PRAIRIEVILLE

Tree House in the Park	$$ MAP	Full breakfast
16520 Airport Rd., Port Vincent,	4 rooms, 3 pb	Dinner included
70769	Visa, MC, •	Hot tubs, gazebo
800-532-2246	S-no/P-no/H-no	heated swimming pool
Fran & Julius Schmieder		kyak & pirogues
All year		

*Cajun cabin in the swamp. Rooms have private entrance, queen waterbed, TV/VCR, hot tub on deck under stars. Comp. first supper. Cypress trees, moss, ponds. **3rd night free***

SHREVEPORT

2439 Fairfield, A B&B	$$$ B&B	Full breakfast
2439 Fairfield Ave., 71104	4 rooms, 4 pb	Hot tubs, fountain
318-424-2424	Visa, AmEx, *Rated*, •	private garden, gazebo
Jimmy & Vicki Harris	C-ltd/S-no/P-no/H-no	balconies, library
All year		

1905 Victorian, p/baths w/whirlpools, p/balconies overlook English gardens w/gazebo, fountain, Victorian swing. Full English breakfast served. Sitting room

Fairfield Place B&B Inn	$$$ B&B	Full breakfast
2221 Fairfield Ave., 71104	9 rooms, 6 pb	Sitting room
318-222-0048	Visa, MC, AmEx, *Rated*,	
Janie Lipscomb	C-ltd/S-ltd/P-ltd/H-no	
All year		

Casually elegant 1900s inn. European and American antiques, gourmet breakfast. Ideal for business travelers and tourists.

ST. FRANCISVILLE

Barrow House Inn	$$$ B&B	Continental breakfast
P.O. Box 1461, 70775	7 rooms, 5 pb	Full breakfast $5
524 Royal St.	*Rated*, •	Dinner (res), comp. wine
504-635-4791	C-ltd/S-yes/P-no/H-no	sitting room, bicycles
Shirley & Lyle Dittloff		cassette walking tours
All year		

Circa 1809, located in historic district. Rooms with balconies and period antiques. Cassette walking tours for guests. Honeymoon packages. Arnold Palmer golf course nearby.

WHITE CASTLE

Nottoway Plantation Inn	$$$ B&B	Full breakfast
P.O. Box 160, 70788	13 rooms, 13 pb	Restaurant, comp. wine
30970 Highway 405	Visa, MC, *Rated*, •	Swimming pool
504-545-2730	C-yes/S-yes/P-no/H-ltd	sitting room
Cindy Hidalgo, Faye Russell	French	piano, tennis nearby
All year exc. Christmas		

Fresh flowers in your room, chilled champagne, a wake-up call consisting of hot sweet potato biscuits, coffee and juice delivered to your room. Also a guided tour of mansion.

More Inns . . .

Mt. Hope Plantation B&B, 8151 Highland Rd., Baton Rouge, 70808, 504-766-8600
Homeplace, Rt 2, Box 76A, Bunkie, 71322, 318-826-7558
The Country House, 825 Kidder Rd., Carencro, 70520, 318-896-6529
La Maison de Champagne, 825 Kidder Rd., Carenero, 70520, 318-896-6529
Tezcuco Plantation Village, 3138 Hwy. 44, Darrow, 70725, 504-562-3929
Asphodel Village, Rt. 2, Box 89 Hwy 68., Jackson, 70748, 504-654-6868
Milbank - Historic House, 102 Bank St., Box 1000, Jackson, 70748, 504-634-5901
Seven Oaks Plantation, 2600 Gay Lynn Dr., Kenner, 70065, 504-888-8649
Bois de Chenes Inn, 338 N. Sterling St., Lafayette, 70501, 318-233-7816
Mouton Manor Inn, 310 Sidney Martin Rd, Lafayette, 70507, 318-237-6996

Victoria Inn, Hwy 45, Box 545B, Lafitte, 70067, 504-689-4757
River Run B&B, 703 Main St., Madisonville, 70447, 504-845-4222
Jefferson House B&B, 229 Jefferson St., Natchitoches, 318-352-3957
Estorge-Norton House, 446 E. Main St., New Iberia, 70560, 318-365-7603
Annabelle's House B&B, 1716 Milan, New Orleans, 70115, 504-899-0701
Bougainvillea House, 841 Bourbon St., New Orleans, 70116, 504-525-3983
Chimes Cottages, 1360 Moss St., New Orleans, 70152, 504-525-4640
Columns Hotel, 3811 St. Charles Ave., New Orleans, 70115, 504-899-9308
Creole B&B, 3650 Gentilly Blvd., New Orleans, 70122
Dauzat Guest House, 337 Burgundy St., New Orleans, 70130, 504-524-2075
Delta Queen Steamboat Co., Robin St. Wharf, New Orleans, 70130, 800-543-1949
Dufour-Baldwin House, 1707 Esplanade Ave., New Orleans, 70116, 504-945-1503
French Quarter Maisonnette, 1130 Chartres St., New Orleans, 70116, 504-524-9918
Grenoble House Inn, 329 Dauphine St., New Orleans, 70112, 504-522-1331
Hedgewood Hotel, 2427 St. Charles Ave., New Orleans, 70130, 504-895-9708
Historic B&B Home, P.O. Box 52257, New Orleans, 70152, 800-749-4640
Historic Inns/New Orleans, 911 Burgundy St., New Orleans, 70116, 504-524-4401
Hotel Maison de Ville, 727 Toulouse St., New Orleans, 70130, 504-561-5858
Hotel St. Pierre, 911 Burgundy St., New Orleans, 70116, 504-524-4401
Hotel Ste. Helene, 508 Rue Chartres, New Orleans, 70130, 504-522-5014
Hotel Villa Convento, 616 Ursulines St., New Orleans, 70116, 504-522-1793
House on Bayou Road, The, 2275 Bayou Rd., New Orleans, 70119, 504-945-0992
Jensen's B&B, 1631 Seventh St., New Orleans, 70115
Josephine Guest House, 1450 Josephine St., New Orleans, 70130, 504-524-6361
Lafitte Guest House, 1003 Bourbon St., New Orleans, 70116, 504-581-2678
Longpre Garden's Gsthouse, 1726 Prytania, New Orleans, 70130, 504-561-0654
MacArthy Park Guest House, 3820 Burgundy St., New Orleans, 70117, 505-943-4994
Maison Orleans, 608 Kerlerac St., New Orleans, 70116
Mazant Guest House, 906 Mazant St., New Orleans, 70117
Mechling's Guest House, 2023 Esplande Ave., New Orleans, 70116, 504-943-4131
Melrose B&B, 937 Esplanade Ave., New Orleans, 70116, 504-944-2255
Noble Arms Inn, 1006 Royal St., New Orleans, 70116, 504-524-2222
Old World Inn, 1330 Prytania, New Orleans, 70130, 504-566-1330
Parkview Guest House, 7004 St. Charles, New Orleans, 70118, 504-861-7564
Terrell House Mansion, 1441 Magazine St., New Orleans, 70130, 504-524-9859
Pointe Coupee B&B, Office 605 E. Main St., New Roads, 70760, 504-638-6254
Estorge House, 427 N. Market St., Opelousas, 70570, 318-948-4592
Bedico Creek Inn, 665 C C. Rd, Ponchatoula, 70454, 504-845-8057
Tree House in the Park, 16520 Airport Rd., Prairieville, 70769, 504-622-2850
Cottage Plantation, Route 5, Box 425, Saint Francisville, 70775, 504-635-3674
Myrtles Plantation, P.O. Box 1100, Hwy 61, Saint Francisville, 70775, 504-635-6277
St. Francisville Inn, P.O. Box 1369, Saint Francisville, 70775, 504-635-6502
Columns on Jordan, The, 615 Jordan, Shreveport, 71101, 318-222-5912
Butler Greenwood B&B, HC 69, Box 438, St. Francisville, 70775, 800-749-1928
Old Castillo Hotel, The, 220 Evangeline Blvd, St. Martinville, 70582, 318-394-4010
Oak Alley Plantation, Route 2 Box 10, Hwy. 18, Vacherie, 70090, 504-265-2151
Old Lyons House, 1335 Horridge St., Vinton, 70668, 318-589-2903
Viroqua Heritage Inn, 220 E. Jefferson, Viroqua, 70665, 608-637-3306
Wakefield Plantation, P.O. Box 41, Wakefield, 70784
Camellia Cove, 205 West Hill St, Washington, 70589, 318-826-7362
De La Morandiere, P.O. Box 327, Washington, 70589, 318-826-3510
La Chaumiere, 202 S Main St, Washington, 70589, 318-826-3967
Glencoe Plantation, P.O. Box 178, Wilson, 70789, 504-629-5387

La Maison Marigny, New Orleans, LA

Maine

BAR HARBOR ───

Balance Rock Inn
21 Albert Meadow, 04609
207-288-2610 800-753-0494
Nancy & Michael Cloud
May—October 27

$$$ B&B
14 rooms, 14 pb
Most CC, *Rated*, •
C-ltd/S-ltd/P-no/H-no
French

Continental breakfast
Full breakfast $
Aftn. tea, sitting room
hot tubs, fireplaces
oceanside heated pool

Turn-of-the-century oceanfront mansion w/ lovely rooms & spectacular ocean views. Ideal spot for romantic vacations. In-room amenities vary. Walk to downtown. **Free champagne**

───

Bayview Inn
111 Eden St. (Route 3), 04609
207-288-5861 800-356-3585
Mr. & Mrs. John Davis, Jr.
All year

$$$ EP
6 rooms, 6 pb
Visa, MC, AmEx, *Rated*,
•
C-ltd/S-yes/P-no, French,
Spanish

Continental plus $
Lunch, dinner, bar
Sitting room, library
piano, pool, badminton
croquet, games, kayaks

Luxury 8-acre waterfront estate reminiscent of the gracious chateaux of southern France. Elegant, intimate hotel, townhouses also available.

───

Black Friar Inn
10 Summer St., 04609
207-288-5091
Barbara & Jim Kelly
May—October

$$$ B&B
6 rooms, 6 pb
Visa, MC, *Rated*,
C-ltd/S-no/P-no/H-no

Full breakfast
Aft. tea & refreshments
Sitting room
fly fishing trips
Sea Kayak School-May

Rebuilt in 1981 with antiques & architectural finds from Mt. Desert Island. Victorian & country flavor. Near Acadia National Park, shops, restaurants. 2 day min stay Jul-Oct.

───

Breakwater - 1904
45 Hancock St., 04609
207-288-2313 800-238-6309
Margot & Russell Snyder
Late April - New Year's

$$$ B&B
6 rooms, 6 pb
Visa, MC, AmEx, *Rated*,
•
C-ltd/S-no/P-no

Full breakfast
Aft. tea, snacks
Comp. wine
sitting room, library
billiard table

Oceanfront English Tudor estate w/breathtaking views, gardens and uncommon elegance in a relaxed atmosphere. National Registry of Historic Places.

───

Castlemaine Inn, The
39 Holland Ave., 04609
207-288-4563 800-338-4563
Norah E. O'Brien
All year

$$ B&B
12 rooms, 12 pb
Visa, MC, AmEx, *Rated*,
C-ltd/S-ltd/P-no

Continental plus
All A/C, all cable TV
2 day minimum July
August & holidays

The inn is nestled on a quiet side street in Bar Harbor village, surrounded by the magnificent Acadia National Park. Rooms are well-appointed. AAA 3-Diamond rating.

───

Cleftstone Manor
92 Eden St., 04609
207-288-4951
Pattie & Don Reynolds
April—October

$$$ B&B
16 rooms, 16 pb
Visa, MC, *Rated*, •
C-ltd/S-no/P-no/H-no
Spanish

Full breakfast
Comp. tea, wine & cheese
Sitting room, library
games, formal gardens
restaurant nearby

Recapture timeless splendor in charming Victorian 33-rm cottage amidst formal gardens. Lavish buffet. Lace curtains, goose-down comforters, fireplaces. **Fruit basket**

BAR HARBOR ——————————————————————————

Graycote Inn
40 Holland Ave., 04609
207-288-3044 800-GRA-COTE
Joe & Judy Losquadro
May–November

$$$ B&B
12 rooms, 12 pb
Visa, MC, *Rated*,
C-ltd/S-ltd/P-no/H-no

Full breakfast
Comp. wine & snacks
Sitting room, fireplaces
king or queen-size beds
fireplaces, balconies

Elegantly restored Victorian inn located near Acadia Nat'l Park & Frenchman's Bay. Numerous shops, fine restaurants in walking distance. **Reduced rates off-season**

Hearthside B&B
7 High St., 04609
207-288-4533
Susan & Barry Schwartz
All year

$$$ B&B
9 rooms, 9 pb
Visa, MC, *Rated*,
C-ltd/S-no/P-no/H-no

Continental plus
Comp. wine, cookies
Evening refreshments
3 rooms w/fireplaces
2 bath w/whirlpool jets

Small, gracious hostelry in quiet in-town location; elegant & comfortable; furnished w/blend of antiques & traditional furniture. Visit Bar Harbor & Acadia Nat'l Park.

Holbrook House Inn
74 Mt. Desert St., 04609
207-288-4970
Jack & Jeani Ochtera
Mid-May–mid-October

$$$ B&B
12 rooms, 12 pb
AmEx, Visa, MC, *Rated*,
C-ltd/S-ltd/P-no/H-no

Full breakfast
Afternoon refreshments
Old fashion porch-parlor
library, inn rooms
beautiful furnishings

A bright and airy restored Victorian summer home on Bar Harbor's Historic Corridor. Close to shops, restaurants, ocean and park. Off-street parking. **4th night free, ltd**

Ledgelawn Inn, The
66 Mount Desert St., 04609
207-288-4596 800-274-5334
Nancy & Michael Cloud
April–November

$$$ B&B
33 rooms, 33 pb
MC, Visa, AmEx, •
C-yes/S-yes/P-no/H-no

Continental plus
Bar service, comp. tea
Sitting room, library
piano, pool, sauna
modern exercise room

A graceful turn-of-the-century mansion with lots of charm, antiques, sitting areas, fireplaces, hot tub; in a quiet location only 5 minutes walk to downtown. **Comp. champagne**

Manor House Inn
106 West St., 04609
207-288-3759 800-437-0088
Malcom Noyes
May–mid-October

$$$ B&B
14 rooms, 14 pb
Visa, MC, AmEx, *Rated*,
C-ltd/S-no/P-no/H-no

Continental plus
Afternoon tea
Sitting room, fireplaces
swimming pool, piano
gardens, tennis courts

Many special touches. Restored Victorian, National Register, antique furniture. Bedrms inc. parlor, bath. Near Acadia National Park. **4th night free off-season wkdys.**

Mira Monte Inn
69 Mt. Desert St., 04609
207-288-4263 800-553-5109
Marian Burns
Early May–late October

$$$ B&B
11 rooms, 11 pb
Visa, MC, AmEx, *Rated*,
•
C-ltd/S-yes/P-no/H-ltd

Continental plus
Comp. wine & cheese
Juice, snacks
sitting room, piano
all rms: phones, A/C, TV

Renovated Victorian estate; period furnishings, fireplaces, one-acre grounds; quiet, in-town location, two king beds, walk to waterfront. **honeymoon 4/7 day pkgs: 50% off**

BAR HARBOR

Primrose Inn
73 Mt. Desert St., 04609
207-288-4031 800-543-7842
Bronwen & George Kaldro
May-October

$$$ B&B
13 rooms, 13 pb
Most CC, *Rated*, •
C-yes/S-ltd/P-no/H-ltd

Continental plus
Aft. tea
Sitting room

1878 Victorian guest house on "Historic Corridor." Antique furnishings, some rooms w/whirl-pool, porch, fireplace. Near Acadia and downtown.

Town Guest House
12 Atlantic Ave., 04609
207-288-5548 800-458-8644
Joe & Paulette Paluga
May–October

$$$ EP/B&B
9 rooms, 9 pb
Visa, MC, AmEx, *Rated*,
•
C-yes/S-no/P-no/H-no

Continental plus
Sitting room

Victorian inn offers old-fashioned comfort with modern conveniences. Enjoy period furniture, marble sinks, porches, working fireplaces, private baths in our gracious rooms.

BASS HARBOR

Bass Harbor Cottages Inn
P.O. Box 40, 04653
Rt. 102 A
207-244-3460
Constance L. Howe
All year

$$ EP
3 rooms, 3 pb
Visa, MC, *Rated*,
C-yes/S-no/P-no/H-no

Kitchen available
In room refrigerators
TVs in cottages
porch overlooks harbor
near Acadia Nat'l Park

Our small, intimate inn offers privacy, tranquility & views of the harbor. A staircase leads to the water's edge.

Pointy Head Inn
HCR 33, Box 2A, Route 102A,
04653
207-244-7261
Doris & Warren Townsend
Mid-May–October

$$ B&B
6 rooms, 3 pb
C-ltd/S-no/P-no/H-no

Full breakfast
Sitting room with TV
two organs
porch, deck

Old sea captain's home on the ocean in Bass Harbor. 1 mile from Bass Harbor Headlight in Acadia National Park. A haven for artists and photographers.

BATH

Fairhaven Inn at Bath
RR 2, Box 85, N. Bath Rd., 04530
207-443-4391
George & Sallie Pollard
All year

$$ B&B
6 rooms, 6 pb
Rated, •
C-ltd/S-yes/P-no/H-no

Full breakfast
Tea, soda
Piano, library, bicycles
hiking trail, cross-country
skiing
winter snowshoeing

Old country inn surrounded by 27 acres of meadows, woods, lawns. Antique bed sets, quilts, etc. Hiking, swimming, golf nearby. Gourmet breakfasts available. **Winter disc't**

Inn at Bath, The
969 Washington St., 04530
207-443-4294
Nick Bayard
All year

$$ B&B
5 rooms, 5 pb
Most CC, *Rated*, •
C-yes/S-ltd/P-ltd/H-no

Full breakfast
Comp. wine, aftn. tea
Sitting room, Library
Fireplaces
A+C in all guest rooms

Historical elegance—comfortable 1810 Greek Revival home with private baths, antiques and fireplaces. Near Maritime Museum, ocean beaches and Freeport.

BELFAST

Jeweled Turret Inn, The	$$ B&B	Full breakfast
16 Pearl St., 04915	7 rooms, 7 pb	Aftn. tea by res., ltd
207-338-2304 800-696-2304	*Rated*, •	Sitting rooms, parlors
Carl & Cathy Heffentrager	C-ltd/S-ltd/P-no/H-no	antiques
All year		tennis & pool nearby

Intimate, charming, romantic. Unique architectural features; turrets, verandas, fireplaces, beautiful woodwork. Walk to town, shops & harbor. On National Register.

Penobscot Meadows Inn	$ B&B	Continental plus
M.A.: 90 Northport Ave.,	7 rooms, 7 pb	Lunch, dinner
Route 1, 04915	Visa, MC, *Rated*,	Bar
207-338-5320 FAX:338-5321	C-yes/S-yes/P-yes/H-ltd	sitting room
Dini & Bernie Chapnick	French, Spanish, Portug.	
All year		

Beautifully restored inn on Penobscot Bay convenient for touring mid-coast Maine; gourmet dining features homemade breads, pasta, ice cream & pate. AAA/Mobil 3 diamonds/stars.

BETHEL

Chapman Inn B&B, The	$$ B&B	Full breakfast
P.O. Box 206, 04217	10 rooms, 4 pb	Comp. coffee or tea
On the Common	Visa, MC, AmEx, •	Sauna, cable TV, beach
207-824-2657	C-yes/S-yes/P-ltd/H-no	sitting & game room, VCR
Sandra & George Wight		dorm facilities
All year		

In heart of historic district. Large, sunny rooms. Breakfast featuring fresh fruits and whole grains. Recreation nearby. Family and weekly rates. **Free gift, mention book**

Hammons House, The	$$ B&B	Full breakfast
P.O. Box 16, 04217	4 rooms	Comp. wine
Broad St.	Visa, MC	Porches, art gallery
207-824-3170	C-yes/S-no/P-no/H-no	patio, conservatory
Sally & Dick Taylor	German	2 rm. suite w/priv. bath
All year		

Comfort and elegance of historic circa 1859 home; antique furnishings, beautiful gardens, delicious breakfasts. Convenient to restaurants, shops, skiing, golf.

BINGHAM

Mrs. G's B&B	$$ B&B	Full breakfast
P.O. Box 389, 04920	4 rooms, 2 pb	Dinner by reservation
Meadow St.	•	Comp. wine
207-672-4034	C-yes/S-yes/P-no/H-no	horseshoes, badminton
Frances M. Gibson	Italian	nearby tennis
May—October		

Old Victorian home with rocking chairs on front porch. Walking distance to churches, shopping, restaurants. Situated on scenic Kennebec River. A lovely loft can hold 10.

BOOTHBAY HARBOR

Admiral's Quarters Inn	$$ EP/B&B	Continental breakfast
105 Commercial St., 04538	7 rooms, 7 pb	Unsurpassed harbor view
207-633-2474	Visa, MC, *Rated*,	comp. coffee
Jean E. Duffy	C-ltd/S-yes/P-no/H-ltd	decks, sea views
All year		

Commanding a view of the Harbor unsurpassed by all, this large old sea captain's house & newly-bought adjacent house have pretty rooms, private baths and decks for viewing.

BOOTHBAY HARBOR

Anchor Watch B&B
P.O. Box 535, 04538
3 Eames Rd.
207-633-7565
Diane Campbell
All year

$$ B&B
4 rooms, 4 pb
Rated, •
C-ltd/S-yes/P-no/H-no

Full breakfast
Efficiency appt. avail.
Fresh strawberries from
courtyard (in season)
3 rooms with ocean views

*Scenic shore; winter ducks feed near the rocks; flashing lighthouses; lobstermen hauling traps, walk to restaurants, shops, boats. **Stay 2 nights—free harbor tour, ltd***

Atlantic Ark Inn, The
64 Atlantic Ave., 04538
207-633-5690
Donna Piggott
May–October

$$ B&B
6 rooms, 6 pb
C-ltd/S-ltd/P-no/H-no

Full gourmet breakfast
Comp. wine or sherry
Iced tea, iced coffee
One rm. w/ jacuzzi for 2
sitting room, near town

Quaint & intimate, this small inn offers lovely harbor views, antiques, oriental rugs, mahogany beds, flowers. Suite luxurious: 16 windows, private balcony, panoramic view.

Howard House, The
Route 27, 04538
207-633-3933 207-633-6244
Jim & Ginny Farrin
All year

$ B&B
15 rooms, 15 pb
Rated, •
C-yes/S-yes/P-no/H-ltd

Full breakfast buffet
Private balconies
non-smoking rooms avail.

*Unique chalet design on 20 wooded acres; sparkling clean modern rooms with private balconies; one mile from downtown Boothbay Harbor. **10% discount—ask***

Kenniston Hill Inn
P.O. Box 125, 04537
Route 27
207-633-2159 800-992-2915
David & Susan Straight
All year

$$ B&B/MAP
10 rooms, 10 pb
Visa, MC, *Rated*, •
C-ltd/S-no/P-no/H-ltd

Full breakfast
Fireside dining
Sitting room, fireplaces
fishing, boating, skiing
tennis, golf, swimming

*Oldest inn in Boothbay (c. 1786) on 4 peaceful acres offering country antiques, fireplaces & sitting rooms, full country breakfast. **10% off daily room rate***

BRIDGTON

Noble House B&B, The
P.O. Box 180, 04009
37 Highland Ridge Rd.
207-647-3733
The Starets Family
Mid Oct - Mid June res.

$$ B&B
9 rooms, 6 pb
•
C-ltd/S-ltd/P-no/H-no

Full breakfast
Sitting room, library
baby grand piano, organ
canoe, lake, lawn games

Majestic turn-of-the-century home on beautiful Highland Lake; four-season activities; antique and craft shops, summer theater, skiing, family suites, personal attention.

Tarry-a-While B&B Resort
RD 3, Box 68, Highland Ridge
Rd., 04009
207-647-2522
Hans & Barbara Jenni
May–October

$$$ B&B
36 rooms, 26 pb
Rated
C-yes/S-yes/P-no/H-no
German

Continental plus buffet
3 sandy beaches, library
free canoes, pedal boats
rowboats, tennis, bikes

*Several cottages with 4 rooms each. Rooms w/private baths have A/C, heaters. Schloss-Victorian with majestic views. Switzer Stubli Restaurant on premises. **Off-season upgrade***

BRUNSWICK

Dove B&B, The
16 Douglas St., 04011
207-729-6827
Diana Dove
All year

$ B&B
2 rooms,
•
C-yes/some Spanish

Continental plus
Sunroom
badminton
9 miles to L.L. Bean

Stately old trees grace this newly restored colonial B&B near Maine coast & beaches. Near Bowdoin College. Homemade muffins & hospitality our specialties. **7th night free.**

Samuel Newman House B&B
7 South St., 04011
207-729-6959
Guenter Rose
All year

$$ B&B
7 rooms
Visa, MC, *Rated*
C-yes/S-no/P-no/H-no

Continental plus
Comp. tea
Sitting room
airport limo service
no smoking policy

A handsome federal-style house built in 1821, next to Bowdoin College, near the coast; 10 miles from Freeport. Airport limo service from Portland Airport.

BUCKSPORT

Old Parsonage Inn
P.O. Box 1577, 04416
190 Franklin St.
207-469-6477
Judith & Brian Clough
All year

$ B&B
3 rooms, 1 pb
C-yes/S-ltd

Full breakfast
Kitchenette unit
Sitting room
walk to restaurants
and waterfront

Historic home, winding stairway, private entrance, furnished with antiques and reproductions. Centrally located coastal village. **3rd night 50% off.**

CAMDEN

Abigail's B&B
8 High St., 04843
207-236-2501
Donna & Ed Misner
All year

$$ B&B
3 rooms, 3 pb
Visa, MC, •
C-yes/S-no/P-no/H-no

Full breakfast
Afternoon tea
Sitting room
Porch, library
Near hiking/golf/tennis

Historic Federal w/country elegance, hospitality. 2 new Carriage House Suites. Walk to harbor, shops, restaurants. Fireplaced parlors, wicker-filled porch. **10% off week stay**

Blackberry Inn
82 Elm St., 04843
207-236-6060 800-833-6674
Edward & Vicki Doudera
All year

$$ B&B
10 rooms, 10 pb
Visa, MC
C-yes/S-no/P-no/H-no
French, Italian

Full gourmet breakfast
Comp. wine & cheese
Sitting rooms, library
A/C, fireplaces
outdoor courtyard

A wonderfully ornate Victorian home furnished in period style. New Garden Rooms offer romantic luxury. 2-bedroom Carriage House is perfect for families. Dinner by request.

Blue Harbor House Inn
67 Elm St., 04843
207-236-3196 800-248-3196
Jody Schmoll & Dennis Hayden
All year

$$$ B&B
10 rooms, 10 pb
Visa, MC, *Rated*, •
C-yes/S-no/P-ltd/H-no

Full gourmet breakfast
Picnic lunch, dinner
Comp. wine, aftn. snack
TV, old movies, VCR
1/4-acre yard, bicycles

Restored circa 1835 homestead, antique furnishings, authentic country charm, cozy, comfortable accommodations, warm friendly hospitality. **2 nights comp. dinner for 2**

CAMDEN ——————————————————————————————————

Camden Harbour Inn
83 Bayview St., 04843
207-236-4200
Sal Vella & Patti Babij
All year

$$$ B&B
22 rooms, 22 pb
Most CC, *Rated*, •
C-ltd/S-yes/P-no/H-yes

Full breakfast from menu
Dinner, bar service
Parlour, porch, patio
lounge with fireplace
meeting facilities

Historic 1874 Victorian inn with spectacular panorama of harbor, bay and mountains. Fine dining; cocktails in the Thirsty Whale. Meeting facilities. Winter weekend specials.

Edgecombe-Coles House
HCR 60 Box 3010, 64 High St.,
04843
207-236-2336 FAX:236-6227
Terry & Louise Price
All year

$$$ B&B
6 rooms, 6 pb
Visa, MC, AmEx, DC,
C-ltd/S-yes/P-no/H-no

Full breakfast
Comp. eve. port, sherry
Sitting room, piano
library, bicycles
tennis courts

*Distinctive country inn with breathtaking views of Penobscot Bay. Antique furnishings, private baths, hearty breakfasts. Maine's most beautiful seaport. **3rd night 50%, ltd.***

Elms Bed & Breakfast, The
84 Elm St., Route 1, 04843
207-236-6250
Joan A. James
All year

$$ B&B
6 rooms, 4 pb
Visa, MC
C-ltd/S-no/P-no/H-no

Full gourmet breakfast
Cottage gardens, library
antiques throughout
carriage house rooms

Gracious 1806 Colonial w/candles aglow at the windows to welcome you to pretty bed chambers, sumptuous candlelight breakfasts and "A TRADITION OF HOSPITALITY"

Hartstone Inn
41 Elm St., 04843
207-236-4259
Sunny & Peter Simmons
All year

$$$ EP/B&B
10 rooms, 10 pb
Most CC, *Rated*, •
C-ltd/S-yes/P-no/H-no

Full breakfast
Dinner, picnic sails
Comp. tea, cookies
sitting room, fireplaces
library, TV room

Stately Victorian inn, centrally located in picturesque village, steps away from harbor. Hearty breakfasts, romantic dinners, friendly, relaxed atmosphere.

Hawthorn Inn
9 High St., 04843
207-236-8842 FAX:236-6181
Pauline & Bradford Staub
All year

$$ B&B
9 rooms, 9 pb
Visa, MC, *Rated*, •
C-ltd/S-no/P-no/H-no

Full breakfast buffet
Afternoon tea
2 sitting rooms
piano, hot tub in suites
volleyball

*Refurbished Victorian home with light, airy rooms. Views of either harbor or mountains. Just a 5-minute walk to shops and restaurants. **Honeymoon gift basket***

A Little Dream
66 High St., 04843
207-236-8742
Joanna Ball, Bill Fontana
All year

$$$ B&B
5 rooms, 5 pb
Visa, MC, AmEx
C-ltd/S-no/P-no/H-no
Italian, some Fr. & Ger.

Full breakfast
Comp. sherry
Sitting room
antique books

Lovely luxury B&B in a turn-of-the-century turreted Victorian. Rooms with waterview, decks, or fireplace. Featured in Country Inns Magazine & Glamour Magazine.

CAMDEN ───

Lord Camden Inn
24 Main St., 04843
207-236-4325 800-336-4325
Bill Hughes
All year

$$$ B&B
31 rooms, 28 pb
Visa, MC, AmEx, *Rated*,
•
C-yes/S-yes/P-no/H-ltd

Continental breakfast
Tennis available
bicycles next door
All rooms A/C

Restored 1893 Main Street building has 31 Colonial furnished rooms with private baths, TVs and phones. 3 new luxury suites. Open year-round.

Maine Stay
22 High St., 04843
207-236-9636
Peter, Donny, & Diana
All year

$$$ B&B
8 rooms, 4 pb
Visa, MC, *Rated*, •
C-ltd/S-yes/P-no/H-no
French

Full breakfast
2 parlors w/fireplaces
piano, TV room
deck

Built in 1802, the inn is situated in the high street historic district on two acres of lovely grounds only two blocks from the harbor and village center.

Norumbega Inn
61 High St., Route 1, 04843
207-236-4646
Murray Keatinge
All year

$$$ B&B
12 rooms, 12 pb
•
C-ltd/S-yes/P-no/H-no

Full breakfast to room
Guest refrigerator
comp. tea, wine, snacks
3 sitting rooms

Camden's "stone castle," built 1886. Magnificent oak woodwork, spectacular views of Penobscot Bay and islands. Four acres of private grounds.

Spouter Inn, The
U.S. Rt 1, Box 176, Lincolnville
Beach, 04849
207-789-5171
Paul & Catherine Lippman
All year

$$ B&B
4 rooms, 4 pb
Most CC, *Rated*,
C-ltd/S-no/P-no/H-no

Full breakfast
Aft. tea, snacks
Comp. wine, sitting room
library, beach
sea kayak, jacuzzi

Ocean views from every room in restored 1832 Colonial. Private baths, fireplaces, antiques. Located 100 ft. from ocean. Walk to restaurants and shops.

Swan House
49 Mountain St. (Rt 52), 04843
207-236-8275
Lyn & Ken Kohl
May—October

$$$ B&B
6 rooms, 6 pb
Visa, MC
C-ltd/S-no/P-no/H-ltd

Full breakfast
Sitting room
outdoor gazebo

Located in a quiet neighborhood, a short walk from Camden's Harbor. Hearty breakfasts and country antiques. Enjoy the private backyard gazebo.

Windward House B&B
6 High St., 04843
207-236-9656
Jon & Mary Davis
All year

$$ B&B
5 rooms, 5 pb
Visa, MC
C-ltd/S-no/P-no/H-no

Full gourmet breakfast
Comp. port, sherry
Sitting rooms, library
suite available
garden room

In Harbor Village; spacious historic 1854 colonial fully restored, beautifully decorated, furnished with fine antiques. Gracious hospitality. Full gourmet breakfast.

CAPE ELIZABETH ————————————————————————

Inn by the Sea	$$$ EP	Restaurant - meals $
40 Bowery Beach Rd., Route 77,	43 rooms, 43 pb	Snacks, bar service
04107	*Rated*, •	Library, bicycles
207-799-3134	C-yes/S-yes/P-no/H-yes	tennis court, pool
Maureen McQuade	French	croquet, volleyball
All year		

Luxury suites in chippendale cherry or white pine & natural wicker. Overlooking Atlantic, full kitchen, living/dining area. Natural estuaries.

CASTINE ————————————————————————

Manor, The	$$$ B&B	Continental plus
Box 276, Battle Ave., 04421	12 rooms, 10 pb	La Conque Restaurant/bar
207-326-4861	Visa, MC, •	Sitting room, library
Sara & Paul Brouillard	C-yes/S-yes/P-ltd/H-no	lounge, billiard room
All year exc. Christmas	French, Spanish	piano, bicycles, cottage

Elegant turn-of-the-century mansion. Very quiet, yet close to restaurants and shops. Gourmet dining on-site, 5 acres of lawns. National Register.

COREA ————————————————————————

Black Duck on Corea Harbor	$$ B&B	Full breakfast
P.O. Box 39, 04624	5 rooms, 3 pb	Sitting room, library
Crowley Island Rd.	•	bicycles
207-963-2689	C-ltd/S-no/P-no/H-no	hiking trails
Barry Canner, Bob Travers	Danish, ltd French	
All year		

Casual elegance, antiques and art. Overlooking working lobster harbor. Village charm with rural atmosphere. Near national park and bird sanctuary. **10% off for 7+ nights**

DAMARISCOTTA ————————————————————————

Brannon-Bunker Inn	$$ B&B	Continental plus
HCR 64 Box 045E, #45 Route	9 rooms, 4 pb	Kitchen facilities
129, 04543	Visa, MC, *Rated*, •	Sitting room
207-563-5941	C-yes/S-no/P-no/H-ltd	porch
Jeanne & Joe Hovance		antique shop on premises
All year		

Country B&B; charming rooms furnished with antiques; close to all mid-coast recreational facilities including ocean, beach, boating & golf; antiquing!

Elizabeth's B&B	$ B&B	Continental plus
Box 004, HC 61, Bristol Rd. (Rte.	2 rooms, 2 pb	Homemade breads
130), 04543	*Rated*, •	Sitting room
207-563-1919	C-ltd/S-no/P-no/H-no	on a hill with choice of
Elizabeth B. Bates	Spanish, French, German	water or garden view
All year		

Charming home furnished with country antiques in coastal village, overlooking tidal Damariscotta River. Sun deck. Warm, personal attention. **Fifth night free**

DEER ISLE ————————————————————————

Pilgrim's Inn	$$$ B&B/MAP	Full breakfast
Box 69, Main St., 04627	13 rooms, 8 pb	Supper, tea, coffee, bar
207-348-6615	*Rated*, •	Sitting room, piano
Jean & Dud Hendrick	C-ltd/S-no/P-yes/H-no	bicycles, library, deck
Mid-May—mid-October		patio grill area, garden

Idyllic location on Deer Isle. Elegant yet informal colonial inn, creative cuisine, rustic antique-furnished barn. Commons rooms with 8' fireplaces. **Special mug**

DENNYSVILLE

Lincoln House Country Inn	$$$ MAP	Full breakfast
Routes 1 & 86, 04628	11 rooms, 4 pb	Dinner included
207-726-3953	Visa, MC, AmEx, *Rated*,	Bar, sitting room
Mary & Jerry Haggerty	•	grand piano, library
Open mid-May - mid-Oct.	C-yes/S-yes/P-no/H-yes	fireplaces

Lovingly restored colonial w/95 acres of hiking, birding & fishing. Centerpiece of N.E. corner of coastal Maine. Int'lly acclaimed. National Register. **3rd night 50% lodging**

EASTPORT

Todd House	$ B&B	Continental plus
1 Capen Av, Todd's Head, 04631	7 rooms, 3 pb	Library, fireplace
207-853-2328	•	yard with barbecue
Ruth M. McInnis	C-yes/S-ltd/P-yes/H-yes	picnic facilities
All year		

Step into the past in our revolutionary-era Cape with wide panorama of Passamaquoddy Bay. Breakfast in common room before huge fireplace.

Weston House B&B	$$ B&B	Full breakfast
26 Boynton St., 04631	5 rooms	Comp. wine, tea, snacks
207-853-2907	C-ltd/S-ltd/P-no/H-no	Picnic lunch & dinner
Jett & John Peterson		sitting room, library
All year		croquet, "secret garden"

1810 Federal located on a hill overlooking Passamaquoddy Bay. On National Register of Historic Places. Furnished with antiques, clocks and family treasures. **3rd night 50%**

ELIOT

High Meadows B&B	$$ B&B	Full breakfast
Route 101, 03903	5 rooms, 3 pb	Afternoon wine, tea
207-439-0590	C-ltd/S-yes/P-no/H-no	Sitting room
Elaine Raymond		Barn available for
April–December		parties and weddings

1736 colonial house in the country. Walking & cross-country ski trails. 6.5 miles to historic Portsmouth, New Hampshire; shopping, theater & fine dining.

FREEPORT

181 Main Street B&B	$$$ B&B	Full breakfast
181 Main St., 04032	7 rooms, 7 pb	Comp. coffee, tea, etc.
207-865-1226	Visa, MC, *Rated*,	Sitting room
Ed Hassett & David Cates	C-ltd/S-ltd/P-no/H-no	library
All year	French	in-ground pool

Cozy, antique-filled 1840 cape, in town, with ample parking, hearty breakfasts. Walk to L.L. Bean and luxury outlets.

Bagley House, The	$$$ B&B	Full breakfast
RR 3, Box 269C, 04032	5 rooms, 5 pb	Lunch picnics on request
207-865-6566 800-765-1772	Most CC, -Rated-, •	Sitting room, library
S. O'Connor & S. Backhouse	C-yes/S-no/P-no/H-no	cross-country skiing
All year		(winter)
		6-acre yard, barbecue

Peace, tranquillity and history abound in this magnificent 1772 country home. A warm welcome awaits you from us & two resident dogs. Minutes from downtown Freeport.

FREEPORT ————————————————————————————————

Country at Heart B&B
37 Bow St., 04032
207-865-0512
Roger & Kim Dubay
Exc. Thanksgiving, Xmas

$$ B&B
3 rooms, 3 pb
•
C-yes/P-no/H-no

Full breakfast
Afternoon tea, snacks
Sitting room, fireplace
walk to many restaurants
reproduction furnishings

Enjoy a stay in our 1870 home in 1 of 3 country decorated rooms. Handsome crafts & antiques. 2 blks from L.L. Bean & dozens of outlet stores. **7th night free.**

Harraseeket Inn
162 Main St., 04032
207-865-9377 800-342-6423
The Gray Family
All year

$$$ B&B
6 rooms, 6 pb
Visa, MC, AmEx, *Rated*,
•
C-ltd/S-ltd/P-no/H-no

Full breakfast
Restaurant, tavern
Afternoon tea, library
sitting rooms, fireplace
ballroom, dining rooms

Luxury B&B. Private baths (jacuzzi or steam), cable TV, elegant Maine buffet country breakfast. Two blocks north of L.L. Bean. Walk to famous factory outlet shops.

Isaac Randall House, The
5 Independence Dr., 04032
207-865-9295
Jim & Glynrose Friedlander
All year

$$ B&B
8 rooms, 6 pb
•
C-yes/S-ask/P-ask/H-ask
Spanish, French

Full breakfast
Comp. beverages/snacks
Sitting room, library
dining porch, piano
A/C in all rooms

A gracious country inn circa 1823, elegantly and comfortably furnished with antiques. Pond, woods, picnic areas. Walk to L.L. Bean. **10% Disc't on sailing cruises**

Kendall Tavern B&B
213 Main St., 04032
207-865-1338
Jim Whitley
All year

$$$ B&B
7 rooms, 7 pb
Visa, MC, AmEx, *Rated*,
C-ltd/S-no/P-no/H-no

Full breakfast
Sitting room
hot tubs

Walk to L.L. Bean, outlet shops, and fine dining. Close to many points of interest along beautiful Maine coast.

Porter's Landing B&B
70 South St., 04032
207-865-4488
Peter & Barbara Guffin
All year

$$$ B&B
3 rooms, 3 pb
Visa, MC, *Rated*, •
C-ltd/S-no/P-no/H-no

Full breakfast
Afternoon tea, snacks
Sitting room, library
comp. juices/fruit drink
fireplace, refrigerator

1870s carriage house in historic maritime district; quiet, peaceful country setting less than one mile from L.L.Bean. Rated as excellent by the ABBA.

White Cedar Inn
178 Main St., 04032
207-865-9099
Phil & Carla Kerber
All year

$$$ B&B
6 rooms, 6 pb
Visa, MC
C-ltd/S-no/P-no/H-no

Full breakfast
Outdoor grill
Sitting room, Air Cond.
picnic table
brick patio

Recently restored 100-year-old home with large uncluttered antique-furnished rooms. Located just 2 blocks from L.L. Bean.

FRYEBURG

Admiral Peary House
9 Elm St., 04037
207-935-3365 800-237-8080
Nancy & Ed Greenberg
May 15—Oct, Dec 15—Mar

$$$ B&B
4 rooms, 4 pb
Visa, MC, *Rated*, •
C-ltd/S-no/P-no/H-no
French

Full breakfast
Aft. tea, Comp. beverage
Sitting room, library
bicycles, tennis court
hot tub, billiards, A/C

Charming historical home in a picturesque White Mountain village. Clay tennis court, skiing, canoeing, hiking, spacious grounds and perennial gardens.

GREENVILLE

Greenville Inn
P.O. Box 1194, 04441
Norris St.
207-695-2206
The Schnetzer's
May1-Oct31, Dec15-Mar15

$$$ B&B
9 rooms, 7 pb
Visa, MC, Disc.,*Rated*,
C-ltd/S-yes/P-ltd/H-ltd
German

Continental plus
Dinner, restaurant, bar
Gourmet dining & lounge
sitting room

Restored lumber baron's mansion with many unique features on a hill in town overlooking Moosehead Lake and Squaw Mountain. 8 miles to skiing at Squaw Mountain.

HANCOCK POINT

Crocker House Country Inn
Hancock Point Rd., 04640
207-422-6806
Richard S. Malaby
May—Thanksgiving

$$ B&B
11 rooms, 11 pb
Most CC, *Rated*,
C-ltd/S-yes/P-ltd/H-no

Full breakfast
Restaurant, bar, dinner
Sitting room

Quiet traditional coastal inn offering simple elegant dining. A little out of the way, but way out of the ordinary. Recently renovated.

ISLE AU HAUT

Keeper's House, The
P.O. Box 26, 04645
Robinson Point
207-367-2261
Jeff & Judi Burke
May—October

$$$ AP
4 rooms
C-yes/S-no/P-no/H-no
Spanish

Full breakfast
Lunch, dinner included
Snacks
hiking
ocean swimming

Operating lighthouse station on island in Acadia National Park. Tiny fishing village, primitive spectacular natural surroundings. Arrive on mailboat. **50% off 2nd night, ltd**

KENNEBUNK

Arundel Meadows Inn
P.O. Box 1129, 04046
Route 1, Arundel ME 04046
207-985-3770
Mark Bachelder, Murray Yaeger
All year

$$$ B&B
7 rooms, 7 pb
Visa, MC, *Rated*, •
C-ltd/S-no/P-no/H-ltd

Full gourmet breakfast
Afternoon tea
Set-ups, library
sitting room

Rooms individually decorated with art, antiques. Some with fireplaces; all with private baths. Gourmet breakfasts and teas. Near shops and beaches. **5 nites & over 10% off**

Sundial Inn
P.O. Box 1147, 04043
48 Beach Ave.
207-967-3850
Laurence & Patricia Kenny
All year

$$ B&B
34 rooms, 34 pb
Visa, MC, AmEx, *Rated*,
C-ltd/S-ltd/P-no/H-yes
French

Continental plus
Afternoon tea (winter)
Sitting room
whirlpool tubs
beach

Directly on Kennebunkport beach. Completely renovated with country Victorian antiques and designer linens. Beautiful ocean views. An elevator for your convenience.

KENNEBUNK BEACH ───────────────────

Ocean View, The	$$$ B&B	Continental plus
72 Beach Ave., 04043	9 rooms, 9 pb	Comp. coffee, tea, fruit
207-967-2750 207-967-2681	C-ltd/S-ltd/P-no/H-no	Sitting room, library
Bob, Carole, Mike, Rob, Chris		exclusive boutique
April–October		"Painted Lady" on beach

Oceanfront rooms with sight, sounds & smell of Atlantic at our doorstep. Rooms are well coordinated, cheerful, fresh flowers everywhere. Steps to beach, shopping, galleries.

KENNEBUNKPORT ───────────────────

1802 House B&B Inn	$$ B&B	Full breakfast
P.O. Box 646 A, 15 Locke St.,	8 rooms, 8 pb	Comp. tea, cider
04046	Visa, MC, AmEx, *Rated*,	or lemonade
207-967-5632 800-932-5632	•	hearthside
Ron & Carol Perry	C-ltd/S-yes/P-no/H-no	sitting room
All year		

One of Kennebunkport's most popular inns; charming colonial decor, next to beautiful 18-hole Cepe Arundel Golf Course. Fireplaced rooms newly remodeled. Honeymoon suite.

Captain Fairfield Inn	$$$ B&B	Full breakfast
P.O. Box 1308, 04046	9 rooms, 9 pb	Afternoon tea
Pleasant & Green St.	Visa, MC, *Rated*, •	Sitting room, library
207-967-4454	C-ltd/S-no/P-no/H-no	lovely park-like gardens
Dennis & Bonnie Tallagnon	some French	and grounds

Beautiful Federal 1813 sea captain's mansion. Walking distance to town and sea. Some rooms have fireplaces. Chef-owner prepares wonderful breakfasts. **10% discount-week stay**

Captain Jefferds Inn, The	$$$ B&B	Full breakfast
P.O. Box 691, 04046	15 rooms, 15 pb	Aft. tea
Pearl Street	Visa, MC, *Rated*,	Library, garden
207-967-2311	C-yes/S-no/P-yes/H-yes	breakfast on terrace
April - December		3 suites, sitting room

Especially beautiful, quiet, private. In "House Beautiful" and "Country Living" 12/92.

Captain Lord Mansion, The	$$$ B&B	Full breakfast
P.O. Box 800, 04046	16 rooms, 16 pb	Afternoon tea, sweets
Pleasant & Green Sts.	Most CC, *Rated*, •	Snacks, gift shop
207-967-3141 800-522-3141	C-ltd/S-ltd/P-no/H-no	sitting room, piano
Bev Davis, Rick Litchfield		beach towels, umbrellas
All year		

An intimate Maine coast inn. Furnished with genuine antiques. AAA 4-Diamond. Mobil 3-Star. Conference room for large meetings and TV. **10% off deluxe fireplace rooms.**

Chetwynd House Inn, The	$$$ B&B	Full multi-course brkfst
P.O. Box 130, 04046	4 rooms, 2 pb	Comp. tea
Chestnut St.	•	Sitting room, library
207-967-2235 800-833-3354	C-ltd/S-ltd/P-no/H-no	
Susan Knowles Chetwynd	French, Italian	
All year		

Pristine rooms. Handsome, lovely furnishings. Antique pieces. Rich mahogany and cherry woods. Poster beds. Tea tables. Outstanding for guest reunions. **3rd night free, Ltd**

KENNEBUNKPORT

Dock Square Inn, The
P.O. Box 1123, 04046
3 Temple St.
207-967-5773
Frank & Bernice Shoby
March—December

$$$ B&B
6 rooms, 6 pb
Visa, MC, *Rated*, •
C-ltd/S-ltd/P-no/H-no
Italian

Full gourmet breakfast
Goodies always available
Sitting room
bicycles, A/C all rooms
color cable TV

Gracious Victorian country inn—former shipbuilder's home located in the heart of historic Kennebunkport village. Warm congenial atmosphere. **Special celebrations: wine/fruit**

English Meadows Inn
141 Port Rd., Route 35, 04043
207-967-5766
Charlie Doane
April—October

$$$ B&B
15 rooms, 5 pb
Rated
C-ltd/S-no/P-yes/H-no
French

Full breakfast
Aft. tea, lemonade
Room service for brkfast
sitting room, piano
airport/station pickup

1860 Victorian farmhouse. Stroll to beaches, town, restaurants. Inn furnished throughout with antiques and local artworks. Extra-special breakfasts. **Off-season rates**

Inn on South Street, The
P.O. Box 478A, South St., 04046
207-967-5151 207-967-4639
Jacques & Eva Downs
February—December

$$$ B&B
4 rooms, 4 pb
MC, Visa, *Rated*, •
C-ltd/S-no/P-no/H-no
German, Spanish, Russian

Full breakfast
Comp. tea, wine, juice
Sitting room
fireplace, garden
whirlpool tub in suite

Enjoy beautifully appointed rooms in a romantic 19th-century home. Convenient, quiet location. Sumptuous breakfast, fireplaces, gardens, fresh flowers. **3rd night disc't-Ltd**

Kennebunkport Inn, The
P.O. Box 111, 04046
One Dock Square
207-967-2621 800-248-2621
Rick & Martha Griffin
All year

$$ EP
34 rooms, 34 pb
Visa, MC, AmEx, *Rated*,
•
C-yes/P-no/H-no
French

Continental Nov-April
Full bkfst May 15-Oct 15
Pub, restaurant
pool, color TV
golf & tennis nearby

Country inn in old sea captain's home. All rooms w/private baths. Gourmet dining, turn-of-the-century bar, piano bar. Historic district. **3rd night free Nov-April**

Kylemere House, 1818
P.O. Box 1333, 04046
South St.
207-967-2780
Ruth & Helen Toohey
May 1-mid December

$$$ B&B
4 rooms, 4 pb
AmEx, Visa, MC, *Rated*,
•
C-ltd/S-no/P-no/H-no

Full gourmet breakfast
Comp. wine, beverages
Sitting rm., porch, lawn
featured in Glamour 4/90
Regis & Kathie Lee Show

Charming federal inn in historic area located within a short walk to shops and beach. Warm, inviting rooms, traditional hospitality and "down east" breakfast. **Discounts, ask**

Maine Stay Inn & Cottages
P.O. Box 500 A-PL,
34 Maine St., 04046
207-967-2117 800-950-2117
Lindsay & Carol Copeland
All year, FAX: 967-8757

$$$ B&B
17 rooms, 17 pb
Most CC, *Rated*, •
C-yes/S-ltd/P-no/H-no
some French & German

Full breakfast
Afternoon tea, snacks
Sitting room, lawn games
swing set, garden, porch
4 cottages w/fireplace

Victorian inn known for exceptional warmth, hospitality and great breakfasts. Elegant inn rooms, charming garden cottages, spacious lawn, cable TV. **2 night pkg. Nov-June**

The Tides Inn By-The-Sea, Kennebunkport, ME

KENNEBUNKPORT

Old Fort Inn
P.O. Box M, Old Fort Ave., 04046
207-967-5353 800-828-3678
Sheila & David Aldrich
FAX:967-4547

$$$ B&B
16 rooms, 16 pb
Visa, MC, AmEx, *Rated*,
•
C-ltd/S-ltd/P-no/H-no

Full breakfast
Cable TV, phone in room
tennis, swimming pool
jacuzzi tubs, bicycles

A luxurious resort in a secluded charming setting. The inn has yesterday's charm with today's conveniences. Within walking distance to the ocean.

Tides Inn By-The-Sea, The
RR 2, 737 Goose Rocks Beach,
04046
207-967-3757
M. Henriksen & K. Blomberg
May - Mid-October

$$$ EP
22 rooms, 20 pb
Visa, MC, Disc.,
C-yes/S-ltd/P-no/H-no

Restaurant
Breakfast & Dinner $
Bar service
sitting room
3 miles of sandy beach

Seaside Victorian Inn, magnificent ocean views, unpretentious, fine seaside dining, delicious homemade food, pub room, beach, "relaxed atmosphere bordering on inefficiency."

Welby Inn
P.O. Box 774, 04046
Ocean Ave.
207-967-4655
David Knox, Betsy Rogers-Knox
All year

$$ B&B
7 rooms, 7 pb
AmEx, *Rated*
C-ltd/S-no/P-no/H-no

Full breakfast
Eve. homemade Amaretto
Guest pantry
sitting room, piano
bicycles

Gracious turn-of-the-century home in historic Kennebunkport. Walk to beach, marina and shops. Deep-sea fishing and harbor cruises available.

White Barn Inn
P.O. Box 560C, 37 Beach St.,
04046
207-967-2321 Fax-967-1100
L. Bongiorno & L. Cameron
All year

$$$ B&B
24 rooms, 24 pb
Visa, MC, AmEx, *Rated*,
•
C-yes/S-yes/P-no/H-ltd

Continental, full $
Dinner, bar, aftn. tea
Fireplaces, whirlpool
entertainment, bicycles
near beach & town square

Elegant farmhouse Inn with 5-diamond restaurant. Dramatically set in the original, architecturally preserved barn. Member of Relais and Chateau. 5 diamond restaurant.

KITTERY

Melfair Farm B&B	$$ B&B	Full breakfast
11 Wilson Rd., 03904	5 rooms, 1 pb	Comp. iced tea, lemonade
207-439-0230	*Rated*, •	Large sitting room
Claire Cane	C-yes/S-yes/P-no/H-no	piano, TV
March–December	French	near shopping, beaches

1871 New England farmhouse, 9 acres of pastoral setting. Theater, gourmet dining in nearby historical Portsmouth, NH. **3rd night 30% off**

LITCHFIELD

Inn @ Bachelder's Tavern	$$	Full breakfast
P.O. Box 445, 04350	4 rooms, 4 pb	Gourmet 5 star rest.
Exit 28 off I-95	C-yes/S-yes/P-yes/H-ltd	Swimming pool, bar
207-268-4965		sitting room, boating
Virginia Albert		golf nearby, skiing
All year		

This old stage coach stop was built in 1808. Granite hitching posts still flank the inn. Located in Maine's beautiful lake country. **Discount on dinner at tavern**

NAPLES

Augustus Bove House, The	$ B&B	Full breakfast
RR 1, Box 501, Corner of Rts. 302	12 rooms, 5 pb	Honeymoon/Anniv. tray
& 114, 04055	Visa, MC, AmEx, *Rated*,	Comp. coffee, tea
207-693-6365	•	sitting room
David & Arlene Stetson	C-yes/S-ltd/P-yes/H-ltd	veranda, lawn
All year		

Recently restored, offers authentic colonial accomodations in a relaxing atmosphere. Located between two lakes & 20 min. from mountain skiing. **Off season specials avail. Ask**

Inn at Long Lake	$$ B&B	Continental plus
P.O. Box 806, 04055	16 rooms, 16 pb	Comp. coffee & tea
Lake House Rd.	Most CC, *Rated*, •	Comp. hot chocolate
207-693-6226 800-437-0328	C-yes/S-ltd/P-no/H-no	sitting room, library
Maynard & Irene M. Hinks	Some french, spanish	Great Room w/fireplace
All year		

Restored 16-room inn nestled in Sebago Lakes region, year-round activities, shopping, fine dining. Romantic elegance, Maine hospitality. **3rd night 50% off; mid-week disc'ts**

Lamb's Mill Inn	$$$ B&B	Full breakfast
Box 676 Lamb's Mill Rd., 04055	6 rooms, 6 pb	Afternoon tea, snacks
207-693-6253	•	Sitting room, library
Laurel Tinkham, Sandra Long	C-ltd/S-no/P-no/H-no	hot tubs, outside stone
All year		fire pit & gas grills

Charming country inn, 1/2 mi from Naples Village, in heart of western Maine's lakes/mountains region. Ewe hike, ewe bike, ewe ski, ewe zzzz... **Midwk 15% off, 6th night free.**

NEW HARBOR

Bradley Inn, The	$$$ B&B	Continental plus
HC 61, Box 361, Rt. 130, 04554	16 rooms, 16 pb	Restaurant, bar service
207-677-2105	Visa, MC, AmEx, *Rated*,	Dinner, sitting room
Chuck & Merry Robinson	C-yes/S-no/P-no/H-ltd	library, bicycles
April 1-January 2	Some German	tennis court

Charm, elegance and convenience in spacious guest rooms. Also enjoy Ships, the three star restaurant and pub. **1993 Rates for reservations prior to 5/15/94. 5% off**

NEW HARBOR

Gosnold Arms
HC 61, Box 161, Route 32,
Northside Rd., 04554
207-677-3727
The Phinney Family
Mid-May—October

$$$ B&B
26 rooms, 19 pb
Visa, MC, *Rated*,
C-yes/S-ltd/P-no/H-ltd

Full breakfast
Dinner
Cocktails
sitting room
small wharf

Charming country inn and cottages. All-weather dining porch overlooking harbor. Beaches, lobster pounds, parks nearby.

NEWCASTLE

Captain's House B&B, The
P.O. Box 242, 04553
19 River Rd.
207-563-1482
Susan Rizzo, Joe Sullivan
All year

$$ B&B
5 rooms
C-yes/S-yes/P-no/H-no

Full breakfast from menu
Comp. tea
Dinner (winter)
sitting room

Spacious colonial home overlooking the Damariscotta River offers sunny rooms furnished with antiques and delicious full Maine breakfast. Omelettes a specialty.

Mill Pond Inn
RFD1, Box 245, Route 215,
Damariscotta, 04553
207-563-8014
Bobby & Sherry Whear
All year

$$ B&B
5 rooms, 5 pb
Visa, MC
C-ltd/S-yes/P-no/H-ltd

Full breakfast
Comp. wine
Swimming/boating in lake
canoe & mountain bikes
hammock, horseshoes

Small, private inn with a water view from four rooms, across the road from Damariscotta Lake. Guided fishing trips available with "registered Maine fishing guide."

Newcastle Inn, The
River Rd., 04553
207-563-5685 800-832-8669
Ted & Chris Sprague
All year

$$$ B&B, MAP
15 rooms, 15 pb
Visa, MC, *Rated*, •
C-ltd/S-no/P-no/H-ltd

Gourmet 4-course brkfast
Evening reception bar
Dinner, aftn. beverages
sitting room w/fireplace
screened-in porch

Fine dining and a pampering environment in an intimate, full-service, country inn on the Damariscotta River.

NORTH ANSON

Olde Carrabassett Inn, The
Union St., 04958
207-635-2900
Walt & Sylvia Bailey
All year

$ B&B
3 rooms, 1 pb
C-ltd/S-no/P-no/H-no

Full breakfast
Swimming pool, hot tub
tennis nearby, sitt. rm.
3 acres to walk

Best of Maine's scenic countryside. Restored 19th century inn. Delightful breafasts, ski, hike, golf, white water raft. Borders North Anson Gorge.

OGUNQUIT

Beauport Inn
P.O. Box 1793, 03907
102 Shore Rd.
207-646-8680
Dan Pender
All year

$$ B&B
4 rooms, 4 pb
Visa, MC
C-ltd/S-no

Continental plus
Sitting room
piano, TV room
antique shop

Restored cape furnished with antiques. Pine paneled sitting room with fireplace. Walk to beach, Marginal Way and Perkins Cove.

OGUNQUIT

Gazebo, The	$$$ B&B	Full gourmet breakfast
P.O. Box 668, 03907	9 rooms, 7 pb	Sitting room
Rt. 1 N.	Visa, MC	dining room
207-646-3733	C-ltd/S-yes/P-no/H-no	heated swimming pool
Tony Fontes		
All year exc. January		

150-year-old restored farmhouse serving full gourmet breakfast. Short walk to Ogunquit Beach. Afternoon tea and pate. 5 rooms w/queen beds, 1 king, 1 twin.

Gorges Grant Hotel	$$ B&B/MAP	Full breakfast $
P.O. Box 2240, Route 1, Route 1,	56 rooms, 56 pb	Restaurant, bar
North, 03907	Most CC, •	Hot tubs
207-646-7003	C-yes/S-yes/P-no/H-yes	indoor & outdoor pool
Patty & Steve Farrar		large saltwater aquarium

Elegant, small, modern hotel operated w/an inn flavor. Located in Ogunquit near (within short trolley ride) one of the world's best beaches. **10% off restaurant upon arrival**

Hartwell House	$$$ B&B	Full breakfast
P.O. Box 393, 03907	17 rooms, 17 pb	Afternoon tea daily
118 Shore Rd.	Most CC, *Rated*, •	Swimming, tennis, A+C
207-646-7210 800-235-8883	C-ltd/S-no/P-no/H-no	banquet/conference fac.
J & T Hartwell, A & R Adams		golf privileges, fishing
All year		

Elegantly furnished in early American & English antiques. Set amid 2 acres of sculpted gardens, perfect for relaxing. Swim, stroll, fish, golf. **Seasonal dining packages**

Rockmere Lodge	$$$ B&B	Continental plus
P.O. Box 278, 03907	7 rooms, 5 pb	Aft. tea, comp. wine
40 Stearns Rd.	Visa, MC	Sitting room, library
207-646-2985	C-yes/S-no/P-no/H-no	beach chairs
Andy Antoniuk & Bob Brown		cool drinks for beach
All year		

Seaside, shingled cottage in out-of-the-way location. Very quiet. Listen to the ocean and relax. Walking distance to everything.

PORTLAND

Inn at Parkspring	$$ B&B	Continental plus
135 Spring St., 04101	7 rooms, 5 pb	Comp. brandy & tea
207-774-1059 800-437-8511	Major credit cards,	Sitting room
Judi Lowell-Riley	C-ltd/S-yes/P-no/H-ltd	
All year		

Unique three-story 1845 townhouse in the heart of Portland. Fresh flowers, imported chocolates, fluffy towels—Portland's "Smallest Grand Hotel." **3rd night 25% off, Nov-Ap.**

Inn on Carleton	$$$ B&B	Full breakfast
46 Carleton St., 04102	7 rooms, 3 pb	Afternoon tea
207-775-1910 800-639-1779	Visa, MC, Disc., *Rated*,	Sitting room
Phil & Sue Cox	C-yes/S-no/P-no/H-no	
All year		

Old world charm & elegance in Portland's historic West End District. Walk to Old Port, art museum & many museum houses, antiques shops.

PORTLAND ───────────────────────────────

West End Inn	$$$ B&B	Full breakfast
146 Pine St., 04102	4 rooms, 4 pb	Afternoon tea, snacks
207-772-1377	Most CC, *Rated*, •	Comp. wine, library
Hilary & Tom Jacobs	C-ltd/S-no/P-no/H-no	sitting room
April-December		

Very comfortable, relaxing home atmosphere in the heart of the city in historical district. Art Museum, theaters and Old Port within walking distance. Rated 3 stars by AAA.

PROSPECT HARBOR ───────────────────────────

Oceanside Meadows Inn	$$ B&B	Full breakfast
P.O. Box 90, 04669	7 rooms, 1 pb	Sitting room
Route 195, Corea Rd.	Visa, MC, DC	library, games, VCR
207-963-5557 207-846-5301	C-yes/S-no/P-yes/H-no	ocean & sandy beach
Norm & Marge Babineau		
All year		

Charming 19th-century home; sandy beach and ocean across street; beautiful gardens. One hour from Bar Harbor and Acadia National Park. Great place for biking.

RANGELEY ───────────────────────────────

Rangeley Inn	$$ EP	Full menu for breakfast
P.O. Box 160, 04970	50 rooms, 50 pb	Restaurant - dinner
Main St.	Most CC, *Rated*, •	Bar service
207-864-3341 800-666-3687	C-yes/S-yes/P-no/H-yes	library, hot tubs
Fay & Ed Carpenter		sitting room
All year, Fax: 864-3634		

Old-fashioned country inn 1500 ft. above sea level, in the lakes and mtn. resort area of western Maine. Come visit. AAA rated 3 diamonds; Mobil 3 star.

ROCKPORT ───────────────────────────────

Twin Gables B&B	$$$ B&B	Full breakfast
P.O. Box 189, 04856	2 rooms, 2 pb	Aft. tea & lemonade
4 Spear St. at Beauchamp	C-ltd/S-no/P-no/H-no	Snacks, sitting room
207-236-4717	Limited French	library
Don & Nina Woolston		flowers, candy
June - mid October		

Warm and welcoming 17 room, 1855 home. Gourmet breakfast, beautiful coastal area.

SEARSPORT ───────────────────────────────

Homeport Inn	$$ B&B	Full breakfast
Box 674, E. Main St., 04974	11 rooms, 7 pb	Mermaid lounge & bar
207-548-2259 800-742-5814	Most CC, *Rated*, •	Soda fountain, garden
Edith & George Johnson	C-yes/S-ltd/P-no/H-yes	antique shop, ocean view
All year		bicycles, golf, tennis

*Listed on the Historic Register. Ideal mid-coast location for an extended stay to visit coast of Maine. Victorian cottage also available by the week. **5% off weekly stay.***

Thurston House B&B Inn	$ B&B	Full breakfast
P.O. Box 686, 04974	4 rooms, 2 pb	Snacks (sometimes)
8 Elm St.	Visa, MC, *Rated*, •	Sitting room
207-548-2213	C-ltd/S-no/P-no/H-ltd	library, shade garden
Carl & Beverly Eppig		tennis courts nearby
All year		

*Circa 1830 Colonial in quiet village setting. Easy stroll to everything, including Maritime Museum, tavern, beach park on Penobscot Bay. **6th night free***

SORRENTO

Bass Cove Farm B&B	$$ B&B	Continental plus
HC 32, Box 132, Route 185,	3 rooms, 1 pb	Exercise room, library
04677	Visa, MC	porch, gardens
207-422-3564	C-ltd/S-no/P-no	sitting room
Mary Solet & Michael Tansey		
All year		

Coastal Maine farmhouse in active summer colony. Convenient to Acadia Nat'l. Park. Comfortable beds, delicious breakfast. Explore, shop, relax. **4-7 days stay, discounts**

SOUTH WEST HARBOR

Lambs Ear Inn, The	$$$ B&B	Full breakfast
P.O. Box 30, 04679	6 rooms, 6 pb	Peace & quiet
Clark Point Rd.	Visa, MC, *Rated*, •	sitting room
207-244-9828	C-ltd/S-no/P-no/H-ltd	
Elizabeth & George Hoke		
May 1 - October 15		

The inn was built in 1857. Comfortable and serene, in the village overlooking South West Harbor. Surrounded by Acadia National Park.

SOUTHPORT

Albonegon Inn	$$ B&B	Continental breakfast
Capitol Island, 04538	15 rooms, 3 pb	Afternoon tea
207-633-2521	Visa, MC	Sitting room, piano
Kim & Bob Peckham	C-yes/Spanish	tennis court, beaches
July—mid October		"grill" your own dinner

A very special place to relax. On a private island, perched on the edge of the ocean. Spectacular views! Hike, bird-watch, swim, beachcomb, tennis, sail. Golf nearby.

SOUTHWEST HARBOR

Harbour Cottage Inn	$$ B&B	Continental breakfast
P.O. Box 258, 04679	8 rooms, 8 pb	Full breakfast, snacks
Clark Pt. & Dirigo Rds.	Most CC, *Rated*, •	Sitting room w/piano
207-244-5738	C-ltd/S-no/P-no/H-no	some rms. w/whirlpool
Ann & Mike Pedreschi		
All year		

Surrounded by beautiful, spectacular Acadia National Park w/hiking, biking and cross-country skiing. All rooms are individually designer decorated. **10% discount 7+ nights**

Harbour Woods Lodging	$$ B&B	Full breakfast
P.O. Box 1214, 04679	3 rooms, 3 pb	Snacks
410 Main St.	*Rated*, •	Sitting room, sunroom
207-244-5388	C-ltd/S-no/P-no/H-no	Acadia National Park
M. Eden, J. Paviglionite		hiking/swimming/cruises
All year		

Spacious rooms w/harbor or garden views. Sunroom w/guest refrigerator. Thick towels, fresh flowers, candlelight, soft music, imaginative breakfasts. **3rd night 50% off, ltd**

Island House, The	$$ B&B	Full breakfast
P.O. Box 1006, 04679	5 rooms, 2 pb	Comp. beverages
Clark Point Rd.	*Rated*	Sitting room/fireplace
207-244-5180	C-ltd/S-no/P-no	library, large garden
Ann Gill		fishing docks, harbor
May—October		

A gracious, restful, seacoast home on the quiet side of Mt. Desert Island. An efficiency apartment available. Near wharves; 5 min. to Acadia National Park. **Discounts, ask**

SOUTHWEST HARBOR ──────────────────────────

Kingsleigh Inn	$$ B&B	Full breakfast
P.O. Box 1426, 04679	8 rooms, 8 pb	Afternoon tea
100 Main St.	Visa, MC, *Rated*,	Sitting room w/fireplace
207-244-5302	C-ltd/S-ltd/P-no/H-no	library
Tom & Nancy Cervelli		
All year		

A cozy intimate inn overlooking the harbor. Filled with many antiques, wing-back chairs and four-poster beds. Rooms with harbor views. AAA 3-Diamond.

Lindenwood Inn	$ B&B	Full breakfast
P.O. Box 1328, 04679	9 rooms, 9 pb	Guest cottage available
98 Clark Point Rd.	C-ltd/S-no/P-no/H-no	Sitting room
207-244-5335		balconies, harbor views
Jim King		TV, decks, shops, wharf
All year		

A friendly, cozy restored sea captain's home on quiet side of Mount Desert Island. Stroll to wharf, restaurants. Enjoy the island's attributes all year.

Penury Hall	$ B&B	Full breakfast
Main St., Box 68, 04679	3 rooms	Comp. wine, coffee, tea
207-244-7102	C-ltd/S-yes/P-no/H-no	Sitting room, sauna
Toby & Gretchen Strong		picnic day sails
All year		canoe & windsurfer avail

Comfortable rambling Maine home for us and our guests. Decor reflects hosts' interests in art, antiques, books, gardening, sailing. Water sports paradise.

SPRUCE HEAD ──────────────────────────

Craignair Inn	$$ B&B	Full breakfast
533 Clark Island Rd., 04859	16 rooms	Restaurant, coffee & tea
207-594-7644	Visa, MC, *Rated*, •	Wine service, parlor
Terry & Norman Smith	C-yes/S-yes/P-yes/H-no	library, flower garden
All year		coastal activities

Area is alive w/history of quarrying days. 4 acre shorefront. Delightful swimming in abandoned granite quarry. The old church & store still stand. **25% restaurant disc'ts.**

STONINGTON ──────────────────────────

Burnt Cove B&B	$$ B&B	Continental plus
RFD 1, Box 2905, Whitman Rd.,	2 rooms	Box lunches
04681	Visa, MC	shops, restaurants
207-367-2392	C-ltd/S-no/P-no/H-no	fishing village
Bob Williams, Diane Berlew		
May–October		

Waterfront location on Penobscot Bay island; working lobster wharves; multitude of birds; nature conservancy trails. TV, water view available. **Pay for 6, get 7th night free.**

SULLIVAN HARBOR ──────────────────────────

Sullivan Harbor Farm	$$ B&B	Full breakfast
Box 96, U.S. Route 1, 04664	5 rooms	Sitting room, library
207-422-3735	Visa, MC	3 guestrooms
Joel Frantzman	C-yes/S-yes/P-no/H-no	2 cottages
All year		

Country B&B in lovely 1820 house. Gardens, beach access, charm. Rooms w/antiques and fine artwork. Close to Acadia National Park. Owners w/local knowledge. **Complimentary wine**

SUNSET

Goose Cove Lodge/Deer Isle	$$$ B&B/MAP	Full breakfast
P.O. Box 40, 04683	21 rooms, 21 pb	Full bkfst./dinner (MAP)
Goose Cove Road	Visa, MC, *Rated*, •	BYOB, sitting rm, piano
207-348-2508	C-yes/S-ltd/P-no/H-yes	bicycles, entertainment
Dom and Joanne Parisi	French, German, Spanish	beaches, sailboats, Kyak
May—mid-October		

Rustic retreat—sand beaches, rocky shores, spruce forest with moss-covered trails and open ocean at the End of Beyond. B&B in the spring and fall. MAP in the summer.

TENANTS HARBOR

East Wind Inn	$$ EP	Full breakfast $
P.O. Box 149, 04860	26 rooms, 12 pb	Comp. beverages
One Mechanic St.	Visa, MC, AmEx, *Rated*,	All meals, sitting room
207-372-6366 800-241-8439	•	entertainment, piano
Timothy Watts	C-ltd/S-yes/P-ask/H-ltd	conference room
Jan - March, closed		

Authentic country inn. Fishing boats unload at wharf. Antiques, telephones, color TV and piano. Productive meeting site with well-equipped conference rooms.

VINALHAVEN

Fox Island Inn	$ B&B	Continental breakfast
P.O. Box 451, 04863	10 rooms, 1 pb	Sitting room
Carver St.	C-ltd/S-ltd/P-no/H-no	piano
207-863-2122		
Gail Reinertsen		
May—October		

A restored century-old townhouse on an unspoiled Maine island. A short walk to the picturesque harbor and fishing village of Vinalhaven.

WATERFORD

Kedarburn Inn	$$ B&B	Full breakfast
Route 35, Box 61, Valley Rd.,	7 rooms, 3 pb	Dinner, Sunday brunch
04088	Visa, MC, *Rated*, •	Afternoon tea, bar
207-583-6182	C-yes/S-yes/P-yes/H-no	sitting rm., piano, lake
Margaret & Derek Gibson	French	quilt lessons & packages
All year		

A wonderful old home built in 1858, situated on a beautifully landscaped knoll in the center of historic Waterford Village. A romantic country setting. **3rd night 20% off**

WEST BOOTHBAY HARBOR

Lawnmeer Inn, The	$$ EP	Full breakfast $
Box 505, Rt #27, 04575	32 rooms	Dinner
207-633-2544 800-633-7645	Visa, MC, *Rated*, •	Restaurant, bar
Jim & Lee Metzger	C-yes/S-yes/P-ask/H-no	sitting room, library
May—October	some French	complimentary coffee

"The only thing that we overlook is the water."

WEST GOULDSBORO

Sunset House B&B	$ B&B	Full breakfast
HCR 60, Box 62, Route 186,	7 rooms	Fresh water pond for
04607	Visa, MC, •	swimming, fishing
207-963-7156 800-233-7156	C-yes/S-no/P-no/H-no	great biking, sunporch
Carl & Kathy Johnson		
All year		

Late Victorian country farm inn on the coast; water views; beautiful sunsets. Near Acadia Nat'l Park. Observe bald eagle, osprey, loons in natural environment. **3rd night 50%**

YORK

Dockside Guest Quarters
P.O. Box 205, 03909
Harris Island Rd.
207-363-2868
The David Lusty Family
May 1 - Nov. 1, ltd.

$$ EP
21 rooms, 19 pb
Visa, MC, *Rated*, •
C-yes/S-no/P-ltd/H-ltd

Continental plus $
Lunch, dinner, bar room
Restaurant, sitting room
porches, lawn games
marina, boat rentals

Unsurpassed location along edge of harbor. Tranquil, beautiful scenery abounds. Rms. tastefully decorated for warmth & comfort. AAA 3-diamonds.

YORK HARBOR

Canterbury House
Box 881, 432 York St., 03911
207-363-3505
James T. Pappas
All year

$$ B&B
7 rooms, 2 pb
Visa, MC, Disc, *Rated*, •
C-ltd/S-ltd/P-ltd/H-no
Greek, French

Full breakfast
Aft. tea
Sitting room
porch overlooking harbor
picnic lunch available

Spacious, bright, meticulously renovated to enhance its turn-of-the-century magnificance, Canterbury House is dedicated to a renewal of the quality of life from yesterday.

York Harbor Inn
P.O. Box 573, 03911
York St., Route 1A
207-363-5119 800-343-3869
Joseph & Garry Dominguez
All year

$$ B&B
32 rooms, 26 pb
Visa, MC, AmEx, *Rated*, •
C-yes/S-yes/P-no/H-ltd

Continental plus
Lunch, dinner, bar
Sitting room, piano
bicycles, ocean swimming
conf./banquet facilities

Quiet, authentic country inn (circa 1637) listed in Nat'l Register. Overlooks ocean & York Harbor Beach. A+C & phones. AAA rated 3 diamond. **10% Senior Citizen's discount**

YORK—CAPE NEDDICK

Cape Neddick House, The
P.O. Box 70, 03902
1300 Rt.1, PO Box 70
207-363-2500
Dianne & John Goodwin
All year

$$ B&B
6 rooms, 6 pb
Rated
C-ltd/S-ltd/P-no/H-no

Full breakfast
Comp. wine, tea, coffee
Parlor & living room
bicycles, guitar
horseshoes, picnic area

Coastal cntry 4th-gen. Victorian home. Close to beach, antiques, outlet shops, boutiques. Cultural, historic opportunities. Award-winning Apple Butter Nut Cake. **Wine/cheese**

More Inns . . .

Olde Berry Inn, Kennebunk Rd., Box 2, Alfred, 04002, 207-324-0603
Cloverleaf Cottages, RFD 1, Box 75, Bailey Island, 04003
Atlantean Inn, 11 Atlantic Ave., Dept., Bar Harbor, 04609, 207-288-3270
Bay Ledge Inn and Spa, 1385 Sand Point Rd., Bar Harbor, 04609, 207-288-4204
Heathwood Inn, Bar Harbor, 800-582-3681
Maples Cottage Inn, 16 Roberts Ave., Bar Harbor, 04609, 207-288-3443
Pachelbel Inn, 20 Roberts Ave, Bar Harbor, 04609, 207-288-9655
Ridgeway Cottage Inn, 11 High St., Bar Harbor, 04609, 207-288-9682
Shady Maples, RFD #1, Box 360, Bar Harbor, 04609, 207-288-3793
Stratford House Inn, 45 Mt. Desert St., Bar Harbor, 04609, 207-288-5189
The Tides, 119 West St., Bar Harbor, 04609, 207-288-4968
Thornhedge Inn, 47 Mt. Desert St., Bar Harbor, 04609, 207-288-5398
Moosehorn B&B, Route 1, Box 322, Baring, 04694, 207-454-8883
Glad II, 60 Pearl St., Bath, 04530, 207-443-1191
Levitt Family B&B, 50 Pearl St., Bath, 04530
Hiram Alden Inn, 19 Church St., Belfast, 04915, 207-338-2151
Horatio Johnson House, 36 Church St., Belfast, 04915, 207-338-5153
Londonderry Inn, SR 80, Box 3, Belfast, 04915, 207-338-3988
Northport House B&B Inn, 197 Northport Ave., Belfast, 04915, 207-338-1422
Bakers B&B, Route 2, Box 2090, Bethel, 04217, 207-824-2088
Bethel Inn and Count, P.O. Box 26, Bethel, 04217, 800-654-0125
Douglass Place, Route 2, Box 90, Bethel, 04217, 207-824-2229
Four Seasons Inn, P.O. Box 390, Bethel, 04217, 207-824-2755

L'Auberge Country Inn, P.O. Box 21, Bethel, 04217, 207-824-2774
Norseman Inn, HCR-61 Box 50, Bethel, 04217, 207-824-2002
Pointed Fir B&B, Paradise Rd., Box 745, Bethel, 04217, 207-824-2251
Sudbury Inn, Lower Main St., Bethel, 04217, 207-824-2174
Sunday River Inn, Sunday River Rd., Bethel, 04217, 207-824-2410
Lodge, 19 Yates, Biddefordpool, 04006, 617-284-7148
Arcady Down East, South St., Blue Hill, 04614, 207-374-5576
Blue Hill Farm Country Inn, Route 15, Box 437, Blue Hill, 04614, 207-374-5126
Blue Hill Inn, P.O. Box 403, Blue Hill, 04614, 207-374-2844
John Peters Inn, P.O. Box 916, Blue Hill, 04614, 207-374-2116
Boothbay Harbor Inn, 37 Atlantic Ave. Box 4, Boothbay Harbor, 04538, 207-633-6302
Captain Sawyer's Place, 87 Commercial St., Boothbay Harbor, 04538, 207-633-2290
Green Shutters Inn, P.O. Box 543, Boothbay Harbor, 04538, 207-633-2646
Harbour Towne Inn, P.O. Box 266, Boothbay Harbor, 04538, 207-633-4300
Hilltop Guest House, 44 McKown Hill, Boothbay Harbor, 04538, 207-633-2941
Seafarer B&B Inn, The, 38 Union St., Boothbay Harbor, 04538, 207-633-2116
Thistle Inn, P.O. Box 176, Boothbay Harbor, 04538, 207-633-3541
Topside, McKown Hill, Boothbay Harbor, 04538, 207-633-5404
Welch House Inn, 36 McKown St., Boothbay Harbor, 04538, 207-633-3431
Westgate B&B, 18 West St., Boothbay Harbor, 04538, 207-633-3552
Mountainside B&B, P.O. Box 290, Bridgton, 04009, 207-647-5091
North Woods B&B, 55 N. High St., Bridgton, 04009, 207-647-2100
Old Cape of Bristol Mills, P.O. Box 129, Rte. 130, Bristol Mills, 04539, 207-563-8848
Breezemere Farm Inn, P.O. Box 290, Brooksville, 04617, 207-326-8628
Aaron Dunning House, 76 Federal St., Brunswick, 04011, 207-729-4486
Captain Daniel Sto, 10 Water St., Brunswick, 04011
Harborgate B&B, RD 2-2260, Brunswick, 04011, 207-725-5894
Harriet Beecher Stowe Hse, 63 Federal St., Brunswick, 04011, 207-725-5543
Walker Wilson House, 2 Melcher Place, Brunswick–Topsham, 04086, 207-729-0715
A Little Dream, 66 High St., Camden, 04843, 207-236-8742
Belmont, The, 6 Belmont Ave., Camden, 04843, 207-236-8053
Chestnut House, 69 Chestnut St., Camden, 04843, 207-236-6137
Goodspeed's Guest House, 60 Mountain St., Camden, 04843, 207-354-8077
High Tide Inn, Camden, 04843, 207-236-3724
Hosmer House B&B, 4 Pleasant St., Camden, 04843, 207-236-4012
Mansard Manor, 5 High St., Camden, 04843, 207-236-3291
Owl and The Turtle, 8 Bay View St., Camden, 04843, 207-236-4769
Whitehall Inn, Rt. 1 N. at 52 High St., Camden, 04843, 207-236-3391
Green Acres Inn, RFD #112, Canton, 04221, 207-597-2333
Crescent Beach Inn, Route 77, Cape Elizabeth, 04107, 207-799-1517
Sea Chimes B&B, RD 1, Shore Rd., Cape Neddick, 03902, 207-646-5378
Wooden Goose Inn, P.O. Box 195, Cape Neddick, 03902, 207-363-5673
Newagen Seaside Inn, Box H, Southport Island, Cape Newagen, 04552, 207-633-5242
Sugarloaf Inn, Carrabassett Valley, Carrabassett Valley, 04947, 207-237-2701
Castine Inn, P.O. Box 41, Main St., Castine, 04421, 207-326-4365
Holiday House, P.O. Box 215, Castine, 04421, 207-326-4335
Pentagoet Inn, The, P.O. Box 4, Main St., Castine, 04421, 207-326-8616
Agawam Kezar Lodge, Center Lovell, 04016
Center Lovell Inn, P.O. Box 261, Center Lovell, 04016, 207-925-1575
Farrington's, Off Route 5, Center Lovell, 04016
Westways on Kezar Lake, Box 175, Route 5, Center Lovell, 04016, 207-928-2663
Chebeague Island Inn, P.O. Box 492, South Rd., Chebeague Island, 04017, 207-846-5155
Ricker House, P.O. Box 256, Cherryfield, 04622, 207-546-2780
Cornish Inn, P.O. Box 266, Cornish, 04020, 207-625-8501
Down Easter Inn, Bristol Rd Rt. 130, Damariscotta, 04543
Eggemoggin Inn, RFD Box 324, Deer Isle, 04650, 207-348-2540
Laphroaig B&B, Rt. 15, Box 67, Deer Isle Village, 04627, 207-348-6088
Atlantic Seal B&B, RFD 2, Box 3160, Dexter, 04930
Ben-Loch Inn, RFD #1 Box 1020, Dixmont, 04932, 207-257-4768
Foxcroft B&B, 25 W. Main St., Dover-Foxcraft, 04426, 207-564-7720
Linekin Village B&B, Route 65, Box 776, East Booth Bay, 04544, 207-633-3681
Five Gables Inn, P.O. Box 75, East Boothbay, 04544, 207-633-4551
Ocean Point Inn, Shore Rd., East Boothbay, 04544, 207-633-4200
Lucerne, East Holden
East River B&B, P.O. Box 205 High St., East Machias, 04630, 207-255-8467
Mariner Bed & Breakfast, P.O. Bx 40, East Machias, 04630
Artists Retreat, 29 Washington St., Eastport, 04631, 207-853-4239
Ewenicorn Farm B&B, 116 Goodwin Rd., Rt. 10, Eliot, 03903, 207-439-1337
Victoria's B&B, 58 Pine St., Ellsworth, 04605, 207-667-5893
Inn at Cold Stream Pond, P.O. Box 76, Enfield, 04433, 207-732-3595
Blackberry Farm B&B, RR3 Box 7048, Farmington, 04938, 207-778-2035
Coveside, Five Islands, 04546, 207-371-2807
Grey Havens Inn, Box 82, Five Islands, 04546, 207-371-2616
Daigle's B&B, 96 E. Main St., Fort Kent, 04743
Atlantic Seal B&B, P.O. Box 146, 25 Main, Freeport, 04078, 207-865-6112
Captain Josiah Mitchell, 188 Main St., Freeport, 04032
Holbrook Inn, 7 Holbrook St., Freeport, 04032, 207-865-6693
Old Red Farm, Desert of Maine Rd., Freeport, 04032, 207-865-4550
Oxford House Inn, 105 Main St., Fryeburg, 04037, 207-935-3442
Country Squire B&B, RR 1 Box 178 Mighty, Gorham, 04038, 207-839-4855
Chesuncook Lake House, Chesuncook Vil. Rt.76 , Greenville, 04441
Trebor Inn, The, P.O. Box 299, Guilford, 04443, 207-876-4070

Le Domaine Restaurant/Inn, P.O. Box 496, US Rt. 1, Hancock, 04640, 207-422-3395
Harpswell Inn, RR1 Box 141, Harpswell (South), 04079, 207-833-5509
Tolman House Inn, P.O. Box 551, Tolman Rd, Harrison, 04040, 207-583-4445
Inn at Canoe Point, Box 216C, Route 3, Hulls Cove, 04644, 207-288-9511
Island B&B, Box 275,Ltl. Cranberry , Isleford, 04646, 207-244-9283
Dark Harbor House Inn, Box 185, Islesboro, 04848, 207-734-6669
Islesboro Inn, Islesboro, 04848, 207-734-2222
Tootsie's B&B, Trynor Sq., RFD 1,Box 2, Jonesport, 04649
Alewife House, 1917 Alewive Rd., Rt 35, Kennebunk, 04043, 207-985-2118
Battlehead Cove, P.O. Box 449, Kennebunk, 04046, 207-967-3879
Kennebunk Inn, 45 Main St., Kennebunk, 04043, 207-985-3351
Waldo Emerson Inn, 108 Summer St, Kennebunk, 04043, 207-985-7854
Aiello & Co. B&B, P.O. Box 1143, Kennebunkport, 04046
Breakwater Inn, Ocean Ave., Kennebunkport, 04046, 207-957-3118
Bufflehead Cove, P.O. Box 499, Kennebunkport, 04046, 207-967-3879
Clarion Nonantum Inn, Ocean Ave., Box 2626, Kennebunkport, 04046, 207-967-4050
English Robin, Route 1, Box 194, Kennebunkport, 04046, 207-967-3505
Farm House, RR 1, Box 656, Kennebunkport, 04046, 207-967-4169
Flakeyard Farm, RFD 2, Kennebunkport, 04046, 207-967-5965
Green Heron Inn, The, Box 2578, Kennebunkport, 04046, 207-967-3315
Harbor Inn, P.O. Box 538A, Kennebunkport, 04046, 207-967-2074
Inn at Harbor Head, RR 2, Box 1180, Kennebunkport, 04046, 207-967-5564
Kilburn House, P.O. Box 1309, Kennebunkport, 04046, 207-967-4762
Lake Brook Guest House, RR 3, Box 218, Kennebunkport, 04046, 207-967-4069
Port Gallery Inn, P.O. Box 1367, Kennebunkport, 04046, 207-967-3728
Schooners Inn & Restaurant, P.O. Box 1121, Kennebunkport, 04046, 207-967-5333
Seaside Inn & Cottages, P.O. Box 631, Kennebunkport, 04046, 207-967-4461
Village Cove Inn, P.O. Box 650, Kennebunkport, 04046, 207-967-3993
Country Cupboard, RFD 1, Box 1270, Kingfield, 04947, 207-265-2193
Herbert, The, P.O. Box 67, Kingfield, 04947, 207-265-2000
Three Stanley Avenue, P.O. Box 169, Kingfield, 04947, 207-265-5541
Winter's Inn, P.O. Box 44, Kingfield, 04947, 207-265-5421
Gundalow Inn, 6 Water St., Kittery, 03904, 207-439-4040
Harbour Watch B&B, R.F.D. 1 Box 42, Kittery Point, 03905, 207-439-3242
Whaleback Inn B&B, Box 162, Pepperrell Rd., Kittery Point, 03905, 207-439-9560
Lamoine House, Rt. 184 Box 180, Lamoine, 04605
Green Woods, R.F.D. No. 2, Lincolnvile, 04849, 207-338-3187
Cedarholm Cottages, HC 60, Box 569, Lincolnville, 04849, 207-236-3886
Red House, HC 60 Box 540, Lincolnville, 04849, 207-236-4621
Sign of the Owl, Route 1 Box 85, Lincolnville, 04849, 207-338-4669
Youngtown Inn & Restaurant, RR 1, Box 4246, Lincolnville, 04849, 207-763-4290
Home Port Inn, 45 Main St., Lubec, 04652, 207-733-2077
Hugel Haus B&B, 55 Main St., Lubec, 04652, 207-733-4965
Overview, The, RD 2, Box 106, Lubec, 04652, 207-733-2005
Clark Perry House, 59 Court St., Machias, 04654, 207-255-8458
Halcyon Days B&B, 7 Freemont St,, Machias, 04654, 207-255-4662
Monhegan House, Monhegan, 04852, 207-594-7983
Island Inn, On the Harbor, Monhegan Island, 04852, 207-596-0371
Shining Sails Inc., Box 344, Monhegan Island, 04852, 207-596-0041
Sky Lodge, P.O. Box 99, Moose River, 04945
Feather Bed Inn, Box 65, Mount Vernon, 04352, 207-293-2020
Charmwoods, Naples, 04055, 207-693-6798
Songo B&B, Songon Locks Rd., Naples, 04055, 207-693-3960
Glidden House, RR 1 Box 740, Newcastle, 04553, 207-563-1859
Markert House, P.O. Box 224, Glidden, Newcastle, 04553, 207-563-1309
Lake Sebasticook B&B, 8 Sebasticook Ave., Newport, 04953, 207-368-5507
Oliver Farm Inn, Box 136 Old Route 1, Nobleboro, 04555, 207-563-1527
Norridgewock Colonial Inn, Upper Main St, Rt 2 &20, Norridgewock, 04957, 207-634-3470
Channelridge Farm, 358 Cross Point Rd., North Edgecomb, 04556, 207-882-7539
Pulpit Harbor Inn, Crabtree Point Rd., North Haven Island, 04853, 207-867-2219
Olde Rowley Inn, P.O. Box 87, North Waterford, 04267, 207-583-4143
Aimhi Lodge, R.R. #3, North Windham, 04082
Sebago Lake Lodge, White Bridge Rd., North Windham, 04062, 207-892-2698
Grey Rock Inn, Northeast Harbor, 04662, 217-276-9360
Pressey House-1850, 85 Summer St., Oakland, 04963, 207-465-3500
Admiral's Inn, 70 S. Main St., Ogunquit, 03907, 207-646-7093
Admiral's Loft, 97 Main St., Ogunquit, 03907, 207-646-5496
Bayberry, The, 26 Shore Rd., Ogunquit, 03907
Berwick, Box 261, Ogunquit, 03907, 207-646-4062
Blue Shutters, 6 Beachmere Pl., Ogunquit, 03907, 207-646-2163
Blue Water Inn, Beach St., Ogunquit, 03907, 207-646-5559
Clipper Ship Guest House, 46 N. Main St., Ogunquit, 03907, 207-646-9735
Colonial Inn, 71 Shore Rd.,PO Box 895, Ogunquit, 03907
Gorges Grant Hotel, P.O. Box 2240, Route 1, Ogunquit, 03907, 207-646-7003
Juniper Hill Inn, Route 1 North, Ogunquit, 03907, 207-646-4501
Leisure Inn, 19 School St., Ogunquit, 03907, 207-646-2737
Marimor Motor Inn, 66 Shore Rd., Ogunquit, 03907, 207-646-7397
Morning Dove B&B, The, P.O. Box 1940, Ogunquit, 03907, 207-646-3891
Ogunquit House, P.O. Box 1883, Ogunquit, 03907, 207-646-2967
Old Village Inn, 30 Main St., Ogunquit, 03907, 207-646-7088
Parson's Post House Lodge, 30 Shore Rd., Ogunquit, 03907
Puffin Inn, Box 2232, Ogunquit, 03907, 207-646-5496

Seafair Inn, Box 1221, Ogunquit, 03907, 207-646-2181
Shore House, 15 1/2 Shore Rd., Ogunquit, 03907, 207-646-6619
Strauss Haus, Shore Rd., Ogunquit, 03907, 207-646-7756
Terrace By the Sea, 11 Wharf Ln., Ogunquit, 03907, 207-646-3232
Trellis House, P.O. Box 2229, Ogunquit, 03907, 207-646-7909
Yardarm Village Inn, Box 773, 130 Shore Rd., Ogunquit, 03907, 207-646-7006
Ye Olde Perkins Place, Shore Rd., Ogunquit, 03907
Yellow Monkey Guest House, 44 Main St., Ogunquit, 03907, 207-646-9056
Claibern's B&B, P.O. Box B, Oxford, Otisfield, 04270, 207-539-2352
Little River Inn, HC 62, Box 178, Pemaquid, 04558, 207-677-2845
Bradley Inn @ Pemaquid Pt., H.C.61, Box 361, Pemaquid Pt.—New Harbor, 04554, 207-677-2105
Victorian House, Route 26, Poland Spring, 04274, 207-998-2169
Ocean House, Box 66, Port Clyde, 04855, 207-372-6691
Pomegranate Inn, 49 Neal St., Portland, 04102, 297-772-1006
Country Club Inn, Country Club Dr., Rangeley, 04970
Davis Lodge, Route 4, Rangeley, 04970, 207-864-5569
Farmhouse Inn, P.O. Box 496, Rangeley, 04970, 207-864-5805
Northern Pines Health Rsrt, Raymond, 04071, 207-655-7624
Old Granite Inn, 546 Main St., Rockland, 04841, 207-594-7901
Rosemary Cottage, Russell Ave., Rockport, 04856, 207-236-3513
Sign of the Unicorn House, P.O. Box 99, Rockport, 04856, 207-236-4042
Allen's Inn, 279 Main St., Sanford, 04073, 207-324-2160
Oakland House, Herricks Rd., Sargentville, 04673, 207-359-8521
Higgins Beach Inn, Scarborough, 04074, 207-883-6684
Carriage House Inn, P.O. Box 238, Searsport, 04974, 207-548-2289
McGilvery House, P.O. Box 588, Searsport, 04974, 207-548-6289
Stonewycke Inn, P.O. Box 589, Searsport, 04974, 207-548-2551
William & Mary Inn, U.S. Rte. 1, PO Box 813, Searsport, 04974, 207-548-2190
Edgewater Farm B&B, Box 464, Small Pt. Rd., Sebasco Estates, 04565, 207-389-1322
Rock Gardens Inn, Sebasco Estates, 04565, 207-389-1339
Sebasco Lodge, Sebasco Estates, 04565, 207-389-1161
Brick Farm B&B, RFD 1, Skowhegan, 04976, 207-474-3949
Coveside Inn, Cove Rd. Christmas, South Bristol, 04568
Buck's Harbor Inn, P.O. Box 268, South Brooksville, 04617, 207-326-8660
Migis Lodge, Route 302, South Casco, 04077, 207-655-4524
Thomas Inn & Playhouse, P.O. Box 128, South Casco, 04077, 207-655-7728
Bluff House Inn/Restaurant, P.O. Box 81, Rt. 186, South Gouldsboro, 04678, 207-963-7805
Alfred M. Senter B&B, Box 830, South Harpswell, 04079, 207-833-2874
Senter B&B, Route 123, South Harpswell, 04079, 207-833-2874
Weskeag Inn, Route 73, P.O. Box 213, South Thomaston, 04858, 207-596-6676
Claremont, Southwest Harbor, 04679, 207-244-5036
Harbor Lights Home, Route 102, Southwest Harbor, 04679, 207-244-3835
Island Watch B&B, P.O. Box 1359, Southwest Harbor, 04679, 207-244-7229
Moorings Inn, The, Shore Rd., Southwest Harbor, 04679, 207-244-5523
Widow's Walk, Box 150, Stratton, 04982, 207-246-6901
Surry Inn, P.O. Box 25, Route 172, Surry, 04684, 207-667-5091
Time & Tide B&B, RR 1 Box 275B, Surry, 04684, 207-667-3382
Mill Pond House, Box 640, Tenants Harbor, 04860, 207-372-6209
Pointed Fir, The, HCR 35, Box 625, Tenants Harbor, 04860
Crab Apple Acres Inn, Route 201, The Forks, 04985, 207-663-2218
Bedside Manor Guest House, HCR 35 Box 100, Thomaston, 04861, 207-354-8862
Cap'n Frost's B&B, 241 W. Main St., Thomaston, 04861, 207-354-8217
Gracie's B&B, 52 Main St., Thomaston, 04861, 207-354-2326
River House B&B, HCR 35, Box 119, Thomaston, 04861, 207-354-8936
Middaugh B&B, 36 Elm St., Topsham, 04086, 207-725-2562
Shepard Hill B&B, Shepard Hill Rd., Union, 04862, 207-785-4121
Farrell-Michaud House, 231 Main St., Van Buren, 04785
Libby House, Water St., Vinalhaven, 04853
Blackford Inn, The, P.O. Box 817, Waldoboro, 04572, 207-832-4714
Broad Bay Inn & Gallery, P.O. Box 607, Main St., Waldoboro, 04572, 207-832-6668
Le Vatout, Route 32, Box 375, Waldoboro, 04572, 207-832-4552
Letteney Farm Vacations, RFD 2, Box 166A, Waldoboro, 04572, 207-832-5143
Medomak House, Box 663, Friendship, Waldoboro, 04572, 207-832-4971
Roaring Lion B&B, The, Main St., P.O. Box 756, Waldoboro, 04572, 207-832-4038
Tide Watch Inn, Pine St., P.O. Box 94, Waldoboro, 04572, 207-832-4987
Bittersweet Inn, Clarks Cove Rd., Walpole, 04573, 207-563-5552
Windward Farm, Young's Hill Rd., Washington, 04574, 207-845-2830
Artemus Ward House, Waterford, 04088, 207-583-4106
Lake House, P.O. Box 82, Waterford, 04088, 800-223-4182
Waterford Inne, The, P.O. Box 149, Waterford, 04088, 207-583-4037
Kawanhee Inn Lakeside, Route 142, RR 1 Box 100, Weld, 04285, 207-585-2243
Weld Inn, The, P.O. Box 8, Weld, 04285, 207-585-2429
Grey Gull Inn, 321 Webhannet Dr., Wells, 04090, 207-646-7501
Haven, The, RR 4 Box 2270, Wells, 04090, 207-646-4194
Purple Sandpiper House, R.R. #3 Box 226, Wells, 04090, 207-646-7990
Bayview Inn B&B, RR4, 2131 Webhannet Dr., Wells Beach, 04090, 207-646-9260
Bakke B&B, RD#1,Box 505A,Foster Pt, West Bath, 04530, 207-442-7185
New Meadows Inn, Bath Rd., West Bath, 04530, 207-443-3921
King's Inn, P.O. Box 92, West Bethel, 04286, 207-836-3375
Vicarage East Ltd, Box 368A, West Harpswell, 04079, 207-833-5480
Colonial Winterport Inn, P.O. Box 525, Winterport, 04496, 207-223-5307
Stacked Arms B&B, The, RR 2, Box 146, Wiscasset, 04578, 207-882-5436

Homewood Inn, P.O. Box 196, Yarmouth, 04096, 207-846-3351
Summer Place, RFD 1 Box 196, York, 03909, 207-363-5233
Wild Rose of York, 78 Long Sands Rd., York, 03909, 207-363-2532
Bennetts, 3 Broadway, York Beach, 03910, 207-363-5302
Edwards Harbourside Inn, Stage Neck Rd., York Beach, 03910, 207-363-3037
Homestead Inn B&B, P.O. Box 15, York Beach, 03910, 207-363-8952
Jo-Mar B&B on the Ocean, P.O. Box 838, York Beach, 03910, 207-363-4826
Lighthouse Inn, Box 249, Nubble Rd., York Beach, 03910, 207-363-6072
Lilac Inn, Box 1325, 3 Ridge Rd., York Beach, 03910, 207-363-3930
Nautilus B&B, 7 Willow Ave., Box 916, York Beach, 03910, 207-363-6496
Tide Watch, The, 46 Shore Rd., York Beach, 03910, 207-363-4713
Inn at Harmon Park, York St. & Harmon, York Harbor, 03911, 207-363-2031

Maryland

ANNAPOLIS

Barn on Howard's Cove, The
500 Wilson Rd., 21401
410-266-6840
Graham & Libbie Gutsche
All year

$$ B&B
2 rooms
Rated
C-yes/S-no/P-no/H-no

Full breakfast
Snacks
Sitting room
near pool, tennis, dock
deep water docking avail

1850 restored barn on Severn River. Antiques, quilts, gardens, deep water docking. Near historic Annapolis. Farm breakfasts. Bedrooms overlooking river.

Chesapeake Bay Lighthouse
1423 Sharps Point Rd., 21401
410-757-0248
Bill & Janice Costello
All year

$$$ B&B
5 rooms, 5 pb
Visa, MC, •
C-ltd/S-no/P-no/H-no

Continental plus
Snacks
Comp. wine special occ.
300 ft. pier

An exact replica of the Thomas Point Lighthouse on the Chesapeake Bay. It's a working lighthouse called the Sharps Point Lighthouse.

College House Suites
One College Ave., Historic
District, 21401
410-263-6124
Don & Jo Anne Wolfrey
All year

$$$ B&B
2 rooms, 2 pb
Rated, •
C-ltd/S-no/P-no/H-no

Continental plus
Suites w/sitting room
A/C, Cable TV
courtyard, fireplace

Town home nestled between the USNA & St. John's College. Walk to Colonial Harbor, U.S. Naval Academy, historic sites. Private entrance. 2 night minimum. AAA approved.

Gibson's Lodgings
110 Prince George St., 21401
410-268-5555
Claude & Jeanne Schrift
All year

$$ B&B
20 rooms,
•
C-yes/S-no/P-no/H-yes

Continental plus
Comp. evening wine
Piano, conference fac.
daily maid service
parking

Located in historic district, near City Docks, adjacent to U.S. Naval Academy. Antique furnishings throughout. Offstreet parking. Daily maid service. Unique conf. facilities.

ANNAPOLIS

William Page B&B Inn
8 Martin St., 21401
410-626-1506 800-364-4160
Robert Zuchelli, Greg Page
All year

$$ B&B
5 rooms, 3 pb
Rated, •
C-ltd/S-no/P-no/H-no

Full breakfast
Afternoon tea, snacks
Wet bar set-up
sitting room
tennis and pool nearby

Circa 1908, furnished in genuine antiques and period reproductions. Featuring suite with private bath and whirlpool. Free off-street parking.

ANNAPOLIS—EDGEWATER

Riverwatch
145 Edgewater Dr., 21037
410-974-8152
Karen Dennis, Donald Silawksy
All year

$$ B&B
2 rooms, 2 pb
•
C-ltd/S-no/P-no/H-no

Continental plus
Hot tubs, boat dock
waterfront balconies
sitting room

Luxurious waterfront B&B with spectacular river view. King-queen beds, exquisite contemporary and oriental decor. Just minutes from historic Annapolis.

BALTIMORE

Admiral Fell Inn
888 S. Broadway, 21231
410-522-7377 800-292-INNS
Dominik Eckenstein
All year

$$$ B&B
38 rooms, 38 pb
Most CC, *Rated*, •
C-yes/S-yes/P-no/H-yes
German, French, Spanish

Continental breakfast
Full service restaurant
English-style pub
meeting facilities
free drop-off service

Restored inn on waterfront in historic Fell's Pt. Water taxi to Inner Harbor attractions. Packages, Disc'ts. Under 16 stay free. **10% discount when reservation made by guest**

Betsy's B&B
1428 Park Ave., 21217
410-383-1274
Betsy Grater
All year

$$$ B&B
3 rooms, 3 pb
Visa, MC, AmEx, *Rated*,
•
C-ltd/S-ltd/P-no/H-no

Full breakfast
Hot tub (by reservation)
piano, TV, bicycles
swim club privileges

Charming, 100-yr-old townhouse w/hallway floor in alternating oak/walnut strips, handsome brass rubbings. 3 blks to light rail, Inner Harbor, Oriole Park. **10% off wkdays**

Biltmore Suites Hotel, The
205 W. Madison St., 21201
410-728-6550 800-868-5064
Robert Dionne
All year

$$ B&B
27 rooms, 27 pb
Most CC, *Rated*, •
C-yes/S-yes/P-no/H-no

Continental breakfast
Free evening reception
Comp. stretch limo
library
courtyard/backyard

Historic inn, rooms & suites appointed with period antiques and private baths. Short walk to Inner Harbor and Orioles Park. **3rd night free when space available**

Celie's Waterfront B&B
1714 Thames St., 21231
410-522-2323 800-432-0184
Celie Ives
All year, Fax: 522-2324

$$$ B&B
7 rooms, 7 pb
Most CC, *Rated*, •
C-ltd/S-no/P-no/H-yes

Continental breakfast
Refrigerators, A/C
Private phones, TV
bedroom fireplaces
whirlpools, parking

New urban inn in Fell's Point historic, maritime community. Near Harborplace, business district & Orioles Park by water taxi. Harborview, roofdeck, garden & conference center.

BALTIMORE

Paulus Gasthaus, The
2406 Kentucky Ave., 21213
401-467-1688
Lucie & Ed Paulus
All year

$$ B&B
2 rooms, 1 pb
•
C-ltd/S-no/P-no/H-no
German, some French

Full breakfast
Comp. sherry in room
Sitting rm, outsd. patio
near golf, fitness trail
free parking

Best of two worlds: Tudor-style European home, lovely residential neighborhood. Quality accommod., Gemuetlichkeit, near Inner Harbor. Guests choose German or Amer. breakfast.

Union Square House B&B
23 S. Stricker St., 21223
410-233-9064 FAX-233-4046
Patrice & Joe Debes
Dec. 23 - Jan 1 closed

$$$ B&B
3 rooms, 3 pb
Visa, MC, AmEx, *Rated*,
•
C-ltd/S-ltd/P-ltd/H-no

Full breakfast
Afternoon tea, snacks
Comp. wine, sitting rm.
color TV in room
some fireplaces

Genteel Victorian townhouse in historic Union Square. 15 blocks west of Inner Harbor/Stadium area. Period furnishings and air-conditioning. **1 week stay, 7th night free**

BERLIN

Atlantic Hotel, The
2 N. Main St., 21811
410-641-0189
Stephen Jacques
All year

$$ B&B
16 rooms, 16 pb
Visa, MC, •
C-yes/S-yes/H-yes

Continental breakfast
Afternoon tea, cheese
Restaurant, bar, dinner
outdoor cafe, sitting rm
lounge, parlor, library

Restored Victorian hotel, circa 1895, centrally located in historic Berlin. 16 bedrooms with antique furnishings, private baths and air-conditioning. Fine dining.

CAMBRIDGE

Sarke Plantation Inn
6033 Todd Point Rd., 21613
410-228-7020
Genevieve Finley
All year

$$ B&B
5 rooms, 3 pb
AmEx
C-ltd/S-yes/P-ltd/H-no

Continental breakfast
Swimming pool, stereo
sitting room, piano
pool table, fireplaces

Spacious & scenic country, waterfowl abundant on waterfront. Breakfast in "sidewalk cafe" with paintings by local artists. Summer house for cards and games. **3rd night 50%**

CENTREVILLE

Academy B&B, The
100 Academy Lane, 21617
410-758-2791
Bill & Teresa Newman
All year

$$ B&B
3 rooms, 3 pb
Visa, MC, •
C-yes/S-yes/P-yes/H-no

Continental plus
Aft. tea, snacks
Comp. wine
croquet, sun bathing
garden

The Centreville Male Academy (built 1804), one of Maryland's oldest schoolhouses, now transformed into a charming Eastern Shore B&B. Lovely gardens. **3rd night 50% off**

CHESAPEAKE CITY

Inn at the Canal
P.O. Box 187, 21915
104 Bohemia Ave.
410-885-5995
Mary & Al Ioppolo
All year

$$ B&B
6 rooms, 6 pb
Most CC, *Rated*, •
C-ltd/S-no/P-no/H-no

Full breakfast
Comp. iced tea, cider
Sitting room
waterside porch

Elegant waterside Victorian in quaint historic district on banks of Chesapeake and Delaware Canal. Fine shops and restaurants all within walking distance. **2nd night 50%, ltd**

CHESTERTOWN

White Swan Tavern, The
231 High St., 21620
410-778-2300
Mary Susan Maisel
All year

$$$ B&B
5 rooms, 5 pb
Rated
C-yes/S-yes/P-no/H-ltd

Continental breakfast
Comp. wine, eve. sherry
Comp. fruit basket
sitting room, terrace
bicycles, king bed

18th-century inn nestled in Maryland's historic eastern shore. Genuine antiques, homemade continental breakfast, tea, complimentary wine & fruit.

CUMBERLAND

Inn at Walnut Bottom
120 Greene St., 21502
301-777-0003 800-286-9718
Sharon Ennis Kazary
All year

$$ B&B
12 rooms, 10 pb
Visa, MC, AmEx, *Rated*,
•
C-yes/S-no/P-no/H-ltd

Full breakfast
Restaurant-full service
Afternoon tea, snacks
sitting room, library
TV rm., bicycles, phones

Charming traditional country inn & Arthur's Restaurant. Beautiful mountain city w/ scenic railroad, historic district & extraordinary recreation area. **10% discount w/ mention**

FREDERICK

Middle Plantation Inn
9549 Liberty Rd., 21701
301-898-7128
Shirley & Dwight Mullican
All year

$$$ B&B
3 rooms, 3 pb
Rated, •
C-ltd/S-no/P-no/H-no

Continental plus
Sitting room, garden
hen house, brook
four golf courses nearby

A rustic stone and log B&B, furnished with antiques, television and A/C. Near Gettysburg, Antietam, Harper's Ferry, Washington D.C., and Baltimore. **$15 disc't w/out breakfast**

Spring Bank—A B&B Inn
7945 Worman's Mill Rd., 21701
301-694-0440
Beverly & Ray Compton
All year

$$$ B&B
5 rooms, 1 pb
Most CC, *Rated*, •
C-ltd/S-no/P-no/H-no

Continental breakfast
Double parlors, library
view from observatory
10 acres for roaming

On National Register of Historic Places. Antiques. Near Baltimore, Washington, D.C., and Civil War battlefields. Exceptional dining in Frederick Historic District 2 mi. away.

Spring Bank, Frederick, MD

Gaithersburg Hospitality, Gaithersburg, MD

GAITHERSBURG

Gaithersburg Hospitality	$$ B&B	Full breakfast
18908 Chimney Place, 20879	4 rooms, 2 pb	Aft. tea, snacks
301-977-7377	•	Comp. wine
Joe & Suzanne Danilowicz	C-yes/S-ltd/P-no/H-no	library, sitting room
All year	Polish	tennis, pool nearby

A relaxed and comfortable B&B experience with delicious, sumptupus breakfast and cheerful personal attention await you.

HAGERSTOWN

Beaver Creek House B&B	$$$ EP/B&B	Full breakfast
20432 Beaver Creek Rd., 21740	5 rooms, 3 pb	Afternoon tea, snacks
301-797-4764	*Rated*, •	Comp. sherry in room
Don & Shirley Day	C-ltd/S-no/P-no/H-no	sitting room, library
All year		restaurants nearby

Antique-filled Victorian country home near I-70 and 81. Clean, hospitable, relaxed; near historic sites, golf, antique and outlet shopping. **$10 disc't mid-week**

Lewrene Farm B&B	$ B&B	Full breakfast
9738 Downsville Pike, 21740	6 rooms, 3 pb	Bedside snack
301-582-1735	Visa, MC	Sitting room, whirlpool
Lewis & Irene Lehman	C-yes/S-no/P-no/H-no	gazebo, large farm
All year	Spanish, some German	quilts for sale, piano

Quiet farm, cozy colonial home w/fireplace, antiques, candlelight breakfasts, Historic Antietam Battlefield, Harper's Ferry, outlets, restaurants. **3rd night 10% off**

HAVRE DE GRACE

Spencer Silver Mansion	$$ B&B	Full breakfast
200 S. Union Ave., 21078	4 rooms, 1 pb	Two parlors, fireplace
410-939-1097	*Rated*, •	porch, reading nook, TV
Carol & Jim Nemeth	C-yes/S-ltd/P-no/H-no	guided tours, sitt. rm.
All year	German	

In the heart of the historic district, our 1896 mansion takes you to the turn of the century. Antique-filled Victorian-style rooms, informative hosts. **3rd nite 50% off**

HAVRE DE GRACE

Vandiver Inn
301 S. Union Ave., 21078
410-939-5200 800-245-1655
Mary McKee
All year

$$ B&B
8 rooms, 8 pb
Visa, MC, AmEx, *Rated*,
•
C-ltd/S-ltd/P-no/H-yes

Full breakfast
2 rooms private porch &
entrance
large front porch

1886 Victorian mansion. Surrounded by historic sites, antiquing, museums, marinas. Dinner served on Friday & Saturday evenings. 2 blocks from Chesapeake Bay.

LUTHERVILLE

Twin Gates B&B Inn
308 Morris Ave., Suburb of
Baltimore, 21093
301-252-3131 800-635-0370
Gwen & Bob Vaughan
All year

$$$ B&B
7 rooms, 5 pb
Rated, •
C-ltd/S-no/P-no/H-no

Full gourmet breakfast
Comp. wine, tea
Free winery tours
library

Victorian mansion in serene northern suburb. 20 min. to convention center, Harbor Place & Nat'l Aquarium. Excellent seafood restaurants, winery tours. **Free bottle wine, ltd**

NEW MARKET

National Pike Inn
P.O. Box 299, 21774
9 W. Main St.
301-865-5055
Tom & Terry Rimel
All year

$$$ B&B
6 rooms, 3 pb
Visa, MC, *Rated*,
C-ltd/S-ltd/P-no/H-no

Continental plus
Basket of fruit, snacks
Coffee, tea, sitting rm
private garden courtyard
shopping, tennis, golf

Our Colonial decor and warm hospitality will make your stay memorable! Explore historic architecture, antique shopping, and dine in excellence. **3rd nite 50% off**

OAKLAND

Oak & Apple B&B, The
208 N. Second St., 21550
301-334-9265
Jana & Ed Kight
All year

$$ B&B
4 rooms, 2 pb
Visa, MC, •
C-ltd/S-no/P-no/H-no

Continental plus
Aft. tea, snacks
Sitting room, bicycles
sunporch w/swing
fireplaces

Colonial revival mansion circa 1915 in historic district of quaint mountain village. Elegant yet relaxed, surrounded by scenic and recreational paradise.

OLNEY

Thoroughbred B&B
16410 Batchellor Forest, 20832
301-774-7649
Helen M. Polinger
All year

$$ B&B
15 rooms, 7 pb
Visa, MC, *Rated*, •
C-yes/S-no/P-no/H-ltd

Continental breakfast
Hot tubs, pool table
swimming pool, library
golf nearby, sitting rm.

Beautiful country estate on 18-hole, 72 par golf course. 12 mi. to DC, 6 mi. to Metro. Some rooms w/fireplaces & whirlpool tubs. **$5 discount if pay by cash or check**

OXFORD

Robert Morris Inn
P.O. Box 70, 21654
314 N. Morris St.
410-226-5111
Jay Gibson
All year

$$$ EP
33 rooms, 33 pb
Visa, MC, *Rated*, •
C-ltd/S-yes/P-no/H-ltd

Full breakfast (W-Sun) $
Continental (M-Tu)
Restaurant (excl. Tues.)
bar service

Historic Chesapeake Bay romantic inn located in charming Oxford, MD. Featuring the best crab cakes on the eastern shore. Tennis, fishing, boating, and golfing all nearby.

SNOW HILL

River House Inn, The	$$$ B&B	Full breakfast
201 E. Market St., 21863	9 rooms, 9 pb	Lunch, dinner, snacks
410-632-2722	Visa, MC, *Rated*, •	Comp. wine/tea, porches
Larry & Susanne Knudsen	C-yes/S-no/P-no/H-no	A/C, fishing, boating
All year		country club golf, bikes

Come relax at our elegant 1860s riverfront country home in historic Snow Hill. Enjoy Maryland's eastern shore, beaches and bay. **Free bottle of wine.**

SOLOMONS ISLAND

Davis House	$$ B&B	Full breakfast
P.O. Box 759, 20688	6 rooms	Afternoon tea
Charles & Maltby Sts.	*Rated*	Comp. sherry
410-326-4811	C-ltd/S-ltd/P-no/H-no	sitting room
Jack & Runa Howley	Spanish, Swedish, French	library
All year		

Charming Victorian, furnished comfortably and stylishly, in front of the harbor, achieving a quality as the best of European inns. Golf, tennis, wind surfing, sailing nearby.

ST. MICHAELS

Kemp House Inn	$$ B&B	Continental plus
P.O. Box 638, 21663	8 rooms, 6 pb	Bicycles
412 Talbot St.	Visa, MC, *Rated*, •	queen-sized beds
410-745-2243	C-yes/S-yes/P-yes/H-no	private cottage avail.
Diane & Steve Cooper		
All year		

1805 Georgian house with four-poster beds and working fireplaces in historic eastern shore village; close to restaurants, museums, harbor.

Parsonage Inn	$$ B&B	Full gourmet breakfast
210 N. Talbot (Rt. 33), 21663	8 rooms, 7 pb	Comp. ice tea, tea
301-745-5519 800-394-5519	Visa, MC, *Rated*, •	Parlor, library
Peggy & Bill Parsons	C-yes/S-no/H-yes	bicycles, shops, museums
All year		fireplaces, restaurants

Unique brick Victorian, part of historic district. Walking distance to maritime museums. Laura Ashley linens. **Midwk: 20% off 2nd night, 25% off 3rd night.**

THURMONT

Cozy Country Inn	$ B&B	Continental plus
103 Frederick Rd., 21788	21 rooms, 21 pb	Restaurant, lunch
301-271-4301	Visa, MC, DC, *Rated*,	Dinner, full breakfast
Gerald G. Freeze	C-yes/S-ltd/P-no/H-ltd	snacks, bar service
All year		sitting room, hot tubs

Unique, historic country inn & cottages. Charming decor commemorating dignitaries who have visited Cozy & nearby Camp David. **Discounts for seniors**

TILGHMAN ISLAND

Black Walnut Point Inn	$$$ B&B	Continental plus
P.O. Box 308, 21671	7 rooms, 7 pb	Comp. wine
Black Walnut Rd.	*Rated*	Sitting room, bicycles
410-886-2452	C-ltd/S-ltd/P-no/H-yes	tennis, pool, shoreline
M. Thomas Ward/Brenda C.		57-acre wildlife reserve
Ward		
All year		

The inn at the end of the road. Key West sunsets. Hammocks by the bay. Quiet and peaceful. **Complimentary bottle of champagne for anniversary**

Chesapeake Wood Duck Inn, Tilghman Island, MD

TILGHMAN ISLAND

Chesapeake Wook Duck Inn	$$$ B&B	Full breakfast
P.O. Box 202, 21671	6 rooms, 6 pb	Aft. tea, snacks
Gibsontown Rd.	Visa, MC, *Rated*, •	Comp. wine, sitting room
410-886-2070	C-ltd/S-yes/P-no/H-no	sun room, bicycles
Stephanie & Dave Feith		access to country club
All year		

Southern hospitality on The Chesapeake Bay. 1890 Victorian overlooking Dogwood Harbor in quaint Waterman's Village. Porches, decks, fireplaces, antiques.

VIENNA

Tavern House, The	$$ B&B	Full breakfast
P.O. Box 98, 21869	3 rooms	Aftn. tea, comp. wine
111 Water St.	Visa, MC, •	Sitting room
410-376-3347	C-ltd/S-yes/Spanish,	tennis courts nearby
Harvey & Elise Altergott	German	
All year		

Restored Colonial tavern on Nanticoke River. Simple elegance; stark whites, detailed woodwork. Looking out over river and marshes. Great for bicycling and bird-watching.

More Inns . . .

Annapolis B&B, 235 Prince George Sr., Annapolis, 21401, 301-269-0669
Bay View B&B, 2654 Ogleton Rd., Annapolis, 21403, 301-268-0781
Casa Bahia, 262 King George St., Annapolis, 21404
Charles Inn, 74 Charles St., Annapolis, 21401, 301-268-1451
Heart of Annapolis B&B, 185 Duke of Gloucester , Annapolis, 21404, 301-267-2309
Hunter House, 154 Prince George St., Annapolis, 21404
Jonah Williams Inn, 101 Severn Ave., Annapolis, 21403, 301-269-6020
Mary Rob B&B, 243 Prince George St., Annapolis, 21401, 301-268-5438
Maryland Inn, Church Circle, Annapolis, 21401, 800-638-8902
Reynolds Tavern, 4 Church Cr., Annapolis, 21401, 800-638-8902
Robert Johnson House, 23 State Cir., Annapolis, 21401, 800-638-8902
Shaw's Fancy B&B, 161 Green St., Annapolis, 21401, 410-263-0320
State House Inn, 15 State Cir., Annapolis, 21401, 800-638-8902
Agora, 824 E. Baltimore St., Baltimore, 21202, 301-234-0515
Bolton Hill B&B, 1534 Bolton St., Baltimore, 21217, 301-669-5356
Eagles Mere B&B, 102 E. Montgomery, Baltimore, 21230, 301-332-1618
Inn at Government House, 1125 North Calvert St., Baltimore, 21202, 301-752-7722
Mr. Mole B&B, 1601 Bolton St., Baltimore, 21217, 410-728-1179

Mulberry House, 111 W. Mulberry St., Baltimore, 21201, 301-576-0111
Society Hill Hotel, 58 W. Biddle St., Baltimore, 21201, 410-837-3630
Society Hill—Hopkins, 3404 St. Paul St., Baltimore, 21218, 410-235-8600
Lantern Inn B&B, PO Box 29, 115 Ericsson, Betterton, 21610, 401-348-5809
Catoctin Inn & Antiques, 3613 Buckeystown Pike, Buckeystown, 21717, 301-874-5555
Inn at Buckeystown, 3521 Buckeystown Pike, Buckeystown, 21717, 301-874-5755
Upsteam Guest House, 3604 Dustin Rd, Box 240, Burtonsville, 20866, 301-421-9163
Winslow Home, 8217 Caraway St., Cabin John, 20818, 301-229-4654
Commodore's Cottage B&B, 215 Glenburn Ave., Cambridge, 21613, 800-228-6938
Glasgow Inn, 1500 Hambrooks Blvd., Cambridge, 21613, 301-228-0575

The Inn at Walnut Bottom, Cumberland, MD

Lodgecliffe on Choptank, 103 Choptank Ter., Cambridge, 21613
Blue Bird on the Mountain, 14700 Eyler Ave., Cascade, 21719
Inwood Guest House, Box 378, Route 1, Cascade, 21719, 301-241-3467
Brampton, 25227 Chestertown Rd., Chestertown, 21620, 410-778-1860
Flyway Lodge, Rt.1, Box 660, US Rt.21, Chestertown, 21620, 301-778-5557
Great Oak Manor, Route 2 Box 766, Chestertown, 21620, 301-778-5796
Hill's Inn, 114 Washington Ave., Chestertown, 21620, 301-778-INNS
Imperial Hotel, The, 208 High St., Chestertown, 21620, 410-778-5000
Inn at Mitchell House, Box 329, R.D. 2, Chestertown, 21620, 301-778-6500
Radcliffe Cross, Route 3, Box 360, Chestertown, 21620, 301-778-5540
Widow's Walk Inn, 402 High St., Chestertown, 21620, 410-778-6455
Chevy Chase B&B, 6815 Connecticut Ave., Chevy Chase, 20815, 301-656-5867
Loblolly Landings & Lodge, 2142 Liners Rd., Church Creek, 21622, 410-397-3033
Sportman's Retreat, The, 2142 Liners Rd., Church Creek, 21622, 410-397-3033
Red Lamp Post B&B, 849 Braddock Rd., Cumberland, 21502, 301-777-3262
Sophie Kerr House, Route 3, Box 7-B, Denton, 21629, 301-479-3421
Bishop's House B&B, The, P.O. Box 2217, Easton, 21601, 410-820-7290
McDaniel House, The, 14 North Aurora St., Easton, 410-822-3704
Tidewater Inn, Dover & Harrison Sts., Easton, 21601, 301-822-1300
Victorian Lady, 710 Edgewood Rd., Edgewood, 21040, 410-676-4661
Hayland Farm, 5000 Sheppard Ln., Ellicott City, 21043, 301-531-5593
White Duck B&B, The, 3920 College Ave., Ellicott City, 21043, 410-992-8994
Broom Hall B&B, 2425 Pocock Rd., Fallston, 21047, 301-557-7321
Trailside Country Inn, US 40, Flintstone, 21530, 301-478-2032
Tran Crossing, 121 E. Patrick St., Frederick, 21701, 301-663-8449
Turning Point Inn, 3406 Urbana Pike, Frederick, 21701, 301-874-2421
Tyler-Spite House, 112 W. Church St., Frederick, 21701, 301-831-4455
Freeland Farm, 21616 Middletown Rd., Freeland, 21053, 301-357-5364
Kitty Knight House, Route 213, Georgetown, 21930, 301-648-5777
Nicholl's House, 19217 Fox Chapel Dr., Germantown, 20874
Claudia Brey, 7260 S. Ora Ct., Greenbelt, 20770
Sunday's B&B, 39 Broadway, Hagerstown, 21740, 800-221-4828
Ches' Bayvu, 4720 Paul Hance Rd., Huntington, 20639
Country Inn, P.O. Box 397, McHenry, 21541, 301-387-6694
Marameade, The, 2439 Old National Pike, Middletown, 21769, 301-371-4214
Castle, P.O. Box 578, Route 36, Mount Savage, 21545, 301-759-5946
Strawberry Inn, The, P.O. Box 237, New Market, 21774, 301-865-3318
Angels in the Attic, P.O. Box 70, North Beach, 20714, 410-257-1069
Westlawn Inn, 7th St. & Chesapeake, North Beach, 20714, 301-855-8410
Mill House, The, 102 Mill Ln., North East, 21901, 301-287-3532
Oak & Apple B&B, 208 N. 2nd St., Oakland, 21550, 301-334-9265
Red Run Inn, Route 5, Box 268, Oakland, 21550, 301-387-6606
1876 House, P.O. Box 658, Oxford, 21654, 301-226-5496
Elmwood c. 1770 B&B, P.O. Box 220, Princess Anne, 21853, 301-651-1066
Washington Hotel & Inn, Somerset Ave., Princess Anne, 21853, 301-651-2525
Strawberry Factory, Route 20, Gratitude, Rock Hall, 21661, 301-639-7068
Hambleton Inn, 202 Cherry St., Box 299, Saint Michaels, 21663, 301-245-3350
Inn at Perry Cabin, Saint Michaels, 21663, 301-745-5178
Two Swan Inn, P.O. Box 727, Saint Michaels, 21663, 301-745-2929
Victoriana Inn, 205 Cherry St., Box 449, Saint Michaels, 21663, 410-745-3368
Inn at Antietam, P.O. Box 119, Sharpsburg, 21782, 301-432-6601
Piper House B&B Inn, Antietam Battlefield, Sharpsburg, 21782, 301-797-1862
Northwood Inn, 10304 Eastwood Ave., Silver Spring, 20901
Quality International, 10750 Columbia Pike, Silver Spring, 20901, 301-236-5032
Snow Hill Inn, 104 E. Market St., Snow Hill, 21863, 301-632-2102
Back Creek Inn B&B, P.O. Box 520, Solomons, 20688
By-The-Bay B&B, PO Box 504, Calvert St., Solomons, 20688
Capt.& Ms J's Guest House, P.O. Box 676, Solomons, 20688, 301-326-3334
Wades Point Inn On The Bay, P.O. Box 7, St. Michaels, 21663, 410-745-2500
Gramercy, 1400 Greenspring Valley, Stevenson, 21153, 410-486-2405
Kent Manor Inn, Kent Island, Box 815, Stevensville, 21666, 301-643-5757
\ntrim 1844, 30 Trevanion Rd., Taneytown, 21787, 410-756-6812

Antrim Plantation, 30 Trevanian Rd., Taneytown, 21787
Glenburn, 3515 Runnymede Rd., Taneytown, 21787, 410-751-1187
Harrison's Country Inn, P.O. Box 310, Tilghman, 21671, 301-886-2123
Sinclair House B&B, Box 145, Tilghman Island, 21671, 410-886-2147
Wood Duck Inn B&B, P.O. Box 202, Tilghman Island, 21671, 410-886-2070
Newel Post, The, 3428 Uniontown Rd., Uniontown, 21157, 301-775-2655
Governor's Ordinary, P.O. Box 156, Vienna, 21869, 301-376-3530
Nanticoke Manor House, P.O. Box 248, Vienna, 21869, 301-376-3530
Avondale, 501 Stone Chapel Rd., Westminster, 21157
Judge Thomas House 1893, 195 Willis St., Westminster, 21157, 301-876-6686
Westminster Inn, 5 South Center St., Westminster, 21157, 301-876-2893
Winchester Country Inn, 430 S. Bishop St., Westminster, 21157, 301-876-7373
Christmas Farm, Rte. 33, Wittman, 21676, 301-822-4470
Rosebud Inn, 4 N. Main St., Woodsboro, 21798, 301-845-2221

Lewrene Farm B&B, Hagerstown, MD

Massachusetts

AMHERST

Allen House Victorian Inn
599 Main St., 01002
413-253-5000
Alan & Ann Zieminski
All year

$ B&B
5 rooms, 5 pb
Rated
C-ltd/S-no/P-no/H-no

Full breakfast
Aft. English tea & snack
Library
sitting room
veranda

Authentic antique-filled 1886 Victorian on 3 acres. Spacious bed chambers, private baths. Historic Preservation Award winner. Opposite Emily Dickinson Homestead. **Weekly rates**

BARNSTABLE

Charles Hinkley House
P.O. Box 723, 02630
Rt 6A, Olde King's Hwy
508-362-9924
Les & Miya Patrick
All year

$$$ B&B
4 rooms, 4 pb
Rated, •
C-ltd/S-no/P-no/H-yes

Full breakfast
Comp. sherry
Sitting room
4 rooms with fireplaces
on National Register

Intimate country inn where great expectations are quietly met. Fireplace suites with four-poster beds. Short stroll from Cape Cod Bay. "Most photographed inn in Cape Cod."

Thomas Huckins House
P.O. Box 515, 02630
2701 Main St., Route 6A
508-362-6379
Burt & Eleanor Eddy
All year

$$$ B&B
3 rooms, 3 pb
Visa, MC
C-ltd/S-yes/P-no/H-no

De Luxe Continental
Sitting room
fireplaces
2 bedroom suite

B&B in historic 1705 house on Cape Cod's picturesque northside. Fireplaces, antiques, canopy beds, privacy and charm. Walk to ocean and village.

BARNSTABLE VILLAGE ────────────────────────────────

Beechwood $$$ B&B   Full breakfast
2839 Main St., 02630   6 rooms, 6 pb   Afternoon tea
508-362-6618   Most CC, *Rated*, •   Sitting room, veranda
Anne & Bob Livermore   C-ltd/S-ltd/P-no/H-no croquet
All year   Perrenial garden

A romantic Victorian inn along the historic "Old King's Way." Spacious period-furnished guest rooms offer fireplaces and views of Cape Cod Bay. Walk to shops, beaches.

Cobb's Cove Inn $$$ B&B   Full breakfast
P.O. Box 208, 02630   6 rooms, 6 pb   Dinner, comp. wine, tea
31 Powder Hill Rd.   •   Whirlpool tubs, robes
508-362-9356 FAX:362-9356 C-ltd/S-ltd/P-no/H-no toiletries, piano
Evelyn Chester & Henri Jean French   sitting room, library
All year

Secluded getaway inn for couples. Two fabulous honeymoon suites with water views. Located on Cape Cod's unspoiled North Shore overlooking Cape Cod Bay.

BARNSTABLE–CAPE COD ───────────────────────────────

Ashley Manor $$$ B&B   Full gourmet breakfast
P.O. Box 856, 02630   6 rooms, 6 pb   Comp. wine/sherry/port
3660 Old Kings Hwy(Rt 6A) Visa, MC, AmEx, *Rated*, Flowers, fruit, snacks
508-362-8044   •   sitting room, croquet
Donald & Fay Bain   C-ltd/S-ask/P-no/H-no bikes, tennis, garden
All year

1699 mansion in the historic district; rooms and suites have antiques, fireplaces, and private baths; walk to beach, village and harbor. All suites have canopy beds.

BOSTON ───

Beacon Hill B&B $$$ B&B   Full breakfast
27 Brimmer St., 02108   3 rooms, 3 pb   Restaurants nearby
617-523-7376   •   Sitting room
Susan Butterworth   C-yes/S-no/P-no/H-no   garage nearby
All year   French

1869 Victorian townhouse. Fireplaces, riverview. Gas-lit, historically preserved downtown neighborhood. Boston Common, "Cheers" bar, Freedom Trail, Convention Center easy walk

BOSTON–BROOKLINE ──────────────────────────────────

Anthony's Town House $ EP   Restaurant/stores nearby
1085 Beacon St., 02146   14 rooms   Near major league sports
617-566-3972   *Rated*, •   all hospitals, sitt. rm.
Barbara Anthony   C-yes/S-yes/P-no/H-no historical sites, TV
All year

Turn-of-the-century brownstone townhouse; spacious rooms in Victorian atmosphere; family-operated for over 50 years; on trolley line, 10 min. to Boston. **Special winter rates**

Beacon Inn $$ B&B   Continental breakfast
1087 Beacon St., 02146   25 rooms, 6 pb   Lobby fireplaces
617-566-0088   Visa, MC, •   original woodwork
Maureen Keaney/Megan Rockett C-yes/S-yes/P-no/H-no
All year

Large, comfortable furnished, sunny rooms provide pleasant accommodations at a surprisingly affordable price. Near subway line.

BREWSTER —————————————————————————————

Bramble Inn & Restaurant	$$$ B&B	Continental plus
P.O. Box 807, 02631	8 rooms, 8 pb	Lunch, dinner
2019 Main St., Route 6A	*Rated*, •	Sitting room
508-896-7644	C-ltd/S-yes/P-no/H-ltd	near beach, tennis
Ruth & Cliff Manchester		
April–December		

Romantic country inn in historic district of Cape Cod. Beach, tennis courts, and close to golf, fishing, and museums. **7th night free**

Brewster Farmhouse Inn	$$ B&B	Full breakfast
716 Main St., 02631	5 rooms, 4 pb	Aft. tea, snacks
508-896-3910 800-892-3910	Most CC, Rated-	Comp. wine, sitting room
March - December	C-ltd/S-no/P-no/H-no	library, bicycles
	Spanish	heated swimming pool

Impeccably furnished, unparalleled services & amenities, fireplaced gathering room, full gourmet breakfasts, creative afternoon teas, walk to Cape Cod Bay.

Captain Freeman Inn	$$ B&B	Full breakfast
15 Breakwater Rd., 02631	12 rooms, 9 pb	Menu gardens
508-896-7481 800-843-4664	Most CC, *Rated*, •	Sitting room
Carol Covitz	C-ltd/S-no/P-no/H-no	bicycles, badminton
All year		swimming pool, croquet

A quiet country inn in a charming old sea captain's mansion; spacious rooms, canopy beds and romantic porch. 3 luxury suites w/fireplace, TV, A/C, refrig. & jacuzzi. **10% off**

Isaiah Clark House	$$$ B&B	Full breakfast
P.O. Box 169, 02631	7 rooms, 7 pb	Comp. tea and snacks
1187 Main St.	Visa, MC, *Rated*, •	Library, sitting rm, A/C
508-896-2223 800-822-4001	C-ltd/S-ask/P-no/H-no	cable TV, records, tapes
Charles & Ida DiCesare	French, Italian	bicycles
Mid-February–December		

Charming 1780 captain's house set on five lush acres. Near the beach and all the Cape attractions. Warm New England hospitality. Cookies & milk at bedtime. **3rd night 25% off**

Old Manse Inn, The	$$ B&B	Full breakfast
P.O. Box 839, 02631	9 rooms, 9 pb	Gourmet dinner, bar
1861 Main St.	Visa, MC, AmEx, *Rated*,	Aftn. tea, coffee
508-896-3149	•	library, patio, garden
Sugar & Doug Manchester	C-ltd/S-yes/P-no/H-yes	some rms. A+C, TV
March–December		

Enjoy salt air from room in antique sea captain's home. Walk to Cape Cod's attractions. Gourmet dining by reservation; award-winning food. **3rd night 50% w/guide.**

Old Sea Pines Inn	$ B&B	Full breakfast
P.O. Box 1026, 02631	14 rooms, 9 pb	Beverage on arrival
2553 Main St	Most CC, *Rated*, •	Restaurant
508-896-6114	C-ltd/S-yes/P-no/H-no	sitting room w/fireplace
Stephen & Michele Rowan	Italian, German	parlor, deck
April–December 22		

Newly redecorated turn-of-the-century mansion furnished with antiques. Near beaches, bicycle trails, quality restaurants and shops. **Complimentary beverages upon arrival.**

CAMBRIDGE

Cambridge House B&B, A
2218 Massachusetts Ave., 02140
617-491-6300
Ellen Riley & Tony Femmino
All year

$$$ B&B
13 rooms, 11 pb
Visa, MC, AmEx, *Rated*,
•
C-ltd/S-no/P-no/H-no
Italian

Full breakfast
Comp. wine & cheese
Lemonade, coffee, tea
cookies
sitting room

"Boston's finest gem" —Country Inns Magazine; "Famous for breakfast" —Glamour Magazine; "Boston's premier B&B" —BBC; "Our vote goes to Cambridge House" —L.A. Times.

Irving House, The
24 Irving St., 02138
617-547-4600
Rachael Solem
All year

$$
44 rooms, 8 pb
Visa, MC, AmEx, •
C-yes/S-no/P-ask/H-ltd
Spanish, some French

Continental plus
Sitting room
library
bicycles

Friendly accommodations in the heart of Cambridge. Off-street parking included. 10 min. walk to Harvard Square. Children under the age of 7 are free.

CAPE COD

Captain Isaiah's House
33 Pleasant St., Bass River,
02664
508-394-1739
Marge & Alden Fallows
Late June—early Sept

$ B&B
8 rooms, 2 pb
C-ltd/S-yes/P-no/H-no

Continental breakfast
Sitting room
fireplaces
whale watching nearby

Charming, restored old sea captain's house in historic Bass River area. Most rooms have fireplaces. Breakfast with home-baked breads, coffee cake. **Free potted plants**

CAPE COD—BARNESTABLE

Honeysuckle Hill
591 Main St., 02668
508-362-8418 800-441-8418
Barbara Rosenthal
All year

$$$ B&B
3 rooms, 3 pb
Most CC, *Rated*, •
C-ltd/S-yes/P-ltd/H-ltd
French, Italian

Full gourmet breakfast
Afternoon tea & pastries
Great room, TV, library
croquet, bicycles, piano
cookies by bed

Charming Victorian inn with feather beds, full country breakfasts, afternoon teas and homemade cookies at bedside. Near lovely Sandy Neck beach.

CAPE COD—YARMOUTH PORT

Liberty Hill Inn-Cape Cod
77 Main St., Route 6A, 02675
508-362-3976 800-821-3977
Jack & Beth Flanagan
All year

$$ B&B
5 rooms, 5 pb
Visa, MC, *Rated*, •
C-yes/S-yes/P-no/H-no

Full breakfast
Gourmet lunch
Candlelight dinner
sitting room, cable TV
maid service, telephone

Elegant country inn in gracious Greek Revival Manor house, circa 1825. Shopper's paradise, a romantic hideaway, antique furnishings. 3 rms. w/air-conditioning. **Free bottle wine**

CENTERVILLE

Copper Beech Inn
497 Main St., Cape Cod, 02632
508-771-5488
Joyce Diehl
All year

$$$ B&B
3 rooms, 3 pb
Visa, MC, *Rated*,
C-ltd/S-no/P-no/H-no

Full breakfast
Bicycles
6 blocks to beach
sitting room

1830 sea captain's house on the Nat'l. Register of Historic Places; offering air-conditioned comfort and the charm of yesteryear. Enjoy one of the 10 best beaches in America.

CHATHAM —————————

Bradford Inn & Motel

P.O. Box 750, 02633	$$$ B&B	Full breakfast from menu
26 Cross St.	25 rooms, 25 pb	Snacks, restaurant, bar
508-945-1030 800-562-4667	Most CC, *Rated*, •	Sitting room, library
William P. & Audrey E. Gray	C-ltd/S-yes/P-no	heated swimming pool
All year		tennis courts nearby

In Chatham's Historic District. Abundant amenities: fireplaces, 4-poster canopy beds, A/C, refrig., cable TV. Rated 3 Diamond-AAA/3 Star-Mobil. **Comp. dinner wine/newspaper.**

Captains House Inn

369-377 Old Harbor Rd., 02633	$$$ B&B	Continental plus
508-945-0127	14 rooms, 14 pb	Comp. afternoon tea
David & Cathy Eakin	Visa, MC, AmEx, *Rated*,	Sitting room
February 15—November	C-ltd/S-ltd/P-no/H-no	boat trips
		AAA 4-Diamond (1987)

Antiques & Williamsburg wallpapers. Charming guest rooms have 4-poster beds, fireplaces. Private 2-acre estate of lawns and gardens. Quiet and elegant.

Cranberry Inn at Chatham

359 Main St., 02633	$$$ B&B	Continental plus
508-945-9232 800-332-4667	18 rooms, 18 pb	Tap Room, liquor license
Richard Morris, Peggy DeHan	MC, Visa, AmEx, *Rated*,	Rooms w/phone, TV, A/C
March—mid-December	•	patio, front porch
	C-ltd/S-ltd/P-no/H-no	poster beds, suites

In heart of Chatham's picturesque seaside village & Historic District. Relaxed & intimate atmosphere, fireplaces, antiques. **Special Mid-week & off-season rates**

Cyrus Kent House Inn

63 Cross St., 02633	$$$ B&B	Continental plus
508-945-9104 800-945-9115	10 rooms, 10 pb	Porch, deck, gardens
Jodie Doman	Visa, MC, AmEx, *Rated*,	ample parking, phones
All year	C-ltd/S-yes/P-no/H-no	art & antique gallery

A sea captain's house reborn in the heart of the quaint seaside village of Chatham.Picturesque stroll to Main St. shops, beaches, restaurants.

Moses Nickerson House Inn

364 Old Harbor Rd., 02633	$$$ B&B	Full breakfast
508-945-5859 800-628-6972	7 rooms, 7 pb	Comp. wine, cheese/fruit
Elsie & Carl Piccola	Visa, MC, AmEx, *Rated*,	Sitting room near beach
All year	•	fresh flowers, antiques
	C-ltd/S-yes/P-no/H-no	turndown service

Elegant sea captain's home built 1839. Canopy beds, fireplaces, romantic, quiet. Walk to village & beaches. Glass-enclosed breakfast room overlooking garden. **Off-seas. disc't**

Old Harbor Inn

22 Old Harbor Rd., 02633	$$$ B&B	Continental plus
508-945-4434 800-942-4434	6 rooms, 6 pb	Restaurants nearby
Sharon & Tom Ferguson	Visa, MC, AmEx, *Rated*,	Sitting rm. w/ fireplace
All year	C-ltd/S-ltd/P-no/H-no	sun room, deck
		near golf, boating

English country decor. Queen/Twin beds. Delectable buffet breakfast. Walk to quaint seaside village attractions. Pleasurable memory-making awaits. Afternoon teas.

CONCORD

Hawthorne Inn
462 Lexington Rd., 01742
508-369-5610
Gregory Burch, Marilyn Mudry
All year

$$$ B&B
7 rooms, 7 pb
Rated, •
C-yes/S-ltd/P-no/H-no

Continental plus
Tea & coffee at check-in
Sitting room
yard, small pond, garden
bicycles

On the "Battle Road" of 1775, furnished with antiques, quilts and artwork with the accent on New England comfort and charm.

CUMMINGTON

Cumworth Farm
472 W. Cummington Rd., Route
112, 01026
413-634-5529
Ed & Mary McColgan
All year

$$ B&B
6 rooms
Rated
C-yes/S-ltd

Full breakfast
Afternoon tea
Comp. wine, snacks
sitting room, hot tub
piano, bicycles

Big, 200-year-old farmhouse; sugarhouse on premises; sheep; berries—pick your own in season. Close to cross-country skiing, hiking trails. Quiet getaway, sweeping views.

Swift River Inn
151 South St., 01026
413-634-5751 800-532-8022
Daniel Harper
All year, FAX: 634-5300

$$$ B&B
22 rooms, 22 pb
Most CC, *Rated*, •
C-yes/S-no/P-no/H-yes

Continental breakfast
Restaurant, all meals
Snacks, bar service
library, bicycles
swimming pool,
cross-country ski

Former turn-of-the-century gentleman's daily farm restored for lodging, dining & recreation. Family fun for all seasons: hiking, biking, fishing, children's programs, tennis.

DENNIS

Isiah Hall B&B Inn
152 Whig St., 02638
508-385-9928 800-736-0160
Marie Brophy
April—mid-October

$$ B&B
11 rooms, 10 pb
AmEx, Visa, MC, *Rated*,
•
C-ltd/S-yes/P-no/H-ltd

Continental plus
Comp. tea & coffee
Library, gift shop
2 sitting rooms, gardens
innkeeping seminars

Enjoy our relaxing quiet country ambience and hospitality in the heart of Cape Cod. Walk to beach, village, Playhouse and restaurants. **Spring Value Packages available**

DENNISPORT

Rose Petal B&B, The
P.O. Box 974, 02639
152 Sea St.
508-398-8470
Dan & Gayle Kelly
All year

$ B&B
4 rooms
Visa, MC, *Rated*, •
C-yes/S-ltd/P-no/H-no
some French

Full breakfast
Comp. wine, snacks
Guest refrg. on sunporch
gas grill, lawn furnit.
sitting room, TV, piano

Inviting 1872 home, attractive yard, lovely accommodations, superb breakfasts with homemade pastries. In residential neighborhood, few blocks to sandy beach or Village center.

EAST ORLEANS

Farmhouse at Nauset, The
163 Beach Rd., 02653
508-255-6654
Dot Standish
All year

$ B&B
9 rooms, 5 pb
Visa, MC
C-ltd/S-yes/P-no/H-no

Continental plus
Sitting room
Brkfst on oceanview deck
picnic tables

19th C. farmhouse beautifully restored. Enjoy a unique blend of country life in a seashore setting. Short walk to Nauset Beach. **10% discount on 7 nights**

The Rose Petal B&B, Dennisport, MA

EAST ORLEANS

Nauset House Inn
P.O. Box 774, 02643
143 Beach Rd.
508-255-2195
D & L Johnson, C & J Vessella
April—October

$$ EP
14 rooms, 8 pb
Visa, MC
C-ltd/S-ltd/P-no/H-no

Full breakfast avail. $
Wine & hors d'oeuvres
Commons room
piano, conservatory
dining room

Intimate 1810 inn, unique turn-of-the-century conservatory, warm ambience, a short walk to the sea.

Parsonage Inn, The
P.O. Box 1501, 02643
202 Main St.
508-255-8217
Ian & Elizabeth Browne
All year

$$ B&B
8 rooms, 8 pb
Visa, MC, *Rated*,
C-ltd/S-no/P-no/H-no

Continental plus
Guest refrigerator
Appetizers, parlor
piano, dining room
suite w/TV, AC, fridge

Experience a 1770 antique-furnished Cape home. Savor breakfast on the patio, walk to restaurants. Biking, golfing, tennis, fishing, Nauset beach nearby. Warm, friendly hosts.

Ship's Knees Inn
P.O. Box 756, 02643
186 Beach Rd.
508-255-1312
Jean & Ken Pitchford
All year

$ B&B
25 rooms, 11 pb
Rated, ●
C-ltd/S-yes/P-no/H-no

Continental breakfast
Sitting room
swimming pool
tennis courts

A restored sea captain's house; surrounded by the charm of yesterday while offering the convenience of today. **3rd night 50% off**

EASTHAM ──

Over Look Inn, The	$$$ B&B	Full breakfast
P.O. Box 771, 02642	8 rooms, 8 pb	Dinner occasional
3085 County Rd., Route 6	*Rated*, •	Aft. tea, sitting room
508-255-1886 800-356-1121	C-ltd/S-ltd/P-no/H-ask	bicycles, library
The Aitchison Family		tours, rentals, packages
All year, Fax:260-0345		

Victorian country inn within walking distance of Cape Cod National Seashore. Bike paths & nature trails. Delicious breakfast; tranquil wooded setting. Cottage available.

Whalewalk Inn, The	$$$ B&B	Full gourmet breakfast
220 Bridge Rd., 02642	12 rooms, 12 pb	Comp. hors d'ouevres
508-255-0617	*Rated*, •	Bar, sitting room, patio
Carolyn & Richard Smith	C-ltd/S-ltd/P-no/H-no	fireplaces, lawn games
April–November		rooms, suites, cottage

Restored 1830s whaling master's home. Elegance, hospitality. Uniquely decorated. On quiet road by bay, ocean. Near beach. OUR 1993 INN OF THE YEAR! **3rd night 50%—Ltd**

EDGARTOWN ───

Arbor, The	$$$ B&B	Continental breakfast
P.O. Box 1228, 02539	10 rooms, 8 pb	Comp. wine, beverages
222 Upper Main St.	Visa, MC, *Rated*, •	Parlor, fresh flowers
508-627-8137	C-ltd/S-ask/P-no/H-no	garden, courtyard
Peggy Hall		lovely cottage available
May–October		

Turn-of-the-century home in historic Edgartown. Walk to town & harbor. Rooms are delightfully and typically New England. Enchanting one-bedroom cottage available by the week.

Ashley Inn	$$$ B&B	Continental breakfast
P.O. Box 650, 02539	10 rooms, 8 pb	Sitting room
Edgartown, 129 Main St.	Visa, MC, AmEx, •	tea room, grounds
508-627-9655 800-477-9655	C-ltd/S-yes/P-no/H-no	badminton, hammock
Fred Hurley, Jude Cortese		
All year		

Attractive 1800s sea captain's home with country charm, decorated with period antiques, brass & wicker. A leisurely stroll to shops, beaches, fine foods. **3rd night 50% off.**

Captain Dexter House	$$$ B&B	Continental plus
P.O. Box 2798, 02539	11 rooms, 11 pb	Comp. wine
35 Pease's Point Way	Visa, MC, AmEx, *Rated*,	Hot cider (winter)
508-627-7289	•	lemonade (warm weather)
Lori & Len	C-ltd/S-ltd/P-no/H-no	sitting room
All year		

Lovely 1840s home; romantic antique-filled guest rooms with canopied beds and working fireplaces. Expansive landscaped gardens. Near the harbor, shops and restaurants.

Chadwick Inn, The	$$ B&B	Continental plus
P.O. Box 1035, 02539	21 rooms, 21 pb	Comp. sherry
67 Winter St.	Visa, MC, AmEx, •	Sitting room
508-627-4435 508-627-5656	C-ltd/S-yes/P-no/H-yes	library
Peter & Jurate Antioco	French	
All year		

In stately Edgartown Historic District, 1840s Greek Revival buildings, gardens, brick courtyard. Rooms furnished with antiques, canopy beds, fireplaces and terraces.

EDGARTOWN —————————————————————————

Colonial Inn of Marthas	$$ B&B	Continental plus
P.O. Box 68, 02539	Visa, MC, AmEx, *Rated*,	Restaurant, bar
38 N. Water St.	•	Sitting room, library
508-627-4711 800-627-4701	C-yes/S-yes/P-no/H-yes	by tennis, riding, golf
Linda Malcouronne	Portuguese	sailing, fishing, beach
April-Dec, FAX: 627-5904		

Charming, lovingly refurbished inn w/brass beds offers affordable luxury. Some rooms w/refrigerators. Near museums, galleries, shops. **Upgrade when available at check-in**

Edgartown Inn, The	$ EP	Full breakfast $
P.O. Box 1211, 02539	22 rooms, 13 pb	Garden house renovation
56 North Water St.	*Rated*	
508-627-4794	C-ltd/S-yes/French	
Susanne Chlastawa-Faraca		
April—October		

192 year old historic inn where Nathaniel Hawthorne, Daniel Webster & John Kennedy stayed. Serving homemade cakes and breads for breakfast in the garden.

Point Way Inn	$$ B&B	Continental plus
P.O. Box 5255, 02539	15 rooms, 15 pb	Comp. wine/lemonade/tea
104 Main St.	Visa, MC, AmEx, *Rated*,	Honor bar, snacks
508-627-8633	•	sitting room, library
Linda & Ben Smith	C-yes/S-yes/H-ltd	croquet, gardens, gazebo
All year		

Located near center of town; 11 rooms w/ working fireplaces. Inn is a former whaling captain's mansion. A comp. courtesy car is available to guests. **3rd. night 50% off, ltd.**

Shiretown Inn	$ B&B	Continental breakfast
P.O. Box 921, 02539	34 rooms, 34 pb	Full breakfast $3
North Water St.	Visa, MC, AmEx, Disc., •	Restaurant - dinner
800-541-0090	C-yes/S-yes/P-no/H-yes	bar service
Sonya Lima		sailing, fishing
April - November		

1700s whaling captain's house. Listed in National Register Historic Places. Center of Edgartown. 1 block Chappaquiddick Ferry, Town Wharf, Harbor. **3rd night 50% off w/book**

EDGARTOWN-MARTHA'S VINYD ——————————————————

Governor Bradford Inn, The	$$$ B&B	Full breakfast
128 Main St., 02539	16 rooms, 16 pb	Comp. wine, aftn. tea
508-627-9510	Most CC, *Rated*, •	Candlelit dinner avail.
Ray & Brenda Raffurty	C-ltd/S-yes/P-no/H-yes	sitting room
All year		library

A gracefully restored whaling captain's home in the seaport village of Edgartown, on the island of Martha's Vineyard. Spacious rooms have king-size poster or brass beds.

ESSEX ————————————————————————————

George Fuller House	$$ B&B	Full breakfast
148 Main St., 01929	6 rooms, 5 pb	Comp. coffee, tea
508-768-7766	Visa, MC, AmEx, *Rated*,	Sitting room, fireplaces
Cindy & Bob Cameron	•	learn to sail/charter in
All year	C-yes/S-ltd/P-no/H-no	30-foot yacht (midweek)

Federalist-style w/antique furnishings, 4 firepl's, TV, marsh view. Near antique shops, seafood restaurants. 30-ft yacht for sailing/charters. **3rd night 50%**

FAIRHAVEN ────────────────────────────────

Edgewater B&B	$$ B&B	Continental breakfast
2 Oxford St., 02719	5 rooms, 5 pb	Comp. tea, coffee
508-997-5512	•	Sitting room
Kathy Reed	C-ltd/S-yes/P-no/H-no	library, spacious lawns
All year		2 suites w/fireplaces

Gracious waterfront mansion overlooking Bedford Harbor. Spacious accommodations; 2 suites w/fireplaces. 5 min. from I-195. Close to historic areas, beaches, factory outlets.

FALMOUTH ────────────────────────────────

Capt. Tom Lawrence House	$$$ B&B	Full gourmet breakfast
75 Locust St., 02540	6 rooms, 6 pb	Comp. tea
508-540-1445	Visa, MC, *Rated*, •	Sitting room, library
Barbara Sabo-Feller	C-ltd/S-yes/P-no/H-no	piano, TV
All year	German	porch, large yard

Redecorated Victorian captain's home close to village center, beaches, golf, island ferries. Breakfast w/homemade bread from organic grain. **Ask about honeymooner specials**

Palmer House Inn, The	$$ B&B	Full gourmet breakfast
81 Palmer Ave., 02540	8 rooms, 8 pb	High tea Sun., Oct - Apr
508-548-1230 800-4RB-ANDB	Most CC, *Rated*, •	Sitting room, piano, TV
Ken & Joanne Baker	C-ltd/S-no/P-no/H-no	fireplace, open porches
All year, FAX:540-1878		biking, golf, tennis

Step back in time to Grandmother's day in this charming Victorian. Antiques; gourmet breakfast; bicycles; near shops, beaches, restaurants, island ferries. Let us pamper you.

Peacock's Inn on the Sound	$$$ B&B	Full gourmet breakfast
P.O. Box 201, 02541	10 rooms, 10 pb	Library, cable TV, bikes
313 Grand Ave., 02540	Visa, MC, *Rated*, •	country-style dining rm.
508-457-9666	C-ltd/S-no/P-no/H-no	golf, tennis, ferry
Phyllis & Bud Peacock		
All year		

Country cottage charm, spacious rooms w/spectacular ocean view, fireplaces, providing rest, relaxation or endless activities. Steps from beach. **10% off week reservations.**

Village Green Inn	$$$ B&B	Full gourmet breakfast
40 W. Main St., 02540	5 rooms, 5 pb	Seasonal beverages
508-548-5621	*Rated*, •	Comp. wine, guest parlor
Linda & Don Long	C-ltd/S-no/P-no/H-no	fireplaces, open porches
All year		piano, cable TV, bikes

Old Victorian ideally located on Falmouth's historic green. 19th-c. charm & warm hospitality in lovely spacious rooms/fireplaces. **Comp. ferry tickets to Martha's Vinyard, ltd**

Woods Hole Passage B&B	$$ B&B	Full breakfast
186 Woods Hole Rd., 02540	5 rooms, 5 pb	Sitting room, patio
508-548-9575	Visa, MC, *Rated*, •	library, garden
Cristina Mozo	C-ltd/S-no/P-no/H-no	short walk to beach
All year	Spanish	

100-year-old carriage house & renovated barn; spacious grounds, old trees, raspberries and blueberries. Close to spring and summer fun of the Cape. **$20 off dinner, off-season**

Grafton Inn, Falmouth, MA

FALMOUTH — CAPE COD

Grafton Inn	$$$ B&B	Full gourmet breakfast
261 Grand Ave. S., 02540	11 rooms, 9 pb	Comp. wine & cheese
508-540-8688 800-642-4069	Visa, MC, *Rated*, •	Sitting room
Liz & Rudy Cvitan	C-ltd/S-no/P-no/H-yes	bicycles, cottage
Feb.-Dec., Fax: 540-1861	Croatian	porch

Oceanside—on the beach; panoramic view; delectable croissants from France. Convenient to ferry, shops, restaurants. Gallery throughout.

Mostly Hall B&B Inn	$$$ B&B	Full gourmet breakfast
27 Main St., 02540	6 rooms, 6 pb	Coffee, tea, sherry
508-548-3786 800-682-0565	Visa, MC, *Rated*,	Sitting room, piano
Caroline & Jim Lloyd	C-ltd/S-no/P-no/H-no	gazebo, veranda, porch
Mid Feb—mid Jan	German	bicycles, gardens

Falmouth's first summer residence built in 1849 for New Orleans bride. Spacious corner rooms. Queen-sized four-poster canopy beds. A/C. Near beaches, shops, ferries.

FALMOUTH—WEST FALMOUTH

Elms, The	$$ B&B	Full gourmet breakfast
P.O. Box 895, 02574	9 rooms, 7 pb	Comp. sherry
495 W.Falmouth Hwy Rt 28A	C-ltd/S-ltd/P-no/H-no	Living room, study
508-540-7232		gardens, gazebo
Betty & Joe Mazzucchelli		bicycles
All year		

*Refurbished Victorian home built in the 1800s, filled w/antiques, plants. Boasting cool breezes from Buzzard's Bay. 1/2 mi. to beach. **Free bottle of wine for honeymooners.***

GREAT BARRINGTON ───────────────────────────────────

Baldwin Hill Farm B&B
RD 3, Box 125, Baldwin Hill Rd,
Egremont, 01230
413-528-4092
Richard & Priscilla Burdsall
All year

$$ B&B
4 rooms, 1 pb
Visa, MC, *Rated*, •
C-ltd/S-no/P-no/H-no

Full country breakfast
Afternoon tea, snacks
2 sitting rooms, library
screened porch, pool
fireplace, cross-country
skiing

Spacious Victorian farmhouse. 360 degree views of mountains. 500 acres for nature hikes. Restaurants nearby. Hiking, tennis, golf, boating, fishing. Friendly and elegant.

Bread & Roses
Star Rt 65, Box 50, Route 71,
01230
413-528-1099
Elliot & Julie Lowell
All year

$$$ B&B
5 rooms, 5 pb
C-ltd/S-no/P-no/H-no
French

Full breakfast
Aft. tea
Golf, tennis nearby
swimming nearby

The Lowells have a unique gift for making their guests part of their "home." The inn is light-hearted and charming, the hospitality welcoming.

Round Hill Farm
Nonsmokers
17 Round Hill Rd., 01230
413-528-6969
A. Blair & R. Tillinghast
All year

$$ B&B
3 rooms, 2 pb
Visa, MC, AmEx, *Rated*,
C-ltd/S-no/P-no/H-no
French, German, Spanish

Full breakfast
Swimming, hiking
skiing
bicycles, tennis court

Luxurious converted barn, spacious accommodations, private baths. Spectacular views, access to 300 groomed acres, tennis, swimming, near Tanglewood. Delicious breakfast.

Seekonk Pines Inn
142 Seekonk Cross Rd., corner
of Rte 23, 01230
413-528-4192 800-292-4192
Linda & Christian Best
All year

$$ B&B
6 rooms, 6 pb
Rated
C-yes/S-no/P-no/H-no
German

Full breakfast
Hot cider, beverages
Sitting room, bicycles
pool, piano, kitchenette
near skiing, hiking

Country estate; close to Tanglewood. Hosts are artists/singers. Original artwork, homemade jams, produce for sale. Low-fat, low-cholesterol diets. Peaceful. **3rd nite 50%-Ltd**

Turning Point Inn
RD 2 Box 140, 3 Lake Buel Rd.,
01230
413-528-4777
Irving & Jamie Yost
All year

$$$ B&B
8 rooms, 6 pb
MC, Visa, AmEx
C-yes/S-no/P-no/H-no

Full breakfast
Comp. tea, coffee, juice
4-room cottage with bath
piano, fireplaces
bicycles, cottage

We offer a natural environment: whole grain vegetarian breakfast; no smoking; hiking, skiing; comfort in 18th-century inn near Tanglewood, next to ski slopes.

Windflower Inn
684 S. Egremont Rd., 01230
413-528-2720 800-992-1993
Liebert & Ryan Family
All year

$$$ MAP
13 rooms, 13 pb
Rated, •
C-yes/S-ltd/P-no/H-ltd

Full breakfast
Dinner, afternoon tea
Snacks, bar service
sitting room, library
swimming pool

Elegant small country Inn. Beautiful rooms, some with fireplaces. Summer dining on our screened porch. Produce from our organic garden. **Special ski & off-season packages**

HAMILTON

Miles River Country Inn
P.O. Box 149, 01936
823 Bay Rd.
508-468-7206
Gretel & Peter Clark
All year

$$ B&B
8 rooms, 3 pb
Rated
C-yes/S-no/P-no/H-no
Spanish, French, German

Full breakfast
Aft. tea
Library, gardens
paths in woods, field
wildlife, beaches

*200 year old country Colonial on large estate. Summer breakfast on shaded garden terraces or winter evenings by your bedroom's fireplace. **Discount for long term stay***

HARWICH PORT

Captain's Quarters B&B Inn
85 Bank St., 02646
508-432-1991 800-992-6550
Susan & Ed Kennedy
All year

$$ B&B
5 rooms, 5 pb
Visa, MC, AmEx, *Rated*,
•
C-ltd/S-no/P-no/H-ltd

Continental plus
Some TVs & ceiling fans
cottage, walk to beach
tennis/pool near, porch

Classic 1850s Victorian with wraparound porch, turret, queen brass beds or twins, lace-trimmed sheets. Walk to beach, shops, dining, bike rentals. Perfect for honeymooners!

Harbor Walk Guest House
6 Freeman St., 02646
508-432-1675
Marilyn & Preston Barry
May–October

$ B&B
6 rooms, 4 pb
•
C-ltd/S-no/P-ltd/H-no
some French

Continental plus
Canopy beds
library, sitting room
tennis & ocean nearby

Victorian charmer, featuring antiques, homemade quilts and queen canopy beds. Walk to beach and most photographed harbor on Cape Cod. Summer sports paradise.

HARWICH PORT—CAPE COD

Dunscroft By-the-Sea Inn
24 Pilgrim Rd., 02646
508-432-0810 800-432-4345
Alyce & Wally Cunningham
All year

$$$ B&B
10 rooms, 10 pb
Rated, •
C-ltd/S-ltd/P-no/H-no

Full breakfast
Comp. wine, juices
Library, piano, terrace
sun porch, private beach
A/C, canopies, sleigh

Located 300 feet from a beautiful private beach on Nantucket Sound; walk to restaurant and shops. Exclusive residential area. Honeymoon cottage, romance package available.

HARWICH WEST

Cape Cod Sunny Pines
P.O. Box 667, 02671
77 Main St.
800-356-9628
Eileen & Jack Connell
All year

$$$ B&B
8 rooms, 8 pb
Most CC, *Rated*, •
C-ltd/S-yes/P-no/H-no

Full Irish breakfast
Restaurant - all meals
Aft. tea, snacks
bar service, sitting rm.
swimming pool, library

*Irish hospitality in Victorian ambiance. Sunny Pines now a full-service inn but remains small, friendly and intimate. Authentic Irish Pub. **10% discount on full tavern bill***

HOLYOKE

Yankee Pedlar Inn
1866 Northampton St., 01040
413-532-9494
Larry Audette
All year

$$ B&B
47 rooms, 47 pb
Most CC, *Rated*,
C-yes/S-ltd/P-no/H-ltd
French, Polish, Spanish

Continental breakfast
Lunch, dinner, bar
Piano
entertainment

Old Victorian mansion, antiqued bedrooms, many dining rooms including French restaurant and herb garden. Continental menu, live entertainment, outdoor cafe.

HYANNIS ───

Inn on Sea Street, The	$$ B&B	Full breakfast
358 Sea St., 02601	9 rooms, 7 pb	Fruit & cheese
508-775-8030	Visa, MC, AmEx, *Rated*,	Sitting room
Lois Nelson, J.B. Whitehead.	C-ltd/S-yes/P-no/H-no	library
April–November		Cottage

Elegant Victorian inn, steps from the beach and Kennedy Compound. Antiques, canopy beds, fireplace, home-baked delights. Full gourmet breakfast, fruit and cheese.

───

Sea Breeze Inn	$$ B&B	Continental breakfast
397 Sea St., 02601	14 rooms, 12 pb	Kitchen privileges
508-771-7213	*Rated*, ●	Sitting room
Patricia & Martin Battle	C-yes/S-yes/P-no/H-no	bicycles, canopy beds
All year		cable TV, A/C

Quaint, nautical atmosphere, private setting, beach & Hyannisport Harbor 900 ft., near center of Hyannis. All Cape Cod towns & points of interest within 1 hour.

HYANNIS PORT ───

Simmons Homestead Inn, The	$$$ B&B	Full breakfast
	9 rooms, 9 pb	Comp. wine and cheese
P.O. Box 578, 02647	Visa, MC, AmEx, *Rated*,	Sitting room, library
288 Scudder Ave.	●	wraparound porch
508-778-4999 800-637-1649	C-yes/S-ltd/P-no/H-no	huge yard, beaches
Bill Putman		
All year		

Beautifully restored 1820 sea captain's home abounds in art, priceless antiques, canopy beds. Lovely grounds. One of the most pleasant inns on the Cape.

LEE ──

Haus Andreas	$$ B&B	Continental plus
RR1, Box 435, Stockbridge Rd.,	7 rooms, 5 pb	Guest pantry
01238	Visa, MC, *Rated*,	Heated pool, tennis
413-243-3298	C-ltd/S-yes/P-no/H-no	bicycles, lawn sports
Gerhard & Lilliane Schmid	French, German	sitting room, piano
All year		

*Historic revolutionary setting, heated pool, golf, tennis, luxury, comfort, local fine restaurants. Complimentary breakfast. Relax in Old World charm. **7 days stay 10% off.***

LENOX ───

Birchwood Inn	$$ B&B	Full breakfast
P.O. Box 2020, 01240	12 rooms, 10 pb	Comp. tea, wine & cheese
7 Hubbard St.	Visa, MC	Sitting room, library
413-637-2600 800-524-1646	C-ltd/S-ltd/P-no/H-ltd	6 fireplaces
Joan, Dick & Dan Toner		lake nearby
All year		

*This 200 year old colonial is on the historic register. Beautifully appointed, with fireplaces . Guided hiking/biking tours. Weekend dinner packages. **3rd night free, ltd.***

───

Blantyre	$$$ B&B	Continental, full avail.
P.O. Box 995, 01240	23 rooms, 23 pb	Restaurant, bar
Rt. 20, East St.	Most CC, *Rated*, ●	Comp. wine, snacks
413-637-3556 413-298-3806	C-ltd/S-yes/P-no/H-yes	tennis, pool, hot tubs
Roderick Anderson	French, German	croquet, bikes, hiking
Mid May–early November		

A gracious country house hotel surrounded by 85 acres of grounds. The hotel has a European atmosphere and exceptional cuisine.

LENOX

Brook Farm Inn
15 Hawthorne St., 01240
413-637-3013
Joseph & Anne Miller
All year

$$$ B&B
12 rooms, 12 pb
Visa, MC, *Rated*,
C-ltd/S-no/P-no/H-no

Continental plus
Comp. tea with scones
Library, sitting room
swimming pool, garden
poetry library

100-year-old-inn w/the grace of its Victorian past & comfort of the present. There is poetry here: 650 volumes & 60 poets on tape w/players available. **10% disc't 7+ days.**

Cornell Inn
197 Main St., 01240
413-637-0562 800-637-0562
David A. Rolland
All year

$$ B&B
18 rooms, 18 pb
Visa, MC, •
C-ltd/S-yes/P-no/H-yes

Continental plus/Sun buf
Lunch, dinner, tavern
Sitting rooms, sundeck
restaurant bar & lounge
health spa

Large Victorian home w/country charm & modern conveniences. Close to all Berkshire sites. Full-service inn. Condo-style Carriage House w/all comforts of home. **Packages**

Forty-Four St. Ann's Ave.
P.O. Box 718, 01240
44 St. Ann's Ave.
413-637-3381
Barbara & Milton Kolodkin
Memorial Day - Labor Day

$$$ B&B
3 rooms, 3 pb
C-ltd/S-yes/P-no/H-no
French

Continental plus
Air conditioned rooms
porches - 1 screened
spacious yard w/flowers

Close to Tanglewood Music Festival & village. Elegant breakfasts; quiet location; professional, knowledgeable hosts who help you enjoy the Berkshires. Lower midweek rates.

Gables Inn, The
103 Walker St., 01240
413-637-3416
Mary & Frank Newton
All year

$$ B&B
17 rooms, 17 pb
Most CC, *Rated*,
C-ltd/S-yes/P-no/H-no
Spanish

Continental plus
Comp. wine
Sitting room, library
tennis courts
swimming pool

Built in 1885, this gracious "cottage" was the home of Edith Wharton at the turn of the century. Lovingly furnished in period style. 2 new suites: Teddy & Edith Wharton suites

---

Garden Gables Inn
P.O. Box 52, 01240
141 Main St.
413-637-0193
Mario & Lynn Mekinda
All year

$$ B&B
14 rooms, 12 pb
Visa, MC, *Rated*,
C-ltd/S-ltd/P-no/H-no
German, French

Full breakfast
Comp. port and sherry
Library, fireplace, pool
whirlpools, porches
sitting room, tennis

220-year-old gabled inn located in center of Lenox on four wooded acres. Furnished with antiques. One mile to Tanglewood and many other attractions. Phones in all rooms.

Gateways Inn
71 Walker St., 01240
413-637-2532 FAX:637-2532
Vito Perulli, Brenda Mayberry
All year, Fax:637-2532

$$$ B&B
8 rooms, 8 pb
Most CC, *Rated*,
C-ltd/S-no/P-no/H-no
French, German, Italian

Continental plus, lunch
Dinner, Restaurant, bar
Sitting room w/TV
telephones in room
A/C, fireplaces, tennis

Gateways Inn is Berkshire's only four-star restaurant. Elegant, luxurious townhouse in heart of Lenox.

LENOX ──────────────────────────────────────

Rookwood Inn	$$ B&B	Full breakfast buffet
P.O. Box 1717, 01240	19 rooms, 19 pb	Afternoon tea & cakes
19 Old Stockbridge Rd.	AmEx, *Rated*, •	Sitting room, tennis
413-637-9750 800-223-9750	C-yes/S-no/P-no/H-yes	library, verandas
Tom & Betsy Sherman		fireplaces, lawn
All year		

1885 "Painted Lady" country inn. Gracious & relaxing with antiques throughout, period decorations. Wonderful beds, quiet, ideal location, buffet breakfast.

Summer Hill Farm	$$ B&B	Full breakfast
830 East St., 01240	7 rooms, 5 pb	
413-442-2057	*Rated*	
Michael & Sonya Wessel	C-yes/S-ltd/P-ltd/H-no	
All year		

200 year old Colonial on 20 acres, furnished with English antiques and oriental rugs. Rural setting close to all local amenities.

Underledge Inn	$$ B&B	Continental plus
76 Cliffwood St., 01240	8 rooms, 8 pb	Sitting room
413-637-0236	Visa, MC	library, piano
Marcie & Cheryl Lanoue	C-ltd/S-ltd/P-no/H-no	5 fireplaces
All year		

Underledge offers elegance and country charm. Large parlour bedrooms with fireplaces, decorated with an air of bygone days. Breakfast in unique solarium.

Village Inn, The	$$ EP	Restaurant, bar
P.O. Box 1810, 01240	32 rooms, 32 pb	Sitting room, library
16 Church St.	Most CC, *Rated*, •	lakes, mountain trails
413-637-0020 800-253-0917	C-ltd/S-yes/P-no/H-yes	parks & museums nearby
Clifford Rudisill, Ray Wilson	Spanish, French, German	
All year. FAX:637-9756		

Historic 1771 inn reflecting charm & warmth of colonial New England. Rooms furnished in country antiques. Afternoon tea with homemade scones. **3rd night 50% off Nov.-May**

Walker House Inn	$$ B&B	Continental plus
64 Walker St., 01240	8 rooms, 8 pb	Comp. wine, aftn. tea
413-637-1271 800-235-3098	*Rated*	Sitting room, piano
Peggy & Richard Houdek	C-ltd/S-no/P-ask/H-ltd	library video theatre
All year	Spanish, French	opera/film wkends, bikes

Our guests feel like special pampered friends. Lovely country atmosphere on 3 acres. Walk to shops, restaurants. 100-in. video screen shows films, plays. **3rd night 50%—Ltd**

MARBLEHEAD ──────────────────────────────────────

Harbor Light Inn	$$$ B&B	Continental plus
58 Washington St., 01945	20 rooms, 20 pb	Aft. tea, Comp. wine
617-631-2186	Visa, MC, AmEx,	Sitting room
Peter Conway	C-yes/S-yes/P-no/H-no	hot tubs
All year		swimming pool

The north shore's premier B&B inn. Elegant 18th century Federalist mansion. Double jacuzzis, sundecks, pool, in heart of Historic Harbor District. Close to everything.

The Village Inn, Lenox, MA

MARBLEHEAD

Harborside House	$$ B&B	Continental plus
23 Gregory St., 01945	2 rooms,	Harbor Sweets candy
617-631-1032	•	Living room w/fireplace
Susan Livingston	C-ltd/S-no/P-no/H-no	deck overlooking harbor
All year		period dining room

C. 1850 colonial home offers antiques/modern amenities. Homemade baked goods. Sunny porch, flower gardens. Walk to historic sites, shops, beach, restaurants. **10% off 3+ nites**

Sea Street B&B	$$ B&B	Continental plus
9 Gregory St., 01945	4 rooms, 4 pb	Snacks
617-631-1890 800-572-7335	Visa, MC, AmEx, •	Sitting room
Margaret Bacon	C-yes/S-ltd/P-no/H-no	tennis, beaches &
All year		sailing nearby

Turn-of-the-century country home in historic seacoast village w/sparkling harbor views. Beaches, shops, restaurants, sailing and cross-country skiing nearby. **10% Off 2+ night**

Spray Cliff on the Ocean	$$$ B&B	Continental plus
25 Spray Ave., 7 Summer St.,	5 rooms, 5 pb	Comp. wine, sherry
Salem, 01945	Most CC, *Rated*, •	Sitting room, gardens
508-744-8924 800-626-1530	C-ltd/S-no/P-no/H-no	walk to beach
Dick & Diane Pabich		suite w/ fireplace, deck
All year		

English Tudor mansion set high above the Atlantic. Views extend forever. Elegant bedrooms, cozy relaxed atmosphere; garden terrace. Come unwind. **3rd night 25% off.**

Stillpoint	$$ B&B	Continental plus
27 Gregory St., 01945	3 rooms, 1 pb	Near shops, restaurants
617-631-1667 800-882-3891	Visa, MC, •	beaches, historic sites
Sarah Lincoln-Harrison	C-ltd/S-no/P-no/H-no	sitting room, library
All year	French, Spanish	

Nicely appointed 1840's home, quiet refreshing ambiance; antiques, fireplace, piano. Breakfast on deck, with excellent views of harbor and lighthouse. **3rd night 50% off, ltd.**

Walker House, Lenox, MA

MARTHA'S VINEYARD

Bayberry, The
P.O. Box 654, 02575
Old Courthouse, W.Tisbury
508-693-1984
Rosalie H. Powell
All year

$$$ B&B
5 rooms, 3 pb
Visa, MC, •
C-ltd/S-no/P-no/H-ltd

Full gourmet breakfast
Comp. tea, wine
Sitting room, gardens
piano, croquet, hammock
beach pass and towels

Gourmet brkfast served by fireplace in charming country home on historic Martha's Vineyard Island. Antique furnishings, canopy beds, friendly atmosphere. **4th weeknight 50%.**

Thorncroft Inn
P.O. Box 1022, 02568
278 Main St.
508-693-3333
Karl & Lynn Buder
All year

$$$ B&B
19 rooms, 19 pb
Rated, •
C-ltd/S-ltd/P-no/H-no

Full breakfast
Afternoon tea
Evening turndown service
morning paper at door
3.5 acres of grounds

Romantic, noncommercial atmosphere; fine antiques; private baths; fireplaces; central A/C; luxury suites w/ jacuzzi; balconies; canopied four-poster beds. Prvt. hot tub avail.

MENEMSHA

Menemsha Inn & Cottages
Box 38, North Road, 02552
508-645-2521
Nancy & Richard Steves
May 1 - November 30

$$$ B&B
27 rooms, 27 pb
Rated
C-yes/S-yes/P-no/H-no

Continental plus
Tennis court
walk to beach
sitting room

A unique cottage-inn facility located on 10.5 secluded acres of gardens, woodlands, ocean vistas and moss-covered stone walls.

MIDDLETON

Blue Door, The
20 East St., 01949
508-777-4829
Ethel Marino
All year

$$$ B&B
2 rooms, 2 pb
•
C-ltd/P-no/H-no

Continental plus
Dinner
Sitting room, hot tubs
horse shoes, bocci
some fireplaces

Take a step back in time- a romantic, historic home with antique furnishings, gazebo, goldfish pond & gardens. Minutes to major highways. **3rd night 50% off**

NANTUCKET

Brant Point Inn
6 N. Beach St., 02554
508-228-5442
Thea & Peter Kaizer
All year

$$$ B&B
8 rooms, 8 pb
Visa, MC, AmEx
C-ltd/S-yes

Continental breakfast
Sitting room, porch
Belgium fireplace
fishing charters arrang.

Ideally located, this post & beam inn is minutes from Nantucket's finest beaches & the historic town. All modern amenities to assure a relaxing & comfortable visit. Welcome!

Carriage House
5 Rays Court, 02554
508-228-0326
Jeanne McHugh & son, Haziel
All year

$$ B&B
7 rooms, 7 pb
Rated, •
C-ltd/S-no/P-no/H-no
Fr., Ger., Span., Jap.

Continental plus
Guest refrigerator
Sitting room, library
patio, beach towels

Converted carriage house on the prettiest country lane; beautifully quiet, yet right in town. B&B and more, since 1974. Tennis, boating and unspoiled beaches nearby.

Centerboard Guest House
P.O. Box 456, 02554
8 Chester St.
508-228-9696
Reggie Reid
All year

$$$ B&B
7 rooms, 7 pb
Visa, MC, AmEx, *Rated*,
•
C-ltd/S-no/P-no/H-no

Continental plus
Comp. refreshments
Beach towels
library, sitting room
suite, jacuzzi

A Victorian guest house of quiet country elegance; lovingly renovated & restored in 1986-87; located in historic district, Nantucket Center; beaches nearby. **7th night free.**

Century House, The
10 Cliff Rd., 02554
508-228-0530
Gerry Connick & Jean Heron
All year

$$ B&B
9 rooms, 9 pb
Rated, •
C-yes/S-ltd/P-no/H-no
Fr, Rus, Ger, Jap, Chi

Continental plus
Happy hour setups
Afternoon tea, munchies
sitting room, veranda
H. Miller player piano

Historic sea captain's B&B inn serving Nantucket travelers since the mid-1800s; minutes to beaches, restaurants, galleries, shops; antique appointments, Laura Ashley decor.

Cobblestone Inn
5 Ash St., 02554
508-228-1987
Robin Hammer-Yankow
All year

$$$ B&B
5 rooms, 5 pb
Rated, •
C-yes/S-no

Continental plus
Living room
sun porch, yard

Circa 1725 home on a quiet cobblestoned street in Nantucket's historic district. Relax in our yard/sun porch/living room. Walk to shops, museums, restaurants. Open year-round.

Corner House Circa 1790
P.O. Box 1828, 02554
49 Centre St.
508-228-1530
John & Sandy Knox-Johnston
February 15 - December

$$ B&B
14 rooms, 14 pb
Visa, MC, Disc.,*Rated*, •
C-ltd/S-ltd/P-no/H-ltd
French, German

Continental plus
Afternoon tea
Sitting rooms, bch towel
screen porch w/wicker
secluded garden terrace

Especially comfortable & attractive 18th century village inn, brought very gently into the 20th century. Antiques, canopy beds, cozy fires. **3rd night free, ltd.**

NANTUCKET ───────────────────────────────────────

Eighteen Gardner St. Inn
18 Gardner St., 02554
508-228-1155 800-435-1450
Mary Schmidt
April–October 15

$$$ B&B
14 rooms, 10 pb
Rated, •
C-ltd/S-yes/P-no/H-no

Continental breakfast
Comp. wine
Sitting room
working fireplaces
bikes, some rms A+C

Restored 1835 whaling captain's home. Canopy queen beds; antiques. Original floorboards, period wallpapers. "Casual elegance & attentive service." 3rd night free off-season

---

Four Chimneys Inn
38 Orange St., 02554
508-228-1912
Bernadette Mannix
May–late December

$$$ B&B
10 rooms, 10 pb
Most Cred.Cds., *Rated*,
C-ltd/S-yes/P-no/H-no

Continental breakfast
Comp. hors d'oeuvres
Sitting room, antiques
secluded garden
porches

Distinctively Nantucket. Be a guest in a 1835 sea captain's mansion, the largest on this faraway island. Return to gracious living and hospitality.

Jared Coffin House
29 Broad St., 02554
800-248-2405
Philip Whitney Read
All year

$$$ B&B
Most CC, *Rated*, •
C-ltd/S-yes/P-ltd/H-no

Full breakfast
Full menu, bar service
Sitting room
piano, meeting rooms
entertainment

Historically interesting collection of six buildings make up the inn. Convenient location in town near everything. Two excellent restaurants. Mobil 3-star rating.

Martin House Inn
61 Centre St., 02554
508-228-0678
Channing & Ceci Moore
All year

$$$ B&B
13 rooms, 9 pb
Visa, MC, AmEx, *Rated*,
C-yes/S-yes/P-no/H-no

Continental plus
Complimentary sherry
Sitting/dining room
fireplace/veranda/piano
fireplaced rooms

Stately 1803 Mariner's home in Nantucket's historic district. Four-poster canopy beds, 13 airy rooms. Spacious living room, dining room, verandah.

Parker Guest House, The
4 E. Chestnut St., 02554
508-228-4625 800-248-4625
Paul & Beverly Sheets
All year

$$ B&B
6 rooms, 6 pb
Visa, MC, AmEx, *Rated*,
•
C-yes/S-no/P-no/H-no

Continental plus
Snacks Wed. & Sat. eves
Comp. wine Wed. & Sat.
sitting room, A/C
CCTV, fridge, coffee

Small, friendly guest house in the heart of historic Nantucket town. Minutes from theaters, galleries, shops, museums, fine dining. 3rd night 50% off mid-Sept.–mid-May

---

La Petite Maison
132 Main St., 02554
508-228-9242
Holli Martin
April 15–January 15

$$ B&B
4 rooms, 1 pb
MC, Visa, *Rated*,
C-ltd/S-yes/H-ltd
French

Continental plus
Afternoon tea
Sitting room
dining room w/fireplace
Cottage/apt./studio

Charming, antique-furnished European-style guest house, quiet town location. Continental breakfast on sun porch; peaceful garden; friendly atmosphere. 10% off wkdays, ltd

NANTUCKET

Quaker House Inn & Rest.
5 Chestnut St., 02554
508-228-0400 508-228-9156
Caroline & Bob Taylor
Memorial Day–September

$$$ EP
9 rooms, 9 pb
Visa, MC, *Rated*, •
C-ltd/S-ltd/P-no/H-no

Full breakfast $
Restaurant
Dinner, beer, wine
sitting room
some rooms with A/C

Located in the heart of Nantucket's historic district. Guest rooms have private baths, queen-size beds, and decorated in 19th-century antiques. Charming candlelit dinners.

Seven Sea Street Inn
7 Sea St., 02554
508-228-3577
Matthew & Mary Parker—Owners
All year

$$$ B&B
8 rooms, 8 pb
Visa, MC, AmEx, *Rated*,
C-ltd/S-no/P-no/H-no

Continental plus
Sitting rooms
Jacuzzi
widow's walk

Red oak post and beam guest house with authentic Nantucket ambiance. Romance, comfort and warmth best describe our colonial inn. **10% off 3+ nights, ltd.**

Stumble Inne
109 Orange St., 02554
508-228-4482
Mal, Mary Kay & Carol Condon
All year

$$$ B&B
13 rooms, 10 pb
Visa, MC, AmEx, *Rated*,
•
C-ltd/S-yes/P-no/H-no

Continental plus
Afternoon tea
Sitting room
spacious grounds
Comp. wine, parking

Nantucket's friendliest bed & breakfast. Delightful Laura Ashley decor. Hearty breakfast in a gracious dining room. Near activities & sites. **2nd night free, ltd.**

Tuckernuck Inn
60 Union St., 02554
508-228-4886 800-228-4886
Ken & Phyllis Parker
All year

$$$ B&B
18 rooms, 17 pb
Visa, MC, AmEx, *Rated*,
•
C-ltd/S-no/P-no/H-yes

Continental plus
Full breakfast $
Comp. wine, snacks
sitting room, library
full service dining, ltd

Wonderful in-town location; panoramic harbor view from our widow's walk; spacious lawn w/recreational facilities; Colonial ambiance. **50% off high season rate Oct 15-May 15th**

Woodbox Inn, The
29 Fair St., 02554
508-228-0587
Dexter Tutein
June—mid-October

$$$ EP
9 rooms, 9 pb
Rated
C-yes/S-yes/P-ltd/H-yes
French, German

Full breakfast $
Dinner
Sitting room
fireplaces

"Probably the best place to stay on Nantucket." Oldest inn (1709) in Nantucket, furnished with period antiques. Breakfast 8:30-10:30; dinner—continental cuisine—7 and 9 p.m.

NEWBURYPORT

Windsor House, The
38 Federal St., 01950
508-462-3778 FAX:465-3443
Judith & John Harris
All year

$$$ B&B/MAP
6 rooms, 3 pb
Visa, MC, *Rated*, •
C-yes/S-yes/P-yes/H-no

Full English breakfast
Aftn. tea, evening meal
Common rooms, organ
shops, museums

Federalist mansion/ship's chandlery in restored historic seaport furnished in period antiques; explore our beaches & wildlife refuge. **3rd night 50% off**

The Knoll, Northampton, MA

NEWTON

Sage and Thyme B&B
65 Kirkstall Rd., 02160
617-332-0695
Edgar & Hertha Klugman
All year

$$ B&B
2 rooms,
•
C-yes/S-no/P-no/H-no
Ger., Ital., Sp., Fr.

Full breakfast
Comp. coffee, juice
A/C in rooms

Classic colonial in a quiet neighborhood. Downtown Boston only 5 miles away. Outstanding breakfasts and congenial hosts and cats. Cozy quilts in winter. **8th night free, ltd**

NORTH EASTHAM

Penny House Inn
P.O. Box 238, 02651
4885 County Rd., Rte 6
508-255-6632 800-554-1751
William & Margaret Keith
All year

$$$ B&B
12 rooms, 12 pb
Visa, MC, *Rated*, •
C-ltd/S-yes/P-no/H-no
French

Full breakfast
Comp. wine, aftn. tea
Sitting room
library, fireplace
gathering place

Experience original Cape Cod charm & serenity in this 1751 bow roof rambling Cape conveniently near all Nat'l Seashore Park activities. **Restaurant coupons for 2 night stay.**

NORTHAMPTON

Knoll, The
230 N. Main St., Florence, 01060
413-584-8164
Leona (Lee) Lesko
All year

$ B&B
3 rooms
C-ltd/S-no/P-no/H-no

Full breakfast

Large Tudor house in quiet rural setting on 16 acres. Near 5 colleges: Smith, Amherst, Mt. Holyoke, University of Massachusetts, Hampshire.

NORTHFIELD

Northfield Country House
P.O. Box 617, 01360
RR1, School St.
413-498-2692 800-498-2692
Andrea Dale
All year

$$ B&B
7 rooms
Rated
C-ltd/S-yes/P-no/H-no

Full gourmet breakfast
Dinner (by reservation)
Sitting room, piano
cross-country skiing, tennis
court
swimming pool

English manor house softened by firelight & flowers. Personally decorated bedrooms w/antiques. 3 rooms w/romantic fireplaces. Center of New England activities. **3rd night 50%**

OAK BLUFFS

Dockside Inn, The
Circuit Ave. Extension, 02557
508-693-2966 800-245-5979
Lee & Diane Malloy
Mid May - Mid October

$$$ B&B
20 rooms, 20 pb
Misa, MC, Disc, *Rated*, •
C-yes/S-yes/P-no/H-yes

Continental breakfast
Bicycles, A/C
TV, Kitchen suites
sitting room

A romantic Victorian Inn on the harbor. Built in 1989 with all the charm of the 1800s and all the amenities of today.

Oak Bluffs Inn, The
P.O. Box 2477, 02557
Circuit & Pequot Ave.
508-693-7171 800-955-6235
Maryann Leeds
All year

$$$ B&B
10 rooms, 10 pb
Visa, MC, AmEx, •
C-yes/S-yes/P-no/H-no

Continental plus
Afternoon tea
Sitting room, flowers
60-ft. observation tower
large wraparound porch

A Victorian masterpiece. Reflects the romance and elegance of the past yet fresh and colorful. Near beaches, nightlife and gingerbread cottages. **3rd night free—offseason.**

Oak House, The
P.O. Box 299CG, Seaview &
Peguot Aves., 02557
508-693-4187
Betsi Convery-Luce
May—mid-October

$$$ B&B
10 rooms, 10 pb
Visa, MC, *Rated*, •
C-ltd/S-yes/P-no/H-no

Continental plus
Afternoon tea
Sitting room, piano
sun porch, bicycles
near town, ferry, beach

Romantic Victorian inn on the beach. Richly restored 1872 Governor's home. Oak paneling, wide porches, balconies, leaded windows, water views. **Free bottle of champagne**

PETERSHAM

Winterwood at Petersham
P.O. Box 176, 01366
19 North Main St.
508-724-8885
Jean & Robert Day
All year

$$$ B&B
6 rooms, 6 pb
Visa, MC, AmEx, •
C-yes/S-ltd/P-no/H-no

Continental plus
Restaurant
Bar service
sitting room, library
fireplaces

Sixteen-room Greek revival mansion—built as private summer home—on National Register of Historic Homes. Beautifully appointed and professionally decorated.

PLYMOUTH

Foxglove Cottage
101 Sandwich Rd., 02360
508-747-6576 FAX:747-7622
Mr. & Mrs. Charles K. Cowan
All year

$$ B&B
2 rooms, 2 pb
Visa, MC, AmEx, •
C-ltd/S-no/P-no/H-no

Full breakfast
Picnic lunch baskets
Dinner, sitting room
video library, bicycles
breakfast on deck

Restored Circa 1820 Cape in pastoral setting, minutes from Plimoth Plantation & the May-flower. Day trips to Cape Cod and Islands. "A touch of tranquility." **10% off 4+ nights**

PRINCETON

Harrington Farm, The
178 Westminster Rd., 01541
508-464-5600 800-736-3276
John Bomba
All year

$$ B&B
5 rooms, 2 pb
Visa, MC, Disc.,*Rated*, •
C-yes/S-no/P-ltd/H-no

Continental plus
Dinner
TV
sitting room
bicycles

1763 farmhouse on western slope of Mt. Wachusett. A century of innkeeping tradition, farm breakfast, skiing, hiking, breathtaking sunsets. **3rd night 50% off**

PROVINCETOWN ───────────────────────────────────────

Bradford Gardens Inn $$ B&B   Full gourmet breakfast
178 Bradford St., 02657   12 rooms, 12 pb   townhouses available
508-487-1616   Visa, MC, AmEx, *Rated*,   landscaped gardens
M. Susan Culligan   •   maid service, fireplace
April–December   C-ltd/S-ltd/P-no/H-no
                                    French

1820 Colonial antique-filled inn. Most rooms and cottages have fireplaces. Situated in beautiful gardens. Within a short walk to town center. Exceptionally clean & friendly.

Cape Codder Guest House $ B&B/EP   Continental breakfast
570 Commercial St., 02657   14 rooms, 1 pb   Private sandy beach
508-487-0131   Visa, MC   sun deck, seaside garden
Deborah Dionne   C-yes/S-ltd/P-ask/H-ltd   1 apt. with private bath
Mid-April–October

Old-fashioned comfort in quiet area; private beach, sun deck; whale-watching and bicycling nearby; informal friendly atmosphere; resident marine biologists! Daily maid

---

Captain Lysander Inn $$$ B&B   Continental breakfast
96 Commercial St., 02657   12 rooms, 10 pb   Front deck w/ocean view
508-487-2253   Visa, MC, *Rated*,   walk to shops
Edwards Family   C-yes/S-yes/P-no/H-ltd   near beaches, sitting rm
All year

Stately sea captain's home with large, gracious rooms. Across street from ocean. 5 minutes from shops and restaurants.

Lamplighter Inn $$ B&B   Continental breakfast
26 Bradford St., 02657   10 rooms, 8 pb   Courtyard, flower garden
508-487-2529 FAX:487-0079   Most CC, *Rated*, •   maid service, phone
M. Novik, J. Czarnecki   C-ltd/S-yes/P-no/H-no   parking, rooftop deck
All year

Antique sea captain's home w/wonderful Cape Cod views. Clean, airy rooms, suites. Near Nat'l Seashore, restaurants, shopping, whale-watching, museums. **Off-season discounts**

Land's End Inn $$$ B&B   Continental breakfast
22 Commercial St., 02657   14 rooms, 14 pb   Restaurants
508-487-0706   C-ltd/S-yes/P-no/H-no   Sitting room, near shops
David Schoolman   panoramic views
All year   some queen-size beds

Victorian summer house set high on a hill overlooking Provincetown with panoramic views of Cape Cod. With a homelike and friendly atmosphere. Oriental wood carvings, antiques.

Somerset House $$ B&B   Continental breakfast
378 Commercial St., 02657   13 rooms, 10 pb   Library, antiques
508-487-0383   Visa, MC, AmEx, *Rated*,   original paintings
Don & Sandy   C-yes/S-yes/P-no/H-no   lithographs

An historic 3 story Victorian house built in 1850. Located in the center of town, across the street from the beach. Many plants and flowers enhance the decor.

REHOBOTH ───────────────────────────────

Perryville Inn	$$ B&B	Continental plus
157 Perryville Rd., 02769	5 rooms, 4 pb	Comp. wine, tea, coffee
508-252-9239	Visa, MC, AmEx, *Rated*,	2 sitting rooms
Tom & Betsy Charnecki	•	piano, balloon rides
All year	C-yes/S-ltd/P-no/H-no	bicycles

Newly renovated 19th-century spacious farmhouse in quiet country setting. Centrally located between Boston, Newport, Providence. On National Register of Historic Homes.

ROCKPORT ───────────────────────────────

Addison Choate Inn	$$$ B&B	Continental plus
49 Broadway, 01966	10 rooms, 10 pb	Afternoon iced tea
508-546-7543 800-245-7543	C-ltd/S-ltd/P-no/H-yes	Pool, near beaches
Knox & Shirley Johnson	German	sitting room, library
All year		stable house apartments

Remarkably fine small country inn. Cruise the coast on our private yacht the "Sweetwater." Antiques, flowers, a surprise on your pillow!

Inn on Cove Hill, The	$ B&B	Continental breakfast
37 Mt. Pleasant St., 01966	11 rooms, 9 pb	Canopy beds
508-546-2701	*Rated*	antiques, garden
John & Marjorie Pratt	C-ltd/S-no/P-no/H-no	panoramic view, porch
April—October		

This 18th-century inn overlooks a historic harbor. Breakfast is served on fine china in the garden or in your room. Short walk to shops, Art Association, rocky seafront.

Mooringstone for Nonsmokrs	$$$ B&B	Continental plus
12 Norwood Ave., 01966	3 rooms, 3 pb	Air conditioning
508-546-2479	Visa, MC, AmEx, •	cable TV, refrigerators
David & Mary Knowlton	C-ltd/S-no/P-no/H-ltd	microwaves, toaster oven
May—October		

Quiet, central to beach, shops, & restaurants. Comfortable ground floor rooms w/parking.
Special long term discounts, ask

Old Farm Inn	$$ B&B	Continental plus
291 Granite St., Rt 127, Route	13 rooms, 13 pb	Comp. sherry, port
127, Pigeon Cove, 01966	Visa, MC, *Rated*, •	Sitting room, bicycles
508-546-3237 800-233-6828	C-yes/S-yes/P-no/H-ltd	2 bedroom house avail.
Susan & Bill Balzarini		queen or king beds
April—December		

Relax by the fire, nap under a tree, wander on the rocky coastline. Unwind at our friendly, cozy, country farmhouse. Cottage with 2 bedrooms also available.

Pleasant Street Inn	$$$ B&B	Continental plus
17 Pleasant St., 01966	8 rooms, 8 pb	Sitting room
508-546-3915 800-541-3915	Visa, MC, AmEx, •	veranda
Roger & Lynne Norris	C-ltd/S-ltd/P-no	2 bedroom apartment
All year		

A recently renovated inn situated on a knoll overlooking the village; within walking distance to shops, restaurants, beaches and galleries.

ROCKPORT ─────────────────────────────────

Rocky Shores Inn/Cottages
65 Eden Rd., 01966
508-546-2823 800-348-4003
Renate & Gunter Kostka
April–October

$$$ B&B (Inn)
22 rooms, 22 pb
Rated, •
C-ltd/S-ltd/P-no/H-no
German

Continental plus
Sitting room
rooms with ocean views
walk to beaches

Inn and cottages with unforgettable views of Thatcher Island lights and open sea. Inn has 7 fireplaces & beautiful woodwork. Complimentary breakfast included for inn guests.

Sally Webster Inn, The
34 Mt. Pleasant St., 01966
508-546-9251
T. Traynor, D. Muhlenburg
All year

$$ B&B
8 rooms, 8 pb
Visa, MC, *Rated*,
C-ltd/S-yes/P-no/H-no

Continental plus
Comp. wine for special
occasions
sitting room, piano
suite which sleeps 5

Historic, colonial home built in 1832. Antique decor. Walk to village and sea. Welcome to the charm of yesteryear. **Anniversary or birthday free bottle of wine if notified.**

Seacrest Manor
131 Marmion Way, 01966
508-546-2211
L. Saville, D. MacCormack, Jr
Exc. December–February

$$$ B&B
8 rooms, 6 pb
C-ltd/S-ltd/P-no/H-no
some French

Full breakfast
Afternoon tea
Library, sitting room
gardens, sun deck
bicycles

Decidedly small, intentionally quiet inn. Beautiful peaceful setting; prizewinning gardens overlooking woods & sea. Scenic trolley stop, Apr.-Nov. OUR 1988 INN OF THE YEAR!

Yankee Clipper Inn
P.O. Box 2399, 01966
96 Granite St.
508-546-3407 800-545-3699
Bob & Barbara Ellis
All year exc. Dec 24-27

$$$ B&B
27 rooms, 27 pb
Rated, •
C-yes/S-ltd/P-no/H-no

Full breakfast
Gourmet dinner
Sitting room, weddings
small conference fac.
swimming pool, bicycles

Beautiful oceanfront grounds in picturesque Rockport. 3 converted estate buildings. Rooms furnished in antiques, named after clipper ships. **Midwk specials May 21-Nov 1**

SALEM ─────────────────────────────────

Amelia Payson House
16 Winter St., 01970
508-744-8304
Ada May & Donald Roberts
All year

$$$ B&B
4 rooms, 4 pb
Visa, MC, AmEx
C-ltd/S-no

Continental plus
Restaurant nearby

Beautifully decorated rooms in elegantly restored 1845 Greek Revival-style home; 5-min. stroll finds restaurants, museums, shopping & train station. **Ask for special rates**

Coach House Inn, The
284 Lafayette St., Routes 1A &
114, 01970
508-744-4092 800-688-8689
Patricia Kessler
All year

$$ B&B
11 rooms, 10 pb
Visa, MC, AmEx, *Rated*,
•
C-yes/S-yes/P-no/H-no

Continental breakfast

Return to elegance. Enjoy the intimacy of a small European-type inn. Victorian fireplaces highlight the charming decor of each room.

SALEM

Salem Inn, The
7 Summer St., 01970
508-741-0680 800-446-2995
Diane & Richard Pabich
All year

$$$ B&B
23 rooms, 23 pb
Most CC, *Rated*, •
C-yes/S-yes/P-no/H-no

Continental plus
Comp. wine, restaurant
Private garden, phones
color TV, A/C, courtyard
special packages avail.

Spacious, luxuriously appointed rooms in elegantly restored Federal mansion. Some efficiencies & suites. In the heart of historic district. 3rd night 25% off

Stephen Daniels House
One Daniels St., at 55 Essex St.,
01970
508-744-5709
Catherine Gill
All year

$$ B&B
5 rooms, 3 pb
Rated, •
C-yes/S-yes/P-yes/H-no

Continental plus
Comp. tea
Sitting rooms
walk-in fireplaces
private garden, bicycles

300-year-old house furnished with canopy beds, antiques throughout, fireplaces in every room. Lovely flower-filled English garden, private for guests. Discount after 4+ days

Stepping Stone Inn, The
19 Washington Square N., 01970
508-741-8900 800-338-3022
John Brick
All year

$$$ B&B
8 rooms, 8 pb
Visa, MC, AmEx, •
C-yes/S-no/P-no

Continental breakfast
Sitting room
private functions avail.

Step into the past at our elegant inn located in Heritage Trail; continental breakfast in a candlelit dining room; 8 unique guest rooms; rated "best" by The Washington Post.

SANDWICH

Bay Beach B&B
Box 151, 1-3 Bay Beach Lane,
02563
508-888-8813
Emily & Reale Lemieux
May 1 - Nov. 15

$$$ B&B
3 rooms, 3 pb
Visa, MC, *Rated*, •
C-ltd/S-no/P-no/H-ltd
French

Continental plus
Aft. tea, comp. wine
Sitting room, CD player
bicycles, cable, phones
exercise room, jacuzzi

Location! Location! Location! Extraordinary ocean-front in private setting. Non-smoking, adults only. Unparalleled amenities. The gem of Cape Cod. Exclusive!

Captain Ezra Nye House
152 Main St., 02563
508-888-6142 800-388-CAPT
Harry & Elaine Dickson
All year, FAX: 888-2940

$$ B&B
6 rooms, 4 pb
Most CC, *Rated*, •
C-ltd/S-no/P-no/H-no
Spanish

Full breakfast
Comp. wine
Sitting room, library
2 canopy beds
working fireplaces

1829 Federal home in heart of historic Sandwich; near museums, antique shops, the ocean and Heritage Plantation. Bedside goodies, champagne for special occasions

Isaiah Jones Homestead
165 Main St., 02563
508-888-9115 800-526-1625
Shirley Jones Sutton
All year

$$ B&B
5 rooms, 5 pb
Most CC, *Rated*, •
C-ltd/S-no

Continental plus
Hot tea
Lemonade, iced tea
phone available
room with whirlpool tub

Victorian B&B w/queen-sized beds, one room with double & twin, furnished with museum-quality antiques. Breakfast features low cholesterol cooking. 3rd night 50% off

SANDWICH

Village Inn at Sandwich
P.O. Box 951, 02563
4 Jarves St.
508-833-0363 800-922-9989
Patricia & Winfried Platz
April—December 23

$$ B&B
6 rooms, 6 pb
Visa, MC, AmEx, *Rated*,
•
C-ltd/S-no/P-no/H-no
German

Continental plus
Comp. wine
Feather comforters
wraparound porch
rocking chairs

1830s Federal-style home in the heart of the village. Wraparound porch surrounded by fragrance of roses. Walking distance to boardwalk, beach and restaurants.

SCITUATE

Allen House, The
18 Allen Place, 02066
617-545-8221
Christine & Iain Gilmour
April—Feb.

$$ B&B
4 rooms, 2 pb
Visa, MC, AmEx, •
C-ltd/S-no/P-no/H-no
French, German, Spanish

Full breakfast
Comp. afternoon tea
Sitting room

Gourmet cook-owner serves "Fantasy Breakfast" on Victorian porch overlooking harbor in unpretentious fishing town 25 miles south of Boston. **Discounts available, ask**

SIASCONSET

Summer House, The
P.O. Box 313, 02564
S. Bluff, 17 Ocean Ave. at
Magnolia
508-257-4577 FAX:257-4590
Susan E. Manolis
May 20—October 20

$$$ B&B
8 rooms, 8 pb
Visa, MC, AmEx, •
C-yes/S-yes/P-no/H-yes
French

Continental plus
Lunch, dinner, snacks
Restaurant, bar
Jacuzzi tubs in room
ocean view, beach pool

Eight ivy-&-rose covered cottages on a bluff overlooking the Atlantic. Enjoy dinner or drinks in front of a roaring fire while Sal is at the piano. Casual, relaxed and fun.

SOUTH CHATHAM

Ye Olde Nantucket House
P.O. Box 468, 02659
2647 Main St.
508-432-5641
Steve & Ellen Londo
All year

$$ B&B
5 rooms, 5 pb
Visa, MC, •
C-ltd/S-yes

Continental plus
Homebaked goods

Delightful 19th-century home with friendly, informal atmosphere. Close to Nantucket Sound beach. Fresh breads, muffins and crepes daily. Single occupancy discount.

SOUTH EGREMONT

Weathervane Inn
P.O. Box 388, 01258
Rt. 23, Main St.
413-528-9580
Anne & Vincent Murphy
All year

$$$ B&B/MAP
10 rooms, 10 pb
Visa, MC, *Rated*, •
C-ltd/S-yes/P-no/H-yes

Full breakfast
Bar, dinner by menu
Cordial in room
sitting room, library
swimming pool

200-year-old hostelry with modern amenities. Hearty breakfasts and superb dining will make your stay memorable. **3rd night 50% off, off-season**

SOUTH YARMOUTH

Four Winds
345 High Bank Rd., 02664
508-394-4182
Mary & Walt Crowell
All year

$$ B&B
5 rooms, 4 pb
C-yes/S-yes

Continental plus
Fireplaced parlour
fishing, swimming, golf
tennis, shopping nearby

Four Winds is a 1712 sea captain's home in historic South Yarmouth near saltwater beaches and golf courses.

STERLING

Sterling Inn
P.O. Box 609, 01564
240 Worcester Rd.
508-422-6592 508-422-6333
Mark & Patricia Roy
All year

$ B&B
8 rooms, 6 pb
Visa, MC, AmEx, *Rated*,
C-ltd/S-ltd/P-no/H-ltd

Continental breakfast
Lunch, dinner, bar
Afternoon cheese & fruit
sitting room, piano
entertainment

Turn-of-the-century setting, unique to the area. Near skiing. Private dining rooms. One hour to Boston. **3rd night 30% off**

STOCKBRIDGE

Merrell Tavern Inn
Route 102, Main St., South Lee,
01260
413-243-1794 800-243-1794
Charles & Faith Reynolds
All year

$$ B&B
9 rooms, 9 pb
Visa, MC *Rated*, •
C-yes/S-ltd/P-no/H-no

Full breakfast
Air conditioned
Sitting room
guest parlor/TV room
telephones

New England setting of the 1800s in the heart of the Berkshire region. Fireplaces, canopy beds. 1 mile from Main St., Stockbridge. **3rd night free Nov.-May**

STURBRIDGE

Col. Ebenezer Crafts Inn
P.O. Box 187, 01566
66 Fiske Hill Rd.
508-347-3313 800-782-5425
David C. Lane
All year

$$ B&B
8 rooms, 8 pb
Most CC, *Rated*, •
C-yes/S-yes/P-no/H-no

Continental plus
Comp. tea, breads
Swimming pool
sitting room, piano
2 suites

1786 gracious home, under the management of Publick House, is Sturbridge's most beautiful inn. Sweeping views of gentle Massachusetts hills and gracious accommodations.

Sturbridge Country Inn
P.O. Box 60, 01566
530 Main St.
508-347-5503
Mr. MacConnell
All year

$$ B&B
9 rooms, 9 pb
Visa, MC, AmEx, *Rated*,
•
C-yes/S-yes/P-no/H-yes

Continental breakfast
Restaurant, bar
Lunch, dinner
comp. champagne
hot tubs

Close to Old Sturbridge Village lies our grand Greek Revival structure. Each room has period reproductions, fireplaces, and whirlpool tubs. **Jan-Ap, Sun-Th 2 for 1**

TRURO

Parker House
P.O. Box 1111, 02666
Route 6-A, Truro Center
508-349-3358
Stephen Williams

$$ B&B
2 rooms
C-ltd/S-no/P-no/H-no

All year

Continental breakfast
Ocean and bay beaches
national park
tennis

A warmly classic 1850 Cape house with many antiques. Close to beaches and charm of Wellfleet and Provincetown.

VINEYARD HAVEN

Captain Dexter House
P.O. Box 2457, 02568
100 Main St.
508-693-6564
Tom & Kim
All year

$$/$$$ B&B
8 rooms, 8 pb
Visa, MC, *Rated*, •
C-ltd/S-yes/P-no/H-no

Continental plus
Comp. sherry
Library, fireplaces
sitting room, parking
fresh flowers

Beautifully restored 1843 sea captain's home. Furnished with fine antiques. Some rooms have fireplaces and canopied beds. Walk to beach.

VINEYARD HAVEN ─────────────────────────────

Hanover House, The	$$$ B&B	Continental plus
P.O. Box 2107, 02568	15 rooms, 15 pb	Refrigerator, BBQ grills
10 Edgartown Rd.	Most CC, *Rated*, •	Bike racks
508-693-1066	C-yes/S-ltd/P-no/H-ltd	picnic tables
Kay & Ron Nelson		tennis nearby
All year		

Located on beautifully landscaped grounds just a short walk to town and ferry. The inn offers old Island charms with 20th century comforts. 3 rooms with kitchenettes.

Lambert's Cove Country Inn	$$$ B&B	Continental plus
RR 1, Box 422, Lambert's Cove	15 rooms, 15 pb	Restaurant, dinner
Rd., 02568	Visa, MC, AmEx, •	Sunday brunch
508-693-2298	C-yes/S-yes	sitting room, library
M. Kowalski, R. Wilson		Lambert's Cove Beach
All year		

Quiet and secluded 1790 inn with spacious lawns, gardens, apple orchard & tennis court amid a country setting of tall pines. Delicious dinners and Sunday brunch.

Lothrop Merry House, The	$$$ B&B	Continental breakfast
P.O. Box 1939, 02568	7 rooms, 4 pb	Beach front
Owen Park	Visa, MC	Terrace
508-693-1646	C-yes/S-no/P-no/H-no	boat cruises
John & Mary Clarke		canoe, sailing
All year		

Charming 18th-century guest house. Harbor, view, beach front. Walk from ferry. Fireplaces, antiques. Home-baked continental breakfast served. **3rd night 50% off Nov.—May 1.**

WARE ─────────────────────────────

Wildwood Inn, The	$ B&B	Full breakfast
121 Church St., 01082	7 rooms, 4 pb	Lemonade, cider
413-967-7798	Visa, MC, AmEx, *Rated*,	Sitting room, canoe
F. Fenster, R. Watson	•	tennis courts
All year	C-ltd/S-no/P-no/H-no	swimming hole

Relax! American primitive antiques, heirloom quilts, firm beds. Enjoy Sturbridge, Deerfield, Amherst. Canoe, swim, bike, hike. We'll spoil you. ABBA approved.

WAREHAM ─────────────────────────────

Mulberry B&B	$ B&B	Continental plus
257 High St., 02571	3 rooms	Full breakfast on occ.
508-295-0684	AmEx, Disc., •	Aft. tea, snacks
Frances Murphy	C-yes/S-no/P-no/H-no	sitting room, library
All year		bicycle routes w/maps

Charming 1840s Cape Cod style home built by blacksmith. Used as a general store by B&B owner's grandfather. Restful location, close to Boston. **3rd night 50% off, off season**

WEST HARWICH ─────────────────────────────

Cape Cod Sunny Pines	$$$ B&B	Full breakfast
P.O. Box 667, 02671	8 rooms, 8 pb	Restaurant, pub, lunch
77 Main St.	Visa, MC, Disc, *Rated*, •	Dinner, aft. tea, snacks
508-432-9628 800-356-9628	C-yes/S-yes/P-ltd/H-no	bar service, sitting rm
Eileen & Jack Connell		library, hot tubs, pool
April 1 - January 15		

Irish hospitality in Victorian ambiance. Cape Cod Victorian built in 1900. Modern amenities, oriental carpets, lace & linens. Homemade food, candlelight. **Comp. wine w/dinner**

WEST HARWICH ――――――――――――――――――――――――――――

Cape Cod Sunny Pines B&B	$$$ B&B/MAP	Gourmet Irish breakfast
P.O. Box 667, 02671	8 rooms, 8 pb	Restaurant, Irish pub
77 Main St.	Most CC, *Rated*, •	Comp. wine, tea
508-432-9628 800-356-9628	C-ltd/S-ltd/P-no/H-no	porch, A/C, cable TV
Eileen & Jack Connell		pool, spa, gardens
April–November		

Irish hospitality in Victorian ambiance. Gourmet Irish breakfast by candlelight and Irish music. Relax in the New Claddagh Tavern and tearoom. **2nd night free bottle of wine**

Lion's Head Inn	$$ B&B	Full gourmet breakfast
P.O. Box 444, 02671	6 rooms, 6 pb	Comp. tea, wine
186 Belmont Rd.	Visa, MC, *Rated*, •	Sitting room w/fireplace
508-432-7766 800-321-3155	C-ltd/S-yes/P-no/H-ltd	swimming pool, patio
Fred, Deborah & Ricky Denton		private woods, cottages
All year		

Built as a Cape half-house in 1800; former sea captain's home; charming inn with a sense of history; furnished in period antiques; central Cape Cod location. Walk to beach.

WOODS HOLE ――――――――――――――――――――――――――――

Marlborough, The	$$ B&B	Full gourmet breakfast
320 Woods Hole, Box 238,	5 rooms, 5 pb	Dinner (off season)
02543	MC, Visa, •	Afternoon tea, wine
508-548-6218	C-ltd/S-no/P-ltd/H-no	sitting room, A/C, pool
Diana M. Smith	some French	paddle tennis court
All year		

Charming inn located close to island ferries and cozy day trips to all of southeast New England. Antique shop on premises. **3rd night 50% off October-May**

YARMOUTH PORT ――――――――――――――――――――――――――――

One Centre Street Inn	$$ B&B	Full breakfast (winter)
1 Centre St., 02675	6 rooms, 4 pb	Continental plus (summ.)
508-362-8910	Visa, MC, *Rated*, •	Comp. wine, tea
Stefanie & Bill Wright	C-ltd/S-ltd/P-no/H-no	piano, bicycles
All year		flower & herb gardens

Vintage antique-furnished sea captain's home, 1 mi. to Cape Cod Bay or village. Fireplace avail. Delicious brkfast in brkfast room or garden deck. **10% off w/guide book.**

Wedgewood Inn	$$$ B&B	Full breakfast
83 Main St., 02675	6 rooms, 6 pb	Afternoon tea
508-362-5157 508-362-9178	Most CC, *Rated*, •	Common room
Milt & Gerrie Graham	C-ltd/S-ltd/P-no/H-ltd	screened porches, A/C
All year		gazebo & gardens

Romantic inn in historic area of Cape Cod. Near beaches & restaurants. Antiques, fireplaces, wide board floors, canopy beds. **Off-season rates Nov. 1-Memorial Day**

More Inns . . .

Anchorage, 122 South Shore Dr., Bass River, 02664, 617-398-8265
Belvedere B&B Inn, 167 Main St., Bass River, 02664, 508-398-6674
Old Cape House, 108 Old Main St., Bass River, 02664, 617-398-1068
Canterbury Farm B&B, Fred Snow Rd., Becket, 01223, 413-623-8765
Stonehedge B&B, 119 Sawyer Hill Rd., Berlin, 01503, 617-838-2574
Bernardston Inn, Church St., Bernardston, 01337, 413-648-9282
Billerica B&B, 88 Rogers St., Billerica, 01862, 508-667-7317
Baird Tavern B&B, Old Chester Rd., Blandford, 01008, 413-848-2096
Tirnanoag—McKenna Place, Chester Rd., Blandford, 01008, 413-848-2083
B&B Above the Rest, 50 Boatswains Way, #105, Boston, 02150, 617-884-7748
Emma James House, The, 47 Ocean St., Boston, 02124, 617-288-8867
Lenox Hotel, Boyleston St. at Copley, Boston
Newbury Guest House, 261 Newbury St., Boston, 02116, 617-437-7666
Terrace Townehouse, 60 Chandler St., Boston, 02116, 617-350-6520
Cape Cop Canalside B&B, 7 Coastal Way, Bourne, Cape Cod, 02532, 508-759-6564
Bleu Auberge, 5 Scar Hill Rd., Boylston, 01505, 617-869-2666
French's B&B, 5 Scar Hill Rd., Boylston, 01505
Cape Cod Ocean Gold B&B, 74 Locust Lane, Brewster, 02631, 508-255-7045
Inn of the Golden Ox, 1360 Main, Brewster, 02631, 617-896-3111
Poore House, 2311 Main St., Brewster, 02631, 800-233-6662
Brookline Manor Guest Hous, 32 Centre St., Brookline, 02146, 617-232-0003
William Wood House, 71 Perry St., Brookline, 02146, 617-566-2237
1797 House, Charlemont Rd., Buckland, 01338, 413-625-2697
Scott House, Hawley Rd., Buckland, 01338, 413-625-6624
Cambridge House B&B, A, 2218 Massachusetts Ave, Cambridge, 02140, 617-491-6300
Carver House, 638 Main St., Centerville, 02632, 617-775-9414
Inn at Fernbrook, 481 Main St., Centerville, 02632, 508-775-4334
Long Dell, 436 South Main St., Centerville, 02632
Old Hundred House, 1211 Craigville Beach R, Centerville, 02632, 617-775-6166
Terrace Gardens Inn, 539 Main St., Centerville, 02632, 617-775-4707
Forest Way Farm, Route 8A (Heath), Charlemont, 01339, 413-337-8321
Gingerbread B & Brunch, RR 2 Box 542A Stafford , Charlton, 01507, 617-248-7940
Bow Roof House, 59 Queen Anne Rd., Chatham, 02633, 617-945-1346
Queen Anne Inn, 70 Queen Anne Rd., Chatham, 02633, 617-945-0394
Seafarer Motel, Main St., Chatham, 02633, 617-432-1739
Chatham Town House Inn, 11 Library Ln., Chatham/Cape Cod, 02633, 508-945-2180
Pleasant Pheasant B&B, 296 Heath St., Chestnut Hill, 02167, 617-566-4178
Actor's Row, 90 Howard Gleason Rd., Cohasset, 02025, 617-383-9200
Grandmother's House, RR1 Box 37, Colrain, 01340, 413-624-3771
Maple Shade Farm B&B, Rt.1, Box 469, Colrain, 01340
Colonel Roger Brown House, 1694 Main St., Concord, 01742, 800-292-1369
Colonial Inn, The, 48 Monument Square, Concord, 01742, 508-369-9200
Hilltop B&B, Truce Rd., Conway, 01341, 413-369-4928
Poundsworth B&B, Old Cricket Hill Rd., Conway, 01341
James & Ellen Allen B&B, 60 Nickerson Ln, Box 22, Cotuit, 02635, 617-428-5702
Salty Dog Inn, 451 Main St., Cotuit, 02635, 508-428-5228
Acworth Inn, The, P.O. Box 256, Cummaquid, 02637, 800-362-6363
Hidden Brook, RR 1, Box 238C, Cummington, 01026, 413-634-5653
Hill Gallery, Cole St., Cummington, 01026, 413-238-5914
Inn at Cummington Farm VII, RR 1, Box 234, Cummington, 01026, 413-634-5551
Allen House Inn/Restaurant, P.O. Box 27, Main St., Cuttyhunk, 02713, 508-996-9292
Dalton House, 955 Main St., Dalton, 01226, 413-684-3854
Yellow Gabled House B&B, 307 N. Main St., Deerfield, 01373, 413-665-4922
Four Chimneys Inn, 946 Main St., Dennis, 02638, 617-385-6317
Weatherly House, 36 New Boston Rd., Dennis, 02638, 508-385-7458
"By-the-Sea" Guests, 57 Chase Ave., Box 50, Dennisport, 02639, 617-398-8685
Winsor House Inn, P.O. Box 287 SHS, Duxbury, 02331, 617-934-0991
Ocean Gold Cape Cod B&B, 74 Locust Lane, Route 2, East Brewster, 02631, 617-255-7045
Peterson's B&B, 226 Trotting Park, East Falmouth, 02536, 508-540-2962
Arey's Pond Relais, P.O. Box 1387, East Orleans, 02653, 508-240-0599
Spring Garden Motel, 578 Rte. 6A, Box 867, East Sandwich, 02537, 508-888-0710
Wingscorton Farm Inn, Olde Kings Hwy, Rt. 6A, East Sandwich, 02537, 508-888-0534
Great Pond House, P.O. Box 351, Eastham, 02642,
 508-255-2867
Charlotte Inn, S. Summer St., Edgartown, 02539,
 617-627-4751
Daggett House, P.O. Box 1333, Edgartown, 02539,
 508-627-4600
Edgartown Heritage Hotel, 227 Upper Main St.,
 Edgartown, 02539, 617-627-5161
Katama Guest House, RFD #108,166 Katama Rd.,
 Edgartown, 02539, 617-627-5158
Meeting House Inn, 40 Meeting House Way,
 Edgartown, 02539, 508-627-8626
Victorian Inn, The, P.O. Box 947, Edgartown,
 02539, 508-627-4784
Shiverick Inn, The, P.O. Box 640,
 Edgartown/Martha's Vinyd, 02539, 508-627-3797
Amherst, 30 Amherst Ave., Falmouth, 02540,
 617-548-2781
Coonamesset Inn, Falmouth, 508-548-2300
Elm Arch Inn, Elm Arch Way, Falmouth, 02540,
 617-548-0133

Summer Hill Farm, Lenox, MA

Gladstone Inn, 219 Grand Ave. S., Falmouth, 02540, 508-548-9851
Hastings By the Sea, 28 Worcester Ave., Falmouth, 02540, 617-548-1628
Moorings Lodge, 207 Grand Ave. S., Falmouth, 02540, 617-540-2370
Seawinds, The, P.O. Box 393, Falmouth, 02541, 508-548-3459
Wyndemere House, 718 Palmer Ave., Falmouth, 02540, 617-540-7069
Outermost Inn, The, RR 1, Box 171, Gay Head, 02535, 508-645-3511
Blue Shutters Inn, 1 Nautilus Rd., Gloucester, 01930, 617-281-2706
Williams Guest House, 136 Bass Av., Gloucester, 01930, 617-283-4931
Whale Inn, Rt. 9, Main St., Box 6, Goshen, 01032, 413-268-7246
Elling's Guest House B&B, R.D. #3, Box 6, Great Barrington, 01230
Littlejohn Manor, Newsboy Monument, Rt 23, Great Barrington, 01230, 413-528-2882
Thornewood Inn, 453 Stockbridge Rd., Great Barrington, 01230, 413-528-3828
Brandt House, The, 29 Highland Ave., Greenfield, 01301, 413-774-3329
Miles River Country Inn, P.O. Box 149, Hamilton, 01936, 508-468-7206
Mill House Inn, P.O. Box 1079, Hancock, 01237
Two Deerfoot B&B, 2 Deerfoot Trail, Harvard, 01451, 508-456-3669
Victorian Inn at Harwich, P.O. Box 340, Harwich, 02645, 508-432-8335
Winstead, The, 328 Bank St., Harwich, 02645, 508-432-4586
Bayberry Shores, 255 Lower County Rd., Harwich Port, 02646, 508-432-0337
Beach House Inn, The, 4 Braddock Ln., Harwich Port, 02646, 508-432-4444
Country Inn, 86 Sisson Rd. (Rte. 39), Harwich Port, 02646, 508-432-2769
Grey Gull Guest House, 547 Main St., Harwich Port, 02646, 508-432-0222
Harbor Breeze, 326 Lower County Rd., Harwich Port, 02646, 508-432-0337
Inn on Bank Street, 88 Bank St., Harwich Port, 02646, 508-432-3206
No. 10 Bed & Breakfast, 10 Cross St., Harwich Port, 02646, 508-432-9313
Beach House Inn, 4 Braddock Ln., Harwichport, 02646, 508-432-4444
Ripley House, 347 Main St., Hingham, 02043
Alpine Haus, Mashapaung Rd., Box 782, Holland, 01550, 413-245-9082
Acorn House, 240 Sea St., Hyannis, 02601, 617-771-4071
Captain Sylvester Baxter, 156 Main St., Hyannis, 02601, 508-775-5611
Elegance By-The-Sea, 162 Sea St., Hyannis, 02601, 508-775-3595
Pistachio Cove, 229 County Rd., Lakeville, 02347, 617-763-2383
AMC - Bascom Lodge, P.O. Box 686, Lanesboro, 01237, 413-743-1591
1777 Greylock House, 58 Greylock St., Lee, 01238, 413-243-1717
Chambery Inn, Main St., Lee, 01238, 413-243-2221
Kingsleigh 1840/ A B&B, 32 Park St., Lee, 01238, 413-243-3317
Ramsey House, 203 W. Park St., Lee, 01238, 413-243-1598
Tollgate Inn, HC 63, Box 98A, Lee, 01238, 413-243-0715
Rockwood Inn, Box 1717, Lennox, 01240
Amity House, 15 Cliffwood St., Lenox, 01240, 413-637-0005
Apple Tree Inn, 224 West St., Lenox, 01240, 413-637-1477
Candlelight Inn, 53 Walker St., Lenox, 01240, 413-637-1555
Cliffwood Inn, 25 Cliffwood St., Lenox, 01240, 413-637-3330
East Country Berry Farm, 830 East St., Lenox, 01240, 413-442-2057
Seven Hills Inn, 100 Plunkett St., Lenox, 01240, 800-869-6518
Strawberry Hill, P.O. Box 718, Lenox, 01240, 413-637-3381
Wheatleigh Inn, Lenox, 01240, 413-637-0610
Whistler's Inn, 5 Greenwood St., Lenox, 01240, 413-637-0975
Ashley's B&B, 6 Moon Hill Rd., Lexington, 02173, 617-862-6488
Halewood House, 2 Larchmont Ln., Lexington, 02173, 617-862-5404
Sherman-Berry House B&B, 163 Dartmouth St., Lowell, 01851, 508-459-4760
10 Mugford Street B&B, 10 Mugford St., Marblehead, 01945, 617-639-0343
Lindsey's Garret, 38 High St., Marblehead, 01945, 800-882-3891
Osterville Fairways Inn, 1198 Race Ln., Marstons Mill, 02648, 617-428-2747
Farmhouse, State Rd., Martha's Vineyard, 02568, 617-693-5354
Harborview Hotel, Edgartown, Martha's Vineyard, 508-627-4333
Shiverick Inn, The, Martha's Vineyard, 508-627-3797
Tisbury Inn, Vineyard Haven, Martha's Vineyard, 508-693-2200
Beach Plum Inn, Box 98, Menemsha, 02552, 617-645-9454
Strawberry Banke Farm B&B, on Skyline Trail, Middlefield, 01243, 413-623-6481
Bay Breeze Guest House, P.O. Box 307, Monument Beach, 02553
1739 House, 43 Centre St., Nantucket, 02554
Anchor Inn, 66 Centre St., Nantucket, 02554, 508-228-0072
Beachside, N. Beach St., Nantucket, 02554, 617-228-2241
Brass Lantern, 11 N. Water St., Nantucket, 02554, 508-228-4064
Carlisle House Inn, 26 N. Water St., Nantucket, 02554, 508-228-0720
Chestnut House, 3 Chestnut St., Nantucket, 02554, 617-228-0049
Cliff Lodge B&B, 9 Cliff Rd., Nantucket, 02554, 617-228-9480
Cliffside Beach Club, P.O. Box 449, Nantucket, 02554, 617-228-0618
Dolphin Guest House, 10 N. Beach St., Nantucket, 02554, 617-228-4028
Easton House, Box 1033, Nantucket, 02554, 617-228-2759
Fair Gardens, 27 Fair St., Nantucket, 02554, 617-228-4258
Fair Winds, 29 Cliff Rd., Nantucket, 02554
Four Ash Street, 4 Ash St., Nantucket, 02554, 617-228-4899
Great Harbor Inn, 31 India St., Nantucket, 02554
Greider Guest House, 43 Orange St., Nantucket, 02554
Hawthorn House, 2 Chestnut St., Nantucket, 02554, 617-228-1468
House of the Seven Gables, 32 Cliff Rd., Nantucket, 02554, 617-228-4706
Hussey House - 1795, 15 N. Water St., Nantucket, 02554, 617-228-0747
India House, 37 India St., Nantucket, 02554, 617-228-9043
Ivy Lodge, 2 Chester St., Nantucket, 02554, 617-228-6612
Le Languedoc Inn, 24 Broad St., Nantucket, 02554, 617-228-2552

Nantucket Landfall, 4 Harbor View Way, Nantucket, 02554, 617-228-0500
Nesbitt Inn, 21 Broad St., Nantucket, 02554, 617-228-0156
Paul West House, 5 Liberty St., Nantucket, 02554
Periwinkle Guest House, 9 N. Water St., Nantucket, 02554, 617-228-9267
Roberts House, India & Centre Sts., Nantucket, 02554, 617-228-9009
Rueben Joy Guest House, 107 Main St., Nantucket, 02554, 617-228-6612
Safe Harbor Guest House, 2 Harbor View Way, Nantucket, 02554, 508-228-3222
Ships Inn, 13 Fair St., Nantucket, 02554, 508-228-0040
Spring Cottage B&B Suites, 98 Orange St., Nantucket, 02554, 508-325-4644
Ten Hussey, Ten Hussey St., Nantucket, 02554
Ten Lyon Street Inn, 10 Lyon St., Nantucket, 02554, 617-228-5040
Union Street Inn, 7 Union St., Nantucket, 02554, 508-228-9222
Wake Up On Pleasant Street, 31 Pleasant St., Nantucket, 02554, 617-228-0673
West Moor Inn, Off Cliff Rd., Nantucket, 02554, 617-228-0877
Wharf Cottages, New Whale St., Nantucket, 02554, 617-228-4620
Sherburne Inn, 10 Gay St., Nantucket Island, 02554, 508-228-4425
Durant Sail Loft Inn, One Merrill's Wharf, New Bedford, 02740, 508-999-2700
Melville House, The, 100 Madison St., New Bedford, 02740, 508-990-1566
Morrill Place Inn, 209 High St., New Buryport, 01950, 508-462-2808
Old Inn on the Green, The, Star Route 70, Route 57, New Marlborough, 01230, 413-229-3131
Red Bird Inn, P.O. Box 592, New Marlborough, 01230, 413-229-2433
Morrill Place Inn, 209 High St., Newburyport, 01950, 617-462-2808
Ted Barbour, 88 Rogers St., North Billrtivs, 01862, 617-667-7317
Autumn Inn, 259 Elm St., Northampton, 01060, 413-584-7660
Centennial House, 94 Main St., Northfield, 01360, 413-498-5921
Squaheag House, RR #1, Northfield, 01360, 413-498-5749
Arend's Somoset on the Sou, Box 847, Oak Bluffs, 02557
Attleboro House, 11 Lake Ave., Oak Bluffs, 02557, 617-693-4346
Beach House B&B, The, P.O. Box 417, Oak Bluffs, 02557, 508-693-3955
Capricorn House, P.O. Box 855, Oak Bluffs, 02557
Circuit House, Box 2422, 150 Circuit A, Oak Bluffs, 02557, 617-693-5033
Island Country Club Inn, Beach Rd., Oak Bluffs, 02557
Narragansett House, 62 Narragansett Ave., Oak Bluffs, 02557, 617-693-3627
Nashua House, Kennebee and Park Ave., Oak Bluffs, 02557, 617-693-0043
Pequot House, 19 Pequot Ave, Box 1146, Oak Bluffs, 02557
Ship's Inn, Box 1483, Oak Bluffs, 02557, 617-693-2760
Onset Pointe Inn, The, POBox 1450, 9 Eagle Way, Onset, 02558, 508-295-8442
Boggastowe Farm, Shattuck St, Pepperell, 01463
Chalet d'Alicia B&B, E. Windsor Rd., Peru, 01235, 413-655-8292
Stall, The, East Windsor Rd., Peru, 01235, 413-655-8008
Country Hearts B&B, 52 Broad St., Pittsfield, 01201
White Horse Inn B&B, 378 South St, Rts 7 & 2, Pittsfield, 01201, 413-443-0961
Rolling Meadow Farm, H.C. 15A Pleasant St., Plainfield, 01070, 415-634-2166
Another Place Inn, 240 Sandwich St., Plymouth, 02360, 548-746-0126
Colonial House Inn, 207 Sandwich St., Plymouth, 02360, 617-746-2087
Hawthorne Hill B&B, 3 Wood St., Plymouth, 02360, 508-746-5244
Morton Park Place, 1 Morton Park Rd., Plymouth, 02360, 508-747-1730
Two-Sixty-Four Sandwich St, 264 Sandwich St., Plymouth, 02360, 508-747-5490
Admiral's Landing, 158 Bradford St., Provincetown, 02657
Asheton House, 3 Cook St., Provincetown, 02657, 508-487-9966
Bed 'n B'fast, 44 Commercial St., Provincetown, 02657, 508-487-9555
Crosswinds Inn, 140 Bradford St., Provincetown, 02657, 508-487-3533
Elephant Walk Inn, 156 Bradford St., Provincetown, 02657
Fairbanks Inn, The, 90 Bradford St., Provincetown, 02657, 508-487-0386
Red Inn, 15 Commercial St., Provincetown, 02657, 508-487-0050
Rose and Crown Guest House, 158 Commercial St., Provincetown, 02657, 508-487-3332
Sunset Inn, 142 Bradford St., Provincetown, 02657, 617-487-9810
Twelve Center Guest House, 12 Center St., Provincetown, 02657, 617-487-0381
Victoria House, 5 Standish St., Provincetown, 02657, 617-487-1319
Wave's Landing Guest House, 158 Bradford St., Provincetown, 02657, 617-487-9198
White Wind Inn, 174 Commercial St., Provincetown, 02657, 508-487-1526
Windamar House, 568 Commercial St., Provincetown, 02657, 617-487-0599
Middlerise B&B, Route 41, Box 17, Richmond, 01254
Beach Knoll Inn, 30 Beach St., Rockport, 01966, 508-546-6939
Cable House, 3 Narwood Ave., Rockport, 01966, 508-546-3895
Eden Pines Inn, Eden Rd., Rockport, 01966, 508-546-2505
Lantana House, 22 Broadway, Rockport, 01966, 508-546-3535
Leiden Tree Inn, 26 King St., Rockport, 01966, 508-546-2494
Rockport Lodge, 61 South St., Rockport, 02108, 508-546-2090
Seafarer Inn, 86 Marmion Way, Rockport, 01966, 508-546-6248
Seven South St.—The Inn, 7 South St., Rockport, 01966, 508-546-6708
Tuck Inn, 17 High St., Rockport, 01966, 617-546-6252
General Rufus Putnam House, 344 Main St., Rt. 122-A, Rutland, 01543, 508-886-4256
Captain Farris House, 308 Old Main St., S. Yarmouth, 02664, 508-760-2818
Bed & Breakfast, One Hawes Rd., Box 205, Sagamore Beach, 02562, 508-888-1559
Widow's Walk B&B, 152 Clark Rd., Sagamore Beach, 02562, 508-888-3888
Inn at Seven Winter St., Seven Winter St., Salem, 01970, 617-745-9520
Nathaniel Bowditch House, 2 Kimball Court, Salem, 01970, 000-745-7755
Suzannah Flint House, 98 Essex St., Salem, 01970, 508-744-5281
New Boston Inn, Routes 57 & 8, Sandisfield, 01255, 413-258-4477
Dillingham House, 71 Main St., Sandwich, 02563, 508-833-0065
Isaiah Jones Homestead, 165 Main St., Sandwich, 02563, 508-888-9115

Ocean Front, 273 Phillips Rd., Sandwich, 02563
Seth Pope House 1699 B&B, 110 Tuppee Rd., Sandwich, 02563
Six Water Street, P.O. Box 1295, Sandwich, 02563, 508-888-6808
Centuryhurst Antiques B&B, P.O. Box 486, Sheffield, 01257, 413-229-8131
Colonel Ashley Inn, RR #1 Box 142, Bow Wow , Sheffield, 01257, 413-229-2929
Stagecoach Hill Inn, Route 41, Sheffield, 01257, 413-229-8585
Staveleigh House, P.O. Box 608, Sheffield, 01257, 413-229-2129
Unique B&B, Under Mountain, Box 7, Sheffield, 01257, 413-229-3363
Country Comfort, 15 Masonic Ave., Shelburne Falls, 01370, 413-625-9877
Parson Hubbard House, Old Village Rd., Shelburne Falls, 01370, 413-625-9730
Orchard Terrace, 330 No. Main St., So. Deerfield, 01373, 413-665-3829
Westview Landing, Box 141, South Chelmsford, 01824
Westview Landing, POBox 4141, 4 Westview, South Chelmsford, 01824, 508-256-0074
Little Red House, The, 631 Elm St., South Dartmouth, 02748, 508-996-4554
Egremont Inn, P.O. Box 418, South Egremont, 01258, 413-528-2111
House on the Hill, P.O. Box 51, 968 Main, South Harwich, 02661, 617-432-4321
Federal House, Route 102, South Lee, 01260, 413-243-1824
Hillbourne House B&B, Route 28, Box 190, South Orleans, 02662, 617-255-0780
Wayside Inn, South Sudbury, 01776, 617-443-8846
Langhaar House, P.O. Box 191, Southfield, 01259, 413-229-2007
Berkshire Thistle B&B, The, Rte. 7, P.O. Box 2105, Stockbridge, 01262, 413-298-3188
Inn at Stockbridge, Stockbridge, 01262, 413-298-3337
Olde Lamplighter, Church St., Stockbridge, 01262, 413-298-3053
Amerscot House, 61 West Acton Rd., Stow, 01775, 508-897-0666
Bethlehem Inn, 508 Stallion Hill, Sturbridge, 01566
Chamberlain, P.O. Box 187, Sturbridge, 01566, 617-347-3313
Country Motor Lodge, P.O. Box 187, Sturbridge, 01566, 617-347-3313
Commonwealth Inn, P.O.Box 251, Fiskdale, Sturbridge—Fiskdale, 01566, 508-347-5503
Checkerberry Corner B&B, 5 Checkerberry Circle, Sudbury, 01776, 508-443-8660
Sudbury B&B, 3 Drum Ln., Sudbury, 01776, 617-443-2860
Maquires, The, 431 Hampden St., Swampscott, 01900
Wood Farm, 40 Worcester Rd., Townsend, 01469, 508-597-5019
Golden Goose, P.O. Box 336, Tyringham, 01264, 413-243-3008
Capron House, 2 Capron St., Uxbridge, 01569
Gazebo B&B, Edgartown Rd., Vineyard Haven, 02568, 617-693-6955
High Haven House, Box 289, Summer St., Vineyard Haven, 02568, 617-693-9204
Ocean Side Inn, Main St., Box 2700, Vineyard Haven, 02568, 617-693-1296
Post House, The, PO Box 717, 47 Causeway, Vineyard Haven, 02568, 508-693-5337
Sea Horse Guests, RFD Box 373, Vineyard Haven, 02568, 617-693-0594
South Wind, Box 810, Vineyard Haven, 02568, 617-693-5031
Tuckerman House, 45 William St, Box 194, Vineyard Haven, 02568, 617-693-0417
Tern Inn, The, 91 Chase St., W. Harwich, 02671, 508-432-3714
Mariners Cove B&B, 15 Seconsett Pt. Rd., Waquoit, 02536, 508-548-3821
1880 Inn B&D, The, 14 Pleasant St., Ware, 01082, 413-967-7847
Inn at Duck Creeke, The, P.O. Box 364, Wellfleet, 02667, 617-349-9333
Rose Cottage, 24 Worcester,Rts 12 & 1, West Boylston, 01583, 617-835-4034
Brookfield House Inn, P.O. Box 796, West Brookfield, 01585, 617-867-6589
Beach House, 61 Uncle Stephen's Rd., West Dennis, 02670, 617-398-8321
Lighthouse Inn, West Dennis, 02670, 508-398-2244
Old Silver Beach B&B, 3 Cliffwood Lane, Box 6, West Falmouth, 02574, 617-540-5446
Sjöholm Inn B&B, P.O. Box 430, West Falmouth, 02574, 508-540-5706
Barnaby Inn, P.O. Box 151, West Harwich, 02671, 508-432-6789
Cape Winds By The , 28 Shore Rd., West Harwich, 02671
Sunny Pines B&B Inn, 77 Main St, West Harwich, 02671, 508-432-9628
Stump Sprouts Guest Lodge, West Hill Rd., West Hawley, 01339, 413-339-4265
Williamsville Inn, Route 41, West Stockbridge, 01266, 413-274-6118
Cove House/Studio House, Box 25, West Tisbury, 02575
Manor House, 57 Maine Ave., West Yarmouth, 02673, 617-771-9211
Outlook Farm, Route 66, Westhampton, 01027, 413-527-0633
Sunnyside Farm, 11 River Rd., Whately, 01093, 413-665-3113
Victorian, 583 Linwood Ave., Whitinsville, 01588, 617-234-2500
B&B with Barbara & Bo, 15 Three Rivers Rd., Wilbraham, 01095, 413-596-6258
Carl & Lottie Sylvester, 9 South St., Williamsburg, 01096, 413-268-7283
Twin Maples, 106 South St., Williamsburg, 01098, 413-268-7925
Field Farm Guest House, 554 Sloan Rd., Williamstown, 01267, 413-458-3135
House On Main Street, 1120 Main St., Williamstown, 01267, 413-458-3031
Le Jardin, 777 Coldspring Rd., Williamstown, 01267, 413-458-8032
Orchards, The, Williamstown, 01267, 800-225-1517
River Bend Farm, 643 Simonds Rd., Williamstown, 01267, 413-458-5504
Steep Acres Farm, 520 White Oaks Rd., Williamstown, 01267, 413-458-3774
Upland Meadow House, 1249 Northwest Hill Rd., Williamstown, 01267
Woods Hole Passage B&B, 186 Woods Hole Rd., Woods Hole, 02540, 508-548-9575
Country Cricket Inn, Huntington Rd. Rt 112, Worthington, 01098, 413-238-5366
Franklin Burr Homestead, HC63 B196, Kinne Brook, Worthington, 01098, 413-238-5826
Heritage, The, Buffington Hill Rd., Worthington, 01098, 413-238-4230
Inn Yesterday, Huntington Rd., Rt. 11, Worthington, 01098, 413-238-5529
Worthington Inn, Route 143, Old North Rd, Worthington, 01098, 413-238-4441
Colonial House Inn, Rt. 6A, 277 Main St., Yarmouth Port, 02675, 508-362-4348
Olde Captain's Inn, 101 Main St., Route 6, Yarmouth Port, 02675, 508-362-4496
Joshua Sears Manor, 4 Summer St & Route 6A, Yarmouthport, 02675, 508-362-5000
Old Yarmouth Inn, 223 Main St., Yarmouthport, 02675

Michigan

ANN ARBOR

Urban Retreat B&B, The
2759 Canterbury Rd., 48104
313-971-8110
Andrè Rosalik, Gloria Krys
All year

$$ B&B
2 rooms, 1 pb
Rated
C-ltd/S-yes/P-no/H-no

Full breakfast
Sitting room
patio, gardens
air-conditioned

Comfortable 1950s ranch home on quiet tree-lined street; furnished with antiques; adjacent to 127-acre meadowland park; minutes from major universities.

BAY CITY

Stonehedge Inn B&B
924 Center Ave. (M-25), 48708
517-894-4342
Ruth Koerber
All year

$$ B&B
7 rooms
Most CC, *Rated*, •
C-ltd/S-ltd/P-no/H-no

Continental plus
Comp. wine, tea, snacks
Sitting room
library

Elegant journey into the past; 1889 English Tudor home has original stained glass windows, nine fireplaces and a magnificent open staircase. Breakfast in formal dining room.

BROOKLYN

Dewey Lake Manor B&B
11811 Laird Rd., 49230
517-467-7122
The Phillips Family
All year

$$ B&B
4 rooms, 4 pb
Visa, MC, *Rated*, •
C-ltd/S-ltd/P-ltd/H-no
Some Japanese

Continental plus
Picnic lunch, snacks,tea
Sitting room with piano
croquet, cross-country
skiing
bonfires, ice skating

The 1870s Italianate home sits on the shore of Dewey Lake. Guests can enjoy 18 acres and an aura of yesteryear. Many antique shops nearby. Enjoy romance. **3rd night 25% off**

CADILLAC

American Inn B&B
312 E. Cass (E-M55), 49601
616-779-9000
Mike & Cathy Feister
All year

$$ B&B
5 rooms, 5 pb
Visa, MC, AmEx, *Rated*,
•
C-yes/S-ltd/P-no/H-no

Continental plus
Hot tubs, sauna
Cable/HBO, phones
sitting room

Charming turn of the century home. Tastefully appointed guest rooms. Luxurious suite w/private spa. Walk to lakes, downtown. Year-round activities.

CHAMPION

Michigamme Lake Lodge
P.O. Box 97, 49814
800-358-0058
Frank & Linda Stabile
All year

$$$ B&B
9 rooms, 6 pb
Visa, MC, •
C-ltd/S-no/P-no/H-no

Continental plus
Afternoon tea
Sitting room, porch
gift shop, canoes
1700 ft. of lake & beach

On the lake, sandy beach, canoes, stroll gardens and birch groves. Built in the 1930s. Quiet and secluded. Furnished with antiques. On National and State Register.

CHARLEVOIX

Bridge Street Inn, The	$$ B&B	Full breakfast
113 Michigan Ave., 49720	9 rooms, 3 pb	Close to beaches
616-547-6606	*Rated*, •	restaurants, shopping
Vera & John McKown	C-ltd/S-no/P-no/H-no	& boating
All year		

Recapture grace & charm of a gentler era in this 1895 colonial revival home. 3 stories deco-rated w/unique, interesting antiques. Each room w/different decor. **3rd night 50%**

COLDWATER

Chicago Pike Inn	$$$ B&B	Full breakfast
215 E. Chicago St., 49036	8 rooms, 8 pb	Dinner (house bookings)
517-279-8744	*Rated*	Afternoon tea, snacks
Rebecca Schultz	C-ltd/S-ltd/P-no/H-no	sitting room
All year		library, bicycles

Lodging in Victorian elegance. 8 beautifully restored rooms surrounded by peace & tranquil-ity. Located in historic district. 2 new carriage house rms. w/whirlpool, priv bath.

FENNVILLE

Heritage Manor Inn B&B	$$ B&B	Full breakfast
2253 Blue Star Hwy., 49408	18 rooms, 18 pb	Comp. juices, snacks
616-543-4384	Visa, MC, Disc., •	Sitting room, canoeing
Ken & Ione Rahrig	C-yes/S-yes/P-no/H-yes	11 hot tubs, indoor pool
All year		Gazebo for weddings, BBQ

Romantic country inn. Jacuzzi/fireplace suites, whirlpool. Near Lake MI, beaches, fishing, hiking, horseback trails, flowers. Specializing in weddings, honeymoon, anniv. pkgs.

Hidden Pond B&B	$$ B&B	Full breakfast
P.O. Box 461, 49408	2 rooms, 2 pb	Snacks, comp. sherry
5975 - 128th Ave.	*Rated*, •	Sitting room, library
616-561-2491	C-ltd/S-ltd/P-no/H-no	guest use of home
Priscilla & Larry Fuerst		bicycles
All year		

28 acres of wooded, ravined land for your relaxation. Full gourmet breakfast. Beaches, Saugatuck, Holland & Fennville 10 minutes away. Lovely quiet retreat. **15% off 3+ nights**

FENNVILLE—SAUGATUCK

Kingsley House B&B, The	$$$ B&B	Full breakfast
626 W. Main St., 49408	5 rooms, 5 pb	Comp. tea, cocoa, coffee
616-561-6425	*Rated*, •	Sitting rooms, firepl's.
David & Shirley Witt	C-ltd/S-no	bicycles, porch swing
All year		3 suites w/whirlpool tub

Elegant Queen Anne 1886 Victorian home. Country setting near beaches, cross-country ski-ing. "Top 50 Inn in America" by InnTimes. Family antiques. **Bottle of wine, 4th night 50% off.**

FLINT

Avon House B&B	$ B&B	Full breakfast
518 Avon St., 48503	3 rooms	Formal dining room
313-232-6861	C-yes/S-yes/P-no/H-no	Sitting room, A/C
Arletta E. Minore		Stienway grand piano
All year		extended stay rates

Enchanting Victorian home-walking distance to College & Cultural Center w/art (Art Fair Site) & entertainment. Driving distance to Manufacturers's Marketplace. **Discounts, ask**

GLEN ARBOR ─────────────────────────

Sylvan Inn
P.O. Box 648, 49636
6680 Western Ave.
616-334-4333
Jenny & Bill Olson
May–February

$$ B&B
14 rooms, 7 pb
Visa, MC, *Rated*, •
C-ltd/S-no/P-no/H-yes

Continental plus
Sitting room
hot tubs
sauna

Luxuriously renovated 1885 historic inn situated in the heart of Sleeping Bear National Lakeshore. Easy access to fine dining, shopping, swimming, biking, skiing.

HOLLAND ─────────────────────────

Dutch Colonial Inn
560 Central Ave., 49423
616-396-3664
Bob & Pat Elenbaas
All year

$$ B&B
5 rooms, 5 pb
Most CC, *Rated*,
C-ltd/S-no/P-no/H-no

Full breakfast
Afternoon tea, snacks
Sitting room, A/C
bicycles
whirlpool tubs

Lovely 1928 Dutch Colonial home. Touches of elegance and antiques. Lovely common room w/fireplace. Whirlpool tubs for two in private baths; honeymoon suite. **10% off 4+ nights**

Parsonage 1908 B&B, The
6 E. 24th St., 49423
616-396-1316
Bonnie McVoy-Verwys
May–October

$$$ B&B
4 rooms
Rated, •
C-ltd/S-no/P-no/H-no

Full breakfast
Sitting room
TV, games
golf, tennis nearby

European-style B&B in town famous for May tulip festival. Marvelous alternative to motels for traveling businesswomen. Convenient to several major cities. **Free gift.**

INTERLOCHEN ─────────────────────────

Between the Lakes
4570 Case Blvd., 49643
616-276-9216 FAX:276-7752
Barbara & Gordon Evans
Inn will open August '94

$$ B&B
5 rooms, 3 pb
Visa, MC, •
C-ltd/S-no/P-no/H-yes

Continental plus
Afternoon tea
Sitting room
library, piano
indoor heated lap pool

This home reflects our Foreign Service in Asia and Africa. Stay fit in our lap pool, and walk to the Interlochen Center for the Arts. **10% discount for students and seniors.**

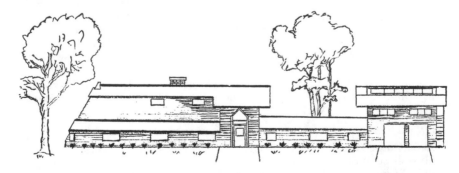

Between the Lakes, Interlochen, MI

KALAMAZOO

Hall House B&B
106 Thompson St., 49006
616-343-2500
Bob & Liz Costello
All year

$$ B&B
4 rooms, 4 pb
Most CC, *Rated*,
C-ltd/S-ltd/P-no/H-no

Full breakfast
Afternoon snack
sitting rms., fireplaces
AC, TV, piano

Exceptional overnight accommodations in a renovated Georgian Colonial Revival, near the city, on the edge of the Kalamazoo college campus. **3rd. night 50% off**

LAKESIDE

Pebble House, The
15093 Lakeshore Rd., 49116
616-469-1416
Jean & Ed Lawrence
All year

$$$ B&B
8 rooms, 6 pb
Rated
C-ltd/S-yes/P-no/H-ltd

Full breakfast
Screen house w/hammocks
fireplace, bicycles
tennis courts, walkways

Ca. 1910 decorative block & beach pebble house. Arts & Crafts furniture & decorative items. Fireplace, woodstove, rocking chairs and a lake view. Like going home to Grandma's.

MACKINAC ISLAND

Cloghaun
P.O. Box 203, 49757
Market St.
906-847-3885 313-331-7110
Dorothy & James Bond
Open May-September

$$ B&B
10 rooms, 8 pb
Rated
C-yes/S-no/P-no

Continental plus
Large front porch
2 rms. w/balconies
library

Cloghaun, built in 1884, is a large Victorian home filled with antiques and ambience of elegance of another generation. **Discount pass for ferry transportation**

Haan's 1830 Inn
P.O. Box 123, 49757
Huron St.
906-847-6244 414-248-9244
Nicholas, Nancy, Vernon, Joy
Mid-May—mid-October

$$$ B&B
7 rooms, 5 pb
Rated
C-yes/S-ltd/P-no/H-no

Continental plus
Parlor, porches
antique furnishings

Restored Greek Revival home on Historic Register. Across street from Hennepin Bay. 4 blocks from Fort Mackinac and downtown. Featured in Summer 1990 Innsider Magazine.

MANISTEE

Inn Wick-A-Te-Wah
3813 Lakeshore Dr., 49660
616-889-4396
Len & Marge Carlson
All year

$$ B&B
4 rooms, 1 pb
Visa, MC, *Rated*, •
C-ltd/S-ltd/P-no/H-no

Full breakfast
Comp. wine, fruit
Snacks, sitting room
inner tubes, bicycles
sunfish (sailing)

Gorgeous view to Portage Lake and Lake Michigan Channel. All water sports, golf, and snow skiing nearby. Lovely, airy rooms with period furnishings. **10% off 4 days midweek.**

MENDON

Mendon Country Inn B&B
P.O. Box 98, 49072
440 W. Main St.
616-496-8132
Dick & Dolly Buerkle
All year

$$ B&B
18 rooms, 18 pb
Most CC, *Rated*, •
C-ltd/S-ltd/P-no/H-yes
A little Spanish

Continental plus
Hot tubs, sauna
evening dessert
bicycles, tennis court

1843 Stagecoach Inn. 9 antique-filled rooms, 9 jacuzzi suites w/fireplaces. Close to Amish, golfing, canoes, wineries. Rural setting.

NEW BUFFALO

Sans Souci Euro Inn
19265 S. Lakeside Rd., 49117
616-756-3141 FAX:756-5511
Angelika Siewert
All year

$$$ B&B
8 rooms, 8 pb
Visa, MC, AmEx, •
C-ltd/S-ltd/P-no/H-yes
German, Spanish

Full buffet breakfast
TV, VCR, audio systems
private lakes, swim/fish
near Lake Michigan, golf

Exceptional accomm. in 88/89 converted farmbuildings. Contemp. warm eurodecor. Privacy. Reunite, meet here. Vacation homes w/kitchens. A little piece of heaven! **Family pkgs.**

NORTHPORT

Old Mill Pond Inn, The
202 West 3rd St., 49670
616-386-7341
David Chrobak
June–October

$$ B&B
4 rooms, 2 pb
C-ltd/S-yes/P-no/H-no

Continental plus
Sitting room

Restored ninety-year-old house decorated with period furniture and an extensive collection of art objects from around the world. Gay friendly.

PENTWATER

Pentwater Inn
P.O. Box 98, 49449
180 E. Lowell St.
616-869-5909
Sue and Dick Hand
All year

$$ B&B
5 rooms, 3 pb
Rated
C-ltd/S-yes/P-no/H-no
German

Full breakfast
Comp. wine
Sitting room, spa
organ, Ping-Pong table
tandem bicycle

Quiet residential area, good for retreats & family reunions, close to town. Beautiful beach, charter boats, good fishing; skiing, snowmobiling, shopping. **7th night free**

PORT HURON

Victorian Inn, The
1229 7th St., 48060
313-984-1437
The Secorys & The Petersons
All year

$$ B&B
4 rooms, 2 pb
Most CC, *Rated*,
C-ltd/S-yes/P-no/H-no

Continental plus
Restaurant, pub
Lunch, dinner
near museum, downtown
civic center, marina

The Victorian Inn features fine dining with creative cuisine and guest rooms presenting a timeless ambiance in authentically restored Victorian elegance.

PORT SANILAC

Raymond House Inn, The
P.O. Box 438, 48469
111 S. Ridge (M-25)
810-622-8800
Gene Denison
April - December

$$ B&B
7 rooms, 7 pb
•
C-ltd/S-no/P-no/H-no

Full breakfast
Comp. sherry, snacks
A/C in most rooms
sitting room, deck
Antique Shop

120-year-old Victorian home on Michigan's Historic Register, furnished in antiques; on Lake Huron; marina, boating, shipwreck scuba diving, fishing, swimming.

RAPID RIVER

Buck Stop B&B, The
P.O. Box 156, 49878
Hiawatha National Forest
906-446-3360
Charles & Sue Muntwyler
All year

$$ B&B
2 rooms
Visa, MC, Discover,
C-yes/S-ltd/P-ltd/H-no

Full breakfast
Aft. tea, snacks
Fireplaces, oil lamps
whirlpool, fishing
private trails, hunting

Very secluded, lakeside, ranch-style home in Hiawatha Nat'l Forest. Rooms w/stunning view of lake & forest wildlife. Peace, quiet & serenity. **6th night free**

ROCHESTER HILLS

Paint Creek B&B	$ B&B	Full breakfast
971 Dutton Rd., 48306	3 rooms,	Snacks
313-651-6785	•	Library, sitting room
Loren & Rea Siffring	C-yes/S-no/P-ltd/H-no	hike, bike cross-country ski
All year		

Unique setting on 3.5 wooded acres above wetlands & trout stream. Adjacent to hiking, biking trail. Close to Palace and Silverdome. Restaurants, shopping & Oakland University.

SAUGATUCK

Kemah Guest House	$$$ B&B	Continental
633 Pleasant, 49453	5 rooms, 2 pb	Non-alcoholic socials
616-857-2919	Visa, MC, *Rated*, •	Sitting room
Cindi & Terry Tatsch	C-ltd/Spanish	library
All year		

Turn-of-the-century mansion sports a combination of Old World flavor, art deco and a splash of southwestern airiness. **Nov.-March 2nd night 50% off excluding holidays.**

Maplewood Hotel	$$ B&B	Full breakfast
P.O. Box 1059, 49453	15 rooms, 15 pb	Restaurant
428 Butler St.	Visa, MC, AmEx, *Rated*,	Hors d'oeuvres, bar
616-857-1771	•	sitting room, library
C. Simon & S. Burnell	C-ltd/S-no/P-ltd/H-ltd	pool, jacuzzi, tennis
All year		

Gracious Greek revival hotel is a gleaming tribute to the 19th century. Inside, crystal chandeliers, antiques and period furniture make the hotel a perennial favorite.

Red Dog B&B, The	$$ B&B	Continental plus
P.O. Box 956, 49453	7 rooms, 4 pb	Sitting room
132 Mason St.	Visa, MC, *Rated*, •	bicycles
616-857-8851	C-yes/S-no/P-no/H-no	
D.Indurante/K.Richter/G.Kott		
All year		

A comfortable place to stay in the heart of Saugatuck. Steps away from restaurants, shopping, golf, beaches, watersports, boardwalk and year-round activities.

Sherwood Forest B&B	$$ B&B	Continental plus
P.O. Box 315, 49453	5 rooms, 5 pb	Afternoon tea, snacks
938 Center St.	Visa, MC, *Rated*,	Sitting room, bicycles
616-857-1246	C-ltd/S-no/P-no/H-no	heated pool, skiing
Keith & Susan Charak		jacuzzi, cottage
All year		

Victorian home, wraparound porch, public beach access, heated swimming pool. Just minutes from the charming shops of Saugatuck. **Spring & fall, wkdays, 2nd night 50% off, ltd**

Twin Gables Country Inn	$$ B&B	Continental plus buffet
P.O. Box 881, 49453	10 rooms, 10 pb	Refreshments, fireplace
900 Lake St.	Visa, MC, *Rated*, •·	Whirlpool, hot tub, pool
616-857-4346	C-ltd/S-ltd/P-no/H-yes	A/C, bicycles, pond
Denise & Michael Simcik	Italian, French, Maltese	garden park, ski equip.
All year		

Country charm overlooking Kalamazoo Lake. Each guestrm. in a delightful theme decor. Short walk to downtown. 3 cottages furnished in antiques also available. **Wkdays low rates**

SAUGATUCK ─────────────────────────────────────

Wickwood Country Inn, The
P.O. Box 1019, 49453
510 Butler St.
616-857-1097 616-857-1465
Julee & Bill Rosso-Miller
All year

$$$ B&B
11 rooms, 11 pb
Visa, MC, AmEx, *Rated*,
•
C-ltd/S-yes/P-no/H-yes

Continental breakfast
Comp. hors d'oeuvres
Courtyard
screened gazebo, patio
4 common rooms

Truly elegant comfort in stately home on beautiful Lake Michigan yachting harbor. Laura Ashley decor, antiques, stunning common rooms. Owned by cookbook author (Silver Palate)

SAULT STE. MARIE ─────────────────────────────

Water Street Inn
140 E. Water St., 49783
906-632-1900 800-236-1904
Phyllis & Greg Walker
All year

$$$ B&B
4 rooms
Visa, MC, *Rated*,
C-ltd/S-no/P-no/H-no
Spanish

Full breakfast
Snacks
Sitting room, library
porch, gazebo
marble fireplaces

*1900s Queen Anne overlooking St. Mary's River promises a special visit every season. Breakfast in elegant dining room. Tiffany windows, woodwork. **Off-season discounts***

SOUTH HAVEN ─────────────────────────────────

Arundel House
56 North Shore Dr., 49090
616-637-4790
Patricia & Tom Zapal
All year

$ B&B
8 rooms, 5 pb
Visa, MC, Discover,
C-ltd/S-ltd/P-no/H-no
French

Continental plus
Aft. tea
Library
sitting room

Historic inn, registered w/ Michigan Historic Society. Furnished with Victorian antiques. Walk to shops, restaurants and Lake Michigan beaches.

Old Harbor Inn
515 Williams St., 49090
616-637-8480 800-433-9210
Gwen DeBruyn
All year

$$ EP
37 rooms, 37 pb
Most Cred. Cds. *Rated*,
•
C-yes/S-yes/P-no/H-yes

Restaurant
Comp. paper, hot tubs
fishing, boating, golf
tennis, beaches, sailing

*Nestled on banks of the Black River, Old Harbor Inn offers guests the charm & grace of a quaint coastal village. Luxury suites, fireplaces, kitchenettes, pool. **10% off midwk***

Victoria Resort B&B
241 Oak St., 49090
616-637-6414 800-473-7377
Bob & Jan
All year

$ B&B
14 rooms, 14 pb
Visa, MC, Disc., •
C-yes/S-ltd/P-no

Continental plus
Tennis court, hot tubs
swimming pool, sitt. rm.
playground near, bicycle

*An old-fashioned family place with rooms, suites w/ whirlpool tubs and cottages. Close to the beach and town, on 3 acres. **25% discount except June-August***

Yelton Manor B&B
140 North Shore Dr., 49090
616-637-5220
Elaine & Rob
All year

$$$ B&B
17 rooms, 17 pb
Visa, MC, AmEx, *Rated*,
C-ltd/S-no/P-no/H-no

Full breakfast
Evening hors d'oeuvres
Fireplaces in 8 rooms
library, screened porch
jacuzzis in 11 rooms

Luxuriously appointed romantic escape. Some rooms have panoramic lake views. The ultimate environment for elite executive conference. Walk to lake, marina, shops.

TRAVERSE CITY

Linden Lea On Long Lake	$$ B&B	Full breakfast
279 S. Long Lake Rd., 49684	2 rooms, 1 pb	Comp. wine, snacks
616-943-9182	*Rated*, •	Sitting room
Jim & Vicky McDonnell	C-ltd/S-no/Spanish	lake frontage, rowboat
All year		sandy beach, raft

Wooded lakeside retreat with private sandy beach, rowboat & raft. Comfortable country furnishings, window seats, antiques & beveled glass throughout. Heavily wooded. Peaceful.

Warwickshire Inn	$$ B&B	Full breakfast
5037 Barney Rd., 49684	3 rooms, 3 pb	Comp. beverages
616-946-7176	•	Sitting room
Dan & Roberta Warwick	C-ltd/S-ltd/P-no/H-no	A/C in rooms
All year		

Antique-filled circa 1900 country farm home overlooking Traverse City. Spacious, comfortable rooms. Warm congeniality in a rural setting.

UNION PIER

Inn at Union Pier	$$$ B&B	Full breakfast
P.O. Box 222, 49129	15 rooms, 15 pb	Snacks & beverages
9708 Berrien St.	Most CC, *Rated*,	Great room, library
616-469-4700	C-ltd/S-no/P-no/H-yes	bikes, outdoor hot tub
Joyce Erickson & Mark Pitts		Lake Michigan beach
All year		

Elegantly refurbished inn blending barefoot informality with gracious hospitality. In "Harbor Country," known for Lake Michigan beaches, antiques, galleries, and wineries.

More Inns ...

Briaroaks Inn, 2980 N. Adrian Hwy., Adrian, 517-263-1659
Smith-Whitehouse B&B, 401 E. Porter St., Albion, 49224, 517-629-2220
Torch Lake B&B, 10601 Coy St., Alden, 49612, 616-331-6424
Torch Timbers B&B, 9260 S.E. Torch Lake Dr, Alden, 49612, 616-331-4050
Linda's Lighthouse Inn, 5965 Point Tremble, Algonac, 48001, 313-794-2992
Delano Inn, 302 Cutler, Allegan, 49010, 616-673-2609
Winchester Inn, 524 Marshall St., Allegan, 49010, 616-673-3621
Olde Bricke House, P.O. Box 211, Allen, 49227, 517-860-2349
Candlelight Cottage B&B, 910 Vassar, Alma, 48801, 517-463-3961
Saravilla B&B, 633 N. State St., Alma, 48801, 517-463-4078
Gladstone House, 2865 Gladstone, Ann Arbor, 48104, 313-769-0404
Hexagon House, 7301 Warren Rd., Ann Arbor, 48105, 313-668-1616
Reynolds House, 5259 W Ellsworth Rd, Ann Arbor, 48103, 313-995-0301
Wood's Inn, 2887 Newport Rd, Ann Arbor, 48103, 313-665-8394
Homestead B&B, 9279 Macon Rd., Ann Arbor–Saline, 48176, 313-429-9625
Pinewood Lodge, Box 176, M-28 West, Au Train, 49806, 906-892-8300
Point Augres Hotel, 3279 S. Point Ln., AuGres, 48703, 517-876-7217
Greencrest Manor, 6174 Halbert Rd, Battle Creek, 49017, 616-962-8633
Old Lamp-Lighter, The, 276 Capital Ave., N.E., Battle Creek, 49017, 616-963-2603
William Clements Inn, 1712 Center (M-25), Bay City, 48708, 517-894-4600
Florence B&B, P.O. Box 1031, Bay View, 49770, 616-348-3322
Gingerbread House, The, P.O. Box 1273, Bay View, 49770, 616-347-3538
Terrace Inn, 216 Fairview Ave., Bay View, 49770, 616-347-2410
Bellaire B&B, 212 Park St, Bellaire, 49615, 616-533-6077
On-The-Lake B&B, P.O. Box 870, Bellaire, 49615, 616-533-6167
Richardi House, The, 402 N. Bridge St, Bellaire, 49615, 616-533-6111
Bolins' B&B, 576 Colfax Ave, Benton Harbor, 49022, 616-925-9068
Brookside Inn, US 31, Beulah, 49617, 616-882-9688
Windermere Inn, 747 Crystal Dr., Beulah, 49617, 616-882-7264
Big Bay Lighthouse B&B, No. 3 Lighthouse Rd., Big Bay, 49808, 906-345-9957
Taggart House B&B, 321 E. Maple St., Big Rapids, 49307, 616-796-1713
PJ's B&B, 722 N. 29th St., Bilings, 59101, 406-259-3300
Silver Creek, 4361 US-23, South, Black River, 48721, 517-471-2198
Celibeth House B&B, Route 1, Box 58A, Blaney Park, 49836, 906-283-3409
H. D. Ellis Inn, 415 W. Adrian, US 223, Blissfield, 49228, 517-486-3155
Hathaway House, Blissfield, 517-486-2141
Hiram D. Ellis Inn, 415 W. Adrian St., Blissfield, 49228, 517-486-3155
Duley's State Street Inn, 303 State St, Boyne City, 49712, 616-582-7855

Chicago Street Inn, 219 Chicago St., Brooklyn, 49230, 517-592-3888
Essenmacher's B&B, 204 Locust Ln., Cadillac, 49601, 616-775-3828
Bostrom-Johnson House, 1109 Calumet Ave., Calumet, 49913, 906-337-4651
Calumet House B&B, P.O. Box 126, Calumet, 49913, 906-337-1936
Garden Gate B&B, 315 Pearl St., Caro, 48723, 517-673-2696
Country Charm Farm, 5048 Conkey Rd, Caseville, 48725, 517-856-3110
Jarrold Farm, Box 215A, County Rd 643, Cedar, 49621, 616-228-6955
Victoria Creek B&B, 8702 Co. Rd. 645, Cedar, 49621, 616-228-7246
Bridgewalk B&B, P.O. Box 577, Central Lake, 49622, 616-544-8122
Darmon Street B&B, P.O. Box 284, Central Lake, 49622, 616-544-3931
Twala's B&B, Torch Lake, Rte 2, Box 84B, Central Lake, 49648, 616-599-2864
Michigamme Lake Lodge, P.O. Box 97, Champion, 49814, 906-339-4400
Aaron's Windy Hill Guest, 202 Michigan (US-31), Charlevoix, 49720, 616-547-2804
Bay B&B, Route 1, Box 136A, Charlevoix, 49720, 616-599-2570
Belvedere House, 306 Belvedere Ave., Charlevoix, 49720, 616-547-4501
Channel View Inn, 217 Park, Charlevoix, 49720, 616-147-6180
Charlevoix Country Inn, 106 W. Dixon Ave., Charlevoix, 49720
Patchwork Parlour B&B, 109 Petoskey Ave US 31 , Charlevoix, 49720, 616-547-5788
Algomah Wheelhouse Inn, 333 North Huron, Cheboygan, 49721, 616-627-3543
Bonnymill Inn, 710 Broad St., Chesaning, 48616
Clinton Inn, 104 W. Michigan Ave., Clinton, 49236, 517-456-4151
Chandelier Guest House, 1567 Morgan Rd., Clio, 48420, 313-687-6061
Batavia Inn, 1824 W Chicago Rd, Coldwater, 49036, 517-278-5146
Our Old House B&B, 285 Mill St., Constantine, 49403, 616-435-5365
Crystal Inn B&B, 600 Marquette Ave, Crystal Falls, 49920, 906-875-6369
Oakbrook Inn, 7256 E. Court St., Davison, 48423, 313-658-1546
Dearborn Inn, 200301 Oakwood Blvd., Dearborn, 48124, 313-271-2700
Village Green, P.O. Box 1731, Dearborn, 48121, 313-561-6041
Blanche House Inn, 506 Parkview, Detroit, 48214, 313-822-7090
Bannicks B&B, 4608 Michigan Rd., M-9, Dimondale, 48821, 517-646-0224
Rosemont Inn, 83 Lake Shore Dr., Douglas, 49406, 616-857-2637
Dundee Guest House, The, 522 Tecumseh (M-50), Dundee, 48131, 313-529-5706
Easterly Inn, P.O. Box 366, East Jordan, 49727, 616-536-3434
Coleman Corners B&B, 7733 Old M-78, East Lansing, 48823, 517-339-9360
East Tawas Junction B&B, 514 West Bay, East Tawas, 48730, 517-362-8006
Sunrise B&B, Box 52, Eastport, 49627, 616-599-2706
Torch Lake Sunrise B&B, P.O. Box 52, Eastport, 49627, 616-599-2706
Cairn House B&B, 8160 Cairn Hwy, Elk Rapids, 49629, 616-264-8994
Widows Walk, 603 River St., Elk Rapids, 49629, 616-264-5767
Ellsworth House, Dixon, Rt 1 204 Lake St, Ellsworth, 49729, 616-588-7001
House on the Hill, P.O. Box 206, Lake St., Ellsworth, 49729, 616-588-6304
Lavender Hill B&B, Rt 1. Box 92, Ellsworth, 49729, 616-588-7755
Lotus Inn, 2310 Lotus Dr., Erie, 48133, 313-848-5785
B&B at Lynch's Dream, 22177 80th Ave., Evart, 49631, 616-734-5989
Crane House, 6051 - 124th Ave., Fennville, 49408, 616-561-6931
J. Paules' Fenn Inn, 2254 S 58th St, Fennville, 49408, 616-561-2836
Kingsley House, The, 626 West Main St., Fennville, 49408, 616-561-6425
Porches B&B, The, 2297 Lakeshore Dr, Fennville, 49408, 616-543-4162
Pine Ridge, N-10345 Old US 23, Fenton, 48430, 313-629-8911
Courtyard, The, G-3202 W. Court St., Flint, 48532, 313-238-5510
Botsford Inn, 28000 Grand River Ave., Framington Hills, 48824, 313-474-4800
B&B at The Pines, 327 Ardussi St., Frankenmuth, 48734, 517-652-9019
Bavarian Town B&B, 206 Beyerlein St, Frankenmuth, 48734, 517-652-8057
Frankenmuth Bender Haus, 337 Trinklein St, Frankenmuth, 48734, 517-652-8897
Franklin Haus, 216 S. Franklin St., Frankenmuth, 48734, 517-652-3383
Kueffner Haus B&B, 176 Parker St, Frankenmuth, 48734, 517-652-6839
Hotel Frankfort, Main St., Frankfort, 49635, 616-882-7271
Morningside B&B, Box 411, 219 Leelanau, Frankfort, 49635, 616-352-4008
Trillium, 611 S. Shore Dr., Frankfort, 49635, 616-352-4976
Village Park B&B, 60 West Park, Fruitport, 49415, 616-865-6289
Byrd House, The, 11483 E. G Ave., Galesburg, 49053, 616-665-7052
Summer House, P.O. Box 107, State St, Garden, 49835, 906-644-2457
Heritage House B&B, 521 E. Main St., Gaylord, 49735, 517-732-1199
Norden Hem Resort, P.O. Box 623, Gaylord, 49735, 517-732-6794
Walker's White Gull B&B, 5926 Hwy M-22, Glen Arbor, 49636, 616-334-4486
White Gull Inn, P.O. Box 351, Glenn Arbor, 49636, 616-334-4486
Kal-Haven B&B, 23491 Paulson Rd., Gobles, 49055
Country Inn of Grand Blanc, 6136 S. Belsay Rd., Grand Blanc, 48439, 313-694-6749
Boyden House Inn B&B, 301 South 5th St., Grand Haven, 49417, 616-846-3538
Harbor House Inn, 114 S. Harbor Dr., Grand Haven, 49417, 800-841-0610
Highland Park Hotel B&B, 1414 Lake Ave., Grand Haven, 49417, 616-842-6483
Washington Street Inn, 608 Washington St, Grand Haven, 49417, 616-842-1075
Lakeview Inn, P.O. Box 297, Grand Marais, 49839, 906-494-2612
Fountain Hill B&B, 222 Fountain, NE, Grand Rapids, 49503, 616-458-6621
Heald-Lear House, 455 College Ave, SE, Grand Rapids, 49503, 616-451-4859
Gibson House, The, 311 W Washington, Greenville, 48838, 616-7546691
Winter Inn, 100 N. Lafayette, Greenville, 48838
Wellock Inn, 404 S. Huron Ave., Harbor Beach, 48441, 517-479-3645
Four Acres B&B, 684 W. Bluff Dr., Harbor Springs, 49740, 616-525-6076
Harbour Inn, Beach Dr., Harbor Springs, 49740, 616-526-2107
Kimberly Country Estate, 2287 Bester Rd, Harbor Springs, 49740, 616-526-7646
Main Street B&B, 403 E Main St, Harbor Springs, 49740, 616-526-7782

Red Geranium Inn, 508 E. Main St. (M-72), Harrisville, 48740, 517-724-6153
Widow's Watch B&B, P.O. Box 245, Harrisville, 48740, 517-724-5465
Rooms At "The Inn", 515 State St., Hart, 49420, 616-873-2448
Farmstead B&B, 13501 Highland Rd., Hartland, 49353, 313-887-6086
McIntyre B&B, 13 E. 13th St., Holland, 49423, 616-392-9886
Old Holland Inn, 133 W. 11th St., Holland, 49423
Old Wing Inn, 5298 E. 147th Ave., Holland, 49423, 616-392-7362
Side Porch B&B, The, 120 College St., Holly, 48442, 313-634-0740
Grist Guest House, 310 E. Main St., Homer, 49245, 517-568-4063
Hansen's Guest House, 102 W. Adams, Homer, 49245, 517-568-3001
Wellman Accommodations, 205 Main St., Horton, 49246, 517-563-2231
Charleston House B&B, 803 W. Lakeshore Dr., Houghton, 49931, 906-482-7790
Sutton's Weed Farm B&B, 18736 Quaker Rd, Hudson, 49247, 517-547-6302
Old Octagon House, 595 - 24th Ave, Hudsonville, 49426, 616-896-9941
Betsie Valley B&B, 4440 US-31 South, Interlochen, 49643, 616-275-7624
Interlochen Aire, 4550 State Park Hwy., Interlochen, 49643, 616-276-6941
Union Hill Inn, 306 Union, Ionia, 48846, 616-527-0955
Pine Willow B&B, 600 Selden Rd, Iron River, 49935, 906-265-4287
Chaffin's Balmoral Farm, 1245 W. Washington Rd., Ithaca, 48847, 517-875-3410
Munro House B&B, 202 Maumee St., Jonesville, 49250, 517-849-9292
Bartlett-Upjohn House, 229 Stuart Ave, Kalamazoo, 49007, 616-342-0230
Kalamazoo House, 447 W. South St., Kalamazoo, 49007, 616-343-5426
Stuart Avenue Inn B&B, 405 Stuart Ave., Kalamazoo, 49007, 616-342-0230
Belknap's Garnet House, 237 Stuart Ave., Kearsarge, 49942, 906-337-5607
B & B In The Pines, 1940 Schneider Park Rd., Lake City, 49651, 616-839-4876
Centennial Inn, Rt. 1, Box 251, Lake Leelanau, 49653, 616-271-6460
Centennial Inn, 251 Alpers Rd, Lake Leelanau, 49653, 616-271-6460
Creative Holiday Lodge, 1000 Calumet St., Lake Linden, 49945, 906-296-0113
Sunset Cove, 10391 Edgelake Dr., Lakeland, 48143, 313-231-3802
White Rabbit Inn, 14634 Red Arrow Hwy, Lakeside, 49116, 616-469-4620
Stagecoach Stop B&B, Box 18, 4819 Leonard Rd, Lamont, 49430, 616-677-3940
Bungalow B&B, Route 1, Box 123, Lanse, 49946, 906-524-7595
Maplewood B&B, 15945 Wood Rd., Lansing, 48906, 517-485-1426
Hart House, 244 W Park St, Lapeer, 48446, 313-667-9106
Keweenaw House B&B, 209 Pewabic St., Laurium, 49913, 906-337-4822
Laurium Manor B&B, 320 Tamarack St, Laurium, 49913, 906-337-2549
Oak Cove Resort, 58881 46th St., Lawrence, 49064, 616-674-8228
Springbrook B&B, 28143 Springbrook Dr., Lawton, 49065, 616-624-6359
Highlands, The, P.O. Box 101, Leland, 49654, 616-256-7632
Manitou Manor, P.O. Box 864, Leland, 49654, 616-256-7712
Riverside Inn, 302 River St., Leland, 49654, 616-256-9971
Gorton House, Wolf Lake Dr., Lewiston, 49756, 517-786-2764
Lakeview Hills Country Inn, P.O. Box 365, Lewiston, 49756, 517-786-2000
Centennial B&B, P.O. Box 54, Lexington, 48450, 313-359-8762
Governor's Inn B&B, P.O. Box 471, Lexington, 48450, 313-359-5770
West Wind B&B, 7156 Huron Ave., Lexington, 48450, 313-359-5772
West Wind B&B, P.O. Box 344, Lexington, 48450, 313-359-5772
McGee Homestead B&B, 2534 Alden Nash NE, Lowell, 49331, 616-897-8142
1880 Inn On The Hill, 716 E Ludington Ave, Ludington, 49431, 616-845-6458
B&B at Ludington, 2458 S. Beaune Rd., Ludington, 49431, 616-843-9768
Doll House Inn, 709 E. Ludington Ave., Ludington, 49431, 616-843-2286
Hamlin Lake Cottage B&B, 7035 Harvey Rd., Ludington, 49431
Inland Sea Getaway, 5393 S. Lakeshore Dr., Ludington, 49431, 616-845-7569
Inn at Ludington, The, 701 E. Ludington Ave., Ludington, 49431, 616-845-7055
Ludington House, 501 E. Ludington Ave., Ludington, 49431, 616-845-7769
Snyder's Shoreline Inn, 903 W. Ludington Ave., Ludington, 49431
Bay View at Mackinac, P.O. Box 448, Mackinac Island, 49757, 615-298-2759
Bogan Lane Inn, P.O. Box 482, Mackinac Island, 49757, 906-847-3439
Inn on Mackinac, Mackinac Island, 49757
Metivier Inn, Box 285, Mackinac Island, 49757, 906-847-6234
Cedar Bend Farm, 1021 Doerr Rd., Mancelona, 49659, 616-587-5709
1879 E.E. Douville House, 111 Pine St., Manistee, 49660
E. E. Douville House, 111 Pine St., Manistee, 49660, 616-723-8654
Gubalt's B&B, 450 Cedar St., Manistee, 49660, 616-723-2006
Manistee Country House, 1130 Lakeshore Rd., Manistee, 49660, 616-723-2367
Margaret's B&B, 230 Arbutus, Box 344, Manistique, 49854, 906-341-5147
Country Cottage B&B, 135 E. Harbor Hwy., Maple City, 49664, 616-228-5328
Leelanau Country Inn, 149 E. Harbor Highway, Maple City, 49664, 616-228-5060
Heather House, 409 N. Main St., Marine City, 48039, 313-765-3175
Blueberry Ridge B&B, 18 Oak Dr., Marquette, 49855, 906-249-9246
McCarthy's Bear Creek Inn, 15230 "C" Dr. N., Marshall, 49068, 616-781-8383
National House Inn, 102 S. Parkview, Marshall, 49068, 616-781-7374
Helmer House Inn, Route 3, County Rd. 417, McMillan, 49853, 906-586-3204
Blue Lake Lodge B&B, P.O. Box 1, Mecosta, 49332, 616-972-8391
Arizona East, 3528 Thornville Rd, Metamora, 48455, 313-678-3107
Cottage On The Bay B&B, HCR-1, Box 960, Michigamme, 49861, 906-323-6191
Castle B&B, The, 1298 W. Sugnet, Midland, 48640, 517-8359398
Jay's B&B, 4429 Bay City Rd., Midland, 48640, 517-631-0470
Hibbard Tavern, 115 E Summit, Milford, 48042, 313-685-1435
Morning Glory Inn, 8709 Old Channel Trail, Montague, 49437, 616-894-8237
Country Chalet, 723 S. Meridian Rd., Mount Pleasant, 48858, 517-772-9259
Blue Country B&B, 1415 Holton Rd (M-120), Muskegon, 49445, 616-744-2555

Village B&B, 1135 Fifth St., Muskegon, 49440, 616-726-4523
Tall Oaks Inn Bed & Breakf, Box 6, Grand Beach, New Buffalo, 49117, 616-469-0097
Macleod House, The, Rt 2, Box 943, Newberry, 49868, 906-2933841
Woods & Hearth B&B, 950 S. Third St., Niles, 49120, 616-683-0876
Yesterday's Inn, 518 N. 4th, Niles, 49120, 616-683-6079
Birch Brook, 310 S. Peterson Park Rd, Northport, 49670, 616-386-5188
Mapletree Inn B&B, Rt. 1, Box 169-F, M-22, Northport, 49670, 616-386-5260
North Shore Inn, 12794 County Rd. 640, Northport, 49670
Plum Lane Inn, P.O. Box 74, Northport, 49670, 616-386-5774
Vintage House B&B, Box 424, 102 Shabwasung, Northport, 49670, 616-386-7228
Wood How Lodge, Route 1 Box 44E, Northport, 49670, 616-386-7194
Atchison House, 501 W. Dunlap St., Northville, 48167, 313-349-3340
Stonegate Inn, 10831 Cleveland, Nunica, 49448, 616-837-9267
Frieda's B&B, 13141 Omena Point Rd., Omena, 49674, 616-386-7274
Haus Austrian, 4626 Omena Point Rd., Omena, 49674, 616-386-7338
Omena Shores B&B, P.O. Box 15, Omena, 49674, 616-386-7311
Lake Breeze House, 5089 Main St., Onekama, 49675, 616-889-4969
Onekama, Lake Breeze House, Onekama, 49675, 616-889-4969
Huron House, 3124 N. US-23, Oscoda, 48750, 517-739-9255
Mulberry House, 1251 Shiawassee St., Owasso, 48867, 517-723-4890
Sylverlynd, 3452 McBride Rd., Owosso, 48667, 517-723-1267
Victorian Splendor, 426 N. Washington St., Owosso, 48867, 517-725-5168
Carrington's Country House, 43799 60th Ave., Paw Paw, 49079, 616-657-5321
Candlewyck House B&B, The, 438 E. Lowell St., Pentwater, 49449, 800-348-5827
Historic Nickerson Inn, P.O. Box 109, Pentwater, 49449, 616-869-6731
Pentwater Abbey, P.O. Box 735, Pentwater, 49449, 616-869-4409
Bear & The Bay, 421 Charlevoix Ave., Petoskey, 49770, 616-347-6077
Bear River Valley, 03636 Bear River Rd., Petoskey, 49770, 616-348-2046
Benson House, 618 E. Lake St., Petoskey, 49770, 616-347-1338
Cozy Spot, 1145 Kalamazoo, Petoskey, 49770, 616-347-3869
Gull's Way, 118 Boulder Lane, Petoskey, 49770, 616-347-9891
Pebble Beach, 496 Rosedale Ave., Petoskey, 49770, 616-347-1903
Stafford's Bay View Inn, P.O. Box 3 G, Petoskey, 49770, 616-347-2771
Bunn-Pher Hill, 11745 Spencer Lane, Pinckney, 48169, 313-8789236
1882 John Crispe House B&B, 404 E. Bridge St., Plainwell, 49080, 616-685-1293
Mayflower B&B Hotel, 827 W. Ann Arbor Trail, Plymouth, 48170, 313-453-1620
Garfield Inn, 8544 Lake St., Port Austin, 48467
Lake Street Manor B&B, 8569 Lake St. (M-53), Port Austin, 49467, 517-738-7720
Questover Inn, 8510 Lake St., Port Austin, 48467, 517-738-5253
Webber House, 527 James St., Portland, 48875, 517-647-4671
Spring Brook Inn, P.O. Box 390, Prudenville, 48651, 517-366-6347
Village Rose B&B, 161 N. Monroe, Rockford, 49341, 616-866-7041
Country Heritage B&B, 64707 Mound Rd., Romeo, 48065, 313-752-2879
Tall Trees, Route 2, 323 Birch Rd., Roscommon, 48653, 517-821-5592
Double J Resort Ranch, P.O. Box 94, Rothbury, 49452, 616-894-4444
Brockway House B&B, 1631 Brockway, Saginaw, 48602, 517-792-0746
Heart House, 419 N. Michigan, Saginaw, 48602, 517-753-3145
Montague Inn, 1581 S. Washington Ave., Saginaw, 48601, 517-752-3939
Murphy Inn, 505 Clinton Ave., Saint Clair, 48079, 313-329-7118
Colonial House Inn, 90 N. State St., Saint Ignace, 49781, 906-643-6900
Homestead B&B, 9279 Macon Rd, Saline, 48176, 313-429-9625
Bayside Inn, 618 Water St., Saugatuck, 49453, 616-857-1870
Beechwood Manor, 736 Pleasant St., Saugatuck, 49453, 616-857-1587
Fairchild House, P.O. Box 416, Saugatuck, 49453, 616-857-5985
Marywood Manor, 236 Mary St., Saugatuck, 49453, 616-857-4771
Newnham Inn, Box 1106, 131 Griffith S, Saugatuck, 49453, 616-857-4249
Park House, The, 888 Holland St., Saugatuck, 49453, 616-857-4535
Wickwood Country Inn, P.O. Box 1019, Saugatuck, 49408, 616-857-1465
Kirby House, The, Box 1174, 294 W.Center , Saugatuck (Douglas), 49453, 616-857-2904
Rummel's Tree Haven, 41 N. Beck St., Sebewaing, 48759, 517-883-2450
Elmhurst B&B, 5520 Marshville Rd., Shelby, 49455, 616-861-4846
A Country Place B&B, Rt. 5, Box 43, N. Shore, South Haven, 49090, 616-637-5523
Country Place B&B, Rt. 5, Box 43, South Haven, 49090, 616-637-5523
Elmhurst Farm Inn, Rt. 4, Box 261, South Haven, 49090, 616-637-4633
Last Resort B&B Inn, 86 N. Shore Dr, South Haven, 49090, 616-637-8943
N. Beach Inn & Restaurant, 51 North Shore Dr., South Haven, 49090, 616-637-6738
Ross B&B House, 229 Michigan Ave., South Haven, 49090, 616-637-2256
Seymour House, The, 1248 Adams Rd., South Haven, 49090, 616-227-3918
Alberties Waterfront, 18470 Main St-N. Shores, Spring Lake, 49456, 616-846-4016
Seascape B&B, 20009 Breton, Spring Lake, 49456, 616-842-8409
Shifting Sands, 19343 N. Shore Dr., Spring Lake, 49456, 616-842-3594
McCann House, The, P.O. Box 241, St. James, 49782, 616-448-2387
South Cliff Inn B&B, 1900 Lakeshore Dr., St. Joseph, 49085, 616-983-4881
Clifford Lake Hotel, 561 W. Clifford Lake, Stanton, 48888, 517-831-5151
Christmere House Inn, 110 Pleasant St., Sturgis, 49091, 616-651-8303
Lee Point Inn on W. Grand, Rt. 2, Box 374B, Suttons Bay, 49682, 616-271-6770
Open Windows B&B, P.O. Box 698, Suttons Bay, 49682, 616-271-4300
Pink Palace Farms, 6095 Baldwin Rd., Swartz Creek, 48473, 313-655-4076
Sarah's Countryside B&B, 1461 S. Lorenz, Tawas City, 48763, 517-362-7123
Boulevard Inn, 904 W. Chicago Blvd., Tecumseh, 49286, 517-423-5169
Bowers Harbor B&B, 13972 Peninsula Dr., Traverse City, 49684, 616-223-7869
Cherry Knoll Farm, 2856 Hammond Rd., E., Traverse City, 49684, 616-947-9806

Cider House B&B, 5515 Barney Rd., Traverse City, 49684, 616-947-2833
L'DA RU B&B, 4370 N. Spider Lake Rd., Traverse City, 49684, 616-946-8999
Mission Pt. B&B, 20202 Center Rd., Traverse City, 49684, 616-223-7526
Neahtawanta Inn, 1308 Neahtawanta Rd., Traverse City, 49684, 616-223-7315
Peninsula Manor, 8880 Peninsula Dr., Traverse City, 49684, 616-223-7526
Queen Anne's Castle, 500 Webster, Traverse City, 49684, 616-946-1459
Stonewall Inn, The, 17898 Smokey Hollow Rd., Traverse City, 49684, 616-223-7800
Tall Ship Malabar, 13390-D W. Bayshore Dr., Traverse City, 49684, 616-941-2000
Victoriana 1898, The, 622 Washington St., Traverse City, 49684, 616-929-1009
Wooden Spoon B&B, 316 W. 7th St., Traverse City, 49684, 616-947-0357
Bear Haven, 2947 - 4th St., Trenton, 48183, 313-675-4844
Victorian Villa Inn, The, 601 N. Broadway St., Union City, 49094, 517-741-7383
Gordon Beach Inn, 16240 Lakeshore Rd., Union Pier, 49129, 616-469-3344
Pine Garth Inn, P.O. Box 347, Union Pier, 49129, 616-469-1642
Masters House B&B, 2253 North Shore, Walloon Lake, 49796, 616-535-2294
Walloon Lake Inn, P.O. Box 85, Walloon Lake Village, 49796, 616-535-2999
Basic Brewer B&B, 5174 Royce, Webberville, 48892, 517-468-3970
Lake Webb House, P.O. Box 127, Weld, 48285
Curtis B&B, 4262 S. M-76, West Branch, 48661, 517-345-1411
Green Inn, 4045 West M-76, West Branch, 48661, 517-345-0334
Rose Brick Inn, 124 E. Houghton Ave., West Branch, 48661, 517-345-3702
Shack Country Inn, The, 2263 W. 14th St., White Cloud, 49349, 616-924-6683
River Haven, 9222 St. Joe River Rd., White Pigeon, 49099, 616-483-9104
Timekeepers Inn, 303 Mears Ave., Whitehall, 49461, 616-894-5169

Minnesota

ANNANDALE

Thayer Inn "Victorian B&B"
60 West Elm St., Highway 55 at
Elm St., 55302
800-944-6595
Sharon & Warren Gammell
All year

$ B&B
13 rooms, 13 pb
Visa, MC, Discover, •
C-yes/S-yes/P-ltd/H-no

Full breakfast
Restaurant - all meals
Aft. tea, snacks
comp. wine, bar service
sitting room, sauna

Enjoy Victorian ambiance amidst gracious antique furnishings in restored 1895 inn. Surrounded by lakes, near Mall of America & Twin Cities. **10% off 1st night, mention ad**

CHASKA

Bluff Creek Inn
1161 Bluff Creek Dr., 55318
612-445-2735
Gary & Anne Delaney
All year

$$$ B&B
5 rooms, 2 pb
Visa, MC, *Rated*,
C-ltd/S-ltd/P-ask/H-ltd

Full breakfast
Comp. dessert
Catered gourmet dinners
summer kitchen, parlor
min. from Arboretum

*Enjoy 19th century charm & hospitality in this restored country inn in Minnesota River Valley.
Canterbury Downs. Hollyhock Cottage: large whirlpool suite w/fireplace & deck.*

CROOKSTON

Elm Street Inn
422 Elm St., 56716
218-281-2343 800-568-4476
John & Sheryl Winters
All year

$$ B&B
4 rooms, 2 pb
Visa, *Rated*, •
C-yes/S-no/P-no/H-no
Spanish, French

Full breakfast
Lunch, dinner, Snacks
Sitting room, library
bicycles, pool next door
wine license, fax

*Lovingly restored 1910 home w/antiques. Candlelight breakfast, romantic dinners w/wine
service. Limo to casino, sunporch & gift shop. Murder mystery dinners.* **free bottle wine**

Bakketopp Hus B&B, Fergus Falls, MN

FERGUS FALLS

Bakketopp Hus B&B	$$ B&B	Full breakfast
RR 2, Box 187A, 56537	3 rooms, 3 pb	Aft. tea, snacks
218-739-2915	*Rated*	Sitting room
Dennis & Judy Nims	C-ltd/S-no/P-no/H-no	hot tubs
All year		

Wooded hillside lake view. Listen to loons at dusk, enjoy flowers in tiered gardens or relax in spa. Golf, antiques & restaurants nearby.

GRAND MARAIS

Gunflint Lodge	$$ EP,MAP,AP	Full breakfast
Box 100 GT, 750 Gunflint Trail,	18 rooms, 18 pb	Lunch, dinner, tea
55604	Visa, MC, AmEx, *Rated*,	Sauna, outdoor hot tubs
800-328-3325	•	sitting room, sauna
Bruce & Susan Kerfoot	C-yes/S-yes/P-yes/H-yes	dog sled rides in winter
All year		

Family style Northwest country inn, adjacent to famed Boundary Waters Canoe Area, hiking, fishing, wilderness activities program. Cross-country skiing.

Pincushion Mountain B&B	$$ B&B	Full breakfast
220 Gunflint Trail, 55604	4 rooms, 4 pb	Sauna, hiking, biking
218-387-1276 800-542-1226	Visa, MC, Disc, *Rated*, •	cross-country skiing
Scott Beattie	C-ltd/S-no/P-no/H-no	44 acres, sitting room
All year except April		

B&B sits on ridge of Sawtooth Mountains overlooking north shore of Lake Superior 1,000 feet below. Hiking, mountain biking, cross-country ski trails at doorstep. Bike and ski rentals.

HASTINGS

Thornwood Historic Inns	$$$ B&B	Full breakfast
315 Pine, 620 Ramsey, 55033	15 rooms, 15 pb	Lunch, dinner
612-437-3297 800-992-4667	Most CC, *Rated*, •	Snacks, library
Dick & Pam Thorsen	C-yes/S-no/P-no/H-yes	central AC
All year		quiet, private

*Two 1880 National Register Mansions, restored to grandeur but including double whirlpools, wood-burning fireplaces, breakfast to your schedule. **3rd night 50% off except Oct.***

LANESBORO

Mrs. B's Historic Inn
P.O. Box 411, 55949
101 Parkway
507-467-2154 800-657-4710
Bill Sermeus & Mimi Abell
All year

$$
10 rooms, 10 pb
Rated, •
C-ltd/S-ltd

Full breakfast
Dinner by resv.
Comp. sherry, chocolate
sitting room, library
tennis & golf nearby

Nestled deep in Root River Valley; 1872 limestone bldg. in village on National Register. Serene; rural; famous regional cuisine. Restaurant operates Wed-Sun, 5 course dinners.

LUTSEN

Lindgren's B&B
P.O. Box 56, 55612
County Road 35
218-663-7450
Bob & Shirley Lindgren
All year

$$$ B&B
4 rooms, 4 pb
Visa, MC, *Rated*, •
C-ltd/S-ltd/P-no/H-no

Full breakfast
Snacks
Restaurant nearby
sauna, horseshoes
volleyball court

Gracious and very charming 1920s log home on walkable shores of Lake Superior. Gourmet breakfast served fireside with full lake view. Golf, hike, ski, bike, fish, skyride.

MARSHALL

Babette's Inn
113 Park Ave./Marshall, 308 S.
Tyler St./Tyler, 56258
507-247-3962
Jim & Alice Johnson
All year

$$ B&B
3 rooms, 3 pb
Visa, MC
C-yes/S-ltd/P-no/H-no

Full breakfast
Gourmet dinner
Sleep & dine package
comp. coffee/tea
gift shop

Historic home in Danish-American village. Antiques, foreign films, vintage bicycles, special occasion gourmet dinners enhance the small town experience.

MINNEAPOLIS

1900 Dupont
1900 Dupont Ave. S., 55403
612-374-1973
Chris Viken
All year

$$ B&B
4 rooms, 2 pb
•
S-no/P-no/H-no

Continental plus
Library

Gracious antique-filled 1896 home with 3-story center staircase, library and solarium. Neighborhood of mansions. Walking distance to downtown, restaurants.

Elmwood House
1 East Elmwood Pl., 55423
612-822-4558 612-869-3152
Barbara & Bob Schlosser
All year

$$ B&B
2 rooms
Visa, MC, *Rated*
C-yes/S-no/P-no/H-no

Continental plus
Sitting room

1887 Norman chateau. Historical home on National Register. 3 miles from downtown. 10 miles from Mall of America and airport. Near walks and nature trails. **7th night free**

Evelo's B&B
2301 Bryant Ave. S., 55405
612-374-9656
Sheryl & David Evelo
All year

$ B&B
3 rooms
AmEx
C-yes/S-no/P-no/H-no

Continental plus
TV, refrigerator
coffee maker
air conditioning

1897 Victorian, period furnishings. Located on bus line, walk to Guthrie Theater, Minneapolis Art Institute, children's theater. Near historic Lake District.

MINNEAPOLIS

Nan's B&B	$ B&B	Full breakfast
2304 Fremont Ave. S., 55405	3 rooms	Beautiful porch
612-377-5118 800-214-5118	Visa, MC, •	antique furnishings
Nan Zosel & Jim Zosel	C-yes/S-yes/P-ask/H-no	sitting room w/woodstove
All year		

Comfortable urban 1890s Victorian family home; near best theatres, galleries, shopping in Minneapolis. Friendly, informative hosts. **Weekly rate: 1 night free.**

NEW PRAGUE

Schumacher's New Prague	$$$ EP	Restaurant, bar
212 W. Main St., 56071	11 rooms, 11 pb	Breakfast, lunch, dinner
612-758-2133 FAX:758-2400	Most CC, *Rated*, •	Comp. wine, piano
John & Kathleen Schumacher	C-ltd/S-yes/P-no/H-ltd	front porch, gift shop
All year		whirlpools, fireplaces

Eleven European-decorated sleeping rooms named after the months of the year. Restaurant serves Czechoslovakian and German cuisine seven days a week. AAA 3-Star, Mobil 3-Star.

RUSHFORD

Meadows Inn B&B	$$$ B&B	Full breakfast
P.O. Box 703, 55971	5 rooms, 4 pb	Aft. tea, comp. wine
900 Pine Meadow Lane	Visa, MC, Dis. *Rated*,	Sitting room, bicycles
507-864-2378	C-yes/S-no/P-no/H-no	tennis court, jacuzzi
Nancy Johnson		pool, bridal suite
All year		

Luxurious European charm in pastoral setting of hills, pine forest and meadows. Gateway to state Root River Bike Trail. **3rd night 50% off**

SPRING VALLEY

Chase's	$$ B&B	Full farm breakfast
508 N. Huron Ave., 55975	5 rooms, 5 pb	Comp. tea
507-346-2850	Visa, MC, *Rated*, •	Library, sitting room
Bob & Jeannine Chase	C-yes/S-no/P-no/H-no	fishing, quiet, solitude
May–October		golf, bike, hike

Antiques throughout Chase's 19th-century mansion. Sleep in solitude, breakfast in quietness. Scenic southeastern Minnesota bluff country. Amish area.

ST. PAUL

Chatsworth B&B	$$ B&B	Continental plus
984 Ashland Ave., 55104	5 rooms, 3 pb	Tea, coffee, cocoa
612-227-4288	*Rated*	Sitting room
Donna & Earl Gustafson	C-ltd	library
All year		2 rooms with whirlpools

Peaceful retreat in city near Governor's Mansion. Whirlpool baths, down comforters, lace curtains. Excellent restaurants and unique shops within walking distance.

ST. PETER

Park Row B&B	$$ B&B	Full breakfast
525 W. Park Row, 56082	4 rooms	Snacks, refreshments
507-931-2495	Discover, *Rated*, •	Sitting room
Ann L. Burckhardt	C-ltd/S-no/P-no/H-no	library
February–December		

Queen Anne home in quiet college town, beautifully decorated. Down comforters. Cookbook collection. Innkeeper is food writer, loves to talk about travel and cookery.

STILLWATER

Lowell Inn
102 N. Second St., 55082
612-439-1100
The Palmer Family
All year

$$$ B&B
21 rooms, 21 pb
Visa, MC, *Rated*, •
C-yes/S-yes/P-no/H-yes
German

Full breakfast
Lunch, dinner, bar
Jacuzzi

Colonial country inn nestled in history-filled Stillwater, Minnesota near the bluff of St. Croix River. Elegant dining and accommodations. **Complimentary bottle of wine**

Rivertown Inn B&B, The
306 W. Olive St., 55082
612-430-2955 800-562-3632
Chuck & Judy Dougherty
All year

$ B&B
13 rooms, 13 pb
Visa, MC, *Rated*, •
C-ltd/S-no/P-no/H-no

Full breakfast
Comp. wine on weekends
Sitting areas, A/C
screen porch, gazebo
whirlpool bath, bicycles

Guest rooms decorated w/fine antiques; all with private baths, some with double whirlpools & fireplaces. 4 blocks from Historic Main St. **2nd night 50% mid-wk**

VERGAS

Log House on Spirit Lake
P.O. Box 130, 56587
East Sprit Lake
218-342-2318
Yvonne & Lyle Tweten
May–October

$$ B&B
4 rooms, 4 pb
Visa, MC, *Rated*, •
C-ltd/S-ltd/P-no/H-no
French

Full breakfast
Dinner w/notice, snacks
sitting room
tennis nearby

Romantic, elegant adult retreat in restored 1889 loghouse overlooking lake. Tranquility & pampered comfort with the charm of a bygone era. 2 rooms have a whirlpool/fireplace.

More Inns . . .

Afton House Inn, Hwy 95, Afton, 612-436-8883
Fountain View Inn, 310 N. Washington Ave., Albert Lea, 56007, 507-377-9425
Carrington House B&B, Route 5, Box 88, Alexandria, 56308, 612-846-7400
Robards House, The, 518 Lincoln Ave., Alexandria, 56308, 612-763-4073
Rainy River Lodge, Baudette, 56623, 218-634-2730
Pine Springs Inn, 448 Center Ave. N., Blooming Prairie, 55917, 507-583-4411
Breezy Point Resort, P.O. Box 70, Breezy Point Place, 56472, 218-562-7811
Inn on the Farm, 6150 Summit Dr., N., Brooklyn Center, 55430, 612-569-6330
Inn on the Green, Rt. 1 Box 205, Caledonia, 55921, 507-724-2818
Basswood Hill's Farm, Route 1, Box 331, Cannon Falls, 55009, 507-778-3259
Quill & Quilt, B&B, 615 W. Hoffman St., Cannon Falls, 55009, 507-263-5507
Carousel Rose Inn, 217 W. Third St., Carver, 55315, 612-448-5847
Lund's Guest House, 500 Winona St. SE, Chatfield, 55923, 507-867-4003
Pillow, Pillar & Pine, 419 Main St., Cold Spring, 56320, 612-332-6774
Wilkinson-Thorson, 327 Houston Ave., Crookston, 56716
Hallet House, P.O. 247, Crosby, 56441, 218-546-5433
Lo-Kiandy Inn, Box 33, Crosslake, 56442, 218-692-2714
Walden Woods B&B, Route 1, Box 193, Deerwood, 56444, 612-692-4379
Eden Bed & Breakfast, RR 1, Box 215, Dodge Center, 55927, 507-527-2311
Ellery House, 28 S. 21st Ave. E., Duluth, 55812, 218-724-7639
Fitzger's Inn, 600 E. Superior St., Duluth, 55802, 218-722-8826
Mansion, 3600 London Rd., Duluth, 55804, 218-724-0739
Mathew S. Burrows 1890 Inn, 1632 E. 1st St., Duluth, 55812, 218-724-4991
Stanford Inn, 1415 Superior St., Duluth, 55805, 218-724-3044
Three Deer Haven, Hwy 169, Ely, 55731, 218-365-6464
Christopher Inn, 201 Mill St., Excelsior, 55331, 612-474-6816
Murray Street Gardens B&B, 22520 Murray St., Excelsior, 55331, 612-474-8089
Cherub Hill, 101 NW 1st. Ave., Faribault, 55021, 507-332-2024
Hutchinson House B&B, 305 NW 2nd St., Faribault, 55021, 507-332-7519
Peter's Sunset Beach Hotel, Rt. 2, Box 118, Glenwood, 56334, 612-634-4501
Cedar Knoll Farm, Rt. 2, Box 147, Good Thunder, 56037, 507-524-3813
Lakeside B&B, 113 W. 2nd St., Graceville, 56420, 612-748-7657
Bear Track Outfitting Co., Box 51, Grand Marais, 55604
Clearwater Lodge, 355-B Gunflint Trail, Grand Marais, 55604, 218-388-2254
East Bay Hotel, Box 246, Grand Marais, 55604, 218-387-2800
Naniboujou Lodge, Star Route 1, Box 505, Grand Marais, 55604, 218-387-2688
Superior Overlook B&B, Box 963, Grand Marais, 55604, 218-387-1571
Young's Island, Gunflint Tr. 67-1, Grand Marais, 55604, 218-388-4487

Hazlewood c/o Thorwood, 705 Vermillion, Hastings, 55033, 612-437-3297
River Rose c/o Thorwood, 705 Vermillion, Hastings, 55033, 612-437-3297
Thorwood Inn, 4th & Pine, Hastings, 55033, 612-437-3297
Triple L Farm, Rt. 1, Box 141, Hendricks, 56136, 507-275-3740
Lawndale Farm, Rt. 2, Box 50, Herman, 56248, 612-677-2687
B&B Lodge, Rt. 3, Box 178, Hinckley, 55037, 612-384-6052
Bunk House, The, 501 S. Jefferson, Houston, 55943, 507-896-2080
Trovall's Inn, Box 98, Hwy. 61, Hoveland, 55606, 218-475-2344
Jacob's Inn, 108 2nd Ave. NW, Kasson, 55944, 507-634-4920
Evergreen Knoll Acres, Rt. 1, Box 145, Lake City, 55041, 612-345-2257
Pepin House, 120 S. Prairie St., Lake City, 55041, 612-345-4454
Rahilly House, 304 S. Oak St., Lake City, 55041, 612-345-4664
Red Gables B&B Inn, 403 N. High St., Lake City, 55041, 612-345-2605
Victorian Bed & Breakfast, 620 South High St., Lake City, 55041, 612-345-2167
Sherwood Forest Lodge, 7669 Interlachen Rd., Lake Shore-Brainerd, 56401, 218-963-2516
Carrolton Country Inn, RR 2, Box 139, Lanesboro, 55949, 507-467-2257
Scanlan House B&b, 708 Park Ave. S., Lanesboro, 55949, 507-467-2158
Cosgrove, 228 S. Second St., Le Sueur, 56058, 612-665-2763
Birdwing Spa, Litchfield, 55355, 612-693-6064
Pine Edge Inn, 308 First St. SE, Little Falls, 56345, 612-632-6681
Caribou Lake B&B, N512 Co. Rd., Box 156, Lutsen, 55612, 218-663-7489
Mabel House B&B, 117 S. Main, Mabel, 55954, 507-493-5768
Grand Old Mansion, 501 Clay St., Mantorville, 55955, 507-635-3231
Asa Parker House B&B, 17500 St. Croix Trail N, Marine on the St. Croix, 55047, 612-433-5248
Savanna Portage Inn, HCR 4, Box 96, McGregor, 55760, 258-426-3500
Country House, The, Rt. 3 Box 110, Miltona, 56354, 218-943-2928
Le Blanc House, 302 University Ave., Minneapolis, 55413, 612-379-2570
Nicollet Island Inn, 95 Merriam, Nicollet Is, Minneapolis, 55401
American House, The, 410 E. Third St., Morris, 56267, 612-589-4054
Park Street Inn, The, Rt. 1, Box 254, Nevis, 56467], 612-599-4763
Schuyten Guest House, 257 Third Ave., Newport, 55055, 612-459-5698
Red Pine B&B, 15140 400th St., North Branch, 55056, 612-583-3326
Archer House, 212 Division St., Northfield, 55057, 507-645-5661
Lowell House, RR 2 Box 177, 531 Wood, Old Frontenac, 55026, 612-345-2111
Kettle Falls Hotel, Box 1272, Int'l Falls, Orr, 55771, 218-374-3511
Northrop House, 358 East Main St., Owattona, 55060
Dickson Viking Huss B&B, 202 E. 4th St., Park Rapids, 56470, 218-732-8089
Dorset Schoolhouse, P.O. Box 201, Park Rapids, 56470, 218-732-1377
Stonehouse B&B, HCR 2, Box 9, Pequot Lakes, 56472, 218-568-4255
Black Cow Inn, The, 535 6th St., Pine City, 55063, 612-629-7421
Calumet Inn, 104 W. Main, Pipestone, 56164, 507-825-5871
Inn Town Lodge, 205 Franklin St., Preston, 55965, 507-765-4412
Jail House, The, 109 Houston 3 NW, Preston, 55965, 507-765-2504
Sunnyside at Forestville, RR 2, Box 119, Preston, 55965, 507-765-3357
Rum River Country B&B, Rt. 6, Box 114, Princeton, 55371, 612-389-2679

Gunflint Lodge, Grand Marais, MN

Bunt's B&B, Lake Kabetogama, Ray, 56669, 218-875-3904
Candlelight Inn, The, 818 W. 3rd St., Red Wing, 55066, 612-388-8034
Pratt Taber Inn, 706 W. 4th, Red Wing, 55066, 612-388-5945
St. James Hotel, 406 Main St., Red Wing, 55066, 612-388-2846
Swanson-Johnson Inn, Rt. 2, Box 77, Red Wing, 55066, 612-388-3276
Canterbury Inn B&B, 723 2nd St. SW, Rochester, 55902, 507-289-5553
Prairie House Round Lake, RR 1, Box 105, Round Lake, 56167, 507-945-8934
Grant House, Box 87, Rush City, 55069, 612-358-4717
Sunwood Inn, Bandana Sq. 1010 Banda, Saint Paul, 55108
Palmer House Hotel, 500 Sinclair Lewis Ave., Sauk Centre, 56378, 612-352-3431
Country B&B, 32030 Ranch Tr., Shafer, 55074, 612-257-4773
Guest House B&B, 299 Outer Dr., Silver Bay, 55614, 218-226-4201
Inn At Palisade, The, 384 Hwy. 61 E., Silver Bay, 55614, 218-226-3505
Woodland Inn, The, Rt. 4, Box 68, Sleepy Eye, 56085, 507-794-5981
Spicer Castle, P.O. Box 307, Spicer, 56288, 612-796-5870
Touch Of The Past, 102 3rd Ave. SE, Spring Grove, 55974, 507-498-5146
Anchor Inn, Hwy. 4, RR, Spring Lake, 56680, 218-798-2718
Victorian Lace Inn, 1512 Whitewater Ave., St. Charles, 55972, 507-932-3054
Lamb's B&B, 29738 Island Lake Rd., St. Joseph, 56374, 612-363-7924
Como Villa, 1371 W. Nebraska Ave., St. Paul, 55108, 612-647-0471
Miller B&B, 887 James Ave., St. Paul, 55102, 612-227-1292
Prior's On Desoto, 1522 Desoto St., St. Paul, 55101, 612-774-2695
University Club, The, 420 Summit Ave., St. Paul, 55102, 612-222-1751
Kings Oakdale Park G.H., 6933 232nd Ave NE, Stacy, 55029, 612-462-5598
Heirloom Inn B&B, The, 1103 S. Third St, Stillwater, 55082, 612-430-2289
Outing Lodge at Pine Pt., 11661 Myeron Rd., Stillwater, 55082, 612-439-9747

Overlook Inn B&B, 210 E. Laurel, Stillwater, 55082, 612-439-3409
Wm. Sauntry Mansion, 626 N. Fourth St, Stillwater, 55082, 612-430-2653
Hudspeth House B&B, 21225 Victory Ln., Taylors Falls, 55084, 612-465-5811
Old Jail Company B&B, The, 100 Government Rd, Taylors Falls, 55084, 612-465-3112
Old Taylors Falls Jail, 102 Government Rd., Taylors Falls, 55084, 612-465-3112
Anderson House, 333 W. Main St., Wabasha, 55981, 612-565-4524
Chase On The Lake Lodge, P.O. Box 206, Walker, 56484, 218-547-1531
Peacecliff, HCR 73, Box 998D, Walker, 56484, 218-547-2832
Carriage House B&B, 420 Main, Winona, 55987, 507-452-8256
Hotel and Zach's, 3rd & Johnson, Winona, 55987, 507-452-5460

Mississippi

HOLLY SPRINGS

Hamilton Place
105 E. Mason Ave., 38635
601-252-4368
Linda & Jack Stubbs
All year

$$ B&B
3 rooms, 3 pb
Visa, MC
C-yes/S-yes/P-no/H-yes

Full breakfast
Sitting room, library
bicycles, swimming pool
antique shop

Antebellum home furnished with heirloom antiques. On National Historic Register; antique shop on premises; breakfast served in formal dining room or gazebo.

LONG BEACH

Red Creek Colonial Inn
7416 Red Creek Rd., 39560
601-452-3080 800-729-9670
Rebecca & Daniel Peranich
All year

$ B&B
3 rooms, 3 pb
•
C-yes/S-ltd/P-ltd

Continental plus
Coffee
afternoon tea

Three-story "raised French cottage" with 6 fireplaces, 64-foot porch, and many antiques. Situated amidst 11 acres of live oaks and magnolias near beaches.

LORMAN

Rosswood Plantation
Route 552, 39096
601-437-4215 800-533-5889
Jean & Walt Hylander
Exc. Jan. & Feb.

$$$ B&B
4 rooms, 4 pb
Visa, MC, Disc, *Rated*, •
C-yes/S-ltd/P-no/H-ltd

Full breakfast
Civil War library, piano
pool, whirlpool/spa
sitting room, TV, VCR

Classic 1857 mansion on a working plantation near Natchez. Ideal for honeymoons. Canopied beds, fine antiques, all conveniences. National Register. AAA rates 3 diamonds.

NATCHEZ

Briars Inn & Gardens, The
P.O. Box 1245, 39120
31 Irving Ln.
601-446-9654 FAX:445-6037
Newton Wilds & Robert Canon
All year

$$$ B&B
13 rooms, 13 pb
Visa, MC, AmEx, *Rated*,
•
C-ltd/S-yes/P-no/H-yes

Full 5-course breakfast
Bar service, snacks
Sitting room, library
swimming pool, porch
gardens

Circa 1812, unique retreat into 19th century splendor with modern amenities. National Register. 19 acres of gardens overlooking Mississippi River. Entirely antique-furnished.

NATCHEZ ————————————————

Hope Farm	$$$ B&B	Plantation breakfast
147 Homochitto St., 39120	4 rooms, 4 pb	Comp. refreshments
601-445-4848	*Rated*, •	Sitting room
Mrs. Ethel G. Banta	C-ltd/S-yes/P-no/H-no	library
All year		

Fine old southern mansion, circa 1775, on 20 acres including 10 acres of formal gardens. Antiques throughout.

Linden, circa 1790	$$$ B&B	Full southern breakfast
1 Linden Pl., 39120	7 rooms, 7 pb	Sitting room
601-445-5472	*Rated*, •	piano
Jeanette S. Feltus	C-ltd/S-yes/P-no/H-yes	
All year		

Antebellum home furnished with family heirlooms. Park-like setting of mossy live oaks. Occupied by same family since 1849. **Free bottle of wine**

PORT GIBSON ————————————————

Oak Square Plantation	$$$ B&B	Full breakfast
1207 Church St., 39150	11 rooms, 11 pb	Comp. wine & tea
601-437-4350 800-729-0240	Most CC, *Rated*, •	Victorian parlor
Mr. & Mrs. William Lum	C-yes/S-ltd/P-no/H-ltd	piano, TV, courtyard
All year		fountain, gazebo

Antebellum mansion in the town General Ulysses S. Grant said was "too beautiful to burn." Heirloom antiques. Canopied beds. Nat'l Register. AAA 4-diamond rated.

VICKSBURG ————————————————

Cedar Grove Mansion-Inn	$$$ B&B	Full breakfast
2200 Oak St., 39180	20 rooms, 20 pb	Restaurant 6pm-9pm
601-636-2800 800-862-1300	Visa, MC, *Rated*, •	Cocktails, mint juleps
Ted Mackey	C-ltd/S-ltd/H-yes	hot tubs, roof garden
All year	Spanish	pool, tennis, croquet

Antebellum mansion, ca. 1840. Exquisitely furnished w/many original antiques, gaslit chandeliers. Tennis court, croquet, river view roof garden. Relive "Gone With the Wind."

More Inns ...

Mount Holly, Box 140, Chatham, 38731, 601-827-2652
Amzi Love B&B, 305 S. 7th St., Columbus, 39701, 601-328-5413
Antebellum Homes, 906 - 3rd Ave., Columbus, 39701, 601-329-3533
Cartney-Hunt House, 408 S. 7th St., Columbus, 39701, 601-327-4259
Madison Inn, 822 Main St., Corinth, 38834, 601-287-7157
Springfield Plantation, Rt. 1 Box 201, Hwy 553, Fayette, 39069, 601-786-3802
Sassafras Inn B&B, P.O. Box 612, Hernando, 38632, 800-882-1897
Millsaps Buie House, 628 N. State St., Jackson, 39202, 601-352-0221
Burn, The, 712 N. Union St., Natchez, 39120, 601-442-1344
D'Evoreaux, D'Evoreaux Dr., Natchez, 39120
Dunleith, 84 Homochitto, Natchez, 39120, 601-446-8500
Elgin Plantation House, 81 Dunbar Rd., Natchez, 39120, 601-446-6100
Lenoir Plantation, P.O. Box 1341, Natchez, 39120
Melrose, 136 Melrose Ave., Natchez, 39120, 601-446-9408
Monmouth Plantation, P.O. Box 1736, Natchez, 39120, 601-442-5852
Mount Repose, P.O. Box 347, Natchez, 39121
Pleasant Hill, 310 S. Pearl St., Natchez, 39120, 601-442-7674
Ravennaside, 601 S. Union St., Natchez, 39120, 601-442-8015
Shields Town House, P.O. Box 347, Natchez, 39121
Silver Street Inn, 1 Silver St., Natchez, 39120, 601-442-4221
Stanton Hall, 401 High St., Natchez, 39120
Texada, P.O. Box 347, Natchez, 39121
Twin Oaks, P.O. Box 347, Natchez, 39121
Weymouth Hall, P.O. Box 1091, Natchez, 39121, 601-445-2304
ISOM Place, 1003 Jefferson Ave., Oxford, 39655
Oliver-Britt House, 512 Van Buren Av., Oxford, 38655, 601-234-8043
Gibson's Landing, P.O. Box 195, Port Gibson, 39150, 601-437-3432

Anchuca, 1010 First East St., Vicksburg, 39180, 601-636-4931
Balfour House, 1002 Crawford St., Vicksburg, 39180
Cherry Street Cottage, 2212 Cherry St., Vicksburg, 39180
Corners, The, 601 Klein St., Vicksburg, 39180, 601-636-7421
Duff Green Mansion, The, P.O. Box 75, Vicksburg, 39180, 601-636-6968
Gray Oaks, 4142 Rifle Range Rd., Vicksburg, 39180, 601-638-4424
Tomil Manor, 2430 Drummond St., Vicksburg, 39180, 601-638-8893

Missouri

ARROW ROCK

Borgman's B&B	$ B&B	Continental plus
706 Van Buren, 65320	4 rooms	Lunch, dinner (arranged)
816-837-3350	C-yes/S-no/P-no/H-yes	Sitting room, porch
Kathy & Helen Borgman		victrola
All year		summer repertory theater

Enjoy antiques, crafts, theater, and history in the warmth of this century-old home in historic Arrow Rock, at the head of the Santa Fe Trail.

DownOver Inn	$ B&B	Continental plus
602 Main St., 65320	3 rooms, 3 pb	Cottage w/kitchen & bath
816-837-3268	C-yes/S-yes/P-no/H-yes	Sitting room, piano
John & Joy Vinson		porch, The Old Library
April 15–December 15		playpen toys for kids

Distinctively decorated guest cottage and rooms. Enjoy Missouri small-town atmosphere. See "Tom Sawyer" which was filmed in Arrow Rock. Rare & collectable book shop on-site.

CARTHAGE

Grand Avenue Inn	$$ B&B	Full breakfast
1615 Grand Ave., 64836	4 rooms, 1 pb	Snacks
417-358-7265	Visa, MC, *Rated*, ●	Sitting room, library
Betty Nisich & Paula Hunt	C-ltd/S-no/P-no/H-no	swimming pool
All year		2 hours from Branson, MO

Victorian inn on National Register, furnished in antiques. Close to Precious Moments Chapel, Red Oak II, on Historic Route 66. **After 3rd night comp. dinner for 2**

EXCELSIOR SPRINGS

Crescent Lake Manor B&B	$$ B&B	Full breakfast
1261 St. Louis St., 64024	4 rooms	BBQ/picnic area
816-637-2958	C-ltd/S-ltd/P-no	Tennis court
Mary Elizabeth Leake		swimming pool
All year		horse shoes, badminton

3-story brick Colonial Estate is a half-hour's drive to Kansas City. Georgian charm w/spacious, garden-like grounds. 21 acres of rolling, brook-fed terrain.

HANNIBAL

Fifth Street Mansion B&B	$$ B&B	Full breakfast
213 S. Fifth St., 63401	7 rooms, 7 pb	Comp. tea
314-221-0445 800-874-5661	*Rated*, ●	Sitting room
Mike & Donalene Andreotti	C-ltd/S-yes/P-no/H-no	special event weekends
All year		beer & wine licensed

Italianate Victorian brick mansion; National Historic Register home near historic district. Special events like mystery weekends, craft workshops, and art shows.

Crescent Lake Manor B&B, Excelsior Springs, MO

HANNIBAL ————————————————————————

Garth Woodside Mansion	$$ B&B	Full breakfast
RR 1 off Route 61, 63401	8 rooms, 8 pb	Comp. tea or hot cider
314-221-2789	Visa, MC, *Rated*	Library, tour planning
Diane & Irv Feinberg	C-ltd/S-ltd	turndown service
All year		guest nightshirts

Mark Twain was a guest at this 39-acre country estate. Original Victorian furnishings, flying staircase. Pampered elegance, hospitality. **Nov.-March 2nd night free, ltd**

HERMANN ————————————————————————

Birk's Goethe St. Gasthaus	$$ B&B	Full breakfast
P.O. Box 255, 65041	9 rooms, 7 pb	Comp. coffee
700 Goethe St.	Visa, MC, *Rated*, •	Dining area, lounge
314-486-2911 314-486-3143	C-ltd/S-no/P-no/H-no	piano, sitting room
Elmer & Gloria Birk		porch with gazebo
Exc. Dec 25–Jan 1		

Original owner owned 3rd largest winery in the world, still in operation. Victorian furnishings, tubs w/gold-plated feet. Mystery Dinner Theater. Grand place to stay.

KANSAS CITY ————————————————————————

Behm's Carriage House B&B	$$$ B&B	Full breakfast
4320 Oak, 64111	5 rooms, 5 pb	Comp. wine & cheese
816-753-4434	Visa, MC	Living room, frplc, TV
Shirley Behm	C-yes/S-ltd/P-no/H-no	jacuzzi, side porch
All year		yard, airport shuttle

1910 Georgian colonial, fully restored w/elegantly appointed suites. Walk to Country Club Plaza & Nelson-Atkins Art Museum.

KANSAS CITY

Doanleigh Wallagh Inn
217 E. 37th St., 64111
816-753-2667 FAX:753-2408
Ed & Carolyn Litchfield
All year

$$$ B&B
5 rooms, 5 pb
Visa, MC, AmEx, *Rated*,
•
C-yes/S-ltd/P-no/H-no

Full breakfast
Facilities for meetings
parties, weddings, piano
phone & TV in rms. organ

Located between the Plaza and Crown Center. Georgian style home–European and American antiques, romantic, comfortable elegance, Midwestern hospitality, unpretentious.

Kelley's B 'n B
P.O. Box 17602, 64123
321 N. Van Brunt Blvd.
816-483-8126
Jim & Mary Jo Kelley
All year

$ B&B
3 rooms
C-yes/S-ltd/P-ltd/H-no

Full family-style bkfst
Cont. bkfst. if pref.
High chair, crib
babysitting arranged

Large family home, minutes from all activities–sports, culture, parks, conventions. Comfortable rooms w/ceiling fans & decor handcrafted like Grandma's. **6th night free**

Milford House B&B
3605 Gillham Rd., 64111
816-753-1269
Ian & Pat Mills
All year

$$$ B&B
4 rooms, 4 pb
Visa, MC, AmEx, •
C-ltd/S-no/P-no/H-no

Full breakfast
Snacks
Sitting room, piano
tennis courts
phones & TVs in rooms

100-year-old home situated in heart of Kansas City. Combination of Queen Anne and Dutch Colonial style. 4 luxurious guest rooms. Afternoon tea our specialty! **Free wine bottle**

Southmoreland on the Plaza
116 E. 46th St., 64112
816-531-7979
Susan Moehl & Penni Johnson
All year

$$$ B&B
12 rooms, 12 pb
Visa, MC, AmEx, *Rated*,
•
C-ltd/S-ltd/P-no/H-yes

Full breakfast
Comp. wine, snacks
Library, frplc, solarium
decks, jacuzzi, croquet
airport shuttle, mod/FAX

Only B&B on Country Club Plaza, Kansas City's cultural, shopping, entertainment area. Elegantly restored Colonial revival; special services for business & vacation traveler.

PLATTE CITY

Basswood Country Inn
15880 Interurban Rd., 64079
816-431-5556 800-242-4775
Don & Betty Soper
All year

$$ B&B
7 rooms, 7 pb
Visa, MC, *Rated*, •
C-yes/S-yes/P-no/H-ltd
American Sign Language

Continental breakfast
Fishing lakes, trails
craft & gift store, deck
shuffleboard, horseshoes

Historic Basswood Lakes; former millionaire's estate. 6 suites plus mother-in-law cottage. Elegant country French; prvt. baths, patios, refrig., microwaves, TV. **3rd nite 50%**

POINT LOOKOUT

Cameron's Crag
P.O. Box 526, 65726
Acacia Club Rd.
417-335-8134 800-933-8529
Kay Cameron
All year

$$ B&B
3 rooms, 3 pb
Visa, •
C-ltd/S-no/P-no/H-no

Full breakfast
Video library
views, private entrance
hot tubs, cable TV/VCR

Contemporary hideaway on bluff overlooking Branson, MO (3 miles away). Fantastic views from rooms! Two private tubs. King and queen beds. **Continental dinner w/4 nights, ltd**

Southmoreland on the Plaza, Kansas City, MO

ROCHEPORT

School House B&B
P.O. Box 88, 65279
504 Third St.
314-698-2022
Vicki & John Ott
All year

$$ B&B
9 rooms, 7 pb
Visa, MC, *Rated*, •
C-yes/S-no/P-no/H-no
French, Spanish

Full breakfast
Bicycles, swing, library
basketball court
nature/bike trails

Historic 3-story brick school building magnificently restored into a 9 guestroom inn. Furnished w/antiques & school memory charm. Local winery, shops/cafes. **3rd night 50% off**

SEDALIA

Sedalia House Country B&B
Rt 4, Box 25, 65301
816-826-6615
Daniel R. Ice
All year

$ B&B
4 rooms, 1 pb
Visa, MC
C-yes/S-ltd/P-ltd/H-no

Full breakfast
Aft. tea, snacks
Sitting room
hiking trails, hunting
working farm activities

Turn-of-the-century colonial home situated on 300 acre working farm providing a peaceful atmosphere and gracious contry living.

SPRINGFIELD

Walnut Street Inn
900 E. Walnut St., 65806
417-864-6346 800-593-6346
Karol & Nancy Brown
All year

$$ B&B
14 rooms, 14 pb
Most CC, *Rated*, •
C-yes/S-no/P-no

Full breakfast
Dinner with reservation
Comp. wine & cheese, bar
high tea, sitting room
tennis nearby

1894 Victorian showcase inn in Historic District. Walk to 8 performance theatres, many cafes, boutiques, university, antique shops. **2nd night free midwk except holidays**

ST. CHARLES

Boone's Lick Trail Inn	$$ B&B	Full breakfast
1000 So. Main St., 63301	5 rooms, 5 pb	1 suite, 4 guestrooms
314-947-7000	Most CC, *Rated*, •	sitting room
All year	C-yes/S-no/P-no/H-ltd	

Dressed in regional antique finery, warmed with cheery hospitality, in Missouri's largest Historic District. Biking trail, casinos nearby.

ST. JOSEPH

Harding House B&B	$ B&B	Full breakfast
219 N. 20th St., 64501	5 rooms, 2 pb	Dinner wknds/lunch wkdys
816-232-7020	Visa, MC, AmEx, •	Comp. wine/tea, tea room
Glen & Mary Harding	C-yes	sitting room, library
All year		antique pump organ

Gracious turn-of-the-century home, furnished w/antiques, offers warm hospitality. Famous lemon bread, homemade coffee cake. **Comp. special occ. champagne/juice. 10% off meals**

ST. LOUIS

Geandaugh House B&B	$$ B&B	Full breakfast
3835-37 S. Broadway, 63118	4 rooms, 4 pb	Aft. tea
314-771-5447	Visa, MC, *Rated*, •	Sitting room
Gea & Wayne Popp	C-yes/S-no/P-no/H-yes	extras for spec. occ.
All year	Some Port., Fr., Ger.	

Historical home 5 min. from downtown. Lovingly restored & filled w/family heirlooms, antiques & collectibles. Guest sample Early American recipes. **3rd night 50% off**

Lafayette House	$$ B&B	Full breakfast
2156 Lafayette Ave., 63104	4 rooms, 2 pb	Snacks
314-772-4429	Visa, MC, *Rated*, •	Sitting room
Sarah & Jack Milligan	C-yes/S-yes/P-no/H-no	library, cable TV, VCR
All year		crib available, A/C

An 1876 Victorian mansion "in the center of things to do in St. Louis." Suite available. We have resident cats. Furnished in antiques but with modern conveniences.

Soulard Inn, The	$$ B&B	Full breakfast
1014 Lami, 63104	4 rooms,	Aft. tea, snacks
314-773-3002	•	Sitting room
Raymond Ellerbeck2	C-ltd/S-yes/H-no	bicycles
All year		

The Soulard Inn is one of the oldest buildings in St. Louis. Only moments away from blues & jazz music & restaurants. **3rd night 50% off**

Winter House, The	$$ B&B	Continental plus
3522 Arsenal St., 63118	3 rooms, 3 pb	Comp. refreshments
314-664-4399	Most CC *Rated*, •	Sitting room, AC
Sarah & Kendall Winter	C-yes/S-ltd/P-no/H-no	suite w/balcony
All year except Xmas		near shops & restaurants

1897 Victorian 10-room house with turret. Hand-squeezed O.J. and live piano at breakfast by reservation. Near Missouri Botanical Gardens and fine restaurants.

ST. LOUIS—BONNE TERRE

Mansion Hill Country Inn	$$$ EP	Continental breakfast
11215 Natural Bridge, Mansion	5 rooms, 2 pb	Tour at Bonne Terre Mine
Hill Dr., 63044	Visa, MC, Disc.,*Rated*,	sitting room, library
314-731-5003 314-358-5311	C-yes/S-ltd/H-no	golf, scuba diving
Douglas & Catherine Goergens		
All year		

Relaxed getaway in turn-of-the-century English-style mansion on 130 acres with 45-mile view of Ozark Mountain foothills. Fishing, golf, cross-country ski, scuba at Bonne Terre Mine.

TRENTON

Hyde Mansion B&B	$$ B&B	Full breakfast
418 E. 7th St., 64683	5 rooms, 5 pb	Comp. beverages, snacks
816-359-5631	Visa, MC, AmEx	Sitting room, library
Robert & Carolyn Brown	C-ltd/S-ltd/P-no/H-no	Baby Grand piano, patio
All year		screened porch, bicycles

Inviting hideaway in rural America, 1949 mansion refurbished for your convenience. Close to Amish country, serves full breakfast.

WARRENSBURG

Cedarcroft Farm B&B	$ B&B	Full breakfast
431 S.E. "Y" Hwy., 64093	2 rooms	Lunch, dinner by arrang.
816-747-5728 800-368-4944	Visa, MC, Disc.,*Rated*, •	Comp. tea & goodies
Sandra & Bill Wayne	C-yes/S-ltd/P-no/H-no	sitting room, parlor
All year		hiking, horseback riding

Country hospitality, country quiet, more-than-you-can-eat country cooking at 1867 farmhouse on 80 scenic acres, Civil War reenactor hosts. Only 1 hr. from Kansas City.

WASHINGTON

Washington House B&B	$$ B&B	Full breakfast
P.O. Box 527, 63090	4 rooms, 4 pb	Comp. bottle of wine
3 Lafayette	*Rated*	Cheese, teas, coffees
314-239-2417	C-yes/H-yes	sitting room
Chuck & Kathy Davis		
All year		

Our historic 1837 inn on the Missouri River features antique furnishings and decor, queen-size canopy beds, river views, country breakfasts. Balcony and terrace on riverside.

More Inns ...

Cedar Grove B&B/Antiques, Cedar Grove, Arrow Rock, 65320, 816-837-3441
Miss Nelle's B&B, Arrow Rock
Lindenhof Country Inn, Augusta
Bethel Colony B&B, Bethel
1909 Depot, Oak St. at Allen St., Bonne Terre, 63628, 314-731-5003
Dauphine Hotel, Bonnots Mill
Country Gardens B&B, HCR 4, Box 2202, Branson, 65616, 417-334-8564
Gaines Landing B&B, P.O. Box 1369, Branson, 65616, 800-825-3145
Ozark Mountain Country B&B, P.O. Box 295, Branson, 65616, 800-695-1546
Memory Lane B&B, California
Ramblewood B&B, 402 Panoramic Dr., Camdenton, 65020, 314-346-3410
B&B on the Square, P.O. Box 320, Carthage, 64836, 417-358-1501
Brewer's Maple Lane Farm, Rt.1, Carthage, 417-358-6312
Brewer's Maple Lane Farms, RR #1, Carthage, 64836, 417-358-6312
Hill House, Carthage
Leggett House, Carthage
Maple Lane Farms, RR 1, Carthage, 64836
Saint Charles House, 338 S Main St, Charles, 63301, 314-946-6221
Russell Carroll House, Clarksville
Fannie Lee B&B, Condordia
Eminence Cottage & Brkfst, P.O. Box 276, Eminence, 65466, 314-226-3642
River's Edge B&B Resort, HCR 1, Box 11, Eminence, 65466, 314-226-3233
Loganberry Inn, 310 W. 7th St., Fulton, 65251, 314-642-9229
Lingerlong B&B, Gravois Mills

Bordello House, 111 Bird, Hannibal, 63401, 314-221-6111
Victorian Guest House, #3 Stillwell, Hannibal, 63401, 314-221-3093
Alice's Wharf, Hermann
Beard's Little Haus, Hermann
Bide-A-Wee B&B, Hermann
Captain Wohlt Inn, Hermann
Das Brownhaus, 125 E. 2nd St., Hermann, 65041, 314-486-3372
Der Klingerbau Inn, 108 E. 2d St., Hermann, 65041, 314-486-2030
Die Gillig Heimat, Hermann
John Bohlken Inn, Hermann
Kolbe Guest Haus, Hermann
Mollye C's B&B, Hermann
Reiff House B&B, Hermann
Schmidt Guesthouse, 300 Market, Hermann, 65041, 314-486-2146
Schneider's B&B, Hermann
Seven Sisters, Hermann
White House Hotel-1868-, 232 Wharf St., Hermann, 65041, 314-468-3200
William Klinger Inn, P.O. Box 29, Hermann, 65041, 314-486-5930
Benner House B&B, 645 Main St., Historic Weston, 64098, 816 386 2616

Grand Avenue Inn, Carthage, MO

Arthur's Horse & Carriage, 601 W. Maple, Independence, 64050, 816-461-6814
Woodstock Inn B&B, 1212 W. Lexington, Independence, 64050, 816-833-2233
Trisha's B&B, 203 Bellevue, Jackson, 63755, 314-243-7427
Home Place, The, Route 2, Box 70, Jamesport, 64648
Richardson House B&B, P.O. Box 227, Jamesport, 64648, 816-684-6664
Visages B&B, 327 N. Jackson, Joplin, 64801, 417-624-1397
Dome Ridge, 14360 N.W. Walker Rd., Kansas City, 64164, 816-532-4074
Faust Townhouse, 8023 N. Stoddard, Kansas City, 64152, 816-741-7480
Pridewell, 600 W. 59th St., Kansas City, 64112, 816-931-1642
Shawnee Bluff, Route 72, Box 14-2, Lake Ozark, 65049, 314-365-2442
Grandpa's Farm, Box 476, HCR 1, Lampe, 65681, 417-779-5106
Parkview Farm, RR #1, Box 54, Lathrop, 64465, 816-664-2744
Lakeview Hills Country Inn, One Lakeview Dr., Lewiston, 49756, 517-786-2000
Graystone, Lexington
Linwood Lawn B&B Inn, Route 2, Box 192, Lexington, 64067
Peppermint Spings Farm, P.O. Box 240, Hwy FF, Lonedell, 314-629-7018
Aunt Nene's B&B, Lucerne
St. Agnes Hall B&B, Macon
White Squirrel Hollow Inn, Marionville
Dickey House B&B, The, 331 S. Clay St., Marshfield, 65706, 417-468-3000
Gramma's House, Route 3, Box 410, Marthasville, 63357, 314-433-2675
Gramma's House B&B, 1105 Hwy D, Marthasville, 314-433-2675
Hylas House B&B Inn, 811 S. Jefferson, Mexico, 65265, 314-581-2011
Jack's Fork Country Inn, Route 1 Box 347, Mountain View, 65548, 805-934-1000
Augustin River Bluff Farm, RR 1, Box 42, New Haven, 63068, 314-239-3452
Country View B&B, Route 3, Box 593, Nixa, 65714, 417-725-1927
Schwegmann House B&B Inn, 3251 Rock Springs Rd., Pacific, 63009, 314-239-5025
Down to Earth Lifestyles, 12500 N. Crooked Rd., Parkville, 64152, 816-891-1018
Boone's Lick Trail Inn, 1000 S. Main St., Saint Charles, 63301, 314-947-7000
Schuster-Rader Mansion, 703 Hall St., Saint Joseph, 64501, 816-279-9464
Music Box Inn, 703 North Kirkwood Rd., Saint Louis, 63122, 314-822-0328
River Country B&B, 1900 Wyoming, Saint Louis, 63118, 324-965-4328
Seven Gables Inn, 26 N. Meramec, Saint Louis, 63105, 314-863-8400
Fenwick Guest Cottage, Sainte Genevieve
Hotel Sainte Genevieve, Main & Merchant Sts., Sainte Genevieve, 63670, 314-883-2737
Inn St. Gemme Beauvais, 78 N. Main, Box 231, Sainte Genevieve, 63670, 314-883-5744
Southern Hotel, 146 S. Third St., Sainte Genevieve, 63670, 314-883-3493
Steiger Haus, 1021 Market St., Sainte Genevieve, 63670, 314-883-5881
Fletcher Residence B&B, Sedalia
Honey Branch Cave & Park, Sparta
Kimmswick Korner Inn, Front & Market, St Louis, 314-467-1027
Lemp Mansion Inn, 3322 DeMenil Pl., St Louis, 314-664-8024
Old Convent Guesthouse, 2046 Sidney St., St Louis, 314-772-3531
Saint Charles House B&B, 338 S. Main St., St. Charles, 63301, 314-946-6221
B&B in St. Louis, Lemp & Wyoming, St. Louis, 314-533-9299
Caverly Farm & Orchard B&B, 389 N. Mosley Rd., St. Louis, 63141
Coachlight B&B, P.O. Box 8095, St. Louis, 63141, 314-367-5870
Doelling Haus, 4817 Towne South, St. Louis, 63128, 314-894-6796
Eastlake Inn, 703 N. Kirkwood, St. Louis, 314-965-0066
Geandaugh House, 3835-37 S. Broadway, St. Louis, 63118, 314-771-5447
Parkside Cottage, 2156 Lafayette Ave., St. Louis, 63104, 314-772-1304
Saint Charles House B&B, 338 S. Main, St. Louis, 314-946-6221
Mansion At Elfindale, The, 1701 S. Fort, Ste. Genevieve, 65807, 417-831-5400
Whip Haven Farm, R.R. 1, Box 395, Sullivan, 63080, 314-627-3717
Camel Crossing B&B, Warrensburg
John A. Adams Homestead, Route 3, Box 130, Warrensburg, 64093

Hopp's Hillside B&B, West Plains
Apple Creek B&B, Weston
Hatchery, The, 618 Short St., Weston, 64098, 816-386-5700
Zanoni Mill Inn, P.O. Box 2, Zanoni, 65784, 417-679-4050

Montana

BIG SKY

Lone Mountain Ranch
P.O. Box 160069, 59716
Lone Mountain Access Rd.
406-995-4644
Bob & Vivian Schaap
All year

$$$ AP
20 rooms, 20 pb
Visa, MC, AmEx,
C-yes/S-no/P-no/H-ltd

All meals included
Winter sleighride dinner
Bar, sitting room, piano
hot tub, jacuzzi, horses
weekly rates

Historic guest ranch offering family vacations and Nordic ski vacations near Yellowstone National Park. Beautiful log cabins with fireplaces, conveniences.

BIGFORK

Burggraf's Countrylane B&B
Rainbow Dr., on Swan Lake,
59911
406-837-4608 800-525-3344
Natalie & RJ Burggraf
April–January

$$$ B&B
5 rooms, 5 pb
Visa, MC
C-ltd/S-ltd/P-no/H-yes

Full breakfast
Comp. wine/cheese/fruit
Picnic baskets avail.
lake, snowmobile rental
boat rental, jacuzzi

True log home nestled in heart of Rocky Mountains; 7 acres on the shores of Swan Lake; panoramic view; country breakfast. Boating or canoeing. **Disc't for 4 or more nights**

O'Duachain Country Inn
675 Ferndale Dr., 59911
406-837-6851 800-837-7460
Margot & Tom Doohan
All year

$$$ B&B
5 rooms
Visa, MC, *Rated*, •
C-yes/S-ltd/P-ltd/H-no

Full gourmet breakfast
Comp. sherry in room
Sitting room
hot tubs, water sports
help w/tour plans

Elegant, rustic log home nestled in the woods and mountain meadows, antique furniture, original artwork, two huge stone fireplaces and manicured grounds. South of Kalispell.

BOZEMAN

Torch & Toes B&B
309 S. 3rd Ave., 59715
406-586-7285
Ron & Judy Hess
All year

$$ B&B
4 rooms, 2 pb
Visa, MC, *Rated*, •
C-yes/S-no/P-no/H-no

Full breakfast
Comp. sherry
Sitting room, library
bicycles
porch swing

A friendly cat, a gourmet breakfast and unique collections of dolls, mouse traps, and brass rubbings make for a pleasant stay. Nearby skating, band concerts, and market.

Voss Inn
319 S. Willson, 59715
406-587-0982
Bruce & Frankee Muller
All year

$$ B&B
6 rooms, 6 pb
Visa, MC, DC, *Rated*, •
C-ltd/S-ltd/P-no/H-no

Full breakfast
Afternoon tea, sherry
Sitting room, piano
trips to Yellowstone
Park guided by owner

Warmly elegant historic Victorian mansion beautifully decorated w/period wallpaper, furniture. Walk to university, museums, restaurants, shopping. **Champagne to honeymooners**

EUREKA

Trail's End B&B
57 Trail's End Rd., 59917
406-889-3486
Warren & Betty Taylor
All year

$$ B&B
5 rooms
Visa, MC
C-ltd/S-no/P-no/H-no

Full breakfast
Fishing all year
Hunting

Three level log home. Walk to three lakes. 2 miles from boat ramp on Lake Koocanusa. **Senior citizens discount, ask**

GREAT FALLS

Sovekammer B&B, The
1109 Third Ave. N., 59401
406-453-6620
Dean & Irene Nielsen
All year

$$ B&B
4 rooms, 4 pb
Personal checks,*Rated*,
•
C-ltd/S-no/P-no/H-no

Full Danish breakfast
Dessert/coffee evenings
Sitting room, bicycles
front porch and swing

Colorful, old-fashioned inn in historic downtown. Walk to CM Russell Museum. Perfect stop between Yellowstone and Glacier Park! Complimentary desert & coffee in the evening.

KALISPELL

Switzer House Inn
205 Fifth Ave. East, 59901
406-257-5837
Heather B. Brigham
April & Sept. closed/ask

$$$ B&B
4 rooms
Visa, MC, *Rated*,
C-ltd/S-no/P-no/H-no

Full breakfast
Snacks, Comp. wine
Sitting room, library
picnics for small fee
catered dinners, piano

1910 Queen Anne Revival home, located in historic side of city. Furnished with period pieces, 5 blocks to downtown restaurants, antique shops, theaters. Cat in residence.

RED LODGE

Willows Inn
P.O. Box 886, 59068
224 S. Platt Ave.
406-446-3913
Elven, Kerry & Carolyn Boggio
All year

$ B&B
6 rooms, 4 pb
Visa, MC, •
C-yes/S-no/P-no/H-no
Finnish, Spanish

Continental plus
Comp. aftn. refreshments
TV parlor w/VCR & movies
games/books, local menus
ski racks, sun decks

Charming Victorian. Delicious homebaked pastries. Spectacular mountain scenery. Yellowstone Park; ski, fish, hike, golf, bike. 2 cottages. **Free wine: honeymoon/anniversary.**

ST. IGNATIUS

Mandorla Ranch B&B
6873 Allard Rd., 59865
406-745-4500 800-852-6668
Mr. & Mrs. Ray Knapp
All year

$$ B&B
5 rooms, 3 pb
C-yes/S-no/P-ltd/H-yes
French, Greek

Full breakfast
Bicycles, hot tubs
horses, hiking, fishing
mt. biking, sitting rm.

Mission Mountain retreat. Perfect for honeymoons, family reunions, small meetings. Designer log home, 360' views, ranch animals, hearty western breakfasts & hospitality.

THREE FORKS

Sacajawea Inn
P.O. Box 648, 59752
5 N. Main St.
406-285-6515 800-821-7326
Jane & Smith Roedel
All year

$$ EP/B&B
34 rooms
Most CC, *Rated*, •
C-yes/S-ltd/P-ask/H-ask
Spanish, French

Continental
Restaurant, bar service
All meals available
library, dining room
conference facilities

Casual elegance of a bygone era in this 1910 National Historic Landmark. Excellent fishing, hunting, biking. Between Glacier & Yellowstone Parks. **3rd night 50%, ltd**

WEST YELLOWSTONE

Sportsman's High B&B	$$ B&B	Full breakfast
750 Deer St., 59758	5 rooms, 5 pb	Sitting room, Fax
406-646-7865 800-272-4227	Visa, MC	library, wildlife
Diana & Gary Baxter	C-ltd/S-no/P-no/H-no	hot tub, mountains
All year		

8 miles from Yellowstone Park you'll find country charm at its best amidst aspen and pines, with close and personal views of mountains. **4th night free Oct.-June, Ltd.**

WHITEFISH

Castle B&B	$$ B&B	Full breakfast
900 S. Baker Ave., 59937	3 rooms	Library, piano
406-862-1257	Visa, MC, •	fireplace, TV
Jim & Pat Egan	C-ltd/S-no/P-no/H-no	video room, sauna
All year		

Historic home in beautiful setting. Minutes from Big Mountain ski area and Glacier National Park. Tennis, golf, boating, hiking nearby.

Kandahar Lodge	$$$ EP/MAP	Full breakfast
P.O. Box 1659, 59937	50 rooms, 50 pb	Restaurant
Big Mountain Rd.	Most CC, *Rated*, •	Sitting room
406-862-6098	C-yes/S-yes/P-no/H-no	two hot tubs
Buck & Mary Pat Love		two saunas
All year		

Beautiful rock and cedar lodge in Alpine setting. Ski to the door. Close to Glacier Park. European atmosphere, restaurant. Rustic yet elegant.

More Inns . . .

Johnson's Petty Creek Rnch, Mail Box 195, Alberton, 59820, 406-864-2111
Gustin Orchard, East Lake Shore, Big Fork, 59911, 406-982-3329
Grand, The, P.O. Box 1242, Big Timber, 59011
Lazy K Bar Ranch, Box 550, Big Timber, 59011, 406-537-4404
Gustin Orchard B&B, E. Lake Shore, Bigfork, 59911, 406-982-3329
Jubilee Orchards Lake Reso, Sylvan Dr., Bigfork, 59911, 406-837-4256
Schwartz's B&B, 890 McCaffery Rd., Bigfork, 59911, 406-837-5463
Feather Cove Inn, 5530 Vermilion Rd., Billings, 59105, 406-373-5679
PJ's B&B, 722 N. 29th St., Billings, 59101, 406-259-3300
Lehrkind Mansion, 719 N. Wallace, Bozeman, 59715, 406-586-1214
Silver Forest Inn, 15325 Bridger Canyon Rd, Bozeman, 59715, 406-586-1882
Sun House B&B, 9986 Happy Acres West, Bozeman, 59715, 406-587-3651
Cliff Lake Lodge, P.O. Box 573, Cameron, 59720, 406-682-4982
Holland Lake Lodge, S.R. Box 2083, Condon, 59826, 800-648-8859
Bunky Ranch Outfitters, P.O. Box 215, Conner, 59827, 406-821-3312
Triple Creek Inn, 5551 W. Fork Srage Rt., Darby, 59829, 406-821-4664
Bison Creek Ranch, Box 144, East Glacier, 59434
Grave Creek B&B, P.O. Box 551, Eureka, 59917, 406-882-4658
Gallatin Gateway Inn, P.O. Box 376, Gallatin Gateway, 59730
Chalet, The, 1204 — 4th Ave. N., Great Falls, 59401, 406-452-9001
Murphy's House B&B, 2020 Fifth Ave. North, Great Falls, 59401
Three Pheasant Inn, 626 Fifth Ave. N., Great Falls, 59401, 406-453-0519
Sanders-Helena B&B, The, 328 N. Ewing, Helena, 59601, 406-442-3309
Upcountry Inn, 2245 Head Ln., Helena, 59601, 406-442-1909
Schoolhouse and Teacherage, 9 Mile, Huson, 59846, 406-626-5879
Whispering Pines, Box 36, Huson, 59846, 406-626-5664
Huckleberry Inn, 1028 3rd Ave. W., Kalispell, 59901, 406-755-4825
Stillwater Inn B&B, 206 Fourth Ave. East, Kalispell, 59901, 800-398-7024
Switzer House Inn B&B, 205 5th Ave. East, Kalispell, 59901, 406-257-5837

Switzer House Inn, Kalispell, MT

Whitney Mansion, The, 538 Fifth Ave., Kalispell, 59901, 800-426-3214
Bernard Burgess B&B, P.O. Box 218, Kila, 59920
Shoreline Inn, POBox 568, 696 Lakeside, Lakeside, 59922, 800-645-0255
Beverly Fachner, Heath Star Route, Lewistown, 59457
Bobtail B&B, 4909 Bobtail Rd., Libby, 59923, 406-293-3926
Kootenai Country Inn, The, 264 Mack Rd., Libby, 59923, 406-293-7878
Davis Creek, Rt. 38, Box 2179, Livingston, 59047, 406-333-4353
Virgelle Merc., Rural Route 1, Loma, 59460, 800-426-2926
Hargrave Cattle House, Thompson River Valley, Marion, 59925, 406-858-2284
Goldsmith Inn, 809 E. Front, Missoula, 59802, 406-721-6732
Nevada City Hotel, Nevada City, 59755, 406-843-5377
Bighorn Lodge, 710 Bull River Rd., Noxon, 59853, 406-847-5597
Bayview B&B, 1221 Bayview Dr., Polson, 59860, 406-883-6744
Hammond's B&B, 10141 East Shore, Polson, 59860, 406-887-2766
Hawthorne House B&B, 304 Third Ave. East, Polson, 59860, 406-883-2723
Ruth's B&B, 802 7th. Ave, Polson, 59860, 406-883-2460
Maxwell's Mountain Home, 606 S. Broadway, Red Lodge, 59068, 406-446-3052
Pitcher Guest House, P.O. Box 3450, Red Lodge, 59068, 406-446-2859
Yoders B&B, 5611 West Kootenai Rd., Rexford, 59930, 406-889-3466
Mission Mountain B&B, RR Box 183 A, Saint Ignatius, 59865, 406-745-4331
Double Arrow Lodge, Seeley Lake, 59868, 800-468-0777
Emily A. The, P.O. Box 350, Seeley Lake, 59868, 406-677-3474
King's Rest B&B, 55 Tuke Ln., Sheridan, 59749, 406-842-5185
Osprey Inn, 5557 Hwy 93 So., Somers, 59932, 800-258-2042
Country Caboose B&B, 852 Willoughby Rd., Stevensville, 59870, 106-777-3145
Camp Creek Inn, 7674 Hwy 93 South, Sula, 59871, 406-821-3771
Hidden Hollow Hideaway, Box 233, Townsend, 59644, 406-266-3322
Bull Lake Guest Ranch, 15303 Bull Lake Rd., Troy, 59935, 406-295-4228
Colonial House B&B, 13655 Turah Rd., Turah, Missoula, 59825, 406-258-6787
Mountain Timbers Lodge, Box 94, West Glacier, 59936, 800-841-3835
Foxwood Inn, Box 404, White Sulphur Springs, 59645, 406-547-3918
Duck Inn, 1305 Columbia Ave., Whitefish, 59937, 406-862-DUCK
Edgewood, The, 12 Dakota Ave., Whitefish, 59937, 406-862-WOOD
Garden Wall, 504 Spokane Ave., Whitefish, 59937, 406-862-3440
Hibernation House, P.O. Box 1400, Whitefish, 59937, 406-862-3511

Nebraska

OMAHA

Offurt House
140 North 39th St., 68131
402-553-0951
Jeannie Swoboda
All year

$$ B&B
7 rooms, 5 pb
Visa, MC, AmEx, *Rated*,
•
C-yes/S-yes/P-ltd/H-no
A little Italian

Continental plus
Comp. wine
Dinner, lunch/groups
Sitting room, library
deep claw-foot tubs

Mansion built in 1894 furnished with antiques. Centrally located near historic "Old Market" area of shops, restaurants. Sun porch, bar on 1st floor. **15% off after five nights**

More Inns . . .

Pheasant Hill Farm, HCR 68, Box 12, Bartley, 69020
Behrens Inn, 605 E. 3rd St., Beemer, 68716, 402-528-3212
Thompson House, Route 1, Brownville, 68321, 402-825-6551
Cottonwood Inn B&B, The, P.O. Box 446, Chappell, 69129, 308-874-3250
Butte Ranch, P.O. Box 39A, Crawford, 69339, 308-665-2364
Fort Robinson Inn, Box 392, Crawford, 69339, 308-665-2660
Wrought Iron Tourist Home, 238 Ash, Crawford, 69339, 308-665-1900
Johnston-Muff House, 1422 Boswell, Crete, 68333, 402-826-4155
Parson's House, The, 638 Forest Ave., Crete, 68333, 402-826-2634
George's, The, Rt. 1, Box 50, Dixon, 68732, 402-548-2625
Plantation House B&B, Rt.2, Box 17, Elgin, 68636, 402-843-2287
Parker House B&B, 515 4th St., Fairbury, 68352, 402-729-5516
B&B of Fremont, 1624 E. 25th St., Fremont, 68025, 402-727-9534
Monument Heights B&B, 2665 Grandview Rd., Gering, 69341, 308-635-0109
Meadow View Ranch, HC 91 Box 29, Gordon, 69343
Spring Lake Ranch, H.C. 84, Box 103, Gordon, 69343, 308-282-0835
Bed & Breakfast, 2617 Brahma St., Grand Island, 68801, 308-384-0830
Kirschke House B&B, The, 1124 W. 3rd, Grand Island, 68801, 308-381-6851
Bundy's Bed & Breakfast, RR #2 Box 39, Gretna, 68028

Sowbelly B&B Hide-a-way, Box 292, Harrison, 69346, 308-668-2537
Hansen's Homestead B&B, P.O. Box 77, Hemingford, 69348, 308-487-3805
Century B&B, P.O. Box 13, Holdrege, 68949, 308-995-6750
George W. Frank Jr. House, 621 W. 27th, Kearney, 68847, 308-237-7545
Walden West, RR #4, Fawn Woods Lake, Kearney, 68847, 308-237-7296
Memories, 900 N. Washington, Lexington, 68850, 308-324-3290
Capitol Guesthouse B&B, 720 S. 16th St., Lincoln, 68508, 402-476-6669
Danish Farm B&B, P.O. Box 2333, Lincoln, 68502, 402-423-3480
Rogers House, 2145 "B" St., Lincoln, 68502, 402-476-6961
Yellow House on the Corner, 1603 N. Cotner, Lincoln, 68505, 402-466-8626
Clown 'N Country, RR Box 115, Madrid, 69150, 308-326-4378
Twisted Pine Ranch B&B, Box 84, Merriman, 69218, 308-684-3482
Prairie View, Rt. 2, Box 137, Minden, 68959, 308-832-0123
Peppercricket Farm B&B, RR1, Box 304, Nebraska City, 68410
Whispering Pines B&B, 21st St. & 6th Ave., Nebraska City, 68410, 402-873-5850
Watson Manor Inn, P.O. Box 458, North Platte, 69103, 308-532-1124
Mary Mahoney's Thissen B&B, 6103 Burt St., Omaha, 68132, 402-553-8366
Willow Way B&B, Rt. 2, Box A20, Osmond, 68765, 402-748-3593
My Blue Heaven, 1041 5th St., Pawnee City, 68420, 402-852-3131
Gingerbread Inn, P.O. Box 247, Paxton, 69155, 308-239-4265
Rose Garden Inn, 305 N. 3rd, Plainview, 68769, 402-582-4708
Meadowlark Manor B&B, The, 241 W. 9th Ave., Red Cloud, 68970, 402-746-3550
Richardson House, 202 N. Webster St., Red Cloud, 68970, 402-746-3264
Old Boarding House, The, 1300 11th Ave., Sidney, 69162, 308-254-3685
Esch Haus, Rt. 1, Spalding, 68665, 308-497-2628
Swedish Inn, 520 Main St., Stromsburg, 68666, 402-423-3480
Deer Run B&B, RR1, Box 142, Tekamah, 68061, 402-374-2423
Flying A Ranch B&B, P.O. Box 142, Trenton, 69044, 308-334-5574
Stone House Inn, 559 N. Main, Valentine, 69201, 402-376-1942
Town & Country B&B, P.O. Box 624, Valentine, 69201, 402-376-2193
Journey's End B&B, P.O. Box 190, Waterloo, 68069, 402-779-2704
Swanson's B&B, Rt.2, Wayne, 68787, 402-584-2277
Grey Gull, 321 Webhannet Dr., Wells, 04090, 207-646-7501
Hotel Wilber, 203 S. Wilson, Wilber, 68465, 402-821-2020

Nevada

ELY

Steptoe Valley Inn
P.O. Box 151110, 89315
220 E. 11th St.
702-289-8687
Jane & Norman Lindley
June–September

$$ B&B
5 rooms, 5 pb
Visa, MC, AmEx, *Rated*,
C-ltd/S-no/P-no/H-no
Spanish

Full breakfast
Juice and cheese
Sitting room, library
rose garden, back porch
private balconies, TVs

Romantic, historic structure near railroad museum, reconstructed 1990. Elegant dining room/library. Rooms have country-cottage decor. Self-guided jeep tours.

IMLAY–UNIONVILLE

Old Pioneer Garden B&B
79 Main St., 89418
702-538-7585
Lew & Mitzi Jones
All year

$$ B&B
11 rooms, 3 pb
●
C-ltd/S-ok/P-ltd/H-yes

Full breakfast
Other meals arranged
Sitting room
home movies
Nevada Junket antiques

Ranch operating since 1861. We're proud of our pristine pure air, abundant fruit trees and trout stream through the property. Antique shop in the barn.

INCLINE VILLAGE —————————————————————————

Haus Bavaria	$$ B&B	Full breakfast
P.O. Box 3308, 89450	5 rooms, 5 pb	Comp. wine
593 N. Dyer Circle	Visa, MC, AmEx, *Rated*,	Large family room
702-831-6122 800-GO TAHOE	•	TV, fireplace
Bick Hewitt	C-ltd/S-no/P-no/H-no	
All year		

There is much to do and see in this area, from gambling casinos to all water sports and golf, hiking, tennis and skiing at 12 different nearby sites. ***Off season rates***

WASHOE VLLY–CARSON CITY —————————————————————

Deer Run Ranch B&B	$$$ B&B	Full breakfast
5440 Eastlake Blvd., 89704	2 rooms, 2 pb	Comp. wine, beverages
702-882-3643	Visa, MC	Snacks, refrigerator
David & Muffy Vhay	C-ltd/S-no/P-ask/H-no	sitting room, library
Exc. Thanksgiving & Xmas	limited Spanish	TV, VCR, private entry

Western ambiance in a unique architect-designed and built ranch house near Reno and Carson City overlooking Washoe Lake. Pottery, pond, swimming pool, privacy, great brkfsts.

More Inns ...

Elliot Chartz House, 412 N. Nevada, Carson City, 89701, 702-882-5323
Winters Creek Ranch B&B, 1201 U.S. 395 N., Carson City, 89701, 702-849-1020
Oasis B&B, 540 W. Williams, Fallon, 89406
Nenzel Mansion, 1431 Ezell St., Gardenerville, 89410, 702-782-7644
Sierra Spirit Ranch, 3000 Pinenut Rd., Gardnerville, 89410, 702-782-7011
Genoa House Inn, P.O. Box 141, Genoa, 89411, 702-782-7075
Orchard House, 188 Carson St., Genoa, 89411, 702-782-2640
Wild Rose Inn, 2332 Main St., Genoa, 89411
Gold Hill Hotel, P.O. Box 710, Gold Hill, 89440, 702-847-0111
Breitenstein House, Lamoille, 89828, 702-753-6356
B&B South Reno, 136 Andrew Ln., Reno, 89511, 702-849-0772
Hardwicke House, P.O. Box 96, Silver City, 89429, 702-847-0215
Windybrush Ranch, Box 85, Smith, 89430, 702-465-2481
Blue Fountain B&B, 1590 "B" St., Sparks, 89431, 702-359-0359
Chollar Mansion, 565 S. D St., Box 889, Virginia City, 89440
Edith Palmer's Country Inn, Box 756, South B St., Virginia City, 89440, 702-847-0707
Savage Mansion, P.O. Box 445, Virginia City, 89440, 702-847-0574
Winters Creek Inn, 1201 US Hwy. 395, Washoe Valley, 89704
Robin's Nest Inn, 130 E. Winnemucca, Winnemucca, 89445, 702-623-2410
Harbor House, 39 N. Center St., Yerington, 89447
Robric Ranch, P.O. Box 2, Yerrington, 89447, 702-463-3515

New Hampshire

ANDOVER ————————————————————————————————

English House, The	$$ B&B	Full breakfast
P.O. Box 162, 03216	7 rooms, 7 pb	Comp. sherry, aftn. tea
Main St.	Visa, MC, *Rated*,	Sitting room
603-735-5987	C-ltd/S-no/P-no/H-yes	homemade jams
Ken & Gillian Smith	French, German	breads & muffins
All year		

Elegant comfort of an old English country house set in the scenic beauty of New England. Breakfast and afternoon tea are rare treats.

ASHLAND

Glynn House Victorian Inn
P.O. Box 719, 03217
43 Highland St.
603-968-3775 800-637-9599
Betsy & Karol Paterman
All year

$$ B&B
4 rooms, 4 pb
Rated, •
C-ltd/S-yes/P-no/H-no
Polish, Russian

Full breakfast
Comp. wine, snacks
Sitting room, bicycles
tennis, lake
golf & skiing nearby

Fine example of Victorian Queen Anne architecture situated among lakes and mountains. Antiques, gourmet brkf. and hospitality are our specialities. **Free bottle of champagne**

BARTLETT

Country Inn at Bartlett
P.O. Box 327, 03812
Route 302
603-374-2353 800-292-2353
Mark Dindorf
All year

$$ B&B
17 rooms, 10 pb
Visa, MC, AmEx, *Rated*,
•
C-yes/S-ltd/P-ltd

Full breakfast
Comp. tea/coffee, snacks
Sitting room
outdoor hot tub
cross-country ski trails

A B&B inn for hikers, skiers & outdoors enthusiasts in the White Mountains. New addition of 2-rm. cottage. Expert hiking & trail advice. **3rd night free midwk, ltd**

Notchland Inn, The
General Delivery, Rte. 302,
Hart's Location, 03812
603-374-6131
John & Pat Bernardin
All year

$$$ B&B
11 rooms, 11 pb
Visa, MC, AmEx,
C-ltd/S-ltd/P-no/H-ltd

Full breakfast
Dinner
Sitting room, library
hot tubs, sauna
cross-country skiing

A traditional country inn where hospitality hasn't been forgotten. Working fireplaces in every room, gourmet meals and spectacular mountain views. Hiking & swimming nearby.

BETHLEHEM

Adair - A Country Inn
Old Littleton Rd., 03574
603-444-2600
Pat & Hardy Banfield
All year

$$$ B&B
8 rooms, 8 pb
Visa, MC, AmEx, *Rated*,
•
C-yes/S-ltd/P-no/H-no

Full breakfast
Aft. tea
Sitting room, library
fireplaces, gardens
tennis court, 200 acres

Elegant country estate on 200 acres in the heart of the White Mountains. Extensive gardens, dramatic views. Delightful bistros nearby.

BRADFORD

Bradford Inn, The
RR 1, Box 40, Main St., 03221
603-938-5309 800-669-5309
Conni & Tom Mazol
All year

$$$ MAP (EP/B&B)
12 rooms, 12 pb
Visa, MC, *Rated*, •
C-yes/S-yes/P-yes/H-yes
Arabic

Full breakfast
Restaurant, dinner incl.
Sitting room, library
meeting facility, bikes
award-winning apple pie

There's simply "nothing to do," Fireplace, good books, three ski areas, & 2 lovely lakes nearby. Banquets available. Recent period renovations. **50% off 2nd dinner entree**

CAMPTON

Mountain Fare Inn
P.O. Box 553, 03223
Mad River Rd.
603-726-4283
Susan & Nick Preston
All year

$ B&B
8 rooms, 5 pb
Rated, •
C-yes/S-no/P-ask/H-no

Full breakfast
Dinner (groups, winter)
Snacks, sitting room
hiking, biking, golf
cross-country & downhill
skiing

1840s white clapboard mountain village home. Truly New Hampshire. Skiers, hikers, travelers: come share fun & beauty. Hosts are ski resort coaches. **3rd night 30% off, ltd**

CAMPTON

Osgood Inn B&B
P.O. Box 419, 03223
Cross St.
603-726-3543
Dexter & Patricia Osgood

$$ B&B
4 rooms
C-yes/S-no/P-no/H-no
Open all year
   except Thanksgiving

Full breakfast
Aft. tea, snacks
Sitting room, gardens
porch, yard, birds
ski area 10 miles

Charming gracious village inn. Close to major ski areas, shops, tourist attractions. Wonderful breakfasts, handmade quilts. Restful and quiet.

CENTER HARBOR

Kona Mansion Inn
P O. Box 458, Kona Rd
Moultonboro/03254, 03226
603-253-4900
The Crowley family
May 25—October 12

$$ EP/B&B
14 rooms, 14 pb
Visa, MC, *Rated*,
C-yes/S-ask/P-ask/H-ltd

Full breakfast avail. $
Dinner, bar service
Sitting room
tennis courts, golf
private beach on lake

Kona Mansion, built in 1900, is a peaceful get away from today's hectic pace. Serving superb cuisine. **10% room discount**

CENTRE HARBOR

Red Hill Inn
RFD 1, Box 99M, Route 25B &
College Rd., 03226
603-279-7001
Rick Miller & Don Leavitt
All year

$$ B&B
21 rooms, 21 pb
AmEx, Visa, MC, *Rated*,
•
C-yes/S-yes/P-no/H-no

Full breakfast
Lunch (summer), dinner
Bar, Sunday brunch
library, lake swimming
small conference center

Lovely restored mansion on fifty private acres overlooking Squam Lake (Golden Pond) and White Mountains. Excellent country gourmet cuisine, antiques.

CHARLESTOWN

Maple Hedge B&B Inn
P.O. Box 638, 03603
Main St., Route 12
603-826-5237
Joan De Brine
May 1 - November 1

$$$ B&B
5 rooms, 5 pb
Visa, MC, *Rated*, •
C-ltd/S-ltd/P-no/H-no

Full breakfast
Aft. tea, comp. wine
Sitting room, library
horseshoes, croquet
badminton

Luxurious accommodations in historic home set among lovely gardens & 200 year old maples. Memorable 3 course breakfasts.

CHICHESTER

Hitching Post B&B, The
RFD #2, P.O. Box 948, US-40 &
202, Chichester, 03263
603-798-4951
Lis & Gil Lazich
Feb—Nov and by res.

$ B&B
4 rooms,
•
C-ltd/S-ltd/P-no/H-no
Scan., Slav., Fr., Sp.

Full gourmet breakfast
Comp. tea/wine
Parlor, piano
library, VCR
color TV

Cozy 1787 Colonial; on US 4 & 202, heart of NH's Antique Row. 7.5 miles east of Concord; "en route to anywhere else"—lakes, mountains, or ocean. **Disc't to AARP & longer stay**

CONWAY

Darby Field Inn, The
P.O. Box D, Bald Hill Rd., 03818
603-447-2181 800-426-4147
Marc & Maria Donaldson
All year

$ B&B/$$ MAP
16 rooms, 14 pb
Visa, MC, AmEx, *Rated*,
•
C-ltd/S-yes/P-no/H-no
Spanish

Full breakfast
Dinner, bar
Sitting room, piano
15 miles of cross-country
skiing
pool, entertainment

Cozy little country inn overlooking the Mt. Washington Valley & Presidential Mountains. Candlelight dinners; surrounding mountains and rivers, ski trails. **3rd night 50%-Ltd**

CONWAY ─────────────────────────────────────

Mountain Valley Mannor B&B	$ B&B	Full breakfast
P.O. Box 1649, 03818	4 rooms, 2 pb	Afternoon tea, snacks
148 Washington St.	Visa, MC, Disc.,*Rated*,	Comlimentary beverages
603-447-3988	•	sitting room, library
Bob, Lynn, Amy & Lord Frisky	C-yes/S-no/P-no/H-no	swimming pool, cable TV
All year		

Friendly restored Victorian at the Kankamaugus Hwy, 200 yds. from 2 historic Kissing Bridges, walk to restaurants & outlets. Environmentally clean. **5th. night free**

CORNISH ─────────────────────────────────────

Chase House, The	$$$ B&B	Full breakfast
RR 2, Box 909, Route 12-A, 03745	7 rooms, 7 pb	Parlor, library w/fp
603-675-5391 FAX:675-5010	Visa, MC, *Rated*, •	Canoeing, hiking
Hal & Marilyn Wallace	C-ltd/S-no/P-no/H-yes	cross-country skiing, skating
Dec.-March, May-October		

National Historic Landmark, meticulously restored 1775 Federal-style, on Connecticut River w/160 acres near Killington/Woodstock. Bicycle tours, downhill skiing.

Home Hill Country Inn	$$$ B&B	Continental
RR 3, Box 235, River Rd., 03745	9 rooms, 9 pb	Restaurant, dinner
603-675-6165	Visa, MC	Bar service, sitting rm.
Roger Nicolas	C-ltd/S-ltd/P-no/H-no	library, tennis court
All year	French	swimming pool, hiking

A secluded country escape. Exquisite food, tennis, swimming and cross-country skiing in the Upper Connecticut River Valley.

EATON CENTER ─────────────────────────────────

Inn at Crystal Lake, The	$$ B&B/$$$ MAP	Full country breakfast
Route 153, Box 12, 03832	11 rooms, 11 pb	Dinner, bar, parlor, TV
603-447-2120 800-343-7336	Visa, MC, D, AmEx, •	Fireplace,lounge, pianos
Walter & Jacqueline Spink	C-yes/S-ltd/P-no/H-no	lake swimming & canoes
All year		hiking & cross-country ski nearby

Newly restored country inn—Greek revival with Victorian influence. Relaxing ambience, extraordinary international cuisine presented with elegant appeal. **3rd night 30% off**

FRANCONIA ─────────────────────────────────────

Blanche's B&B	$$ B&B	Full breakfast
351 Easton Valley Rd., 03580	5 rooms	Dinner for groups
603-823-7061	Visa, MC, AmEx, *Rated*,	Sitting room, books
Brenda Shannon & John Vail	C-yes/S-no/P-no/H-no	woods for hiking
All year		

Thoughtfully restored farmhouse; peaceful rural setting. Decorative painting throughout including unusual stenciling and wall glazing. Good home-cooked breakfasts.

Bungay Jar B&B	$$ B&B	Full breakfast
P.O. Box 15, 03580	6 rooms, 4 pb	Dinner for groups by res
Easton Valley Rd.	Visa, MC, *Rated*	Afternoon tea, snacks
603-823-7775	C-ltd	library, antiques, sauna
Kate Kerivan, Lee Strimbeck		swimming hole, balconies
All year		

5.5 miles south of Franconia Village. Crackling fire; mulled cider; popovers; homemade snacks. Mountain views on 8 private, quiet wooded acres with garden walks to river.

FRANCONIA

Franconia Inn
1300 Easton Rd., 03580
603-823-5542 800-473-5299
The Morris Family
Mem. Day—Oct, 12/15-4/1

$$ B&B/MAP
35 rooms, 34 pb
Most CC, *Rated*, •
C-yes/S-yes/P-no/H-no

Full breakfast
Restaurant, full bar
Lounge w/movies, library
bicycles, heated pool
piano, sitt. rm., tennis

Located in the Easton Valley—Mt. Lafayette and Sugar Hill. Riding stable, ski center. All rooms & bathrooms beautifully decorated. Sleigh rides, horseback riding, soaring.

Horse and Hound Inn, The
205 Wells Rd., 03580
603-823-5501 800-450-5501
Jim Cantlon, Bill Steele
May—March

$$ B&B/MAP
12 rooms, 6 pb
Discover, *Rated*, •
C-yes/S-yes/P-no/H-no

Full breakfast
Restaurant
Dinner 6-9 pm (exc. Tue)
sitting room

Fine traditional inn on a quiet road amid hiking & cross-country trails. Nearest inn to ski lifts. Fine dining, menu changes daily. 2 dogs & 2 cats welcome you. **3rd night 50% off**

Inn at Forest Hills, The
P.O. Box 783, 03580
Rt 142
603-823-9550
Joanne & Gordon Haym
All year

$$ B&B
8 rooms, 5 pb
Visa, MC, *Rated*, •
C-ltd/S-no/P-no/H-no

Full breakfast
Snacks, Comp. wine
Sitting room
solarium, 3 fireplaces
dinner by request, ltd.

Charming, historic 18 room Tudor Manor house nestled among majestic scenery and year-round attractions of the White Mountains.

Lovett's Inn
Route 18, Profile Rd., 03580
603-823-7761 800-356-3802
Anthony & Sharon Avrutine
Exc. April & November

$$ EP/$$$ MAP
30 rooms, 22 pb
Visa, MC, AmEx, *Rated*,
•
C-yes/S-ltd/P-no

Full breakfast
Restaurant, bar, dinner
Afternoon tea, library
sitting room, bicycles
cable TV, hiking

Beautiful 1784 historic inn w/fireplaced cottages & gourmet restaurant. Spectacular Franconia Notch. Swimming, biking, cross-country/downhill skiing. Breathtaking views. **Comp. wine.**

FRANKLIN

Atwood Inn, The
Rte. 3A, 03235
603-934-3666
Phil & Irene Fournier
All year

$$ B&B
7 rooms, 7 pb
Most CC, *Rated*,
C-ltd/S-no/P-no/H-no
French & Greek

Full breakfast
Aft. tea, snacks
Sitting room w/TV
tennis court nearby
library

Our guests say, "charmingly furnished; scrumptious breakfasts; warm hospitality; romantic fireplaces; everything we imagined a New England B&B to be"!

GILFORD

Gunstock Country Inn
580 Cherry Valley Rd., Route
11A, 03246
603-293-2021
Denley W. Emerson
All year

$$ EP/$$$ MAP
27 rooms, 27 pb
Visa, MC, AmEx, •
C-yes/S-ltd/H-yes

Dinner (Tues.-Sat.)
Restaurant
Bar service
sitting room, sauna
pool, hot tubs, tanning

Romantic inn with country antique furnishings, candlelight dining, olympic pool and fitness room. View of Lake Winnipesaukee and Ossipee Mountain Range. Winter skiing.

The Atwood Inn, Franklin, NH

GLEN

Bernerhof Inn
P.O. Box 240, 03838
Rte 302
603-383-4414 800-548-8007
Sharon & Ted Wroblowski
All year

$$$ B&B
9 rooms, 9 pb
Visa, MC, AmEx, *Rated*,
C-ltd/S-no/P-no/H-no

Full breakfast
Lunch ltd, dinner, tea
Snacks, restaurant
bar, sitting room
sauna

An elegant small hotel featuring antique rooms, many with private spa tubs. Host of the renowned "A Taste of the Mountains Cooking School." **3rd night 50% off, Ltd**

GORHAM

Gorham House Inn B&B
P.O. Box 267, 03581
55 Main St.
603-466-2271 800-453-0023
Ron Orso and Maggie Cook
All year

$$ B&B
3 rooms
Visa, MC, Disc.,*Rated*, •
C-yes/S-ltd/P-yes

Full breakfast
Hot or iced tea, snacks
Sitting room
library
skiing/ wkly rentals

1891 Victorian on town common. Closest B&B to White Mountain National Forest & Mount Washington. Fine restaurants, golf, hiking, skiing, sightseeing nearby.

HAMPSTEAD

Stillmeadow B&B
P.O. Box 565, 03841
545 Main St.
603-329-8381
Lori & Randy Offord
All year

$$ B&B
4 rooms, 4 pb
AmEx, *Rated*
C-yes/S-no/P-no/H-no
some Fr.,Ger.,Span.

Full breakfast (wkends)
Continental plus (wkdys)
Comp. wine and cookies
croquet, gardens, bikes
near lake & cross-country
skiing

Discover Southern New Hampshire's best kept secret. Memorable, charming getaway. Inviting Greek Revival Colonial with 5 chimneys and 3 staircases. **15% off for 1 week stays.**

HAMPTON

Curtis Field House, The
735 Exeter Rd., 03842
603-929-0082
Mary F. Houston
Open May–October

$$ B&B
3 rooms, 2 pb
Visa, MC, *Rated*,
C-ltd/S-ltd/P-no

Full breakast
Dinner (on request)
Afternoon tea
sitting room, library
tennis courts, pool

Royal Bairy Wills Cape-country setting. Near Phillips Exeter, antiques, historical area, ocean. Breakfast served on terrace. Lobster dinners on request. **10% off 3+ nights.**

Inn at Elmwood Corners
252 Winnacunnet Rd., 03842
603-929-0443 800-253-5691
John & Mary Hornberger
All year

$$ B&B
7 rooms, 2 pb
Visa, MC, *Rated*
C-yes/S-ltd

Full breakfast
Dinner for guests
Cookies, iced tea
sitting room/library
wraparound porch

Memorable breakfasts in an 1870 home filled with quilts and country charm. 1.5 miles from the ocean; short walk to a quaint village.

HAMPTON BEACH

Oceanside, The
365 Ocean Blvd., 03842
603-926-3542
Skip & Debbie Windemiller
Mid-May–mid-October

$$$ B&B
10 rooms, 10 pb
Most CC, *Rated*, •
C-ltd

Continental plus
Bar service
sitting room, library
beach chair & towels

Directly across from sandy beach; beautiful ocean views. Active, resort-type atmosphere during mid-summer. Recently renovations, many antiques. **20-30% discounts, ask**

HAVERHILL

Haverhill Inn
P.O. Box 95, 03765
Dartmouth College Hwy
603-989-5961
Stephen Campbell, Anne Baird
All year

$$$ B&B
4 rooms, 4 pb
C-ltd/S-no/P-no/H-ltd
French

Full breakfast
Comp. sherry, tea
Piano, library
sitting room
canoeing

An elegant federal colonial w/working fireplaces in every room. Newly rebuilt kitchen. Incomparable views of Vermont & New Hampshire hills. Cross-country ski trails, canoeing trips.

HENNIKER

Colby Hill Inn
P.O. Box 778, 03242
The Oaks
603-428-3281 800-531-0330
Ellie & John Day & Laurel Day
All year

$$$ B&B
16 rooms, 16 pb
Visa, MC, AmEx, *Rated*,
C-ltd/S-ltd/P-no/H-ltd

Full breakfast
Dinner, bar
Comp. beverages. cookies
sitting room, library
croquet, badminton, pool

1800 country inn on 5 acres in a quiet village. Antique-filled rooms, smiling hosts, fine dining. Swimming, hiking, skiing, canoeing, kayaking, fishing and cycling all nearby.

Meeting House Inn, The
35 Flanders Rd., 03242
603-428-3228
J. & B. Davis, P. & C. Bakke
All year

$$ B&B
6 rooms, 6 pb
Visa, MC, AmEx, *Rated*,
C-ltd/S-no/P-no/H-no

Full breakfast
Lunch, dinner, lounge
Hot tub, sauna
bicycles
sitting room

A country retreat with cozy rooms and attention to detail. "Your place to return to again and again." **25% off after three nights**

HILLSBOROUGH

Stonebridge Inn
365 W. Main St., 03244
603-464-3155
Clara & George Adame
All year

$ B&B
4 rooms, 4 pb
Visa, MC
C-yes/S-yes/P-no/H-no

Continental brekafast
Sitting room

A mid-1800s colonial farmhouse, lovingly restored and redecorated to create the kind of small country inn you've always hoped to find.

HOLDERNESS

Inn on Golden Pond, The
P.O. Box 680, 03245
Route 3
603-968-7269
Bill & Bonnie Webb
All year

$$$ B&B
9 rooms, 9 pb
Visa, MC, *Rated*, •
C-ltd/S-no/P-no/H-no

Full breakfast
Piano

Located on 55 wooded acres across the street from Squam Lake, setting for "On Golden Pond." Close to major attractions, skiing.

Manor on Golden Pond, The
P.O. Box T, Rt. 3 & Shepard Hill
Rd., 03245
603-968-3348 800-545-2141
David & Bambi Arnold
All year

$$$ B&B
27 rooms, 27 pb
Rated, •
C-ltd/S-no/P-no/H-no
French, Spanish

Full breakfast
Restaurant, bar service
Dinner, Aft. tea
sitting room, library
tennis, swimming pool

Elegant 1903 English mansion overlooking "Golden Pond." Spectacular views, spacious grounds, private beach, romantic dining. Charming accommodations. Relax & Enjoy!

INTERVALE

Wildflowers Guest House
P.O. Box 802, 03845
N. Main St., (Route 16)
603-356-2224
Eileen Davies & Dean Franke
May–October

$$ B&B
6 rooms, 2 pb
C-yes/S-yes/P-no/H-no

Continental plus
Sitting room
panoramic views

Century-old country home offering simplicity and charm of yesteryear; cozy parlor with woodstove; dining room with fireplace. Panoramic views of mountains.

JACKSON

Dana Place Inn
P.O. Box L, Route 16, Pinkham
Notch, 03846
603-383-6822 800-537-9276
The Levine Family
All year

$$$ B&B/MAP
35 rooms, 31 pb
Visa, MC, AmEx, *Rated*,
•
C-yes/S-yes/P-no/H-no
French

Full breakfast in season
Dinner, pub
Piano, river swimming
indoor pool, cross-country
skiing
tennis courts, jacuzzi

Historic country inn at base of Mt. Washington. Cozy rooms, fine dining, afternoon tea. Indoor heated pool, jacuzzi, tennis, hiking, skiing. **3rd night 50% off, ltd**

Ellis River House
P.O. Box 656, 03846
Route 16
603-383-9339 800-233-8309
Barry & Barb Lubao & family
All year

$$ B&B
18 rooms, 15 pb
Visa, MC, AmEx, Disc., •
C-yes/S-yes/P-ask/H-ask
Polish

Full country breakfast
Tea, coffee, cookies
Sitting rm., atrium, A/C
cable TV, VCR, fishing
some 2 person jacuzzis

Turn-of-the-century house w/balconies overlooking Ellis River. Honeymoon cottage. Home-made breads; jacuzzi spa. cross-country skiing, outdoor heated pool. **Champagne for newlyweds**

JACKSON

Inn at Jackson
P.O. Box H, Thornhill Rd., 03846
603-383-4321 800-289-8600
Lori Tradewell
All year

$$ B&B
9 rooms, 9 pb
Most CC, *Rated*, •
C-yes/S-ltd/P-no/H-no

Full breakfast
Hot tub, jacuzzi
3 rooms w/fireplaces
sitting room, library
phone in lobby

Stanford White mansion in the heart of the White Mountains. Adjacent to Jackson ski touring trails. Spacious rooms, several common rooms, porch diningroom.

Paisley and Parsley B&B
Box 572, Five Mile Circuit Rd.,
03846
603-383-0859
Bea & Chuck Stone
Dec–Apr, Jun 20–Nov 20

$$ B&B
3 rooms, 3 pb
Visa, MC, *Rated*, •
C-ltd/S-no/P-no/H-yes
some French

Full breakfast
Afternoon tea, snacks
Sitting room, library
hot tub, bicycles
near skiing, golf, fish

Mountain village with spectacular view of Mt. Washington. Private phones and entrances. Charming new home, folk art, fine antiques, herb garden. Quiet location. **3rd night 50%**

Village House, The
P.O. Box 359, 03846
Route 16A
603-383-6666
Robin Crocker
All year

$ B&B
15 rooms, 8 pb
Visa, MC, •
C-yes/S-yes/P-no/H-no

Full breakfast (winter)
Cont. plus (summer-fall)
Aft. snack, TV, balcony
pool, tennis courts
living room w/fireplace

7 acres, beautiful village setting. 10 well-decorated rooms. Near fine dining, hiking, golfing. Fantastic cross-country downhill skiing. Rooms w/TV, kitchens. Family accommodations.

JAFFREY

Benjamin Prescott Inn
Route 124 E., 03452
603-532-6637
Jan & Barry Miller
All year

$$ B&B
11 rooms, 9 pb
Visa, MC, *Rated*, •
C-ltd/S-ltd/P-no/H-no

Full breakfast
Comp. tea, coffee
Sitting room
bicycles

Relax… Indulge… Less than two hours from Boston, the inn offers the opportunity to reset your pace and explore the Monadnock region.

Galway House B&B, The
247 Old Peterboro Rd., 03452
603-532-8083
Joe & Marie Manning
August 15–June

$$ B&B
2 rooms
C-yes/S-no/P-no/H-no

Full breakfast
Library, sun deck
Woodland setting
cross-country skiing

Four season inn run in the "old country tradition"—a warm bed, a warm hearth, a full country breakfast at a moderate price. The Currier & Ives corner of NH. **10% skiing disc't**

Lilac Hill Acres B&B
5 Ingalls Rd., 03452
603-532-7278
Frank & Ellen McNeill
All year

$$ B&B
6 rooms, 1 pb
C-ltd/S-ltd/P-no/H-no

Full breakfast
Comp. tea
Sitting room
piano, pond

Five-star service in a beautiful setting. Enjoy a bit of life on the farm with a warm personal touch. Join us year-round.

Dana Place, Jackson, NH

JEFFERSON

Applebrook B&B	$ B&B	Full breakfast
P.O. Box 178, 03583	12 rooms, 4 pb	Dinner by reservation
Route 115A	Visa, MC, Disc, *Rated*, •	Sitting room, library
603-586-7713 800-545-6504	C-yes/S-no/P-yes/H-no	outdoor hot tub
Sandra J. Conley/Martin Kelly	All year	Dorm avail. for groups

Hike, golf, ski from comfortable Victorian farmhouse. Taste our mid-summer raspberries while enjoying mountain views. Stained glass & goldfish pool. **50% off 3rd night**

Jefferson Inn, The	$ EP, $$ B&B	Full breakfast
RFD 1, Box 68A, Route 2, 03583	13 rooms, 13 pb	Afternoon tea
603-586-7998 800-729-7908	Visa, MC, AmEx, *Rated*,	Conference room
Greg Brown, Bertie Koelewijn	•	swimming pond, tennis
Exc. November & April	C-ltd/S-ltd/Dutch,	2-bedroom family suite
	German, French	

Uniquely furnished Victorian near Mount Washington; outdoor paradise including hiking, golf, theater, swimming pond; wraparound porch; 360-degree views; evening tea.

LACONIA

Cartway House Inn	$$ B&B	Full breakfast
Old Lakeshore Rd/Gilfor, 03246	9 rooms	Comp. tea, wine
603-528-1172	MC, •	Sitting room
Gretchen & Tony Shortway	C-yes/S-yes/P-yes/H-no	
All year	Italian, French, Spanish	

1791 renovated farmhouse, French country dining room overlooking mountains and lake. Near all attractions, ski area, lake. Casual comfort.

LINCOLN

Red Sleigh Inn B&B, The	$$ B&B	Full hearty breakfast
P.O. Box 562, 03251	8 rooms	Comp. tea, wine
Pollard Rd.	Visa, MC, Disc.	Sitting room, library
603-745-8517	C-ltd/S-ltd/P-no/H-no	indoor/outdoor pool
Bill & Loretta Deppe		sauna, hot tubs, BBQs
All year		

The mountains surrounding us abound in ski touring trails. Bedrooms are tastefully decorated with many antiques. Panoramic view of surrounding mountains.

LISBON

Ammonoosuc Inn	$$ B&B	Continental plus
Bishop Rd., 03585	9 rooms, 9 pb	Lunch, snacks
603-838-6118	Visa, MC, AmEx, •	Restaurant, bar
Steve & Laura Bromley	C-yes/S-yes/P-no/H-no	sitting room, pool2
All year		fishing, canoeing

1888 farmhouse, guesthouse w/private baths, swimming pool, tennis, 9-hole golf course. Public dining room, lunch and cocktails on porch overlooking river. **Comp. wine w/dinner**

LITTLETON

Beal House Inn, The	$ B&B	Continental plus
247 West Main St., Jct. of US 302	13 rooms, 9 pb	Dinner, tea, snacks
& NH Rt 18, 03561	Visa, MC, *Rated*, •	Restaurant, wine, beer
603-444-2661	C-yes/S-no/P-no/H-no	sitting room, library
Catherine/John Fisher-Motheu	French	billiards, view, porch
All year		

1833 inn in the White Mountains. True Belgian waffles by morning fire. Robust European fare in evening. Year-round mountain adventures in between! **Comp. dessert with dinner**

MARLBOROUGH

Peep-Willow Farm B&B	$ B&B	Full breakfast
51 Bixby St., 03455	3 rooms, 1 pb	Comp. wine
603-876-3807	•	Snacks
Noel Aderer	C-yes/S-no/P-ask/H-yes	sitting room
All year		

I raise thoroughbred horses—you can help with chores (no riding), watch the colts play and enjoy the view all the way to Vermont's Green Mountains.

MOUNT SUNAPEE

Blue Goose Inn B&B, The	$$ B&B	Full breakfast
Route 103 B, Box 117, 03772	5 rooms, 3 pb	Dinner on request
603-763-5519	Visa, MC, *Rated*, •	Sitting room, bicycles
Meryl & Ronald Caldwell	C-yes/S-yes/P-no/H-yes	lake, downhill skiing
All year		picnicking, lawn games

Adjacent to Mt. Sunapee State Park; 19th-century farmhouse on 3.5 acres. Picnicking, grill, bikes available. Mystery weekends. Non-smoking policy. **Area events discounts**

NEW IPSWICH

Inn at New Ipswich, The	$$ B&B	Full hearthside brkfast
P.O. Box 208, 03071	7 rooms, 5 pb	Tea, coffee, snacks
11 Porter Hill Rd.	Visa, MC, •	Sitting room, library
603-878-3711	C-ltd/S-no/P-no/H-no	game chest, 6 fireplaces
Ginny & Steve Bankuti	Hungarian	porch, stone walls
All year		

Graceful, lovingly maintained 1790 farmhouse w/fruit trees. Hearty hospitality. Near cross-country & downhill skiing, antiquing, concerts, arts & crafts, hiking. **4th night free**

NEW LONDON

Maple Hill Farm	$$ B&B	Full breakfast
RR1 Box 1620, 200 Newport Rd.,	10 rooms, 2 pb	Dinner by reservation
03257	•	Sitting room
603-526-2248 800-231-8637	C-yes/S-yes/P-yes/H-ltd	bicycles
Dennis & Roberta Aufranc		
All year		

160-yr-old farmhouse, newly restored, serving country breakfast, near golf, cross-country & alpine skiing, all other recreation. Country gourmet dinner: $15-25 pp. **10% off 3+ nights.**

NEWPORT

Inn at Coit Mountain	$$$ B&B	Full gourmet breakfast
HCR 63, Box 3, Route 10, 523 N.	5 rooms, 1 pb	Lunch, dinner, tea
Main St., 03773	Visa, MC	Sitting room, library
603-863-3583 800-367-2364	C-yes/S-ltd/H-yes	sleigh rides
Dick & Judi Tatem		airport pickup
All year		

Elegant country home with French charm and rooms with fireplaces. Year-round activities in the Lake/Mount Sunapee region. **7th night free**

NORTH CONWAY ─────────────────────────────────────

1785 Inn, The
P.O. Box 1785, 03860
3582 White Mountain Hwy
603-356-9025 800-421-1785
Becky & Charlie Mallar
All year

$$ B&B
13 rooms, 8 pb
Visa, MC, AmEx, *Rated*,
●
C-yes/S-ltd/P-ltd/H-ltd
French

Full breakfast
Restaurant, lounge, pool
2 sitting rooms, piano
classical guitar Sat-Sun
ski/honeymoon packages

Newly redecorated historic inn at The Scenic Vista overlooking the Saco River Valley. Award winning cross-country skiing trails. Won several food & wine accolades. **20% off Mar-June**

Buttonwood Inn, The
P.O. Box 1817, 03860
Mt. Surprise Rd.
603-356-2625 800-258-2625
Ann & Hugh Begley
All year

$ B&B
9 rooms, 3 pb
Most CC, *Rated*, ●
C-ltd/S-yes/P-no/H-no

Full breakfast
Comp. wine
Sitting room, library
40-foot swimming pool
TV, lawn sports, skiing

Tucked away on Mt. Surprise. Quiet & secluded yet only 2 mi. to town-excellent dining, shopping. Near all outdoor activities. Apres-ski gameroom w/firepl. **Restaurant disc't**

Center Chimney—1787, The
P.O. Box 1220, 03860
River Rd.
603-356-6788
Farley Ames Whitley
All year

$ B&B
4 rooms
Rated
C-yes/S-yes/P-no/H-no

Continental breakfast
Comp. hot cider (winter)
Sitting room, library
cable TV, piano
fireplaces, whirlpool

Charming early Cape, woodsy setting, just off Saco River and Main St. Easy walking to shops, restaurants; year-round sports. **$5 off/night after 3rd night midweek.**

Cranmore Mountain Lodge
P.O. Box 1194, 03860
859 Kearsarge Rd.
603-356-2044 800-356-3596
Dennis & Judy Helfand
All year

$$ B&B
16 rooms, 16 pb
Most CC, *Rated*, ●
C-yes/S-yes/P-no/H-no
Danish

Full breakfast
Dinner, poolside BBQs $
Fireplace room
piano, hot tub
swimming, tennis

Authentic country inn in heart of White Mts. Hearty country breakfast. Tennis court, pool, jacuzzi, tobogganing, skating, cross-country skiing. 2-bdrm townhouse also avail.

Nereledge Inn
P.O. Box 547, 03860
River Road, North Conway
603-356-2831
Valerie & Dave Halpin
All year

$$ B&B
9 rooms, 3 1/2 pb
Visa, MC, AmEx
C-yes/S-no/P-no/H-no

Full breakfast
Dinner for groups
2 sitting rooms, games
piano, Saco River
June fly-fishing school

Cozy 1787 inn, five minutes walk from village, close to skiing areas, fishing, golf, climbing, canoeing. Home-cooked meals including country-style breakfast.

Old Red Inn & Cottages
P.O. Box 467, 03860
Routes 16 & 302
603-356-2642
Don & Winnie White
All year

$$ B&B
17 rooms, 15 pb
Visa, MC, AmEx, Disc.
C-yes/S-yes/P-ltd/H-no
French

Full breakfast
Kitchenettes
Living room w/woodstove
piano, herb garden
flower gardens

Four-season 1810 country inn with 10 cottages and award-winning gardens. Walking distance to village. Spectacular mountain views—Mt. Washington seen from canopied bed suite!

NORTH CONWAY ————————————

Scottish Lion Inn & Restr. | $ B&B | Full breakfast
P.O. Box 1527, 03860 | 8 rooms, 8 pb | Lunch, dinner, bar
Rt. 16 1 mi. N. of Conway | Most CC, *Rated*, • | Sitting room, library
603-356-6381 800-258-0370 | C-yes/S-yes/P-no/H-no | hot tub, bicycles, A/C
Michael & Janet Procopio | Ital., Hawaiin, Phillip. | cross-country skiing, hiking
All year exc. Christmas

A country inn in the Scottish tradition. Over sixty scotches and an American Scottish Highland menu. Skiing out backdoor 70 km. All attractions are minutes away.

Stonehurst Manor | $$ EP/MAP | Full breakfast $
P.O. Box 1937, 03860 | 25 rooms, 23 pb | Dinner incl., tea/coffee
Route 16 | Visa, MC, AmEx, *Rated* | Library, piano, bar
603-356-3271 800-525-9100 | C-yes/S-yes/P-no/H-yes | swimming pool, hot tub
Peter Rattay | German | tennis courts
All year

Turn-of-the-century mansion with old oak and stained glass. Relax by our fireplace in the library. Mount Washington Valley.

Wyatt House English Inn | $$ B&B | Full candlelit breakfast
P.O. Box 777, 03860 | 6 rooms, 4 pb | Aft. tea, snacks
603-356-7977 800-527-7978 | Visa, MC, Disc. *Rated*, • | Comp. sherry
Bill & Arlene Strickland | C-ltd/S-ltd/P-no/H-no | sitting room, library
All year | | swim in Sacto River

Panoramic mountain & river views. Rooms furnished w/antiques. Candlelit, gourmet breakfast served on English Wedgewood & Irish lace. Stroll to Sacto River to swim & fish.

NORTH CONWAY—INTERVALE ————————————

Forest—A Country Inn, The | $ B&B | Full breakfast
P.O. Box 37, 03845 | 11 rooms, 11 pb | Dinner by rsvp.
Route 16A | Visa, MC, AmEx, *Rated*, | Aftn. tea, wine in room
603-356-9772 800-448-3534 | • | swimming pool, piano, TV
Ken & Rae Wyman | C-yes/S-no/P-no/H-no | cross-country skiing, skating
All year exc. April

Century-old inn furnished w/antiques; nestled in peaceful woodlands by White Mountains attractions. Sleigh rides, fireplcs. Suites, family pkgs. **3rd night 50% off, ltd**

NORTH WOODSTOCK ————————————

Wilderness Inn B&B | $ B&B/$$ MAP | Full gourmet breakfast
RFD 1, Box 69, Route 3 & | 7 rooms, 5 pb | Dinner with reservation
Kaucamagus Hwy, 03262 | Visa, MC, AmEx, *Rated*, | Aftn. tea, cider, cocoa
603-745-3890 800-200-WILD | • | swimming hole, 3 porches
Rosanna & Michael Yarnell | C-yes/S-yes/P-no/H-no | cottage w/deck available
All year | Fr.,Ital.,Hindi, Amharic

"The quintessential country inn." Circa 1912, located in quaint New England town. Inn & rooms furnished w/antiques & oriental carpets. 3 mi. to Loon Mountain skiing.

Woodstock Inn | $ B&B | Full breakfast
80 Main St., 03262 | 19 rooms, 11 pb | Outdoor jacuzzi, lounge
603-745-3951 800-321-3985 | Most CC, *Rated* | 3 rms. w/jacuzzis
Scott & Eileen Rice | C-yes/S-yes/P-no/H-no | 2 fireplace rooms
All year

100-year-old Victorian & 2 adjacent bldgs., individually appointed rms. Town's original train station serve pub-style meals. Complete breakfast and candlelit fine dining.

NORTHWOOD

Meadow Farm B&B
Jenness Pond Rd., 03261
603-942-8619
Janet & Douglas Briggs
All year

$$ B&B
3 rooms
C-yes/S-ltd/P-ltd/H-no

Full breakfast
Private beach
canoeing, sitting room
antiquing

Restored charming 1770 colonial home—50 acres of fields, woods. Private beach on lake. Enjoy walks, canoeing, cross-country skiing. Memorable breakfasts.

OSSIPEE

Acorn Lodge
P.O. Box 144, 03864
Duncan Lake
603-539-2151 407-737-3199
Julie & Ray Terry
June—October 15

$ B&B
4 rooms, 4 pb
C-yes/S-ltd/P-no/H-yes

Continental breakfast
Lake, boats, canoes
bicycles, sitting room
badminton, fishing

*Grover Cleveland's hideaway, furnished with antiques and new beds. Breakfast on veranda overlooking Duncan Lake. Cottage available by the week. **3rd night 50% off, ltd***

PLYMOUTH

Northway House
R.F.D. #1, U.S. Rte. 3 North,
03264
603-536-2838
Micheline & Norman
McWilliams
All year

$ B&B
3 rooms
C-yes/S-yes/P-ltd/H-no
French

Full breakfast
Comp. wine
Sitting room
cable TV
near skiing, shops

*Hospitality plus awaits the traveler in this charming colonial. Close to lakes and mountains. Gourmet breakfast. Reasonable rates, children welcome. **3rd night 50% off***

PORTSMOUTH

Governor's House B&B
32 Miller Ave., 03801
603-431-6546
John & Nancy Grossman
All year

$$ B&B
4 rooms, 4 pb
Visa, MC, •
C-ltd/S-no/P-no/H-no

Full breakfast
Aft. tea, snacks
Sitting room, library
tennis court
gardens

Experience turn-of-the-century living. Four intimate rooms; gourmet breakfast. Walk to all that historic Portsmouth has to offer.

Inn at Strawbery Banke
314 Court St., 03801
603-436-7242 800-428-3933
Sarah Glover O'Donnell
All year

$$$ B&B
7 rooms, 7 pb
Visa, MC, AmEx, *Rated*
C-ltd/S-no/P-no/H-ltd

Full breakfast
Sitting room
outdoor garden
bicycles

This colonial inn charms travelers with its beautiful rooms & outdoor garden. Located in heart of old Portsmouth with its quaint shops, working port, parks, historical homes.

Martin Hill Inn
404 Islington St., 03801
603-436-2287 800-445-2286
Jane & Paul Harnden
All year

$$$ B&B
7 rooms, 7 pb
Visa, MC, *Rated*
C-ltd/S-no/P-no/H-no

Full breakfast
All rooms have writing
tables and sofas or
separate sitting areas

1810 colonial has beautifully appointed rooms with period antiques. Elegant yet comfortable Walk to downtown Portsmouth and waterfront. Lovely gardens.

PORTSMOUTH

Sise Inn	$$$ B&B	Continental plus
40 Court St., 03801	34 rooms, 34 pb	Afternoon tea, snacks
603-433-1200	Most CC, *Rated*, •	Sitting room
Carl G. Jensen	C-yes/S-yes/P-no/H-yes	
All year	Danish	

All rooms & suites feature private baths, remote controlled cable color TV and video cassette players, telephones and alarm clock radios.

RYE

Cable House, The	$ B&B	Continental plus
20 Old Beach Rd., 03870	7 rooms, 2 pb	Sitting room
603-964-5000	C-ltd/S-yes/P-no/H-no	
Kay Kazakis	Greek	
May 15–September 30		

Named historical site, walk to beach. Landfall of first direct cable between Europe and the USA. $200/wk: 6th & 7th nights free

Rock Ledge Manor B&B	B&B	Full breakfast
1413 Ocean Blvd, Route 1A,	4 rooms, 4 pb	Sitting room
03870	*Rated*	piano
603-431-1413	C-ltd/S-no/P-no/H-no	
Norman & Janice Marineau		
All year		

Seacoast getaway on the ocean, period furnishings, full memorable bkft. served in mahogany-ceilinged bkft. room. Near all NH & ME activities, U. of NH. Discounts, ask

SNOWVILLE

Snowvillage Inn	$$ B&B/$$$ MAP	Full country breakfast
Box 176 L, Stuart Rd., 03849	18 rooms, 18 pb	Dinner, bar, tea/cookies
603-447-2818 800-447-4345	Most CC, *Rated*	Sauna, fireplace, piano
Peter, Trudy & Frank Cutrone	C-ltd/S-ltd/P-no/H-ltd	tennis court, sitting rm
All year exc. April	German	hike from door, skiing

Seclusion & peace amidst mountain magic. Warm old-country elegance, great food, gardens, dine in chalet w/breathtaking view of Mt. Washington, glorious sunsets.

SUNAPEE

Haus Edelweiss B&B	$ B&B	Full breakfast
P.O. Box 368, 03782	5 rooms, 1 pb	Comp. wine, snacks
13 Maple St.	Visa, MC, *Rated*, •	Sitting room, TV
603-763-2100 800-248-0713	C-ltd/S-no/P-no/H-no	front/back sitting porch
John & Jennifer Dixon	French, Spanish	books, games, packages
All year		

Lovely, spacious Victorian at Sunapee Harbor near Mt. Sunapee. Leisurely, unsurpassed breakfasts. Hiking, skiing, and swimming nearby. Discounts, ask

Seven Hearths Inn	$$$ B&B	Full breakfast
26 Seven Hearths Ln., 03782	10 rooms, 10 pb	Restaurant, bar
603-763-5657	Visa, MC, *Rated*, •	Afternoon tea, snacks
Laraine Pedrero	C-yes/S-yes/P-no/H-yes	sitting room, library
All year		pool, A/C in rooms

Beautiful country inn on five private acres. Year round resort area, minutes from beach and ski areas. Guests are welcomed to their rooms with fresh flowers & bowls of fruit.

SUTTON MILLS

Village House, The	$ B&B	Full breakfast
Box 151 Grist Mill Rd., 03221	3 rooms	Aft. tea, snacks
603-927-4765	•	Comp. wine, sitting room
Peggy & Norm Forand	C-ltd/S-no/P-no/H-no	library, board games
All year		yard games

1857 country Victorian in Lake Sunapee area. Recently redecorated. Antiques & old quilts in rooms. Convenient to attractions & restaurants. **3rd night 50% off**

TAMWORTH

Whispering Pines B&B	$$ B&B	Full breakfast
Rte 113A & Hemenway Rd., 03886	4 rooms, 1 pb	Afternoon/evening snacks
603-323-7337	Most CC, *Rated*	Private sitting room
Karen & Kim Erickson	C-ltd/S-no/P-ltd/H-no	private porch
All year		

Country farmhouse nestled into State Forest. Hiking, cross-country skiing from door. Local village summer theater. Lakes and mountains. Resort area.

WENTWORTH

Hilltop Acres B&B	$$ B&B	Continental plus
P.O. Box 32, 03282	145 rooms	Afternoon tea, snacks
East Side & Buffalo Rd.	Visa, MC, *Rated*, •	Sitting room, library
603-764-5896	C-yes/S-ltd/P-no/H-no	lawn games, cable TV
Marie A. Kauk	German	recreation room, piano
All year		

Country hospitality; charming, comfortable rooms; large pine-paneled recreation room with antique piano, fireplace; peaceful outdoor setting; pine forest and flowing brook.

WHITEFIELD

Spalding House Inn, The	$$$ B&B/AP	Full breakfast
RR# 1, Box 57, Mountain View Rd., 03598	42 rooms, 42 pb	Dinner w/AP plan
603-837-2572	Visa, MC, *Rated*, •	Aft. tea, bar service
D. Cockre & M. Flinder	C-yes/S-yes/P-yes/H-no	sitting room, library
June - October		tennis court, pool

A premier country inn in the heart of the White Mtns. Set on 200 acres w/manicured lawns and perennial gardens. Glorious views, magnificent food & a slow, relaxed way of life.

WINNISQUAM

Tall Pines Inn	$$ B&B	Full country breakfast
P.O. Box 327, 03289	3 rooms, 1 pb	Dinner by reservation
752 Old Rt.3	Visa, MC, *Rated*, •	Snacks, sitting room
603-528-3632 800-722-6870	C-ltd/S-ltd/P-no/H-no	lake, boating, woodstove
Kent & Kate Kern		swimming, fishing
All year		

Beautiful four-season destination in New Hampshire "Lakes Region." Super views. Boat rental and sandy beach. Winter skiing. Superb fall foliage. **3rd night 50% off**

WOLFEBORO

Tuc'Me Inn B&B	$$ B&B	Full breakfast
P.O. Box 657, 03894	6 rooms, 2 pb	Sitting room
68 N. Main St.	Visa, MC, *Rated*, •	library
603-569-5702	C-yes/S-ltd/P-no/H-no	2 screened porches
E., T. & T. Foutz, I. Evans		
All year		

Early 1800s Colonial inn. Homey atmosphere, tastefully furnished. "Cook's whims" breakfast. Two-block walk to downtown and beautiful Lake Winnipesaukee. **5+ nights discount.**

The Tuc Me Inn, Wolfeboro, NH

More Inns ...

Mt. Cardigan B&B, Knowles Hill Rd., Alexandria, 03222, 603-744-5803
Stone Rest B&B, 652 Fowler River Rd., Alexandria, 03222, 603-744-6066
Darby Brook Farm, Hill Rd., Alstead, 03602, 603-835-6624
Breezy Point Inn, RFD-1, Box 302, Antrim, 03440, 603-478-5201
Steele Homestead, The, RR1, Box 78, Antrim, 03440
Uplands Inn, Miltimore Rd., Antrim Center, 03440, 603-588-6349
Country Options, P.O. Box 736, Ashland, 03217, 603-968-7958
Rose & The Bear B&B, Sanborn Rd., Ashland, 03217
David's Inn, Bennington Sq., Bennington, 03442, 603-588-2458
Bells B&B, The, P.O. Box 276, Bethlehem, 03574, 603-869-2647
Gables of Park and Main, Box 190 Main St., Bethlehem, 03574, 603-869-3111
Highlands Inn, P.O. Box 118C, Bethlehem, 03574, 603-869-3978
Mulburn Inn, The, Main St., Bethlehem, 03574, 603-869-3389
Mountain Lake Inn, P.O. Box 443, Route 114, Bradford, 03221, 603-938-2136
Mount Washington Hotel, Bretton Woods, 03575, 603-278-1000
Pasquaney Inn, Star Route 1 Box 1066, Bridgewater, 03222, 603-744-2712
Victorian B&B, 16 Summer St., Rt. 104, Bristol, 03222, 603-744-6157
Campton Inn, The, RR 2, Box 12, Campton, 03223, 603-726-4449
Campton Inn, The, RR 2, Box 12, Campton Village, 03223, 603-726-4449
Village Guest House, P.O. Box 222, Campton Village, 03223, 603-726-4444
Inn on Canaan St., The, P.O. Box 92, Canaan, 03741, 603-523-7310
Towerhouse Inn, One Parker St., Canaan, 03741
Sleepy Hollow B&B, RR #1, Baptist Hill Rd., Canterbury, 03224, 603-267-6055
Lavender Flower Inn, P.O. Box 328, Main St., Center Conway, 03813, 603-447-3794
Hitching Post Village Inn, Old Route 16, Center Ossipee, 03814, 603-539-4482
Corner House Inn, P.O. Box 204, Center Sandwich, 03227, 603-284-6219
Dearborn Place, Box 997, Route 25, Centre Harbor, 03226, 603-253-6711
Staffords in the Field, Box 270, Chocorua, 03817, 603-323-7766
Goddard Mansion, 26 Hillstead Rd., Claremont, 03743
Poplars, 13 Grandview St., Claremont, 03743, 603-543-0858
Wyman Farm, RFD 8, Box 437, Concord, 03301, 603-783-4467
Eastman Inn, Main St., Conway, 03860, 603-356-6707
Home Hill Country Inn, RFD 2, Cornish, 03781, 603-675-6165
Inn at Danbury, Route 104, Danbury, 03230, 603-768-3318
Patchwork Inn, P.O. Box 107, Maple St., East Andover, 03231, 603-735-6426
Delford Inn, Centre St., East Sullivan, 03445, 603-847-9778
Haley House Farm, RFD #1, N. River Rd., Epping, 03857, 603-679-8713
Moose Mountain Lodge, Moose Mountain, Etna, 03750, 603-643-3529
Inn of Exeter, 90 Front St., Exeter, 03833, 603-772-5901
Fitzwilliam Inn, Fitzwilliam, 03447, 603-585-9000
Francestown B&B, Main St., Francestown, 03043, 603-547-6333
Inn at Crotched Mountain, Mountain Rd., Francestown, 03043, 603-588-6840
Cannon Mt. Inn and Cottage, Easton Rd., Route 116, Franconia, 03580, 603-823-9574
Main St. B&B of Franconia, Main St., Franconia, 03580, 603-823-8513
Pinestead Farm Lodge, Route 116, RFD 1, Franconia, 03580, 603-823-5601
Shepherd's Inn, Forest Hills Rd. Rt.142, Franconia, 03580, 603-823-8777

Sugar Hill Inn, Route 117 (Sugar Hill), Franconia, 03580, 603-823-5621

Freedom House B&B, Box 338, 1 Maple St., Freedom, 03836, 603-539-4815

Hall's Hillside B&B, R.D. #4 Box GA372, Gilford, 03246, 603-293-7290

Historic Tavern Inn, P.O. Box 369, Gilmanton, 03237, 603-267-7349

Greenfield B&B Inn, P.O. Box 400, Greenfield, 03047, 603-547-6327

Blue Heron Inn, 124 Landing Rd., Hampton, 03842, 603-926-9666

John Hancock Inn, Main St., Hancock, 03449, 603-525-3318

Westwinds of Hancock, P.O. Box 635, Route 1, Hancock, 03449, 603-525-4415

Trumbull House, Box C-29, Hanover, 03755, 603-643-1400

Harrisville Squires' Inn, Box 19, Keene Rd., Harrisville, 03450, 603-827-3925

Hanscom House, Box 191, Henniker, 03242

New England Inn, P.O. Box 100, Intervale, 03845, 603-356-5541

Old Field House, Intervale, 03845

Riverside Country Inn, Route 16A, Box 42, Intervale, 03845, 603-356-9060

Christmas Farm Inn, Route 16B, P.O. Box 176, Jackson, 03846, 603-383-4313

Covered Bridge Motor Lodge, Box 277B, White Mt. Hwy, Jackson, 03846, 603-383-9151

Inn at Thorn Hill, Box A, Thorn Hill Rd., Jackson, 03846, 603-383-4242

Iron Mountain House, Jackson, 03846

Jackson House B&B, P.O. Box 378, Jackson, 03846

Whitney's Inn, Route 16B, Jackson, 03846, 603-383-6886

Nestlenook Farm & Resort, Dinsmore Rd., Jackson Village, 03846, 603-383-9443

Wildcat Inn & Tavern, Box T, Main St., Jackson Village, 03846, 603-383-4245

Gould Farm, P.O. Box 27, Jaffrey, 03452, 603-532-6996

Jaffrey Manor Inn, 13 Stratton Rd., Jaffrey, 03452, 603-532-8069

Mill Pond Inn, 50 Prescott Rd., Jaffrey, 03452, 603-532-7687

Woodbound Inn, Woodbound Rd., Jaffrey, 03452, 603-532-8341

Monadnock Inn, Main St., Box 103, Jaffrey Center, 03454, 603-532-7001

Davenport Inn, RFD 1 Box 93A, Jefferson, 03583, 603-586-4320

Stag Hollow Inn, Route 115, Jefferson, 03583, 603-586-4598

Noah Cooke Inn, Route 2, Box 300, Keene, 03431, 603-357-3117

289 Court, 289 Court St., Kenne, 03431, 603-357-3195

Hickory Stick Farm, RFD #2, Laconia, 03246, 603-524-3333

Tin Whistle Inn, 1047 Union Av., Laconia, 03246, 603-528-4185

Ferry Point House, R-1 Box 335, Laonia, 03246, 603-524-0087

1895 House, 74 Pleasant St., Littleton, 03561, 603-444-5200

Edencroft Manor, Route 135, Dalton Rd., Littleton, 03561, 603-444-6776

Inn at Loudon Ridge, Box 195, Loudon, 03301, 603-267-8952

Dowd's Country Inn, On the Common, Lyme, 03768, 603-795-4712

Dowds Country Inn, P.O. Box 58, Lyme, 03768, 603-795-4712

Loch Lyme Lodge, RFD 278, Lyme, 03768, 603-795-2141

Lyme Inn, The, Route 10, On the Common, Lyme, 03768, 603-795-2222

Marjorie's House, Route 10, Lyme, 03768

Thatcher Hill Inn, Thatcher Hill Rd., Marlborough, 03455, 603-876-3361

Hathaway Inn, RFD 4, Red Gate Ln., Meredith, 03253, 603-279-5521

Nutmeg Inn, The, 80 Pease Road, RFD 2, Meredith, 03253, 603-279-8811

Tuckernuck Inn, The, RFD 4, Box 88, Meredith, 03253, 603-279-5521

Ram in the Thicket, Maple St., Milford, 03055, 603-654-6440

Olde Orchard Inn, RR, Box 256, Moultonboro, 03254, 603-476-5004

New London Inn, P.O. Box 8, 140 Main St, New London, 03257, 603-526-2791

Pleasant Lake Inn, N. Pleasant St., New London, 03257

Isaac Merrill House Inn, P.O. Box 8, New Town, 03847, 603-356-9041

Helga's B&B, 92 Packers Falls Rd., Newmarket, 03857, 603-659-6856

Indian Shutters Inn, Route 12, North Charlestown, 03603, 603-826-4445

Merrill Farm Resort, RFD Box 151, Route 16, North Conway, 03860, 603-447-3866

New England Inn, P.O. Box 428, Route 16A, North Conway, 03860, 603-356-5541

Schoolhouse Motel, P.O. Box 302, North Conway, 03860, 800-638-6050

Scottish Lion Inn & Restr., P.O. Box 1527, North Conway, 03860, 603-356-6381

Sunny Side Inn, Seavey St., North Conway, 03860, 603-356-6239

Cascade Lodge/B&B, Main St., P.O. Box 95, North Woodstock, 03262, 603-745-2722

Three Rivers House, RR#1 Box 72, Rte.3, North Woodstock, 03262, 603-745-2711

Aviary, Bow Lake, Box 268, Northwood, 03261, 603-942-7755

Nostalgia B&B, Box 520, Route 1, Northwood, 03261, 603-942-7748

White Goose Inn, P.O. Box 17, Route 10, Orford, 03777, 603-353-4812

Crab Apple Inn, The, RR 4, Box 1955, Plymouth, 03264, 603-536-4476

Govenor's House B&B, 32 Miller Ave., Portsmouth, 03801, 603-431-6546

The Chase House, Cornish, NH

The Village House, Jackson, NH

Leighton Inn, 69 Richards Ave., Portsmouth, 03801,
603-433-2188
Sheafe Street Inn, 3 Sheafe St., Portsmouth, 03801,
603-436-9104
Theatre Inn, 121 Bow St., Portsmouth, 03801,
603-431-5846
Grassy Pond House, Rindge, 03461, 603-899-5166
Tokfarm Inn, Box 1124, RR 2, Rindge, 03461,
603-899-6646
Ferry Point House, Lower Bay Rd., Sanbornton,
03269
Hide-Away Lodge, P.O. Box 6, New London,
Springfield, 03257, 603-526-4861
Stoddard Inn, Route 123, Stoddard, 03464,
603-446-7873
Province Inn, P.O. Box 309, Strafford, 03884,
603-664-2457
Hilltop Inn, The, Sugar Hill, 03585, 603-823-5695
Ledgeland, RR1, Box 94, Sugar Hill, 03585, 603-823-5341
Sunset Hill House, Sunset Rd., Sugar Hill, 03585, 603-823-5522
Dexter's Inn & Tennis Club, P.O. Box 703 B, Sunapee, 03782, 603-763-5571
Inn at Sunapee, The, P.O. Box 336, Sunapee, 03782, 603-763-4444
Loma Lodge, RFD #1 Box 592, Sunapee, 03782, 603-763-4849
Old Governor's House, P.O. Box 524, Sunapee, 03782, 603-763-9918
Times Ten Inn, Route 103B, Box 572, Sunapee, 03782, 603-763-5120
Suncook House, 62 Main St., Suncook, 03275, 603-485-8141
Tamworth Inn, P.O. Box 189, Main St., Tamworth, 03886, 603-323-7721
Whispering Pines B&B, Rt. 113A, Hemenway Rd., Tamworth, 03886, 603-323-7337
Birchwood Inn, Route 45, Temple, 03084, 603-878-3285
Black Swan Inn, 308 W. Main St., Tilton, 03276, 603-286-4524
Country Place, RFD 2, Box 342, Tilton, 03276, 603-286-8551
Tilton Manor, 28 Chestnut St., Tilton, 03276, 603-286-3457
Thimbleberry B&B, Parker Rd., Twin Mountain, 03595
Thirteen Colonies Farm, RFD Route 16, Union, 03887, 603-652-4458
Black Iris B&B, P.O. Box 83, Warren, 03279, 603-764-9366
Silver Squirrel Inn, Snow's Brook Rd., Waterville Valley, 03223
Snowy Owl Inn, P.O. Box 407, Waterville Valley, 03215, 603-236-8383
Hobson House, Town Common, Wentworth, 03282, 603-764-9460
Mountain Laurel Inn B&B, P.O. Box 147, Wentworth, 03282, 603-764-9600
Chesterfield Inn, Route 9, West Chesterfield, 03466, 800-365-5515
Strolling Woods on Webster, SW on Lake Shore Dr., West Franklin, 03235
West Ossipee House, Covered Bridge House, West Ossipee, 03890, 603-539-2874
Kimball Hill Inn, P.O. Box 74, Whitefield, 03598, 603-837-2284
Stepping Stones B&B, RFD #1, Box 208, Wilton Center, 03086, 603-654-9048
Tall Pines Inn, P.O. Box 327, Winnisquam, 03289, 800-722-6870
Wolfeboro Inn, P.O. Box 1270, Wolfeboro, 03894, 603-569-3016

Colby Hill Inn, Henniker, NH

New Jersey

AVON-BY-THE-SEA

Avon Manor Inn, The	$$$ B&B	Full breakfast
109 Sylvania Ave., 07717	8 rooms, 6 pb	Aft. tea, Comp. wine
908-774-0110	Most CC, *Rated*, •	Sitting room, library
Jim & Kathleen Curley	C-yes/S-no/P-no/H-no	tennis court
All year		air-conditioned

*Romantic seaside inn furnished w/period antiques & wicker. Queen size beds, living room w/fireplace. 1 block to beach & boardwalk. Wraparound veranda. **Free wine w/3 nights***

Cashelmara Inn	$$$ B&B	Full breakfast
P.O. Box 223, 07717	14 rooms, 14 pb	Wine available
22 Lakeside Ave.	Visa, MC, AmEx, *Rated*	Sitting room
201-776-8727 800-821-2976	C-yes/S-no/P-no/H-no	
Martin Mulligan/Mary Wiernasz		
All year		

Oceanfront, lakeside charming Victorian inn with period antiques. Cozy rooms with private baths. Hearty breakfast served on oceanside veranda.

BAY HEAD

Bay Head Gables
200 Main Ave., 08742
908-892-9844
Don Haurie & Ed Laubusch
Wkends only in Winter

$$$ B&B
11 rooms, 11 pb
Most CC, *Rated*, •
C-ltd/S-no/P-no/H-no

Full breakfast
Snacks, Comp. wine
Sitting room
75 yds. to ocean
A/C guestrooms

A 3-story Georgian Colonial overlooking ocean. Elegant Victorian to ultra contemporary—to please the most discriminating guest. Memorable breakfasts. AAA rates 3 diamonds.

Conover's Bay Head Inn
646 Main Ave., 08742
908-892-4664
Beverly, Carl, & Tim Conover
Exc. wkdys/Dec 15-Feb 15

$$$ B&B
12 rooms, 12 pb
Visa, MC, AmEx, *Rated*
C-ltd/S-no/P-no/H-no

Full breakfast
Comp. tea Oct-April
Sitting rm., dining rm.
library, parlor, porch
small conference room

Romantic seashore hideaway furnished with antiques, handmade pillows, bedcovers, crocheted washcloths, old family pictures. Quiet town on ocean at the bay head. **$10.00 off**

BERNARDSVILLE

Bernards Inn, The
27 Mine Brook Rd., Route 202,
07924
908-766-0002
Alice M. Rochat
All year

$$$ B&B
21 rooms, 20 pb
Visa, MC, AmEx, DC
C-yes/S-yes/P-no/H-no
Spanish, German

Continental breakfast
Restaurant, bar, ent'l
snacks, sitting room
near Nat'l Historic Park
250 grand ballroom

In the gracious style of a European hotel, the Bernards Inn offers elegant accommodations, exemplary food, and impeccable service in an unhurried atmosphere. **Champagne**

CAPE MAY

7th Sister Guesthouse
10 Jackson St., 08204
609-884-2280
JoAnne & Bob Myers
All year

$$ EP
6 rooms, 1 pb
C-ltd/S-yes/P-no/H-no
Spanish, French, German

Guest refrigerator
Piano, library, sunporch
rooms 100 ft. from beach
restaurants, sitt. room

Ocean view, wicker-filled rooms with a hint of eccentricity. Paintings by the owner/innkeeper, JoAnne Echevarria Myers, hang throughout.

The Avon Manor Inn, Avon-By-The-Sea, NJ

CAPE MAY

Abbey B&B, The
34 Gurney St., Columbia Ave.,
08204
609-884-4506
Jay & Marianne Schatz
April–December

$$$ B&B
14 rooms, 14 pb
Visa, MC, *Rated*, •
C-ltd/S-ltd/P-no/H-no

Continental (summer)
Full brkfast (spr./fall)
Comp. wine, snacks
2 parlors, piano, harp
off-street parking

*Elegantly restored villa, with period antiques. Genuine merriment and a warm atmosphere are always present. A/C avail. One block from Atlantic Ocean. **10% off week stay.***

Abigail Adams B&B by Sea
12 Jackson St., 08204
609-884-1371
Kate Emerson
All year

$$$ B&B
5 rooms, 3 pb
Visa, MC, •
C-ltd/S-no/P-no/H-no

Full gourmet breakfast
Continental plus (summ.)
Comp. tea
sitting room, porch

*Intimate, elegant country charm, ocean views all located in historic Cape May w/in 100 ft of beach. Walk to Victorian shopping mall & restaurants. **3rd night 50% off-season.***

Albert Stevens Inn, The
127 Myrtle Ave., 08204
609-884-4717
Diane & Curt Diviney Rangen
All year

$$ B&B/MAP
6 rooms, 6 pb
Visa, MC, AmEx, *Rated*,
•
C-ltd/S-no/P-ask/H-no
French

Full breakfast
Comp. Dinner (Nov–Mar)
Evening tea, sherry
Stress-Reduction Center
large, lighted jacuzzi

*1889 country Queen Anne Victorian nestled on Cape May's quiet side. Genuine antiques, crystal, porcelain & original artifacts from Dr. Albert Stevens. **3rd night 50% Jan-Apr.***

Barnard-Good House
238 Perry St., 08204
609-884-5381
Nan & Tom Hawkins
April–November 15

$$$ B&B
5 rooms, 5 pb
Visa, MC, *Rated*
C-ltd/S-ltd/P-no/H-no

Full 4-course breakfast
Wine, snacks (sometimes)
Sitting room
antique organ
Prvt baths, A/C in rooms

Victorian splendor in landmark-dotted town. Breakfast is a taste bud thrill… sumptuous, gourmet and lovingly created for you. Awarded best breakfast in N.J.

Bedford Inn
805 Stockton Ave., 08204
609-884-4158
Cindy & Al Schmucker
March–December

$$ B&B
11 rooms, 11 pb
Visa, MC, *Rated*, •
C-ltd/S-no/P-no/H-no

Full breakfast
Comp. sherry, beverages
Sitting room, parlor
set-up service
enclosed sun porch

*Elegant 1880 Italianate seaside inn w/unusual double staircase; offering lovely, antique-filled rms, suites. Near beach & historic shopping district. **Midwk disc't Sept-June.***

Bell Shields House
501 Hughes St., 08204
609-884-8512
Lorraine Bell
February–October

$$$ B&B
6 rooms, 1 pb
C-yes/S-ltd/P-no/H-no

Full breakfast
Wraparound porch, TV
beach passes, sitt. room
parking area

Restored Victorian house in middle of historic district. 2 blocks from beach and Victorian shopping mall. Delicious home-cooked breakfasts. Decorated with antiques.

CAPE MAY —————————————————————————————

Brass Bed Inn, The
719 Columbia Ave., 08204
609-884-8075
John & Donna Dunwoody
All year

$$ B&B
8 rooms, 6 pb
Visa, MC, *Rated*
C-ltd/S-ltd/P-no/H-no

Full breakfast
Afternoon tea & snacks
Sitting room, library
veranda, rocking chairs
near beach, theater, A/C

An 8-guestroom Gothic Revival "cottage" w/ wraparound veranda & lovely gardens. Rooms authentically furnished w/outstanding collection of brass beds. **Free specl. occ. wine.**

Captain Mey's B&B Inn
202 Ocean St., 08204
609-884-7793
M. Lacanfora & C. Fedderman
All year

$$$ B&B
9 rooms, 2 pb
Visa, MC, *Rated*
C-ltd/S-ltd/P-no/H-no
Dutch, Italian

Full country breakfast
Comp. wine, refreshments
Victorian parlor, A/C
parking, beach equipment
veranda, courtyd brkfast

Turn-of-the-century inn. Spacious rooms, antiques, Delft Blue collection, Dutch artifacts, European accents. Evning turndown service w/ mints. **10% off midwk Apr-June**

Colvmns by the Sea
1513 Beach Dr., 08204
609-884-2228
Marilyn & Tony Codario
April–December

$$$ B&B
11 rooms, 11 pb
Visa, MC, *Rated*
C-ltd/S-ltd/P-no/H-no
German

Full gourmet breakfast
Comp. wine, tea & snacks
Sitting room, hot tub
beach chairs/towels
bicycles free

Large, airy rooms, most w/ocean views. Elegant turn-of-the-century mansion, decorated w/Victorian antiques. Rockers & hot tub on veranda. **3rd night 50%—midwk off-season.**

Duke of Windsor B&B Inn
817 Washington St., 08204
609-884-1355 800-826-8973
Bruce & Fran Prichard
All year

$$ B&B
9 rooms, 7 pb
Visa, MC, *Rated*
C-ltd/S-no/P-no/H-no

Full breakfast
Sitting rooms, veranda
organ, bicycles
Christmas grand tour

Grand in scale and bold in Victorian character. Warm & friendly atmosphere, antiques. Near beaches, restaurants, shopping area, historical area, tennis courts. Some rooms A/C.

Gingerbread House, The
28 Gurney St., 08204
609-884-0211
Fred & Joan Echevarria
All year

$$$ B&B
6 rooms, 3 pb
Rated
C-ltd/S-yes/P-no/H-no

Continental plus
Aftn. tea w/baked goods
Wicker-filled porch
parlor with fireplace
Victorian antiques

The G.B.H. offers period furnished rooms—comfortable accommodations within walking distance to all major sights and restaurants. Half block from the beach.

Humphrey Hughes House, The
29 Ocean St., 08204
609-884-4428
Lorraine & Terry Schmidt
All year

$$$ B&B
12 rooms, 12 pb
Rated
C-ltd

Full breakfast
Afternoon tea
Sitting room
library
piano

Our inn is one of the most authentically restored bed & breakfast inns. Hospitality, Victorian charm, & casual, yet elegant, creature comforts are the hallmarks of our house.

CAPE MAY

John F. Craig House, The
609 Columbia Ave., 08204
609-884-0100
Frank & Connie Felicette
All year

$$$ B&B
9 rooms, 7 pb
Visa, MC, AmEx, *Rated*
C-ltd/S-ltd/P-no/H-no
Some French

Full breakfast
Aft. tea, snacks
Sitting room, library
parking, beach tags
some rooms with A/C

Victorian inn, period furnishings/decor. Wrap-around veranda, enclosed sunporches. Delicious breakfast and tea served in elegant dining rm. **15% off for 1 wk. stays**

Leith Hall Seashore Inn
22 Ocean St., 08204
609-884-1934
Elan & Susan Zingman-Leith
All year

$$$ B&B
7 rooms, 7 pb
C-ltd/S-no/P-no/H-no
French, Yiddish

Full breakfast
Afternoon English tea
Sitting room, library
beach chairs, towels
Victorian suite w/view

Elegantly restored 1880s home in the heart of the Victorian district. Only half block from the beach, with ocean views. **3rd night 50% off, ltd.**

Mainstay Inn & Cottage
635 Columbia Ave., 08204
609-884-8690
Tom & Sue Carroll
April–November

$$$ B&B
13 rooms, 9 pb
Rated
C-ltd/S-no/P-no/H-no

Full breakfst (spr/fall)
Cont. breakfast (summer)
Afternoon tea
piano
3 sitting rooms

Two wealthy 19th-century gamblers spared no expense to build this luxurious villa. Sumptuous Victorian furnishings, garden, afternoon tea. Adding 2 bdrm units for Spring '94.

Mason Cottage, The
625 Columbia Ave., 08204
609-884-3358
Dave & Joan Mason
May–October

$$$ B&B
9 rooms, 9 pb
Visa, MC, *Rated*, •
C-ltd/S-no/P-no/H-no

Continental plus
Afternoon tea
Sitting room, veranda
games, reading material
parlor, bike rack

An elegant seaside inn located on a quiet, tree-lined street in the center of historic district, 1 block to beach & close to other Victorian attractions. **disc'ts 4-7 nights**

Mooring Guest House
801 Stockton Ave., 08204
609-884-5425
Harry & Carol Schaefer
April 3–December 30

$$$ B&B
12 rooms, 12 pb
Visa, MC
C-ltd/S-no/P-no/H-no

Full breakfast
Afternoon tea
Sitting room
mid–week discounts
Sept-Jan, March–June

Victorian mansard structure furnished in original period antiques. One block to ocean and easy walking distance to five different restaurants.

Perry Street Inn
29 Perry St., 08204
609-884-4590
John & Cynthia Curtis
April–November

$$ B&B
20 rooms, 13 pb
Visa, MC, *Rated*, •
C-ltd/S-yes/H-yes

Full gourmet breakfast
Afternoon tea, snacks
Sitting room
bicycles
ocean front porch

National historic landmark city. Victorian guest house & modern efficiency suites. Beach block; close to unique shopping, fine restaurants. **10% off "Mystery Weekend" package**

Mainstay Inn, Cape May, NJ

CAPE MAY

Poor Richard's Inn
17 Jackson St., 08204
609-884-3536
Richard & Harriett Samuelson
Valentines–New Years

$$ B&B
9 rooms, 4 pb
C-ltd/S-yes/P-no/H-no

Continental breakfast
Sitting room
oriental rock garden
near beach

Classic gingerbread guest house offers accommodations w/eclectic Victorian & country decor; friendly, unpretentious atmosphere. **10-25% disc't off-season. Mention Lanier book.**

Queen Victoria, The
102 Ocean St., 08204
609-884-8702
Joan & Dane Wells
All year

$$$ B&B
12 rooms, 12 pb
Visa, MC, AmEx, *Rated*
C-ltd/S-ltd/P-no/H-ltd
French

Full buffet breakfast
Afternoon tea
Sitting room, bicycles
kitchen & whirlpool
2 luxury suites, bikes

A country inn located in the center of the nation's oldest seaside resort; specialty is comfort & service. Morning and evening room cleanings. Large breakfast. A/C in rooms.

Sea Holly B&B Inn
815 Stockton Ave., 08204
609-884-6294
Christy & Chris Igoe
All year

$$$ B&B
8 rooms, 8 pb
Visa, MC, Disc., *Rated*
C-ltd/S-ltd/P-no/H-no

Full breakfast
Comp. sherry, tea, etc.
Sitting room, books, A/C
beach equipment & tags
rockers, veranda, bikes

Elegant 3-story 1875 Victorian Gothic; some ocean view rooms; period antiques; known for Christy's breakfast treats–have written cookbook! **Champagne/balloons spec. occas.**

Springside
18 Jackson St., 08204
609-884-2654
Meryl & Bill Nelson
All year

$$ B&B
4 rooms
Visa, MC, •
C-ltd/S-no/P-no/H-no

Continental breakfast
King-sized beds, library
1/2 block from beach
1/2 block from mall

1890 Victorian beach house with bright, airy guest rooms with ocean views. Many creature comforts–big beds, ceiling fans, rockers on veranda, books and good music.

CAPE MAY _____

Stetson B&B Inn
725 Kearney Ave., 08204
609-884-1724
Carol & Lou Elwell
Jul-Aug, wkends Sep—Jun

$$$ B&B
7 rooms, 7 pb
Visa, MC, *Rated*
C-ltd/S-no/P-no/H-no

Full breakfast
Afternoon tea
Sitting room
on-site parking
beach tags, A/C

1915 seaside cottage with oceanview sun/shade porches. Cozy parlor fireplace. Country English decor. Teatime is anytime! **Jan-Mar 50% off 2nd night.**

White Dove Cottage
619 Hughes St., 08204
609-884-0613 800-321-3683
Frank Smith
All year

$$$ B&B
6 rooms, 6 pb
Rated, •
C-ltd/S-no/P-no/H-no

Full breakfast
Aft. tea
Comp. wine
sitting room
two blocks from ocean

Elegant 1866 B&B located in center of Historic District on tree-lined, gas-lit street. A memorable occasion—a delightful retreat. AAA 3 star rating.

White House Inn
821 Beach Ave., 08204
609-884-5329 800-729-7778
Sue Marleton
April—October 20

$$$ B&B
8 rooms
•
C-ltd/S-ltd/P-no/H-no
some French

Continental plus
Suite w/pvt. bath avail.
porch, ocean view
beach tags, sitting room

A bed & breakfast inn on the beach w/a Victorian atmosphere. Away from the center of the city, yet close to shops, restaurants, everything. **Off season midweek, all rooms $60**

Wilbraham Mansion
133 Myrtle Ave., 08204
609-884-2046
Elaine Robbins
All year

$$$ B&B
8 rooms, 8 pb
Visa, MC, *Rated*, •
C-ltd/S-ltd/P-no/H-no

Full breakfast
Afternoon tea
Comp. wine
sitting rooms
swimming pool

This high Victorian mansion takes you back in time with parlors, porches, original antiques and a breathtaking indoor heated swimming pool accented with stained glass.

Windward House
24 Jackson St., 08204
609-884-3368
Sandy & Owen Miller
All year

$$$ B&B
8 rooms, 8 pb
Visa, MC, *Rated*
C-ltd/S-ltd/P-no/H-no

Full breakfast
Afternoon tea, sherry
Sitting rm, library, A/C
ocean view sundeck
bicycles, beach passes

Edwardian shingle cottage; sun/shade porches; spacious antique-filled guest rooms; massive oak doors w/stained & leaded glass. Some rooms w/TV. Parking. ½ blk to beach.

Wooden Rabbit B&B Inn, The
609 Hughes St., 08204
609-884-7293
Greg & Debby Burow
All year

$$ B&B
3 rooms, 3 pb
Visa, MC
C-ltd/S-no/P-no/H-no

Full breakfast
Afternoon tea
Sitting room
sun room, guest phone
air-conditioned rooms

Horse-drawn carriages roll through our quiet, shaded neighborhood—colorful Victorian homes; fine restaurants; antiques; sandy beaches. Country ambiance; family hospitality.

White Dove Cottage, Cape May, NJ

CAPE MAY

Woodleigh House
808 Washington St., 08204
609-884-7123
Buddy & Jan Wood
All year

$$$ B&B
4 rooms, 4 pb
•
C-ltd

Continental plus
Comp. wine
Sitting room, porches
courtyards, bicycles
1 bedroom apt. available

Nestled in Cape May's historic district, surrounded by porches and courtyards. This attractive example of "Country Victorian" is charmingly hosted. **Midweek 4th night free.**

CHATHAM

Parrot Mill Inn at Chatham
47 Main St., 07928
201-635-7722
Betsy Kennedy
All year

$$$ B&B
11 rooms, 10 pb
Visa, MC, AmEx, *Rated*,
•
C-yes/S-no/P-no/H-no

Continental breakfast
Afternoon tea
Sitting room

English country elegance. Tastefully decorated bedrooms with private baths, situated ideally near major corporate offices and universities. **Free bottle of wine**

CLINTON

Leigh Way B&B
66 Leigh St., 08809
908-735-4311
Terry Schlegal
April–December

$$ B&B
5 rooms, 4 pb
Visa, MC, AmEx, •
C-ltd/S-no/P-no/H-no
French

Continental plus
Restaurant nearby
Sitting room, fireplace
fishing, sailing
tennis nearby

Lovingly restored inn with cozy fireplace, porch swing and ferns. Authentic Victorian (c. 1862) located in picture-book Clinton, where small town America is alive and well.

FLEMINGTON

Cabbage Rose Inn, The
162 Main St., 08822
908-788-0247
Pam Venosa & Al Scott
All year

$$$ B&B
5 rooms, 5 pb
Visa, MC, AmEx, *Rated*,
•
C-ltd/S-no/P-no/H-no

Continental plus/full
Afternoon refreshments
Comp. sherry
sitting room, gazebo
sunporch, piano, firepl.

Victorian romance & roses galore! Fabulous shopping, restaurants, galleries, wineries, theater, Delaware River. Warmest hospitality. "Romance & Roses" pkg. **3rd night 50% off**

FLEMINGTON

Jerica Hill—A B&B Inn
96 Broad St., 08822
908-782-8234
Judith S. Studer
All year

$$$ B&B
5 rooms, 5 pb
Visa, MC, AmEx, *Rated*,
•
C-ltd/S-no/P-no/H-no

Continental plus
Sherry, refreshments
Picnic & wine tours
hot air balloon flights
all rms. A+C

Gracious Victorian in heart of historic Flemington. Spacious, sunny guest rooms, antiques, living room with fireplace, wicker-filled screened porch. **3rd night 50% off**

FRENCHTOWN

Hunterdon House, The
12 Bridge St., 08825
908-996-3632 800-382-0375
Clark F. & Karen Johnson
All year

$$$ B&B
7 rooms, 7 pb
Visa, AmEx, *Rated*, •
C-ltd/S-no/P-no/H-no

Full breakfast
Comp. fruit & cheese
Comp. cordials, desserts
housekeeping service
sitting room

Small town Civil War-era mansion furnished in Victoriana. Distinctive guest rooms & emphasis on special touches for comfort and elegance. **3rd night 50% off, ltd.**

HOPE

Inn at Millrace Pond, The
P.O. Box 359, 07844
Route 519
908-459-4884
G. Carrigan & R. Gooding
All year

$$$ B&B
17 rooms, 17 pb
Visa, MC, AmEx, *Rated*,
•
C-ltd/S-ltd/P-no/H-no

Continental breakfast
Sun. lunch & dinner menu
Restaurant, bar service
sitting room, riding
tennis court

Historic 1769 Grist Mill complex authentically restored reflects the atmosphere of colonial America. Hiking, canoeing, antiques, Waterloo Village, wineries, bicycling.

MONTCLAIR

Marlboro Inn, The
334 Grove St., 07042
201-783-5300
Joanna Rees
All year

$$$ B&B
Visa, MC, AmEx, DC, •
C-yes/S-yes/P-no/H-yes
Spanish Italian

Continental breakfast
Full breakfast $
Full menu
sitting room
piano

Turn-of-the-century Tudor mansion on a 3-acre estate, featuring luxury bedrooms and suites, each with private bath. Featuring chef Eric Gallanter.

NORTH WILDWOOD

Candlelight Inn
2310 Central Ave., 08260
609-522-6200
Paul DiFilippo, Diane Buscham
All year exc. January

$$$ B&B
9 rooms, 7 pb
Most CC, *Rated*, •
C-ltd/S-no/P-no/H-no
French

Full breakfast
Comp. wine, refreshments
Sitting room, piano
hot tub, sun deck
getaway specials

Seashore B&B with genuine antiques, fireplace, wide veranda. Getaway specials and murder mystery parties available. Close to beach and boardwalk. **3rd night 50% off wkdays**

OCEAN CITY

New Brighton Inn, B&B
519 Fifth St., 08226
609-399-2829
Daniel & Donna Hand
All year

$$$ B&B
4 rooms, 2 pb
Visa, MC, AmEx, *Rated*
C-ltd/S-ltd/P-no/H-no

Full breakfast
Afternoon tea
Sitting room, library
slate patio, bicycles
each room A/C, TV

Magnificently restored seaside Victorian filled w/antiques. Close to beach, boardwalk, shopping district, restaurants. A charming, romantic inn. **Free deserts, ask**

OCEAN CITY

Northwood Inn B&B	$$$ B&B	Continental plus (wkdys)
401 Wesley Ave., 08226	8 rooms, 6 pb	Full breakfast (wknds)
609-399-6071	Visa, MC, *Rated*	Aftn. tea/snacks, piano
Marj & John Loeper	C-ltd/S-no/P-no/H-no	porches, roof-top deck
All year		game room, beach passes

Elegantly restored 1894 Victorian with 20th-century comforts. Three blocks to beach and boardwalk. Between Atlantic City and Cape May. 1990 Beautification Award winner.

OCEAN GROVE

Pine Tree Inn	$$ B&B	Continental plus
10 Main Ave., 07756	13 rooms, 3 pb	Reflexology, jinshin
908-775-3264	C-ltd/S-no/P-no/H-no	fresh flowers, TV lounge
Karen Mason		pillow mints, bicycles
All year		

*Small inn furnished w/Victorian antiques & collectibles. Room & porch ocean views. Home-made muffins. Steps to boardwalk & beach. Historic seaside town. **3rd night free midwk.***

ORANGE GROVE

Cordova	$ B&B	Continental plus
26 Webb Ave., 07756	20 rooms, 3 pb	Guest kitchen
908-774-3084 212-751-9577	•	Sat. night wine & cheese
Doris Chernik	C-yes/S-ltd/P-no/H-no	sitting room, bicycles
Mem. Day—Labor Day	French, Russian	yard, BBQ, picnic tables

*Century-old Victorian inn, located in lovely historic beach community. You feel like one of the family, experience Old World charm, many amenities. **Midwk specials***

PRINCETON

Peacock Inn	$$$ B&B	Continental plus
20 Bayard Ln., 08540	17 rooms, 15 pb	French restaurant, bar
609-924-1707 FAX:921-3183	Visa, AmEx, MC, •	Lunch, dinner, snacks
M. Walker, C. Lindsay	C-yes/S-yes/P-yes/H-no	afternoon tea, bicycles
All year	Czech, Spanish, French	sitting room, garden

*Located in the heart of Princeton; walk to University, antique shops. 4 star restaurant w/special prices for Inn guests. Breakfast a plus. **3rd night 50% off***

Red Maple Farm	$$ B&B	Full country breakfast
Raymond Rd., 08540	3 rooms	Lunch, dinner, snacks
908-329-3821	*Rated*	Tea, sitting room
Robert Churchill	C-ltd/S-no/P-no/H-no	library, tennis nearby
All year	Some French	lg. in-ground swim. pool

*Charming, gracious 1740 Historic Register Colonial farm. A 2 acre country retreat minutes from Princeton University and Rte 1 business. **Wine & cheese or tea & homemade snacks***

SEA GIRT

Holly Harbor Guest House	$$$ B&B	Full buffet breakfast
112 Baltimore Blvd., 08750	12 rooms	Open porch
908-449-9731 800-348-6999	AmEx, •	ocean swimming
Bill & Kim Walsh	C-yes/S-no/P-no/H-no	beach badges
All year	German	

*Enjoy the friendly atmosphere in our redecorated turn-of-the-century inn nestled in quiet seashore community, eight houses from ocean. **3rd night 50% off.***

SPRING LAKE

Ashling Cottage
106 Sussex Ave., 07762
908-449-3553 800-237-1877
Goodi & Jack Stewart
March–December

$$ B&B
10 rooms, 8 pb
Rated
C-ltd/S-ltd/P-no/H-no
German

Full breakfast buffet
Complimentary wine
AAA rated 3 diamonds
TV, VCR, sitting room
library, games, bicycles

Victorian gem furnished w/oak antiques & solarium breakfast room, a block from the ocean, in a storybook setting. Rowboating on Spring Lake. **15% off mkwk except July & Aug**

Chateau Inn
500 Warren Ave., 07762
908-974-2000 FAX:974-0007
Scott P. Smith
All year

$ EP/B&B Winter
35 rooms, 35 pb
Rated, •
C-yes/S-yes/P-no/H-ltd

Cont. breakfast to room
Comp. wine
22 marble baths
9 fireplaces, bicycles
cable color TV/VCRs

Turn-of-the-century inn, nestled between two parks, overlooking lake. Air-conditioning, TV, refrigerators, 9 fireplaces, phones. Conference room for 40. AAA-rated 3 diamonds.

Normandy Inn, The
21 Tuttle Ave., 07762
908-449-7172
Michael & Susan Ingino
All year

$$$ B&B
18 rooms, 18 pb
Rated, •
C-yes/S-ltd/P-no/H-no

Full breakfast
Comp. wine
Sitting room
bicycles, front porch
side enclosed porch

A country inn at the shore, decorated with lovely Victorian antiques, painted with 5 different Victorian colors. Hearty breakfast included.

A Sea Crest By The Sea
19 Tuttle Ave., 07762
908-449-9031
John & Carol Kirby
All year

$$ B&B
12 rooms, 12 pb
Visa, *Rated*
C-ltd/S-no/P-no/H-no

Full breakfast
Afternoon tea
Sitting room, library
bicycles, local trolley
croquet, beach towels

Luxury by the sea; English and French antiques; queen-size beds; one block from beach and boardwalk. Afternoon tea; entertainment by restored player piano. A seaside holiday.

STANHOPE

Whistling Swan Inn
P.O. Box 791, 07874
110 Main St.
201-347-6369
Paula Williams, Joe Mulay
All year

$$ B&B
6 rooms, 6 pb
Visa, MC, AmEx, *Rated*,
•
C-ltd/S-no/P-no/H-no

Full breakfast buffet
Comp. sherry, cookies
Sitting room
clawfoot tubs for two
bicycles

Northwestern New Jersey's finest Victorian B&B guest house; 1.5 mi. from Waterloo Village, International Trade Zone, 20 mi. to Delaware River. **3rd night 50% Nov thru Apr-Ltd**

STOCKTON

Stockton Inn, The
P.O. Box C, One Main St., 08559
609-397-1250
Andy McDermott, Bruce Monti
All year exc. Christmas

$$ B&B
11 rooms, 11 pb
Visa, MC, AmEx, *Rated*
C-ltd/S-yes/P-no/H-no

Continental plus
Restaurant, bar
Sunday brunch
Alfresco dining
8 suites

Unique country inn in riverside town. Distinctive lodging; garden & fireside dining. 3 mi. to Lambertville-New Hope galleries, theaters, antiquing. **Suite retreat disc't-ask.**

STOCKTON

Woolverton Inn	$$ B&B	Full breakfast weekends
6 Woolverton Rd., 08559	13 rooms, 4 pb	Continental M-F, snacks
609-397-0802	Visa, MC	Sitting room, piano, tea
Louise Warsaw	C-ltd/S-ltd/P-no/H-yes	library, fireplaces
All year exc. Dec 20-26	French	bicycles, lawn games

1793 stone manor house set amidst formal gardens & stately trees, overlooking Delaware River Valley, famed for antiques & fine food. **3rd night 50% off, excl. holidays.**

WOODBINE

Henry Ludlam Inn	$$$ B&B	Full 4-course breakfast
1336 Rt. 47, Cape May County,	6 rooms, 2 pb	Picnic baskets, wine
08270	*Rated*, •	Dinner winter (Sat)
609-861-5847	C-ltd/S-ltd/P-no/H-no	sitting room, fireplaces
Ann & Marty Thurlow		piano, gazebo, lake
All year		

1804 home overlooking Ludlam Lake. All chambers decorated w/antiques, feather beds. Fishing, canoeing, delicious country brkfasts. Fireside winter picnics. **3rd night 50% Ltd**

More Inns ...

Josiah Reeve House B&B, P.O. Box 501, Alloway, 08001, 609-935-5640
Hudson Guide Farm, Andover, 07821, 201-398-2679
Hermitage Guest House, 309 First Ave, Asbury Park, 07712, 201-776-6665
Sands B&B Inn, 42 Sylvania Ave., Avon-by-the-Sea, 07717, 201-776-8386
Old Mill Inn, P.O. Box 423, Basking Ridge, 07920, 201-221-1100
Bay Head Sands B&B, 2 Twilight Rd., Bay Head, 08742, 908-899-7016
Bentley Inn, The, 694 Main Ave, Bay Head, 08742, 201-892-9589
Bayberry Barque B&B Inn, 117 Centre St., Beach Haven, 08008, 609-492-5216
Green Gables, 212 Centre St., Beach Haven, 08008, 609-492-3553
Magnolia House, The, 215 Centre St., Beach Haven, 08008, 609-492-0398
Pierrot-by-the-Sea B&B, 101 Centre St., Beach Haven, 08008, 609-492-4424
St. Rita Hotel, 127 Engleside Ave., Beach Haven, 08008, 609-492-9192
Victoria B&B, 126 Amber St., Beach Haven, 08008, 609-492-4154
Seaflower, The, 110 Ninth Ave., Belmar, 07719, 908-681-6006
Alexander's Inn, 653 Washington St., Cape May, 08204, 609-884-2555
Angel of the Sea, 5 Trenton Ave., Cape May, 08204, 609-884-3369
Buttonwood Manor, 115 N. Broadway, Cape May, 08204
Carroll Villa B&B Hotel, 19 Jackson St., Cape May, 08204, 609-884-9619
Cliveden Inn B&B, 709 Columbia Ave., Cape May, 08204, 609-884-4516
Delsea, 621 Columbia Ave., Cape May, 08204, 609-884-8540
Dormer House, 800 Columbia Ave., Cape May, 08204, 609-884-7446
Dormer House International, 800 Columbia Ave., Cape May, 08204, 609-884-7446
Hanson House, 111 Ocean St., Cape May, 08204, 609-884-8791
Heirloom B&B Inn, 601 Columbia Ave., Cape May, 08204, 609-884-1666
Holly House, 20 Jackson St., Cape May, 08204, 609-884-7365
Inn of Cape May, The, P.O. Box 31, Cape May, 08204, 800-257-0432
John Wesley Inn, 30 Gurney St., Cape May, 08204, 609-884-1012
Linda Lee, 725 Columbia Ave., Cape May, 08204, 609-884-1240
Manor House, 612 Hughes St., Cape May, 08204, 609-884-4710
Manse Inn, 510 Hughes St., Cape May, 08204, 609-884-0116
Prince Edward, The, 38 Jackson St., Cape May, 08204, 609-884-2131
Sand Castle, The, 829 Stockton Ave., Cape May, 08204, 609-884-5451
Sevilla, The, 5 Perry St., Cape May, 08204
Summer Cottage Inn, 613 Columbia Ave., Cape May, 08204, 609-884-4948
Victorian Lace Inn, 901 Stockton Ave., Cape May, 08204, 609-884-1772
Victorian Rose, 719 Columbia Ave., Cape May, 08204, 609-884-2497
Washington Inn, 801 Washington St., Cape May, 08204
Publick House Inn, 111 Main St., Box 85, Chester, 07930, 201-879-6878
Country Meadows B&B, RR#3 Box 3174, Cream Ridge, 08514, 609-758-9437
National Hotel, 31 Race St., Frenchtown, 08825, 201-996-4871
Queen Anne Inn, 44 West End Ave., Haddonfield, 08033, 609-428-2195
Studio of John F. Peto, 102 Cedar Ave., Island Heights, 08732, 201-270-6058
Chimney Hill Farm B&B, 207 Goat Hill Rd., Lambertville, 08530, 609-397-1516
Coryell House, 44 Coryell St., Lambertville, 08530, 609-397-2750
Inn @ Lambertville Station, 11 Bridge St., Lambertville, 08530, 609-397-4400
York Street House, 42 York St., Lambertville, 08530, 609-397-3007
Winchester Hotel, One S. 24 St., Longport, 08403, 609-822-0623
Jeremiah J. Yercance House, 410 Riverside Ave., Lyndhurst, 07071, 201-438-9457
Garden Suite, 42 Ridgedale, Madison, 07940, 201-765-0233
Goose N. Berry Inn B&B, 190 N. Main St., Manahawkin, 08050, 609-597-6350
Chestnut Hill on Delaware, P.O. Box N, Milford, 08848, 201-995-9761

Adelmann's, The, 1228 Ocean Ave., Ocean City, 08226, 609-399-2786
Barnagate B&B, 637 Wesley Ave., Ocean City, 08226, 609-391-9366
Beach End Inn, 815 Plymouth Pl., Ocean City, 08226, 609-398-1016
Enterprise B&B Inn, The, 1020 Central Ave., Ocean City, 08226, 609-398-1698
Manor, The, Atlantic Ave., Ocean City, 08226, 609-399-4509
Top o'the Waves, 5447 Central Ave., Ocean City, 08226, 609-399-0477
Amherst Inn, The, 14 Pitman Ave., Ocean Grove, 07756, 201-988-5297
House By The Sea, The, 14 Ocean Ave., Ocean Grove, 07756, 908-775-2847
Keswick Inn, 32 Embury Ave., Ocean Grove, 07756, 201-775-7506
Isaac Hilliard House B&B, 31 Hanover St., Pemberton, 08068, 609-894-0756
Seven Springs Farm B&B, 12 Perryville Rd., Pittstown, 08867
Candy Lindsay, 19 Corson Rd., Princeton, 08540
Shaloum Guest House, 119 Tower Hill, Red Bank, 07701, 201-530-7759
Ma Bowman's B&B, 156 Harmersville Peck-, Salem, 08079, 609-935-4913
Beacon House B&B, The, 100 & 104 Beacon Blvd., Sea Girt, 08750, 908-449-5835
Hollycroft, 506 North Blvd., South Belmar, 07719, 201-681-2254
Colonial Ocean House, First and Sussex Aves., Spring Lake, 07762
Grand Victorian Hotel, The, 1505 Ocean Ave., Spring Lake, 07762, 908-449-5327
Hewitt Wellington Hotel, 200 Monmouth Ave., Spring Lake, 07762, 908-974-1212
Johnson House Inn, 25 Tuttle Ave., Spring Lake, 07762, 908-449-1860
Kenilworth, The, 1505 Ocean Ave., Spring Lake, 07762, 201-449-5327
Moulton House, 120 Ludlow Ave., Spring Lake, 07762
Sandpiper Inn, 71 Atlantic Ave., Spring Lake, 07762, 201-449-6060
Stone Post Inn, 115 Washington Ave., Spring Lake, 07762, 201-449-1212
Victoria House, 214 Monmouth Ave., Spring Lake, 07762, 201-974-1882
Villa Park House, 417 Ocean Rd., Spring Lake, 07762, 908-449-3642
Warren Hotel, 901 Ocean Ave., Spring Lake, 07762, 201-449-8800
Stewart Inn, Stewartsville

New Mexico

ALBUQUERQUE

Casita Chamisa B&B	$$ B&B	Continental plus
850 Chamisal Rd. NW, 87107	3 rooms, 2 pb	Homemade coffee cakes
505-897-4644	Visa, MC, AmEx, •	Sitting room, patio
Kit & Arnold Sargeant	C-yes/S-no/P-ask/H-no	decks, indoor pool
Exc. Oct. 15 – Nov. 1		near tennis, horses

2 Bedroom country guesthouse and 19th century adobe house 15 minutes to downtown. Near museums, art galleries, aerial tram, Indian petroglyphs, skiing. Archaeologist-owner.

Sarabande B&B	$$$ B&B	Full breakfast
5637 Rio Grande Blvd NW, 87107	3 rooms, 3 pb	Aftn. tea, comp. wine
505-345-4923	Visa, MC, •	Tennis courts, bicycles
M. Magnussen & B. Vickers	C-ltd/S-no/P-no/H-yes	fireplace, jogging path
All year		riding, spa, 50'lap pool

Nestled in Los Ranchos, a pastoral village: the best of old New Mexico charm. Linger & reminese by the courtyard fountain or country kitchen. **Free champagne to honeymooners.**

CHIMAYO

La Posada de Chimayo	$$$ B&B	Full breakfast
P.O. Box 463, 87522	6 rooms, 4 pb	Comp. wine
El Rincon Rd. (C.R.#0101)	*Rated*	Private sitting rooms
505-351-4605	C-ltd/S-yes/P-ask/H-no	fireplace
Sue Farrington	Spanish	hiking
All year		

A traditional adobe guest house in beautiful northern New Mexico; brick floors, viga ceilings, corner fireplaces, Mexican rugs. 30 miles to Santa Fe & Taos.

Casa La Resolana, Corrales, NM

CORRALES

Casa La Resolana
7887 Corrales Rd., 87048
505-898-0203
Nancy & Jerry Thomas
All year

$$ B&B
3 rooms, 2 pb
•
C-ltd/S-ltd/P-no/H-no

Continental plus
Full breakfast, Aft. tea
Snacks, sitting room
hot tubs
golf packages

Southwest adobe, magnificent mountain & bosque views, pastoral setting w/spacious suites, winter skiing, golfers paradise. **10% discount for 3 night stay**

EL PRADO

Salsa del Salto B&B Inn
P.O. Box 1468, 87529
Hwy 150, Taos, NM
505-776-2422
Mary Hackett, Dadou Mayer
All year

$$$ B&B
6 rooms, 6 pb
Visa, MC, *Rated*, •
C-ltd/S-ask/P-no/H-no
French, German, Spanish

Full breakfast
Afternoon tea, snacks
Sitting room, library
bikes, tennis, hot tubs
pool, ski packages

Exquisite Southwest inn perfectly located halfway between historic Taos and Taos Ski Valley. Private pool and tennis court. Gourmet breakfast.

ESPANOLA

Casa Del Rio
P.O. Box 92, 87532
Hwy. 84 #19946
505-753-6049
Eileen & Mel Vigil
All year

$$$ B&B
2 rooms, 2 pb
Most CC, *Rated*
C-ltd/S-no/P-ltd/H-no
Spanish

Full breakfast
Picnic basket, dinner
Wakeup tray to room

A Gold Medallion certified B&B that offers intimate luxury in a country setting; appointed with handmade crafts, rugs, furniture. situated halfway between Taos and Santa Fe.

FARMINGTON

Silver River Adobe Inn
P.O. Box 3411, 87401
3151 West Main
505-325-8219
Diana Ohlson & David Beers
All year

$$ B&B
3 rooms, 3 pb
Visa, MC, •
C-ltd/S-no/P-no/H-yes

Continental plus
Dinner, ask
River walk
wildlife

New Mexico adobe with large timbers. Day trips to Chaco Canyon, Mesa Verde, Aztec ruins, Salmon ruins, Canyon de Chelly. **6th night free**

LAS CRUCES

Lundeen Inn of the Arts
618 S. Alameda Blvd., 88005
505-526-3327 FAX:526-3355
Gerald & Linda Lundeen
All year

$ B&B
18 rooms, 15 pb
Most CC, *Rated*, •
C-ltd/S-ltd/P-no/H-no
Spanish

Full breakfast
Afternoon social hour
Comp. coffee, tea, wine
sitting room, library
patio & gazebo

Artistic lodging, rooms decorated representing famous artists, authentic antiques. 5 min. from NMSU & Old Mesilla, art lectures. **Weekly & monthly rates available.**

LINCOLN

Casa de Patron B&B Inn
P.O. Box 27, 88338
Hwy. #380 East
505-653-4676
Jeremy & Cleis Jordan
All year

$$ B&B
5 rooms, 5 pb
Visa, MC, Disc.,*Rated*
C-yes/S-no/P-no/H-ltd

Continental plus
Snacks, dinner by req.
Sitting room
hiking trail

Billy the Kid spent nights here, sometimes as a house guest and sometimes as a guest of the Sheriff!

MESILLA

Mesón de Mesilla
P.O. Box 1212, 88046
1803 Avenida de Mesilla
505-525-9212 505-525-2380
Chuck Walker
All year

$$ B&B
13 rooms, 13 pb
Most CC, *Rated*, •
C-yes/S-yes/P-ask/H-no
Spanish

Full breakfast
Restaurant, lunch (W-F)
Dinner (Tue-Sat), bar
comp. wine, bicycles
swimming pool (in seas.)

Tranquil setting; gourmet breakfasts; restaurant on premises. Walk to old Mesilla Plaza; ride bicycles; swim in season. Quiet Old World charm.

PILAR

Plum Tree B&B, The
Box A-1, State Rd. 68, 2886 State
Rd. 68, 87531
505-758-0090 800-999-7586
Eva C. Behrens
All year

$ B&B
5 rooms, 3 pb
Visa, MC, •
C-yes/S-ltd/P-ltd/H-yes

Continental plus
Kitchen
Sitting room, hot tub
Located in Nat'l forest
Lovely garden, orchard

At the Plum Tree you can hike, bird-watch, rock hunt, swim, cross-country ski, raft, learn to kayak, see petroglyphs, study art, enjoy wholesome food. Nature program in the fall.

SANTA FE

Adobe Abode
202 Chapelle, 87501
505-983-3133
Pat Harbour
All year

$$$ B&B
5 rooms, 5 pb
Visa, MC, Disc, *Rated*, •
C-ltd/S-ltd/P-no/H-yes
Spanish

Continental plus
Snacks, comp. sherry
Sitting rm. w/ fireplace
morning paper, cable TV
off-street parking

Restored, historic adobe 3 blocks from the Plaza, with a sophisticated mix of Southwest decor and European touches. Beautiful gourmet breakfast!

Alexander's Inn
529 E. Palace Ave., 87501
505-986-1431
Carolyn Lee/Mary Jo Schneider
All year

$$$ B&B
5 rooms, 3 pb
Visa, MC, *Rated*, •
C-ltd/S-no/P-no/H-no
French

Continental plus
Afternoon tea, beverages
Sitting room w/fireplace
lovely terrace, porches
lilacs & roses in garden

Cozy, quiet & romantic, yet just minutes from the Plaza. Full continental breakfast served by fireside or on terrace. Private casita avail. **Off-season midwk 2nd night free**

SANTA FE ———————————————————————————————————

Arius Compound
P.O. Box 1111, 87504
1018½ Canyon Rd.
505-982-2621 800-735-8453
Len & Robbie Goodman
All year, FAX: 989-8280

$$$ EP
3 rooms, 3 pb
Visa, MC, AmEx
C-yes/S-yes/P-ask/H-no

1 or 2 bedroom suites
Full kitchens
Hot tub
near shops & restaurants

1 & 2 bedroom guest houses on historic adobe compound. Classic Sante Fe charm; corner fireplaces, complete kitchens, garden patios and fountains, fruit trees. Outdoor hot tub.

Canyon Road Casitas
652 Canyon Rd., 87501
505-988-5888 800-279-0755
Trisha Ambrose
All year

$$$ B&B
2 rooms, 2 pb
Most Crd. Cds., *Rated*, •
C-yes/S-no/P-no/H-ltd
Spanish

Continental breakfast
Comp. wine, snacks
Guest robes
private walled courtyard
original artwork

Awarded most spectacular B&B in N.M. by Rocky Mountain B&B. Decorated in the finest of Southwestern decor. European down quilts/pillows/feather beds. **Comp. bottle of wine.**

Casa De La Cuma B&B
105 Paseo de la Cuma, 87501
505-983-1717
Art & Donna Bailey
All year

$$$ B&B
5 rooms, 5 pb
Rated, •
C-ltd/S-ltd/P-no/H-no
Spanish

Continental plus
Comp. beverages
TV, Solarium, garden
patio w/ barbecue
avail. as rental house

Mountain views! Walking distance to downtown Plaza, shopping, restaurants, galleries, library, museums, banks. City sports facilities across street. **Weekly discounts**

Dunshee's B&B
986 Acequia Madre, 87501
505-982-0988
Susan Dunshee
All year

$$$ B&B
1 rooms, 1 pb
Visa, MC
C-yes/S-no/P-no/H-no

Full breakfast
Homemade cookies, tea
Sitting room
refrig., microwave, TV
patio, porch

Romantic hideaway in adobe home in historic zone, two-room suite furnished with antiques, folk art, fresh flowers, two fireplaces.

Four Kachinas Inn
512 Webber St., 87501
505-982-2550 800-397-2564
John Daw & Andrew Beckerman
All year

$$$ B&B
4 rooms, 4 pb
Visa, MC, *Rated*, •
C-ltd/S-no/P-no/H-yes

Continental plus
Afternoon tea
Sitting room

Only four blocks from historic Plaza; furnished with handcrafted furniture, Navajo rugs & Indian art; breakfast served in your room.

Grant Corner Inn
122 Grant Ave., 87501
505-983-6678
Louise Stewart & Pat Walter
All year

$$ B&B
13 rooms, 7 pb
Visa, MC, *Rated*, •
C-ltd/S-yes/P-no/H-yes
Spanish

Full breakfast
Comp. wine & cheese
Gourmet picnic lunches
private club access
(pool, sauna, tennis)

Elegant colonial home located in the heart of downtown Santa Fe, nine charming rooms furnished with antiques; friendly, warm atmosphere.

SANTA FE ———————————————————————————

Inn of the Animal Tracks
707 Paseo de Peralta, 87501
505-988-1546
Daun Martin & Barney Martin
All year

$$$ B&B
5 rooms, 5 pb
Visa, MC, AmEx, *Rated*,
•
C-yes/S-no/P-no/H-yes

Full breakfast
Lunch ($)
Comp. high tea
sitting room
cable T.V.

Full of humor and Southwest charm. Historic adobe-style inn. 3 blocks from city's 17th-century Plaza and close to ski slopes. Hearty breakfast and afternoon teas.

Inn on the Alameda
303 E. Alameda, 87501
505-984-2121
Fritz Mercer
All year

$$$ B&B
47 rooms, 47 pb
Most CC, *Rated*, •
C-yes/S-yes/P-yes/H-yes
Spanish

Continental plus buffet
Sitting room, library
hot tubs, conf. facility
drinks in main lounge

Between gallary-filled Canyon Rd. & Historic Plaza. Spanish-style accents, romantic kiva fireplaces, open-air courtyard. Handmade armoires, chairs & beds.

Manzano House
661 Garcia St., 87501
505-983-2054
John Orvy Zinn
All year

$$$ EP
3 rooms, 3 pb
•
C-yes/S-yes/P-no/H-yes

Fully equipped kitchens
Comp. wine, soda
Fully furnished adobes
some woodstoves
some fireplaces

Three charming adobe homes; unique alternative to traditional hotel/motel. In historic zone, close to Plaza, Complimentary wine/sodas.

El Paradero
220 W. Manhattan, 87501
505-988-1177
Ouida MacGregor, Thom Allen
All year

$$ B&B
14 rooms, 8 pb
Visa, MC, *Rated*, •
C-ltd/S-ltd/P-ltd/H-ltd
Spanish

Full gourmet breakfast
Comp. tea & snacks, wine
Gourmet picnic lunches
TV rm, living rm, piano
2 suites available

180-year-old adobe in quiet downtown location. Gourmet breakfasts, warm atmosphere, detailed visitor information. True southwestern hospitality. **Bottle of wine w/reservation**

Preston House, The
106 Faithway St., 87501
505-982-3465
Signe Bergman
All year

$ B&B
14 rooms, 14 pb
Visa, MC, *Rated*
C-ltd/S-ltd/P-no/H-no

Continental plus
Afternoon tea & dessert
Sitting room
lawn

Historic 100-year-old Queen Anne house on National Register with fireplaces and antiques; quiet location 3 blocks from Plaza.

Pueblo Bonito B&B Inn
138 W. Manhattan, 87501
505-984-8001
Herb & Amy Behm
All year

$$ B&B
14 rooms, 14 pb
Most CC, *Rated*, •
C-yes/S-ltd/P-no/H-ltd

Continental plus to room
Aft. tea, snacks
Laundry, cable TV
tours, sightseeing arr.
airport pickup

Secluded historic adobe; 5-minute walk from Santa Fe Plaza. Traditional New Mexico living and decor. 15 guest rooms with private bath and fireplace. Landscaped grounds.

Hacienda Del Sol, Taos, NM

SANTA FE

Territorial Inn
215 Washington Ave., 87501
505-989-7737
Lela McFerrin
All year

$$$ B&B
10 rooms, 8 pb
Visa, MC, *Rated*, •
C-ltd/S-ltd/P-no/H-yes

Continental plus
Comp. brandy, cookies
Sitting room
hot tubs

Elegantly furnished 100-year old home. One block from Historic Plaza.

SANTA FE—ALGODONES

Hacienda Vargas
P.O. Box 307, 87001
1431 Hwy 313
505-867-9115 800-723-2194
Pablo & Julia DeVargas
All year

$$ B&B
4 rooms, 4 pb
Visa, MC, *Rated*, •
C-ltd/S-ltd/P-no/H-no
Spanish, German

Full breakfast
Hot tubs, sitting room
golf courses nearby
murder mystery weekends

Romantic, secluded and historic adobe hacienda. F/P, private jacuzzi, private baths & entrances, majestic views. **Romance packages w/champagne & flowers—$20**

TAOS

Hacienda Del Sol
P.O. Box 177, 87571
109 Mabel Dodge Ln.
505-758-0287
John & Marcine Landon
All year

$$ B&B
7 rooms, 5 pb
Visa, MC, *Rated*, •
C-yes/S-no/P-no/H-ltd

Full breakfast
Comp. wine, snacks
Library, guest robes
fireplaces, gallery
outdoor hot tub

180-yr-old large adobe hideaway purchased by Mabel Dodge for Indian husband, Tony. Adjoins vast Indian lands yet close to Plaza. Tranquillity, mountain views. Comp. newspaper.

La Posada de Taos B&B
P.O. Box 1118, 87571
309 Juanita Ln.
505-758-8164
Nancy & Bill Swan
All year

$$ B&B
5 rooms, 5 pb
•
C-yes/S-yes/P-yes/H-yes

Full breakfast
Sitting room
piano
Japanese garden

Mountain views from this provincial adobe inn in artists' colony of Taos. Visit Indian pueblos and art galleries. Hearty breakfasts.

TAOS

El Rincón B&B	$ B&B	Continental breakfast
114 Kit Carson, 87571	12 rooms, 12 pb	Complimentary wine
505-758-4874	Visa, MC, AmEx, *Rated*,	VCRs & Stereos in rooms
Nina C. Meyers, Paul Castillo	•	hot tubs
All year	C-yes/S-yes/P-yes/H-yes	
	Spanish	

Historic home in the heart of Taos. Fine art collection and all modern amenities. **Free bottle of wine for special occasions**

Stewart House Gallery/Inn	$$$ B&B	Full breakfast
P.O. Box 2326, 87571	4 rooms, 4 pb	Sitting room
#46 Ski Vly Rd., Hwy 150	Visa, MC, *Rated*, •	library, hot tubs
505-776-2913 FAX:776-1399	C-ltd/S-no/P-no/H-no	private patios
Mildred & Don Cheek		
All year		

Mountain views & sunsets. Private patios. 5 miles to historic Taos Plaza & world-famous Taos Pueblo. Skiing, fishing, rafting, hiking nearby. On TV's "Great Country Inn's

TAOS SKI VALLEY

Amizette Inn & Restaurant	$$ B&B	Full breakfast
P.O. Box 756, 87525	12 rooms, 11 pb	Sauna
Hwy 150, Ski Vally Rd.	Visa, MC, AmEx, •	hot tub
505-776-2451 800-446-8267	C-yes/S-yes	mountain hiking trails
Patrick E. Walsh		
All year		

Inn located at 9,000 feet, borders wilderness area and trout stream. Approximately 18 miles NE of Taos. Paved road, very accessible, yet very much off the beaten path!

More Inns . . .

Adobe and Roses B&B, 1011 Ortega NW, Albuquerque, 87114, 505-898-0654
Bottger Mansion, The, 110 San Felipe NW, Albuquerque, 87104, 505-243-3639
Casas de Sueños, B&B Inn, 310 Rio Grande Blvd. SW, Albuquerque, 87104, 505-247-4560
Corner House, The, 9121 James Place NE, Albuquerque, 87111,
Inn at Paradise, The, 10035 Country Club Ln., Albuquerque, 87114, 505-898-0161
Las Palomas Valley B&B, 2303 Candelaria Rd. NW, Albuquerque, 87107, 505-345-7228
W.E. Mauger Estate, The, 701 Roma Ave., Albuquerque, 87102, 505-242-8755
Sierra Mesa Lodge, P.O. Box 463, Alto, 88312, 505-336-4515
Monte Verde Ranch B&B, Box 173, Angel Fire, 87710, 505-377-6928
La Casa Muñeca, 213 N. Alameda, Carlsbad, 88220, 505-887-1891
Rancho do Chimaya, P.O. Box 11, Chimaya, 87522,
Casa Escondida B&B, P.O. Box 142, Chimayo, 87522, 505-351-4805
Hacienda Rancho de Chimayo, P.O. Box 11, Chimayo,
Casa del Gavilan, P.O. Box 518, Cimarron, 87714, 505-376-2246
All Season's B&B, Swallow Pl., Box 144, Cloudcroft, 88317, 505-682-2380
Lodge at Cloudcroft, P.O. Box 497, Cloudcroft, 88317, 505-682-2566
Casa la Resolana, 7887 Corales Rd., Corrales, 87048,
Corrales Inn B&B, P.O. Box 1361, Corrales, 87048, 505-897-4422
Yours Truly, P.O. Box 2263, Corrales, 87048, 505-898-7027
Costilla B&B, P.O. Box 186, Costilla, 87524, 505-586-1683
La Casita Guesthouse, P.O. Box 103, Dixon, 87527, 505-579-4297
Blue Star Healing & Vaca., P.O. Box 800, El Prado, 87529, 505-758-4634
La Puebla House B&B, Route 3, Box 172-A, Espanola,
O'Keefe Country, P.O. Box 92, Espanola, 87532,
Galisteo Inn, Box 4, Route 69, Galisteo, 87540, 505-982-1506
La Casita, Route 10, Box 440, Glenwood, 88039,
Los Olmos Guest Ranch, P.O. Box 127, Glenwood, 88039, 505-539-2311
Hilltop Hacienda, 2520 Westmoreland, Las Cruces, 88001, 505-382-3556
Carriage House B&B, 925 Sixth St., Las Vegas, 87701, 505-454-1784
Plaza Hotel, 230 Old Town Plaza, Las Vegas, 87701, 505-425-3591
Wortley Hotel, Box 96, Lincoln, 88338, 505-653-4500
Casa del Rey, 305 Rover, Los Alamos, 87544, 505-672-9401
Lone Pine B&B, 3065 Arizona Ave., Los Alamos, 87544, 505-662-3015
Los Alamos B&B, P.O. Box 1212, Los Alamos, 87544, 505-662-6041
Orange Street B&B, 3496 Orange St., Los Alamos, 87544, 505-662-2651
Walnut Executive Suite, P.O. Box 777, Los Alamos, 87544, 505-662-9392
Elms, P.O. Box 1176, Mesilla Park, 88001, 505-524-1513

Monjeau Shadows Inn, Bonito Route, Nogal, 88341, 505-336-4191
Broken Drum Guest Ranch, Route 2 Box 100, Pecos, 87552, 505-757-6194
Hacienda de Las Munecas, P.O. Box 564, Placitas, 87043, 505-867-3255
Vogt Ranch B&B, The, Box 716, Ramah, 87321, 505-783-4362
Don Pasqual Martinez B&B, P.O. Box 1205, Rancho de Taos, 87557,
Adobe & Pines Inn, P.O. Box 837, Ranchos De Taos, 87557, 800-723-8267
Ranchos Ritz B&B, P.O. Box 669, Ranchos de Taos, 87557, 505-758-2640
Whistling Waters, Talpa Route, Box 9, Ranchos de Taos, 87557,
Red Violet Inn, 344 N. Second St., Raton, 87740, 505-445-9778
El Western Lodge, Box 301, Gilt Edge, Red River, 87558, 505-754-2272
Chinguague Compound, P.O. Box 1118, San Juan Pueblo, 87566, 505-852-2194
Pine Cone Inn B&B, Box 94, 13 Tejano Canyo, Sandia Park, 87047, 505-281-1384
Dancing Ground of the Sun, 711 Paseo de Peralta, Santa Fe, 87501, 505-986-9797
Don Gaspar Compound, 617 Don Gaspar, Santa Fe, 87501, 505-986-8664
Inn of the Victorian Bird, P.O. Box 3235, Santa Fe, 87501, 505-455-3375
Jean's Place B&B, 2407 Camino Capitan, Santa Fe, 87505,
La Posada de Santa Fe, 330 E. Palace Ave., Santa Fe, 87501, 800-727-5276
Polly's Guest House, 410 Camino Don Miguel, Santa Fe, 87501, 505-983-9481
Rancho Jacona, Route 5, Box 250, Santa Fe, 87501, 505-455-7948
Sunrise Springs, Rt. 2, Box 203, Santa Fe, 87501, 505-471-3600
Sunset House, 436 Sunset, Santa Fe, 87501, 505-983-3523
Triangle Inn, P.O. Box 3235, Santa Fe,
Water Street Inn, 427 W. Water St., Santa Fe, 87501,
Hotel St. Francis, 210 Don Gaspar Ave., Sante Fe, 87501, 505-983-5700
Adobe Walls Motel, East Kit Carson Rd., Taos, 505-758-3972
American Artists House, P.O. Box 584, Taos, 87571, 505-758-4446
Brooks Street Inn, P.O. Box 4954, Taos, 87571, 505-758-1489
Casa Benarides B&B, 137 Kit Carson Rd., Taos, 87571, 505-758-1772
Casa Europa Inn & Gallery, 157 Upper Ranchitos Rd., Taos, 87571, 505-758-9798
Casa de Las Chimeneas, 405 Cordoba, Box 5303, Taos, 87571, 505-758-4777
Casa de Milagros B&B, P.O. Box 2983, Taos, 87571, 800-243-9334
Dasburg House & Studio, Box 2764, Taos, 87571, 505-758-9513
Historic Taos Inn, The, 125 Paseo del Pueblo N., Taos, 87571, 505-758-2233
Hotel Edelweiss, P.O. Box 83, Taos, 87571, 505-776-2301
Las Palomas Conf. Center, P.O. Box 6689, Taos, 87571, 505-758-9456
Laughing Horse Inn, P.O. 4904, Taos, 87571, 505-758-8350
Mabel Dodge Lujan House, P.O. Box 3400, Taos, 87571, 505-758-9456
Rancho Rio Pueblo Inn, Box 2331, Taos, 87571, 505-758-4900
Sagebrush Inn, S. Santa Fe Rd., Hwy 68, Taos, 87571, 800-428-3626
San Geronimo Lodge, P.O. Box 2491, Taos, 87571, 505-758-7117
Silvertree Inn, P.O. Box 1528, Taos, 87571, 505-758-3071
Zia House, Box 5017, Taos, 87571, 505-751-0697
Rancho Encantado, State Rd. 592, Tesuque, 87501, 505-982-3537
Rancho Arriba B&B, P.O. Box 338, Truchas, 87578, 505-689-2374
Vallecitos Retreat, P.O. Box 226, Vallecitos, 87581, 505-582-4226

New York

ADDISON

Addison Rose B&B
37 Maple St., 14801
607-359-4650
Bill & Mary Ann Peters
All year

$$ B&B
3 rooms, 1 pb
Rated
C-ltd/S-no/P-no/H-no

Full breakfast
Afternoon tea
Antiques
near golf, hiking
skiing, lakes & streams

Discover "Victorian elegance in the heart of the country" in this restored, period-furnished "painted lady." Minutes from Corning and Finger Lakes Wineries.

ALBANY

Mansion Hill Inn
115 Philip St., at Park Ave.,
12202
518-465-2038 800-477-8171
MaryEllen & Steve Stofelano
All year

$$$ B&B
12 rooms, 12 pb
Visa, MC, AmEx, DC, •
C-yes/S-yes/P-yes/H-yes
Sp., Ital., Ger., Fr.

Full breakfast
Restaurant, bar
Health club privileges
golf and tennis nearby

An urban inn, established in a residential neighborhood. The inn is comprised of three Victorian-era buildings around the corner from Governor's Mansion. **2nd. night free Ltd.**

ALBION

Friendship Manor B&B	$ B&B	Continental plus
349 S. Main St., 14411	4 rooms, 1 pb	Aft. tea, snacks
716-589-7973	*Rated*, •	Sitting room, library
John & Marylin	C-yes/S-no/P-no/H-no	bicycles, tennis court
All year		pool, grill & tables

Historical rural town. Ride on Erie Canal, fish in lake Ontario. Homemade fudge & pastries or ice cream filled waffle cone. Pick your own fresh fruit. **3rd night 50% off**

Friendship Manor B&B	$$ B&B	Continental plus
349 S. Main St., 14411	4 rooms, 1 pb	Lunch, dinner by request
716-589-7973	*Rated*	Aft. tea, snacks
All year	C-yes/S-no/P-no/H-no	sitting room
		tennis, bikes, pool

Rural setting in Historic Cobblestone area. Fisherman's paradise, antiquing a joy, ride or walk to Historic Erie Canal, Albion Historic Court House. **3rd night 50% off**

ALEXANDRIA BAY

Bach's Alexandria Bay Inn	$$ B&B	Full breakfast
2 Church St., 13607	7 rooms, 7 pb	Aftn. tea, comp. wine
315-482-9697	Visa, MC, *Rated*, •	Sitting room, library
Virginia Bach, Robert J. Bach	C-ltd/S-ltd/P-no/H-no	boat tours, fishing
All year	Spanish, some French	hiking, antique shopping

A beautiful Victorian inn in the Thousand Islands. Glorious antiques & Laura Ashley bedding fill guest rooms. Gourmet breakfast in dining room or on porches. **7th night free.**

AMENIA

Troutbeck Country Inn	$$$ AP	All meals included
Box 26, Leedsville Rd., 12501	31 rooms, 26 pb	Open bar
914-373-9681 FAX:373-7080	AmEx, *Rated*, •	Public rooms, piano
Jim Flaherty	C-ltd/S-yes/P-no/H-no	tennis courts, library
All year	Span., Port., Ital., Fr.	year-round swimming pool

Historic English country estate on 422 acres, with indoor and outdoor pools, fine chefs, . 12,000 books, lovely grounds. A quiet retreat. **10% off winter, ltd**

AUBURN

Springside Inn	$$ MAP	Continental plus
P.O. Box 327, 13021	8 rooms, 5 pb	Dinner included
41-43 W. Lane Rd.	Visa, *Rated*, •	Restaurant, bar, lake
315-252-7247	C-yes/S-no/P-no/H-no	bicycles, swim, fish
William Dove		wine & cheese on arrival
All year		

Charming guest rooms. Breakfast in a basket prepared for each room. Summer Dinner Theater combines gourmet dining with Broadway entertainment. Wedding. **3rd. night 50% off**

AVERILL PARK

Gregory House Rest., The	$$$ B&B	Continental breakfast
P.O. Box 401, 12018	12 rooms, 12 pb	Restaurant (Tues-Sun)
Route 43	Most CC, *Rated*, •	Bar, comp. sherry, pool
518-674-3774 800-497-2977	C-ltd/S-yes/P-no/H-no	common room w/fireplace
Melissa & Christopher Miller		direct dial phones in rm
All year		

Country charm centrally located—near Albany, Troy, Saratoga, Tanglewood, mountains, lakes & skiing. Vermont & Berkshires 45 min. away. **Comp. glass of wine w/dinner**

BAINBRIDGE

Berry Hill Farm B&B	$$ B&B	Full country breakfast
RD1, Box 128, Ward-Loomis Rd.,	3 rooms, 1 pb	Herb/flower garden, shop
13733	*Rated*, •	nature trails, cross-country
607-967-8745	C-yes/S-ltd/P-no/H-no	ski
Jean Fowler, Cecilio Rios	Span, Fr, German, Ital	swimming & beaver ponds
All year		

Comfortably restored 1820s farmhouse on hilltop surrounded by acres of woods, meadows, extensive perennial flower gardens. Antiques. Near tennis, golf. **2+ nights, free plant**

BOLTON LANDING

Hilltop Cottage B&B	$ B&B	Full breakfast
P.O. Box 186, 12814	4 rooms, 2 pb	
6883 Lakeshore Dr.	Visa, MC, *Rated*, •	
518-644-2492	C-ltd/S-ltd/P-no/H-no	
Anita & Charlie Richards	German	
All year		

Beautiful Lake George—Eastern Adirondack region. Clean, comfortable. Renovated farmhouse. Walk to beach, restaurants, marinas. Friendly hosts familiar w/area. **7th nite free**

BROOKLYN

B&B on the Park	$$$ B&B	Full breakfast
113 Prospect Park West, 11215	6 rooms, 4 pb	Sitting room
718-499-6115	Visa, MC, *Rated*	Victorian antiques
Liana Paolella	C-yes/S-ltd/P-no/H-no	stained glass, woodwork
All year	French	

Beautifully appointed 1892 Victorian townhouse—a refuge minutes from Manhattan. Situated in Park Slope, a historic district of Brooklyn. Fabulous full breakfasts.

BURDETT

Red House Country Inn, The	$$ B&B	Full breakfast
4586 Picnic Area Rd., Finger	6 rooms, 2 pb	Comp. wine, tea, coffee
Lakes Nat'l Forest, 14818	Visa, MC, AmEx, *Rated*,	Large in-ground pool
607-546-8566	•	sitting room, piano
Sandy Schmanke & Joan Martin	C-ltd/S-ltd/P-no,	nature trails
All year		

Within national forest; 28 miles of trails. Beautiful rooms in this gorgeous setting. Near famous Watkins Glen, east side of Seneca Lake. Over 30 wineries nearby.

BURLINGTON FLATS

Chalet Waldheim	$$$ B&B	Continental plus
RD 1, Box 51-G-2, 13315	2 rooms	Afternoon tea, snacks
607-965-8803	*Rated*	Comp. wine
Franzi & Heinz Kuhne	C-ltd/S-no/P-no/H-yes	sitting room, antiques
May—December	German	patio, deck, pond

Unique, quiet chalet; authentic antiques; private entrance; 75 acres of trails; gourmet breakfast; 12 mi. to Cooperstown, golf & Lake Otsego. **15% senior disc't 3+ nights**

CAIRO

Cedar Terrace Resort	$$ EP/B&B	Restaurant
R 2, Box 407, Main St., 12413	30 rooms, 30 pb	Lunch, dinner
518-622-9313	Visa, MC, *Rated*, •	Bar service
Joseph P. Errante	C-yes/S-yes/P-no/H-ltd	sitting room, library
All year	Italian, German	tennis, swimming pool

Beautiful, small resort with lovely grounds. Near major attractions and ski areas. Full service May-Oct., B&B only Nov.-April. **Weekly rates available**

CAMILLUS

Green Gate Inn
Two Main St., 13031
315-672-9276
Lori Edwardsen
All year

$$ B&B
6 rooms, 6 pb
Visa, MC, AmEx, *Rated*,
•
C-yes/S-no/P-no/H-no

Continental plus
Restaurant, comp. wine
Lunch, dinner
2 rms w/jacuzzi

Elegantly restored historic country inn offering excellence in fine dining & gracious lodging. Furnished in genuine antiques. Gateway to Finger Lakes Region. **Free bottle wine**

CANANDAIGUA

Acorn Inn B&B, The
4508 Rt 64 S., Bristol Center,
14424
716-229-2834
Louis & Joan Clark
All year

$$$ B&B
4 rooms, 4 pb
Rated, •
C-ltd/S-no/P-ltd/H-yes

Full breakfast
Swimming hiking nearby
golf, skiing nearby
sitting room, library

1795 Stagecoach Inn furnished with period antiques & canopy beds. Fireplace, gardens. Nearby outdoor activities. Gourmet breakfast. Warm hospitality. **3rd night 50% off**

Habersham Country Inn
6124 Routes 5 & 20, 14425
716-394-1510
Robyn Prince
All year

$$$ B&B
5 rooms, 5 pb
Visa, MC, Disc., •
C-yes/S-no/P-no/H-no

Full gourmet breakfast
Afternoon tea
Comp. wine
sitting room

Charming 18th-century Federal-style inn; comfortable period decor; bridal suite; gourmet breakfast; gift shop. Close to lake, skiing and wineries.

Lakeview Farm B&B
4761 Rt. 364, Rushville, 14544
716-554-6973
Howard & Betty Freese
All year

$$ B&B
2 rooms
AmEx, *Rated*, •
C-ltd/S-ltd/P-no/H-no

Full breakfast
Comp. tea, coffee, A/C
Sitting room, lounge
pond, lawn games
walking trails

2 antique-furnished rooms in country home overlooking Canandaigua Lake. 170 acres. Near beach, restaurants, and Finger Lakes attractions. **Special rates for extended stays**

CANDOR

Edge of Thyme, The
P.O. Box 48, 13743
6 Main St.
607-659-5155 800-722-7365
Frank and Eva Mae Musgrave
All year

$$ B&B
Visa, MC, *Rated*, •
C-yes/S-no/P-no/H-no

Full breakfast
High tea by appt.
Sitting rms w/fireplaces
piano, indoor games
lawn games, gift shoppe

Gracious Georgian home, antiques, gardens, arbor, leaded glass windowed porch. Finger Lakes, Cornell, Ithaca College, Watkins Glen, Corning, wineries nearby.

CAZENOVIA

Brae Loch Inn
5 Albany St., U.S. Rt. 20, 13035
315-655-3431 800-655-3431
Jim & Val Barr
All year, FAX: 655-4844

$$$ B&B
12 rooms, 12 pb
Most CC, *Rated*, •
C-yes/S-yes/P-no/H-yes

Continental breakfast
Restaurant, bar
Banquet fac., catering
meeting rooms, lounge
phones in all rooms

Victorian inn built in 1805, decorated in Scottish motifs, Victorian antiques, tartan plaids. Waitresses wear kilts and tams. Unique Scottish gifts. **3rd night 50% off, ltd**

CAZENOVIA

Brewster Inn, The
P.O. Box 507, 13035
6 Ledyard Ave.
315-655-9232
Richard & Catherine Hubbard
All year

$ B&B
17 rooms, 17 pb
Most CC, *Rated*
C-yes/S-ltd/P-no/H-ltd

Continental breakfast
Restaurant - dinner
Bar service
lake, sitting room
4 rooms w/jacuzzi

Excellent food/wine list. Unspoiled, "non-touristy" town w/quaint shops & outdoor activities: swimming, cross-country skiing, Chittenango Falls Park. Quiet & relaxing.

CHAPPAQUA

Crabtree's Kittle House
11 Kittle Rd., 10514
914-666-8044
John & Dick Crabtree
All year

$$$ B&B
11 rooms, 11 pb
Visa, MC, AmEx, DC
C-yes/S-yes/P-yes/H-yes
Spanish

Continental breakfast
Lunch, dinner
Restaurant, bar
Snacks

Built in 1790, award-winning wine list, American-Continental cuisine. Jazz band Thurs. & Fri. w/dancing. Music Sat. also, Sunday champagne brunch.

CHAUTAUQUA

Plumbush—A Victorian B&B
P.O. Box 864, 14722
Route 33
716-789-5309
George & Sandy Green
All year

$$ B&B
5 rooms, 5 pb
Visa, MC, •
C-ltd/S-no/P-no/H-no

Continental plus
Comp. tea and cookies
Sitting room, library
music room with piano
bicycles

Restored 1860s Italian villa country home; 125 acres; wildlife; cross-country skiing; nearby lake, antiques, wineries; 1 mi. to Chautauqua Institute. Peak season 2/3 night min.

CHEMUNG

Halcyon Place B&B
P.O. Box 244, 14825
197 Washington St.
607-529-3544
Yvonne & Douglas Sloan
All year

$ B&B
3 rooms, 1 pb
Rated
C-ltd/S-ltd/P-no/H-no
Some German

Full breakfast
Homemade herb cheese
Lemon herb tea bread
bicycles, wineries
jazz & classical music

1825 Greek Revival home offers peace, tranquility and gracious hospitality for the discerning traveler. Period antiques. Full gourmet breakfast served.

CHESTERTOWN

Balsam House, The
Box 171, Atateka Dr., Friends
Lake, 12817
518-494-2828 800-441-6856
Bruce Robbins, Helena Edmark
Exc. April—mid-April

$$$ B&B/MAP
20 rooms, 20 pb
Rated
C-yes/S-yes/P-no/H-no

Continental plus/Full
Country French cuisine
Entertainment
bicycles, piano

Dramatically restored Victorian country inn, filled w/antiques & wicker from 1900s. Fine wine list, superb dining, casual elegance, southern hospitality. **10% off for 5 days+**

CLARENCE

Asa Ransom House
10529 Main St., Route 5, 14031
716-759-2315
Judy & Bob Leuz
All year exc. January

$$$ B&B
9 rooms, 9 pb
Visa, MC, Disc.,*Rated*, •
C-ltd/S-ltd/P-no/H-ltd

Full breakfast
Dinner, bar, snacks
Sitting room, library
most rooms w/fireplace
herb garden, bicycles

Village inn furnished with antiques, period reproductions; gift shop, herb garden, regional dishes, homemade breads & desserts. **Ask about wkday "Getaway Package"**

Halcyon Place B&B, Chemung, NY

CLAYTON—1000 ISLANDS

Thousand Islands Inn
P.O. Box 69, 13624
335 Riverside Dr.
315-686-3030 800-544-4241
Susan & Allen Benas
Memorial Day-late Sept

$$ EP
13 rooms, 13 pb
Most CC, *Rated*
C-yes/S-yes/P-no/H-no

Full breakfast $
All meals served
Piano
near public tennis
courts and pool

The last full-service inn in the Islands. 1000 Islands salad dressing originated here in the early 1900s. Original recipe still used. 1993 was our 96th year!

COLDEN

Back of the Beyond
7233 Lower E. Hill Rd., 14033
716-652-0427
Bill & Shash Georgi
All year

$$ B&B
3 rooms
C-yes/S-no/P-no/H-no

Full country breakfast
Comp. beverages & snacks
Kitchen, fireplace
pool table, gift shop
swimming pond,
cross-country ski

Charming mini-estate 50 mi. from Niagara Falls, hiking, organic herb, flower & vegetable gardens. Brkfast served on deck/living rm. **Kids under 10 free.**

COOPERSTOWN ───

Angelholm B&B	$$ B&B	Full breakfast
P.O. Box 705, 13326	4 rooms, 4 pb	Deluxe & aftn. tea
14 Elm St.	Visa, MC, *Rated*	Sitting room, library
607-547-2483 FAX:547-2309	C-ltd/S-no/P-no/H-no	porch, piano, TV room
Jan & Fred Reynolds		
All year		

Historic 1815 colonial in town, with off-street parking. Walking distance to shops, restaurants and Hall of Fame Museum. All new Oriental rugs and furniture.

Chestnut Street Guesthouse	$$ B&B	Continental plus
79 Chestnut St., 13326	3 rooms, 1 pb	Restaurants nearby
607-547-5624	AmEx	Sitting room
John & Pam Miller	C-yes/S-no/P-no/H-no	walk to 3 museums
All year		tennis nearby

Park your car and enjoy the beauty of our delightful village. Warm hospitality and a lovely home await you. Please come share it with us.

Inn at Cooperstown, The	$$$ B&B	Continental breakfast
16 Chestnut St., 13326	17 rooms, 17 pb	1986 NY State Historic
607-547-5756	Most CC, *Rated*, •	Preservation award
Michael Jerome	C-yes/S-yes/P-no/H-yes	winner, sitting room
All year		

Restored Victorian inn providing genuine hospitality; close to Baseball Hall of Fame, Fenimore House and Farmer's Museum; open all year.

Litco Farms B&B	$$ B&B	Full breakfast
P.O. Box 1048, 13326	4 rooms, 2 pb	Sitting room
Route 28, Fly Creek	*Rated*, •	library, pool
607-547-2501	C-yes/S-yes/P-no/H-no	cross-country ski trails
Jim & Margaret Wolff		
All year		

Families & couples enjoy 20'x40' pool, 70 acres & nature trails. Handmade quilts by resident quilter. Warm hospitality; marvelous breakfasts. **Restaurant discounts**

CROTON-ON-HUDSON ──────────────────────────────────────

Alexander Hamilton House	$$ B&B	Full gourmet breakfast
49 Van Wyck St., 10520	5 rooms, 5 pb	Fireplaces, bicycles
914-271-6737	Visa, MC, AmEx, *Rated*,	gardens, swimming pool
Barbara Notarius	•	bridal chamber w/jacuzzi
All year	C-yes/S-no/P-no/H-no	
	French, Russian	

1889 Victorian furnished w/oriental rugs, antiques & other treasures. First B&B in Westchester County. Close to West Point and NYC by train. **3+ nights—special flowers**

DE BRUCE ───

De Bruce Country Inn	$$$ MAP	Full breakfast
Box 286 A, Rd. 1, 12758	15 rooms, 15 pb	Restaurant, bar, dinner
914-439-3900 212-226-0342	C-yes/S-yes/P-yes/H-no	Library, sauna, pool
All year	French	private preserve
		trout pond, art gallery

Within the Catskill Forest Preserve with its trails, wildlife, famous trout stream, our turn-of-the-century inn offers superb dining overlooking the valley.

DEPOSIT

Alexander's Inn
770 Oquaga Rd., 13754
607-467-6023 FAX:467-6098
Alexander Meyer
All year

$ B&B
5 rooms, 3 pb
C-yes/S-ltd/P-ltd/H-no
German, French

Full breakfast, snacks
Dinner by appointment
Bicycles, tennis nearby
sitting room, library
sauna, hot tubs, pool

Beautiful lake, elegant & relaxing meeting place for world travellers. Golf, fishing. Day trips to Catskills, Finger Lakes, Niagara Falls. Breakfast all you can eat.

White Pillars Inn, The
82 Second St., 13754
607-467-4191 607-467-4189
Ms. Najla R. Aswad
All year

$$ B&B
5 rooms, 3 pb
Most CC, *Rated*, •
C-ltd/S-no/P-no/H-no

Full 5-course breakfast
Dinner by resv.
Comp. wine, desserts
sitting room, library
in-room phones & TV's

Lavishly furnished 1820 Greek Revival mansion. Gourmet breakfast is the highlight of your stay. Antiquing, cycling or just a perfect place to do nothing at all.

DOVER PLAINS

Old Drovers Inn
P.O. Box 675, 12522
Old Route 22
914-832-9311
Alice Pitcher, Kemper Peacock
All year

$$$ B&B
4 rooms, 4 pb
Visa, MC, DC, *Rated*, •
C-ltd/S-yes/P-yes/H-ltd

Continental plus (wkday)
Full breakfast (wkend)
Restaurant, bar service
sitting room, library
near tennis, golf, etc.

Authentic, early American inn only 75 mi. north of NYC. Fireplaces, antiques, beautiful grounds, exquisite food, the ultimate romantic experience. **Request discount certif.**

DRYDEN

Sarah's Dream Village Inn
P.O. Box 1087, 13053
49 W. Main St., (Rt. 13)
607-844-4321
Judi Williams, Ken Morusty
All year

$$ B&B
7 rooms, 7 pb
Visa, MC, AmEx, Disc., •
C-ltd/S-no/P-no/H-no

Full breakfast
Comp. tea and snacks
Sitting room, library
airport pickup, gardens
room trays for weddings

On Nat'l Register of Historic Places. 1828 Greek Revival furnished w/antiques. Not pretentious. Nearby: golfing, sailing, skiing, antiquing. Antique/decor shop. **4th night 50%**

EAGLE BAY

Big Moose Inn
on Big Moose Lake, 13331
315-357-2042
Doug & Bonnie Bennett
Exc. April, Nov–Dec 26

$ B&B
12 rooms, 12 pb
credit cards accepted
C-yes/S-yes/P-no/H-ltd

Continental (wkdys)
All meals (wknds), bar
Sitting room
floating gazebo, canoes
some rms. w/fireplace

Located on Big Moose Lake. Excellent dining. Overlooking the lake. Hiking trails, canoes, winter sports enthusiasts galor. **Special rates wkdays & off-season**

EAST HAMPTON

Pink House, The
26 James Ln., 11937
516-324-3400
Sue Calden, Ron Steinhilber
All year

$$$ B&B
5 rooms, 5 pb
credit cards accepted
C-ltd/S-no/P-no/H-no
Spanish

Full breakfast
Sitting room
porch
swimming pool

A distinctive B&B located in the historic district of E. Hampton. Newly renovated with marble bathrooms, lush bathrobes & special emphasis on personal service.

ELIZABETHTOWN

Stony Water
RR 1, P.O. Box 69, Roscoe Rd., 12932
518-873-9125
Winifred Thomas/Sandra Murphy
All year

$$ B&B
4 rooms, 3 pb
Visa, MC, *Rated*, •
C-yes/S-no/P-no/H-yes

Full breakfast
Lunch, dinner
Afternoon tea, snacks
sitting room, library
piano, trails, fishing

Stony Water's tranquil setting on 87 wooded acres provides a perfect refuge from the complexities of today's world. 2 bedroom cottage also available. **7th Night Free**

ELKA PARK

Redcoat's Return, The
Dale Ln., 12427
518-589-6379 518-589-9858
Tom & Margaret Wright
Nov 23–Mar, May 23–Oct

$$$ B&B
14 rooms, 7 pb
Visa, MC, AmEx, *Rated*
C-yes/S-yes/P-no/H-no

Full breakfast
Dinner, tea
Sitting room
cocktail lounge
gazebo, croquet, patio

Cozy English-style country inn, scenically nestled in the heart of the Catskill Game Preserve. Abundant seasonal activities; excellent cuisine.

FLEISCHMANNS

River Run
Main St., 12430
914-254-4884
Jeanne Palmer & Larry Miller
All year

$$ B&B
9 rooms, 6 pb
Visa, MC, *Rated*, •
C-yes/S-ltd/P-yes/H-no

Full breakfast
Fireplace, stained glass
beautiful grounds, piano
front porch/trout stream

Exquisite country village Victorian, at the edge of the Catskill Forest. Enjoy magnificent hiking trails, superb skiing, antiquing, auction, fishing, golf & tennis.

FOSTERDALE

Fosterdale Heights House
205 Mueller Rd., 12726
914-482-3369
Roy Singer
All year

$$ B&B
11 rooms, 5 pb
Visa, MC
C-ltd/S-yes/P-no/H-no

Full breakfast
Dinner, snacks, pond
Sitting room, library
billiard room, piano
cross-country skiing,
canoeing

Historic 1840 European-style country estate. Catskill Mountains, less than 2 hours from New York City. Gentle, quiet. Bountiful country breakfast. **$2.00 off dinner entre**

FULTON

Battle Island Inn
RD #1, Box 176, Rt. 48 N., 13069
315-593-3699
Richard & Joyce Rice
All year

$$ B&B
6 rooms, 6 pb
Visa, MC, *Rated*
C-yes/S-no/P-no/H-no

Full breakfast
Sitting room
four acres of large
flower and herb gardens

1840s farm estate furnished with period furnishings. Gourmet breakfast served in our elegant Empire Period dining room. Located across from golf course, cross-country skiing.

GARRISON

Bird & Bottle Inn, The
Route 2, Box 64, Old Albany Post Rd., 10524
914-424-3000
Ira Boyar
All year

$$$ B&B/MAP
4 rooms, 4 pb
Visa, MC, AmEx, *Rated*,
•
C-ltd/S-ltd/P-no/H-no

Full breakfast
Dinner (MAP), bar

Established in 1761, the inn's history predates the Revolutionary War. Each room has period furniture, a working fireplace & four-poster or canopy bed. **Free bottle of wine.**

GREENFIELD

Wayside Inn
104 Wilton Rd., 12833
518-893-7249
Karen & Dale Shook
All year

$$ B&B
4 rooms, 4 pb
Visa, MC, *Rated*, •
C-ltd/S-no/P-no/H-no

Full breakfast
Bicycles
sitting room

1789 Stagecoach/Tavern, 10 acres w/stream, pond, wildflowers, herb gardens, working pottery, unique arts center. Come a stranger—leave a friend.

GREENVILLE

Greenville Arms
P.O. Box 659, 12083
RD 1, Box 2, South St.
518-966-5219
Eliot & Letitia Dalton
May 1 - December 1

$$$ B&B
14 rooms, 14 pb
Visa, MC, Disc.*Rated*, •
C-ltd/S-ltd/P-no/H-ltd

Full breakfast from menu
Dinner with reservation
Library, piano, pool
living/sitting rooms
art workshops, croquet

Victorian country inn in small village in Hudson River Valley. Former house of William Vanderbilt settled on 6 acres of shade trees and gardens. **Comp. split of champagne**

HADLEY

Saratoga Rose
4174 Rockwell St., 12835
518-696-2861 800-942-5025
Nancy & Anthony Merlino
All year

$$ B&B
5 rooms, 5 pb
Visa, MC, AmEx
C-ltd/S-ltd/P-no/H-no

Full breakfast
Restaurant, bar, dinner
Comp. wine, library
in-room dining, bicycles
gift & antique shop

Romantic Victorian inn/restaurant. Near Saratoga, Lake George, skiing, recreational activities. Some rms w/firepl. & jacuzzi. Gourmet meals. **Dinner disc'ts, coupons**

Greenville Arms, Greenville, NY

HAMMONDSPORT

Another Tyme B&B
P.O. Box 134, 14840
7 Church St.
607-569-2747
Carolyn Clark
All year

$$ B&B
3 rooms, 1 pb
Visa, MC, *Rated*
C-ltd/S-no/P-no/H-no

Full breakfast
Afternoon tea & snacks
sitting room

The past is recaptured in the three comfortable guest rooms. The grace and charm of another tyme plus a gourmet breakfast.

Blushing Rose B&B, The
11 William St., 14840
607-569-3402 800-982-8818
Ellen & Bucky Laufersweiler
All year

$$$ B&B
4 rooms, 4 pb
Rated, •
C-ltd/S-no/P-no/H-no

Full country breakfast
Afternoon refreshment
bicycles, sitting room
lake nearby

An 1843 Victorian Italianate located in heart of a historic village. Enjoy museums, wineries, Corning, swimming, boating or just strolling. **Corporate Discounts**

HAMPTON BAYS

House on the Water
P.O. Box 106, 11946
33 Rampasture Rd.
516-728-3560
Hostess: Mrs. UTE
May–November

$$$ B&B
2 rooms, 2 pb
Rated, •
C-ltd/S-ltd/P-no/H-no
German, Spanish, French

Full breakfast
Comp. coffee & tea
Kitchen privileges
barbecue, windsurfer
sail/pedal boats, bikes

Seven miles to Southampton Village. Museum, art gallery, stores. Short drive to beaches. Breakfast on terrace, relax in garden, kitchen privileges (snacks). **Discounts, ask**

HEMPSTEAD BY GARDEN CITY

Country Life B&B
237 Cathedral Ave., 11550
516-292-9219
Richard & Wendy Duvall
All year

$$ B&B
4 rooms, 4 pb
Rated, •
C-yes/S-no/P-no/H-ltd
Spanish, German, French

Full breakfast
Stereo, patio, backyard
color TV & A/C in rooms
bicycles, sitting room

Charming old Dutch colonial; close to New York City, beaches, airports and public transportation, Fifth Avenue of Long Island, tourist sights, Hofstra & Adelphi Universities.

HILLSDALE

Swiss Huttek Country Inn
Route 23, MA/NY border, 12529
518-325-3333 413-528-6200
Mr./Mrs. Gert & Cynthia Alper
April 15–March

$$$ MAP,EP avail
16 rooms, 16 pb
Visa, MC, *Rated*
C-yes/S-yes/P-yes/H-yes
German

Full breakfast
Lunch, dinner, noon tea
Restaurant, bar service
sitting room
tennis, pool, skiing

Swiss chef & owner. French continental decor. Indoor/outdoor patio dining. Nestled in a hidden valley among firs & hemlocks. All rooms w/phones. Daily bar menu, bistro style.

HOPEWELL JUNCTION

Bykenhulle House
21 Bykenhulle Rd., 12533
914-221-4182
Bill & Florence M. Beausoleil
All year

$$$ B&B
5 rooms, 5 pb
Visa, MC, •
C-ltd/S-no/P-no/H-no

Full breakfast
Aft. tea
Library, sitting room
jacuzzi in 2 rooms

Luxurious Georgian manor house; 5 guestrooms with private baths, some with jacuzzis or fireplaces. Great restaurants and antiquing nearby. **3rd night 50% off**

ITHACA ───────────────────────────────

Hanshaw House B&B Inn | $$ B&B | Full breakfast
15 Sapsucker Woods Rd., 14850 | 4 rooms, 4 pb | Comp. wine, aftn. tea
607-273-8034 | Visa, MC, AmEx, *Rated* | Snacks, sitting room
Helen Scoones | C-yes/S-no/P-no/H-no | patio, pond, gardens
All year | | overlooking woods, A/C

Elegantly remodeled 1830s farmhouse overlooking pond & woods. Furnished w/antiques, colorful chintzes, goose down comforters, gardens. **Winter special—Restaurant discount**

Peregrine House Inn | $$ B&B | Full breakfast
133 Giles St, 140 College Ave, | 8 rooms, 4 pb | Afternoon tea
14850 | Visa, MC, *Rated*, • | Comp. wine, snacks
607-272-0919 | C-ltd/P-no, | sitting room
Nancy Falconer | | TV in rooms
All year

1874 Brick Victorian inn furnished with antiques, pretty linens, terry robes. In the heart of city, near Cornell campus. Air conditioned.

Rose Inn | $$$ B&B | Full breakfast
P.O. Box 6576, 14851 | 16 rooms, 16 pb | Gourmet dinner by resv.
Rt. 34 N. | AmEx, *Rated*, • | Antique shop, parlor
607-533-7905 FAX:533-4202 | C-ltd/S-no/P-no/H-no | 80 seat conference room
Charles & Sherry Rosemann | German, Spanish | piano, bikes, jacuzzis
All year

1850s Italianate mansion with 3-story circular mahogany staircase. Furnished with period pieces. 20 landscaped acres, orchard. One of Uncle Ben's "Ten Best Inns in America."

KEENE ───────────────────────────────

Bark Eater Inn, The | $$$ B&B | Full breakfast
Alstead Mill Rd., 12942 | 17 rooms, 4 pb | Comp. tea, wine
518-576-2221 | AmEx, • | Sitting room
Joe - Pete Wilson | C-yes/S-yes/P-yes, | piano
All year

Country inn from the stagecoach days, nestled in quiet valley in heart of Adirondack Mountains. Gracious hosts and gourmet food compliment your stay.

KINGSTON ───────────────────────────────

Rondout B&B | $$ B&B | Full breakfast
88 W. Chester St., 12401 | 2 rooms, 1 pb | Comp. wine, snacks
914-331-2369 | • | Sitting room, piano
Adele & Ralph Calcavecchio | C-yes/S-ltd/Some Ital. & Fr. | library
All year | | glassed-in porch

Spacious, pleasant 1906 mansion near the Hudson River. Year-round recreation, historic sites. Near trains, buses and airports. Hearty breakfast, evening refreshments.

LAKE LUZERNE ───────────────────────────────

Lamplight Inn B&B, The | $$$ B&B | Full breakfast
P.O. Box 70, 12846 | 10 rooms, 10 pb | Comp. tea & coffee
2129 Lake Ave. (9N) | Visa, MC, AmEx, *Rated*, | Sitting rm. w/fireplaces
518-696-5294 800-262-4668 | • | porch w/swing, gardens
Gene & Linda Merlino | C-ltd/S-ltd/P-no/H-no | lake swimming
All year

Romantic 1890 Victorian, 5 fireplaced bedrooms, antiques, comfortable atmosphere. Spacious sun porch breakfast room. OUR 1992 INN OF THE YEAR! **3rd night 50% off, Ltd**

LAKE PLACID

Highland House Inn
3 Highland Place, 12946
518-523-2377 FAX:523-1863
Ted & Cathy Blazer
All year

$$ B&B
7 rooms, 7 pb
Visa, MC, *Rated*, •
C-yes/S-yes

Full breakfast
Coffee, tea, cocoa
Sitting room, bicycles
pool, tennis, cottage
outdoor hot tub spa, TVs

Renowned for blueberry pancakes. Glass enclosed garden dining year round. Central village location. Uniquely appealing. **Two free ski lift tickets included, ask**

Interlaken Inn/Restaurant
15 Interlaken Ave., 12946
518-523-3180 800-428-4369
Roy & Carol Johnson
Exc. April & November

$$$ MAP
11 rooms, 11 pb
Visa, MC, *Rated*, •
C-ltd/S-yes/P-no/H-no

Full breakfast, dinner
Restaurant, bar
Comp. wine, high tea
sitting room, croquet
carriage house sleeps 6

Adirondack inn; heart of Olympic country; quiet setting-half block from Main St. btwn Mirror Lake & Lake Placid. Balconies, carriage house avail. Great food! **3rd night 50%.**

Stagecoach Inn
370 Old Military Rd., 12946
518-523-9474
Lyn Witte
All year

$$ B&B
9 rooms, 5 pb
•
C-ltd/S-yes/P-ltd/H-ltd

Full breakfast
Front porch w/swing
rocking chairs
sitting room

An Adirondack experience since 1833. Quiet, convenient location. Rooms decorated with quilts, wicker and antiques. Outstanding "great room."

LEWISTON

Little Blue House, The
115 Center St., 14092
716-754-9425
Margot & Michael Kornfeld
All year

$$ B&B
3 rooms, 1 pb
Personal checks OK
C-ltd/S-no/P-no/H-no

Continental plus
Snacks
Sitting room
cable TV in each room

Set in the historic village of Lewiston, this antique-filled 1906 home creates a romantic mood in a warm, sophisticated environment. 6 mi. to Niagara Falls. **3rd night 50% off**

LIVINGSTON MANOR

R.M. Farm
P.O. Box 391, 12758
Lenape Lake Rd.
914-439-5511
Gina Molinet
All year

$$ B&B
4 rooms
Rated
C-yes

Full breakfast
Comp. tea and coffee
Sitting room, library
lake fishing, cross-country
skiing hunting, pond
swimming

Charming rooms and panoramic views are yours at this mountaintop farm amidst the Catskill's finest resources. Bird-watching, hunting, swimming, skiing; on 270 acres.

LOCKPORT

Hambleton House B&B
130 Pine St., 14094
716-439-9507
The Hambleton Family
All year

$$ B&B
3 rooms, 1 pb
Rated, •
C-ltd/S-ltd/P-no/H-no

Continental plus
Snacks
Sitting room

Gracious, historic city home where Lockport carriage maker resided in the 1850s. Each room a delicate blending of the past and present. Walk to city's main street.

Hambleton House B&B, Lockport, NY

LOCKPORT

National Centennial House	$$ B&B	Continental plus
111 Ontario St., 14094	3 rooms, 3 pb	Refreshments, snacks
716-434-8193	•	Afternoon tea
Billie & Marvin Pascoe	C-ltd/S-no/P-no/H-no	sitting room, library
All year		

Gorgeous historic mansion with wonderful black walnut and chestnut woodwork. 1 block from Erie Barge Canal. Superb ambiance. 20 miles from Buffalo, Niagara Falls and Lewiston.

LYNBROOK

Rick's B&B Inn	$$ B&B	Full breakfast
128 Union Ave., 11563	5 rooms, 3 pb	Aft. tea, comp. wine
516-593-6721	checks, *Rated*, •	Sitting room, bicycles
Rick Rogers	C-yes/S-ltd/P-yes/H-no	TV & A/C in all rooms
All year		sun porch, free parking

Turn of the century old Dutch home restored and furnished with antiques. Charming old fashion inn. Comfortable and inviting. Restaurants one block away. **Weekly rates**

MOUNT TREMPER

Mount Tremper Inn	$$ B&B	Full breakfast
P.O. Box 51, 12457	23 rooms	Elegant parlor, library
Rt. 212 & Wittenberg Rd.	*Rated*	game room, reading room
914-688-5329	C-ltd/S-ltd/P-no/H-no	comp. sundries
Lou Caselli, Peter LaScala		
All year		

1850 Victorian mansion with Victorian antiques, classical music, gourmet breakfast, wrap-around porch, large fireplace. Near Woodstock and all ski slopes.

MUMFORD

Genesee Country Inn, The
P.O. Box 340, 14511
948 George St.
716-538-2500
Glenda Barcklow/Kim
Rasmussen
All year

$$$ B&B
12 rooms, 12 pb
Most CC, *Rated*, •
C-ltd/S-no/P-no/H-ltd

Full breakfast
Afternoon tea, snacks
Common rooms, fireplaces
canopy beds, gift shop
A/C, fly fishing, TVs

17-room 1833 stone mill specializing in hospitality and quiet, comfortable retreats. Unique natural setting—woods, gardens, waterfalls. Near Village-Museum. **Winter Specials**

NAPLES–SOUTH BRISTOL

Landmark Retreat
6006 Route 21, 14512
716-396-2383
Ann Albrecht, Lottie Benker
All year

$ B&B
6 rooms, 1 pb
Visa, MC, •
C-ltd/S-yes/P-yes/H-yes
German

Full breakfast
Afternoon tea, snacks
Sitting room, library
gazebo, patios, A/C
picnic facilities

Country setting w/peaceful scenery and spectacular view of Canandaigua Lake. Near golf, fishing, skiing & wineries. Marble fireplace. **10% off senior, group or extended stays**

NEW ROCHELLE

Rose Hill Guest House
44 Rose Hill Ave., 10804
914-632-6464
Marilou Mayetta
All year

$$ B&B
2 rooms

•
C-yes/S-yes/P-ltd/H-no

Continental plus
Comp. wine, tea
Sitting room, library
VCR, cable TV
bicycles

Beautiful Norman Rockwell home 20 min. from Manhattan or Greenwich. Enjoy "Big Apple" & country living in one. Horseback riding, golfing, sailing, etc. **Weekly stay discount.**

NEW YORK

Incentra Village House
32 8th Ave., 10014
212-206-0007
Gaylord Hoftiezer
All year

$$$ EP
10 rooms, 10 pb
Visa, MC, AmEx, •
C-yes/S-yes/P-yes/H-no

Most rooms have kitchens
Sitting room
fireplaces, A/C

The Incentra Village House is a renovated 1841 townhouse centrally located in Greenwich Village. Most rooms are decorated in the period and include a fireplace & kitchenette.

NIAGARA FALLS

Cameo Inn & Cameo Manor
3881 Lower River Rd., 14174
716-745-3034 716-754-2075
Greg & Carolyn Fisher
All year

$$ B&B
8 rooms, 4 pb
Visa, MC, Disc., •
C-yes/S-no/P-no/H-no

Full breakfast
Antiquing, fishing
bicycling, cross-country ski
relax by river, library

Choose Victorian elegance in a romantic river setting or a secluded English manor, both just minutes from Niagara Falls. **3rd night 50% off year 'round.**

NORTH HUDSON

Pine Tree Inn B&B
P.O. Box 10, 12855
Route 9
518-532-9255 800-645-5605
Peter & Patricia Schoch
All year

$ B&B
5 rooms
Rated
C-ltd/S-ltd/P-no/H-no

Full breakfast
Dinner by resv. (winter)
Comp. tea & coffee
sitting room

Adirondack sturdy, converted 1920 hotel, country-comfortable furnishings (circa 1740-1856). Near Schroon Lake, Fort Ticonderoga and Lake Placid.

NORTH RIVER

Garnet Hill Lodge	$$ MAP	Full breakfast
13th Lake Rd., 12856	19 rooms, 19 pb	Dinner incl., bar
518-251-2444	*Rated*, •	Sitting room, piano
George & Mary Heim	C-yes/S-ltd/P-no/H-ltd	tennis courts
Exc. June & November		beach, lake swimming

Mountain retreat with freshly baked breads, cross-country skiing, hiking trails on premises. Alpine skiing and Adirondack Museum nearby.

OGDENSBURG

Maple Hill Country Inn	$$ B&B	Full breakfast
Route 2, Box 21, Riverside Dr.,	4 rooms	Dinner on request
13669	C-yes/S-yes/P-yes/H-no	Comp. tea, wine, snacks
315-393-3961		library, sitting room
Marilyn Peters-Jones		winter tours
All year		

"More than a nice place to stay." We offer comfortable rooms, views of St. Lawrence River and hearty breakfast. Getaway weekends. Antiques & collectibles sale. **3rd. night 50%**

OLIVEREA

Slide Mtn. Forest House	$$ B&B/MAP	Full breakfast
805 Oliverea Rd., 12410	21 rooms, 17 pb	Lunch & dinner avail. $
914-254-5365 914-254-4269	Visa, MC	Restaurant, bar, pool
Ursula & Ralph Combe	C-yes/S-yes/P-no/H-no	sitting room, hiking
All year	German	tennis courts, fishing

Fresh air, nature & a touch of Old World charm await you at our German/American Catskill Mountains Inn. Congenial family atmosphere. **3rd nite 50% off midweek only**

PHOENIX

Main Street House B&B	$$ B&B	Full breakfast
1110 Main St., 13135	3 rooms, 3 pb	Aft. tea, snacks
315-695-5601	C-ltd/S-ltd/P-no/H-no	Comp. wine
Lois & Joe Merritt		sitting room, hot tubs
All year		swimming pool

Queen Anne home w/Victorian furnishings, terry robes, breakfast in Victorian dining room or sun porch overlooking garden. Antique shop on premises.

PINE CITY

Rufus Tanner House	$$ B&B	Full breakfast
1016 Sagetown Rd., 14871	4 rooms, 4 pb	Lunch & Dinner w/notice
607-732-0213	Visa, Mc, *Rated*, •	Afternoon tea, snacks
Bill Knapp & John Fribson	C-yes/S-no/P-no/H-no	sitting room
All year		fireplaces

1864 Greek Revival farmhouse, 4 rooms, 1 with jacuzzi. Homemade syrup. Quiet country, near Elmira and Corning. Weekend packages, private baths. **10% off for more than 3 nites**

PITTSFORD

Oliver Loud's Inn	$$$ B&B	Continental breakfast
1474 Marsh Rd., 14534	8 rooms, 8 pb	Restaurant, welcome tray
716-248-5200 FAX:248-9970	Most CC, *Rated*, •	Comp. cocktails/dessert
Vivienne Tellier	C-ltd/S-ltd/P-no/H-yes	snacks, sitting room
All year	French, Spanish	jogging, cross-country skiing

English country house charm and service in meticulously restored c. 1810 stagecoach inn on banks of Erie Canal. 12 minutes from downtown Rochester. **Corporate rates**

PORT JEFFERSON ─────────────────────────────────

Captain Hawkins Inn $$$ B&B   Continental plus
321 Terryville Rd., 11776   9 rooms, 6 pb   Comp. wine on arrival
516-473-8211   Visa, MC, *Rated*, •   Afternoon tea, snacks
Ralph & Anne Cornelius   C-ltd/S-ltd/P-no/H-ltd sitting room
All year   hot tubs, swimming pool

Quiet relaxed atmosphere; furnished in antiques and reproductions. Three villages, golf and tennis nearby; short ride to Long Island wine country; ferry to New England.

POUGHKEEPSIE ─────────────────────────────────

Inn at the Falls $$$ B&B   Continental breakfast
50 Red Oaks Mill Rd., 12603 36 rooms, 36 pb
914-462-5770   *Rated*, •
Arnold & Barbara Sheer   C-yes/S-yes/P-no/H-yes
All year

QUEENSBURY ─────────────────────────────────

Crislip's B&B $$ B&B   Full breakfast
RD 1, Box 57, Ridge Rd., 12804 3 rooms, 3 pb   Sitting room
518-793-6869   Visa, MC, AmEx, *Rated*
Ned & Joyce Crislip   C-yes/S-no/P-ask/H-no
All year

Queensbury-Glens Falls. Located minutes from Saratoga & Lake George. Landmark Federal home provides spacious accommodations, complete w/antiques, 4-poster beds, private baths.

RHINEBECK ─────────────────────────────────

Village Victorian Inn $$$ B&B   Full gourmet breakfast
31 Center St., 12572   5 rooms, 5 pb   Lunch & dinner (request)
914-876-8345   Visa, MC, AmEx, *Rated*, Afternoon tea, snacks
Judy & Richard Kohler   •   comp. wine
All year   C-ltd/S-no/P-no/H-no   sitting room
                             Italian

1860 Victorian home. Beautifully furnished w/period antiques, lace, canopy beds. Gourmet breakfasts, afternoon tea. 90 minutes from New York City.

ROCHESTER ─────────────────────────────────

Dartmouth House B&B $$ B&B   Full candlelight brkfast
215 Dartmouth St., 14607   3 rooms, 3 pb   Comp. beverages
716-271-7872 716-473-0778   AmEx, *Rated*, •   Sitting room, porches
Ellie & Bill Klein   C-ltd/S-no/P-no/H-no   grand piano, organ
All year   bicycles, A/C, TV

Spacious Tudor home nearby everything. Quiet, architecturally fascinating, residential neighborhood. Hosts are well traveled & love people! Great breakfasts! Walk to museums.

Strawberry Castle B&B $$$ B&B   Full breakfast
1883 Penfield Rd., Penfield, 3 rooms, 3 pb   Sitting room, piano
14526   Visa, MC, AmEx, *Rated*, swimming pool, patio
716-385-3266   •   bicycles
Charles & Cynthia Whited   C-ltd/S-yes/P-no/H-no
All year

Landmark Victorian mansion on three acres. Large rooms and suites with antique furnishings. Small town advantages with convenience to Finger Lakes area. **7th night free**

ROCHESTER—FAIRPORT

Woods Edge B&B	$$ B&B	Full breakfast
P.O. Box 444, 14450	3 rooms, 3 pb	Afternoon tea, snacks
151 Bluhm Rd.	*Rated*, •	Sitting room, library
716-223-8877	C-yes/S-no/P-no/H-no	bicycles, hiking
Betty & Bill Kinsman		tennis court 1 mile away
All year		

Country hideaway nestled in secluded location of fragrant pines and wildlife. King/queen-sized beds. Only 20 minutes from downtown Rochester, near exit 45 of NYS I-90.

ROME

Maplecrest B&B	$$ B&B	Full breakfast
6480 Williams Rd., 13440	3 rooms, 1 pb	Beverage on arrival
315-337-0070	•	Fridge use, center AC
Diane & Henry Saladino	C-ltd/S-no/P-no/H-no	sitting room, bicycles
All year	Italian	grill, picnic facilities

Modern split-level home. Formal country breakfast. Close to historic locations. Adirondack foliage, lakes, and skiing. Near Griffiss Air Force Base. **Business/long term rates**

SARATOGA SPRINGS

Adelphi Hotel, The	$$$ B&B	Continental breakfast
365 Broadway, 12866	20 rooms, 20 pb	Summer dinners, bar
518-587-4688	Visa, MC, AmEx, *Rated*	Entertainment
Gregg Siefkert, Sheila Parker	C-yes/S-yes/P-no/H-no	sitting room
May—November		library, piano

Charming accommodations. Opulently restored high Victorian hotel located in the historic district of the renowned resort and spa of Saratoga Springs.

Apple Tree B&B	$$ B&B	Full breakfast
49 W. High St., Ballston Spa,	4 rooms, 4 pb	TV/VCR, hot tubs
12020	Visa, MC, AmEx, *Rated*,	beautiful gardens
518-885-1113	•	historic district
Dolores & Jim Taisey	C-ltd/S-no/P-no/H-no	
All year		

Second Empire Victorian w/romantic ambiance. Close to SPAC, Spa Park & Saratoga attractions. Delightful breakfast, private baths w/whirlpool. **20% discount 3 nights off season**

Chestnut Tree Inn	$$ B&B	Continental plus
9 Whitney Place, 12866	10 rooms, 7 pb	Afternoon tea, lemonade
518-587-8681	Visa, MC, •	Comp. wine, snacks
Cathleen & Bruce DeLuke	C-ltd/S-no/P-no/H-no	sitting room, antiques
Mid-April—October		porch, spas

Restored turn-of-the-century Saratoga guest house. In town; walk to racetrack and downtown. Furnished with antiques. Including large wicker porch.

Inn on Bacon Hill, The	$$ B&B	Full breakfast
P.O. Box 1462, 12866	4 rooms, 2 pb	Comp. bev. & snacks
518-695-3693	Visa, MC, *Rated*, •	Sitting room, piano
Andrea Collins-Breslin	C-ltd/S-no/P-no/H-no	library, screened gazebo
All year		close to ski areas

10 minutes from Saratoga Springsi- elegant 1862 restored Victorian. Rural setting, warm hospitality, sumptuous breakfasts, central A/C. Innkeeping course offered.

SARATOGA SPRINGS

Saratoga B&B	$$ B&B	Full Irish breakfast
434 Church St., 12866	8 rooms, 8 pb	Sitting room
518-584-0920	Visa, MC, AmEx, *Rated*,	piano, bicycles
Kathleen & Noel Smith	•	
All year	C-ltd/S-yes/P-ltd/H-yes	
	French	

Splendidly appointed rooms w/ fireplaces. Kings, queens, suites. Lush lawns, towering pines. Saratoga elegance w/ finest in modern amenities. Conviviality. **20% disc't mdwk**

Six Sisters B&B	$$ B&B	Full breakfast
149 Union Ave., 12866	4 rooms, 4 pb	Comp. beverage
518-583-1173 FAX:587-2470	*Rated*, •	Sitting room, porch
Kate Benton & Steve Ramirez	C-ltd/S-no/P-no,	A/C, restaurant nearby
All year		spa packages

Beautifully appointed 1880 Victorian, recommended by Gourmet. Luxurious suites: prvt. baths, king beds. Near Skidmore, conventions, SPAC, racetracks, downtown. **10% disc't Ltd**

Union Gables B&B	$$$ B&B	Continental plus
55 Union Ave., 12866	12 rooms, 12 pb	Hot tub outdoors
518-584-1558	Visa, MC, AmEx, *Rated*	telephones, TVs, A/C
Jody & Tom Roohan	C-yes/S-ltd/P-yes/H-no	sitting room, bicycles
All year		

Restored turn of the century Queen Ann Victorian. Gigantic front porch. Great downtown location. Walk to everything.

Westchester House B&B, The	$$ B&B	Continental plus
P.O. Box 944, 12866	7 rooms, 7 pb	Comp. beverages
102 Lincoln Ave.	Visa, MC, AmEx, *Rated*,	Sitting room, library
518-587-7613	•	wraparound porch, piano
Bob & Stephanie Melvin	C-ltd/S-ltd/P-no/H-no	A/C, games, cross-country
All year	French, German	skiing

Gracious, award-winning, Queen Anne Victorian, Painted Lady combines old-world ambience w/up-do-date comforts. Walk to all historic Saratoga offers. **Disc't. rates, ltd**

SHELTER ISLAND HEIGHTS

Belle Crest House, The	$$$ B&B	Full breakfast
P.O. Box 891, 11965	10 rooms, 6 pb	Dinner, aftn. tea & cake
163 N. Ferry Rd.	Visa, MC, •	Comp. wine & cheese
516-749-2041 718-441-2274	C-yes/S-yes/H-yes	sitting room, library
Yvonne & Herbert Loinig	German, French	bicycles, tennis courts
All year		

Excellent accommodations—European hospitality and charm. Dining room is perfect for private parties. Riding, sailing, fishing are some of the many recreational activities.

SKANEATELES

Cozy Cottage Guest House	$ B&B	Continental plus
4987 Kingston Rd., 13060	3 rooms	Snacks
315-689-2082	*Rated*	Sitting room
Elaine N. Samuels	C-ltd/S-no/P-ask/H-no	hiking, biking
All year		cross-country skiing

Five mi. from Skaneateles Lake. Five acres. Newly remodeled ranch. Experienced hostess offers friendship, casual comfortable ambiance, antiques. **10% off after 5 days**

SOUTHOLD

Goose Creek Guesthouse	$$ B&B	Full country breakfast
P.O. Box 337, 11971	3 rooms, 1 pb	Tea, snacks
1475 Waterview Dr.	•	Homegrown vegetables &
516-765-3356	C-yes/S-no/P-ltd/H-no	fruit
Mary Mooney-Getoff	Spanish	sitting room, library
All year		

Pre-Civil War farmhouse, secluded in 7 acres of woods, near golf, beaches and ferries. Gourmet country breakfasts, garden-fresh food. **3rd night 50% off**

STANFORDVILLE

Lakehouse Inn	$$$ B&B	Full breakfast
Shelley Hill Rd., 12581	8 rooms, 8 pb	Afternoon appetizers
914-266-8093	Visa, AmEx, MC, *Rated*,	7-acre lake
Judy & Rich Kohler	•	swimming, boating
All year	C-yes/S-no/P-no/H-no	fishing

Private country estate overlooking the lake. Rooms with jacuzzis and fireplaces. Scrumptious breakfasts, afternoon appetizers. Swimming, boating & fishing.

SYRACUSE

Russell-Farrenkopf B&B	$$ B&B	Continental plus
209 Green St., 13203	4 rooms, 1 pb	Restaurant nearby
315-472-8001	C-ltd/S-no/P-no/H-no	Sitting room
Joan Farrenkopf		library
Jan & Feb closed		breakfast in solarium

Near university, downtown & restaurants. Subperb architectural restoration decorated w/hand-grained floors and woodwork, ceiling medallions, marble fireplaces.

TANNERSVILLE

Eggery Inn, The	$$ B&B	Full breakfast from menu
County Rd. 16, 12485	15 rooms, 15 pb	Wine list
518-589-5363	AmEx, Visa, MC, *Rated*,	Dinner for groups
Abe & Julie Abramczyk	•	cable TV in rooms
All year	C-ltd/S-ltd/P-no/H-ltd	player piano, AAA app.

Majestic setting, panoramic views, dining in a garden setting, fireplaces atmosphere and individualized attention. Near Hunter Mountain ski slopes. **4 nites or more 10% off**

TRUMANSBURG

Taughannock Farms Inn	$$$ B&B	Continental plus
2030 Gorge Rd. (Rte.89), at	7 rooms, 7 pb	Restaurant, bar
Taughannock Falls Park, 14886	*Rated*	Guest houses, sitting rm
607-387-7711	C-ltd/S-ltd/P-no/H-no	music box, lake swimming
C. Keith & Nancy A. le Grand	Dutch, German, French	gardens, hiking trails
March 15–December 15		

Majestically situated high on a slope with commanding views of forests & Lake Cayuga. Near 200-foot Taughannock waterfall. Hiking trails, boat rentals, picnic grounds, marina.

UTICA

Iris Stonehouse B&B	$ B&B	Full breakfast
16 Derbyshire Place, 13501	3 rooms, 1 pb	Snacks
315-732-6720 800-446-1456	Visa, MC, AmEx, *Rated*,	Sitting room
Shirley & Roy Kilgore	•	central A/C
All year	C-ltd/S-no/P-no/H-no	

City charm, close to everything. Full breakfast served from menu. Central A/C for hot days; blazing fireplace for cold days. Easy access to I-90, exit 31 and route 5, 8 & 12.

VERNON

Lavender Inn
5950 State Rt 5, 13476
315-829-2440
Rose Degni and Lyn Doring

$$ B&B
3 rooms, 3 pb
Most CC, *Rated*, •
C-yes/S-ltd/P-no/H-no

Full breakfast, ltd.
Lunch & dinner available
TV & VCR in parlor, A/C
meeting facilities
herb & flower gardens

1799 Federal style home offers a quiescent respite for the weary traveler. Antiques, quilts, pine plank floors. Craft study weekends taught by hosts. Many activities nearby.

VICTOR

Golden Rule B&B
6934 Rice Rd., 14564
716-924-0610
Karen & Dick deMauriac
All year

$$ B&B
2 rooms
Rated
C-ltd/S-no/P-no/H-no

Full breakfast
Aft. tea, picnic area
Sitting room, hammock
swimming pool
lawn games

A uniquely renovated and enlarged 1865 country schoolhouse furnished with many antiques. Sumptuous gourmet candlelight breakfast. Many area attractions. **10% discount, ask**

WARRENSBURG

Country Road Lodge
HCR 1 Box #227, Hickory Hill
Rd., 12885
518-623-2207
Steve & Sandi Parisi
All year

$$ B&B
4 rooms, 2 pb
Rated, •
C-ltd/S-ltd/P-no/H-no

Full breakfast
Sitting room
piano, library
birdwatching, hiking

Quiet, idyllic setting along Hudson River at the end of a country road. Discreetly sociable host. No traffic or TV. In the southern Adirondack Mountains, near Lake George, etc

Merrill Magee House, The
2 Hudson St., 12885
518-623-2449
Ken & Florence Carrington
All year

$$$ B&B
13 rooms, 10 pb
Most CC, *Rated*, •
C-ltd/S-yes/P-no/H-yes

Full breakfast
Restaurant, bar, dinner
Comp. coffee, tea, cocoa
sitting room, library
swimming pool, hot tubs

Elegant Victorian setting w/decidedly 20th-C. comforts in the center of a charming Adirondack Mountain village. Family suite avail. w/TV, fridge, pvt. bath. **Comp. champagne.**

White House Lodge
53 Main St., 12885
518-623-3640
James & Ruth Gibson
All year

$$$ B&B
3 rooms
Visa, MC
C-ltd/S-ltd/P-no/H-no

Continental breakfast
Comp. wine, cookies
Homemade cakes, pies
sitting room, television
front porch

Pre-Civil War mansion, four miles from beautiful Lake George. Eight miles from Gore Mountain. Queen village of the Adirondacks.

WATER MILL

Seven Ponds
P.O. Box 98, 11976
261 Seven Ponds Rd.
516-726-7618
Carol Conover
All year

$$$ B&B
3 rooms, 3 pb
C-ltd/S-ltd/P-no/H-no
Spanish

Continental plus
Full bkfst by request
Sitting room, comp. wine
swimming pool
one room with jacuzzi

Comfortable, cozy atmosphere in secluded wooded setting. Central a/c, fireplace, pool and deck. Biking distance to famous Hampton beaches.

WESTFIELD

Westfield House	$$ B&B	Full breakfast
P.O. Box 505, 14787	6 rooms, 6 pb	Comp. wine, snacks
E. Main Rd., Route 20	Visa, MC, *Rated*, •	Sitting room, bicycles
716-326-6262	C-ltd/S-no/P-no/H-yes	needlework shop
Betty & Jud Wilson		small meeting facilites
All year		

Elegant red brick Gothic Revival inn situated behind maple trees overlooking vineyards. Near antique shops, recreational and cultural activities. **Special holiday weekends**

William Seward Inn, The	$$$ B&B	Full gourmet breakfast
RD #2, Box 14, S. Portage Rd.,	14 rooms, 14 pb	Dinner & wet bar avail.
Rte. 394, 14787	Visa, MC, Disc.,*Rated*, •	Sitting room, library
716-326-4151	C-ltd/S-no/P-no/H-yes	king/queen beds
Jim & Debbie Dahlberg		4 rms. w/ double jacuzzi
All year		

Country mansion w/ period antiques; close to major antique center, wineries, ski slopes & cross-country, & charming Lake Chatauqua. **Special weekend packages**

WESTHAMPTON BEACH

1880 House	$$$ B&B	Full breakfast
P.O. Box 648, 11978	3 rooms, 3 pb	Comp. sherry & muffins
2 Seafield Ln.	*Rated*, •	Sitting room, piano
516-288-1559 800-346-3290	C-ltd/S-no/P-no/H-no	tennis court, library
Elsie P. Collins		swimming pool
All year		

Country hideaway w/3 suites furnished in antiques. Gourmet brkfast served in lovely decorated dining rm or enclosed porch overlooking pool. **3rd night 50%**

WEVERTOWN

Mountainaire Adventures	$$ B&B	Full breakfast
Route 28, Glen-Dillon Hill Rd.,	8 rooms, 6 pb	Comp. hot drinks, videos
12886	Visa, MC, •	Bar, sitting room
518-251-2194 800-950-2194	C-yes/S-yes/P-yes/H-yes	bicycles, sauna
Douglas Cole		hot tubs
All year		

Adirondack inn and chalet with mountain views. Near Gore Mountain Ski area and Lake George. Private adventure tours! Canoe rentals. **3rd day $10. off**

More Inns . . .

Lange's Grove Side, Rt. 23/P.O. Box 79, Acra, 12405, 518-622-3393
New Mohican House, Old Rt 23/P.O. Box 79, Acra, 12405, 518-622-3393
Providence Farm, 11572 Hiller Rd., Akron, 14001, 716-759-2109
Pine Haven, 531 Western Ave., Albany, 12203, 518-482-1574
Pine Haven B&B, 531 Western Ave., Albany, 12203, 518-482-1574
Alder Creek Bed & Breakfas, Route 12, P.O. Box 5, Alder Creek, 13301, 315-733-0040
S. S. Suellen B&B, 24 Otter St., Alexandria Bay, 13607,
Appel Inn, Box 18, RD#3, Altamont, 12009, 518-861-6557
21 House, Montauk Hwy. Box 149, Amagansett, 11930, 800-888-8888
Mill-Garth-Mews Inn, P.O. Box 700, Amagansett, 11930, 516-267-3757
Marshfield B&B, RR 1, Box 432, Amenia, 12501, 914-868-7833
Henry J. Dombrowski, 8404 Old Lake Shore Rd., Angola, 14006, 716-549-1055
Green Acres, RD 1, Route 474, Ashville, 14710, 716-782-4254
Fay's Point Beachhouse, RD 1, Box 1479, Auburn, 13021,
Irish Rose, 102 South St., Auburn, 13021,
Aurora Inn, Main St., Aurora, 13026, 315-364-8842
Ananas Hus B&B, Route 3, Box# 301, Averill Park, 12018, 518-766-5035
Mulligan Farm B&B, 5403 Barber Rd., Avon, 14414, 716-226-6412
Avon Manor, The, 109 Slyvania Ave., Avon-By-The-Sea, 07717, 201-775-9770
House On Saratoga Lake, 143-51 Manning Rd., Ballston Spa, 12020, 518-584-5976
Sugarbush, RR #1 Box 227, Barneveld, 13304,

All Breeze Guest Farm, Haring Rd., Barryville, 12719, 914-557-6485
Reber's Motel on the Hill, 5 Route 97, Barryville, 12719, 914-557-8111
Bearsville B&B, P.O. Box 11, Bearsville, 12409,
Vrede Landgoed, Dug Rd., RD #2, Beaver Dams, 14812, 607-535-4108
Beaverbrook House, Duell Rd., Bengall, 12545, 914-868-7677
Sedgewick Inn, Berlin, 518-658-2334
Sedgwick Inn, The, Route 22, Berlin, 12022, 518-658-2334
Potter's Resort, Jct Rts 28 & 30, Blue Mountain Lake, 12812, 518-352-7331
Cold Brook Inn, P.O. Box 251, Boicerille, 12412, 914-657-6619
Candlelight Cottages, Route 9N Box 133 N, Bolton Landing, 12814, 518-644-3321
Port Jerry Resort, H.C.R. Box 27, Bolton Landing, 12814, 518-644-3311
Richard M. Hayes, Box 537, Bolton Landing, 12814, 518-644-5941
Greenmeadow, RD #3, Alder Creek Rd., Boonville, 13309, 315-733-0040
Four Seasons B&B, 470 W. Lake Rd., Rt.54A, Branchport, 14418, 607-868-4686
Bivona Hill B&B, Academy Rd., Brookfield, 13314, 315-899-8921
Gates Hill Homestead, Off Dugway Rd., Brookfield, 13314, 315-733-0040
A.J. Bluestone, 432 Eighth St., Brooklyn, 11215, 718-499-1401
Brooklyn B&B, 128 Kent St, Brooklyn, 11222, 718-383-3026
Alan Dewart B&B, 701 Seneca St., Buffalo, 14210,
Bryant House, 236 Bryant St., Buffalo, 14222,
Tonjes Farm, Tonjes Rd., Callicoon, 12723, 914-482-5357
Cambridge Inn B&B, 16 West Main St, Cambridge, 12816, 518-677-5741
Maple Ridge Inn, Rt. 372, Rt. 1,Box 391C, Cambridge, 12816, 518-677-3674
Tara Farm B&B, Kiernan Rd., Campbell Hall, 10916, 914-294-6482
Inn at Shaker Mill Farm, Cherry Ln., Canaan, 12029, 518-794-9345
Mountain Home B&B, Box 280, Canaan, 12029, 518-392-5136
Thornberry Inn, Stony Kill Rd., Canaan, 12029, 518-781-4939
Nottingham Lodge Bed & Bre, 5741 Bristol Valley, Rt, Canandaigua, 14424, 716-374-5355
Thendara Inn & Restaurant, 4356 East Lake Rd., Canandaigua, 14424, 518-394-4868
Wilder Tavern Country Inn, 5648 N. Bloomfield Rd., Canandaigua, 14425, 716-394-8132
Country House, Box 146, 37 Mill St., Canaseraga, 14822, 607-545-6439
Locustwood Inn, 3563 Route 89, Canoga, 13148, 315-549-7132
Featherbed Shoals, RD 1, Box 11, Cape Vincent, 13618,
Eastwood House, 45 So. Main St., Castile, 14427, 716-493-2335
Ludwig's Kozy Kove, Box 866, Cayuga, 13034, 315-889-5940
Lincklaen House, 79 Albany St., Cazenovia, 13035, 315-655-8171
Gasho Inn, Route 32, Box M, Central Valley, 10917, 914-928-2277
Banner House Inn, Chateaugay Lake, 12920,
Athenaeum Hotel, Chautauqua, 14722,
Chautauqua Inn, 16 N. Terrace, Box 454, Chautauqua, 14722,
Longfellow Inn, 11 Roberts Ave., Box Y, Chautauqua, 14722, 716-357-2285
Rose Cottage, The, 2 Roberts Ave, Chautauqua, 716-357-5375
Shenango Inn, 20 Ramble, P.O. Box 34, Chautauqua, 14722,
St. Elmo Hotel, P.O. Box Y, Chautauqua, 14722, 716-357-3566
Summer House, 22 Peck St., Chautawqua, 14722, 716-357-2101
Halcyon Place B&B, P.O. Box 244, Chemung, 14825,
Chester Inn, The, Box 163, Main St, Chestertown, 12817, 518-494-4148
Friends Lake Inn, Friends Lake Rd., Chestertown, 12817, 518-494-4751
Maplewood, P.O. Box 40, Chichester, 12416, 914-688-5433
Melody Inn, The, Box 130, East Lake Rd., Cleveland, 13042,
Clinton House, 21 W. Park Row, Clinton, 13323, 315-853-5555
Victorian Carriage House, 46 William St., Clinton, 13323, 315-853-8389
Bed & Breakfast, Sunset Trail, Clinton Corners, 12514, 914-266-3922
Orchard House, Rt. 44/55 Box 413, Clintondale, 12515, 914-883-6136
Gables Bed & Breakfast, Th, 62 West Main St., Cobleskill, 12043, 315-733-0040
Hudson House, Country Inn, 2 Main St., Cold Spring, 10516, 914-265-9355
Olde Post Inn, The, 43 Main St., Cold Spring, 10516, 914-265-2510
One Market Street, One Market St., Cold Spring, 10516, 914-265-3912
Pig Hill Inn B&B, 73 Main St., Cold Spring, 10516, 914-265-9247
Creekside, R.D.1, Box 206, Cooperstown, 13326,
Hickory Grove Inn, Rd. 2, Box 898, Cooperstown, 13326, 607-547-8100
Inn at Brook Willow Farm, CR 33, RD 2, Box 5, Cooperstown, 13326,
J. P. Sill House B&B, 63 Chestnut St., Cooperstown, 13326,
Phoenix Inn at River Road, RD #3, Box 150, Cooperstown, 13326, 607-547-8250
Serendipity, RD 2, Box 1050, Cooperstown, 13326, 607-547-2106
Stockbridge Inn B&B, RD 2 Box 536, Cooperstown, 13326, 607-547-5069
Tunnicliff Inn, 34-36 Pioneer St., Cooperstown, 13326, 607-547-9611
Wynterholm, 2 Chestnut St., Cooperstown, 13326, 607-547-2308
Inn at Edge of the Forest, 11 E. Dayton Dr., Corinth, 12822, 518-654-6656
"1865" White Birch B&B, 69 E. 1st. St., Corning, 14830, 607-962-6355
Delevan House, 188 Delevan Ave., Corning, 14830, 607-962-2347
Laurel Hill B&B, 2670 Powderhouse Rd., Corning, 14830, 607-936-3215
Rosewood Inn, 134 E. First St., Corning, 14830, 607-962-3253
Country View B&B, 1500 Route 392, Cortland, 13045, 607-835-6517
33 South, 33 South St., Cuba, 14727, 716-968-1387
Helen's Tourist Home, 7 Maple St., Cuba, 14727,
1819 Red Brick Inn, RD 2 Box 57A, Dandee, 14837, 607-243-8844
Scott's Oquaga Lake, Oquaga, Deposit, 13754,
Adrianna, 44 Stewart St., Dolgeville, 13329, 315-733-0040
Mill Farm, 66 Cricket Hill Rd., Dover Plains, 12522,
Margaret Thatchers B&B, 9 James St., Box 119, Dryden, 13053, 518-844-8052
Spruce Haven, 9 James St.l Box 119, Dryden, 13053,

Country Manor B&B, 4798 Dundee-Himrod Rd., Dundee, 14837, 607-243-8628
Glenora Guests, 65 N. Glenora Rd., Dundee, 14837, 607-243-7686
Lakeside Terrace B&B, RD 1, P.O. Box 197, Dundee, 14837, 607-292-6606
Willow Cove, 77 S. Glenora Rd., RD 4, Dundee, 14837, 607-243-8482
Roycroft Inn, 40 S. Grove St., East Aurora, 14052, 716-652-9030
Holloway House, Routes 5 & 20, East Bloomfield, 14443, 716-657-7120
Highland Springs, Allen Rd., East Concord, 14055, 716-592-4323
1770 House, 143 Main St., East Hampton, 11937, 516-324-1770
Bassett House, 128 Montauk Hwy., East Hampton, 11937, 516-324-6127
Centennial House, 13 Woods Ln., East Hampton, 11937, 516-324-9414
Hedges House, 74 James Ln., East Hampton, 11937, 516-324-7100
Huntting Inn, 94 Main St., East Hampton, 11937, 516-324-0410
Maidstone Arms, 207 Main St., East Hampton, 11937, 516-324-5006
Mill House Inn, 33 North Main, East Hampton, 11937, 516-324-9766
Caffrey House, Squires Ave., East Quogue, 11942, 516-728-1327
Eaton B&B, PO Box 4, Rte. 26, Eaton, 13334,
Eden Inn B&B, 8362 N. Main St., Eden, 14057, 716-992-4814
Windswept B&B, County Rd. 16, Elka Park, 12427, 518-589-6275
Ellicottville Inn, 4-10 Washington St., Ellicotville, 14731, 716-699-2373
Breinlinger's B&B, RD 3, Box 154 W. Hill, Elmira, 14903, 607-733-0089
Strathmont—A B&B, 740 Fassett Rd., Elmira, 14905, 607-733-1046
Platt's Rustic Mountain, Star Route 49, Ensampment, 82325,
Brown's Village Inn B&B, Box 378, Stafford St., Fair Haven, 13064, 315-947-5817
Frost Haven Resort B&B, West Bay Rd., Fair Haven, 13064, 315-947-5331
Issac Turner House, 739 Main St., Fair Haven, 13064, 315-947-5901
Woods-Edge B&B, Box 444, Fairport, 14450, 716-223-8877
Mansard Inn, Rd 1, Box 633, Falconer, 14733,
Beard Morgan House B&B, 126 E. Genesee St., Fayetteville, 13066, 315-637-4234
Runaway Inn, Main St., Fleischmanns, 12430, 111-914-5660
Inn at Lake Joseph, RD 5, Box 85, Forestburgh, 12777, 914-791-9506
1870 House B&B, 20 Chestnut St., Franklinville, 14737, 716-676-3571
White Inn, 52 E. Main St., Fredonia, 14063, 716-672-2103
Tounley House, 304 Peruville Rd., Freeville, 13068,
Merry Maid Inn B&B, 53 W. Main St., Friendship, 14739, 716-973-7740
Salt Hill Farm, 5209 Lake Rd, Galway, 12074, 518-882-9466
American House B&B Inn, 39 Main St., Geneseo, 14454, 716-243-5483
Cobblestones, The, 1160 Routes 5 & 20, Geneva, 14456, 315-789-1890
Geneva on the Lake, P.O. Box 929, Geneva, 14456, 315-789-7190
Inn at Belhurst Castle, P.O. Box 609, Geneva, 14456, 315-789-0359
Crislip's B&B, P.O. Box 57, Glens Falls, 12801, 518-793-6869
East Lake George House, 492 Glen St., Glens Falls, 12801, 378-656-9452
Teepee, The, RD #1, Box 543. Rte 438, Gowanda, 14070, 716-532-2168
Grafton Inn, Rt. 2 & Babcock Lake Rd, Grafton, 12082, 518-279-9489
Grant Inn, Stormy Hill Rd., Grant, 13324, 315-826-7677
Greenfield Pole Club, Birchall Rd., Box 83, Greenfield Park, 12435, 916-647-3240
Bartlett House Inn, The, 503 Front St., Greenport, 11944, 516-477-0371
Homestead, The, Red Mill Rd., Greenville, 12083, 518-966-4474
Benn Conger Inn, 206 W. Cortland St., Groton, 13073, 607-898-5817
Missert's Bed & Breakfast, 66 Highland Ave., Hamburg, 14075, 716-649-5830
Colgate Inn, Hamilton, 13346, 315-824-2134
Bowman House, 61 Lake St., Hammondsport, 14840, 607-569-2516
Cedar Beach Bed & Breakfas, 642 West Lake Rd., Hammondsport, 14840, 607-868-3228
Lake Keuka Manor, 626 W. Lake Rd., Hammondsport, 14840, 607-868-3276
Pleasant Valley B&B, RD #3, Box 69, Hammondsport, 14840,
Wheeler B&B, RD #2 Box 455, Hammondsport, 14810, 607-776-6756
Twin Forks B&B, P.O. Box 657, Hampton Bays, 11946, 516-728-5285
Gill House Inn, Harbor Rd., Henderson Harbor, 13651, 315-938-5013
Bellinger Woods, 611 W. German St., Herkimer, 13350, 315-866-2770
House on the Hill, Box 86 Old Route 213, High Falls, 12440, 914-687-9627
David Harum House, 80 S. Main St., Homer, 13077, 607-749-3548
Le Chambord Inn, Route 52, Box 3, Hopewell Junction, 12533, 914-221-1941
Williams Inn, 27 Main St., Hornell, 14843, 516-324-7400
Burch Hill Bed & Breakfast, 2196 Burch Hill Rd., Horseheads, 14845, 607-739-2504
Muse, The, 5681 Middle Rd., Horseheads, 14845, 607-739-1070
Cavern View, RD 1, Box 23, Howes Cave, 12092, 518-296-8052
Inn at Blue Stores, Box 99, Star Rt., Rt. 9, Hudson, 12534, 518-537-4277
Washington Irving Lodge, P.O. Box 675, Rt. 23A, Hunter, 12442, 518-589-5560
Fala B&B, E. Market St., Hyde Park, 12538, 914-229-5937
Chesham Place, 317 W. Main St., Ilion, 13357, 315-894-3552
Cinnamon Bear B&B, P.O. box 538, Inlet, 13360,
Buttermilk Falls B&B, 110 E. Buttermilk Falls, Ithaca, 14850, 607-272-6767
Elmshade Guest House, 402 S. Albany St., Ithaca, 14850, 607-273-1707
Glendale Farm B&B, 224 Bostwick Rd., Ithaca, 14850, 607-272-8756
Hillside Inn, 518 Stewart Ave, Ithaca, 607-272-9507
Hound & Hare B&B, The, 1031 Hanshaw Rd., Ithaca, 14850, 607-257-2821
Peirce House B&B, 218 S. Albany St., Ithaca, 14850, 518-273-8043
Terence Forbes B&B, 168 Pleasant Grove Rd., Ithaca, 14850,
Welcome Inn B&B, 529 Warren Rd., Ithaca, 14850, 607-257-0250
Kinship B&B, RD 1, Box 23, Rt. 38N, Ithaca—Berkshire, 13736, 607-657-4455
Austin Manor B&B, 210 Old Peruville Rd., Ithaca—Groton, 13073, 607-898-5786
High Meadow B&B, 3740 Eager Rd, Jamesville, 13078, 315-492-3517
Book & Blanket B&B, The, P.O. Box 164, Jay, 12941, 518-946-8323

Champagne's High Peaks Inn, Route 73, P.O. Box 701, Keene Valley, 12943, 518-576-2003
Trail's End, Trail's End Rd., Keene Valley, 12943, 518-576-9860
Maybrook Lodge, #2 P.O. Box 80, Kerhonkson, 12446, 914-626-9823
Cherry Valley Ventures, 6119 Rt. 20, Lafayette, 13084, 518-677-9723
Corner Birches B&B Guests, 86 Montcalm St., Lake George, 12845, 518-668-2837
McEnaney's Lincoln Log, Route 9, Lake George, 12845, 518-668-5326
Timothy's B&B, Bx. 2500, RR2, Lake George, 12845, 518-668-5238
Blackberry Inn B&B, 59 Sentinel Rd., Lake Placid, 12946, 518-523-3419
Lake Placid Manor, Whiteface Inn Rd., Lake Placid, 12946, 518-523-2573
South Meadow Farm Lodge, HCR 1, Box 44, Lake Placid, 12946, 518-523-9369
Spruce Lodge, 31 Sentinel Rd., Lake Placid, 12946, 518-523-9350
Hummingbird Hill, Route 8, Lake Pleasant, 12108,
Bay Horse Bed & Breakfast, 813 Ridge Rd., Lansing, 14882, 607-533-4612
Edson House, 7856 Griswold Circle, Le Roy, 14482, 715-758-2340
Horned Dorset Inn, Leonardsville, 13364, 315-855-7898
Beaverkill Valley Inn, Beaverkill Rd., Lew Beach, 12753, 914-439-4844
Buttermilk Bear, 37 Milligan St., Little Falls, 13365, 315-823-3378
Napoli Stagecoach Inn, Napoli Corners, Little Valley, 14755, 716-938-6735
Lanza's Country Inn, RD 2, Box 446, Livingston Manor, 12758, 914-439-5070
Iris Farm, 162 Hook Rd., Macedon, 14502, 315-986-4536
Killarney B&B, PO Box 337, Maine, 13802,
Merryhart Victorian Inn, 12 Front St., Box 363, Marathon, 13803, 607-849-3951
Three Bear Inn, 3 Broom St., Box 507, Marathon, 13803, 607-849-3258
Margaretville Mountain Inn, Margaretville Mountain, Margaretville, 12455, 914-586-3933
Inn at Hobnobbin Farm, P.O. Box 176, Route 17, Mayville, 14757, 716-753-3800
Village Inn B&B, 111 S. Erie St., Mayville, 14757, 716-753-3583
Maple Shade B&B, RD 1, Milford, 13807,
Calico Quail Inn, Route 44, Box 748, Millbrook, 914-677-6016
Cottonwood Inn & Motel, Route 44, Millbrook, 12545, 914-677-3919
Simmons Way Village Inn, Main St., Route 44, Millerton, 12546, 518-789-6235
Minerva Hill Lodge, Route 28N, Minerva, 12851, 518-251-2710
Country Hills, RD # Box 80, Route 28, Mohawk, 13407, 315-866-1306
Shepherd's Neck Inn, Montauk, 516-668-2105
B&B at Twin Fawns, 166 Otto Stahl Rd. RD 1, Mt. Vision, 13810, 607-293-8009
The Historian, Route 5, Box 224, Nelliston, 13410, 315-733-0040
The Globe, 45 Pearl St., New Harford, 13413, 315-733-0040
Audrey's B&B, 219 Mountain Rest Rd., New Paltz, 12561, 914-255-1103
Mohonk Mountain House, Lake Mohonk, New Paltz, 12561, 914-255-1000
Nana's B&B, 54 Old Ford Rd., New Paltz, 12561, 914-255-5678
Nieuw Country Loft, 41 Allhuson Rd., New Paltz, 12561, 914-ALL-OLD
Ujjala's B&B, 2 Forest Glen Rd., New Paltz, 12561,
A Village B&B, 131 E. 15th. St #2N, New York, 10003, 212-387-9117
Abode B&B, P.O. Box 20022, New York, 10028, 212-472-2000
Chelsea Pines Inn, 317 W. 14th St., New York, 10014, 212-929-1023
James House, The, 131 E. 15th. St, New York, 10003, 212-213-1484
Decker Pond Inn, 1076 Elmira Rd., Newfield, 14867, 607-273-7133
Historic Cook House, 167 Main St., Newfield, 14867, 607-564-9926
What Cheer Hall, P.O. Box 417, N. Main, Newport, 13416, 316-845-8312
Linen'n'Lace B&B Home, 659 Chilton Av., Niagara Falls, 14301, 518-285-3935
Old Niagara House B&B, 337 Buffalo Av., Niagara Falls, 14303, 716-285-9408
Rainbow Guest House, 423 Rainbow Blvd., So., Niagara Falls, 14092, 716-282-1135
Red Coach Inn, Two Buffalo Ave., Niagara Falls, 14303, 716-282-1459
Chateau L'Esperance, Star Rte. - Hwy. 11B, Nicholville, 12965, 315-328-4669
Copperfield Inn, North Creek, 12853, 518-251-5200
Highwinds Inn, Barton Miners Rd, North River, 12856, 518-251-3760
Jerry's Accommodations, 168 Cottage Walk, Ocean Beach, 11770, 516-583-8870
Ocean Beach Inn/Restaurant, Bay Walk, Ocean Beach, 11770, 516-583-5558
Salty Dog B&B, The, Rt.2, Ogdensburg, 13669, 315-393-1298
Way Back Inn, 247 Proctor Ave., Ogdensburg, 13669, 315-393-3844
B&B of Long Island, Inc., P.O. Box 392, Old Westbury, 11568, 516-334-6231
Castle Inn, 3220 W. State Rd., Olean, 14760, 518-422-7853
Alpine Inn, Alpine Rd., Oliverea, 12462, 914-254-5026
Catskill Mountain Lane, Route 47, Oliverea, 12462, 914-254-5498
Valley View, Country Rt. 47, Oliverea, 12462, 914-254-5117
Pollyanna, The, 302 Main St., Oneida, 13421, 315-733-0040
Agnes Hall Tourist Home, 94 Center St., Oneonta, 13820, 607-432-0655
Cathedral Farms Inn, RD 1, Box 560, Oneonta, 13820, 607-432-7483
Walnut Street B&B, 18 Walnut St., Oneonta, 13820,
Tummonds House, 5392 Walworth/Ontario, Ontario, 14519, 315-524-5381
Windy Shores B&B, 2629 Lake Rd., Ontario, 14519, 315-524-2658
Chestnut Grove Inn, R.D.7, Box 10, Oswego, 13069, 315-342-2547
Whitegate, P.O. Box 917, Oxford, 13830, 607-843-6965
Ithaca, Federal House B&B, The, P.O. Box 4914, 14852, 607-533-7362
Dannfield, 50 Canada Rd., Painted Post, 14870, 607-962-2740
Palenville House B&B, P.O. Box 465, Palenville, 12463, 518-678-5649
Canaltown B&B, 119 Canandaigua St., Palmyra, 14522, 315-597-5553
Springbrook Farms B&B, CR 38, RD 2, Parish, 13131,
Arrowhead Ranch, Parksville, 12768, 914-292-6267
Halcyon Manor, 380 Bay Av., Patchogue, 11772, 516-289-9223
Finton's Landing, 661 E. Lake Rd., Penn Yan, 14527, 315-536-3146
Fox Run Vineyards B&B, 670 Route 14, RD 1, Penn Yan, 14527, 315-536-2507
Heirlooms B&B, 2756 Coates Rd., Penn Yan, 14527, 315-536-7682

Wagener Estate B & B, 351 Elm St., Penn Yan, 14527, 315-536-4591
Sunrise Farm, RD 1, Box 433A, Pine Bush, 12566,
Rufus Tanner House, 1016 Sagetown Rd., Pine City,
  14871, 607-732-0213
Belleayre Youth Hostel, P.O. Box 665, Pine Hill,
  12465, 914-254-4200
Birch Creek B&B, P.O. Box 583, Pine Hill, 12465,
  914-254-5222
Colonial Inn, Main St., Pine Hill, 12465, 914-254-5577
Pine Hill Arms, Pine Hill, 12462, 918-254-9811
Hammertown Inn, RD 2, Box 25, Pine Plains, 12567,
  518-398-7539
Sunny Side Up B&B, RD 1, Box 58, Butler Rd,
  Plattsburgh, 12901, 518-563-5677
Danford's Inn, 25 E. Broadway, Port Jefferson, 11777,
  516-928-5200
Genesee Falls Hotel, P.O. Box 396, Portageville,
  14536, 716-493-2484
Hideaway Hotel, Huntersfield Rd., Prattsville, 12468,
  518-299-3616
Sequoia Inn, 7686 N. Jefferson St., Pulaski, 13302,
  315-298-4407
Way Inn, 7377 Salina St., Pulaski, 13142, 315-298-6073
Box Tree Hotel, P.O. Box 477, Purdy's, 10578,
  914-277-3677

The Brewster Inn, Cazenovia, NY

Shepherd's Croft, 263 Mountain Ave., Purling, 12470,
  518-622-9504
Living Springs Retreat, Rt. 3, Bryant Pond Rd., Putnam Valley, 10579, 914-526-2800
Red Hook Inn, 31 S. Broadway, Red Hook, 12571, 914-758-8445
Stor Felen, RD #2, Box 9, Remsen, 13438,
Tibbitt's House Inn, 100 Columbia Turnpike, Rensselaer, 12144, 518-472-1348
Beekman Arms, Route 9, Rhinebeck, 12572, 914-876-7077
Delamater House, 44 Montgomery St., Rhinebeck, 12572, 914-876-7077
Hellers, The, 46C River Rd., Rhinebeck, 12572, 914-876-3468
Lakehouse, Box 723, Rhinebeck, 12572, 914-266-8093
Mary Sweeney B&B, "Bantry," Asher Rd., Rhinebeck, 12572, 914-876-6640
Montgomery Inn Guest House, 67 Montgomery St., Rhinebeck, 12572, 914-876-3311
Whistle Wood Farm, 11 Pells Rd., Rhinebeck, 12572, 914-876-6838
Rhinecliff B&B, Box 167,William & Grinn, Rhinecliff, 12574, 914-876-3710
Canadarago Lake House, E. Lake Rd., Richfield Springs, 13439, 315-858-1761
Country Spread B&B, P.O. Box 1863, Richfield Springs, 13439, 315-858-1870
Summerwood B&B, P.O. Box 388, Richfield Springs, 13439, 315-858-2024
Rose Mansion & Gardens, 625 Mt. Hope Ave., Rochester, 14620, 716-546-5426
Mansion, The, Rt29,W of Saratoga, Rock City Falls, 12863, 518-885-1607
Little Schoolhouse, The, RD #2, 6905 Dix Rd., Rome, 13440,
Antrim Lodge Hotel, Roscoe, 12776, 607-498-4191
Astoria Hotel, 25 Main St., Rosendale, 12472, 914-658-8201
Pickwick Lodge, Round Top, 12473, 518-622-3364
Klartag Farms B&B, W. Branch Rd., Rushford, 14777, 716-437-2946
Burke's Cottages, Lake Shore Dr., Sabael, 12864, 516-281-4983
Five Acre Farm, RD #3, Box 60, Saint Johnsville, 13452, 315-733-0040
Mill At Bloomvale Falls, Rt. 82, Salt Point, 12578, 914-266-4234
Inn at Saratoga, 231 Broadway, Saratoga Springs, 12866, 518-583-1890
Washington Inn, South Broadway, Saratoga Springs, 12866, 518-584-9807
High Woods Inn, 7472 Glasco Turnpike, Saugerties, 12477, 914-246-8655
House on the Quarry, 7480 Pine Rd., Saugerties, 12477, 914-246-8584
Sacks Lodge, Saugerties, 12477, 914-246-8711
Secret Garden, 6071 Malden Tpk., Saugerties, 12477, 914-246-3338
Hayfield House B&B, 2805 Oneida St., Sauquoit, 13456,
Julia's Farm House, Elk Creek Rd., Schenevus, 12155,
Marsh House, P.O. Box 250, Schoharie, 12157, 518-295-7981
Woods Lodge, Schroon Lodge, 12870, 518-532-7529
Gould, 108 Fall St., Seneca Falls, 13148, 518-568-5801
Auberge des Quatre Saisons, Route 42, Shandaken, 12480, 914-688-2223
Copper Hood Inn, Route 28, Shandaken, 12480, 914-688-9962
Two Brooks B&B, SR 108, Route 42, Shandaken, 12480, 914-688-7101
Bowditch House, 166 N. Ferry Rd., Shelter Island, 11965, 516-749-0075
Chequit Inn, 23 Grand Ave., Shelter Island, 11965, 516-749-0018
Shelter Island Resort, P.O. Box 3039, Shelter Island, 11965, 516-749-2001
Belle Crest House, The, P.O. Box 891, Shelter Island Heights, 11965, 516-749-2041
Sherwood Inn, 26 W. Genesee St., Skaneateles, 13152, 315-685-3405
Maxwell Creek Inn, 7563 Lake Rd., Sodus, 14551, 315-483-2222
Carriage House Inn, Wickham Blvd & Ontario, Sodus Point, 14555, 315-483-2100
Silver Waters Guesthouse, 8420 Bay St., Sodus Point, 14555, 315-483-8098
Town & Country B&B, P.O. Box 208, Pine St., South Dayton, 14138, 716-988-3340
Eleanor's, 3 Washington Ave., South Nyack, 10960, 914-353-3040
Old Post House Inn, 136 Main St., Southampton, 11968, 516-283-1717
Zeiser's Oak Mtn. Lodge, Route 30, Speculator, 12164, 518-548-7021
Gold Mountain Chalet, Tice Rd. Box 456, Spring Glen, 12483, 914-395-5200
Leland House, 26 E. Main St., Springville, 14141, 518-592-7631
Scenery Hill, N. Cross Rd., Staatsburg, 12580, 914-889-4812
Bluebird B&B, 21 Harper St., Stamford, 12167, 607-652-3711

Lanigan Farmhouse, Box 399, RD 1, Stamford, 12167, 607-652-7455
Sixteen Firs, 352 St. Paul Ave., Staten Island, 10304, 212-727-9188
Millhof Inn, Route 43, Stephentown, 12168, 518-733-5606
Bakers B&B, RD 2 Box 80, Stone Ridge, 12484, 914-687-9795
Hasbrouck House Inn, Route 209, Box 76, Stone Ridge, 12484, 914-687-0055
Three Village Inn, 150 Main St., Stony Brook, 11790, 516-751-0555
Ivy Chimney, 143 Pidama St., Syracuse, 13224,
Washington Irving Lodge, Route 23A, Tannersville, 12485, 518-589-5560
Moose River House, PO Box 184, Thendara,
Le Muguet, 2553 Church St., Three Mile Bay, 13693, 315-649-5896
Ranchouse at Baldwin, Baldwin Rd., Ticonderoga, 12883, 518-585-6596
Conifer Hill Bed & Breakfa, RD 2, Box 309, Route 22, Trumansburg, 14886, 607-387-5849
Sage Cottage, Box 626, Trumansburg, 14886, 607-387-6449
Green Gables B&B, 24 Wawbeek Ave., Tupper Lake, 12986, 518-359-7815
Greenway Terrace Motel, 18-19 Moody Rd., Rte 30, Tupper Lake, 12986, 518-359-2852
Towpath Inn, Route 26 and West Rd., Turin, 13473, 315-348-8122
Adam Bowman Manor, 197 Riverside Dr., Utica, 13502,
Audreys Farmhouse B&B Corp, RD 1, Box 268A, Wallkill, 12561, 914-895-3440
Gypsy Lady, N. Bennington, Rt. 6, Walloomsac, 12090, 518-686-4880
Castle Hill B&B, Box 325, near Route 9D, Wappingers Falls, 12590, 914-298-8000
Bent Finial Manor, 194 Main St, Warrensburg, 12885, 518-677-5741
Donegal Manor B&B, 117 Main St, Warrensburg, 12885, 518-623-3549
Stacey's Country Inn, 62 Big Island Rd., Warwick, 10990, 914-986-7855
Ocean View Farm, 342 Lopers Path, Water Mill, 11976,
Evergreens, 1248 Waterloo-Geneva Rd, Waterloo, 13165, 315-539-8329
Historic James R. Webster, 115 E. Main St., Waterloo, 13165, 315-539-3032
James Russell Webster Inn, 115 East Main St, Waterloo, 13165, 315-539-3032
Starbuck House B&B, 253 Clinton St., Watertown, 13601, 315-788-7324
B&B of Waterville, 211 White St., Waterville, 13480, 315-841-8295
Center House Farm B&B, Box 64 RD #2, Watkins Glen, 14891, 607-535-4317
Chalet Leon, 3835 Rt. 414 Box 388, Watkins Glen, 14891, 518-546-7171
Denonville Inn, 1750 Empire Blvd., Webster, 14580, 518-671-1550
Adirondack Mountain Chalet, G.G. Commons, Box 341, Wells, 12190, 518-924-2112
Buena Vista Manor, Route 9W, Box 144, West Camp, 12490, 914-246-6462
Glen Atty Farm, Box 578, West Shokan, 12494, 914-657-8110
Haus Elissa B&B, P.O. Box 95, West Shokan, 12494, 914-657-6277
Five Gables, 489 E. Main St., West Winfield, 13491, 315-822-5764
Old Stone House, Box 229, West Winfield, 13491,
Victoria Lodge, 502 E. Main St., West Winfield, 13941, 315-822-6290
Brewer House Inn, 112 E. Main St., Westfield, 14787, 716-326-2320
Sunshine Valley House, Spruceton Rd., Westkill, 12492,
Inn on the Library Lawn, #1 Washington St., Westport, 12993, 518-962-8666
Apple Orchard Inn, Route 4, Whitehall, 12789,
Skene Manor, Mountain St. off Rt. 4, Whitehall, 12887, 518-499-1112
Woven Waters, HC 73 Box 193E Rt. 41, Willet, 13863, 607-656-8672
Whiteface Chalet, Springfield Rd., Wilmington, 12997, 518-946-2207
Chez Renux, 229-C Budd Rd., Woodbourne, 12788, 914-434-1780
Fannie Schaffer Vegetarian, P.O. Box 457 M, Woodridge, 12789, 914-434-4455
One More Time, 141 Tinker St., Woodstock, 12498, 914-679-8701
Twin Gables of Woodstock, 73 Tinker St., Woodstock, 12498, 914-679-9479

North Carolina

ABERDEEN ——————————————————————————————

Inn at the Bryant House
214 N. Poplar St., 28315
919-944-3300 800-453-4019
Bill & Abbie Gregory
All year

$ B&B
8 rooms, 6 pb
Visa, MC, AmEx, *Rated*,
•
C-yes/S-ltd/P-no/H-no
German

Continental plus
Snacks, comp. wine
Sitting room, library
picnic area

Georgian inn on the National Historic Registry. Close to Pinehurst golfing, PGA Hall of Fame, antique shops and historic sites.

ASHEVILLE

Albemarle Inn
86 Edgemont Rd., 28801
704-255-0027
Kathy & Dick Hemes
All year

$$$ B&B
11 rooms, 11 pb
Visa, MC, *Rated*, •
C-ltd/S-no/P-no/H-no

Full breakfast
Comp. wine, snacks
Sitting rooms, pool
TV & phone in all rooms
golf & tennis nearby

Unmatched hospitality in a comfortably elegant Greek Revival mansion. Exquisite carved oak staircase, balcony and panelling. Beautiful residential area. Delicious breakfasts.

Applewood Manor B&B
62 Cumberland Circle, 28801
704-254-2244
Maryanne Young & Susan Poole
All year

$$$ B&B
4 rooms, 4 pb
Visa, MC, Disc.,*Rated*, •
C-ltd/S-no/P-no/H-no

Full gourmet breakfast
Afternoon tea
Sitting room, library
free use of fitness club
badminton, croquet

Balconies, fireplaces, private baths, delicious breakfasts & afternoon tea...just to mention a few of the pleasures. Come romance yourselves w/a stay. Cottage for 4 available.

Beaufort House
61 N. Liberty St., 28801
704-254-8334
Jacqueline & Robert Glasgow
All year

$$ B&B
10 rooms, 10 pb
Visa, MC, •
C-yes/S-no/P-no/H-no

Continental plus
Aft. tea
Sitting room
bicycles
hot tubs

*National Historic property. Lovely tea garden & manicured lawns. All homemade baked goods. VCR & cable in each room. Free movies. **15% off Mon.-Th.***

Black Walnut B&B Inn, The
288 Montford, 28801
704-254-3878
Jeanette & Adam Syprzak
All year

$$$ B&B
4 rooms, 4 pb
Visa, MC, Disc., •
C-yes/S-ltd/P-no/H-no
A little Polish

Full breakfast
Snacks, fireplace
Sitting room
tennis & golf nearby
guest cottage

Turn-of-the-Century shingle-style home in heart of historic district. Minutes from downtown & Biltmore Estate. Welcoming refreshments.

Blake House Inn
150 Royal Pines Dr., Arden,
South Asheville, 28704
704-684-1847
Bob, Eloise & Pati Roesler

$$ B&B
5 rooms, 5 pb
Visa, MC, *Rated*
C-ltd/S-no/P-no/H-yes

Full breakfast
Restaurant (Wed-Sun)
Comp. wine, bar
sitting room, bicycles
tennis & pool nearby

*Mountains cradle town with protective embrace. Wine and dine in intimate country inn on edge of town. Cordon Bleu chef, prepares fabulous meals. **Free dessert & wine, ltd***

Cedar Crest Victorian Inn
674 Biltmore Ave., 28803
704-252-1389
Jack & Barbara McEwan
All year

$$$ B&B
10 rooms, 8 pb
Visa, MC, *Rated*
C-ltd/S-ltd/P-no/H-no

Continental plus
Afternoon refreshments
Evening beverages/sweets
sitting room, piano
A/C, phones, desks

The essence of Victorian, opulent carved woodwork, beveled glass, period antiques, fireplaces. Breakfast and tea on veranda. Four blocks to Biltmore Estate. Winter discounts.

ASHEVILLE ————————————————————————————————————

Colby House, The
230 Pearson Dr., 28801
704-253-5644 800-982-2118
Everett & Ann Colby
All year

$$ B&B
4 rooms, 4 pb
Rated, •
C-ltd/S-no/P-no/H-no

Full breakfast
Refreshments all day
Library, fireplaces
lovely gardens

Historic Dutch Tudor home of charm and elegance. Full gourmet breakfast varies daily. Hosts personal attention to every guests' needs.

Corner Oak Manor
53 St. Dunstans Rd., 28803
704-253-3525
Karen & Andy Spradley
All year

$$$ B&B
4 rooms, 4 pb
Most CC., *Rated*
C-ltd/S-no/P-no/H-no

Full breakfast
Picnic baskets
Snacks, sitting rm. AC
baby grand piano
fireplace, hot tub

Elegant & comfortable; full gourmet breakfast; queen-size beds; outdoor deck w/jacuzzi; flowers/chocolates. Minutes from Biltmore Estate & Blue Ridge Parkway. **3rd. night 50%**

Flint Street Inns
100 & 116 Flint St., 28801
704-253-6723
Rick, Lynne & Marion Vogel
All year

$$$ B&B
8 rooms, 8 pb
Visa, MC, AmEx, *Rated*,
•
C-ltd/S-yes/P-no/H-no

Full southern breakfast
Comp. wine, cider, etc.
Sitting room, fireplaces
English style garden
A/C, bicycles for guests

Charming, turn-of-the-century-style residences, located in historic district. Comfortable walking distance to town, restaurants, and shops.

Inn on Montford
296 Montford Ave., 28801
704-254-9569
Ripley Hotch, Owen Sullivan
All year

$$$ B&B
4 rooms, 4 pb
Visa, MC, AmEx, *Rated*,
•
C-ltd/S-no/P-no/H-no
French

Full breakfast
Afternoon tea
Sitting room, library
fireplaces in all rooms
bicycles

Arts and crafts style home in historic district. Perfect setting for the owner's collection of porcelains, antiques, oriental rugs. **3rd night 50% off**

Lion & the Rose B&B, The
276 Montford Ave., Montford
Historic Dist., 28801
704-255-7673
Jeanne Donaldson
All year

$$$ B&B
4 rooms, 4 pb
Visa, MC, *Rated*
C-ltd/S-ltd

Full breakfast
Comp. wine, aftn. tea
TV and card rooms
suite available
lovely verandas

Classic, elegantly restored & furnished English Queen Anne 1898 townhome. Full gourmet breakfasts, varied daily. Four deluxe suites. "Pampering" in tasteful Victorian style.

Old Reynolds Mansion, The
100 Reynolds Heights, 28804
704-254-0496
Fred & Helen Faber
Exc. weekdays Dec—Mar

$$ B&B
10 rooms, 7 pb
Rated
C-ltd/S-yes/P-no/H-no

Continental breakfast
Comp. wine
Afternoon beverages
sitting room, verandas
swimming pool, A/C

A restored 1850 antebellum mansion in a country setting. Wide verandas, mountain views, woodburning fireplaces, huge old swimming pool. On the National Register.

ASHEVILLE ───────────────────────────────

Ray House B&B, The	$$B&B	Continental breakfast
83 Hillside St., 28801	4 rooms, 2 pb	Library/music room
704-252-0106	*Rated*	grand piano
Alice Curtis	C-yes/S-yes/P-ltd/H-no	
All year	French	

The Ray House is located in the city, yet hidden among spruces and native trees. Interior has the feeling of an English country home.

Reed House	$$ B&B	Continental plus
119 Dodge St., 28803	3 rooms, 1 pb	Sitting room, cottage
704-274-1604	Visa, MC	piano, pool table
Marge Turcot	C-yes/S-yes/P-no/H-no	play area for children
May–October		

Children welcome in our Victorian home in Biltmore: fireplace in your room, breakfast on the porch, relaxing rocking chairs everywhere. Listed in the National Register.

Richmond Hill Inn	$$$ B&B	Full gourmet breakfast
87 Richmond Hill Dr., 28806	21 rooms, 21 pb	Gourmet restaurant
704-252-7313 800-545-9238	Visa, MC, AmEx, *Rated*,	Extensive library
Susan Michel	•	turn-down, phone, TV
All year	C-yes/S-no/P-no/H-ltd	conference facilities

Historic Victorian inn built in 1889, magnificently renovated, with gracious service and fine dining in restaurant. Elegant setting for meetings and small weddings. 5 cottages

Wright Inn, The	$$$ B&B	Full breakfast (inn)
235 Pearson Dr., 28805	9 rooms, 9 pb	Afternoon tea, snacks
704-251-0789 800-552-5724	Visa, MC, *Rated*	sitting room
E. & B. Siler, S. Robertson	C-ltd/S-no/P-no/H-no	carriage house
All year		

The elegantly restored Wright Inn offers the discriminating traveler the opportunity to step back to the peaceful and gracious time at the turn of the century.

BALSAM ───────────────────────────────

Balsam Mountain Inn	$$$ B&B	Full breakfast
P.O. Box 40, 28707	34 rooms, 34 pb	Restaurant
Balsam Mountain Inn Rd.	Visa, MC, *Rated*, •	Game room, porches
704-456-9498	C-yes/S-yes/P-no/H-yes	26 acres, springs
Merrily Teasley, Bill Graham		rhododendron forest
All year		

Rest, read, ramble, romp and revel in the easy going hospitality of our southern mountains. Magical enchantment awaits at our historic inn. **10% disc't after four days**

BEAUFORT ───────────────────────────────

Cedars at Beaufort, The	$$$ B&B	Full breakfast
305 Front St., 28516	11 rooms, 11 pb	Restaurant, bicycles
919-728-7036	Visa, MC, *Rated*, •	Sail boat, power boats
Hugh & Marie Grady	C-ltd/S-ltd/P-no/H-no	harbor tours
All year	Spanish, French	outer banks ferry

Restored shipbuilder's home c. 1768, in the historic seacoast village of Beaufort on the outer banks.

BEAUFORT ─────────────────────────────────────

Delmar Inn
217 Turner St., 28516
919-728-4300
Tom & Mabel Steepy
All year

$$$ B&B
3 rooms, 3 pb
Visa, MC, *Rated*, •
C-ltd/S-ltd/P-no/H-no

Continental plus
Comp. wine, ltd
Snacks, sitting room
library, bicycles
tennis, beach furniture

Authentically furnished guestrooms in charming Civil War home. Enjoy a delightful evening & lavish breakfast. Historic homes tour, 2nd yr. **5th night 50% off, AAA disc't**

───

Langdon House B&B
135 Craven St., 28516
919-728-5499
Jimm Prest
All year

$$ B&B
4 rooms, 4 pb
Rated
C-ltd/S-ltd/P-no/H-no

Full breakfast
Dinner reservations
Refreshments
sitting room, bicycles
fishing & beach supplies

Friends who help you make the most of your visit. Restored 18th-century home in historic seaside hamlet on the outer banks. Wonderful breakfasts—waffles are our specialty!

───

Pecan Tree Inn
116 Queen St., 28516
919-728-6733
Susan & Joe Johnson
All year

$$ B&B
7 rooms, 7 pb
Visa, MC, *Rated*, •
C-ltd/S-no/P-no/H-no

Continental plus
Soda & juices
Jacuzzi in 1 room
sitting room, library
bicycles, beach chairs

Antique-filled 1866 Victorian home in the heart of Beaufort's Historic District. Half a block from waterfront. Bridal suite with jacuzzi. **5th night free**

BLACK MOUNTAIN ──────────────────────────────

B&B Over Yonder
P.O. Box 269, 28711
Rt 1, 433 N. Fork Rd.
704-669-6762
Wilhelmina K. Headley
May—November

$ B&B
5 rooms, 5 pb
Rated, •
C-ltd/S-no/P-no/H-no

Full breakfast
Comp. wine (occ.), snacks
Sitting room, library
wildflower gardens
near tennis, pool, golf

Secluded & comfortable on wooded hillside. Brkfast of mountain trout served on rock terraces surrounded by flowers, views of highest peaks in eastern U.S. **$5 off 4th night.**

───

Black Mountain Inn
718 W. Old Hwy 70, 28711
704-669-6528 800-735-6128
June Bergeron-Colbert
April—December

$$ B&B
7 rooms, 7 pb
•
C-ltd/S-no/P-no/H-no

Full breakfast buffet
Sitting room

Turn-of-the-century mountain home, nestled on three acres, a restful retreat for body and soul. Full breakfast buffet.

BLOWING ROCK ─────────────────────────────────

Maple Lodge B&B
P.O. Box 1236, 28605
Sunset Dr.
704-295-3331
Marilyn Bateman
April—February

$$ B&B
10 rooms, 10 pb
•
C-ltd/S-no/P-no/H-no

Full breakfast
Comp. sherry & fruit
Two parlors
stone fireplace
piano, tennis courts

In the heart of the village, a small inn furnished in country antiques, handmade quilts, family heirlooms. Full, queen, king, some canopies. Full buffet breakfast.

BLOWING ROCK

Ragged Garden Inn
P.O. Box 1927, 28605
Sunset Dr.
704-295-9703
Joe & Joyce Villani
Exc. January 6–March

$$ B&B
9 rooms, 9 pb
Visa, MC, AmEx, *Rated*
C-ltd/S-yes/P-no/H-no

Continental plus
Comp.
champagne/newlywed
Cottage for family avail
beautiful walled garden

*Near Blue Ridge Parkway and majestic Grandfather Mountain. People come here for the fantastic cool summers and the scenery. **After 3rd. night 10% off.***

BOONE

Grandma Jean's B&B
209 Meadowview Dr., 28607
704-262-3670
Dr. Jean Probinsky
April–October

$ B&B
4 rooms, 2 pb
•
C-yes/S-yes/P-no/H-no
Spanish

Continental plus
Comp. wine, snacks
Porch swing, hammock
country garden

Old-fashioned country-style hospitality. The perfect stopover place. Within minutes to Appalachian State University, the scenic Blue Ridge Parkway, and the Tweetsie Railroad.

BREVARD

Inn at Brevard, The
410 E. Main St., 28712
704-884-2105
Eileen & Batrand Bourget
March–December

$$ B&B
13 rooms, 11 pb
Rated
C-ltd/S-ltd/P-no/H-no

Full breakfast
Lunch, dinner ltd.
Sunday brunch
sitting room, color TV
cocktails, aft. tea

*Antique furnishings, gracious hospitality, restful beauty. Main building recently placed on the National Register of Historic Places. **3rd night 50%***

Red House Inn, The
412 W. Probart St., 28712
704-884-9349
Lynne Ong
All year

$ B&B
5 rooms, 3 pb
•
C-ltd/S-no/P-no/H-no

Full breakfast
Comp. wine
Sitting room
porches
off-street parking

*Lovingly restored antebellum home. Former trading post, courthouse, school and more. Near park, outlets, theater and sights. Completely furnished in antiques. **3rd. night 50%***

BRYSON CITY

Chalet Inn, The
Route 2, Box 99, Bryson
City/Dillsboro, 28789
704-586-0251
George & Hanneke Ware
April - December

$$ B&B
6 rooms, 4 pb
C-yes/S-no/P-no/H-no
German, Dutch, French

Full breakfast
Snacks, comp. wine, tea
Great room w/library
private balconies/views
brook, hiking trails

Authentic Alpine Chalet (Gasthaus) nestled in mountain cove of Blue Ridge Mts. Secluded with 19-mile views, but convenient to attractions. Picnic area, children's playground.

Folkestone Inn
101 Folkestone Rd., 28713
704-488-2730
Norma & Peter Joyce
All year

$$ B&B
9 rooms, 9 pb
C-ltd

Full English breakfast
Comp. snacks, wine
Sitting room, library
porch, rocking chairs
balconies, antiques

Friendly atmosphere, gracious country living. Situated in a peaceful, secluded rural mountain setting. Walk to 3 waterfalls; hiking; fishing; tubing. 5 rooms w/porches, decks.

BRYSON CITY ───────────────────

Fryemont Inn	$$$ MAP	Full breakfast
P.O. Box 459, 28713	36 rooms, 36 pb	Full dinner included
Fryemont Rd.	Visa, MC	Full service launge
704-488-2159 800-845-4879	C-yes/S-yes/P-no/H-no	library, sitting room
Sue & George Brown		swimming pool
April–November		

Located on a mountain shelf overlooking the Great Smoky Mountains National Park. A tradition in mountain hospitality since 1923. Price includes dinner!

Nantahala Village	$$ EP	Restaurant
4 Hwy 19 West, 28713	54 rooms, 54 pb	All meals available
704-488-2826 800-438-1507	Most CC, *Rated*, •	Sitting room, Rec. hall
John Burton & Jan Letendre	C-yes/S-ltd/P-no/H-ltd	tennis court, volleyball
April – December		rafting, horsebackriding

Family mountain resort; 200 acres in the Nantahala Mountains, Western N.C., great base for a wide variety of sightseeing activities.

Randolph House Country Inn	$$ B&B, $$$ MAP	Full country breakfast
	6 rooms, 3 pb	Dinner, tea on request
P.O. Box 816, 28713	Visa, MC, AmEx, •	Wine, set-ups
223 Fryemont Rd.	C-ltd/S-yes/P-no/H-yes	sitting room
704-488-3472		library, piano
Bill & Ruth Randolph Adams		
April–November		

Country inn c.1895, original furnishings; located in Smoky Mountains, near Appalachian trails, whitewater rafting; ruby mines. Country gourmet food. **10% restaurant discount.**

BURNSVILLE ───────────────────

Nu Wray Inn	$$ B&B	Full breakfast
P.O. Box 156, 28714	26 rooms, 26 pb	Lunch, picnic boxes
Town Square	Visa, MC, AmEx, *Rated*	Aft. snacks, 2 parlors
704-682-2329 800-368-9729	C-yes/S-no/P-no/H-yes	family-style dinners
Chris & Pam Stickland		library, porch, antiques
All year		

Historic Country inn...since 1833. Quaint town square setting, nestled in the Blue Ridge Mountains. Near Asheville, Parkway, Crafts, & Golf.

CAROLINA BEACH ───────────────────

Bayberry Inn by-the-sea	$$ B&B	Full breakfast
313 Carolina Beach Ave., 28428	11 rooms, 11 pb	Aft. tea, comp. wine
919-458-9663	Visa, MC, AmEx, *Rated*,	Sitting room, fridge
Allan & BJ Schneider	•	bicycles, tennis nearby
All year	C-yes/S-ltd/P-no/H-no	beach, beach towels

Year 'round seaside community. Breakfast on porch overlooking marina. Beautiful beaches, historic fort, aquarium. Fisherman/golfers paradise. **3+ nights 15% discount**

CASHIERS ───────────────────

Millstone Inn	$$$ B&B	Full breakfast
P.O. Box 949, 28717	11 rooms, 11 pb	Comp. sherry
Hwy 64 West	Visa, MC	Sitting room, porch
704-743-2737	C-ltd/S-yes/P-no/H-no	library, games
Heinz Haibach	Spanish, German	hiking
Easter–Thanksgiving		

Rustic elegance in a romantic setting. Surrounded by native forestland and flora. Breathtaking mountain views. The Millstone Inn exudes privacy.

CHARLOTTE —————————————————————————————————

Inn on Providence B&B, The $$ B&B   Full breakfast
6700 Providence Rd., 28226   5 rooms, 3 pb   Afternoon tea
704-366-6700   Visa, MC, *Rated*   Sitting room
Dan & Darlene McNeill   C-ltd/S-no/P-no/H-no   library
All year   swimming pool

Experience the grandeur of this large southern homestead and enjoy our attention to detail.
Breakfast served on the veranda overlooking the pool.

McElhinny House $$ B&B   Continental plus
10533 Fairway Ridge Rd., 28277 2 rooms, 2 pb   Afternoon tea
704-846-0783   Visa, MC, *Rated*   Sitting room
Mary & Jim McElhinney   C-yes/S-ltd/P-no/H-no
All year   French, German, Italian

Special welcome to international travelers; French, Italian and German-speaking host. Adja-
cent to three golf courses. Cable TV. **3rd night 50% off**

Morehead Inn, The $$$ B&B   Continental plus
1122 E. Morehead St., 28204   11 rooms, 11 pb   Comp. wine, tea
704-376-3357 FAX:335-1110   Most CC, *Rated*, •   Meeting/social functions
Bill Armstrong, Doug Spain   C-yes/S-ltd/P-no/H-ltd   piano, whirlpool, bikes
All year   Span., Fr., Ital., Port.   YMCA fitness privileges

Restored estate in historic district; furnished w/American & English art; quiet elegance. Chur-
chill Galleries on-site: exclusive antiques. 48 hour cancellation policy.

Still Waters $$ B&B   Full breakfast
6221 Amos Smith Rd., 28214   3 rooms, 3 pb   Sport court, tennis
704-399-6299   Visa, MC, *Rated*, •   basketball, volleyball
Janet & Rob Dyer   C-yes/S-no/P-no/H-no   boat ramp, dock, gazebo
All year

Log resort home on two wooded acres overlooking Lake Wylie. Near Charlotte downtown
and airport. Full breakfast featuring homemade bread. **2nd night 50% off.**

CHIMNEY ROCK ————————————————————————————————

Gingerbread Inn, The $$ B&B   Continental breakfast
P.O. Box 187, 28720   4 rooms   Sitting room
Hwy 74   C-yes/S-yes/P-no/H-no
704-625-4038
Tom & Janet Sherman
All year

Our rooms are furnished with charming country furniture and home-sewn quilts. Relax in
rocking chairs on deck overlooking the Rocky Broad River.

CLINTON ——————————————————————————————————

Shield House, The $ B&B   Continental breakfast
216 Sampson St., 28328   7 rooms, 7 pb   Comp. coffee, sodas
919-592-2634 800-462-9817   Visa, MC, AmEx, •   Sitting room
A. Green, J. & G. McLamb   C-ltd/S-ltd/P-no/H-no   tennis & golf nearby
All year   2-bedroom bungalow avail

Reminiscent of Gone With The Wind. Elegant furnishings; outstanding architectural features.
Listed in National Register. I-40 10 miles; I-95 29 miles. **10% off/seniors, Ltd**

CLYDE

Windsong: A Mountain Inn	$$$ B&B	Full breakfast
120 Ferguson Ridge, 28721	6 rooms, 6 pb	Dessert coffee
704-627-6111	Visa, MC, *Rated*, •	Lounge with wet bar
Donna & Gale Livengood	C-ltd/S-no/P-no/H-no	pool table, llama herd
January-closed		tennis courts, pool

Secluded, contemporary rustic log inn set high in the Smoky Mountains. Rooms have fireplaces, tubs and private deck. Breathtaking views. Near National Park and Maggie Valley.

DILLSBORO

Jarrett House, The	$ EP	Full breakfast wkends $
P.O. Box 219, 28725	22 rooms, 18 pb	Restaurant, all meals $
100 Haywood St.	C-ltd/S-no/P-no/H-yes	Sitting room
704-586-0265		large porches
Jim & Jean Hartbarger		
April - December		

One of the oldest inns in Western NC. Generous porches & dozens of rocking chairs. Designated a National Historic Place in 1984. Country-stlye restaurant. **Weekly rates**

Squire Watkins Inn	$$ B&B	Full squire's breakfast
P.O. Box 430, 28725	5 rooms, 5 pb	Comp. coffee & tea
W. Haywood Rd.	*Rated*	Sitting room, piano
704-586-5244	C-ltd/S-ltd/P-no/H-no	solarium
Tom & Emma Wertenberger		porch swing & rockers
All year		

Small mountain Bed and Breakfast Inn for lovers of romance, comfort, relaxation, scenic hikes, great breakfasts and small towns.

DUCK

Sanderling Inn Resort	AP	Full buffet breakfast
1461 Duck Rd., 27949	60 rooms, 60 pb	Restaurant, comp. wine
919-261-4111	*Rated*, •	All meals included
Christine J. Berger	C-yes/S-yes/P-no/H-yes	bar service, sitting rm.
All year		library, hot tubs

Private porches, bathrobes, kitchenettes or wetbars, whirlpool, tennis, swimming, health club, jogging trail, sauna, oceanfront. **Welcome gift**

DURHAM

Arrowhead Inn	$$ B&B	Full breakfast
106 Mason Rd., 27712	8 rooms, 6 pb	Comp. tea
919-477-8430	Vis/MC/AmEx, *Rated*, •	Sitting room
Jerry, Barbara & Cathy Ryan	C-yes/S-ltd/P-no/H-yes	piano, patio
January–December 22	French	air conditioned

1775 manor house offers tasteful period rooms with modern conveniences. New log cabin on our 4 acres. Written up in USA Today & 19 newspapers.

Blooming Garden Inn, The	$$$ B&B	Full gourmet breakfast
513 Holloway St., 27701	5 rooms, 5 pb	Comp. wine, tea, snacks
919-687-0801 919-688-1401	Visa, MC, AmEx, *Rated*,	Sitting rooms, library
Frank & Dolly Pokrass	•	145 foot porch, antiques
All year	C-yes/S-no/P-no/H-no	jacuzzis for 2 in suites

Vibrant colors transform this authentically restored Victorian home into a cozy, memorable retreat in downtown historic Durham. Flower gardens. **Extended stay 20-50% off.**

EDENTON

Lords Proprietors' Inn
300 N. Broad St., 27932
919-482-3641
Arch, Jane, & Martha Edwards
All year

$$$ B&B/MAP
20 rooms, 20 pb
Rated, •
C-yes/S-yes/P-no/H-no

Full breakfast
Tea, homemade cookies
Dinner served on weekday
sitting room, bicycles
private pool privileges

Three restored houses in the historic district of "the South's prettiest town." Furnished by area antique dealers with all for sale. Full-service Inn.

Trestle House Inn
Route 4, P.O. Box 370,
Soundside Rd., 27932
919-482-2282
Carol & Bill Brothers
All year

$$ B&B
4 rooms, 4 pb
Visa, MC, AmEx, •
C-ltd/S-ltd/P-no/H-no

Continental plus
BYOB
Sitting room, billiards
steam, exercise room, TV
shuffleboard, fishing

Immaculate accommodations. Tranquil setting overlooking private 15-acre fishing lake and 60 acres of trees. Five miles from historic Edenton.

FRANKLIN

Buttonwood Inn
190 Georgia Rd., 28734
704-369-8985
Liz Oehser
May–December

$$ B&B
4 rooms, 3 pb
Rated, •
C-ltd/S-ltd/P-no/H-no

Full breakfast
Sitting room, TV
golf nearby

Completely surrounded by tall pines, small and cozy Buttonwood will appeal to the person who prefers simplicity and natural rustic beauty. **3rd night 10% off**

Country Time B&B
506 Potts Branch Dr., 28734
704-369-3648
Greg & Darlene Kimsey
All year

$$ B&B
4 rooms, 2 pb
Visa, MC
C-ltd/S-no/P-no/H-no

Full breakfast
Screened & front porches
sitting room, TV room

Country hideaway. Restful, quiet & cool. Large porches, spacious lawn, mountain view. Spring blooms and fall foliage are spectacular. **7th night free, weekly rate**

Franklin Terrace, The
67 Harrison Ave., Highway 28
N., 28734
704-524-7907 800-633-2431
Ed & Helen Henson
May–October

$$ B&B
7 rooms, 7 pb
Visa, MC, •
C-ltd/S-ltd/P-no/H-no

Full breakfast
Comp. refreshments
Antiques & gifts shop

All rooms furnished with antiques. First floor houses dessert shop with cheesecakes, home-made pies & cakes—also antique shop. In town. Beautiful views.

GERMANTOWN

MeadowHaven B&B
P.O. Box 222, 27019
NC Highway 8
919-593-3996
Samuel & Darlene Fain
All year

$$
3 rooms, 3 pb
Visa, MC, *Rated*
C-ltd/S-ltd/P-no/H-no
Some Spanish

Full breakfast
Sitt. rm., hot tub/sauna
indoor heated pool
game room, fishing pond

Contemporary retreat on 25 country acres. Near Winston-Salem, Hanging Rock State Park, Sauratown Mountain. Fresco, winery, golf, canoeing, picnicing.

GREENSBORO ───────────────────────────────────

Biltmore Greensboro Hotel	$$ B&B	Complimentary wine
111 W. Washington St., 27401	23 rooms, 23 pb	Wine tastings w/15 wines
800-332-0303	Most CC, *Rated*, •	stretch limo available
Cheryl Parham	C-yes	meeting space
All year		

Historic inn, recently revovated, rooms and suites appointed with period antiques and private baths. Near antique shopping and the Coliseum. **3rd night free (space available)**

HENDERSONVILLE ───────────────────────────────

Claddagh Inn, The	$$ B&B	Full breakfast
755 N. Main St., 28792	14 rooms, 14 pb	Dinner, comp. tea/sherry
704-697-7778 800-225-4700	Most Cred.Cds. *Rated*, •	Sitting room, library
Vickie & Dennis Pacilio	C-yes/S-yes/P-no/H-no	TV, phone & A/C in rooms
All year		tennis, shuffleboard

On National Register of Historic Places. Beautiful country inn located in downtown Hendersonville, provides a homelike atmosphere where love and lasting friendships prevail.

Waverly Inn, The	$$$ B&B	Full breakfast
783 N. Main St., 28792	16 rooms, 16 pb	Comp. wine, beverages
704-693-9193 800-537-8195	Most CC, *Rated*, •	Sitting room, A/C
J & D Sheiry, D. Olmstead	C-yes/S-yes/P-no/H-ltd	telephones in all rms.
All year		tennis courts, social hr

A landmark near downtown shopping park, quaint restaurants. On National Register. Beautiful antiques. Spotlessly clean. AAA Approved. **3rd night 50% off**

HICKORY ──────────────────────────────────────

Hickory B&B, The	$$ B&B	Full country breakfast
464 7th St. SW, 28602	5 rooms, 2 pb	Afternoon tea
704-324-0548 800-654-2961	*Rated*, •	Library, piano
Suzanne & Bob Ellis	C-ltd/S-no/P-no/H-no	flowers
All year		

A restful night in our home, followed by a specially cooked breakfast, guarantees contentment. Come see us. Decorated with country furnishings & Southern hospitality.

HIGHLANDS ────────────────────────────────────

Colonial Pines Inn	$$ B&B	Full breakfast
Route 1, Box 22B, Hickory St. at	7 rooms, 7 pb	Afternoon refreshments
4½ St., 28741	Visa, MC	Sitting room, kitchen
704-526-2060	C-ltd/S-ltd/P-no/H-no	grand piano
Chris & Donna Alley		picnic area
All year		

Two acres of lawn and trees, w/mntn. view from veranda. Antique furnishings and country charm. Newly renovated guest house with fireplace, sleeps up to 6. **Winter rates**

Highlands Inn, The	$$ B&B	Continental plus
P.O. Box 1030, 28741	28 rooms, 28 pb	Restaurant, lunch
Corner of 4th & Main Sts.	Visa, MC, AmEx, *Rated*	Dinner, comp. snacks
704-526-9380 704-526-5036	C-ltd/S-ltd/P-no/H-yes	sitting room, library
Rip & Pat Benton		aviary room, golf priv.
April–November		

Located in heart of historic Highlands. Near all outdoor activities. Breathtaking mountain views, waterfalls, shops. On Nat'l Registry of Historic Places.

HIGHLANDS

Long House B&B	$$ B&B	Full breakfast
P.O. Box 2078, 28741	4 rooms, 4 pb	Snacks
Highway 64 East	Visa, MC	Sitting room
704-526-4394 800-833-0020	C-ltd/S-no/H-no	near golf, hiking paths
Lynn & Valerie Long		fishing
All year		

Rustic mountain home at the 4000-foot level in the Blue Ridge Mountains. Country comfort, large deck, and wonderful breakfast.

Old Edwards Inn, The	$$ B&B	Continental plus
P.O. Box 1030, 28741	20 rooms, 20 pb	Restaurant, lunch
Corner of 4th & Main Sts	Visa, MC, AmEx, *Rated*	Dinner, comp. snacks
704-526-5036 704-526-9380	C-ltd/S-ltd/P-no/H-no	sitting room, golf priv.
Rip & Pat Benton		Victorian side yards
April–November		

Located in the heart of historic Highlands. Close to all outdoor activities. Breathtaking mountain views, waterfalls and beautiful shops. Golf available.

HILLSBOROUGH

Hillsborough House Inn	$$$ B&B	Continental plus
P.O. Box 880, 27278	5 rooms, 5 pb	Snacks
209 E. Tryon St.	Visa, MC, *Rated*, •	Library, swimming pool
919-644-1600	C-ltd/S-no/P-no/H-no	7 acres nature paths
Katherine Webb		separate suite w/kitchen
Closed Xmas - New Years		

Italianate mansion with a dream of a front porch (80 ft.) on 7 acres in the Historic District. Eclectic, gracious and very convenient.

KILL DEVIL HILLS

Cherokee Inn B&B	$$ B&B	Continental breakfast
500 N. Virginia Dare Tr, 27948	6 rooms, 6 pb	Wraparound porches
919-441-6127 800-554-2764	Most CC, *Rated*, •	overhead ceiling fans
Bob & Kaye Combs	C-ltd/S-ltd/P-no/H-no	Sr. citizen discount
March - November		

Beach house with rustic cypress interior. Small, private, quiet. Atlantic Ocean 600 feet away. Near historic sites, shops and restaurants. **Senior discount**

LAKE JUNALUSKA

Providence Lodge	$$ MAP	Full breakfast
207 Atkins Loop, 28745	16 rooms, 8 pb	Dinner included
704-456-6486 704-452-9588	C-yes/S-no/P-no/H-ltd	Sitting room, fireplace
Ben & Wilma Cato		porch, clawfoot tubs
June–September		near tennis, pool, golf

A touch of yesterday in an old, very rustic mountain lodge—where our family-style meals are our claim to fame. Near canoeing, paddleboats, shuffleboard. **3rd. night 50% off**

LAKE LURE

Lodge on Lake Lure, The	$$$ B&B	Full breakfast
Route 1, Box 529A, Charlotte	11 rooms, 11 pb	complimentary wine
Dr., 28746	Visa, MC, AmEx, *Rated*,	Sitting room, library
704-625-2789 800-733-2785	•	piano, lake swimming
Jack & Robin Stanier	C-ltd/S-no/P-no/H-no	tennis, golf nearby
April–November		

Adult getaway in the Blue Ridge Mountains. Giant stone fireplace, breathtaking view of mountains and lake. Only public facility actually on Lake Lure.

LILLINGTON

Waverly's of Lillington
P.O. Box 25, 27546
106 W. Front St.
919-893-6760 800-272-7116
Carey & Waverley Kelly
All year

$$ B&B
4 rooms, 3 pb
Visa, MC, AmEx, Others, •
C-yes/S-no/P-no/H-yes

Full breakfast
Lunch, dinner, snacks
Afternoon tea, florist
restaurant, sitting room
bicycles, carriage rides

Large Victorian home featuring wrap-around verandah. Antique furnishings with fourposter beds. Complimentary wine and cheese upon arrival. Gifts. **6th. night Free**

LITTLE SWITZERLAND

Big Lynn Lodge
P.O. Box 459, 28749
Highway 226-A
704-765-4257 800-654-5232
Gale & Carol Armstrong
April 15—October

$$$ MAP
40 rooms, 40 pb
Visa, MC, Disc.,*Rated*, •
C-yes/S-yes/P-no/H-ltd
German

Full breakfast
Dinner included, fruit
Sitting room, library
player piano lounge
billards, shuffleboard

Old-fashioned country inn. Dinner and breakfast included with room. Cool mountain air. Elevation 3200 ft. Breathtaking view. Come and relax. Suites with whirlpools available.

MANTEO

Tranquil House Inn
P.O. Box 2045, 27954
405 Queen Elizabeth St.
919-473-1404 800-458-7069
Don & Lauri Just
All year

$$ B&B
28 rooms, 28 pb
Visa, MC, AmEx, •
C-yes/S-yes/P-no/H-yes

Full breakfast
Afternoon tea
Comp. wine, snacks
sitting room, library
bicycles

Minutes from the beach but a world apart. We offer accommodations in the tradition of the old Nags Head Inns. Condo also available. Conference facilites. **20% off 5+ nights**

MARS HILL

Baird House, Ltd. B&B Inn
P.O. Box 749, 28754
41 S. Main St.
704-689-5722
Yvette K. Wessel
All year exc. December

$ B&B
5 rooms, 2 pb
•
C-yes/S-no/P-no/H-no
French

Full breakfast
Sitting room
fireplaces

In a tiny village nestled in the hills of western North Carolina; traditional furnishings, open hearths, parlor, porches and garden.

MILTON

Woodside Inn
Box 197, Hwy. 57 South, 27379
919-234-8646
Lib & Tom McPherson
All year

$$ B&B
4 rooms, 4 pb
Visa, MC, •
C-yes/S-yes/P-ltd/H-ltd

Full breakfast
Lunch, dinner avail.
Comp. wine, snacks
sitting room
library

Greek revival plantation house provides elegant yet relaxed atmosphere, Southern cuisine, period furnishings. Spacious wooded grounds for relaxed strolling & Piedmont vistas.

MOREHEAD CITY

Morehead Manor B&B
107 N. 10th St., 28557
919-726-9233
Bob & Brenda Thorne
Memorial Day—Labor Day

$ B&B
8 rooms, 3 pb
Visa, MC, *Rated*, •
C-ltd/S-no/P-no/H-no

Full breakfast
Comp. beverages
Porches, courtyard

Comfortable old inn close to sandy beaches, three porches, a cozy courtyard, cool coastal breezes. Walk to restaurants. Group rentals off season.

MOUNT AIRY

Pine Ridge Inn
2893 West Pine, Hwy 89, 27030
919-789-5034
Ellen & Manford Haxton
All year

$$ B&B
7 rooms, 5 pb
Visa, MC, AmEx, *Rated*,
•
C-yes/S-yes/P-no/H-yes

Full breakfast
All meals available
Comp. tea, wine & cheese
sitting room, piano
hot tub, swimming pool

Elegant luxury at foot of Blue Ridge Mountains. A country inn with all the amenities of a grand hotel. All meals available on request. **3rd. night 50% off**

MURPHY

Huntington Hall B&B
500 Valley River Ave., 28906
704-837-9567 800-824-6189
Bob & Kate Delong
All year

$ B&B
5 rooms, 5 pb
Visa, MC, AmEx, *Rated*,
•
C-yes/S-yes/P-no/H-ltd

Full breakfast
Complimentary wine
Sitting room, library
public pool & tennis

A Bed & Breakfast well done! Circa 1881, former mayor's home, delightful country Victorian. Sumptous breakfast, cool mountain breezes await you! Murder Mystery wkend package.

NAGS HEAD

First Colony Inn, The
6720 S. Virginia Dare, 27959
919-441-2343 800-368-9390
Alan & Camille Lawrence
All year, FAX: 441-9234

$$$ B&B
26 rooms, 26 pb
Visa, MC, Disc, *Rated*, •
C-yes/S-ltd/P-no/H-yes

Continental plus buffet
Aftn. tea, comp. wine
Sitting room, library
verandas, pool, croquet
ocean beach, fishing

With verandas along all four sides. Furnished with antiques, wonderful big beds. Ocean views on second and third floors. Direct ocean access to uncrowded private beach.

Ocean Inn
303 Admiral St., 27959
800-262-6082
John & Susan Pettibone
May–August

$$ B&B
14 rooms, 14 pb
Most CC, *Rated*, •
C-yes/S-ltd/P-no/H-no
Spanish, French

Continental plus, snacks
Restaurant & Bar nearby
Sitting room, comp. wine
bicycles, hot tub, pool
ocean across the street

Romantic island B&B. Old island charm/paradise, all modern conveniences. Close to ocean yet secluded and quiet. Nags Head the way it used to be. **3rd night 50% off**

(800) 421-8466   (919) 441-8466

NEW BERN

Harmony House Inn
215 Pollock St., 28560
919-636-3810
A.E. & Diane Hansen
All year

$$$ B&B
9 rooms, 9 pb
Visa, MC, AmEx, *Rated*,
•
C-yes/S-no/P-no/H-no

Full breakfast
Comp. soft drinks/juices
Victorian pump organ
parlor, porch with
swings & rocking chairs

Unusually spacious circa 1850 home, rocking chairs on porch, lovely yard. In the historic district, near Tryon Palace, shops, fine restaurants.

OCRACOKE

Berkley Center Country Inn
P.O. Box 220, 27960
Rt. 12
919-928-5911
Ruth & Wes Egan
March–November

$$ B&B
11 rooms, 9 pb
Rated, •
C-yes/S-yes/P-no/H-yes

Continental breakfast
Sitting room
bicycles

Beautifully restored estate on harbor of outer banks fishing village located in U.S. National Seashore. 19 miles of uncommercialized beach.

OLD FORT

Inn at Old Fort, The
P.O. Box 1116, 28762
W. Main St.
704-668-9384
Debbie & Chuck Aldridge
All year

$ B&B
4 rooms, 4 pb
C-yes/S-ltd/P-no/H-no

Continental plus
Snacks
Parlor and library
cable TV, large porch
breakfast on garden deck

1880s Victorian cottage furnished with antiques. Large porch for rocking; terraced lawn and gardens; 3.5 acres overlooking Blue Ridge town. Near Asheville, Lake Lure.

PISGAH FOREST

Key Falls Inn
151 Everett Rd., 28768
704-884-7559
C. & P. Grosvenor, J.Fogleman
All year

$$ B&B
5 rooms, 5 pb
Visa, MC, AmEx, •
C-ltd/S-ltd/P-no/H-no
Spanish

Full breakfast
Afternoon tea, lemonade
Sitting room, cable TV
VCR, trail to waterfall
tennis, fishing pond

Charming, restored Victorian farmhouse furnished w/antiques, on 28 acres near Brevard. Porches, mountain view, waterfall, wooded setting & sumptuous brkfasts. **7th nite free.**

Pines Country Inn, The
719 Hart Rd., Pisgah Forest,
28768
704-877-3131
Tom & Mary McEntire
May–October

$$ B&B/MAP
22 rooms, 19 pb
C-yes/S-yes/P-no/H-ltd

Full breakfast
Dinner (MAP, Wed-Sat)
Sitting room
piano
great biking & hiking

Quiet, homey country inn. Fantastic view. Accommodations in the Inn or the 4 cabins and cottages. Where guests are treated like family at Grandma's house.

PITTSBORO

Fearrington House Inn
2000 Fearrington, 27312
919-542-2121
Jenny & R.B. Fitch
All year

$$$ B&B
23 rooms, 23 pb
Visa/MC, *Rated*, •
C-ltd/S-ltd/P-no/H-yes

Continental breakfast
Lunch, dinner
Aft. tea
sitting room
swimming pool

Classic countryside elegance in suites furnished with English antiques. Charming courtyard and gardens. Delicately prepared regional cuisine. Member of Relais & Chateaux.

ROBBINSVILLE

Blue Boar Lodge
200 Santeetlah Rd., 28771
704-479-8126
Roy & Kathy Wilson
April–December

$$$ MAP
9 rooms, 9 pb
Visa, MC
C-yes/S-yes/P-no/H-no

Full breakfast
Dinner included
Sitting room, game room
lake swimming
boat rental, fishing

Secluded hideaway in the Smoky Mountains; near beautiful hiking trails and lake activities; family-style meals.

Snowbird Mountain Lodge
275 Santeetlah Rd., 28771
704-479-3433
Eleanor & Jim Burbank
April 15–November 6

$$$ AP
21 rooms, 21 pb
Most CC, *Rated*
C-ltd/S-ltd/P-no/H-ltd

Full breakfast
Lunch & dinner included
Sitting room
piano

Located in the heart of the National Forest. Fishing, hiking, mountain stream swimming, canoeing, whitewater rafting, shuffleboard, and horseback riding.

SALISBURY

Rowan Oak House
208 S. Fulton, 28144
704-633-2086 800-786-0437
Bill & Ruth Ann Coffey
All year

$$ B&B
4 rooms, 2 pb
Rated, •
C-ltd/S-ltd
Spanish

Full breakfast
Comp. snacks
Library, sitting room
bicycles, antiques
jacuzzi tub in one room

"Lavish, luxurious and unique" describes our Queen Anne home with antiques, flowers, porches, gardens, and historic Salisbury's small town atmosphere. AAA approved!

SALUDA

Orchard Inn, The
P.O. Box 725, 28773
Highway 176
704-749-5471 800-581-3800
Ann & Ken Hough
All year

$$$ B&B
10 rooms, 10 pb
Visa, MC
C-ltd/S-yes/P-no/H-no

Full breakfast
Lunch, dinner, fruit
Library, living room
walking paths

Orchard Inn is a real country inn featuring quiet living with all the comforts and informal elegance of a mountain country house.

SOUTHERN PINES

Knollwood House
1495 W. Connecticut Ave, 28387
919-692-9390
Louisa Jackson
All year

$$ B&B
4 rooms, 4 pb
Rated, •
C-yes/S-yes/P-no/H-no

Full breakfast
Comp. hors d'oeuvres
Late night goodies
golf nextdoor
sitting room with games

A luxurious English manor house with 18th century antiques & contemp. comforts in the heart of golf country. Wine & foodstuffs from Paris every week. **4th. nite free, Ltd. ask**

SPRUCE PINE

Richmond Inn B&B
101 Pine Ave., 28777
704-765-6993
Bill Ansley, Lenore Boucher
All year

$$ B&B
7 rooms, 7 pb
Visa, MC, *Rated*, •
C-yes/S-no/P-no/H-no
French, German

Full breakfast
Comp. tea, wine
Sitting room, piano
stone terrace porch

In the heart of the most spectacular mountain scenery. Close to Blue Ridge Parkway. Luxurious accommodations, Anglo/North Carolinian hosts. Cottages available.

TARBORO

Little Warren B&B
304 E. Park Ave., 27886
919-823-1314
Patsy & Tom Miller
All year

$$ B&B
3 rooms, 3 pb
AmEx, Disc., *Rated*, •
C-ltd/S-yes/P-no/H-no
Spanish

Continental plus or Full
Comp. wine, beer, etc.
Sitting room
tennis courts
Antique store downtown

Large, gracious, Edwardian home renovated, appointed w/antiques & collectibles. In quiet neighborhood, historic district. Depply set wraparaound porch overlooking Town Common.

TRYON

Pine Crest Inn
200 Pine Crest Ln., 28782
800-633-3001 704-859-9135
Jeremy & Jennifer Wainwright
All year

$$$ B&B
30 rooms, 30 pb
Visa, MC, AmEx, *Rated*, •
C-yes/S-yes/P-no/H-no
French

Full breakfast
Lunch Sun, dinner M-Sat
Restaurant, bar, snacks
sitting room, fireplaces
library, club privileges

Peaceful Blue Ridge getaway. Main inn, cabins, cottages on 3 acres, most w/fireplace. Gourmet restaurant, wine list. Near golf, tennis. Magnificent sightseeing. AAA 4 diamond.

TRYON ───────────────────────────────────────

Stone Hedge Inn	$$ B&B	Full breakfast
P.O. Box 366, 28782	6 rooms, 6 pb	Restaurant, dinner
300 Howard Gap Rd.	Visa, MC, •	Swimming pool
704-859-9114	C-ltd/S-yes/P-no/H-yes	hiking
Ray & Anneliese Weingartner	German	
All year		

Restaurant and lodge with Bavarian-type setting. Continental dining with German favorites.
7th night free/midwk rates

VALLE CRUCIS ─────────────────────────────────

Mast Farm Inn	$$$ MAP	Continental plus
P.O. Box 704, 28691	12 rooms, 8 pb	Dinner included
State Road 1112	Visa, MC, *Rated*, •	Sitting room
704-963-5857	C-ltd/S-no/P-no/H-yes	setups
Francis & Sibyl Pressly	Portugese	
May—Oct, Dec 26—Mar 15		

Inn on 18-acre farm in beautiful mountain valley near Boone. Ski, golf, fish, white water rafting. Country cooking. Vegetables from our farm.

WAYNESVILLE ──────────────────────────────────

Belle Meade Inn	$$ B&B	Full breakfast
P.O. Box 1319, 28786	4 rooms, 4 pb	Afteronn tea, snacks
804 Balsam, Hazelwood	Visa, MC, Disc., •	Library
704-456-3234	C-ltd/S-no/P-no/H-no	bicycles
Larry Hanson, William Shaw		golfing, National Park
April—December		

Nestled in mountains, this elegant home from yesteryear offers distinctive breakfasts. Near golfing, Biltmore House & Smoky Mountain Nat'l Park. **10% AARP, 10% off 5+ nights.**

Grandview Lodge	$$$ MAP	Full breakfast
809 Valley View Ci., 28786	15 rooms, 15 pb	Dinner incl., lunch
704-456-5212 800-255-7826	*Rated*, •	Restaurant (resv)
Stan & Linda Arnold	C-yes/S-yes/Polish,	library, piano, golf
All year	Russian, German	tennis, shuffleboard

Inn located on rolling land, w/ an orchard & arbor. Breakfast features homemade jams & jellies. Dinner includes fresh vegetables, baked breads & desserts. **3rd nite 50%, Ltd.**

Hallcrest Inn	$$ MAP	Full breakfast
299 Halltop Circle, 28786	12 rooms, 12 pb	Dinner included
704-456-6457 800-334-6457	MC, Visa, *Rated*, •	Tea/coffee/cocoa/juice
M.& T.Burson, D.& C.Mitchell	C-yes/S-ltd/P-no/H-no	library, living room
June—October		

Small country inn in 100-year-old farmhouse with adjacent modular unit. Family-style dining around lazy-susan tables and beautiful view of the mountain.

Heath Lodge	$$ MAP	Full breakfast
900 Dolan Rd., 28786	22 rooms, 22 pb	Gourmet dinner included
704-456-3333 800-HEATH-99	*Rated*, •	Sitting room, library
Robert & Cindy Zinser	C-yes/S-yes/P-no/H-ltd	outdoor deck w/hot tub
All year	Spanish	color TV in rm, 2 pianos

Secluded on a wooded hillside, this mountain inn offers unique lodging with beamed ceilings and country furnishings. Bountiful breakfasts and gourmet dinners.

WAYNESVILLE

Palmer House B&B
108 Pigeon St., 28786
704-456-7521
Kris Gillet, Jeff Minick
All year

$$ B&B
7 rooms, 7 pb
•
C-ltd/S-yes/P-no/H-ltd

Full breakfast
Bedtime chocolates
sitting room, piano
book & game library

Rambling old house with small-town charm in the Smoky Mountains. Our bookstore on Main St. offers a 10% discount to guests. Delicious breakfasts. **10% off at bookstore**

Swag, The
Route 2, Box 280-A, 28786
704-926-0430
Deener Matthews
Late May - October

$$$ AP
14 rooms, 14 pb
Visa, MC, *Rated*
C-ltd/S-yes/P-no/H-ltd

Full breakfast
Lunch & dinner included
Library, piano, sauna
racquetball, hiking
croquet field above pond

At 5,000 feet, hand-hewn log lodge. Elegant, intimate hideaway. Fourteen unique bedrooms, excellent cuisine, breathtaking views. Executive retreat, honeymoon haven.

WEAVERVILLE

Dry Ridge Inn
26 Brown St., Weaverville,
28787
704-658-3899
Paul & Mary Lou Gibson
All year

$$ B&B
9 rooms, 5 pb
Visa, MC, *Rated*, •
C-yes/S-ltd/Dutch

Full breakfast
Comp. wine
Sitting room
bicycles, art gallery
gift shop

Convenient to Asheville and Blue Ridge Parkway with small town charm. Large comfortable guest rooms; antiques and homemade quilts. **3rd night 30% off**

WILMINGTON

Anderson Guest House
520 Orange St., 28401
919-343-8128
Connie Anderson
All year

$$ B&B
2 rooms, 2 pb
C-ltd/S-yes/P-yes/H-no

Full breakfast
Comp. wine, mixed drinks
Afternoon tea
restaurant nearby
baby-sitting service

1851 Italianate townhouse; separate guest quarters overlooking private garden. Furnished with antiques, ceiling fans, fireplaces. Drinks upon arrival. Delightful breakfasts.

Catherine's Inn
N. 410 Orange St., 28210
919-251-0863 800-476-0723
Catherine & Walter AcKiss
All year

$$ B&B
3 rooms, 3 pb
Visa, MC, AmEx *Rated*,
•
C-yes/S-yes/P-no/H-no

Full breakfast
Comp. wine, snacks, tea
Bar service
sitting room, library
swimming pool

In heart of the historical district. Experience warm gracious hospitality, tasty breakfasts. Near Wilmington attractions. **Free wine & fresh flowers—brides, annniv., b'days.**

Inn at St. Thomas Court
101 S. Second St., 28401
919-343-1800 800-525-0909
T.K. Scott, M.L. Compton
All year

$$ B&B
23 rooms, 23 pb
Visa, MC, AmEx, *Rated*,
•
C-yes/S-yes/H-yes

Continental plus
in suites—kitchen inc.
Concierge, conservatory
billiard room, courtyard
sailing charters/school

Elegant accommodations for discriminating travelers, located in romantic Historic District. Walk along Cape Fear River paths to fine restaurants, museums and specialty shops.

WILMINGTON

Market Street B&B	$$ B&B	Full breakfast
1704 Market St., 28403	3 rooms, 3 pb	Sitting room, sun room
919-763-5442 800-242-5442	Visa, MC, *Rated*	central air conditioning
Jo Anne Jarrett	C-ltd/S-no/P-no/H-no	off-street parking
All year		

Early 20th century Georgian-style mansion on National Register of Historic Places. Beaches and golfing only minutes away.

WILSON

Miss Betty's B&B Inn	$$ B&B	Full breakfast
600 W. Nash St., 27893	12 rooms, 12 pb	4 parlors, antique shop
919-243-4447 800-258-2058	Most CC, *Rated*	A/C, golf, swimming pool
Betty & Fred Spitz	C-ltd/S-yes/P-no/H-yes	4 golf courses, suites
All year		

Located in "antique capital of North Carolina," main inn (c.1858) and guest house (c.1900) provide Victorian elegance & beauty w/all modern conveniences. Main N-S Rt. I-95.

WINSTON—SALEM

Colonel Ludlow Inn	$$$ B&B	Full breakfast
Summit & W. 5th St., 27101	13 rooms, 13 pb	King bed, some firplcs.
919-777-1887 FAX:777-1890	Visa, MC, AmEx, *Rated*,	swim spa, exercise room
C. Creasman & M. Sullivan	•	gardens, fountains
All year	C-ltd/S-yes/P-no/H-no	

Two beautifully restored 1887 National Register homes. Deluxe rooms & suites, each w/2-person jacuzzi in romantic alcove. Near downtown, shops, fine restaurants.

Lady Anne's Victorian B&B	$$ B&B	Full breakfast
612 Summit St., 27101	4 rooms, 3 pb	Afternoon tea, snacks
919-724-1074	Visa, MC, AmEx, •	Sitting room, hot tubs
Shelley Kirley & Steve Wishon	C-ltd/S-no/P-no/H-no	cable TV, stereo, tapes
All year		room refrig., coff. mak.

1890 Victorian. Some suites w/antiques, private porch, bath, 2-person whirlpool. Full break-fast & evening dessert. Close to everything. **Disc't to tour Old Salem**

More Inns . . .

Walker Inn, 39 Junaluska Rd., Andrews, 28901, 704-321-5019
Doctor's Inn, 716 S. Park St., Asheboro, 27203, 919-625-4916
Aberdeen Inn B&B, 64 Linden Ave., Asheville, 28801, 704-254-9336
Acorn Cottage B&B, 25 St. Dunstans Circle, Asheville, 28803, 704-253-0609
Bridle Path Inn, 30 Lookout Rd., Asheville, 28804, 704-252-0035
Cairn Brae, 217 Patton Mountain Rd., Asheville, 28804, 704-252-9219
Carolina B&B, 177 Cumberland Ave., Asheville, 28801, 704-254-3608
Grove Park Inn, Asheville,
Bakersville B&B, Route 4, Box 427, Bakersville, 28705, 704-688-3451
Spiced Apple Inn B&B, Route 1, Box 82, Bakersville, 28705,
Balsam Lodge B&B, P.O. Box 279, Balsam, 28707, 704-456-6528
Archers Inn, Route 2, Box 56-A, Banner Elk, 28604, 704-898-9004
Banner Elk Inn B&B, The, P.O. Box 1953, Banner Elk, 28604, 704-898-6223
Mountview Chateau, Route 1, Box 426, Banner Elk, 28604, 704-963-6593
Old Mill Inn & Antiques, P.O. Box 252, Bat Cave, 28710, 704-625-4256
Orig. Hickory Nut Gap Inn, P.O. Box 246, Bat Cave, 28710, 704-625-9108
Stonehearth Inn, P.O. Box 242, Bat Cave, 28710, 704-625-4027
Bath Guest House, So. Main St., Bath, 27808, 919-923-6811
Beaufort Inn, 101 Ann St., Beaufort, 28516, 919-728-2600
Captains' Quarters, 315 Ann St., Beaufort, 28516, 919-728-7711
Inlet Inn, 601 Front at Queen Sts., Beaufort, 28615, 919-728-3600
Shotgun House, 406 Ann St., Beaufort, 28516, 919-728-6248
River Forest Manor, 600 E. Main St., Belhaven, 27810, 919-943-2151
Black Forest Lodge, Laurel Lane, Route 1, Black Mountain, 27811,
Blackberry Inn, P.O. Box 965, Black Mountain, 27811, 704-669-8303
Red Rocker Inn, 136 N. Dougherty St., Black Mountain, 28711, 704-669-5991
Farm House, P.O. Box 126, Blowing Rock, 28605,

Gideon Ridge Inn, P.O. Box 1929, Blowing Rock, 28605, 704-295-3644
Hound Ears Lodge and Club, P.O. Box 188, Blowing Rock, 28605, 704-963-4321
Meadowbrook Inn, P.O. Box 2005, Blowing Rock, 28605, 704-295-4300
Sunshine Inn, P.O. Box 528, Sunset Dr, Blowing Rock, 28605, 704-295-3487
Overlook Lodge, Box 132, Boone, 28607,
Womble Inn, 301 W. Main St., Brevard, 28712, 704-884-4770
Deep Creek Lodge, 810 W. Deep Creek, Bryson City, 28713,
Hemlock Inn, Bryson City, 28713, 704-488-2885
West Oak Bed & Breakfast, Fryemont Rd., Bryson City, 28713, 704-488-2438
Hamrick Inn B&B, 7787 Hwy 80 South, Burnsville, 28714, 704-675-5251
Mountain Springs Cottages, P.O. Box 2, Hwy #151, Candler, 28715, 704-665-1004
Tom Jones B&B Inn, P.O. Box 458, Carthage, 28327, 919-947-3044
High Hampton Inn, P.O. Box 338, Hwy. 107S, Cashiers, 28717, 704-743-2411
Caroline Inn, Box 1110, Chapel Hill, 27514, 919-933-2001
Hillcrest House, 209 Hillcrest Rd., Chapel Hill, 27514, 919-942-2369
Inn at Bingham School, P.O. Box 267, Chapel Hill, 27514, 919-563-5583
Pineview Inn & Conf. Ctr., Route 10,Box 265, Chapel Hill, 27514, 919-967-7166
Windy Oaks, Route 7, Box 587, Chapel Hill, 27514, 919-942-1001
Elizabeth B&B, The, 2145 E. 5th St., Charlotte, 28204, 704-358-1368
Hampton Manor, 3327 Carmel Rd., Charlotte, 28211, 704-542-6299
Homeplace B&B, The, 5901 Sardis Rd., Charlotte, 28270, 704-365-1936
New England Inn, 3726 Providence Rd., Charlotte, 28211, 704-362-0005
Overcarsh House, 326 West Eighth St., Charlotte, 28202, 704-334-8477
Dogwood Inn, P.O. Box 70, Hwy 64 &74, Chimney Rock, 28720, 704-625-4403
Esmeralda Inn, Box 57, Chimney Rock, 28720, 704-625-9105
Tanglewood B&B Inn & Lodge, P.O. Box 1040, Clemmons, 27012, 919-766-0591
Dillsboro Inn, 2 River Rd., Box 490, Dillsboro, 28725, 704-586-3898
Governor Eden Inn, 304 N. Broad St., Edenton, 27932, 919-482-2072
Granville Queen Inn, 108 S. Granville St., Edenton, 27932, 919-482-5296
Jason House Inn, Granville St., Edenton, 27932, 919-482-3400
River City B&B, 1004 W. Williams Circle, Elizabeth City, 27909, 919-338-3337
Crepe Myrtle Inn, 501 Ocean Dr., Emerald Isle, 28557, 919-354-4616
Pines Guest Lodge, 1003 Arberdale Dr., Fayetteville, 28304, 919-864-7333
Historic Woodfield Inn, P.O. Box 98, Flat Rock, 28731, 704-693-6016
Heritage Country Inn, 7 Bates Branch Rd., Franklin, 28734, 704-524-7381
Lullwater Farmhouse Inn, Route 5, Box 540, Franklin, 28734, 704-524-6532
Olde Mill House, 44 McClure Mill Rd., Franklin, 28734, 704-524-5226
Poor Richard Summitt Inn, E. Rogers St., Franklin, 28734, 704-524-2006
MeadowHaven B&B, NC Hwy. 8, P.O. Box 222, Germanton, 27019, 919-593-3996
Glendale Springs Inn, R 16, Milepost 259, Glendale Springs, 28629, 919-982-2102
Mountain View Lodge, P.O. Box 90, Glendale Springs, 28629, 919-982-2233
Henry Weil B&B, 200 W. Chestnut St., Goldsboro, 27530, 919-735-9995
College Hill B&B, 922 Carr St., Greensboro, 27407, 919-274-6829
Greenwich Inn, 111 W. Washington St., Greensboro, 27401, 919-272-3474
Plaza Manor, 511 Martin St., Greensboro, 27406, 919-274-3074
Heather House, P.O. Box 61, 102 Church, Hayesville, 28904, 704-389-3343
La Grange Plantation Inn, Route 3, Box 610, Henderson, 27536, 919-438-2421
Pool Rock Plantation, Route 5, Box 62, Henderson, 27536, 919-492-6399
Echo Mountain Inn, 2849 Laurel Park Hwy., Hendersonville, 28739, 704-693-9626
Havenshire Inn, Route 13, Box 366, Hendersonville, 28739, 704-692-4097
Reverie, 1197 Greenville Hwy, Hendersonville, 28739, 704-693-8255
Hidden Crystal Inn, School Rd., Hiddenite, 28636, 704-632-0063
Premier B&B, The, 1001 Johnson St., High Point, 27262, 919-889-8349
Chandler Inn, P.O. Box 2156, Highlands, 28741, 704-526-5992
Phelp's House, Route 1, Box 55, Highlands, 28741, 704-526-2590
Colonial Inn, 153 W. King St., Hillsborough, 27278, 919-732-2461
Inn At Teardrop, 175 W. King St., Hillsborough, 27278, 919-732-1120
Taylor House Inn B&B, 14 N. 17th St., Historic Wilmington, 28401, 919-763-7581
Figurehead Bed & Breakfast, 417 Helga St., Kill Devil Hills, 27948, 919-441-6929
Brookside Lodge, P.O. Box 925, Lake Junaluska, 28745, 704-456-8897
Sunset Inn, 300 N. Lakeshore Dr., Lake Junaluska, 28745, 704-456-6114
Fairfield Mountains, Route 1, Buffalo Rd., Lake Lure, 28746, 704-625-9111
Lake Lure Inn, P.O. Box 6, Hwy 74, Lake Lure, 28746, 704-625-2525
Earthshine Mountain Lodge, Route 1, Box 30AA, Lake Toxaway, 28747, 704-862-4207
Greystone Inn, The, Greystone Ln., Lake Toxaway, 28747, 704-966-4700
Greystone Inn, The, Lake Toxaway, 800-824-5766
Burgiss Farm B&B, Rte. 1, Box 300, Laurel Springs, 28644, 919-359-2995
Lawrences, Route 1, Box 641, Lexington, 27292, 704-249-1114
Alpine Inn, Hwy 226-A, Little Switzerland, 28749, 704-765-5380
Boxley B&B, 117 E. Hunter St., Madison, 27025, 919-427-0453
Catalooche Ranch, Rt. 1, Box 500, Maggie Valley, 28751,
Smokey Shadows Lodge, P.O. Box 444, Maggie Valley, 28571,
Snuggle Inn, US Hwy 19, P.O. Box 416, Maggie Valley, 28751, 704-926-3782
Scarborough Inn, Hwy 64/264, Box 1310, Manteo, 27954, 919-473-3979
Marshall House, S. Hill St P.O. Box 865, Marshall, 28753,
Blooming Garden Inn, 209 W. Holt St., Mebane, 27302,
Buntie's B&B, 322 Houston St., Monroe, 28110, 704-289-1155
Glen Rock Inn, 421 Kentucky Rd., Montreat, 28756,
Oak Ridge Farm B&B, Rt. 5, Box 111,NC HWY 1, Mooresville, 28115, 704-663-7085
Dill House, 1104 Arendell St., Morehead City, 28557, 919-726-4449
Forever Christmas Inn, 2 Courtland, Box 865, Mountain Home, 28758, 704-692-1133
William E Merritt House, 618 N. Main, Mt. Airy, 27030,

Winborne House, 333 Jay Trail, Murphreesboro, 27855,
Hilltop House B&B, 104 Campbell St., Murphy, 28906, 704-837-8661
Hoover House, 306 Natural Springs Dr., Murphy, 28906, 704-837-8734
Carefree Cottages, Rt. 1 Box 748, Nags Head, 27959, 919-441-5340
Colony Beach Inn, P.O. Box 87, Nags Head, 27959, 919-441-3666
Griffin-Pace House, Rt. 4, Box 300, Hwy 58N, Nashville, 27856, 919-459-4746
Aerie, The, 509 Pollock St., New Bern, 28560, 919-636-5553
King's Arms Inn, The, 212 Pollock St., New Bern, 28560, 919-638-4409
New Berne House Inn B&B, 709 Broad St., New Bern, 28560, 800-842-7688
Blackbeard's Lodge, P.O. Box 37, Ocracoke, 27960, 919-928-3421
Boyette House, Box 39, Ocracoke, 27960, 919-928-4261
Ships Timbers B&B, Box 10, Ocracoke, 27960, 919-928-6141
Island Inn, Box 7, Ocracoke Island, 27960, 919-928-4351
Oscar's House, Box 206, Ocracoke Island, 27960, 919-928-1311
Tar Heel Inn, The, P.O. Box 176, Oriental, 28571, 919-249-1078
Chinquapin Inn, P.O. Box 145, Penland, 28765, 704-765-0064
Pilot Knob, P.O. Box 1280, Pilot Mountain, 27041, 919-325-2502
Pine Cone Manor B&B, P.O. Box 1208, Pinebluff, 28373, 919-281-5307
Holly Inn, Box 23, Cherokee Rd., Pinehurst, 28374,
Magnolia Inn, Box 266, Pinehurst, 28374, 919-295-6900
Patterson's Carriage Shop, Hwy 10, P.O. Box 268, Polkville, 28136, 704-538-3929
Trent River Plantation, P.O. Box 154, Pollocksville, 28573, 919-224-3811
Oakwood Inn, 411 N. Bloodworth St., Raleigh, 27604, 919-832-9712
Old House B&B, Old US 70, P.O. Box 384, Ridgecrest, 28770, 704-669-5196
Red Lion Inn, Star Route, Box 200, Rosman, 28772, 704-884-6868
Bear Creek Lodge, Route 1, Box 335, Saluda, 28773, 704-749-2272
Oaks, The, P.O. Box 1008, Saluda, 28773, 704-749-9613
Fairfield Sapphire Valley, 4000 Hwy. 64, W., Sapphire, 28774,
Doe Creek Inn, Hwy 17, Shallotte, 28459, 919-754-7736
Eli Olive's Inn, P.O. Box 2544, Smithfield, 27577, 919-934-9823
Jefferson Inn, 150 W. New Hampshire, Southern Pines, 28387, 919-692-6400
Dosher Plantation House, Route 5, Box 100, Southport, 28461, 919-457-5554
River's End B&B, 120 W. Moore St., Southport, 28461, 919-457-9939
Bella Columns, Route 2, Box 228-B, Sparta, 28675,
Turby-Villa, East Whitehead St., Sparta, 28675, 919-372-8490
Fairway Inn B&B, The, 110 Henry Ln., Spruce Pine, 28777, 704-765-4917
Pinebridge Inn, 101 Pinebridge Ave., Spruce Pine, 28777, 704-765-5543
Madelyn's B&B, 514 Carroll St., Statesville, 28677, 704-872-3973
Bedside Manor, Route 1, Box 90A, Sugar Grove, 28679, 704-297-1120
Mt. Pleasant B&B, 310 Journey's End, Swansboro, 28584, 919-326-7076
Scotts Keep B&B, 308 Walnut St., Swansboro, 28584, 919-326-1257
Todd House, 6 Live Oak St., Tabor City, 28463, 919-653-3778
Phyllis Bardley, Route 6, Box 12, Taylorsville, 28681,
Melrose Inn, 211 Melrose, Tryon, 28782, 704-859-9419
Mill Farm Inn, P.O. Box 1251, Tryon, 28782, 704-859-6992
Bluestone Lodge, P.O. Box 736, Valle Crucis, 28691, 704-963-5177
Inn at the Taylor House, Hwy 194, Box 713, Valle Crucis, 28691, 704-963-5581
Mountainview Chateau, P.O. Box 723, Valle Crucis, 28691, 704-963-6593
Chapel Brook B&B, Route 1, Box 290-D, Vilas, 28692, 704-297-4304
C.W. Pugh's B&B, P.O. Box 427, Wanchese, 27981, 919-473-5466
Traub's Inn, 116 W. Macon St., Warrenton, 27589, 919-257-2727
Squire's Vintage Inn, Route 2 Box 130R, Warsaw, 28398, 919-296-1831
Pamlico House B&B, 400 E. Main St., Washington, 27889, 919-946-7184
Forsyth, The, 305 Walnut St., Waynesville, 28786, 704-456-3537
Haywood Street House B&B, 409 South Haywood St., Waynesville, 28786, 704-456-9831
Way Inn, 299 S. Main St., Waynesville, 28786, 704-456-3788
Weldon Place Inn, 500 Washington Ave., Weldon, 27890, 919-536-4582
Dock Street Inn, 522 Dock St., Wilmington, 28401, 919-763-7128
Five Star Guest House, The, 14 N. Seventh St., Wilmington, 28401, 919-763-7581
Graystone Guesthouse, 100 S. Third St., Wilmington, 28401, 919-762-0358
James Place B&B, 9 S. 4th St., Wilmington, 28401, 919-251-0999
Murchison House B&B Inn, 305 S. 3rd St., Wilmington, 28401, 919-343-8580
Stemmerman's 1855 Inn, 138 S. Front St., Wilmington, 28401,
Worth House, The, 412 S. Third St., Wilmington, 28401, 919-762-8562
Pilgrims Rest Inn, 600 W. Nash St., Wilson, 27893, 919-243-4447
Brookstown Inn B&B, 200 Brookstown St., Winston-Salem, 27101, 919-725-1120
Lowe-Alston House B&B, 204 Cascade Ave., Winston-Salem, 27127, 919-727-1211
Wachovia B&B, Inc., 513 Wachovia, Winston-Salem, 27101, 919-777-0332
Edgewater Inn, 10 W. Columbia St., Wrightsville Beach, 28480, 919-256-2914

Pine Crest Inn, Tryon, NC

North Dakota

LUVERNE

Volden Farm B&B	$$ B&B	Full breakfast
RR 2, Box 50, 58056	3 rooms, 1 pb	Lunch, dinner, Aft. tea
701-769-2275	*Rated*	Snacks, Comp. wine
Jim & JoAnne Wold	C-yes/S-no/P-no/H-ltd	sitting room, library
All year	Russian, ltd.	bicycles, billiards

Unexpected and out of the ordinary. Volden Farm will renew and satisfy. Good food & conversation w/ wide prarie and ski await you. ABBA rating 2+.

VALLEY CITY

Bonhus House Guest Inn	$ B&B	Continental plus
341 Third Ave. NW, Off I-94,	4 rooms, 1 pb	Lunch, Snacks
58072	C-yes/S-no/P-no/H-no	Dinner avail. by reserv.
701-845-2229		sitting room, library
The Bonhus Ladies		fresh flowers
All year		

Victorian elegance located in the scenic Sheyenne River Valley. Special events catered. Antiques. Fishing, hunting, skiing, golfing nearby. College. Winter show.

More Inns . . .

White Lace, 807 N. 6th St., Bismark, 58501, 701-258-4142
Log Manor B&B Inn, P.O. Box 159, Bottineau, 58318, 701-263-4596
Logging Camp Ranch B&B, P.O. Box 27, Bowman, 58623, 701-279-5702
Kirkland B&B 1886, RR 2, Box 18, Carrington, 58421, 701-652-2775
Dakotah Friend B&B, P.O. Box 280A, Devils Lake, 58301, 701-662-6327
Bohlig's B&B, 1418 3rd Ave. S., Fargo, 58103, 701-235-7867
Beiseker Mansion, The, P.O. Box 187, Fessenden, 58438, 701-547-3411
511 Reeves, 511 Reeves Dr., Grand Forks, 58201, 701-772-9663
Lord Byron's B&B, 521 S. 5th St., Grand Forks, 58201, 701-775-0194
Merrifield House, P.O. Box 151, Grand Forks, 58201, 701-775-4250
Country Charm B&B, RR3, Box 71, Jamestown, 58401, 701-251-1372
Farm Comfort, Kemare, 58746, 701-848-2433
Lady Bird B&B Inn, P.O. Box 177, Leonard, 58052, 701-645-2509
Kaler B&B, Rt 2, Box 151, Lidgerwood, 58053,
Kaler's B&B, 9650 Highway 18, Lidgerwood, 58053, 701-538-4848
Grandma's House Farm B&B, P.O. Box 12, Luverne, 58056, 701-845-4994
Midstate B&B, P.O. Box 28, McClusky, 58463, 701-363-2520
Rough Rider Hotel, Medora, 58505,
Minnewaukan B&B Inn, 230 2nd St. E., Minnewaukan, 58351, 701-473-5731
Broadway Inn B&B, 433 N. Broadway, Minot, 58701, 701-838-6075
D-Over-L B&B, P.O. Box 187, Minot, 58701, 701-722-3326
Dakotah Rose B&B, 510 4th Ave. NW, Minot, 58701, 701-838-3548
Lois & Stan's B&B, 1007 11th Ave. NW, Minot, 58701, 701-838-2244
Prairie View B&B, Route 2, Box 87, New Salem, 58563, 701-843-7236
Twin Pine B&B, P.O. Box 30, Northwood, 58267, 701-587-6075
Rocking Chair B&B Inn, P.O. Box 236, Reeder, 58649, 701-853-2204
Pleasant View B&B Inn, P.O. Box 211, Regent, 58650, 701-563-4542
Jacobson Mansion, Route 2, Box 27, Scranton, 58653, 701-275-8291
Triple T Ranch, Route 1, Box 93, Stanley, 58784, 701-628-2418
Tower City Inn B&B, 502 Church St., Tower City, 58071, 701-749-2660
Hagenhus B&B Inn, 406 W. 2nd St., Velva, 58790, 701-338-2714
Adama Fairview Bonanza B&B, 17170 82nd St. SE, Wahpeton, 58075, 701-274-8262
Eva's B&B, HCR's Box 10, Wing, 58494, 701-943-2461

Ohio

BUCYRUS

Hide Away B&B
1601 St. Rt. 4, 44820
419-562-3013
Steve & Debbie Miller
All year

$$ B&B
4 rooms, 1 pb
Visa, MC, *Rated*
C-yes/S-ltd/P-no/H-no

Full breakfast, snacks
Lunch, dinner w/res.
Sitting room, library
hot tubs, swimming pool
bike & hiking trails

*Elegant country manor nestled among majestic century-old oak trees. Gracious guestrooms, gourmet breakfasts, antiques, golf, jacuzzi, pool. **2nd night 25%, 3rd night 50% off***

CENTERVILLE

Yesterday B&B
39 S. Main St., 45458
513-433-0785 800-225-0485
Barbara & Tom Monnig
closed varied vacations

$$ B&B
3 rooms, 3 pb
Rated, •
C-ltd/S-ltd/P-no

Continental plus
Fruit bowl in parlor
Sitting room, porch
one suite available
vintage linen shop

Beautifully restored Victorian home in historic district. Short drive to downtown Dayton, Air Force Museum, King's Island Amusement Park, antique centers.

DANVILLE

White Oak Inn, The
29683 Walhonding Rd., 43014
614-599-6107
Ian & Yvonne Martin
All year

$$$ B&B
10 rooms, 10 pb
Visa, MC, *Rated*
C-ltd/S-no/P-no/H-no

Full breakfast (wkends)
Dinner with notice
Afternoon snacks, sherry
common room, porch
screen house, lawn games

Large country home nestled in wooded area. Outdoor enthusiasts' paradise. Comfortable antique decor; 3 fireplace rooms. Homemade breads, desserts. Near Amish country/antiques.

Yesterday B&B, Centerville, OH

DELLROY ────────────────────────────────

Candleglow B&B $$$ B&B   Full breakfast
4247 Roswell Rd., S.W., 44620   3 rooms, 3 pb   Aft. tea
216-735-2407   C-ltd/S-no/P-no/H-no   Snacks
Audrey Genova   sitting room
All year   library

Spacious Century house furnished in comfortable, 18th century furnishings. Close to Atwood Lake. Swimming, boating, tennis, golf available.

DOVER ─────────────────────────────────

Mowrey's Welcome Home $$ B&B   Continental plus
4489 Dover-Zoar Rd. NE,   3 rooms, 1 pb   Library, grand piano
Dover-Zoar Rd., 44622   C-ltd/S-ltd/P-no/H-no   123 species of native
216-343-4690   trees on 28 acres
Paul & Lola Mowrey
All year

Retired-teacher hosts welcome you. Enjoy solitude, porches, views, fireplaces, antiques. Near museums, historic villages, interesting shops, large Amish settlement.

KINSMAN ───────────────────────────────

Hidden Hollow B&B $ B&B   Full breakfast
9340 State Route 5 NE, 44428 4 rooms, 3 pb   Comp. wine, eve. snacks
216-876-8686   C-yes/S-yes/P-ask/H-no   Sitting room
Bob & Rita White   large balcony
All year   swimming pool

Secluded and lovely setting. We are perched on a hillside overlooking a scenic valley. Breakfast by the pool or on the balcony overlooking Hidden Hollow. Gourmet snacks.

MOUNT VERNON ──────────────────────────

Russell-Cooper House, The $$$ B&B   Full breakfast
115 E. Gambier St., 43050   6 rooms, 6 pb   Comp. wine, tea, soda
614-397-8638   *Rated*, •   Tea room for party/mtgs.
Maureen & Tim Tyler   C-ltd/S-ltd/P-no/H-no   porch, museum & shop
All year   recreational assistance

Victorian elegance abounds, restored Gothic mansion! Antiques, memorabilia, delightful breakfasts. Ohio's colonial city. Special weekends w/dinner. **10% off 2 cons. nites, Ltd**

OLD WASHINGTON ────────────────────────

Zane Trace B&B $ B&B   Continental breakfast
P.O. Box 115, 43768   4 rooms   Refrigerator availabe
225 Old National Rd.   *Rated*   Sitting room
614-489-5970 301-757-4262   C-ltd/S-yes/P-no/H-ltd   heated swimming pool
Ruth & Max Wilson   picnics
May–October

On historic national trail, this 1859 Victorian brick home has charm a plenty. Near Zane Grey Museum. **3rd night 50% off; 10% off for seniors- every day**

PAINESVILLE ───────────────────────────

Rider's 1812 Inn $$ B&B   Full breakfast
792 Mentor Ave., 44077   10 rooms, 8 pb   Restaurant, bar, pub
216-942-2742   Visa, MC, AmEx, *Rated*, Sitting room, library
Elaine Crane, Gary Herman   •   English pub games, bikes
All year   C-yes/S-ltd/P-ltd/H-no   nearby golf, Lake Erie
                             Spanish

Living history—authentic 1812 stagecoach inn. Breakfast in bed, antiques, A/C in all rms. We welcome you; come plan explorations of Ohio Western Reserve. **3rd night 50%, ltd.**

PICKERINGTON

Central House B&B
27 W. Columbus St., Old Village
Area, 43147
614-837-0932
Judy & Rob Wagley
All year

$$ B&B
4 rooms, 4 pb
C-ltd/S-no/P-no/H-ltd

Full breakfast
Comp. wine, aftn. tea
Sitting room
library, herb gardens
tennis courts nearby

Total restoration of 1860 small-town hotel. Redecorated w/country antiques, Victorian ambiance. Many unique shops in historic village by Columbus. Natural wholefood cooking.

POLAND

Inn At The Green
500 S. Main St., Youngstown,
44514
216-757-4688
Ginny & Steve Meloy
All year

$$ B&B
5 rooms, 4 pb
Visa, MC, *Rated*, •
C-ltd/S-no/P-no/H-no

Continental breakfast
Comp. wine
Oriental rugs, deck
patio, antiques, garden
Sitting rm., fireplaces

Authentically restored Victorian townhouse in preserved Western Reserve village near Youngstown. Convenient to Turnpike and I-80. **3rd night 50%**

SANDUSKY

Wagner's 1844 Inn
230 E. Washington St., 44870
419-626-1726
Walt & Barb Wagner
All year

$$ B&B
3 rooms, 3 pb
Visa, MC, *Rated*, •
C-ltd/S-ltd/P-no/H-no

Continental plus
Comp. wine, chocolates
Billard room with TV
air-conditioning

Elegantly restored Victorian home. Listed on National Register of Historic Places. Near Lake Erie attractions. Air-conditioned rooms. **50% off 2nd night, Nov.-Apr.**

ZOAR

Cobbler Shop B&B Inn
P.O. Box 650, 44697
House #22, Corner of 2nd &
Main Sts.
216-874-2600
Sandy Worley
All year

$$ B&B
4 rooms, 2 pb
Visa, MC, AmEx, •
C-ltd/S-ltd/P-no/H-no

Full breakfast
Comp. wine, snacks, tea
Sitting room

Original structure in historic village, furnished in 18th- and 19th-century antiques; close to local museum and a number of charming shops. **25% off 4th. night**

Inn at Cowger House, The
#9 Fourth St., Box 527, 44697
216-874-3542
Ed/Mary Cowger
All year

$$ B&B
3 rooms, 3 pb
Rated, •
C-ltd/S-yes/P-no/H-no

Full country breakfast
Lunch & dinner by rsvp.
Entertainment
honeymoon suite with
fireplace & jacuzzi

A little bit of Williamsburg. 1817 log cabin with 2-acre flower garden maintained by the Ohio Historic Society.

More Inns . . .

Portage House, 601 Copley Rd., Akron, 44320, 216-535-1952
Frederick Fitting House, 72 Fitting Ave., Bellville, 44813, 419-886-2863
Rockledge Manor, Route 3, Possum Run Rd., Bellville, 44813, 419-892-3329
McNutt Farm II/Outdoorsman, 6120 Cutler Lake Rd., Blue Rock, 43720, 614-674-4555
Elegant Inn B&B, The, 215 Walnut St., Bryan, 43506, 419-636-2873
Charm Countryview Inn, The, P.O. Box 100, Charm, 44617, 216-893-3003
Chillicothe B&B, 202 S. Paint St., Chillicothe, 45601, 614-772-6848
Old McDill-Anderson Place, 3656 Polk Hollow Rd., Chillicothe, 45601, 614-774-1770

Prospect Hill B&B, 408 Boal St., Cincinnati, 45210, 513-421-4408
Castle Inn, 610 S. Court St., Circleville, 43113, 614-477-3986
Glidden House, 1901 Ford Dr., Cleveland, 44106, 216-231-8900
Tudor House, P.O. Box 18590, Cleveland, 44118, 216-321-3213
Roscoe Village Inn, 200 N. Whiteman St., Coshocton, 43812
50 Lincoln, 50 E. Lincoln St., Columbus, 43215, 614-291-5056
Slavka's B&B, 180 Reinhard Ave., Columbus, 43206, 614-443-6076
Victorian B&B, 78 Smith Place, Columbus, 43201, 614-299-1656
1890 B&B, 663 N. Whitewoman St., Coshocton, 43812, 614-622-1890
Studio 12 B&B, 2850 Bailey Rd., Cuyahoga Falls, 44221
Prices' Steamboat House, 6 Josie St., Dayton, 45403, 513-223-2444
Aunt Bee's Bed & Breakfast, 5538 S. Section Line Rd, Delaware, 43015, 614-881-4412
Camelot at Heater's Run, 676 Taggart Rd., Delaware, 43015
Dripping Rock Farm, 4247 Roswell Rd. SW, Dellroy, 44620, 216-735-2987
Pleasant Journey Inn, 4247 Roswell Rd. SW, Dellroy, 44620, 216-735-2987
Whispering Pines B&B, P.O. Box 340, Dellroy, 44620, 216-735-2824
Hill View Acres B&B, 7320 Old Town Rd., East Fultonham, 43735, 614-849-2728
Otto Court B&B, 5653 Lake Rd., Geneva-On-The-Lake, 44041, 216-466-8668
Buxton Inn, 313 E. Broadway, Granville, 43023
Granville Inn, 314 E. Broadway, Granville, 43023, 614-587-3333
Mertz Place, The, 240 Mirabeau St., Greenfield, 45123, 513-981-2613
Candle Wick B&B, 245 E. Main St., Hillsboro, 45133, 513-393-2743
Chanticleer B&B, The, 11885 E. Rt. 50, Hillsboro, 45133, 513-365-1308
Beach House, 213 Kiwanis Ave., Huron, 44839, 419-433-5839
Captain Montague's B&B, 229 Center St., Huron, 44839, 419-433-4756
Beatty House, S. Shore Dr., Kelley's Island, 43438, 419-746-2379
Cricket Lodge B&B, Lakeshore Dr., Kelley's Island, 43438, 419-746-2263
Poor Richards Inn, 317 Maple, Lakeside, 43440
Quiet Country B&B, 14758 TWP Rd. 453, Lakeville, 44638, 216-378-3882
Summer House, The, 16934 Edgewater Dr., Lakewood, 44107, 216-226-6934
Golden Lamb, 27 S. Broadway, Lebanon, 45036
Grandma Betty's B&B, 35226 Rte 78, Lewisville, 43754
White Fence Inn, 8842 Denmanu Rd., Lexington, 44904, 419-884-2356
Bells, Located in downtown, Logan, 43138, 614-385-4384
Deep Woods Cabin B&B, Logan, 43133, 614-332-6084
Inn at Cedar Falls, The, 21190 State Rt. 374, Logan, 43138, 614-385-7489
Log Cabin, 7657 TWP Rd. 234, Logan, 43138, 614-385-8363
Pines, Logan, 43133, 614-385-7012
Blackfork Inn, 303 N. Water St., Loudonville, 44842, 419-994-3252
Pleasant Valley Lodge, 1983 Pleasant Valley Rd, Lucas, 44843, 419-892-2443
Old Stone House Inn, 133 Clemons St., Marblehead, 43440, 419-798-5922
Clair E, 127 Ohio St., Marietta, 45750, 614-374-2233
Folger's Bantam Farm B&B, Route 6, Mitchell Ln., Marietta, 45750, 614-374-6919
House Of Seven Porches,The, 331 - 5th St., Marietta, 45750, 614-373-1767
True Brook Inn, 9637 State Rt. 534, Mesopotamia, 44439, 800-832-8690
Coach House Inn B&B, The, 304 St. Rt. 113 W., Milan, 44846, 419-499-2435
Adams Street B&B, 175 W. Adams St., Millersburg, 44654, 216-674-0766
Inn at Honey Run, The, 6920 Country Rd. #203, Millersburg, 44654, 216-674-0011
Oak Hill B&B, 16720 Park Rd., Mount Vernon, 43050, 614-393-2912
Wind's Way B&B, 3851 Edwards Rd., Newtown, 45244, 513-561-1933
St. George House, 33941 Lorain Rd., North Ridgeville, 44039, 216-327-9354
Bayberry Inn B&B, 25675 St., Route 41 N., Peebles, 45660, 513-587-2221
Centennial House, 5995 Center St., Box 67, Peninsula, 44264, 216-657-2506
Peninsula B&B, 5964 Center St., Peninsula, 44264
Pickwinn B&B Guesthouse, 707 N. Downing St., Piqua, 45356, 513-773-8877
Old Island House Inn, 102 Madison St., Port Clinton, 43452, 419-734-2166
Buckeye B&B, P.O. Box 130, Powell, 43065, 614-548-4555
Arlington House, The, P.O. Box 395, Put-In-Bay, 43456
Fether B&B, 1539 Langram Rd., Put-In-Bay, 43456, 419-285-5511
Vineyard, The, P.O. Box 283, Put-In-Bay, 43456
Baird House, The, 201 N. 2nd. St., Ripley, 45167, 513-392-4918
Inn at Brandywine Falls, 8230 Brandywine Rd., Sagamore Hills, 44067
Big Oak, 2501 S. Campbell St., Sandusky, 44870
Bogart's Corner B&B, 1403 E. Bogart Rd., Sandusky, 44870, 419-627-2707
Pipe Creek B&B, 2719 Columbus Ave., Sandusky, 44870, 419-626-2067
Red Gables, The, 421 Wayne St., Sandusky, 44870, 419-625-1189
Sanduskian, The, 232 Jackson St., Sandusky, 44870, 419-626-6688
Birch Way Villa, 111 White Birch Way, South Amherst, 44001, 216-986-2090
3 B's Bed-n-Breakfast, 103 E. Race St., Spring Valley, 45370, 513-862-4278
Zelkova Inn, 2348 S. County Rd. #19, Tiffin, 44883, 419-447-4043
Willowtree Inn, 1900 W. State Route 571, Tipp City, 45371, 513-667-2957
Mansion View Inn B&B, 2035 Collingwood Ave., Toledo, 43620, 419-244-5676
Allen Villa B&B, 434 S. Market St., Troy, 45373, 513-335-1181
Governor's Lodge, SR 552, Waverly, 45690, 614-947-2266
Locust Lane Farm B&B, 5590 Kessler Cowlesvlle, West Milton, 45383, 513-698-4743
Murphin Ridge Inn, 750 Murphin Ridge Rd., West Union, 45693, 513-544-2263
Priscilla's B&B, 5 South West St., Westerville, 43081
Haueisens, The, 3317 Friendsville Rd., Wooster, 44691, 216-345-8105
Howey House, 340 N. Bever St., Wooster, 44691, 216-264-8231
Worthington Inn, 649 High St., Worthington, 43085, 614-885-2600
Haven @ 4th & Park, P.O. Box 467, Zoar, 44697, 216-874-4672
Weaving Haus, P.O. Box 431, Zoar, 44697, 216-874-3318

Oklahoma

EDMOND

Arcadian Inn, The
328 East First, 73034
405-348-6347 800-299-6347
Martha & Gary Hall
All year

$$ B&B
5 rooms, 5 pb
Visa, MC, AmEx
C-ltd/S-no/P-no/H-no

Full breakfast
Dinner by reservation
Sitting room
hot tubs

Luxurious, romantic setting, sumptious homemade breakfast. Intimate getaway for couples, perfect for the business traveler. Specializing in preferential treatment.

GUTHRIE

Harrison House
124 W. Harrison St., 73044
405-282-1000 800-375-1001
Claude & Jane Thomas
All year

$$ B&B
35 rooms, 35 pb
AmEx, Visa, MC, *Rated*,
•
C-yes/S-yes/P-ltd/H-yes

Continental plus
The Sand Plum restaurant
Sitting room, gift shops
TVs in parlors
games, elevators

35 room historic inn, nestled in the heart of a giant Historic District. Surrounded by live theater, museums, trolley rides and turn-of-the-century homes.

OKLAHOMA CITY

Grandison B&B Inn, The
1841 NW 15th St., 73106
405-521-0011
Claudia & Bob Wright
All year

$ B&B
5 rooms, 5 pb
Most CC
C-ltd/S-ltd/P-ltd/H-no

Full breakfast
Lunch by reservation
Dinner by reservation

Country Victorian in the heart of Oklahoma City. 1912 original Grapevine Motif stained glass. You'll feel like you've stepped back in time.

More Inns . . .

Clayton Country Inn, Route 1, Box 8, Clayton, 74536, 918-569-4165
Memories B&B, 120 West Queen, Coalgate, 74538, 405-927-3590
Goff House, The, 506 S. Evans Ave., El Reno, 73036, 405-262-9334

The Arcadian Inn, Edmond, OK

Guthrie B&B Association, 1016 W. Warner, Guthrie, 73044, 405-282-0012
Prairie View B&B, RR 2, Box 163 A, Guymon, 73942, 405-338-3760
Graham-Carroll House, 501 N. 16th St., Muskogee, 74401, 918-683-0100
Queen's House, 525 N. 16th St., Muskogee, 74401, 918-687-6767
Country House B&B, 10101 Oakview Rd., Oklahoma City, 73112, 405-840-3157
Flora's B&B, 2312 NW 46th, Oklahoma City, 73112, 405-840-3157
Newton & Joann, 23312 W.W. 46, Oklahoma City, 73112
Willow Way, 27 Oakwood Dr., Oklahoma City, 405-427-2133
Inn at Woodyard Farms, The, Rt. 2, Box 190, Pawhuska, 918-287-2699
Davarnathey Inn, 1001 W. Grand, Ponca City, 74601, 405-765-9922
Kerr Country Mansion, The, 1507 S. McKenna, Poteau, 74953, 918-647-8221
Jarrett Farm, Route 1, Box 1480, Ramona, 74061
Thomasville, 4115 N. Denver, Stillwater, 74075, 405-372-1203
Artesian B&B, 1022 W. 12th St., Sulphur, 73086, 405-622-5254
Drake House, 617 S. 93rd. E. Ave., Tulsa, 74112, 918-835-0752

Oregon

ASHLAND

Buckhorn Springs
2200 Buckhorn Springs, 97520
503-488-2200
B. & L. Sargent, C. Fowler
April—December

$$ B&B
13 rooms, 10 pb
Visa, MC, Disc., •
C-yes/S-no/P-no/H-yes

Full breakfast
Box lunches, dinner
Restaurant, appetizers
creek, hiking trails
gardens, birdwatching

Historic mineral springs resort 20 min. from Ashland's Shakespearean Festival. Newly renovated, period-decorated guestrooms & restaurant. Creekside cabins. **3rd night, 50%.**

Country Willows B&B
1313 Clay St., 97520
503-488-1590
Bill & Barbara Huntley
All year

$$$ B&B
5 rooms, 5 pb
Visa, MC, *Rated*, •
C-ltd

Full breakfast
Snacks
Sitting room
library
swimming pool

Quiet 5-acre hideaway only min. to Shakespearean Festival. Panoramic view of mountains. Hiking trails, rafting, fishing. Home-baked bread. **25% off Nov.1-May 15**

Cowslip's Belle B&B
159 N. Main St., 97520
503-488-2901 800-888-6819
Jon & Carmen Reinhardt
All year

$$ B&B
4 rooms, 4 pb
Visa, MC, *Rated*, •
C-ltd/S-no/P-no/H-no

Full breakfast
Comp. tea, coffee
Snacks, library
sitting room
airport pick-up

Come enjoy our scrumptious breakfast, cozy down comforters, lovely antiques, stained glass, quilts, teddy bears & choclate truffles. 1913 Craftsman home and carriage house.

Hersey House B&B
451 N. Main St., 97520
503-482-4563
Gail Orell, Lynn Savage
Late April—October

$$$ B&B
4 rooms, 4 pb
Visa, *Rated*, •
C-ltd/S-ltd/P-no/H-no

Full breakfast
Comp. tea, wine, snacks
Edible flowers w/meal
sitting rm, player piano
balcony, near theatres

Elegantly restored turn-of-the-century Victorian w/family antiques, china, silver, linens, queen beds, central A/C, lovely English garden. Hersey Bungalow sleeps 4-6.

ASHLAND ───

Iris Inn, The
59 Manzanita St., 97520
503-488-2286
Vicki Lamb
All year

$$ B&B
5 rooms, 5 pb
Visa, MC
C-ltd/S-no/P-no/H-no
Spanish

Full breakfast
Comp. wine
Lemonade, iced tea
sitting room
nightly turn-down

Lovely restored 1905 home; spacious, flower-filled yard for relaxing; 4 blocks to Oregon Shakespeare Festival; elegant & creative breakfasts.

Laurel Street Inn
174 N. Main St., 97520
503-488-2222
Marilyn Krichman
All year

$$ B&B
3 rooms, 3 pb
C-ltd/S-no/P-no/H-no

Full breakfast
Snacks
Comp. sherry
sitting room
library

Intimate retreat behind massive rock walls; lovely gardens, antiques, superb night's sleep & scrumptious breakfast. Real hospitality for Shakespeare lovers.

Shrew's House
570 Siskiyou Blvd., 97520
503-482-9214
Laurence & Laura Shrewsbury
All year

$$ B&B
3 rooms, 3 pb
Visa, MC, *Rated*
C-ltd/S-no/P-no/H-no

Full breakfast
Comp. coffee, tea
Sitting room, library
swimming pool
secluded porches

Luxurious comfort two blocks to town, featuring private suites with wet bars, refrigerators, jacuzzis, covered porches, swimming pool and health conscious breakfast.

Woods House B&B, The
333 N. Main St., 97520
503-488-1598 800-435-8260
Francoise A./Lester S. Roddy
All year

$$ B&B
6 rooms, 6 pb
Visa, MC, *Rated*, •
C-ltd/S-no/P-no/H-no

Full breakfast
Afternoon tea
Comp. sherry
sitting room

1908 Craftsman offers six sunny rooms, fine linens, antiques, roses, laces, full breakfasts, terraced gardens. Walk to theatres, shops, restaurants. **3rd night free, Ltd**

ASTORIA ───

Grandview B&B
1574 Grand Ave., 97103
503-325-5555 800-488-3250
Charleen Maxwell
All year

$ B&B
8 rooms, 6 pb
Most CC, *Rated*, •
C-ltd

Continental plus
Lunch & dinner for conf.
Sitting room
books in room, bicycles
liquor not permitted

Light, airy, cheerful Victorian close to superb Maritime Museum, Lightship, churches, golf, clam-digging, fishing, beaches and rivers. Sleeps 21. **2nd night free Nov 1-May 23**

Inn-Chanted B&B
P.O. Box 904, 97103
707-8th St.
503-325-5223
Richard & Dixie Swart
All year

$$$ B&B
2 rooms, 2 pb
Visa, MC, Disc.,*Rated*
C-yes/S-no/P-no/H-no

Full breakfast
Comp. refreshments
Decks overlooking river
near tennis, restaurants

1883 Victorian overlooking majestic Columbia River. Historic district, near antique shops, museums. Doll, train display. Choice of gourmet breakfasts. **Wedding/Anniv. special**

BANDON

Lighthouse Inn B&B
P.O. Box 24, 97411
650 Jetty Rd.
503-347-9316
Linda & Bruce Sisson
All year exc. July 4

$$$ B&B
4 rooms, 4 pb
Visa, MC, •
C-ltd/S-no/P-no/H-no

Continental plus
Comp. teas, hot cocoa
Sitting room, bicycles
hot tub in one room
on the beach

Located on the beach across from historic lighthouse. Panoramic views, quiet location. Walk to fine restaurants. A non-smoking inn. **2nd night 50% off, ltd.**

Sea Star Guesthouse
370 - 1st St., 97411
503-347-9632
David & Monica Jennings
All year

$$ B&B
4 rooms, 4 pb
Visa, MC, AmEx
C-yes/S-no/P-no/H-no

Full breakfast
Lunch, dinner
Comp. wine, laundry
restaurant
decks, skylights

Coastal getaway on harbor in "Oldtown" with bistro. Romantic retreat with European flair. Beachwalks, natural beauty, theater, galleries. **3rd night 50% off**

BEND

Farewell Bend B&B
29 N.W. Greeley, 97701
503-382-4374
Lorene Bateman
All year

$$ B&B
2 rooms, 2 pb
Rated, •
C-ltd/S-no/P-no/H-no

Full breakfast
Aftn. tea, comp. wine
Sitting room
library, deck
terry bath robes

Restored 70-year-old Dutch Colonial; gourmet breakfast and hand-made quilts. Skiing, fishing, golfing. Recreation center of Pacific NW. Near downtown Bend. **1 wk stay 10% off**

BROOKINGS

Chetco River Inn
21202 High Prairie Rd., 97415
503-469-8128 800-327-2688
Sandra Brugger
Exc. Thanksgiving & Xmas

$$$ B&B
3 rooms, 3 pb
Visa, MC, *Rated*, •
C-ltd/S-ltd/P-no/H-no

Full breakfast
Lunch, dinner with resv.
Beverages & cookies
Sitting room, library
games, hiking, river

Relax in peaceful seclusion of our private 35-acre forest, bordered on 3 sides by the Chetco River. Enjoy "Old World" hospitality & "New World" comfort. **3rd night 50% off**

Holmes Sea Cove B&B
17350 Holmes Dr., 97415
503-469-3025
Lorene & Jack Holmes
All year

$$$ B&B
3 rooms, 3 pb
Visa, MC, •
C-ltd/S-no/P-no/H-no

Continental plus
Tea, coffee, cocoa
Trail to private park
creek and beach
airport pickup

Delightful seacoast hideaway. Three cozy rooms with spectacular ocean views, private entrances, baths. Cottage available. Tasty continental plus breakfast served in rooms.

EUGENE

Atherton Place B&B
690 W. Broadway, 97402
503-683-2674
Marne Krozek
All year

$$ B&B
3 rooms, 2 pb
•
C-ltd/S-no/P-no/H-no

Full breakfast
Snacks
Sitting room
library, ceiling fans
bicycles, cable TV

Spacious 1928 Dutch Colonial home. Library, sun porch, upstairs sitting room. Centrally located to downtown, U of O. Three course breakfast. **10% off 5+ nights**

EUGENE

Duckworth B&B Inn
987 E. 19th Ave., 97403
503-686-2451
Peggy & Fred Ward
All year

$$ B&B
3 rooms, 1 pb
Rated, •
C-ltd/S-no/P-no/H-no

Full breakfast
Afternoon tea
Sitting rm, player piano
bicycles, 600+ videos
TV & VCR in rms. library

English-style 1926 home, decorated in English and American antiques. Gardens with willow furniture and stone paths. A stroll from Univ. of Oregon. **3rd night 20% disc't.**

Kjaer's House in the Woods
814 Lorane Hwy, 97405
503-343-3234
George & Eunice Kjaer
All year exc. Christmas

$$ B&B
2 rooms, 1 pb
Rated, •
C-yes/S-no/P-no/H-no
German

Full breakfast
Afternoon tea, snacks
Sitting room, library

1910 Craftsman home in parklike setting among tall firs. Furnished with antiques and provides urban convenience with suburban tranquillity. **3rd night 50% off.**

Maryellen's Guest House
1583 Fircrest, 97403
503-342-7375
Maryellen & Bob Larson
All year

$$ B&B
2 rooms, 2 pb
Visa, MC, *Rated*, •
C-ltd/S-ltd/P-no/H-no

Full breakfast
Snacks
Bicycles, hot tubs
swimming pool
sitting room

Our guests are pampered! The suites are private and spacious, one with double showers and deep soaking tub. Outdoors enjoy swimming pool & hot tub jacuzzi. **6th night free**

Oval Door, The
988 Lawrence at 10th, 97401
503-683-3160 FAX:485-5339
Judith McLaine
All year

$$ B&B
4 rooms, 4 pb
Visa, MC, *Rated*, •
C-ltd/S-yes/P-ask/H-no
French, German, Portug.

Full gourmet breakfast
Full breakfast (Sunday)
Dinner by prior res.
comp. wine, sitting room
library, bicycles

An elegant home in a quiet neighborhood, only blocks from city's center. Whirlpool bath; continental plus breakfast; congenial hosts. **3rd night 50%.**

FLORENCE

Johnson House
P.O. Box 1892, 97439
216 Maple St.
503-997-8000
Jayne & Ronald Fraese
All year

$ B&B
6 rooms, 3 pb
Visa, MC, *Rated*, •
C-ltd/S-no/P-no/H-no
French, Swedish

Full breakfast
Afternoon tea
sitting room

Beautifully restored 1892 Victorian; down comforters; genuine antiques throughout; turn-of-the-century charm; in Old Town one block from bayfront.

GOLD BEACH

Heather House B&B
190 11th St., 97444
503-247-2074
Bob & Katy Cooper
All year

$$ B&B
4 rooms, 2 pb
Visa, MC, •
C-ltd/S-no/P-no/H-no

Full breakfast
Afternoon tea
Sitting room, library
airport pick-up avail.
by arrangement

Enjoy the exceptional climate of Oregon's Southern Coast in this lovely house that offers breathtaking ocean views from most rooms. **3rd night 50% off.**

GOLD BEACH ——————————————

Tu Tu Tun Lodge, The
96550 N. Bank Rogue, 97444
503-247-6664
Dirk & Laurie Van Zante
May–October

$$$ EP
18 rooms, 18 pb
Visa, MC, *Rated*, •
C-yes/S-yes/P-yes/H-yes

Full breakfast $
Lunch, dinner, bar
Library, sitting room
swimming pool, games
2 outdoor hot tubs

Secluded lodge nestled on banks of the Rogue River with "Country Inn" hospitality, gourmet meals, white water excursions, guided fishing. Remodeled rms, player piano, fireplace.

GOVERNMENT CAMP ——————————————

Falcon's Crest Inn
P.O. Box 185, 97028
87287 Gov't Camp Loop Hwy
503-272-3403 800-624-7384
Robert & Melody Johnson
All year

$$$ B&B
5 rooms, 5 pb
Most CC, *Rated*, •
C-ltd/S-no/P-no/H-no

Full breakfast
Restaurant, lunch
Dinner, snacks
beer & wine
hot tubs, sauna

Elegance, Mt. Hood style. In the heart of Mt. Hood Nat'l. Forest. Downhill & cross-country skiing. Gourmet restaurant on premises. Year round recreation. **Ski packages.**

GRANTS PASS ——————————————

AHLF House B&B
762 NW 6th St., 97526
503-474-1374
Ken & Cathy Neuschafer
All year

$$ B&B
4 rooms, 4 pb
Rated
C-ltd/S-no/P-no/H-no

Full breakfast
Eve. dessert & beverage
Sitting room
bicycles
amid lawns and trees

1902 Queen Anne Victorian furnished with fine collectibles and antiques is a step back in time. Close to town and Rogue River recreation trips. **3rd night 50% off**

Lawnridge House B&B
1304 NW Lawnridge, 97526
503-476-8518
Barbara Head
All year

$ B&B
2 rooms, 2 pb
Rated, •
C-ltd/S-ltd/Spanish, some
French

Full breakfast
Refrigerator, comp. wine
Filled bookshelves
secluded deck & porch
Alfresco dining

1909 historic home w/antique furnishings, canopy beds, fireplace, beamed ceilings, dark wood floors, oriental rugs, color cable TV, phone, A/C. **3rd night free Nov-March, ltd**

Martha's B&B Inn
764 N.W. 4th St., 97526
503-476-4330
Glenn & Evelyn Hawkins
All year

$$ B&B
3 rooms, 3 pb
Visa, MC, •

Full breakfast
Afternoon tea, snacks
Sitting room, library

Victorian farmhouse, large front porch with antiques, wicker rockers. In historic district. Herb garden. Gourmet breakfast. Close to everything. **3rd night, 50% off.**

Riverbanks Inn B&B
8401 Riverbanks Rd., 97527
503-479-1118
Myrtle Franklin
Apr. 1–Oct. 31

$$$ B&B
5 rooms, 3 pb
Visa, MC, *Rated*, •
C-yes/S-no/P-no/H-no
some Spanish

Full breakfast
Ponds, oriental garden
massage, artists studio
Zen House, jacuzzi suite

Woods; paths to the Rogue River; ponds with wild ducks and bass. A restful retreat; fanciful rooms such as Casablanca. Also a river cottage and fishing lodge. **3rd nite 50%**

JACKONVILLE ──────────────────────────────────

Jacksonville Inn
P.O. Box 359, 97530
175 E. California St.
503-899-1900
Jerry & Linda Evans
All year

$$$ B&B
9 rooms, 9 pb
Most CC, *Rated*, •
C-yes/S-yes/P-ltd/H-no
Greek

Full breakfast
Restaurant, bar service
Lunch, dinner, snacks
luxurious cottage with
many amenities avail.

Built in 1863 and located in center of historic village. 8 rooms and one cottage. Private baths and award-winning restaurant with over 700 wines. Steam shower available.

Tauvelle House B&B, The
P.O. Box 1891, 97530
455 N. Oregon
503-899-8938 800-846-8422
John & Patricia Valleta
March–December

$$ B&B
5 rooms, 5 pb
Visa, MC, *Rated*
S-no

Full breakfast
Comp. wine
Formal parlor dinning rm
TV room, library
swiming pool, hot tub

*Walk to Britt Festival, historic Jacksonville, Victorian Christmas. Enjoy Shakespeare Festival, whitewater rafting and snow skiing. Experience elegance! **Jan.-March 10% off***

MYRTLE CREEK ──────────────────────────────────

Sonka's Sheep Station Inn
901 NW Chadwick Ln., 97457
503-863-5168
Louis & Evelyn Sonka
All year

$$ B&B
4 rooms, 2 pb
C-yes/S-no/P-no/H-no

Full breakfast
Comp. tea, cookies
Sitting room
bicycles

Working sheep ranch; house furnished in sheep country motif and antiques. Quiet setting along river. Guests may partake of ranch activities as hosts and guests agree.

NEWBERG ──────────────────────────────────

Secluded B&B
19719 NE Williamson Rd., 97132
503-538-2635
Del & Durell Belanger
All year

$ B&B
2 rooms, 1 pb
Rated
C-yes/S-no/P-no/H-no

Full gourmet breakfast
Comp. tea & coffee
Living room w/fireplace
library, A/C, VCR
hiking trails

Located in the heart of wine country! Antiques in every room; gourmet breakfast served; large library. Hiking trails and seasonal wildlife. Air-conditioned home.

Spring Creek Llama Ranch
14700 NE Spring Ck. Ln., 97132
503-538-5717
Dave & Melinda Van Bossuyt
All year

$ B&B
2 rooms, 2 pb
Rated, •
C-yes/S-no/P-no/H-no
Spanish

Full breakfast
Snacks
Library
Llama farm experience

*Spacious and contemporary. Comfortable rooms. Completely secluded in a picturesque and peaceful setting of forest and pasture. Trails, friendly 11amas. **3+ nights 20% off, ltd***

NEWPORT ──────────────────────────────────

Ocean House B&B
4920 NW Woody Way, 97365
800-562-2632 503-265-7779
Bob & Bette Garrard
All year

$$ B&B
4 rooms, 4 pb
Visa, MC
C-ltd/S-no/P-no/H-no

Full breakfast
Snacks, coffee, tea
Sitting room, library
beach trail, garden
gallery; golf nearby

*Near the center of coastal activities & fun. Large comfortable home w/beautiful surroundings overlooks gardens & surf. Near Yaquina Head Lt. House. **Special winter rates, Ask.***

OREGON CITY

Jagger House B&B
512 Sixth St., 97045
503-657-7820
Claire Met
All year

$$ B&B
3 rooms, 1 pb
Visa, MC, •
C-ltd/S-no/P-no/H-no

Full breakfast
Snacks
Sitting room
gazebo in garden
close to 5 museums

Cozy country comfort in 1880 house at "end of Oregon Trail." Antiques, reproductions. Private. Innkeeper is a history/old house buff. **7th night free**

OTIS

Salmon River B&B
5622 Salmon River Hwy, Near
Lincoln City, 97368
503-994-2639
Marvin & Pawnee Pegg
All year exc. holidays

$ B&B
4 rooms, 2 pb
Visa, MC, Disc., •
C-yes/S-no/P-no/H-no

Full breakfast
Private entry
sitting room, fireplace

Near ocean and 5-mile lake; warm winters, cool summers; huckleberry hotcakes and home-made fruit syrups; quiet wooded setting. **3rd night 50% off Oct.-April**

PORT ORFORD

Home by the Sea B&B
P.O. Box 606, 97465
444 Jackson St.
503-332-2855
Alan & Brenda Mitchell
All year, FAX: 332-7585

$$ B&B
2 rooms, 2 pb
Visa, MC, personal cks.
C-ltd/S-no/P-no/H-no
Macintosh

Full breakfast
Comp. tea
Refrigerator, laundry
beach access, ocean view
cable TV, phones, spa

Enjoy dramatic views of the ocean and miles of unspoiled public beaches in this quiet fishing village. Tennis and golf nearby.

PORTLAND

General Hooker's B&B
125 SW Hooker St., 97201
503-222-4435 800-745-4135
Lori Hall
FAX:295-6727, All year

$$ B&B
4 rooms, 2 pb
Visa, MC, AmEx, *Rated*,
•
C-ltd/S-no/P-no/H-no

Continental plus
Comp. wine & beverages
Sitting room, library
A/C, roof deck
cable TV & VCR in rooms

Casually elegant Victorian in quiet, historic neighborhood within walking distance of City Center. Host is knowledgeable 4th generation Portlander. Resident Abyssinian cat.

John Palmer House B&B Inn
4314 N. Mississippi Ave, 97217
503-284-5893
Mary, Richard & David Sauter
All year

$ B&B
4 rooms, 1 pb
Visa, MC, *Rated*, •
C-ltd/S-no/P-no/H-no
Sign Language

Full breakfast
Dinner (Tue-Sat)
Aft. tea by reservation
bathrobes, massages
bicycles, library, piano

High tea, gourmet summer breakfasts on the veranda. Flowers, wines, beer, chocolates. Victorian sleepwear may be rented for the stay. **3+ nights-50% off horse & carriage tours**

MacMaster House
1041 SW Vista Ave., 97205
503-223-7362
Cecilia Murphy
All year

$$$ B&B
7 rooms, 2 pb
Visa, MC, AmEx
C-ltd/S-no/P-no/H-no

Very full breakfast
Comp. beverages
Sitting room
library
tennis nearby

Historic Colonial mansion near Washington Park. Convenient to rose gardens, cafes, galleries, boutiques. Lovely neighborhood for walking and jogging. Fireplace rooms.

PORTLAND ─────────────────────────────────────

Portland Guest House $$ B&B   Full breakfast
1720 N.E. 15th Ave., 97212   7 rooms, 5 pb   Comp. beverages
503-282-1402   Visa, MC, AmEx, *Rated*, Room phones, antiques
Susan Gisvold   •   jogging routes
All year   C-yes/S-no/P-no   bus & light rail tickets

1890 Victorian in historic Irvington. All rooms have vintage linens & great beds. Luscious breakfasts. Closest B&B to Convention Center, Coliseum, Lloyd Center Mall.

ROSEBURG ─────────────────────────────────────

House of Hunter $$ B&B   Full breakfast
813 S.E. Kane St., 97470   5 rooms, 3 pb   Comp. bev, VCR, TV
503-672-2335   Visa, MC, *Rated*   Phone, fridge, patio
Walt & Jean Hunter   C-ltd/S-no/P-no/H-no   near golf & downtow
All year   laundry facil., A/C

Restored 2-story historic home, both antiques & modern. Awaken to coffee outside door, full gourmet breakfast in dining room. Enjoy grandroom w/fireplace. **5+ nights 10% off**

SANDLAKE ─────────────────────────────────────

Sandlake Country Inn $$ B&B   Full breakfast
8505 Galloway Rd., 97112   4 rooms, 3 pb   Comp. spiced cider
503-965-6745   Visa, MC, *Rated*, •   Sitting room, robes
Margo & Charles Underwood   C-ltd/S-no/P-no/H-yes   garden spa, hammock
All year   rm w/jacuzzi, firepl, pb

Romantic, peaceful hideaway especially designed for making marriage memories. Flowers, bikes, antiques. Coastal forest setting. Gourmet breakfasts served in your room or deck.

SEAL ROCK ─────────────────────────────────────

Blackberry Inn B&B $$ B&B   Full breakfast
P.O. Box 188, 97376   4 rooms, 4 pb   Comp. tea & cookies
6575 Hwy 101   Visa, MC, *Rated*, •   Sitting room, library
503-563-2259   C-ltd/S-no/P-no/H-no   color TV, victrola
Barbara Tarter   nature trail, crabbing
Exc. Nov 15–Dec

Pamper yourself on the Oregon Coast. Fluffy comforters, antiques, hot tub, quiet beach, gourmet breakfast, farm critters, nature trails.

TILLAMOOK ─────────────────────────────────────

Blue Haven Inn $$ B&B   Full breakfast
3025 Gienger Rd., 97141   3 rooms, 1 pb   Dinner
503-842-2265   •   Sitting room
Joy & Ray Still   C-ltd/S-no/P-no/H-no   library
All year

Peaceful, quiet country setting surrounded by tall evergreens; gourmet breakfast served in formal dining room. Furnished with antiques (which are also for sale).

WALLOWA LAKE ─────────────────────────────────────

Tamarack Pines Inn $$ B&B   Full breakfast
60073 Wallowa Lake Hwy.,   5 rooms, 5 pb   Snacks
97846   Visa, MC, *Rated*, •   Sitting room
503-432-2920   C-ltd/S-no/P-no/H-no   near backpacking, horses
Robert & Linda Claassen   near Wallowa Lake
All year

Charming mountain home in a relaxing forest setting including trout pond, dramatic view of Mt. Howard and Wallowa Lake nearby.

More Inns . . .

Farm "Mini Barn" House, 7070 Springhill Dr. N., Albany, 97321, 503-928-9089
Arden Forest Inn, 261 W. Hersey, Ashland, 97520, 503-488-1496
Ashland Colony Inn, 725 Terra, Ashland, 97520, 503-482-2668
Ashland Guest Villa, 634 Iowa St., Ashland, 97520, 503-488-1508
Ashland Valley Inn, 1193 Siskiyou Blvd., Ashland, 97520, 503-482-2641
Ashland's Main St. Inn, 142 W. Main St., Ashland, 97520, 503-488-0969
Asland's Knight's Inn, 2359 Hwy. 66, Ashland, 97520, 503-482-5111
Auburn Street Cottage, 549 Auburn St., Ashland, 97520, 503-482-3004
Bayberry Inn, 483 N. Main St., Ashland, 97520, 503-482-1252
Best Western Bard's Inn, 132 N. Main St., Ashland, 97520, 503-482-0049
Bluebell House, 325 N. Main St., Ashland, 97520
Cedarwood Inn of Ashland, 1801 Siskiyou Blvd., Ashland, 97520, 503-488-2000
Chanticleer Inn, 120 Gresham St., Ashland, 97520, 503-482-1919
Columbia Hotel, 262 1/2 E. Main, Ashland, 97520, 503-482-3726
Country Walrus Inn, 2785 E. Main St., Ashland, 97520, 503-488-1134
Edinburgh Lodge B&B, 586 E. Main St., Ashland, 97520, 503-488-1050
Fadden's Inn, 326 Main St., Ashland, 97520, 503-488-0025
Fiddle Family Inn, 111 B St., Ashland, 97520
Fox House Inn, 269 "B" St., Ashland, 97520, 503-488-1055
Hillside Inn, 1520 Siskiyou Blvd., Ashland, 97520, 503-482-2626
Lithia Rose Lodging, 163 Granite St., Ashland, 97520, 503-482-1882
McCall House, 153 Oak St., Ashland, 97520, 503-482-9296
Morical House, 668 N. Main St., Ashland, 97520, 503-482-2254
Mt. Ashland Inn, 550 Mt. Ashland Rd., Ashland, 97520, 503-482-8707
Neil Creek House, 341 Mowetza Dr., Ashland, 97520, 503-482-1334
Oak Hill Country B&B, 2190 Siskiyou Blvd., Ashland, 97520, 503-482-1554
Oak Street Station B&B, 239 Oak St., Ashland, 97520, 503-482-1726
Parkside, 171 Granite St., Ashland, 97520, 503-482-2320
Queen Anne, 125 N. Main St., Ashland, 97520, 503-482-0220
Redwing B&B, 115 N. Main St., Ashland, 97520, 503-482-1807
Romeo Inn, 295 Idaho St., Ashland, 97520, 503-488-0884
Royal Carter House, 514 Siskiyou Blvd., Ashland, 97520
Shutes Lazy S, 200 Mowetza Dr., Ashland, 97520, 503-482-5498
Stone House, 80 Hargadine St., Ashland, 97520, 503-482-9233
Studio's Inn, The, 550 E. Main, Ashland, 97520, 503-488-5882
Treon's Country Homestay, 1819 Colestin Rd., Ashland, 97520, 503-482-0746
Wimer Street Inn, 75 Wimer St., Ashland, 97520, 503-488-2319
Winchester Inn, 35 S. 2nd St., Ashland, 97520, 503-488-1113
Astoria Inn B&B, 3391 Irving Ave., Astoria, 97103
Columbia River Inn B&B, 1681 Franklin Ave., Astoria, 97103, 503-325-5044
Powder River B&B, HCR 87, Box 500, Baker, 97814, 503-523-7143
Cliff Harbor Guest House, P.O. Box 769, Bandon, 97411, 503-347-3956
Floras Lake House, P.O. Box 1591, Bandon, 97411, 503-347-9205
Lighthouse Inn B&B, P.O. Box 24, Bandon, 97411, 503-347-9316
Seabird Inn, 3165 Beach Loop Dr., Bandon, 97411
Yankee Tinker B&B, The, 5480 SW 183rd Ave., Beaverton, 97007, 503-649-0932
Gazebo B&B, 21679 Obsidian Ave., Bend, 97702, 503-389-7202
Heidi Haus, 62227 Wallace Rd., Bend, 97701, 503-388-0850
House at Water's Edge, 36 NW Pinecrest Court, Bend, 97701, 503-382-1266
Lara House, 640 N.W. Congress, Bend, 97701, 503-388-4064
Mirror Pond House, 1054 NW Harmon Blvd., Bend, 97701, 503-389-1680
Sea Dreamer Inn, 15167 McVay Ln. Box 184, Brookings, 97415, 503-469-6629
Ward House B&B, 516 Redwood St., Box 86, Brookings, 97415, 503-469-5557
Cannon Beach Hotel, P.O. Box 943, Cannon Beach, 97110, 503-436-1392
Tern Inn B&B, 3663 S. Hemlock, Box 95, Cannon Beach, 97110, 503-436-1528
Inn at the Locks, P.O. Box 39, Cascade Locks, 97104, 702-374-8222
Oregon Caves Chateau, P.O. Box 128, Cave Junction, 97523, 503-592-3400
Hudson House, 37700 Hwy 101 S, Cloverdale, 97112, 503-392-3533
Sandlake Country Inn, 8585 Galloway Rd., Cloverdale, 97112, 503-965-6745
Wheeler's B&B, Box 8201, Coburg, 97401, 503-344-1366
Coos Bay Manor, 955 South Fifth St., Coos Bay, 97420, 503-269-1224
This Olde House B&B, 202 Alder St., Coos Bay, 97420, 503-267-5224
A B&B at Spark's Hearth, 2515 S.W. 45th, Corvallis, 97333
Abed & Breakfast at Sparks, 2515 SW 45th St., Corvallis, 97333, 503-757-7321
Huntington Manor, 3555 NW Harrison Blvd., Corvallis, 97330, 503-753-3735
Madison Inn B&B, 660 SW Madison Ave., Corvallis, 97333, 503-757-1274
Wedgwood Inn, 563 SW Jefferson Ave., Corvallis, 97333, 503-758-7377
Ivanoffs' Inn, 3101 Bennett Creek Rd., Cottage Grove, 97424
Lea House Inn, 433 Pacific Hwy., Cottage Grove, 97424, 503-942-0933
Channel House B&B, P.O. Box 56, Depoe Bay, 97341, 503-765-2140
Gracie's Landing, 235 S.E. Bay View Ave., Depoe Bay, 97341, 800-228-0448
McGillivray's Log Home B&B, 88680 Evers Rd., Elmira, 97437, 503-935-3564
Aristea's Guest House, 1546 Charnelton St., Eugene, 97401, 503-683-2062
B & G's B&B, 711 W. 11th Ave., Eugene, 97402, 503-343-5739
Backroads B&B, 85269 Lorane Hwy., Eugene, 97405, 503-485-0464
Campus Cottage B&B Inn, 1136 E. 19th Ave., Eugene, 97403, 503-342-5346
Chambers House B&B Inn, 1006 Taylor St., Eugene, 97402, 503-686-4242
Getty's Emerald Garden B&B, 640 Audel Ave., Eugene, 97404, 503-688-6344

Gile's Guest Haus, 690 W. Broadway, Eugene, 97402, 503-683-2674
Lorane Valley B&B, 86621 Lorane Hwy, Eugene, 97405, 503-686-0241
Guest House at Gardiner by, 401 Front St., Gardiner, 97441, 503-271-4005
Dragovich House, P.O. Box 261, Gates, 97346, 503-897-2157
Bien Venue B&B, 95629 Jerry Flat Rd., Gold Beach, 97444, 503-247-2335
Endicott Gardens, 95768 Jerry's Flat Rd., Gold Beach, 97444, 503-247-6513
Hig Seas Inn, 105 Walker St. Box 3, Gold Beach, 97441
Nicki's Country Place, 31780 Edson Creek, Gold Beach, 97444, 503-247-6037
Willowbrook Inn B&B, 628 Foots Creek Rd., Gold Hill, 97525, 503-582-0075
Glemens House B&B, 612 Northwest Third St., Grants Pass, 97526, 503-476-5564
Mt. Baldy B&B, 678 Troll View Rd., Grants Pass, 97527, 503-479-7998
Paradise Ranch Inn, 7000 Monument Dr., Grants Pass, 97526, 503-479-4333
Washington Inn, 1002 NW Washington Blvd, Grants Pass, 97526, 503-476-1131
Wilson House Inn, The, 746 N.W. Sixth St, Grants Pass, 97526, 503-479-4754
Birch Leaf Lodge, RR 1, Box 91, Halfway, 97834, 503-742-2990
Clear Creek Farm B&B, Route 1, Box 138, Halfway, 97834, 503-742-2238
Columbia Gorge Hotel, 4000 Westcliff Dr., Hood River, 97031, 503-386-5566
Columbia Gorge Hotel, 4000 Westcliff Dr., Hood River, 97031, 503-386-5566
Hackett House, 922 State St., Hood River, 97031, 503-386-1014
Lakecliff Estate B&B, P.O. Box 1220, Hood River, 97031, 503-386-5918
State Street Inn, B&B, 1005 State St., Hood River, 97031, 503-386-1899
Davidson House, 887 Monmouth St., Independence, 97351, 503-838-3280
Out of the Blue B&B, 386 Monmouth St., Independence, 97351, 503-838-3636
Livingston Mansion B&B Inn, Box 1476, Jacksonville, 97530, 503-899-7107
McCully House Inn, P.O. Box 13, Jacksonville, 97530, 503-899-1942
Old Stage Inn, The, 883 Old Stage Rd, Jacksonville, 97530, 800-US-STAGE
Orth House, 105 W Main St, Jacksonville, 97530, 503-899-1900
Reames House B&B, 540 E California St, Jacksonville, 97530, 503-899-1868
Touvelle House, The, P.O. Box 1891, Jacksonville, 97530, 503-899-8938
Bed, Bread & Trail, Route 1, Box 365, Joseph, 97846, 503-432-9765
Chandler's Bed, Bread, & T, Box 639, 700 E. Main, Joseph, 97846, 503-432-9765
Wallowa Lake Lodge, Joseph, 97846, 503-432-4082
Lands Inn B&B, Star Route 1, Kimberly, 97848, 503-934-2333
Klamath Manor B&B, 219 Pine St., Klamath Falls, 97601, 503-883-5459
Thompson's B&B By the Lake, 1420 Wild Plum Ct., Klamath Falls, 97601, 503-882-7938
Wasthaven Bed & Breakfast, 2059 Lakeshore Dr., Klamath Falls, 97601
Pitcher Inn B&B, 608 "N" Ave., La Grande, 97850, 503-963-9152
Stange Manor, 1612 Walnut, La Grande, 97850, 503-963-2400
Big Blue House B&B, 53223 Riverview Dr., La Pine, 97739, 503-536-3879
A Gran-Mother's Home, 12524 SW Bonnes Ferry, Lake Oswego, 97034, 505-244-4361
Marjon Bed & Breakfast Inn, 44975 Leaburg Dam Rd., Leaburg, 97489, 503-896-3145
Beach Retreat, 1736 N.W. 37th, Lincoln City, 97367
Palmer House B&B Inn, 646 NW Inlet, Lincoln City, 97367, 503-994-7932
Lakeside Cottage, 234 Pioneer S., Box 26, Lowell, 97452, 503-937-2443
Orchard View Inn, 16540 N.W. Orchard View, McMinnville, 97128, 503-472-0165
Steiger Haus B&B, 360 Wilson St., McMinnville, 97128, 503-472-0821
Youngberg Hill Farm B&B, 10660 Youngberg Hill Rd, McMinnville, 97128, 503-472-2727
Cedar Lodge Motor Inn, 518 N. Riverside, Medford, 97501, 503-773-7361
Nendels Inn, 2300 Crater Lake Hwy., Medford, 97504, 503-779-3141
Petera Ahn Reuthlinger, 7770 Griffin Creek Rd., Medford, 97501, 503-535-7423
Under the Greenwood Tree, 3045 Bellinger Ln., Medford, 97501, 503-776-0000
Waverly Cottage, 305 N. Grape, Medford, 503-779-4716
Morrison's Rogue River, 8500 Galice Rd., Merlin, 97532, 503-476-3825
Birch Tree Manor B&B, 615 S. Main St., Hwy 11, Milton—Freewater, 97862, 503-938-6455
Broetiea House, 3101 S.E. Courtney Rd., Milwaukie, 97222, 503-659-8860
Littlefield House, 401 N. Howard, Newberg, 97132, 503-538-9868
Owl's View B&B, 29585 NE Owls Ln., Newberg, 97132, 503-538-6498
Oar House, 520 SW 2nd St., Newport, 97365, 503-265-9571
Sylvia Beach Hotel, 267 N.W. Cliff St., Newport, 97365, 503-265-5428
Highlands B&B, 608 Ridge Rd., North Bend, 97459, 503-756-0300
Sherman House B&B, 2380 Sherman Ave., North Bend, 97459, 503-756-3496
Pringle House B&B, P.O. Box 578, Oakland, 97462, 503-459-5038
Sleepy Hollow B&B, 4320 Stearns Ln., Oakland, 97462, 503-459-3401
Three Capes B&B, 1685 Maxwell Mnt. Rd., Oceanside, 97134, 503-842-6126
Fellows House, 416 S. McLoughlin, Oregon City, 97045, 503-656-2089
Inn Of The Oregon Trail, 416 S. McLoughlin, Oregon City, 97045, 503-656-2089
Gwendolyn's B&B, 735 8th, P.O. Box 913, Port Orford, 97465, 503-332-4373
Petchekovitch and Son B&B, 106 W. 6th St., Port Orford, 97465, 503-332-9055
Allenhouse B&B, 2606 N.W. Lorejoy St., Portland, 97210, 503-227-6841
Cape Cod B&B, 5733 SW Dickinson St., Portland, 97219, 503-246-1839
Clinkerbrick House, 2311 N.E. Schuyler, Portland, 97212, 503-281-2533
Corbett House B&B, 7533 SW Corbett Ave., Portland, 97219, 503-245-2580
Heron Haus, 2545 NW Westover Rd., Portland, 97210, 503-274-1846
Lion & The Rose, The, 1810 N.E. 15th, Portland, 97212, 503-287-9245
Lombard Guest House, 2911 N. Russet, Portland, 97217
Mumford Manor, 1130 S.W. King, Portland, 97205
Baldwin Inn B&B, 126 W. First St., Prineville, 97754, 503-447-5758
Tennyson Manor, P.O. Box 825, Rogue River, 97537, 503-582-2790
Umpqua House, The, 7338 Oakhill Rd, Roseburg, 97470, 503-459-4700
Woods B&B, The, 428 Oakview Dr., Roseburg, 97470, 503-672-2927
Harbison House, 1845 Commercial S.E., Salem, 97302, 503-581-8118
State House B&B, 2146 State St., Salem, 97301, 503-588-1340

Auberge des Fleurs, 39391 SE Lusted Rd., Sandy, 97055, 503-663-9449
Beachwood, 671 Beach Dr., Seaside, 97138, 503-738-9585
Boarding House, 208 N. Holladay Dr., Seaside, 97138, 503-738-9055
Chocolates for Breakfast, 606 N. Holiday, Seaside, 97138, 503-738-3622
Custer House, 811 First Ave., Seaside, 97138, 503-738-7825
Gilbert House, 341 Beach Dr., Seaside, 97138, 503-738-9770
Hartman's Hearth, 208 N. Holladay Dr., Seaside, 97138, 503-738-9055
Rita Mae's B&B, 486 Necanicum Dr., Seaside, 97138, 503-738-8800
Riverside Inn B&B, 430 S. Holladay Dr., Seaside, 97138, 503-738-8254
Victoriana B&B, 606 12th Ave., Seaside, 97138, 503-738-8449
Walker House, 811 First Ave., Seaside, 97138, 503-738-5520
Historic Shanitio Hotel, P.O. Box 86, Shanitio, 97057, 503-489-3441
Lake Creek Lodge, Star Route, Sisters, 97759, 503-595-6331
Pioneer B&B, Star Route, Spray, 97874, 503-462-3934
Horncroft, 42156 Kingston-Lyons Dr, Stayton, 97383, 503-769-6287
Steamboat Inn, Steamboat, 97447, 503-496-3495
Bigelow B&B, 308 E. Fourth St., The Dalles, 97058, 503-298-8239
Williams House Inn, 608 W. 6th St., The Dalles, 97058, 503-296-2889
McKenzie River Inn, 49164 McKenzie Hwy, Vida, 97488, 503-822-6260
Mountain Shadows B&B, Box 147, Welches, 97067, 503-622-4746
King Salmon Lodge, Ferry Rd., Westport, 97016
Key's B&B, 5025 SW Homesteader Rd., Wilsonville, 97070, 503-638-3722
Willows B&B, 5025 SW Homesteader Rd., Wilsonville, 97070
Valley Creek Cottage, 4231 Placer Rd/Box 124, Wolf Creek, 97497
Wolf Creek Tavern, P.O. Box 97, Wolf Creek, 97497, 503-866-2474
Adobe, Yachats, 97498, 503-547-3141
Bird's Nest Inn B&B, Yachats, 97498, 503-547-3683
Oceanaire Rest B&B, 95354 Hwy 101, Yachats, 97498, 503-547-3782
Oregon House Inn, 94288 Hwy 101, Yachats, 97498, 503-547-3329
Sea Quest B&B, P.O. Box 448, Yachats, 97498, 503-547-3782
Ziggurat B&B, P.O. Box 757, Yachts, 97498, 503-547-3925
Flying M Ranch, 23029 NW Flying M Rd., Yamhill, 97148, 503-662-3222

Pennsylvania

ADAMSTOWN

Adamstown Inn
P.O. Box 938, 19501
62 W. Main St.
717-484-0800 800-594-4808
Tom & Wanda Berman
All year

$$ B&B
4 rooms, 2 pb
Visa, MC, *Rated*, •
C-ltd/S-ltd/P-no/H-no

Continental plus
Afternoon tea, snacks
Sitting room
jacuzzi's in 2 rooms
public tennis and pool

Small charming Victorian inn in the antique district & Pennsylvania Dutch countryside. Min. from Reading/Lancaster factory outlets. Morning coffee/tea. **10% off 4+ nights**

AIRVILLE

Spring House
Muddy Creek Forks, 17302
717-927-6906
Ray Constance Hearne
All year

$$ B&B
5 rooms, 3 pb
•
C-yes/S-no/P-no/H-yes
Spanish

Full breakfast
Comp. wine, tea, cookies
Sitting room, piano
bicycles
creek swimming

18th-century stone house in river valley settlement near Lancaster, York. Feather beds, gourmet country breakfast. Hiking, fishing, wineries. **Comp. wine & cheese upon arrival**

ALLENTOWN

Coachaus
107-111 N. Eighth St., 18101
215-821-4854 800-762-8680
Barbara Kocher/Francine Danko
All year

$$$ B&B
24 rooms, 24 pb
Most CC, *Rated*, •
C-ltd/S-ltd/P-ltd/H-no

Full breakfast
Comp. wine
Sitting room
TV, room phones
air conditioning, FAX

Gaciously restored & appointed; blessed w/amenities of the finest hotels. Fine dining, shops, theater nearby. 1,2,3 bedrms w/private bath & kitchen. **3rd night 40% off**

BEACH LAKE

Beach Lake Hotel	$$$ B&B	Full breakfast
P.O. Box 144, 18405	6 rooms, 6 pb	Restaurant, bar, dinner
Main & Church	Visa, MC, *Rated*, •	Fruit bowls, tea, coffee
717-729-8239 800-382-3897	C-ltd/S-ltd/P-no/H-no	A/C in guest rooms
Erika & Roy Miller	Polish	antique store
All year		

*1850s general store lovingly restored to Victorian splendor. Gourmet dinners. Your Pocono hideaway near the Delaware River. **3rd night free***

BIRD-IN-HAND

Greystone Manor B&B	$$ B&B	Full breakfast
P.O. Box 270, 17505	13 rooms, 13 pb	Anniv/free botl. of wine
2658 Old Philadelphia Pke	Visa, MC, •	Lobby, A/C
717-393-4233	C-ltd/S-no/P-no/H-yes	color cable TV
Tracy Rice, Sally Davis		quilts & crafts shop
All year		

Victorian mansion and carriage house located on 2 acres close to Amish farms. Unique, air-conditioned rooms with private baths. Quilts & crafts shop in basement.

Village Inn, The	$$ B&B	Continental plus
Box 253, 2695 Old Philadel.	11 rooms, 11 pb	Evening snacks
Pike, 17505	Most CC, *Rated*	Sitting room
717-293-8369	C-ltd/S-ltd/P-no/H-no	bus tour of Dutch Cntry.
Richmond & Janice Young		hot tubs in 2 suites
All year		

Beautifully restored historic inn located in Pennsylvania Dutch Country. Country setting. Victorian-style architecture and furnishings. Individually decorated deluxe rooms.

BLOOMSBURG

Inn at Turkey Hill, The	$$ MAP	Continental plus
991 Central Rd., I-80 Exit 35 S,	18 rooms, 18 pb	Sunday brunch, dinner
17815	Most CC, *Rated*, •	Bar service
717-387-1500	C-yes/S-yes/P-yes/H-yes	library, fax machine
Andrew B. Pruden		tennis courts nearby
All year		

Nestled amid Pennsylvania's rolling hills & farmlands, the inn extends warmth, comfort, charm & hospitality. The inn is, as one guest says, "an unexpected find." AAA 4 diamond

Irondale Inn B&B	$$$ B&B	Full breakfast
100 Irondale Ave., 17815	4 rooms	Comp. wine, snacks, tea
717-784-1977 717-387-0203	C-ltd/S-ltd/P-no/H-no	Lunch & dinner on requ.
Linda Wink		sitting room, library
All year		outdoor hot tub, patio

*Walk to Bloomsburg University. Just off Route 80. 7 fireplaces, sun porch, lush lawns, goldfish pond, gardens, great food. **3rd nite free w/ mention of Guide Sun.-Th.***

BRACKNEY

Indian Mountain Inn B&B	$$$ B&B	Full gourmet breakfast
RD 1 Box 68, Tripp Lake Rd.,	8 rooms, 8 pb	Box lunch, dinner by res
18812	Visa, MC, AmEx, *Rated*,	Restaurant, bar, game rm
717-663-2645 800-435-3362	•	sitting room, hot tubs
Nancy & Dan Strnatka	C-yes/S-ltd	lakes, swimming, boating
All year, FAX:663-3123		

*Nestled high in the Endless Mountains. Hundreds of acres for cross-country skiing, hunting, fishing, hiking. Near Binghamton, N.Y. Dining room, liquor license. **3rd night free midwk***

CANADENSIS

Brookview Manor B&B Inn	$$ B&B	Full breakfast
Rt. 447, RR 1, Box 365, 18325	6 rooms, 6 pb	Aft. tea, snacks
717-595-2451	Most CC, *Rated*, •	Sitting room, library
Nancie & Lee Cabana	C-ltd/S-ltd/P-no/H-no	pool table, ping pong
All year		lawn games, waterfall

On 400 picturesque acres, wrap-around porch, panoramic view of the forest. Hiking trails, golf, skiing, excellent dining nearby.

Dreamy Acres	$ B&B	Continental plus
P.O. Box 7, 18325	6 rooms, 4 pb	Sitting room, piano
Rt. 447 & Seese Hill Rd.	*Rated*	color cable TV, VCRs
717-595-7115	C-ltd/S-yes/P-no/H-no	air-conditioning
William E. & Esther Pickett		
All year		

Dreamy Acres is situated in the "Heart of the Pocono Mountain Vacationland" close to stores, gift shops, churches and recreational facilities.

Pine Knob Inn	$$$ MAP	Full breakfast
P.O. Box 295, 18325	27 rooms, 18 pb	Dinner included, bar
Rt. 447	Visa, MC, •	Sitting room, tennis
717-595-2532	C-ltd/S-no/P-no/H-no	Steinway grand piano
Dick & Charlotte Dornich		swimming pool, hiking
All year		

The inn is in a lovely country setting in the Pocono Mountains. Antiques and art abound. Nightly turndown service. Best of all, the food is scrumptious!

CARLISLE

Line Limousin Farmhouse	$ B&B	Full breakfast
2070 Ritner Highway, 17013	4 rooms, 2 pb	Golf driving range
717-243-1281	C-ltd/S-no/P-no/H-no	sitting room
Bob & Joan Line		
All year		

Lovely, quiet brick farmhouse. 2 bedrooms w/king beds, private bath, AC & TV. Easy to find from exit 12 of I81. NO SMOKING.

CHRISTIANA

Winding Glen Farm Home	$ B&B	Full breakfast
107 Noble Rd., 17509	5 rooms	Sitting room
215-593-5535	C-yes/S-ltd/P-no/H-ltd	piano
Minnie & Robert Metzler		slide shows
All year		

Working dairy farm situated in beautiful valley. Stores and quilt shops nearby. Handcrafted furniture made on premises.

COOKSBURG

Clarion River Lodge	$$ B&B	Continental breakfast
P.O. Box 150, 16217	20 rooms, 20 pb	Full bkfst. available
River Rd., Cook Forest	Visa, MC, AmEx, *Rated*,	Restaurant, beverages
800-648-6743 814-744-8171	•	sitting room, library
Ellen C. O'Day	C-ltd/S-yes	adjacent to river
All year		

*Small romantic inn along gentle Clarion River in northwestern Pennsylvania's great forest. Year-round outdoor activities. Fine lodging, dining & spirits. **3rd night 50%, Ltd***

COOKSBURG ───────────────────────────────

Gateway Lodge & Restaurant
Route 36 Box 125, Cook Forest, 16217
814-744-8017 800-843-6862
Joseph & Linda Burney
All year

$$$ EP/B&B
8 rooms, 3 pb
Rated
C-ltd/S-yes/P-ltd/H-ltd

Full breakfast $
Dinner, lunch, snacks
Piano, buggy rides
sitting room, hot tubs
swimming pool, sauna

Colonial log cabin inn w/large stone fireplace. Fine dining by lantern light. Heavy quilts on hand-hewn beds. Activities all year. Indoor heated pool. Tea time daily 4-5 p.m.

CRESCO ───────────────────────────────

La Anna Guest House
RD 2, Box 1051, 18326
717-676-4225
Kay Swingle & Julie Wilson
All year

$ B&B
3 rooms
C-ltd/S-yes/P-ltd/H-no

Continental breakfast
Sitting room
piano, cross-country skiing
fishing, swimming, golf

Private Victorian home nestled in Pocono Mt. village welcomes guests. Furnished with antiques. Skating ponds, waterfalls, woodland walks.

DOYLESTOWN ───────────────────────────────

Inn at Fordhook Farm, The
105 New Britain Rd., 18901
215-345-1766
E. Romanella, B. Burpee Dohan
All year

$$$ B&B
6 rooms, 4 pb
Visa, MC, AmEx, *Rated*,
•
C-ltd

Full farm breakfast
Afternoon tea
Snacks
sitting room
library

*Burpee (seed) family estate w/60 acres of meadows & woodlands. 1760s home with grand-father clocks, majestic mirrors, fireplaces and balconies. **Jan-March 2nd night 50% off***

DUSHORE ───────────────────────────────

Cherry Mills Lodge
RR 1, Box 1270, Route 87 South, 18614
717-928-8978
Florence & Julio
All year

$$ B&B
8 rooms, 1 pb
Disc, •
C-yes/S-ltd/P-no/H-no

Full breakfast
Packed lunches for hikes
Wine w/ dinner, fishing
fireplaces, porches
sauna, ponds, streams

*Historic 1865 country hotel, antique furnished. Secluded 27 acres, mountain trout stream, hiking, biking. Nearby Victorian Eagles Mere, 2 state parks. **3rd night 50% off.***

EAGLES MERE ───────────────────────────────

Eagles Mere Inn
P.O. Box 356, 17731
Mary & Sullivan Avenues
717-525-3273 800-426-3273
Susan & Peter Glaubitz
All year

$$$ MAP
17 rooms, 17 pb
Visa, MC, AmEx, *Rated*,
•
C-yes/S-no/P-no/H-no

Full breakfast
5-course dinner incl.
Bar, sitting room, piano
tennis, swimming pool
golf, skiing, hunting

Charming country inn located in a quiet Victorian town high in the Endless Mountains. Superb food. Beautiful lake with sandy beach nearby. Undisturbed nature.

───────────────────────────────

Shady Lane B&B
P.O. Box 314, 17731
Allegheny Ave.
717-525-3394
Pat & Dennis Dougherty
All year

$$$ B&B
8 rooms, 8 pb
Rated, •
C-ltd/S-no/P-no/H-yes

Full breakfast
Comp. wine, aft. tea
Two sitting rooms
tennis court, lake
golf, skiing, ice skate

Picturesque mountaintop resort close to excellent hiking, swimming, fishing, skiing and tobogganing. Eagles Mere: "the town time forgot." Summer craft and antique shops.

EAST BERLIN

Bechtel Mansion Inn
400 West King St., 17316
717-259-7760 800-331-1108
Ruth Spangler/C. & M. Bechtel
All year

$$ B&B
9 rooms, 7 pb
Visa, MC, AmEx, *Rated*,
•
C-yes/S-ltd/P-no/H-no

Full breakfast
Complimentary tea
Sitting room, library
A/C, meeting rm, garden
downhill & cross-country
skiing

*Restored Victorian mansion w/fine antiques, in Pennsylvania German Nat'l Historical District. Popular w/honeymooners, Civil War & architecture buffs. **3rd night 40% off, Ltd***

EAST STROUDSBURG

Inn at Meadowbrook, The
RD 7, Box 7651, Cherry Lane
Rd., 18301
717-629-0296 800-441-7619
Bob & Kathy Overman
All year

$$ B&B
18 rooms, 12 pb
Visa, MC, *Rated*, •
C-ltd/S-yes/P-no/H-no

Full breakfast
Dinner
Sitting room
tennis, swimming pool
bicycles

*Forty acres of meadows and woods located in the heart of the Poconos. Close to skiing and major attractions. **2nd. night midweek free (non-holiday)***

ELIZABETHTOWN

West Ridge Guest House
1285 West Ridge Rd., 17022
717-367-7783
Alice P. Heisey
All year

$$ B&B
9 rooms, 9 pb
Visa, MC, AmEx, *Rated*,
•
C-yes/S-no/P-no

Full breakfast
Hot tubs
TV, phones
tennis court

Country setting. Each room decorated in a different decor. Some rooms with decks and fireplaces. Fishing pond.

Bechtel Mansion Inn, East Berlin, PA

EPHRATA ───

Hackman's Country Inn B&B $$ B&B — Continental plus
140 Hackman Rd., 17522 — 4 rooms, 2 pb — Porch, lawn
717-733-3498 — Visa, MC — sitting room
Kathryn H. Hackman — C-ltd/S-no/P-no/H-no
All year

Charming 1857 farmhouse on 90 acres in quaint Lancaster County. Breakfast by walk-in fireplace in keeping room. Spacious rooms with bubble glass windows & patchwork quilts.

Inns at Doneckers, The — $$ B&B — Continental plus buffet
318-324 N. State St., 409 N. State — 31 rooms, 29 pb — Restaurant, fireplaces
St., 17522 — Most CC, *Rated*, • — Comp. tea, jacuzzis, TV
717-733-9502 — C-yes/S-yes/P-no/H-yes — sitting room, library
Jan Grobengieser — porch, Farmer's Market
All year

Unique getaway w/country simplicity & genteel luxury. Elegance w/antiques & folk art; fine dining, splendid shopping. 2 carriage suites, decks. **Begin-the-Week Getaways, Ltd**

Smithton Inn, The — $$ B&B — Full breakfast
900 W. Main St., 17522 — 9 rooms, 9 pb — Comp. tea, snacks
717-733-6094 — Visa, MC, *Rated* — Sitting room, fireplaces
Dorothy Graybill — C-yes/S-no/P-ltd/H-ltd — whirlpool baths
All year — library, canopy beds

Picturesque 1763 Penn. Dutch Country Inn. Fireplaces in parlor, dining and guest rooms. Chamber music; canopy four-poster beds, refrigerator, quilts and candles in each room.

ERWINNA ───

Evermay on-the-Delaware — $$$ B&B — Continental plus
River Rd., 18920 — 16 rooms, 16 pb — Comp. sherry in parlor
215-294-9100 — Visa, MC, • — Cordial in rm., bar, tea
Ronald Strouse, Fred Cresson — C-ltd/S-ltd/P-no/H-yes — restaurant (weekends)
All year exc. Dec 24 — sitting room, piano

Romantic Victorian inn on 25 acres of gardens, woodlawn paths and pastures. Elegant dinner served Friday-Sunday & holidays. Rooms face the picturesque Delaware River.

Golden Pheasant Inn — $$$ B&B — Continental breakfast
763 River Rd. (Rt. 32), 18920 — 5 rooms, 1 pb — Restaurant, bar, canoes
215-294-9595 — Visa, MC, *Rated* — Dinner (Tues-Sun)
Barbara & Michel Faure — C-ltd/S-ltd/P-no, French, — Delaware Canal & River
All year — Spanish, Italian — wine in room, solarium

1857 fieldstone inn situated between river and canal. Five rooms furnished with incredible blend of antiques. Quiet. Plant-filled solarium for romantic candlelight dining.

EXTON ───

Duling-Kurtz House & Inn — $ B&B — Continental plus
146 S. Whitford Rd., 19341 — 15 rooms, 15 pb — Restaurant, bar
215-524-1830 — Most CC, *Rated* — Lunch, dinner
Tish Morescalchi — C-yes/S-yes/P-no/H-yes — sitting room
All year — Ger, Fr, Span, Ital — golf courses

Charming 1830s stone house and stable, elegantly furnished with period reproductions furniture. Landscaped grounds with covered gazebo and flowing stream.

Quo Vadis B&B, Franklin, PA

FOGELSVILLE

Glasbern
Box 250, RD 1, Pack House Rd., 18051
215-285-4723
Beth & Al Granger
All year

$$$ B&B
23 rooms, 23 pb
Visa, MC, AmEx, *Rated*
C-ltd/S-yes/P-no/H-ltd

Full breakfast
Lunch, dinner, bar
Fireplaces, conf. room
hiking trails
pool, 16 whirlpools

A simple elegance pervades this 19th-century bank barn, situated in a hidden pastoral valley. Creatively renovated. 100 acres of trails, streams, and ponds.

FRANKLIN

Quo Vadis B&B
1501 Liberty St., 16323
814-432-4208
Kristal & Stanton Bowmer-Vath
All year

$$ B&B
6 rooms, 6 pb
Most CC, *Rated*, •
C-ltd/S-no/P-no/H-no

Full breakfast
Snacks
Sitting room
library
near restaurants

1867 Queen Anne House in historic district, Victorian elegance, heirloom antiques and quilts of same family. Walking tour, museums, bike trails.

GAP

Fassitt Mansion B&B
6051 Philadelphia Pike, Rte 340
White Horse, 17527
717-442-3139 800-653-4139
Tara & Ed Golish
All year

$$ B&B
4 rooms, 2 pb
Visa, MC, Disc.,*Rated*, •
C-ltd/S-no/P-no/H-no

Full breakfast
Afternoon tea
Sitting room, library
bicycle tours

1845 country mansion with 12-foot ceilings, antiques, handmade Amish quilts. Surrounded by rolling hills & farmland. Conveniently located in Lancaster County. **3rd night 50%.**

GETTYSBURG ————————————————————————————————————

Brafferton Inn, The $$$ B&B   Full breakfast
44 York St., 17325   10 rooms, 10 pb   Coffee, tea
717-337-3423   Visa, MC, *Rated*, •   Library, atrium, piano
Jane & Sam Back   C-ltd/S-no/P-no/H-yes   hat collection, old mags
All year   primitive mural

*Stone and clapboard inn circa 1786 near the center square of Gettysburg. The rooms have
stenciled designs, antiques. Walk to battlefield and restaurants.*

Hickory Bridge Farm $$$ B&B   Full breakfast
96 Hickory Bridge Rd.,   7 rooms, 6 pb   Saturday dinner
Orrtanna, 17353   Visa, MC, *Rated*   Sitting room
717-642-5261   C-yes/S-yes/P-no/H-no   bicycles, fishing
Hammetts & Martins   pond swimming
All year

*Relax in the country by enjoying a cozy cottage by the stream, a hearty breakfast at the
farmhouse, and dine in restored PA barn during the weekends.*

Keystone Inn B&B $$ B&B   Full breakfast from menu
231 Hanover St., 17325   4 rooms, 2 pb   Lemonade, coffee, tea
717-337-3888   Visa, MC   Sitting room
Wilmer & Doris Martin   C-yes/S-ltd/P-no   library, antiques
All year   tennis courts nearby

*Unique decor—lots of natural chestnut and oak; comfort our priority. Area rich in history;
antique lover's paradise. Country breakfast!* **Weekday 4 nights, pay for 3.**

Tannery B&B, The $$ B&B   Continental plus
P.O. Box 4565, 17325   5 rooms, 5 pb   Comp. wine, snacks
449 Baltimore St.   Visa, MC, *Rated*   Sitting room, library
717-334-2454   C-ltd/S-no/P-no/H-no   rocking chairs on
Charlotte W. Swope   front porch, golf nearby
All year

*Built in 1868 of Gothic structure, The Tannery is located within walking distance of historical
sites, museums, and restaurants.*

GETTYSBURG—HANOVER ————————————————————————————

Beechmont Inn $$ B&B   Full breakfast
315 Broadway, Route 194, 17331   7 rooms, 7 pb   Comp. wine, snacks
717-632-3013 800-553-7009   Most CC, *Rated*, •   Afternoon tea
Monna Hormel   C-ltd/S-ltd/P-no/H-no   sitting room, library
All year   honeymoon/golf packages

*Federal period elegance; echoes of Civil War memories; a refuge from the 20th century
rush—a bridge across time. Near Gettysburg, antiquing. Whirlpool tub, fireplace avail.*

GLEN ROCK ————————————————————————————————————

Dogwood @ Spoutwood $$ B&B   Full breakfast
Farm   2.5 rooms   Comp. wine
RD 3, Box 66, 17327   •   Library, sitting room
717-235-6610   C-yes/S-no/P-no   hot tub in season
Rob & Lucy Wood   display gardens
All year

*Cottage, antique-furnished w/equipped kitchen on herb/dried flower farm. Gardening, culi-
nary and dried flower crafting classes (request schedule).* **15% disc't on classes**

GORDONVILLE—INTERCOURSE

Osceola Mill House
313 Osceola Mill Rd., 17529
717-768-3758
Robin & Sterling Schoen
Exc. Christmas & Easter

$$$ B&B
3 rooms
C-ltd/S-no/P-no/H-no
German

Full gourmet breakfast
Comp. beverages
Sitting room
bicycles nearby
fireplaces, antiques

Historic stone mill house built 1766. Located in scenic Lancaster County surrounded by Amish farms. Private cottage w/private bath, wood-burning stove, kitchen, patio avail.

HAWLEY

Academy Street B&B
528 Academy St., 18428
717-226-3430 609-395-8590
Judith & Sheldon Lazan
May—October

$$ B&B
7 rooms, 4 pb
Visa, •
C-ltd/S-yes/P-no/H-no

Full breakfast buffet
Comp. wine, coffee, cake
Afternoon tea
sitting room, TV
A/C in rooms

Magnificent Victorian in Poconos near Lake Wallenpaupack. European gourmet breakfast, afternoon coffee and cheesecake. Near restaurants, all activities.

Settlers Inn, The
4 Main Ave., 18428
717-226-2993 800-833-8527
Grant & Jeanne Genzlinger
All year

$$ B&B
18 rooms, 18 pb
Most CC, *Rated*, •
C-yes/S-yes/P-ltd/H-no

Full breakfast
Lunch, dinner, bar
Eve. cheese & crackers
sitting room, library
tennis, bicycles, piano

Delightful country inn of Tudor architecture, with gift shops and art gallery. Lake Wallenpaupack and shopping are nearby. Air conditioned rooms. **3rd night 50% off.**

HESSTON

Aunt Susie's Country Vac.
RD 1, Box 225, 16647
814-658-3638
John Wilson
All year

$$ B&B
8 rooms, 2 pb
Rated
C-yes/S-no/P-no/H-no
French, German

Continental plus
Afternoon tea
Snacks, sitting room
houses with kitchens
boat parking, bed linens

Experience country living in a warm friendly atmosphere; antiques, oil paintings. 28-mile-long Raystown Lake for recreation. Quaint village of Hesston. Inn, cottages & houses.

HOLICONG

Barley Sheaf Farm
P.O. Box 10, 18928
Route 202, 5281 York Rd.
215-794-5104
Ann & Don Mills
Exc. Xmas, wkdys to 2/14

$$$ B&B
9 rooms, 9 pb
C-ltd/S-yes/P-no/H-yes
French

Full farm breakfast
Swimming pool
sitting room

30-acre working farm—raise sheep. Rooms all furnished in antiques. Good antiquing and historic sights in area.

HOLICONG—NEW HOPE

Ash Mill Farm
P.O. Box 202, 18928
5358 Old York Rd.,Rte 202
215-794-5373
Patricia & Jim Auslander
All year

$$$ B&B
6 rooms
Visa, MC, AmEx, *Rated*,
•
C-ltd/S-yes/P-no/H-no

Full gourmet breakfast
Afternoon tea
Evening brandy
sitting room
near tennis & swimming

18th-century manor house on 10 acres of countryside, adjacent to Peddlers' Village & convenient to all of Bucks County. Featured in Gourmet Magazine. **4th night free, mid-week**

INTERCOURSE

Carriage Corner B&B
P.O. Box 371, 17534
3705 E. Newport Rd.
717-768-3059 800-209-3059
Gwen & Gordon Schutt
All year

$$ B&B
4 rooms, 2 pb
Visa, MC, *Rated*, •
C-yes/S-no/P-no/H-no

Full breakfast
Aft. tea, use of fridge
Sitting room
central A/C
cable TV in rooms

At the hub of the Amish area, our B&B offers a relaxing country atmosphere. Dinner with an Amish family arranged. Special diets will be accommodated. **3rd night 50% off**

JIM THORPE

Harry Packer Mansion
P.O. Box 458, 18229
Packer Hill
717-325-8566
Robert & Patricia Handwerk
All year

$$$ B&B
13 rooms, 8 pb
Visa, MC, •
C-ltd/S-no/P-no/H-no

Full breakfast
Sitting room, library
tennis, water sports
murder mistery weekends

Magnificent Victorian mansion in historic district with period furnishings, original woodwork and stained glass. Gracious and friendly atmosphere with sports activities near.

KENNETT SQUARE

Meadow Spring Farm B&B
201 E. St. Rd., 19348
215-444-3903
Anne Hicks & Debbie Ayelrod
All year

$$ B&B
6 rooms, 3 pb
AmEx
C-yes/S-yes/P-no/H-no

Full breakfast
Dinner upon request
Comp. wine, tea, snacks
hot tubs, game room
pool, pond for fishing

1836 farmhouse on working farm with sheep, pigs & cows; filled with antiques, dolls & teddy bears. Full country breakfast served on porch, spacious dining room or by the pool.

Scarlett House B&B
503 W. State St., 19348
215-444-9592
A. Ascosi & S. Lalli-Ascosi
All year

$$ B&B
4 rooms, 2 pb
Rated
C-ltd/S-no/P-no/H-no

Continental plus
Afternoon tea, snacks
Sitting room, library
Victorian parlor, piano
A/C, fireplaces, porch

Elegantly restored Victorian located minutes from Longwood Gardens, Winterthur and Brandywine Valley attractions. Old-fashioned hospitality, gracious atmosphere, antiques.

LAHASKA

Golden Plough Inn
P.O. Box 218, 18931
Rte. 202 & Street Rd.
215-794-4004 215-794-4003
Earl & Donna Jamison
All year

$$$ B&B
60 rooms, 60 pb
Most CC, *Rated*, •
C-yes/S-yes/P-no/H-yes

Continental plus
Restaurant - all meals
Snacks, Comp. champagne
sitting room, jacuzzis
fireplaces, cable TV

Luxurious guestrooms & suites individually furnished English country style. Adjacent to Peddler's Village: shopping, dining, entertainment. **Seasonal & mid-week packages, ask**

LANCASTER

Apple Bin Inn, The
2835 Willow St. Pike, Willow
Street, 17584
717-464-5881 800-338-4296
Debbie & Barry Hershey
All year

$$ B&B
4 rooms, 2 pb
Visa, MC, *Rated*
C-ltd/S-no/P-no/H-no

Full breakfast
Afternoon tea, snacks
Sitting room, patios
A/C & cable TV in rooms
bike storage and maps

Warm colonial charm with a country flavor. Antiques, reproductions. Located near Amish community, antique and craft shops, excellent restaurants and historical sites.

LANCASTER ─────────────────────────────────

B&B—The Manor
P.O. Box 416, 17537
830 Village Rd., Lampeter
717-464-9564
Jackie Curtis/MaryLou Paolini
All year

$$ B&B
5 rooms, 2 pb
Visa, MC
C-yes/S-no/P-no/H-yes

Full breakfast
Lunch, dinner
Snacks, sitting room
A/C, swimming pool
winter & group discounts

Cozy farmhouse centrally located in scenic Amish country. Deluxe swimming pool, full gourmet breakfast. Children welcome, group discount rates. **6+ nights 10% off**

───

Gardens of Eden
1894 Eden Rd., 17601
717-393-5179
Marilyn & Bill Ebel
All year

$$ B&B
4 rooms, 2 pb
Visa, MC, •
C-yes/S-no/P-no/H-no

Continental plus
Full breakfast, snacks
Amish dinner, sitting rm
canoes, rowboats, tours
tea & fruit upon arrival

Eden exists along the Conestoga River where wild flowers, herbs, and perennials bloom among the trees and lawns of this circa 1867 Iron Masters mansion. Summer rental avail.

───

Hollinger House
2336 Hollinger Rd., 17602
717-464-3050
Gina & Jeff Trost
All year

$$ B&B
7 rooms, 5 pb
Most Cred.Cds. *Rated*
C-ltd/S-ltd/P-no/H-no

Full breakfast
Picnic basket, aft. tea
Snacks, comp. wine
sitting room, library
tennis, swim nearby

Your special haven. Natural, friendly, romantic & comfortable. 1870 Adams period brick home. Large wraparound porch, lavish breakfast, near attractions. **Seasonal disc'ts.**

───

King's Cottage, A B&B Inn
1049 E. King St., 17602
717-397-1017 800-747-8717
Karen & Jim Owens
All year

$$$ B&B
8 rooms, 8 pb
Visa, MC, *Rated*, •
C-ltd/S-no/P-no/H-no
Spanish

Full breakfast
Afternoon tea, cordials
Sitting room, library
water garden, Dinner w/
Amish family available

Enjoy National Register award-winning architecture, elegance. Central location, near Amish farms, restaurants, antiques, outlets, quilts, historic sites. Mobil 3-star.

───

Lincoln Haus Inn B&B
1687 Lincoln Hwy E., 17602
717-392-9412
Mary K. Zook
All year

$ B&B
8 rooms, 8 pb
Personal checks,*Rated*,
•
C-ltd/S-no/P-no/H-ask
Dueisch, German

Full breakfast (rooms)
No alcohol on premises
honeymoon suite avail.
Amish crafts nearby

Unique suburban home, built in the late 1800s, with rooms and apartments. Natural oaks woodwork, antiques. Owner is a member of the old order Amish church. **7th night free**

───

Witmer's Tavern—1725 Inn
2014 Old Philadelphia P, 17602
717-299-5305
Brant E. Hartung
All year

$$ B&B
2 rooms, 2 pb
Personal Checks OK, •
C-yes/S-ltd/P-no/H-no

Continental plus
Popcorn poppers
Antique shop, sitting rm
air field, honeymoon rm.
National Register

Lancaster's only pre-Revolutionary inn still lodging travelers. Fireplaces, antiques, quilts & fresh flowers in romantic rooms. **Champagne or cake for special occasions**

LANCASTER—COLUMBIA

Columbian, The	$$ B&B	Full breakfast
360 Chestnut St., 17512	6 rooms, 6 pb	Comp. beverages
717-684-5869 800-422-5869	Visa, MC, •	Sitting room, A/C, TV in
Linda & John Straitiff	C-ltd/S-no/P-no/H-no	all rms, fireplace in 1
All year		wrap-around sun porch

*Restored turn-of-the-century Colonial Revival mansion decorated w/antiques in Victorian or country style. Hearty breakfast, fresh fruit, homemade breads. **10% off Sun.-Th.***

LANCASTER—LAMPETER

Walkabout Inn, The	$$$ B&B	Full Aussie breakfast
P.O. Box 294, 17537	5 rooms, 5 pb	Afternoon tea, gardens
837 Village Rd.	Visa, MC, AmEx, *Rated*,	Library, antique shop
717-464-0707	•	playground/picnic area
Richard & Margaret Mason	C-ltd/S-no/P-no/H-no	movies on Amish culture
All year		

*Country-restored 1925 Mennonite home, landscaped in a quaint village setting. Dinner tour w/Amish family arranged. Picturesque English gardens, fountain. **Restaurant coupons.***

LANCASTER—NOTTINGHAM

Little Britain Manor	$ B&B	Full breakfast
20 Brown Rd., Village of Little	4 rooms	Dinner by request
Britain, 19362	C-yes	2 rooms with A/C
717-529-2862		help with tours
Fred & Evelyn Crider		
All year		

A home away from home country farm furnished with antiques and country flair. See up close the unique culture of the Amish people and markets.

LEWISBURG

Inn on Fiddler's Tract	$$ B&B	Continental plus
RD 2, Box 573A, Buffalo Rd.,	5 rooms, 5 pb	Comp. wine
17837	Visa, MC, AmEx, *Rated*,	Party dining by adv.res.
717-523-7197 800-326-9659	•	library, on premises
Tony & Natalie Boldurian	C-ltd/S-ltd/P-no/H-no	hiking & cross-country
All year		skiing

Located on 33 acres, this 1810 stone mansion welcomes you to enjoy the tranquillity of the Susquehanna Valley and the charm of Victorian Lewisburg.

Pineapple Inn	$$ B&B	Full country breakfast
439 Market St., 17837	6 rooms, 2 pb	Comp. tea, snacks
717-524-6200	Most Cred. Crds, -Rate-	All rooms A/C, tea room
Charles & Deborah North	C-ltd/S-ltd/P-no/H-no	piano, sitting room
All year	German	tennis, pool nearby

*This c.1857 home of Federalist design is decorated w/period antiques. Just blocks from Bucknell University. Upside-Down Shoppe. **10% discount 4+ nights.***

LITITZ

Swiss Woods B&B	$$ B&B	Full breakfast
500 Blantz Rd., 17543	5 rooms, 5 pb	Lunch (picnic baskets)
717-627-3358 800-594-8018	Visa, MC, *Rated*, •	Comp. tea and cake
Werner & Debrah Mosimann	C-ltd/German	sitting room
All year		bicycles

A chalet nestled in the woods overlooking Speedwell Fodge Lake. Swiss specialties and European decor. Queen beds and down comforters. Two rooms with jacuzzis.

LUMBERVILLE

1740 House
River Rd., 18933
215-297-5661
Robert John Vris
All year

$$ B&B
24 rooms, 24 pb
•
C-ltd/S-yes/P-no

Continental plus—buffet
Restaurant, aftn. tea
Sitting room, library
bicycles, swimming pool
tennis & cross-country ski

If you can't be a house guest in Buck's County, be ours—24 attractively furnished rooms overlooking the Delaware River. Horseback riding, canoeing, antiquing, etc. nearby.

MARIETTA

River Inn, The
258 West Front St., 17547
717-426-2290
Joyce & Bob Heiserman
All year

$$ B&B
3 rooms, 3 pb
Visa, MC, Disc.
C-ltd/S-ltd/P-no/H-no

Full breakfast
Beverages
Library, bicycles
guided boat fishing
color cable TV

200-year-old Colonial on Historic Register with fireplaces, antiques, reproduction furnishings. Herb garden & porch breakfasts. Centrally located. **3+ nights, 25% off**

MERCER

Magoffin Inn
129 S. Pitt St., 16137
412-662-4611 800-841-0824
Judy Forrester
All year

$$ B&B
7 rooms, 7 pb
Visa, MC, AmEx, *Rated*
C-yes/S-no/P-no/H-no

Full breakfast
Dinner available
Cordial, snacks
library
tennis courts, pool

1884 Queen Anne Victorian. Affordable elegance in ideal location. Outdoor activities abound: boating, fishing, golf, cross-country skiing. Near I-79 and I-80. **10% off dinner**

MERCERSBURG

Mercersburg Inn, The
405 S. Main St., 17236
717-328-5231 FAX:328-3403
John Mohr
All year

$$$ B&B
15 rooms, 15 pb
Visa, MC, *Rated*, •
C-yes/S-ltd/H-no
Spanish

Full breakfast
6-course dinner wkends $
Bar, TV in game room
golf/skii/tennis nearby
phones in all rooms

Elegant, restored mansion in south central Pennsylvania. 90 minutes from Washington, D.C. Gourmet dining by candlelight. Handmade canopy beds, antiques & crackling fireplace.

Steiger House, The
33 North Main St., 17236
717-328-5757
Ron & Nancy Snyder
All year

$$ B&B
2 rooms, 2 pb
Visa, MC
C-yes/S-no/P-no/H-no

Full breakfast
Snacks
Comp. wine
sitting room
7 fireplaces

Circa 1820 home in historic Mercersburg, Pa. Boyhood home of President James Buchanan. Nearby restaurants & White Tail ski resort. **$5.00 discount on room**

MERTZTOWN

Longswamp B&B
RD2, Box 26, 19539
215-682-6197
Elsa & Dean Dimick
All year

$$ B&B
10 rooms, 6 pb
•
C-yes/S-ltd/P-no/H-ltd
French

Full breakfast
Comp. wine & cheese, etc
Picnics, sitting room
library, piano, bicycles
horseshoes, bocce court

Historic country farmhouse near Amish country and skiing. Tempting delicacies prepared by area chef. Book and music collection for guests' use. **3rd night 50% off**

MILFORD

Black Walnut B&B
P.O. Box 1024, 18337
RD2 Box 9285-Firetower Rd
717-296-6322 800-866-9870
Stewart & Effie Schneider
All year

$$ B&B
14 rooms, 8 pb
Visa, MC, AmEx, *Rated*
C-ltd/S-ltd/P-no/H-no

Full breakfast
Restaurant, comp. sherry
Pool table, lawn games
piano, pond, hot tub
riding lessons, trails

Large secluded estate for an exclusive clientele. Tudor-style stone house with historic marble fireplace, charming bedrooms with antiques and brass beds. Riding stable also.

Cliff Park Inn & Golf Crs.
RR 4, Box 7200, Cliff Park Rd.,
18337
717-296-6491 800-225-6535
•
Harry W. Buchanan
All year, FAX:296-3982

$$$ B&B/MAP/AP
18 rooms, 18 pb
Most Cred. Cds. *Rated*,
•
C-yes/S-yes/P-no/H-ltd
French, Spanish

Full breakfast
Restaurant, bar
Sitting room
library, 8 rooms with
fireplace & jacuzzi

Historic country inn surrounded by long-established golf course & school on secluded 600-acre estate. Midweek golf packages. Cross-country skiing. Gourmet dining. Mobil 3-Star rating.

MONTGOMERYVILLE

Joseph Ambler Inn
1005 Horsham Rd., North Wales,
19454, 18936
215-362-7500
Steve & Terry Kratz
All year

$$$ B&B
28 rooms, 28 pb
Most CC, *Rated*, •
C-yes/S-yes/P-no/H-ltd
French, German

Full breakfast
Restaurant
3 sitting rooms
banquet/meeting room

1735 estate house set on 13 acres and furnished with antiques, four-poster beds, walk-in fireplace. Children welcome. **50% off 2nd night.**

MONTOURSVILLE

Carriage House—Stonegate
RD 1, Box 11A, 17754
717-433-4340
Harold & Dena Mesaris
All year

$$ B&B
2 rooms
Rated, •
C-yes/S-yes/P-yes

Full breakfast
Continental plus (summr)
Snacks, bar service
sitting room, library
bicycles

Total privacy along the banks of Mill Creek, 30 yards from the main house in the beautiful Loyalsock Creek Valley. Tubing in creeks and hiking nearby

MOUNT JOY

Cameron Estate Inn
RD 1, Box 305, 1895 Donegal
Springs Rd., 17752
717-653-1773
Janice Rote
All year

$$ B&B
18 rooms, 16 pb
Most Crd. Cds. *Rated*, •
C-ltd/S-yes/P-no/H-yes

Continental breakfast
Lunch, dinner, bar
Sitting room, games
swimming, tennis
bicycles, hiking

Country hideaway furnished in Federal style. Close to Pennsylvania Dutch country, where the Amish people live. Intimate rooms and large suites.

Cedar Hill Farm
305 Longenecker Rd., 17552
717-653-4655
Russel & Gladys Swarr
All year

$$ B&B
5 rooms, 5 pb
Most CC, *Rated*
C-yes/S-no/P-no/H-no

Continental plus
Central air-conditioning
porch, private balcony
roam this working farm

Host born in this 1817 Fieldstone farmhouse. Quiet area overlooks stream. Near Lancaster's Amish country & Hershey. Near farmer's markets & quaint villages. **Weekly discount.**

MOUNT JOY

Hillside Farm B&B
607 Eby Chiques Rd., 17552
717-653-6697
Gary & Deb Lintner
All year

$$ B&B
5 rooms, 3 pb
Rated
C-ltd/S-no/P-no/H-no

Full breakfast
Sitting room, library
baby grand piano

1863 farmhouse in Amish Country, furnished with dairy farm antiques and milk bottles. Very secluded, near creek & waterfall. Biking, hiking, outlets, antique shops, wineries.

MUNCY

Bodine House, The
307 S. Main St., 17756
717-546-8949
David & Marie Louise Smith
All year

$$ B&B
4 rooms, 4 pb
Visa, MC, AmEx, •
C-ltd/S-no/P-no/H-yes

Full breakfast
Complimentary wine
Sitting room, library
bicycles

Restored townhouse circa 1805 with period antiques & reproductions. Located in Nat'l Historic District. Full breakfast served by candlelight. **10% discount for 3+ nights**

NARVON—CHURCHTOWN

Churchtown Inn
2100 Main St., Rte. 23, 17555
215-445-7794
H. & S. Smith, J. Kent
All year

$ B&B
8 rooms, 6 pb
Visa, MC, AmEx, *Rated*
C-ltd/S-ltd/P-no, German

Full 5-course breakfast
Dinner with Amish family
Glass garden room, piano
game rm., carriage house
theme weekends

In the heart of Pennsylvania Dutch country. Historic circa 1735 stone federal colonial. Antiquing, farm markets and outlets. On National Historic Register. **7th night free**

NEW HOPE

Aaron Burr House Inn
80 W. Bridge St., corner of
Chestnut St., 18901
215-862-2343
Dinie & Carl Glassman
All year

$$$ B&B
6 rooms, 6 pb
AmEx, *Rated*, •
C-ltd/S-no/P-no/H-yes
French, Spanish

Continental plus
Comp. liqueur, snacks
Afternoon tea, library
2 new fireplace suites
white wicker porch, pool

Discover "safe haven" in vintage village Victorian inn—Aaron Burr did after his famous pistol duel w/Alexander Hamilton in 1804! Innkeeping seminars. **3rd night disc't., ltd**

Back Street Inn
144 Old York Rd., 18938
215-862-9571 800-841-1874
Bob Puccio
All year

$$$ B&B
7 rooms, 7 pb
Visa, MC, *Rated*, •
C-ltd/S-yes/German

Full gourmet breakfast
Sitting room
swimming pool
croquet

New Hope is a village of vitality and romance. 10 min. stroll into center of town. Swimming pool, A/C rooms & full gourmet breakfast in garden room. **3rd night 50% off, ltd**

Centre Bridge Inn
Box 74 Star Route, Routes 32 &
263, 18938
215-862-9139 215-862-2048
Stephen R. DuGan
All year

$$ B&B
9 rooms, 9 pb
Visa, MC, *Rated*
C-ltd/S-yes/P-no/H-no

Continental plus
Dinner, bar
Sitting room w/fireplace
riverside deck

Charming riverside country inn furnished with lovely period antiques; cozy Old World restaurant with walk-in fireplace and alfresco dining in season.

NEW HOPE

Hotel du Village
N. River Rd., at Phillips Mill Rd., 18938
215-862-9911 215-862-5164
Barbara & Omar Arbani
All year

$$$ B&B
20 rooms, 20 pb
AmEx, *Rated*, •
C-ltd/S-yes/P-no/H-yes
French, Spanish

Continental plus
Dinner, bar
Swimming pool
tennis courts
sitting room

Intimate country dining & lodging in Bucks County, Pennsylvania.

Wedgewood Inn of New Hope
111 W. Bridge St., 18938
215-862-2570
Carl & Dinie Glassman
All year

$$$ B&B
18 rooms
Rated, •
C-yes/S-ltd/P-ltd/H-ltd
Fr, Hebr, Dutch, Ger, Fr

Continental plus
Aftn. tea & refreshments
Victorian gazebo, parlor
horsedrawn carriage ride
club w/tennis, swimming

Victorian mansion. Wedgewood china, fresh flowers & original art. Innkeepers make your stay as pleasant as surroundings. OUR 1989 INN OF THE YEAR! **Midwk disc't off-season**

Whitehall Inn, The
RD 2, Box 250, 1370 Pineville Rd., 18938
215-598-7945
Mike & Suella Wass
All year

$$$ B&B
6 rooms, 4 pb
Most CC, *Rated*, •
C-ltd/S-no/P-no/H-no

Full candlelight brkfast
High tea, comp. sherry
Pool & rose garden
library, sun room
piano & pump organ

Experience our four-course candlelit breakfast using European china and crystal and heirloom sterling silver. Formal tea; fireplaces; working dressage horse farm.

NEW HOPE—WRIGHTSTOWN

Hollileif B&B
677 Durham Rd., 18940
215-598-3100
Richard & Ellen Butkus
All year

$$$ B&B
4 rooms, 4 pb
Visa, MC, *Rated*, •
C-ltd/S-no/P-no/H-no
some Spanish

Full gourmet breakfast
Comp. wine, refreshments
Afternoon tea, snacks
volleyball, croquet
badminton, horseshoes

Let us pamper you in our romantic 18th-century home; on 5.5 beautiful country acres; trees, gardens, stream; charming country furnishings. **4th night free, ltd**

NORTH EAST

Brown's Village Inn
51 E. Main St., 16428
814-725-5522
Ruth & Bill Brown
All year

$$ B&B
3 rooms, 3 pb
Visa, MC, *Rated*
C-yes/S-yes/P-ltd, Dutch, French

Full breakfast wkends.
Lunch/dinner, restaurant
Afternoon tea, snacks
sitting room, library
golf, tennis, beach near

A restored 1832 federal-style house now is home for a fine restaurant and antique-appointed guest rooms. Only 1 mile to the Lake Erie shore. Experience a bit of yesteryear.

PARADISE

Maple Lane Farm B&B
505 Paradise Ln., 17562
717-687-7479
Edwin & Marion Rohrer
All year

$ B&B
4 rooms, 2 pb
C-yes/S-no/P-no/H-no

Continental plus
Organ, front porch
spacious lawns
sitting room

Maple Lane Farm has air conditioning, antiques. Near Amish homesteads, museums, farmer's markets. Farm guest house plus 120-cow dairy, streams and woodland.

PHILADELPHIA

Shippen Way Inn
418 Bainbridge St., 19147
215-468-1271 800-245-4873
Ann Foringer & Raymond Rhule
All year

$$ B&B
9 rooms, 9 pb
Visa, MC, AmEx, *Rated*,
•
C-yes/S-ltd/P-no/H-ltd

Continental plus
Afternoon tea
Comp. wine
sitting room

Friendly family owned and operated Inn with a country feel in the city. Colonial herb and rose garden. Fireplaces.

Thomas Bond House
129 S. Second St., 19106
215-923-8523 800-845-BOND
Jack Van Zandt
All year

$$$ B&B
12 rooms, 12 pb
Visa, MC, AmEx, *Rated*,
•
C-yes/S-yes/P-no/H-no

Continental plus (wkdys)
Full breakfast (wkends)
Comp. wine and cheese
fresh-baked cookies
whirlpool tubs, parlor

Colonial period (c. 1770), listed in National Register. Individually decorated rms w/hair dryer, TV, phone. In Independence National Historical Park. Next to historic shrines

PITTSBURGH

Priory—A City Inn, The
614 Pressley St., 15202
412-231-3338 FAX:231-4838
Mary Ann Graf
All year

$$$ B&B
24 rooms, 24 pb
AmEx, Visa, MC, *Rated*,
•
C-yes/S-yes/P-no/H-yes

Continental plus
Comp. tea, port, sherry
Sitting room, library
fireplace, courtyard
comp. limo service

Newly restored historic Victorian Priory—antiques; courtyard or city view; neighborhood atmosphere; close to city. National Register district. TV and phone in rooms.

POCONO MOUNTAINS

Nearbrook B&B
RD 1, Box 630, Rt. 447,
Canadensis, 18325
717-595-3152
Barb & Dick Robinson
All year

$ B&B
3 rooms, 1 pb
C-ltd/P-ask/H-no

All you can eat brkfast
Wooden train set, games
games, piano, sleds
piano/art lessons-adults

Rock garden paths, roses, woods, mountain stream. Relaxing breakfast on porch. 7 restaurants nearby. Hiking & skiing. Weekly rates. Parties for groups. **7th night free**

Nearbrook B&B, Pocono Mountains, PA

POINT PLEASANT—NEW HOPE

Tattersall Inn
P.O. Box 569, 18950
Cafferty & River Rds.
215-297-8233
Gerry & Herb Moss
All year

$$$ B&B
6 rooms, 6 pb
Most CC, *Rated*, •
C-yes/S-ltd/P-no/H-no

Continental plus
Apple cider, snacks
Library, sitting room
piano

Bucks County historic mansion circa early 1800s. Antique phonograph collection. River canoeing & tubing, antique shops, art galleries. **2nd night 50% off Sun-Wed, no holidays**

POTTSTOWN

Coventry Forge Inn
RR 7 - Coventryville, 1.5 mi. W.
of Rt100 on 23, 19464
215-469-6222
June and Wallis Callahan
All year

$$ B&B
5 rooms, 5 pb
Most Crd. Cds., *Rated*
C-yes/S-yes/P-no/H-no

Continental breakfast
Restaurant, bar
Dinner available
sitting room, library

Superb French restaurant in Chester County horse country. Brandywine Valley & Amish country nearby. Excellent antiquing.

QUAKERTOWN—BUCKS COUNTY

Sign of The Sorrel Horse
243 Old Bethlehem Rd., 18951
215-536-4651
M. Gaumont-Lanvin, J. Atkin
All year

$$$ EP/B&B
5 rooms, 5 pb
Visa, MC, AmEx, *Rated*
C-ltd/S-no/P-yes/H-no
French, German

Continental breakfast
Restaurant, bar, dinner
Comp. sherry & fruits
sitting room, bicycles
skiing, fishing, boating

Built in 1749 as a stagecoach stop; secluded on 5 manicured acres; gracious country inn; five antique-filled guest rooms. A little bit of France in Bucks County.

QUARRYVILLE

Runnymede Farm
Guesthouse
1030 Robert Fulton Hwy., R.222
S., 17566
717-786-3625
Herb & Sara Hess

$ B&B
3 rooms
Rated
C-yes/S-no/P-no/H-no

All year

Full country breakfast
Snacks
Piano
sitting room
pleasant porch

Enjoy old-fashioned hospitality when you vacation in our clean, comfortable farm home. Full country breakfast. Bicycling, hiking, picnicking.

RIDGWAY

Faircroft B&B
Box 17, Montmorenci Rd.,
Rt.948 N, 15853
814-776-2539
John & Lois Shoemaker
All year

$ B&B
3 rooms, 2 pb
Rated
C-ltd/S-no/H-no

Full breakfast option
Comp. beverages, snacks
Sitting room, fireplace
hiking trails, hunting
fishing, swimming, golf

Two miles from Route 219. Warm, comfortable, 1870 farmhouse on 75 acres. Antiques, Swedish foods. Next to Allegheny National Forest.

SCOTTDALE

Pine Wood Acres B&B
Rt 1, Box 634, 15683
412-887-5404
Ruth A. Horsch
All year

$$ B&B
3 rooms, 1 pb
Visa, MC, •
C-yes/S-no/P-no/H-no

Full breakfast
Snacks
Wildlife, gardens
porch, patio

A country get-away in another world. Antiques, herbs, flowers. Near Wright's Fallingwater, bike trails, hiking, rafting, ski resorts, historic sites.

SLIPPERY ROCK ─────────────────

Applebutter Inn	$$ B&B	Full gourmet breakfast
152 Applewood Ln., 16057	11 rooms, 11 pb	Comp. beverages & snacks
412-794-1844	Visa, MC, *Rated*	Dinner avail. next door
Gary & Sandra McKnight	C-yes/S-no/P-no/H-yes	sitting room, library
All year		near university, parks

Restored 1844 farmstead with fireplaces, canopy beds and genuine antiques; gourmet breakfasts; warm quiet atmosphere. Meeting/conference rm for 16—TV/VCR, phone, modem.

SMOKETOWN ─────────────────

Homestead Lodging	$ B&B	Continental
184 E. Brook Rd., Route 896,	4 rooms, 4 pb	A/C, microwave availble
17576	Visa, MC, *Rated*	color TV w/stereo radio
717-393-6927	C-yes/S-yes/H-yes	Amish country tours
Robert & Lori Kepiro		
All year		

Quiet country lodging in hand-stenciled rooms.Gift shop with local handcrafts. Located beside Amish farm. Walk to restaurants and outlets. Gift shop, tennis court.

SOLEBURY ─────────────────

Hollyhedge English Estate	$$$ B&B	Full breakfast
Box 213, 6987 Upper York Rd.,	15 rooms, 15 pb	Afternoon tea, snacks
18963	Visa, MC, AmEx, •	Library, sitting room
215-862-3136	C-yes/S-ltd/P-ask	piano, tennis courts
Joseph & Amy Luccaro		swimming pool
All year exc. Xmas		

Join us in a warm, friendly atmosphere. Relax and enjoy our sumptuous breakfasts and the charm of Hollyhedge Estate. **3rd night 50% off**

SOMERSET ─────────────────

Bayberry Inn B&B	$ B&B	Continental plus
611 N. Center Ave., Route 601,	11 rooms, 11 pb	Snacks
15501	Most CC, *Rated*, •	Sitting room, library
814-445-8471	C-ltd/S-no/P-no/H-no	central A/C
Robert & Marilyn Lohr		TV room with VCR/stereo
All year		

One and one-half blocks from turnpike exit, near Georgian Place outlet mall. Seven Springs and Hidden Valley ski resorts, whitewater rafting, "Fallingwater."

SOUTH STERLING ─────────────────

French Manor, The	$$$ MAP	Full breakfast, Bar serv
Box 39, Huckleberry Rd., 18460	8 rooms, 8 pb	Lunch sometimes, Dinner
717-676-3244	Most CC, *Rated*, •	Aft. tea, Bar service
Ron & Mary Kay Logan	C-ltd/S-no/P-no/H-ltd	snacks, restaurant
All year	French	tennis court, hot tubs

High atop Huckleberry Hill, French Manor commands a magnificent view of the surrounding countryside and forested hills. Sitting room, library, pool. **Picnic lunch w/2 nights**

Sterling Inn, The	$$$ MAP	Full breakfast
Rt. 191, 18460	54 rooms, 54 pb	Lunch, dinner, Aft. tea
717-676-3311 800-523-8200	Most CC, *Rated*, •	Snacks, restaurant
Ron & Mary Kay Logan	C-yes/P-no/H-yes	bar service, sitting rm.
All year	French	library, tennis court

The country inn you've always looked for but never thought you'd find. Pretty country rooms & suites w/fireplaces. Indoor pool, hot tubs, outdoor activities. **Comp. glass wine**

STARLIGHT

Inn at Starlight Lake, The	$$$ B&B/MAP	Full breakfast
P.O. Box 27, 18461	27 rooms, 21 pb	Lunch, dinner, full bar
717-798-2519 800-248-2519	Visa, MC, *Rated*, •	Sitting room, piano
Jack & Judy McMahon	C-yes/S-yes/P-no/H-no	tennis courts, boating
Exc. late Mar–Apr 16		bicycles, ski trails

A beautiful clear lake; setting of pastoral tranquillity; excellent food and spirits; recreation for every season; congenial & informal atmosphere. Suite with whirlpool for 2.

STRASBURG

Decoy B&B, The	$ B&B	Full breakfast
958 Eisenberger Rd., 17579	4 rooms, 4 pb	Sitting room
717-687-8585 800-726-2287	*Rated*	library, A/C
Deborah & Hap Joy	C-yes/S-no/P-no/H-no	bicycles tours
All year		

Spectacular view; quiet rural location in Amish farm country. Former Amish home. Bike touring paradise. Two cats in residence!

Strasburg Village Inn	$$ B&B	Full breakfast
One W. Main St., Centre Square,	11 rooms, 11 pb	Continental brkfst (Sun)
17579	Visa, MC, •	Two sitting rooms
717-687-0900 800-541-1055	C-yes/S-yes/P-no/H-no	porch & patio
Alice & Ed Felter		jacuzzis in 2 suites
All year		

Circa 1788. Elegantly appointed rooms in heart of Amish Country & Strasburg's national historic district; adjacent to original Strasburg Country Store & Creamery.

WASHINGTON CROSSING

Woodhill Farms Inn	$$$ B&B	Full breakfast (weekend)
150 Glenwood Dr., 18977	6 rooms, 6 pb	Continental plus (M-F)
215-493-1974 800-982-7619	Visa, MC, *Rated*, •	Sitting room, king beds
John & Donna Behun	C-ltd/S-no/P-no/H-no	Sunken tub, garden
All year	Slovak	use as small conf. ctr.

Nestled on 10 wooded acres. Enjoy delicious breakfasts in rural, relaxing Bucks County. New York, Philadelphia, nearby Princeton; New York—90 min. Complimentary refreshments.

WEST CHESTER

Bankhouse B&B	$$$ B&B	Full breakfast
875 Hillsdale Rd., 19382	2 rooms	Snacks
215-344-7388	*Rated*	Sitting room, porch
Diana & Michael Bove	C-ltd/S-no/P-no/H-no	library, A/C
All year		private entrances

Charming 18th-century "bankhouse" located across from a 10-acre horse farm. Convenient to Longwood Gardens, Winterthur, etc. Quiet country setting. **10% off 4+ nights stay.**

Lenape Springs Farm	$$ B&B	Full breakfast
P.O. Box 176, 19366	4 rooms, 4 pb	Tea, coffee, sodas, eves
580 West Creek Rd.	*Rated*, •	Rooms overlook gardens
215-793-2266	C-yes/S-ltd/P-no/H-no	creek
Bob & Sharon Currie		
All year		

You are not just guests, but you are our guests when you stay on our small farm in the heart of Brandywine Valley. **10% discount to senior citizens**

WILKES-BARRE

Ponda-Rowland B&B Inn
RR1, Box 349, Dallas, 18612
717-639-3245 800-854-3286
Jeanette & Cliff Rowland
All year

$$ B&B
3 rooms, 3 pb
Most CCs *Rated*, •
C-yes/S-no/P-no

Full candlelight brkfast
Picnics
Satellite TV, fireplace
wildlife sanctuary
walking, hiking

130-acre farm in the Endless Mtns. Beautiful mountain and forest scenery. Farm includes 30-acre wildlife refuge, canoeing and swimming. 6% senior, 20% 4th night disc'ts.

WILLIAMSPORT

Reighard House, The
1323 E. 3rd St., 17701
717-326-3593 FAX:323-4734
Susan L. Reighard
Exc. Christmas, New Year

$$ B&B
6 rooms, 6 pb
Most CC, *Rated*, •
C-yes/S-no/P-no/H-no

Full breakfast
Afternoon tea
Comp. wine, beer, snacks
sitting room, library
club membership at YMCA

1905 stone and brick Victorian house; formal parlor, music room, formal dining room. Six large bedrooms with private baths, color TV, phone, carpeting, air conditioning.

WOODBURY

Waterside Inn B&B
RD #1, Box 52, 16695
814-766-3776
Barbara Leighty
All year

$$ B&B
6 rooms, 2 pb
Visa, MC
C-yes/S-no/P-no/H-yes

Full breakfast
Hiking trails, birding
fishing, hunting
air-conditioned, library

Two beautiful, antique-filled homes both used as a bed & breakfast—one 1853 stone house and a 1980 cape cod house. Sitting room available.

WRIGHTSVILLE

Roundtop B&B
6995 Roundtop Ln., 17368
717-252-3169 800-801-0184
Jodi & Tyler Sloan
All year

$$ B&B
6 rooms, 1 pb
Rated
C-yes/S-yes/P-no/H-no

Full gourmet breakfast
Sitting room
library
hiking

Romantic 1880 stone home—unique setting—100 acres woodland, most spectacular view of Susquehanna River anywhere.

YORK

Briarwold B&B
5400 Lincoln Hwy., 17406
717-252-4619
Marion Bischoff
All year

$$ B&B
3 rooms
•
C-yes/S-yes/P-no/H-no

Full breakfast
Comp. tea, coffee
Sitting room
library
A/C bedrooms

1830s house of Colonial architecture, furnished with lovely antiques. 3 acres of grass and trees. Close to Amish country, Gettysburg, and many attractions. Hospitality plus.

Smyser-Bair House B&B
30 S. Beaver St., 17401
717-854-3411
The King Family
All year

$$ B&B
4 rooms, 1 pb
Visa, MC, •
C-yes/S-no/P-no/H-no

Full breakfast
Afternoon tea
Large parlor, library
player piano, A/C
convenient parking

Magnificent Italianate Victorian townhouse in historic district. Antiques, warm hospitality, breakfasts made from nearby market produce. Near Lancaster and Gettysburg.

More Inns . . .

Salisbury House, 910 E. Emmause Ave., Allentown, 18103, 215-791-4225
Swatara Creek Inn B&B, Box 692, RD #1, Annville, 17003, 717-865-3259
Weatherbury Farm, RD #1, Box 250, Avella, 15312
Hurryback Riverhouse B&B, RR 2, Box 2176A, Bangor, 18013, 215-498-3121
East Shore House, P.O. Box 12, Beach Lake, 18405, 717-729-8523
Morning Dove Manor, P.O. Box 33, Beach Lake, 18405
Bedford House, 203 W. Pitt St., Bedford, 15522, 814-623-7171
Jean Bonnet Tavern, R.D.2, Box 724, Bedford, 15522, 814-623-2250
Grandmaw's Place Bunk, RD 2, Box 239, Benton, 17814, 717-925-2630
Vietersburg Inn B&B, 1001 E. Main St., Berlin, 15530, 814-267-3696
Sunday's Mill Farm B&B, R.D.2, Box 419, Bernville, 19506, 215-488-7821
Bethlehem Inn, 476 N. New St., Bethlehem, 18018, 215-867-4985
Wydnor Hall Inn, Rd 3, Bethlehem, 18015, 215-867-6851
Little House, The, RD3, Box 341, Boyerton, 19512, 215-689-4814
Twin Turrets Inn, 11 E. Philadelphia Ave., Boyertown, 19512, 215-367-4513
Bluebird Hollow B&B, RD 4, Box 217, Brookville, 15825, 814-856-2858
Buck Hill Inn, Buck Hill Falls, 18232, 800-233-8113
Buffalo Lodge, R.D.1, Box 277, Buffalo Mills, 15534, 814-623-2207
Bethany Guest House, 325 So. Main St., Cambridge Springs, 16403, 814-398-2046
Canadensis Old Village Inn, P.O. Box 404, Canadensis, 18325, 717-595-2120
Laurel Grove Inn, Canadensis, 18325, 717-595-7262
Old Village Inn, RR 1, Box 404, Canadensis, 18325, 717-595-2120
Overlook Inn, RD 1, Box 680, Canadensis, 18325, 717-595-7519
Pump House Inn Inc., RR1 Box 430, Skytop Rd., Canadensis, 18325, 717-595-7501
Fern Hall, Box 1095, RD 1, Crystal, Carbondale, 18407, 717-222-3676
Barn of Fleecydale Mill, Carversville, 18913
Historic Cashtown Inn, The, Old Route 30, Box 103, Cashtown, 17310, 717-334-9722
Cedar Run Inn, Cedar Run, 17727, 717-353-6241
Brandywine River Hotel, P.O. Box 1058, Chadd's Ford, 19317, 215-388-1200
Chadds Ford Inn, Rts. 1 & 100, Chadds Ford, 19317, 215-388-1473
Hedgerow B&B, 268 Kennett Pike, Chadds Ford, 19317, 215-388-6080
Hill House, Creek Rd., Chadds Ford, 19317
Sevenoaks Farm B&B, 492 New Galena Rd., Chalfont, 18914, 215-822-2164
Tara—A Country Inn, 3665 Valley View Rd., Clark, 16113, 412-962-3535
C & L B&B, 1327 Fairview Rd., Clark's Summit, 18411
Conifer Ridge Farm, RD 2, P.O. Box 202A, Clearville, 15535, 814-784-3342
River's Edge Cafe B&B, 203 Yough St., Confluence, 15424, 814-395-5059
Garrott's B&B, RD 1, Box 73, Cowansville, 16218, 412-545-2432
Cranberry B&B, Box 1009, Cranberry Township, 16033, 412-776-1198
Melanie Ann's B&B, 120 Center St., Danville, 17821
Pine Barn Inn, #1 Pine Barn Pl., Danville, 17821, 717-275-2071
Duck Hill Farm, R.D. 1, Downingtown, 19335
Pear & Patridge Inn, Dept. NT Old Easton Rd., Doylestown, 18901, 215-345-7800
Pine Tree Farm, 2155 Lower State Rd., Doylestown, 18901, 215-348-0632
Heritage Guest House, Rte 87 & 487, Dushore, 18614
Shady Lane Lodge, Alleghany Ave., Eaglesmere, 17731
Lafayette Inn, The, 525 W. Monroe St., Easton, 215-253-4500
Noon-Collins Inn, 114 East High St., Ebensburg, 15931, 814-472-4311
John Butler House B&B, The, 800 Rock Run Rd., Elizabeth, 15037, 412-751-6670
Inn at Elizabethville, 30 W. Main St., Elizabethville, 17023
Elm Country Inn, P.O. Box 37, Elm, 17521, 717-664-3623
Emig Mansion, Box 486, 3342 N.George, Emigsville, 17318, 717-764-2226
Clearview Farm B&B, 355 Clearview Rd., Ephrata, 17522, 717-733-6333
Gerhart House B&B, 287 Duke St., Ephrata, 17522, 717-733-0263
Issac Stover House, P.O. Box 68, Erwinna, 18920
Historic Fairfield Inn, 15 W. Main St., Box 196, Fairfield, 17320, 717-642-5410
Herb Cottage Inn, Lincoln Hwy E., Rt. 30, Fayetteville, 17222, 717-352-7733
Franklin B&B, 1501 Liberty St., Franklin, 16323, 814-432-4208
Ben-Mar Farm Lodging, R. D. 1, Box 106, Gap, 17527
Maplewood Farm B&B, P.O. Box 239, Gardenville-Bucks County, 18926, 215-766-0477
Abraham Spangle Inn, 264 Baltimore St., Gettysburg, 17325
Appleford Inn, 218 Carlisle St., Gettysburg, 17325, 717-337-1711
Cozy Comfort Inn, 264 Baltimore St., Gettysburg, 17325, 717-337-3997
Dobbin House Tavern Gettys, 89 Steinwehr Ave., Gettysburg, 17325, 717-334-2100
Herr Tavern Publick House, 900 Chambersburg Rd., Gettysburg, 717-334-4332
Historic Farnsworth House, 401 Baltimore St., Gettysburg, 17325, 717-334-8838

The Irondale Inn, Booomsburg, PA

Old Appleford Inn, 218 Carlisle St., Gettysburg, 17325
Swinn's Lodging, 31 E. Lincoln Ave., Gettysburg, 17325, 717-334-5255
Doubleday Inn, 104 Doubleday Ave., Gettysburg Battlefield, 17325
Goose Chase, 200 Blueberry Rd., Gettysburg–Gardners, 17324, 717-528-8877
Crier In The Country, Route 1, Glen Mills, 19342, 215-358-2411
Sweetwater Farm, 50 Sweetwater Rd., Glen Mills, 19342, 215-459-4711
Spoutwood Farm, RD 3, Box 66, Glen Rock, 17327, 717-235-6610
Huntland Farm B&B, RD #9, Box 21, Greensburg, 15601, 412-834-8483
Phillips 1890 House B&B, 32 Eagle St., Greenville, 16125, 412-588-4169
Log Cabin B&B, Box 393, Rt. 11, Hallstead, 18822, 717-879-4167
Gibson's B&B, 141 W. Caracas Ave., Hershey, 17033
Horetsky's Tourist Home, 217 Cocoa Ave., Hershey, 17033, 000-533-5783
Pinehurst Inn B&B, 50 Northeast Dr., Hershey, 17033, 717-533-2603
Shady Elms Farm B&B, Box 188, R.D1, Hickory, 15340, 412-356-7755
Yoder's B&B, RD 1, Box 312, Huntingdon, 16652, 814-643-3221
Villamayer, 1027 East Lake Rd., Jamestown, 16134, 412-932-5194
Willowood Inn, 215 West Lake Rd., Jamestown, 16134, 412-932-3866
Inn at Jim Thorpe, The, 24 Broadway, Jim Thorpe, 18229, 717-325-2599
Meadowbrook School B&B, 160 Engbert Rd., Johnstown, 15902, 814-539-1756
Kane Manor B&B, 230 Clay St., Kane, 16735, 814-837-6522
Hawk Mountain Inn, RD 1, Box 186, Kempton, 19529, 215-756-4224
Buttonwood Farm, 231 Pemberton Rd., Kennett Square, 19348, 215-444-0278
Campbell House B&B, 160 E. Doe Run Rd., Kennett Square, 19348, 215-347-6756
Bucksville House, R.D.2, Box 146, Kintnersville, 18930, 215-847-8948
Groff Tourist Farm Home, 766 Brackbill Rd., Kinzer, 17535, 717 442 8223
Lahaska Hotel, Route 202, Lahaska, 18931, 215-794-0440
Peddler's Village, P.O. Box 218, Lahaska, 18931
Buona Notte B&B, 2020 Marietta Ave., Lancaster, 17603
Candlelite Inn B&B, 2574 Lincoln Hwy East, Lancaster, 17572, 717-299-6005
Dingeldein House, 1105 E. King St., Lancaster, 17602, 717-293-1723
Landyshade Farms, 1801 Colebrook Rd., Lancaster, 17601, 717-898-7689
Lime Valley Cottage, 1107 Lime Valley Rd., Lancaster, 17602, 717-687-6118
Meadowview Guest House, 2169 New Holland Pike, Lancaster, 17601, 717-299-4017
New Life Homestead, 1400 E. King St., Lancaster, 17602
Inn at Twin Linden, 2092 Main St., Route 23, Lancaster–Churchtown, 17555, 215-445-7619
Limestone Inn B&B, 33 E. Main St., Lancaster–Strasburg, 17579, 717-687-8392
Liberty Hill B&B, 245 East Patterson St., Lansford, 18232
Ligonier Country Inn, P.O. Box 46, Rt. 30 E, Laughlintown, 15655, 412-238-3651
Loom Room, RD 1, Box 1420, Leesport, 19533, 215-926-3217
Millport Manor, 924 Log Cabin Rd., Leola, 17540, 717-627-0644
Turtle Hill Road B&B, 111 Turtle Hill Rd., Leola, 17540
Brookpark Farm B&B, 100 Reitz Blvd., Rt. 45, Lewisburg, 17837, 717-524-7733
Lewisburg Hotel, 136 Market St., Lewisburg, 17837, 717-523-1216
Grant House B&B, 244 W. Church St., Ligonier, 15658, 412-238-5135
Town House, 201 S. Fairfield St., Ligonier, 15658, 412-238-5451
Royalview Dairy Farm, Box 93, Lincoln University, 19352
Alden House, 62 E. Main St., Lititz, 17543, 717-627-3363
General Sutter Inn, 14 E. Main St., Lititz, 17543, 717-626-2115
Historic Gen. Sutter Inn, 14 East Main St., Lititz, 17543, 717-626-2115
Black Bass Hotel, 3774 River Rd., Rt. 32, Lumberville, 18933, 215-297-5770
Eaglesmere, RR 3, Box 2350, Malvern, 19355, 215-296-9696
Herr Farmhouse Inn, 2256 Huber Dr., Manheim, 17545, 717-653-9852
Jonde Lane Farm, R.D.7, Box 363, Manheim, 17545
Rose Manor, 124 S. Linden St., Manheim, 17545, 717-664-4932
Vogt Farm, 1225 Colebrook Rd., Marietta, 17547, 717-653-4810
Three Center Square Inn, P.O. Box 428, Maytown, 17550, 717-426-3036
Guest Home, 1040 Lincoln Way, McKeesport, 15132, 412-751-7143
Fairville Inn, Rt 52, Kennett Pk,Box 2, Mendenhall, 19357, 215-388-5900
Stranahan House B&B, The, 117 E. Market St., Mercer, 16137, 412-662-4516
Ye Olde Hotel, 124 W. Third St., Mifflinville, 18631
Pine Hill Farm B&B, P.O. Box 1001, Milford, 18337, 717-296-7395
Milheim Hotel, Main St., Milheim, 16854, 814-349-5994
Sunbury Street B&B, 310 E. Sunbury, Box 555, Millerstown, 17062, 717-589-7932
Walnut Hill B&B, 113 Walnut Hill Rd., Millersville, 17551, 717-872-2283
Windy Hill Bed & Breakfast, Candy Rd, RD1, Box 1085, Mohnton, 19540, 215-775-2755
Montrose House, The, 26 S. Main St., Montrose, 18801, 717-278-1124
Elvern Country Lodge, RR 2, Box 2099A, Mount Bethel, 18343
Mount Gretna Inn, Kauffman at Pine, Mount Gretna, 17064, 717-964-3234
Brenneman Farm - B&B, RD 1, Box 310, Mount Joy, 17552, 717-653-4213
Country Stay B&B, The, 2285 Bull Moose Rd., Mount Joy, 17552, 717-367-5167
Donegal Mills Plantation, Box 257, Mount Joy, 17552, 717-653-2168
Nolt Farm Guest Home, S. Jacob St. Farm, Mount Joy, 17552, 717-653-4192
Country Road B&B, HER 1, Box 9A, Grange R, Mount Pocono, 18344, 717-839-9234
Mountville Antiques B&B, 407 E. Main St., Rt. 4, Mountville, 17554, 717-285-5956
Tulpehocken Manor Inn, Route 422, RD 2, Myerstown, 17067
Waltman's B&B, RD 1, Box 87, New Albany, 18833, 717-363-2295
Tressler House B&B, The, P.O. Box 38, New Bloomfield, 17068, 717-582-2914
Farm Fortune, 204 Lime Kiln Rd., New Cumberland, 17070, 717-774-2683
Hacienda Inn, 36 W. Mechanics St., New Hope, 18938, 215-862-2078
Inn at Phillips Mill, North River Rd., New Hope, 18938, 215-862-9919
Logan Inn, 10 W. Ferry St., New Hope, 18938, 215-862-5134
Behm's B&B, 166 Waugh Ave., New Wilmington, 16142, 412-946-8641

Tavern, Box 153, On the Square, New Wilmington, 16142, 412-946-2020
White Cloud, RD 1, Box 215, Newfoundland, 18445, 717-676-3162
Central Bridge Inn, River Rd., NewHope, 18938
Temperance House, The, 5-11 S. State St., Newport, 18940, 215-860-0474
Flower Cottage B&B, 515 W. 6th St., Oil City, 16301
Salvino's Guest House, P.O. Box 116, Orbisonia, 17243, 814-447-5616
John Hayes House, 8100 Limestone Rd., Oxford, 19363, 215-932-5347
Neffdale Farm, 604 Strasburg Rd., Paradise, 17562, 717-687-7837

The Pine Knob, Canadensis, PA

Rayba Acres Farm, 183 Black Horse Rd., Paradise, 17562, 717-687-6729
Verdant View Farm, 429 Strasburg Rd., Paradise, 17562, 717-687-7353
Pleasant Grove Farm, R. D. 1, Box 132, PeachBottom, 17563
Abigail Adams B&B, 1208 Walnut St., Philadelphia, 19107, 215-893-9393
Germantown B&B, 5925 Wayne Ave., Philadelphia, 19144, 215-848-1375
Hotel La Reserve, 1804 Pine St., Philadelphia, 19103, 215-735-0582
Independence Park , 235 Chestnut St., Philadelphia, 19106
Society Hill Hotel, 301 Chestnut St., Philadelphia, 19106, 215-925-1919
Steele Away B&B, 7151 Boyer St., Philadelphia, 19119, 215-242-0722
Village Guest House B&B, 808 S. 2nd St., Philadelphia, 19147, 215-755-9770
Valley Forge B&B, 137 Forge Hill Ln., Phoenixville, 19460, 215-933-6460
Cole's Log Cabin B&B, RD 1, Box 98, Pine Bank, 15354, 412-627-9151
Forge, The, RD 1, Box 438, Pine Grove, 17963, 717-345-8349
Columbus Inn, The, 400 Landmarks Bldg., Pittsburgh, 15219, 412-471-5420
Oakwood, 235 Johnston Rd., Pittsburgh, 15241, 412-835-9565
Lenape Springs Farm B&B, P.O. Box 176, Pocopson, 19366, 215-793-2266
Inn of Innisfree, Box 108, Point Pleasant, 18950, 215-297-8329
Fairway Farm, Vaughan Rd., Pottstown, 19464, 215-326-1315
Hunter House B&B, 118 S. Fifth St., Reading, 19602, 215-374-6608
Inn at Centre Park, 730 Centre Ave., Reading, 19601, 215-374-8557
Bianconi's B&B, 727 East End Ave, Regent Square, 15221, 412-731-2252
Riegelsville Hotel, 10-12 Delaware Rd., Riegelsville, 18077, 215-749-2469
Carousel Inn, RR #2, Box 280, Rockwood, 15557, 814-926-2666
Wee Three Guest Haus, 233 Hartman Bridge Rd., Ronks, 17572, 717-687-8146
Towne House Inn, 138 Center St., Saint Marys, 15857, 814-781-1556
Century Inn, S, Scenery Hill, 15360, 412-945-6600
Blue Lion Inn, The, 350 S. Market St., Selinsgrove, 17870, 717-374-2929
Greissinger's Farm, 2397 Springdale Ln., Sewickley, 15143, 412-741-2597
Haag's Hotel, Main St., Shartlesville, 19554, 215-488-6692
Eagle Rock Lodge, River Rd., Box 265, Shawnee-On-Delaware, 18356, 717-421-2139
Field & Pine B&B, RD 5, Box 161, Shippensburg, 17257
Discoveries B&B, RD #1, Box 42, Sigel, 15680, 814-752-2632
Smoketown Village, 2495 Old Phila. Pike, Smoketown, 17576, 717-393-5975
Heart of Somerset, 130 W. Union St., Somerset, 15501, 814-445-6782
Nethercott Inn B&B, The, P.O. Box 26, Starrucca, 18462, 717-727-2211
Wye Oak Farm Tourists, RD #1, Box 152, Strasburg, 17579, 717-687-6547
Kaufman House, Box 183, Route 63, Sumneytown, 18084, 215-234-4181
April Valley B&B, RR 1, Box 141, Susquehanna, 18847, 717-756-2688
Jefferson Inn, RD 2, Box 36, Route 171, Thompson, 18465, 717-727-2625
Pace One, Glen Mills & Thornton, Thornton, 19373, 215-459-3702
Victorian Guest House, 118 York Av., Towanda, 18848, 717-265-6972
Silver Oak Leaf B&B, The, 196 Canton St., Troy, 16947, 717-297-4315
Tyler Hill B&B, P.O. Box 62, Route 371, Tyler Hill, 18469, 717-224-6418
Bridgeton House, P.O. Box 167, Upper Black Eddy, 18972, 215-982-5856
Tara, 1 Bridgeton Hill, Upper Black Eddy, 18972, 215-982-5457
B&B of Valley Forge, P.O. Box 562, Valley Forge, 19481, 800-344-0123
Valley Forge Mountain B&B, Box 562, Valley Forge, 19481
Bennett's B&B, 1700 Pennsylvania Ave E, Warrcn, 16365, 814-723-7358
Altheim B&B, 104 Walnut St., Waterford, 16441
Point House, P.O. Box 13, Waterville, 17776, 717-753-8707
Jesse Robinson Manor, 141 Main St., Wellsboro, 16901, 717-724-5704
Kaltenbach's B&B, Stony Ford Rd. 6, Wellsboro, 16901, 717-724-4954
Crooked Windsor, 409 S. Church St., West Chester, 19382, 215-692-4896
Dilworthtown Inn, Old Wilmington Pike, West Chester, 19382, 215-399-1390
Faunbrook B&B, 699 W. Rosedale Ave., West Chester, 19382, 215-436-5788
Highland Manor B&B, 855 Hillsdale Rd., West Chester, 19382, 215-686-6251
Marshalton Inn, Route 162, West Chester, 19380, 215-692-4367
Green Gables B&B, 2532 Willow St. Pike, Willow Street, 17584, 717-464-5546
Woodbury Inn, Main St., Woodbury, 16695, 814-766-3647
Woodward Inn, Box 177, Woodward, 16882, 814-349-8118
Wyalusing Hotel, 111 Main St., Wyalusing, 18853, 717-746-1204
Wycombe Inn, P.O. Box 204, Wycombe, 18980, 215-598-7000
Fairhaven, RD 12 Box 445, Keller, York, 17406, 717-252-3726
Inn at Mundis Mills, RD 22, Box 15, York, 17402, 717-755-2002
Twin Brook Inn, Box 1042, RD 24, Kreut, York, 17409, 717-757-5384

Rhode Island

BLOCK ISLAND

1661 Inn & Hotel Manisses
P.O. Box I, 1 Spring St, 02807
401-466-2421
Joan & Justin Abrams
May–October

$$$ B&B
25 rooms, 16 pb
AmEx, Visa, MC, *Rated*,
•
C-ltd/S-yes/P-no/H-yes

Full buffet breakfast
Lunch, dinner, full bar
Comp. brandy in room
ocean view deck
sitting room

Island country inn overlooking Atlantic Ocean–full buffet breakfast, wine & nibble hour, flaming coffees served on ocean view deck. **3rd night 50% off, off-season**

Blue Dory Inn, The
Box 488, Dodge St., 02807
401-466-5891 800-992-7290
Ann Loedy
All year

$$ B&B
13 rooms, 13 pb
Visa, MC, AmEx, *Rated*, ocean
•
C-yes/S-yes/P-no/H-ltd
Spanish, German

Continental plus
Bicycles, sitting room

Sam, resident feline

Charming Victorian inn with Block Island's beautiful crescent beach at our back door. Antique furnishings. Walk to beach, shops, restaurants. **3rd. night free, Ltd. ask.**

Hotel Manisses, 1661 Inn
P.O. Box I, 02807
401-466-2836 401-466-2421
J.& J. Abrams, R.& S. Draper
All year

$$$ B&B
18 rooms, 18 pb
Visa, MC, Amex, *Rated*,
•
C-ltd/S-yes/P-no/H-yes
Spanish, Portuguese

Full buffet breakfast
Lunch & dinner, full bar
Comp. wine, appetizers
elegant lobby, sitting
phones in all rooms

1872 Victorian hotel–fully restored–some rooms with jacuzzi. Gourmet dining, High Tea served daily. Seafood Raw Bar.

Rose Farm Inn
Roslyn Rd., P.O. Box E, 02807
401-466-2021
Judith B. Rose
May–October

$$$ B&B
10 rooms, 8 pb
Visa, MC, AmEx
C-ltd/S-ltd/P-no/H-no

Continental plus
Whirlpool baths, decks
some canopies, bicycles
stone porch, gardens

Sea & country setting. Furnished with antiques, queen or king size beds, some with canopy. Bicycle or stroll to waterfront shops & sights. **5% discount on room rate**

Sheffield House, The
P.O. Box C-2, High St., 02807
401-466-2494
Claire & Steve McQueeny
All year

$$ B&B
7 rooms, 5 pb
Visa, MC, AmEx, •
C-ltd/S-yes/P-no/H-yes

Continental plus
Comp. wine, snacks, tea
Bicycles & tennis nearby
beaches, hiking trails
bird sanctuaries, nature

1886 Victorian home in the historic district; walk to beach, shops, restaurants. Quiet, gracious home furnished in family antiques & collections. **3rd. night 50% off, Ltd.**

BLOCK ISLAND ————————————————————————

Spring House Hotel, The	$$ B&B	Continental plus
P.O. Box 902, 02807	50 rooms, 50 pb	Comp. wine,lunch, dinner
902 Spring St.	Visa, MC, AmEx, •	Restaurant, bar, library
401-466-5844	C-yes/S-yes/P-no/H-no	sitting room, bicycles
Vincent J. McAloon		volleyball, horseshoes

Elegant Victorian hotel on 15-acre promontory overlooking seascape. Wide verandas, sweeping green lawns, quiet pond with swans. Many natural wonders. **3rd night 50% off, Ltd**

BRISTOL ————————————————————————

William's Grant Inn	$$$ B&B	Full breakfast
154 High St., 02809	5 rooms, 3 pb	Aft. tea, comp. sherry
401-253-4222	Most CC, *Rated*, •	Sitting room, library
Michael & Mary Weaver Rose	C-ltd/S-ltd/P-no/H-ltd	bicycles
All year		box lunches for picnics

On a quiet tree-lined street you'll find William's Grant Inn. Filled with family antiques and artist's fine work. **Third night 50% off**

GREEN HILL ————————————————————————

Fairfield-by-The-Sea B&B	$$ B&B	Gourmet cont./cont. plus
527 Green Hill Beach Rd, 02879	2 rooms	Comp. wine
401-789-4717	•	Sitting room
Jeanne Ayers Lewis	C-ltd/S-ltd	library
All year		tennis courts

Artist's contemporary house filled with art and books. Near ocean, great restaurants, historical places, Block Island, Newport, and Mystic. Fireplaces. **Off season lower rates**

MIDDLETOWN ————————————————————————

Country Goose B&B, The	$$ B&B	Continental
563 Greenend Ave., 02840	3 rooms	Wine & cheese on arrival
401-846-6308	Visa, MC, *Rated*	Sitting room, bicycles
Paula Kelley	C-ltd/S-yes/P-no/H-no	large yard, volleyball
All year		near tennis & beach

Country setting minutes from Newport. Front porch with wicker for comfortable relaxation. Family heirlooms and antiques. **Comp. wine & cheese upon arrival & midweek rates**

NARRAGANSETT ————————————————————————

Richards, The	$$ B&B	Full gourmet breakfast
144 Gibson Ave., 02882	3 rooms, 2 pb	Comp. sherry in room
401-789-7746	C-ltd/S-no/P-no/H-no	Library w/fireplace
Nancy & Steven Richards		tennis courts nearby
All year		fireplaces in bedrooms

Gracious accommodations in a country setting. Awaken to the smell of gourmet coffee and freshly baked goods. Walk to the beach. Suite w/king bed, sitting room, private bath.

Sea Gull Guest House	$ EP	Bar service
50 Narragansett Ave., 02882	5 rooms	Tennis courts nearby
401-783-4636	Visa, MC, *Rated*, •	near gambling casino
Kimber Wheelock	C-yes/S-yes/P-no/H-no	ocean beach 1 block
All year		

Large rooms cooled by ocean breezes. Close to everything. Swim, sun, sail and fish in comfort that you can afford. **Stay 7 nights, pay for only 6. Midweek special, ask**

NARRAGANSETT

White Rose B&B	$ B&B	Full breakfast
22 Cedar St., 02882	4 rooms	Refrigerator, comp. wine
401-789-0181	*Rated*	Sitting room with TV
Pat & Sylvan Vaicaitis	C-ltd/S-no/P-no/H-no	bikes, 1 block to ocean
All year	Some French & Spanish	fishing, tennis nearby

A classic Victorian where the upbeat atmosphere is simple and elegant. Enjoy the breeze of the front porch or soak up the sun in our large yard.

NEWPORT

Admiral Benbow Inn	$$ B&B	Continental plus
8 Fair St., 93 Pelham St., 02840	15 rooms, 15 pb	Breakfast/conf. room
401-846-4256 800-343-2863	Visa, MC, AmEx, •	air conditioning
Cathy	C-yes/S-no/P-yes/H-no	telephone service, Fax
February–December		

Brass beds, antiques and atmosphere, deck and spectacular view of Narragansett Bay. A treasure on our island. **Free wine on Birthdays, Anniversaries, etc.**

Admiral Farragut Inn	$$$ B&B	Full breakfast
8 Fair St., 31 Clarke St., 02840	8 rooms, 8 pb	Afternoon tea
401-846-4256	Visa, MC, AmEx, •	Sitting room
Dee	C-yes/S-ltd/P-no/H-yes	air conditioning
All year		telephones, Fax

Carefully restored 1702 colonial, furnished with English antiques. All hand-made pencil four-poster beds, comfortable accommodations. A truly unique inn. **free wine spec. occasions**

Admiral Fitzroy Inn	$$$ B&B	Full breakfast
398 Thames St., 02840	18 rooms, 18 pb	Afternoon tea, snacks
401-846-4256 800-343-2836	Visa, MC, AmEx, *Rated*,	Refrigerator, cable TV
Evelyn & Lynn	•	telephone & coffee maker
All year exc. January	C-yes/S-yes/P-no/H-yes	in room, hair dryer, A/C

Small hotel located in town near harbor. Harborviews, gracious, attentive service. Large, comfortable rooms ind. decorated w/hand-painted walls. **Free wine/special occasions**

Brinley Victorian Inn	$$ B&B	Continental breakfast
23 Brinley St., 02840	17 rooms, 12 pb	Wine & lobster dinner
401-849-7645 800-999-8523	*Rated*, •	Sitting room
John & Jennifer Sweetman	C-ltd/S-yes/P-no/H-no	landscaped courtyard
All year		A/C, gardens

Romantic Victorian uniquely decorated w/antiques, period wallpapers. Brick courtyard planted w/Victorian flowers. Park & walk to historic sites/beaches.

Cliff View Guest House	$$ B&B	Continental plus
4 Cliff Terrace, 02840	4 rooms, 2 pb	Sitting room
401-846-0885	Visa, MC	piano
Pauline & John Shea	C-ltd/S-yes/P-no/H-no	
May 1–November 1		

Two-story Victorian (circa 1871-1890). East side has view of Atlantic Ocean. Two porches, open sun deck. Walk to beach or Cliff Walk.

NEWPORT —————————————————————————————————

Cliffside Inn
2 Seaview Ave., 02840
401-847-1811 800-845-1811
Annette & Norbert Mede
May–October

$$$ B&B
12 rooms, 12 pb
Visa, MC, AmEx, *Rated*,
•
C-ltd/S-no/P-no/H-no

Full breakfast
Afternoon appetizers
Living rm, porch, piano
5 rms w/whirlpool
6 rms w/AC, 4 w/fireplcs

Gracious Victorian home near beach & Cliff Walk. Each room individually & tastefully decorated w/antiques. **Call for packages**

Commodore Perry
8 Fair St., Side door 348 Thames
St., 02840
401-846-4256 800-343-2863
All year

$$ Pension
9 rooms
Visa, MC, AmEx, •
C-yes/S-no/P-yes

3 meals available
Ark Restaurant
Cable TV, A/C, Fax
Tea & coffee fixings
3rd floor walkup

The inn is located above the Ark Restaurant and is decorated in Japanese motif. Very much in the hustle and bustle of Newport.

Halidon Hill Guest House
Halidon Ave., 02840
401-847-8318
Helen & Paul Burke
All year

$$ B&B
6 rooms, 3 pb
AmEx, •
C-yes/S-yes/P-no/H-yes
Russian, Fr. Span., ltd.

Continental plus
Swimming pool
sitting room

Modern, spacious rooms, ample on-site parking, inground pool/deck area, walk to Hammersmith Farm, minutes to beach. Convenient to shopping areas, restaurants, mansions.

Hydrangea House Inn
16 Bellevue Ave., 02840
800-945-4667
All year

$$ B&B
6 rooms, 6 pb
Visa, MC, *Rated*, •
C-yes/S-no/P-no/H-no

Full breakfast
Snacks
Sitting room

Within Newport's "Walking District." A gratifying hot breakfast buffet served in our contemporary art gallery. Air-conditioned, private parking. AAA rated 2 stars.

Inn at Old Beach, The
19 Old Beach Rd., 02840
401-849-3479
Cynthia & Luke Murray
All year

$$$ B&B
7 rooms, 7 pb
Visa, MC, AmEx
C-ltd/S-no/P-no/H-no

Continental plus
Comp. bottle champagne
Gazebo, fish pond, patio
Sitting room, fireplaces
garden, some A/C & TVs

An intimate Inn built in 1879 with elegant accommodations; close to beaches, fabled mansions, cliff-walk, restaurants and historic harborfront.

Melville House, The
39 Clarke St., 02840
401-847-0640
Vincent DeRico, David Horan
March–December

$ B&B
7 rooms, 5 pb
Visa, MC, AmEx, *Rated*,
•
C-ltd/P-no/H-no

Continental plus
Comp. sherry, tea, snack
Sitting room
library, bicycles
off-street parking

1750 colonial inn, heart of historic district, close to shops, restaurants, wharfs. Homemade granola, yogurt, and muffins for breakfast. National Register of Historic Places.

NEWPORT ─────────────────────────────────────

Merritt House Guests c1850 $$$ B&B   Full breakfast
57 - 2nd St., 02840   2 rooms, 1 pb   Hot or iced tea
401-847-4289   *Rated*, •   Sitting room
Angela R. Vars   C-ltd   private dining room
All year   patio, glider in yard

Historic home (circa 1850) in Point Section, close to bay & center of city, beaches & mansions. Nominated one of 100 Best B&B Homes in North America. **Restaurant discounts**

Mill Street Inn $$$ B&B   Continental breakfast
75 Mill St., 02840   23 rooms, 23 pb   Afternoon tea
401-849-9500 800-392-1316   Most CC, *Rated*   Sun deck with view
Robert & Paula Briskin   C-yes/S-yes/H-yes   parking
All year

Located in a 19th-century mill w/ panoramic view of Narragansett Bay. We combine affordable luxury w/ impeccable service. **Packages available throughout year, 10% AAA discount**

Pilgrim House Inn $$ B&B   Continental plus
123 Spring St., 02840   10 rooms, 8 pb   Comp. sherry, shortbread
401-846-0040 800-525-8373   Visa, MC, *Rated*, •   Deck
Pam & Bruce Bayuk   C-ltd/S-yes/P-no/H-no   living room w/fireplace
All year

Beautifully restored Victorian home in center of downtown historic district; magnificent rooftop deck with panoramic view of Newport Harbor. **Midweek 3 night special.**

Spring Street Inn $$ B&B   Full breakfast
353 Spring St., 02840   5 rooms, 5 pb   Afternoon tea
401-847-4767   Visa, MC, •   Sitting room
Parvin & Damian Latimore   C-ltd/S-yes/P-no/H-no   parking, bus loop
All year   two blocks from harbour

Charming restored Empire Victorian house, c.1858; free on-site parking; harbour view apartment w/balcony (sleeps 2-4). Free bus loop nearby. **25% off 3rd night midwk + wine**

Stella Maris Inn $$ B&B   Continental plus
91 Washington St., 02840   8 rooms, 8 pb   Aft. tea, Comp. wine
401-849-2862   C-ltd/S-no/P-no/H-no   Sitting room, library
Dorothy & Ed Madden   Minimal French
All year

1861 Victorian mansion. Newly renovated, water view rooms, fireplaces, spacious porch and gardens, antique decor, homemade muffins, walk to town. Elegant & romantic.

Villa Liberté $$ B&B   Continental breakfast
22 Liberty St., 02840   15 rooms, 15 pb   Dinner, Tavern Fare
401-846-7444 800-392-3717   Visa, MC   "Harpo's" Lounge, bar
Leigh Anne Mosco   C-yes/S-yes/P-no/H-no   sun deck, room service
All year exc. January   suites w/kitchens

Elegance with the intimacy of a guest house. Suites, rooms, apartments in a 1910 "House of the evening." Ideally located off Historic Bellevue Avenue in the heart of Newport.

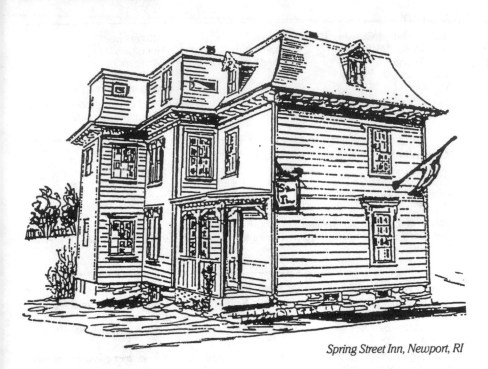

Spring Street Inn, Newport, RI

NEWPORT

Willows of Newport, The
8 & 10 Willow St., Historic Point
District, 02840
401-846-5486
Pattie Murphy
February–January 3

$$$ B&B
5 rooms, 5 pb
Rated, •
C-ltd/S-ltd/P-no/H-no

Continental breakfast
Black-Tie-Brkfast-in-Bed
Victorian parlor
wet bar
secret victorian garden

Elegant breakfast in bed—cut flowers, mints on your pillow. Private parking and private bath, air conditioning. Featured nationally on PM Magazine.

NEWPORT—MIDDLETOWN

Lindsey's Guest House
6 James St., 02842
401-846-9386
Anne Lindsey
All year

$$ B&B
3 rooms, 1 pb
Visa, MC, *Rated*, •
C-yes/H-yes

Continental plus
Tennis nearby, sitt. rm.
large yard, deck
ceiling fans in all rms

Quiet, 10 min. walk to beaches and restaurants. One mile Bellevue Avenue mansions. Two miles downtown Newport harborfront. Off-street parking. **3rd night 50% off, ltd**

PROVIDENCE

Old Court B&B, The
144 Benefit St., 02903
401-751-2002
Becky Aijala
All year

$$$ B&B
10 rooms, 10 pb
Most CC, *Rated*, •
C-ltd/S-yes/P-no/H-no
French

Continental plus
Comp. tea
Kitchen, washer/dryer
antiques, apt. available
wet bars in some rooms

Built in 1863, Italianate in design and in ornate details; combines tradition with contemporary standards of luxury; filled with antique furniture, chandeliers. Private baths.

PROVIDENCE

State House Inn
43 Jewett St., 02908
401-785-1235
Monica & Frank Hopton
All year

$$$ B&B
10 rooms, 10 pb
Visa, MC, AmEx, *Rated*,
•
C-yes/S-no/P-no/H-no

Full breakfast
Snacks
Sitting room

Charming country B&B decorated with shaker and colonial furnishings with all the privacy and amenities frequent travelers desire. 3rd night 50% off.

WAKEFIELD

Larchwood Inn, The
521 Main St., 02879
401-783-5454 FAX:783-1800
Francis & Diann Browning
All year

$ EP
19 rooms
Most CC, *Rated*, •
C-yes/S-yes/P-yes/H-no
Spanish, French

All meals available $
Restaurant, bar
Cocktail lounge
sitting room

Intimate country inn in New England townhouse style. Circa 1831. Conveniently located near Newport, Mystic Seaport, Block Island and Univ. of Rhode Island.

WESTERLY

Shelter Harbor Inn
10 Wagner Rd., Route 1, 02891
401-322-8883
Jim & Debbye Dey
All year

$$$ B&B
24 rooms, 24 pb
Most CC, *Rated*, •
C-yes/S-yes/P-no/H-no

Full breakfast
Lunch, dinner, bar
Library, paddle tennis
hot tub, croquet court
private beach, gardens

A charming country inn where the emphasis is on relaxation, superlative food, and a warm friendly atmosphere. Just a mile from the Rhode Island shore.

Woody Hill B&B
330 Woody Hill Rd., 02891
401-322-0452
Ellen L. Madison
All year

$$ B&B
5 rooms, 5 pb
•
C-yes/S-no/P-no/H-ltd

Full country breakfast
Extensive library
porch with swing, pool
winter hearth cooking

Near beaches and Mystic Seaport, secluded country atmosphere. In-ground pool. Handmade quilts, antiques, wide-board floors, gardens, casual Colonial feeling. 7th night free

WYOMING

Cookie Jar B&B, The
64 Kingston Rd., Route 138, just
off I95, 02898
401-539-2680 800-767-4262
Dick & Madelein Sohl
All year

$$ B&B
3 rooms, 1 pb
Rated, •
C-yes/S-no/P-no/H-no

Full breakfast
Snacks
Library, 3 acres has
fruit trees, grape vines
berries, grass & gardens

Outside, a simple farmhouse—unusually attractive inside. Living room was a 1732 blacksmith shop—almost in original condition. Swimming pool & golf nearby. 3rd night 50% off

More Inns . . .

Atlantic Inn, Box 188, Block Island, 02807, 401-466-2005
Barrington Inn, P.O. Box 397, Block Island, 02807, 401-466-5510
Driftwind Guests, High St., Block Island, 02807, 401-466-5548
Gables Inn, P.O. Box 516, Block Island, 02807, 401-466-2213
Gothic Inn, P.O. Box 458, Block Island, 02807, 401-466-2918
Guest House, P.O. Box 24, Center Rd., Block Island, 02807, 401-466-2676
Inn at Old Harbour, The, Water St., Block Island, 02807
Island Home, PO Box 737, Beach Ave., Block Island, 02807
Island Manor Resort, Chapel St., Block Island, 02807, 401-466-5567
Lewis Farm, Cooneymas Rd., Block Island, 02807, 401-466-2428
Mill Pond Cottages, Old Town Rd., Block Island, 02807, 401-466-2423
New Shoreham House Inn, P.O. Box 356, Water St., Block Island, 02807, 401-466-2651
Old Town Inn, Old Town Rd, P.O. Box 3, Block Island, 02807, 401-466-5958

Samuel Peckham Tavern, New Harbor, Block Island, 02807

Sea Breeze Inn, Spring St., Box 141, Block Island, 02807, 401-466-2275

Seacrest Inn, 207 High St., Block Island, 02807, 401-466-2882

White House, The, Spring St., Block Island, 02807, 401-466-2653

Willow Grove, P.O. Box 156, Block Island, 02807, 401-466-2896

Joseph Reynolds House, 956 Hope St., Bristol, 02809, 401-254-0230

Country Acres B&B, Box 551, Carolina, 02812, 401-364-9134

General Stanton Inn, P.O. Box 222, Charleston, 02813, 401-364-8888

"Hathaways", Box 731, Charlestown, 02813, 401-364-6665

Lindsey's Guest House, Middletown, RI

Inn the Meadow, 1045 Shannock Rd., Charlestown, 02813, 401-789-1473

King Tom Farm, P.O. Box 1440, Charlestown, 02807, 401-364-3371

Windswept Farm Inn, Rt. 1, Post Rd, Box 154, Charlestown, 02807, 401-364-6292

Mary W. Murphy, 59 Walcott Ave., Jamestown, 02835, 401-423-1338

Nordic Lodge, Pasquiset Pond Rd., Kenyon, 02836, 401-783-4515

Hedgerow B&B, 1747 Mooresfield Rd., Kingston, 02881, 401-783-2671

Ballyvoreen, 75 Stone Church Rd., Little Compton, 02837, 401-635-4396

Finnegan's Inn at Shadow L, 120 Miantonomi Ave., Middletown, 02840, 401-847-0902

Peckham's Guest Home, 272 Paradise Av., Middletown, 02840, 401-846-2382

Whimsey Cottage, 42 Briarwood Ave, Middletown, 02840, 401-841-5824

Andrea Hotel, 89 Atlantic Ave., Misquamicut, 02891, 401-348-8788

Ocean View, Atlantic Ave., Misquamicut Beach, 02891, 401-596-7170

Meadowland B&B Ltd., 765 Old Baptist Rd., N. Kingstown, 02852, 401-294-4168

1900 House, The, 59 Kingstown Rd., Narragansett, 02882, 401-789-7971

Chestnut House, 11 Chestnut St., Narragansett, 02882, 401-789-5335

Duck Harbor, 295 Boston Neck Rd., Narragansett, 02882, 401-783-3495

Going My Way, 75 Kingstown Rd., Narragansett, 02882, 401-789-3479

Grinnell Inn, 83 Narragansett Ave., Narragansett, 02882

House of Snee, 191 Ocean Rd., Narragansett, 02882, 401-783-9494

Ilverthorpe Cottage, 41 Robinson St., Narragansett, 02882, 401-789-2392

Kenyon Farms, P.O. Box 648, Narragansett, 02882, 401-783-7123

Mon Reve, 41 Gibson Ave., Narragansett, 02882, 401-783-2846

Murphy's B&B, 43 South Pier Rd., Narragansett, 02882, 401-789-1824

Narragansett Pier Inn, 7 Prospect Ave., Narragansett, 02882, 401-783-8090

Phoenix House, 29 Gibson Ave., Narragansett, 02882, 401-783-1918

Pier House Inn, 113 Ocean Rd., Narragansett, 02882, 401-783-4704

Pleasant Cottage B&B, 104 Robinson St., Narragansett, 02882, 401-783-6895

Southwest Wind Acres, 8 Lindsley Rd., Narragansett, 02882, 401-783-5860

Stone Lea, 40 Newton Ave., Narragansett, 02882, 401-783-9546

Twenty-Three Perkins, 23 Perkins, Narragansett, 02882, 401-783-9158

1855 Marshall Slocum House, 29 Kay St., Newport, 401-841-5120

Aboard Commander's Quarter, 54 Dixon St., Newport, 02840, 401-849-8393

Anna's Victorian, 5 Fowler Av., Newport, 02840, 401-849-2489

Bellevue House, 14 Catherine St., Newport, 02840, 401-847-1828

Blue Stone, 33 Russell Ave., Newport, 02840, 401-846-5408

Castle Keep, 44 Everett, Newport, 02840, 401-846-0362

Cliff Walk Manor, 82 Memorial Blvd, Newport, 02840, 401-847-1300

Covell Guest House, 43 Farewell St., Newport, 02840, 401-847-8872

Elm Tree Cottage, 336 Gibbs Av., Newport, 02840, 401-849-1610

Flag Quarters B&B, 54 Malbone Rd., Newport, 02840, 401-849-4543

Francis Malbone House, The, 392 Thames St, Newport, 02840, 401-846-0392

Guest House International, 28 Weaver Ave., Newport, 02840, 401-847-1501

Hammett House Inn B&B, 505 Thames St., Newport, 02840

Harborside Inn, Christie's Landing, Newport, 02840, 401-846-6600

Inn at Castle Hill, Ocean Dr., Newport, 02840, 401-849-3800

Inn of Jonathan Bowen, 29 Pelham St., Newport, 02840, 401-846-3324

Inntowne, 6 Mary St., Newport, 02840, 401-846-9200

Ivy Lodge, 12 Clay St., Newport, 02840, 401-849-6865

Jailhouse Inn, 13 Marlborough St., Newport, 02840, 401-847-4638

John Banister House, 56 Pelham St., Newport, 02840, 401-846-0050

La Forge cottage, 96 Pelham St., Newport, 02840, 401-847-4400

Ma Gallagher's, 348 Thames St., Newport, 02840, 401-849-3975

Mount Vernon Inn, 24 Mount Vernon St., Newport, 02840, 401-846-6314

Ocean Cliff, Ocean Dr., Newport, 02840, 401-849-9000

Old Dennis House, 59 Washington St., Newport, 02840, 401-846-1324

One Bliss, One Bliss Rd., Newport, 02840, 401-846-5329

Rhode Island House, 77 Rhode Island Ave., Newport, 02840, 401-849-7765

Samuel Honey House, 12 Francis St., Newport, 02840, 401-847-2669

Sea Quest, 9 Cliff Terrace, Newport, 02840, 401-846-0227

Thames Street Inn, 400 Thames St., Newport, 02840, 401-847-4459

Victorian Ladies, The, 63 Memorial Blvd., Newport, 02840, 401-849-9960

Wayside, 406 Bellevue Ave., Newport, 02840, 401-847-0302

William Fludder House, 30 Bellevue Ave., Newport, 02840, 401-849-4220

Sunset Cabins, 1172 W. Main Rd., Portsmouth, 02871, 401-683-1874

Twin Spruce Tourist, 515 Turnpike Ave., Portsmouth, 02871
Newport Collection, The, 445 Putman Pike, Smithfield, 02828, 800-947-4667
Admiral Dewey Inn, 668 Matunuck Beach Rd., South Kingstown, 02879, 401-783-2090
Blueberry Bush, 128 South Rd., South Kingstown-Wakefiel, 02879
Highland Farm, 4145 Tower Hill Rd., South Kingstown-Wakefiel, 02879
Stone Bridge Inn, 1 Lawton Ave., Tiverton, 02878, 401-624-6601
"Almost Heaven" B&B, 49 W. St., Wakefield, 02879, 401-783-9272
Open Gate Motel, 840 Quaker Ln., Warwick, 02886, 401-884-4490
Hartley's Guest House, Larkin Rd., Watch Hill, 02891
Inn at Watch Hill, Bay St., Watch Hill, 02891, 401-596-0665
Ocean House, 2 Bluff Ave, Watch Hill, 02891, 401-348-8161
Watch Hill Inn, 50 Bay St., Watch Hill, 02891, 401-348-8912
Weekapaug Inn, Weekapaug, 02891, 401-322-0301
Cornerstone Inn, Route 1, Westerly, 02891, 401-322-3020
Grandview B&B, 212 Shore Rd., Westerly, 02891, 401-596-6384
Harbour House, Bay St., Westerly, 02891
Inn on the Hill, 29 Summer St., Westerly, 02891, 401-596-3791
J. Livingston's Guesthouse, 39 Weekapang Rd., Westerly, 02891, 401-322-0249
Seven Granite St. B&B, 7 Granite St., Westerly, 02891, 401-596-6384
Villa, The, 190 Shore Rd., Westerly, 02891, 401-596-1054
Moran's B&B, The, 130 W. Main St., Wickford, 02852, 401-294-3497
Sparrow's Nest, 470 Annaquatucket Rd., Wickford, 02852, 401-295-1142
Away Stop, 161 New London Trnpike, Wyoming, 02898, 401-539-7233

South Carolina

AIKEN

New-Berry Inn B&B	$$ B&B	Full breakfast
240 New Berry St. SW, 29801	6 rooms, 6 pb	Comp. coffee, beverages
803-649-2935	Visa, MC, AmEx, DC, •	Snacks, sitting room
Wendy & Dave Mason	C-yes/S-yes/P-no/H-yes	golf, hiking, and
All year		horseback riding nearby

Quiet relaxed atmosphere of the South. New England-style home. Five large rooms with private baths and antiques. Historic area. Golf, hiking, horse country. **Govt./Corp. rates**

BEAUFORT

Bay Street Inn	$$$ B&B	Full breakfast
601 Bay St., 29902	6 rooms, 6 pb	Sherry, fruit, chocolate
803-524-0050	Visa, MC, *Rated*,	Library, bicycles
Jeff & Leslee Peth	C-ltd/S-yes/P-no/H-no	air conditioned
All year	French	bridal suite

Antebellum cotton planter's home furnished with antiques; beautiful water views & fireplaces in every room; beaches, restaurants, golf and tennis nearby.

Old Point Inn	$$ B&B	Full breakfast
212 New St., 29902	4 rooms, 4 pb	Comp. wine
803-524-3177	Visa, MC, AmEx	Library, piano
Joan and Joe Carpentiere	C-ltd/S-ltd/P-no/H-no	Garden, FAX
All year		bicycles

1898 Queen Anne, heart of historic district near shops, restaurants, park. Relax on verandas, nap in our hammock; enjoy low country hospitality.

BEAUFORT

Rhett House Inn, The	$$$ B&B	Full breakfast, Aft. tea
1009 Craven St., 29902	10 rooms, 10 pb	Comp. sherry in rooms
803-524-9030	Visa, MC, *Rated*, •	Sitting room, library
Marianne & Stephen Harrison	C-ltd/S-no/P-no/H-no	dinner by reservation
All year	Spanish	phones in room, A/C, TV

Restored, historic antebellum mansion. Beautifully landscaped gardens. Courtyard w/fountain. Walk to everything. Enjoy hammocks on a wide veranda. Mobil-4 stars. **Comp. wine**

TwoSuns Inn B&B	$$$ B&B	Full breakfast
1705 Bay St., 29902	5 rooms, 5 pb	Aftn. tea, comp. wine
803-522-1122 800-532-4244	Visa, MC, AmEx, *Rated*,	Sitting room, bicycles
Carrol and Ron Kay	•	public tennis courts
All year, FAX: 522-1122	C-ltd/S-no/P-no/H-yes	computer, fax, cable TV

Enjoy the bay from our veranda, explore the charm of Historic Beaufort (founded in 1711) and relax with gracious hospitality. Handwoven items available from Carrol.

BLACKSBURG

White House Inn	$$ B&B	Full breakfast
607 West Pine St., 29702	5 rooms, 4 pb	Snacks, comp. wine
803-839-3000 800-352-6077	Visa, MC, *Rated*	Sitting room, library
Jim White & Jo Ann Miller	C-ltd/S-no/P-no/H-no	tennis nearby
All year	Some Spanish	goldfish pond in yard

Greek Revival completely renovated, elegant antiques & collections. Private baths & fireplaces, near historic battlegrounds, gourmet breakfasts. **15% discount 3 nights**

CHARLESTON

1837 B&B/Tearoom	$$ B&B	Full gourmet breakfast
126 Wentworth St., 29401	8 rooms, 8 pb	Beer or wine avail. ($)
803-723-7166	AmEx, Visa, MC, *Rated*	Comp. mint tea or coffee
Sherri Weaver, Richard Dunn	C-ltd/S-no/P-no/H-no	piazzas, rocking chairs
All year	French	Canopied rice beds

Gracious southern home owned by 2 artists, centrally located in Charleston's historic district. Gourmet breakfast in dining room or on piazza. Walk to Old Market, restaurants.

Ann Harper's B&B	$$ B&B	Full breakfast
56 Smith St., 29401	2 rooms, 1 pb	Small garden
803-723-3947	C-ltd/S-ltd/P-no/H-no	off-street parking
Ann D. Harper		
All year		

Charming circa 1870 home located in Charleston's historic district. The owner, a retired medical technologist, enjoys serving a full Southern breakfast each morning.

Ashley Inn B&B	$$ B&B	Full breakfast
201 Ashley Ave., 29403	7 rooms, 7 pb	Aft. tea, snacks
803-723-1848	Visa, MC, *Rated*	Comp. wine
Sally & Bud Allen	C-ltd/S-ltd/P-no/H-no	sitting room
All year		bicycles

Sleep until the fragrance of southern cooking lures you to garden breakfast. Fireplaces, private baths & bikes assure the best Charleston experience. **Comp. aft. sherry & tea**

Ashley Inn B&B, Charleston, SC

CHARLESTON ―――――――――――――――――――――――――――――――

Barksdale House Inn, The	$$$ B&B	Continental breakfast
27 George St., 29401	10 rooms, 10 pb	Comp. tea, wine
803-577-4800	Visa, MC, *Rated*, ●	Sitting room
George & Peggy Sloan	C-ltd/S-yes/P-no/H-no	whirlpool baths, decks
All year exc. Christmas		bicycle rental

Circa 1778, elegant inn with whirlpool baths, fireplaces, built-in dry bars, elaborate furnishings and antiques; adjacent to the historic shopping district. **Bottle/wine**

Battery Carriage House Inn	$$$ B&B	Continental breakfast
20 S. Battery, 29401	11 rooms, 11 pb	Comp. wine
803-723-9881 800-775-5575	Most CC, *Rated*, ●	3 whirlpool baths
Katherine Hastie	C-ltd/S-ltd/P-no/H-no	4 steam showers
All year		

Very romantic, elegant. Located in garden of historic mansions on the Battery; silver tray breakfast, friendly and professional staff. **Champagne on arrival**

Belvedere B&B, The	$$$ B&B	Continental breakfast
40 Rutledge Ave., 29401	3 rooms, 3 pb	Sherry
803-722-0973	*Rated*	Sitting room, newspaper
David Spell & Rick Zender	C-ltd/S-yes/P-no/H-no	TV, A/C, bicycles
All year		porch with lake view

We offer hospitable accommodations in our gracious mansion overlooking beautiful Colonial Lake. We provide bicycles, sherry and other extras. **2 nights, free print of Inn**

Brasington House B&B	$$$ B&B	Full breakfast
328 E. Bay St., 29401	4 rooms, 4 pb	Comp. wine
803-722-1274 FAX:722-6785	Visa, MC, *Rated*	Sitting room, books
Dalton & Judy Brasington	C-ltd/S-no/P-no/H-no	
All year		

200 year old antebellum house elegantly furnished w/antiques. Located in Historic District. Breakfast in formal dining room, wine and liquors included. Gracious hospitality.

CHARLESTON ————————————————————————————

Cannonboro Inn
184 Ashley Ave., 29403
803-723-8572
Sally & Bud Allen
All year

$$ B&B
6 rooms, 6 pb
Visa, MC, *Rated*, •
C-ltd/S-no/P-no/H-no

Full breakfast
Comp. sherry, tea
Sitting room, library
garden, tennis courts
comp. touring bikes

Antebellum home c.1850 in Charleston's historic district. Enjoy a full breakfast served on a circular piazza overlooking a low country garden. All rooms have fireplaces.

Country Victorian B&B
105 Tradd St., 29401
803-577-0682
Diane Deardurff Weed
All year

$$$ B&B
2 rooms, 2 pb
•
C-ltd/S-no/P-no/H-no

Continental plus
Afternoon tea, snacks
Parking, bicycles
TV, restaurants nearby
piazzas

Private entrances, antique iron and brass beds, old quilts, antique oak and wicker furniture. Situated in the historic district. Walk to everything. Many extras.

John Rutledge House Inn
116 Broad St., 29401
803-723-7999 800-476-9741
Linda Bishop
All year

$$$ B&B
19 rooms, 19 pb
Visa, MC, AmEx, *Rated*,
•
C-yes/S-ltd/P-no/H-yes

Continental plus/full $
Comp. wine/brandy/sherry
Bar, sitting room
hot tubs, concierge
turndown service

John Rutledge, a signer of US Constitution, built this elegant home in 1763. Visit and re-live history. Downtown location near shopping & historic sites. AAA 4 diamond.

King George IV Inn
32 George St., 114 Rutledge
Ave., 29401
803-723-9339 803-722-7551
Jean, B.J., Mike
All year

$$ B&B
8 rooms, 8 pb
Visa, MC, •
C-yes/S-no/P-ask/H-ltd

Continental breakfast
Comp. coffees & teas
Three levels of porches
parking, refrigerators
A/C, TV, television

Circa 1790s Federal-style old Charleston home. Lovely wide-planked hardwood floors, original six-ft. oak doors, 10-ft. ceilings & fireplaces. Walk to shopping & restaurants.

Kings Courtyard Inn
198 King St., 29401
803-723-7000 800-845-6119
Laura Howard
All year

$$$ B&B
58 rooms, 58 pb
Visa, MC, AmEx, *Rated*,
•
C-yes/S-yes/P-no/H-yes

Continental plus/full $
Comp. wine/sherry/brandy
Sitting room, parking
hot tub, bicycles
conference/party room

1853 historic inn, rooms with period furnishings, canopied beds, fireplaces, overlook two inner courtyards. Concierge service, evening turndown with brandy and chocolate.

Kitchen House (c 1732)
126 Tradd St., 29401
803-577-6362
Lois Evans
All year

$$$ B&B
3 rooms, 3 pb
Visa, MC, *Rated*, •
C-ltd/S-yes/P-no/H-no

Continental plus
Kitchen, afternoon tea
Comp. sherry
sitting room, cable TV
concierge service

Restored, pre-Revolutionary house in the historic district. Patio & herb garden. Featured in Colonial Homes Magazine. Honeymoon packages. **Free bottle wine w/mention of book.**

CHARLESTON —————————————————————————————

Lodge Alley Inn
195 E. Bay St., 29401
800-722-1611 803-722-1611
Norma M. Armstrong
All year

$$$ EP
93 rooms, 93 pb
Visa, MC, AmEx, *Rated*,
•
C-yes/S-yes/P-no/H-yes
French, Italian

Morning coffee
Lunch, dinner, bar
Restaurant, sitting room
hot tubs some rooms
Comp. valet parking

Antebellum Inn located within the heart of the historic district. Furnished in 18th century decor. Some rooms with fireplace & jacuzzi. Nightly turn-down with chocolates.

———————————————————————————————————

Maison Du Pré
317 E. Bay St., at George St.,
29401
803-723-8691 800-662-INNS
Lucille/Bob/Mark Mulholland
All year

$$$ B&B
15 rooms, 15 pb
Most CC, *Rated*, •
C-yes/S-yes/P-no/H-no

Continental breakfast
Low country tea party
(wine, hors d'oeuvres)
drawing room
porch, patio, bicycles

Ideally located in Charleston's historic district. 15 guest rm. w/ private baths. Antiques, carriage rides. Honeymoon suites, kitchen suites, executive suites. **Golf packages**

———————————————————————————————————

Middleton Inn
Ashley River Rd., 29414
803-556-0500 FAX:556-0500
Brenda Burns
All year, Fax: 556-0500

$$$ B&B
52 rooms, 52 pb
Visa/MC/AmEx, *Rated*,
•
C-yes/S-yes/P-yes/H-yes

Full/continental
Tennis courts, pool
nature trails, canoes
Middleton Gardens

Secluded contemporary Inn adjacent to America's Oldest Landscaped Gardens. Fireplaces & large tile bathtubs. Incredible view of Ashley River.

———————————————————————————————————

Palmer Home, The
87 Wentworth St., 5 E. Battery,
29401
803-722-4325
Dr. Olivia Palmer
All year

$$$ B&B
3 rooms, 3 pb
C-yes/S-no/P-no/H-no

Continental breakfast
Sitting room, piano
sauna
swimming pool

One of the fifty famous homes in the city; furnished in period antiques; piazzas overlook harbor and Fort Sumter where Civil War began.

———————————————————————————————————

Rutledge Victorian Inn
114 Rutledge Ave., 29401
803-722-7551
BJ, Jean, Mike
All year

$$ EP/B&B
11 rooms
MC, Visa
C-yes/S-ltd

Continental breakfast
24-hour refrshmnt. table
Porch with rocking chair
TV, A/C, refrigerator
parking, student rates

Century-old Victorian house in Charleston's historic district. Rooms quaint, antique decor. Beautiful porch. Reasonable rates for historic district. **Complimentary goodies**

———————————————————————————————————

Thirty Six Meeting St. Inn
36 Meeting St., 29401
803-722-1034
Anne & Vic Brandt
All year

$$ B&B
9 rooms, 9 pb
Visa, MC, *Rated*, •
C-yes/S-no/P-no/H-yes

Continental plus
Comp. wine on request
Bicycles
walled garden
kitchenettes

1740 Charleston Single House in heart of Historic District. Suites elegantly furnished with mahogony rice beds, kitchenetts. **free bottle wine or 50% off carriage ride**

CHARLESTON ————————————————————————————————

Twenty-seven State St. B&B $$$ B&B/EP   Continental plus
27 State St., 29401   5 rooms, 5 pb   Bicycles, sitting room
803-722-4243   *Rated*, •   tennis nearby
Paul & Joye Craven   C-yes/S-no/P-no/H-no morning paper, flowers
All year

Charming & unique with pronounced old world influence. In French Quarter of the original walled city. 2 suites B&B, 2 suites EP. Some with fireplaces.

Victoria House Inn $$$ B&B   Continental plus
208 King St., 29401   16 rooms, 16 pb   Suites available
803-720-2944 800-933-5464   Visa, MC, AmEx, *Rated*,   Bar service
Larry Spelts   •   some hot tubs
All year   C-yes/S-ltd/P-no/H-yes

Victorian inn built in 1889. Document wallpapers and paint colors. Furnished with antiques and historically accurate reproductions. Located in a historic district.

Villa de La Fontaine B&B $$$ B&B   Full breakfast
138 Wentworth St., 29401   6 rooms, 6 pb   Canopy beds
803-577-7709   Visa, MC, AmEx   Garden, terraces
Aubrey Hancock, Bill Fontaine C-ltd   tennis nearby
All year   off-street parking

Southern colonial mansion, circa 1838, in historic district; half-acre garden; fountain and terraces. Furnished with 18th-century museum pieces. Walk to places of interest.

COLUMBIA ————————————————————————————————

Claussen's Inn $$$ B&B   Continental plus
2003 Greene St., 29205   29 rooms, 29 pb   Comp. wine/sherry/brandy
803-765-0440 800-622-3382   *Rated*, •   Morning paper
Dan O. Vance   C-yes/S-yes/P-no/H-yes turn-down service with
All year   chocolate & brandy

Restored old bakery building close to the university, shops, dining, entertainment. Some rooms have kitchenettes.

GEORGETOWN ————————————————————————————————

1790 House $$ B&B   Full breakfast
630 Highmarket St., 29440   6 rooms, 6 pb   Afternoon tea, snacks
803-546-4821   Visa, MC, *Rated*, • Sitting room, gardens
John & Patricia Wiley   C-ltd/S-ltd/P-no/H-yes bikes, central air/heat
All year   cottage with jacuzzi

200-year-old plantation-style inn; lovely gardens. Spacious rooms. In historic district. Walk to shops, restaurants, tours. Near Myrtle Beach & Charleston. **3rd night 50% off**

Du Pre House $$ B&B   Full breakfast
921 Prince St., 29440   5 rooms, 5 pb   Lunch, dinner, aft. tea
803-546-0298   Visa, MC, *Rated*   Snacks, comp. wine
Michael, Roberta, Michelle   C-yes/S-ltd/P-no/H-no sitting rooms, bicycles
All year   in-ground swimming pool

Enjoy personalized family vacation in Historic South. Fireplaces, verandas, picnic lunch/dinner by request. Walk to waterfront. **10% off for seniors, 15% off off-season**

GEORGETOWN

Five Thirty Prince St. B&B
530 Prince St., 29440
803-527-1114
Nancy M. Bazemore
All year

$$ B&B
3 rooms, 2 1/2 pb
Rated, •
C-ltd/S-ltd/P-ask/H-no

Full breakfast
Bar, snacks, comp. beer
Sitting rooms, sun porch
rocking chairs, veranda
private garden patio

*75-year-old home is nestled in charming circa 1729 National Register Georgetown Historic District. Large rooms with ceiling fans. **3rd night 25% off***

Shaw House, The
613 Cyprus Ct., 29440
803-546-9663
Mary & Joe Shaw
All year

$ B&B
3 rooms, 3 pb
Rated, •
C-yes/S-yes/P-no/H-ltd

Full breakfast
Comp. wine, tea, coffee
Sitting room
piano
bicycles

Spacious rooms furnished with antiques. Bird-watching from glassed-in den overlooking Willowbank Marsh. Walk to Historic District. Hostess loves pleasing her guests.

GREENWOOD

Inn on the Square
104 Court St., 29646
803-223-4488
Xmas closed

$$ B&B, ltd.
48 rooms, 48 pb
Visa, MC, AmEx, Ds, DC, •
C-yes/S-yes/P-no/H-yes

Continental plus wkends
Restaurant, all meals $
Comp. wine, bar service
swimming pool
tennis & library nearby

Greenwood's premier hotel. Ideally located for business or pleasure. Full-service dining room, English-style pub. Comp. coffee, juice, newspaper. Spacious rooms

MCCLELLANVILLE

Laurel Hill Plantation
P.O. Box 190, 29458
8913 N. Hwy 17
803-887-3708
Jackie & Lee Morrison
All year

$$$ B&B
4 rooms, 4 pb
Rated, •
C-ltd/S-ltd/P-no/H-no

Full breakfast
Comp. wine, snacks
Sitting room
fishing boat trip
freshwater fish pond

*Located with a fantastic waterfront view of Cape Romain and the Atlantic Ocean, this 1850s plantation home is furnished with country antiques. **3rd night 50% off***

MONCKS CORNER

Rice Hope Plantation
206 Rice Hope Dr., 29461
800-569-4038
Doris Kasprak
All year

$$ B&B
5 rooms, 3 pb
Visa, MC, *Rated*
C-yes/S-no/P-no/H-no

Continental plus
Lunch, dinner, Aft. tea
Snacks, comp. wine
restaurant, sitting room
bicycles, tennis court

Less than 1 hour from Charleston. Large mansion set among live oaks overlooking the river. Calm, quiet, friendly atmosphere.

MYRTLE BEACH

Serendipity, an Inn
407 N. 71st Ave., 29572
803-449-5268
Cos & Ellen Ficarra
All year

$$ B&B
15 rooms, 15 pb
Visa, MC, AmEx, *Rated*,
•
C-yes/S-ltd/P-no/H-no
Spanish, Italian

Continental plus
Grill
Heated pool, bicycles
color TV & A/C in rooms
garden room, sitting rm.

Lovely Spanish mission style, surrounded by lush tropical vegetation. Winners of Myrtle Beach "Keep America Beautiful" Award. Two blocks to ocean. Daily maid service.

PAWLEYS ISLAND

Litchfield Plantation	$$$ B&B	Continental plus
P.O. Box 290, 29575	4 rooms, 4 pb	Restaurant
River Road	Visa, MC, AmEx, •	Sitting room, library
803-237-4286 800-869-1410	C-yes/S-yes/P-no/H-no	tennis court, hot tubs
All year		sauna, swimming pool

Escape thru our avenue of moss-draped oaks to the Plantation House (c.1750) of this 600 acre plantation. Ocean front beach club, golf, tennis, fine dining. Also cottages.

PENDLETON

Liberty Hall Inn	$$ B&B	Continental plus
621 S. Mechanic St., 29670	10 rooms, 10 pb	Dinner, bar
803-646-7500 800-643-7944	Most CC, *Rated*	Phones in all rooms
Tom & Susan Jonas	C-ltd/S-ltd/P-no/H-no	Comp. wine, Fax
All year		no cribs available

Lodge and dine in this classic 1840 Piedmont home, authentically restored, furnished in period antiques. In charming Pendleton National Historic District.

SALEM

Sunrise Farm B&B	$$ B&B	Full breakfast
P.O. Box 164, 29676	4 rooms, 4 pb	Snacks
325 Sunrise Dr.	*Rated*, •	Sitting room
803-944-0121	C-ltd/S-no/P-no/H-no	off-season discounts
Jean Webb		
All year		

Charming country Victorian farmhouse set on 74 acre cattle farm. Close to Blue Ridge Mts., parks, waterfalls and nature trails. **3rd night 50% off**

More Inns . . .

Abbewood B&B, 509 N. Main St., Abbeville, 29620, 803-459-5822
Belmont Inn, 106 E. Pickens St., Abbeville, 29620, 803-459-9625
Painted Lady, The, 307 N. Main St., Abbeville, 29620, 803-459-8171
Briar Patch, The, 544 Magnolia Ln., Aiken, 29801, 803-649-2010
Brodie Residence, The, 422 York St., Aiken, 29801, 803-648-1445
Chancellor Carroll House, 112 Gregg Ave., Aiken, 29801, 803-649-5396
Hair Residence, 544 Magnolia Lane S.E., Aiken, 29801
Holley Inn, 235 Richland Ave.,W., Aiken, 29801, 803-648-4265
Hollie Berries Inn, 1560 Powderhouse Rd. S., Aiken, 29801, 803-648-9952
Pine Knoll Inn, 305 Lancaster St. SW, Aiken, 29801, 803-649-5939
Willcox Inn, The, 100 Colleton Ave., Aiken, 29801, 803-649-1377
Evergreen Inn, 1109 South Main St., Anderson, 29621, 803-225-1109
River Inn, 612 E. River St., Anderson, 29624, 803-226-1431
Trescot Inn, 500 Washington St., Beaufort, 29902, 803-522-8552
Twelve Oaks Inn, P.O. Box 4126, Beaufort, 29902, 803-525-1371
Belton Inn, 324 S. Main St., Belton, 29627, 803-338-6020
Breeden House Inn, The, 404 East Main St., Bennettsville, 29512, 803-479-3665
Foxfire B&B, The, 416 N. Main St., Bishopville, 29010, 803-484-5643
Law Street Inn, 200 South Main St., Bishopville, 29010, 800-253-5474
Floyd Hall Inn B&B, 111 Dexter St., Blackville, 29817, 803-284-3736
Fripp House Inn, P.O. Box 857, Bridge St, Bluffton, 29910, 803-757-2139
Branchville Country Inn, 1 Carroll St., Branchville, 29432, 803-274-8894
Latimer Inn, P.O. Box 295, Calhoun Falls, 29628, 803-391-2747
Aberdeen, 1409 Broad St., Camden, 29020, 803-432-2524
Carriage House, The, 1413 Lyttleton St., Camden, 29020, 803-432-2430
Fair Oaks, 1308 Fair St., Camden, 29020, 803-432-1499
Greenleaf Inn, 1308/10 Broad St., Camden, 29020, 803-425-1806
Inn on Broad, 1308/10 Broad St., Camden, 29020, 803-425-1806
Anchorage Inn, 26 Vendue Range, Charleston, 29401, 803-723-8300
Ansonborough Inn, 21 Hasell St., Charleston, 29401, 803-723-1655
Bed and Breakfast, 36 Meeting St., Charleston, 29401
Capers Motte House, 69 Church St., Charleston, 29401, 803-722-2263
Church St. Inn, 177 Church St., Charleston, 29401, 803-722-3420
Coach House, 39 East Battery, Charleston, 29401, 803-722-8145
Colonial Lake B&B, 32 Rutledge Ave., Charleston, 29401, 803-722-6476
Elliott House Inn, 78 Queen St., Charleston, 29401, 803-723-1855
Elliott House Inn, 78 Queen St., Charleston, 29401, 803-723-1855
Hayne House, The, 30 King St., Charleston, 29401, 803-577-2633

Holland's Guest House, 15 New St., Charleston, 29401, 803-723-0090
Indigo Inn, One Maiden Ln., Charleston, 29401, 803-577-5900
Jasmine House, 8 Cumberland, Charleston, 29401, 803-577-5900
Kings Inn, 136 Tradd St., Charleston, 29440
Loundes Grove Inn, 266 St. Margaret St., Charleston, 29403, 803-723-3530
Planters Inn, 112 N. Market St., Charleston, 29401, 803-722-2345
Sword Gate Inn, 111 Tradd St., Charleston, 29401, 803-723-8518
Thirty Six Meeting Street, 36 Meeting St., Charleston, 29401, 803-722-1034
Two Meeting Street Inn, 2 Meeting St., Charleston, 29401, 803-723-7322
Vendue Inn, 19 Vendue Range, Charleston, 29401, 803-577-7970
Vendue Inn, 19 Vendue Range, Charleston, 29401, 803-577-7970
501 Kershaw, 501 Kershaw St., Cheraw, 29520, 803-537-7733
505 Market St., 505 Market St., Cheraw, 29520, 803-537-9649
Spears B&B, 501 Kershaw St., Cheraw, 29520, 803-537-7733
Nord-Lac, P.O. Box 1111, Clemson, 29633, 803-639-2939
Henry Bennett House B&B, 301 Red Bluff St., Clio, 29525, 803-586-2701
Chesnut Cottage B&B, 1718 Hampton St., Columbia, 29201, 803-256-1718
Richland St. B&B, 1425 Richland St., Columbia, 29202, 803-779-7001
Coosaw Plantation, P.O. Box 160, Dale, 29914, 803-723-6516
Croft Magnolia Inn, 306 Cashua Street, Darlington, 29532, 803-393-1908
Yellow Gables, 1121 Danzler Rd., Duncan, 29334, 803-439-8164
Carnoosie Inn, 407 Columbia Rd., Edgefield, 29824, 800-622-7124
Inn On Main, The, 303 Main St., Edgefield, 29824, 803-637-3678
Plantation House, The, Ct. House Square, Edgefield, 29824, 803-637-3789
Cassina Point Plantation, P.O. Box 535, Edisto Island, 29438, 803-869-2535
Ehrhardt Hall, 400 South Broadway, Ehrhardt, 29081, 803-267-2020
John Lawton House, 159 3rd St. E, Estill, 29918, 803-625-3240
Pleasant Valley, P.O. Box 446, Fort Mill, 29715, 803-547-7551
Ashfield Manor, 3030 S. Island Rd., Georgetown, 29440, 803-546-5111
Shipwright's B&B, 11 Cypress Ct., Georgetown, 29440, 803-527-4475
Grace Place B&B, 115 Grace St., Greenwood, 29646, 803-229-0053
Ambiance B&B, 8 Wren Dr., Hilton Head, 29928, 803-671-4981
Halcyon, Harbormaster 604, Hilton Head Island, 29928, 803-785-7912
Home Away B&B, 3 Pender Ln., Hilton Head Island, 29928, 803-671-5578
Sugerfoot Castle, 211 S. Main St., Honea Path, 29654, 803-369-6565
Almost Home B&B, 1236 Oceanview Rd., James Island, 29412, 803-795-8705
Cox House Inn, P.O. Box 486, Johnston, 29832, 803-275-4552
Wade-Beckham House, Box 348, Lancaster, 29720, 803-285-1105
Holly Hill, Route 1, Box 223, Landrum, 29356, 803-457-4010
Bailie Hall B&B, 104 Bethea St., Latta, 29536, 803-752-7376
Two Sisters Inn, 814 S. Harper, Laurens, 29360, 803-984-4880
Able House Inn, 205 Church St., Leesville, 29070, 803-532-2763
Lake Murray House, 2252 Old Cherokee Rd., Lexington, 29072, 803-957-3701
Stella's Guest Home, P.O. Box 564, Little River, 29566, 803-249-1871
Chauga River House, Cobb's Bridge Rd., Long Creek, 29658, 803-647-9587
Magnolia Grove B&B, 201 Holliday Dr., Manning, 29102, 803-435-4722
Cantey Redidence, 108 Wilcox Ave., Marion, 29571, 803-423-5578
Windsong, Rt 1, Box 300, Mayesville, 29104, 800-453-5004
McClellan's B&B, P.O. Box 4, McClellanville, 29458, 803-887-3371
Village B&B, 333 Mercantile Rd., McClellanville, 29458, 803-887-3266
Annie's Inn, P.O. Box 311, Montmorenci, 29839, 803-649-6836
Guilds Inn, 101 Pitt St., Mt. Pleasant, 29464, 803-881-0510
Tara Oaks B&B, 1199 Long Point Rd., Mt. Pleasant, 29464, 803-884-7082
Webster's Manor, 115 E. James St., Mullins, 29574, 803-464-9632
Brustman House, 400-25th Ave. S., Myrtle Beach, 29577, 803-448-7699
Cain House B&B, 206 29th Ave. S., Myrtle Beach, 29577, 803-448-3063
College St. Tourist B&B, 1710 College St., Newberry, 29108, 803-321-9155
Bloom Hill, 772 Pine Log Rd., North Augusta, 29841, 803-593-2573
Russell Street Inn, 491 Russell St., Orangeburg, 29115, 803-531-2030
Southern Belle B&B, Rt. 2, Box E, Pamplico, 29583, 803-493-1975
Manor House At Litchfield, P.O. Box 290, Pawley's Island, 29585, 803-237-9322
Sea View Inn, P.O. Box 210, Pawley's Island, 29858, 803-237-4253
Colonial House Inn, 206 Griffin St., Pickens, 29671, 803-875-5236
Schell Haus, The, 4913 SC 11, Pickens, 29671, 803-878-0078
Lakewood Plantation, Rt. 2, P.O. Box 3, Ridgeland, 29936, 803-726-5141
Book & The Spindle, The, 626 Oakland Ave., Rock Hill, 29730, 803-328-1913
East Main Guest House, 600 E. Main St., Rock Hill, 29730, 803-366-1161
Hunter House B&B, 201 E. College St., Simpsonville, 29681, 803-967-2827
Gray House, The, 111 Stones Throw Ave., Starr, 29684, 803-352-6778
Palmettos, P.O. Box 706, Sullivan's Island, 29482, 803-883-3389
B&B Of Summerville, 304 S. Hampton St., Summerville, 29483, 803-871-5275
Gadsden Manor Inn, Box 1710, Summerville, 29484, 803-875-1710
Sumter B&B, 6 Park Ave., Sumter, 29150, 803-773-2903
Laurel Springs Country Inn, 1137 Moorefield Hwy., Sunset, 29685, 803-878-2252
Inn at Merridun, The, 100 Merrridun Pl., Union, 29379, 803-427-7052
Liberty Lodge, Rt. 1, P.O. Box 77, Walhalla, 29691, 803-638-8639
Walhalla B&B & Antiques, 503 Main St., Walhalla, 29691, 803-638-9032
Brakefield B&B, 214 High St., Winnsboro, 29180, 803-635-4242
Kings Mountain St. Inn, 225 Kings Mountain St., York, 29745, 803-684-7013

South Dakota

CANOVA

Skoglund Farm	$ MAP	Full breakfast
Route 1, Box 45, 57321	6 rooms	Dinner included
605-247-3445	•	Sitting room, piano
Alden & Delores Skoglund	C-yes/S-ltd/P-yes/H-no	bicycles
All year	Swedish	

Enjoy overnight on the South Dakota prairie. Return to your childhood—animals, country walking, home-cooked meals. **Children 5 & under are free**

CUSTER

Custer Mansion B&B	$ B&B	Full breakfast
35 Centennial Dr., 57730	6 rooms, 2 pb	Restaurant, aftn. tea
605-673-3333	*Rated*, •	Sitting room, bicycles
Mill & Carole Seaman	C-yes/S-no/P-no/H-no	tennis, golf nearby
All year	Spanish	hiking in Black Hills

Historic 1891 Victorian home on 1 acre in heart of unique Black Hills. Western hospitality & delicious, home-baked food. On National Register Historic Places. **6th night free.**

LEAD

Deer Mountain B&B	$$ B&B	Full breakfast
HC 37 - Box 1214, #1 Aspen	4 rooms, 2 pb	Dinner w/adv. notice
Dr/Deer Mt. Rd., 57754	Visa, MC, •	Snacks, pool table
605-584-2473	C-yes/S-ltd/P-yes/H-no	box lunch avail.
Vonnie, Bob, Carrie Ackerman		sitting room, hot tubs
All year		

Unique log home. Skiing & snowmobiling minutes away. Near historic Deadwood gambling town. Mt. Rushmore, hunting, fishing all close by. **3rd night 25% off**

RAPID CITY

Carriage House B&B	$$ B&B	Full breakfast
721 West Blvd., 57701	5 rooms, 2 pb	Library, sitting room
605-343-6415	Visa, MC	piano
Betty & Joel King	C-ltd/S-no/P-no/H-no	video & music libraries
All year		

Located on historic West Boulevard, the inn has English Country interior with antiques, hardwood floors & oil paintings. Relax on veranda or balcony.

SALEM

Jacobson Farm	$ B&B	Full breakfast
RR 2, Box 428, 57058	3 rooms, 2 pb	Restaurant nearby
605-247-3247	•	Sitting room, snacks
The Jacobsons	C-yes/S-ltd/P-no/H-no	swimming pool nearby
May-October		attractions nearby

Lots of country hospitality at a quiet hide-away. Breakfast served on the sun deck if desired and weather permitting. Handmade quilts and crafts available. **3rd night 50% off**

WEBSTER

Lakeside Farm B&B	$ B&B	Full breakfast
RR 2, Box 52, 57274	2 rooms	Other meals possible
605-486-4430	C-yes/S-no/P-no/H-no	Comp. coffee, tea, snack
Glenn & Joy Hagen		sitting room, bicycles
All year		piano

Sample a bit of country life with us. A family-owned/operated dairy farm. Northeastern South Dakota lakes area. Fresh air. Open spaces. Fresh milk. Homemade cinnamon rolls.

YANKTON

Mulberry Inn	$ B&B	Continental breakfast
512 Mulberry St., 57078	6 rooms, 2 pb	Full breakfast $
605-665-7116	Visa, MC, AmEx, *Rated*	Comp. wine, snacks
Millie Cameron	C-yes/S-ltd/P-ltd	parlors, fireplaces
All year		porch, parlors

Built in 1873. Beautiful hand-carved door, high ceilings and marble fireplaces. Very warm and homey with a quiet atmosphere. Missouri River. **3rd night 25% off**

More Inns...

Mrs. Doris E. Pier, Route 4, Box 251, Brookings, 57006
Real Ranch, HCR 2, Box 112, Buffalo, 57720
Riverview Ridge B&B, HC 69, Box 82A, Chamberlain, 57325, 605-734-6084
Bavarian Inn, P.O. Box 152, Custer, 57730, 605-673-2802
Blue Bell Lodge & Resort, HCR 83, Box 63V, Custer, 57730
Hidden Fortune B&B, Box 748, Custer, 57730, 605-666-4744
Rock Crest Lodge, P.O. Box 687, Custer, 57730, 605-673-4323
State Game Lodge, Custer, 57730, 605-255-4541
Sylvan Lake Lodge, Box 752, Custer, 57730, 605-574-2561
Adams House, 22 Van Buren, Deadwood, 57732, 605-578-3877
Harer Lodge & B&B, Route 1, Box 87A, Gettysburg, 57442, 605-765-2167
Heart of the Hills B&B, 517 Main St., Hill City, 57745, 605-574-2704
Homestead, The, Box 635, Hill City, 57745, 605-574-4226
Palmer Gulch Lodge, Box 295 V, Hill City, 57745, 605-574-2525
Pine Rest Cabins, P.O. Box 377, Hill City, 57745, 605-574-2416
Robins Roost Cabins, HCR 87, Box 62, Hill City, 57745, 605-574-2252
Cascade Ranch B&B, P.O. Box 461, Hot Springs, 57747, 605-745-3397
Prairie's Edge B&B, P.O. Box 11, Interior, 57750, 605-433-5441
B&B Inn, Box 154, Keystone, 57751, 605-666-4490
Elk Haven Resort, Hwy 16A, Box 717K, Keystone, 57751, 605-666-4856
Triple R Dude Ranch, Box 124, Keystone, 57751, 605-666-4605
Cheyenne Crossing B&B, HC 37, Box 1220, Lead, 57754, 605-584-3510
49'er, The, HCHR 63, Box 305, Lemmon, 57638, 701-376-3280
Cross Roads Inn, Box 970, Jct. Hwy 18/73, Martin, 57551, 605-685-1070
Fitch Farms, Box 8, Milesville, 57553, 605-544-3227
Guest House B&B, 215 W. 2nd Ave., Miller, 57362, 605-853-2863
Landmark Country Inn, HCR 77, Box 2, Murdo, 57559, 605-669-2846
Roghair Herefords B&B, HCR 74 Box 16, Okaton, 57562, 605-669-2529
Thorson's Homestead, HCR 2 Box 100, Philip, 57567, 605-859-2120
Cow Creek Lodge, HCR 37, Box 134, Pierre, 57501, 605-264-5450
Spring Creek Resort, 610 N. Jackson, Pierre, 57501, 605-224-8336
Audrie's Cranbury Corner, RR 8, Box 2400, Rapid City, 57702, 605-342-7788
B&B H-D Lodge, RR 8, Box 3360, Rapid City, 57702, 605-341-7580
Black Forest Inn, HC 33, Box 3123, Rapid City, 57702, 605-574-2000
Hillside Country Cottages, HC 33, Box 1901, Rapid City, 57702, 605-342-4121
Willow Springs Cabin, HCR 39 Box 108, Rapid City, 57702, 605-342-3665
Pine Crest Inn, 4501 W. 12th St., Sioux Falls, 57106, 605-336-3530
Christensen's Country Home, 432 Hillsview, Spearfish, 57783, 605-642-2859
Flying Horse B&B, 630 - 8th St., Spearfish, 57783, 605-642-1633
Kelly Inn, 540 E. Jackson, Spearfish, 57783, 605-642-7795
Luxury Lodge, P.O. Box 437, Spearfish, 57783, 605-642-2728
Western Dakota Ranch, HCR 1, Wall, 57790, 605-279-2198

Tennessee

CHATTANOOGA ——————————————————————————————

Alford House B&B $$ B&B   Continental plus
5515 Alford Hill Dr., Route 4,   3 rooms   Afternoon tea, snacks
37419   ●   Sitting room, gazebo
615-821-7625   C-yes   child care service
Robert Alford   trails up Lake Mountain
All year

3 story home bordering the National Forest, below historic Point Park. 10 min. to Tennessee Aquarium. Antiques, bridal baskets. Coffee served early & healthy "lite" breakfast.

DANDRIDGE ——————————————————————————————

Sugar Fork B&B $$ B&B   Full breakfast
743 Garrett Rd., 37725   3 rooms, 2 pb   Afternoon tea & coffee
615-397-7327 800-487-5634   Visa, MC   Snacks, newspaper
Mary & Sam Price   C-yes/S-yes/P-no/H-ltd   sitting room, fireplace
All year   porch w/lake view, dock

A unique setting on Douglas Lake in historical Dandridge. Fishing and water sports. Convenient to Smoky Mountains & Knoxville. Southern hospitality.

DUCKTOWN ——————————————————————————————

White House B&B, The $$ B&B   Full breakfast
P.O. Box 668, 37326   3 rooms, 1 pb   Aft. tea, snacks
104 Main St.   Visa, MC, *Rated*, ●   Cable TV in den
615-496-4166   C-ltd/S-ltd/P-no/H-no   wrap around porches
Mardee & Dan Kauffman   rocking chairs
All year

Small town atmosphere & unique heritage. Visit the Ducktown Mining Museum for history of the industry from 1800s. Embrace the elegance of the past & the convenience of today.

FRANKLIN ——————————————————————————————

Lyric Springs Country Inn $$$ B&B   Continental plus
P.O. Box 120428, 37064   3 rooms, 3 pb   Other meals, ask
7306 S. Harpeth Rd.   Visa, MC, *Rated*, ●   Snacks, sitting room
615-329-3385 800-621-7824   C-ltd/S-no/P-no/H-yes   library, swimming pool
All year   stable horses, ride

Treasure trove of 1940's textiles, in Homes & Gardens, home of famous songwriter. Charm & pampering in an antique-filled home. 25 mi. from Music City (Nashville).

GATLINBURG ——————————————————————————————

7th Heaven Log Home Inn $$ B&B   Full breakfast
3944 Castle Rd., 37738   4 rooms, 4 pb   Lunch, dinner
615-430-5000   Visa, MC, *Rated*, ●   Guest kitchen, billiards
Ginger & Paul Wolcott   C-ltd/S-yes/P-no/H-no   game room, tennis
All year   gazebo, hot tubs, pool

Large, beautiful log home located on the 7th green of golf resort with the Smoky Mountain National Park just across the road. **4 room group discount 10%**

GATLINBURG

Buckhorn Inn	$$$ B&B	Full breakfast
2140 Tudor Mtn. Rd., 37738	11 rooms, 11 pb	Dinner
615-436-4668	Visa, MC	Sitting room, fireplace
John & Connie Burns	C-ltd/S-ltd/P-no/H-no	self-guided nature trail
All year		small conference center

Sits on 35 acres of meadows, woodlands, & breathtaking views of highest peaks in Smokies. Great Smoky Mountains Nat'l Park within 1 mile. **7th night free**

Butcher House-Mountains	$$$ B&B	Full European breakfast
1520 Garrett Ln., 37738	Visa, MC, *Rated*	Afternoon tea, snacks
615-436-9457	C-ltd/S-no/P-no/H-no	Sitting room w/TV
Hugh & Gloria Butcher	Ital, some Span. & Frch.	deck
All year		Dessert offered in eve.

Cradled 2800 feet above Gatlinburg. Swiss chalet furnished with many museum quality antiques. One mile from the slopes. Original gourmet recipes. **Theater & Restaurant Disc't**

Eight Gables Inn B&B	$$$ B&B	Full breakfast
219 N. Mtn. Trail, 37738	10 rooms, 10 pb	Afternoon tea
615-430-3344	Visa, MC, AmEx, *Rated*,	sitting room, TV lounge
Helen Smith	•	spacious rooms, hot tubs
All year	C-ltd/S-ltd/P-no/H-no	

Exquisite spacious guest rooms individually decorated. Wraparound porch with rocking chairs. Spacious rooms, dramatic surroundings, southern hospitality. **3rd night 50% off**

GERMANTOWN

Highland Place B&B	$ B&B	Full breakfast
7755 Hunters Run, 519 N.	3 rooms, 1 pb	Snacks
Highland/Jackson, 38301	Visa, MC, *Rated*, •	Library, gardens
901-427-1472	C-ltd/S-no/P-no/H-no	screened porch, patio
Glenn & Janice Wall		rec. room w/pool table
All year		

Highland Place is a stately 1911 home in a garden setting, furnished with antiques, offering comfortable accommodations and Southern hospitality. **4th night free, Ltd**

GREENEVILLE

Hilltop House B&B Inn	$$ B&B/MAP	Full breakfast
Route 7, Box 180, 37743	3 rooms, 3 pb	Afternoon tea
615-639-8202	Most CC, -Rated, •	Sitting room, library
Denise M. Ashworth	C-ltd/S-no/P-no/H-no	hiking trails
All year		trout fishing, rafting

Comfortable country home with panoramic mountain views and English antiques. Visit historic towns, hike mountain trails with local hiking club. Gourmet meals. **6th night free**

JONESBOROUGH

Hawley House B&B	$$ B&B	Full breakfast
114 E. Woodrow Ave., 37659	4 rooms, 3 pb	Afternoon tea, snacks
615-753-8869	C-ltd/S-ltd/P-no/H-no	Sitting room
Marcy & R.I.C. Hawley		wrap-around porch
All year		rocking chairs

Celebrate the 200th birthday of Jonesborough's oldest dwelling in the heart of the Historic District. Antique-filled rooms, southern hospitality. **3rd night 50% off, Ltd**

LOUDON

Mason Place B&B, The
600 Commerce St., Close to
Knoxville, 37774
615-458-3921
Bob & Donna Siewert
All year

$$$ B&B
5 rooms, 5 pb
Visa, MC, •
C-ltd/S-ltd/P-no/H-ltd

Full breakfast plus
Afternoon tea, snacks
Comp. wine, bar service
Sitting room, library
tennis court, pool

Antebellum plantation home on Nat'l registry. Quaint Civil War Town. Feather beds, 10-fire-places, lovely pool, candlelight breakfast. Near Knoxville, I-75 & I-40.

MONTEAGLE

Adams Edgeworth Inn
Monteagle Assembly, 37356
615-924-2669 FAX:924-3236
Wendy & David Adams
All year

$$ B&B
12 rooms, 12 pb
Visa, MC, *Rated*, •
C-ltd/S-ltd/P-no/H-ltd
French

Full gourmet breakfast
Candle-lit dining
Gift shop, library
Verandas, swim, hike
entertainment, conf. rm.

Ancient Victorian village on mountain top. Canopy beds, fireplaces, antiques, prize-winning gardens, 1200 wild acres wilderness w/trails, Sewanee U. 6 mi. **3rd night 50% off**

North Gate Lodge
P.O. Box 858, 37356
Monteagle Assembly #103
615-924-2799
Nancy & Henry Crais
All year

$$ B&B
7 rooms, 7 pb
•
C-yes/S-no/P-no/H-no

Full breakfast
Picnic lunches, snacks
Sitting room
summer Chatauqua
program

Sumptuous breakfasts & warm hospitality are trademarks of this 1890s boarding house. Explore Assembly's historic community & Monteagle Mountain's trails, waterfalls & forest.

MURFREESBORO

Clardy's Guest House
435 E. Main St., 37130
615-893-6030
Robert & Barbara Deaton
All year

$ B&B
3 rooms, 2 pb
Rated, •
C-yes/S-yes/P-no/H-no

Continental breakfast
Comp. beverages
Sitting room w/cable TV
porch

Built in 1898 during opulent and decorative times, the house is completely furnished with beautiful antiques. Murfreesboro is the South's antique center. **3rd night 50% off**

NASHVILLE

Drake Farm - Lumsley Creek
P.O. Box 875, 37072
5508 Brick Church Pike
615-859-2425 800-586-7539
Rose Mary Drake
All year

$$ B&B
2 rooms
Visa, MC, AmEx, •
C-yes/S-no/P-yes/H-no
German

Full breakfast
Lunch/Dinner (arranged)
Afternoon tea, snacks
sitting room, library
hammock/swings, antiques

Antebellum farmhouse circa 1850, 15 miles from downtown Nashville in Goodlettsville, offers a perfect blend of peaceful rural seclusion. Accessible to city attractions

Monthaven B&B
1154 W. Main St.,
Hendersonville, 37075
615-824-6319
Hugh Waddell, Lisa Neideffer
All year

$$$ B&B
2 rooms, 2 pb
Visa, MC, AmEx, •
C-ltd/S-no/P-yes/H-yes

Continental plus
Lunch, dinner, bar
Afternoon tea, snacks
sitting room, bicycles
tennis & pool nearby

On National Register; Monthaven offers both serene tranquillity of middle Tennessee & conve-nience; 15 mi. to downtown. True "Southern charm." Log cabin avail. **3rd night free**

ROGERSVILLE

Hale Springs Inn
110 W. Main St., Town Square,
37857
615-272-5171
Capt. & Mrs. Netherland-Brown
All year

$ B&B
10 rooms, 10 pb
Visa, MC, AmEx, •
C-yes/S-yes/P-ltd/H-no

Continental breakfast
Restaurant
Central A/C and heat
fireplaces, guided tours
formal gardens & gazebo

Restored 1824 brick. Fronts Village Green with other antebellum buildings. Antiques, poster beds, working fireplaces, plush large rooms—near Gatlinburg.

RUGBY

Newbury House Inn
P.O. Box 8, 37733
Hwy 52, Historic Rugby
615-628-2441
Historic Rugby
All year

$$ B&B
8 rooms, 3 pb
Visa, MC, *Rated*
C-ltd/S-ltd/P-no/H-ltd

Full breakfast
Restaurant, tea & coffee
Victorian parlor
period library
games, fireplace

Unique 1880s Victorian village offers lodging in restored and antique-filled Newbury House and Pioneer Cottage, home-style restaurant. Borders Big South Fork Nat'l Park.

SEVIERVILLE

Blue Mountain Mist Country
1811 Pullen Rd., 37862
615-428-2335
Norman & Sarah Ball
All year

$$$ B&B
12 rooms, 12 pb
Rated, •
C-ltd/H-yes

Full breakfast
Afternoon tea/coffee
Snacks, hot tubs
sitting room, TV room
5 country cottages

See the early morning mist rise from rolling meadows framed by the Great Smokies. Huge Victorian porch, hearty breakfast and country charm. **15% off 5+ nights.**

SHELBYVILLE

Cinnamon Ridge B&B
799 Whitthorne St., 37160
615-685-9200
Bill & Pat Sherrill
All year

$$ B&B
5 rooms, 5 pb
Visa, MC, *Rated*, •
C-ltd/S-no/P-no/H-no

Full breakfast
Afternoon tea, snacks
Sitting room
rockers on front porch
over-sized shaded deck

Experience the quiet opulence and exquisite amenities of years gone by. Colonial home rich with nostalgia and southern hospitality. **3rd night 50% off**

TOWNSEND

Richmont Inn
220 Winterberry Ln., 37882
615-448-6751
Susan & Jim Hind
All year

$$$ B&B
10 rooms, 10 pb
Rated, •
C-ltd/S-no/P-no/H-yes

Full French/Swiss bkfast
Candlelight dessert
Luxury rooms, spa-tubs
king beds, fireplaces
sitting areas, balconies

Appalachian barn beautifully furnished: 18th-century English antiques, French paintings. Breathtaking mountain views! 10 min. to Great Smokies National Park. ABBA Excellent.

Tuckaleechee Inn
160 Bear Lodge Dr., 37882
615-448-6442 800-487-6059
Cary & Sandy Plummer
All year

$$ B&B
10 rooms, 10 pb
Visa, MC, AmEx, •
C-yes/S-no/P-no/H-no

Full breakfast
Hot tubs
Swimming pool

In the foothills of the Smokies, the most popular park in the country. Specialize in church groups. Perfect for families!

More Inns . . .

Manor, The, P.O. Box 240, Altamont, 37301, 615-692-3153
Woodlee House, P.O. Box 310, Altamont, 37301, 615-692-2368
Falls Mill Log Cabin, Rt. 1 Box 44, Belvidere, 37306, 615-469-7161
Magnolia Manor B&B, 418 N. Main St., Bolivar, 38008, 901-658-6700
Herbert's B&B, Box 2166, Brentwood, 615-373-9300
Abbey Road, 1551 Abbey Rd., Brownsville, 38012, 901-772-5680
Harmony Hill Inn, Rt. 3 Box 1937, Chuckey, 37641, 615-257-3893
Brown Manor, 215 - 20th St. NE, Cleveland, 37311, 615-476-8029
Scarecrow Country Inn, 1720 E. Spring St., Cookeville, 38501, 615-526-3431
Mill Dale Farm and B&B, Route 5, Dandridge, 37725, 615-397-3470
McEwen Farm Log Cabin B&B, P.O. Box 97, Bratton Ln, Duck River, 38454, 615-583-2378
White House, The, P.O. Box 668, 104 Main, Ducktown, 37326, 615-496-4166
Old Cowan Plantation, Rt 9, Box 17, Fayetteville, 37334, 615-433-0225
Bottle Hollow Lodge, P.O. Box 92/Shelbyville, Flat Creek, 37160, 615-695-5253
Barbara W. Humes B&B, 1207 Holly Hill Dr., Franklin, 37064
Magnolia House B&B, 1317 Columbia Ave., Franklin, 37064, 615-794-8178
Windsong, 3373 Sweeney Hollow Rd, Franklin, 37064
Colonel's Lady, Rt. 1, Box 273, Gatlinburg, 37738, 615-436-5432
LeConte Lodge, P.O. Box 350, Gatlinburg, 37738, 615-436-4473
Pride Hollow, Route 1, Box 86, Gordonsville, 38563, 615-683-6396
Big Spring Inn, 315 N. Main St., Greenville, 37743, 615-638-2917
Phelp's House Inn, Route 1, Box 55, Highlands, 28741, 704-526-2590
Branner-Hicks House, Rt. 1, Box 4, Jefferson City, 37760, 615-475-2302
Hart House, The, 207 East Holston Ave., Johnson City, 37601, 615-926-3147
Touch of Thyme B&B, 501 E. Watauga Ave., Johnson City, 37601, 615-926-7570
Jonesborough B&B, P.O. Box 722, Jonesborough, 37659, 615-753-9223
Robertson House B&B Inn, 212 E. Main St., Jonesborough, 37659, 615-753-3039
Compton Manor, 3747 Kingston Pike, Knoxville, 37919, 615-523-1204
Middleton, The, 800 West Hill Ave., Knoxville, 37902, 615-524-8100
Grandma's House, Route #1 Pollard Rd., Kodak, 37764, 615-933-3512
Dogwood Acres B&B Inn, Rt. 4, Box 628, La Follette, 37766, 615-566-1207
Granville House, 229 Pulaski St., Lawrenceburg, 38464, 615-762-3129
Snapp Inn B&B, 1990 Davy Crockett Rd., Limestone, 37681, 615-257-2482
Silver Leaf 1815, Rt. 1, Box 122, Lyles, 37098, 615-726-1470
Lynchburg B&B, P.O. Box 34, Mechanic, Lynchburg, 37352, 615-759-7158
White Oak Creek B&B, Rt. 2, Box 184, McEven, 37101, 615-582-3827
Lowenstein-Long House, 217 N. Waldran, Memphis, 38105, 901-527-7174
Hidden Acres Farm B&B, Hwy. 67, Rt. 3, Box 39, Mountain City, 37683, 615-727-6564
Chateau Graeme B&B, 2200 Lebanon Rd., Nashville, 37214, 615-883-1687
Hachland Hill Inn, 5396 Rawlings Rd., Nashville, 37080, 615-255-1727
Parish Patch Farm & Inn, 625 Cortner Rd., Normandy, 37360, 615-857-3017
Aurora Inn—B&B, 8253 Hwy. 52, Orlinda, 37141, 615-654-4266
Homestead House Inn, P.O. Box 218, Pickwick Dam, 38365, 901-689-5500
Hilton's Bluff B&B Inn, 2654 Valley Heights Dr., Pigeon Forge, 37863, 615-428-9765
Grey Gables B&B, P.O. Box 5252, Hwy. 52, Rugby, 37733, 615-628-5252
Ross House, P.O. Box 398, Savannah, 38372, 901-925-3974
Cove Country Inn, Route 6, Box 197, Sevierville, 37862, 615-453-3997
Kero Mountain Resort, Route 11, Box 380, Sevierville, 37862, 615-453-7514
Milk & Honey Country, 2803 Old Country Way, Sevierville, 37862, 615-428-4858
Mockingbird Country Inn, 1243 Allensville Rd., Sevierville, 37862, 615-428-1398
The Gallery House, P.O. Box 5274, Sevierville, 37864, 615-428-6937
Victoria Rose Tea Room, 217 Cedar St., Sevierville, 37862, 615-428-0759
Von-Bryan Inn, 2402 Hatcher Mtn. Rd., Sevierville, 37862, 615-453-9832
Country Inn, Rt. 3, Chris Haven Dr., Seymour, 37865, 615-573-7170
Leawood-Williams Estate, P.O. Box 24, Shiloh, 38376, 901-689-5106
Flow Blue Inn, P.O. Box 495, Sweetwater, 37874, 615-442-2964
Xanadu Farm, 8155 Horton Hwy., Triune, 37014, 615-395-4040
Tullahoma B&B, 308 N. Atlantic St., Tullahoma, 37388, 615-455-8876
Turkey Penn Resort, Rt. 1, Vonore, 37885, 615-295-2400
Blackberry Farm, West Millers Cove Rd., Walland, 37886
Walking Horse Hotel, P.O. Box 266, Wartrace, 37183
Nolan House Inn, The, P.O. Box 164, Waverly, 37185, 615-296-2511

Texas

ABILENE ─────────────────────────────────

Bolin's Prairie House B&B	$$ B&B	Full breakfast
508 Mulberry, 79601	4 rooms	Sitting room, den
915-675-5855	Visa, MC, AmEx, DC, Dis	high ceilings
Ginny Bolin	C-ltd/S-no/P-no/H-no	hardwood floors
All year		

Built in 1902. Completely renovated. Relax in spacious rooms accented with antiques. Great breakfast served on china and lace. Brochure available.

AUSTIN ─────────────────────────────────

Carrington's Bluff B&B	$$ B&B	Full breakfast
1900 David St., 78705	17 rooms, 15 pb	Comp. coffee, soda
512-479-0638	AmEx, *Rated*, •	Afternoon tea
Gwen & David Fullbrook	C-ltd/S-no/P-no/H-no	sitting room
All year		

English country inn located on tree-covered acre in the heart of the city. Antique-filled rooms and fabulous breakfasts. **10% off weekdays**

Chequered Shade B&B, The	$$ B&B	Full breakfast
2530 Pearce Rd., 78730	3 rooms, 2 pb	Library, bicycles
512-346-8318	Visa, MC, AmEx	antiques, porches, patio
Millie Scott	C-ltd/S-ltd/P-no/H-no	
All year		

Secluded inn by the lake with panoramic views. Fifteen minutes from restaurants and shopping. Plenty of wildlife in the area. Complimentary champagne on arrival.

Fairview, A B&B	$$$ B&B	Full breakfast
1304 Newning Ave., 78704	6 rooms, 6 pb	Comp. wine
512-444-4746	Most CC, *Rated*	Sitting room, library
Duke & Nancy Waggoner	C-ltd/S-ltd/P-no/H-no	tennis close by
All year		cable TV, phones in rms.

1910 Austin landmark. 1 acre of landscaped grounds in downtown area. Quiet, relaxing, spacious. Antique furnishings. **Weekly rates & extended stay rates**

McCallum House, The	$$$ B&B	Full breakfast
613 W. 32nd, 78705	5 rooms, 5 pb	Private kitchens
512-451-6744 FAX:451-6744	Visa, MC, *Rated*, •	Sitting area in room
Roger & Nancy Danley	C-ltd/S-no/P-no/H-no	some rooms w/pvt. porch
All year		color TV in rooms

Explore beautiful Austin from this historic, antique-filled late Victorian. We're ten blocks from UT-Austin, 20 blocks from Capitol and downtown. **2 nights 15% off Sun-Th.**

Peaceful Hill B&B	$$ B&B	Full breakfast
10817 Ranch Rd. 2222, 78730	2 rooms, 2 pb	Porch swing, hammock
512-338-1817 800-369-2805	Visa, MC	grand stone fireplace
Mrs. Peninnah Thurmond	C-yes/S-ltd/P-no/H-no	25X20 living rm. rockers
All year		

Hill country getaway overlooking panoramic view of city. Swimming, tennis, 18-hole golf-2 miles- at River Place C.C. 15 min. to city; 5 min. to Lake Travis & the Oasis.

Fairview, A B&B, Austin, TX

AUSTIN

Southard-House	$$ B&B	Continental plus (wkdys)
908 Blanco, 78703	5 rooms, 5 pb	Full breakfast (wkends)
512-474-4731	Visa, MC, AmEx, *Rated*,	Comp. wine
Jerry & Rejina Southard	•	sitting room, porches
All year	C-ltd/S-yes/P-no/H-no	garden, gazebo

Elegant historic home. Clawfoot tub, cutwork linens. Dine by a roaring fire. Caring hosts in the grand Texas style. Downtown.

Wild Flower Inn, The	$$ B&B	Full breakfast
1200 W. 22½ St., 78705	4 rooms, 2 pb	Afternoon tea, snacks
800-747-9231 512-477-9639	Visa, MC, AmEx, *Rated*	Sitting room, deck
Kay Jackson, Claudean Schultz	C-ltd/S-no/P-no/H-no	nearby public tennis
All year		hiking & biking trails

Lovely old home furnished with antiques; located on tree-shaded street; delicious full breakfast served on deck overlooking garden; near University of Texas and State Capitol.

BOERNE

Borgman's Sunday House	$ B&B	Full breakfast
B&B	12 rooms, 12 pb	Restaurant nearby
911 S. Main, 78006	Visa, MC, AmEx, Disc., •	private baths, A/C
210-249-9563	C-yes/S-ltd/P-no/H-ltd	cable TV, telephone
Mike & Mary Jewell		
All year		

Texas Hill Country. Unique rooms, most furnished with antiques. Craft and antique shops nearby, also nature walk. 25 miles from San Antonio.

CANYON

Hudspeth House & Spa, The
1905 - 4th Ave., 79015
806-655-9800
Dave & Sally Haynie
All year

$$ B&B
8 rooms, 5 pb
Visa, MC, *Rated*, •
C-yes/S-ltd

Full gourmet breakfast
Lunch & dinner (reserv.)
Comp. wine/tea/lemonade
gazebo, veranda, hot tub
health & fitness center

*Relaxed historic 1909 B&B: gourmet breakfast, antiques, original stained glass. Close to musical drama "Texas," state park, Panhandle Plains Museum & WTSU. **3rd night 50% off***

DALLAS

Hotel St. Germain
2516 Maple Ave., 75201
214-871-2516
Claire Heymann
All year

$$$ B&B
7 rooms, 7 pb
Most CC, *Rated*, •
C-ltd/S-yes/P-no/H-yes
Spanish, French

Continental plus
Restaurant, bar
Comp. wine, aftn. tea
sitting room, library
spa, hot tubs, concierge

Elegant, Old World hotel with full services. Furnished entirely in antiques, fireplaces, canopied beds. Breakfast on china & silver. Sumptuous "Dangerous Liaisons" atmosphere.

EL PASO

Sunset Heights B&B Inn
717 W. Yandell Ave., 79902
915-544-1743 800-767-8513
R. Barnett & R. Martinez
All year

$$ B&B
6 rooms, 6 pb
Visa, MC, AmEx, *Rated*, •
C-ltd/S-no/P-no/H-no
Spanish

Full breakfast
Snacks, comp. wine
Sitting room, hot tubs
swimming pool
other meals by arrange.

*Victorian elegance (1905); Tiffany doors. National Historic Home. Panorama of El Paso and Juarez. For discriminating travelers & gourmet diners. **Multi-room/night disc't***

ENNIS

Raphael House
500 W. Ennis Ave., 75119
214-875-1555
Brian & Dana Cody Wolf
All year

$$ B&B
6 rooms, 6 pb
Most CC, *Rated*
C-ltd/S-ltd/P-no/H-no
Spanish

Full 3-course breakfast
Lunch & dinner available
Afternoon tea, snacks
sitting room, library
hot tub, sauna, pool

*1906 mansion w/ original antiques .".. perhaps the most romantic B&B in Texas," says Park Cities'People. Tennis, golf, health club nearby. Carriage House. **3rd nite 50%, ltd.***

FORT DAVIS

Hotel Limpia
Box 822, Main St. on the
Square, 79734
915-426-3237 800-662-5517
Lanna & Joe Duncan
All year

$$ EP
20 rooms, 20 pb
Visa, MC, AmEx
C-yes/S-yes/P-yes/H-yes
Spanish

Family-style restaurant
Meals can be in-rm., Bar
Sitting room, library
glassed-in verandas and
porches, rocking chairs

Historic hotel built in 1912. 1-mile high in the Davis mountains. Beautiful scenery. Close to Big Bend National Park, McDonald Observatory, museums, rafting, swimming, golf.

FORT WORTH

Miss Molly's Hotel B&B
109½ W. Exchange Ave., 76106
817-626-1522
Susan & Mark Hancock
All year

$$ B&B
8 rooms, 1 pb
Visa, MC, AmEx, *Rated*, •
C-yes/S-no/P-no/H-no

Continental plus
Comp. wine, tea, snacks
Sitting room, antiques
claw-foot tubs, quilts
stained glass skylight

A 1910 bordello with light "Old West" rooms located in the historic Stockyards, home of Billy Babs—World's largest honky-tonk. Many activities nearby.

FREDERICKSBURG

Country Cottage Inn
249 E. Main, 78624
210-997-8549
Ms. Jeffery Webb
All year

$$ B&B
7 rooms, 7 pb
Visa, MC, •
C-yes/S-no/P-no/H-no

Full breakfast
Comp. wine on arrival
Fireplaces, bathrobes
kitchens, porch swings
cable TV, room phones

Historic Texas stone home; built in 1850 by German pioneers; handcrafted woodwork, rafters, 24" walls; antique furnishings, king beds, jacuzzis; National Register.

Delforge Place, The
710 Ettic St., 78624
210-997-5612 210-997-6212
Betsy & George Delforge
All year

$$$ B&B
4 rooms, 4 pb
Visa, MC, Disc, •
C-ltd/S-no/P-no, French,
Spanish

Full breakfast
Lunch, picnic baskets
Afternoon tea, snacks
comp. wine
sitting rm, near tennis

1898 Victorian in town. Historical antiques, many reminiscent of Clipper-ship era. World class breakfast. Warm, friendly ambiance. **Business rates, ask**

John Walter Complex, The
231 W. Main St., Includes
Annie's Cabin, 78624
210-997-5612
Regina Eldrige
All year

$$$ B&B
4 rooms, 3 pb
Visa, MC, Disc, *Rated*, •
C-yes/S-ltd/P-no/H-no
German

Continental breakfast
Historic District
courtyard areas

Main House: Beautiful grounds, early immigrant settlers log and fachwerk construction. Annie's Cabin: Enchanting, time-worn decor! Fireplace. **7th night free**

Settler's Crossing
231 W. Main, Gastehaus
Schmidt, 78624
210-997-5612
Gastehaus Schmidt
All year

$$$ B&B
9 rooms, 4 pb
Visa, MC, Disc, *Rated*, •
C-yes/S-ltd/P-no/H-no

Continental plus
Donkeys, sheep
whirlpool tub, fireplace
2 log houses

Historic complex of 4 homes on 35 acres. Built 1787 to 1925. Professionally decorated in 18th/19th century antiques. Sleeps 21. **7th night free**

GALVESTON

Queen Anne B&B
1915 Sealy Ave., 77550
409-763-7088 713-779-0188
John McWilliams, Earl French
All year

$$$ B&B
4 rooms
Visa, MC
C-ltd/S-no/P-no/H-no

Full breakfast
Snacks, comp. wine
Sitting room
sun porch

Four-story 1905 Queen Anne Victorian, walk to shops and restaurants, stained glass windows, pocket doors, unbelievable floors, large rooms, beautiful. **3rd night 50% off**

Trube Castle Inn
1627 Sealy Ave., 77550
409-765-4396 800-662-9647
Nonette O'Donnell
All year

$$$ B&B
2 rooms, 2 pb
Visa, MC, AmEx, *Rated*,
•
C-ltd/S-ltd/P-no/H-no

Full breakfast
Private stocked refrig.
Two suites, jacuzzi
sitting room, library
TV, VCR, balconies

1890 replica of Danish Royal Castle, meticulously restored, museum quality antiques. Unsurpassed luxury near all island attractions. **3rd night 50% off**

GALVESTON ———————————

Victorian Inn
511 - 17th St., 77550
409-762-3235
Marcy Hanson
All year

$$$ B&B
5 rooms, 3 pb
Visa, MC, AmEx
C-ltd/S-yes/P-no/H-no

Continental plus
Comp. wine, snacks
Near historical district
flowers, balconies
retreats, weddings

The blending of yesteryear and today. Massive Italianate villa with stained glass, maple floors, carved oak fireplaces. Rooms have king-size brass beds, antiques & balconies.

GLEN ROSE ———————————

Inn on the River
P.O. Box 1417, 76043
205 S.W. Bernard
817-897-2101
Amy D. Guinn
All year

$$$ B&B
22 rooms, 22 pb
Visa, MC, AmEx, Disc., •
C-ltd/S-ltd/P-no/H-ltd
Spanish

Full breakfast
Dinner on Fri. & Sat.
Library, sitting room
swimming pool
riverside grounds

Restored historical structure near town square with Paluxy River frontage. Delicious food. Relaxing atmosphere. Great Blue Heron meeting house available.

Lodge at Fossil Rim, The
Rt 1, Box 210, 76043
817-897-7452
Lisa & Artie Ahier
All year

$$$ B&B
5 rooms, 3 pb
Most CC, *Rated*, •
C-yes/S-ltd/P-no/H-no

Full breakfast
Dinner Fri. & Sat.
Bar service, ltd.
swimming pool, star gaze
wildlife viewing drives

The lodge is situated in a secluded area of Fossil Rim Wildlife Center which is dedicated to the breeding of endangered species. **20% disc't for Seniors midwk**

Ye Ole Maple Inn
P.O. Box 1141, 76043
1509 Vanzant
817-897-3456
Roberta Maple
All year

$$ B&B
2 rooms, 2 pb
•
C-ltd/S-no/P-no/H-yes

Full breakfast
Snacks
River w/swimming, tubing

Quilt country getaway. Inviting porch swing and rockers. Great breakfast and desserts. Unique sightseeing attraction and golf course nearby.

HOUSTON ———————————

Durham House B&B Inn
921 Heights Blvd., 77008
713-868-4654
Marguerite Swanson
All year

$$ B&B
6 rooms, 6 pb
Visa, MC, AmEx, *Rated*,
•
C-ltd/German

Full breakfast
Comp. wine, refreshments
Sitting room, gazebo
tandem bicycles
Murder mystery evenings

Authentic Victorian on Nat'l Register of Historic Places. Antique furnishings. Romantic getaway/wedding location. Near downtown Houston. Carriage house avail. **6th night free**

Sara's B&B Inn
941 Heights Blvd., 77008
713-868-1130 800-593-1130
Donna & Tillman Arledge
All year

$$ B&B
11 rooms, 10 pb
Most CC, *Rated*, •
C-ltd/S-ltd/P-no/H-no

Continental plus
Cold drinks, coffee, tea
Sitting room, large deck
hot tub, bicycles

Old-time hospitality in the heart of Houston. Twelve distinctive bedrooms are furnished with antiques. Only four miles from downtown Houston.

JEFFERSON

Pride House	$$$ B&B	Full breakfast
409 Broadway, 75657	10 rooms, 10 pb	Comp. coffee, tea
903-665-2675	Visa, MC, *Rated*, •	Sitting room, A/C
Ruthmary Jordan	C-ltd/S-yes/P-no/H-yes	rooms have ceiling fans
All year		stained glass windows

Experience Victorian charm and traditional deep Southern legendary hospitality in the oldest B&B in Texas: 2-story Pride House, c. 1889. **Midwk pay one night, next one free.**

KEMAH

Captain's Quarters	$ B&B	Full breakfast
701 Bay Ave., 77565	9 rooms, 9 pb	Aft. tea, snacks
713-334-4141	Visa, MC, AmEx, *Rated*,	Comp. wine, sitting rm.
Mary Patterson	•	bicycles, tennis nearby
All year	C-ltd/S-no/P-no/H-yes	nearby swimming pool

Located on Galveston Bay. All private baths & antiques. Some rooms w/fireplaces. Walk to shops, restaurants and boat rentals. **3rd night 50% off**

Captians Quarters	$	Full breakfast
701 Bay Ave., NASA/Galveston	8 rooms, 8 pb	Aft. tea
area, 77565	Visa, MC, *Rated*, •	Snacks, sitting room
713-334-4141 713-474-2042	C-ltd/S-no/P-no/H-no	tennis/pool nearby
Mary Patterson		Comp. wine
All year		

Fantastic view of Galveston Bay with 8 elegantly furnished rooms, antiques, private baths, fireplaces. Walk to restaurants, shops. **3rd night 50% off**

LEANDER

Trails End B&B	$$ B&B	Full breakfast
12223 Trails End Rd.#7, 78641	Visa, MC, •	Dinner, snacks
512-267-2901	C-yes/S-no/P-no/H-no	Sitting room, library
Jo Ann & Tom Patty		bicycles, hiking
All year		swimming pool

Austin-Lake Travis area. Truly unique, elegant, comfortable country B&B. Porches, decks w/panoramic view of hill country. Fireplaces, hospitality. **10% off 3rd night**

MARBLE FALLS

La Casita B&B	$$ B&B	Full breakfast
1908 Redwood Dr., Granite	1 rooms, 1 pb	Comp. wine on arrival
Shoals, 78654	*Rated*, •	Refrigerator, sink
210-598-6443	C-yes/S-ltd/P-no/H-ltd	library, queen-sized bed
Joanne & Roger Scarborough		flowers, swimming
All year exc. Christmas		

Private, hill country cottage west of Marble Falls, wildlife and wildflowers, near Lake LBJ, river cruises & vineyards. **Small wedding, birthday, anniversary packages**

NACOGDOCHES

Llano Grande Plantation	$$ B&B	Continental plus
Route 4, Box 9400, 75961	3 rooms, 3 pb	Private kitchen
409-569-1249	*Rated*	Sitting room
Charles & Ann Phillips	C-ltd/S-no/P-no/H-no	historic tours
All year		library

Deep in the pine woods you will find the charming 1840s restored homestead of Tol Barret, who in 1866 drilled Texas' first producing oil well. **3rd night for $50 plus tax.**

NEW BRAUNFELS

Prince Solms Inn
295 E. San Antonio St., 78130
512-625-9169
Carmen Morales

$$ B&B
26 rooms, 26 pb
C-yes/S-yes/P-yes/H-no
Spanish

Continental breakfast
Lunch, dinner, bar
Entertainment

Late 18th-century converted to motel in 1806, furnished with reproduction antique furnishings—turn-of-the-century; completely renovated and restored. **Lower weekly rates**

SAN ANTONIO

Adams House B&B
231 Adams St., 78210
210-224-4791 800-666-4810
Betty Mays Lancaster
All year

$$ B&B
3 rooms, 3 pb
Visa, MC, AmEx
C-ltd/S-ltd/P-no/H-no
Spanish

Full gourmet breakfast
Aft. tea, snacks
Comp. wine, sitting room
library, computer, fax

Three story brick; King William Historic District, near Riverwalk/downtown; furnished in period antiques; spacious verandas; Gourmet breakfast served in dining room.

Bullis House Inn
P.O. Box 8059, 78208
621 Pierce St.
210-223-9426 FAX:299-1479
Steve & Alma Cross
All year

$ B&B
7 rooms, 2 pb
Most CC., *Rated*, •
C-yes/S-yes/P-no/H-no
Spanish

Continental plus
Guest kitchen, snacks
Child care (fee), phones
library, veranda, pool
king/queen/full beds

Historic 3 story, white mansion, minutes from Alamo, Riverwalk, downtown. Chandeliers, fireplaces, decorative 14-ft. ceilings, geometrically patterned floors of fine woods.

Chabot Reed Carriage House $$$ B&B
403 Madison, 78204
210-734-4243
Sister & Peter Reed
All year

2 rooms, 2 pb
•
C-yes/S-no/P-no/H-yes
Spanish

Full breakfast

Beautiful, Victorian mansion built in 1876. Close to Riverwalk, luxurious, comfortable rooms with a sense of history & sophistication, surrounded by lovely gardens.

Falling Pines B&B Inn
300 W. French Pl., 78212
210-733-1998 800-880-4580
Grace & Bob Daubert
All year

$$$ B&B
4 rooms, 4 pb
Rated, •
C-ltd/S-no/P-no/H-no

Full breakfast
Comp. wine/brandy in rm.
Sitting room, library
tennis courts
bicycles

Near downtown, riverwalk (5 minutes), three-story mansion in historic district with towering trees in parklike setting. Pristine restoration.

Norton Brackenridge House $$$ B&B
230 Madison, 78204
210-271-3442 800-221-1412
Carolyn & Nac
All year

5 rooms, 5 pb
Visa, MC, AmEx, *Rated*,
•
C-ltd/S-yes/P-no/H-no

Full breakfast
King & full-size beds
Veranda
off-street parking
6 blocks to downtown

Lovely blend of comfort and nostalgia. Original pine floors, double-hung windows, high ceilings and antique furniture. **One night off for 7 day stay.**

SAN ANTONIO

San Antonio Yellow Rose
229 Madison St., 78204
210-229-9903 800-950-9903
Jennifer & Cliff Tice
All year

$$ B&B
5 rooms, 5 pb
Most CC, *Rated*, •
C-ltd/S-no/P-no/H-no

Full breakfast
Aft. tea, snacks
Comp. wine
sitting room

Located King William Historic District, 2 blocks to Riverwalk, walk to Alamo, Convention Center, antiques, off street parking.

SAN MARCOS

Crystal River Inn
326 W. Hopkins, 78666
512-396-3739
Mike & Cathy Dillon
All year

$ B&B
12 rooms, 10 pb
Visa, MC, AmEx, *Rated*,
•
C-ltd/S-ltd/P-no/H-yes

Full breakfast
Comp. brandy, chocolates
Fireplaces, courtyard
piano, fountain, bikes
2rm suites, 4rm cottage

Romantic, luxurious Victorian captures matchless spirit of Texas Hill Country. Fresh flowers, homemade treats. Garden cottage available: fireplace. **3rd. night 50%, Ltd.**

TYLER

Mary's Attic B&B
413 S. College, 417 S. College,
75702
903-592-5181
Mary Mirsky
All year

$$ B&B
5 rooms, 3 pb
Visa, MC, AmEx
C-ltd/S-no/P-no/H-no

Continental plus
Antique shop next door

The completely restored 1920 bungalow and annex garage apartment are located on the brick streets in the historical district of Tyler. American and English antiques.

Rosevine Inn B&B
415 S. Vine, 75702
903-592-2221
Bert & Rebecca Powell
All year

$$ B&B
5 rooms, 5 pb
Rated, •
C-ltd/S-no/P-no/H-no
French

Full breakfast
Comp. wine, cheese tray
Sitting room, library
spa, outdoor hot tub
courtyard, gameroom

Original bed and breakfast in the rose capital of the world. Pleasant accommodations with delicious breakfast. Friendly hosts make you feel at home.

WACO

Thornton's B&B
908 Speight, 76706
817-756-0273
Davis & Jenifer Thornton
All year

$$ B&B
4 rooms, 4 pb
Visa, MC, •
C-ltd/S-no/P-no/H-ltd

Full breakfast
Aft. tea, snacks
Sitting room, library

Decorated with antiques & Texas Hill Country art. Quiet & comfortable bedrooms. Near Baylor University and IH-35. Easy to find.

WAXAHACHIE

Bonnynook B&B
414 W. Main St., 75165
214-938-7207 800-486-5936
Vaughn & Bonnie Franks
All year

$$ B&B
4 rooms, 4 pb
Most CC, *Rated*, •
C-ltd/S-yes/P-no/H-no

Full gourmet breakfast
Comp. wine, dinner
Picnic basket, snacks
whirlpool tubs in 2 rms
patio, piano, antiques

1887 Victorian home, located near Square in a historic national district. Each room is a different experience; plants & fresh flowers, a country garden. **10% off wkdays**

WIMBERLEY ─────────────────────────────────

Old Oaks Ranch B&B	$$ B&B	Continental plus
P.O. Box 912, 78676	3 rooms, 3 pb	Full breakfast (Sunday)
County Rd. 221	Visa, MC, *Rated*, •	Sitting room
512-847-9374 FAX:847-9374	C-ltd/S-no/P-no/H-no	one 2-bedroom cottage
Susan & Bill Holt		Two 1-bedroom cottages
All year		

Quiet, country inn furnished with Victorian antiques. Hiking. Cows, geese, wild birds, deer. Picturesque. Close to resort area. Golf & tennis available. **5th night free**

─────────────────────────────────

Southwind B&B	$$ B&B	Full breakfast
Route 2, Box 15, 78676	3 rooms, 3 pb	Hot tub
512-847-5277 800-508-5277	•	Sitting room
Carrie Watson	C-ltd/S-no/P-no/H-no	library, porch
All year	Spanish	rocking chairs on porch

Rocking chairs on porch; 25 scenic hill country acres; hearty southwestern breakfasts; homemade bread and muffins. Convenient to Austin (40 min.) and San Antonio (1 hour).

WINNSBORO ─────────────────────────────────

Thee Hubbell House	$$ B&B	Full breakfast
307 W. Elm, 75494	10 rooms, 10 pb	Candlelight dinner (res)
903-342-5629	Visa, MC, AmEx, *Rated*,	Sitting room, library
Dan & Laurel Hubbell	•	veranda, gallery, garden
All year	C-ltd/S-ltd/P-ltd/H-ltd	piano, jacuzzi, gazebo

1888 historic Georgian home, restored and furnished in period antiques. Plantation or continental breakfast. Centrally located to other tourist areas. **Honeymoon pkgs**

More Inns . . .

Brook House B&B, The, 609 W. 33rd St., Austin, 78705, 512-459-0534
Pfeiffer House, 1802 Main St., Bastrop, 78602, 512-321-2100
Pink Lady Inn, 1307 Main St., Bastrop, 78602, 512-321-6273
Nueces Inn, P.O. Box 29, Beeville, 78104, 713-362-0868
High Cotton Inn, 214 S. Live Oak, Bellville, 77418, 800-321-9796
Annie's B&B Country Inn, P.O. Box 928, Big Sandy, 75755, 214-636-4355
Secrets Bed & Breakfst, Pecan St., Brenham
Williams Point, 16 Lakeside Dr., Burnet, 78611, 512-756-2074
Landmark Inn, P.O. Box 577, Castroville, 78009, 512-538-2133
John C. Rogers House, 416 Shebyville, Center, 75935, 409-598-3971
Pine Colony Inn, 500 Shelbyville St., Center, 75935, 409-598-7700
Browning Plantation, Rt. 1, Box 8, Chappell Hill, 77426, 409-836-6144
Gingerbread House, Gingerbread St., Box 94, Chireno, 75937, 409-362-2365
Anglin Queen Anne, 723 N. Anglin, Cleburne, 76031, 817-645-5555
Cleburne House, 201 N. Anglin, Cleburne, 76031, 817-641-0085
Gast Haus Lodge, Box 423, 952 High St., Comfort, 78013, 512-995-2304
Sand Dollar Hospitality, 3605 Mendenhall, Corpus Christi, 78415, 512-853-1222
Smith House, 306 W. Aspen, Crosbyton, 79322, 806-675-2178
Reiffert-Mugge Inn, 304 W. Prairie St., Cuero, 77954, 512-275-2626
Inn on Fairmount, P.O. Box 190244, Dallas, 75219, 214-522-2800
Hill Top Cafe & Guesthouse, Fredericksburg Rt,Bx 88, Doss, 78618, 512-997-8922
Farris 1912, 201 N. McCarty, Eagle Lake, 77434, 409-234-2546
Red Rooster Square, Route 3, Box 3387, Edom, 75756, 214-852-6774
Gardner Hotel, 311 E. Franklin Ave., El Paso, 79901, 915-532-3661
Room with a View, 821 Rim Rd., El Paso, 79902, 915-534-4400
New Canaan Farm, P.O. Box 1173-1, Elkhart, 75839, 214-764-2106
Country Place Hotel, P.O. Box 39, Fayetteville, 78940, 409-378-2712
Old Texas Inn B&B, P.O. Box 785, Fort Davis, 79734
Stockyards Hotel, Main & Exchange Sts., Fort Worth, 76106, 817-625-6427
Baron's Creek Inn, 110 E. Creek St., Fredericksburg, 78624, 512-997-9398
J Bar K Ranch B&B, HC 10, Box 53-A, Fredericksburg, 78624, 210-669-2471
Rose Cottage & Guesthouse, 231 W. Main, Fredericksburg, 78624, 210-997-5612
Schmidt Barn, The, 231 W. Main, Fredericksburg, 78624, 210-997-5612
Terrill's B&B, 242 W. Main St., Apt. A, Fredericksburg, 78624, 512-997-8615
Dickens Loft, 2021 Strand, Galveston, 77550, 409-762-1653
Gilded Thistle, The, 1805 Broadway, Galveston, 77550, 409-763-0194
Hazelwood House, 1127 Church, Galveston, 77550, 713-762-1668
Key Largo, 5400 Seawall Blvd., Galveston, 77550, 800-833-0120

La Quinta Inn, 1402 Seawall Blvd., Galveston, 77550, 800-531-5900
Mather-Root Home, 1816 Winnie, Galveston, 77550, 713-439-6253
Michael's-A B&B Inn, 1715 - 35th St., Galveston, 77550, 409-763-3760
Tremont House, 2300 Ship's Mechanic Rd, Galveston, 77550, 800-874-2300
Virginia Point Inn, 2327 Avenue K, Galveston, 77550
White Horse Inn, 2217 Broadway, Galveston, 77550
Matali B&B Inn, 1727 Sealy, Galveston Island, 77550, 409-763-4526
Catnap Creek B&B, 417 Glen Canyon Dr., Garland, 75040, 214-530-0819
Lodge at Fossil Rim, The, P.O. Box 2189, Glen Rose, 76043, 817-897-7452
White House Inn, P.O. Box 992, Goliad, 77963, 512-645-2701
St. James Inn, 723 St. James, Gonzales, 78629, 512-672-7066
Nutt House, Town Square, Granbury, 76048, 817-573-5612
Farlton House of 1895, 211 N. Pleasant St., Hillsboro, 76645, 817-582-7216
Tarlton House, 211 N. Pleasant St., Hillsboro, 76645, 817-582-7216
Barbara's B&B, 215 Glenwood Dr., Houston, 77007
Highlander, The, 607 Highland St., Houston, 77009, 713-861-7545
La Colombe d'Or, 3410 Montrose Blvd., Houston, 77226, 713-524-7999
Patrician B&B Inn, The, 1200 Southmore Ave., Houston, 77004, 713-523-1114
Robin's Nest, 4104 Greeley St, Houston, 77006, 713-528-5821
Woodlake House, 2100 Tanglewilde, #371, Houston, 77063
Joy Spring Ranch B&B, Route 1, Box 174-A, Hunt, 78024, 512-238-4531
River Bend B&B, P.O. Box 158, Hunt, 78024, 512-238-4681
Austin Cottage, P.O. Box 488, Jefferson, 75657, 903-938-3153
Bluebonnet Inn B&B, 307 Soda St., Jefferson, 75657, 903-665-8572
Captain's Castle, 403 E Walker, Jefferson, 75657, 903-665-2330
Cottage, The, 307 Soda St., Jefferson, 75657
Excelsior House, 211 W. Austin St., Jefferson, 75657, 214-665-2513
Gingerbread House, 601 E. Jefferson, Jefferson, 75657, 214-665-8994
Hale House, 702 S. Line St., Jefferson, 75657, 903-665-8877
Magnolias Inn, 209 E. Broadway, Jefferson, 75657, 214-665-2754
McKay House B&B Inn, 306 E. Delta St., Jefferson, 75238, 214-348-1929
Roseville Manor, 217 West Lafayette, Jefferson, 75657, 800-665-7273
Stillwater Inn, 203 E. Broadway, Jefferson, 75657, 214-665-8415
William Clark House, 201 W. Henderson, Jefferson, 75657, 214-665-8880
Mimosa Hall, Route 1, Box 635, Karnack, 75661, 214-679-3632
Tea & Crumpets, 19131 Lookout Mt Ln., Katy, 77449
Mary Jane Robinson, P.O. Box 4529, Lago Vista, 78645
Granny's Hse c/o Ledbetter, P.O. Box 212, Ledbetter, 78946, 409-249-3066
Ledbetter Bed & Breakfast, P.O. Box 212, Ledbetter, 78940, 409-249-3066
Badu House, 601 Bessemer, Llano, 78643, 915-247-4304
Fort Russell Inn, U.S. 67, Marfa
Lash-Up B&B, 215 N. Austin, Marfa, 915-729-4487
Cotten's Patch, 703 E. Rusk, Marshall, 75670, 214-938-8756
Ginocchio Hotel, 707 N. Washington St., Marshall, 75670, 214-935-7635
Gregg-Plumb Home, 1006 E. Bowie, Marshall, 75670, 214-935-3366
La Maison Malfacon, 700 E. Rusk, Marshall, 75670, 214-935-6039
Meredith House, 410 E. Meredith St., Marshall, 75670, 214-935-7147
Weisman-Hirsch-Beil Home, 313 S. Washington, Marshall, 75670, 214-938-5504
Haden Edwards Inn, 106 N. Lanana, Nacogdoches, 75961, 409-564-9999
Tol Barret House, The, Rt. 4, Box 9400, Nacogdoches, 75961
Castle B&B, 1403 E. Washington, Navasota, 77868, 409-825-8051
Comfort Common, 240 S. Seguin Ave., New Braunfels, 78130, 512-995-3030
Gruene Mansion Inn, 1275 Gruene Rd., New Braunfels, 78130, 512-629-2641
Hill Country Haven, 227 S. Academy St., New Braunfels, 78130, 512-629-6727
Hotel Faust, 240 S. Seguin, New Braunfels, 78130, 512-625-7791
Lipan Ranch, Rt 1 Box 21C, Paint Rock, 76866, 915-468-2571
Hermitage, The, P.O. Box 866036, Plano, 75086, 214-618-2000
Tarpon Inn, P.O. Box 8, Port Aransas, 78373
Yacht Club Hotel, P.O. Box 4114, Port Isabel, 78578, 512-943-1301
La Borde House, 601 E. Main St., Rio Grande, 78582, 512-487-5101
Chain-O-Lakes, P O Box 218, Romayor, 77368, 713-592-2150

Trail's End B&B, Leander, TX

Thomas J. Rusk Hotel, 105 E. Sixth St., Rusk, 75785, 214-683-2556
Belle Of Monte Vista, 505 Belknap Pl., San Antonio, 78212
Bonner Garden, 145 E. Agarita, San Antonio, 78212
Cardinal Cliff, 3806 Highcliff, San Antonio, 78218, 512-655-2939
Mrs. Cauthorn's Inn, 217 King William St., San Antonio, 78204, 512-227-5770
Sartor House, 217 King William, San Antonio, 78204, 512-227-5770
Terrell Castle B&B, 950 E. Grayston St., San Antonio, 78206
San Juan Hotel, P.O. Box 114, San Juan, 78589
Aquarena Springs Inn, P.O. Box 2330, San Marcos, 78666, 512-396-8900
B&B on the Bay, 7629 Olympia Dr.Houston, Seabrook, 77586, 713-861-9492
Oxford House, The, 563 North Graham St., Stephenville, 76401, 817-965-6885
Lajitas on the Rio Grande, Box 400, Terlingua, 79852, 915-424-3471
Main House, 3419 Main St., Texarkana, 75503, 903-793-5027
Hotel Turkey, Box 37, Turkey, 79261, 806-423-1151
Casa De Leona B&B, P.O. Box 1829, Uvalde, 78802, 512-278-8550
Big Thicket Guest House, Box 91, Village Mills, 77663, 409-834-2875
Weimar Country Inn, P.O. Box 782, Weimar, 78962, 409-725-8888
Rio Grande B&B, P.O. Box 16, Weslaco, 78596, 512-968-9646
Guest House B&B, 2209 Miramar St., Wichita Falls, 76308
Yesteryear Bed & Breakfast, 208 West Myrtle, Winnsboro, 75494
Hygeia Health Retreat, 439 Main St., Yorktown, 78164, 512-564-3670

Utah

CEDAR CITY

Paxman Summer House	$$ B&B	Continental plus
170 North 400 West, 84720	4 rooms, 4 pb	Sitting room
801-586-3755	MC, *Rated*, •	swimming pool
Karlene Paxman	C-ltd/S-ltd/P-ltd/H-no	tennis courts
All year		

Comfortable Victorian home, one block from Utah's Shakespearean Festival. Near Zion, Dixie and Bryce National Parks. Swimming, golf and tennis.

GLENDALE

Smith Hotel	$ B&B	Continental plus
P.O. Box 106, 84729	7 rooms, 7 pb	Afternoon tea, snacks
Highway 89	Visa, MC	Sitting room
801-648-2156	C-ltd/S-no/P-no/H-no	screened porch
Shirley Phelan		
April—October		

Historic 1927 hotel; lovely view of nearby bluffs from the guest porch. Located in beautiful Long Valley between Zion and Bryce Canyon National Parks. **3rd nite $10 off**

MIDWAY

Homestead Resort, The	$$$ B&B	Continental plus
P.O. Box 99, 84049	117 rooms, 117 pb	Restaurant & bar
700 North Homestead Dr.	Most CC, *Rated*, •	Sitting rm, water sports
801-654-1102 800-327-7220	C-ltd/S-ltd/P-no/H-yes	tennis, skiing, golf
Britt R. Mathwich	German, Spanish	hot tubs, sauna, pool
All year		

Classic country inn located in gorgeous Heber Valley. Great country fare. Celebrated personal service. Charming accommodations. Fitness retreat. Conference space seats 250.

MOAB

Canyon Country B&B	$$ B&B	Full breakfast
590 North 500 West, 84532	5 rooms, 3.5 pb	Afternoon tea, hot tub
801-259-5262 800-435-0284	Most CC, *Rated*, ●	Library, bikes, walk or
Jeanne Lambla	C-ltd/S-no/P-no	bike to local museums
All year		shops, restaurants, etc.

Casual Southwestern home. A warm decor, freshly cut flowers in your room, a large yard with patio & travel library all combine to provide a "home away from home" atmosphere.

Pack Creek Ranch	$$$ AP	Full breakfast
P.O. Box 1270, 84532	10 rooms, 10 pb	All meals included
La Sal Pass Rd.	Visa, MC, AmEx, Disc., ●	Bar service, hot tubs
801-259-5505	C-yes/S-yes/P-yes/H-no	sauna, swimming pool
Ken & Jane Sleight		trail rides & pack trips
All year		

Cozy log cabins on old homestead site. Quiet country setting w/open spaces. Good food, great hiking. Close to canyonlands & Arches National Parks. Low winter rates w/out meals

PARK CITY

Blue Church Lodge, The	$$ B&B	Continental
P.O. Box 1720, 84060	11 rooms, 11 pb	Hot tubs, gameroom
424 Park Ave.	Visa, MC, ●	kitchens, fireplaces
801-649-8009	C-yes/S-yes/P-ltd/H-no	ski lockers, sitting rm.
Nancy Schmidt		
Ski season		

Elegantly designed condos w/antique country charm, 1-4 bedrooms. Listed National Register Historic Places. Walk to Main Street and town lift.

Imperial Hotel	$$ B&B	Continental plus
P.O. Box 1628, 84060	10 rooms, 10 pb	Aft. tea, snacks
221 Main St.	Visa, MC, AmEx, *Rated*,	Pub & art gallery
801-649-1904 800-669-8824	●	jacuzzi & ski lockers
Ted & Marianne Dumas	C-yes/S-no/P-no/H-no	near all activities
All year		

Superbly restored 1904 hotel in heart of Park City. Private baths w/large roman tubs, phone, cable TV & HBO. On National Register of Historic Homes.

Old Miners' Lodge B&B	$ B&B	Full country breakfast
P.O. Box 2639, 84060	10 rooms, 10 pb	Evening refreshments
615 Woodside Ave.	Most CC, *Rated*, ●	Organ, fireplace
801-645-8068 800-648-8068	C-yes/S-no/P-no/H-no	sitting room, library
Hugh Daniels & Susan Wynne		hot tub, games
All year		

An original miner's lodge—antique-filled rooms, feather beds, full breakfast, complimentary refreshments and fine hospitality; an unforgettable experience!

Washington School Inn	$$$ B&B	Full breakfast
P.O. Box 536, 84060	15 rooms, 15 pb	Comp. wine, tea, snacks
543 Park Ave.	Visa, MC, AmEx, *Rated*,	Sitting room
801-649-3800 800-824-1672	●	hot tub, sauna
N. Beaufait , D. Covington	C-ltd/S-ltd/P-no/H-ltd	steam showers
All year		

Original schoolhouse is now an unique country inn, antique furnishings, in the center of Park City. Many activities, including skiing.

ROCKVILLE

Handcart House B&B
P.O. Box 630146, 84763
244 W. Main St
801-772-3867
Rick & Lynda Sentker
All year

$$ B&B
4 rooms, 4 pb
Visa, MC, AmEx
C-ltd/S-no/P-ask/H-no

Full breakfast
Snacks
Sitting room with
satellite TV, VCR

Adjacent to Zion National Park, reminiscent of early Mormon pioneer homes. Antiques, handmade quilts give feeling of past. Private baths, satellite TV please modern tastes.

SALT LAKE CITY

Anton Boxrud B&B
57 South 600 East, 84102
801-363-8035 800-524-5511
Mark Brown, Keith Lewis
All year

$ B&B
6 rooms, 3 pb
Visa, MC, *Rated*, •
C-ltd/S-no/P-no/H-no

Continental breakfast
Hot tubs (winter)
sitting room

The interior of this "Grand Old Home" is replete with beveled and stain-glass windows, burled woodwork, hardwood floors and pocked doors. Come be pampered.

Brigham Street Inn
1135 E. South Temple, 84102
801-364-4461 FAX:521-3201
John & Nancy Pace
All year

$$$ B&B
9 rooms, 9 pb
Visa, MC, AmEx, *Rated*,
•
C-yes/S-yes/P-no/H-no

Continental breakfast
Comp. tea, coffee
Entertainment, piano
jacuzzi in 1 suite
sitting room, library

Nat'l historic site, served as designers' showcase in May '82. Winner of many architectural awards. Near 7 major ski areas. Unique executive hotel. AAA/MOBIL 4 diamonds/stars.

SANDY

Mountain Hollow B&B Inn
10209 S. Dimple Dell Rd, 84092
801-942-3428
Doug & Kathy Larson
All year

$$ B&B
9 rooms
Visa, MC, *Rated*, •
C-ltd/S-no/P-no/H-no

Expanded Continental
Sitting room
library
game room, hot tub

Mountain hideaway, antiques, stream, spa, recreation room, movies, room TVs, cathedral living room, relaxing atmosphere, close to downtown and skiing. One suite available.

SPRINGDALE

Harvest House
P.O. Box 125, 84767
29 Canyon View Dr.
801-772-3880
Steve & Barbara Cooper
All year

$$ B&B
4 rooms, 4 pb
Visa, MC, *Rated*
C-ltd/S-no/P-no/H-no

Full breakfast, snacks
Dinner/winter only
Sitting room, library
tennis court, comp. bev.
private decks, hot tub

Comfortably furnished country home, nestled in Zion National Park. Remarkable views throughout. Quiet, clean, charming, relaxing. Spectacular breakfast! AAA-3 stars.

ST. GEORGE

Greene Gate Village Inn
76 W. Tabernacle, 84770
801-628-6999 800-635-6999
M. & B. Greene/J. & S. Greene
All year

$ B&B
12 rooms, 9 pb
Visa, MC, *Rated*, •
C-yes/S-no/P-yes/H-yes

Full breakfast
Lunch, Dinner
Soft drinks on arrival
sitting room, hot tubs
tennis courts, pool

*Restored original pioneer home in an unique village close to downtown but in a quiet neighborhood. Close to Zion, Grand Canyon. **3rd night free.***

ST. GEORGE

Seven Wives Inn
217 N. 100 West, 84770
801-628-3737 800-600-3737
The Curtises and Bowcotts
All year

$$ B&B
12 rooms, 12 pb
Most CC, *Rated*, •
C-yes/S-no/P-no/H-ltd

Full gourmet breakfast
Comp. fruit
Bicycles, hot tub, pool
sitting room, organ
golf & tennis nearby

1870s pioneer home on National Register, furnished throughout in antiques, in heart of St. George—close to national parks. Honeymoon suite w/whirlpool tub room.

More Inns . . .

Old Hotel B&B, The, 118 East 300 South St., Blanding, 84511, 801-678-2388
Bluff B&B, P.O. Box 158, Bluff, 84512, 801-672-2220
Calabre B&B, PO Box 85, Bluff, 84512, 801-672-2252
Recapture Lodge & Pioneer , Box 36, Bluff, 84512, 801-672-2281
Meadeau View Lodge, P.O. Box 356, Cedar City, 84762, 801-682-2495
Willow Glen Inn B&B, 3308 N. Bulldog Rd., Cedar City, 84720, 801-586-3275
Woodbury Guest House, 237 S. 300 W., Cedar City, 84720, 801-586-6696
Ephraim Homestead, 135 W. 100 N., Ephraim, 84627, 801-283-6367
Inn Of The Three Bears, 135 S. Bear Lake Blvd., Garden City, 84028, 801-946-8590
Homeplace, The, PO Box 41, 200 S. Main, Glendale, 84729, 801-648-2194
Dearden's B&B, 202 West 100 North, Hemefer, 84033
Jackson Fork Inn, 7345 East 900 South, Huntsville, 84317, 801-745-0051
Pah Temple Hot Springs, 825 N. 800 E. 35-4, Hurricane, 84737, 801-635-2879
Miss Sophie's B&B, 30 N. 200 W., Kanab, 84741, 801-644-5952
Nine Gables Inn, 106 W. 100 North, Kanab, 84741, 801-644-5079
Zion Overlook B&B, P.O. Box 852, La Verkin, 84745, 801-877-1061
Vue De Valhalla, 2787 Nordic Valley Rd, Liberty, 84310
Road Creek Inn, P.O. Box 310, Loa, 84747, 801-836-2485
Center Street B&B Inn, 169 E. Center St., Logan, 84321, 801-752-3443
Manti House Inn, 401 N. Main St, Manti, 84642, 801-835-0161
Yardley B&B Inn, 190 W. 200 S., Manti, 84642, 801-835-1861
Inn On The Creek, 375 Rainbow Ln., Midway, 84049, 801-654-0892
Castle Valley Inn, CVSR Box 2602, Moab, 84532, 801-259-6012
Cedar Breaks Condos B&B, Center & 4th East, Moab, 84532, 801-259-7830
Matterhorn Guest House, 3601 E. Matterhorn Heig, Moab, 84532, 801-259-6979
Rose Tree B&B, 505 Rose Tree Ln., Moab, 84532, 801-259-6015
Sandi's B&B, 450 Walker St., Moab, 84532, 801-259-6359
Sistelita, CVSR 2105, 484 Amber Ln, Moab, 84532
Slick Rock Inn, 286 South 400 East, Moab, 84532, 801-259-2266
Sunflower Hill B&B, 185 North, 400 West, Moab, 84532
Peterson's B&B, P.O. Box 142, Monroe, 84754, 801-527-4830
Crist Mill Inn, The, P.O. Box 29, Monticello, 84535
Mansion House, 298 S. State St. #13, Mount Pleasant, 84647, 801-462-3031
Whitmore Mansion B&B, The, P.O. Box 73, Nephi, 84648, 801-623-2047
Rogers Rest B&B, 914 29th St., Ogden, 84403, 801-393-5824
505 Woodside, B&B Place, P.O. Box 2446, Park City, 84060, 801-649-4841
Snowed Inn, 3770 N. Hwy 224, Park City, 84060, 801-649-5713
Star Hotel B&B, P.O. Box 777, Park City, 84060, 801-649-8333
Sundance, P.O. Box 837, Provo, 84601, 801-225-4100
Whitney House, The, 415 S. University Ave.,
  Provo, 84601, 801-377-3111
Old Church B&B, The, 180 W. 400 S., Richfield,
  84701, 801-896-6705
Blue House B&B, The, 125 East Main, Rockville,
  84763, 801-772-3912
Dave's Cozy Cabin Inn, 2293 East 6200 South,
  Salt Lake City, 84121, 801-278-6136
Pinecrest B&B, 6211 Emigration Canyon , Salt
  Lake City, 84108, 801-583-6663
Saltair B&B, 164 S. 900 E., Salt Lake City, 84012,
  801-533-8184
Spruces B&B, 6151 S. 900 East, Salt Lake City,
  84121, 801-268-8762
Quail Hills Guesthouse, 3744 E. N.Little Cttnwd,
  Sandy, 84092, 801-942-2858
Escalante B&B, 733 North Main St., Spanish
  Fork, 84660, 801-798-6652
Under the Eaves House, PO Box 29, Zion Park
  Bl, Springdale, 84767
Zion House B&B, Box 323, Springdale, 84767,
  801-772-3281
Shady Corner B&B, 194 S. 600 E., St. George,
  84770, 801-673-7383
Cedar Crest B&B, POBox T, Palisade Lake,
  Sterling, 84665, 801-835-6352
Your Inn Toquerville, POBox 276, 650 Springs,
  Toquerville, 84774, 801-635-9964

The Imperial Hotel, Park City, UT

Vermont

ARLINGTON

Arlington Inn
P.O. Box 369, 05250
Historic Route 7A
802-375-6532 800-443-9442
Robert & Marsha Artig
All year

$$ B&B
13 rooms, 13 pb
Most CC, *Rated*
C-yes/S-yes/French

Continental plus
Lunch (summer/fall)
Cookies and cider
Restaurant, bar
sitting rm; tennis court

Antique-filled rooms in one of Vermont's finest Greek revival homes. Located in Norman Rockwell country. Winner of 1988 Travel Holiday Dining Award & Taste of Vermont Award.

Hill Farm Inn
RR 2, Box 2015, Hill Farm Rd,
Sunderland, 05250
802-375-2269 800-882-2545
John & Regan Chichester
All year

$$ B&B
13 rooms, 8 pb
Most CC, *Rated*, •
C-yes/S-no/P-ltd/H-no

Full country breakfast
Comp. afternoon snacks
Sitting room, piano
fireplace, fruit baskets
guide to the area in rm.

1790 & 1830 farmhouses, an inn since 1905; pleasant mountain views, hearty home cooking, fish the Battenkill, hike country roads.

Inn at Sunderland, The
RR 2, Box 2440, Route 7A,
05250
802-362-4213 800-441-1628
Tom & Peggy Wall
All year exc. April

$$$ B&B
10 rooms, 10 pb
Visa, MC, AmEx, *Rated*,
•
C-ltd/S-ltd/P-no/H-yes

Full breakfast
Afternoon cheese/cider
Sitting room, bicycles
fly fishing clinic/guide
country club privileges

Country elegance in a B&B inn; beautifully restored Victorian farmhouse with antiques and fireplaces, double-decker porch with Green Mountains view. **3rd. night 50%, Ltd.**

Shenandoah Farm
Route 313, Box 3260, Battenkill
Dr., 05250
802-375-6372
Woody Masterson
All year

$$ B&B
5 rooms, 3 pb
Rated, •
C-yes/S-yes/P-no/H-no

Full breakfast
Comp. wine, tea
Sitting room
piano, library
fishing/canoeing/tubing

Beautifully restored 1820 colonial furnished with antiques, overlooking Battenkill River and rolling meadows. Near skiing, golf, tennis. **3rd. night 50% off**

West Mountain Inn
Box 481, Route 313 & River Rd.,
05250
802-375-6516
Wes & Mary Ann Carlson
All year

$$$ MAP
15 rooms, 15 pb
Visa, MC, AmEx, *Rated*,
•
C-yes/S-ltd/P-no/H-yes
French

Full breakfast
Dinner included, bar
Fruit, chocolate llama
sitting room, piano
dining room, flowers

150-acre hillside estate; hike or ski woodland trails. Fish the Battenkill. Hearthside dining, charming rooms. Relax and enjoy the 11amas, goats and rabbits.

BELMONT ———————————————————————————————————

Leslie Place, The	$$ B&B	Continental plus
Box 62, 05730	4 rooms, 2 pb	Spacious rooms, sitt. rm
802-259-2903 800-352-7439	Visa, MC	swimming & hiking nearby
Mary K. Gorman	C-yes/S-no/P-no/H-no	separate apt. available
All year		

New England farmhouse peacefully set on 100 acres; mountain views, open meadows; near Weston. Perfect retreat near ski areas, restaurants, theater, shops. **3rd nite 50%, Ltd**

Parmenter House	$$ B&B	Continental plus
P.O. Box 106, 05730	4 rooms, 4 pb	Comp. wine, refreshments
Healdville Rd.	Visa, MC, •	Sitting room, bikes
802-259-2009 800-785-7468	C-yes/S-no/P-no/H-no	2 children free
Joe & Robyn Phelan		lake swimming
All year		

Antique-furnished country Victorian in idyllic lakeside village. Summer sports, cross-country skiing, sleigh rides. Near Weston Priory. **Midwk disc't, ltd.**

BENNINGTON ———————————————————————————————

Molly Stark Inn	$$ B&B	Full gourmet breakfast
1067 E. Main St., 05201	6 rooms, 6 pb	Champagne dinner avail.
802-442-9631 800-356-3076	Most CC, *Rated*, •	Den with woodstove, TV
Reed Fendler	C-ltd/S-no/P-no/H-no	hardwood floors, antique
All year		quilts, claw foot tubs

Charming 1860 Victorian on Main Street, one mile from center. Decorated with country American, antiques, classical music playing. Champagne/dinner package. **3rd night 50% off.**

BRANDON ————————————————————————————————————

Moffett House B&B, The	$$ B&B	Full breakfast
69 Park St., 05733	6 rooms, 3 pb	Comp. tea
802-247-3843	*Rated*	Library, bicycles, golf
Elliot & Nancy Phillips	C-yes/S-yes/P-ltd/H-no	tennis, skiing, gardens
All year		wine & cheese on arrival

Splendid Victorian bed & breakfast, perfect for a romantic getaway or family fun. Enjoy an elegant country breakfast and activities ranging from skiing to rocking.

BRIDGEWATER CORNERS ———————————————————————————

October Country Inn	$$$ B&B/$$$ MAP	Full breakfast
P.O. Box 66, 05035	10 rooms, 7 pb	Dinner (MAP), fireplace
Upper Rd.	*Rated*, •	Homebaked aftn. treats
802-672-3412 800-648-8421	C-yes/S-no/P-no/H-ltd	sitting room, sun deck
Richard Sims, Patrick Runkel		pool, antique stove
Dec–mid-April, May–Nov		

19th-century Vermont farmhouse. Meals include garden vegetables, freshly baked breads, desserts. Comfortable rooms, cozy living room. **Discounts, ask**

BROOKFIELD ———————————————————————————————————

Green Trails Country Inn	$$ B&B	Full breakfast
By the Floating Bridge, 05036	15 rooms, 9 pb	Dinner with notice, tea
802-276-3412 800-243-3412	*Rated*, •	3 sitting rms, fireplace
Pat & Peter Simpson	C-yes/S-no/P-no/H-no	swimming, biking, canoes
May–March	Swedish	cross-country skiing,
		antiques

National Register of Historic Places. Located by the Floating Bridge. Warm hospitality, decorated w/quilts—like going to Grandma's. Featured on Today Show. **3rd nite 50% off**

BURLINGTON

Howden Cottage B&B
32 N. Champlain St., 05401
802-864-7198
Bruce M. Howden
All year

$ B&B
2 rooms
Visa, MC
C-ltd/S-no/P-no/H-no

Continental breakfast
Sitting room
sinks in rooms
suite w/private bath

Howden Cottage offers cozy lodging and warm hospitality in the atmosphere of a private home. Owned and operated by a local artist, Bruce M. Howden. Reservations, please!

CHARLOTTE

Inn at Charlotte, The
RR1, Box 1188, State Park Rd.,
05445
802-425-2934
Letty Ellinger
All year

$$ B&B
6 rooms, 6 pb
Visa, MC
C-ltd/S-no/P-no/H-no
Philippine (Tagalog)

Full breakfast
Picnic lunch basket
Dinner on adv. request
comp. wine, appetizers
tennis courts, pool

Beautiful courtyard/flower gardens. Spacious rooms w/country furniture. Breakfast poolside. Picnic baskets & dinner available on request. ***Free bottle wine w/3 nights***

CHELSEA

Shire Inn
P.O. Box 37, 05038
Main St.
802-685-3031
Karen & Jay Keller
All year

$$$ B&B
6 rooms, 6 pb
Visa, MC, *Rated*
C-ltd/S-no/P-no/H-no

Full breakfast
Dinner by reservation
Sitting room
fireplaces
bicycles

Elegant country atmosphere; antique furnishings. Gracious candlelight dining. On White River. Cross-country skiing in winter. ***3rd night 50%***

CHESTER

Chester House
P.O. Box 708, 05143
Main St., Village Green
802-875-2205
Irene & Norm Wright
All year

$$ B&B
4 rooms, 4 pb
Rated, •
C-ltd/S-yes

Full breakfast
Sitting room, library
jacuzzi
fireplaces in rooms

A southern Vermont B&B inn of extraordinary charm & hospitality. Beautifully restored, antique-furnished c.1780 home in the Nat'l Register of Historic Places. ***4+ night disc't***

Greenleaf Inn
P.O. Box 188, 05143
Depot St.
802-875-3171
Elizabeth & Dan Duffield
All year

$$ B&B
5 rooms, 5 pb
Visa, MC, *Rated*
C-ltd/S-yes/P-no/H-no

Full breakfast
Picnic box lunch $
Beverages, art gallery
2 large living rooms
library, bicycles nearby

Lovely 1880s village inn. Comfortable, large, airy rooms. Private baths. Big, fluffy towels. Spotlessly clean. Beautifully furnished throughout. ***Discount with group rental***

Henry Farm Inn
P.O. Box 646, 05143
Green Mountain Trnpk
802-875-2674 800-723-8213
Jean & Keu Tanch
All year

$$ B&B
7 rooms, 7 pb
Rated, •
C-yes/S-ltd/P-no/H-ltd

Full breakfast
Tea, coffee, cookies
Sitting room
library
pond, hiking

1750s farmhouse in charming country setting in the glorious Green Mountains. Full country breakfast each morning. Extensive grounds available for your pleasure. ***3rd night 50%***

CHESTER

Hugging Bear Inn & Shoppe
Box 32, Main St., 05143
802-875-2412 800-325-0519
G., D., & P. Thomas
All year

$$$ B&B
6 rooms, 6 pb
Visa, MC
C-yes/S-no/P-no/H-no
Russian

Full breakfast
Afternoon bev., snacks
Sitting room
library
bicycles

Elegant Victorian in National Historic District, on the Village Green, thousands of Teddy Bears throughout, thousands in the shoppe. (3,609 at last count!) FUN!

Madrigal Inn & Arts, The
61 Williams River Rd., 05143
802-463-1339 800-854-2208
Ray & Nancy Dressler
All year

$$$ B&B
11 rooms, 11 pb
Visa, MC, •
C-yes/S-no/P-ltd/H-yes

Full breakfast
Lunch/dinner by res.
Aft. tea, snacks
arts & crafts center
sitting room, library

Beauty inside & out. 11 romantic guest rooms w/baths. 60 acres mountain/meadow landscape. Warm hospitality. 5K cross-country skiing trails. Arts & crafts workshop/classes. **10% off bill**

Rowell's Inn
RR 1, Box 267D, Route 11,
Simonsville, 05143
802-875-3658
Lee & Beth Davis
All year exc. April

$$$ MAP
5 rooms, 5 pb
Rated
C-ltd/S-yes/P-no/H-no

Full breakfast
Dinner included
Afternoon teas
tavern
sitting room

1820 stagecoach hotel on National Register of Historic Places. Antique furnishings, hearty food. Rowell's Tavern offers Robert Haas wines and a variety of English beer.

CHITTENDEN

Tulip Tree Inn
Chittenden Dam Rd., 05737
802-483-6213
Ed & Rosemary McDowell
Exc. Apr, Nov to Thksgvg

$$$ MAP
8 rooms, 8 pb
Visa, MC, *Rated*, •
C-ltd/S-ltd/P-no/H-no
German

Full breakfast
Dinner included
Full bar & wine cellar
sitting room, library
some rooms w/jacuzzis

Small, antique-filled country inn, hidden away in the Green Mountains. Gracious dining, homemade breads and desserts, liquor license, wine list. One of Uncle Ben's 10 best.

CUTTINGSVILLE

Buckmaster Inn B&B
RR1, Box118, Shrewsbury,
Lincoln Hill Rd., 05738
802-492-3485
Sam & Grace Husselman
All year

$$ B&B
3 rooms, 1 pb
C-ltd/S-ltd/P-no/H-ltd
Dutch

Full breakfast
Comp. tea & cookies
Sitting room, fireplace
porches, library
organ, bicycles

1801 historic stagecoach stop with spacious rooms, charm of family heirlooms in Green Mountains. Nature paradise, relaxing atmosphere. **7th night free**

Maple Crest Farm
Box 120, Lincoln Hill, 05738
802-492-3367
William, Donna & Russ Smith
All year

$$ B&B
6 rooms, 2 pb
C-ltd/S-yes/P-no/H-ltd

Full breakfast
Afternoon tea
Sitting room
piano, hiking
cross-country skiing

Dairy farm located in beautiful mountain town of Shrewsbury. Lovingly preserved for five generations of Vermont tradition Rutland area. Our 22th anniversary this year!

DANBY

Quail's Nest B&B
P.O. Box 221, 05739
Main St.
802-293-5099
Chip & Anharad Edson
All year

$$ B&B
5 rooms, 3 pb
Visa, MC, *Rated*
C-ltd/S-no/P-no/H-no

Full breakfast
Comp. tea & snacks
Sitting room w/fireplace
library, horseshoes
deck & garden, bicycles

Nestled among the Green Mountains in a quiet Vermont village; home-baked breakfasts followed by relaxing country fun! **10% off 5+ nights**

Silas Griffith Inn
RR 1, Box 66F, S. Main St., 05739
802-293-5567
Paul & Lois Dansereau
All year

$$ B&B
17 rooms, 11 pb
Visa, MC, AmEx, *Rated*,
•
C-yes/S-yes

Full breakfast
Restaurant, bar, dinner
Aftn. beverages, cookies
sitting room, library
swimming pool

Lovingly restored Victorian mansion and carriage house. Relax in antique-filled rooms; enjoy a quiet 19th-century village. Spectacular Green Mountain views.

DORSET

Barrows House
Route 30, 05251
802-867-4455 800-639-1620
Jim & Linda McGinnis
All year, FAX:867-0132

$$$ MAP
28 rooms, 28 pb
Rated, •
C-yes/S-yes/P-ltd/H-ltd
German

Full breakfast
Lunch, dinner, bar
Swimming pool, sauna
tennis courts, bicycles
sitting room, piano

Eight buildings in picturesque Dorset, close to hiking, fishing, golf, horseback riding, shopping, cross-country ski shop. Playroom for children. **3rd night 50% off, ltd.**

Little Lodge at Dorset
P.O. Box 673, 05251
Route 30
802-867-4040
Allan & Nancy Norris
All year

$$$ B&B
5 rooms, 5 pb
C-yes/S-no/P-no/H-no

Continental plus
Afternoon tea
Sitting room w/fireplace
skating pond
some rooms, A/C

Delightful old house on hillside near picturesque village. Lovely antiques, inviting barnboard den, guests' refrigerator, friendly atmosphere.

Marble West Inn
P.O. Box 847, 05251
Dorset West Rd.
802-867-4155 800-453-7629
Wayne & June Erla
All year

$$$ B&B/MAP
8 rooms, 8 pb
Visa, MC, AmEx, *Rated*,
•
C-ltd/S-no/P-no/H-no

Full breakfast
Dinner, Aft. tea
Refreshments
wine & beer service
sitting room, library

Historic 1840 Greek Revival elegant country inn. Polished oak floors, oriental rugs, grand piano. Candlelight dining. Warm, friendly atmosphere. **25% off Mar & April B&B**

ENOSBURG FALLS

Berkson Farms
RR 1, Box 850, Rt. 108 W.
Berkshire Rd., 05450
802-933-2522
Susan & Terry Spoonire
All year

$$ B&B/$$$ AP
4 rooms, 1 pb
C-yes/S-yes/P-yes/H-no

Full breakfast
Lunch, dinner
Sitting room, bicycles
working dairy farm
farm animals

Homey 150-year-old farmhouse on working dairy farm. Relax on 600 acres surrounded by animals, nature and warm hospitality.

FAIR HAVEN

Maplewood Inn & Antiques
RR 1, Box 4460, Route 22A
South, 05743
802-265-8039 800-253-7729
Cindy & Doug Baird
All year

$$ B&B
5 rooms, 5 pb
Visa, MC, Disc, *Rated*, •
C-ltd/S-ltd

Continental plus buffet
Comp. wine, tea, coffee
BYOB tavern, chocolates
sitting room, toiletries
library, TV in room, A/C

Romantic, elegantly appointed, suites & many common areas. Firepl, bicycles, antiques, brewing supply shop. In lakes region close to everything. We pamper you! **10% off rsvp**

FAIRFAX

Inn at Buck Hollow Farm
RR 1, Box 680, 05454
802-849-2400
Dody Young, Brad Schwartz
All year

$$ B&B
4 rooms
Visa, MC, *Rated*, •
C-yes/S-no/P-no/H-no

Full breakfast
Beer & wine
Sun room, jacuzzi, pool
fenced-in play area
cross-country skiing,
antique shop

Our intimate inn features canopy beds, antique decor, beamed ceilings, heated pool, fireplace, jacuzzi and 400 spectacular acres. Satellite TV in rooms. **3+ nights 10% off**

FAIRLEE

Silver Maple Lodge/Cottage
RR 1, Box 8, S. Main St., 05045
802-333-4326 800-666-1946
Scott & Sharon Wright
All year

$ B&B
15 rooms, 7 pb
Visa, MC, *Rated*, •
C-yes/S-yes/P-no/H-no

Continental breakfast
Sitting room, lawn games
picnic area, cottages
bicycle & canoe rental

Quaint country inn located in a scenic resort area; convenient to antique shops, fishing, golf, swimming, tennis & winter skiing. Ballooning pkgs avail. **3rd night 50% off.**

GAYSVILLE

Cobble House Inn
P.O. Box 49, 05746
Childrens Camp Rd.
802-234-5458
Beau & Phil Benson
All year

$$$ B&B
6 rooms, 6 pb
Visa, MC, *Rated*
C-ltd/S-no/P-no/H-ltd

Full breakfast
Romantic restaurant
Afternoon hors d'oeuvres
2 sitting rooms, river
swimming, cross-country
skiing

Victorian mansion, 1864. Mountain views on the White River; country breakfasts; gourmet dinners; antique furnishings; private baths. Golf tours arranged.

Laolke Lodge
P.O. Box 107, 05746
Laury Hill Rd.
802-234-9205
Ms Olive Pratt
All year

$ MAP
5 rooms
C-yes/S-yes/P-ltd/H-no

Full breakfast
Evening meal
Sitting room, piano
pool, color TV, tennis
river swimming, tubing

Family-style vacations in modern, rustic log cabin. Home cooking. Near skiing, horseback riding, hunting, boating, and other Vermont attractions. **3rd night 50% off**

GRAFTON

Farmhouse 'Round the Bend
P.O. Box 57, 05146
Pickle St., Route 121 E.
802-843-2515
Tom Chiffriller

$$ B&B
3 rooms, 3 pb
C-ltd/S-ltd/P-no/H-no

All year

Continental plus
Afternoon tea
Sitting room
catering, badminton
horse shoes, croquet

Warm country atmosphere. Open sunny porch. Scrumptious breakfast. Short walk to most picturesque village in Vermont. **3 nights or more $5 off rate**

HANOVER–WILDER

Stonecrest Farm B&B
P.O. Box 504, 05088
119 Christian St.
802-295-2600 603-643-1400
Gail Sanderson
All year

$$$ B&B
5 rooms, 3 pb
Visa, MC, *Rated*, •
C-ltd/S-no/P-no/H-no
Some German, French

Continental plus wkdys
Full breakfast wkends
Snacks, comp. wine
sitting room
inn to inn canoe trips

Country setting 3.5 miles from Dartmouth College. Gracious 1810 home offers antiques, down comforters, terraces. All outdoor activities. **1 night free w/wk stay**

HYDE PARK

Fitch Hill Inn, The
RFD 1, Box 1879, Fitch Hill Rd.,
05655
802-888-3834
Richard A. Pugliese
All year

$$ B&B/MAP avail
4 rooms, 2 pb
Rated, •
C-ltd/S-no/P-ltd/H-no
German

Full breakfast
Lunch & dinner on requ.
Sitting room
piano
library

18th-century farmhouse near Stowe and Northeast Kingdom. Extensive views of mountains, country antique decor, home cooking, informal atmosphere. **3rd night 50% off, ltd.**

JEFFERSONVILLE

Smuggler's Notch Inn, The
P.O. Box 280, 05464
Church St.
802-644-2412 800-845-3101
Virginia & Jeff Morgan
All year

$ MAP
11 rooms, 11 pb
Visa, MC, *Rated*, •
C-yes/S-yes/P-yes/H-no
French, Spanish

Full breakfast
Dinner included, bar
Sitting room, bicycles
tennis ct, swimming pool
hot tub in guest room

Over 100 years of service to the Smugglers' Notch area. Maple floors, tin ceilings, screened porch, village setting. Enjoy our relaxing atmosphere. **3rd night package, ask**

JERICHO

Homeplace B&B
RR 2 Box 367, Old Pump Rd.,
05465
802-899-4694
Hans & Mariot Huessy
All year

$$ B&B
4 rooms
Rated, •
C-ltd/S-no/P-no/H-no
German

Full breakfast
Comp. wine, beer, juice
Sitting room, library
Perenial gardens, trails
tennis courts nearby

Quiet spot in a 100-acre wood, 1.5 miles from Jericho. Farm animals welcome you to their sprawling home. European antiques, Vermont craftwork and charm. **6th night free**

KILLINGTON

Mountain Meadows Lodge
RR 1 Box 4080, Thundering
Brook Rd., 05751
802-775-1010 800-370-4567
The Stevens Family
Ex. 4/15-6/1;10/15-11/21

$ B&B
17 rooms, 17 pb
Visa, MC, *Rated*, •
C-yes/S-ltd/P-no/H-ltd

Full breakfast
Dinner, coffee, tea
Swimming pool
sitting room
mountain getaway pkges

A casual, friendly family lodge in a beautiful secluded mountain and lake setting. Complete cross-country ski center. Converted 1856 farmhouse and barn.

Vermont Inn, The
Route 4, Cream Hill Rd., 05751
802-775-0708 800-541-7795
Susan & Judd Levy
Memorial Day–April 15

$$$ MAP
16 rooms, 12 pb •
Visa, MC, AmEx, *Rated*,
C-ltd/S-no/P-no/H-ltd
French, Spanish

Full breakfast (winter)
Continental plus (summ.)
Dinner included, bar
library, piano, pool
tennis, sauna, whirlpool

Award-winning cuisine; fireside dining (winter), spectacular mountain views, secluded romantic stream. Minutes to Killington and Pico ski areas. **3rd night 50% off**

LONDONDERRY ───────────────────────────────────────

Highland House, The	$$ B&B	Full breakfast
RR#1 Box 107, Route 100, 05148	17 rooms, 15 pb	Dinner Wed-Sun
802-824-3019	Visa, MC, AmEx, *Rated*	Tea (winter), sitting rm
Michael & Laurie Gayda	C-ltd/S-ltd/P-no/H-yes	pool, tennis court
Exc. April, Thanksgiving		cross country skiing

An 1842 country inn with swimming pool and tennis court. Set on 32 acres. Classic, candlelight dining. Located in the heart of the Green Mountains.

LUDLOW ───────────────────────────────────────

Andrie Rose Inn, The	$$$ B&B/MAP	Full breakfast buffet
13 Pleasant St., 05149	14 rooms, 14 pb	5-course cndlght. dinner
802-228-4846 800-223-4846	Visa, MC, AmEx, *Rated*,	Comp. cheese/fruit/bread
Jack & Ellen Fisher	•	down comforters, bar
All year	C-ltd/S-no/P-no/H-no	hot tubs, bicycles

Elegant c.1829 country village inn at base of Okemo Ski Mtn. Antiques. Luxury suites: whirlpl. tub, firepl. Near skiing, lakes, golf, shops. In Top 50 US Inns—Inn Times 1991.

Black River Inn	$$$ B&B/MAP	Full breakfast
100 Main St., 05149	10 rooms, 8 pb	4-course dinner
802-228-5585	Visa, MC, AmEx, *Rated*,	Full beverage service
Rick & Cheryl DelMastro	•	TV-game rm., sitting rm.
All year	C-ltd/S-yes/P-no/H-no	jacuzzi

Charming 1835 country inn w/antique furnished rooms, feather pillows & down comforters, brandy at bedside. Near skiing, swimming, golf, fishing, biking. **5th night free**

Combes Family Inn, The	$$$ B&B/MAP	Full breakfast
RFD 1, Box 275, 05149	11 rooms, 11 pb	Dinner
802-228-8799	Visa, MC, AmEx, *Rated*,	Sitting room, piano
Ruth & Bill Combes	•	bicycles
All year exc. 4/15—5/15	C-yes/S-ltd/P-ltd/H-yes	
	French	

The Combes Family Inn is a century-old farmhouse located on a quiet country back road.

Governor's Inn, The	$$$ B&B/MAP	Full 5-course breakfast
86 Main St., 05149	8 rooms, 8 pb	6-course dinner, bar
802-228-8830 800GOVE-RNOR	Visa, MC, AmEx, *Rated*,	Restaurant, picnic lunch
Deedy & Charlie Marble	•	fireside hors d'oeuvres
All year exc. April	C-ltd/S-no/P-no/H-no	afternoon tea, library

Stylish, romantic, Victorian inn c.1890. Furnished w/family antiques. Beautiful firepl's. Generous hospitality; quiet town. 1987 INN OF THE YEAR! **Packages available**

Okemo Inn, The	$$$ B&B/MAP	Full country breakfast
RFD#1, Box 133, Locust Hill Rd.	11 rooms, 11 pb	Candlelight dinner
Rt.103 N, 05149	Most CC, •	Fireside cocktail lounge
802-228-8834 800-328-8834	C-ltd/S-yes/P-no/H-no	library, TV room, piano
Ron & Toni Parry		pool, sauna, bicycles
All year		

Fine food and lodging—lovely 1810 country inn, antiques set the mood. Convenient to all-season sports and activities. Biking and walking tours arranged. **3rd night 50% off**

MANCHESTER

Birch Hill Inn	$$$ B&B/MAP	Full breakfast
P.O. Box 346, 05254	6 rooms, 6 pb	A la carte dinner incl.
West Rd.	Visa, MC, AmEx, *Rated*,	Swimming pool, tea
802-362-2761	•	sitting room, piano
Jim & Pat Lee	C-ltd/S-ltd/P-no/H-no	trout pond
Exc. Nov–Xmas, Apr–May		

Small country inn, more than 15 kilometers of private cross-country ski trails. Panoramic views, country cuisine; swimming pool; large fireplace.

Manchester Highlands Inn	$$$ B&B	Full breakfast
P.O. Box 1754 CG, Highland	15 rooms, 15 pb	Dinner by arrangement
Ave., 05255	Visa, MC, AmEx, *Rated*,	Sitting rm., bar, snacks
802-362-4565 800-743-4565	•	game rm, featherbeds
Patricia & Robert Eichorn	C-yes/S-yes/P-no/H-no	biking, piano, pool
Exc. midweek Apr & Nov		

Romantic Victorian inn, charming rooms. Resident cat. Homemade country brkfast-in-bed. Tennis, hiking, skiing, antiquing. Manchester's best-kept secret! ***3rd nite 50%-Ltd***

MANCHESTER CENTER

Brook-n-Hearth	$$ B&B	Full breakfast
P.O. Box 508, 05255	3 rooms, 3 pb	Gas BBQ grill, sodas
Star Routes 11 & 30	AmEx	Sitting room, VCR
802-362-3604	C-yes/S-ltd/P-no/H-no	player piano, A+C all rm
Larry & Terry Greene		library, swimming pool
Exc. early Nov & May		

Cozy early American decor, close to everything. Wooded pastoral setting, lawn games, walking or cross-country skiing trails by brook.

MANCHESTER VILLAGE

1811 House	$$$ B&B	Full breakfast
P.O. Box 39, 05254	14 rooms, 14 pb	Bar, comp. sherry
Route 7A	Most CC, *Rated*, •	Sitting room, library
802-362-1811 800-432-1811	C-ltd/S-ltd/P-no/H-no	canopy beds, fireplaces
Marnie & Bruce Duff		gardens w/pond, mtn view
All year		

Unequaled charm in a Revolutionary War-era building furnished with English & American antiques. Walk to golf, tennis, swimming; near sailing, hiking, skiing. Central A/C.

Inn at Manchester, The	$$ B&B	Full breakfast
Route 7A, Box 41, 05254	19 rooms, 14 pb	Comp. wine (Sat. nights)
802-362-1793	Visa, MC, AmEx, *Rated*,	Sitting room, library
Stan & Harriet Rosenberg	•	piano, swimming pool
All year	C-ltd/S-ltd/P-no/H-no	3 lounge areas, porch

Beautiful Victorian mansion restored by owners. Antique furniture. Delicious brkfasts. Golf, tennis, shopping, antiquing nearby. Country elegance. ***3rd night 50% off, ltd***

Reluctant Panther Inn, The	$$$ B&B	Continental breakfast
Box 678, West Rd., Off Rt. 7A,	13 rooms, 13 pb	Restaurant, bar
05254	Visa, MC, AmEx, *Rated*,	Wine upon arrival
800-822-2331	•	sitting room
Mame & Robert Bachofen	C-ltd/S-ltd/P-no/H-no	conference facilities
Mem Day-Oct, 12/10–4/10		

Enhance your romance with select lodging and elegant dining. Thirteen unusually decorated rooms for adults. Eight have fireplaces. Room rate includes a la carte dinner.

MANCHESTER VILLAGE

Village Country Inn
P.O. Box 408, 05254
Route 7A
802-362-1792 800-370-0300
Anne & Jay Degen
All year

$$$ MAP
30 rooms, 30 pb
Visa, MC, *Rated*, •
C-ltd/S-yes/P-no/H-ltd

Full breakfast
Candlelight dinner incl.
Tavern, sitting room
fireplaces in common rms
tennis court, pool

"A French Auberge" located in the heart of the Green Mountains. Beautiful country French decor, antiques, baskets & flowers. gracious rooms & 13 special suites.

MIDDLEBURY

Brookside Meadows Country
RD 3, Box 2460, Painter Rd.,
05753
802-388-6429 800-442-9887
Linda & Roger Cole
All year

$$$ B&B
5 rooms, 4 pb
Rated, •
C-ltd/S-ltd/P-ltd/H-ltd

Continental plus
Comp. wine
Sitting room, piano
2 bedroom suite w/bath
private entr., woodstove

Comfortable, gracious home in rural area, only 2.5 miles from town and Middlebury College. Near Shelburne Museum. Hiking, cross-country skiing on property.

Middlebury Inn, The
Rt. 7, P.O. Box 798, 14
Courthouse Sq., 05753
802-388-4961 800-842-4666
Frank & Jane Emanuel
All year

$$$ EP
75 rooms
Visa, MC, *Rated*, •
C-yes/S-ltd/P-ltd/H-yes

Continental breakfast
Restaurant, bar
Afternoon tea
sitting room, library
private bath, bath phone

Elegant 1827 historic landmark. Distinctively decorated rooms. Gracious dining. Walk to college, unique shops, historic sites in picturesque Middlebury. Year-round activities.

Swift House Inn
25 Stewart Lane, Rt. 7, 05753
802-388-9925
John & Andrea Nelson
All year

$$$ B&B
14 rooms, 14 pb
Most CC, *Rated*
C-yes/S-yes/P-no/H-no

Continental breakfast
Restaurant, bar
Sitting room, library
formal gardens
whirlpool tubs in 3 rms

Warm and gracious lodging and dining in an elegant 1815 federalist estate furnished with antiques. Four of the bedrooms have working fireplaces.

MIDDLETOWN SPRINGS

Middletown Springs Inn
Box 1068, On The Green, 05757
802-235-2198
Jayne & Eugene Ashley
Exc. 2 weeks in April

$$ B&B/MAP
9 rooms, 9 pb
Visa, MC, *Rated*, •
C-ltd/S-ltd/P-no/H-no

Full country breakfast
Comp. snacks
Dinner, bar, piano
sitting room, library
cross-country skiing from
door

Elegant 1879 Victorian mansion on Village Green. Authentically decorated, quality antiques. Gracious hospitality, small village. A special place. **4th night 50%**

NEWFANE

Four Columns Inn, The
P.O. Box 278, 05345
West Street
802-365-7713
Pamela & Jacques Allembert
All year

$$$ EP/MAP
15 rooms, 15 pb
Visa, MC, AmEx, *Rated*
C-yes/S-no/P-yes/H-no
French

Continental plus
Restaurant, bar
Afternoon tea
sitting room
swimming pool

The Four Columns Inn has the only 4 diamond restaurant rated by AAA in Vermont. And the Inn is just as fine! No smoking inn.

NORTH HERO

North Hero House
P.O. Box 106, 05474
Route 2, Champlain Islands
802-372-8237 800-488-4376
John R. Sherlock
June 15–October

$$ EP
23 rooms, 21 pb
Most CC, *Rated*
C-yes/S-yes/P-no/H-yes
Spanish, French

Full breakfast $
Restaurant, coffee, tea
Lounge, sitting room
tennis, lake swimming
bicycles, sauna

Lake Champlain island inn (1890). Magnificent views mountains. Crystal-clear water for marvelous swimming, boating & fishing. **3rd night 50% off September & October**

NORTHFIELD

Northfield Inn
27 Highland Ave., 05663
802-485-8558
Aglaia & Alan Stalb
All year

$$$ B&B
8 rooms, 8 pb
Visa, MC, *Rated*, •
C-ltd/S-no/P-no/H-no
Greek

Full breakfast
Lunch & dinner by arr.
Comp. wine, snacks
cross-country & alpine
skiing
bicycles, nearby tennis

Victorian comfort and congeniality. Private baths, antiques, brass beds and feather bedding. Hearty breakfast, beautiful porches, magnificent hillside setting. **7th night free**

ORWELL

Historic Brookside Inn
Route 22A, PO Box 36, 05760
802-948-2727
Joan & Murray Korda & Family
All year

$$$ B&B
6 rooms, 2 pb
Rated, •
C-yes/S-yes/P-no/H-yes
Fr., Sp., Ger., Ital.

Full country breakfast
Lunch, dinner, wine
Sitting room, library
music room, antique shop
cross-country skiing, skating

Enjoy country elegance in our National Register Greek revival mansion, set on 300 acres and furnished in period antiques. Antique shop on premises. **3rd night 50% off, ltd**

PERU

Johnny Seesaw's
P.O. Box 68, 05152
Route 11
802-824-5533
Gary & Nancy Okun
All year exc. April–May

$$ B&B/MAP
30 rooms, 27 pb
Visa, MC, •
C-yes/S-yes/P-yes/H-ltd

Full breakfast
Dinner (MAP winter)
Afternoon tea, full bar
tennis, swimming pool
library, sitting room

Unique country lodge, rooms with private baths, cottages with king beds and fireplaces, licensed pub, full dining room, quarter mile east of Bromley Mountain.

POULTNEY

Lake St. Catherine Inn
P.O. Box 129, 05764
Cones Point Rd.
802-287-9347 800-626-LSCI
Patricia & Raymond Endlilch
May–October

$$$ MAP
35 rooms, 35 pb
Rated, •
C-yes/S-yes/P-no/H-yes

Full breakfast
5-course dinner, bar
Piano, bicycles
free use of sailboats
paddleboats & canoes

Rural country inn located among tall pines on the shores of Lake St. Catherine. Swimming, boating, fishing & country dining. 3-bedrm cottage available. Rates inc. gratuities.

PROCTORSVILLE

Golden Stage Inn
P.O. Box 218, 05153
Depot St.
802-226-7744
Kirsten Murphy, Marcel Perret
Exc. April & November

$$$ MAP
10 rooms, 6 pb
Visa, MC, *Rated*, •
C-yes/S-yes/P-no/H-no
Swiss, German, French

Full breakfast
Candlelight dinner, bar
Hors d'oeuvres by fire
sitting room, pool
flower gardens

Country inn on 4 acres, Swiss specialties, sumptuous deserts, own baking, vegetable garden, colorful flowers, library, hiking, biking, skiing nearby. Dinner included.

PUTNEY

Hickory Ridge House
RFD 3, Box 1410, Hickory Ridge
Rd., 05346
802-387-5709
Jacquie Walker/Steve Anderson
All year

$ B&B
7 rooms, 3 pb
Visa, MC
C-ltd/S-no/P-no/H-yes
French, German, Russian

Full breakfast
Mulled cider in winter
Coffee, tea, cocoa
sitting room, piano
swimming hole

Gracious 1808 brick Federal with six fireplaces, rolling meadows, woods to explore on foot or skis. Our own breads, eggs, jams and honey for breakfast. **10% off 4+ nights.**

Putney Inn, The
P.O. Box 181, 05346
Depot Rd.
802-387-5517 800-653-5517
All year

$$ B&B/MAP
25 rooms, 25 pb
Most AA, *Rated*
C-yes/S-yes/P-yes/H-yes

Full breakfast
Restaurant - all meals
Afternoon tea, snacks
bar service, sitting rm.
hiking, canoeing

Charming 1790s farmhouse w/luxury of privacy. Lodging in adjacent building to hand-hewn, post-and-beam dining room. Exceptional food. **3rd night 50% off**

QUECHEE

Quechee B&B
P.O. Box 80, 05059
Rt. 4/753 Woodstock Rd.
802-295-1776
Susan Kaduboski
All year

$$$ B&B
8 rooms, 8 pb
Visa, MC, *Rated*, •
C-ltd/S-ltd/P-no/H-no
Spanish

Full breakfast
Lawn furniture
outdoor sitting area
sitting room

Historic 1795 Colonial with easy access to all four season sports, fine dining, natural and historic attractions, antiquing & shopping. Spectacular cliffside views.

**Quechee Inn-Marshland
Farm**
P.O. Box BB, Clubhouse Rd.,
05059
802-295-3133 800-235-3133
Hal Lothrop
All year

$$$ MAP
24 rooms, 24 pb
Visa, MC, AmEx, *Rated*,
•
C-yes/S-yes/P-no/H-ltd

Continental plus
Dinner included, bar
Wine list, sitting room
club membership (sauna
swimming, tennis)

The beautifully restored 18th-C. farmstead of Vermont's first lieutenant governor; nearby private Quechee Club for golf, tennis, boating, etc. **3rd night 50% off room rate**

ROYALTON

Fox Stand Inn & Restaurant
Route 14, 05068
802-763-8437
Jean & Gary Curley
All year

$$ B&B
5 rooms
Visa, MC, *Rated*
C-yes/S-yes/P-no/H-no

Full breakfast
Lunch, dinner
Licensed restaurant
river swimming

Restored 1818 handsome brick building, family-owned and operated inn. Economical rates include full breakfast. Fishing, golf, cross-country skiing nearby.

S. WOODSTOCK

Kedron Valley Inn
Route 106, 05071
802-457-1473
Max & Merrily Comins
All year

$$$ B&B/MAP
29 rooms, 29 pb
Visa, MC, DC, *Rated*, •
C-yes/S-yes/P-yes/H-yes
French, Spanish

Full country breakfast
Dinner, bar
Sitting room, swim pond
piano, TV's, quilts
A/C dining patio

Distinguished country 1822 inn. Full riding stables, hiking, cross-country skiing. Nouvelle cuisine w/local products. Canopy beds, fireplaces. "Adults only" beach. 1991 INN OF THE YEAR!

The Inn at Saxtons River, Saxtons River, VT

SAXTONS RIVER

Inn at Saxtons River, The
27 Main St., Box 448, 05154
802-869-2110
March closed

$$$ B&B
16 rooms, 16 pb
Visa, MC, •
C-yes/S-ltd/P-no/H-no

Full breakfast
Lunch, dinner, aft. tea
Snacks, bar service
sitting room, TV room
bicycles, tennis court

16 individually appointed rooms, full gourmet dining room, full bar & garden, sitting rm. w/piano entertainment, TV lounge, full bkfst. w/room, nearby tennis & golf.

SHELBURNE

Inn at Shelburne Farms
Shelburne Farms, 05482
802-985-8498
Kevin O'Donnell
May - October

$$$ B&B/MAP
24 rooms, 17 pb
Visa, AmEx, MC, DC
C-yes/S-ltd/P-no/H-no

Full breakfast
Restaurant - all meals
Aft. tea, snacks
bar service, sitting rm.
library, tennis court

Recall the elegance of another era. 24 guest rooms with 19th century furnishings. Spectacular lakeshore setting on 1,000-acre farm with mountain views.

STOCKBRIDGE

Stockbridge Inn B&B, The
Rt. 100N, P.O. Box 45, 05772
802-746-8165
Jan Hughes
All year

$$ B&B
5 rooms, 3 pb
Rated, •
C-ltd/S-ltd/P-no/H-no

Full breakfast
Afternoon refreshments
Library
living room w/woodstove
beamed ceilings

*Restored 1780 farmhouse complete w/ period antiques & firm mattresses. Guided night hikes into the Green Mountain National Forest using natural lighting. **3rd night free, ltd.***

STOWE ───

Andersen Lodge—Austrian
3430 Mountain Rd., 05672
802-253-7336 800-336-7336
Dietmar & Trude Heiss

$$ B&B/$$$ MAP
17 rooms, 16 pb
Most CC, *Rated*, •
C-yes/S-yes/P-ltd/H-no
German, French

Full breakfast
Dinner available
Piano, game room, spa
jacuzzi, tennis court
heated pool, golf nearby

Set in relaxing surroundings with lovely view of mountains. Trout fishing, horseback riding, mountain hiking. Owners and hosts of Austrian background. Austrian chef.

───

Brass Lantern, Inn at the
717 Maple St., Route 100 N,
05672
802-253-2229 800-729-2980
Andy Aldrich
All year

$$ B&B
9 rooms, 9 pb
Most CC, *Rated*, •
C-yes/S-no/P-no/H-no

Full country breakfast
Picnic lunch, bar
Afternoon tea, snacks
sitting room with piano
library, fireplaces, A/C

1800s farmhouse and carriage barn with antiques, handmade quilts, stenciled walls, and views. 1989 Award winning restoration by innkeepers. Sports, dining, theater packages.

───

Butternut Inn at Stowe
2309 Mountain Rd., 05672
802-253-4277 800-3-BUTTER
Jim & Deborah Wimberly
6/15–10/20, 12/18–4/20

$$$ B&B/MAP
18 rooms, 18 pb
Visa, MC, *Rated*, •
C-ltd/S-no/P-no/H-no

Full country breakfast
Dinner (winter)
Comp. sherry, aftn. tea
sitting rm., piano, pool
sun room, courtyard

Landscaped grounds, mountain views, by stream. Hospitality—a family tradition. Country decor. Poolside brkfast, fireside dining. **Honeymoon/anniv. special retreat package.**

───

Fiddler's Green Inn
4859 Mountain Rd., Route 108,
05672
802-253-8124 800-882-5346
Bud McKeon
All year

$ B&B
7 rooms, 6 pb
Visa, MC, AmEx, •
C-ltd/S-yes/P-no/H-no

Full breakfast
Dinner in ski season
beverages & snacks
guest living room
tennis nearby

Cozy New England inn situated on Vermont babbling brook. Hearty country breakfast. Hiking in Green Mountains or cross-country skiing from our doorstep. Near golf & antiquing.

───

Gables Inn, The
1457 Mountain Rd., 05672
802-253-7730 800-GAB-LES1
Sol, Lynn, & Josh Baumrind
All year

$$ B&B/$$$ MAP
16 rooms, 16 pb
Rated, •
C-yes/S-ltd/P-no/H-ltd

Full breakfast
Sitting room, fireplace
piano, swimming pool
hot tub, jacuzzis, A/C

Classic country inn—antiques, wide plank floors, panoramic view. Great breakfast on lawn or porch (summer). Near golf, hiking, skiing, tennis, bicycling. **4th night free**

───

Golden Kitz Lodge
1965 Mountain Rd., Route 108,
05672
802-253-4217 800-KITS-LOV
Sam/Alice/Margie Jones
All year

$ EP
16 rooms, 8 pb
Visa, MC, AmEx, CB, Dis, •
C-yes/S-ltd/P-ltd/H-ltd

Full breakfast $
Après-ski wine, snacks
Sitting room, porch
piano, art studio
bicycles, rec. room

Share legendary international family treasures in warm, cozy, caring comfort. Lively recreation room. Sporty fun, games & flirty dancing to records. **Multi-day discounts**

STOWE ───────────────────────────────────────

Green Mountain Inn	$$$ EP	Restaurant, bar
P.O. Box 60, 05672	62 rooms, 62 pb	Lunch, dinner, snacks
Main St.	Visa, MC, AmEx, *Rated*,	Full service health club
802-253-7301 800-445-6629	•	pool, massage, aerobics
Patti Clark	C-yes/S-ltd/P-ltd, French	beauty salon, shops
All year		

Beautifully renovated 1833 inn listed in the Register of Historic Places. Antique furnished with every modern convenience. Heart of Stowe Village. **Stowe Village discount card**

Guesthouse Christel Horman	$ B&B	Full breakfast
RR #1 Box 1635, 4583 Mountain	8 rooms, 8 pb	Comp. tea
Rd., 05672	Visa, MC, *Rated*, •	Sitting room
802-253-4846 800-821-7891	C-ltd/S-yes/P-no/H-no	swimming pool
Christel Horman	German	2 bicycles
Nov 15–Ap; Jun–end Oct		

Quiet, charming European guest house. Large comfortable double rooms, private bathrooms and cozy guest living room. Near Mount Mansfield skiing. **10% off 3-5 nights midweek.**

Logwood Inn & Chalets	$$ B&B	Full Vermont breakfast
199 Edson Hill Rd., 05672	23 rooms, 18 pb	Swimming pool, library
800-426-6697 802-253-7354	Visa, MC, •	tennis court, game room
Melanie & Sam Kerr	C-yes/S-yes/P-ltd/H-ltd	sitting room, piano, A/C
All year		

A warm welcome, tree-filled quiet oasis by mountain stream in scenic Stowe, Main lodge, balconies, apartment, 2 chalets. A Stowe tradition since 1941.

Siebeness Inn, The	$$ B&B	Full breakfast
3681 Mountain Rd., 05672	10 rooms, 10 pb	Comp. beverages & snacks
802-253-8942 800-426-9001	Most CC, *Rated*, •	Lounge, hot tub
Sue & Nils Andersen	C-yes/S-no/P-no/H-no	pool, cross-country skiing
All year		golf & tennis nearby

Charming country inn, newly renovated with antiques and quilts. Outstanding food served with mountain view. cross-country skiing from door Dinner fall & winter. **3 nts mid-week 10% off**

Ski Inn	$ B&B/$$$ MAP	Continental breakfast
Route 108, Mountain Rd., 05672	10 rooms, 5 pb	Full breakfast (winter)
802-253-4050	•	Dinner (winter MAP)
The Heyer Family	C-ltd/S-yes/P-ltd/H-no	
All year	some French	

This comfortable inn, noted for good food and good conversation, is a great gathering place for interesting people. MAP available in the winter.

Ten Acres Lodge	$$ B&B	Full breakfast buffet
14 Barrows Rd., 05672	16 rooms, 16 pb	Quiet seas. cont. bkfst
802-253-7638 800-327-7357	Visa, MC, AmEx, *Rated*,	Dinner, bar, cider, tea
Curt & Cathy Dann	•	tennis court, sitting rm
All year	C-yes/S-ltd/P-ltd/H-no	swimming pool, hot tub

Stowe's favorite country inn & restaurant for over 40 yrs. Ski trails, hiking, golf in New England ski capital. Hill house & cottages available. **2nd night 50% non-peak, ltd**

STOWE

Timberhölm Inn
452 Cottage Club Rd., RR 1 Box
810, 05672
802-253-7603 800-753-7603
Kay & Richard Hildebrand
All year

$$$ B&B
10 rooms, 10 pb
Visa, MC, •
C-yes/S-ltd/P-no/H-no

Full breakfast
Après-ski soup
Outdoor hot tub
large common room
game room

Secluded off-road cozy country inn. Magnificent mountain view, spacious deck. Huge field-stone fireplace. **5th night free**

Ye Olde England Inne
433 Mountain Rd., 05672
802-253-7558 802-253-7064
Christopher & Linda Francis
All year

$$$ B&B
23 rooms, 23 pb
Visa, MC, *Rated*, •
C-yes/S-yes/P-ltd/H-no
French, Arabic

Gourmet English Bkfst.
Dinner, Aft. tea
Library, piano, pool
pub, murder mystery wknd
polo & gliding packages

Classic English luxury, Lara Ashley rooms/cottages. Four posters, fireplaces & jacuzzi's. Gourmet dining in Copperfield's. Mr. Pickwick's Polo Pub. **Call for specials**

TOWNSEND

Townsend Country Inn
RR 1, Box 3100, 05353
800-569-1907
Joseph & Donna Peters
Open May - March

$$ EP
6 rooms
Most CC, *Rated*
C-yes/S-no/P-no/H-yes

Continental plus
Restaurant
Lunch, June - October
dinner, bar service
sitting room

A truly unique country inn, surrounded by spectacular pro golf courses, state parks and 3 major ski & golf resort areas.

TYSON

Echo Lake Inn
Route 100, 05056, Box 154,
Ludlow, 05149
802-228-8602 800-356-6844
Phil & Kathy Cocco
All year exc. April

$$ MAP
26 rooms, 13 pb
Visa, MC, AmEx, •
C-yes/S-yes/P-no/H-no

Full breakfast from menu
Dinner from menu, bar
Swimming, tennis
fishing, hiking
sitting room, piano

Serene setting in Green Mountains, on Echo Lake. Unique menu, homemade pasta, desserts. Antique beds in private rooms. Minutes to major ski areas. **4th. night free. Ltd**

VERGENNES

Strong House Inn
RD#1, Box 1003, 82 W. Main St.,
(Rt. 22A), 05491
802-877-3337
Mary & Hugh Bargiel
Ex. Nov/mid Mar–mid Apr

$$ B&B
7 rooms, 2 pb
Visa, MC, AmEx, *Rated*,
•
C-ltd/S-ltd/P-ltd/H-ltd

Full country breakfast
Dinner with notice
Aftn. beverage & snack
sitting room w/fireplace
piano, catering avail.

Comfortably elegant lodging in a tastefully decorated historic home. Wonderful breakfasts. Convenient to Middlebury, Burlington, Lake Champlain. Suites w/cable & living room.

WAITSFIELD

Hyde Away Inn
RR 1, Box 65, Route 17, 05673
802-496-2322 800-777-HYDE
Bruce & Margaret Hyde
All year

$ B&B/MAP
16 rooms, 3 pb
Visa, MC, AmEx, •
C-yes/S-yes/P-no/H-no

Full breakfast $
Restaurant, bar
Afternoon tea, snacks
sitting room, library
bicycles, skiing, toys

Comfortable, cozy, rustic circa 1820 converted farmstead. Families encouraged. Mountain bike center. Outrageous downhill & cross-country skiing. **10% off 3+ nights, ltd.**

WAITSFIELD —————————————————————————

Inn at Mad River Barn, The
P.O. Box 88, 05673
Route 17
802-496-3310
Betsy Pratt
All year

$ B&B
15 rooms, 15 pb
Visa, MC, AmEx, *Rated*,
•
C-yes/S-yes/P-no/H-ltd

Full breakfast
Dinner (Dec.-Apr.), bar
Afternoon tea
sitting room, steam bath
use of resort pool, golf

Classic Vermont country lodge. Spacious rooms with private baths. Grand stone fireplace. Excellent hiking on our trails. One mile from ski area. **3rd night 50% off.**

———————————————————————————————————

Inn at Round Barn Farm
RR 1, Box 247, E. Warren Rd.,
05673
802-496-2276
J. & D. Simko, A. DeFreest
All year

$$$ B&B
10 rooms, 6 pb
Visa, MC, AmEx, *Rated*,
•
C-ltd/S-no/P-no/H-no
Hungarian

Full breakfast
Comp. wine, tea, snacks
Sitting room, library
bicycles, 60-ft lap pool
cross-country ski
center/rentals

Sugarbush's most noted landmark; elegant inn; 85 acres for quiet walks, gourmet picnics, Bach, Mozart, and simple pleasures of unspoiled Vermont. **Special champagne & flowers**

———————————————————————————————————

Lareau Farm Country Inn
P.O. Box 563, 05673
Route 100
802-496-4949 800-833-0766
Susan & Dan Easley
All year

$$ B&B
14 rooms, 11 pb
Visa, MC, •
C-yes/S-ltd/P-no/H-no

Full breakfast
Après-ski hors d'oeuvres
Dinner, wine & beer $
sitting room, fireplace
porches, picnic lunches

Picturesque Vermont farmhouse, now an inn, nestled in a picturesque meadow beside the Mad River, our 150-year-old farmhouse is minutes from skiing and shopping.

———————————————————————————————————

Millbrook Inn
RFD Box 62, Route 17, 05673
802-496-2405
Joan & Thom Gorman
All year exc. April-May

$$ B&B\$$$ MAP
7 rooms, 4 pb
Visa, MC, AmEx, •
C-ltd/S-no/P-ask/H-ltd

Full breakfast from menu
Full dinner from rest.
Comp. refreshments
3 sitting rooms, piano

Charming hand-stenciled guest rooms with handmade quilts, country gourmet dining in our small candlelit restaurant, friendly, unhurried atmosphere.

———————————————————————————————————

Newtons' 1824 House Inn
Route 100, Box 159, 05673
802-496-7555 800-420-0000
Joyce & Nick Newton
All year

$$$ B&B
6 rooms, 6 pb
Most CC, *Rated*, •
C-ltd/S-no/P-no/H-no
Spanish

Full gourmet breakfast
Dinner by special order
Comp. sherry, tea
library, swimming hole
cross-country skiing, tennis,
golf

Relaxed elegance, pristine countryside, oriental rugs, chandeliers, firepls. "Best breakfast" say guests! Near Sugarbush Resort horseback riding. **20% off 5 days/10% wkdys**

———————————————————————————————————

Tucker Hill Lodge
RD 1, Box 147 (Rt. 17), 05673
802-496-3983 800-543-7841
Susan & Giorgio Noaro
All year

$$ B&B/MAP
22 rooms, 16 pb
Visa, MC, AmEx, •
C-yes/S-yes/P-no/H-no

Full breakfast
Dinner, bar service
Restaurant (exc. April
May, Nov),sitting room
tennis courts, pool

Cozy country inn with award-winning New American/French restaurant. In Sugarbush/Mad River Valley, near skiing, hiking, biking, canoeing and golf.

WAITSFIELD ───────────────────────────────────

Valley Inn, The
Route 100, RR 1, Box 8, 05673
802-496-3450 800-638-8466
Bill & Millie Stinson
All year

$$ B&B/MAP
20 rooms, 20 pb
Visa, MC, AmEx, *Rated*,
•
C-yes/S-no/P-no/H-yes
French

Full breakfast
Dinner included (MAP)
Sitting room, sauna
group-tour packages
soaring packages

An Austrian-style inn near Sugarbush and Mad River Ski Areas. Winter sports paradise, outstanding summer antiquing, golf and gliding.

Waitsfield Inn, The
Rt. 100 Box 969, 05673
802-496-3979
Steve & Ruth Lacey
Exc. Nov, Apr 15—Mem Dy

$$ MAP/B&B
14 rooms, 14 pb
Most CC, *Rated*, •
C-ltd/S-ltd/P-no/H-no

Full breakfast
Dinner, bar
Sitting room
piano, down comforters
fireplace

A romantic and restful inn w/ wonderfully comfortable guest rooms, two especially cozy fireside lounges & exquisite cuisine. Surrounded by mountains. **3rd night 50% off, ltd.**

WARREN ───────────────────────────────────

Beaver Pond Farm Inn
RD Box 306, Golf Course Rd.,
05674
802-583-2861
Betty & Bob Hansen
All year exc. May

$$ B&B
6 rooms, 4 pb
Visa, MC, AmEx, •
C-ltd/S-yes/P-no/H-no
French

Full breakfast
Comp. sherry, brandy
Sitting room, library
weddings, Thanksg. pkg.
hiking, swimming, skiing

Beautifully restored Vermont farmhouse adjacent to golf course. Spectacular views from spacious deck; hearty breakfasts. Summer golf/winter skiing pkgs. **Mid-week discounts**

Sugartree—A Country Inn
RR 1, Box 38, Sugarbush Access
Rd., 05674
802-583-3211 800-666-8907
Frank & Kath Partsch
All year

$$ B&B
10 rooms, 10 pb
Most CC, *Rated*, •
C-ltd/S-no/P-no/H-yes

Full country breakfast
Living room w/fireplace
all rooms have brass
antiques, or canopy beds

Beautifully decorated with unique country flair and antiques. Enchanting gazebo amid flower gardens. Breathtaking views of ski slopes or fall foliage. **3rd night free, ltd**

WATERBURY ───────────────────────────────────

Grünberg Haus B&B
RR 2, Box 1595, Route 100
South, 05676
802-244-7726 800-800-7760
Chris Sellers, Mark Frohman
All year

$$ B&B
10 rooms, 5 pb
Most CC, *Rated*, •
C-ltd/S-no/P-no/H-no

Full musical breakfast
Dinner, comp. wine
Self-serve pub, piano
tennis court, jacuzzi
sauna, flock of chickens

Tyrolian chalet on 10 acres in Green Mtns. Our guests are friends. Hiking trails, gardens, decks. cross-country ski center. Live piano music—requests taken. **Free tour Ben & Jerrys**

Inn at Blush Hill
RR 1, Box 1266, Blush Hill Rd.,
05676
802-244-7529 800-736-7522
Pamela & Gary Gosselin
All year

$$ B&B
6 rooms, 6 pb
Most CC, *Rated*, •
C-ltd/S-ltd/P-no/H-ltd

Full breakfast
Aftn. tea
Library, firepl., piano
lawn games, swim/boating
electric mattress pads

Cozy, 1790s brick farmhouse, near 9-hole golf course, 15 min. to Sugarbush, Bolton, Stowe. Canopy queen bedrm, fireplaces. Adjacent to Ben & Jerry's. **Free tour of B & J's**

The Weathervane Lodge, West Dover, VT

WATERBURY CENTER

Black Locust Inn, The
RR 1, Box 715, 05677
802-244-7490 800-366-5592
Anita & George Gajdos
All year

$$ B&B
6 rooms, 6 pb
Visa, MC, *Rated*, •
C-ltd/S-no/P-no/H-ltd
Hungarian

Full breakfast
Afternoon tea
Comp. wine, snacks
sitting room, library
lawn games, croquet

Beautifully decorated 1832 farmhouse set on hill surrounded by Green Mountains and Worcester Range. Cross-country skiing, hiking, biking, fishing and antiquing nearby.

WEST DOVER

Austin Hill Inn
P.O. Box 859, 05356
Route 100
802-464-5281 800-332RELAX
Robbie Sweeney
All year

$$$ B&B
12 rooms, 12 pb
Visa, MC, AmEx, *Rated*
C-ltd/S-ltd/P-no/H-no

Full breakfast - menu
Dinner, bar service
Afternoon tea, snacks
sitting room, library
swimming pool, bicycles

Casual elegance, gracious service; antiques, wine list, fine dining. Welcoming wine & cheese. Murder mystery & quilting weekends. Comfort a priority. 3rd night 50%, ltd

---

Weathervane Lodge B&B
HCR 63, Box 57, Dorr Fitch Rd.,
05356
802-464-5426
Liz & Ernie Chabot
All year

$$ B&B
10 rooms, 5 pb
•
C-yes/S-yes/P-no/H-no
French

Full breakfast
Comp. beverages, snacks
BYOB bar, sitting room
lounge, piano, fireplc's
Bike & walking trails

Mountainous country inn: Colonial antiques, lounge, recreation rooms w/fireplaces. cross-country skiing, tennis, golf, swimming; bring children. 3rd night 50% off, ltd.

West Dover Inn
P.O. Box 506, 05356
Route 100
802-464-5207 800-732-0745
Don & Madeline Mitchell
All year exc. Apr–June

$$$ B&B
12 rooms, 12 pb
Visa, MC, AmEx, *Rated*
C-ltd/S-yes/P-no/H-no

Full breakfast
Dinner plan (exc. Wed.)
Bar, lounge, library
4 fireplace suites
bicycles, organ

Historic inn. Handsomely appointed guest rooms with cozy quilts, antiques. Fine country dining. Golf, skiing, swimming, antiquing nearby. Register of Historic Places.

WEST TOWNSHEND

Windham Hill Inn
RR 1, Box 44, off Route 30, 05359
802-874-4080
Grigs & Pat Markham
Ex. Apr & Nov(open Thgv)

$$$ MAP
15 rooms, 15 pb
Visa, MC, *Rated*, •
C-ltd/S-no/P-no/H-yes

Full breakfast
6-course dinner, cordial
Bar, 3 sitting rooms
library, swimming pond
hiking, ski trails

Restored 1825 farmhouse & barn set on 160 acres, offers warm guest & public rooms, elegant dining. 1988, 1989 & 1992 One of Ten Best Inns—Innsider. **Pkg./midwk rates avail.**

WESTON

1830 Inn on the Green, The
PO Box 104, Route 100, 05161
802-824-6789
Sandy & Dave Granger
All year

$$ B&B
4 rooms, 3 pb
Visa, MC, *Rated*
C-ltd/S-ltd

Full breakfast
Afternoon tea
Comp. wine
bedtime sweets
sitting room

A small, romantic inn located on the Village Green. Recognized by the National Register of Historic Places.

Colonial House, The
RR 1, Box 138 IG, Route 100, 05161
802-824-6286 800-639-5033
Betty & John Nunnikhoven
All year

$$ B&B
15 rooms, 9 pb
Visa, MC, *Rated*
C-yes/S-ltd/P-ltd/H-ltd

Full breakfast
Dinner
Tea, coffee, baked goods
sitting room

Your country cousins are waiting with a warm welcome, old-fashioned meals and a relaxing living room for you while you visit the attractions of southern Vermont.

WILLIAMSTOWN

Autumn Crest Inn
Clark Rd., 05679
802-433-6627 800-339-6627
All year

$$$ B&B, MAP
18 rooms, 18 pb
Visa, MC, AmEx, *Rated*, •
C-ltd/S-ltd/P-yes/H-yes

Full breakfast
Dinner, restaurant, bar
Sitting room, library
tennis, swimming pond
hiking, cross-country ski
from door

Central Vermont's best kept secret. Outstanding romantic dinners. 46 acres to explore. Inn over 180 years old, magnificently restored. **4 Nights 10% Off, 5 Nights 15%**

WILMINGTON

Nutmeg Inn
P.O. Box 818, 05363
Route 9W, Rt 9W Molly Stark Trail
802-464-3351
Del & Charlotte Lawrence
All year

$$$ B&B
16 rooms, 16 pb
AmEx, *Rated*, •
C-ltd/S-ltd/P-no/H-ltd

Full breakfast from menu
Dinner, 3 dining rooms
Sitting room, piano, TVs
2-room suites w/firepl.
Central A/C, phones

"Charming and cozy" early American farmhouse with informal homelike atmosphere. Spotless guest rooms—delicious "country-style" meals. Enjoy complimentary afternoon tea/coffee

Red Shutter Inn
P.O. Box 636, 05363
Route 9 West
802-464-3768 800-845-7548
Max & Carolyn Hopkins
Exc. early Nov & April

$$$ B&B
9 rooms, 9 pb
Visa, MC, *Rated*
C-ltd/S-yes

Full breakfast
Restaurant, bar service
Snacks, alfresco dining
fireplaces, guest suites
whirlpool bath, packages

Hillside inn & renovated Carriage House at village edge w/candlelight dining. Fireplace suites. Golf, hike, ski amid mountains & valleys **Midwk discounts available, ask**

WILMINGTON

Trail's End, A Country Inn	$$$ B&B	Full breakfast (menu)
Smith Rd., 05363	15 rooms, 15 pb	Comp. sherry, beverages
802-464-2727 800-859-2585	*Rated*	Snacks, library, pool
Bill & Mary Kilburn	C-yes/S-yes/P-no/H-no	fireplace/jacuzzi suites
April & May closed, ask		clay tennis court

Friendly inn tucked along a country road with English flower gardens, hiking trails, trout pond. Dramatic 2-story fireplace and loft. Skiing and golf nearby.

White House of Wilmington	$$$ MAP	Full breakfast
Route 9, Box 757, 05363	12 rooms, 12 pb	Dinner (inc.), bar
802-464-2135 800-541-2135	Most CC, *Rated*	Sitting room, piano
Robert Grinold	C-ltd/S-yes/P-no/H-no	hot tub, sauna
All year	French	indoor & outdoor pools

"One of the most romantic inns..." N.Y. Times. Turn of the century mansion, elegant accommodations, fireplaces. cross-country skiing. Downhill skiing & golf packages. AAA 2 diamonds.

WINDSOR

Juniper Hill Inn	$$$ B&B	Full breakfast
RR 1, Box 79, Juniper Hill Rd.,	16 rooms, 16 pb	Dinner by reservation
05089	Visa, MC, *Rated*, •	Bar service, library
802-674-5273 800-359-2541	C-ltd/S-no	hiking, skiing, snowshoe
Robert & Susanne Peall		canoe & bicycle packages
Exc. Nov-Dec 15, Mar-Apr		

A stately 28-room mansion on 14 private acres. Rooms with romantic fireplaces available. Antiques, museums, covered bridges in summer; relaxing in winter. **Discounts, ask**

WOODSTOCK

Charleston House, The	$$ B&B	Full breakfast
21 Pleasant St., 05091	7 rooms, 7 pb	Aft. tea, snacks
802-457-3843	Visa, MC, AmEx, *Rated*,	Sitting room, library
Bill & Barbara	•	bicycles
All year	C-ltd/S-no/P-no/H-no	

Classic home in historic village. Listed in National Register. All private baths. Bikes available. Two blocks to center village. **Mid-week discounts**

Charleston House, The	$$$ B&B	Full breakfast
21 Pleasant St., 05091	7 rooms, 7 pb	Afternoon tea
802-457-3843	Visa, MC, AmEx, *Rated*,	Snacks
Bill & Barbara Hough	•	sitting room
All year	C-ltd/S-no/P-no/H-no	bicycles

A National Registry classic brick townhome in the village. Charleston Rice four-poster queen beds, private baths, and full breakfast. **Midweek discounts.**

Woodstocker B&B, The	$$ B&B	Full breakfast buffet
61 River St., Route 4, 05091	7 rooms, 7 pb	Afternoon tea
802-457-3896	Visa, MC, *Rated*, •	Sitting room
L. Deignan, R. Formichella	C-yes/S-no/P-no/H-yes	hot tub
All year exc. April		library

We enjoy making our guests feel at home. Within easy walking distance of shops and restaurants. Cross-country and downhill skiing close by.

More Inns . . .

Auverge Alburg, RD 1, Box 3, Alburg, 05440, 802-796-3169
Thomas Mott Homestead, RFD 2, Box 149B, Alburg, 05440, 800-348-0843
Ye Old Graystone B&B, RFD 1, Box 76, Alburg, 05440, 802-796-3911
Hillside, RR #1, Box 196, Andover, 05143, 802-875-3844
Inn at Highview, The, East Hill Rd., Andover, 05143, 802-875-2724
Evergreen, Sandgate, Box 2480, Arlington, 05250, 802-375-2272
Sycamore Inn, RD 2, Box 2485, Rt. 7A, Arlington, 05250, 802-362-2284
Silver Lake House, The, P.O. Box 13, North Rd., Barnard, 05031
Old Homestead, The, Box 35, Barnet, 05821
Woodruff House, 13 East St., Barre, 05641, 802-476-7745
Barton Inn, P.O. Box 67, Main St., Barton, 05822, 802-525-4721
Horsefeathers B&B, 16 Webb Terrace, Bellows Falls, 05101
Four Chimneys Inn, 21 West Rd., Bennington, 05201, 802-447-3500
Mt. Anthony Guest House, 226 Main St., Bennington, 05201, 802-447-7396
South Shire Inn, 124 Elm St., Bennington, 05201, 802-447-3839
Eastwood House, River St., Bethel, 05032, 802-234-9686
Greenhurst Inn, RD2, Box 60, Bethel, 05032, 802-234-9474
Poplar Manor, RD 2, Rts. 12 & 107, Bethel, 05032, 802-234-5426
Alpenrose Inn, P.O. Box 187, Bondville, 05340, 802-297-2750
Bromley View Inn, Route 30, Bondville, 05340, 802-297-1459
Merry Meadow Farm, Lower Plain, Route 5, Bradford, 05033, 802-222-4412
Beauchamp Place, US Route 7, Brandon, 05733, 802-247-3905
Brandon Inn, 20 Park Green, Brandon, 05733, 802-247-5766
Churchill House Inn, RD #3, Box 3265 PL, Brandon, 05733, 802-247-3078
Gazebo Inn, 25 Grove St., Route 7, Brandon, 05733, 802-247-3235
Inn at Tiffany Corner, RD 3, Blof Course Rd., Brandon, 05733, 802-247-6571
Old Mill Inn, Stone Mill Dam Rd., Brandon, 05733
Long Run Inn, RD 1 Box 560, Bristol, 05443, 802-453-3233
Mill Brook B&B & Gallery, P.O. Box 410, Brownsville, 05037, 802-484-7283
Haus Kelley B&B, Old West Bolton Rd., Burlington, 05490
Truax Tourist Home, 32 University Terrace, Burlington, 05401, 802-862-0809
Fitch House, Route 1, Box 30, Calais, 05648
Yankee's Northview B&B, Lightening Ridge Rd., Calais, 05667, 802-454-7191
Green Meadows B&B, Mt. Philo Rd., POB 1300, Charlotte, 05445, 802-425-3059
Inn Victoria, P.O. Box 788, Chester, 05143, 802-875-4288
Night With A Native B&B, P.O. Box 327, Route 103, Chester, 05143
Stone Hearth Inn, The, Route 11 West, Chester, 05143, 802-875-2525
Mountain Top Inn, Mountain Top Rd., Chittenden, 05737, 802-483-2311
On the Lamb B&B, 60 Depot Rd., Colchester, 05446
Craftsbury Inn, Main St., Craftsbury, 05826, 802-586-2848
Inn on the Common, P.O. Box 75, Main St., Craftsbury Common, 05827, 802-586-9619
Derby Village Inn B&B, 46 Main St., Derby Line, 05830, 802-873-3604
Cornucopia of Dorset, Route 30, Dorset, 05251, 802-867-5751
Dovetail Inn, Route 30, Main St., Dorset, 05251, 802-867-5747
Maplewood Colonial Inn, Route 30, P.O. Box 1200, Dorset, 05251, 802-867-4470
Village Auberge, P.O. Box 970, Dorset, 05251, 802-867-5715
Doveberry Inn, HCR 63 Box 9, Dover, 05356, 802-464-5652
Schneider Haus, Route 100, Duxbury, 05676, 802-244-7726
Inwood Manor, RD 1 Box 127, East Barnet, 05821, 802-633-4047
Burke Green Guest House, RR 1, Box 81, East Burke, 05832, 802-467-3472
Garrison Inn, The, P.O. Box 177, East Burke, 05832, 802-626-8329
Nutmegger, The, Box 73, Mountain Rd., East Burke, 05832
Old Cutter Inn, Burke Mt. Access Rd., East Burke, 05832, 802-626-5152
Cooper Hill Inn, Cooper Hill Rd., Box 14, East Dover, 05341, 802-348-6333
Whispering Pines, East Fairfield, 05448, 802-827-3827
Brick House, Box 128, East Hardwick, 05836, 802-472-5512
October Pumpkin B&B, Route 125 E., Box 226, East Middlebury, 05740
Robert Frost Mountain B&B, Box 246, East Middlebury, 05740
Waybury Inn, Route 125, East Middlebury, 05740, 802-388-4015
Fair Haven Inn, Fair Haven, 05743, 802-265-3833
Haven, est. 1948, One Fourth St., Fair Haven, 05743, 802-265-3373
Vermont Marble Inn, 12 W. Park Place, Fair Haven, 05743, 802-265-4736
Hillside View Farm, South Rd., Fairfield, 05455
Aloha Manor, Lake Morey, Fairlee, 05045, 802-333-4478
Old Town Farm Inn, Route 10, Gassetts, 05143, 802-875-2346
Blueberry Hill, RFD 3, Goshen, 05733, 802-247-6535
Eaglebrook of Grafton, Main St., Grafton, 05146
Hayes House, Grafton, 05146, 802-843-2461
Old Tavern at Grafton, The, Main St., Box 009, Grafton, 05250, 802-843-2231
Stronghold Inn, HCR 40, Route 121, Grafton, 05146, 802-843-2203
Highland Lodge, RR 1, Box 1290, Greensboro, 05841, 802-533-2647
Guildhall Inn B&B, P.O. Box 129, Route 102, Guildhall, 05905, 802-676-3720

Shelburne House, Shelburne, VT

Kincraft Inn, P.O. Box 96, Hancock, 05748, 802-767-3734
Carolyn's Bed & Breakfast, 15 Church St., Hardwick, 05843
Kahagon at Nichols Pond, Box 728, Hardwick, 05843, 802-472-6446
House of Seven Gables, P.O. Box 526, Hartford, 05047, 802-295-1200
Tyler Place-Lake Champlain, P.O. Box 45, Highgate Springs, 05460, 802-868-3301
Three Mountain Inn, Box 180, Main St. Rt.30, Jamaica, 05343, 802-874-4140
Jay Village Inn, Route 242, Mountain Rd, Jay, 05859, 802-988-2643
Village Inn, Rt. 242, Jay, 05859, 802-988-2643
Woodshed Lodge, Jay, 05859, 802-988-4444
Windridge Inn B&B, Main St., Rt. 15 & 108, Jeffersonville, 05464, 802-644-8281
Eaton House B&B, P.O. Box 139, Jericho, 05465, 802-899-2354
Henry M. Field House, RR 2, Box 395, Jericho, 05465, 802-899-3984
Saxon Inn, RR2, Box 4295, S. Orr, Jericho, 05465, 802-899-3015
Cortina Inn, HCR 34, US Route 4, Killington, 05751, 800-451-6108
Grey Bonnet Inn, Killington, 05751, 800-342-2086
Inn at Long Trail, The, P.O. Box 267, Killington, 05751, 802-775-7181
Nordic Inn, Rt. 11, P.O. Box 96, Landgrove, 05148, 802-824-6444
Blue Gentian Lodge, Box 129 RR #1, Londonderry, 05148, 802-824-5908
Country Hare, Rt. 11 & Magic Mtn Rd., Londonderry, 05148, 802-824-3131
Village Inn, RFD Landgrove, Londonderry, 05148, 802-824-6673
Flower Cottage, Lower Waterford, 05848, 802-748-8441
Rabbit Hill Inn, Route 18, Lower Waterford, 05848, 802-748-5168
Jewell Brook Inn, 82 Andover St., Rt. 10, Ludlow, 05149
Red Door, 7 Pleasant St., Ludlow, 05149, 802-228-2376
Wildflower Inn, Darling Hill Rd., Lyndonville, 05851, 802-626-8310
Sky Line Inn, Box 325, Manchester, 05254, 802-362-1113
Wilburton Inn, P.O. Box 468, Manchester, 05254
Inn at Willow Pond, P.O. Box 1429, Route 7, Manchester Center, 05255, 802-362-4733
Longwood Inn, Route 9, P.O. Box 86, Marlboro, 05344, 802-257-1545
Red Clover Inn, RR 2, Woodward Rd., Mendon, 05701, 802-775-2290
A Point of View, South Munger St., Middlebury, 05753
Inn on Trout River, Box 76, Main St., Montgomery Center, 05471, 800-338-7049
Black Lantern Inn, Route 118, Montgomery Village, 05470, 802-326-4507
Inn at Montpelier, 147 Main St., Montpelier, 05602, 802-223-2727
Nunts Hideaway, Route 111, Morgan, 05872, 802-895-4432
Seymour Lake Lodge, Route 111, Morgan, 05853, 802-895-2752
Austria Haus, Box 2, Austria Haus Rd., Mount Holly, 05758, 802-259-2441
Hortonville Inn, Box 14, Mount Holly, 05758
Hound's Folly, Box 591, Mount Holly, 05758, 802-259-2718
Inn at Quail Run, The, HCR 63, Box 28-Smith Rd, Mount Snow—Wilmington, 05363, 800-343-7227
Horn Farnsworth B&B, RR 1, Box 170A, New Haven, 05472
A Century Past, P.O. Box 186, Route 5, Newbury, 05051, 802-866-3358
West River Lodge, RR 1, Box 693, Newfane, 05345, 802-365-7745
Charlies Northland Lodge, Route 2, Box 88, North Hero, 05474, 802-372-8822
Stone House Inn, Box 47, Route 5, North Thetford, 05054, 802-333-9124
Rose Apple Acres Farm, RR 1, Box 300, North Troy, 05859, 802-988-4300
Norwich Inn, The, P.O. Box 908, Norwich, 05055, 802-649-1143
Valley House Inn, 4 Memorial Square, Orleans, 05860, 802-754-6665
Gwendolyn's, Route 106, P.O. Box 225, Perkinsville, 05151, 802-263-5248
Inn at Weathersfield, The, Rte. 106, P.O. Box 165, Perkinsville, 05151, 802-263-9217
Wiley Inn, Route 11, P.O. Box 37, Peru, 05152, 802-824-6600
Inn at Pittsfield, The, Box 675, Route 100, Pittsfield, 05762, 802-746-8943
Swiss Farm Lodge, P.O. Box 630, Pittsfield, 05762, 802-748-8341
Fox Bros. Farm, Corn Hill Rd., Pittsford, 05763, 802-483-2870
Hawk Inn & Mountain Resort, P.O. Box 64, Plymouth, 05056, 800-685-4295
Snowy Owl Lodge, HCR 70, Rt 100A, Box106, Plymouth, 05056, 802-672-5018
Salt Ash Inn, Jct. Rts. 100 & 100A, Plymouth Union, 05056, 802-672-3748
Lake House Inn, Route 244, P.O. Box 65, Post Mills, 05058, 802-333-4025
Stonebridge Inn, Route 30, Poultney, 05764, 802-287-9849
Castle Inn, Box 157, Proctorsville, 05153, 802-226-7222
Okemo Lantern Lodge, P.O. Box 247, Proctorsville, 05153, 802-226-7770
Mapleton Farm B&B, RD 2, Box 510, Putney, 05346
Misty Meadow, RD 1, Box 458, Putney, 05346
Parker House, 16 Main St., Box 0780, Quechee, 05059, 802-295-6077
Abel Barron House, 37 Main, P.O. Box 532, Quechee Village, 05059, 802-295-1337
Three Stallion Inn, RD #2 Stock Farm Rd., Randolph, 05060, 802-728-5575
Peeping Cow B&B, The, Route 106, P.O. Box 178, Reading, 05062, 802-484-5036
Old Coach Inn, RR 1 Box 260, Readsboro, 05350, 802-423-5394
Black Bear Inn, The, P.O. Box 26, Richmond—Bolton Valley, 05477, 802-434-2126
Chipman Inn, The, Route 125, Ripton, 05766, 802-388-2390
Harveys Mt. View Inn, Rochester, 05767, 802-767-4273
Liberty Hill Farm, Liberty Hill Rd., Rochester, 05767, 802-767-3926
New Homestead, Rochester, 05767, 802-767-4751
Bellevue, 9 Parsons Ln., Saint Albans, 05478, 802-527-1115

Grünberg Haus, Waterbury, VT

Echo Ledge Farm Inn, P.O. Box 77, Route 2, Saint Johnsbury, 05838, 802-748-4750
Red Barn Guest House, Hatfield Ln., Saxton's River, 05154
Shoreham Inn, Route 74W, Main St., Shoreham Village, 05770, 802-897-5081
Londonderry Inn, Box 301-12, Rt. 100, South Londonderry, 05155, 802-824-5226
Inn at South Newfane, Dover Rd., South Newfane, 05351, 802-348-7191
Watercours Way, Route 132, South Strafford, 05070, 802-765-4314
Green Mountain Tea Room, RR 1 Box 400, Route 7, South Wallingford, 05773, 802-446-2611
Hartness House Inn, 30 Orchard St., Springfield, 05156, 802-885-2115
Stockbridge Inn B&B, The, P.O. Box 45, Rt. 100 N, Stockbridge, 05772, 802-746-8165
1860 House B&B Inn, The, P.O. Box 276, Stowe, 05672, 802-253-7351

Austin Hill Inn, West Dover, VT

Baas' Gastehaus, Edson Hill, RR1, Box 22, Stowe, 05672
Bittersweet Inn, RR 2, Box 2900, Stowe, 05672
Edson Hill Manor, 1500 Edson Hill Rd., Stowe, 05672, 802-253-7371
Fontain B&B, Route 100, Box 2480, Stowe, 05672, 802-253-9285
Foxfire Inn, RR2, Box 2180, Stowe, 05672, 802-253-4887
Grey Fox Inn, Stowe, 05672, 802-253-8921
Hob Knob Inn, Mountain Rd., Stowe, 05672, 802-253-8549
Innsburck Inn, RR1, Box 1570, Stowe, 05672, 802-253-8582
Nichols Lodge, Box 1098, Stowe, 05672, 802-253-7683
Raspberry Patch B&B, The, 606 Randolph Rd., Stowe, 05672, 802-253-4145
Scandinavia Inn & Chalet, Stowe, 05672, 802-253-8555
Spruce Pond Inn, Stowe, 05672, 802-253-4828
Stowe-Away Lodge, Mountain Rd., Box 1360, Stowe, 05672, 802-253-7574
Stowehof Inn, P.O. Box 1108, Stowe, 05672, 802-253-9722
Sun & Ski Motor Inn, Mountain Rd., Stowe, 05672, 802-253-7159
Yodler, The, Route 1, Box 10, Stowe, 05672
Eastbrook B&B, River Rd., Sunderland, 05250
Maitland-Swan House, The, P.O. Box 72, School St., Taftsville, 05073, 800-959-1404
Fahrenbrae Hilltop Retreat, Box 129, Thetford Hill, 05074, 802-785-4304
Emersons' Guest House, 82 Main St., Vergennes, 05491, 802-877-3293
Battleground, The, Route 17, Waitsfield
Honeysuckle's Inn, P.O. Box 828, Waitsfield, 05673, 802-496-6200
Knoll Farm Country Inn, RFD 1, Box 179, Waitsfield, 05673, 802-496-3939
Mountain View Inn, Route 17, RFD Box 69, Waitsfield, 05673, 802-496-2426
Old Tymes Inn, Route 100, P.O. Box 165, Waitsfield, 05673
Snuggery Inn, Box 65, RR#1, Waitsfield, 05673, 802-496-2322
White Rocks Inn, RR1, Box 297, Wallingford, 05773, 802-446-2077
Pitcher Inn, P.O. Box 408, Warren, 05674
Sugarbush Inn, Access Rd., Warren, 05674
Thatcher Brook Inn, RD 2 Box 62, Waterbury, 05676, 802-244-5911
Four Winds Country Inn, River Rd., West Arlington, 05250
Inn on Covered Bridge Gree, RD 1, Box 3550, West Arlington, 05250
Hunts' Hideaway, RR 1, Box 570, West Charleston, 05872, 802-895-4432
Deerhill Inn & Restaurant, P.O. Box 136, West Dover, 05356, 802-464-3100
Inn at Sawmill Farm, Box 8 (#100), West Dover, 05356, 802-464-8131
Shield Inn, Box 366, Route 100, West Dover, 05356, 802-464-3984
Snow Den Inn & Gallery, Route 100, Box 625, West Dover, 05356, 802-464-9355
Waldwinkel Inn, West Dover, 05356, 802-464-5281
Silver Fox Inn, RFD 1, Box 1222, West Rutland, 05777, 802-438-5555
Darling Family Inn, The, Route 100, Weston, 05161, 802-824-3223
Inn at Weston, Route 100, P.O. Box 56, Weston, 05161, 802-824-5804
Wilder Homestead Inn, RR1, Box 106D, Weston, 05161, 802-824-8172
Rosewood Inn, P.O. Box 31, Williamstown, 05679, 802-433-5822
Partridge Hill, P.O. Box 52, Williston, 05495, 802-878-4741
Brook Bound Building, Coldbrook Rd., Wilmington, 05363, 802-464-3511
Darcroft's Schoolhouse, Rt. 100, Wilmington, 05363, 802-464-2631
Hermitage Inn & Brookbound, P.O. Box 457, Wilmington, 05363, 802-464-3511
Misty Mountain Lodge, Wilmington, 05356, 802-464-3961
Nordic Hills Lodge, Wilmington, 05356, 802-464-5130
On the Rocks Lodge, Wilmington, 05363, 802-464-8364
Golden Maple Inn, P.O. Box 35, Wolcott, 05680, 802-888-6614
Applebutter Inn B&B, P.O. Box 24, Woodstock, 05091
Canterbury House, The, 43 Pleasant St., Rte. 4, Woodstock, 05091
Carriage House, 15 Route 4 West, Woodstock, 05091, 802-457-4322
Deer Brook Inn, HCR 68, Box 443, Rt. 4, Woodstock, 05091, 802-672-3713
Jackson House at Woodstock, Route 4 West, Woodstock, 05091, 802-457-2065
Lincoln Covered Bridge Inn, RR 2, Box 40, Route 4, Woodstock, 05091, 802-457-3312
Thomas Hill Farm B&B, Rose Hill, Woodstock, 05091, 802-457-1067
Three Church Street B&B, 3 Church St., Woodstock, 05091, 802-457-1925
Village Inn of Woodstock, 41 Pleasant St., Woodstock, 05091, 802-457-1255
Winslow House, 38, Route 4 West, Woodstock, 05091, 802-457-1820
Woodstock Inn & Resort, 14 The Green, Woodstock, 05091, 800-448-7900

Virginia

AMHERST

Dulwich Manor B&B Inn
Rte 5, Box 173A, Rt 60 East,
24521
804-946-7207
Bob & Judy Reilly
All year

$$ B&B
6 rooms, 4 pb
Rated, •
C-yes/S-ltd/P-no/H-no

Full breakfast
Afternoon tea/request
Complimentary wine
bar service, study w/TV
whirlpool, A/C in rooms

English style manor, Blue Ridge Mt. views, beautifully appointed, sumptous breakfast. Surrounded by natural and historic beauty. Outdoor hot tub.

BOSTON

Thistle Hill B&B
Route 1, Box 291, 22713
703-987-9142 FAX:987-9122
Charles & Marianne Wilson
All year

$$$ B&B
5 rooms, 5 pb
Visa, MC, *Rated*, •
C-yes/S-no/P-no/H-yes

Full breakfast
Lunch/dinner on request
Deck, balcony, hot tub
picnics, library, spa
conference/party accom.

Modern amenities in rural parklike setting. Antique-furnished home offers A/C, gazebo, cottages. Near Skyline Dr. in Blue Ridge foothills of VA. Antique shop.

BOYCE

River House, The
Route 2, Box 135, 22620
703-837-1476 FAX:837-2399
Cornelia S. Niemann
All year

$$$ B&B
5 rooms, 5 pb
Visa, MC, *Rated*, •
C-yes/S-yes/P-yes/H-yes
French

Full breakfast
Fruit, beverages/liqueur
Sitting room, library
phones, FAX available
special comedy weekends

1780 Fieldstone rural getaway, convenient to scenic, historical, rec. areas, superb restaurants. Houseparties; small workshops; family reunions. **3rd night 50%**

CASTLETON

Blue Knoll Farm
Route 1, Box 141, Route 676,
22716
703-937-5234
Gil & Mary Carlson
All year

$$$ B&B
4 rooms, 4 pb
Visa, MC, *Rated*,
C-ltd/S-ltd/P-no/H-ltd

Full breakfast
Comp. fruit/snacks/bev.
Sitting room, porches
one room with jacuzzi
antique woodstove, pond

Charming 19th-century farmhouse in the foothills of Blue Ridge Mountains. 65 miles west of Washington, D.C., near Skyline Dr. and 5 star inn at Little Washington Restaurant.

CHARLES CITY

Edgewood Plantation
4800 John Tyler Hwy., Route
5/Williamsburg, 23030
804-829-2962
Juilian & Dot Boulware
All year

$$$ B&B
8 rooms, 4 pb
Visa, MC, *Rated*, •
C-ltd/S-yes

Full breakfast
Comp. refreshments
Antique and gift shops
formal gardens, gazebo
hot tubs, pool, fishing

Sweetness, romance, uniqueness & charm fill each antique bedroom, dining room, country kitchen. Pre-Civil War 1849 historical house. Business facility. **Mid-wk disc'ts, ltd**

Clifton—The Country Inn, Charlotteville, VA

CHARLES CITY

North Bend Plantation B&B
Route 1, Box 13A, 12200
Weyanoke Rd., 23030
804-829-5176
George & Ridgely Copland
All year

$$$ B&B
4 rooms, 4 pb
Rated, •
C-ltd/some French

Full breakfast
Comp. wine, lemonade
Sitting room, library
game room w/pool table
piano, swimming pool

*Virginia Historic Landmark circa 1819 in James River Plantation area. 25 min. to historic Williamsburg. Private, peaceful, 250 acres of farmland. **Comps. at local rest.***

CHARLOTTESVILLE

200 South Street Inn
200 South St., 22902
804-979-0200 800-964-7008
Brendan Clancy
All year

$$$ B&B
20 rooms, 20 pb
Visa, MC, AmEx, *Rated*,
•
C-yes/S-yes/P-no/H-yes
French

Continental plus
Lunch M-F, dinner wkends
Restaurant, comp. wine
sitting room, fireplaces
library, whirlpool tubs

Restored residences in downtown historic district near landmarks, shops, restaurants. Room options include whirlpool tubs, fireplaces, canopy beds. English & Belgian antiques.

Clifton - The Country Inn
Rt 13, Box 26, 22901
804-971-1800
Craig & Donna Hartman
All year

$$$ B&B
14 rooms, 14 pb
Visa, MC, AmEx, *Rated*,
C-yes/S-no/P-no/H-yes

Full breakfast
Dinner $, aft. tea
Snacks, comp. wine
restaurant, bar service
sitting room, library

One of Country Inn magazines 12 best—February 1993! Award-winning gourmet cuisine, fireplace, antiques in every room. Near Jefferson's Monticello. Tennis, pool & bicycles.

CHARLOTTESVILLE

Inn at Monticello, The
Route 19, Box 112, 22902
804-979-3593
Carol & Larry Engel
All year except X-mas

$$$ B&B
5 rooms, 5 pb
Visa, MC, *Rated*, •
C-ltd/S-no/P-no/H-no
some French

Full breakfast
Comp. local beer & wine
Sitting room, hammock
covered porch, croquet
tennis court nearby

19th century manor, perfectly located 2 miles from Thomas Jefferson's beloved "Monticello." Antiques, canopy beds, fireplaces. Golf, tennis, canoeing, wine-tasting nearby.

Inn at the Crossroads, The
Rt. 2, Box 6, RR 692, 22959
804-979-6452
Lynn L. Neville, Tee Garrison
All year

$$ B&B
5 rooms, 1 pb
Visa, MC, *Rated*, •
C-ltd/S-no/P-no/H-no

Full breakfast
Catered supper or dinner
Two sitting rooms
Champagne for honey/annv

Landmark 1820s tavern in foothills of mountains; close to historic Charlottesville. All outdoor activities nearby. Wonderful breakfasts. **Champagne for special occasions**

Silver Thatch Inn
3001 Hollymead Rd., 22901
804-978-4686
Rita & Vince Scoffone
All year

$$$ B&B
7 rooms, 7 pb
Visa, MC, *Rated*, •
C-ltd/S-no/P-no/H-no

Continental plus
Dinner, comp. wine
Restaurant, bar service
tennis courts
swimming pool

Circa 1780 historic Southern inn with romantic lodging rooms and full evening dining. Located in one of Virginia's prettiest towns.

Upland Manor
304 14th St., Rt.# 15,
Nellysford/22958, 22903
804-361-1101
Debbie Summers
All year

$$ B&B
10 rooms, 10 pb
Visa, MC, *Rated*, •
C-yes/S-no/P-no/H-yes

Continental plus
Aft. tea, snacks
Sitting room
golf, tennis, swimming
restaurants

An historic country escape conveniently located between the beautiful Blue Ridge Mountains and Thomas Jefferson's Charlottesville. **3rd night 50% off**

CHINCOTEAGUE

Island Manor House
4160 Main St., 23336
804-336-5436
Charles Kalmykow/Carol Rogers
All year

$$ B&B
6 rooms, 1 pb
Visa, MC
C-ltd/S-yes/P-no/H-no

Full breakfast
Afternoon tea
Sitting room
new garden room
brick courtyard fountain

Elegantly furnished in Federal period antiques. Four minutes from Chincoteague National Wildlife Refuge and seashore. **Special mid-week packages available**

Miss Molly's Inn
4141 Main St., 23336
804-336-6686
David & Barbara Wiedenheft
Valentines - New Years

$$ B&B
7 rooms, 5 pb
Rated, •
C-ltd/S-no/French, Dutch,
German

Full breakfast
English afternoon tea
Sitting room
no smoking!

A charming Victorian home overlooking the Bay. Marguerite Henry stayed here while writing her childhood classic "Misty of Chincoteague."

CHINCOTEAGUE

Watson House
4240 Main St., 23336
804-336-1564
The Derricksons & The Sneads
March–November

$$ B&B
6 rooms, 6 pb
Visa, MC, *Rated*,
C-ltd/S-ltd/P-no/H-no

Full breakfast
Aftn. tea
Bicycles, beach nearby
beach chairs & towels
wildlife refuge nearby

Beautifully restored Victorian. Furnished w/antiques. Breakfast and tea on the veranda. View of Chincoteague Bay and beach nearby. AAA–3 diamond. **4th night 50% off, mdwk**

CLARKSVILLE

Needmoor Inn
P.O. Box 629, 801 Virginia Ave., 23927
804-374-2866
Lucy & Buddy Hairston
All year

$ B&B
4 rooms, 3 pb
Rated, •
C-yes/S-ltd/P-ltd/H-no

Full gourmet breakfast
Aftn. tea, snacks
Comp. wine, bicycles
library, airport pickup
herb garden

Heartfelt hospitality in the heart of Virginia's Lake Country. 1889 homestead amid 1.5 acres of fruit trees. 3 blks away from all water sports. Massage therapist in residence.

CLUSTER SPRINGS

Oak Grove Plantation B&B
P.O. Box 45, 24535
Highway 658
804-575-7137
Pickett Craddock
May–September

$$ B&B
2 rooms
Rated, •
C-yes/S-no/P-no/H-no
Spanish

Full gourmet breakfast
Dinner
Sitting room
library
bicycles

Come enjoy our antebellum country home built by our ancestors in 1820. 400 acres w/trails, creeks and wildlife. Children welcome; midwk childcare package. **3rd night 50% off.**

COVINGTON

Milton Hall B&B Inn
RR 3, 207 Thorny Ln., 24426
703-965-0196
John & Vera Eckert
All year

$$$ B&B
6 rooms, 5 pb
Visa, MC, *Rated*, •
C-yes/S-yes/P-yes/H-no

Full breakfast
Dinner, box lunch
Bar service, comp. wine
aftn. tea, sitting room
library, patio, jacuzzi

English country manor c.1874 set on 44 wooded acres w/gardens. This Historic Landmark adjoins Nat'l Forest, mountains, lakes, springs. Near hunting, fishing. **3rd night 50%**

CULPEPER

Fountain Hall B&B
609 S. East St., 22701
703-825-8200 800-476-2944
Kathi & Steve Walker
All year

$$ B&B
5 rooms, 5 pb
Most CC, *Rated*, •
C-ltd/S-no/P-no/H-ltd

Continental plus
Complimentary beverages
3 sitting rooms, books
fireplaces, VCR, porches
golf nearby, bicycles

Gracious accommodations for business and leisure travelers. Centrally located in quaint historic Culpepper, between Washington, D.C., Charlottesville & Skyline Drive.

DRAPER

Clayton Lake Homestead Inn
P.O. Box 7, 24324
Rt 651, Brown Rd.
703-980-6777
Don & Judy Taylor
All year

$$ B&B
5 rooms, 1 pb
Visa, MC, AmEx, *Rated*, •
C-yes/S-no/P-no/H-no

Full breakfast
Aft. tea, snacks
Sitting room

Lovely home situated on its own beach with three hundred and fifty feet of waterfront

FREDERICKSBURG

Fredericksburg Colonial
1707 Princess Anne St., 22401
703-371-5666
Robert S. Myers
All year

$$ B&B
32 rooms, 32 pb
Visa, MC, *Rated*, •
C-yes/S-yes/P-yes/H-yes

Continental breakfast
Conference room avail.
honeymoon/anniversary
Colonial Suites

Rooms furnished in Victorian decor. Enjoy our antiques, prints, and museum. Inn located in historic district. Antique shops, restaurants nearby.

Kenmore Inn
1200 Princess Anne St., 22401
703-371-7622 800-437-7622
Ed & Alice Bannan
All year

$$$ B&B
13 rooms, 12 pb
Visa, MC, *Rated*, •
C-yes/S-yes/P-ltd/H-yes

Continental plus
Restaurant, wine tasting
Patio garden for dining
sitting rm., lounge, A/C
antiques, bicycles

On the historic walking tour, elegant guest rooms considered to be among Virginia's 5 most exclusive restaurants. **Free VA wine tasting, breakfast in bed, free beverages.**

Richard Johnston Inn
711 Caroline St., 22401
703-899-7606
Susan Thrush
All year

$$$ B&B
11 rooms, 7 pb
Vis, MC, AmEx, *Rated*,
C-yes/S-no/P-no/H-yes

Continental
Comp. tea, wine
Library
sitting room
air conditioned

Directly across from the Olde Towne Visitors Center. The Rappahanock River is just across from the courtyard. Enjoy a private fireplace and antiques.

La Vista Plantation
4420 Guinea Station Rd., 22408
703-898-8444
Michele & Edward Schiesser
All year

$$$ B&B
2 rooms, 2 pb
Visa, MC, *Rated*, •
C-yes/S-no/P-ltd/H-no

Full breakfast
Comp. soda and juice
Sitting room, library
bicycles, A/C, kitchen
TV, phone, wicker furn.

Lovely 1838 classical revival country home on 10 acres outside historic Fredericksburg. Antiques; prvt fireplaces; old trees; pond. **7th night free**

FRONT ROYAL

Chester House
43 Chester St., 22630
703-635-3937 800-621-0441
Bill & Ann Wilson
All year

$$ B&B
6 rooms, 2 pb
Visa, MC, *Rated*, •
C-ltd/S-ltd/P-no/H-no

Continental plus
Comp. wine, snacks
Living & dining room
lawns, gardens
television parlor

Quiet, elegant, relaxed atmosphere home reminiscent of a bygone era. Amidst formal boxwood garden and shade trees. Golf, tennis, horseback riding, hiking, canoeing nearby.

Constant Spring Inn
413 S. Royal Ave., 22630
703-635-7010
Joan & Bob Kaye
Exc. 2 weeks in Jan

$$ B&B
9 rooms, 9 pb
Visa, MC, •
C-yes/S-ltd/P-no/H-ltd

Full breakfast
Comp. beverages
Sitting room, bicycles
conf. room, FAX, copying
fitness studio

Three blocks from Skyline Drive; parklike setting; heart of history land. Located atop a hill with a view of the countryside. 80 minutes to Washington, D.C. **3rd night 25% off**

FRONT ROYAL

Killahevlin
1401 North Royal Ave., 22630
703-636-7335
John & Susan Lang
All year

$$$ B&B
4 rooms, 4 pb
Visa, MC, *Rated*, •
C-ltd/S-no/P-no/H-no

Continental plus
Aft. tea, snacks
Comp. wine
sitting room, hot tubs
gazebos, screened porch

Historic Edwardian mansion on Civil War encampment hill. Mountain views, working fireplaces, private baths w/jacuzzi tubs. Prepare to be pampered.

GORDONSVILLE

Sleepy Hollow Farm B&B
16280 Blue Ridge Turnpk, 22942
703-832-5555
Beverley Allison
All year

$$ B&B
7 rooms, 6 pb
Visa, MC, *Rated*,
C-yes/S-yes/P-ask/H-no
Spanish, French

Full breakfast
Comp. wine, beverages
Sitting room, conf. room
croquet field, gazebo
pond fishing & swimming

Old farmhouse & cottage furnished in antiques, accessories. One bdrm w/fireplace & jacuzzi. In beautiful countryside, near James Madison's Montpelier. **3+ nights 10% off**

GOSHEN

Hummingbird Inn, The
P.O. Box 147, Wood Ln., 24439
703-997-9065 800-397-3214
Jeremy & Diana Robinson
All year

$$ B&B
4 rooms, 4 pb
Visa, MC, *Rated*, •
C-ltd/S-ltd/P-no/H-no

Full breakfast
Lunch (groups), dinner
Comp. snacks
sitting room, solarium
porches, fireplaces

Nestled in mountain splendor, country Victorian mansion in historic Shenandoah Valley. Antique furnishings. Near historic sites, Lexington, horse center, Blue Ridge Parkway.

HARRISONBURG

Joshua Wilton House Inn
412 S. Main St., 22801
703-434-4464
Craig & Roberta Moore
All year

$$$ B&B
5 rooms, 5 pb
Visa, MC, AmEx, •
C-ltd/S-no/P-no/H-no

Full breakfast
Restaurant - dinner
Snacks, comp. wine
bar service, sitting rm
bicycles

One hundred year-old Victorian mansion furnished with antiques and reproductions. Fine dining restaurant and cafe for casual dining.

HILLSVILLE

Bray's Manor B&B Inn
Rt 2, Box 760C, 24343
703-728-7901
Dick & Helen Bray
March–January

$$ B&B
4 rooms, 2 pb
Visa, MC, *Rated*, •
C-yes/S-no/P-no/H-no

Full breakfast
Snacks, soft drinks
Sitting room with TV
parlor, library

Beautiful southwest Virginia; 12 miles north of Blue Ridge Parkway; croquet; badminton; rambling porch for sitting, sipping; near golf and crafts.

HOT SPRINGS

Vine Cottage Inn
P.O. Box 918, Rt. 220, 24445
703-839-2422 800-666-VINE
Wendell & Pat Lucas
All year

$$$ B&B
14 rooms, 8 pb
Visa, MC, Ch, *Rated*,
C-yes/S-yes/P-no/H-no

Continental plus
Sitting room, library
large veranda w/rockers
tennis nearby

A charming and relaxing turn-of-the-century inn located in a renowned mountain spa. Outdoorsmen delight in golfing, skiing, hunting, hiking, fishing and swimming.

LEESBURG

Fleetwood Farm B&B
Route 1, Box 306-A, 22075
703-327-4325 FAX:777-8236
Carol & Bill Chamberlin
All year

$$$ B&B
2 rooms, 2 pb
Rated, •
C-ltd/S-no

Full country breakfast
Comp. wine, snacks, tea
Living room w/TV, stereo
library, games, jacuzzi
cook-out fac., canoe

1745 hunt country manor house. Beautiful rooms each with private baths, air-conditioning, fireplaces, antiques. Horseback riding nearby. A Virginia Historic Landmark.

LEXINGTON

Llewellyn Lodge—Lexington
603 S. Main St., 24450
703-463-3235 800-882-1145
Ellen & John Roberts
All year

$$ B&B
6 rooms, 6 pb
Most CC, *Rated*, •
C-ltd/S-yes/P-no/H-no

Full breakfast
Comp. beverages
Sitting room
tennis courts, pool
and golf nearby

Charming half-century-old colonial with a warm friendly atmosphere, where guests can relax after visiting this historic Shenandoah town. Gourmet breakfast.

LINCOLN

Springdale Country Inn
22078
703-338-1832 800-388-1832
Nancy & Roger Fones
All year

$$$ B&B
9 rooms, 3 pb
Most CC, *Rated*, •
C-ltd/S-no/P-no/H-yes

Full breakfast
Lunch, dinner, snacks
Comp. wine, aftn. tea
sitting room, library
once/month family wkends

Restored historic landmark, 45 miles west of Washington, D.C., special event and meeting facilities. Seats 50, sleeps 20. Easily accessible. **15% off 2nd night, 20% off 3rd.**

LYNCHBURG

Madison House B&B, The
413 Madison St., 24504
804-528-1503 800-828-6422
Irene & Dale Smith
All year

$$ B&B
4 rooms, 4 pb
Rated, •
C-ltd/S-no/P-no/H-no

Full gourmet breakfast
Afternoon tea w/scones
2 rm. suite, telephones
sitting room, snacks
library, central A/C

Lynchburg's finest Victorian B&B, 1880 antique-filled elegant mansion. Historic District known as "quality row." Wonderful breakfast and English high tea. **Baseball tickets**

MANASSAS—WASH. D.C.

Sunrise Hill Farm B&B
5590 Old Farm Lane,
Washington D.C. area, 22110
703-754-8309
Frank & Sue Boberek
All year

$$ B&B
2 rooms, 1 pb
Visa, MC, *Rated*, •
C-ltd/P-no/H-no

Full gourmet breakfast
Horseback riding
near hiking, antiquing
tennis, golf, horses

Civil War treasure located within the heart of 6500 acre Manassas/Bull Run National Battlefields just 35 minutes west of Washington DC. Civil War Battle parks.

MIDDLEBURG

Middleburg Country Inn
P.O. Box 2065, 22117
209 E. Washington St.
703-687-6082 800-262-6082
John & Susan Pettibone
All year

$$$ MAP
8 rooms, 8 pb
Most CC, *Rated*, •
C-yes/S-ltd/P-no/H-yes
Spanish, French

Full breakfast
Dinner, Aft. tea, snacks
Comp. wine, bar, library
sitting room, hot tubs
bicycles, horse events

Where horse is king! Romantic historic inn, 18th century antique charm, luxurious baths, canopy beds, fireplaces. Sleep where George Washington camped. **3rd. night 50% off**

MIDDLEBURG

Welbourne
Route 743, 22117
703-687-3201
Nathaniel & Sherry Morison
All year

$$$ B&B
10 rooms, 10 pb
•
C-yes/S-yes/P-yes/H-ltd
French

Full breakfast
Comp. wine
Piano
sitting room

Antebellum home occupied by the same family for seven generations. In heart of Virginia's fox-hunting country. Virginia historic landmark.

MIDDLETOWN

Wayside Inn, The
7783 Main St., 22645
703-869-1797 FAX:869-6038
Maggie Edwards
All year

$$ EP
22 rooms, 22 pb
Most CC, *Rated*, •
C-yes/S-yes/P-no/H-yes

Full breakfast
Lunch, dinner appetizers
Bar service
sitting room, piano
entertainment

In Shenandoah Valley, offering Civil War history with southern cooking. Rooms are decorated in different historic styles with antiques for sale. **Restaurant discount**

MOLLUSK

Guesthouses at Greenvale
Route 354, Box 70, 22517
804-462-5995
Pam & Walt Smith
All year

$$$ B&B
6 rooms, 6 pb
•
C-ltd/S-ltd/P-no

Continental
Living rms., kitchens
Sitting room, library
veranda, pool, beach
docks, boating, bicycles

Waterfront guesthouses on 13 acres. Privacy & tranquility w/pool, dock, private beach. Beautiful sunsets & birdwatcher's paradise. Fishing & crabbing.

MONTEREY

Highland Inn
P.O. Box 40, Main St., 24465
703-468-2143
Michael Strand & Cynthia Peel
All year

$ B&B
17 rooms, 17 pb
Visa, MC, *Rated*, •
C-yes/S-yes/P-no

Continental breakfast
Breakfast, dinner
Restaurant, bar
porches
library

Relaxing country getaway with wraparound porches, antiques, private baths, country cooking, and a tavern. Lots of charm. Fishing (fresh trout), hunting and skiing.

MONTROSS

Montross Inn & Restaurant
P.O. Box 908, Courthouse
Sqaure, 22520
804-493-9097 800-321-0979
Eileen & Michael Longman
All year

$$ B&B/$$$ MAP
6 rooms, 6 pb
Visa, MC, Disc, *Rated*, •
C-yes/S-yes/P-ask/H-no

Continental plus
Restaurant, English pub
Bedside brandy, truffles
retail wine & gift shop
phone & cable TV in rms

Country inn dating back in part to 1683, offers antiques, fine dining, and elegant accommodations. Located in historic area near Stratford Hall. **25% off 2nd night midwk**

MOUNT JACKSON

Widow Kip's Country Inn
Route 1, Box 117, 22842
703-477-2400
Betty Luse
All year

$$ B&B
6 rooms, 6 pb
Rated, •
C-yes/S-ltd/P-yes/H-no

Full breakfast
Comp. sherry
Picnics & snacks, VCR
sitting room, fireplaces
bicycles, swimming pool

1830 gracious colonial on 7 acres overlooking Shenandoah. Seven fireplaces. Victorian furnishings. Near golf and skiing.

NEW CHURCH—E. SHORE ———————————————————————————

Garden & The Sea Inn, The	$$$ B&B	Continental plus
P.O. Box 275 Rt 710, 4188 Nelson	5 rooms, 5 pb	Dinner, afternoon tea
Rd., 23415	Most CC, *Rated*, •	Comp. wine, restaurant
804-824-0672	C-ltd/S-ltd/P-no/H-no	sitting room, beach near
Victoria Olian & Jack Betz	French	outdoor patio/garden
April 1—October 31		

Eastern shore near Chincoteqague and Assateague. Elegant, Euorpean-style inn with French-style gourmet restaurant. Luxurious rooms, beautiful beach nearby. **4th nt. free, ask**

NEW MARKET ———————————————————————————————————

A Touch of Country B&B	$$ B&B	Full breakfast
9329 Congress St., 22844	6 rooms, 6 pb	Comp. beverages
703-740-8030	Visa, MC, •	Sitting room with TV
Dawn Kasow, Jean Schoellig	C-ltd/S-ltd/P-no/H-no	
All year		

A comfortable 1870s restored home decorated with antiques, collectibles, and a country flavor. Located in the beautiful Shenandoah Valley.

ONANCOCK ————————————————————————————————————

Colonial Manor Inn	$ EP	Morning coffee
P.O. Box 94, 23417	14 rooms, 5 pb	Glass-enclosed porch
84 Market St.	C-yes/S-yes/P-no/H-no	Victorian gazebo, A/C
804-787-3521		cable TV, sitting room
June & Jerry Evans		
All year		

Family-owned business since 1936. Cozy, at-home kind of friendly atmosphere in a historic little town on the water; fine restaurants nearby. **2nd night 50% off, ltd**

ORANGE ——————————————————————————————————————

Hidden Inn	$$$ B&B	Full country breakfast
249 Caroline St., 22960	10 rooms, 10 pb	Aftn. tea
703-672-3625 Fax-672-5029	Visa, MC, *Rated*, •	Dinner by reservation
Ray & Barbara Lonick	C-yes/S-no/P-no/H-no	sitting room, jacuzzi
All year		A/C, fireplaces

Comfortably furnished country inn tucked away in rural community. Convenient to D.C., Charlottesville, Blue Ridge Mountains. Super breakfasts!

PETERSBURG ——————————————————————————————————

Mayfield Inn	$$ B&B	Full breakfast
P.O. Box 2265, 23804	4 rooms, 4 pb	Afternoon tea
3348 W. Washington St.	Visa, MC, •	Two sitting rooms
804-861-6775 804-733-0866	C-yes/S-ltd/P-no/H-no	swimming pool
Jamie Caudle/Cherry Turner		
All year		

A 1750 house, completely and very beautifully restored, set on four tranquil acres. Close to historic Petersburg and battlefields. **2+ nights 10%, 4+ nights 20% off**

RICHMOND ————————————————————————————————————

Emmaneul Hotzler House	$$$ B&B	Full breakfast
2036 Monument Ave., 23220	4 rooms, 4 pb	Natural cereals
804-355-4885 804-353-6900	Visa, MC, •	Living room, library
Lyn Benson & John Richardson	C-ltd/S-no/P-no/H-no	fireplace in 2 of rooms
All year		jacuzzi in large room

Elegant 1914 Italian Renaissance in historic district with natural mahogany raised paneling, wainscoting, leaded glass windows, coffered ceilings with dropped beams.

RICHMOND ───

Mr. Patrick Henry's Inn	$$$ B&B	Full breakfast
2300 E. Broad St., 23223	4 rooms, 4 pb	Restaurant, bar
804-644-1322 800-932-2654	Most CC, *Rated*, •	Lunch, dinner
Lynn & Jim News	C-yes/S-yes/P-no/H-no	sitting room, fireplaces
All year		kitchenettes, balconies

*A pre-Civil War inn. Walking distance to many tourist attractions. Featuring a gourmet restaurant, English pub & garden patio. Suites include fireplaces. **3rd night 50% off.***

William Catlin House, The	$$$ B&B	Full breakfast
2304 E. Broad St., 23223	5 rooms, 4 pb	Fireplaces, antiques
804-780-3746	Visa, MC, DC, *Rated*, •	oriental rugs
Robert & Josephine Martin	C-ltd/S-yes/P-no/H-no	crystal chandeliers
All year		

Retire in a four-poster bed in front of a romantic, burning fireplace—wake up to freshly brewed coffee served in your room.

ROANOKE ───

Mary Bladon House, The	$$ B&B	Full breakfast
381 Washington Ave. SW, 24016	3 rooms, 3 pb	Afternoon tea
703-344-5361	Visa, MC, *Rated*, •	Sitting room
Bill & Sheri Bestpitch	C-yes/S-no/P-no/H-no	A/C in rooms
All year		24 hr answering service

Romantic Victorian setting with period antiques and local arts and crafts. Walking distance to historic downtown area, shops and restaurants.

ROCKY MOUNT ─────────────────────────────────────

Claiborne House, The	$$ B&B	Full breakfast
119 Claiborne Ave., 24151	5 rooms, 5 pb	Aft. tea, snacks
704-483-4616	Visa, MC, *Rated*,	Sitting room, library
Margaret & Jim Young	C-yes/S-ltd/P-no	tennis court, boat ride
March 1 - December 31		fishing packages

Elegant Victorian w/charming English garden. Luxurious antique-appointed rooms. Rich coffee outside your door before romantic, candlelit breakfast.

SCOTTSVILLE ──────────────────────────────────────

High Meadows Vineyard Inn	$$$ B&B/MAP	Full breakfast
Route 4, Box 6, Route 20 South,	12 rooms, 12 pb	Candlelight dining
24590	*Rated*, •	Nightly winetasting
804-286-2218 800-232-1832	C-yes/S-ltd/P-ltd/H-no	library, hot tub, pond
Peter Sushka, Mary Jae Abbitt	French	gazebo, bikes, vineyard
All year		

*Enchanting historical landmark south of Charlottesville. Large, tastefully appointed rooms; fireplaces; period antiques. Private 50 acres for walking & picnics. **3rd night 50%***

SMITH MOUNTAIN LAKE ──────────────────────────────

Manor at Taylor's Store	$$ B&B	Full breakfast
Route 1, Box 533, 24184	6 rooms, 4 pb	Comp. tea & lemonade
703-721-3951 800-248-6267	Visa, MC, *Rated*, •	Exercise rm, movies
Lee & Mary Lynn Tucker	C-ltd/S-ltd/P-no/H-yes	swimming, fishing
All year	some German	canoeing, hiking, hottub

Explore this secluded 120 acre estate w/6 prvt. lakes, an elegantly furnished historic manor house, warm hospitality & wonderful food. Private family cottage. Hot Air Balloon.

SMITHFIELD

Isle of Wight Inn	$$ B&B	Full breakfast
1607 S. Church St., 23430	10 rooms, 10 pb	Snacks, tea, soft drinks
804-357-3176	Visa, MC, AmEx, *Rated*,	Sitting room, bicycles
Harts, Earls, S. Blackwell	•	jacuzzi, walking tour
All year	C-yes/S-ltd/P-no/H-yes	golf and fishing nearby

Luxurious inn & antiques shop. Famous for Smithfield hams & old homes dating from 1750. Saint Lukes church 1632. Near Colonial Williamsburg & Jamestown. **50% off 3rd night.**

Smithfield Station Inn	$$ B&B	Continental(Mon.-Fri.)
P.O. Box 486, 23431	15 rooms, 15 pb	Restaurant, all meals
415 S. Church St.	Visa, MC, AmEx, *Rated*,	Bar service, snacks
804-357-7700	•	historic siteseeing
Ron & Tina Pack	C-yes/S-yes/P-no/H-no	
All year		

Romantic waterfront Inn modeled after Victorian Coast Guard Station. Full Service Restaurant and Marina. Smithfield Historic District. Boaters paradise. **Packages available**

SPERRYVILLE

Conyers House Inn, The	$$$ B&B	Hearty gourmet breakfast
Route 1, Box 157, Slate Mills Rd.,	9 rooms, 7 pb	Comp. wine & cake
22740	*Rated*, •	Candlelight dinner
703-987-8025	C-ltd/S-ltd/P-ask/H-ltd	fireplaces, wood stoves
Sandra & Norman Brown	Fr., Ger., Ital., Arabic	piano, porches, horses
All year		

18th-century former country store graciously furnished w/ heirlooms & antiques. Outstanding hiking; foxhunting & trail rides. Candlelit dinner by rsvp. **10% off 3+ nights**

STAFFORD

Rennaisance Manor B&B	$$ B&B	Continental plus
2247 Courthouse Rd., 22554	4 rooms, 2 pb	Aftn. tea, comp. sherry
703-720-3785	•	Library
The Bernard's & The Houser's	C-yes/S-no/P-no/H-no	local artist's gallery
All year	German	formal garden, gazebo

Resembles Mount Vernon in architecture & decor; fountain, brick walk & bridge. Near Fredericksburg, Washington DC; Potomac & Rappahonock Rivers. **Week rates 15% off.**

STANLEY

Jordan Hollow Farm Inn	$$$ MAP	Full breakfast, dinner
Route 2, Box 375, 22851	16 rooms, 16 pb	Restaurant & bar
703-778-2285 703-778-2209	Visa, MC, DC, *Rated*, •	Sitting room, game room
Jetze & Marley Beers	C-yes/S-yes/P-yes/H-no	library, canoeing
All year	Dutch, German, French	riding, pool, trails

A 200-year-old restored colonial horse farm. Friendly, informal atmosphere w/spectacular views. Caverns, Skyline Drive, canoeing. Carriage rides. **3rd night 50% off, ltd**

STAUNTON

Ashton Country House	$$ B&B	Full breakfast
1205 Middlebrook Rd., 24401	4 rooms, 4 pb	Afternoon tea, snacks
703-885-7819 800-296-7812	*Rated*, •	Sitting room
S. Kennedy, S. Polanski	C-ltd/S-no/P-ask/H-no	live piano music wkends
All year		accompanies tea

1860's Greek Revival on 20 aces. One mile from town. Professional musician & professional chef entertain and care for you. Delicious! Delightful! **3rd night 50% off**

STAUNTON

Frederick House
P.O. Box 1387, 28 N. New St., 24401
703-885-4220 800-334-5575
Joe & Evy Harman
All year

$$ B&B
14 rooms, 14 pb
Most CC, *Rated*, •
C-yes/S-no/P-no/H-no

Full breakfast
Sitting room
library
conference facilities

Located in the oldest city west of the Blue Ridge Mountains of Virginia. Historic Staunton contains Woodrow Wilson birthplace, shops and restaurants. **10% Sr citizen discount**

Hilltop House
1810 Springhill Rd., 24401
703-886-0042
John & Sonna Reinheimer
All year

$ B&B
2 rooms
Rated, •
C-ltd/S-no/P-no/H-no

Full breakfast
Dinner for theme wkend
Aft. tea, snacks
comp. wine, BYOB setups
library, lg. front porch

Hilltop House offers panoramic 360 degree views of the Blue Ridge, Allegheny & Shenandoah Mts., and dishes up southern hospitality at its very best. **40% off/rent both rms.**

Sampson Eagon Inn, The
238 East Beverley St., 24401
703-886-8200 800-597-9722
Laura & Frank Mattingly
All year

$$ B&B
5 rooms, 5 pb
Rated, •
C-ltd/S-no/P-no/H-ltd

Full breakfast
TV/VCR and sitting area
in each accommodation
FAX available as needed

An elegant alternative in in-town historic lodging. The inn features spacious, antique furnished accommodations complemented by gracious personal service.

STEELE'S TAVERN

Sugar Tree Inn
Highway 56, 24483
703-377-2197
Sarah & Hal Davis
March - November

$$$ B&B
11 rooms, 11 pb
Visa, MC, •
C-yes/S-ltd/P-no/H-yes

Full breakfast
Dinner by resv., pub
Sitting room
library, porches, rocker
creek & waterfall

Mountain inn of hand-hewn logs, high in the Blue Ridge on 28 wooded acres. Fireplace in every room-perfect for romantic getaways.

STRASBURG

Hotel Strasburg
201 S. Holliday St., 22657
703-465-9191 800-348-8327
Gary & Carol Rutherford
All year

$$ B&B
24 rooms, 24 pb
Most CC, *Rated*, •
C-yes/S-yes/P-no/H-no

Continental plus
Restaurant, bar service
Snacks, meeting rooms
sitting room, near beach
jacuzzi in some rooms

Charming Victorian restoration, rooms w/ period antiques, some jacuzzi suites. Great food & atmosphere. Antique capital of Virginia. **Call for golf & theater packages**

SYRIA

Graves' Mountain Lodge
Rte. 670, 22743
703-923-4231
Spring, Summer & Fall

$ AP
45 rooms
C-yes/S-ltd/P-ltd

Full breakfast
Lunch, dinner included
Tennis court
swimming pool, fishing
hiking, horseback riding

Rustic, charming inn located in shadow of Blue Ridge Mtns. Three abundant meals/day in Lodge. Activities range from fishing to horseback riding to relaxing.

TREVILIANS

Prospect Hill Plantation
Route 3, Box 430, Route 613, 23093
703-967-0844 800-277-0844
Sheehan Family
All year

$$$ B&B/MAP
10 rooms, 10 pb
Visa, MC, *Rated*, •
C-ltd/S-yes/P-no/H-no

Full breakfast in bed
Dinner, afternoon tea
Comp. wine or cider
library, fireplaces
jacuzzi, pool, bicycles

1732 plantation. Bedrooms w/fireplaces in manor house and grooms' quarters. 15 miles to Charlottesville. Continental dining, peace & quiet countryside. **10% off Mon-Thu. Ltd**

TROUTVILLE

WoodsEdge Guest Cottage
2800 Ridge Trail, 24175
703-473-2992
Ferrel & Fred Phillips
All year

$$$ B&B
1 rooms, 1 pb
Visa, MC
C-yes/S-no/P-no/H-no

Continental plus
Housekeeping cottage
full kitchen, sitt. rm.
accommodates families

On fourteen private acres overlooking the Alleghany Mountains. Delightfully furnished with antiques. Porch with rocking chairs. Scenic golf course adjacent. **3rd night 50%**

WARM SPRINGS

Inn at Gristmill Square
Box 359, Route 645, 24484
703-839-2231
The McWilliams Family
All year exc. March 1-15

$$$ B&B
15 rooms, 14 pb
Visa, MC, *Rated*, •
C-yes/S-yes/P-yes/H-ltd

Continental breakfast
Lunch, dinner, bar
Sauna
swimming pool
tennis courts

Casual country hideaway, historic original mill site dating from 1800s. Each room individually decorated. Fine dining and distinguished wine cellar. **3rd night 50% off**

WASHINGTON

Caledonia Farm B&B 1812
Route 1, Box 2080, 22627
703-675-3693
Phil Irwin
All year

$$$ B&B
3 rooms, 1 pb
Most CC, *Rated*, •
C-ltd/S-no/P-ask/H-yes
German, Danish

Full breakfast
Comp. wine
Bikes, lawn games, VCR
evening fun hayrides
68 miles to D.C.

Beautifully restored 1812 stone farm home adjacent to Shenandoah National Park/Blue Ridge Mountains. Virginia Landmark, on National Register. AAA rates 3 diamonds.

Fairlea Farm B&B
P.O. Box 124, 22747
Mt. Salem Ave.
703-675-3679 703-675-1064
Susan, Walt & Casey Longyear
All year

$$ B&B
4 rooms, 4 pb
•
C-yes/S-ltd/P-yes/H-no
French

Full breakfast
Sitting room, hiking
near tennis & library
antique shops, horses

Spectacular mountain views, a 5-min. stroll to The Inn at Little Washington. Warm hospitality & sumptuous breakfast in fieldstone manor house, overlooking sheep & cattle farm.

Foster-Harris House, The
P.O. Box 333, 22747
Main St.
703-675-3757 800-666-0153
Phyllis Marriott
All year

$$$ B&B
4 rooms, 4 pb
Visa, MC, *Rated*, •
C-ltd/S-no/P-no/H-no
Spanish, German

Full breakfast
Comp. sweets & beverages
Sitting room, queen beds
fireplace stove
whirlpool

Restored Victorian (circa 1900) house in historic "Little" Washington, Virginia. Antiques, fresh flowers, mountain views, 3 blocks from 5-star restaurant. **3rd nite $10.00 off**

WASHINGTON

Gay Street Inn
P.O. Box 237, Gay Street, 22747
403-675-3288
Donna & Robin Kevis
All year

$$$ B&B
3 rooms, 3 pb
•
C-yes/S-ltd/P-ltd/H-yes

Full breakfast
Picnic lunch, Aft. tea
Set ups for drinks
sitting room, library
river-canoeing, rafting

In Blue Ridge Mtns. in historic country town. 1850s farm house w/friendly, relaxing atmosphere. Furnished w/period New England funiture. **10% discount 2nd night, ltd.**

Heritage House
P.O. Box 427, 22747
Main & Piedmont St.
703-675-3207
Jean & Frank Scott
All year

$$$ B&B
4 rooms, 4 pb
Visa, MC, *Rated*, •
C-ltd/S-no/P-no/H-yes

Full gourmet breakfast
Comp. beverages & snacks
Parlor w/fireplace
walk to restaurant

153-year-old Colonial home in quaint village George Washington surveyed as a 17-year-old. 12 miles from Skyline Dr.; near vineyards, antiques. **Special rates off season, ltd.**

WHITE POST

L'Auberge Provencale
P.O. Box 119, 22663
Rt. 1, Box 203, Boyce
703-837-1375 800-638-1702
Alain & Celeste Borel
Exc. Jan—mid-Feb

$$$ B&B
10 rooms, 10 pb
Most CC, *Rated*, •
C-ltd/S-yes/P-no/H-no
French

Full gourmet breakfast
Dinner, bar service
Refreshments, flowers
library, sitting room
bicycles, gardens

Master chef from France presents nationally acclaimed cuisine. Extensive wine list. Elegant accomm. w/fireplaces, private entrances. FAX:837-2004. **Special goodies in room**

WILLIAMSBURG

Applewood Colonial B&B
605 Richmond Rd., 23185
804-229-0205 800-899-2753
Fred Strout
All year

$$ B&B
4 rooms, 4 pb
Visa, MC, *Rated*, •
C-yes

Continental plus
Afternoon tea
Sitting room
fireplaces

Elegant colonial decor. Walking distance to colonial Williamsburg & College of William & Mary. Fireplaces, antiques, apple collection & lots of comfort. **Free bottle of cider**

Cedars B&B, The
616 Jamestown Rd., 23185
804-229-3591 800-296-3591
Debbie Howard
All year

$$$ B&B
9 rooms, 4 pb
•
C-yes/S-ltd/P-no/H-yes

Continental breakfast
Afternoon tea
Screened porch
parlor with fireplace

Brick Georgian colonial house, air-conditioned, antiques and canopy beds. Room for 22 guests, plus brick cottage with fully equipped kitchen for 6-8. **Sr. citizen 10% discount**

Colonial Capital B&B
501 Richmond Rd., 23185
804-229-0233 800-776-0570
Barbara & Phil Craig
All year

$$$ B&B
5 rooms, 5 pb
Visa, MC, AmEx, *Rated*,
•
C-ltd/S-ltd/P-no/H-no

Full gourmet breakfast
Parlor, books, solarium
games, videos, bicycles
free on premise parking

Antique-furnished Colonial Revival (c.1926) only three blocks from Historic Area. Cozy canopied beds and breakfast with class. Afternoon tea and wine.

WILLIAMSBURG

Fox Grape B&B
701 Monumental Ave., 23185
800-292-3699 804-229-6914
Pat & Bob Orendorff
All year

$$ B&B
4 rooms, 4 pb
Visa, MC, Disc, *Rated*, •
C-yes/S-ltd/P-no/H-no

Continental plus
Sitting room

Two story Colonial with large porch, features antiques, counted cross stitch, duck decoy collection, cup plate collection, canopy beds.

Indian Springs B&B
330 Indian Springs Rd., 23185
804-220-0726 800-262-9165
Kelly & Paul Supplee
All year

$$ B&B
4 rooms, 4 pb
Rated, •
C-yes/S-no/P-no/H-yes

Full breakfast
Afternoon tea, snacks
Restaurant nearby
sitting room, library
game room, veranda

Short walk to historic district, College of William & Mary. Family-operated restaurant nearby. Enjoy seasonal snack served in Carriage House. Hospitality abides!

Legacy of Williamsburg
930 Jamestown Rd., 23185
804-220-0524 800-962-4722
Mary Ann & Ed Lucas
All year

$$$ B&B
3 rooms, 3 pb
Visa, MC, AmEx, *Rated*,
C-ltd/S-no

Full breakfast
Comp. wine, soft drinks
VCR tapes available
library, billiards
6 fireplaces, bicycles

True 18th C. tradition: Canopy beds. Prvt baths. Gardens. Best location for walking. Unforgettable breakfast. The Inn place to stay in Williamsburg. **Comp. wine, fresh fruit.**

Liberty Rose B&B
1022 Jamestown Rd., 23185
800-545-1825
Brad & Sandi Hirz
All year

$$$ B&B
5 rooms, 5 pb
Visa, MC, *Rated*, •
C-ltd

Full breakfast
Comp. bev., chocolates
Sitting room, gift shop
Suite w/many amenities
TVs, VCRs, movies in rms

"Williamsburg's most romantic B&B." Charming home renovated in perfect detail. An acre of magnificent trees. Delightful antiques, wallpapers, lace. **Silk rose takehome gift**

Newport House B&B
710 South Henry St., 23185
804-229-1775
Cathy & John Millar
All year

$$$ B&B
2 rooms, 2 pb
•
C-yes/S-no/P-no/H-no
French

Full breakfast
Sitting room
Library, Harpischord
Ballroom for receptions

Designed in 1756. Completely furnished in period. 5 minute walk from historic area. Colonial dancing every Tuesday evening. VA B&B Assoc. and ABBA member.

Piney Grove at Southall's
P.O. Box 1359, 16920 Southall
Plantation, 23187
804-829-2480
The Gordineer Family
All year

$$$ B&B
6 rooms, 4 pb
Rated, •
C-yes/S-no/P-no/H-no
German

Full breakfast
Picnic lunches (request)
Comp. wine, mint juleps
sitting room, library
swimming pool

Nat'l Registry property in James River Plantation Country—20 mi. to Williamsburg. 2 authentically restored & antique-filled antebellum houses. **Wine & Plantation tickets incl**

WILLIAMSBURG ————————————————————————————

Williamsburg Manor B&B	$$$ B&B	Full breakfast
600 Richmond Rd., 23185	5 rooms, 5 pb	Dinner by reservation
804-220-8011 800-422-8011	*Rated*, •	Library/sitting room
Michael & Laura MacKnight	C-ltd/S-no/P-no/H-no	fireplace, TV, AC
All year		catering/floral service

1927 Georgian brick colonial restored to original elegance. 5 bedrooms w/exquisite pieces. Walk to historic area. Award winning chef. Adjacent to College of William & Mary.

———————————————————————————————————————

Williamsburg Sampler B&B	$$$ B&B	Full "Skiplunch" brkfast
922 Jamestown Rd., 23185	4 rooms, 4 pb	18th Cty. carriage house
804-253-0398 800-722-1169	*Rated*, •	Antiques/pewter/samplers
Helen & Ike Sisane	C-ltd/S-no/P-no/H-no	parking, AAA 3 diamonds
All year		

Williamsburg's finest plantation style colonial home. Richly furnished. Guests have included decendents of Charles Dickens & John Quincy Adams. **Disc't to Historic Area**

WINTERGREEN ————————————————————————————

Trillium House	$$$ B&B	Full breakfast
P.O. Box 280/Nellysford,	12 rooms, 12 pb	Afternoon tea, bar
Wintergreen Dr., 22958	Visa, MC, *Rated*, •	Dinner Fri & Sat
804-325-9126 800-325-9126	C-yes/S-ltd/P-no/H-yes	sitting room, library
Ed & Betty Dinwiddie		near tennis, pool, golf
All year		

Birds entertain at breakfast at this owner-designed inn in year-round Wintergreen Resort. Fall and spring foliage are specialties.

Williamsburg Manor B&B, Williamsburg, VA

WOODSTOCK

Azalea House B&B	$ B&B	Full breakfast
551 S. Main St., 22664	3 rooms, 3 pb	Snacks
703-459-3500	Visa, MC, AmEx	Sitting room
Margaret & Price McDonald	C-ltd/S-no/P-no/H-no	library
All year		

Attractive, comfortable rooms with mountain viewing. Located in the rolling hills of the Shenandoah Valley. Nearby restaurants, vineyards, caverns, hiking.

Inn at Narrow Passage	$$ B&B	Full breakfast
P.O. Box 608, US 11 S., 22664	12 rooms, 8 pb	Sitting room, conf. fac.
703-459-8000	Visa, MC, *Rated*, •	fireplace, swimming
Ellen & Ed Markel	C-ltd/S-ltd/P-no/H-no	fishing, rafting
All year		

Historic 1740 log inn on the Shenandoah River. Fireplaces, colonial charm, close to vineyards. Civil War sites, hiking, fishing and caverns. AAA 3 diamond rating.

More Inns ...

Lone Willow Inn, 337 Valley St., Abingdon, 24210
Maplewood Farm, Route 7, Box 272, Abingdon, 24210
River Garden B&B, RR 6, Box 650, Abingdon, 24210, 703-676-0335
Summerfield Inn, 101 W. Valley St., Abingdon, 24210, 703-628-5905
Little River Inn, P.O. Box 116, Rt. 50, Aldie, 22001, 703-327-6742
Alexandria Lodgings, P.O. Box 416, Alexandria, 22313, 703-836-5575
Spinning Wheel B&B, The, 509 S. Fairfax St., Alexandria, 22314
Bunree, P.O. Box 53, Amissville, 22002, 703-937-4133
Bluestone Inn, 2101 Crystal Plaza #246, Arlington, 20202
Crystal B&B, 2620 S. Fern St., Arlington, 22202, 703-548-7652
Memory House, 6404 N. Washington Blvd, Arlington, 22205, 703-534-4607
Sky Chalet Country Inn, Route 263 West, Basye, 22810, 703-856-2147
Peaks of Otter Lodge, P.O. Box 489, Bedford, 24523, 703-586-1081
Per Diem B&B, 401 Clay St. SW, Blacksburg, 24060, 703-953-2604
Old Mansion B&B, Box 845, Bowling Green, 22427
Hyde Park Farm, Route 2, Box 38, Burkeville, 23922, 804-645-8431
Country Antiques B&B, Route 2, Box 85, Charles City, 23030, 804-829-5638
Oxbridge Inn, 316—14th St. NW, Charlottesville, 22903
Palmer Country Manor, Route 2, Box 1390, Charlottesville, 22963, 800-253-4306
Woodstock Hall, Route 3, Box 40, Charlottesville, 22903, 804-293-8977
Sims-Mitchell House B&B, P.O. Box 429, Chatham, 24531, 800-967-2867
Main Street House, P.O. Box 126, Chincoteague, 23336, 804-336-6030
Channel Bass Inn, 100 Church St., Chincoteague Island, 23336, 804-336-6148
Victorian Inn, 105 Clark St., Chincoteaque, 23336, 804-336-1161
Year of the Horse Inn, 600 S. Main St., Chincoteuque, 23336, 804-336-3221
Oaks, The, 311 E. Main St., Christiansburg, 24073, 703-381-1500
Buckhorn Inn, E Star Route, Box 139, Churchville, 24421, 703-337-6900
Kinderton Manor, RR 1, Box 19A, Clarksville, 23927, 804-374-4439
Mary's Country Inn, Rt. 2, Box 4, Edinburg, 22824, 703-984-8286
Little's B&B, 105 Goodwyn St., Emporia, 23847, 804-634-2590
Bailiwick Inn, 4023 Chain Bridge Rd., Fairfax, 22030, 703-691-2266
School House, The, P.O. Box 31, Flint Hill, 22627, 703-675-3030
Stone House Hollow, P.O. Box 2090, Flint Hill, 22627, 703-675-3279
Brookfield Inn, P.O. Box 341, Floyd, 24091, 703-763-3363
McGrath House, 225 Princess Anne St., Fredericksburg, 22401, 703-371-4363
Spooner House, The, 1300 Caroline St., Fredericksburg, 22401, 703-371-1267
Doubleday Inn, 104 Doubleday Ave., Gettysburg, 17325, 717-334-9119
Hamilton Garden Inn, 353 W. Colonial Highway, Hamilton, 22068, 703-338-3693
Kingsway B&B, 3581 Singers Glen Rd., Harrisonburg, 22801, 703-867-9696
Irish Gap Inns, Rt. 1, Box 40, Vesuvius, Irish Gap, 24483, 804-922-7701
Irvington House, Box 361, Irvington, 22480, 804-438-6705
King Carter Inn, P.O. Box 425, Irvington, 22480, 804-438-6053
Inn at Levelfields, P.O. Box 216, Lancaster, 22503, 804-435-6887
Laurel Brigade Inn, 20 W. Market St., Leesburg, 22075, 703-777-1010
Norris House Inn, The, 108 Loudoun St. SW, Leesburg, 22075, 703-777-1806
Alexander-Withrow House, 3 W. Washington, Lexington, 24450, 703-463-2044
Fassifern B&B, Route 5, Box 87, Lexington, 24450, 703-463-1013

Isle of Wight Inn, Smithfield, VA

McCampbell Inn, 11 N. Main St., Lexington, 24450, 703-463-2044

Oak Spring Farm, Rte 1, Box 706, Raphine, Lexington/Staunton area, 24472, 703-377-2398

Boxwood Hill, 128 South Court, Luray, 22835, 703-743-9484

Hawksbill Lodge, Luray, 22835, 703-281-0548

Ruffner House Inn, The, Box 620, Route 4, Luray, 22835, 703-743-7855

Langhorne Manor B&B, 313 Washington St., Lynchburg, 24504, 804-846-4667

Lynchburg Mansion B&B, 405 Madison St., Lynchburg, 24504, 804-528-5400

Olive Mill Bed & Breakfast, Route 231, Banco, Madison City, 22711, 703-923-4664

Beaver Creek Plantation, Route 2, Box 9, Martinsville, 24112

Ravenswood Inn, P.O. Box 250, Mathews, 23109, 804-725-7272

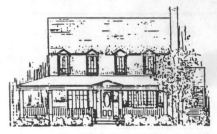

Fox Grape B&B, Williamsburg, VA

Riverfront House B&B, P.O. Box 310, Rt. 14 E., Mathews, 23109, 804-725-9975

Shenandoah Valley Farm, Route 1, Box 142, McGaheysville, 22840, 703-289-5402

Evans Farm Inn, 1696 Chain Bridge Rd. , McLean, 22101, 703-356-8000

Spangler B&B, Route 2, Box 108, Meadows of Dan, 24120, 703-952-2454

Luck House, P.O. Box 919, Middleburg, 22117, 703-687-5387

Middleburg Inn and Suites, Box 984, Middleburg, 22117

Red Fox Inn & Tavern, P.O. Box 385, Middleburg, 22117, 703-687-6301

Fort Lewis Lodge, HCR 3, Box 21A, Millboro, 24460, 703-925-2314

Stuartfield Hearth, Route 1, Box 199, Mitchells, 22729, 703-825-8132

Pumpkin House Inn, Ltd., Route 2, Box 155, Mount Crawford, 22841, 703-434-6963

Acorn Inn, P.O. Box 431, Nellysford, 22958

Meander Inn, The, P.O. Box 443, Nellysford, 22958, 804-361-1121

Sunset Hill, Route 1, Box 375, Nellysford, 22958, 804-361-1101

Upland Manor, Route 1, Box 375, Nellysford, 22958, 804-361-1101

B&B Larchmont, 1112 Buckingham Ave., Norfolk, 23508, 804-489-8449

Historic Country Inns, P.O. Box 11265, Norfolk, 23517, 703-463-2044

Rockledge Mansion 1758, 410 Mill St., Occoquan, 22125, 703-690-3377

Spinning Wheel B&B, The, 31 North St, Onancock, 23417, 804-787-7311

Mayhurst Inn B&B, P.O. Box 707, Orange, 22960, 703-672-5597

Shadows B&B Inn, Route 1, Box 535, Orange, 22960, 703-672-5057

Ashby Inn, Route 1, Box 2/A, Paris, 22130, 703-592-3900

Folly Castle Inn B&B, 323 W. Washington St., Petersburg, 23803, 804-733-6463

High Street Inn, 405 High St., Petersburg, 23803, 804-733-0505

Springdale Country Inn, Route #2, Box 356, Purcellville, 22132

Hanover Hosts B&B, Box 25145, Richmond, 23260

Linden Row, First & Franklin Sts., Richmond, 23219

The Catlin-Abbott House, 2304 East Broad St., Richmond, 23223

Grandin Hall c/o T. Turner, 1007 Dominion Bank Bldg, Roanoke, 24011

Old Manse B&B, The, 530 E Main St., Salem, 24153

Chester B&B, Route 4, Box 57, Scottsville, 24590, 804-286-3960

Holland-Duncan House, Route 5, Box 681, Smith Mountain Lake, 24121, 703-721-8510

Swift Run Gap B&B, Skyline Dr. & Rt. 33 E., Stanardsville, 22973, 804-985-2740

Milton House, P.O. Box 366, Main St., Stanley, 22851, 703-778-3451

Belle Grae Inn, 515 W. Frederick St., Staunton, 24401, 703-886-5151

Hilltop House, 1810 Springhill Rd., Staunton, 24401, 703-886-0042

Thornrose House, 531 Thornrose Ave., Staunton, 24401, 703-885-7026

Surrey House, Surrey, 23883, 804-294-3191

Lambsgate B&B, Route 1, Box 63, Swoope, 24479, 703-337-6929

Prospect Hill Plantation, Route 3, Box 150, Trevilians, 23093, 703-967-0844

Fox Hill Inn, 16 S., P.O. Box 88, Troutdale, 24378, 703-677-3313

1763 Inn, Rt. 1 Box 19 D, Upperville, 22176, 703-592-3848

Gibson Hall Inn, P.O. Box 25, Upperville, 22176, 703-592-3514

Sugar Tree Inn, P.O. Box 548, Hwy 56, Vesuvius, 24483, 703-377-2197

Angie's Guest Cottage, 302 - 24th St., Virginia Beach, 23451, 804-428-4690

Burton House, The, P.O. Box 182, Wachapreague, 23480, 804-787-4560

Meadow Lane Lodge, Route 1, Box 110, Warm Springs, 24484, 703-839-5959

Three Hills Inn, P.O. Box 99, Warm Springs, 24484, 703-839-5381

Inn at Little Washington, Box 300, Middle & Main , Washington, 22747, 703-675-3800

Sycamore Hill House, Route 1, Box 978, Washington, 22747, 703-675-3046

Brass Lantern Lodge, 1782 Jamestown Rd., Williamsburg, 23185, 804-229-9089

Himmel B&B, 706 Richmond Rd., Williamsburg, 23185

Wood's Guest Home, 1208 Stewart Dr., Williamsburg, 23185, 804-229-3376

Candlewick Inn, 127 N. Church St., Woodstock, 22664, 703-459-8008

Country Fare, 402 N. Main St., Woodstock, 22664, 703-459-4828

River'd Inn, Route 1, Box 217A1, Woodstock, 22664, 703-459-5369

Washington

ANACORTES

Albatross B&B
5708 Kingsway W., Fidalgo
Island, 98221
206-293-0677
Barbie & Ken
All year

$$ B&B
4 rooms, 4 pb
Visa, MC, *Rated*, •
C-ltd/S-ltd/P-ltd/H-yes
Spanish, some French

Full breakfast
Restaurant 1 block away
King & queen beds
Library
Washington travel videos

*Cape Cod-style house across from marina. Large deck w/view. Charter boats, fine fishing, crabbing. Close to Washington Park and Sunset Beach. **Reduced rate on sailboat cruise***

A Burrow's Bay B&B
4911 MacBeth Dr., 98221
206-293-4792
Beverly & Winfred Stocker
All year

$$$ B&B
1 rooms, 1 pb
Visa, MC
C-yes/S-no/P-no/H-yes

Continental plus
Afternoon tea/coffee
Sitting room
library

Sweeping view of San Juan Islands—near marina and international and island ferries. Private suite has its own entry, deck, fireplace and bath (sleeps 6).

Channel House
2902 Oakes Ave., 98221
206-293-9382 800-238-4353
Dennis & Pat McIntyre
All year

$$ B&B
6 rooms, 6 pb
Visa, MC, *Rated*, •
C-ltd/S-no/P-no/H-no

Full breakfast
Coffee/tea/cocoa/cookies
Sitting room
library, hot tub
bicycle rentals

Gateway to the San Juan Islands; built in 1902; Victorian-style mansion; all antiques throughout. All rooms view San Juans and Puget Sound. Separate Rose Cottage.

Hasty Pudding House B&B
1312 8th St., 98221
206-293-5773 800-368-5588
Mike & Melinda Hasty
All year

$$ B&B
4 rooms, 3 pb
Most CC, *Rated*, •
C-ltd/S-no/P-no/H-no

Full breakfast
Sitting room, fireplace

Romantic 1913 Craftsman home. Antique decor. Walk to restaurants, park, shops and marina. Luscious breakfast served in our charming dining room.

ANDERSON ISLAND

Inn at Burg's Landing, The
8808 Villa Beach Rd., 98303
206-884-9185
Ken & Annie Burg
All year

$$ B&B
3 rooms, 3 pb
Most CC, *Rated*,
C-yes/S-no/P-no/H-no

Full breakfast
Lunch, dinner w/notice
Outdoor gazebo
golf nearby
deck & hot tub

*Magnificent log home loaded with country charm, on the beach with a spectacular view of Mt. Ranier and Puget Sound. **3rd night 50% off***

ASHFORD

Mountain Meadows Inn B&B
28912 SR 706E, 98304
206-569-2788
Chad Darrah
All year

$$ B&B
3 rooms, 3 pb
Visa, *Rated*
C-ltd/S-no/P-no/H-yes

Full country breakfast
Tea, coffee, s'mores
Library, VCR, pvt. lake
rooms with kitchens
6 mi. to Mt. Rainier Prk

Quiet country elegance; full veranda porch; pondside relaxation atmosphere; campfire by night; reflection all day; hearty mountain brkfast; hiking trails, fishing, campfires.

BAINBRIDGE ISLAND

Bombay House B&B, The
8490 NE Beck Rd., 98110
206-842-3926 800-598-3926
Bunny Cameron & Roger
Kanchuk
All year

$$ B&B
5 rooms, 3 pb
AmEx, •
C-ltd/S-yes/P-no/H-no

Continental plus
Comp. tea, wine
Sitting room
piano
library

*Comfortable country atmosphere near shore. Furnished w/ antiques. Fresh flowers & romantic atmosphere. Near fishing, boating, golf, tennis, park. **2nd night 50%, ltd.***

BELLEVUE

Bellevue B&B
830 - 100th Ave. SE, 98004
206-453-1048
Cy & Carol Garnett
All year

$$ B&B
2 rooms, 2 pb
Visa, MC, *Rated*, •
C-ltd/S-no/P-no/H-yes

Full breakfast
Sitting room
cable TV, telephone
microwave, laundry

*Hilltop, mountain & city views from private unit or single room. Gourmet coffee. Central location near Lake Washington. In Seattle "Best Places." **7th night free***

BELLINGHAM

Schnauzer Crossing B&B
4421 Lakeway Dr., 98226
206-733-0055 206-734-2808
Vermont & Donna McAllister
All year

$$$ B&B
3 rooms, 3 pb
Visa, MC, *Rated*,
C-yes/P-ltd, Some Fr.,
Span., Ger.

Full gourmet breakfast
Sitting room, library
lake view, outdoor spa
new cottage added 1991

A luxury bed & breakfast set amidst tall evergreens overlooking Lake Whatcom. Master suite with jacuzzi. Cottage has fireplace, VCR, private deck, jacuzzi, skylights.

BREMERTON

Willcox House
2390 Tekiu Rd. NW, 98312
206-830-4492
Cecilia & Phillip Hughes
All year

$$$ B&B
5 rooms, 5 pb
Visa, MC, *Rated*, •
C-ltd/S-no/P-no/H-no

Full breakfast
Lunch, dinner
Comp. wine and cheese
library, game room
with pool table

Secluded 1930s estate on Hood Canal; quiet relaxation in an elegant, historic mansion with landscaped grounds, private pier and beach.

CASHMERE

Cashmere Country Inn
5801 Pioneer Dr., 98815
509-782-4212
Patti & Dale Swanson
All year

$$$ B&B
5 rooms, 5 pb
Visa, MC, AmEx, *Rated*,
•
C-ltd/S-no/P-no/H-no

Full breakfast
Snacks
Sitting room, library
bicycles, hot tubs
swimming pool, croquet

Delightful 1907 farmhouse w/five lovely bedrooms, cozy fireplace, queen beds country gardens, sunny dining room, pool, hot tubs, and a small orchard. A delightful getaway.

CATHLAMET

Country Keeper B&B Inn
P.O. Box 35, 98612
61 Main St.
206-795-3030 800-551-1691
Barbara & Tony West
All year

$$ B&B
4 rooms
Visa, MC, *Rated*
C-ltd/S-no/P-no/H-no

Full breakfast
Comp. wine
Tea & coffee
sitting room, library
near golf, tennis & pool

Our stately 1907 home overlooks the scenic Columbia River and Puget Island. Candlelit breakfasts in elegant dining room. Historic area. Marina, ferry, and game reserve nearby.

Gallery B&B, The
Little Cape Horn, 98612
206-425-7395 FAX:425-1351
Carolyn & Eric Feasey
All year

$$ B&B
4 rooms, 2 pb
AmEx, *Rated*,
C-ltd/S-no/P-ask/H-no

Full breakfast-ltd.
Comp. cookies
Sitting room
hot tub, beach
windsurfing, fishing

Very private country elegance. Contemporary home on private beach. Breakfast served overlooking fascinating ship channel of Columbia River. **3rd night 50% off**

COUPEVILLE

Captain Whidbey Inn, The
2072 W. Capt. Whidbey, 98239
206-678-4097 800-366-4097
Captain John C. Stone
All year

$$$ B&B
32 rooms, 20 pb
Most CC., *Rated*, •
C-ltd/S-ltd/P-ltd/H-no
French, German, Spanish

Continental breakfast
All meals, bar
Sitting room
bicycles, library
sailboats & rowboats

Historic log inn, est. 1907. On the shores of Penn Cove. Antique furnished. Fine restaurant and quaint bar. Sailboats, rowboats & bikes.

DEER HARBOR

Palmer's Chart House
P.O. Box 51, 98243
Orcas Island
206-376-4231
Majean & Donald Palmer
All year

$ B&B
2 rooms, 2 pb
•
C-ltd/S-ltd/P-no/H-no
Spanish

Full breakfast
Library, private deck
travel slide shows
flower beds, gardens

Quiet, intimate and informal atmosphere. Your hosts know how to pamper you. Fishing, hiking, golf, biking nearby. Day sails and overnight sails on a private 33-foot yacht.

EASTSOUND

Kangaroo House B&B
P.O. Box 334, 98245
5 N. Beach Rd.
206-376-2175
Jan & Mike Russillo
All year

$$ B&B
5 rooms
Visa, MC
C-yes/S-ltd/P-no/H-no

Full breakfast
Comp. beverages & snacks
Sitting room
fireplace

Small country inn; stone fireplace in sitting room; gourmet breakfast in sunny dining room. Furnished in antiques. Close to town and beach.

Outlook Inn on Orcas Isle
P.O. Box 210, 98245
Main St.
206-376-2200
Mary Beth Lamont
All year

$ EP
29 rooms, 11 pb
Visa, MC, AmEx, *Rated*,
•
C-yes/S-yes/P-no/H-no

Continental breakfast
some private phones

Lovely turn-of-the-century inn completely refurbished, full of memorabilia. Home-style dining. Perfect island hideaway. **50% off room rate winter season**

EASTSOUND

Turtleback Farm Inn
Route 1, Box 650, Crow Valley
Rd, Orcas Isl, 98245
206-376-4914
William & Susan Fletcher
All year

$$ B&B
7 rooms, 7 pb
Visa, MC, *Rated*, •
C-ltd/S-no/P-no/H-yes

Full breakfast
Comp. tea & coffee
Bar, comp. sherry
games, living room
fireplace

Romantic pastoral retreat-outdoor adventures. 80 acres of meadows, forests and ponds. Furnished with fine antiques. Quiet comfort and warm hospitality. On Orcas Island.

FRIDAY HARBOR

Roche Harbor Resort
P.O. Box 4001, 98250
4950 Tarte Mem. Dr.
206-378-2155
Bradford Augustine
April - November

$$ EP
60 rooms, 44 pb
•
C-yes/S-yes/P-no/H-no

Restaurant
Swimming pool
boat rentals
tennis court

107 year old country inn is the centerpiece of a full service resort. Quiet in spring & fall, very busy in summer.

Tucker House B&B
260 "B" St., 98250
206-378-2783 800-742-8210
Skip & Annette Metzger
All year, FAX:378-6437

$$$ B&B
6 rooms, 3 pb
Visa, MC, •
C-yes/S-yes/P-yes/H-yes

Full breakfast
Kitchens & private
Baths available
hot tub
childen welcome

Newly remodeled turn-of-the-century home. Rooms with private baths & entrances. Breakfast in solarium. Walk to ferry, airport, shops & restaurants. **10% off 2+ nights**

GREENBANK

Guest House Cottages
3366 S. Hwy. 525, Whidbey
Island, 98253
206-678-3115
Mary Jane & Don Creger
All year

$$$ B&B
7 rooms, 7 pb
Most CC, *Rated*, •
C-ltd/S-no/P-no/H-ltd

Continental plus
Exercise room, pool, spa
retreat & honeymoon spot
rated 4 diamond by AAA

An unique, romantic experience. We aren't your usual B&B. Very pvt. cottages on 25 ac. wooded & pastoral. Jacuzzi, TV/VCR, full kitchens, feather beds, pool, hot tub.

KIRKLAND

Shumway Mansi
11410 - 99th Place NE, 98033
206-823-2303
Harris & Blakemore Families
All year

$$ B&B
8 rooms, 8 pb
Visa, MC, *Rated*, •
C-ltd/S-no/P-no/H-ltd

Full breakfast buffet
Evening snack, drinks
Sitting room, piano
athletic club privileges
weddings, receptions

Four-story mansion circa 1910. Beautiful views of lake and bay. Delicious breakfasts and afternoon treats. Walk to beach, shops, galleries. AAA-3 stars.

LA CONNER—MOUNT VERNON

White Swan Guest House
1388 Moore Rd., 98273
206-445-6805
Peter Goldfarb
All year

$$$ B&B
3 rooms
Rated, •
C-ltd/S-no/P-no/H-no

Continental plus-country
Cookies
Sitting room
library, outdoor patio
private garden cottage

A "storybook" Victorian farmhouse six miles from the historic waterfront village of La Conner. 1 hour north of Seattle. English gardens, farmland. A perfect romantic getaway.

LACONNER

Katy's Inn
P.O. Box 869, 503 S. Third St., 98257
206-466-3366
Anne Uruburu/Lynnell Diamond
All year

$$ B&B
4 rooms
Visa, MC, *Rated*, •
C-ltd/S-ltd/P-no/H-no

Full breakfast
Aft. tea
Sitting room
library
rocking chairs on porch

Charming 1876 Victorian w/lovely antiques. Down comforters, extensive library, delicious breakfast. Rooms open onto veranda overlooking historic village.

LANGLEY

Country Cottage of Langley
215 6th St., 98260
206-221-8709
Bob & Mary DeCelles
All year

$$$ B&B
4 rooms, 4 pb
Visa, MC
C-ltd/S-no/P-no/H-no

Continental plus in rm.
Scenic dining room
view deck, gazebo

Restored 20s farmhouse and separate guest cottage on 2 acres of gardens. Views of village, mountains and sea. Breakfast, private baths.

Eagles Nest Inn
3236 E. Saratoga Rd., 98260
206-321-5331
Nancy & Dale Bowman
All year

$$$ B&B
4 rooms, 4 pb
Visa, MC, Disc.,*Rated*
S-no

Full breakfast
Snacks
Chocolate chip cookies
sitting room, TV/VCR
library, hot tub

Casual elegance in country setting on Whidbey Island two miles from seaside village of Langley. Breathtaking view of Saratoga Passage. AAA rates three diamonds.

Log Castle
3273 E. Saratoga Rd., 98260
206-221-5483
Senator Jack & Norma Metcalf
All year

$$$ B&B
4 rooms, 4 pb
Visa, MC, •
C-ltd/S-no/P-no/H-no

Full breakfast
Cider, homemade cookies
Sitting room
guest canoe & rowboat

Unique waterfront log lodge on Whidbey Island. Turret bedrooms, secluded beach, fantastic view of mountains, 50 miles north of Seattle.

LEAVENWORTH

Haus Rohrbach Pension
12882 Ranger Rd., 98826
509-548-7024
Robert & Kathryn Harrild
All year

$$ B&B
12 rooms, 8 pb
Most CC, *Rated*, •
C-yes/S-no/P-no/H-no

Full breakfast
Desserts offered
Sitting room
swimming pool
hot tub

One-of-a-kind, European-style country inn, unequaled in the Pacific Northwest. Alpine-setting pool and hot tub. Year-round outdoor activities. Suites w/fireplace and whirlpool

LOPEZ ISLAND

Edenwild Inn
P.O. Box 271, 98261
Lopez S. Rd. & Eads Lane
206-468-3238
Sue Aran
All year

$$$ B&B
8 rooms, 8 pb
Visa, MC, *Rated*, •
C-yes/S-no/P-no/H-yes

Full breakfast, Ap-Sept
Cont. bkfast Nov-Mar
Comp. wine, Aft. tea
bicycles, volleyball
croquet, kayaking

Elegant country inn located in the heart of Lopez village on Lopez island in the San Juans. Gourmet breakfasts, English gardens, summer patio, beautiful bay sunsets, boating.

LOPEZ ISLAND

Inn at Swifts Bay, The
Route 2, Box 3402, 98261
206-468-3636 FAX:468-3637
R. Hermann & C. Brandmeir
All year

$$$ B&B
5 rooms, 3 pb
Visa, MC, *Rated*, •
C-ltd/Portuguese, Germ.,
Spa.

Full breakfast
Comp. sherry, min. water
Sitting room
video library, hot tub
bicycle rentals

English country comfort in the San Juan Islands. Private separate beach. Delightful breakfasts. Bald eagles, Orca whales. Pastoral and restful.

MacKaye Harbor Inn
Route 1, Box 1940, 98261
206-468-2253
Mike & Robin Bergstrom
All year

$$ B&B
5 rooms, 1 pb
Most CC, *Rated*, •
C-ltd/S-no/P-no/H-no

Full breakfast
Afternoon aperitif
Bicycles & kayaks

Romantic country hideaway on a protected sandy beach. Beautiful sunset views. Personal service, antiques, nostalgia and tranquility. Kayak instruction available.

LUMMI ISLAND

Willows Inn, The
2579 West Shore Dr., 98262
206-758-2620
Victoria & Gary Flynn
Mid Feb - Mid Nov

$$$ B&B
7 rooms, 5 pb
Visa, MC
C-ltd/S-no/P-no/H-ltd

Full breakfast
Afternoon tea, dinner
Sitting room, billiards
restaurant, bar service
honeymoon cottage

Third generation innkeeper offering family hospitality and fine dining at this historic west shore landmark. A most romantic island retreat. Fine dining w/wine & beer.

MONTESANO

Sylvan Haus B&B
P.O. Box 416, 98563
417 Wilder Hill Ln.
206-249-3453
Jo Anne & Mike Murphy
Exc. Nov—Apr (hike in)

$$ B&B
4 rooms, 3 pb
Rated
C-ltd/S-no/P-no

Full gourmet breakfast
Country kitchen, snacks
Restaurant nearby
hot tub, decks, boating
swimming, hiking

A gracious family home surrounded by towering evergreens; secluded high hill overlooking valley. Dining room; 5 decks; hot tub; gourmet breakfast. **3rd night 50% off, Ltd**

OLYMPIA

Harbinger Inn
1136 East Bay Dr., 98506
206-754-0389
Marisa & Terrell Williams
All year

$$ B&B
4 rooms, 1 pb
Visa, MC, AmEx, *Rated*,
C-ltd/S-no/P-no/H-no

Continental plus
Comp. wine
Sitting room
library
queenbed suite available

Restored turn-of-the-century home w/beautiful water view; period furnishings. Conveniently located for boating, bicycling, business and entertainment.

Puget View Guesthouse
7924 - 61st Ave. NE, 98516
206-459-1676
Dick & Barbara Yunker
All year

$$$ B&B
2 rooms, 1 pb
Visa, MC, •
C-yes/S-yes/P-ask/H-no

Continental plus
Private dining area/deck
books, games, canoe
100-acre park next door

Charming waterfront guest cottage suite next to host's log home. Breakfast to your cottage. Peaceful. Picturesque. A "NW Best Places" since 1984. Puget Sound 5 min. off I-5.

PORT ANGELES

Domaine Madeleine	$$$ B&B	Full breakfast
146 Wildflower Ln., 98362	2 rooms, 2 pb	Aft. tea, snacks
206-457-4174	Visa, MC, *Rated*,	Sitting room, library
Madeleine & John Chambers	C-ltd/S-no/P-no/H-no	jacuzzi, lawn games
All year	Fr., Span., Farsi, Ger.	

Serene waterfront estate w/panoramic views; Monet garden replica; unique Euorpean/ Asian antiques; fireplaces; jacuzzi, whales and eagles. AAA 3 diamonds.

PORT TOWNSEND

Ann Starrett Mansion B&B	$$ B&B	Full breakfast
744 Clay St., 98368	10 rooms, 10 pb	Comp.sherry, tea
206-385-3205 800-321-0644	Visa, MC, *Rated*, •	Sitting room
Edel & Bob Sokol	C-ltd/S-yes/P-no/H-ltd	player/baby grand pianos
All year		jacuzzi, hot tub

Port Townsend's only full-service Victorian inn. Internationally renowned for its classic Victorian architecture, frescoed ceilings & free hung three-tiered spiral staircase.

Bishop Victorian Suites	$$$ B&B	Continental breakfast
714 Washington St., 98368	12 rooms, 12 pb	Coffee, tea
206-385-6122 800-824-4738	Visa, MC, AmEx, *Rated*,	Sitting room
Lloyd W. & Marlene M. Cahoon	C-yes/S-yes/P-yes/H-no	parking lot
All year		

Downtown, Victorian-era hotel; beautifully restored. Gracious suites. Mountain and water views. Walk to Port Townsend, Washington's historic Victorian seaport.

Heritage House Inn	$$ B&B	Full breakfast
305 Pierce St., 98368	6 rooms, 3 pb	Coffee/tea/fresh cookies
206-385-6800	Most CC, *Rated*, •	Victorian parlor
P & J Broughton, B & C Ellis	C-ltd/S-no/P-no/H-ltd	bicycles
All year		

Unique combination of Victorian setting, unparalleled view of the bay, classic Italianate inn, quaint charm, warm traditional attention to comfort.

Holly Hill House	$$ B&B	Full breakfast
611 Polk, 98368	5 rooms, 5 pb	Library, sitting room
206-385-5619 800-435-1454	Visa, MC, *Rated*,	1 suite w/king bed
Lynne Sterling	C-ltd/S-no/P-no/H-no	queen-size beds
All year		

Beautifully maintained 1872 Victorian home, in historic uptown. Walking distance to downtown. Bountiful breakfast. Enjoy our Victorian waterfront community.

James House	$$ B&B	Full breakfast
1238 Washington St., 98368	12 rooms, 4 pb	Comp. tea, sherry
206-385-1238	Visa, MC, *Rated*,	Sitting parlors
Carol McGough, Anne Tiernan	C-ltd/S-no/P-no/H-ltd	player piano, fireplaces
All year		porch with swing, garden

1889 Queen Anne Victorian mansion featuring unsurpassed water and mountain views, period antiques. First B&B in the Northwest, still the finest.

PORT TOWNSEND ─────────────────────────────────────

Lizzie's Victorian B&B
731 Pierce St., 98368
206-385-4168
Bill & Patti Wickline
All year

$$ B&B
7 rooms, 4 pb
Visa, MC, *Rated*
C-ltd

Full breakfast
Coffee, tea
Sitting room
tennis courts nearby

Victorian comfort and hospitality amid elegance and class. Close to town, beach and mountains.

Old Consulate Inn/Hastings
313 Walker, at Washington St.,
98368
206-385-6753
The Jacksons, Rob & Joanna
All year

$$$ B&B
8 rooms, 8 pb
Visa, MC, *Rated*, •
C-ltd/S-no/P-no/H-no

Full 7 course breakfast
Refreshments, aftn. tea
Comp. port & sherry
parlors, grand piano
library, billiard room

Victorian decor that creates a nostalgia for great-grandmother's house! Cluttered elegance, romantic bedrooms—quiet and peaceful. Formal dining room.

Quimper Inn
1306 Franklin St., 98368
206-385-1060
Ron & Sue Ramage
All year

$$ B&B
5 rooms, 3 pb
Visa, MC, *Rated*,
C-ltd/S-no/P-no

Full breakfast
Library, sitting room
bicycles
access to health club

1888 historic 3-story home. Large, cheerful rooms with views of Town, the bay and the Olympic Mtns. 2-room suite, 2nd floor balcony.

Quimper Inn, Port Townsend, WA

PORT TOWNSEND

Water Street Hotel
Quincy Street Dock, 98368
206-385-5467 800-735-9810
Chris Sudlow & Dawn Pfeiffer
All year

$$ B&B
15 rooms, 10 pb
Visa, MC, AmEx, *Rated*,
C-yes/S-yes/P-yes/H-no

Continental breakfast
Restaurant in building
pub in bldg.
cable TV

Historic Trust Bldg., renovated 1990. Waterview rooms and suites. In Historic District of secluded waterfront community. Panoramic view of Puget Sound.

SEATTLE

Beech Tree Manor
1405 Queen Anne Ave. N.,
98109
206-281-7037
Virginia Lucero
All year

$ B&B
6 rooms, 3 pb
Visa, MC, *Rated*, •
C-ltd/S-no/P-yes/H-no

Full breakfast
Sitting room, library
antique linen shop
porch with wicker chairs

1904 mansion, near City Center, English decor; scrumptious breakfasts; original art in all rooms; luxuriously comfortable.

Broadway Guest House
959 Broadway East, 98102
206-329-1864
Daryl King & Tim Stiles
All year

$$$ B&B
5 rooms, 5 pb
AmEx, MC, Visa, •
C-yes

Continental plus
Sitting room
library
conference facilities

One of Capitol Hill's gracious mansions circa 1909. Luxury antique-filled rooms, hand-carved woodwork. Carriage House also available.

Capitol Hill Inn
1713 Belmont Ave., 98122
206-323-1955
Katie & Joanne Godmintz
All year

$$ B&B
5 rooms, 3 pb
AmEx, *Rated*, •
C-ltd/S-no/P-no/H-no

Full breakfast
Espresso bar
Sitting room
European antiques

Victorian ambiance within walking distance of Convention Center, downtown, Broadway shops & restaurants. All rooms furnished in European antiques, brass beds & down comforters

Challenger Tugboat
1001 Fairview Ave. N., 98109
206-340-1201 FAX:621-9208
Jerry Brown
All year

$$$ B&B
7 rooms, 4 pb
C-yes/S-yes/P-no/H-yes

Full breakfast
Soft drinks
Sitting room, library
bicycles, fireplace
small boats

On board a fully functional, exceptionally clean, restored tugboat. Near downtown Seattle. Closed circuit TV. Carpeted throughout. Nautical antiques.

Chambered Nautilus B&B Inn
5005 22nd Ave. NE, 98105
206-522-2536
Bunny & Bill Hagemeyer
All year

$$ B&B
6 rooms, 4 pb
Most CC, *Rated*, •
C-ltd/S-ltd/P-no/H-no
German

Full gourmet breakfast
Tea & homemade lollypops
Sitting room with phone
desks in rooms
Fireplaces, grand piano

"Seattle's Finest." Gracious historic in-city retreat near downtown & Univ. of Washington. Nat'l Award-winning family-style brkfasts. **3 nights for price of 2 in Jan & Feb.**

SEATTLE ──────────────────────────────────

Chelsea Station B&B Inn
4915 Linden Ave. N, 98103
206-547-6077
Dick & MaryLou Jones
All year

$$ B&B
6 rooms, 6 pb
Most CC, *Rated*, •
C-ltd/S-no/P-no/H-no

Full breakfast
Eve. snack, comp. tea
sitting room
pump organ

Old World charm, tranquil country setting amidst the city's activity. Each room is a very private answer to a quiet getaway. Banana French toast. **2nd night 50% off, ltd**

Mildred's B&B Inn
1202 15th Ave. E, 98112
206-325-6072
Mildred Sarver
All year

$$$ B&B
3 rooms, 3 pb
Rated, •
C-yes/S-ltd/P-no/H-no

Full breakfast
Afternoon tea or coffee
Sitting room
library, veranda
grand piano

1890 Victorian. Wraparound veranda, lace curtains, red carpets, grand piano, fireplace. City location near bus, electric trolley, park, art museum, flower conservatory.

Pensione Nichols
1923 First Ave., 98101
206-441-7125
All year

$ B&B
12 rooms, 3 pb
Visa, MC, Disc, AmEx,
C-yes/P-ltd/H-no

Continental plus
Sitting room

Seattle's only B&B located in the Pike Place Market. European-styled with a spectacular view.

Prince of Wales B&B
133 13th Ave. E., 98102
206-325-9692 800-327-9692
Carol Norton & Chuck Morgan
All year

$$ B&B
4 rooms, 2 pb
Visa, MC, *Rated*, •
C-ltd/S-no/P-no/H-no

Full breakfast
Morning coffee to room
Sitting room
fireplaces, garden
attic suite w/prvt. deck

Downtown 1.5 miles away; on bus line; walk to convention center; turn-of-the-century ambiance; panoramic views of city skyline, sound and mtns. **10% off 7+ nights**

Salisbury House
750 16th Ave. E., 98112
206-328-8682
Cathryn & Mary Wiese
All year

$$ B&B
4 rooms, 4 pb
Most CC, *Rated*,
C-ltd/S-no/P-no/H-no

Full breakfast
Comp. tea, lemonade
Sitting room, library
porch, down comforters
private baths

Elegant Capitol Hill home. Ideal location for business or pleasure. Take advantage of Seattle's excellent transit system. Minutes to downtown, Univ. of WA, Seattle Univ.

Seattle Guest Cottage
2442 NW Market St. #300, 98107
206-783-2169 206-784-0539
Inge Pokrandt
All year

$$ B&B
3 rooms, 2 pb
Visa, MC, AmEx, *Rated*,
•
C-yes/S-no/P-no/H-yes
German

Breafast food in fridge
Comp. tea, wine
Sitting rm, maid service
color cable TV, phone
kitchen, prvt. entrance

Private suite & cottage near downtown, parks, University. Relaxed atmosphere. Tourist books/materials—hostess knowledgeable about area. **7th night 50% off/free surprises**

SEATTLE

Shafer-Baillie Mansion B&B
907 14th Ave. E., 98112
206-322-4654 FAX:329-4628
Erv Olssen
All year

$$ B&B
13 rooms, 8 pb
AmEx, MC, Visa, •
C-yes/S-no/P-no/H-no

Continental breakfast
Fax, phones, sitting rm.
tennis & pool nearby
downtown: 5 min. library

15,000-square-foot brick mansion on Seattle's "Millionaire's Row." Gourmet breakfast; 12 suites/rooms. Television, refrigerator and antiques in all rooms. **3rd night 33% off.**

Villa Heidelberg B&B
4845 45th Ave., S.W., 98116
206-938-3658
Barb & John Thompson
All year

$$ B&B
4 rooms, 2 pb
Visa, MC, AmEx, *Rated*,
C-ltd/S-ltd/P-no/H-no

Full breakfast
Sitting room

1909 Craftsman country home just minutes from the airport and downtown Seattle. Two blocks to shops, bus and restaurants

Williams House B&B
1505 - 4th Ave. N., 98109
206-285-0810
The Williams Family
All year

$$ B&B
5 rooms, 1 pb
Most CC, *Rated*,
C-yes/S-ltd/P-no/H-no

Continental plus
Coffee, tea, cookies
Sitting room
piano

Views of Seattle, Puget Sound, mountains. One of Seattle's oldest neighborhoods. Very close to Seattle activities, parks, lakes. **October-April 10% off 4+ days stay**

SEQUIM

Greywolf Inn
395 Keeler Rd., 98382
206-683-5889 206-683-1487
Peggy Bill Melang
All year

$$ B&B
5 rooms, 5 pb
Visa, MC, AmEx, *Rated*,
•
C-ltd/S-ltd/P-no

Full breakfast, 4-course
Fireplace, decks
Japanese bathhouse & spa
enclosed courtyard

Secluded country estate nestled in a crescent of evergreens. Sweeping views of Dungeness Valley from French country dining room. Your springboard to adventure. **3rd night 50%**

Margie's Inn on the Bay
120 Forrest Rd., 98382
206-683-7011 800-730-7011
Margie Vorhies
March—October

$$ B&B
6 rooms, 6 pb
Visa, MC, *Rated*, •
C-ltd/S-no/P-no/H-yes

Full breakfast
Comp. sherry
Sitting room
tennis courts
VCR, TV, boats

Country hideaway: large modern ranch-style home on the water. Full breakfast. Golf, fish, hike. Close to John Wayne marina. **10% discount Oct.15/93-March 31/94**

SOUTH CLE ELUM

Moore House Country Inn
P.O. Box 629, 98943
526 Marie St.
509-674-5939 800-22-TWAIN
Eric & Cindy Sherwood
All year

$ B&B
12 rooms, 4 pb
Visa, MC, AmEx, *Rated*,
•
C-yes/S-ltd/P-no/H-no

Full breakfast
Lunch, dinner, hot tubs
Sitting room, bicycles
caboose unit with bath
winter sleigh rides

Old railroad hotel adjacent to Iron Horse State Park. Mountain location makes four seasons of activities possible from our doorstep. Group dinners, receptions, weddings.

SPOKANE

Fotheringham House B&B
W. 2128 Second Ave., 99204
509-838-4363
Howard & Phyllis Ball
All year

$$ B&B
8 rooms, 5 pb
AmEx, Visa, MC, •
C-yes/S-no/P-no/H-no

Continental plus
Comp. tea, cookies
Living room, library
A/C in rooms
near tennis & park

Victorian home located in historic Spokane District. Antique furnishings, queen beds, park across street. Next to restaurant in Victorian mansion.

Marianna Stoltz House
E. 427 Indiana, 99207
509-483-4316
Jim & Phyllis Maguire
All year

$$ B&B
4 rooms, 2 pb
Visa, MC, AmEx, Disc., •
C-ltd/S-no/P-no/H-no

Full breakfast
Veranda

Antique quilts, lace curtains, oriental rugs. Delicious breakfasts. Friendly hosts await you in our centrally located 1908 historic B&B.

SUNNYSIDE

Sunnyside Inn B&B
800 Edison Ave., 98944
800-221-4195
Karen & Donavon Vlieger
All year

$ B&B
8 rooms, 8 pb
Visa, MC, AmEx, •
C-yes/S-no/P-no/H-no

Full breakfast
Snacks, hot tubs
Sitting room
near tennis, golf, and
wineries

Eight luxurious rooms, all with private baths, 7 with private jacuzzi tubs. In the heart of Washington wine country.

VASHON ISLAND

Swallow's Nest Cottages
6030 SW 248th St., Maury
Island, 98070
206-463-2646 800-269-6378
Bob Keller, Robin Hughes
All year

$$ EP
5 rooms, 3 pb
Most CC, *Rated*, •
C-yes/S-no/P-ltd/H-ltd

Breakfast by arrangement
Coffee, tea, cocoa
Kitchen in cottages
some hot tubs/fireplaces
golf nearby

Get away to comfortable country cottages on the bluffs overlooking Puget Sound and Mt. Rainier. Optional breakfast brought you. Swallows visit every summer. **Seasonal specials**

WHITE SALMON

Inn of the White Salmon
P.O. Box 1549, 98672
172 W. Jewett
509-493-2335
Janet & Roger Holen
All year

$$$ B&B
16 rooms, 16 pb
Most CC, *Rated*, •
C-yes/S-ltd/P-ask

Full breakfast
Restaurant nearby
Sitting room, hot tub
phone, TV, A/C in rooms
Parlor w/fireplace

Columbia River Gorge, "the quiet side." Built as an hotel in 1937. Furnished with antiques. World famous breakfast. Windsurfing, hiking, skiing.

Orchard Hill Inn
Route 2, Box 130, 199 Oak
Ridge Rd., 98672
509-493-3024
James & Pamela Tindall
All year

$$ B&B
5 rooms
Visa, MC, *Rated*, •
C-yes/S-yes/P-no/H-no
German

Continental plus
Beer, garden
Sitting room, piano
library, whirlpool bath
6-hole p&c golf course

A secluded homestead on the White Salmon River adjoining the notorious Columbia Gorge. Attractive guest rooms. Bunkhouse. Skiing, kayaking, hiking, etc.

More Inns . . .

River Valley B&B, Box 158, Acme, 98220, 206-595-2686
Dutch Treat House, 1220 31st St., Anacortes, 98221, 206-293-8154
Lowman House B&B, 701 "K" Ave., Anacortes, 98221, 206-293-0590
Old Brook Inn, 530 Old Brook Ln., Anacortes, 98221, 206-293-4768
Sunset Beach B&B, 100 Sunset Beach, Anacortes, 98211
White Gull, 420 Commercial, Anacortes, 98221, 206-293-7011
Alexander's Country Inn, Hwy. 706, Ashford, 98304, 206-569-2300
Ashford Mansion, Box G, Ashford, 98304, 206-569-2739
Growly B&B, 37311 SR 706, Ashford, 98304, 206-569-2339
Jasmer's Guest House, 30005 SR 706 E, Ashford, 98304, 206-569-2682
Beach Cottage, 5831 Ward Ave., NE, Bainbridge Island, 98110, 206-842-6081
Olympic View B&B, 15415 Harvey Rd. NE, Bainbridge Island, 98110, 206-842-4671
North Bay Inn B&B, East 2520 Hwy 302, Belfair, 98528, 206-275-5378
Lions B&B, 803 - 92nd Ave. N.E., Bellevue, 98004, 206-455-1018
Petersen B&B, 10228 S.E. 8th St., Bellevue, 98004, 206-454-9334
Anderson Creek Lodge, 5602 Mission Rd., Bellingham, 98226, 206-966-2126
Castle, The, 1103 - 15th, Bellingham, 98225, 206-676-0974
Circle F, 2399 Mt. Baker Hwy, Bellingham, 98226, 206-733-2509
De Cann House B&B, 2610 Eldridge Ave, Bellingham, 98225, 206-734-9172
North Garden Inn, 1014 N. Garden, Bellingham, 98225, 206-671-7828
Secret Garden, 1807 Lakeway Dr., Bellingham, 98226, 206-671-7850
Loganita, Villa By The Sea, 2825 W. Shore Dr., Bellingham—Lummi Island, 98262, 206-758-2651
Bellingham's DeCann House, 2610 Eldridge Ave., Billingham, 98225
Grand Old House, P.O. Box 667, Hwy. 14, Bingen, 98605, 509-493-2838
Alice Bay B&B, 982 Scott Rd., Bow, 98232
Idyl Inn on the River, 4548 Tolt River Rd., Carnation, 98014, 206-333-4262
Carson Hot Springs Hotel, P.O. Box 370, Carson, 98610, 509-427-8292
Cathlamet Hotel, 67-69 Main St, Cathlamet, 98612, 800-446-0454
Brick House Inn, 304 Wapato Ave., Chelan, 98816
Em's B&B Inn, P.O. Box 206, Chelan, 98816, 509-682-4149
Lake Chelan River House, Route 1, Box 614, Chelan, 98816, 509-682-5122
Mary Kay's Whaley Mansion, Route 1, Box 693, Chelan, 98816, 509-682-5735
North Cascades Lodge, P.O. Box W, Chelan, 98816, 509-682-4711
Summer House, 2603 Center Rd., Chimacum, 98325, 206-732-4017
Ramblin' Rose, 102 W. Railroad, Cle Elum, 98922, 509-674-5224
Beach House, 7338 S. Maxwelton Rd., Clinton, 98236, 206-321-4335
Home by the Sea, 2388 E Sunlight Beach R, Clinton, 98236, 206-221-2964
Tulin House, The, S. 812 Main St., Colfax, 99111, 509-397-3312
Lakeside Manor B&B, 2425 Pend Oreille Lakes, Colville, 99114, 509-684-8741
Cascade Mountain Inn, 3840 Pioneer Ln., Concrete, 98237, 206-826-4333
Colonel Crockett Farm Inn, 1012 S. Fort Casey Rd., Coupeville, 98239, 206-678-3711
Fort Casey Inn, 1124 S. Engle Rd., Coupeville, 98239, 206-678-8792
Inn at Penn Cove, P.O. Box 85, Coupeville, 98239, 206-678-6990
Victorian House, 602 N. Main St., Coupeville, 98239, 206-678-5305
Syndicate Hill B&B, 403 S. 6th St., Dayton, 99328, 509-382-2688
Blue Heron, Route 1, Box 64, Eastsound, 98245, 206-376-2954
Rosario Resort Hotel, Eastsound, 98245, 206-376-2222
Old Mill House B&B, P.O. Box 543, Eatonville, 98328, 206-832-6506
Harrison House, 210 Sunset Ave., Edmonds, 98020, 206-776-4748
Heather House, 1011 "B" Ave., Edmonds, 98020, 206-778-7233
Hudgrens Haven, 9313 - 190th, SW, Edmonds, 98020, 206-776-2202
Murphy's Country B&B, Route 1, Box 400, Ellensburg, 98926, 509-925-7986
Anderson House B&B, P.O. Box 1547, Ferndale, 98248, 206-384-3450
Hill Top B&B, P.O. Box 231, Ferndale, 98248, 206-384-3619
Manitou Lodge, P.O. Box 600, Forks, 98331, 206-374-6295
Miller Tree Inn, P.O. Box 953, Forks, 98331, 206-374-6806
River Inn, Route 3, Box 3858 D, Forks, 98331, 206-374-6526
Cliff House, 5440 Windmill Rd., Freeland, 98249, 206-321-1566
Blair House B&B, 345 Blair Ave., Friday Harbor, 98250, 206-378-5907
Cathy Robinson, P.O. Box 1604, Friday Harbor, 98250, 206-378-3830
Collins House, 225 "A" St., Friday Harbor, 98250, 206-378-5834
Duffy House, 760 Pear Point Rd., Friday Harbor, 98250, 206-378-5604
Duffy House, 760 Pear Point Rd., Friday Harbor, 98250, 206-378-5604
Friday's, P.O. Box 2023, Friday Harbor, 98250, 206-378-5848
Hillside House, 365 Carter Ave., Friday Harbor, 98250, 206-378-4730
Meadows, The, 1980 Cattle Point Rd., Friday Harbor, 98250, 206-378-4004
Moon & Sixpence, 3021 Beaverton Valley, Friday Harbor, 98250, 206-378-4138
Olympic Lights, 4531A Cattle Point Rd., Friday Harbor, 98250, 206-378-3186
San Juan Inn, P.O. Box 776, Friday Harbor, 98250, 206-378-2070
Westwinds Bed & Breakfast, 4909 N. Hannah Hghlnds, Friday Harbor, 98250, 206-378-5283
R.C. McCroskey House, Box 95, Garfield, 99130, 509-635-1459
American Hearth B&B, 7506 Soundview Dr., Gig Harbor, 98335, 206-851-2196
Olde Glencove Hotel, 9418 Glencove Rd., Gig Harbor, 98335, 206-884-2835
Parsonage Bed & Breakfast, 4107 Burnham Dr., Gig Harbor, 98335
Flying L Ranch Inn, 25 Flying L Ln., Glenwood, 98619, 509-364-3488
Three Creeks Lodge, 2120 Hwy 97 Satus Pass, Goldendale, 98620, 509-773-4026
Smith House B&B, 307 Maple St., Hamilton, 98255, 206-826-4214
Inn at Ilwaco, 120 Williams St. N.E, Ilwaco, 98624, 206-642-8686

Bush House, P.O. Box 58, Index, 98256, 206-793-2312
Wildflower B&B Inn, 25237 SE Issaquah Rd., Issaquah, 98027, 206-392-1196
Kalaloch Lodge, HC 80, Box 1100, Kalaloch, 98331, 206-962-2271
Heron in La Conner, Box 716, 117 Maple St., La Conner, 98257, 206-466-4626
Hotel Planter, 715 1st Ave. S., La Conner, 98257
La Conner Country Inn, P.O. Box 573, La Conner, 98257, 206-466-3101
Rainbow Inn B&B, 1075 Chilberg, Box 1600, La Conner, 98257, 206-466-4578
Raymond House, 604 S 2nd, La Conner, 98257
Downey House B&B, The, 1880 Chilberg Rd., LaConner, 98257, 206-466-3207
Whaley Mansion, 415 Third St., Lake Cheelan, 98816, 509-682-5735
Blue House Inn & B&B, 513 Anthes, Langley, 98260, 206-221-8392
Garden Path Inn, The, 111 First St., Box 575, Langley, 98260, 206-321-5121
Inn at Langley, P.O. Box 835, Langley, 98260, 206-221-3033
Lone Lake Cottage & Bkfst., 5206 S. Bayview Rd., Langley, 98260, 206-321-5325
Orchard, 619 3rd St., Langley, 98260, 206-221-7880
Whidbey Inn, P.O. Box 156, Langley, 98260, 206-221-7115
Bavarian Meadows B&B, 11097 Eagle Creek Rd., Leavenworth, 98826, 509-548-4449
Brown's Farm B&B, 11150 Hwy 200, Leavenworth, 98826, 509-548-7863
Cougar Inn, 23379 Hwy. 207, Leavenworth, 98826, 509-763-3354
Edel Haus Pension, 320 Ninth St., Leavenworth, 98826, 509-548-4412
Heaven Can Wait Lodge, 12385 Shugart Flats Rd., Leavenworth, 98826, 206-881-5350
Hotel Europa, 833 Front St., Leavenworth, 98826, 509-548-5221
Old Blewett Pass B&B, 3470 Highway 97, Leavenworth, 98826, 509-548-4475
Old Brick Silo B&B, 9028 E. Leavenworth Rd., Leavenworth, 98826, 509-548-4772
Phippen's B&B, 10285 Ski Hill Dr., Leavenworth, 98826, 800-666-9806
Pine River Ranch, 19668 Highway 207, Leavenworth, 98826, 509-763-3959
River Inn B&B, 8751 Icicle Rd., Leavenworth, 98826, 509-548-1425
Run of the River B&B, 9308 E. Leavenworth Rd., Leavenworth, 98826, 509-548-7171
National Park Inn, Longmire, 98398, 206-569-2565
Betty's Place, P.O. Box 86, Lopez, 98261, 206-468-2470
Otter's Nest, 2724 N. Nugent Rd., Lummi Island, 98262, 206-758-2667
Shorebird House, 2654 N. Nugent Rd, Lummi Island, 98262, 206-758-2177
West Shore Farm B&B, 2781 W. Shore Dr., Lummi Island, 98262, 206-758-2600
Century House B&B, 401 S. B.C. Ave., Lynden, 98264, 206-354-2439
Le Cocq House, 719 W. Edson, Lynden, 98264, 206-354-3032
Maple Valley B&B, 20020 S.E. 228th, Maple Valley, 98038, 206-432-1409
Mazawa Country Inn, Mazawa, 98833, 509-996-2681
Mole House Bed & Breakfast, 3308 W. Mercer Way, Mercer Island, 98040
Abel House B&B Inn, The, 117 Fleet St., So., Montesano, 98563, 206-249-6002
St. Helens Manorhouse, 7476 Hwy 12, Morton, 98356, 206-498-5243
Desert Rose, P.O. Box 166, Moxee City, 98936, 509-542-2237
Ecologic Place, 10 Beach Dr., Nordland, 98358, 206-385-3077
Apple Tree Inn, 43317 SE N. Bend Way, North Bend, 98045, 206-888-3572
Hillwood Gardens B&B, 41812 S. E. 142nd St., North Bend, 98045, 206-888-0799
Inn New England, 400 N. Bend, Box 1349, North Bend, 98045, 206-888-3879
Elfreeda's Place B&B, 5140 Anglers Haven Dr, Oak Harbor, 98277
Hanford Castle, The, Box 23, Oakesdale, 99158, 509-285-4120
Oceanfront Lodge, N. Ocean Shores Blvd., Ocean Shores, 98569, 206-289-3036
Olalla Orchard B&B, 12530 Orchard Ave. S.E., Olalla, 98359, 206-857-5915
Unicorn's Rest, 316 E. 10th St., Olympia, 98501, 206-754-9613
Orcas Hotel, P.O. Box 155, Orcas, 98280, 206-376-4300
Woodsong B&B, P.O. Box 32, Orcas, 98280, 206-376-2340
Packwood Hotel, Route 256, Packwood, 98361, 206-494-5431
Amy's Manor B&B, P.O. Box 411, Pateros, 98846, 509-923-2334
French House B&B, 206 W. Warren, Pateros, 98846, 509-923-2626
Mount Valley Vista B&B, Box 476, Peshastin, 98847, 509-548-5301
Bennett House B&B, 325 E. 6th, Port Angeles, 98362, 206-457-0870
Glen Mar by the Sea, 318 N. Eunice, Port Angeles, 98362, 206-457-6110
Kennedy's Bed & Breakfast, 322 E. 5th, Port Angeles, 98362, 206-457-3628
Lake Crescent Lodge, Star Route 1, Port Angeles, 98362, 206-928-3211
Log Cabin Resort, 6540 E. Beach Rd., Port Angeles, 98362
Sol Duc Hot Springs Resort, P.O. Box 2169, Port Angeles, 98362
Tudor Inn, 1108 S. Oak, Port Angeles, 98362, 206-452-3138
Ogle's B&B, 1307 Dogwood Hill S.W., Port Orchard, 98366, 206-876-9170
Arcadia Country Inn, 1891 S. Jacob Miller Rd, Port Townsend, 98368, 206-385-5245
Irish Acres, P.O. Box 466, Port Townsend, 98368, 206-385-4485
Lincoln Inn, The, 538 Lincoln St., Port Townsend, 98368, 206-385-6677
Manresa Castle Hotel, P.O. Box 564, Port Townsend, 98368, 206-385-5750
Palace Hotel, 1004 Water St., Port Townsend, 98368, 206-385-0773
Quimper Inn, 1306 Franklin St., Port Townsend, 98368, 206-385-1060
Ramage House, 1306 Franklin St., Port Townsend, 98368, 206-385-1086
Ravenscroft Inn Ltd., 533 Quincy St., Port Townsend, 98368, 206-385-2784
Manor Farm Inn, 26069 Big Valley Rd., Poulsbo, 98370, 206-779-4628
Kimbrough House, 505 Maiden Ln., Pullman, 99163, 509-334-3866
Murray House, NW 108 Parkwood Blvd., Pullman, 99163, 509-332-4569
Lake Quinault Lodge, P.O Box 7, S. Shore Rd., Quinault, 98575, 206-288-2571
Hampton House B&B, 409 Silverbrook Rd, Randle, 98377
Cedarym, A Colonial B&B, 1011 - 240th Ave. NE, Redmond, 98053, 206-868-4159
Shirlin Inn, The, 105 Patton St., Richland, 99352, 509-375-0720
Hotel de Haro/Resort, 4950 Tarte Mem. Dr., Roche Harbor, 98250, 206-378-2155
Summer Song B&B, P.O. Box 82, Seabeck, 98380, 206-830-5089
Walton House, 12340 Seabeck Hwy NW, Seabeck, 98380, 206-830-4498

Burton House, P.O. Box 9902, Seattle, 98109, 206-285-5945
College Inn Guest House, 4000 University Way NE, Seattle, 98105, 206-633-4441
Dibble House B&B, 7301 Dibble Ave. N.W., Seattle, 98117, 206-783-0320
Galer Place B&B, 318 W. Galer St., Seattle, 98119, 206-282-5339
Gaslight Inn, 1727 - 15th Ave., Seattle, 98122
Hainsworth House, 2657 37th Ave. SW, Seattle, 98126
Hanson House B&B, 1526 Palm Ave. SW, Seattle, 98116, 206-937-4157
Queen Anne Hill B&B, 1835 7th West, Seattle, 98119, 206-284-9779
Rocking Horse Inn, 2011 10th Ave. East, Seattle, 98102, 206-322-0206
Shelburne Country Inn, The, P.O. Box 250, Seaview, 98644, 206-642-2442
Granny Sandy's Orchard B&B, 405 W. Spruce, Sequim, 98382, 206-683-5748
Groveland Cottage, 4861 Sequim, Sequim, 98382, 206-683-3565
Twin River Ranch B&B, E 5730 Hwy 3, Shelton, 98584, 206-426-1023
B-G's B&B, 405 Hall Rd., Silver Lake, 98645, 206-274-8573
Dennis Fulton B&B, 16609 Olympic View Rd., Silverdale, 98383, 206-692-4648
Countryman B&B, 119 Cedar, Snohomish, 98290, 206-568-9622
Noris House, 312 Ave. D, Snohomish, 98290, 206-568-3825
Country Manner B&B, 1120 First St., Snohowish, 98290, 206-568-8254
Old Honey Farm Country Inn, 8910 384th Ave. S.E., Snoqualmie, 98065, 206-888-9399
Blakely Estate B&B, E. 7710 Hodin Dr., Spokane, 99212, 509-926-9426
Hillside House, E. 1729 18th Ave., Spokane, 99203, 509-534-1426
Town & Country Cottage B&B, N7620 Fox Point Dr., Spokane, 99208, 509-466-7559
Waverly Place B&B, W. 709 Waverly Place, Spokane, 99205, 509-328-1856
Silver Bay Inn, P.O. Box 43, Stehekin, 98852, 509-682-2212
Keenan House, 2610 N. Warner, Tacoma, 98407
Tokeland Hotel, P.O. Box 117, Tokeland, 98590, 206-267-7700
Orchard Country Inn, Box 634, Tonasket, 98855, 509-486-1923
Mio Amore Pensione, P.O. Box 208, Trout Lake, 98650, 509-395-2264
River Bend Inn, Route 2 Box 943, Usk, 99180, 509-445-1476
Edson House, Route 3, P.O. Box 221, Vashon Island, 98070, 206-463-2646
Island Inn B&B, Route 1, Box 950, Vashon Island, 98070, 206-567-4832
Green Gables Inn, 922 Bonsella, Walla Walla, 99362, 509-525-5501
Rees Mansion Inn, 260 E. Birch St., Walla Walla, 99362, 509-529-7845
Forget-Me-Not B&B, 1133 Washington St., Wenatchee, 98801, 509-663-6114
Llama Ranch B&B, 1980 Hwy 141, White Salmon, 98672, 509-395-2264
Rader Road Inn, Box 134, Winthrop, 98862, 509-996-2173
Dammann's Bed & Breakfast, 716 SR 20, Wintrop, 98862
Bear Creek Inn, 19520 N.E. 144th Place, Woodinville, 98072, 206-881-2978
'37 House, 4002 Englewood Ave., Yakima, 98908, 509-965-5537

West Virginia

CHARLES TOWN

Carriage Inn, The	$$ B&B	Full breakfast
417 E. Washington St., 25414	5 rooms, 5 pb	Comp. wine
304-728-8003	Visa, MC, Disc.,	Sitting room
Bob & Virginia Kaetzel	C-ltd/S-ltd/P-no/H-no	fireplaces
All year		walk to restaurants

All rooms w/private baths, tubs and showers. All have queen-sized, canopy beds. 4 rooms have working fireplaces. Full breakfast included.

Cottonwood Inn	$$$ B&B	Full breakfast
RR 2, Box 61-S, Mill Lane &	7 rooms, 7 pb	Comp. tea, coffee, wine
Kabletown Rd., 25414	Visa, MC, Choice,-Rated, •	Picnic lunch, dinner
304-725-3371	C-yes/S-yes/P-no/H-no	sitting room, library
Eleanor & Colin Simpson		trout stream
All year		

Quiet country setting, stocked trout stream, near Harper's Ferry in historic Shenandoah Valley. Bountiful breakfast. Guest rooms have TV and air-conditioning.

CHARLES TOWN

Gilbert House B&B	$$$ B&B	Full gourmet breakfast
P.O. Box 1104, 25414	3 rooms, 3 pb	Comp. tea, etc.
Middleway Historic Dist.	Visa, MC, •	Sitting room, library
304-725-0637	C-ltd/S-ltd/P-no/H-ltd	piano, fireplaces
Bernie Heiler	German, Spanish	bridal suite
All year		

Near Harper's Ferry, magnificent stone house on Nat'l Register in 18th-c. village. Tasteful antiques, art treasures. Leisurely, romantic breakfast. **3rd night 50%, Ltd**

ELKINS

Post House, The	$ B&B	Continental plus
306 Robert E. Lee Ave., 26241	5 rooms, 3 pb	Afternoon tea
304-636-1792	Visa	AMTA certified massage
Jo Ann Post Barlow	C-yes/S-no/P-no/H-no	near 5 ski resorts
All year		

Surrounded by mountain and park recreation, yet in town. Parklike backyard with children's playhouse. Handmade quilts for sale, and certified massage on premises.

Tunnel Mountain B&B	$$ BB	Full breakfast
Route 1, Box 59-1, 26241	3 rooms, 3 pb	Restaurant nearby
304-636-1684	*Rated*	Sitting room w/fireplace
Anne & Paul Beardslee	C-ltd/S-ltd/P-no/H-no	patio, wooded paths, A/C
All year		scenic views, cable TV

Romantic country fieldstone B&B nestled in the scenic West Virginia. Mountains next to National Forest and recreational areas. Antiques, fireplaces, warm hospitality.

HUTTONSVILLE

Hutton House B&B	$$ B&B	Full gourmet breakfast
Rts. 219/250, Box 88, 26273	7 rooms, 3 pb	Lunch, dinner, Aft. tea
800-234-6701	Visa, MC, *Rated*, •	Snacks, Comp. wine
Loretta Murray, Dean Ahren	C-yes/S-no/P-no/H-no	sitting room
All year		

Historic Queen Anne mansion conveniently located near cultural & outdoor attractions. Meticulous restoration yet kitchen friendly atmosphere.

LEWISBURG

General Lewis Inn	$$ EP	Full breakfast $
301 E. Washington St., 24901	26 rooms, 26 pb	Lunch, dinner, bar
304-645-2600	Most CC, *Rated*, •	Sitting room
Rodney Fisher	C-yes/S-yes/P-yes/H-no	A/C in rooms
All year		

1834 country inn furnished with genuine antiques, in Historic District. Fine food, spacious gardens. 200 year old town of Lewisburg has over 50 antebellum structures.

MARTINSBURG

Aspen Hall Inn	$$$ B&B	Full breakfast
405 Boyd Ave., 25401	5 rooms, 5 pb	Afternoon tea, snacks
304-263-4385	Visa, MC, *Rated*, •	Sitting room, library
Lou Anne & Gordon Claucherty	C-ltd/S-no/P-no/H-no	gazebo in garden
All year		rockers/hammock on porch

Luxurious queen-size accommodations, one twin-bed room, scrumptious breakfast served by the fireplace in the dining room. A+C in all rms., one bedrm. w/fireplace.

ROMNEY

Hampshire House 1884
165 N. Grafton St., 26757
304-822-7171
Scott & Jane Simmons
All year

$$ B&B/MAP/AP
7 rooms, 6 pb
Most CC, *Rated*, •
C-ltd/S-no/P-no/H-no

Full breakfast
Lunch, dinner
Comp. wine, snacks
sitting room, library
bikes, near tennis, pool

Completely renovated 1884 home. Period furniture, lamps, fireplaces. Gourmet dining. Quiet Central heat and air. Therapeutic massage available.

SHEPHERDSTOWN

Thomas Shepherd Inn
P.O. Box 1162, 25443
300 W. German St. at Duke
304-876-3715
Margaret Perry
All year

$$$ B&B
6 rooms, 6 pb
Visa, MC, AmEx, *Rated*,
C-ltd/S-ltd/P-no/H-no

Full breakfast
Sherry, coffee, tea
Living room w/fireplace
bicycles & picnics
central A/C

*1868 restored stately home in quaint historic Civil War town. Period antiques, very special breakfasts, fireside beverage, excellent restaurants. **3rd night 50% off***

WHEELING

Yesterdays Ltd. B&B
823 Main St., 808 Main St.,
26003
304-232-0864 800-540-6039
Michael & Lee Anne Flaherty
All year

$$ B&B
26 rooms, 22 pb
Visa, MC, •
C-yes/S-no/P-no/H-no

Continental plus
Restaurant, lunch
Dinner, afternoon tea
sitting room, parking
whirlpool suites

*Lovingly restored Victorian townhouses in historic district overlooking river. Antiques. Brkfast served on elegant china, crystal, silver. Walk to downtown. **3rd night 50%**.*

WINONA

Garvey House B&B
P.O. Box 98, 100 Main St., 25942
304-574-3235 800-767-3235
Valerie Ritter
April—October

$ B&B
4 rooms, 1 pb
Visa, MC, •
C-yes/S-ltd/P-no/H-no

Full breakfast
Dinner by res.
Advance reservation
for 4 or more

*This Garvey House is on a mountainside surrounded by beautiful gardens. Comfortable accommodations & early 1900s atmosphere, gardens, pond and gazebo. **15% room discount, ltd.***

More Inns . . .

Cabin Lodge, Box 355, Route 50, Aurora, 26705, 304-735-3563
Country Inn, The, 207 S. Washington St., Berkeley Springs, 25411, 304-258-2210
Folkestone B&B, Route 2, Box 404, Berkeley Springs, 25411, 304-258-3743
Highlawn Inn, 304 Market St., Berkeley Springs, 25411, 304-258-5700
Janesway B&B, 501 Johnson Mill Rd., Berkeley Springs, 25411
Manor, P.O. Box 342, Berkeley Springs, 25411, 304-258-1552
Maria's Garden & Inn, 201 Independence St., Berkeley Springs, 25411, 304-258-2021
Three Oaks & a Quilt, Duhring St., Bramwell, 24715
Shelly's Homestead, Route 1, Box 1-A, Burlington, 26710, 304-289-3941
Greenbrier River Inn, US Rt.60 nr Lewisburg, Caldwell, 24925, 304-647-5652
Shay Inn, Box 46, Cass, 24927
Hillbrook Inn, Route 2, Box 152, Charles Town, 25414, 304-725-4223
Pennbrooke Farm B&B, Granny-she Run, Chloe, 25235, 304-655-7367
Bright Morning, Route 32, William Ave., Davis, 26260, 304-259-2719
Twisted Thistle B&B, Route 32, Fourth St., Davis, 26260, 304-259-5389
Cheat Mountain Club, P.O. Box 28, Durbin, 26264, 304-456-4627
Cheat River Lodge, Route 1, Box 116, Elkins, 26241, 304-636-2301
Lincoln Crest B&B, P. O. Box 408, Elkins, 26241
Retreat at Buffalo Run, 214 Harpertown Rd., Elkins, 26241, 304-636-2960
Prospect Hill B&B, P.O. Box 135, Gerrardstown, 25420, 304-229-3346
Glen Ferris Inn, US Route 60, Glen Ferris, 25090, 304-632-1111
Oak Knoll B&B, Crawley, Greenbrier County, 24931, 304-392-6903

Fillmore Street B&B, Box 34, Harpers Ferry, 25245, 301-337-8633
Beekeeper Inn, Helvetia, 26224, 304-924-6435
Current B&B, The, HC 64, Box 135, Hillsboro, 24946, 304-653-4722
Cardinal Inn B&B, Route 1 Box 1, Rt. 219, Huttonsville, 26273, 304-335-6149
West Fork Inn, Route 2, Box 212, Jane Lew, 26378, 304-745-4893
Lynn's Inn B&B, Rt. 4 Box 40, Lewisburg, 24901
Minnie Manor, 403 E. Washington St., Lewisburg, 24901
Crawford's Country Corner, Box 112, Lost Creek, 26385, 304-745-3017
Guest House, Low-Gap, Lost River, 26811, 304-897-5707
Lost River Guest House, Low Gap, Lost River, 26811, 304-897-5707
Boydsville Inn, 609 So. Queen St., Martinsburg, 25401
Dunn Country Inn, Route 3, Box 33J, Martinsburg, 25401, 304-263-8646
Valley View Farm, Route 1, Box 467, Mathias, 26812, 304-897-5229
Daniel Fry House B&B, The, Rt 1, Box 152, Middleway, 25430
Hickory Hill Farm, Route 1, Box 355, Moorefield, 26836, 304-538-2511
McMechen House B&B, 109 N. Main St., Moorefield, 26836, 304-538-2417
Chestnut Ridge School B&B, Morgantown, 304-598-2262
Maxwell B&B, Route 12, Box 197, Morgantown, 26505, 304-594-3041
Kilmarnock Farms, Route 1 Box 91, Orlando, 26412, 304-452-8319
Bavarian Inn & Lodge, Route 1, Box 30, Shepherdstown, 25443, 304-876-2551
Fuss 'N Feathers, Box 1088, 210 W. German, Shepherdstown, 25443, 304-876-6469
Little Inn, P.O. Box 219, Shepherdstown, 25443, 304-876-2208
Mecklenberg Inn, 128 E. German St,Box 16, Shepherdstown, 25443, 304-876-2126
Shang-Ra-La B&B, Route 1, Box 156, Shepherdstown, 25443, 304-876-2391
Morgan Orchard, Route 2, Box 114, Sinks Grove, 24976, 304-772-3638
Cobblestone-on-the-Ohio, 103 Charles St., Sistersville, 26175, 304-652-1206
Wells Inn, 316 Charles St., Sistersville, 26175, 304-652-3111
Elk River Touring Center, Slatyfork, 26291, 304-572-3771
Countryside, P.O. Box 57, Summit Point, 25446, 304-725-2614
Stratford Springs Inn, 355 Oglebay Dr., Wheeling, 26003, 304-233-5100
James Wylie House B&B, 208 E. Main St., White Sulphur Springs, 24986, 304-536-9444

Wisconsin

APPLETON

Queen Anne B&B, The
837 E. College Ave., 54911
414-739-7966
Susan & Larry Bogenschutz
All year

$$ B&B
3 rooms, 1 pb
Rated
C-ltd/S-no/P-no/H-no

Full breakfast (wkends)
Continental plus (wkdys)
Fully equipped kitchen
bicycles
sitting room

Historically significant for its architectural style, the Queen Anne bears many reminders of a rich past. Near Lawrence University. **3rd night 50% off**

BARABOO

Baraboo's Gollmar House
422 3rd St., 53913
608-356-9432
Tom & Linda Luck
All year

$$ B&B
4 rooms, 3 pb
Visa, MC, *Rated*,
C-ltd/S-no/P-no/H-no

Full breakfast
Library, sitting room
patio overlooking garden
central A/C

1889 Victorian circus home featuring original furniture, antiques, chandeliers, bevelled glass and Frescos. Guest parlor/library. Romantic guest rooms.

Pinehaven B&B
E. 13083 Hwy. 33, 53913
608-356-3489
Lyle & Marge Getschman
All year

$$ B&B
4 rooms, 4 pb
Visa, MC, *Rated*,
C-ltd/S-no/P-no/H-no

Full breakfast
Fishing, rowing
Guest house
sitting room

Beautiful view of bluffs and small private lake. Tranquil setting. Take a stroll, fish, admire the Belgian draft horses. Relax. Acres to roam.

BAYFIELD

Cooper Hill House
P.O. Box 1288, 54814
33 S. Sixth St.
715-779-5060
Julie & Larry MacDonald
All year

$$ B&B
4 rooms, 4 pb
Visa, MC, *Rated*, •
C-ltd/S-no/P-no/H-no

Continental plus
Sitting room, library
spacious grounds, A/C
swimming & tennis nearby

Comfortable historic home in relaxed Lake Superior coastal community. Near to shops, restaurants, waterfront. Sail, explore the Apostle Islands. **Free skiing w/2 night stay.**

BELLEVILLE

Abendruh B&B Swisstyle
7019 Gehin Rd., 53508
608-424-3808
Mathilde Jaggi
All year

$$ B&B
3 rooms, 2 pb
Visa, MC, *Rated*, •
C-ltd/German, French,
Swiss

Full Swiss breakfast
Afternoon tea, wine
Comp. hors d'oeuvres
sitting room, library
hot tub, fireplaces

True European hospitality. Beautiful, quiet country getaway. Central A/C. Near cross-country skiing, biking, nature trails, many tourist attractions. **Special occasion rates.**

CAMBRIDGE–ROCKDALE

Night Heron Books & B&B
315 E. Water St., 53523
608-423-4141
Pamela Schorr, John Lehman
All year

$ B&B
3 rooms, 1 pb
Rated
C-ltd/P-no/H-no
German

Continental plus
Snacks, Comp. wine
Restaurant, sitting room
bicycles, hot tub
cross-country skiing, trails

Romantic getaway: terrace, hot tub, fireplace, art deco interior, across from the river and 300 acre nature park. Antique and pottery shops. **Free bottle of champagne**

CEDARBURG

Stagecoach Inn B&B
W61 N520 Washington Ave,
53012
414-375-0208
Brook & Liz Brown
All year

$$ B&B
13 rooms, 13 pb
Visa, MC, AmEx, *Rated*,
C-ltd/S-no/P-no/H-no

Continental plus
Full bar, restored pub
Library, sitting room
whirlpools, antiques
tennis court nearby

Restored 1853 stone inn furnished with antiques and Laura Ashley comforters. Historic pub and chocolate shop on the first floor.

Washington House Inn
W62 N573 Washington Ave,
53012
414-375-3550 800-554-4717
Wendy Porterfield
All year

$$ B&B
29 rooms, 29 pb
Rated, •
C-yes/S-yes/P-no/H-yes

Continental plus
Afternoon social
Sitting room, fireplaces
whirlpool baths, sauna
wet bars, bicycles

Country inn in center of historical district. Breakfast in charming gathering room. Shopping, golf, winter sports. Whirlpool baths and wet bars in each rm. **3rd night 50% off**

CHETEK

Lodge at Canoe Bay, The
W16065 Hogback Rd., 54728
800-568-1995
Dan & Lisa Dobrowolski
All year

$$ B&B
7 rooms, 4 pb
Most CC, *Rated*, •
C-ltd/S-no/P-no/H-yes

Continental plus
Snacks
cross-country skiing,
bicycles
sitting room, library
whirlpool tubs

Ultimate in relaxation! Secluded, luxurious lodge, soaring cedar ceilings, massive fireplace. On pristine lake in 280-acre forest. Every amenity, whirlpools.

The Lodge at Canoe Bay, Chetek, WI

EAGLE

Eagle Centre House B&B
W370, S9590 Hwy 67, 53119
414-363-4700
Riene Wells & Dean Herriges
All year exc. Christmas

$$$ B&B
5 rooms, 4 pb
Visa, MC, AmEx, *Rated*,
•
C-ltd/S-no/P-no/H-no

Full breakfast
Comp. wine, cider, etc.
Parlor, tap room
air-conditioning
hiking, riding, skiing

Greek Revival Inn features period antiques. In scenic Kettle Moraine Forest. Half mile from "Old World Wisconsin" Historic Site. Near Milwaukee. **Multiple night discount.**

ELLISON BAY

Griffin Inn & Cottages
11976 Mink River Rd., 54210
414-854-4306
Laurie & Jim Roberts
All year

$$ B&B
7 rooms, 7 pb
Rated
C-ltd/S-no/P-no/H-no

Full country breakfast
Lnch & dinner by request
Evening popcorn/beverage
gathering rooms, library
tennis court, skiing

New England-style country inn on Door County Peninsula, since 1910. Handmade quilts on antique beds. Cross-country ski from our door trail. On five lovely acres. **Winter wkend pkgs, ltd**

EPHRAIM

Hillside Hotel of Ephraim
P.O. Box 17, 54211
9980 Hwy 42
414-854-2417 800-423-7023
Karen & David McNeil
May—October, Jan—Feb

$$ B&B/MAP
12 rooms
Most CC, *Rated*, •
C-yes/S-no/P-no/H-no

Full specialty breakfast
6-course gourmet dinner
Full restaurant, tea
private beach, mooring
charcoaler for picnics

Country-Victorian hotel in resort w/harbor view, original furnishings, spectacular views; near galleries, shops. Deluxe cottages w/whirlpool baths. **3rd night 50% off**

FISH CREEK

Thorp House Inn & Cottages
P.O. Box 490, 54212
4135 Bluff Rd.
414-868-2444
C. & S. Falck-Pedersen
All year

$$ B&B
11 rooms, 11 pb
Rated
C-ltd/S-no/Norwegian

Continental plus
Sitting room w/fireplace
library, bicycles
winter cross-country skiing

Antique-filled historic home backed by wooded bluff, overlooking bay. Walk to beach, park, shops, restaurants. Kids O.K. in cottages, 5 w/fireplace, 1 w/whirlpool. **Specials**

HAMMOND

Summit Farm B&B
1622 110th Ave., 54015
715-796-2617
Grant & Laura Fritsche
All year

$ B&B
2 rooms, 2 pb
Rated
C-yes/S-ltd/P-ltd/H-no

Full breakfast
Snacks, coffee bar
Sitting room, games
books, farm animals
gardens

Eighty-year-old restored gentleman's farm. Gourmet breakfast served in antique-filled rooms. Soak in deep claw-foot bath tubs.

HARTLAND

Monches Mill House
W301 N9430 Hwy E, 53029
414-966-7546
Elaine D. Taylor
May–December

$$ B&B
4 rooms, 2 pb
C-yes/S-yes/P-yes/H-yes
French

Continental
Sitting room
hot tub, bicycles
tennis, canoeing, hiking

House built in 1842, located on the bank of the mill pond, furnished in antiques, choice of patio, porch or gallery for breakfast enjoyment.

HAYWARD

Lumberman's Mansion Inn
P.O. Box 885, 54843
4th & Kansas Sts.
715-634-3012
All year

$$ B&B
6 rooms, 6 pb
Visa, MC, *Rated*, •
C-yes/S-no/P-no/H-no

Full breakfast
Snacks
Sitting room, library
TV/VCRs, fireplaces

Elegant 1887 Victorian, antique furnishings, modern luxuries, immaculate. Gourmet breakfasts featuring regional delicacies. Hospitality & privacy. **4th night free**

HUDSON

Phipps Inn
1005 3rd St., 54016
715-386-0800
Cyndi & John Berglund
All year

$$$ B&B
6 rooms, 6 pb
Visa, MC, *Rated*,
C-ltd/S-no/P-no/H-no

Full breakfast
Snacks, comp. wine
Sitting room
bicycles
whirlpools

Elegant, historic inn. authentic antiques, whirlpools, eight fireplaces & central air-conditioning. Near St. Croix River, 30 minutes to Minneapolis/St. Paul.

KENOSHA

Manor House, The
6536 - 3rd Ave., 53140
414-658-0014
Dr. Clifton Peterson
All year

$$$ B&B
4 rooms, 4 pb
Visa, MC, AmEx, *Rated*,
•
C-ltd/S-ltd/P-no/H-no
French

Continental plus
Meals upon arrangement
Sitting room, library
piano, bicycles
fireplaces in 2 rooms

Georgian mansion overlooking Lake Michigan. Furnished w/ 18th-century antiques. Formal landscaped grounds. Between Chicago and Milwaukee. National Register. **Corporate rates**

LAKE DELTON

Swallow's Nest B&B, The
P.O. Box 418, 53940
141 Sarrington
608-254-6900
Rod & Mary Ann Stemo
All year

$$ B&B
4 rooms, 4 pb
Visa, MC, *Rated*,
C-ltd/S-no/P-no/H-no

Full breakfast
Comp. beverages, candy
Afternoon tea, library
deck, 2-story atrium
gallery, photo studio

Beautifully sited new home w/cathedral windows & ceilings offers quiet seclusion. Relax on screened deck, in library, by fireplace. Near golf, boating, restaurants.

LAKE GENEVA ───────────────────────────────────────

Eleven Gables Inn	$$$ B&B	Full breakfast
493 Wrigley Dr., 53147	12 rooms, 12 pb	Private pier, fishing
414-248-8393	Visa, MC, AmEx, *Rated*,	swimming, boating
A. Fasel Milliette	C-ltd/S-yes/P-no/H-ltd	hiking, cross-country skiing
All year		

Lakeside, nestled in evergreens amid giant oaks. Fireplaces, down comforters, wet bar/kitchenettes, TVs, balconies, courtyards. "Downtown" 2 blocks. **3rd night 50% off, ltd.**

Geneva Inn, The	$$$ B&B	Continental plus
N2009 State Rd. 120, 53147	37 rooms, 37 pb	Restaurant, lunch/dinner
414-248-5680 800-441-5881	Visa, MC, AmEx, DC,	Turndown cognac & choc.
Mr. Richard B. Treptow	C-yes/S-yes/P-no/H-yes	whirlpools, gift shop
All year	German, French, Spanish	atrium, lake swimming

A relaxing retreat on the shores of Lake Geneva. Deluxe accommodations touched with English charm. Restaurant and lounge. Banquet/meeting facilities; marina; gift shop.

T.C. Smith Historic Inn	$$ B&B	Full breakfast buffet
865 Main St., 53147	9 rooms, 5 pb	Afternoon tea, snacks
414-248-1097 800-423-0233	Most CC, *Rated*, •	Sitting room, library
Marks Family	C-yes/S-yes/P-yes/H-no	bicycles, gift shoppe
All year		A/C, TV, bicycle rentals

Relax by fireplaces to experience romance & warmth of Grand Victorian era in downtown lakeview mansion of 1845. On National Register. **Disc't extended stays**

LODI ──

Victorian Treasure B&B	$$ B&B	Full breakfast
115 Prairie St., 53555	4 rooms, 4 pb	Aft. tea, snacks
608-592-5199 800-859-5199	Misa, MC, *Rated*, •	Sitting room, hot tubs
Todd & Kimberly Seidl	C-ltd/S-no/P-no/H-no	games & books, turndown
All year		wrap-around porch

Exceptional 1897 Victorian between Madison & Dells. Evening sweet and turndown. Gourmet breakfast and innkeepers who fuss over details. **50% off 2nd night, midwk**

MADISON ───

Annie's Hill House	$$$ B&B	Full breakfast
2117 Sheridan Dr., 53704	4 rooms, 2 pb	Library, whirlpool, A/C
608-244-2224	Visa, MC, AmEx, *Rated*,	tennis, nature trails
Anne & Larry Stuart	C-ltd/S-ltd/P-ltd/H-no	swimming, cross-country
All year		skiing

Beautiful country garden setting in the city, w/romantic gazebo. Full recreation fac., 10 min to downtown & campus. Woodland whirlpool room for 2 avail. **4th week night free**

Canterbury Inn	$$$ B&B	Continental plus
315 W. Gorham, 53703	6 rooms, 6 pb	Restaurant, all meals
608-258-8899	Visa, MC	Afternoon tea, snacks
Jennifer Sanderfoot	C-yes/S-no/P-no/H-yes	comp. wine, sitting room
All year	French, Spanish	library

A literary B&B located above Canterbury Booksellers Coffeehouse. Six elegant, whimsical rooms each feature a character from Chaucer's "Canterbury Tales."

MADISON

Collins House B&B
704 E. Gorham St., 53703
608-255-4230
Barb & Mike Pratzel
All year

$$ B&B
5 rooms, 5 pb
Visa, MC, *Rated*,
C-yes/S-ltd/P-yes/H-no

Full breakfast
Comp. chocolate truffles
Sitting room w/fireplace
library, movies on video
whirlpools, fireplace

Restored prairie school style. Overlooks Lake Mendota, near university and state capitol.
Elegant rooms, wonderful gourmet breakfasts and pastries.

Mansion Hill Inn
424 N. Pinckney St., 53703
608-255-3999 800-798-9070
Polly Elder
All year

$$$ B&B
11 rooms, 11 pb
Visa, MC, AmEx, *Rated*,
•
C-ltd/S-yes/P-no/H-no

Continental plus
Afternoon tea, snacks
Comp. wine, bar service
sitting room, hot tubs
sauna, valet service

Victorian elegance abounds in our antique-filled guest rooms. Fireplaces, private baths with
whirlpools, valet service. We await your pleasure.

Plough Inn B&B
3402 Monroe St., 53711
608-238-2981
Sharon & Bob Gilson
All year

$$$ B&B
4 rooms, 3 pb
Visa, MC, *Rated*,
C-ltd/S-no/P-no/H-no

Continental (midweek)
Full breakfast (wkends)
New "tap" room added
sitting room

Historic 1850s inn with 3 charming, spacious rooms. Arborview room has fireplace and
whirlpool bath. Across from arboretum, near university campus.

MENOMONIE

Bolo Country Inn
207 Pine Ave., 54751
715-235-5596 800-553-2656
The Neuballers and Walleens
All year

$$ B&B
25 rooms, 25 pb
Most CC, *Rated*, •
C-yes/S-yes/P-yes/H-yes

Continental breakfast
Restaurant
Bar service
Comp. snacks - wkends
horse & carriage rides

Breakfast basket brought to room. Famous Supper Club serves lunch and dinner. Summer
golf, biking, winter cross-country skiing. Theater close by.

OSCEOLA

St. Croix River Inn
305 River St., 54020
715-294-4248 800-645-8820
Bev Johnson
All year

$$$ B&B
7 rooms, 7 pb
Visa, MC, AmEx, *Rated*,
•
C-ltd/S-ltd/P-no/H-no

Full breakfast wkends
Continental bkfast midwk
Sitting rooms
jacuzzis in all suites
seven suites

Elegantly furnished suites—some with fireplaces, all with jacuzzis. Overlooking the beautiful
St. Croix River. Skiing, fishing and sightseeing nearby. **3rd night free**

PLYMOUTH

B. L. Nutt Inn
632 E. Main St., 53073
414-892-8566
Doris Buckman
All year

$ B&B
2 rooms
C-ltd/S-no/P-no/H-no

Continental plus
Complimentary snacks
Sitting room
Renaissance style open
staircase, porches

1875 Italianate landmarked home, quietly located along Mullet River. Close to Road America
race track, Kettle Moraine State Forest and Lake Michigan. Delicious homemade treats

PORT WASHINGTON

Inn at Old Twelve Hundred	$$ B&B	Continental plus
806 W. Grand Ave., 53074	5 rooms, 5 pb	Bicycles, sitting room
414-284-6883	Visa, MC, AmEx, *Rated*,	hot tubs in 2 rooms
Stephanie & Ellie Bresetta	C-ltd/S-ltd/P-no/H-no	fireplaces some rooms
All year		

1890 Queen Anne furnished with antiques, many gracious open and enclosed porches. Blocks from Lake Michigan, minutes to Cedarburg. **3rd night 50% off**

PORTAGE

Breese Waye B&B	$$ B&B	Full breakfast
816 Macfarlane Rd., 53901	4 rooms, 3 pb	Sitting room
608-742-5281	*Rated*	tennis nearby
Keith & Gretchen Sprecher	C-yes/S-yes/P-yes/H-no	pool nearby
All year		

Circa 1880 Victorian home furnished in antiques—summertime breakfast served in Florida Room—winter breakfast in formal dining room. **3rd. night 50% off**

PRINCETON

Gray Lion Inn, The	$ B&B	Continental plus
115 Harvard, 54968	4 rooms, 4 pb	Aft. tea, snacks
414-295-4101	*Rated*	Full breakfast by req.
Maureen & Ed Ellison	C-ltd/S-no/P-no/H-no	sitting room
All year		restaurant nearby

Small town charm, close to everything. Antique malls, summer flea market, Lake trout fishing at beautiful Green Lake, golf, canoeing, cycling.

SPARTA

Franklin Victorian, The	$$ B&B	Full 3-course breakfast
220 E. Franklin St., 54656	4 rooms, 2 pb	Afternoon tea, snacks
608-269-3894 800-845-8767	*Rated*	Sitting room
Jane & Lloyd Larson	C-ltd/S-no/P-no/H-no	library
All year		canoe rental

Relax in quiet, gracious comfort—spacious rooms, fine woods. Delectable breakfasts. Surrounding area abounds with beauty. Recreation all four seasons. Near famous bike trail.

Just-N-Trails B&B/Farm	$$ B&B	Full breakfast
Route 1, Box 274, 54656	3 rooms	Lemonade, apple cider
608-269-4522 800-488-4521	Visa, MC, *Rated*, ●	Specialize in recreation
Donna & Don Justin	C-yes/S-no/P-no/H-no	relaxation & romance
All year		log cabin available

Roam on a 200-acre dairy farm, daydream by a pond. Ride on nearby Elroy-Sparta bike trail, cross-country ski or hike our 20 km. of trails. Relax in our charming country home.

STURGEON BAY

Inn at Cedar Crossing	$$$ B&B	Continental plus
336 Louisiana St., 54235	9 rooms, 9 pb	Restaurant, pub
414-743-4200	Visa, MC, DC, *Rated*,	Comp. beverages, cookies
Terry Wulf	C-ltd/S-ltd/P-no/H-no	dining rms., sitting rm.
All year		Whirlpool in some rooms

1884 inn situated in historic district near shops, restaurants, museum, beaches. Country antique decor, fireplaces, whirlpools, common room. Rated "Top 25 Restaurants."

STURGEON BAY

White Lace Inn	$ B&B	Continental plus
16 N. 5th Ave., 54235	15 rooms, 15 pb	Tea, coffee, chocolate
414-743-1105	Visa, MC, *Rated*,	Sitting room, gazebo
Dennis & Bonnie Statz	C-ltd/S-ltd/P-no/H-ltd	tandem bicycles
All year		fireplaces, whirlpools

A Victorian country inn with romantic decor; 15 charming guest rooms, all with fine antiques, authentic Victorian or poster bed; 10 w/fireplace, 7 w/whirlpool and fireplace.

WATERTOWN

Brandt Quirk Manor	$$ B&B	Full breakfast
410 S. Fourth St., 53094	5 rooms, 3 pb	Library
414-261-7917	Visa, MC, *Rated*	sitting room
Wayne & Elda Zuleger	C-ltd/P-no/H-no	
All year		

1875 mansion tastefully decorated in Victorian motif. Enjoy the antiques, stained-glass windows, Grecian pillars, ceramic and marble fireplaces, marble sinks, plaster accents.

WAUKESHA

Joanie's B&B	$$$ B&B	Full breakfast
615 E. Newhall Ave., 53186	1 rooms, 1 pb	Train ride on grounds
414-542-5698 FAX:542-5598	*Rated*	12 golf courses nearby
Peter & Joan Haupert	C-ltd/S-no/P-no/H-no	sherry in rm., cross-country
All year	Span, Fr, Ger, Russ	ski

World-travelers share their contemporary Frank Lloyd Wright inspired home on 3 wooded acres in historic Waukesha. 20 min. to Milwaukee. Private wing. **Senior disc't 20%**

More Inns . . .

Albany Guest House, 405 S. Mill St., Albany, 53502, 608-862-3636
Sugar river Inn, POBox 39, 304 S.Mill St, Albany, 53502, 608-862-1248
Amberwood Inn, N7136 Hwy. 42, Algoma, 54201, 414-487-3471
King Olaf's Pub & Inn, Hwy 42, Algoma, 54201, 414-487-2090
Gallery House, 215 N. Main St., Box 55, Alma, 54610, 608-685-4975
Laue House Inn, Box 176, Alma, 54610, 608-685-4923
Journey's End, P.O. Box 185, Amherst, 54406, 715-824-3970
Potter's Door Inn, The, 9528 Highway 57, Baileys Harbor, 54202, 414-839-2003
Kaleidoscope Inn, 800-11th Ave., Baldwin, 54002, 715-684-4575
Barrister's House, The, 226 - 9th Ave., Baraboo, 53913, 608-356-3344
Frantiques Showplace, 704 Ash St., Baraboo, 53913, 608-356-5273
House of Seven Gables, Box 204, Baraboo, 53913, 608-356-8387
Apple Tree Inn, Rt. 1, Box 251, Bayfield, 54814, 715-779-5572
Baywood Place B&B, The, 20 N. 3rd St., Bayfield, 54814, 715-779-3690
Greunke's Inn, 17 Rittenhouse, Bayfield, 54814, 715-779-5480
Old Rittenhouse In, P.O. Box 584, Bayfield, 54814, 715-779-5111
Pinehurst Inn, Hwy 13, P.O. Box 222, Bayfield, 54814, 715-779-3676
Cameo Rose B&B, 1090 Henry & Severson, Belleville, 53508, 608-424-6340
Ty-Bach, 2817, Beloit, 53511, 608-365-1039
Roadside Attraction, 703 Railroad St., Blanchardville, 53516, 608-523-2001
Palmquist Farm, River Rd., Brantwood, 54513, 715-564-2558
Hillcrest B&B Inn, 540 Storle Ave., Burlington, 53105, 414-763-4706
Kettlebrook Farm, Inc., W. 541 Hwy. SS, Campbellsport, 53010, 414-533-5387
Mielke-Mauk House B&B, The, W977 County Hwy. F, Campbellsport, 53010, 414-533-8602
Newcastle Pines, N. 1499 Hwy. 45, Campbellsport, 53010, 414-533-5252
Convent House, Route 1, Box 160, Cashton, 54619, 608-823-7906
Geiger House, 401 Denniston, Cassville, 53806, 608-725-5419
Annandale Inn, 569 18th St., Chetek, 54728, 715-837-1974
East Shore Inn, N2577 Lake Shore Dr., Chilton, 53014, 414-849-4230
Willson House, 320 Superior St., Chippewa Falls, 54729, 715-723-0055
ClearView Hills B&B, Route 2, Box 87, Colfax, 54730, 715-235-7180
Son Ne Vale Farm B&B, Route 1, Box 132, Colfax, 54730, 715-962-4342
By the Okeag, 446 Wisconsin St., Columbus, 53925, 414-623-3007
Old Parsonage, 508 Central Ave., Coon Valley, 54623, 608-452-3833
House in the Woods, 200 N. Riverside Dr., Cornell, 54732, 715-239-6511
Village Inn, The, P.O. Box 127, Cornucopia, 54827, 715-742-3941
Courthouse Square B&B, 210 E. Polk St., Crandon, 54520, 715-478-2549
Enchanted Valley Garden, 554 Enchanted Valley Rd, Cross Plains, 53528, 608-798-4554
Past & Present Inn, The, 2034 Main St., Cross Plains, 53528, 608-798-4441
Rectory B&B, The, 1575 Second Ave., Cumberland, 54829, 715-822-3151

Birch Creek Inn, 2263 Birch Creek Rd., De Pere, 54115, 414-336-7575
Circle B Bed & Breakfast, 3804 Vinburn Rd., DeForest, 53532, 608-846-3481
Allyn House, Box 429, Delavan, 53115
Jeremiah Mabie House B&B, 711 Walworth Ave., Delavan, 53115, 414-728-1876
Lakeside Manor Inn, 1809 S. Shore Dr., Delavan, 53115, 414-728-2043
Creamery, Box 22, Downsville, 54735, 715-664-8354
Ryan House, Rt. 2, Box 28, Durand, 54736, 715-672-8563
Brennan Manor, 1079 Everett Rd., Eagle River, 54521, 715-479-7353
Inn at Pinewood, The, POBox 549, 1800 Silver, Eagle River, 54521, 715-479-4414
Greystone Farms B&B, N. 9391 Adams Rd., East Troy, 53120, 414-495-8485
Mitten Farm B&B, W2454 Hwy. J, East Troy, 53120, 414-642-5530
Pine Ridge B&B, 1152 Scout Rd., East Troy, 53120, 414-594-3269
Apple Tree Inn, P.O. Box 677, Eau Claire, 54702, 715-836-9599
Fanny Hill Inn, 3919 Crescent Ave., Eau Claire, 54703, 715-836-8184
Otter Creek Inn, 2536 Hwy 12, Eau Claire, 54701, 715-832-2945
Westlin Winds, 3508 Halsey St., Eau Claire, 54701, 715-832-1110
Country Gardens B&B, 6421 Hwy. 42, Egg Harbor, 54209, 414-743-7434
Ye Olde Manor House B&B, R R 5, Box 390, Elkhorn, 53121, 414-742-2450
"Haus Zur Gemutlichkeit", 1052 Berry Lane N., Ellison Bay, 54210, 414-854-4848
Country Woods B&B, 520 Europe Lake Rd., Ellison Bay, 54210, 414-854-5706
Waarvik's Century Farm, N. 4621 County Rd. H, Elroy, 53929, 608-462-8595
Eagle Harbor Inn, P.O. Box 72, Ephraim, 54211, 414-854-2121
Ephraim Inn, P.O. Box 247, Ephraim, 54211, 414-854-4515
French Country Inn, 3052 Spruce Ln, Box 129, Ephraim, 54211, 414-854-4001
Proud Mary, P.O. Box 193, Fish Creek, 54212, 414-868-3442
Whistling Swan Inn, P.O. Box 193, Main St., Fish Creek, 54212, 414-868-3442
White Gull Inn, Box 175, Fish Creek, 54212, 414-868-3517
Emerald View House B&B, P.O. Box 322, Fontana-On-Geneva Lake, 53125, 414-275-2266
Lamp Post Inn, 408 South Main St., Fort Atkinson, 53538, 414-563-6561
Silver Maples, 1602 16th Ct., Friendship, 53934, 608-564-2388
House on the Hill B&B, Rt.2, Box 72, Genoa City, 53128, 414-279-6466
Parson's Inn B&B, Rock School Rd., Glen Haven, 53810, 608-794-2491
Stonewood Haus, PO Box 10201, Green Bay, 54307, 414-499-3786
Oakwood Lodge, 365 Lake St., Green Lake, 54941, 414-294-6580
Strawberry Hill, Route 1, Box 524-D, Green Lake, 54941, 414-294-3450
McConnell Inn, 497 S. Lawson Dr.,Box 6, Greenlake, 54941, 414-294-6430
Jordan House, 81 S. Main St., Hartford, 53027, 414-673-5643
Mustard Seed B&B, The, 205 California, Hayward, 54843, 715-634-2908
Open Window B&B, Route 5, Box 5194, Hayward, 54843, 715-462-3033
De Winters of Hazel Green, 22nd at Main St., Hazel Green, 53811, 608-854-2768
Wisconsin House Stagecoach, 2105 E. Main, Hazel Green, 53811, 608-854-2233
Hazelhurst Inn, 6941 Hwy 51, Hazelhurst, 54531, 715-356-6571
Mascione's Hidden Valley, Route 2, Box 74, Hillsboro, 54634, 608-489-3443
Old Granary Inn, The, 1760 Sandy Rock Rd., Hollandale, 53544, 608-967-2140
Shady Ridge Farm, 410 Highland View, Houlton, 54082, 715-549-6258
Boyden House, 727 Third St, Hudson, 54016, 715-386-7435
Jefferson-Day House, 1109 - 3rd St., Hudson, 54016, 715-386-7111
Taylor House B&B, 210 E. Iola St., Iola, 54945, 715-445-2204
Jackson Street Inn B&B, 210 S. Jackson St., Janesville, 53545, 608-754-7250
Dusk to Dawn, P.O. Box 191, Rt. 1, Kendall, 54638, 608-463-7547
Black Swan Inn B&B, 6003 7th Ave., Kenosha, 53140, 414-656-0207
Chelsea Rose, 908 Milwaukee St., Kewaunee, 54216, 414-388-2012
Duvall House, 815 Milwaukee St., Kewaunee, 54216, 414-388-0501
Gables, The, 821 Dodge St., Kewaunee, 54216
River Terrace B&B, 521 River Terrace, Kiel, 53042, 414-894-2032
Knapp Haus, 1117 Main St., La Crosse, 54601, 608-784-5272
Martindale House, The, 237 S. 10th St., La Crosse, 54601, 608-782-4224
Sandy Scott, 1520 State St., La Crosse, 54601, 608-784-7145
Trillium, Route 2, Box 121, La Farge, 54639, 608-625-4492
Chateau Madeleine, P.O. Box 27, La Pointe, 54850, 715-747-2463
Woods manor, 165 Front St., Box 7, La Pointe, 54850, 715-747-3102
Chippewa Lodge, 3525 Chippewa Lodge Trl, Lac du Flambeau, 54538, 715-588-3297
Ty-Bach, 3104 Simpson Ln., Lac du Flambeau, 54538, 715-588-7851
Martindale House B&B, The, 237 S. 10th St., LaCrosse, 54601, 608-782-4224
OJ's Victorian Village, P.O. Box 98, Hwy 12, Lake Delton, 53940, 608-254-6568
Elizabethian Inn, 463 Wrigley Dr., Lake Geneva, 53147, 414-248-9131
Pederson Victorian B&B, 1782 Hwy. 120 N., Lake Geneva, 53147, 414-248-9110
Red House Inn B&B, 512 Wells St., Lake Geneva, 53147, 414-248-1009
William's B&B, 830 Williams St., Lake Geneva, 53147, 414-248-1169
Bayberry Inn, 265 S. Main St., Lake Mills, 53551, 414-648-3654
Fargo Mansion Inn, 406 Mulberry St., Lake Mills, 53551, 414-648-3654
Laona Hostel, PO Box 325, 5397 Beech, Laona, 54541, 800-669-2615
Seven Pines Lodge, Lewis, 54851, 715-653-2323
Oak Hill Farm, 9850 Highway 80, Livingston, 53554, 608-943-6006
Shanahan's, S. 7979 Hwy. 23, Loganville, 53943, 608-727-2507
White Shutters, The, W265 County Trunk H., Lomira, 53048, 414-269-4056
Lake House On Monona, The, 4027 Monona Dr., Madison, 53716, 608-222-4601
Harrisburg Inn B&B, PO Box 15, W3334 Hwy 35, Maiden Rock, 54750, 715-448-4500
Victorian Acres B&B, Box 304, Manawa, 54949, 414-596-3643
Mahloch's Cozy B&B, 2104 Madson Rd., Manitowoc, 54220, 414-775-4404
Lauerman Guest House Inn, 1975 Riverside Ave., Marinette, 54143
Edward's Estates, N4775 22nd Ave., Mauston, 53948, 608-847-5246

Audubon, The, Mayville
Stan & Dorothy Slachetka, W6219 Mulberry Ln., Medford, 54451
Dorshel's B&B Guest House, W140 N7616 Lilly Rd., Menomonee Falls, 53051, 414-255-7866
Bolo Country Inn, 207 Pine Ave., Menomonie, 54751
Cedar Trail Guest House, Rt 4, Box 175, Menomonie, 54751
Katy Mayhouse, 2013 Wilson St., Menomonie, 54751, 715-235-1792
American Country Farm B&B, 12112 N. Wauwatosa Rd., Mequon, 53092, 414-242-0194
Homestead, The, 1916 W. Donges Bay Rd., Mequon, 53092, 414-242-4174
Sonnenhof Inn, 13907 N Port Washington, Mequon, 53092, 414-375-4294
Brick House B&B, The, 108 S. Cleveland St., Merrill, 54452, 715-536-3230
Candlewick Inn, 700 W. Main St., Merrill, 54452, 715-536-7744
Grandpa's Gate B&B, E13841 Lower DL, Merrimac, 53561, 608-493-2755
Middleton Beach Inn B&B, 2303 Middlton Beach Rd., Middleton, 53562, 608-831-6446
Chase-on-the-Hill, 3928 N. Highway 26, Milton, 53563, 608-868-6646
Greene House of 819, 819 N. Cass St., Milwaukee, 53202, 414-271-1979
Guest House of 819, 819 N. Cass St., Milwaukee, 53202
Ogden House, 2237 N. Lake Dr., Milwaukee, 53202, 414-272-2740
Pfister Hotel, 424 E. Wisconsin Ave., Milwaukee, 53202, 414-273-8222
Chesterfield Inn, 20 Commerce St., Mineral Point, 53565, 608-987-3682
Duke House B&B, 618 Maiden St., Mineral Point, 53565, 608-987-2821
Knudson's Guest House, 415 Ridge St., Mineral Point, 53565, 608-987-2733
Wilson House Inn, 110 Dodge St., Mineral Point, 53565, 608-987-3600
Wm. A. Jones House, 215 Ridge St., Hwy 1, Mineral Point, 53565, 608-987-2337
Victorian Blue, 314 Jackson St., Mishicot, 54228, 414-755-4907
Mathaniel Treat House, 1222 11th St., Monroe, 53566, 608-325-5656
Nathaniel Treat House, 1222 11th St., Monroe, 53566, 608-325-5656
Victorian Garden B&B, 1720-16th St., Monroe, 53566, 608-328-1720
Westmont Farms B&B, Rt. 3, Box 556, Montello, 53959, 414-293-4456
Inn, 30 Wisconsin Ave., Montreal, 54550, 715-561-5180
H.B. Dahle House, 200 N. 2rd St., Mount Horeb, 53572, 608-437-8894
Bluebell Inn, 122 Hewett St., Neillsville, 54456, 715-743-2929
Krupp Farm Homestead, W. 1982 Kiel Rd., New Holstein, 53061, 414-782-5421
Rambling Hills Tree Farm, 8825 Willever Ln., Newton, 53063, 414-726-4388
Lonesome Jake's Ranch, Route 2, Box 108A, Norwalk, 54648, 608-823-7585
Inn at Pine Terrace, 351 Lisbon Rd., Oconomowoc, 53066, 414-567-7463
Victorian Belle, The, 520 W. Wisconsin Ave., Oconomowoc, 53066, 414-567-2520
Stonewood Haus, 894 Riverdale Dr., Oneida, 54155, 414-499-3786
Inn at Wildcat Mountain, P.O. Box 112, Ontario, 54651, 608-337-4352
Pleasant Lake Inn, Rt2, Box 42B, 2208-60th, Osceola, 54020, 715-294-2545
Marybrooke Inn, 705 W. New York Ave., Oshkosh, 54901, 414-426-4761
Tiffany Inn, 206 Algoma Blvd, Oshkosh, 54901, 414-426-1000
Halfway House B&B, Route 2, Box 80, Oxford, 53952, 608-586-5489
Limberlost Inn, 2483 Hwy 17, Phelps, 54554, 715-545-2685
East Highland B&B, W4342 Hwy. D, Phillips, 54555, 715-339-3492
Bettinger House B&B, 855 Wachter Ave., Plain, 53577, 608-546-2951
Kraemer House B&B Inn, The, 1190 Spruce St., Plain, 53577, 608-546-3161
Cunningham House, 110 Market St., Platteville, 53818, 608-348-5532
52 Stafford (Irish House), P.O. Box 217, Plymouth, 53073, 414-893-0552
Spring Farm, N. 4502 County Rd. S., Plymouth, 53073, 414-892-2101
Tulip House Spring Farm, N4502 County Rd. S., Plymouth, 53073, 414-892-2101
Yankee Hill B&B, 315 Collins St., Plymouth, 53073
Captain's Table, 118 E. Woodruff St., Port Washington, 53074, 414-284-3818
Grand Inn, 832 W. Grand Ave., Port Washington, 53074, 414-284-6719
Port Washington Inn, 308 W. Washington St., Port Washington, 53074, 414-284-5583
Country Aire B&B, N. 4452 County U, Portage, 53901, 608-742-5716
Inn at Grady's Farm B&B, W10928 Hwy 33, Portage, 53901, 608-742-3627
O'Reilly House B&B, 7509 Stiger Rd., Potosi, 53802, 608-763-2386
Jamieson House, 407 N. Franklin St., Poynette, 53955, 608-635-4100
Neumann House B&B, 121 N. Michigan St., Prairie du Chien, 53821, 608-326-8104
Oak Street Inn, 506 Oak St., Prescott, 54021, 715-262-4110
Lochnaiar Inn, 1121 Lake Ave., Racine, 53403, 414-633-3300
Mansards on the Lake, The, 827 Lake Ave., Racine, 53403, 414-632-1135
Parkview B&B, 211 N. Park St., Reedsburg, 53959, 608-534-4333
Cranberry Hill Inn, 209 East Frederick St, Rhinelander, 54501, 715-369-3504
Mansion, 323 S. Central, Richland Center, 53581, 608-647-2808
Knollwood House, N. 8257 950th St., River Falls, 54022, 715-425-1040
St. Germain B&B, 6255 Hwy 70 E, Box 6, Saint Germain, 54558, 715-479-8007
Firefly House, Kingstown Box 349, Saint Vincent, 809-458-4621
Rochester, The, Sheboygan Falls
Forgotten Tymes, Siren, 54872, 715-349-5837
White Apron, The, 414 Maple Dr., Sister Bay, 54234, 414-854-5107
Old Oak Inn & Acorn Lodge, Hwy 131 South, Box 1500, Soldiers Grove, 54655, 608-624-5217
Riley House B&B, 727 Hawthorne Ave., South Milwaukee, 53172, 414-764-3130
Aunt Martha's Guest House, 1602 County Rd. A, Spooner, 54801, 715-635-6857
Green Valley Inn B&B, Route 1, Box 1345, Spooner, 54801, 715-635-7300
Hill Street B&B, 353 Hill St., Spring Green, 53588, 608-588-7751
Stout Trout B&B, The, Rte.1, Box 1630, Springbrook, 54875, 715-466-2790
Amberwood B&B, 320 McKenney St, St. Croix Falls, 54024, 715-483-9355
St. Germain B&B Resort, P.O. Box 6, St. Germain, 54558, 715-479-8007
Stonehouse B&B, 7855 Lost Lake Dr. N., St. Germain, 715-542-3733
Whip-Poor-Will Inn, P.O. Box 64, Star Lake, 54561, 715-542-3600
Birdhouse, The, 1890 Red Pine Ln., Stevens Point, 54481, 715-341-0084

Dreams of Yesteryear, 1100 Brawley St., Stevens Point, 54481, 715-341-4525
Marcyanna's B&B, 440 N. Old Wausau Rd., Stevens Point, 54481, 715-341-9922
Victorian Swan on Water, 1716 Water St., Stevens Point, 54481, 715-345-0595
Great River Farm, Geneva Delivery, Stockholm, 54971
Lakehouse, The, P.O. Box 177, Stone Lake, 54876, 715-865-2811
New Mountain B7b, Rt.1, Box 73C, Stone Lake, 54876, 715-865-2486
Stokstad's B&B, 305 Hwy 51, Stoughton, 53589, 608-884-4941
Lake House, RR 2, Box 217, Strum, 54770, 715-695-3223
Bay Shore Inn, 4205 Bay Shore Dr., Sturgeon Bay, 54235, 414-743-4551
Gandt's Haus und Hof, 2962 Lake Forest Park, Sturgeon Bay, 54235, 414-743-1238
Gray Goose B&B, The, 4258 Bay Shore Dr., Sturgeon Bay, 54235, 414-743-9100
Nautical Inn, 234 Kentucky St., Sturgeon Bay, 54235
Scofield House B&B, 908 Michigan St., Sturgeon Bay, 54235
Country House, The, 7265 Chicken in Woods, Three Lakes, 54562, 715-546-2012
Frenchtown B&B Inn, 822 S.Tomahawk, Box 121, Tomahawk, 54487, 715-453-3499
Abba's Inn B&B, 2822 Lincoln Ave., Two Rivers, 54241, 414-793-1727
Red Forest B&B, 1421 - 25th St., Two Rivers, 54241, 414-793-1794
Riley Bed-n-Breakfast Inn, 8205 Klevenville Riley, Verona, 53593, 608-845-9150
Eckhart-Dyson House, 217 East Jefferson, Viroqua, 54665, 608-637-8644
Serendipity Farm, Route 3 Box 162, Viroqua, 54665, 608-637-7708
Viroqua Heritage Inn B&B, 220 E. Jefferson St., Viroqua, 54665, 608-637-3306
Karlshuegel Inn B&B, 749 N.Church St, Hwy 26, Watertown, 53094, 414-261-3980
Crystal River B&B, E1369 Rural Rd., Waupaca, 54980, 715-258-5333
Rose Ivy Inn, 228 S. Watertown St., Waupun, 53963, 414-324-2127
Rosenberry Inn, 511 Franklin St., Wausau, 54401, 715-842-5733
Stewart Inn, 521 Grant St., Wausau, 54401, 715-848-2864
Kristine Ann's Inn, 303 E. Main, Wautoma, 54982, 414-787-4901
Wolfway Farm, Rural Route 1, Box 18, West Salem, 54669, 608-486-2686
Westby House, State St., Westby, 54667, 608-634-4112
Martha's Ethnic B&B, 226 2nd St., Westfield, 53964, 608-296-3361
Wolf River Lodge, Star Route Hwys 55 & 64, White Lake, 54491, 715-882-2182
James Wylie House B&B, 208 E. Main St., White Sulphur Springs, 24986, 304-536-9444
Greene House Country Inn, Box 214, Rt. 2, Hwy 12, Whitewater, 53190, 414-495-8771
Victoria on Main B&B, 622 West Main St., Whitewater, 53190, 414-473-8400
Birdsong B&B, POBox 391, 930 E.County, Wild Rose, 54984, 414-622-3770
Foxmoor B&B, Fox River Rd., Wilmot, 53192, 414-862-6161
Pahl's Bed & Breakfast, 608 Railroad St., Wilton, 54670, 608-435-6434
Country Shores, 8748 County Rd. B, Winneconne, 54986, 414-582-7655
Bennett House, 825 Oak St., Wisconsin Dells, 53965
Historic Bennett House, 825 Oak St., Wisconsin Dells, 53965, 608-254-2500
House on River Road, 922 River Rd., Wisconsin Dells, 53965, 608-253-5573
Sherman House, 930 River Rd., Box 397, Wisconsin Dells, 53965, 608-253-2721
Thunder Valley, W. 15344 Waubeek Rd., Wisconsin Dells, 53965, 608-254-4145
Nash House, 1020 Oak St., Wisconsin Rapids, 54494, 715-424-2001

Wyoming

CHEYENNE

A. Drummond's Ranch B&B	$$ B&B	Full breakfast
399 Happy Jack Rd., Hwy	3 rooms, 1 pb	Lunch, dinner, snacks
210/Laramie, 82007	*Rated*, •	Sitting room, library
307-634-6042	C-yes/S-no/P-yes/H-no	hot tubs, riding arena
Kent & Taydie Drummond	French	boarding for horses
All year		

Quiet, gracious retreat by state park near I-80. Relax, cross-country ski, fish, hike, mtn. bike, rock climb, bring horse, magnificent view.

CODY

Lockhart B&B Inn	$$ B&B	All-you-can-eat breakfst
109 W. Yellowstone Ave., U.S.	7 rooms, 7 pb	Comp. brandy, coffee
14, 16, 20, 82414	Most CC, *Rated*, •	Elegant "Tea" lunch $
307-587-6074 800-377-7255	C-yes/S-ltd/P-no/H-no	sitting room
Cindy Baldwin		phones, cable TV
All year		

Historic home of famous western author Caroline Lockhart—featuring antiques, old-style comfort and hearty all-you-can-eat breakfast. Western hospitality. AAA-rated inn.

ENCAMPMENT

Rustic Mountain Lodge
Star Route 49, 82325
307-327-5539
Mayvon & Ron Platt
All year

$ B&B
4 rooms
C-yes/S-no/P-yes/H-no

Full country breakfast
Lunch by arrangement
Trail rides, packtrips
fishing, youth programs
ranch activities

Rustic western lodge, comfortable modern, with massive logs, large window, stonework, spacious rooms w/peaceful mountain view and wholesome country atmosphere. Hot tubs

JACKSON

Wildflower Inn, The
P.O. Box 3724, 83001
3725 N. Teton Village Rd.
307-733-4710
Ken, Sherrie & Jessica Jern
All year

$$$ B&B
5 rooms, 5 pb
Visa, MC, *Rated*,
C-yes/S-no/P-no/H-no

Full breakfast
Comp. wine, tea, coffee
Sitting room, deck
library, hot tubs, pond
solarium, wild ducks

Lovely log home situated on 3 acres of aspens, cottonwoods, and of course, wildflowers. 5 sunny guest rooms, some with private decks. Near racquet club, golf club, ski area.

JACKSON HOLE

Teton Tree House
P.O. Box 550, 83014
Wilson, 6159 Heck of a Hill Rd.
307-733-3233
Chris & Denny Becker
All year

$$$ B&B
6 rooms, 6 pb
Most CC, *Rated*, •
C-yes/S-no/P-no/H-no

Full breakfast-low chol.
Comp. wine, beer, juice
Sitting room, fireplace
library, hot tub
slide shows

*Helpful longtime mountain and river guides offer a rustic but elegant 4-story open-beam home on a forested, wildflower-covered mountainside. **7th night free Jan/Apr/Nov***

JACKSON HOLE–WILSON

Fish Creek B&B
P.O. Box 366, 83014
2455 N. Fish Creek Rd.
307-733-2586
Putzi & John Harrington
All year

$$$ B&B
4 rooms, 4 pb
Visa, MC, *Rated*,
C-ltd/S-no/P-no/H-no
French, German, Spanish

Full breakfast
Sitting room, hot tubs
private fly-fishing
cozy log home

Secluded country hideaway, private baths and entrances. Fishing, hiking, skiing and hot-tubbing. Gourmet breakfasts beside beautiful Fish Creek.

LARAMIE

Annie Moore's Guest House
819 University Ave., 82070
307-721-4177 800-552-8992
Ann Acuff & Joe Bundy
All year

$$ B&B
6 rooms
Visa, MC, AmEx, *Rated*,
C-ltd/S-no/P-no/H-no

Continental plus
Comp. juice, coffee, tea
Sitting room
sun deck, Florida room
cat named "Archina"

Beautifully renovated post-Victorian Queen Anne. Cheerful parlor and second-story sun deck. Close to university, museums, downtown. Rocky Mountain recreational delight.

SARATOGA

Wolf Hotel
P.O. Box 1298, 101 E. Bridge, 82331
307-326-5525
Doug & Kathleen Campbell
All year

$ EP
9 rooms, 9 pb
Most CC, *Rated*,
C-yes/S-yes/P-no/H-no

Restaurant, bar
Breakfast, lunch, dinner
Luxury suite available
TV in 5 rooms
blue ribbon trout stream

Hotel built in 1893 as a stage stop. Listed in National Register. Blue Ribbon fishing, golf, hot springs nearby. Dining room (AAA approved) & lounge redone in Victorian style.

510   Wyoming

WAPITI

Elephant Head Lodge | $$ EP | Full breakfast $
1170 Yellowstone Pk Hwy, 82450 | 10 rooms, 10 pb | All meals available
307-587-3980 | Visa, MC, *Rated*, • | Library, TV, bicycles
The Lambs | C-yes/S-yes/P-yes/H-no | horses, tubing, fishing
May–October | | airport pick-up, Q-beds

In spectacular Wapiti Valley, 40 miles west of Cody—11 miles east of Yellowstone Park. Great base for touring Yellowstone, the Tetons. American Plan available.

More Inns . . .

Star Valley B&B, Afton, 83110
Nordic Inn, Box 14, Alpine, 82922
Spahn's Big Horn Mountain, P.O. Box 579, Big Horn, 82833, 307-674-8150
Paradise Guest Ranch, P.O. Box 790, Buffalo, 82834, 307-684-7876
South Fork Inn, Box 834, Buffalo, 82834
This Olde House B&B, 365 N. Main St., Buffalo, 82834, 307-684-5930
Bessemer Bend B&B, 6905 Speas Rd., Casper, 82604, 307-265-6819
Durbin Street Inn, 843 S. Durbin, Casper, 82601, 307-577-5774
Adventurer's Country B&B, 3803 I-80 E. Service Rd, Cheyenne, 82009, 307-632-4087
Rainsford Inn B&B, 219 E. 18th St., Cheyenne, 82001, 307-638-2337
Willard's B&B, 518 Dartmouth Ln., Cheyenne, 82009
Goff Creek Lodge, P.O. Box 155, Cody, 82414, 307-587-3753
Hidden Valley Ranch, 153 Rd., 6MF, S. Fork R, Cody, 82414, 307-587-5090
Shoshone Lodge Resort, P.O. Box 790BB, Cody, 82414, 307-587-4044
Trout Creek Inn, North Fork Rt., Cody, 82414
Akers Ranch B&B, 81 Inez Rd., Douglas, 82633, 307-358-3741
Cheyenne River Ranch, 1031 Steinle Rd., Douglas, 82633, 307-358-2380
Deer Forks Ranch, 1200 Poison Lake Rd., Douglas, 82633, 307-358-2033
Lorraine's B&B Lodge, Box 312, Encampment, 82325, 307-327-5200
Hotel Higgins, P.O. Box 741, Glenrock, 82637, 307-436-9212
Opal's B&B, Box 219, Glenrock, 82637, 307-436-2626
Annette's White House, 239 S. Dakota St., Guernsey, 82214, 307-836-2148
Big Mountain Inn, P.O. Box 7453, Jackson, 83001, 307-733-1981
Spring Creek Ranch, Box 3154, Jackson, 83001, 307-733-8833
Sundance Inn, 135 W. Broadway, Jackson, 83001, 307-733-3444
Moose Meadows B&B, 1225 Green Ln., Jackson Hole, 83001, 307-733-9510
Powderhorn Ranch, P.O. Box 7400, Jackson Hole, 83001, 307-733-3845
Rancho Alegre, 3600 S. Parkloop Rd., Jackson Hole, 83001, 307-733-7988
Country Fare B&B, 904 Main St., Lander, 82520, 307-332-9604
Empty Nest B&B, 1355 S. First, Lander, 82520, 307-332-7516
Wyoming Whale Ranch, Box 115, Lusk, 82225, 307-334-3598
Bunkhouse, P.O. Box 384, Moose, 83012, 307-733-7283
Box K Ranch, Box 110, Moran, 83013, 307-543-2407
Fort William Recreat. Area, P.O. Box 1081, Pinedale, 82941, 307-367-6353
Window On The Winds, Box 135, Pinedale, 82941, 307-367-2600
Bar X Ranch, 109 Rd 8 WC, Clark, Powell, 82435, 307-645-3231
Ferris Mansion B&B, 607 W. Maple, Rawlins, 82301, 307-324-3961
Cottonwood Ranch B&B, 951 Missouri Valley Rd., Riverton, 82501, 307-856-3064
Dodge Creek Ranch, 402 Tunnel Rd., Rock River, 82083, 307-322-2345
Sha Hol Dee B&B, 116 Pilot Butte Ave., Rock Springs, 82901, 307-362-7131
Brooksong B&B Home, Star Rt. Box 9L, Saratoga, 82331, 307-326-8744
Hood House B&B, 214 N. 3rd. St., Saratoga, 82331, 307-326-8901
Savery Creek Thoroughbred, Ranch, Box 24, Savery, 82332, 307-383-7840
Y L Hideaway Holiday, P.O. Box 24, Savery, 82332, 307-383-7840
Clucas Ranch B&B, 1710 Hwy. 14, Shell, 82441, 307-765-2946
Kilbourne Kastle B&B, 320 S. Main, Sheridan, 82801, 307-674-8716
Mountain Shadows Ranch, Box 110BB, Wapiti, 82450, 307-587-2143
Blackbird Inn, 1101 11th St., Wheatland, 82201, 307-322-4540
Heck of A Hill Homestead, P.O. Box 105, Wilson, 83014, 307-733-8023
Snow Job, P.O. Box 371, Wilson, 83014, 307-739-9695
Teton View B&B, P.O. Box 652, Wilson, 83014, 307-733-7954

Puerto Rico

CONDADO–SAN JUAN ────────────────────────

Wind Chimes
53 Calle Taft, 00911
809-727-4153
All year

$$ B&B
12 rooms, 12 pb
Visa, MC, AmEx, •
C-ltd/S-yes/P-no/H-no
Spanish

Continental breakfast
Sitting room, bicycles
beach nearby, tours
Air Cond., cable TV

A charming Spanish-style villa with airy rooms, ceiling fans and private tile baths. Enjoy Caribbean trade winds on tropical patio. Walk to Casinos, restaurants, & shops.

CULEBRA ISLAND ────────────────────────

Casa Llave
P.O. Box 60, Calle Escudero 142,
 00775
809-742-3559
Dorothy & Richard Kiegler
All year

$ B&B
2 rooms, 2 pb
C-ltd/S-no/P-no/H-yes

Full breakfast
Private bayside yard
picnic tables/chairs

On the bay, easy walk to shops and restaurants. Ideal for beaching, scuba divers and just plain relaxing.

MARICAO ────────────────────────

La Hacienda Juanita B&B
P.O. Box 777, 00606
Road 105, KM 23.5
809-838-2550
Abraham Radames & Luis
Rivera
All year

$$ EP
21 rooms, 21 pb
Visa, MC, AmEx, *Rated*,
•
C-yes/S-yes/P-no/H-yes
Spanish

Restaurant - all meals $
Bar service
Sitting room, library
tennis court, hot tubs
swimming pool, vollyball

Birdwatchers paradise. Rainforest, high in the cool tropical mountains. Built 160 years ago as a coffee plantation's main lodge. **Free bottle wine & 3rd night 50% off**

PUERTO REAL ────────────────────────

Fajardo Inn
P.O. Box 4309, 00740
52 Parcelas Beltran
809-863-5195
Kim & Patricia Amrud
All year

$ B&B
10 rooms, 10 pb
Visa, MC
C-yes/S-yes/P-no/H-no
French

Continental plus
Snacks, bar service
Sitting room, bicycles
air conditioned
cable TV, phone

Spacious, quiet rooms in friendly tropical environment. Close to beach, rainforest, water sports, nature reserve. Home-made muffins, pastry & exotic fruits on balcony.

SAN JUAN ────────────────────────

El Canario Inn
1317 Ashford Ave., Condado,
00907
809-722-3861 800-533-2649
Jose Colon
All year, FAX:722-0391

$$ B&B
25 rooms, 25 pb
Visa, MC, AmEx *Rated*,
•
C-yes/S-yes/P-no/H-no
English, Spanish

Continental plus
Swimming pool, jacuzzi
patios, rooms with A/C
cable TV, phones, wicker

In heart of Condado, near beach, casinos, boutiques and fine restaurants. Freshwater jacuzzi pool, tropical patio and sun deck for sun, fun, and relaxation.

SAN JUAN

Tres Palmas Guest House
2212 Park Blvd., Puntas Las
Marias, 00913
809-727-4617 FAX:727-5434
Elving Torres & Zulma Roman
All year

$$ B&B
10 rooms, 9 pb
Visa, MC, AmEx, •
C-ltd/S-ltd/P-no/H-no

Continental plus
Refrigerators in rooms
Sitting room, cable TV
sun deck, tropical pool
beach, apartments avail.

Beachfront; casinos and gourmet restaurants five minutes away; airport and historic Old San Juan ten minutes. Daily maid service. Welcome drink on arrival.

More Inns . . .

Hotel Monte Rio, H St., Adjuntas, 00601
Duffys' Inn, #9 Isla Verde Rd., Carolina, 00913, 809-726-1415
Ceiba Country Inn, P.O. Box 1067, Ceiba, 00635, 809-885-0471
El Prado Inn, 1350 Luchetti St., Condado, San Juan, 00907, 809-728-5526
Posada La Hamaca, 68 Castelar St., Culebra, 00645, 809-742-3516
Villa Boheme, P.O. Box 218, Culebra Island, 00645, 809-742-3508
Palmas del Mar, P.O. Box 2020, Humacao, 00661, 809-852-6000
La Casa Mathiesen, 14 Calle Uno, Villamar, Isla Verde, 00913, 809-727-3223
La Playa, 6 Amapola, Isla Verde, 00630, 809-791-1115
Parador Martorell, P.O. Box 384, Luquillo, 00673, 809-889-2710
Beach House, 1957 Italia, Ocean Park, 00913, 809-727-5482
Buena Vista by-the-Sea, 2218 Gen.Del Valle, Ocean Park, Santurce, 00913, 809-726-2796
Safari on the Beach, Yardley Place #2, Ocean Park-San Juan, 00911, 809-726-0445
Galeria San Juan, Blvd. del Valle 204-206, Old San Juan, 00901
Hotel Caribe Playa, HC 764 Buzon 8490, Patillas, 00723, 809-839-6339
Fajardo Inn, P.O. Box 4309, Puerto Real, 00740, 809-863-5195
Horned Dorset Primavera Ho, Apartado 1132, Rincon, 00743, 809-823-4030
Tamboo Resorts, H-C 01 4433, Rincon, 00743, 809-823-8550
Parador Oasis, P.O. Box 144, San German, 00753, 809-892-1175
Arcade Inn Guest House, 8 Taft St. - Condado, San Juan, 00911, 809-725-0668
El Canario by the Sea, 4 Condado Ave., San Juan, 00907, 809-722-8640
Green Isle Inn, 36 Cale Uno - Villamar, San Juan, 00913, 809-726-4330
Hosteria del Mar, 5 Cervantes St., San Juan, 00907, 809-724-8203
Jewel's by the Sea, Seaview 1125-Condado, San Juan, 00907, 809-725-5313
La Condesa Inn-Guest House, 2071 Cacique St., San Juan, 00911, 809-727-3698
San Antonio Guest House, 1 Tapia, Ocean Park, San Juan, 00752, 914-727-3302
Bananas Guesthouse, P.O. Box 1300 Esperanza, Vieques, 00765, 809-741-8700
La Casa del Frances, Box 458, Esperanza, Vieques, 00765, 809-741-3751
New Dawn's Caribbean, P.O. Box 1512, Vieques, 00765, 809-741-0495
Sea Gate Guest House, Barriada Fuerts, Vieques, 00765, 809-741-4661

Virgin Islands

CHRISTIANSTED—ST. CROIX

Pink Fancy Inn
27 Prince St., Christiansted,
00820
809-773-8460 800-524-2045
Sam Dillon
All year, FAX:773-6448

$$$ B&B
13 rooms, 13 pb
Rated, •
C-yes/S-yes/P-yes/H-no

Continental
Comp. 24 hr. bar
Library, A/C
24 hr. freshwater pool
phones in rms, FAX avail

Meticulously restored 1780 Danish townhouse—uniquely private oasis. Shopping, beach, 25 restaurants w/in 5-min. walk. Ceiling fans, kitchenettes. **24 hr complimentary bar.**

ST. THOMAS

Danish Chalet Inn
P.O. Box 4319, 00803
9E-9J Nordseidevj
809-774-5764 800-635-1531
Frank & Mary Davis
All year, FAX: 777-4886

$$ B&B
15 rooms, 6 pb
Visa, MC, *Rated*, •
C-yes/S-yes/P-no/H-no
English

Continental breakfast
Bar service ($1 drinks)
Sitting room, library
spa, jacuzzi, sun deck
beach towels

Family inn overlooking Charlotte Amalie harbor, 5 minutes to town, duty-free shops, restaurants. Cool breezes, honor bar, sun deck, jacuzzi. 15 min. to beaches. **10% discount**

Galleon House Hotel
P.O. Box 6577, 00804
31 Kongens Gade
809-774-6952 800-524-2052
Donna J. Francis
All year

$$ B&B
14 rooms, 13 pb
•
C-yes/S-yes/P-no/H-no
English

Continental plus
Refrigerators
A/C in rooms, pool
snorkel gear
veranda, beach towels

Visit historical Danish town. Superb view of harbor with city charm close to everything. Duty-free shopping, beach activities in 85-degree weather.

Island View Guest House
P.O. Box 1903, 00803
11-1C Contant
809-774-4270 800-524-2023
Norman Leader, Barbara Cooper
All year FAX:774-6167

$$ B&B
15 rooms, 13 pb
Rated, •
C-ltd/S-yes/P-no/H-no

Continental, full avail.
38 seat dinner dining rm
Hors d'oeuvres (Friday)
sandwiches, bar, gallery
swimming pool

Overlooking St. Thomas harbor, honor bar and freshwater pool. Spectacular harbor view from all rooms. Convenient to town and airport. **7 nights dinner for 2**

More Inns ...

Maison Greaux Guest House, P.O. Box 1856, Charlotte Amalie, 00803, 809-774-0063
Mark Saint Thomas, The, Blackbeard's Hill, Charlotte Amalie, 00802, 809-774-5511
Villa Madeleine, P.O. Box 24190, Gallows Bay, St. Croix, 00824, 800-548-4461
Cruz Inn, Box 566, Cruz Bay, Saint John, 00830, 809-776-7688
Estate Zootenvaal, Hurricane Hole, Saint John, 00830, 809-776-6321
Gallows Point, Box 58, Saint John, 00830, 809-776-6434
Intimate Inn of St. John, P.O. Box 432, Cruz Bay, Saint John, 00830, 809-776-6133
Raintree Inn, Box 566, Saint John, 00830, 809-776-7449
Selene's, P.O. Box 30, Cruz Bay, Saint John, 00830, 809-776-7850
Heritage Manor, P.O. Box 90, Saint Thomas, 00804, 809-774-3003
Hotel 1829, P.O. Box 1567, Saint Thomas, 00801, 809-774-1829
Inn at Mandahl, P.O. Box 2483, Saint Thomas, 00803, 809-775-2100
Kyalami, Estate Elizabeth No. 27, Saint Thomas, 00837, 809-774-9980
Mafolie Hotel, P.O. Box 1506, Saint Thomas, 00801, 809-774-2790
Pavilions & Pools Hotel, Route 6, Saint Thomas, 00802, 800-524-2001
Pelican Beach Club, Box 8387, Saint Thomas, 00801, 809-775-6855
Twiins Guest House, 5 Garden St,Charlotte A, Saint Thomas, 00801, 809-776-0131
Villa Elaine, 66 Water Island, Saint Thomas, 00802, 809-774-0290

Alberta

BANFF

Kananaskis Guest Ranch
P.O. Box 964, Hwy. 1X, Seebe,
T0L 0C0
403-673-3737 FAX:762-3953
The Brewster Family
May–October 15

$$$ B&B
31 rooms, 31 pb
Visa, MC, *Rated*, •
C-yes/S-yes/P-no/H-yes

Full breakfast
Lic. dining room, lounge
Seminar facility, golf
whirlpool, horses
Western barbecues

Turn-of-the-century guest ranch; private cabins & chalet units; antique furniture. Operated by 5th-generation Brewsters. 45 miles west of Calgary, 30 miles east of Banff.

CANMORE

Georgetown Inn, The
P.O. Box 3151, 1101 Bow Valley
Trail, T0L OMO
403-678-3439
Doreen, Barry & Jones Family
All year

$$$ B&B
14 rooms, 14 pb
•
C-yes/S-ltd/P-no/H-yes
French

Full breakfast
Restaurant lunch, tea $
Dinner $, snacks, bar
sitting room, library

Unspoiled wilderness! Let us introduce you to Canada's mountain heritage.

CLARESHOLM

Anola's B&B
P.O. Box 340, 9 mi. east on Hwy
520, T0L 0T0
403-625-4389
Anola & Gordon Laing
All year

$ B&B
3 rooms, 2 pb
Rated, •
C-ltd/S-no/P-no/H-yes

Full breakfast
Evening tea & muffins
Comp. wine with cottage
library, bikes, hot tub
museum, grain farm

Relax in our country cottage guest house. Perfect for honeymooners. Antique furnishings and Franklin stove. Visit Granddad's museum. Close to Head-Smashed-Inn Buffalo Jump.

HINTON

Black Cat Guest Ranch
P.O. Box 6267L, T7V 1X6
403-865-3084 FAX:865-1924
Amber & Perry Hayward
All year

$$$ AP
16 rooms, 16 pb
Visa, MC, •
C-yes/S-yes/P-no/H-no

Full breakfast
Lunch, dinner
Sitting room, piano
adult oriented
patio, outdoor hot tub

A year-round lodge facing the front range of the Rockies, featuring trail rides and hiking in summer, cross-country skiing in winter. ***First horseback ride 50% off***

More Inns ...

Blue Mountain Lodge, P.O. Box 2763, Banff, T0L OCO, 403-762-5134
Crazee Akerz Farm, RR #1, Bentley, T0C 0J0, 403-843-6444
Bedside Manor B&B, Box 1088, Blairmore, T0K OEO, 403-628-3954
M&M Ranch, Box 707, Bragg Creek, T0L 0K0
Barb's B&B, 1308 Carlyle Rd. SW, Calgary, T2V 2T8
Murphy's Midtown B&B, 707 Royal Ave. SW, Calgary, T2S 0G3
Robin's Nest, The, Box 2, Site 7, RR 8, Calgary, T2J 2T9
Scenic Waters B&B, Box 33, Site 20, RR 2, Calgary, T2P 2G5, 403-286-4348
Canadian Rocky Mountain, Box 95, Canmore, T0L 0M0, 403-678-6777
Cougar Creek Inn B&B, P.O. Box 1162, Canmore, T0L OMO, 403-678-4751
Haus Alpenrose Lodge, 629 - 9th St., Box 723, Canmore, T0L 0M0, 403-678-4134
Spring Creek B&B, Box 172, Canmore, T0L OMO, 403-678-6726
Lane's B&B, Box 974, Claresholm, T0L 0T0
Ausen Hus B&B, RR 2, Didsbury, T0M 0W0, 403-335-4736
Edmonton Hostel, 10422 - 91st St., Edmonton, T0L OMO, 403-429-0140
Virginia's Weedend B&B, 5815-107 St., Edmonton, T6H 2X6
Dimm's Ranch B&B, Box 228, Granum, T0L 1A0

Gwynalta Farm, Gwynne, T0C 1L0, 403-352-3587
Kentucky Ranch, RR #2, High River, T0L 1B0
Hilltop B&B, RR #1, Millarville, T0L 1K0
Broadview Farm, RR #2, Millet, T0C 1Z0, 403-387-4963
Broadway Farm B&B, Box 294, Nanton, T0L 1R0
Squire Ranch, The, RR #1, Nanton, T0L 1R0
Timber Ridge Homestead, Box 94, Nanton, T0L 1R0, 403-646-5683
Welcome Acres B&B, Box 7, Site 2, RR 1, Okotoks, T0L 1T0
Wildflower Country House, Box 8, Site 1, R.R.2, Okotoks, T0L 1T0
Allison House, Box 1351, Pincher Creek, T0K 1W0
Castle Haus Inn, General Delivery, Pincher Creek, T0K 1W0
Cow Creek Ranch, Box 522, Pincher Creek, T0K 1W0
Cowan's Patch, P.O. Box 69, Priddis, T0L 1W0
Rafter Six Ranch Resort, Seebe, T0L 1X0, 403-673-3622
Rose's Rest B&B, 221 John St., Turner Valley, T0L 2A0

British Columbia

BRENTWOOD BAY

Brentwood Bay/Verdier B&B	$$ B&B	Full breakfast
Box 403, 7247 W. Saanich Rd.,	13 rooms, 9 pb	Sitting room
V0S 1A0	•	piano
604-652-2012 800-665-9151	C-yes/S-no/P-no/H-ltd	
Evelyn Hardy	Ukrainian, Arabic	
All year		

Come for the 1994 Commonwealth Games in Victoria, BC. ***3rd night 50% off***

CAMPBELL RIVER

April Point Lodge	$$$ EP	Full breakfast
Box 1, 900 April Pt. Rd,	36 rooms, 36 pb	Restaurant, bar
Quathiaski Cove, V9W 4Z9	Most CC, *Rated*, •	Sitting room, piano
604-285-2222 FAX:285-2411	C-yes/S-yes/P-ltd/H-ltd	entertainment (summer)
The Peterson Family	Fr., Rus., Ger, Japanese	saltwater pool, fishing
April 15–October 15		

Personal service is our pride. More than one staff member per guest. Saltwater pool, many languages spoken. One- to five-bedroom deluxe guest houses. Fishing resort.

CHEMAINUS

Pacific Shores Inn	$$ EP	All suite Inn
Box 958, 9847 Willow St., V0R	3 rooms, 3 pb	Full kitchens
1K0	MC	Washer/dryer 2 units
604-246-4987	C-yes/S-no/P-no/H-yes	bicycles
Dave & Sonia Haberman		cable TV/VCR
All year		

3 blocks from the ocean. 23' off-shore cruiser available for private charter, time and weather permitting.

FORT STEELE

Wild Horse Farm	$$ B&B	Full breakfast
Box 7, Hwy 93/95, V0B 1N0	3 rooms, 3 pb	Sitting room, antiques
604-426-6000	•	player piano
Bob & Orma Termuende	C-yes/S-ltd/P-ltd/H-no	games table
May–October		

Spacious early 1900s log-faced country manor nestled in the Rocky Mountains; extensive lawns, gardens, trees on grounds. Across from Fort Steele Historic Park.

GABRIOLA ISLAND

Surf Lodge Ltd.
RR1, Site 1, 885 Berry Point Rd.,
V0R 1X0
604-247-9231
All year

$ EP
18 rooms, 18 pb
Visa, MC, *Rated*, •
C-yes/S-yes/P-no/H-no

Breakfast, Box Lunch
Dinner, Meals $
Sitting rm. w/fireplace
swimming pool
bicycles

Seaside setting with olympic class sunset-watching from our dining room, deck and licensed lounge. Tennis, golf, fishing charters nearby.

HORNBY ISLAND

Sea Breeze Lodge
Fowler Rd., V0R 1Z0
604-335-2321
Brian & Gail Bishop
All year; AP 6/15–9/15

$$$ AP
11 rooms, 11 pb
Rated
C-yes/S-yes/P-yes/H-ltd
Spanish

Full breakfast
Lunch & dinner also incl
Sitting room, piano
grass tennis courts
hot tub, fishing guide

Sea Breeze Lodge—mentioned in 1983 edition of West World. Near the ocean. Breakfast, homemade pastries. Off season cottages set for housekeeping. Some fireplaces.

MILL BAY

Pine Lodge Farm B&B
3191 Mutter Rd., V0R 2P0
604-743-4083
Clifford & Barbara Clarke
All year

$$$ B&B
7 rooms, 7 pb
•
C-ltd/S-ltd/P-no/H-no

Full farm breakfast
Sitting room
2 bedroom cottage avail.
antique sales, museum

Our lodge is on a 30-acre farm with panoramic ocean views. Each room is furnished with exquisite antiques and stained glass windows. Museum open to public. Antique sales.

NANOOSE BAY

Lookout at Schooner Cove
Box 71 Blueback Dr. RR2, 3381
Dolphin Dr., V0R 2R0
604-468-9796 FAX:468-9796
Marj & Herb Wilkie
All year

$$ B&B
3 rooms, 2 pb
Rated, •
C-ltd/S-ltd/P-no/H-no
Australian, English

Full breakfast
Comp. wine (sometimes)
Sitting room, library
fishing charter avail.
suite avail/3 night min.

Spectacular views of Georgia Strait, watch boats, eagles, cruise ships, Orca whales. Country breakfast on deck. Golf, fishing, marina nearby. Quiet. **Disc't for longer stays**

NORTH VANCOUVER

Helen's B&B
302 E. 5th St., V7L 1L1
604-985-4869
Helen Boire
All year

$$ B&B
3 rooms, 1 pb
Visa, •
C-ltd/S-yes/P-no/H-no
French

Full 3-course breakfast
Complimentary wine
Fantastic views
color TVs in rooms
antique decor

Lovely, comfortable Victorian home. Views to ocean and city. Only five blocks to sea. Near all transport and attractions. Member of Chamber of Commerce.

Nelsons', The
470 West St. James Rd., V7N 2P5
604-985-1178
Roy & Charlotte Nelson
March–November

$$ B&B
4 rooms, 3 pb
C-ltd/S-no/P-no/H-no

Full breakfast
Afternoon tea
Sitting room with TV
swimming pool

Gracious residence offering seclusion and relaxation in garden setting. Easily accessible to Vancouver attractions and island ferries.

NORTH VANCOUVER

Platt's B&B
4393 Quinton Place, V7R 4A8
604-987-4100
Nancy & Elwood Platt
All year

$ B&B
2 rooms, 1 pb
C-ltd/S-no/P-no/H-no
English

Full breakfast
Homemade bread & jams

Quiet parklike area, homemade bread and jams. 15 minutes to heart of town and our famous Stanley Park.

Sue's Victorian GuestHouse
152 E. 3rd, V7L 1E6
604-985-1523
A. & N. Desmarias/S. Chalmers
All year

$ EP
3 rooms, 1 pb
C-ltd/S-no/P-no/H-no
English

Limited use of kitchen
Guests have a fridge
Color TV/video in rms.
phone for local calls

Restored 1904 home, four blocks from harbour, centrally located for transportation, shopping, restaurants and tourist attractions. **7th night free & off season monthly rates**

VickeRidge B&B
3638 Loraine Ave., V7R 4B8
604-985-0338
Barrie Vickers
All year

$ B&B/MAP
3 rooms, 1 pb
Rated, •
C-yes/S-no/P-no/H-no
French

Full breakfast
Dinner by prior arrang.
Comp. wine, snacks
sitting room, library
honeymoon package

Gracious accommodations, superb breakfasts, quiet alpine village, convenient to downtown, cruise ships, cultural and recreational activities. **Passes to attractions**

OSOYOOS

Haynes Point Lakeside
3619 - 87th St., RR #1, V0H 1V0
604-495-7443
John & June Wallace
All year

$ B&B
2 rooms, 1 pb
Rated
C-ltd/S-no/P-no/H-no

Full breakfast
Beverage on arrival
Sitting room, books
bicycles, tennis court
bathroom jet tub

Experience an unforgetable Okanagan holiday! Summer & winter paradise. Sun, water sports, golf, wine tours, ski slopes, beautiful scenery. Congenial hosts.

PORT ALBERNI

Lakewood B&B
Site 339, C5, RR3, 9778 Stirling
Arm Cr., V9Y 7L7
604-723-2310
Dick & Jane Visee
All year

$ B&B
3 rooms, 2 pb
C-ltd/S-no/P-no/H-no
Dutch

Full breakfast
Coffee
Library, sitting room
lake for swimming

We welcome adult travelers to our preaceful waterfront home. Garden setting overlooking beautiful Sproat Lake. **Off-season rates**

SALT SPRING ISLE—GANGES

Cranberry Ridge B&B
RR #2, S. 14 B.5, 269 Don Ore
Dr., V0S 1E0
604-537-4854
Gloria Callison & Roger Lutz
All year

$$$ B&B
3 rooms, 3 pb
Visa, MC, *Rated*, •
C-ltd/S-no/P-no/H-no

Full breakfast
4-6 person hot tub
large sun deck, sitt. rm
magnificent views

3 large rooms w/private powder rooms and private entrances, 1 w/fireplace, 2. Fantastic views. Great Canadian hospitality. Full home-cooked breakfast with homebaked goods.

SOOKE ————————————————————————————————————

Ocean Wilderness	$$ B&B	Full breakfast
109 W. Coast Rd., RR 2, V0S 1N0	9 rooms, 9 pb	Dinner
604-646-2116	Visa, MC, *Rated*, •	In-room bar & fridge
Marion Rolston	C-yes/P-yes	beach, gardens
All year		hot tub in gazebo

Nine elegant rooms featuring canopied beds on forested oceanfront acreage. Country breakfast, garden. Several soaktubs. Gazebo jacuzzi overlooking ocean.

Ocean Wilderness Country	$$$ B&B	Full breakfast
109 West Coast Rd., RR# 2, V0S 1N0	9 rooms, 9 pb	Dinner by arrangement
604-646-2116	Visa, MC, *Rated*, •	Snacks, bar fridge
Marion Paine	C-yes/S-no/P-yes/H-yes	sitting room, hot tubs
All year		beach

5 wooded acres w/beach; whales, seals; hot tubs in romantic rooms w/canopied beds. Honeymoon? Birthday? Plant a Douglas Fir "Memory Tree." **Winter, 3rd night free**

Sooke Harbour House	$$$ B&B	Full breakfast
1528 Whiffen Spit Rd., RR #4, V0S 1N0	15 rooms, 15 pb	Light buffet lunch incl.
604-642-3421 FAX:642-6988	Most CC, *Rated*, •	Dinner, bar, entertnmnt.
Fredrica & Sinclair Philip	C-yes/S-ltd/P-yes/H-yes	sitting room, piano
All year	French	jacuzzi, bikes, hot tubs

Charmingly furnished oceanview guestrooms. Outstanding imaginative gourmet restaurant serves local sea, land produce. Guests say romantic, relaxing, magical, memorable.

SUMMERLAND ————————————————————————————————

Lakeside Inn B&B	$ B&B	Full breakfast menu
Site 104, RR 4, C 1, 7219 Nixon Rd., V0H 1Z0	3 rooms, 1 pb	Hot tubs, sitting room
604-494-1825	Visa, MC, *Rated*,	pottery & gallery
Mary & Ernie Ursuliak	C-yes/S-ltd/P-no/H-no	
All year		

On lakeshore, modern 2+-story home. Safe swimming, sandy beach, wharf, guest livingroom, hot tub, menu. Pottery studio and gallery on premises.

VANCOUVER ————————————————————————————————

Diana's Luxury B&B	$$ B&B	Full breakfast
1019 E. 38th Ave., V5W 1J4	10 rooms, 2 pb	Comp. tea, coffee
604-321-2855 FAX:321-3411	Visa, MC, Travelers Ck., •	Sitting room, sundeck
Diana Piwko	C-ltd/S-yes/P-yes/H-yes	jacuzzi, garden patio
All year	Polish,Russ,Yugos,Czech	TV, games, bicycles

Luxury home in central area. Free airport pickup. Comfortable, friendly atmosphere. Downtown Vancouver accommodations avail. Babysitting avail. **Free champagne/honeymooners**

Johnson Heritage House B&B	$$ B&B	Full breakfast
2278 W. 34th Ave., V6M 1G6	3 rooms, 1 pb	Front & back decks, TV
604-266-4175	Cash or cheque, •	library, sitting room
Sandy & Ron Johnson	C-ltd/S-no/P-no/H-no	rock garden, VCR
All year	French, ltd	

A restored character home in one of Vancouver's finest neighborhoods. Brass beds & carousel horses, antique decor. **7th night free, Oct.-March**

VANCOUVER

Kenya Court Guest House
2230 Cornwall Ave., V6K 1B5
604-738-7085
D. M. Williams
All year

$$$ B&B
5 rooms, 5 pb
Personal ckecks OK,
C-ltd/S-no/P-no/H-no
Italian, French, German

Full breakfast
Comp. tea, coffee
Sitting room, library
tennis courts
glass solarium

Heritage guest house overlooking Kitsiland Beach, mountains, English Bay. Gourmet breakfast served in glass solarium with panoramic view. Minutes from downtown, Granville Isl.

Manor Guest House, The
345 W. 13th Ave., V5Y 1W2
604-876-8494
Brenda Rabkin
All year

$$$ B&B
9 rooms, 5 pb
Visa
C-ltd/S-ltd/P-no/H-no
French, German

Full breakfast
Galley kitchen use
parlor/music room
English garden, decks

An Edwardian heritage manor. Convenient to everything. Spacious rooms, fine breakfasts and helpful hosts make your stay memorable. Sitting room

Rose Guest House, The
3453 Prince Albert St., V5V 4H6
604-876-4419 604-872-1800
Kathryne Holm
All year

$$ B&B
2 rooms
Visa, •
C-ltd/S-no/P-no/H-no

Full breakfast
Coffee/tea on patio
Sitting room
library, TV, videos
piano/instruments

*Gracious home in residential area, close to exciting downtown. Your travel-certified Vancouver-born hostess is eager to help you plan excursions. **10% off seniors & repeats***

West End Guest House, The
1362 Haro St., V6E 1G2
604-681-2889 FAX:688-8812
Evan Penner
All year

$$$ B&B
7 rooms, 7 pb
Visa, MC, *Rated*,
C-ltd/S-no/P-no/H-no
English, French

Full breakfast
Bedside sherry (5-7pm)
Sitting room with TV
parking, library, piano
room phones, bicycles

Walk to Stanley Park, beaches, enjoy quiet ambiance of our comfortable historic inn. Popular w/romantic couples. Fireplace, antiques, robes. Turndown w/snack.

VICTORIA

Battery Street Guest House
670 Battery St., V8V 1E5
604-385-4632
Pamela Verduyn
All year

$$ B&B
6 rooms, 2 pb
C-ltd/S-no/P-no/H-no
Dutch

Full breakfast
Sitting room
walk to park and ocean

Comfortable guest house (1898) in downtown Victoria. Centrally located; walk to town, sites, Beacon Hill Park, ocean. Ample breakfast. Host speaks Dutch as a first language.

Captain's Palace
309 Belleville St., V8V 1X2
604-388-9191
Florence Prior, Helen Beirnes
All year

$$ B&B
18 rooms, 18 pb
Visa, MC, AmEx, *Rated*,
•
C-ltd/S-no/P-no/H-no

Full breakfast from menu
Welcoming cocktail
Morning coffee

*Unique accommodations overlooking harbor in Heritage Mansion. Private baths, TV. 5 minute walk to City Center. Old world charm, modern service. **Complimentary champagne***

VICTORIA ───

Dashwood Seaside Manor
B&B
1 Cook St., V8V 3W6
604-385-5517 800-667-5517
Derek Dashwood
All year, Fax: 383-1760

$$$ B&B
14 rooms
Visa, MC, AmEx, *Rated*,
•
C-yes/S-no/P-ltd/H-no

Full breakfast
Comp. wine
Sitting room
library
tennis court nearby

Victoria's only seaside B&B inn. 1912 Edwardian mansion, adjacent park, near town. 14 suites, each your own home w/fabulous views. **3rd night 50% off, except July & August**

Elk Lake Lodge B&B
5259 Patricia Bay Hwy, V8Y 1S8
604-658-8879 FAX:658-4558
Marty & Ivan Musar
Open May 1 - October 15

$$ B&B
5 rooms, 5 pb
Visa, MC, *Rated*, •
C-ltd/S-no/P-ltd/H-no

Full breakfast
Afternoon tea, coffee
Library and T.V.
large lounge
hot tub on patio

Formerly a unique 1910 monastery and church. Antique furnishings with bedrooms and living room overlooking Elk Lake. Ten min. from the city cntr, ferries. **3rd night 50% off**

Heritage House B&B
3808 Heritage Ln., V8Z 7A7
604-479-0892
Larry & Sandra Gray
All year

$$ B&B
5 rooms, 2 pb
Visa, MC, *Rated*,
C-ltd/S-no/P-no/H-no

Full breakfast
Snacks, comp. wine
Murder Mystery specials
sitting room, library
2-day minimum stay

1910 Craftsman Style, designated "Heritage Home" on³⁄₄ acre. Beautifully decorated. Gardens, lounging veranda, complimentary house wine served. Convenient to ferries.

Holland House Inn
595 Michigan St., V8V 1S7
604-384-6644
Lance Olsen & Robin Birsner
All year

$$$ B&B
10 rooms, 10 pb
Most CC, *Rated*, •
C-ltd/S-no/P-no/H-yes

Full breakfast
Sherry, tea, coffee, etc
Sitting room
library
fresh flowers

A unique 19-room luxury inn furnished throughout with eclectic furnishings and original, contemporary art. Winter months include string quartets once/month. AAA—3 diamonds.

Little Garden Farm, The
5373 Pat Bay Hwy. #2, V8Y 1S9
604-658-8404 FAX:658-4604
Paul & Elizabeth Gregory
All year

$$ B&B
4 rooms, 3 pb
Visa, MC, •
C-ltd/S-ltd/P-no/H-no
French

Full country breakfast
Afternoon tea, snacks
Restaurants nearby
sitting room, parlour
bicycles, piano, animals

Country-style B&B; lakeside swimming, parks & windsurfing; hearty home cooking; character rooms; close to Butchart Gardens and downtown Victoria. **Restaurant coupons, ltd.**

Oak Bay Guest House
1052 Newport Ave., Oak Bay,
V8S 5E3
604-598-3812
Marvin & Dolores Baschman
March — October

$$ B&B
11 rooms, 9 pb
Visa, MC, *Rated*,
C-ltd/S-no/P-no/H-no

Full breakfast
Sitting room
library

Charming, peaceful character home furnished with antiques. Beautiful gardens, close to scenic walks, beaches, golf and minute's drive into Victoria.

VICTORIA ───

Our Home on the Hill B&B $$ B&B   Full breakfast
546 Delora Dr., V9C 3R8   3 rooms, 1 pb   Comp. coffee, tea
604-474-4507   •   Sitting room
Grace & Arnie Holman   C-yes/S-no/P-no/H-no   hot tub
All year

Enjoy peaceful seclusion; cozy, antique-accented bedrooms; a hearty breakfast; near beaches, parks and trails, 20 minutes from Victoria. **7th night free**

Portage Inlet House B&B $$ B&B   Full English breakfast
993 Portage Rd., V8Z 1K9   4 rooms, 3 pb   Organically grown food
604-479-4594   Visa, MC, •   Private entrances
Jim & Pat Baillie   C-yes/S-ltd/P-no/H-yes   garden, water views
All year   "honeymoon" cottage

Acre of waterfront, 3 miles from city centre, located at mouth of salmon stream. Organic food; hearty breakfast. Ducks, swans, eagles, heron and other wildlife on property.

Prior House B&B Inn $$$ B&B   Full breakfast
620 St. Charles St., V8S 3N7 6 rooms, 6 pb   Afternoon tea
604-592-8847   Visa, MC, *Rated*, •   Comp. wine
Candis L. Cooperrider   C-ltd/S-no/P-no/H-no   sitting room
All year   library

Grand English manor built for king's representative. Fireplaces, antiques, ocean vistas and gardens. Recapture romance in elegant beauty. **2 for 1, Jan. & Feb.**

Raven Tree Iris Gardens $$ B&B   Full breakfast
1853 Connie Rd., R.R. #2, V9B 4 rooms, 4 pb   Afternoon tea
5B4   Visa, MC, •   Complimentary wine
604-642-5248   C-ltd/S-ltd/P-no/H-no   sitting room
D. Knight
Easter to September

Gracious English Tudor set in 10 acres of gardens and woodland paths. Located between Victoria and spectacular west coast beaches. 35 miles of bike trails and hiking nearby.

Sonia's B&B by the Sea $$ B&B   Full breakfast
175 Bushby St., V8S 1B5   4 rooms, 4 pb   Tea & coffee
604-385-2700 800-667-4489 C-ltd/S-no/P-yes/H-no   Sitting room
Sonia & Brian McMillan   deck overlooking ocean
April–September   one suite over ocean

Sonia offers marvelous stories, quality lodgings at a good value. Her breakfasts are as bountiful as the hospitality. Innkeeper born and raised in Victoria, can suggest sites.

Sunnymeade House Inn $$ B&B   Full breakfast
1002 Fenn Ave., Cordova Bay by 5 rooms, 1 pb   Restaurant, bar
the Sea, V8Y 1P3   Visa, MC, *Rated*,   Afternoon tea, candy
604-658-1414   C-ltd/S-no/P-no   sitting room, flowers
Jack & Nancy Thompson   garden, tennis courts
All year

Village by the Sea. Walk to shops, restaurants, beach. Country-style B&B inn. Beautiful decor and furnishings; 15 minutes to Butchart Gardens and Ferry. Golf course nearby.

VICTORIA

Swallow Hill Farm B&B
4910 William Head Rd., RR#1,
V9B 5T7
604-474-4042
Gini & Peter Walsh
All year

$$ B&B
2 rooms, 2 pb
Visa, MC, *Rated*, •
C-yes/S-no/P-no/H-no

Full farm breakfast
Comp. tea/coffee
Sitting room, bicycles
books & games for guests
many activity brochures

Mountain & sea views. Delicious homebaked breakfasts. Friendly conversation. Guest rooms w/antiques. Central to S. Vancouver Is. **10% off 7+ nights, picnics, romantic wkend**

Top O' Triangle Mountain
3442 Karger Terrace, V9C 3K5
604-478-7853 FAX:478-2245
Henry & Pat Hansen
All year

$$ B&B
3 rooms, 3 pb
Visa, MC, •
C-yes/S-ltd/P-no/H-yes
Danish

Full breakfast
Refreshments on arrival
Sitting room, TV in rms.
2 room suite avail.
Comp. coffee, tea

Warm, solid cedar home tucked in among the firs. Breathtaking view. Clean, comfortable beds. Hospitality and good food are our specialties. We make guests "at home."

Wellington B&B
66 Wellington Ave., V8V 4H5
604-383-5976 FAX:385-0477
Inge & Sue Ranzinger
All year

$$ B&B
4 rooms, 4 pb
MC, •
C-ltd/S-no/P-no/H-no
German, Spanish

Full breakfast
Refrigerator, ice
Sitting room, library
sun porch, sun deck
tennis court nearby

A touch of class! Quiet street, close to ocean, park and downtown. Beautifully designed bright rooms with queen & king beds. **Winter specials—3rd night free**

VICTORIA—SIDNEY

Graham's Cedar House B&B
1825 Landsend Rd., R.R. #3,
V8L 5J2
604-655-3699 FAX:655-1422
Kay & Dennis Graham
All year

$$ B&B
3 rooms, 3 pb
•
C-ltd/S-no/P-no/H-no

Full breakfast
Afternoon tea, snacks
Comp. sherry, sit. rm.
private entrances, decks
sitting area, TV, bath

Chalet luxury on quiet acreage. Strolling, gardens, magnificent trees. Minutes to Rutchart Gardens, Victoria, ferries, airport, Sidney. **7th night free—Off season rates.**

WEST VANCOUVER

Creekside B&B
1515 Palmerston Ave., V7V 4S9
604-926-1861 604-328-9400
John Boden & Donna Hawrelko
All year

$$$ B&B
2 rooms, 2 pb
Visa, MC, •
C-ltd/S-no/P-no/H-no
Ukrainian

Full breakfast, snacks
Complimentary wine
Color TV, fireplace
2 person jacuzzi tubs
stocked fridge in rooms

Private, natural, woodsy creekside hideaway. Close to parks, skiing, beaches and ocean. Honeymoon suite available. 2 day minimum. **Restaurant & other 50% coupons**

WHISTLER

Golden Dreams B&B
6412 Easy St., V0N 1B6
604-932-2667 800-668-7055
Ann & Terry Spence
All year, Fax: 932-7055

$$ B&B
3 rooms, 1 pb
Visa, MC, •
C-yes/S-no/P-no/H-no

Full breakfast
Comp. sherry
Private jacuzzi, TV, VCR
theme rooms
fireside lounge

1 mile N. of Whistler Village ski lifts on valley trail & bus route Nutritious home-cooking, large patio/deck with guest fridge & B.B.Q. Families welcome!

More Inns . . .

Nolan House, Box 135, Atlin, V0B 1A0, 604-651-7585
Aguilar House, Bamfield, V0R 1B0, 604-728-3323
Betty Cartwright, Box 5A Site 80 R.R., Black Creek, V0R 160
Bobbing Boats, Box 88, 7212 Peden Ln., Brentwood Bay, V0S 1A0, 604-652-9828
Patterson Guest House, 7106 18th Ave., Burnaby, V3N 1H1
Haida Inn, 1342 Island Hwy, Campbell River, V9W 2E1, 604-287-7402
Pacific Shores Inn, P.O. Box 958, Chemainus, V0R 1K0, 604-246-4987
Greystone Manor, RR 6, Site 684/C2, Courtenay, V9N 8H9, 604-338-1422
Blackberry Inn, The, RR1, Box 29, Cowichan Bay, V0R 1N0
Denman Island Guest House, Box 9, Denman Rd., Denman Island, V0R 1T0, 604-335-2688
Sea Canery Guest House B&B, PO Box 31, Denman Island, V0R 1T0
Country Gardens B&B, 1665 Grant Rd., RR 5, Duncan, V9L 4T6, 604-748-5865
Fairburn Farm, RR 7, Duncan, V9L 4W4, 604-746-4637
Grove Hall Estate B&B, 6159 Lakes Rd., Duncan, V9L 4J6, 604-746-6152
Bradshaw's Minac Lodge, On Canim Lake, Eagle Creek, V0K 1L0, 604-397-2416
Kel Kar Acres, 3950 Borland Dr.Box 158, East Kelowna, V0H 1G0
Hummingbird Inn, Sturdies Bay Rd., Galiano Island, V0N 1P0, 604-539-5472
La Berengerie, Montague Harbor Bl., Galiano Island, V0N 1P0, 604-539-5392
Woodstone Country Inn, RR#1, Georgeson Bay Rd., Galiano Island, V0N 1P0, 604-539-2022
Armand Heights B&B, Box 341, Ganges, V0S 1E0, 604-653-9989
Beach House B&B Inn, 930 Sunset Dr., RR 1, Ganges, V0S 1E0, 604-537-2879
Dianne Verzyl, RR 2 S 46 C10, Gibson's, V0N 1V0
Ocean View Cottage B&B, RR 2, Site 46, C10, Gibson's, V0N 1V0, 604-886-7943
Lord Jim's Resort Hotel, RR 1, Ole's Cove Rd., Halfmoon Bay, V0N 1Y0, 604-885-7038
Park Place B&B, 730 Yates Rd., Kamloops, V2B 6C9
Blair House, 1299 Rodondo Place, Kelowna, V1V 1G6, 604-762-5090
Gables Country Inn, 2405 Bering Rd/Box 1153, Kelowna, V1Y 7P8, 604-768-4468
Poplar Point, 345 Herbert Heights Rd., Kelowna, V1Y 1Y4
View to Remember B&B, 1090 Trevor Dr., Kelowna, V1Z 2J8, 604-769-4028
Chilanko Lodge & Resort, Gen. Delivery, Hwy 20, Kleena Kleene, V0L 1M0, 604-Kleena K
Primrose Hill Guest House, 4919-48th Ave., Ladner, V4K 1V4, 604-940-8867
Manana Lodge, Box 9 RR 1, Ladysmith, V0R 2E0, 604-245-2312
Yellow Point Lodge, RR 3, Ladysmith, V0R 2E0, 604-245-7422
Linnaea Farm, Box 112, Mansons Landing, V0P 1K0
Fernhill Lodge, Box 140, Mayne Island, V0N 2J0, 604-539-2544
Gingerbread House, Campbell Bay Rd., Mayne Island, V0N 2J0, 604-539-3133
Oceanwood Country, 22 Dinner Bay Rd., Mayne Island, V0N 2J0, 604-539-5074
Billion $ View B&B, 610 Shorewood Rd., RR#1, Mill Bay, V0R 2P0, 604-743-2387
Brown House B&B, The, 3020 Dolphin Dr, Nanoose Bay, V0N 2J0, 604-468-7804
Oceanside B&B, Box 26, RR2, Blueback, Nanoose Bay, V0R 2R0, 604-468-9241
Wild Rose Stables, RR #1 Site 4 Comp 5, Naramata, V0H 1N0
Heritage Inn, 422 Vernon St., Nelson, V1L 5P4, 604-352-5331
Willow Point Lodge, RR 1, Nelson, V1L 5P4, 604-825-9411
Dutch-Canadian B&B, 201 East 7th Ave, New Westminster, V3L 4H5, 604-521-7404
B&B for Visitors, 10356 Skagit Dr., North Delta, V4C 2K9, 604-588-8866
Hummingbird Hollow B&B, 36125 Galleon Way, North Pender Island, V0N 2M0, 604-629-6392
B&B at Laburnum Cottage, 1388 Terrace Ave., North Vancouver, V7R 1B4, 604-988-4877
Grand Manor, 1617 Grand Blvd., North Vancouver, V7L 3Y2
Thom's Bed & Breakfast, 615 W. 23rd St., North Vancouver, V7M 2C2, 604-986-2168
Fritzville, 34032 Hwy. 97 S. RR #1, Oliver, V0H 1T0
Taliesin Guest House B&B, Box 101, Parson, V0A 1L0, 604-348-2247
Corbett House B&B, Corbett Rd., Pender Island, V0N 2M0, 604-629-6305
Apex Ranch, P.O. Box 426, Penticton, V2A 6K6
Paradise Cove, Box 699, Penticton, V2A 6P1
Feathered Paddle B&B, 7 Queesto Dr., Port Renfrew, V0S 1K0, 604-647-5433
Park Place B&B, 1689 Birch St., Prince George, V2L 1B3, 604-563-6326
Quilchena Hotel, Quilchena, V0E 2R0, 604-378-2611
Cliffside Inn on the Sea, Genl. Delivery, Render Island, V0N 2M0
Ram's Head Inn, Red Mt. Ski Area Box 63, Rossland, V0G 1Y0, 604-362-9577
Cindosa B&B, 3951 - 40th St. NE, Salmon Arm, V1E 4M4, 604-832-3342
Silver Creek Guest House, 6820 - 30th Ave. SW, Salmon Arm, V1E 4M1, 604-832-8870
Hastings House, Box 1110, Ganges, Salt Spring Island, V0S 1E0, 800-661-9255
"Great-Snoring-On-Sea", 10858 Madrona Dr., RR1, Sidney, V8L 3R9, 604-659-9549
Courtyard by the Sea, The, 380 Moses Pt. Rd., Sidney, V8L 4R4
John Gamble B&B, Box 300, Sointala, V0N 3E0
Wayward Wind Lodge, Box 300, Sointala, V0N 3E0, 604-973-6307
Tideview, 1597 Dufour Rd., RR4, Sooke, V0S 1N0
Three Pines Lodge, S. 85, RR 2, Summerland, V0H 1Z0, 604-494-1661
Veto's Vineyard, 9402 Front Beach Rd., Summerland, V0H 1Z0
Hirsch's Place, 10336-145 A St., Surrey, V3R 3S1, 604-588-3326
Clayoquot Lodge, P.O. Box 188, Tofino, V0R 2Z0, 604-725-3284
Burley's Lodge, Box 193, Ucluelet, V0R 3A0, 604-726-4444
Albion Guest House, The, 592 W. 19th Ave., Vancouver, 604-873-2287
An English Garden B&B, 4390 Frances St., Vancouver, V5C 2R3
Green Gables, 628 Union St., Vancouver, V6A 2B9, 604-253-6230
Nelson House, 977 Broughton St., Vancouver, V6G 2A4, 604-684-9793
John & Mary Parker, 11149 Prospect Dr., Vancouver (Delta), V4E 2R4, 604-594-1832
"Castle on the Mountain", 8227 Silver Star Rd., Vernon, V1T 8L6, 604-542-4593

"The Cabin", 7603 Westkal Rd., Vernon, V1B 1Y4, 000-542-3021
Falcon Nest, The, RR 8, Site 7A, Vernon, V1T 8L6, 604-545-1759
Five Junipers, 3704 - 24th Ave., Vernon, V1T 1L9, 604-549-3615
Gisela's Bed & Breakfast, 3907 17th Ave., Vernon, V1T 6Z1, 604-542-5977
Schroth Farm, Site 6, Comp 25, R.R.8, Vernon, V1T 8L6, 604-545-0010
Swan Lake View, RR #5, S-6, C-66, Vernon, V1T 6L8
Twin Willows By The Lake, Site 10, Comp 16, RR 4, Vernon, V1T 6L7, 604-542-8293
Windmill House, S 19A, C2, RR 1, Vernon, V1T 6L4, 604-549-2804
Abigail's Hotel, 906 McClure St., Victoria, V8V 3E7, 604-388-5363
Ambleside B&B, 1121 Faithful St., Victoria, V8V 2R5, 604-383-9948
Arundel Manor B&B, 980 Arundel Dr., Victoria, V9A-2C3, 604-385-5442
Beaconsfield Inn, The, 998 Humboldt St., Victoria, V8V 2Z8, 604-384-4044
Camelot, P O Box 5038, Stn. B, Victoria, V8R 6N3, 604-592-8589
Cherry Bank Hotel, 825 Burdetl Ave., Victoria, V8W 1B3
Craigmyle B&B, 1037 Craigdorroch Rd., Victoria, V8S 2A5, 604-595-5411
Emilie's Bed & Breakfast, 1570 Rockland Ave., Victoria, V8S 1W5, 604-598-8881
Glyn House, 154 Robertson St., Victoria, V8S 3X1
Hibernia B&B, 747 Helvetia Crescent, Victoria, V8Y 1M1, 604-658-5519
Humboldt House, 867 Humboldt St., Victoria, V8V 2Z6, 604-384-8422
Joan Brown's B&B, 834 Pemberton Rd., Victoria, V8S 3R4, 604-592-5929
Maridou House, 116 Elbert St., Victoria, V86 3H7, 604-360-0747
Olde England Inn, 429 Lampson St., Victoria, V8S 2A5, 604-388-4353
Oxford Castle Inn, 133 George Rd., East, Victoria, V9A 1L1, 604-388-6431
Sealake House B&B, 5152 Santa Clara Ave., Victoria, V84 1W4, 604-658-5208
Weathervane B&B, The, 1633 Rockland Ave., Victoria, V8S 1W6, 604-592-0493
Whyte House, 155 Randall St., Victoria, V8V 2E3, 604-389-1598
Wooded Acres B&B, 4907 Rocky Point Rd, Victoria, V98 5B4, 604-478-8172
Beachside B&B, 4208 Evergreen Ave., West Vancouver, V7V 1H1, 604-922-7773
Creekside B&B, 1515 Palmerston Ave., West Vancouver, V7V 4S9, 604-926-1861
Park Royal Hotel, 540 Clyde Ave., West Vancouver, V7T 2J7, 604-932-1924
Lakeview Mansion, 3858 Harding Rd., Westbank, V0H 2A0, 604-768-2205
Durlocher Hof, P.O. Box 1125, Whistler, V0N 1B0, 604-932-1924
Sabey House, Box 341, Whistler, V0N 1B0, 604-932-3498

Manitoba

WINNIPEG

West Gate Manor B&B　　　$ B&B　　　　　　　Full breakfast
71 West Gate, R3C 2C9　　　6 rooms
204-772-9788　FAX:943-8371　Visa, MC, •
John & Louise Clark　　　　C-ltd/S-no/P-no/H-no
All year

Located in historic Armstrong Point area of Winnipeg. Living room is decorated in Victorian splendor. Each guest room reflects it's own period & theme. **Restaurant discounts**

More Inns ...

Dueck's Cedar Chalet, Box 362, Boissevain, R0K 0E0
Ernie & Tina Dyck, Box 1001, Boissevain, R0K 0E0, 204-534-2563
Casa Maley, 1605 Victoria Ave., Brandon, R7A 1C1, 204-728-0812
Bide Awhile, Box 414, Dauphin Beach, R7N 2V2
Solmundson Gesta Hus, Box 76, Hecla, R0C 1K0, 000-279-2088
Deerbank Farm, Box 23, RR 2, Morris, R0G 1K0, 204-746-8395
Geppetto's, Box 2A, RR #1, Richer, R0E 1S0
Beulah Land, Box 26, Treherne, R0G 2V0, 204-723-2828
Plett's B&B, Box 158, Wawanesa, R0K 2G0
Bannerman East, 99 Bannerman Ave., Winnipeg, R2W 0T1, 204-589-6449
Belanger's B&B, 291 Oakwood Ave., Winnipeg, R3L 1E8
Chestnut House, 209 Chestnut St., Winnipeg, R36 1R8, 204-772-9788
Edna O'Hara, 242 Amherst St., Winnipeg, R3J 1Y6, 204-888-6848
Ellie's B&B, 77 Middle Gate, Winnipeg, R3C 2C5
Fillion's B&B, 45 Abingdon Rd., Winnipeg, R2J 3S7
Hawchuk's B&B, 22 Everette Pl., Winnipeg, R2V 4E8, 204-339-7005
Hillman's B&B, 701 Sherburn St., Winnipeg, R3G 2L1
Irish's B&B, 12-341 Westwood Dr., Winnipeg, R3K 1G4
Lobreau's B&B, 137 Woodlawn Ave, Winnipeg, R2M 2P5
Nancy & Geoff Tidmarch, 330 Waverly St., Winnipeg, R3M 3L3, 204-284-3689
Narvey's B&B, 564 Waverley St., Winnipeg, R3M 3L5

Paul & Trudy Johnson, 455 Wallasey St., Winnipeg, R3J 3C5, 204-837-3368
Preweda's B&B, 13 Nichol Ave., Winnipeg, R2M 1Y6
Reimer's B&B, 111 Lake Village Rd., Winnipeg, R3T 4M7
Selci's B&B, 31 Carlyle Bay, Winnipeg, R3K 0H2
Southern Rose Guest House, 533 Sprague St., Winnipeg, R3G 2R9
Thomas & Marie Wiebe, 25 Valley View Dr., Winnipeg, R2Y 0R5, 204-888-0910
Voyageur House, 268 Notre Dame St., Winnipeg, R2H 0C6
Wiebe's B&B, 281 Wallasey St., Winnipeg, R3J 3C2
Zonnehoek B&B, 27 Galbraith Cir., Winnipeg, R2Y 1Z5
Zonneveld's B&B, 144 Yale Ave., Winnipeg, R3M 0L7

New Brunswick

RIVERSIDE

Cailswick Babbling Brook
Albert Co., Route 114, E0A 2R0
506-882-2079
Eunice Cail
All year

$ B&B
5 rooms, 2 pb
C-yes/S-no/P-no/H-no
French

Full country breakfast
Evening snack
Beverages, sweets
sitting room, television
near Hopewell Cape Rocks

Country living. Quiet, serene, restful. Home-cooked meals. Century-old Victorian overlooking Shepardy Bay, lovely grounds. Near Fundy National Park & Hopewell Cape Rocks.

SACKVILLE

Different Drummer, The
Box 188, 146 West Main, E0A
3C0
506-536-1291
Elinor & Ted Philips
All year

$ B&B
8 rooms, 8 pb
Visa, MC
C-yes/S-ltd/P-ltd/H-ltd

Continental plus
Sitting room
TV, library

Victorian house with lovely garden. Four poster and spool beds in sunny bay-windowed rooms, all with private baths. Two new spacious carriage house rooms.

More Inns . . .

Florentine Manor, RR 2, Albert, E0A 1A0, 506-882-2271
Ingle-Neuk Lodge B&B, RR 3 Box 1180, Bathurst, E2A 4G8, 506-546-5758
Poplars—Les Peupliers, RR1 Site 11 Box 16, Beresford, E0B 1H0, 506-546-5271
Dugas Tourist Home, 683 Blvd., St. Pierre, Caraquet, E0B 1K0
Reid Farms Tourist Home, RR 1, Centreville, E0J 1H0, 506-276-4787
Back Porch B&B, 266 Northumberland St., Frederiction, E3B 3J6, 506-454-6875
Happy Apple Acres, RR 4, Hwy 105, Fredericton, E3B 4X5, 506-472-1819
Victoriana Rose B&B, 193 Church St., Fredericton, E3B 4E1, 506-454-0994
Compass Rose, North Head, Grand Manan, E0G 2M0, 506-662-8570
Cross Tree Guest House, Seal Cove, Grand Manan, E0G 3B0, 506-662-8263
Ferry Wharf Inn, North Head, Grand Manan, E0G 2M0, 506-662-8588
Grand Harbour Inn, Box 73, Grand Harbour, Grand Manan, E0G 1X0, 506-662-8681
Manan Island Inn & Spa, P.O. Box 15, Grand Manan, E0G 2M0, 506-662-8624
Rosalie's B&B, Seal Cove, Grand Manan, E0G3B0, 506-662-3344
Shorecrest Lodge, North Head, Grand Manan Island, E0G 2M0, 506-662-3216
Eveleigh Hotel, Evandale, RR1, Hampstead, E0G 1Y0, 506-425-9993
Woodsview II B&B, RR 5, Hartland, E0J 1N0, 506-375-4637
Dutch Treat Farm, RR 1, Shepody, Hopewell Cape, E0A 1Y0, 506-882-2552
Pollocks Heritage Farm, Hopewell Cape, E0A 1Y0
Mactaquac B&B, Mactaquac RR1, Mactaquac, E0H 1N0, 506-363-3630
Governor's Mansion, Main St., Nelson, E0C 1T0, 506-622-3036
Kingfisher Lodge, RR 1, Plaster Rock, E0J 1W0
Northern Wilderness Lodge, Box 571, Plaster Rock, E0J 1W0, 506-356-8327
Shadow Lawn Inn, P.O. Box 41, Rothesay, E0G 2W0, 506-847-7539
Marshlands Inn, Box 1440, Sackville, E0A 3C0, 506-536-0170
PuffInn, P.O. Box 135, Saint Andrews, E0G 2X0, 506-529-4191
Shiretown Inn, Town Square, Saint Andrews, E0G 2X0, 506-529-8877
A Touch of Country, 61 Pleasant St., Saint Stephen, E3L 1A6, 506-466-5056
Pansy Patch, P.O. Box 349, St. Andrews, E0G 2X0, 506-529-3834
Andersons Holiday Farm, Sussex RR 2, Sussex, E0E 1P0, 506-433-3786

Stark's Hillside B&B, RR #4 Waterford, Sussex, E0E 1P0, 506-433-3764
Chez Prime B&B, RR 3, S. 32, Losier St., Tracadie, E0C 2B0, 506-395-6884

Newfoundland

More Inns . . .

Thorndyke Heritage Home, P.O. Box 501, Grand Bank, A0E 1W0, 709-832-0820
Chaulk's Tourist Home, P.O. Box 339, Lewisporte, A0J 3A0, 709-535-6305
Village Inn, Trinity, A0C 2S0, 709-464-3269

Northwest Territories

More Inns . . .

Harbour House, Box 54, 1 Lakeshore Dr., Hay River, X0E 0R0, 403-874-2233
Keewatin Guest Lodge, Box 2001, Keewantin, X0C 0G0
Eric & Eva's B&B, Box 2262, Yellowknife, X1A 2P7, 403-873-5779

Nova Scotia

AMHERST

Amherst Shore Country Inn	$$ EP	Full breakfast ($)
RR #2, Hwy. 366 at Lorneville,	6 rooms, 4 pb	Gourmet dinner, bar
B4H 3X9	Visa, MC, *Rated*, •	Sitting room, piano
902-667-4800 902-542-2291	C-ltd/S-no/P-ltd/H-no	clay tennis court
Donna & Jim Laceby		bicycles, private beach
May—Can. Thanksgiving		

Beautiful panoramic view of the Northumberland Strait. Donna is renowned for the 4-course dinner she serves each evening by reservation only.

CHESTER

Mecklenburgh Inn	$$ B&B	Full breakfast
78 Queen St., B0J 1J0	4 rooms	Picnic lunch
902-275-4638	Visa, *Rated*, •	Sitting room, bicycles
Suzan Fraser	C-yes/S-ltd/P-no/H-no	near tennis, golf
June 1 — October 31	French	Yacht Club, restaurants

Circa 1890 inn in heart of seaside village. Period furnishing; breakfast served before an open fire by young cordonbleu hostess.

HALIFAX

Halliburton House Inn	30 rooms, 26 pb	Continental plus
5184 Morris St., B3J 1B3	*Rated*, •	Restaurant - lunch
902-420-0658	C-yes/S-yes/P-no/H-no	Dinner, Aft. tea
Bruce R. Pretty	French	bar service, library
All year		sitting room, courtyard

Experience the pleasure of stepping into the past by visiting this four star heritage property. Beautiful guest room and gourmet meal. In heart of Halifax.

SYDNEY

Markland Coastal Resort	$$$ B&B	Continental plus
21 Haig St., Dingwall/B0C 1GO,	12 rooms, 12 pb	Restaurant, all meals $
B1S 2Y1	Visa, MC, AmEx, •	Bar service, library
902-564-5226	C-yes/S-yes/P-yes/H-yes	sitting room, bicycles
May 15 - Oct 30	French	swimming pool

Luxury log accommodations where the mtns. touch the sea. Gormet dining room features local fish & lamb. Restore yourself in pristine setting. **Discounts for extended stay**

WOLFVILLE

Blomidon Inn	$$ B&B	Continental
P.O. Box 839, 127 Main St./NS,	26 rooms, 26 pb	Lunch, dinner
B0P 1X0	Visa, MC, *Rated*, •	Comp. aft. tea, 3-5 pm
902-542-2291 FAX:542-7461	C-ltd/S-yes/P-ltd/H-yes	sitting room
Jim & Donna Laceby		tennis, shuffleboard
All year		

A tastefully restored 19th-century sea captain's mansion near the land of Evangeline. Gracious cuisine with fresh offerings from the fertile valley and bountiful sea.

More Inns . . .

Bread and Roses, P.O. Box 177, Annapolis Royal, B0S 1A0, 902-532-5727
Garrison House Inn, P.O. Box 108, Annapolis Royal, B0S 1A0, 902-532-5750
Milford House, RR #4, South Milford, Annapolis Royal, B0S 1A0, 902-532-2617
Poplars B&B, 124 Victoria St., Box 27, Annapolis Royal, B0S 1A0, 902-532-7936
Queen Anne Inn, 494 St. George St., Annapolis Royal, B0S 1A0
Old Manse Inn, 5 Tigo Park, Antigonish, B2G 1L7, 902-863-5696
Telegraph House, Box 8, Baddeck, B0E 1B0, 902-295-9988
Lovett Lodge Inn, P.O. Box 119, Bear River, B0S 1B0, 902-467-3917
1850 House, Box 22, Main St., Canning, Kings County, B0P 1H0, 902-582-3052
Heart of Hart's T. H., N.E. Margaree, Cape Breton, B0E 2H0, 902-248-2765
Markland, The, Cabot Trail, Dingwall, Cape Breton, B0C 1G0, 902-383-2246
Riverside Inn, Margaree Hrb., Cape Breton, B0E 2B0, 902-235-2002
Cobequid Hills Country Inn, Collingwood, B0M 1E0, 902-686-3381
Martin House, 62 Pleasant St., Dartmouth, B2Y 3P5, 902-469-1896
Ellen Eisses, RR #1, Debert, B0M 1G0
Bayberry House, Box 114, Troop Ln., Granville Ferry, B0S 1K0, 902-532-2272
Shining Tides, RR #2, Granville Ferry, B0S 1K0, 902-532-2770
Liscombe Lodge, Liscomb Mills, Guysborough County, B0J 2A0, 902-779-2307
Queen Street Inn, 1266 Queen St., Halifax, B3J 2H4, 902-422-9828
Seabright B&B, Seabright, Halifax County, B0J 3J0, 902-823-2987
Manor Inn, P.O. Box 56, R.R. 1, Hebron, B0W 1X0, 902-742-2487
Highland Heights Inn, Box 19, Iona, B0A 1L0, 902-622-2360
Greta Cross B&B, 81 Peperell St., Louisbourg, B0A 1M0, 902-733-2833
Boscawen Inn, P.O. Box 1343, Lunenburg, B0J 2C0, 902-634-3325
South Shore Country Inn, Broad Cove, Luwenburg County, B0J 2H0, 902-677-2042
Cape Breton Island Farm, RR 2, Mabou, B0E 1X0, 902-945-2077
Camelot, Box 31, Rt. 7, Musquodoboit Harbour, B0J 2L0, 902-889-2198
Annfield Tourist Manor, RR 3, Bras D'or, North Sydney, B0C 1B0, 902-736-8770
Westway Inn, Plympton, B0W 2R0, 902-837-4097
Planter's Barracks Inn, Starr's Point Rd., Port Williams, B0P 1T0
Blue Heron Inn, The, Box 405, Pugwash, B0K 1L0, 902-243-2900
River View Lodge, Box 93, Greenfield, Queens County, B0T 1E0
Cooper's Inn, 36 Dock St., Box 959, Shelbourne, B0T 1W0
Millstones, Box 758, Shelbourne, B0T 1W0
Toddle In B&B, Box 837, Shelbourne, B0T 1W0
Harborview Inn, P.O. Box 35, Smith's Cove, Digby Co., B0S 1S0, 902-245-5686
Lansdowne Lodge, Upper Stewiacke, B0N 2P0, 902-671-2749
Senator Guest House, Route 6, Sunrise Trail, Wallace, B0K 1Y0, 902-257-2417

Gilbert's Cove Farm, RR 3, Weymouth, B0W 3T0, 902-837-4505
Clockmaker's Inn B&B, 1399 King St., Windsor, B0W 3T0, 902-798-5265
Gingerbread House Inn, P.O. Box 819, Wolfville, BPO 1X0, 902-542-1458
Tattingstone Inn, 434 Main St., Wolfville, B0P 1X0
Victoria's Historic Inn, Box 819, 416 Main St., Wolfville, B0P 1X0, 902-542-5744
Churchill Mansion Inn, RR 1, Yarmouth, B5A 4A5, 902-649-2818

Ontario

BALDWIN

Baldwin Mill B&B	$$$ B&B	Full breakfast
24357 Highway 48, R.R.#1,	4 rooms, 2 pb	Dinner, afternoon tea
Sutton West, L0E 1R0	•	Snacks, library
416-722-5743	C-ltd/S-ltd/P-no/H-no	bicycles, hot tubs
Ruth & Jim West		gift shop, games room
May 1 - Oct. 25		

Charmingly restored 1880's grist mill only one hour north of Toronto. Scrumptious breakfasts served overlooking waterfall and dam. Antique furnishings.

BAYFIELD

Little Inn of Bayfield	$$$ EP	Continental breakfast
Main St., N0M 1G0	31 rooms, 31 pb	Lunch, dinner $
519-565-2611 Fax 565-5474	Most CC, *Rated*, •	Sitting room
Pat & Gayle Waters	C-ltd/S-yes/P-no/H-yes	sauna/whirlpool
All year	French, German, Polish	cottage

Ontario's oldest continuously operating Inn—since 1832. Antique-filled bedrooms and quiet parlors. Award-winning dining room. Cross-country ski trails. **Senior disc'ts.**

BLACKSTOCK

Landfall Farm	$ B&B	Full breakfast
3120 Hwy 7A, RR 1, L0B 1B0	4 rooms, 2 pb	Dinner on occasion
416-986-5588 905-986-5588	C-yes/S-ltd/P-ltd/H-no	Sitting room w/fireplace
Merle Heintzman		bicycles, swimming pool
All year		billiards, ping pong

1868 stone farmhouse, designated Heritage Sites. Lawns, swimming pool, pond and antique shop. Tennis, golf, fishing, cross-country skiing, ice skating nearby. **Disc'ts for children**

BRACEBRIDGE

Century House B&B	$ B&B	Full breakfast
155 Dill St., P1L 1E5	3 rooms	Afternoon tea
705-645-9903	*Rated*	Comp. eve. refreshment
Sandy Yudin/Norman Yan	C-ltd/S-ltd/P-no/H-no	sitting room
All year		

Enjoy our restored, air-conditioned century home (and Sandy's waffles) in Ontario's premier recreational lakes area just two hours from Toronto.

COBOURG

Northumberland Heights Inn
RR 5, Northumberland Heights
Rd, K9A 4J8
416-372-7500 FAX:372-4574
Mike & Veronica Thiele
All year

$$ EP
14 rooms, 14 pb
Visa, MC, AmEx, *Rated*,
•
C-yes/S-yes/P-no/H-yes
German, French, Dutch

Full breakfast $
Lunch, dinner, bar
Hot tub, sauna
swimming pool
sitting room, piano

On 100 acres of rolling countryside. Relaxing patio areas, miniature golf, outdoor checkers, trout pond, cross-country skiing, skating. Two-night "Plan" available. Ask about discounts

ELMIRA

Teddy Bear B&B Inn
RR #1, N3B 2Z1
519-669-2379
Gerrie & Vivian Smith
All year

$$ B&B
3 rooms, 3 pb
Visa, MC
C-yes/S-no/P-no/H-no

Full breakfast
Dinner with reservation
Comp. coffee anytime
sitting room, library
bicycles

Hospitality abounds in this outstandingly beautiful countryside inn with Mennonite quilts, crafts, and antiques. Close to Elora, St. Jacob's, and Stratford.

KINGSTON—1000 ISLANDS

Victoria Rose Inn, The
279 King St., Gananoque, K7G
2G7
613-382-3368
J. Chiarandini & C. Franks
All year

$$ B&B
8 rooms, 8 pb
Visa, MC, *Rated*, •
C-yes/S-no/P-no/H-no
Italian

Continental plus
Bicycles, jacuzzi, A/C
gardens, parking
sitting room

Stately mansion built in 1872 elegantly appointed w/Canadian antiques. Veranda overlooks 2 acres of estate grounds. Fine dining and antique shops. 10% off 3 days+ Sun.-Th.

LEAMINGTON

Home Suite Home B&B
115 Erie St. S., N8H 3B5
519-326-7169
Agatha & Harry Tiessen

$$ B&B
Rated
C-ltd/S-no/P-no

Full breakfast
Air-conditioning, deck
enclosed sunporch, pool
hand-made quilts

Enjoy warm hospitality in our turn-of-the-century home. Country & Victorian plush carpeting. Air-conditioned. 40 min. from Detroit. Enroute to Niagara Falls. Fine beaches.

MERRICKVILLE

Sam Jakes Inn
P.O. Box 580, 118 Main St. East,
K0G 1N0
613-269-3711 800-567-4667
Gary B. Clarke
All year

$$$ B&B
30 rooms, 30 pb
Most CC, *Rated*, •
C-ltd/S-no/P-no/H-yes

Full breakfast
Restaurant, tavern
Afternoon tea, snacks
sitting room, gardens
whirlpool, exercise room

Canalside country inn, once home of a prominent village merchant, lets you relive the 1860s in a historic town setting! Inquire about our tours.

NAPANEE

Fairview House B&B
P.O. Box 114, 373 Dundas St.,
West, K7R 3S5
613-354-5142 FAX:354-0609
S. Lucas/K. Pearsall-Lucas
All year

$ B&B
3 rooms
MC, *Rated*
C-yes/S-no/P-no/H-no

Continental plus
Snacks
Library, swimming pool
whirlpool
sitting room

1860's Victorian estate home located in small town atmosphere. Offers guests relaxing escape from hustle & bustle of big city. Stay 2 nights, 3rd night free

NIAGARA-ON-THE-LAKE ───────────────────────────

Kiely House Heritage Inn
P.O. Box 1642, 209 Queen St.,
L0S 1J0
416-468-4588
Ray & Heather Pettit
All year

$$ B&B
12 rooms, 12 pb
Visa, MC, AmEx, *Rated*,
•
C-ltd/S-yes/P-no/H-no

Continental plus
Afternoon tea, snacks
Sitting room, bicycles
verandas, garden
screened porches

Elegant early Victorian inn on one acre garden. Cool verandas; screened porches; many fireplaces. Walking distance to theaters, stores, restaurants. **Disc't Sun-Tues**

OTTAWA ───────────────────────────

Albert House
478 Albert St., K1R 5B5
613-236-4479 800-267-1982
John & Cathy Delroy
All year

$$ B&B
17 rooms, 17 pb
Visa, MC, AmEx, *Rated*,
•
C-ltd/S-yes/P-no/H-no
French, English

Full English breakfast
Tea, coffee, juices
Sitting room
color cable TV in rooms
telephones

Fine restored Victorian residence designed by Thomas Seaton Scott in post-Confederate period. Complimentary breakfast, parking.

Auberge 'The King Edward'
525 King Edward Ave., K1N 7N3
613-565-6700
Richard Gervais
All year

$$ B&B
3 rooms, 1 pb
Visa, MC, *Rated*, •
C-ltd/S-no/P-no/H-no
French

Continental plus
Private deck, bicycles
A/C, cable TV
gardens, parking

Centrally located, the 'King Edward B&B' has been faithfully restored to its formal graciousness & offers a uniqueness of character found in Victorian homes.

Australis Guest House
35 Marlborough Ave., K1N 8E6
613-235-8461
Carol & Brian Waters
All year

$$ B&B
3 rooms, 1 pb
C-yes/S-yes/P-no/H-no

Full breakfast
Afternoon tea
Sitting room, piano
bicycles
off-street parking

An older renovated antique-filled downtown home close to all attractions in an area of embassies, parks and the river. Family suite available. **Many restaurant disc'ts.**

Blue Spruces B&B
187 Glebe Ave., K1S 2C6
613-236-8521
Patricia & John Hunter
All year

$$ B&B
3 rooms, 3 pb
Rated
C-ltd/S-no/P-no/H-no
French

Full breakfast
Afternoon tea
Sitting room
central air-conditioning

Elegant Edwardian home with antiques in downtown Ottawa. Home-cooked breakfasts. We enjoy talking with guests & helping them find memorable parts of Ottawa to explore.

Cartier House Inn
46 Cartier St., K2P 1J3
613-236-4667
Gary Clarke
All year

$$$ B&B
10 rooms, 10 pb
Most CC, *Rated*, •
C-ltd/S-ltd/P-no/H-no
French, Chinese, Dutch

Continental plus
Afternoon tea, TVs
Jacuzzis, AM paper
a non-smoking facility
Relais du Silence member

A "grand luxe" European inn which has been offering tranquillity and an attentive staff since the turn of the century. Near the Parliament, shops, restaurants, nightlife.

OTTAWA

Constance House B&B
62 Sweetland Ave., K1N 7T6
613-235-8888
Esther Peterson & Nickolas
All year

$$ B&B
4 rooms, 1 pb
Visa, MC, AmEx, Enrt., •
S-no/P-no/H-no

Full breakfast
Library, parking
bicycles, sitting room
air conditioning

Award-winning Victorian home offering traditional, friendly comfort in period setting. Close to downtown activities & restaurants, yet nestled in Ottawa's historic Sandy Hill.

Gasthaus Switzerland Inn
89 Daly Ave., K1N 6E6
613-237-0335 Fax:594-3327
Sabina & Josef Sauter
All year

$$$ B&B
25 rooms, 21 pb
Visa, MC, *Rated*, •
C-ltd/S-no/P-no/H-no
German, Serb., French

Full Swiss breakfast
Comp. wine, tea, cafe
Sitting room, TV room
air-conditioned
barbecue, garden

Warm Swiss atmosphere in Canada's beautiful capital; clean, cozy rooms; full Swiss-continental breakfast; close to tourist attractions; free parking. Warm, clean & cheery!

Haydon House
18 Queen Elizabeth Drwy, K2P
1C6
613-230-2697
Mary Haydon
All year

$ B&B
3 rooms
Rated
C-yes/S-yes/P-ltd/H-no
French

Continental plus
Afternoon tea
Sitting room, piano
TV with VHR

Downtown Victorian home, embellished with Canadian pine decor in tranquil residential district beside historic Rideau Canal and scenic parkway.

O'Connor House B&B
172 O'Connor St., K2P 1T5
613-236-4221 800-268-2104
Donna Bradley
All year

$ B&B
34 rooms
Major Cre.Cards,*Rated*,
•
C-yes/S-yes/P-no/H-no
French

Full buffet breakfast
Afternoon tea, snacks
Sitting room, bicycles
ice skates (winter)
tennis packages, A/C

The most centrally located B&B in Ottawa. Friendly, comfortable accommodations. Full all-you-can-eat Canadian breakfast. Free use of bikes & ice skates. **3rd. night 40% off**

Rideau View Inn
177 Frank St., K2P 0X4
613-236-9309 800-268-2082
George W. Hartsgrove
All year, FAX: 237-6842

$$ B&B
7 rooms, 2 pb
Visa, MC, AmEx, *Rated*,
•
C-ltd/S-no/P-no/H-no
English, French

Full breakfast
Coffee, tea, soft drinks
Sitting room
tennis nearby

Large 1907 Edwardian home with very well appointed guest rooms. Walking distance to Parliament Hill, Rideau Canal, fine restaurants, shopping and public transport.

Westminster Guest House
446 Westminster Ave., K2A 2T8
613-729-2707
Kathyn Mikoski / Betty Deavy
All year

$ B&B
3 rooms, 1 pb
C-ltd/S-ltd/P-ltd/H-no
French

Full breakfast
Box lunch, dinner
Evening refreshments
sitting room, piano
fireplace

A turn-of-the-century home in a peaceful setting just a short drive from Parliament Hill. Close to bicycle and walking trails along Ottawa River. **7th night free**

Stone Maiden Inn, Stratford, ON

PORT CARLING

Sherwood Inn
P.O. Box 400, Sherwood Rd,
Glen Orchard, P0B 1J0
705-765-3131 800-461-4233
John & Eva Heineck
All year, Fax: 765-6668

$$$ MAP
29 rooms, 27 pb
Most CC, *Rated*, •
C-yes/S-yes/P-no/H-ltd
German

Full breakfast
Dinner included, lunch
Bar, lounge
tennis, health club
landscaped grounds

A charming country inn but also a luxury resort with just the right touches of elegance and privacy. Among towering pines and at the edge of beautiful Lake Joseph.

ST. JACOBS

Jakobstettel Guest House
16 Isabella St., N0B 2N0
519-664-2208 Fax 664-1326
Ella Brubacher
All year

$$$ B&B
12 rooms, 12 pb
Visa, MC, AmEx, *Rated*,
•
C-ltd/S-no/P-no/H-no
Pennsylvania German

Continental plus
Tea, coffee, snacks
Swimming pool, trail
tennis courts, bicycles
sitting room, library

*Luxurious privacy set amidst 5 acres w/trees. Each room decorated with its own charm and Victorian features. Celebrating 10 yrs. **2nd night $50 off (Winter), $30 off in summer***

STRATFORD

Stone Maiden Inn
123 Church St., N5A 2R3
519-271-7129
Barb & Len Woodward
April 15 - December 15

$$$ B&B
14 rooms, 14 pb
Visa, MC, *Rated*, •
C-ltd/S-yes/P-no/H-ltd

Full breakfast
Snacks
Library, tennis nearby
fireplaces, sitting room
some canopy beds

Superior accommodations amid Victorian elegance. "Bountiful Buffet" breakfasts to pamper you while visiting our Shakespeare Festival from May-November yearly.

TORONTO

Ashleigh Heritage Home $$ B&B   Continental plus
Box 235, Station E, 42 Delaware   4 rooms   Coffee and tea
Ave., M6H 2S7   Visa, •   Sitting room, piano
416-535-4000   C-yes/S-ltd/P-no/H-no   bicycles, library
Gwen Lee   parking, also suites
All year

*Restored 1910 home with interesting architectural details and a large garden. Just minutes
from the University, the museum and government offices.*

Burken Guest House $$ B&B   Continental plus
322 Palmerston Blvd., M6G 2N6   8 rooms   Deck, garden, parking
416-920-7842 FAX:960-9529   Visa, MC, *Rated*, •   TV lounge, phones
Burke & Ken   C-yes/S-no/P-no/H-no   ceiling fans in all rms.
All year   German, French

*Very attractive home in charming downtown residential area. Period furniture, close to Eaton
Centre. Nearby public transportation to downtown. Friendly Old World atmosphere.*

More Inns . . .

Mount Blow Farm B&B, RR #2, Almonte, K0A 1A0
Squirrels, The, Box 729, Almonte, K0A 1A0
Tackaberry's Grant, RR #2, Almonte, K0A 1A0, 613-256-1481
Cataract Inn, 1490 Cataract St., RR#2, Alton, L0N 1A0, 519-927-3033
Horseshoe Inn, RR 2, Alton, L0N 1A0, 519-927-5779
Northridge Farm B&B, RR 2, Baden, N0B 1G0, 519-634-8595
Woodrow Farm, RR #1, Balderson, K0G 1A0, 613-267-1493
Cedarbrook, P.O. Box 62, Belfountain, L0N 1B0, 519-927-5559
Holiday House Inn, P.O. Box 1139, Bracebridge, P0B 1C0, 705-645-2245
Country Guest Home, RR 2, Bradford, L3Z 2A5, 416-775-3576
Glenroy Farm, RR 1, Braeside, K0A 1G0, 613-432-6248
Creditview B&B, 7650 Creditview Rd., Brampton, L6V 3N2, 416-451-6271
Caledon Inn, Caledon East, L0N 1E0, 416-584-2891
Red Door, 754 Queenston Rd., Cambridge, N3H 3K3, 519-653-9767
Cornerbrook Farms, RR2, Cargill, N0G 1J0, 519-366-2629
Blue Gables, 192 Henry St., Carleton Place, K7C 1B1
Hudson House B&B, 7 Lorne St., Carleton Place, K7C 2J9, 613-257-8547
Ottawa Valley B&B, 96 Lake Ave. West, Carleton Place, K7C 1L8
White Trillium B&B, 3681 Vaughan Side. RR 2, Carp, K0A 1L0
Graymore Inn, 2 Sturgeon Bay Rd., Coldwater, L0K 1E0, 705-686-7676
Hatties's Hideaway, RR2, Dobbinton, N0H 1L0, 519-363-6543
McIssac's, The, P.O. Box 263, Drayton, N0G 1P0, 519-638-2190
Glenwood B&B, 42 Osler Dr., Dundas, L9H 4B1, 416-627-5096
Dunwich Farm B&B, RR 1, Dutton, N0L 1J0, 519-762-3006
Sir Sam's Inn, Eagle Lake P.O., Eagle Lake, K0M 1M0, 705-754-2188
Birdland B&B, 1 Grey Owl Dr., Elmira, N3B 1S2, 519-669-1900
Evergreens, The, RR 1, Elmira, N3B 2Z1, 519-669-2471
Elora Mill Inn, 77 Mill St. W., Box 218, Elora, N0B 1S0
Lucky Lancione's, 635 Metler Rd. RR3, Fenwick, L0S 1C0, 416-892-8104
4-Eleven, 411 St. Andrew St. E., Fergus, N1M 1R4, 519-843-5107
Breadelbane Inn, 487 St. Andrew St. W., Fergus, N1M 1P2, 519-843-4770
Inn At The Port, The, RR 3, Goderich, N7A 3X9, 519-529-7986
Kathi's Guesthouse, RR 4, Goderich, N7A 3Y1, 519-524-8587
La Brassine, RR 2, Goderich, N7A 3X8, 519-524-6300
Victoria Inn, The, P.O. Box 40, Gore's Landing, K0K 2E0, 416-342-3261
Ste. Anne's Inn, RR1, Grafton, K0K 2G0, 416-349-2493
Ayr-Wyn Farms, RR3, Hanover, N4N 3B9, 519-364-1540
Lonesome Pines, 192 - 12th Ave., Hanover, N4N 3B9, 519-364-2982
Maitland Manor, RR 2, Harriston, N0G 1Z0, 519-338-3487
Evergreen Lawns, 64 Hilltop Ct., Heidelberg, N0B 1Y0, 519-699-4453
Cedarlane Farm B&B, R.R. 2, Iroquois, K0E 1K0, 613-652-4267
Lamont Guest Home, Kimberley, N0C 1G0, 519-599-5905
Aurel & Marj Armstrong B&B, RR4, Kincardine, N2Z 2X5, 519-395-3301
Prince George Hotel, 200 Ontario St., Kingston, K7L 2Y9, 613-549-5440
Austrian Home, 90 Franklin St. N., Kitchener, N2A 1X9, 519-893-4056
Driftwood Home, 202 Driftwood Dr., Kitchener, N2N 1X6, 519-745-8010
Roots & Wings, 11 Sunbridge Crescent, Kitchener, N2K 1T4, 519-743-4557
Why Not B&B, 34 Amherest Dr., Kitchener, N2P 1C9, 519-748-4577
Linden Meadow Farm, RR #1, Lanark, K0G 1K0
Red Eagle Guest House, The, RR #3, Lanark, K0G 1K0
B&B Macpine Farms, Box 51, Lancaster, K0C 1N0, 613-347-2003

MacPine Farm's B&B, Box 51, Lancaster, K0C 1N0, 613-347-2003
Hart Country Estate, RR #4, Lansdowne, K0E 1L0, 613-659-2873
Ivy Lea Inn, 1000 Isl. Pkwy., Lansdowne, K0E 1L0, 613-659-2329
Steinwald, RR4, Lion's Head, N0H 1W0, 519-795-7894
Lambert House B&B, 231 Cathcart St., London, N6C 3M8, 519-672-8996
Rose House, The, 526 Dufferin Ave., London, N6B 2A2, 519-433-9978
Perennial Pleasures B&B, P.O. Box 304, Lucknow, N0G 2H0, 519-528-3601
Queensborough Hotel, Group Box 8, RR#2, Madoc, K0K 2K0, 613-473-5454
Bea's B&B House, Box 133, Maynooth, K0L 2S0, 613-338-2239
Mcdonald's Corners B&B, Box 81, McDonald's Corners, K0G 1M0
Inn at Manitou, The, McKellar Center Rd., McKellar, P0G 1C0, 416-967-3466
Manitouwabing B&B, Box 236, McKellar, P0G 1C0, 705-389-2440
205 Mill Street B&B, P.O. Box 341, Merrickville, K0G 1N0
Honeybrook Farm, RR 1, Millbank, N0K 1L0, 519-595-4604
Country Garden, RR 1, Milverton, N0K 1M0, 519-595-4495
Country Parsonage Inn B&B, 22 Pacific Ave., Milverton, N0K 1M0, 519-595-8556
Top Of The Morning, Llana Heights, Milverton, N0K 1M0, 519-595-8987
Minden House, P.O. Box 780, Minden, K0M 2K0, 705-286-3263
B&B by the Creek, 1716 Lincolnshire Blvd., Mississauga (Toronto), 416-891-0337
Town & Country B&B, 84 Frank St., Mitchell, N0K 1N0, 519-348-8051
Victoria's Country Garden, 153 Ontario Rd., Mitchell, N0K 1N0, 519-348-9756
Upper Canada B&B, Box 247, Morrisburg, K0C 1X0
Glenalby Dairy Farms, RR 1, New Hamburg, N0B 2G0, 519-625-8353
Pines, The, 124 Shade St., New Hamburg, N0B 2G0, 519-662-3525
Station House, The, 216 Steinman St., New Hamburg, N0B 2G0, 519-662-2957
Waterlot Inn, 17 Huron St., New Hamburg, N0B 2G0, 519-662-2020
White Birches, The, 331 Bleams Rd. W., New Hamburg, N0B 2G0, 519-662-2390
Sterling Lodge, Newboro, K0G 1P0, 613-272-2435
Country Charm, RR 1, Newton, N0K 1R0, 519-595-8789
Gorgeview Guest House, 5087 River Rd., Niagara Falls, L2E 3G7
Angel Inn, Est. 1828, 224 Regent St., Niagara-On-The-Lake, L0S 1J0, 416-468-3411
Moffat Inn, 60 Picton St., Box 578, Niagara-On-The-Lake, L0S 1J0, 416-468-4116
Old Bank House, 10 Front St., Box 1708, Niagara-On-The-Lake, L0S 1J0
Oban Inn, 160 Front St., Niagara-on-the-Lake, L0S 1J0, 416-468-2165
Maple Roch Farm B&B, RR #1, Nobel, P0G 1G0, 705-342-9662
Paines' B&B, Carling Bay Rd., RR1, Nobel, P0G 1G0, 705-342-9266
Union Hotel B&B, Main St., Box 38, RR 1, Normandale, N0E 1W0, 519-426-5568
Willi-Joy Farm, RR #3, Norwich, N0J 1P0, 519-424-2113
A1 Leclerc's Residence, 253-McLeod St., Ottawa, K2P 1A1, 613-234-7577
Auberge Ambiance, 330 Nepean, Ottawa, K1R 5G6, 613-563-0421
Auberge McGee's Inn, 185 Daly Ave., Ottawa, K1N 6E8, 613-237-6089
Beatrice Lyon Guest House, 479 Slater St., Ottawa, K1R 5C2, 613-236-3904
Doral Inn Hotel, 486 Albert St., Ottawa, K1R 5B5, 613-230-8055
Flora House, 282 Flora St., Ottawa, K1R 5S3, 613-230-2152
Gwen's Guest Home, 2071 Riverside Dr., Ottawa, K1H 7X2, 613-737-4129
Moses Sunset Farms B&B, RR6, Owen Sound, N4K 5N8, 519-371-4559
Sunset Farms B&B, RR 6, Owen Sound, N4K 5N8, 519-371-4559
Gillanderry Farms B&B, RR #4, Pakenham, K0A 2X0
Kia Ora Guest House, RR #1, Pakenham, K0A 2X0
Stonebridge B&B, RR #4, Pakenham, K0A 2X0
Belvedere B&B, 18 Belvedere Ave., Parry Sound, P2A 2A1, 705-746-8372
Blackwater Lake B&B, RR #1, Parry Sound, P2A 2W7, 705-389-3746
Cascade 40 B&B, 40 Cascade St., Parry Sound, P2A 1J9, 705-746-8917
Evergreen B&B, P.O. Box 223, Parry Sound, P2A 2X3, 705-389-3554
Jantje Manor B&B, 43 Church St., Parry Sound, P2A 1A3, 705-746-5399
Makin House B&B, The, Box 92, RR #3, Parry Sound, P2A 2W9, 705-732-2994
Otter Lake B&B, RR #2, Parry Sound, P2A 2W8, 705-378-2812
Quilt Patch B&B, RR #2, Parry Sound, P2A 2W8, 705-378-5279
Stone's Bay View B&B, 15 Oak Ave., Parry Sound, P2A 1A3, 705-746-5585
Penetanguishene Area B&B, C.P. 1270, Penetanguishene, L0K 1P0
House on the Corner B&B, 53 Wilson St. West, Perth, N7H 2N3
Perth Manor Heritage Inn, 23 Drummond St. West, Perth, K7H 2J6, 613-264-0050
Rebecca's B&B, P.O. Box 1028, Petrolia, N0N 1R0,
   519-882-0118
Albion, The, P.O. Box 37, Plattsville, N0J 1S0,
   519-684-7434
Gowanlock Farm, RR2, Port Elgin, N0H 2C0,
   519-389-5256
Arrowwood Lodge, P.O. Box 125, Port Severn, L0K
   1S0, 705-538-2354
Kettle Creek Inn, Main St., Port Stanley, N0L 2A0,
   519-782-3388
Spruce Grove Farm, RR 1, Port Stanley, N0L 2A0,
   519-769-2245
Gallagher House, Box 99, West Water St.,
   Portland-On-The-Rideau, K0G 1V0, 613-272-2895
Fieldstone Farm, RR 1, Puslinch, N0B 2J0,
   519-822-3178
Margaret's Guest House, 510 Raglan St. S.,
   Renfrew, K7V 4A4, 613-432-3897
Houseboat Amaryllis Inn, General Delivery,
   Rockport, K0E 1V0, 613-659-3513

Home Suite Home, Leamington, ON

Giggling Otter Inn, 4 Oak St., Rosseau, P0C 1J0, 705-732-1354
Fillimchuk B&B, R.R. #1, Simcoe, N3Y 4J9, 519-428-5165
Green's Corner B&B, R.R. 1, Conc. 9, Simcoe, N3Y 4J9
Chantry House Inn, 118 High St., Southampton, N0H 2L0, 519-797-2646
Crescent Manor, 48 Albert St. N., Southampton, N0H 2L0, 519-797-5637
Hollingborne House, 48 Grey St. N., Southampton, N0H 2L0, 519-797-3202
River House, P.O. Box 212, St. Clements, NOB 2MO, 519-699-4430
Pembroke House Farm, RR 2, St. Marys, N4X 1C5, 519-349-2391
Burnside Guest Home, 139 William St., Stratford, N5A 4X9, 519-271-7076
Shrewsbury Manor, 30 Shrewsbury St., Stratford, N5A 2V5, 519-271-8520
Stone Maiden Inn, 123 Church St., Stratford, N5A 2R3, 519-271-7129
Baldwin Gristmill, The, 24357 Hwy. 48, RR 1, Sutton West, L0E 1R0, 416-722-5743
Unicorn Inn & Restaurant, RR# 1, South Gillies, Thunder Bay, P0T 2V0, 807-475-4200
At-Home-In-The-Beach, 237 Lee Ave., Toronto, M4E 2P4, 416-690-9688
Bonnevue Manor B&B Place, 33 Beaty Ave., Toronto, M6K 3B3, 416-536-1455
English Corner, 114 Bernard Ave., Toronto, M5R 1S3
Orchard View B&B, 92 Orchard View Blvd., Toronto, M4R 1C2, 416-488-6826
Rainier Sabranie's House, 96 Asquith, Rosedale, Toronto, M4W 1J8
Mrs. Mitchell's, Violet Hill, L0N 1S0, 819-925-3672
Union Hotel B&B, The, P.O. Box 38, Vittoria, N0E 1WO, 519-426-5568
Roewood Farm, RR 3, Wallenstein, NOB 2SO, 519-698-2278
Willowbrae Farm, RR 1, Waterloo, N2J 4G8, 519-664-2634
Firella Creek Farm, RR 2, Wellesley, NOB 2TO, 519-656-2974
Paradise Farm, RR 3, Wellesley, NOB 2TO, 519-699-4871
Herlehy Homestead B&B, RR #1, Westport, K0G 1X0
Kilpatrick House, RR #1, Westport, K0G 1X0
Stepping Stone B&B Inn, RR #2, Westport, K0G 1X0
Hillcrest B&B, 394 Gould St., Wiarton, N0H 2T0, 519-534-2262
Maplehurst, 277 Frank St., Wiarton, N0H 2T0, 519-534-1210
McIvor House, RR4, Wiarton, N0H 2T0, 519 534-1709
Windermere House, Windermere, P0B 1P0, 705-769-3611
Old Bridge Inn, Young's Point, K0L 3G0, 705-652-8507
Brentwood On The Beach, RR 2, Zurich, NOM 2TO, 519-236-7137

Prince Edward Island

BAY FORTUNE

Inn at Bay Fortune, The
Souris RR #4, C0A 2B0
902-687-3745
David Wilmer
May 27 - October

$$$ B&B
11 rooms, 11 pb
Visa, MC, •
C-yes/S-yes/P-no/H-yes

Full breakfast
Restaurant, dinner
Bar service, box lunch
sitting room, library
bicycles

PEI's premier dining destination. Formerly summer home of Broadway playwright Elmer Harris & the late actress Colleen Dewhurst. The best on the island!

CHARLOTTETOWN

Barachois Inn
P.O. Box 1022, Church Rd.,
Route 243, C1A 7M4
902-963-2194
Judy & Gary MacDonald
May–October

$$$ B&B
6 rooms, 6 pb
Rated, •
C-yes/S-no/P-no/H-no
English, French

Full breakfast
Comp. tea or coffee
Sitting room
pump organ

Victorian house offers lovely views of bay, river and countryside. Antique furnishings and modern comforts. Walk to seashore.

LITTLE YORK

Dalvay By The Sea Hotel	$$$ B&B/MAP	lunch, dinner
P.O. Box 8, East End National	26 rooms, 26 pb	Restaurant, bar service
Park, COA IPO	Visa, MC, AmEx, *Rated*,	Sitting room, library
902-672-2048	•	bicycles, tennis court
David R. Thompson/Wayne	C-yes/H-yes	croquet green, canoes
Berry	French, Spanish	
June 1–Oct. 1		

Victorian inn located 200 yards from a spectacular beach. Very relaxing, romantic atmosphere. Excellent cuisine. **Honeymoon package—free champagne & flowers.**

MONTAGUE

Partridges' B&B	$ B&B	Full breakfast
Panmure Island, RR2, COA 1RO	7 rooms, 5 pb,	Sitting room, library
902-838-4687	Visa, *Rated*, •	guests may use bicycles
Rod & Gertrude Partridge	C-yes/S-no/P-yes/H-yes	canoe and row boat
All year		

Five minute walk to a beautiful, clean, quiet beach of white sand. Grocery stores, excellent restaurants, lobster fishing & golf all nearby.

MURRAY RIVER

Bayberry Cliff Inn B&B	$ B&B	Full breakfast
RR 4, Little Sands, C0A 1W0	7 rooms, 3 pb	Dinner by reservation
902-962-3395	Visa, MC, *Rated*, •	Library, craft shop
Nancy & Don Perkins	C-yes/Spanish	sitting room
May 15–September		cliff to shore

Two remodeled post & beam barns 50 feet from edge of cliff. Furnishings: antiques, marine paintings. 8 minutes to W.I.'s ferry. Five levels. Perfect for honeymooners.

SOURIS

Matthew House Inn, The	$$ B&B	Continental plus
15 Breakwater St., COA 2B0	8 rooms, 8 pb	Restaurant for guests
902-687-3461	Most CC, *Rated*, •	Full Bkfst $, Comp. wine
L. Anderson & E. Cappelluzzo	C-yes/S-ltd/P-no/H-no	picnic lunch, dinner
June - Mid October		Aft. tea, snacks

Award-winning Victorian Heritage inn overlooking harbor. Secluded beaches, bike trails, sunset cruises. Island's choice for history, hospitality. **20% off gift shop**

VERNON RIVER

Lea's B&B	$ EP	Full breakfast $3.25
COA 2E0	5 rooms, 1 pb	Continental plus $2
902-651-2501 902-651-2051	C-yes/S-yes/P-no/H-no	Hot tub
Ralph & Dora Lea		sitting room, piano
All year		

Small farm with beef cattle, pheasants, rabbits and a bird dog called Tipsy. Bedrooms with two double beds, some with one double bed. Country breakfasts.

More Inns . . .

Stewart's B&B, Vernon P.O., Alberry Plains, C0A 2E0
Lazydays Farm B&B, RR1, Belfast, C0A 1A0, 902-659-2267
Linden Lodge, RR 3, Belfast, C0A 1A0, 902-659-2716
MacLean's B&B, Richmond RR #1, Birch Hill, C0B 1Y0
Churchill Farm T.H., RR3, Bonshaw, C0A 1C0, 902-675-2481
Strathgartney Country Inn, RR #3, Bonshaw, C0A 1C0, 902-675-4711
Goodwin's Tourist Home B&B, RR #1, Borden, C0B 1X0, 902-855-2849
Linden Lane B&B, Brittain Shore Rd., Brackley Beach, C0A 2H0, 000-672-3091
Shaw's Hotel & Cottages, Brackley Beach, C0A 2H0, 902-672-2022
Redcliffe Farm B&B, RR1, Montague, Brooklyn, C0A 1R0, 902-838-2476
Glenhaven B&B, Borden RR #1, Cape Traverse, C0B 1X0

Carleton Cove Farm B&B, Albany RR #2, Carleton Siding, C0B 1A0
MacCullum B&B, Borden P.O., Carleton Siding, C0B 1X0
Kindred Spirits Cntry Inn, Hunter River RR #2, Cavendish, C0A 1N0
MacLure B&B, RR #2 Hunter River, Cavendish, C0A 1N0
Shining Waters Lodge, Hunter River RR2, Cavendish, C0A 1N0
Allix's B&B, 11 Johnson Av., Charlottetown, C1A 3H7, 902-892-2643
Anchors Aweigh B&B, 45 Queen Elizabeth Dr., Charlottetown, C1A 3A8, 902-892-4319
Dundee Arms Inn, 200 Pownal St., Charlottetown, C1A 3W8, 902-892-2496
Elmwood, P.O. Box 3128, Charlottetown, C1A 7N8, 902-368-3310
Jean's B&B, 13 Kirkcaldy Dr., Charlottetown, C1E 1G2
Just Folks B&B, RR 5, Charlottetown, C1A 7J8, 902-569-2089
MacInnes B&B, 80 Euston St., Charlottetown, C1A 1W2
Maple B&B, 28 Maple Ave., Charlottetown, C1A 6E3, 902-894-4488
Pope Avenue B&B, 9 Pope Ave., Charlottetown, C1A 6N4, 902-875-3229
Rosevale Farm B&B, Marshfield, RR 3, Charlottetown, C1A 7J7, 902-894-7821
Woodmere, Marshfield, RR 3, Charlottetown, C1A 7J7, 902-628-1783
Obanlea Farm Tourist Home, RR 4 North River PO, Cornwall, C0A 1H0, 902-566-3067
On-the-Bay B&B, P.O. Box 272, Cornwall, C0A 1H0
Strait View Farm B&B, Rice Pt., RR 2, Cornwall, C0A 1H0, 902-675-2071
Chez-Nous B&B, Ferry Rd., RR 4, Corwan, C0A 1H0, 902-566-2779
Stanhope by the Sea, Route 25, Coxehead, C01 1P0, 902-672-2047
Fralor Farm Tourist Home, RR 1, Kensington, Darnley, C0B 1M0, 902-836-5300
Empty Nest B&B, The, Souris RR #4, Fortune Bridge, C0A 2B0
Miller's Farm B&B, Carlottetown RR3, Frenchford, C1A 7J7
Bradway Inn B&B, RR #1, Hampton, C0A 1J0
Myers Hilltop Farm B&B, Crapaud RR #1, Hampton, C0A 1J0
Wilbert's B&B, Winsloe RR #1, Harrington, C0A 2H0
Brookside Farm House B&B, Charlottetown RR #1, Hazelbrook, C1A 7J6
Beach Point View Inn, RR 5, Kensington, C0B 1M0, 902-836-5260
Blakeney's B&B, 15 MacLean Ave., Box 17, Kensington, C0B 1M0, 902-836-3254
Murphy's Sea View B&B, Route 20, Kensington, C0B 1M0, 902-836-5456
Sherwood Acres Guest Home, RR 1, Kensington, C0B 1M0, 902-836-5430
Woodington's Country Inn, Sea View, RR 2, Kensington, C0B 1M0, 902-836-5518
Breathtaking Waterview B&B, Charlottetown RR #1, Keppoch, C1A 7J6
Little Pond Country Store, Souris RR #4, Little Pond, C0A 2B0
Waugh's Farm B&B, Lower Bedeque, C0B 1C0, 902-887-2320
Thomas Bed & Breakfast, O'Leary RR 3, Mill River, C0B 1V0, 902-859-3209
Carr's Corner Farm Tourist, Route 12, Miscouche, C0B 1T0, 902-436-6287
Boudreault's Tourist B&B, RR #2, Montague, C0A 1R0, 962-838-2560
Brydon's B&B, Heatherdale RR 1, Montague, C0A 1R0, 902-838-4747
Countryman B&B, The, Chestnut St., Montague, C0A 1R0
Pines B&B, The, P.O. Box 486, Montague, C0A 1R0
Pleasant View B&B, Box 89, Montague, C0A 1R0
Kelly's Bed & Breakfast, Box 68, Morell, C0A 1S0, 902-961-2389
Village Bed & Breakfast, Box 71, Morell, C0A 1S0, 902-961-2394
Harbourview B&B, RR 1, Murray Harbour, C0A 1V0, 902-962-2565
Lady Catherine's B&B, Montague RR #4, Murray Harbour North, C0A 1R0
Laine Acres B&B, Cornwall RR2, Nine Mile Creek, C0A 1H0, 902-675-2402
Meadowside Farm B&B, Summerside RR #3, North Bedeque, C1N 4J9
Wright's Bed & Breakfast, Summerside RR#, North Bedeque, C1N 4J9
Smallman's B&B, Knutsford, RR 1, O'Leary, C0B 1V0, 902-859-3469
Sand Dune B&B, Souris RR #2, Priest Pond, C0A 2B0
Mom's B&B, P.O. Box 13, Richmond, C0B 1Y0
Whiffletree Inn, Hunter River RR #3, Rusticoville, C0A 1N0
MacCallum's B&B, Route 2, Saint Peters Bay, C0A 2A0, 902-961-2957
Green Valley B&B, Box 714, Kensington, Spring Valley, C0B 1M0, 902-836-5667
Carriage Hill B&B, Hunter River RR #1, St. Patrick's, C0A 1N0, 902-964-2253
Blue Heron B&B, Breadalbane RR #1, Stanley Bridge, C0A 1E0
By The Bay Country Home, Breadalbane RR #1, Stanley Bridge, C0A 1E0
Creekside Farm B&B, Stanley Bridge, C0A 1E0, 902-886-2713
Gulf Breeze, Stanley Bridge, C0A 1E0, 902-886-2678
Faye & Eric's B&B, 380 Mac Ewen Rd., Summerside, C1N 4X8, 902-436-6847
Silver Fox Inn, 61 Granville St., Summerside, C1N 2Z3, 902-436-4033
Smallman's B&B, 329 Poplar Ave., Summerside, C1N 2B7
VanDykes' B&B, Montague RR #3, Summerville, C0A 1R0
Harbour Lights T. H., RR #2, Tignish, C0B 2B0, 902-882-2479
Doctor's Inn B&B, Tyne Valley, C0B 2C0, 902-831-2164
West Island Inn, Box 24, Tyne Valley, C0B 2C0, 902-831-2495
Abbotswood B&B, Charlottetown RR #1, Upper Tea Hill Crescent, C1A 7J6
MacLeod's Farm B&B, UIGG, Vernon P.O., Vernon, C0A 2E0, 902-651-2303
Blair Hall B&B, Vernon Bridge, C0A 2E0
Dunvegan Farm B&B, RR 2 Uigg, Vernon Bridge, C0A 2E0
Enman's Farm B&B, P.O. RR 2 Vernon Bridge, Vernon Bridge, C0A 2E0, 902-651-2427
Smith's Farm B&B, Millview P.O., Vernon Bridge, C0A 2E0
Dunrovin Lodge B&B, Victoria, C0A 2G0
Victoria Village Inn, Victoria-By-The-Sea, C0A 2G0, 902-658-2288
Dyment Bed & Breakfast, Summerside RR#, Wilmot Valley, C1N 4J9, 902-436-9893
Baba's House Guests B&B, Belle River RR #1, Wood Islands West, C0A 1B0
Amber Lights B&B, P.O. Box 14, Route 26, York, C0A 1P0, 902-894-5868
Vessey's B&B, Highway 25, off Hwy 2, York, C0A 1P0, 902-629-1312

Province of Quebec

AYER'S CLIFF

Auberge Ripplecove Inn
700 Ripple Cove Rd., J0B 1C0
819-838-4296 FAX:838-5541
Jeffrey & Debra Stafford
All year

$$$ MAP
24 rooms, 24 pb
Visa, MC, AmEx, *Rated*,
•
C-ltd/S-yes/P-no/H-no
French

Full breakfast
Restaurant, bar
Comp. wine, sitting room
tennis, pool, sailing
canoes, water skiing

A Charming lakeside inn on 12 private acres. Refined French cuisine. 24 deluxe rooms and suites, many with fireplaces and whirlpool bath. All water sports, tennis, cross-country skiing.

MONT TREMBLANT

Chateau Beauvallon
616 Montee Ryan, Box138, J0T 1Z0
819-425-7275
Judy & Alex Riddell
Exc. mid-Oct–Nov

$ B&B
14 rooms, 7 pb
Rated, •
C-yes/S-yes/P-ltd/H-ltd
French

Full breakfast
Dinner, bar
Comp. tea, coffee
sitting room, piano
lake swimming, bicycles

Country inn w/ home cooking, on a clear quiet mountain lake. Cycling, golf, tennis, windsurfing, all available within two-mile proximity. Children under 12 yr. special price.

MONTREAL

Armor & Manor Sherbrooke
151 Sherbrooke E., H2X 1C7
514-285-0140 Fax-284-1126
Annick Morvan
All year

$ B&B
15 rooms, 7 pb
•
C-yes/S-yes/P-no/H-no
French

Continental breakfast
Comp. coffee

Once a fine Victorian townhouse in downtown Montreal. Fine woodwork in foyer and some guest rooms. **Restaurant discounts**

Auberge De La Fontaine
1301 E. Rachel St., H2J 2K1
514-597-0166
Celine Boudreau, Jean Lamothe
All year

$$$ B&B
21 rooms, 21 pb
Visa, MC, AmEx, •
C-ltd/S-yes/P-no/H-yes
French

Continental plus, buffet
Afternoon tea
Whirlpool in some rooms

Facing Parc La Fontaine (84 acres), located near downtown area. A charming inn where you are welcomed as friends. Public transportation nearby. Warm and friendly staff.

Downtown B&B Bernard
3523 Jeanne-Mance, H2X 2K2
514-845-0431
Bruno Bernard
All year

$$ B&B
5 rooms, 2 pb
Rated
C-ltd/S-yes/P-no/H-no
French

Full breakfast
Kitchen for guests
Color TV, radio, phone

Victorian townhouse in the heart of downtown. Access to different kitchen, delicious breakfasts. Also lovely little apartments for short & long stays.

MONTREAL

Lola's B&B
5 Burton Ave., H3Z 1J6
514-483-6555
Lola Gordon
All year

$$ B&B
2 rooms,
•
C-ltd/S-no/P-no/H-no
French

Full breakfast
Afternoon tea, wine
Sitting room

One double, one twin in upper duplex one mile from heart of downtown and all tourist attractions. Close to metro and bus, shops, restaurants, yet very quiet.

Manoir Ambrose
3422 Stanley St., H3A 1R8
514-288-6922 FAX:288-5757
Lucie Seguin
All year

$ B&B
22 rooms, 17 pb
Visa, MC, *Rated*, •
C-yes/S-yes/P-no/H-no
Eng., Fr., Span., Ger.

Continental breakfast
Phone in each room
cable TV, sitting room
air conditioning

Perfect location of this Victorian-style lodge close to McGill Univ., musee, restaurants, shopping. Quiet surroundings & friendly home atmosphere. **Special off-season rates.**

Montreal Oasis B&B
3000 Breslay Rd., H3Y 2G7
514-935-2312
Lena Blondel
All year

$$ B&B
3 rooms
Visa, MC for res. only, •
C-yes/S-no/P-no/H-no
Swedish, French

Full breakfast
Tea, wine
Bicycles

In the safe, pretty west end of downtown Montreal, close to Fine Arts Museum, Crescent street, shopping, restaurants and cafes.

NEW CARLISLE

Bay View Manor
P.O. Box 21, 395-337 New
Carlisle West, G0C 1Z0
418-752-2725 418-752-6718
Helen Sawyer
All year

$ B&B
6 rooms, 2 pb
Rated
C-yes/P-no, French

Full breakfast
Lunch, dinner
Sitting room, library
tennis courts, pool
near golf, cottage avail

Seaside country haven, yet on a main highway. Fresh farm produce. August Folk Festival. Quilts, handicrafts and home-baking on sale. Cottage at $250 per week also available.

QUEBEC CITY

Le Chateau De Pierre
17 Ave. Ste-Genevieve, G1R 4A8
418-694-0429
Lily Couturier
All year

$$$ EP
15 rooms, 15 pb
Visa, MC, *Rated*,
C-yes/S-ltd/P-no/H-no
French, Spanish

Kitchenettes in 2 units
Color cable TVs
air-conditioned
garage parking

Old English colonial mansion with colonial charm. Fine appointments and distinctive atmosphere. Located in Old Quebec Uppertown. Walk to Citadell, shopping, historical points.

QUEBEC CITY

Maison Marie-Rollet
81, rue Ste-Anne, G1R 3X4
418-694-9271
Fernand Blouin
All year

$$ EP
10 rooms, 10 pb
Visa, *Rated*, •
C-yes/S-yes/P-no/H-no
French

Well situated, in the center of Old Quebec facing the City Hall. Parking across the street. Quiet Victorian house. **20% discount off season**

ST-MARC-SUR-RICHELIEU

Auberge Handfield Inn
555 Richelieu, J0L 2E0
514-584-2226
Conrad Handfield
All year'

$$ EP/MAP (wint)
53 rooms, 53 pb
Most CC, *Rated*, •
C-yes/S-yes/P-no/H-yes
French

Full breakfast $
Restaurant, bar service
Aftn. tea, snacks
pool, horseback riding
tennis courts, marina

Country inn on the River Sibe. Ancestral house, 165 years old. All rooms decorated with antiques. Marina available for traveling sailors.

STE. PETRONILLE

Auberge La Goeliche
22 Rue du Quai, G0A 4C0
418-828-2248
Andree Marchand
All year

$ B&B
19 rooms
Visa, MC, AmEx, •
C-yes/French

breakfast included
Restaurant
Aft. tea, snacks
bar service
sitting room, pool

Overhanging the St. Lawrence River, this castle-like inn offers a breathtaking view of Quebec City, which is only distant by a 15 minute drive.

More Inns . . .

La Maison Otis, 23 R. St. Jean Baptiste, Baie Saint Paul, G0A 1B0, 418-435-2255
La Muse, 39, St-Jean-Baptiste, Baie St-Paule, G0A 1B0, 418-435-6939
Hostellerie Rive Gauche, 1810 boul. Richelieu, Beloeil, J3G 4S4, 514-467-4650
La Pinsonniere, 124 St. Raphael, Cap-A-L'aigh, G0T 1B0, 418-665-4431
Andre Drolet, 102, Vieux Chemin, Cap-Sante, G0A 1L0
Auberge Le Coin Du Banc, Route 132, Coin du Banc-Perce, G0C 2L0, 418-645-2907
Willow Inn, 208 Main Rd., Como, J0P 1A0, 514-458-7006
Auberge La Martre, La Martre, Comte de Mantane, G0E 2H0, 418-288-5533
Maplewood, Malenfant Rd., Dunham, J0E 1M0, 514-295-2519
Henry House, 105 DuParc, St. Simeon, Gaspesie, G0C 3A0, 418-534-2115
Georgeville Country Inn, CP P.O. Box 17, Georgeville, J0B 1T0, 819-843-8683
Hazelbrae Farm, 1650 English River Rd., Howick, J0S 1G0, 514-825-2390
Riversmead B&B, Main Rd., Hudson, J0P 1H0
Willow Place Inn, 208 Main St., Hudson, J0P 1A0, 514-458-7006
Leduc, 1128CH Riviere de Guerr, Huntington, Saint Anicet, J0S 1M0, 514-264-6533
Chez les Dumas, 1415 Chemin Royal, St. , Ile d'Orleans, G0A 3Z0, 418-828-9442
Gite du Passant B&B, 81 Ave. Morel, Kamouraska, G0L 1M0, 418-492-2921
Auberge Laketree, RR 2, Stage Coach Rd., Knowlton, J0E 1V0, 514-243-6604
Chalet Caribou Lodge, Lac Superieur, J0T 1P0, 819-688-5201
Auberge Sauvignon, Route 327, Mont Tremblant, J0T 1Z0, 819-425-2658
Antonio Costa, 101 Northview, Montreal, H4X 1C9, 514-486-6910
B&B de Chez-Nous, 3717 Ste-Famille, Montreal, H2X 2L7, 514-845-7711
Brums Bernard, 3523 Jeanne-Mance, Montreal, H2X 2K2
Montreal Oasis, 3000, de Breslay, Montreal, H3Y 2G7, 514-935-2312
Le Breton, 1609 St. Hubert, Montreal East, H2L 3Z1, 514-524-7273
Auberge Hollandaise, Route 329, Morin Heights, G0R 1H0, 514-226-2009
Hatley Inn, P.O. Box 330, North Hatley, J0B 2C0, 819-842-2451
Hovey Manor, P.O. Box 60, North Hatley, J0B 2C0, 819-842-2421
Batiscan River's Domain, 974 Rte Rousseau Rd., Notre Dame des Anges, G0X 1N0, 418-336-2619
Hotel la Normandie, P.O. Box 129, Perce, Gaspe Peninsula, G0G 2L0, 418-782-2112
Auberge Donohue, 145 Principale, CP 211, Pointe-au-Pic, G0T 1M0, 418-665-4377
Senator's House, P.O. Box 63, Tyne Vally, Port Hill, C0B 2C0, 902-831-2071
Edale Place, Edale Pl., Portneuf, G0A 2Y0, 418-286-3168
France Beaulieu House, 211 Chemin dela Travers, Portneuf, G0A 2Y0, 418-336-2724
Au Chateau Fleur de Lis, 15 Ave. Ste. Genevieve, Quebec City, G1R 4A8, 418-694-1884
Auberge De La Chouette, 71 Rue D'Auteuil, Quebec City, G1K 5Y4, 418-694-0232
Chateau de la Terrasse, 6 Terrasse Dufferin, Quebec City, G1R 4N5, 418-694-9472
Manoir Ste Genevieve, 13 Ave. Ste-Genevieve, Quebec City, G1R 4A7, 418-694-1666
Memory Lane Farm, RR #1, Quyon, J0X 2V0, 819-458-2479
Gite du Mont Albert, Case Postale 1150, Saint Anne des Mont, G0E 2G0, 418-763-2288
Maison sous les Arbres, 145 Chemin Royal, Saint Laurent, G0A 3Z0, 418-828-9442
Pelletier House, 334 de la Seigneurie, Saint Roch Des Aulnaies, G0R 4E0, 418-354-2450
Auberge St-Denis, 61, St-Denis, CP 1229, Saint Sauveur Des Monts, J0R 1R0, 514-227-4766
Auberge St-Simon, Saint Simon
Auberge La Goeliche, 22 Rue du Quai, Sainte Petronille, G0A 4C0, 418-828-2248
Auberge Manoir de Tilly, 3854 Chemin de Tilly, St. Antoine de Tilly, G0S 2C0, 418-886-2407
La Vigie du Pilote, 170 Chemin des Ormes, St.-Jean Isle d'Orleans, G0A 3W0
Hostellerie Les Trois Till, 290 rue Richelieu, St.-Marc-Sur-Richelieu, J0L 2E0, 514-584-2231
Auberge Du Lac Des Sables, 230 St. Venant, C.P.213, Ste.-Agathe, J8C 2A3, 819-326-7016
Auberge Schweizer, 357 Schweizer Rd., Sutton, J0E 2K0, 514-538-2129
Steiner Family, 266 Montee Steiner, Thurso, J0X 3B0, 819-985-2359
Auberge du Vieux Foyer, 3167 Doncaster, Val David, J0T 2N0, 819-322-2686

Parker's Lodge, 1340 Lac Paquin, Val David, J0T 2N0, 819-322-2026
Au Petit Hotel, 3 Ruelle des Ursulines, Vieux—Quebec, G1R 3Y6, 418-694-0965
Perras, 1552 RR 1, Waterloo, J0E 1N0, 514-539-2983

Saskatchewan

More Inns ...

Moldenhauer's Farm, Box 214, Allan, S0K 0C0, 306-257-3578
Ellis Farm, Box 84, Balcarres, S0G 0C0, 306-334-2238
Vereshagin's Country Place, Box 89, Blaine Lake, S0J 0J0, 306-497-2782
Sargent's Holiday Farm, Box 204, Borden, S0K 0N0, 306-997-2230
Tiger Lily Farm, Box 135, Burstall, S0N 0H0, 306-679-4709
Bonshaw House, Box 67, Grenfell, S0G 2B0, 306-697-2654
Magee's Farm, Box 654, Gull Lake, S0N 1A0
Lakeside Leisure Farm, P.O. Box 1, Meota, S0M 1X0, 306-892-2145
Silent Hollow Farms, Box 25, Meskanaw, S0K 2W0, 306-864-3728
Sugden Simmental Vacation , Box 2, Peebles, S0G 3V0, 306-697-3169
Pipestone View Ranch, General Delivery, Percival, S0G 3Y0, 306-735-2858
B & J's B&B, 2066 Ottawa St., Regina, S4P 1P8, 306-522-4575
Turgeon International Hse, 2310 McIntyre St., Regina, S4P 2S2, 306-522-4200
Sweetgrass Farms B&B, Box 218, Rose Valley, S0E 1M0, 306-322-2217
Eaton Manor, Box 591, Tisdale, S0E 1T0
Prairie Acres B&B, Box 1658, Tisdale, S0E 1T0, 306-873-2272
Dee Bar One, Box 51, Truax, S0H 4A0, 306-868-4614
Pleasant Vista Angus Farm, Box 194, Wawota, S0G 5A0, 306-739-2915
Banbury House, The, Wolseley, 306-698-2239

Yukon Territory

More Inns ...

Partridge Creek Farm, Mail Bag 450, Dawson City, Y0B 1G0
White Ram Manor, Box 302, Dawson City, Y0B 1G0, 403-993-5772
Baker's Bed & Breakfast, 84 - 11th Ave., Whitehorse, Y1A 4J2, 403-633-2308
Klondike House, 39 Donjek Rd., Whitehorse, Y1A 3V5, 403-667-4315
Little Salmon Lake, 501 Dezadeash Rd., Whitehorse, Y1A 3X6

Reservation Service Organizations

These are businesses through which you can reserve a room in thousands of private homes. In many cases, rooms in homes are available where there may not be an inn. Also, guest houses are quite inexpensive. RSOs operate in different ways. Some represent a single city or state. Others cover the entire country. Some require a small membership fee. Others sell a list of their host homes. Many will attempt to match you with just the type of accomodations you're seeking and you may pay the RSO directly for your lodging.

Reservation Service Organization by Region—See main RSO listings under the state headings in this section for full description.

North East

Bed & Breakfast, Ltd., New Haven, CT

Covered Bridge, Norfolk, CT

Nutmeg B&B, West Hartford, CT

B&B Accommodations, Washington, DC

B&B League, Washington, DC

A B&B Agency of Boston, Boston, MA

B&B Associates Bay Colony, Boston, MA

Host Homes of Boston, Boston, MA

Greater Boston Hospitality, Brookline, MA

B&B Marblehead, Newtonville, MA

House Guests Cape Cod, Orleans, MA

Bed & Breakfast Cape Cod, West Hyannisport, MA

Berkshire B&B Homes, Williamsburg, MA

Traveller in MD, The, Annapolis, MD

Amanda's B&B, Baltimore, MD

New Hampshire B&B, Guilford, NH

B&B of Princeton, Princeton, NJ

International B&B Club, Buffalo, NY

American Country Collection, Delmar, NY

Elaine's B&B, Elbridge, NY

Adventures B&B, Genesed, NY

Abode Bed & Breakfast, New York, NY

At Home in New York, New York, NY

B&B Network of New York, New York, NY

Bed & Breakfast (& Books), New York, NY

New World B&B, New York, NY

Urban Ventures, New York, NY

B&B Connections, Devon, PA

All About Town, Valley Forge, PA

Anna's Victorian, Newport, RI

Hospitality Network, Newport, RI

South East

Bed & Breakfast Atlanta, Atlanta, GA

Quail Country B&B, Thomasville, GA

New Orleans B&B, New Orleans, LA

Amanda's B&B, Baltimore, MD

All About Town, Valley Forge, PA

Historic Charleston, Charleston, SC

Charleston East B&B, Mount Pleasant, SC

Princely B&B, Alexandria, VA

Guesthouses B&B, Charlottesville, VA

North Central

B&B/Chicago Inc., Chicago, IL

B&B Midwest Reservations, Hoffman Estates, IL

Ozark Mountain Country, Branson, MO

B&B Western Adventure, Billings, MT

International B&B Club, Buffalo, NY

Columbus Bed & Breakfast, Columbus, OH

South Central

Arkansas Ozarks B&B, Calico Rock, AR

Ozark Mountain Country, Branson, MO

Lincoln, Ltd., Meridian, MS

International B&B Club, Buffalo, NY

B&B — About Tennessee, Nashville, TN

Sand Dollar Hospitality, Corpus Christi, TX

The Gilded Thistle, Galveston, TX

B&B Hosts of San Antonio, San Antonio, TX

North West

Accomodations Alaska Style, Anchorage, AK

Alaska Private Lodgings, Anchorage, AK

Kodiak Bed & Breakfast, Kodiak, AK

B&B Western Adventure, Billings, MT

International B&B Club, Buffalo, NY

A Pacific Reservation, Seattle, WA

South West

Bed & Breakfast In Arizona, Phoenix, AZ

Mi Casa Su Casa, Tempe, AZ

Old Pueblo Homestays RSO, Tucson, AZ

Eye Openers B&B, Altadena, CA

B&B of Los Angeles, Long Beach, CA

B&B International, San Francisco, CA

CoHost, America, Whittier, CA

Bed & Breakfast Vail, Vail, CO

Go Native. .Hawaii, Hilo, HI

B&B Honolulu, Honolulu, HI

All Islands B&B, Kailua, Oahu, HI

B&B of New Mexico, Santa Fe, NM

International B&B Club, Buffalo, NY

Eastern Canada

Point Pelee B&B, Leamington, ON

Ottawa B&B Association, Ottawa, ON

Toronto Bed & Breakfast, Toronto, ON

A Bed & Breakfast, Montreal, PQ

B&B Relais Montreal, Montreal, PQ

B&B Bonjour Québec, Quebec, PQ

Western Canada

International B&B Club, Buffalo, NY

Old English B&B Registry, North Vancouver, BC

Town & Country B&B, Vancouver, BC

All Seasons B&B Agency, Victoria, BC

Garden City B&B, Victoria, BC

Northern Network, Dawson City, YU

International

Accomodations Alaska Style, Anchorage, AK

CoHost, America's B&B, Whittier, CA

Bed & Breakfast Vail, Vail, CO

New Orleans B&B, New Orleans, LA

B&B Associates Bay Colony, Boston, MA

Traveller in Maryland, Annapolis, MD

Lincoln, Ltd., Meridian, MS

International B&B Club, Buffalo, NY

At Home in New York, New York, NY

Urban Ventures, Inc., New York, NY

Charleston East B&B, Mount Pleasant, SC

B&B — About Tennessee, Nashville, TN

Toronto Bed & Breakfast, Toronto, ON

B&B Bonjour Québec, Quebec, PQ

Northern Network, Dawson City, YU

ALABAMA

More RSOs ...

B&B Montgomery, P.O. Box 1026, Montgomery. AL 36101 205-264-0056 FAX: 205-262-1872

ALASKA

Accomodations Alaska Style Stay with a Friend 3605 Arctic Blvd. Box 173 Anchorage, AK 99503	907-278-8800 Fax: 907-272-8800 $ Dep. 1 night Visa, MC, AmEx	Directory $2 Alaska 8am-6pm, M-F
Alaska Private Lodgings Anchorage B&B P.O. Box 200047-PL Anchorage, AK 99520	907-258-1717 Fax-907-258-6613 $$ Dep. 1 night Directory $3 Ger,Fr,Sp	Brochure Free Alaska 9am - 6pm M-F Winter varies
Kodiak Bed & Breakfast 308 Cope St. Kodiak, AK 99615	907-486-5367 Fax: 907-486-6567 $$ Dep. 1 night Visa, MC, AmEx Sp	Free Brochure Alaska 24 hours, daily

More RSOs...
Sourdough B&B, 339-BW Cardigan Crl., Anchorage. AK 99503
Fairbanks B&B, P.O. Box 74573, Fairbanks. AK 99707 907-452-4967
Alaska B&B Association, P.O. Box 21890, Juneau. AK 99801 907-586-2959 FAX: 907-463-6788
Ketchikan B&B, P.O. Box 7735, Ketchikan. AK 99801 907-225-3860 907-225-9277

ARIZONA

Bed & Breakfast In Arizona	602-265-9511	Brochure $2
Gallery 3 Plaza	800-266-STAY	Arizona
P.O. Box 8628	$	New Mexico
Phoenix, AZ 85012	Dep. 1 night	10am-3pm M-F
	Visa, MC, AmEx	Sat-Sun ans mach.

Mi Casa Su Casa	602-990-0682	Directory $9.50
P.O. Box 950	800-456-0682	AZ/NM/Ut/NV
Tempe, AZ 85280	$	8am-8pm 7 days
	Dep. $25 or 1 night	
	Fr,Ger,Sp,It,Port,Rom,Ch	

Old Pueblo Homestays RSO	800-333-9776	Free broch. SASE
P.O. Box 13603	Fax: 602-790-2399	Arizona
Tucson, AZ 85132	$	9:30am-9pm daily
	Deposit 50% 4+ days	

More RSOs...
Westways "Private" Resort, P.O. Box 41624, Pheonix. AZ 85080 602-582-3868
Valley o' the Sun B&B, P.O. Box 2214, Scottsdale. AZ 85252 602-941-1281
Florence A. Ejrup RSO, 941 W. Calle Dadivoso, Tucson. AZ 85704
Inter-Bed, 5708 N. Via Lozana, Tucson. AZ 85715 602-323-4045

ARKANSAS

Arkansas Ozarks B&B	501-297-8764	Brochure SASE
Reservation	501-297-8211	Arkansas
HC 61, Box 72	$	9am-5pm Mon-Sat
Calico Rock, AR 72519	Dep. 1 night	
	Visa, MC, Others	
	Fr	

More RSOs...
B&B Reservation Serv., 11 Singleton, Eureka Springs. AR 72632 501-253-9111

CALIFORNIA

Eye Openers B&B	213-684-4428	List $1 with SASE
Reservations	FAX: 818-798-3640	California
P.O. Box 694	$	9am-6pm M-F
Altadena, CA 91003	Dep. $25	10am-12noon Sat.
	Visa, MC	
	Sp,Fr,Ger,Hun,Rus,Heb	

B&B of Los Angeles & Kids	310-498-0552	Brochure $6
Welcome	800-383-3513	California
3924 E. 14th. St	$$	24 hours a day
Long Beach, CA 90804	Deposit 20%	
	Visa, MC	

CALIFORNIA

B&B International	415-696-1690	Free brochure
Fax: 415-696-1699	800-872-4500	Cal., Nevada
P.O. Box 282910	$$	9:00-4:00 Mon-Fri
San Francisco, CA 94128	Dep. 1 night	
	Visa, MC	
	Fr,Ger,It,Ch,Jap,Sp	

Bed & Breakfast San	415-947-1913	Free brochure
Francisco	FAX: 415-921-BBSF	California
P.O. Box 420009	$$$	9:30am-5pm M-F
San Francisco, CA 94142	Dep. 1 night	
	Visa, MC, AmEx	
	Sample list $2	

CoHost, America's B&B	319-699-8427	Listing $3
P.O. Box 9302	$$	CA/Can/Jp/Ger/UK
Whittier, CA 90608	Deposit full pymnt.	7am-7pm daily
	Free broch. SASE	

More RSOs . . .

Unique Housing, 81 Plaza Dr., Berkeley. CA 94705 415-658-3494
B&B Homestay, P.O. Box 326, Cambria. CA 93428 805-927-4613
Pilots International B&B, PO Box 1847, Columbia. CA 95310
Rent A Room B&B, 11531 Varna St., Garden Grove. CA 92640 714-638-1406
B&B Hospitality, 823 La Mirada Ave., Leucadia. CA 92024 619-436-6850
Mendocino Coast Reserv., P.O. Box 1143, Mendocino. CA 95460 707-937-5033
Paradise Vacation Rentals, 45005 Ukiah St, Mendocino. CA 95460
S.S. Seafoam Lodge, P.O. Box 68, Mendocino. CA 95460 707-937-1827
Napa Valley's Finest Ldgs., 1557 Madrid Ct., Napa. CA 94559 707-224-4667 707-257-1051
B&B/Monterey Peninsula, P.O. 1193, Pebble Beach. CA 93953 408-372-7425
B&B Almanac, P.O. Box 295, Saint Helena. CA 94574 707-963-0852
B&B Exchange of Marin, 45 Entrata Ave., San Anselmo. CA 94960 415-485-1971
American Family Inn-B&B SF, P.O. Box 349, San Francisco. CA 94101 415-931-3083
Place to Stay, 14497 New Jersey, San Jose. CA 95124
Megan's Friends B&B Res., 1776 Royal Way, San Luis Obispo. CA 93401 805-544-4406
Wine Country B&B, P.O. Box 3211, Santa Rosa. CA 95403 707-578-1661
Reservations Plus, 1141 Merrimac Dr., Sunnyvale. CA 94807
Calif. Houseguests Int'l., P.O. Box 643, Tarzana. CA 91356 818-344-7878

COLORADO

Bed & Breakfast Vail/Ski	303-949-1212	Brochure $2
Areas	800-748-2666	CO, Worlwide
P.O. Box 491	$$	9am-6pm M-F wint.
Vail, CO 81658	50% deposit summer	Sat 9am-12 noon
	Visa, MC	
	100% dep. winter	
	Ger,Sp	

More RSOs . . .

B&B Cambridge Club, 1550 Sherman St., Denver. CO 80903

CONNECTICUT

New Hampshire B&B	603-279-8348	List $5
329 Lake Dr.	800-582-0853	ME/VT/NH/MA/CT/RI
Guilford, NH 06437	$	9am-9pm 7 days
	Dep. 1 night	
	Fr,Sp,Gr	

CONNECTICUT

Bed & Breakfast, Ltd. P.O. Box 216 New Haven, CT 06513	203-469-3260 $$ Dep. 20% Travelers checks Fr,Sp,Ger	Free broch. SASE CT, MA, RI 4-9:pm M-F Anytime Summ/wknd
Covered Bridge B&B Reserv. Serv. P.O. Box 447, 69 Maple Ave. Norfolk, CT 06058	203-542-5944 800-488-5690 $$ Dep. full Visa, MC, AmEx Free listing SASE Fr	Booklet $3 CT, MA, NY, RI 10am - 6pm M-Sun
Nutmeg B&B Agency P.O. Box 1117 West Hartford, CT 06127	203-236-6698 800-727-7592 $$ Ccard for deposit Visa, MC, AmEx	Brochure $5 Connecticut 9:30am-5pm M-F Also ans. machine

More RSOs . . .

Nautilus B&B, 133 Phoenix Dr., Groton. CT 06340 203-448-1538
Seacoast Landings, 133 Neptune Dr., Groton. CT 06340 203-442-1940
Alexander's B&B Res. Serv., P.O. Box 1182, Sharon. CT 06069 203-364-0505
Four Seasons Int'l B&B, 11 Bridlepath Rd., West Simsbury. CT 06092 203-651-3045

DELAWARE

More RSOs . . .

B&B of Delaware, 3650 Silverside, Wilmington. DE 19810 302-479-9500 800-233-4689

DISTRICT OF COLUMBIA

B&B Accommodations, Ltd. P.O. Box 12011 Washington, DC 20005	202-328-3510 FAX: 202-332-3885 $$ Dep. $50 Visa/MC/AmEx/DC Bal. 2wks prior Fr,Sp	Free brochure Washington, D.C. MD/VA 10am-5pm M-F 10am-1pm Sat
B&B League/ **Sweet Dreams & Toast** P.O. Box 9490 Washington, DC 20016	202-363-7767 $$ Dep. $25 Visa/MC/AmEx/DC	Free brochure Washington, D.C., 9am-5pm M-Th 9am-1pm F

FLORIDA

More RSOs . . .

Key West Res. Serv., 628 Fleming St., Key West. FL 33041 800-327-4831 800-356-3567
B&B Co., P.O. Box 262, Miami. FL 33243 305-661-3270
Magic B&B, 8328 Curry Ford Rd., Orlando. FL 32822 407-277-6602
Open House B&B Registry, P.O. Box 3025, Palm Beach. FL 33480 407-842-5190
B&B Homestays of Florida, 8690 Gulf Blvd., Saint Pete Beach. FL 33706 813-360-1753
B&B Company—Tropical Florida, P.O. Box 262, South Miami. FL 33243 305-661-3270
A & A B&B of Florida, P.O. Box 1316, Winter Park. FL 32790 305-628-3233

GEORGIA

Bed & Breakfast Atlanta, Inc. 1801 Piedmont NE, Suite 208 Atlanta, GA 30324	404-875-0525 800-967-3224 $ Dep. 1 night Visa, MC, AmEx Heb,Fr,Ger,Yid	Brochure SASE GA, Metro Atla. 9am-12, 2-5pm M-F Answering machine
Quail Country B&B, Ltd. 1104 Old Monticello Rd. Thomasville, GA 31792	912-226-7218 912-226-6882 $ Dep. $25	Free brochure Thomasville, GA 9am-9pm 7 days

More RSOs . . .

Georgia B&B, 2472 Lauderdale Dr., Atlanta. GA 30345 404-493-1930
Bed & Breakfast Inns, 117 West Gordon St., Savannah. GA 31401 912-238-0518
R.S.V.P. Savannah B&B, 417 E. Charlton St., Savannah. GA 31401 912-232-7787
Savannah Area Visitors, 222 W. Oglethorpe Ave., Savannah. GA 31499 912-944-0444

HAWAII

Go Native. .Hawaii P.O. Box 11418 Hilo, HI 96721	808-935-4178 800-662-8483 $ Dep. 50% Directory $2 Ger,Sp,Sw,Jap,Kor	Free brochure HI, US. Worldwide 8am-6pm M-Sat Also ans. machine
B&B Honolulu & Statewide 3242 Kaohinani Dr. Honolulu, HI 96817	808-595-7533 800-288-4666 $ Dep. 3 days or 50% Visa, MC	Free brochure Hawaiian Islands 8am-5pm M-F 8am-12noon Sat
Affordable Paradise B&B 226 Pouli Rd. Kailua, HI 96734	808-262-7865 $ 20% deposit Visa, MC, AmEx	Free brochure Hawaian Islands 7am-8pm Mon.-Sat.
All Islands B&B 823 Kainui Dr. Kailua, Oahu, HI 96734	800-542-0344 808-263-2342 $ Dep. 20% Visa, MC, AmEx Fax: 808-263-0308	Free brochure Hawaii 8am-5pm Mon-Fri.

More RSOs . . .

B&B Hawaii, P.O. Box 449, Kapaa, Kauai. HI 96746 808-822-7771 800-733-1632
B&B Maui Style, P.O. Box 98, Puunene. HI 96753 808-879-7865 800-848-5567

IDAHO

More RSOs . . .

B&B of Idaho, 109 W. Idaho St., Boise. ID 83702 208-336-5174
B&B Inland Northwest, P.O. Box 2502, Coeur d'Alene. ID 83814

ILLINOIS

B&B/Chicago Inc. P.O. Box 14088 Chicago, IL 60614	312-951-0085 $$ Visa/MC/AmEx	Free brochure Illinois/Chicago 9am-5pm, M-F
B&B Midwest Reservations P.O. Box 95503 Hoffman Estates, IL 60195	812-378-5855 800-342-2632 $ Dep. $40 Visa, MC, Disc	Free Broch. SASE Illinois, Indiana Ohio 9am-5pm, Mon-Fri Also ans. machine

INDIANA

More RSOs ...

Indiana B&B Assoc., P.O. Box 1127, Goshen. IN 46526
Indiana Amish Country B&B, 1600 W. Market St., Nappanee. IN 46550 219-773-4188
Tammy Galm B&B, P.O. Box 546, Nashville. IN 47448
InnServ Nationwide Res., Route 1, Box 68, Redkey. IN 47373 317-369-2245

KENTUCKY

More RSOs ...

Ohio Valley B&B, Inc., 6876 Taylor Mill Rd., Independence. KY 41051 606-356-7865
Bluegrass B&B, Route 1, Box 263, Versailles. KY 40383 606-873-3208

LOUISIANA

New Orleans B&B **Accommodations** P.O. Box 8163 New Orleans, LA 70182	504-838-0071 504-838-0072 $ Dep. 20% Visa/MC/AmEx/DC	Free brochure Louisiana Europe, New Zeal. 8am-5pm, M-F

More RSOs ...

Southern Comfort B&B Res., 2856 Hundred Oaks, Baton Rouge. LA 70808 504-346-1928
800-749-1928
New Orleans B&B, 671 Rosa Ave., Metairie. LA 70005 504-838-0071 504-838-0072
B&B of Louisiana, P.O. Box 8128, New Orleans. LA 70182
Bed & Breakfast, Inc., 1021 Moss St., New Orleans. LA 70152 504-488-4640 800-749-4640
New Orleans Bed, B&B, P.O. Box 52466, New Orleans. LA 70152 504-897-3867

MARYLAND

Traveller in Maryland, The P.O. Box 2277 Annapolis, MD 21404	410-269-6232 800-736-4667 $$ Dep. 1 night Visa, MC, AmEx	Brochure $5 Maryland, London United Kingdom 9-5 M-Th, 9-1pm F
Amanda's B&B Reservation 1428 Park Ave. Baltimore, MD 21217	410-225-0001 FAX: 410-728-8957 $$ Dep. 1 night Visa, MC, AmEx Description $3 Fr,Ger,It,Arab	Free listing SASE Maryland, PA, DE WV, VA, NJ, DC 8:30-5:30pm M-F 8:30am-noon Sat

More RSOs ...

Annapolis B&B, 235 Prince George St., Annapolis. MD 21401
Green Street B&B, 161 Green St., Annapolis. MD 21401

MASSACHUSETTS

A B&B Agency of Boston 47 Commercial Wharf Boston, MA 02110	617-720-3540 800-248-9262 $$ Dep. 30% Visa, MC Fr,Sp,Ger,Arab,It	Free brochure MA, Camb., Boston 9am-9pm 7 days also ans. machine
B&B Associates **Bay Colony, Ltd.** P.O. Box 57166, Babson Park Boston, MA 02157	617-449-5302 800-347-5088 $$ Dep. 30% Visa/MC/AmEx/DC Directory $6 Fr,Ger,It,Nor,Sp,Gr,Rus	Free brochure Massachusetts 9:30am-5pm M-F
Host Homes of Boston P.O. Box 117, Waban Branch Boston, MA 02168	617-244-1308 FAX: 617-244-5156 $$ Dep. 1 night Visa, MC, AmEx Fr,Ger,Sp,Gr,Jap,Rus	Free broch. SASE MA, Bost. Cape Cd 9am-noon and 1:30pm-4:30pm M-F
Greater Boston Hospitality P.O. Box 1142 Brookline, MA 02146	617-277-5430 $$ Dep. 1 night Visa, MC, AmEx Sp,Fr,Heb,Ger,It,Pol	Brochure SASE Massachusetts 9am - 10pm M-F
B&B of New England 329 Lake Dr. Guildford, MA 06437	203-457-0042 800-582-0853 $ Dep. 1 night	Brochure $5 ME,VT,NH,MA,CT,RI 9am-9pm daily
B&B Marblehead/Northshore P.O. Box 35 Newtonville, MA 02160	617-964-1606 800-832-2632 $$ Deposit 50% AmEx, Visa, MC Free brochure	Directory $3.50 Boston, Cape Cod NH, ME, VT, MA 8:30am-9pm wkdays 9-12 Sat. 7-9pm S
House Guests Cape Cod & **Islands** P.O. Box 1881 Orleans, MA 02653	800-666-HOST 508-896-7053 $ Deposit 50% Visa, MC, AmEx	Listing $3.95 Massachusetts 9am-7pm 7 days
Bed & Breakfast Cape Cod P.O. Box 341 West Hyannisport, MA 02672	508-775-2772 FAX: 508-775-2884 $$ Dep. 25% Visa, MC, AmEx	Brochure SASE MA/Cape Cd/Islnds 8:30am to 6:00pm also ans. machine
Berkshire Bed & Breakfast **Homes** P.O. Box 211 Williamsburg, MA 01096	413-268-7244 $ Dep. 1 night Visa, MC, AmEx	Listing SASE MA, VT, NY, CT 9am-6pm Mon-Fri

More RSOs ...
University B&B, 12 Churchill St., Brookline. MA 02146

B&B Cambridge & Gtr Boston, P.O. Box 665, Cambridge. MA 02140 617-576-1492 617-576-2112
Battina's B&B, P.O. Box 585, Cambridge. MA 02238
Massachusetts B&B Hdqrtrs, P.O. Box 1703, Cotuit. MA 02635
B&B Accom. by Guest House, P.O. Box 8, Dennis. MA 02360
B&B House Guests—Cape Cod, Box AR, Dennis. MA 02638 617-398-0787
Yankee B&B of New England, 8 Brewster Rd., Hingham. MA 02043 617-749-5007
Nantucket Accommodations, Box 426, Nantucket. MA 02554
New England B&B, 1045 Centre St., Newton Center. MA 02159 617-244-2112 617-498-9810
Dukes County Reserv. Serv., P.O. Box 2370, Oak Bluffs. MA 02557
Orleans B&B Assoc., P.O. Box 1312, Orleans. MA 02653 508-255-3824 800-541-6226
Be Our Guest B&B, Ltd., P.O. Box 1333, Plymouth. MA 02362 617-837-9867
Golden Slumber Accom., 640 Revere Beach Blvd., Revere. MA 02151 617-289-1053 800-892-3231
Bed & Breakfast USA, P.O. Box 418, South Egremont. MA 01258 800-255-7213 413-528-2113
Greater Springfield B&B, 25 Bellevue Ave., Springfield. MA 01108
Martha's Vineyard Reserv., P.O. Box 1769, Vineyard Haven. MA 02568

MAINE

More RSOs ...

B&B Down East, Ltd., Box 547, Eastbrook. ME 04634 207-565-3517
Nova Scotia Tourist Info., 129 Commercial St., Portland. ME 04101

MICHIGAN

More RSOs ...

Frankenmuth Area B&B, 337 Trinklein St., Frankenmuth. MI 48734 517-652-8897
Betsy Ross B&B, 701 E. Ludington Ave., Ludington. MI 49431 313-561-6041
Capital B&B, 5150 Corey Rd., Willianston. MI 48895 517-468-3434

MINNESOTA

More RSOs ...

Uptown Lake District B&B, 2301 Bryant Ave., Minneapolis. MN 55405 612-872-7884
B&B Registry Ltd., P.O. Box 8174, Saint Paul. MN 55108 612-646-4238

MISSISSIPPI

Lincoln, Ltd. Mississippi Reserv.	601-482-5483	Free Brochure
	800-633-MISS	MS, AL, TN, LA
P.O. Box 3479, 2303 23rd Ave	$$	9am-5pm M-F
Meridian, MS 39303	Dep. 1 night	also ans. machine
	Visa, MC, AmEx	
	$3.50 Directory	
	Fr,Ger	

More RSOs ...

Natchez Pilgrimage Tours, P.O. Box 347, Natchez. MS 39121 601-446-6631 800-647-6742
Natchez Reservations, 243 John R. Junkin Dr., Natchez. MS 39120 800-824-0355

MISSOURI

Ozark Mountain Country B&B	800-695-1546	Free broch. SASE
	417-334-4720	SW MO, NW AR
P.O. Box 295	$	7:30am-7:30pm
Branson, MO 65616	Dep. 1 night	
	Visa, MC, AmEx	

More RSOs ...

Truman Country B&B, 424 N. Pleasant, Independence. MO 64050 816-254-6657
B&B Kansas City, P.O. Box 14781, Lenexa. MO 66285 913-888-3636
Lexington B&B, 115 N. 18th St., Lexington. MO 64067

MONTANA

B&B Western Adventure
P.O. Box 20972, 806 Poly Dr.
Billings, MT 59104

406-259-7993
$
Dep. 1 night or 50%
Visa, MC
Free brochure

Directory $6
SD/MT/ID/WY
9am-5pm summer
9am-1pm winter

NEBRASKA

More RSOs ...

Swede Hospitality B&B, 1617 Avenue A, Gothenburg. NE 69138 308-537-2680
B&B of the Great Plains, P.O. Box 2333, Lincoln. NE 68502 402-423-3480
B&B of the Midwest, 230 S. Maple, West Point. NE 68788 402-372-5904 800-392-3625

NEW HAMPSHIRE

**Country Inn in
the White Mountains**
P.O. Box 2025
North Conway, NH 03860

800-562-1300
603-356-9460

More RSOs ...

B&B of New England, 121 Bayberry Ln., Strafford. NH 03884 603-664-5492 800-282-5595

NEW JERSEY

B&B of Princeton
P.O. Box 571
Princeton, NJ 08542

609-924-3189
FAX: 609-921-6271
$$
Dep. 1 night

Listing SASE
Princeton, NJ
24 hr. telephone

More RSOs ...

InnNovations, Inc., 118 South Ave. E, Cranford. NJ 07016 201-272-3600
Northern New Jersey B&B, 11 Sunset Trail, Denville. NJ 07834
B&B Adventures, 103 Godwin Ave., Midland Park. NJ 07432 800-992-2632 201-444-7409
Cape Assoc., 340 46th Place, Sea Isle. NJ 08243

NEW MEXICO

B&B of New Mexico
P.O. Box 2805
Santa Fe, NM 87504

505-982-3332
800-648-0513
$$
Dep. 50%+50% 2wk pr
Visa, MC, AmEx

Brochure SASE
New Mexico
9am-5pm M-F

NEW YORK

International B&B Club
504 Amherst St.
Buffalo, NY 14207

716-874-8797
800-373-8797
$
Dep. 1 night
MC, Visa, AmEx

Book $10
9am—9pm M-F

**American Country Collection
B&B**
4 Greenwood Lane
Delmar, NY 12054

518-439-7001
$
Dep. 50%
Visa, MC, AmEx
Free brochure

Directory $7.25
VT, W. MA, E. NY
St. Thomas
Mon. - Fri. 10-5

NEW YORK ———————————————————————

Elaine's B&B & Inn Reservation 4987 Kingston Rd. Elbridge, NY 13060	315-689-2082 $$ Dep. 1 night or 50%	List SASE Central NY/W MA 9:30am-7:30pm
Adventures B&B Reservation Serv. P.O. Box 567, 39 Main St. Genesed, NY 14454	716-243-5540 800-724-1932 $$ Dep. 1 night Visa/MC/DC/Diners	Free brochure NY:Rochester Finger Lakes 9am-5pm Daily
Abode Bed & Breakfast, Ltd. P.O. Box 20022 New York, NY 10028	212-472-2000 $$$ Dep. 25%, 2 ngt min AmEx	Free brochure NY: Manh/Pk Slope 9am-5pm M-F, 11am-2pm Sat
At Home in New York P.O. Box 407, 140 W. 55th St. #9A New York, NY 10185	212-956-3125 FAX: 212-247-3294 $$ Dep. 25% Visa, MC, AmEx Fr,Sp,Ger	Free brochure NY, Nat./Internat 9am-5pm M-F 9am-12pm Sat-Sun
B&B Network of New York 134 W. 32nd St, Ste 602 New York, NY 10001	212-645-8134 $$ Dep. 25%	Free brochure New York 8am-6pm M-F
Bed & Breakfast (& Books) 35 West 92nd St. New York, NY 10025	212-865-8740 $$$ Deposit 25% Fr,Ger	Free list SASE New York City 10am-5pm, Mon-Fri
New World Bed & Breakfast 150 5th Ave., Suite 711 New York, NY 10011	212-675-5600 800-443-3800 $$ Dep. 25% Visa/MC/AmEx/DC	Free brochure Manhattan, NY 9am-5pm M-F
Urban Ventures, Inc. 38 W. 32nd. St., #142 New York, NY 10001	212-594-5650 FAX: 212-947-9320 $$ Dep. 1 night All mayor CrCd	Free list SASE NYC/No. NJ England/France/It 8am-5pm Mon-Fr

More RSOs ...

B&B of Niagara Frontier, 440 LeBrun Rd., Buffalo. NY 14226
B&B USA, Ltd., 129 Grand St., Croton-on-Hudson. NY 10520 914-271-6228 800-255-7213
Alternative Lodging, P.O. Box 1782, East Hampton. NY 11937 516-324-9449
Lodgings Plus B&B, Box 279, East Hampton. NY 11937 212-858-9589
B&B Western New York, 40 Maple Ave., Franklinville. NY 14737 716-676-5704
House Minders & Finders, 53 University Ave., Hamilton. NY 13346 315-824-2311
Leather Stocking Assoc., P.O. Box 3053, Herkimer. NY 13350 315-733-0040
Mid-Island B&B, 518 Mid-Island Plaza, Hicksville. NY 11801 516-931-1234
Finger Lakes B&B Assoc., Box 6576, Ithaca. NY 14851
North Country B&B Reserv., P.O. Box 286, Lake Placid. NY 12946 518-523-9474
B&B Reservation Serv., 162 Hook Rd., Macedon. NY 14502 315-986-4536
B&B in Manhattan, P.O. Box 533, New York. NY 10150 212-472-2528 FAX: 212-988-9818
Bed & Breakfast Bureau, 330 W. 42nd St., New York. NY 10036 212-957-9786 FAX: 212-957-9476

City Lights B&B, Ltd., P.O. Box 20355, New York. NY 10028 212-737-7049 FAX: 212-535-2755
US Virgin Isl. Gov't Travel, 1270 Ave. of the Americas, New York. NY 10020
Island B&B Registry, 5 Exeter Court, Northport. NY 11768 516-757-7398
B&B Res. Ser. of Gtr. NY, P O Box 1015, Pearl River. NY 10965 914-735-4857
Host Homes of North Fork, Box 333, Peconic. NY 11958 516-765-5762
A Reasonable Alternative, 117 Spring St., Port Jefferson. NY 11777 516-928-4034
Tobin's B&B Guide, Rd. 2, Box 64, Rhinebeck. NY 12572
B&B of Columbia County, Box 122, Spencertown. NY 12165 518-392-2358
B&B of Central New York, 4336 Fay Rd., Syracuse. NY 13204
B&B Connection NY, RD 1, Box 325, Vernon. NY 13476 315-824-4888
East End B&B, Inc., P.O. Box 178, West Hampton. NY 11977

NORTH CAROLINA

More RSOs ...

B&B in the Albemarle, P. O. Box 248, Everetts. NC 27825 919-792-4584

NORTH DAKOTA

More RSOs ...

Old West B&B Reserv. Serv., Box 211, Regent. ND 58650

OHIO

Columbus Bed & Breakfast	614-443-3680	Free brochure
769 S. 3rd St.	$$	Columbus, OH
Columbus, OH 43206	Dep. $25	24 hours

More RSOs ...

Private Lodgings, Inc., P.O. Box 18590, Cleveland. OH 44118 216-321-0400
Buckeye B&B, P.O. Box 130, Powell. OH 43065 614-548-4555

OREGON

More RSOs ...

Ashland's B&B Network, P.O. Box 1051, Ashland. OR 97520 503-482-BEDS
Inn Formation, PO Box 1376, Ashland. OR 97520
Southern Oregon Res. Ctr., PO Box 477, Ashland. OR 97520
Bend B&B, 19838 Ponderosa Dr., Bend. OR 97702 503-388-3007
Country Host Registry, 901 NW Chadwick Ln., Myrtle Creek. OR 97457 503-863-5168
B&B Accom.—Oregon Plus, 5733 S.W. Dickinson St., Portland. OR 97219 503-245-0642
Northwest B&B, 610 SW Broadway, Portland. OR 97205 503-243-7616

PENNSYLVANIA

B&B Connections	215-687-3565	Free sample dir.
B&B of Philadelphia	800-448-3619	Philadephia &
P.O. Box 21	$	Suburbs
Devon, PA 19333	Dep. 1 night or 20%	Mon.-Fri. 9am-7pm
	Visa, MC, AmEx	Sat. 9am-5pm
	Fax: 215-995-9524	

All About Town - B&B	215-783-7838	Free brochure
Philadelphia	800-344-0123	Pennsylvania
B&B of Valley Forge	$	9am-9pm 7 days
P.O. Box 562	Dep. 1 night	
Valley Forge, PA 19481	Visa/MC/AmEx/DC	
	Directory $3	
	Sp,Fr,It,Dutch,Ger	

More RSOs ...

B&B of SE Pennsylvania, 146 W. Philadelphia Ave., Boyertown. PA 19512 215-367-4688
Magic Forests Travel Bureau, RD 3, Box 256, Clarion. PA 16214 800-348-9393 814-849-5197
B&B-Lancaster Harrisburg, 463 N. Market St., Elizabethtown. PA 17022 717-367-9408
Pennsylvania Travel Council, 902 N. Second St., Harrisburg. PA 17102 717-232-8880
B&B of Chester County, P.O. Box 825, Kennett Square. PA 19348 215-444-1367
Nissly's Olde Home Inns, 624-632 West Chestnut St., Lancaster. PA 17603 717-392-2311
717-866-4926
B&B Lancaster County, P.O. Box 19, Mountville. PA 17554 717-285-7200
B&B Center City, 1804 Pine St., Philadelphia. PA 19103 215-735-1137
B&B of Philadelphia, 1616 Walnut St., Philadelphia. PA 19103 800-220-1917 215-735-1917
Rest & Repast B&B Serv., P.O. Box 126, Pine Grove Mills. PA 16868 814-238-1484
Guesthouses, Inc., P.O. Box 2137, West Chester. PA 19380 800-950-9130 215-692-4575

RHODE ISLAND

Anna's Victorian Connection	401-849-2489	Free brochure
5 Fowler Ave.	Fax: 401-847-7309	RI, S.MA
Newport, RI 02840	$	9 am - 9 pm daily
	Dep. 50%	10-8 in winter
	All mayor CrCd	
	Fr	

Hospitality Network - New	401-849-1298	Directory $3
England	800-828-0000	Rhode Island
38 Bellevue Ave, Ste. F	$$	South & East MA
Newport, RI 02840	Dep 1 night+1/2 bal	9am-5pm Mon-Fri
	Visa, MC, AmEx	9am-12noon Sat.
	Free broch/SASE	
	Fr,Ger,It,Malay	

More RSOs . . .
B&B International, 21 Dearborn St., Newport. RI 02840
B&B Registry, 44 Everett St., Newport. RI 02840
B&B, Newport, 33 Russell Ave., Newport. RI 02840 401-846-5408
Newport Historic Inns, P.O. Box 981, Newport. RI 02840 401-846-ROOM
Newport Reservation Serv., P.O. Box 518, Newport. RI 02840 401-847-8878
At Home in New England, Box 25, Saunderstown. RI 02874

SOUTH CAROLINA

Historic Charleston B&B	803-722-6606	Free broch. SASE
60 Broad St.	800-743-3583	South Carolina
Charleston, SC 29401	$$	9am-5pm M-F
	Dep. 1 night	
	Visa, MC, AmEx	
	Fr,Sp	

Charleston East B&B League	803-884-8208	List $1
1031 Tall Pine Rd.	$	South Carolina
Mount Pleasant, SC 29464	Dep. 1 night	10am-6pm daily
		answering machine

More RSOs . . .
Bay Street Accom., 601 Bay St., Beaufort. SC 29902
Charleston Society B&B, 84 Murray Blvd., Charleston. SC 29401 803-723-4948

SOUTH DAKOTA

More RSOs ...

Old West & Badlands B&B Assoc., HCR 02, Box 100A, Philip. SD 57567 605-859-2120
605-859-2117

TENNESSEE

B&B — About Tennessee	615-331-5244	Brochure $5
B&B Hospitality Inter.	800-458-2421	TN/Nat./Internat
P.O. Box 110227	$$	9am-5pm M-F
Nashville, TN 37222	Deposit 25%	also ans. machine
	All mayor CrCd	
	Sp,Fr,Ger	

More RSOs ...

Natchez Trace B&B, P.O. Box 193, Hampshire. TN 38461 615-285-2777 800-377-2770
Jonesborough B&B, P.O. Box 722, Jonesborough. TN 37659 615-753-9223

TEXAS

Sand Dollar Hospitality	512-853-1222	Free brochure
3605 Mendenhall Dr.	$$	Texas
Corpus Christi, TX 78415	Deposit 33%	8am—8pm M-Sat
	Fr	

The Gilded Thistle	409-763-0194	9am-5pm daily
1805 Broadway	800-654-9380	
Galveston, TX 77550	$$$	
	Dep. with CreCard	
	MC, Visa	
	Free Brochure	

B&B Hosts of San Antonio	210-222-8846	Free brochure
123 Auditorium Circle	800-356-1605	South Texas
San Antonio, TX 78205	$$	9am-5pm M-F
	Visa/MC/AmEx/Disc	9am-12 noon Sat.

More RSOs ...

B&B Society of Austin, 1702 Gaywood Cove, Austin. TX 78704
B&B Society of Houston, 4432 Holt St., Bellaire. TX 77401 713-666-6372
B&B Texas Style, 4224 W. Red Bird Ln., Dallas. TX 75237 214-298-8586
B&B of Fredericksburg, 102 S. Cherry St., Fredericksburg. TX 78624 512-997-4712
Gästhaus Schmidt, 231 West Main St., Fredericksburg. TX 78624 210-997-5612
B&B - Galveston, 1805 Broadway, Galveston. TX 77550
B&B Society of Texas, 1200 Southmore Ave., Houston. TX 77004 713-523-1114 800-553-5797
NRSO, P.O. Box 850653, Richardson. TX 75085
B&B of Wimberley Texas, P.O. Box 589, Wimberley. TX 78676 512-847-9666 512-847-2837

UTAH

More RSOs ...

B&B Inns of Utah, P.O. Box 3066, Park City. UT 84060 801-645-8068

VERMONT

More RSOs ...

Vermont Travel Info. Serv., Pond Village, Brookfield. VT 05036 802-276-3120
Vermont B&B, P.O. Box 1, East Fairfield. VT 05448 802-827-3827
American B&B, Box 983, Saint Albans. VT 05478

VIRGIN ISLANDS

The Prince Street Inn 402 Prince St. Frederiksted, VI 00840	809-772-9550 $ Dep. 50% Free brochure	Virgin Islands 9am-9pm daily
Hilty House Inn #2 Hermon Hill St. Croix, VI 00824	809-773-2594 $$$ Dep. 50%	Free Brochure Virgin Island 7 days a week

VIRGINIA

Princely B&B Ltd. 819 Prince St. Alexandria, VA 22314	703-683-2159 $$$ Dep. 1 night Fr,Sp,Ger	Free Brochure Alexandria, VA. 10am-6pm M-F
Guesthouses B&B, Inc. P.O. Box 5737 Charlottesville, VA 22903	804-979-7264 $$ Dep. 25% + tax Ccard for deposit Fr,Ger	List $1 SASE Virginia Noon-5pm M-F

More RSOs ...

Blue Ridge B&B, Route 2, Box 3895, Berryville. VA 22611 703-955-1246 800-296-1246
Rockbridge Reserv., Sleepy Hollow, Box 76, Brownsburg. VA 24415 703-348-5698
B&B on the Hill, 2304 East Broad St., Richmond. VA 23223 804-780-3746
Bensonhouse Res. Serv., 2036 Monument Ave., Richmond. VA 23220 804-353-6900
B&B of Roanoke Valley, 1708 Arlington Rd., Roanoke. VA 24015
Travel Tree, P.O. Box 838, Williamsburg. VA 23187 800-989-1571

WASHINGTON

A Pacific Reservation Service 701 N.W. 60th St. Seattle, WA 98107	206-784-0539 FAX: 206-782-4036 $$ Dep. $25 Visa, MC, AmEx Free broch. SASE Ger,Fr,Dan,Nor,Du	List $5 Washington/BC 9am-5pm M-F also ans. machine

More RSOs ...

B&B Guild—Whatcom County, 2610 Eldridge Ave., Bellingham. WA 98225 206-676-4560
B&B Service (BABS), 400 W. Lake Samish Dr., Bellingham. WA 98227 206-733-8642
Whidbey Island B&B Assoc., P.O. Box 259, Langley. WA 98260 206-321-6272
Travellers' B&B, P.O. Box 492, Mercer Island. WA 98040 206-232-2345
West Coast B&B, 11304 20th Place S.W., Seattle. WA 98146
INNterlodging Co-op Serv., P.O. Box 7044, Tacoma. WA 98407 206-756-0343

WEST VIRGINIA

More RSOs ...

Countryside Accom., P.O. Box 57, Summit Point. WV 25446 304-725-2614

WISCONSIN

More RSOs ...

B&B Guest Homes, Route 2, 698 County U., Algoma. WI 54201 414-743-9742
B&B of Milwaukee, 823 N. 2nd. St., Milwaukee. WI 53203 414-277-8066

YUKON

Northern Network of B&B's	403-993-5644	Free brochure
Box 954, 451 Craig St.	Fax: 403-993-5648	Yukon, Alaska
Dawson City, YU Y0B 1G0	$$	British Columbia
	Dep. 1 night	7 days, 24 hours
	Visa, MC, AmEx	

ALBERTA

More RSOs . . .

Banff/Jasper Central Res., 204 Caribou, Banff. AB T0L 0C0
AAA Bed West, 207-35A St. S.W., Calgary. AB T3C 1P6
Welcome West Vacation Ltd., 1320 Kerwood Cres. SW, Calgary. AB T2V 2N6
High Country B&B Bureau, Box 340, Claresholm. AB T0L 0L0 403-931-3514
Big Country B&B Agency, P.O. Box 1027, Duinheller. AB T0J 0Y0
Alberta Hostelling, 10926 - 88th Ave., Edmonton. AB T6G 0Z1 403-433-7798

BRITISH COLUMBIA

Old English B&B Registry	604-986-5069	Free brochure
1226 Silverwood Crescent	Fax: 604-986-8810	British Columbia
North Vancouver, BC V7P 1J3	$$	9am-5pm
	Dep. or CrCd	also ans. machine
	Visa, MC	

Town & Country B&B in B.C.	604-731-5942	Guide $10.50
P.O. Box 74542/2803 W. 4th Ave.	$$	British Columbia
Vancouver, BC V6K 1K2	Dep. 1 night	9am-4:30pm M-F
	Fr,Ger,Sp	evening & wkends

All Seasons B&B Agency, Inc.	604-655-7173	Book $6
P.O. Box 5511, Stn. B	$$	British Columbia
Victoria, BC V8R 6S4	Dep. 20%	9am-5pm Mon-Sat
	Visa, MC	
	Free brochure	
	Fr,Du,Ger	

Garden City B&B	604-479-1986	Free brochure
Reservations	FAX: 604-479-9999	BC, Vanc. Isl.
660 Jones Terrace	$$	7am-9pm daily
Victoria, BC V8Z 2L7	Dep. or CrCd	
	Visa, MC, AmEx	
	Fr,Ger,Sp,Wel,Dan,Jap,Cz	

More RSOs . . .

Born Free B&B of B.C. Ltd., 4390 Frances St., Burnaby. BC V5C 2R3 604-298-8815
Home Away From Home B&B, 1441 Howard Ave., Burnaby. BC V5B 3S2 604-294-1760 FAX: 604-294-0799
Canada-West Accom., P.O. Box 86607, North Vancouver. BC V7L 4L2 604-929-1424 800-873-7976
Western Comfort B&B Regis., 1890 E. Carisbrooke Rd., North Vancouver. BC V7N 1M9
A B & C B&B of Vancouver, 4390 Frances St., Vancouver. BC V5C 2R3 604-298-8815
AAA Bed & Breakfast, 658 E. 29th Ave., Vancouver. BC V5V 2R9 604-875-8888
Alberta & Pacific B&B, P.O. Box 15477, Vancouver. BC V6B 5B2 604-944-1793
Garden City B&B, 660 Jones Terrace, Victoria. BC V8Z 2L7 604-479-1986 FAX: 604-479-9999
Traveller's B&B, 1840 Midgard Ave., Victoria. BC V8P 2Y9 604-477-3069
VIP B&B, 1786 Teakwood Rd., Victoria. BC V8N 1E2 604-477-5604

MANITOBA

More RSOs ...
B&B of Manitoba, 93 Healey Crescent, Winnipeg. MB R2N 2S2 204-256-6151

NEW BRUNSWICK

More RSOs ...
New Brunswick Tourism, P.O. Box 12345, Frederick. NB E3B 5C3

NEWFOUNDLAND

More RSOs ...
Tourist Services Division, Box 2061, Saint John's. NF A1C 5R8

ONTARIO

Point Pelee B&B Reservation 115 Erie St. S. Leamington, ON N8H 3B5	519-326-7169 $ Dep. $20 per night	Free Brochure South Ontario 9am-9pm daily
Ottawa B&B Association 488 Cooper St. Ottawa, ON K1R 5H9	613-563-0161 $ Dep. 1 night Fr,Sp,Ger	Free broch/SASE Ontario 10am-9pm daily also ans. machine
Toronto Bed & Breakfast Inc. Box 269, 253 College St Toronto, ON M5T 1R5	416-588-8800 416-961-3676 $$ Dep. 1 night Visa, MC, AmEx Fr,Ger,It,Pol,Uk,Jap,Swe	Free brochure Ontario England (London) 9-noon, 2-7pm M-F

More RSOs ...
Ontario Vacation Farms Assoc., RR #2, Alma. ON N0B 1A0 519-846-9788
Beachburg & Area B&B Assoc., Box 146, Beachburg. ON K0J 1C0 613-582-3585
Brighton Area B&B Assoc., 61 Simpson St. Box 1106, Brighton. ON K0K 1H0 613-475-0538
Bed & Breakfast Burlington, 5435 Stratton Rd., Burlington. ON L7L 2Z1 416-637-0329
South Renfrew County B&B, c/o B.Collins, Box 67, Calabogie. ON K0J 1H0 613-752-2201
Eastern Ontario Cntry B&B, c/o Roduner Farm RR1, Cardinal. ON K0E 1E0 613-657-4830
Fergus/Elora B&B Assoc., 550 Saint Andrew St. E., Fergus. ON N1M 1R6 519-843-2747
Muskoka B&B Assoc., Box 1431, Gravenhurst. ON P0C 1G0 705-687-4395
Hamilton-Wentworth B&B, 61 E 43rd St., Hamilton. ON L8T 3B7 416-648-0461
Simcoe-Side Country B&B, RR 2, Lakeshore Rd., Hawkestone. ON L0L 1T0 705-487-7191
Kingston Area B&B, P.O. Box 37, Kingston. ON K7M 4V6 613-542-0214
Serena's Place, 720 Headley Dr., London. ON N6H 3V6 519-471-6228
SW Ontario Countryside Vac., RR #1, Millbank. ON N0K 1L0 519-595-4604
All Seasons B&B Assoc., 383 Mississauga Valley, Mississauga. ON L5A 1Y9 416-276-4572
Upper Canada B&B, P.O. Box 247, Morrisburg. ON K0C 1X0
Niagara Regional, 4917 River Rd., Niagara Falls. ON L2E 3G5 416-358-8988
Niagara-on-the-Lake B&B, P.O. Box 1515, Niagara-on-the-Lake. ON L0S 1J0 416-358-8988
Capital B&B Assoc. Ottawa, 2071 Riverside Dr., Ottawa. ON K1H 7X2 613-737-4129
Parry Sound & District B&B, P.O. Box 71, Parry Sound. ON P2A 2X2 705-342-9266
Pelee Island B&B Assoc., c/o Lynn Tiessen, Pelee Island. ON N0R 1M0 519-724-2068
Penetanguishene Area B&B, C.P. 1270, 63 rue Main, Penetanguishene. ON L0K 1P0
705-549-3116
B&B Registry of Peterborough, P.O. Box 2264, Peterborough. ON K9J 7Y8
B&B Prince Edward County, Box 1500, Picton. ON K0K 2T0 613-476-6798
Grey Bruce B&B Association, 435 Wellington, Port Elgin. ON N0H 2T0 519-832-5520
Port Stanley & Sparta Area, 324 Smith St. Box 852, Port Stanley. ON N0L 2A0 519-782-4173
St. Catharines B&B Assoc., 489 Carlton St., Saint Catharines. ON L2M 4W9 416-937-2422

Stratford Area Visitors, 38 Albert St., Stratford. ON N5A 3K3 519-271-5140
Stratford B&B Two, 208 Church St., Stratford. ON N5A 2R6 519-273-4840
B&B Across The City Registry, 1823 Foleyet Cres., Toronto. ON L1V 2X8 416-837-0024
Downtown Toronto Assoc. of B&Bs, P.O. Box 190 Station B, Toronto. ON M5T 2W1
416-690-1724 FAX: 416-690-5730
Metropolitan B&B Registry, 615 Mt. Pleasant, Toronto. ON M4S 3C5 416-964-2566 FAX:
416-537-0233
Prince Edward County B&B, 299 Main St., Wellington. ON K0K 3L0 613-399-2569

PRINCE EDWARD ISLAND

More RSOs ...

Visitors Services Division, P.O. Box 940, Charlottetown.PEI C1A 7MJ
Kensington Area Tourist, RR 1, Kensington. PEI C0B 1M0 902-436-6847

PROVINCE OF QUEBEC

A Bed & Breakfast	514-289-9749	Free brochure
3458 Laval Ave.	FAX: 514-287-7386	Montreal, Quebec
Montreal, PQ H2X 3C8	$	8am-6pm every day
	Dep. 1 night	
	Visa, MC, AmEx	
	Fr,Ger,Sp,Ch,Viet,Pol	
B&B Relais Montreal	514-287-9635	Montreal
Hospitalite	800-363-9635	8am-6pm
3977 Ave Laval	$$	
Montreal, PQ H2W 2H9	Dep. 1 night	
	Visa, MC	
A Montreal Oasis in	514-935-2313	9am-5pm M-F
Downtown	$	
3000 Chemin de Bresley Rd.	Dep. 25%	
Montreal, PQ H3Y 2G7	Visa, MC, AmEx	
	Fr,Sp,Ger,Swed	
B&B Bonjour Québec	418-524-0524	Free brochure
450 Rue Champlain	$	Québec City
Quebec, PQ G1K 4J3	Dep. $10	9am-6pm M-F
	Visa	

More RSOs ...

Mont—Royal Chez Soi, Inc., 5151 Cote-St.-Antoine, Montreal. PQ H4A 1P1
Bonjour Quebec B&B, 450 Rue Champlain, Quebec. PQ G1K 4J3 418-524-0524
Tourism Quebec, CP 20 000, Quebec. PQ G1K 7X2
Gite Quebec, 3729 Ave. le Corbusier, St-Foy. PQ G1W 4R8 418-651-1860

SASKATCHEWAN

More RSOs ...

Saskatchewan Country Vac., Box 89, Blaine Lake. SA S0J 0J0 306-497-2782 306-497-2230

YUKON TERRITORY

More RSOs ...

Tourism Yukon, Box 2703, Whitehorse. YU Y1A 2C6
Yukon B&B, 102-302 Steele St., Whitehorse. YU Y1A 2C5 403-668-2999

B&B Inns with Special Features

Antiques

Many of the inns we list are graced by antiques. These inns have put a special emphasis on antiques and period decor.

Magic Canyon Ranch
Homer, AK

Patton House B&B Inn
Wooster, AR

Greenway House, The
Bisbee, AZ

Whitegate Inn B&B
Mendocino, CA

Martine Inn, The
Pacific Grove, CA

Holden House—1902 B&B Inn
Colorado Springs, CO

Butternut Farm
Glastonbury, CT

Queen Anne Inn
New London, CT

Brunswick Manor
Brunswick, GA

Jesse Mount House
Savannah, GA

Beechwood
Barnstable Village, MA

Inn on Sea Street, The
Hyannis, MA

Addison Choate Inn
Rockport, MA

Spring Bank—A B&B Inn
Frederick, MD

Beaver Creek House B&B
Hagerstown, MD

Spencer Silver Mansion
Havre De Grace, MD

National Pike Inn
New Market, MD

Manor House Inn
Bar Harbor, ME

Hammons House, The
Bethel, ME

English Meadows Inn
Kennebunkport, ME

Maine Stay Inn & Cottages
Kennebunkport, ME

Garth Woodside Mansion
Hannibal, MO

Harding House B&B
St. Joseph, MO

Hamilton Place
Holly Springs, MS

Rosswood Plantation
Lorman, MS

Cedar Crest Victorian Inn
Asheville, NC

Morehead Inn, The
Charlotte, NC

Little Warren B&B
Tarboro, NC

Bungay Jar B&B
Franconia, NH

Bedford Inn
Cape May, NJ

Queen Victoria, The
Cape May, NJ

Sarah's Dream Village Inn
Dryden, NY

Chestnut Tree Inn
Saratoga Springs, NY

Cobbler Shop B&B Inn
Zoar, OH

Adamstown Inn
Adamstown, PA

Hotel Manisses, 1661 Inn
Block Island, RI

Country Victorian B&B
Charleston, SC

Thistle Hill B&B
Boston, VA

Madison House B&B, The
Lynchburg, VA

Conyers House Inn, The
Sperryville, VA

Legacy of Williamsburg
Williamsburg, VA

Inn at Narrow Passage
Woodstock, VA

Governor's Inn, The
Ludlow, VT

Historic Brookside Inn
Orwell, VT

Thorp House Inn & Cottages
Fish Creek, WI

Manor House, The
Kenosha, WI

Yesterdays Ltd. B&B
Wheeling, WV

Pine Lodge Farm B&B
Mill Bay, BC

Architecture

These inns are noted for their unusual and fine architecture.

Elegant Victorian Mansion
Eureka, CA

Chateau Tivoli B&B, The
San Francisco, CA

Bechtel Mansion Inn
East Berlin, PA

King's Cottage, A B&B Inn
Lancaster, PA

Trube Castle Inn
Galveston, TX

Brigham Street Inn
Salt Lake City, UT

Ann Starrett Mansion B&B
Port Townsend, WA

Comfort

Old-fashioned comfort and friendly staff are important to every lodging. These inns have these qualities in abundance.

B&B at Saddle Rock Ranch
Sedona, AZ

Pelican Cove B&B Inn
Carlsbad, CA

Forbestown Inn
Lakeport, CA

Heart's Desire Inn
Occidental, CA

Gatehouse Inn
Pacific Grove, CA

Cinnamon Bear B&B
Saint Helena, CA

Old Yacht Club Inn, The
Santa Barbara, CA

Olive House, The
Santa Barbara, CA

Inn at Chester, The
Chester, CT

Kenwood Inn, The
St. Augustine, FL

Victoria Place B&B
Lawai, Kauai, HI

Davis House
Crawfordsville, IN

RidgeRunner B&B, The
Middlesborough, KY

Honeysuckle Hill
Cape Cod/Barnestable, MA

Point Way Inn
Edgartown, MA

Village Green Inn
Falmouth, MA

Grafton Inn
Falmouth — Cape Cod, MA

Haus Andreas
Lee, MA

Walker House Inn
Lenox, MA

Bayberry, The
Martha's Vineyard Island, MA

Corner House Circa 1790
Nantucket, MA

Seven Sea Street Inn
Nantucket, MA

Northfield Country House
Northfield, MA

Rocky Shores Inn/Cottages
Rockport, MA

Coach House Inn, The
Salem, MA

Kemp House Inn
St. Michaels, MD

Castlemaine Inn, The
Bar Harbor, ME

Hearthside B&B
Bar Harbor, ME

Windward House B&B
Camden, ME

Dock Square Inn, The
Kennebunkport, ME

Old Fort Inn
Kennebunkport, ME

Cape Neddick House, The
York—Cape Neddick, ME

Doanleigh Wallagh Inn
Kansas City, MO

Baird House, Ltd. B&B Inn
Mars Hill, NC

Colonel Ludlow Inn
Winston—Salem, NC

Haverhill Inn
Haverhill, NH

Benjamin Prescott Inn
Jaffrey, NH

Forest—A Country Inn, The
North Conway/ Intervale, NH

Conover's Bay Head Inn
Bay Head, NJ

A Sea Crest By The Sea
Spring Lake, NJ

Normandy Inn, The
Spring Lake, NJ

Lamplight Inn B&B, The
Lake Luzerne, NY

Dartmouth House B&B
Rochester, NY

Country Willows B&B
Ashland, OR

Smithton Inn, The
Ephrata, PA

Tattersall Inn
Point Pleasant/New Hope, PA

Tres Palmas Guest House
San Juan, PR

Adams Edgeworth Inn
Monteagle, TN

Blue Mountain Mist Country
Sevierville, TN

Victorian Inn
Galveston, TX

Old Miners' Lodge B&B
Park City, UT

Cobble House Inn
Gaysville, VT

Golden Kitz Lodge
Stowe, VT

Nutmeg Inn
Wilmington, VT

Schnauzer Crossing B&B
Bellingham, WA

Palmer's Chart House
Deer Harbor, WA

Chelsea Station B&B Inn
Seattle, WA

Swallow's Nest Cottages
Vashon Island, WA

Abendruh B&B Swisstyle
Belleville, WI

Conference

Small conferences can be very productive when held in the inns listed, all of which have the facilities you need and the quiet and opportunity, too, for the fellowship you require.

Cobblestone Inn
Carmel, CA

Valley Lodge
Carmel Valley, CA

Gosby House Inn
Pacific Grove, CA

Power's Mansion Inn
Sacramento, CA

Edward II B&B Inn & Suites
San Francisco, CA

Jackson Court
San Francisco, CA

Conference *(cont'd.)*

Petite Auberge
San Francisco, CA

Hensley House, The
San Jose, CA

Upham Hotel & Cottages
Santa Barbara, CA

Madison Street Inn
Santa Clara, CA

St. George Hotel
Volcano, CA

Oglethorpe Inn
Augusta, GA

English Manor Inns
Clayton, GA

Susina Plantation Inn
Thomasville, GA

Walden Inn
Greencastle, IN

Queen Anne Inn
South Bend, IN

Max Paul. . .An Inn
Wichita, KS

Yankee Clipper Inn
Rockport, MA

Gibson's Lodgings
Annapolis, MD

Robert Morris Inn
Oxford, MD

High Meadows B&B
Eliot, ME

East Wind Inn
Tenants Harbor, ME

York Harbor Inn
York Harbor, ME

Yelton Manor B&B
South Haven, MI

Richmond Hill Inn
Asheville, NC

Jefferson Inn, The
Jefferson, NH

Whistling Swan Inn
Stanhope, NJ

Troutbeck Country Inn
Amenia, NY

Inn at Cooperstown, The
Cooperstown, NY

Genesee Country Inn, The
Mumford, NY

Fountain Hall B&B
Culpeper, VA

Springdale Country Inn
Lincoln, VA

Frederick House
Staunton, VA

Reluctant Panther Inn, The
Manchester Village, VT

Kedron Valley Inn
S. Woodstock, VT

Ten Acres Lodge
Stowe, VT

Moore House Country Inn
South Cle Elum, WA

Jakobstettel Guest House
St. Jacobs, ON

Decor

Distinctive decor and unusual architecture are always a pleasure. Enjoy them in these inns

Baywood B&B Inn
Baywood Park, CA

Hope-Merrill/Hope-
Bosworth
Geyserville, CA

Blackthorne Inn
Inverness, CA

Bluebelle House B&B
Lake Arrowhead, CA

Old World Inn
Napa, CA

Centrella Hotel
Pacific Grove, CA

Morey Mansion B&B Inn
Redlands, CA

Alamo Square Inn
San Francisco, CA

Inn at Union Square, The
San Francisco, CA

Monte Cristo, The
San Francisco, CA

Gables B&B Inn, The
Santa Rosa, CA

Casa Madrona Hotel
Sausalito, CA

Oleander House
Yountville, CA

Lovelander B&B Inn, The
Loveland, CO

Chimney Crest Manor B&B
Bristol, CT

Palmer Inn, The
Mystic-Noank, CT

Watson House, The
Key West, FL

A Hotel. . .The Frenchmen
New Orleans, LA

Ashley Manor
Barnstable, Cape Cod, MA

Bradford Inn & Motel
Chatham, MA

Farmhouse at Nauset, The
East Orleans, MA

Colonial Inn of Marthas
Edgartown, MA

Mostly Hall B&B Inn
Falmouth/Cape Cod, MA

Gables Inn, The
Lenox, MA

Amelia Payson House
Salem, MA

Cleftstone Manor
Bar Harbor, ME

Brannon-Bunker Inn
Damariscotta, ME

Greenville Inn
Greenville, ME

Kemah Guest House
Saugatuck, MI

Walnut Street Inn
Springfield, MO

Winter House, The
St. Louis, MO

Wright Inn, The
Asheville, NC

Shield House, The
Clinton, NC

Manor on Golden Pond, The
Holderness, NH

Gingerbread House, The
Cape May, NJ

Leith Hall Seashore Inn
Cape May, NJ

Old Court B&B, The
Providence, RI

Villa de La Fontaine B&B
Charleston, SC

Decor *(cont'd.)*

William Catlin House, The
Richmond, VA

Inn at Manchester, The
Manchester Village, VT

Franklin Victorian, The
Sparta, WI

Hampshire House 1884
Romney, WV

Little Garden Farm, The
Victoria, BC

Family Fun

Be sure to check this list if you're travelling with your brood of six. The inns below are ideal for a family fun vacation.

Idaho Rocky Mtn. Ranch
Stanley, ID

Swift River Inn
Cummington, MA

Gosnold Arms
New Harbor, ME

Goose Cove Lodge
Sunset, ME

Pentwater Inn
Pentwater, MI

DownOver Inn
Arrow Rock, MO

Kelley's B 'n B
Kansas City, MO

Lone Mountain Ranch
Big Sky, MT

Chalet Inn, The
Whittier, NC

Franconia Inn
Franconia, NH

Cordova, The
Orange Grove, NJ

Litco Farms B&B
Cooperstown, NY

Du Pre House
Georgetown, SC

Danish Chalet Inn
St. Thomas, VI

Barrows House
Dorset, VT

Johnny Seesaw's
Peru, VT

Hyde Away Inn
Waitsfield, VT

A. Drummond's Ranch B&B
Cheyenne, WY

Teton Tree House
Jackson Hole, WY

Golden Dreams B&B
Whistler, BC

Farm Vacation

The inns listed below are working farms.

Howard Creek Ranch
Westport, CA

Ellis River House
Jackson, NH

Sonka's Sheep Station Inn
Myrtle Creek, OR

Winding Glen Farm Home
Christiana, PA

Barley Sheaf Farm
Holicong, PA

Meadow Spring Farm B&B
Kennett Square, PA

Cedar Hill Farm
Mount Joy, PA

Whitehall Inn, The
New Hope, PA

Ponda-Rowland B&B Inn
Wilkes-Barre, PA

Skoglund Farm
Canova, SD

Lakeside Farm B&B
Webster, SD

Fleetwood Farm B&B
Leesburg, VA

Caledonia Farm B&B 1812
Washington, VA

Berkson Farms
Enosburg Falls, VT

Just-N-Trails B&B/Farm
Sparta, WI

Kananaskis Guest Ranch
Banff, AB

Anola's B&B
Claresholm, AB

Swallow Hill Farm B&B
Victoria, BC

Fishing

Nothing like a good catch. These inns are near the haunts of the really big ones. Fishing over, head back to the inn and tell tales to fellow enthusiasts.

Glacier Bay Country Inn
Gustavus, AK

Gustavus Inn
Gustavus, AK

Matheson B&B
Naknek, AK

Matlick House, The
Bishop, CA

Requa Inn
Klamath, CA

Jean's Riverside B&B
Oroville, CA

River Rock Inn
Placerville, CA

Faulkner House, The
Red Bluff, CA

Pleasure Point Inn
Santa Cruz, CA

Outlook Lodge B&B
Green Mountain Falls, CO

Inn at Rock 'n River
Lyons, CO

Harbor Inne & Cottage
Mystic, CT

Fishing *(cont'd.)*

Hopp-Inn Guest House
Marathon, FL

McBride's B&B Guesthouse
Irwin, ID

Black Friar Inn
Bar Harbor, ME

Mill Pond Inn
Newcastle, ME

Dockside Guest Quarters
York, ME

Raymond House Inn, The
Port Sanilac, MI

Buck Stop B&B, The
Rapid River, MI

Langdon House B&B
Beaufort, NC

Gingerbread Inn, The
Chimney Rock, NC

Blue Boar Lodge
Robbinsville, NC

Inn at Coit Mountain
Newport, NH

Old Pioneer Garden B&B
Imlay/Unionville, NV

Thousand Islands Inn
Clayton—1000 Islands, NY

Tu Tu Tun Lodge, The
Gold Beach, OR

Fairfield-by-The-Sea B&B
Green Hill, RI

Highland Inn
Monterey, VA

West Mountain Inn
Arlington, VT

Rowell's Inn
Chester, VT

North Hero House
North Hero, VT

Lake St. Catherine Inn
Poultney, VT

Lareau Farm Country Inn
Waitsfield, VT

Orchard Hill Inn
White Salmon, WA

Griffin Inn & Cottages
Ellison Bay, WI

Fish Creek B&B
Jackson Hole (Wilson), WY

April Point Lodge
Campbell River, BC

Lookout at Schooner Cove
Nanoose Bay, BC

Gardens

Ah, to while away an hour in a lovely garden. What could be more relaxing? These inns are renowned for their lush gardens.

Arizona Inn
TucsonAZ

Holiday House
CarmelCA

Sandpiper Inn at-the-Beach
Carmel by-the-SeaCA

Brewery Gulch Inn
MendocinoCA

Jabberwock, The
MontereyCA

Country Garden Inn
NapaCA

Feather Bed, The
QuincyCA

Harvest Inn
Saint HelenaCA

Victorian Garden Inn
SonomaCA

Country House Inn
TempletonCA

Blue Lake Ranch
DurangoCO

Clark Cottage, Wintergreen
PomfretCT

Merlinn Guesthouse
Key WestFL

Bradford Gardens Inn
ProvincetownMA

Summer House, The
SiasconsetMA

Hartwell House
OgunquitME

Hope Farm
NatchezMS

Cedar Grove Mansion-Inn
VicksburgMS

Blooming Garden Inn, The
DurhamNC

Martin Hill Inn
PortsmouthNH

Woolverton Inn
StocktonNJ

Berry Hill Farm B&B
BainbridgeNY

Back of the Beyond
ColdenNY

Inn at Cowger House, The
ZoarOH

Dogwood @ Spoutwood Farm
Glen RockPA

Back Street Inn
New HopePA

Willows of Newport, The
NewportRI

Rhett House Inn, The
BeaufortSC

Middleton Inn
CharlestonSC

Trail's End, A Country Inn
WilmingtonVT

General Lewis Inn
LewisburgWV

Sunnymeade House Inn
VictoriaBC

Golf

Tee off, walk and relax, then head back to your cozy inn. What could be nicer?

Napa Inn, The
Napa, CA

Kinter House Inn
Corydon, IN

Teetor House, The
Hagerstown, IN

Golf *(cont'd.)*

Old Hoosier House, The
Knightstown, IN

Fairhaven Inn at Bath
Bath, ME

1802 House B&B Inn
Kennebunkport, ME

Red Dog B&B, The
Saugatuck, MI

Buttonwood Inn
Franklin, NC

Old Edwards Inn, The
Highlands, NC

Pine Ridge Inn
Mount Airy, NC

Knollwood House
Southern Pines, NC

Pine Crest Inn
Tryon, NC

Cliff Park Inn & Golf Crs.
Milford, PA

7th Heaven Log Home Inn
Gatlinburg, TN

Inn at Mad River Barn, The
Waitsfield, VT

Valley Inn, The
Waitsfield, VT

Beaver Pond Farm Inn
Warren, VT

Red Shutter Inn
Wilmington, VT

Gourmet

An excellent meal can add a lot to your stay. The inns listed here are particularly celebrated for their fine cuisine.

Harbor House
Elk, CA

Hotel Carter, The
Eureka, CA

Madrona Manor, Country Inn
Healdsburg, CA

McCloud Guest House
McCloud, CA

Copper Beech Inn, The
Ivoryton, CT

Old Lyme Inn
Old Lyme, CT

Stovall House, The
Sautee, GA

La Corsette Maison Inn
Newton, IA

Bramble Inn & Restaurant
Brewster, MA

Old Manse Inn, The
Brewster, MA

Quaker House Inn & Rest.
Nantucket, MA

Harrington Farm, The
Princeton, MA

Penobscot Meadows Inn
Belfast, ME

Camden Harbour Inn
Camden, ME

Crocker House Country Inn
Hancock Point, ME

White Barn Inn
Kennebunkport, ME

Newcastle Inn, The
Newcastle, ME

Wickwood Country Inn, The
Saugatuck, MI

Randolph House Country Inn
Bryson City, NC

Bradford Inn, The
Bradford, NH

Hitching Post B&B, The
Chichester, NH

Inn at Crystal Lake, The
Eaton Center, NH

Colby Hill Inn
Henniker, NH

Stonehurst Manor
North Conway, NH

Woodstock Inn
North Woodstock, NH

Stockton Inn, The
Stockton, NJ

Crabtree's Kittle House
Chappaqua, NY

Balsam House, The
Chestertown, NY

Old Drovers Inn
Dover Plains, NY

Swiss Huttek Country Inn
Hillsdale, NY

Rose Inn
Ithaca, NY

Taughannock Farms Inn
Trumansburg, NY

Golden Pheasant Inn
Erwinna, PA

Academy Street B&B
Hawley, PA

Longswamp B&B
Mertztown, PA

Centre Bridge Inn
New Hope, PA

Shelter Harbor Inn
Westerly, RI

Inn on the River
Glen Rose, TX

Kenmore Inn
Fredericksburg, VA

Montross Inn & Restaurant
Montross, VA

L'Auberge Provencale
White Post, VA

Arlington Inn
Arlington, VT

Middletown Springs Inn
Middletown Springs, VT

Millbrook Inn
Waitsfield, VT

Inn at Swifts Bay, The
Lopez Island, WA

Geneva Inn, The
Lake Geneva, WI

Historic

Inns situated in historic buildings or locales hold a special appeal for many people. The following is a sampling.

Webster House B&B Inn
Alameda, CA

Mine House Inn
Amador City, CA

Coloma Country Inn, The
Coloma, CA

Columbia City Hotel
Columbia, CA

Fallon Hotel
Columbia, CA

Rock Haus Inn
Del Mar, CA

Heirloom B&B Inn, The
Ione, CA

Julian Gold Rush Hotel
Julian, CA

Victorian Farmhouse
Little River, CA

Headlands Inn, The
Mendocino, CA

Washington Square Inn, The
San Francisco, CA

Thistle Dew Inn
Sonoma, CA

Abriendo Inn
Pueblo, CO

Red Brook Inn
Mystic, CT

French Renaissance House
Plainfield, CT

Old Riverton Inn
Riverton, CT

Spring Garden
Laurel, DE

William Penn Guest House
New Castle, DE

St. Francis Inn
St. Augustine, FL

Shellmont B&B Lodge
Atlanta, GA

Bed & Breakfast Inn, The
Savannah, GA

Richards House, The
Dubuque, IA

Standish House B&B
Lanark, IL

Thomas Huckins House
Barnstable, MA

Hawthorne Inn
Concord, MA

Edgartown Inn, The
Edgartown, MA

Penny House Inn
North Eastham, MA

Perryville Inn
Rehoboth, MA

Merrell Tavern Inn
Stockbridge, MA

Lion's Head Inn
West Harwich, MA

White Swan Tavern, The
Chestertown, MD

Jeweled Turret Inn, The
Belfast, ME

Norumbega Inn
Camden, ME

Lincoln House Country Inn
Dennysville, ME

Todd House
Eastport, ME

Weston House B&B
Eastport, ME

Borgman's B&B
Arrow Rock, MO

Briars Inn & Gardens, The
Natchez, MS

Oak Square Plantation
Port Gibson, MS

Inn at Brevard, The
Brevard, NC

Acorn Lodge
Ossipee, NH

Cable House, The
Rye, NH

Captain Mey's B&B Inn
Cape May, NJ

Ashling Cottage
Spring Lake, NJ

Preston House, The
Santa Fe, NM

Bird & Bottle Inn, The
Garrison, NY

Greenville Arms
Greenville, NY

Westchester House B&B, The
Saratoga Springs, NY

Russell-Cooper House, The
Mount Vernon, OH

Inn at Fordhook Farm, The
Doylestown, PA

Beechmont Inn
Gettysburg–Hanover, PA

Osceola Mill House
Gordonville–Intercourse, PA

Ash Mill Farm
Holicong–New Hope, PA

Witmer's Tavern–1725 Inn
Lancaster, PA

Cameron Estate Inn
Mount Joy, PA

Strasburg Village Inn
Strasburg, PA

Ann Harper's B&B
Charleston, SC

Maison Du Pré
Charleston, SC

Palmer Home, The
Charleston, SC

Hale Springs Inn
Rogersville, TN

Country Cottage Inn
Fredericksburg, TX

North Bend Plantation B&B
Charles City, VA

La Vista Plantation
Fredericksburg, VA

Wayside Inn, The
Middletown, VA

High Meadows Vineyard Inn
Scottsville, VA

Isle of Wight Inn
Smithfield, VA

Pink Fancy Inn
Christiansted–St. Croix, VI

Chester House
Chester, VT

1811 House
Manchester Village, VT

Swift House Inn
Middlebury, VT

West Dover Inn
West Dover, VT

Plough Inn B&B
Madison, WI

Historic *(cont'd.)*

Gilbert House B&B
Charles Town, WV

Annie Moore's Guest House
Laramie, WY

Low Price

The following lodgings are particularly noted for modest pricing. It is possible to obtain a room for $40 or less.

Casa Cody B&B Country Inn
Palm Springs, CA

Midwest Country Inn
Limon, CO

Curtis House, Inc.
Woodbury, CT

Smith House B&B
Shoup, ID

Meriwether House B&B
Columbus, KS

Almeda's B&B Inn
Tonganoxie, KS

Anthony's Town House
Boston/(Brookline), MA

Captain Isaiah's House
Cape Cod, MA

Avon House B&B
Flint, MI

Evelo's B&B
Minneapolis, MN

Fryemont Inn
Bryson City, NC

Plum Tree B&B, The
Pilar, NM

Zane Trace B&B
Old Washington, OH

Dreamy Acres
Canadensis, PA

La Anna Guest House
Cresco, PA

Runnymede Farm
Guesthouse
Quarryville, PA

Homestead Lodging
Smoketown, PA

Clardy's Guest House
Murfreesboro, TN

Seven Wives Inn
St. George, UT

Ski Inn
Stowe, VT

Wolf Hotel
Saratoga, WY

Sea Breeze Lodge
Hornby Island, BC

Bayberry Cliff Inn B&B
Murray River, PEI

Lea's B&B
Vernon River, PEI

Armor & Manor Sherbrooke
Montreal, PQ

Bay View Manor
New Carlisle, PQ

Luxury

These establishments are famed for their luxurious appointments and special attention to creature comforts and style.

Carriage House, The
Laguna Beach, CA

Mountain Home Inn
Mill Valley, CA

Villa St. Helena
Saint Helena, CA

Archbishop's Mansion Inn
San Francisco, CA

Sherman House, The
San Francisco, CA

Castle Marne—Urban Inn
Denver, CO

West Lane Inn
Ridgefield, CT

Ballastone Inn &
Townhouse
Savannah, GA

Foley House Inn
Savannah, GA

Gastonian, The
Savannah, GA

Lamothe House
New Orleans, LA

Soniat House
New Orleans, LA

Harraseeket Inn
Freeport, ME

Captain Lord Mansion, The
Kennebunkport, ME

Linden, circa 1790
Natchez, MS

Mainstay Inn & Cottage
Cape May, NJ

Inns at Doneckers, The
Ephrata, PA

Admiral Fitzroy Inn
Newport, RI

Kings Courtyard Inn
Charleston, SC

Hotel St. Germain
Dallas, TX

Mansion Hill Inn
Madison, WI

Captain's Palace
Victoria, BC

Northumberland Heights
Inn
Cobourg, ON

Le Chateau De Pierre
Quebec City, PQ

Nature

Nature lovers, alert! Whether your fancy is ornithology or whale watching, these inns will speak to your heart.

Home B&B/Seekins
Homer, AK

Briar Patch Inn
Sedona, AZ

Cazanoma Lodge
Cazadero, CA

Karen's B&B Yosemite Inn
Fish Camp, CA

Grey Whale Inn, The
Fort Bragg, CA

Marsh Cottage B&B
Inverness/Pt. Reyes Sta., CA

Rancho San Gregorio
San Gregorio, CA

Oak Hill Ranch B&B
Sonora/Tuolumne, CA

Trinidad B&B
Trinidad, CA

Little St. Simons Island
St. Simons Island, GA

Anchor Watch B&B
Boothbay Harbor, ME

Tarry-a-While B&B Resort
Bridgton, ME

Sunset House B&B
West Gouldsboro, ME

Pincushion Mountain B&B
Grand Marais, MN

Cedarcroft Farm B&B
Warrensburg, MO

Burggraf's Countrylane B&B
Bigfork, MT

Willows Inn
Red Lodge, MT

Sportsman's High B&B
West Yellowstone, MT

Folkestone Inn
Bryson City, NC

Trestle House Inn
Edenton, NC

Berkley Center Country Inn
Ocracoke, NC

Key Falls Inn
Pisgah Forest, NC

Pines Country Inn, The
Pisgah Forest, NC

Snowbird Mountain Lodge
Robbinsville, NC

Heath Lodge
Waynesville, NC

De Bruce Country Inn
De Bruce, NY

R.M. Farm
Livingston Manor, NY

Holmes Sea Cove B&B
Brookings, OR

Secluded B&B
Newberg, OR

Swiss Woods B&B
Lititz, PA

Woodhill Farms Inn
Washington Crossing, PA

Alford House B&B
Chattanooga, TN

Lodge at Fossil Rim, The
Glen Rose, TX

Trillium House
Wintergreen, VA

A Burrow's Bay B&B
Anacortes, WA

Mountain Meadows Inn B&B
Ashford, WA

Eagles Nest Inn
Langley, WA

Puget View Guesthouse
Olympia, WA

Black Cat Guest Ranch
Hinton, AB

Sooke Harbour House
Sooke, BC

Outstanding

The following inns are some which, due to attention to detail, amenities and ambiance, are truly outstanding.

Dairy Hollow House
Eureka Springs, AR

Williams House B&B Inn
Hot Springs Nat'l Park, AR

Graham B&B Inn
Sedona, AZ

Carter House
Eureka, CA

Gingerbread Mansion, The
Ferndale, CA

Pelican Inn
Muir Beach, CA

Dunbar House, 1880
Murphys, CA

Beazley House
Napa, CA

Mansions Hotel, The
San Francisco, CA

Seal Beach Inn & Gardens
Seal Beach, CA

Bishopsgate Inn
East Haddam, CT

Kalorama Guest House, The
Washington, DC

Chalet Suzanne Country Inn
Lake Wales, FL

Lahaina Hotel
Lahaina, Maui, HI

Captains House Inn
Chatham, MA

Whalewalk Inn, The
Eastham, MA

Seacrest Manor
Rockport, MA

Stephen Daniels House
Salem, MA

Schumacher's New Prague
New Prague, MN

Swag, The
Waynesville, NC

Snowvillage Inn
Snowville, NH

Abbey B&B, The
Cape May, NJ

Barnard-Good House
Cape May, NJ

Grant Corner Inn
Santa Fe, NM

Outstanding *(cont'd.)*

B&B on the Park
Brooklyn, NY

Adelphi Hotel, The
Saratoga Springs, NY

Coachaus
Allentown, PA

Inn at Turkey Hill, The
Bloomsburg, PA

Wedgewood Inn of New Hope
New Hope, PA

Admiral Benbow Inn
Newport, RI

Battery Carriage House Inn
Charleston, SC

Edgewood Plantation
Charles City, VA

Green Trails Country Inn
Brookfield, VT

Tulip Tree Inn
Chittenden, VT

Black River Inn
Ludlow, VT

Windham Hill Inn
West Townshend, VT

Romance

Ah, romance! These inns offer a hideaway, a peaceful space in which to be together and let the world go by.

Vintage Comfort B&B Inn
Hot Springs, AR

Knickerbocker Mansion
Big Bear Lake, CA

Carriage House Inn
Carmel, CA

Happy Landing Inn
Carmel, CA

Elk Cove Inn
Elk, CA

Murphy's Jenner Inn
Jenner, CA

Channel Road Inn
Los Angeles, CA

Green Gables Inn
Pacific Grove, CA

Seven Gables Inn
Pacific Grove, CA

Cricket Cottage
Point Reyes Station, CA

Jasmine Cottage
Point Reyes Station, CA

East Brother Light Station
Point Richmond, CA

Rancho Caymus Inn
Rutherford, CA

Bartels Ranch/Country Inn
Saint Helena, CA

Deer Run Inn
Saint Helena, CA

Glenborough Inn B&B
Santa Barbara, CA

Simpson House Inn
Santa Barbara, CA

Babbling Brook Inn
Santa Cruz, CA

Cliff Crest B&B Inn
Santa Cruz, CA

Darling House, The
Santa Cruz, CA

Queen Anne B&B Inn
Denver, CO

Riverwind Inn
Deep River, CT

Manor House
Norfolk, CT

Simsbury 1820 House
Simsbury, CT

Courtyard at Lake Lucerne
Orlando, FL

Veranda, The
Senoia, GA

Chateau des Fleurs
Winnetka, IL

Cornstalk Hotel, The
New Orleans, LA

Old Sea Pines Inn
Brewster, MA

Dunscroft By the Sea Inn
Harwich Port, Cape Cod, MA

Thorncroft Inn
Martha's Vineyard, MA

Four Chimneys Inn
Nantucket, MA

Wedgewood Inn
Yarmouth Port, MA

Graycote Inn
Bar Harbor, ME

Ledgelawn Inn, The
Bar Harbor, ME

Rowan Oak House
Salisbury, NC

Gunstock Country Inn
Gilford, NH

Cabbage Rose Inn, The
Flemington, NJ

Hacienda Del Sol
Taos, NM

La Posada de Taos B&B
Taos, NM

Interlaken Inn/Restaurant
Lake Placid, NY

Oliver Loud's Inn
Pittsford, NY

Village Victorian Inn
Rhinebeck, NY

Sandlake Country Inn
Sandlake, OR

Spring House
Airville, PA

Clarion River Lodge
Cooksburg, PA

Brinley Victorian Inn
Newport, RI

Durham House B&B Inn
Houston, TX

Silver Thatch Inn
Charlottesville, VA

Guesthouses at Greenvale
Mollusk, VA

Liberty Rose B&B
Williamsburg, VA

Village Country Inn
Manchester Village, VT

White House of Wilmington
Wilmington, VT

Turtleback Farm Inn
Eastsound, WA

Guest House Cottages
Greenbank, WA

St. Croix River Inn
Osceola, WI

White Lace Inn
Sturgeon Bay, WI

West End Guest House, The
Vancouver, BC

Skiing

These inns share a proximity to downhill or cross-country skiing. Nothing like coming back from an exhilarating day at the slopes to a warm, cozy fire.

Gold Mountain Manor B&B
Big Bear Lake, CA

Royal Gorges Rainbow Lodge
Big Bend, CA

Snow Goose Inn
Mammoth Lakes, CA

Little Red Ski Haus
Aspen, CO

Snow Queen Victorian B&B
Aspen, CO

Mary Lawrence Inn, The
Gunnison, CO

Idaho Country Inn
Sun Valley/Ketchum, ID

Birchwood Inn
Lenox, MA

Cornell Inn
Lenox, MA

Noble House B&B, The
Bridgton, ME

Kandahar Lodge
Whitefish, MT

Country Inn at Bartlett
Bartlett, NH

Bradford Inn, The
Bradford, NH

Mountain Fare Inn
Campton, NH

Darby Field Inn, The
Conway, NH

Chase House, The
Cornish, NH

Meeting House Inn, The
Henniker, NH

Dana Place Inn
Jackson, NH

Village House, The
Jackson, NH

Maple Hill Farm
New London, NH

1785 Inn, The
North Conway, NH

Old Red Inn & Cottages
North Conway, NH

Haus Edelweiss B&B
Sunapee, NH

Tall Pines Inn
Winnisquam, NH

Salsa del Salto B&B Inn
El Prado, NM

River Run
Fleischmanns, NY

Mount Tremper Inn
Mount Tremper, NY

Garnet Hill Lodge
North River, NY

Imperial Hotel
Park City, UT

Washington School Inn
Park City, UT

Mountain Hollow B&B Inn
Sandy, UT

Shire Inn
Chelsea, VT

Greenleaf Inn
Chester, VT

Little Lodge at Dorset
Dorset, VT

Mountain Meadows Lodge
Killington, VT

Brookside Meadows Country
Middlebury, VT

Golden Stage Inn
Proctorsville, VT

Weathervane Lodge B&B
West Dover, VT

Colonial House, The
Weston, VT

Amherst Shore Country Inn
Amherst, NS

Little Inn of Bayfield
Bayfield, ON

Spas

Hot mineral waters are nature's own relaxant. These inns are close to, or are, spas!

Culver's, A Country Inn
Calistoga, CA

Foothill House B&B Inn
Calistoga, CA

Scarlett's Country Inn
Calistoga, CA

Ojai Manor Hotel
Ojai, CA

Palisades Paradise B&B
Redding, CA

Vichy Hot Springs Resort
Ukiah, CA

St. Elmo Hotel
Ouray, CO

Poor Farm Country Inn
Salida, CO

Six Sisters B&B
Saratoga Springs, NY

Hudspeth House & Spa, The
Canyon, TX

Special

These inns all have an extra special, out-of-the-ordinary something that distinguishes them. We hope you'll agree.

Lynx Creek Farm B&B
Prescott, AZ

Wildwood Inn, The
Ware, MA

Keeper's House, The
Isle Au Haut, ME

Mansion Hill Country Inn
St. Louis—Bonne Terre, MO

Casita Chamisa B&B
Albuquerque, NM

Brae Loch Inn
Cazenovia, NY

Special *(cont'd.)*

Inn on Bacon Hill, The
Saratoga Springs, NY

Harry Packer Mansion
Jim Thorpe, PA

Pineapple Inn
Lewisburg, PA

Crystal River Inn
San Marcos, TX

Jordan Hollow Farm Inn
Stanley, VA

Hugging Bear Inn & Shoppe
Chester, VT

Sports

Sports are an integral part of many people's vacation plans. These inns are noted for their sporting facilities or locales. Be sure to call ahead to see if they have the special facility you require.

Westways "Private" Resort
Phoenix, AZ

North Coast Country Inn
Gualala, CA

Tucker Hill Inn
Middlebury, CT

Inn on Lake Waramaug, The
New Preston, CT

1735 House, The
Amelia Island, FL

Over Look Inn, The
Eastham, MA

Davis House
Solomons Island, MD

Gunflint Lodge
Grand Marais, MN

Cherokee Inn B&B
Kill Devil Hills, NC

Notchland Inn, The
Bartlett, NH

Ammonoosuc Inn
Lisbon, NH

Cranmore Mountain Lodge
North Conway, NH

Nereledge Inn
North Conway, NH

Mountainaire Adventures
Wevertown, NY

Gateway Lodge & Restaurant
Cooksburg, PA

Eagles Mere Inn
Eagles Mere, PA

Inn at Starlight Lake, The
Starlight, PA

Homestead Resort, The
Midway, UT

Vine Cottage Inn
Hot Springs, VA

Hill Farm Inn
Arlington, VT

October Country Inn
Bridgewater Corners, VT

Vermont Inn, The
Killington, VT

Okemo Inn, The
Ludlow, VT

Manchester Highlands Inn
Manchester, VT

Northfield Inn
Northfield, VT

Quechee Inn-Marshland Farm
Quechee, VT

Brass Lantern, Inn at the
Stowe, VT

Gables Inn, The
Stowe, VT

Siebeness Inn, The
Stowe, VT

Wildflower Inn, The
Jackson, WY

Sherwood Inn
Port Carling, ON

Vegetarian

These inns can prepare a vegetarian diet for their guests.

Peppertrees B&B Inn
Tucson, AZ

Red Castle Inn, The
Nevada City, CA

Riverhouse B&B
Durango, CO

Nuthatch B&B, The
Indianapolis, IN

Turning Point Inn
Great Barrington, MA

Chatsworth B&B
St. Paul, MN

Blake House Inn
Asheville, NC

Grandview Lodge
Waynesville, NC

General Hooker's B&B
Portland, OR

Golf Resorts International

A wish book and travel guide for the wandering golfer. This guide, written in much the same spirit as the bestselling *Elegant Small Hotels,* reviews the creme de la creme of golf resorts all over the world. Beautifully illustrated, it includes all pertinent details regarding hotel facilities and amenities. Wonderful narrative on each hotel's special charm, superb cuisine and most importantly, those fabulous golf courses. Written from a golfer's viewpoint, it looks at the challenges and pitfalls of each course. For the non-golfer, there is ample information about other activities available in the area, such as on-site health spas, nearby shopping, and more.

Introduction by John Stirling.

Golf Resorts — The Complete Guide

The first ever comprehensive and recently updated guide to over 1,000 golf resorts coast to coast. Includes complete details of each resort facility and golf course particulars. "The Complete Guide to Golf Resorts is a wonderful golf destination guide." — LPGA

Introduction by Fuzzy Zoeller.

Elegant Small Hotels
— A Connoiseur's Guide

This selective guide for discriminating travelers describes over 200 of America's finest hotels characterized by exquisite rooms, fine dining, and perfect service par excellence. Introduction by Peter Duchin. "Elegant Small Hotels makes a seductive volume for window shopping." — *Chicago Sun Times*.

All-Suite Hotel Guide
— The Definitive Directory

The only guide to the all suite hotel industry features over 1,200 hotels nationwide and abroad. There is a special bonus list of temporary office facilities. A perfect choice for business travelers and much appreciated by families who enjoy the additional privacy provided by two rooms.

Condo Vacations
—The Complete Guide

The popularity of Condo vacations has grown exponentially. In this national guide, details are provided on over 3,000 Condo resorts in an easy to read format with valuable descriptive write-ups. The perfect vacation option for families and a great money saver!

Elegant Hotels of the Pacific Rim

Over 140 exquisite hotels and resorts located in the burgeoning Pacific Rim. Especially chosen for their inspired architecture, luxurious ambiance and personal service *par excellence*. A must for the globe trotter!

The Back Almanac
The Best New Thinking on an Age-Old Problem

by Lanier Publishing

Just in the nick of time for the 4 out of 5 Americans suffering with back pain, a practical guide to back pain prevention and care. Delightfully illustrated. Internationally acknowledged experts offer the latest thinking on causes, treatment, and pain-free life, including Danger Signals, Sex and Back Pain, and What If Nothing Works? Resource guide lists back schools, pain centers and specialty items.

Revised

"The editors have amassed a wealth of easy-to-find easy-to-read information ..." —HEALTHLINE

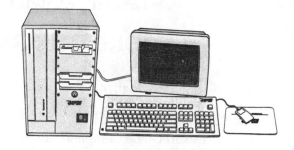

Bed & Breakfast Guide Online™
with Pamela Lanier
on

CompuServe®

You can now access *The Complete Guide to Bed & Breakfasts, Inns and Guesthouses* on your personal computer, online, with CompuServe. In addition, you can discuss your favorite bed and breakfasts with fellow inn-goers, pick up a wonderful recipe for pecan pancakes, share your dream of some day being an innkeeper, or enter a sweepstakes to win a stay at a country inn in the **Inn Forum**™ on CompuServe!

Established in 1979, the CompuServe Information Service provides its worldwide membership of 1.4 million with more than 1,700 databases and services to meet both business and personal interests. CompuServe can be accessed by any modem-equipped personal computer utilizing the CompuServe Information Manager graphical interface or any general communication software.

Special offer to *Complete Guide* readers: call **1-800-524-3388** and ask for operator 237 to receive a free introductory kit. This includes one month free access to basic services and a $15.00 usage credit. CompuServe members pay $8.95 per month for a set of 47 basic services. Members choosing to access CompuServe's 1,700 other areas pay $8.00 per hour for modem speeds of 1200 or 2400 bits per second or $16.00 per hour for accessing at 9.6 or 14.4 kilobits per second.

In addition to the CompuServe Information Service, CompuServe Incorporated provides frame relay, wide and local area networking services, business information services and software to major corporations and government agencies worldwide.

CompuServe is an H&R Block company.

Travel Books from
LANIER GUIDES

ORDER FORM

QTY.	TITLE	EACH	TOTAL
	Golf Courses—The Complete Guide	$14.95	
	Golf Resorts—The Complete Guide	$14.95	
	Golf Resorts International	$19.95	
	Condo Vacations—The Complete Guide	$14.95	
	Elegant Small Hotels	$19.95	
	Elegant Hotels—Pacific Rim	$14.95	
	All-Suite Hotel Guide	$14.95	
	The Complete Guide to Bed & Breakfasts, Inns & Guesthouses	$16.95	
	The Back Almanac	$14.95	
		Sub-Total	$
		Shipping	$2.75 each
		TOTAL ENCLOSED	$

Send your order to:
LANIER PUBLISHING
P.O. Box 20429
Oakland, CA 94620

We accept VISA & MasterCard

Allow 3 to 4 weeks for delivery

Please send my order to:

NAME _____

ADDRESS _____

CITY _____ STATE _____ ZIP_____